N... , CENTRAL, & SOUTHEASTERN EUROPE

BOJKA DJUKANOVIĆ

THE WORLD TODAY SERIES®

2024-2025

23RD EDITION

Graphic Materials Acknowledgments

For their generosity in providing certain visual material for use in this book, special thanks to the following:

European Community Information Services
Delegation of the European Commission, Washington
North Atlantic Treaty Organization
Office of the President of Montenegro
German Information Services, New York
German National Tourist Office, New York
Press and Information Office, Bonn and Berlin
The Royal Norwegian Embassy

The Royal Danish Embassy
The Embassy of Sweden
The Embassy of Finland
The Embassy of Austria
The Embassy of Iceland
The Embassy of Greece

First appearing as *Western Europe 1982*, this annually revised book is published by

Stryker–Post Publications
An imprint of The Rowman & Littlefield Publishing Group, Inc.
4501 Forbes Blvd., Suite 200, Lanham, MD 20706
www.rowman.com

Library of Congress Control Number Available

ISBN 978-1-5381-8586-5 (pbk. : alk. paper)
ISBN 978-1-5381-8587-2 (electronic)

Cover design by Sarah Marizan

Cartographer: William L. Nelson

Typography by Barton Matheson Willse & Worthington
Baltimore, MD 21244

The World Today Series has thousands of subscribers across the United States and Canada. A sample list of users who annually rely on this most up-to-date material includes:

Public library systems
Universities and colleges
High schools
Federal and state agencies
All branches of the armed forces and war colleges
National Geographic Society
National Democratic Institute
Agricultural Education Foundation
ExxonMobile Corporation
Chevron Corporation
CNN

ABOUT THE AUTHOR

Prof. dr Bojka Djukanović is a full professor of British and American civilization and literature in the Faculty of Philosophy of the University of Montenegro. She earned her MA and doctoral degree at the University of Belgrade (Serbia). Her field of research has been the reception of Anglo-Saxon culture in Montenegro. She is also one of the main promoters of education for democratic citizenship and human rights education in Montenegro. Djukanović has been an EDC/HRE coordinator at the Council of Europe, EFA coordinator for Montenegro. She has also been a holder of UNESCO Chair in Education for Democratic Citizenship and Human Rights in the Faculty of Philosophy of the University of Montenegro. Her interests are the British and American historical relations with Montenegro; historical trends and influences of British and American culture and their reception in Montenegro, and travel pieces on Montenegro from the nineteenth century to the modern times. Her works include *the Bibliography of Montenegro in English* (1993), a study *Njegoš and England* (1999), *Apotheosis of Montenegro* (2008), *Historical Dictionary of Montenegro* (2023), as well as a number of shorter studies on the Montenegrin history and culture.

Frankfurter Rundschau

UNABHÄNGIGE TAGESZEITUNG

Montag, 3. Mai 2004 I D-Ausgabe · · · www.fr-aktuell.de · · · D 2972 I Jahrgang 60 I Nr. 102/19 I Preis: 1,30 Euro

Frankfurter Rundschau
60266 Frankfurt am Main
Anzeigenannahme:
Telefon 08 00/202 01 00, Fax 069/131 00 30
Abo-Leserservice:
Telefon 08 00/866 68 66, Fax 069/21 99 - 32 64
Telefon 069/21 99-34 48
www.fr-aktuell.de

Europa ist wieder vereint

Europäische Union nimmt 75 Millionen neue Bürger auf

Weitere Berichte zur EU-Erweiterung
Politik · Seite 3
Kommentar · Seite 3
Schwerpunkt · Seite 5

Klausur

Zuwanderungsgesetz vor dem Scheitern

BERLIN · 2. MAI · VGO · Das Zuwanderungsgesetz steht vor dem Aus. Nachdem die Kompromissverhandlungen am Wochenende ergebnislos abgebrochen worden waren, werden die Grünen voraussichtlich noch in dieser Woche den Ausstieg aus Verhandlungen erklären.

Die 20 Unterhändler von Regierung und Opposition hatten ihre Verhandlungsklausur am Samstagabend abgebrochen, ohne einen neuen Gesprächstermin zu vereinbaren. Bei den 17-stündigen Verhandlungen der Arbeitsgruppe des Vermittlungsausschusses hatte es vor allem über die umstrittenen Sicherheitsfragen keine Annäherung gegeben. Regierung und Opposition wollen für ein mögliches nächstes Treffen schriftliche Vorschläge erarbeiten. Sie wollen dabei jedoch auch prüfen, ob weitere Gespräche sinnvoll sind. Der Verhandlungsführer der Grünen, Volker Beck, kündigte bereits an: „Ich kann meiner Partei nicht raten, diesen Weg weiterzugehen." Eine Entscheidung über das Ende der Verhandlungen könnte am Samstag auf dem Länderrat, dem zweithöchsten Parteigremium der Grünen, fallen.
Thema des Tages, Kommentar S. 3

TAG DER ARBEIT

Gewerkschaften gehen auf Konfrontation zu Rot-Grün

Die Stimmung zwischen Gewerkschaften und den Regierenden in Berlin ist schlecht. Am „Tag der Arbeit" musste sich Rot-Grün scharfe Angriffe gefallen lassen.

VON ULRIKE FÜSSEL
(FRANKFURT A. M.)

Mit markigen Worten haben führende Gewerkschafter bei den traditionellen Mai-Kundgebungen ihrer Organisationen ein deutliches Bild von der Kluft zwischen den Reformplänen der Regierung und den gewerkschaftlichen Vorstellungen gezeichnet. So warf der Vorsitzende des Deutschen Gewerkschafts- da 2010 ist zum Synonym für die Zwei-Drittel-Gesellschaft geworden. „Ein Drittel unserer Bevölkerung einfach abgeschrieben." Die Gewerkschaften würden nicht nachlassen in ihrem Kampf um wirkliche Sozialreformen. Sie verwehrten sich einer „sozialen Abwärtsspirale mit niedrigeren Löhnen, längeren Arbeitszeiten oder Arbeitsbedingungen und Arbeitsrechten aus dem

---

„Nun ist es vollbracht"

EU-Spitzenpolitiker und Neu-Mitglieder feiern die historische Erweiterung des Bündnisses

Hunderttausende Menschen haben am Samstag die größte Erweiterung in der Geschichte der Europäischen Union gefeiert. EU-Spitzenpolitiker würdigten die Aufnahme von zehn neuen Mitgliedern in das Bündnis als „Wiedervereinigung" des Kontinents.

FRANKFURT A.M. · 2. MAI · DPA/AP/RTR/RECK/ME · Der amtierende EU-Ratspräsident und irische Ministerpräsident Bertie Ahern, EU-Kommissionspräsident Romano Prodi und EU-Parlamentspräsident Pat Cox bezeichneten die geschichtliche Bedeutung der EU-Erweiterung am 1. Mai als „Wiedervereinigung Europas". Mit den neuen Mitgliedsstaaten wächst die EU-Bevölkerung von zuvor gut 380 Millionen auf 455 Millionen Menschen.

Bei den offiziellen Erweiterungsfeier in Dublin, zu der die Staats- und Regierungschefs aller 25 EU-Mitgliedsstaaten angereist waren, unterstrichen die drei Spitzenpolitiker die Notwendigkeit, den Verfassungsentwurf wie vereinbart noch in diesem Sommer zu verabschieden. Ahern will noch in dieser Wo- che eine Rundreise durch Europas Hauptstädte beginnen, um in Detailverhandlungen Kompromisslinien abzustecken. Weiterhin umstritten ist die Frage, welches Gewicht die Bevölkerungsstärke einzelner Mitgliedsstaaten bei Mehrheitsentscheidungen erhalten soll.

Am Rande der Feiern ging die irische Polizei mit Wasserwerfern gegen etwa 2000 Globalisierungskritiker vor, die versucht hatten, auf das Festgelände in Dublin vorzudringen. Es kam zu Handgemengen, 28 Demonstranten wurden festgenommen.

Den EU-Beitritt seines Landes sieht Tschechiens früherer Präsident Vaclav Havel als gute Gelegenheit für seine Landsleute, selbstbewusste Europäer zu werden. Sie seien einem Bündnis beigetreten, das nicht durch Kriege entstanden sei, sondern auf dem freien Willen europäischer Länder beruhe.

Ungarns Ministerpräsident Ferenc Medgyessy verkündete, sein Land sei „immer an den Toren Europas" gewesen, durch die EU-Erweiterung nun aber „innerhalb der Tore". In Litauens Hauptstadt Vilnius sagte Präsident Arturas Paulauskas: „Wir haben viele Jahre gebraucht, um diese Reise zurückzulegen. Nun ist es vollbracht".

Bundeskanzler Gerhard Schröder (SPD) würdigte die Erweiterung als Beitrag zum Frieden in Europa. „Die Spaltung des Kontinents und die Trennung seiner Bürger ist endgültig überwunden", sagte Schröder am Samstag bei einer Kundgebung am Dreiländereck in Zittau. Schröder feierte dort mit seinen Amtskollegen Leszek Miller aus Polen und Vladimir Spidla aus Tschechien.

Einen Tag zuvor hatte der Kanzler in einer Regierungserklärung die „historische Mission" der europäischen Einigung herausgestellt, mit der sich jetzt ein Traum vieler Generationen erfüllt habe. Deutschland werde davon auch wirtschaftlich „am meisten profitieren". Gleichzeitig warnte er vor einem „einseitigen Steuerwettbewerb zu Lasten der Nettozahler" in der EU. Auch bei den Unternehmenssteuern müsse es EU-weit einen „Korridor" geben, den einzelne Staaten nicht verlassen dürften, um den Nachbarn Firmen abzuwerben.

Schröder sagte erstmals, dass hier notfalls auf eine formelle „verstärkte Zusammenarbeit" einiger EU-Staaten gesetzt werde, falls eine Einstimmigkeit nicht zu erreichen sei. Im Unterschied zum Kanzler sprach sich CDU-Chefin Angela Merkel klar für weitere soziale Einschnitte aus. Wenn Deutschland nicht „in hohem Maß zum Verlierer" der Erweiterung werden wolle, müsse es sich „den Gesetzmäßigkeiten stellen".

DIE EUROPÄISCHE UNION

1951 gründen Deutschland, Frankreich, Italien und die Benelux-Staaten die Europäische Gemeinschaft für Kohle und Stahl (EGKS).
1957 die Europäische Wirtschaftsgemeinschaft (EWG).
1973 stoßen Dänemark, Irland und Großbritannien zur EG,
1981 Griechenland,
1986 Spanien und Portugal,
1995 folgen noch Österreich, Finnland und Schweden. ap

Finanzpolitik

Koalition rückt von hartem Sparkurs ab

BERLIN · 2. MAI · ME · In Berlin mehren sich die Signale, dass die rot-grüne Koalition von ihrem harten Sparkurs abrückt und die zu erwartenden neuen Haushaltslöcher nicht mehr durch zusätzliche Einsparungen stopfen will. Außenminister Joschka Fischer (Grüne) und der SPD-Finanzpolitiker Joachim Poß unterstützten am Wochenende in Interviews den neuen Kurs von Bundeskanzler Gerhard Schröder (SPD), mit dem auch ein erneutes Verfehlen des EU-Stabilitätsziels 2005 in Kauf genommen wird.

Fischer sagte, „für einen begrenzten Zeitraum" müsse die Konjunkturerholung Priorität haben. Schröder hatte zuvor angekündigt, die Regierung wolle auf keinen Fall durch weitere Sparbeschlüsse die Konjunktur gefährden.

Der stellvertretende CDU-Chef Jürgen Rüttgers forderte den Rücktritt von Finanzminister Hans Eichel (SPD). In Regierungskreisen hieß es, Eichel werde einstweilen im Amt bleiben, er müsse allerdings seine Einsparforderungen zurückschrauben. Zuletzt hatte Verteidigungsminister Peter Struck (SPD) gegen Eichels Sparvorgaben protestiert.
Bericht Seite 4

DIE ECKE

Studienführer

LONDON · 2. MAI · DPA · Ungewöhnliche Konkurrenz hat Prinz William, der Sohn des britischen Thronfolgers, an der schottischen St.-Andrews-Universität erhalten. Der älteste Sohn von Prinz Charles und Prinzessin Di wird in seinem Studium ständig von seinem Leibwächter Bill Noon begleitet. In den Vorlesungen und Seminaren sei Noon stets dabei, berichtete die britische Zeitung News of the World. Der Sicherheitsexperte nehme regen Anteil an den Studien. „Er meldet sich und beantwortet Fragen wie jeder andere Student auch", zitiert das Blatt einen Kommilitonen.

William war schon in der Schule

[Fortsetzung linke Spalte:]
le Spitzengewerkschafter nutzten die Stunde aber zu harscher Kritik an der Regierung. So warf der Vorsitzende der Gewerkschaft Bergbau-Chemie-Energie, Hubertus Schmoldt, der Koalition mangelnde soziale Ausgewogenheit vor. Mit Veränderungen, die oft nicht zu Ende gedacht seien, zerstöre die rot-grüne Koalition Vertrauen, sagte Schmoldt in Marl. So seien die neuen Regeln für die Zumutbarkeit von Arbeit nicht hinzunehmen, wonach Arbeitslose künftig eine Stelle zu nahezu jedem Preis annehmen müssten. „Wir erwarten, dass die Bundesregierung gegen die zunehmende Verarmung di, blockte in Leipzig Forderungen ab, der Niedriglohnsektor müsse ausgeweitet werden. Die Menschen brauchten mehr, nicht weniger Geld, sagte Bsirske.

Nach Angaben der Veranstalter folgten bundesweit rund 500 000 Menschen dem gewerkschaftlichen Aufruf zu Kundgebungen.

Vor dem 1. Mai hatte der neue Vorsitzende der SPD, Franz Müntefering, in einem Schreiben an Betriebsräte anlässlich der EU-Erweiterung um Verständnis geworben. Im erweiterten Europa werde die SPD weiter dafür einstehen, dass die Interessen der arbeitenden

[Fortsetzung Spalte:]
ter ihr Vorsitzender Jürgen Peters in Mannheim an. Peters sagte, eine andere und bessere Politik sei umsetzbar und machbar. Die Unterschriftensammlung solle den Druck für Kurskorrekturen in der Wirtschafts- und Sozialpolitik erhöhen. Das Festhalten an einer höheren Wochenarbeitszeit nannte Peters angesichts der hohen Arbeitslosigkeit „Irrsinn".

Ähnlich deutlich waren auch die Akzente, die der Vorsitzende der IG Bauen-Agrar-Umwelt, Klaus Wiesehügel, in Mülheim (Ruhr) setzte. Wiesehügel wandte sich ge-

CONTENTS

A new generation of Europeans—graduation day at the College of Europe, Warsaw

CENTRAL AND EASTERN EUROPE

. . . in 1877

. . . in 1914

CENTRAL EUROPE

The Danube River at Budapest, Hungary

ACKNOWLEDGMENTS

This book is a revised, updated and extended version of the previous editions prepared by Wayne C. Thompson, professor emeritus of political science at Virginia Military Institute, Lexington, Virginia. He received valuable help in preparing the editions from his students at the College of Europe in Bruges and Warsaw, who carefully and critically read the chapters on their respective countries in the book and offered suggestions for improvement; and from his assistants at the American University in Bulgaria who were very helpful in improving the chapters on the Balkans and southeastern Europe. Professor Krzysztof Jasiewicz and Professor Dieter Mahncke offered advice for the Poland and Germany chapters. Alan Corwin reviewed the chapter on Norway. Marek Payerhin, professor of Political Science at Lynchburg College, kept updating this book for two years. In 2007, Michael Nix made copious editorial changes based on his decades of experience as a Canadian government editor.

My gratitude is due to Dalibor Vukotić, an IT communication expert, and my colleague Professor Olivera Popović for technical assistance and suggestions in preparing this edition.

Introduction: Nordic, Central, and Southeastern Europe

INTRODUCTION

Once again, some three decades after the collapse of communism in Europe, the unification of Germany, and the dissolution of the Soviet Union, Europeans are faced with circumstances that may profoundly alter their livelihood and the political future of their continent. The rise of populist parties and the reawakening of virulent nationalism, the British departure from the European Union and consequent challenges to the very existence of that organization, shifts in the United States' approaches to Europe and NATO, the enormous migrant wave, the surge in terrorist attacks, and the invasion of Ukraine by Russia: Just these monumental developments create a sense of uncertainty among the Europeans, with more than a hint of concern, perhaps even apprehension.

This is not to disregard the hugely positive changes brought about by the events of 1989 and beyond. Because two hostile Europes—created at the Yalta Conference in February 1945 and subsequently hardened by the Cold War—no longer face each other, democratic Europe has doubled its size from 382 to 700 million people. From Reykjavik to Athens, democracies exist in which free elections provide the only legitimate claim to power and which are basically committed to freedom, individual rights, and some variant of capitalism.

Newly independent and sovereign nations have emerged, all in varying states of economic difficulty, some with borders in dispute, ethnic scores to settle, and millions of discontented and frightened citizens. The August 1991 putsch in the former Soviet Union destroyed central authority and dispersed power among its various republics. Western European countries led the way in recognizing the newly independent Baltic States of Estonia, Latvia, and Lithuania, which reached out to the west. Moldova, carved out of Romania at the beginning of World War II, may one day find its way back into union with that state. In the southeast, Yugoslavia came unglued and became the scene of the first full-scale warfare in Europe since 1945.

Political boundaries on the European continent, which extends from the Atlantic Ocean to the Ural Mountains in Russia, have become less sharp and more open. In between there is a 500- to 800-mile strip of countries with a total population of approximately 238 million and extending about 2,400 miles from the Nordic countries southward to the Greek border. All look primarily westward for their trade, almost all feel western in their political and cultural orientation, and most belong to or are demanding for admission to the plentiful western European table, to the European Union (EU), and to

a place under the Atlantic Alliance's security umbrella.

Most European countries are too small to defend themselves alone. Therefore, the majority has joined or seeks to join the North Atlantic Treaty Organization (NATO), also known as the Atlantic Alliance. Created in 1949, NATO links the power of the United States and Canada and the geographic position of Iceland (which has no army) with the military resources of Belgium-Netherlands-Luxembourg (BENELUX), Great Britain, Norway, Denmark, Germany, Italy, Portugal, Türkiye, Greece, France, and Spain. Since 1999 Poland, Hungary, and the Czech Republic are members, joined in April 2004 by Estonia, Latvia, Lithuania, Slovakia, Slovenia, Romania, and Bulgaria. Croatia and Albania entered in 2009, Montenegro in 2017, and Finland in 2023. A few European countries prefer to remain non-aligned, including Ireland, Switzerland, and Austria, though this might change.

In 1991 NATO was transformed into a more political organization seeking to reach out to its former enemies. It created the Euro-Atlantic Partnership Council (EAPC, known until 1997 as the North Atlantic Cooperation Council—NACC), comprising 46 countries by the beginning of the century. The EAPC provides for regular consultations between NATO and the former Soviet republics and central, eastern, and southeastern European nations on subjects ranging from security issues, arms control, and the conversion of defense industries. In 1994 NATO initiated the Partnership for Peace (PfP), which links 19 countries in bilateral treaties with NATO. The purpose is to expand and intensify political and military cooperation and to strengthen stability and peace, primarily through training forces for peacekeeping operations. A special NATO-Ukraine Commission was established by the NATO-Ukraine Charter on a

Distinctive Partnership aiming to deepen cooperation with that important country. It was signed by Ukrainian and Allied Heads of State and Government in Madrid in 1997. At the 2023 NATO Summit in Vilnius (Lithuania), the Commission was replaced by the NATO-Ukraine Council. The Council again is a joint body where Allies and Ukraine meet for crisis consultations and take decisions as equals. The change demonstrated strengthening political ties and Ukraine's increasing integration with NATO.

Many countries regard PfP as a crucial stepping stone to full NATO membership. In principle, the alliance is prepared gradually to accept new members, on the condition that they have solid democratic credentials, including a firm civilian grip on the armed forces, and can make a genuine military contribution to the common defense. The door remains open to a select group of European democracies who ask to join.

NATO planners fear the effects an increase in membership would have on already-complicated decision-making mechanisms, which require unanimity and consensus. Also, Russia is hostile to enlargement, especially insofar as former Soviet republics, especially Ukraine, are concerned. To assuage Moscow's fears, the Atlantic allies signed with Moscow in 1997 a NATO-Russia Founding Act. This is not a legally binding treaty, but it states that NATO has no need, intentions, or plans to create additional capabilities or permanently to station troops or nuclear weapons in the new member states. It led to the creation of a Permanent Joint Committee, strengthened and renamed the NATO Russia Council in May 2002.

These organizations have failed to eliminate the tension between Russia and the West, especially after Russia's unacceptable annexation of Crimea and military meddling in southeast Ukraine which started in 2014. The conflict escalated

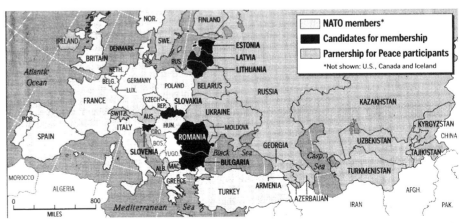

Candidates become members, April 2004, joined in 2009 by Albania and Croatia, and in 2017 by Montenegro

Source: *The Washington Post*

1

Introduction: Nordic, Central, and Southeastern Europe

. . . in 1924

significantly when Russia launched an invasion of Ukraine on February 24, 2022. Russian President Vladimir Putin has challenged the post-Cold War status quo, incensed that the West has expanded NATO and the EU to Russia's borders while ignoring Russia's interests and exploiting its weaknesses. The invasion of Ukraine became the largest attack on a European country since World War II.

NATO's outdated doctrine of containing Soviet power through "forward defense" and "flexible response" was replaced by one that gives NATO a reason to exist in the changed European environment. Smaller, highly mobile, conventional, and multilateral forces are being created that can be deployed on short notice anywhere within NATO territory and that can help manage unpredictable crises and instability in central and eastern Europe, the Balkans, the Mediterranean area and beyond. The NATO Response Force (NRF) comprises up to 40,000 ready and technologically advanced troops whom members provide on a rotating basis. The NRF plans to increase its manpower to over 300,000 troops.

The countries treated in this book are also linked in the 57-member Organization for Security and Cooperation in Europe (OSCE, known until 1994 as the Conference for Security and Cooperation in Europe—CSCE), to which all European states, former Soviet republics, and the United States and Canada belong. It meets irregularly to consider how to defuse threats to peace through mediation, crisis management, and the dispatch of observers, and it makes decisions by consensus. It has a Conflict Prevention Center in Vienna and an Office for Democratic Institutions and Human Rights (ODIHR) in Warsaw.

The 46 members of the Council of Europe, which was created in Strasbourg in 1949, include all the countries discussed in this book, with the exceptions of Kosovo and Kaliningrad Oblast (Russia).

Kosovo, which is still a state with limited recognition (claimed by Serbia as part of its sovereign territory), officially applied for membership in the Council of Europe in 2022. On 24 April 2023, the Committee of Ministers of the Council of Europe approved its request with 33 votes in favor, 7 against and 5 abstaining, allowing the application to progress to the Parliamentary Assembly.

Russia joined the Council of Europe on February 28, 1996, but it was suspended from its rights of representation in the Committee of Ministers and in the Parliamentary Assembly on February 25, 2022 due to the invasion of Ukraine. On March 15, Russia launched a withdrawal procedure from the Council, delivering its formal notification to withdraw effective December 31, 2022. On March 16, 2022 the Committee of Ministers decided to expel Russia with immediate effect.

The Council of Europe assemblies of parliamentarians from the member states serve as a forum for discussing political, economic, social, and cultural issues of interest to all European countries. Its important contribution has been its various conventions, especially its Convention for the Protection of Human Rights and Fundamental Freedoms (known as the European Convention on Human Rights—ECHR), adopted in 1950. All aspirants to EU membership must accept the convention's principles. Since 1991 it has been particularly active in trying to strengthen democracy and human rights in central and eastern Europe. The United States requested and was granted observer status in 1996 in order to be able to promote democracy more effectively in Central and Eastern Europe.

The European Union (EU) is an economic and political union between 27 states located primarily in Europe. It has a total area of 1,634,469 sq. mi. (4,233,255 sq. km.) and an estimated total population of over 448 million. The member states have agreed to pool a portion of their national sovereignty to the union. The attractive logic of European unity has affected countries all over the continent. Most European countries formally applied for EU membership.

Longstanding members of the EU include the BENELUX countries, France, Germany, Italy, the Republic of Ireland, Denmark, Greece, Spain, and Portugal and since 1995 Austria, Finland, and Sweden. In May 2004 they were joined by Estonia, Latvia, Lithuania, Poland, the Czech Republic, Slovakia, Hungary, Slovenia, Malta, and the Greek-speaking part of divided Cyprus. Croatia entered in July 2013. On December 21, 2007, all of these but Cyprus joined the EU's Schengen zone, which eliminates systematic border controls between member states. Romania and Bulgaria were admitted to the EU in 2007. Türkiye was readmitted to candidate status, followed by Montenegro, North Macedonia, Albania, and Serbia. Others joined in the lengthy process of accession. Norway was offered membership in 1972 and 1994, but its voters rejected it both times. Switzerland could join at any time. Entry into the EU is infinitely more complicated than joining NATO. New countries must accept 80,000 pages of EU regulations, half of them relating to agriculture. They must reach consensus with other states on complicated matters, such as banking laws, taxation, and a common currency. In a 2016 referendum, a majority of citizens of the United Kingdom

Introduction: Nordic, Central, and Southeastern Europe

(EU member since 1973) supported the proposition to exit the EU, and in 2017 the UK formally initiated the procedure of withdrawal, a process it completed in 2020. The future of the organization will greatly depend on how it handles this crucial challenge. The electoral victory of pro-EU French president Emmanuel Macron in 2017 and the strong support for the organization in Germany are likely to outweigh the influence of Euroskeptical mavericks, such as the governments of Hungary and Poland.

The European countries treated in this book are also active in such international economic treaties or organizations as the General Agreement on Trade and Tariffs (GATT); the World Trade Organization (WTO), which since 1995 attempts to resolve disputes relating to the GATT Treaty; the International Monetary Fund (IMF), which provides funds for countries with balance-of-payments problems; the International Bank for Reconstruction and Development (World Bank); and the European Bank for Reconstruction and Development (EBRD). Headquartered in London, the EBRD was created after the collapse of communism to help central and eastern European countries make successful transitions to free-market economies.

The Nordic Countries

This survey begins with the prosperous, peaceful, and generally harmonious Nordic countries, which encompass Iceland, Norway, Denmark, Sweden, and Finland. These lands are comfortably set apart from the rest of Europe, and for most of the postwar period, they have enjoyed enviable prosperity and political stability. They are at the top of many international measurements: quality of life, women's opportunities, education, environmental protection, competitiveness, research and development, foreign aid, and absence of corruption.

Most have been spared many of the continent's violent conflicts. They have had the wealth and the leisure to develop generous social welfare systems that are the model for many persons in the former communist countries who yearn for both the wealth of the western world and the economic security offered at a minimal level by their ex-communist regimes. All are in the Nordic Council, which meets regularly to discuss nonmilitary problems they have in common. Two of them—Norway and Finland—border on Russia, and Finland has a half-century of valuable experience in close cooperation with Russians. Finland, Sweden, and Denmark have been especially active and important in supporting the Baltic states, which were the first former Soviet republics to win their independence in 1991.

Transition from Communism

Most of the countries presented in this book had communist regimes until 1989–1991 and have been undergoing the difficult transition to democracy and free-market economies. Residents in all former communist countries had unrealistic expectations about the difficulties in converting planned economies to competitive free- market ones. The dramatic changes from 1989 to 1991 had created an exhilaration of victory and high expectations of quick improvements in people's lives through reforms. Dreams of instant prosperity quickly proved to be illusory. In the painful and protracted transition, eastern Germans and other central and eastern Europeans found themselves in a similar situation.

All countries experienced economic decline at least until 1994. People began to sense that the results they had expected in the short term could be achieved only in the distant future, if at all. Struggling with a wide array of unexpected and unfamiliar problems, their political leaders came to realize that only part of the problems facing their countries had been caused by communism and would not disappear automatically once the old systems had been dismantled. They have had to confront centuries of backwardness, which could take decades to overcome. In the meantime, social services were cut, economic inequality grew, and crime rose dramatically, especially organized crime. To some, it is the market economy, with its emphasis on free enterprise, which enables organized crime to flourish.

Many people who grew up under communism and were threatened by reform lost hope in the free-market experiment. Since socialism remains an attractive idea in principle, they sometimes support socialist parties that would restore the social welfare system, which is still valued in their political culture. The anticommunist governments that first assumed power failed to achieve widespread prosperity. This changed the political environment and fostered the rebirth of discredited communist parties, whose demise almost everybody had predicted. They could succeed only by redefining socialism in more modern terms and by embracing pluralist democracy and, with reservations, a market economy. Their offer of more economic security in a time of painful transition is very appealing.

Many citizens of former communist countries are not willing to disregard their own lives during four decades of dictatorship, as many westerners seem to want them to do. That was the setting in which they went to school, embarked upon careers, had their families, and found their

. . . and today

Introduction: Nordic, Central, and Southeastern Europe

happiness in life. They cannot simply discard their own biographies and say that their earlier lives had been wasted during communist rule.

The Baltic States and Kaliningrad

Estonia, Latvia, and Lithuania can be counted among the winners of the Cold War, although they continue to share a common fear and mistrust of Russia. Through the Baltics one can observe how the west will deal with an uncertain and diminished Russian colossus, which continues to instill fear and wariness in all other Baltic Sea states. This region is the gateway to Russia and contains one of Europe's most complicated geopolitical challenges: how to provide protection for Estonia, Latvia, and Lithuania. Their security is a kind of political and moral litmus test for the extent to which Russia has genuinely changed and has shed its age-old imperial aspirations.

The Soviet Union dominated the Baltic states from 1940 to 1941 and again from 1944 to 1991. All three faced myriad challenges in 1991 and after: They were severed from their traditional markets and had to introduce new currencies, establish from scratch their own military forces, negotiate the departure of former Soviet troops, start cleaning up the environmental damage they had caused, adopt new constitutions and sets of laws, and organize their first democratic elections in a half-century.

This dramatic turn in history did not automatically eradicate the legacies of an overbearing Soviet empire. In order to maintain control over a sprawling multinational state and promote its own socialist industrialization, the Kremlin had intentionally mixed peoples and capriciously changed borders. When Soviet rule ended, sizable Russian minorities were left in both Estonia and Latvia. The Baltic states hold Russia responsible for their loss of independence in 1940; for the disappearance of about a fifth of their populations due to deportation, execution, or exile; for the reminders of Soviet rule in their countries, such as gray, unaesthetic buildings and environmental destruction; and for the fact that they fell far behind the other Nordic countries economically during a half-century of subjugation.

Although Balts strive to work constructively with Russia, they are not inclined to show the kind of fealty to which Russia is accustomed. Many Russians have difficulty adjusting to the new reality and claim the right to obedient ex-dependencies, who should adopt a deferential attitude. Some are not yet ready to tolerate the prospect that the Baltic states are free from Moscow's sphere of influence. Article 61 of the Russian Federation's constitution includes a right of intervention and a role as protectress of 25 million Diaspora Russians, whom it officially calls "compatriots." The Baltic states are troubled by such claims of special privileges in Russia's "near abroad," especially after Russia-Ukraine hostilities since 2014.

These three states have as many differences as similarities. They are all small in geography and population, have a history of repeated foreign domination and of only a few decades of independence in the 20th century, and have experienced humiliation and exploitation by the Soviet Union. Nevertheless, they are three very different nations with separate languages. Estonian is a Finno-Ugric language related to that of Finland, a country with which Estonia has very close relations. Latvian and Lithuanian are ancient Indo-European languages. The three are mutually incomprehensible. There are differing ethnic mixes, as well as cultural heritages. For example, the Catholic Church has played a special role in Lithuania, while religion is less important in Protestant Estonia. Finally, these three countries had little experience or inclination to cooperate closely with each other before the late 1980s. Even today their cooperation, although extensive, is pragmatic and has its limits.

All three newly independent states proceeded rapidly to hold free elections and to establish the kind of institutional and legal conditions that place them within the western political model. They have all developed multiparty systems in which democratic procedures are respected. Despite frequent changes of coalitions and cabinets, they have maintained underlying political stability while demonstrating that power can be transferred peacefully from one coalition government to another. In Latvia and Lithuania but not in Estonia, parties of former communists have been able to win power. However, they relinquished it when they no longer had the voters' support.

They have entered a network of international governmental organizations (IGOs) to internationalize their security concerns until they became NATO members in April 2004. They joined the UN and CSCE (now OSCE) in September 1991 and the Council of the Baltic Sea States (CBSS) in 1992. The 12-member CBSS, which has a rotating presidency, a secretariat, and working groups and committees, also embraces the Nordic states (including non-Baltic Norway and Iceland), Germany, Poland, and Russia. It is a forum to discuss a variety of common issues ranging from the environment and trade to cross border police cooperation. It is of declining importance, even as the Baltic region is watched keenly by the west because of resurgent Russia's energy clout and spending power. The Baltic states entered the North Atlantic Cooperation Council (NACC, now Euro-Atlantic Partnership Council—EAPC) in 1992 and the Council of Europe in 1993.

In 1994 Lithuania became the first to apply officially for NATO membership, followed shortly later by the other two. Lithuania also forged a "strategic partnership" with Poland in 1997 and created with it a joint battalion, LITPOL-BAT, which is interoperable with NATO and prepared to contribute to its security interests. These are only a few of the increasingly tight relationships Poland and Lithuania are forging with each other. Because Lithuania provides the only logical "land bridge" between Russia and its enclave in Kaliningrad, Moscow viewed NATO application as a provocative act. But all three Baltic states noted the wording in the NATO summit declaration in 1994 that "we expect and would welcome NATO expansion." With quiet American encouragement, Denmark became the most visible champion of Baltic applications to NATO. The three quickly joined NATO's Partnership for Peace (PfP) as a concrete means for integrating Baltic defenses, achieving NATO standards and demonstrating the value of their contributions to western security efforts.

Together they created the Baltic Airspace Surveillance Network (BALTNET), a radar monitoring system, steered by Norway. After the three were admitted to NATO, BALTNET was included in NATO's integrated air-defense system, NATINADS, and that of Finland, a country with whom Estonia operates a joint coast guard and marine-surveillance service. The Baltic Squadron (BALTRON), led by Germany and headquartered in Tallinn, Estonia, was interoperable with NATO and organized to clear mines and engage in such international naval exercises as "Open Spirit '98." It also became integrated into NATO's naval forces. The Baltic Battalion (BALTBAT), with support and guidance from Britain and the Nordic countries and with a rotating tri-national command structure, was trained to participate in UN peacekeeping operations, such as in Bosnia with Danish soldiers. Having fulfilled its mission, it was terminated in 2003.

A permanent Baltic Defense College (BALTDEFCOL), supported mainly by the Nordic countries to provide Baltic officers with interoperable training in English, is located in Tartu, Estonia. Upon acceptance into NATO, it became the main education institution to train Baltic soldiers in NATO standards. In 2002 Baltic liaison officers began serving at the headquarters of a multinational corps in Szczecin, Poland, commanded by Poland and including a German and a Danish division. After it suffered a serious cyberattack (sometimes

Introduction: Nordic, Central, and Southeastern Europe

referred to as "Web War 1") from Russia in 2007 in the midst of an emotional dispute over moving a Soviet war monument out of the center of Tallinn, Estonia hosts NATO's Center of Excellence for Cyber Defense in a former Soviet barracks. Estonian experts were dispatched to Georgia in 2008 during its war with Russia to advise on such defense.

Open for cooperation and given potential membership, the military forces of all three countries participated in NATO maneuvers. In 1998 Lithuania hosted 5,000 soldiers, including Americans, Danes, Norwegians, Germans, and Balts, with Russians, Ukrainians, and Belarusians present as observers.

The US communicated that it would like to see Russia and the Baltics develop good neighborly relations. This was made most explicit on January 16, 1998, when the American president endorsed in principle their desire to join the Atlantic Alliance by signing with the three Baltic presidents a "Charter of Partnership." It was not a guarantee of future NATO membership or American protection, and it set no timetable for such membership. But it put on record Washington's "real, profound and enduring interest" in Baltic security and the conviction that the three new democracies had as much right to join NATO as did the three ex-communist countries that joined in 1999: Poland, Hungary, and the Czech Republic. In return, the Baltic nations committed themselves to work toward good relations with all neighbors, including Russia.

Russian leaders expressed no objection when in December 2002 all three Baltic states were offered EU membership for May 2004. However, NATO was another matter. For a long time, they had rejected assurances from Baltic governments that NATO was not directed toward Russia. Russians are divided on how they should react to NATO enlargement. Nevertheless, many moderate and extremist political elements in Russia maintain that NATO presence so close to Russia is undesirable. They directed a stream of threats to the Baltics. But by the time of NATO's November 2002 meeting in Prague, when NATO offered membership to all three, plus Slovakia, Slovenia, Romania, and Bulgaria, the Russian government had accepted Baltic membership in the Atlantic Alliance as inevitable. However, in June 2003 Russia was still worried, insisting "on clear and unambiguous guarantees that arms and armed forces of other countries will not be deployed on the territory of the Baltic States." NATO issued no such assurances, although it has no plans to deploy troops there. Estonia, Latvia and Lithuania joined NATO in Marh 2004.

A particularly delicate problem is posed by the Russian exclave of Kaliningrad, located on the southwest border of Lithuania. It is the northern part of the former East Prussia, containing the earlier German city of Königsberg. After the war, all 1.2 million German citizens were expelled. The region has the potential for economic growth. It has a deepwater harbor that is Russia's only warm-water port in the north, over 90% of the world's amber, rich farmland, modest crude oil reserves, and a well-educated workforce. However, foreign investors were scared away by endemic corruption, powerful organized crime, a drug epidemic, and Russia's highest HIV infection rate. Its future looks a bit brighter as Russia is taking a greater interest in its development. But its prospects remain uncertain and depend on general developments in Russia proper, located 300 miles away across Lithuania and Belarus.

The Baltic Sea has become one of the most important and complicated areas in the new Europe. It links nine European countries, including the continent's most populous (Russia and Germany) and some of its smallest. Democracy is practiced in each, but in some, particularly Russia, it is new and fragile and is accompanied by a weak rule of law and much corruption. Economic and informal ties are thriving all around. Along the western coast are some of the world's most prosperous nations; along the eastern is poverty, especially in Russia. Eyes are on the Baltic states because the ways they grapple with fundamental problems of economic transformation and modernization provide insights and inspiration for other ex-communist countries.

Germany in Central Europe

No western country has such long-standing historical, political, and economic ties to central and eastern Europe as does Germany. For the first time since Germany's initial unification in 1871, this "land of the middle" is surrounded by nine friendly neighbors, more than most countries have. Before 1945 Germany's relationship in and with central Europe (Mitteleuropa) was ambivalent. Germany's central position had always dominated discussions about it. Some Germans perceived Mitteleuropa as a cover for German cultural imperialism. Any notion of it as bringing Germany and the east together in some beneficial way perished in the World War II. Everything changed after that, and many Germans have negative memories of the expulsions, the flight, the homelessness, and the missing loved ones. Most central Europeans also find the earlier notion of Mitteleuropa repugnant because it was identified with German hegemony and violence; therefore, the term practically disappeared from usage.

Germany's defeat in the World War II temporarily diminished its influence in the region. The Yalta Agreement of February 1945 left the area within the Soviet Union's sphere of influence. Once the FRG had recovered from the economic devastation of the war, it rekindled its involvement in the east through trade (Osthandel) and its policy of political cooperation and tension reduction (Ostpolitik). Very quickly the FRG became the "East bloc's" most important trading partner. It is through its economic prowess, not the fact that it has Europe's largest military force outside of Russia, that Germany is so important in the area.

Baltic Defence College, Tartu, Estonia

Introduction: Nordic, Central, and Southeastern Europe

Slovak electoral poster favoring NATO and EU

By 1989 Germany's "economic miracle" had become the model for eastern transformation. At the same time, eastern countries looked at Germany's Basic Law (constitution), political institutions, and central bank (Bundesbank) for examples. A host of semiprivate foundations, including those sponsored by Germany's political parties and subsidized by the state, fanned out to help teach Germany's political, economic, and social values and experiences. Alone among western nations, Germany demonstrated a real commitment to strengthen political stability in the region through economic assistance. It provided far more aid than any other country, including the United States, mostly in the form of loans issued at favorable interest rates.

The economic and political foothold that Germany gradually regained in the four decades after the war gave it a running start in the post-Cold War era. As the central European countries' (and eastern Germany's) trade with the former Soviet Union collapsed, their trade relations were rapidly reoriented westward. Germany's trade with the region jumped by 30% between 1993 and 1995 and soon surpassed its trade volume with the United States. By the end of the century, it exceeded its trade with France, Germany's single-most important trading partner. Germany is the most significant trading partner for Poland, the Czech Republic, and Hungary, conducting a tenth of its foreign commerce with them.

Germany also became the region's main source of foreign investment, even though by 1998 only about 6% of Germany's total flowed into the area; 80% went to only three states: Poland, the Czech Republic, and Hungary. In that year, a fifth of all foreign direct investments in the region were from Germany, compared with 14.6% from the United States, 10.4% from the Netherlands, 7.7% from France, and 7.5% from Austria. This focus on the four Visegrad states (Poland, Czech Republic, Slovakia, and Hungary) reveals the important distinction Germany makes between these countries, which have successfully introduced economic reform and recovery and political stability, and the former Soviet republics (except the Baltics) and Balkan countries, which have not. Germany does more trade with its central European neighbors than with Russia, and this is facilitated by improved roads and telecommunications, plus membership in the EU.

Germany has been one of the most energetic promoters of eastward enlargement of both NATO and the EU. Both of these organizations provide protection both for and from Germany. Because Germany enjoys close ties with the United States, central and eastern Europeans see it as an important bridge to the transatlantic alliance.

NATO is widely regarded in the region as the only credible guarantor of the new democracies' independence from Russia. In 1993 Germany became the first NATO ally to advocate the alliance's eastward enlargement, even before the Clinton administration embraced it. America's leaders soon followed suit partly as a result of intense lobbying on the part of Presidents Lech Wałęsa of Poland and Vaclav Havel of the Czech Republic.

Former chancellor Gerhard Schröder noted in 1999, "Berlin has always served as the bridge to our central and eastern European partners. We are convinced that the European Union should not be limited only to the western part of the continent." For that reason, Germany took the lead in sponsoring early EU membership for Poland, Hungary, and the Czech Republic. For the new democracies to the east, Germany is a source of both assistance and concern. Because of its trade and energy dependence on Russia (it gets 40% of its gas and 35% of its oil from Russia), Germany attempts a difficult balancing act to satisfy both its desire for good relations with Russia and its support for new allies in the Baltics and central Europe who fear a resurgent Russia. There are fears that it tilts too much toward Moscow. Smaller allies are reminded of Bismarck's declaration in 1863: "A good treaty with Russia" is the secret to politics.

Although intended to apply only to Czech circumstances, the words of former President Vaclav Havel expressed in 1995 apply to all central and eastern European nations, who must deal with a new but always large, dynamic, and economically powerful Germany. Referring to the complicated tangle of expectations and fears, combined with the differences in size and prosperity, he said, "Germany is both our inspiration and our pain; a source of understandable traumas and many prejudices and misconceptions, as well as the standards against which we measure ourselves; some see Germany as our greatest hope, others as our greatest danger."

No country influences the transformation of central Europe more than does Germany. Yet its predominance does not

Introduction: Nordic, Central, and Southeastern Europe

extend to the cultural sphere even though its cultural presence is increasing. English has become the undisputedly dominant second language, except in the Czech Republic. There is an increasing demand for business German, and the Goethe Institute estimates that three-quarters of the 20 million foreigners learning German live in east-central Europe. A 2002 EU survey determined that, in the eight new central European member states that joined in 2004, 17% claimed to be able to carry on a conversation in German. The Slovenians had the best command (36%), followed by the Czechs (27%) and the Slovaks (22%). One in five claimed to speak English. Nevertheless, it is American popular culture that reigns, both in the region and in Germany itself.

Austria in Central Europe

Austria sees itself as especially qualified for the role of a "bridge-builder" between East and West. Until its collapse in 1918, the Austro-Hungarian Empire encompassed most of central Europe, much of the Balkans, northeastern Italy, and the western part of Ukraine. From 1945 to 1955, it was occupied by the four victorious allied powers, and it regained its full sovereignty after agreeing to remain a neutral country. It did not join the EU until 1995, and it still remains outside of NATO. At least since the Congress of Vienna in 1814–1815, it has been the location for important international meetings. In 1990 NATO and the Warsaw Pact (the former military alliance binding the Soviet Union

with its eastern European satellites) signed the Conventional Forces in Europe (CFE) Agreement, which reduced conventional weapons between the Atlantic and Urals and established confidence-building measures to give each side advanced notice of troop movements and missile launches. Russia refused to renew the treaty in December 2007.

Since the collapse of communism in Europe, Austrians see themselves in a totally new situation. Before 1989 they were in a kind of cul-de-sac, surrounded on three sides by the communist bloc; now that dead end has been transformed into an intersection with a bustling thoroughfare opening into the east. One Austrian diplomat put it this way: "We used to be on the eastern fringe of Western Europe; now we are in the center of Europe again." Leaving from Vienna, one travels westward to get to the Slovene capital of Ljubljana or the Czech capital of Prague. Austria and Hungary liberalized their border relations so much that in 1989 Hungary dismantled the electronically monitored fences and watchtowers along the Austro-Hungarian border. This opportunity to render a dramatic humanitarian gesture was a key link in the chain of events that led to the unification of Germany.

As communism was collapsing, Austria helped form the Pentagonale, joined by Italy, Hungary, Czechoslovakia, and Yugoslavia, to foster a project-centered approach to issues of international affairs, such as the environment, where more progress can be made through regional

negotiations. The former Yugoslav Republic of Slovenia, which borders on Austria and formerly belonged to the Austro-Hungarian Empire, has strengthened its economic and political ties with Austria. The Slovak capital Bratislava is close to Austria and has been turning more to Vienna than to Prague. Involved in more than 8,000 joint ventures with its eastern neighbors (4,000 in Hungary alone), Austria is becoming more deeply integrated with eastern Europe.

Czech Republic, Slovak Republic, Hungary, and Poland in Central Europe

Central Europe, whose history has been determined by the rivalries of great powers—Germany, Austria-Hungary, and Russia—is more complicated than western Europe. In the 20th century, it was the source of conflict from which the World War II and the Cold War emerged. Culturally it has always belonged to the west, but it was chained to the east after 1945. The US, Britain, and Soviet Union agreed to this division at the Yalta Conference in February 1945, and thereafter the word "Yalta" became in the minds of central Europeans shorthand for the artificial and unwanted division of Europe. The victorious powers imposed a heavily armed deterrence system on the region that precluded any choice on the part of the countries themselves.

There is no universally accepted meaning of the term "central Europe," which has been changing over time. In some ways, it is more a state of mind and expression of sentiment than a geographic reality. Its borders in all directions are open to dispute. The preference for the term "central Europe" is a reflection of the sense of belonging to the west rather than to the east. In 1983 a well-known Czech writer, Milan Kundera, wrote a famous article entitled "The Tragedy of Central Europe." He argued that central Europe had always belonged spiritually and culturally to the west rather than to the east. It had participated completely in the major cultural movements of the west, including the Reformation, the Renaissance, and the Enlightenment. But the area had been "kidnapped, displaced and brainwashed" by the Soviet Union after 1945 and had been forced to become "eastern Europe." Kundera's rejection of the loaded term "eastern Europe" was a direct challenge to the legitimacy of Moscow's control over the region, and he was joined by many dissidents, intellectuals, and Pope John Paul II from Poland.

In the midst and wake of the 1989 revolutions in the Soviet Union's European empire, the term "central Europe" was used by those who wanted an alternative to a Europe split into two blocs and

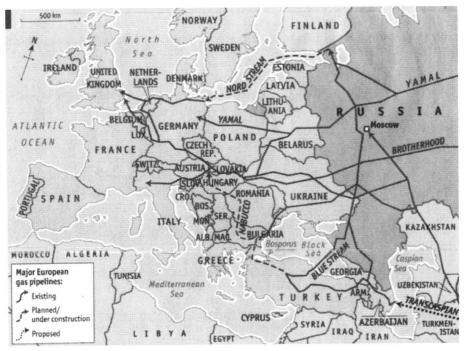

Source: *The Economist*

7

Introduction: Nordic, Central, and Southeastern Europe

who wished to see their small countries as subjects, not mere objects and captives, of European politics. Recognizing this sentiment, former U.S. Assistant Secretary of State Richard Holbrooke declared in 1994 that Poland, the Czech Republic, the Slovak Republic, Hungary, Slovenia, and Croatia would henceforth be called by that designation. Over time, terms "central and eastern Europe" came into vogue among Western countries in order to make the countries of the former Soviet Union feel more wanted in the new Europe.

Slovenians prefer to be ranked in this category, but their relatively well-developed country, as well as Croatia, is treated in this book with ex-Yugoslavia because of its pre-1991 history. The first three and the southern strip of Poland had been parts of the Austro-Hungarian Empire and had enjoyed a limited amount of self-rule and greater tolerance than the subjects of the other empires that exercised control in the region, especially Russia and Ottoman Türkiye. Always aware of being located between Germany and Russia, they have experienced repeated invasion and occupation throughout the centuries. This was facilitated by geographic factors. The area between the Baltic Sea and the northern Carpathian Mountains (which generally extend in a west-east direction in southern Poland, western Ukraine, and northern Romania) is a plain that offers no natural barriers to invasions from the east and west. To this is added the absence of large rivers that could slow down invading armies.

As a prelude to entering the EU, Poland, Hungary, and Czechoslovakia (which in 1993 split into the Czech and Slovak Republics) signed a "Declaration of Cooperation on the Road to Europe Integration" with each other in the Hungarian city of Visegrad. This "Visegrad Group" became the basis for the Central European Free Trade Agreement. This has no organizational structure but is a platform for ongoing consultation aimed at multilateral cooperation, harmonization of social and economic policies, and preparation for EU entry.

All were in the front of the line, along with the Baltic states, Malta, and Cyprus, for admission to the EU, which happened in May 2004. The EU not only holds out the prospect of western European prosperity, but it also offers the small states in the region a kind of equality with larger states they never had experienced before. Poland, the Czech Republic, and Hungary were admitted to NATO in 1999. Membership in the Atlantic Alliance is prized because it offers security from a resurgent Russia, which all of the countries in the region north of the Balkans continue to fear. The EU's and NATO's magnetic

attraction on countries to the east makes the region's western frontier more fluid and blurred than ever before.

The region's new powerhouse is Poland, whose 38 million inhabitants constitute the largest population in the entire region outside of Germany. Before the collapse of the Soviet Union in December 1991, Poland had only three neighbors, none of which exists today: the Soviet Union, Czechoslovakia, and East Germany. Now it has seven. For the first time in a millennium, Poland is at peace with all its neighbors, and for the first time in more than a century, it feels safe on its eastern and western borders. It has developed particularly close relations with Germany, the Czech Republic, and Slovakia. Its rapid political and economic transformation makes it an especially important model and trading partner for Lithuania and Ukraine. It is not afraid to threaten to use its veto in EU councils if it thinks its interests are being disregarded.

Poland has established a link with both Germany and France called the Weimar Triangle, named after the venue of its first meeting in 1991. It wants to widen its Western contacts in order to reduce its possible dependence on Germany. The Weimar Triangle, which brings together the three countries' heads of state and government, ministers, and parliamentary leaders for informal talks on fundamental matters of mutual interest, does just that. The foreign ministers of the three partners also join hands in crisis management, as they had attempted in a turbulent Ukraine in 2014.

Another innovative institution located on the Polish-German border, in Szczecin, is a Northeast Multinational Corps consisting of Polish, German, and Danish troops, commanded by a Polish officer. This military cooperation, supplemented by a dramatic increase in German-Polish exercises and interaction (second only to that between the US and Poland), is symptomatic of a new spirit in Polish-German relations. Together the two countries provide the bulk of NATO forces in the east, even though Poland insists that the US is and will remain its key military partner. NATO membership gives Poland and other central European countries more confidence to deal with their eastern neighbors, especially Russia. Nevertheless, they are mindful of a Russian resurgence. Therefore, Poland unequivocally supported the admission of the Baltic states into NATO.

Southeastern Europe

South of central Europe is a cluster of countries that we call Southeastern Europe, despite the countless differences that exist among them. Most of them are relatively new states that have nevertheless been

shaped by important historical factors as well as by geography. One of Europe's earliest divisions emerged a millennium ago between Roman Catholicism in the west and Orthodox Christianity in the east. The differences between these two religions' ideas led to a fundamental variance in political and social institutions. Most southeastern European countries were Orthodox; only Slovenia and Croatia were Roman Catholic.

Beginning in the 14th century, another defining influence came with the Ottoman Turkish conquest and occupation, which finally ended only in the early 20th century. The Turks imposed their own political and social institutions, which cut the area off from the political and economic developments occurring in the rest of Europe. Among the many cultural legacies such long oriental rule left in the region was Islam, which is the prevailing religion in Albania and Kosovo and a significant minority religion in Bosnia and Herzegovina and North Macedonia. All these cultural, political, and religious features provided barriers from those parts of Europe to the west and north.

The same role was played by geography. The mountainous terrain of the Balkans (whose name is derived from the Turkish word for mountainous area) south of the broad Danube Plain, combined with the enclosure formed by the Black, Aegean, and Adriatic Seas, partially sealed the area off from the west.

There are few navigable rivers that could serve as trade corridors as the Rhine River does in western Europe by connecting five countries to the Atlantic Ocean. The Danube traverses the whole region, but its flow is not toward the west but southeasterly from Germany into the Black Sea. Until 1992 it was not navigable all the way and was iced over during the winter. Also, in the past, the Turks always controlled its lower reaches. The Main-Danube Canal, completed in 1992, has connected the Danube to the Rhine River. But until 2003 man-made barriers prevented the uninterrupted traffic from western Europe to the Black Sea and back: In the 1999 Kosovo war, NATO planes destroyed some of the bridges in Serbia, and the ruins prevented ships from passing them. In 2003 the last debris was cleared from the Danube's navigation channels, and large ships could pass. Other rivers in the region are navigable only for short distances.

Southeastern Europe also has fewer essential raw materials, such as fuel, coal, and iron ore, than does central Europe. The facts that such resources were located in places like northern Bohemia (Czech Republic) and southern Poland and that good transport links connected Budapest with markets and materials helped those

Introduction: Nordic, Central, and Southeastern Europe

Wayne Thompson, author of previous editions of this book, in Gdańsk (Danzig), Poland

areas develop economically. Despite some oil fields in Romania and coalfields in Serbia, the absence of adequate quantities of raw materials hampered the industrialization of southeastern Europe and helps explain the continued economic gap that exists between it and other parts of Europe.

Greece, Türkiye, Romania, Bulgaria, Albania, Russia, Ukraine, Georgia, Moldova, Azerbaijan, and Armenia founded the Black Sea Economic Cooperation Group in 1992, with Poland and Slovakia having observer status. Deeply rooted historical animosities among some of its members, as well as a fragile economic and political environment in the region, have prevented the group from being as effective as its founders had hoped.

In the Balkans, some countries have progressed well in their post-communist transformation, such as Slovenia and Croatia after the death of Franjo Tudjman, and most others have gone or are going through serious difficulties. The 1999 war in Kosovo and the peacekeeping that followed it brought the EU into the region in an unprecedented way. It assumed important responsibility for the reconstruction of the Balkans.

Slovenia and Croatia were the first of the ex-Yugoslav Balkan countries to enter the EU—Slovenia in 2004, and Croatia in 2013. The accession negotiations are under way with Montenegro (since 2012), Serbia (since 2014), North Macedonia (since 2020), and Bosnia and Herzegovina (recognized as a "candidate country" for accession since 2022).

In 2014, the Berlin Process was set up as a platform for high-level cooperation between high official representatives of the Western Balkan countries (Western Balkan Six) and their peers in Berlin Process host countries (Austria, Bulgaria, Croatia, France, Germany, Greece, Italy, Slovenia, Poland as well as the United Kingdom while it was an EU member until January 2020). The Process also involves the EU institutions, international financial institutions, and the region's civil society, youth, and businesses. The Berlin Process aims at utilizing the potential of increased regional cooperation in the Western Balkans to bring the region closer to the EU. The Process fosters specific projects to increase connectivity in the region, as well as good neighborly relations and interpersonal relationships, while subsequently supporting the EU integration.

But closer regional cooperation is also being promoted by the Open Balkan initiative, which originated in the region itself. (See Serbia)

Kosovo, which declared its independence from Serbia in February 2008, appears to have become a long-term protectorate of the EU and NATO. According to international law, Serbia does not recognize the unilateral secession of its territory, which is also contrary to the Constitution of Serbia. As stated by Resolution 1244 of the United Nations Security Council, the entire territory of Kosovo and Metohija, legally speaking, is part of Serbia until a final solution is reached. Nevertheless, the Kosovo government based in Priština has de facto authority over most of the territory, while authorities of Serbia function in the north and Serbian enclaves.

The Eastern Balkan countries Romania and Bulgaria gained admittance to NATO in 2004 and joined the EU in 2007.

In order to present Mediterranean Europe together, Greece and Cyprus (which entered the EU in May 2004, despite its continued division into Greek- and Turkish-speaking sectors) are presented in the Western Europe book of this series. This is not to say that Greece plays no role in the Balkans. On the contrary, as the Balkan country that belongs to both NATO and EU, it bears special responsibility in the area.

The Nordic Countries

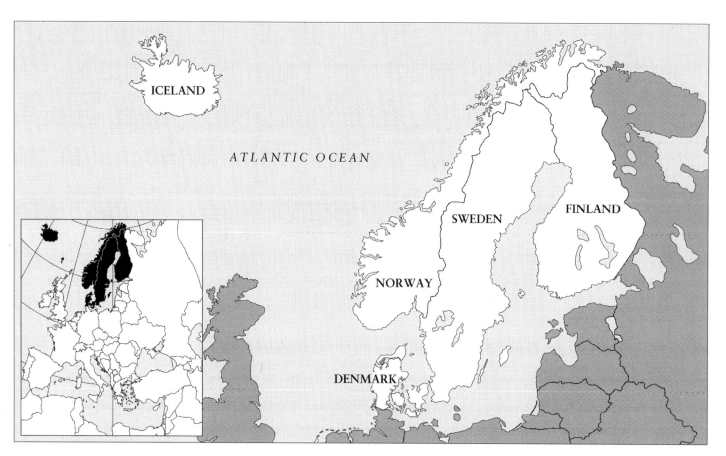

The People

Prosperous, peaceful, harmonious, with a stable, democratic political order and beautiful, unspoiled, and sparsely populated territories on the outskirts of Europe are words that typify this area of the world. These are things that are often associated with the Nordic area, which encompasses Sweden, Norway, Denmark, Iceland, and Finland, or, more narrowly, to Scandinavia, a term generally applied to the first three. Indeed, at first glance, these countries seem to have escaped many of the most severe problems that have afflicted postwar Europe. Yet, a closer look reveals that they share some important economic and social problems with the rest of Europe. Further, they are by no means so isolated from the world as many people often think.

Although the Nordic countries have chosen to take different paths on many matters, they have many things in common. Geographically, they are all located on the same latitude as Alaska and Siberia, but they are warmed by Atlantic currents, which make them more habitable. Also, they are comfortably set apart from Europe, and Iceland, Sweden, Norway (except for a short stretch at the northern tip), and parts of Denmark are separated from Europe by water. Thus, they have been spared many of Europe's violent conflicts. For at least two centuries, their populations have been too small to permit

any grand-scale political activity outside their sphere. They have therefore had the luxury of being able to concentrate on their own affairs and to develop, to a great extent, at their own speed and in their own preferred way.

The 27.6 million citizens of the Nordic countries have minimal language problems among themselves. Except for Finnish, which is related to Estonian and distantly to Hungarian, all other Nordic languages are of northern Germanic origin. To help maintain a lingual tie to the other countries, Finland retains Swedish as an official language together with Finnish. Danes, Swedes, Norwegians, and, to some extent, Icelanders can read each other's languages, and with patience and good-will, they can make themselves understood when speaking, although Danish presents some difficulties to Swedes and Norwegians, and Icelandic presents greater problems to all three. These language ties and proximity enable Nordic officials to cooperate closely.

English is becoming the Nordic countries' lingua franca. At the University of Copenhagen, most doctoral theses in the natural sciences are being published in English, and many universities throughout the region offer a multitude of courses and programs in English. Many large companies, such as Finland's Nokia, use English as their official language. Nevertheless,

laws in most Nordic nations promote the use of the local language in official publications and broadcasting.

The Nordic peoples also share many cultural values. One of the most important is Lutheran Christianity, to which most, at least nominally, belong. Lutheranism in Scandinavia is void of religious fanaticism. Although most citizens are baptized and married in the church and voluntarily pay their church taxes in some countries (no longer in Sweden since 2000), few attend church regularly. All of the Nordic countries are highly secularized in that religious dogma or considerations play a very small role in the everyday lives and politics of the people. By the middle of the 19th century, religious freedom and tolerance were practiced in all Nordic countries and helped to bolster tolerance in the political and social spheres, as well.

Most persons in these countries tend to take a practical, unemotional approach to politics that stresses compromise, stability, and continuity. Compromise is necessary because all have proportional representation electoral systems, which always grant parliamentary seats to a large number of parties. Therefore, a single party almost never wins a majority of parliamentary seats, and the countries must be ruled by either minority or coalition governments. These lands do have fewer social tensions than some other European countries, and over the years, most of their citizens have developed a kind of immunity to totalitarian ideologies or unrealizable political demands.

All of the Nordic countries entered the second half of the 19th century as relatively poor agricultural societies and experienced the Industrial Revolution rather late. Industrialization brought greater wealth, but it also brought many problems. At the same time that they underwent fundamental social and economic changes, they adopted democratic political practices. As a result of many compromises between the traditional ruling elites and the newly developing or increasingly self-confident middle, working, and farming classes, more people were allowed to vote, and the governments became answerable to popularly elected parliaments rather than to the Swedish, Danish, and (after 1905) Norwegian monarchs. In characteristic Nordic style, this process of democratization took place largely without violent revolutions or coups d'etat. These peoples generally have had a good sense of timing in changing outdated practices or structures in order to be able to preserve that which is worth preserving. Also, they have had a genius for solving political, social, and religious issues in such a way that the losers are never left permanently unreconciled to the system and with bitter determination to revive the dispute later.

The Earliest Period

The common ties among these countries did not emerge overnight but in the course of centuries of mutual collaboration. In Denmark there is evidence of human settlements as early as 50,000 BC, and by 10,000 BC, communities began to be established all over Scandinavia. Although some trade gradually developed with the rest of the continent, Europe did not take much notice of the Nordic area. The Romans did not bother with this region at all, except for a small volume of trade in amber. Tacitus did refer to a tribe of people in Sweden known as the Svear, from whom the name Sverige (Sweden) was derived. The Romans also engaged in combat with Cimbri, Vandals, and other Scandinavian groups.

The Vikings
(Norsemen, Northmen, Normans)

This inconspicuous existence ended abruptly in the beginning of the 9th century, when the Vikings burst out of Scandinavia and began venturing in sturdy ships far from their own lands. They sometimes established colonies and traded peacefully, but they often pillaged and plundered, leaving wastelands in their wake. Most Europeans learned to pray for protection from the Viking's ravaging, and the

institution of feudalism was, in part, a response to the widespread willingness of a common people to exchange their liberties for protection.

A notable twist probably occurred in Russia. In the 9th century, warlike Slav tribes were weary of rampant strife. The Vikings were using Russian rivers for trade. The local tribes, according to The Russian Primary Chronicle of the 12th century, actually invited the Vikings to become their rulers. The "Varangian Russes," called Variagi in Russian, were Norman (Norsemen, Northmen, Vikings) who founded the first Russian dynasty. This part of the Chronicle is vigorously disputed in Russia today—the idea that outsiders had to be called in to bring order to the area is offensive. It is indisputable, however, that the Vikings ventured all the way to the Black Sea, Constantinople, and the Mediterranean Sea during this period.

The Vikings sailed to the British Isles, (establishing settlements in England, the Hebrides Islands, Shetlands, and Isle of Man), Ireland (whose capital of Dublin was a Viking fortress), Normandy, and Iceland. From the latter island, Erik the Red discovered and named Greenland in 981 or 982 AD, where he established a settlement on the southwest tip. His son, Leif Eriksson, sailed from Greenland to the northeast coast of North America around the year 1000 AD, beating Christopher Columbus to the New World by about five centuries. In the US, Leif Eriksson Day is celebrated on October 9 of each year. By the middle of the 11th century, the Vikings had reached their peak and dominated most of the sea shipping routes around Europe and Orkney. The boldness and restlessness of such modern Norwegian explorers as Roald Amundsen and Thor

Heyerdahl show that some Scandinavians still have the adventuresome spirit of their forebears.

Christianity

Viking marauding had brought considerable wealth to the Nordic area. But it also caused a serious drain on the tribes' manpower and threatened to make the Nordic lands vulnerable to outside attacks. They began to settle down, and the regional tribal communities gradually gave way to larger kingdoms. Christianity, which had been introduced to Sweden as early as 830 AD, along with other European influences, began to filter more and more into the Nordic area through the peninsula of Jutland. Norway's national hero and symbol of its nationality, St. Olaf, was a commander who brought Christianity to the land in the 11th century. By the 12th century, Christianity had spread to all corners of the area, and with the pope's blessing, the Swedes conducted crusades in Finland, which became a part of the Swedish realm.

Medieval Norway

In the 13th century, Norway, which had been united into one nation by the end of the 9th century, reached the peak of its power. It took possession of Greenland and Iceland. Norwegian culture also reached its high point and was described vividly and imaginatively in the sagas of Snorre Sturlason. The terrible bubonic plague, known in Europe as the Black Death, from 1349–1350 struck the region with full fury. One-half of Norway's population perished. This accelerated the economic and cultural decline of Norway, which became a predominantly peasant nation during the following centuries.

The Nordic Countries

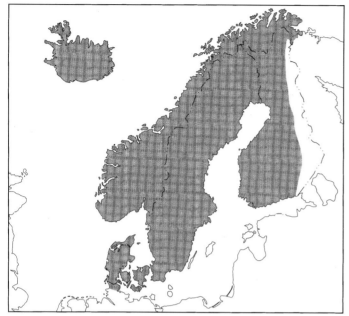

1397: Union of Kalmar (under Denmark)

1523: Swedish independence

Contests for Supremacy

Throughout the ensuing centuries, Denmark and Sweden vied for domination over the Nordic region. Not until the 20th century were Norway, Finland, and Iceland able to win full independence. Every Nordic nation was at one time ruled, at least in part, by another Nordic neighbor. The only exception was Denmark, which had experienced German rule. By the end of the 14th century, it appeared that Denmark would control all of northern Europe. In the late 12th and early 13th centuries, it had already begun to expand to other territories along the northern and southern Baltic coasts. In 1380 it acquired Iceland and the Faroe Islands, and by 1387 its domination extended over Norway. Denmark's political domination over the region was formalized when in 1397 Denmark, Norway, and Sweden merged to form the Union of Kalmar—essentially a Nordic empire. Apart from Iceland and the Faroe Islands, it also comprised the old Norwegian overseas dependencies of the Shetlands and the Orkney Islands, as well as Åland and Finland, which were under Swedish rule during the Middle Ages. Thus, the Union linked all five Nordic nations together in a single kingdom under Danish leadership. It also helped to curtail German commercial predominance in the region, which had threatened to lead to German political domination as well, especially in Sweden.

The Union of Kalmar began to break down after Queen Margrete died in 1412. Swedish nationalism had begun to grow, and by the middle of the 14th century, Swedes had developed a set of laws that applied to the whole nation. In the 15th century, they increasingly resisted Danish domination, and in 1434, a peasant uprising, supported by some noblemen, was directed against Danish rule. This event led to the convocation of the first Riksdag (Swedish parliament) in 1435. King Christian II of Denmark sent an army against the Swedes and in 1520 had himself crowned in Stockholm as the hereditary monarch. There was a good chance that he could pacify the Swedes after he had promised a general amnesty for all opponents.

However, he broke his promise and ordered the decapitation of 80 leading Swedes. This disgusting and politically unwise bloodbath prompted the young Swedish nobleman and first genuine national hero, Gustav Eriksson Vasa, to lead a successful rebellion against the Danes. In 1523 Vasa was declared the first truly Swedish king, taking the name of Gustav I and exercising authority over all of Sweden, except the southernmost provinces, which continued to belong to Denmark until 1658. The Union of Kalmar ceased to exist, although the Swedes and Danes continued for another century and a half to struggle for supremacy in Scandinavia.

The Reign of Gustav I and the Emergence of Sweden

This is generally known as the Vasa period and was extremely important for Sweden's later development. Not only did Gustav I establish Swedish independence, but, like Henry VIII of England, he also severed Sweden's ties with the Catholic Church in 1527, creating the Lutheran State Church, and supported the Reformation. In fact, all over the Nordic

The house of King Gustav I in Delecarlia

area, the Reformation succeeded quickly and with little resistance. Therefore, these countries were left with only tiny religious minorities and were spared the kind of religious divisions and tensions that continued to plague many European countries for centuries. Gustav I also created a centralized national administration, which was essential for Sweden's era as a great European power from 1611 to 1718, generally referred to as the Age of Greatness. During this period, Sweden flourished economically, culturally, politically, and militarily.

Today, it is difficult to imagine that a nation of only a million inhabitants could conduct successful military campaigns against the then, great powers of Denmark, Poland, and Russia. When the Thirty Years' War began to rage in the heart of Europe in 1618, Sweden initially kept out of the struggle and instead continued to concentrate on broadening its foothold in the eastern Baltic. The result of this policy was that the Baltic became a Swedish lake that could be used only under Swedish terms.

By contrast, Denmark rushed headlong into the tragic, ostensibly religious, Thirty Years' War and sought to expand its influence southward. Its military adventures in northern Germany provoked the ravishing of Jutland by marauding Catholic troops. In 1630 a battered Denmark was forced to sue for peace; in the same year, Sweden decided to enter the bloody struggle because of the Catholic armies' advances toward

the Baltic area and the serious reversals that the Protestant princes had suffered in the first half of the war. King Gustavus II Adolphus, grandson of Gustav Vasa, led his Swedish troops brilliantly. He marched them all the way to Bavaria, and by the winter of 1631–1632, he could hold court in Mainz and Frankfurt am Main. He was killed in 1632 while leading his troops to victory against Catholic forces at Lutzen.

His death sapped the initiative and dynamism from Sweden's policy. Nevertheless, when Denmark attempted to take advantage of the new political void in Sweden by launching a renewed attack, the Swedes were able to respond quickly and successfully. The Danes were forced to accept a peace at Brömsebro in 1645, which underscored and solidified Sweden's predominance in Scandinavia. Not only did Denmark lose much of its territory to Sweden, but it also had to renounce its right to levy customs on Swedish goods in Oresund, the narrow strait between the two countries.

Sweden emerged as a great power from the Peace of Westphalia, which formalized the end of the terrible Thirty Years' War in 1648. It received German holdings in Pomerania, the bishoprics of Verden and Bremen, and the island of Rugen. When Denmark sought revenge in the Danish-Swedish War from 1657 to 1660, during which Sweden occupied Jutland and other Danish islands several times, it suffered even further losses. In the Peace of Copenhagen in 1660, Denmark lost all its

Swedish provinces and thereby all control over the Oresund Strait. The borders between Sweden and Denmark, which were established in this settlement, remain essentially unchanged today.

This peace signified the end of Danish dreams of being a great power. It bankrupted the country and laid waste to much of its territory. The outcome of the conflict underscored Sweden's position as the leading power in northern Europe although Denmark occasionally disputed this status in the following decades. Swedish authority extended over Finland, Estonia, Latvia, Ingermanland (Ingria in which St. Petersburg is now located), and several coastal towns, and its empire continued to grow in later years. Sweden fought many wars to expand its empire, but it was fortunate in being able to fight them mostly on foreign soil.

During the 17th century, Sweden also was able to acquire a colony in America that it called Nya Sverige ("New Sweden"). In 1638 it purchased from Indians a large tract that encompassed southeastern Pennsylvania (including the present city of Philadelphia), a chunk of New Jersey, and most of Delaware. The capital of this colony was Christina, which was later renamed Wilmington, in Delaware. Swedish and Finnish Lutheran priests, merchants, soldiers, settlers, and convicts were sent to New Sweden. The residents had relatively good contacts with the local Indians and were possibly the first settlers to introduce a particular Swedish invention into the New World: the log house. In 1655 the Dutch seized the colony following an intense border dispute, but Swedish continued to be spoken in some communities there until the late 18th century, and the Swedish Lutheran Church established its foothold in America.

The Swedes acquired from France the Caribbean Island of Saint Barthélemy in 1784. Very few people settled on this island, whose major population was black slaves, but the capital was named Gustavia after the Swedish king. In 1878 the island was sold back to France. The Swedish also established temporarily a colony called Cabo Corso in what is now Ghana in Africa. The capital was called Carlsborg, and the present-day city of Accra was the site of a Swedish factory. There were very few Swedes in this colony, beyond a governor, soldiers, and merchants.

By the beginning of the 18th century Sweden's empire had so aroused the resentment of Denmark, Russia, Poland, and Saxony (in Germany) that the latter powers decided to help themselves to some of the Swedish holdings. Despite some initial successes by the young king, Karl XII, the Swedes revealed that they had neither the manpower nor the resources

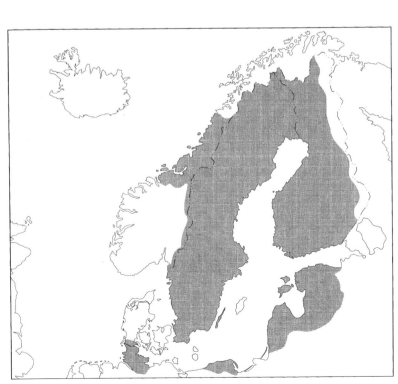

1660: Swedish dominance

The Nordic Countries

to resist for long. The country had become exhausted by constant war, and at least by 1718, Sweden's decline could no longer be denied. Its northern German territories were ceded to Prussia and Hanover by 1720, and during the Great Northern War (1709–1721) the Swedish armies were defeated in Russia, which resulted in Russian occupation of the Baltic countries and of southeastern Finland.

The Napoleonic Wars

These battles at the end of the 18th and beginning of the 19th centuries brought significant territorial changes to the region, and the ideas of the French Revolution influenced political developments in certain Nordic countries, especially Denmark and Norway. In the struggle that gripped all of Europe, Denmark tried in vain to remain neutral. However, the English feared that the country might eventually side with Napoleon, so they challenged the Danish fleet a short distance from Copenhagen in 1801 and forced Denmark to enter a formal non-aggression pact with Britain. Six years later the British again grew nervous. They demanded that Denmark hand over to them its high seas fleet and threatened to shell Copenhagen if this ultimatum was not accepted. The Danes understandably balked at this impudence, but after British ships had bombarded the capital city for four days, the disheartened Danes handed over their navy. Out of spite, they then cast their lot with Napoleon against the British, but Denmark ultimately had to pay a high price for this folly. By 1813 it was bankrupt, and in the Treaty of Kiel a year later, it was compelled to hand Norway over to Sweden, which had fought on the side of the victors.

But the Norwegians, who wanted full independence, went to war against Sweden in order to prevent one form of domination from being exchanged for another. A Norwegian national assembly had adopted one of the most liberal constitutions of its time and had selected a Danish prince as its new king. But a combination of Swedish leniency and military power during the armed confrontation of 1814 persuaded the Norwegians to accept a new arrangement. The newly selected Norwegian king abdicated, and the first Norwegian parliament (Storting) accepted the Swedish monarch as the king of Norway. Sweden assumed overall predominance in foreign policy and the right to appoint a Norwegian viceroy, who performed the normal duties of a prime minister. All Norwegian titles of nobility were abolished.

Norwegians were left with wide powers over their own affairs and with their own constitution, navy, army, customs, and legislature. In effect, Norway had complete liberty and independence within its own boundaries. In the course of the 19th century, Norwegians solidified their sense of national identity and resisted any closer relations with Sweden. Finally, in 1905 they requested in the form of a plebiscite complete independence 99.95% voted in favor. Troops on both sides of the border mobilized. However, after some internal debate, Sweden backed off and granted Norway its independence. The outcome was peaceful largely because Norway's departure from the union did not deprive Sweden of vital resources and wealth, and there were no Swedish communities left on the Norwegian side of the border. At the end of that year, Prince Carl of Denmark was chosen king and took the name Haakon VII.

Sweden's acquisition of Norway in 1814 was mild consolation for its loss of Finland five years earlier. Because Sweden had sided with Britain against the French, Napoleon had granted Russia in the Peace of Tilsit a free hand against Sweden. Thus, in 1809 Russia took Finland, a land it had dominated for a century. This bitter loss of a province that had belonged to Sweden for many centuries cost the Swedish king, Gustav IV, his crown in a bloodless coup. In the same year, the Swedish elite adopted the Instrument of Government (Regeringsformen), which, after the US Constitution, is the second-oldest still- used written document of government in the world and which is one of the four that makes up Sweden's present constitution.

In 1810 the Swedes chose one of Napoleon's field marshals, Jean-Baptiste Bernadotte, as regent. Turning on his former leader, Bernadotte led Sweden into the struggle against France, a decision that secured allied support for the Swedish acquisition of Norway. After the short campaign against that country in 1814, Sweden withdrew from European conflicts and has not been at war since. Bernadotte was crowned king in 1818 with the title of King Karl XIV Johan; he ruled until 1844, and his descendants still hold the throne. It is an irony of history that the king had once been an ardent opponent of the monarchy in France and had even reportedly had the words indelibly tattooed on his arm: "Death to Kings!" It can be assumed that he never wore short sleeves while he occupied the throne of Sweden.

The 19th Century

The 19th century was for the Nordic countries one of major political, economic, and social changes. Except for the war of Prussia and Austria against Denmark, which resulted in Denmark's loss of Schleswig and Holstein, containing about one-third of Denmark's European holdings (see Germany), this was a century of peace for the Nordic area. The French Revolution had produced a spark of democracy all over Europe, and the Nordic countries, especially Norway and Denmark, were touched by that spark. However, unlike many European countries at that time, the northern peoples already had traditions in which some groups had political representation, parliaments had some powers and monarchical authority was limited by constitutions and other barriers.

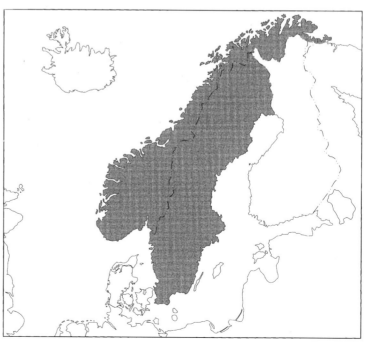

1814: Sweden loses Finland to Russia, gains Norway from Denmark

14

These foundations for modern democracy were strengthened in the course of the 1800s. Following a short outbreak of civil unrest in 1848, Denmark proclaimed a Grundlov (charter) that formally declared the country to be a constitutional monarchy, with guaranteed civil liberties and with a parliament that shared power with the crown. In Norway, municipal self-government was introduced in 1837, and in 1884 the Swedish king recognized the principle of parliamentary government in Norway by agreeing to appoint a prime minister who had the approval of a majority in the Storting. In Sweden, political power passed gradually from an aristocracy of birth to a prosperous elite of common birth, and ultimately to the middle and working classes. By the 1870s all Nordic countries had functioning representative assemblies, although full parliamentary government was not introduced into Norway until 1884, in Denmark until 1901, and in Sweden and Finland until 1917.

Democracy and Industrialization

This progress toward political democracy took place at a time of extremely rapid industrialization. It had come late to the region and created wrenching social problems, such as the breakdown of many rural communities, too-rapid urbanization, excessive population growth, the weakening of family ties, and alcoholism. Nevertheless, the democratic transformation came about without any mass violence. This peaceful change was due in part to the existence in these countries of political institutions and attitudes that could more easily adapt to changing conditions and to increasing demands for greater democratic participation in politics.

More and more citizens were granted the right to vote. Finland achieved universal suffrage in 1906, followed by Norway in 1913, Denmark in 1915, and Sweden in 1921. The absence of mass violence also was due to the steady increase in literacy and to the success of mass movements, such as those for workers' rights or temperance, which could articulate and channel important demands on the political system.

Emigration to America

A further factor that alleviated social tensions in these countries was emigration, which reached massive proportions by the 1860s and which enabled the most desperate to begin new lives elsewhere, especially in the US. The possibility of leaving for the New World helped to diminish militant discontent, which could have been seriously disruptive at a crucial time when these people were adjusting to the modern age. Sweden produced the greatest waves of emigration—in the 1880s at least 325,000 out of a total population of 4.5 million left for the US, and in the following two decades, from 10,000 to 20,000 Swedes left for America each year. By 1900 one-fifth to one-fourth of all native-born Swedes were already living abroad. Nordic immigrants decisively shaped parts of America, particularly the northern-midwestern states around and west of the Great Lakes, where the climate and landscape were very similar to the home country. The lives, problems and successes of these people in America, were movingly portrayed in the three volumes on this subject written by one of Sweden's outstanding novelists, Vilhelm Moberg. Swedish director Jan Troell filmed his story. Edna Ferber's moving *So Big* attested to the hardiness and strength of character of these emigres. This flood to America is also evoked in the Emigrants House museum at Växjö.

Finland experienced waves of emigration to the US and, later, to Sweden. Many Norwegians also set their sights toward the New World. In fact, no country, except for Ireland, sent such a large percentage of its people as emigrants to the US as did Norway. The first shipload landed in New York City in 1825, and from 1866 to 1873, over 100,000 left Norway. In the course of the 19th century, almost a third of all Norwegians resettled in America. From 1900 to 1910, more than 200,000 departed. By 1910, roughly 880,000 Norwegians had left their country for greener pastures in America, especially in the northern Midwest. Today more than 5 million Americans claim to be of Norwegian descent, more than the total population of Norway.

World War I

All Scandinavian countries were able to remain neutral during World War I, but the 1917 revolution in Russia gave the Finns the chance for which many had waited for centuries: the opportunity to declare their country's complete independence. The Danes were able to observe that the wartime threat to shipping was so great that their hold on some faraway islands was simply too tenuous. Thus, Denmark sold its part of the Virgin Islands to the United States in 1917. Denmark also profited from Germany's defeat in the war by winning international approval for a plebiscite in 1920 to determine to which country the population of the province of Schleswig wished to belong. In the north, 75% of the people voted to return to Denmark, but in southern Schleswig, 80% voted to remain with Germany. This latter vote left a small, Danish-speaking minority in Germany that still exists today. For decades afterward, the Danish monarchs would not accept this final loss of southern Schleswig, and they showed their resentment by refusing to set foot in that part of Germany. However, the former Danish queen, Margrete II, discarded this antiquated prejudice of her predecessors and enters the province as a welcomed foreign guest.

Depression and World War II

The citizens of the Nordic countries were not so successful in isolating themselves from the economic shockwaves that were generated by the 1929 stock market crash on Wall Street. Everywhere in the region, the 1930s were lean times, filled with bankruptcies, unemployment, and anxiety. They were also politically and militarily frightening times, with democratic experiments failing in many European countries, and with the European giants, Germany and the Soviet Union, awakening from their own internal chaos and diplomatic and military paralysis.

During this period all four main Nordic countries, like Nazi Germany, introduced eugenics laws, some of which remained in the statutes until 1976. From 1934 to 1974, 62.000 Swedish women were sterilized, often against their will, because they were judged to be rebellious, promiscuous, of low intelligence, or even of mixed blood. The purposes were to prevent "degeneration of the race" and to save the state the heavy cost of welfare for inferior human beings. Officials who believed in the science of racial biology and thought they were helping to construct an enlightened, progressive welfare state openly carried out the policy. Norway and Finland

Statue of Norway's King Haakon VII

The Nordic Countries

confirmed that each did the same to about 1.000 women.

As the clouds of war gathered in the skies over Europe, the Nordic countries tried to maintain a policy of neutrality. All tried to avoid any steps which especially Hitler, the German dictator since 1933, could interpret as being the slightest provocation. They harbored the hope that the League of Nations, the impotence of which had already been demonstrated on repeated occasions, would somehow be able to maintain the peace. Even after the Soviets attacked Finland at the end of 1939, which temporarily drove the Finns into the arms of the Germans and ultimately created an extremely precarious situation from which the Finns have never been able entirely to extract themselves, the Scandinavian countries did not consider themselves to be mortally threatened. Denmark had entered a 10-year nonaggression pact with Germany in May 1939 and declined thereafter to make any military preparations. Norway ordered those military precautions be taken only in the northernmost part of the country, which touches Russia. Sweden peered nervously into the horizon.

The Danish during the War

Denmark's strategic location astride the exits from the Baltic Sea to the North Sea, as well as its proximity to Germany, made the small nation, perched on top of the continent's most dynamic and aggressive power at the time, an irresistible victim. Hitler sent his troops to occupy it in April 1940; with the ominous tones of German heavy bombers in their ears, the Danes offered no significant resistance to the forceful occupation of their country. In return the Germans promised to respect Denmark's independence, integrity, and sovereignty and to allow the Danes to have their own government. It was the only occupied country placed under the authority of the German foreign ministry, and for a while it could hold the only elections in occupied Europe. The Danish government remained in the country, and King Christian X went horseback riding every day in Copenhagen in order to demonstrate that the leaders were still there.

Nevertheless, they had to bend to many unpleasant German demands, and the Germans selection of the Hotel D'Angleterre in the heart of Copenhagen as its military headquarters served as a constant reminder to the Danes of who exactly was in charge. They had to orient their economy exclusively toward German needs, to join the Anti-Comintern Pact, to crack down on communist political activity within Denmark, and ultimately to tolerate the official Nazi persecution of Jews. Hitler called it a "model protectorate."

Denmark is free! 1945

After a wave of strikes and sabotage in August 1943, Germany ordered the deportation of Danish Jews, who were never required to wear a yellow Star of David. But historians believe that the German leader in Denmark, Werner Best, leaked the plans to Danish politicians, who could alert the country's 7,800 Jews to go into hiding. With a haven just a couple of miles across the sea, all but 500 were able to escape to Sweden. Unlike elsewhere in occupied Europe, Danes who helped Jews were not sentenced to death, and thousands hid and helped Jews to flee. The Danish government continued to feed and diplomatically protect several hundred Danish Jews in the Theresienstadt concentration camp. In the end, only 116 Danish Jews, or 1.5% of the total, perished in the Holocaust.

The Danish population practiced a policy of giving the cold shoulder to the occupation forces. Sometimes they chose not to hide their sentiments, such as in 1943, when it became fashionable to wear knitted caps with the colors of the British Royal Air Force. Quite early, a Danish resistance movement sprang up, but for a while, the Danish government opposed it out of fear that its policy of cooperation in order to save the country from destruction would be undermined. However, the government's position became increasingly untenable, and in August 1943, the Danish king and parliament stopped functioning. The center of resistance activity became the Freedom Council, whose membership included former politicians and officers.

The German occupation forces struck back by arresting resistance fighters, police, and Jews, but they could never eradicate the Danish opposition, which enjoyed the sympathy and support of almost all Danes. For this resistance activity, the alliance against Hitler recognized Denmark as a victorious power after the British had liberated the country on May 5, 1945. After the war Denmark punished those Danes who had collaborated too closely with the Germans. Sixty years later, in 2005, half (51%) of Danes admitted in a poll that their relationship with Germans is still influenced by the occupation.

At the same time, the 60th commemoration unleashed vigorous public criticism of all the political parties that had cooperated with the German occupation authorities. Some historians now argue that there was more collaboration than resistance during the war. This tension is also reflected in contemporary Danish literature. Some authors, such as Thorkild Hansen, in his three-volume biography of Knut Hamsun, have dealt with Denmark's experiences under Nazi occupation as seen through the eyes of the resistance movement. By contrast, Ulrik Gräs published in 2000 the first Danish novel, *Berusede by* (Dizzy City), which approaches the occupation period from the point of view of a grandson of a provincial town mayor who, like many of the political establishment during the war, collaborated with the German authorities in order to minimize Danes' suffering.

Britain occupied Denmark's possession of Iceland and the Faroe Islands at the beginning of the war in order to prevent them from falling into enemy hands. In 1941 the US relieved the British in Iceland and, with the approval of local authorities, has retained a military base on the island ever since. The long severance of Iceland from the mother country after the outbreak of the war enabled the Icelanders, who in 1918 had already been granted an autonomy statute for domestic affairs, to declare their complete independence from Denmark in 1944. Greenland was occupied by American troops and was made a temporary protectorate under US authority. After the war it was returned to Danish jurisdiction, although American troops continued to be stationed there by agreement with Denmark.

Norway and the War

Norway, with its long coast facing not only Britain but also the North Sea and North Atlantic, also presented an irresistibly tempting target for German expansion. Unfortunately, Norway had made military preparations only in the north, and its troops were inexperienced and poorly equipped. Therefore, it was not well prepared when Hitler sent his forces against the country on April 9, 1940, the same day on which his troops occupied

16

Denmark. To the Germans' surprise, the Norwegian government rejected the German ultimatum to surrender peacefully and to cooperate, as the Danes had chosen to do. The king, government, and parliament withdrew from Oslo toward the north, from where they conducted war against German troops. Further, Norway was able to transport its entire gold reserves out of the country.

In the confusion of withdrawal to the north, the chief of the Norwegian National Socialist Party (Nasjonal Samling) and former defense minister Vidkun Quisling read a proclamation to the Norwegian people in the afternoon of April 9. Quisling criticized the government for turning down Germany's "peaceful" offer of cooperation, and he declared himself prime minister and foreign minister. His call to the Norwegian troops to lay down their arms merely stiffened the army's resolve to fight. The Norwegians so despised him that the Germans had to dismiss him as prime minister on April 15, although he was reappointed in 1942. The name "Quisling" is now inseparably associated with the very concept of treason against one's own country.

Not until May 5 was the southern part of the country conquered. With the help of Polish land forces and British naval forces, the Norwegians fought bitterly against German troops in the northern part of the country, and the Germans, unused to the bitter cold, suffered considerable losses in taking such strategically important objectives as the port of Narvik from which Swedish iron ore was shipped to Germany. By June 7, the Germans had conquered the northern part and had become the undisputed power in Scandinavia.

Once it was clear that the Germans would win, the Norwegian parliament gave King Haakon VII full powers, and the latter, accompanied by the crown prince and the cabinet, left the country for

Norway's Quisling returning the salute of a German officer

London, where he established a government in exile and directed lively resistance against the occupation forces throughout the war. His family found refuge in the US, and Crown Princess Martha was a frequent guest in the White House. The later king, Harald V, spent the war years in Bethesda, Maryland. Norwegian ships protected allied convoys on their perilous Atlantic crossing, and Norway lost 200 ships and 1,300 seamen from 1940–1942. Americans showed their gratitude in 1945: When Germans sank the SS Henry Bacon in the Arctic Sea, there was not enough space in the lifeboats. American crewmembers relinquished their seats so that the 19 Norwegian refugees aboard would survive.

Within Norway, the German commissioner Josef Terboven governed with the assistance of some cooperative Norwegian civil servants. Others were not cooperative, as so vividly depicted by John Steinbeck in his novel *The Moon Is Down*; active and passive resistance was widespread. A few small units of the Norwegian Army were also evacuated to Britain, and they subsequently absorbed other Norwegians who fled by boat through icy seas or were already abroad. These highly motivated units, as well as local resistance movements, conducted sabotage and small attacks against the alien regime.

Their number grew in 1944, when they were permitted to equip Norwegian refugees in Sweden, who could then join in the attacks against the Germans and Norwegian collaborators. They received a steady stream of weapons, ammunition, and materials from Britain. Unfortunately, these bold actions often provoked Nazi reprisals against civilians, and about 35,000 Norwegians were sent to prisons or concentration camps during the occupation. These included 1,000 teachers who, like most of their colleagues, refused to teach Nazi principles in the schools. Also, 95% of the pastors either were dismissed or they voluntarily gave up their positions because of their almost-universal rejection of the "new order."

Not until May 7, 1945, did the unwanted foreign domination come to an end. On that day the joy and relief of the people, who had won their independence only 40 years earlier, was almost boundless. Quisling was tried and quickly executed in September, and general elections were held in October. In 1946 Trygve Lie of Norway became the first secretary-general of the United Nations; his successor was a Swede, Dag Hammarskjöld.

When Thorbjørn Jagland became prime minister in 1996, his first official act was to commit Norway to pay compensation for property stolen from Jews by the Quisling government during the war. Despite the difficulties of identifying, locating, and allocating the repayments, Norway became the first European country, except Germany, to make this commitment.

In 2002 parliament voted overwhelmingly to remove another black spot by offering compensation for the offspring of Norwegian mothers and German soldiers. These children suffered serious discrimination and scorn in school and at work. They were often forced to live under terrible circumstances after the war, and many of their mothers were deported or interned as collaborators. As an apology the government offered $3,276 to 12,000 of them in 2005, but 154 took their case for adequate compensation to Europe's human rights court two years later.

Sweden

Only Sweden escaped foreign occupation and active participation in the war. However, it was isolated from the outside world, and because of its obvious military inferiority to Germany, it made concessions that created some animosity among Danes and Norwegians. Many Swedes themselves quietly resented these compromises, but most saw no reasonable alternative at the time.

Sweden conducted trade with Nazi Germany, which relied especially on Swedish iron, steel, and ball bearings. In some cases, the Swedish police shared information with the Gestapo (German secret police), and in the early war years, the government tried to muzzle the press to prevent stories unflattering to Nazi Germany. Swedes suppressed most communist activity in their own country in order to please Berlin's leaders. The Swedish government gave in to pressure to permit a German division to move across Swedish territory in order to reach the Russian front. It tolerated German violation of Swedish airspace for military purposes. Finally, the Swedish central bank and the wealthy Wallenberg financial empire bought looted gold from Germany, which provided Germany with additional funds to engage in profitable trade with Sweden and other neutral countries. The Swedish government agreed in 1996 to launch an investigation into allegations that looted Nazi gold had been deposited in Swedish banks; that Holocaust victims had deposited money in Sweden, of which their heirs received only a part; and that Swedes had extended loans and other financial help to Nazi Germany. The Wallenberg family, which continues to dominate Sweden's business sector today, agreed to open its files to examiners.

After denying refuge to fleeing Jews in the early war years, Sweden dispatched the 31-year-old Raoul Wallenberg to Hungary in July 1944 under diplomatic cover

The Nordic Countries

on a mission funded by the United States to distribute Swedish safe-conduct passes to Jews. He courageously bribed, tricked, and bullied Nazi officials in Budapest to spare the lives of 20,000 Hungarian Jews. In January 1945 invading Soviet forces wrongly arrested him on espionage charges while he was traveling to meet their commander. He died mysteriously in Soviet captivity. Not until 2000 did Russian authorities acknowledge publicly that he had been held in a Soviet prison two and a half years until his death, and a Russian investigative committee concluded that in 1947 he had been executed in the infamous Lubyanka prison in downtown Moscow.

Despite these unfortunate compromises, it should not be forgotten that Sweden granted refuge to thousands of Hitler's opponents, who would otherwise have ended in Nazi prisons or death camps. Such important postwar political leaders as Willy Brandt of Germany and Bruno Kreisky of Austria were able to live and work in Sweden during the war. As victorious powers, both Denmark and Norway took part in the occupation of Germany, and Brandt even returned to Germany as a Norwegian citizen and wearing a Norwegian officer's uniform. Undoubtedly, they brought back to their own countries, which between the wars had been severely polarized politically, lasting impressions of Scandinavian moderation, tolerance, and democratic spirit. These were qualities that were badly needed in the new beginning that Europe made after 1945.

Because neutrality had failed to protect all of the Scandinavian countries from armed aggression, Denmark, Norway, and Sweden discussed the possibility of forming a Nordic Defense Community after the war. However, these talks collapsed over the question of whether this alliance should seek the backing of the western powers, as Norway wished, or whether it should try to remain free of all Great Power conflicts, as Sweden wanted. Although there was and remains a strong emotional attachment of the Nordic region to neutrality, Norway, Denmark, and Iceland decided to break with a long tradition and join NATO. Sweden and Finland chose to move away from their strict neutrality in 1994 and join NATO's Partnership for Peace, a form of affiliation short of full membership. In May 2022, following Russia's invasion of Ukraine, both Sweden and Finland officially applied for NATO membership. Finland joined NATO on April 4, 2023, and Sweden has not yet received the requisite unanimous ratification to be an official member. As of December 2023, two remaining countries, Hungary and Turkey, have still not yet ratified Sweden's accession to NATO.

Postwar Attitudes and Cold War

All Nordic countries espouse political values oriented toward the rest of Europe and North America. All had spoken or unspoken fears about Soviet military power and about a possible Soviet military threat to the Nordic area. All are aware that the region has considerable strategic importance. The exits from the Baltic Sea lead through narrow straits between Sweden and Denmark. Two of the countries—Finland and Norway—border on Russia, and Norway and Russia had different opinions as to exactly where the border between their territories in the north should be. Norway is the northern flank of NATO. It is astride the waters that separate the northwestern part of Russia from most other NATO countries and which lead to the Atlantic Ocean, where the NATO countries' most important shipping lanes are located. Finally, all are economically advanced countries with valuable industrial resources and high levels of technology.

Although the Nordic countries share common values and defense needs, they have chosen different roads to military security while retaining a common objective of preserving stability in the region. There is no strategic bloc or single military alliance in the Nordic world. Iceland has no army at all but relies on the American Icelandic Defense Force for its protection. All four other countries have compulsory military service. Norway and Denmark are founding members of NATO, but neither permits the stationing of nuclear weapons or foreign troops on its soil during peacetime. The only exception has been Greenland, where an agreement between the US and Denmark enables the US to station conventional (non-nuclear) forces. In 2014, Sweden and Finland signed "host nation" agreements that allowed NATO troops to deploy in Nordic countries. Nevertheless, given both countries' histories of neutrality and their nonproliferation priorities, how both countries will interact with NATO's nuclear arrangements remains uncertain. In November 2022, Finland's President announced that Finland would not permit the stationing of nuclear weapons on its territory, while in April 2023, Finland's Ministry of Defense announced that it would participate in NATO's Nuclear Planning Group and that it could join support functions for NATO nuclear operations outside its territory. He suggested Finland's possible role in SNOWCAT ("Support of Nuclear Operations with Conventional Air Tactics").

Sweden is also likely to participate in the Nuclear Planning Group. In February 2023, Swedish Minister for Foreign Affairs Tobias Billström issued a statement that: "Like Norway and Denmark in their time, Sweden is joining NATO without reservations. However, like the other Nordic countries, we do not foresee having nuclear weapons on our own territory in peacetime." However, Norway and Denmark prefer not entirely to tie their hands on the question of deploying nuclear weapons on their soil in times of war, even though both plan to defend themselves using conventional weapons.

A central guideline in all Nordic foreign policies is to maintain the established equilibrium and low level of tension in the area. They would never be able to rely on their own strength for protection. This is a rather large area with an extremely small population. If one disregards Greenland, the world's largest island, the Nordic area is still larger than Great Britain, France, Germany, Portugal, and the BENELUX countries combined. But its population, at 27.6 million, is only one-tenth that of those countries. Also,

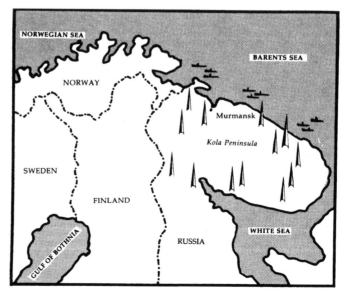

the Nordic countries would have to have enormous navies and mobile land and air forces in order to protect such far-flung possessions as the Faroes, Jan Mayen, Svalbard, Greenland, Bouvet, and Peter I (tiny South Atlantic islands, not far from Norway's claim in Antarctica).

The Kola Peninsula

The collapse of the Soviet Union changed the threat to the Nordic region, which was under the shadow of the Kola Peninsula, an area at the northwestern tip of Russia saturated with nuclear weapons. At Murmansk (60 miles east of the Norwegian border) and the small, ice-free coast next to the northern tip of Norway, Russia has its only naval and air bases with open access to the Atlantic. Sir Winston Churchill described Russia's problem of access to the open sea as "a giant with pinched nostrils." It contains early-warning and air-defense facilities, as well as major naval bases in every fjord between Pechenga on the Norwegian border and Murmansk. The peninsula is the home port of the Northern Fleet, one of four main Russian fleets and the principal naval force in the Arctic. Its headquarters are in Severomorsk (within the Murmansk region), and it is boasting with submarines and surface vessels—aircraft carrier, cruisers, frigates, and amphibious ships.

The nuclear threat to the Nordic region shifted from one of weaponry to one of waste: 71 of the submarines were judged in 1995 to be derelict and still have their nuclear fuel onboard because there is no place else to put it. Two-thirds of the nuclear waste ever dumped into the world's seas lies off Kola, and much more radioactive waste is stored in ships so rickety they cannot be moved from their moorings near downtown Murmansk. The Kola Nuclear Power Station, which provides 60% of the peninsula's power, is one of the world's least safe and suffered a near meltdown in 1993. Norway and the other Nordic nations show a great interest in clearing the area of nuclear waste. Norwegians sought in 1998–1999 to confront another danger to stability in the north: desperation on the part of a million Russians in the impoverished Norway provided tons of food, warm clothing, and medicine.

In 1988 Sweden and Russia settled their long-standing dispute over their economic zones in the Baltic Sea, which separates their mainlands by 200 miles. The agreement, which deals with fishing and exploration rights, gives Sweden 75% of the disputed area and the Russians 25%. In 1993 Russia and the Nordic countries demonstrated their willingness to work together, particularly on environmental protection, by signing an agreement on cooperation in the Barents region.

All Nordic countries exercise restraint. Norway, not the US, or other NATO countries, patrols the Norwegian and Barents Seas. No NATO maneuvers take place in the northernmost Norwegian county of Finnmark, thus always leaving a distance of at least 480 miles (800 km) between any NATO maneuver and the Norwegian-Russian border.

To underscore this, the Norwegians signed an agreement with the US in 1981 providing for the advanced storage of heavy equipment and for Norwegian support of an American marine amphibious brigade, which could be rushed to Norway in an emergency. Reflecting the restraint Norway always exercises, its leaders decided at the same time that the depots would be located in central—not northern—Norway, where any military confrontation would, at least initially, take place. They did permit the construction in 1999 of a powerful American-made radar in Vardo, 40 miles from the Russian border. Its purpose is ostensibly to monitor space debris, but Russia complains that it could track its missile launchings and be linked to an American missile-defense system. Russia is still a major worrying presence on the edge of the Nordic world. How it develops economically, politically, and militarily greatly influences security in the north.

Military Restraint and Preparedness

The fact that the Scandinavian states exercise military restraint does not mean that they are unprepared to contribute to their own defense. All except Iceland had compulsory active military service for males. Sweden decided in 2010 to phase out conscription over several years. Norway's parliament voted overwhelmingly in 2013 to draft women into its armed forces. It is the first European and NATO country to do that. Women already constituted 10% of Norway's force. Conscript service lasts 9 months in Denmark, 12 months in Norway, and 6–12 months in Finland, followed in all three countries by reserve duty. In Finland's case it ends at age 60.

The navies of Sweden, Norway, and Denmark are equipped with submarines, frigates, torpedoes, and fast boats. These craft are designed for the defense of their very long and meandering coastlines, which offer so many hiding places for friendly and enemy ships alike.

A Danish general or admiral always heads a special Baltic Approaches Command, which must try to control the entrances to and exits from the Baltic Sea in wartime. Denmark has a limited number of troops stationed in northern Germany. It has troops in a Northeast Multinational Corps, composed also of Polish and German soldiers, located in Szczecin, on the Polish side of the border with Germany. The air forces of both Denmark and Norway are equipped with American F-16 aircraft, parts of which are produced in Denmark and other NATO countries. In 2006 Norway deployed several of them in Afghanistan, joining 400 Norwegian soldiers already there.

Because it is in NATO, Denmark allowed itself the luxury of spending only about 1% of its GDP for defense, which prompted some critics to speak of "Denmarkization," a term which referred to the alleged inclination of a small country to assume that larger and more powerful countries will come to their rescue in time of emergency, regardless of what the smaller country spent on defense during peacetime. The Danes resented the charge because they do not, in fact, neglect their country's defense. Both Denmark and Norway sent combat and mine-clearing troops to Afghanistan in 2001–2002, and their special forces joined in fierce battles to mop up powerful pockets of al Qaeda and Taliban fighters. To help stabilize and rebuild the war-torn country, Denmark sent 500 troops to Iraq, and 164 Norwegian soldiers were stationed in the British-controlled area around Basra, Iraq. In 2005, Norway withdrew all its military forces from Iraq, but it continued to train senior Iraqi security personnel at the NATO Joint Warfare Center outside Stavanger.

Nordic reactions to the Anglo-American war that unseated Iraq's dictator Saddam Hussein in March-May 2003 differed. Public opinion was solidly critical in all the countries. However, then-Danish prime minister Fogh Rasmussen announced, "As a small European country we would rather rely on a superpower's security guarantees than on a European one based on a French, German and British security balance." Denmark sent a submarine and a ship to support its NATO allies. This was the first time since 1864 that Denmark was a belligerent. It deployed troops to Iraq after the war to supplement the policing efforts of the US, Britain, and Poland. Iceland also approved of the military action, while the other three Nordic countries expressed regret that armed force had been used. Rasmussen became NATO secretary-general. In 2014 he was succeeded by former Norwegian prime minister Jens Stoltenberg.

Although two-thirds of NATO member countries have women in their armed forces, and Belgium, the Netherlands, and Norway allow women in all assignments, only Denmark has made real steps toward imposing full equality in all branches. This move was prompted by passing of a comprehensive equal rights law in 1978, and the military was compelled to comply with it. A four-year

The Nordic Countries

experiment with assigning females to naval combat duties indicated that male-female crews outperform single-sex units and that women recruits are more highly motivated than men. Therefore, Danish women are assigned to all naval billets but submarines, and similar experiments are being made in the army and air force. Because of the country's declining birth rate, women may become a crucial factor in maintaining Danish force levels.

Earlier Sweden's policy of nonparticipation in alliances in peacetime and neutrality (which it still retained upon entry into the EU in 1995) during wartime is still supported by many Swedes. They are willing to underscore this policy by maintaining a strong total defense capacity, backed up by a well-organized civil defense. The aim of such Swedish defense was to raise the costs to an aggressor to such a level that an attacker, though possibly defeating Sweden in the end, would ultimately lose more than it would gain from such an attack. Such preparedness would, the Swedes hoped, dissuade any power from attacking the country in the first place.

There were some real problems with this strategy. If an unprincipled power with vastly superior armaments were to achieve overwhelming victory in Europe, it would be able to attack Sweden successfully after initially ignoring it. Swedish military strength has declined: Its air force has lost half its military aircraft, and its navy has lost a third of its ships and all of its antisubmarine warfare (ASW) helicopters. This became embarrassing when a mysterious foreign submarine was detected in Swedish waters in 2014. All Nordic and Baltic states were alarmed when Russian military planes repeatedly violated their airspace and even conducted simulated missile attacks on Stockholm and Copenhagen.

In 2001 it scaled back its around-the-clock naval operations to a 9 a.m.–5 p.m. shift as a result of budget cuts. This partly explains why the Swedes cannot track submarines effectively and why their antisubmarine force can operate only in one area at a time. Of course, the Swedish military still packs quite a wallop. After the Soviet Union's demise, Sweden continued to modernize its military. However, in 1995 the defense budget was cut so severely that the country was by 2010 left with only 13,000 active-duty soldiers. The defense budget in 2015 had fallen to 1.2% of GDP. Its top commanders feared that Sweden might have to abandon all pretense that it could repel an attacker without calling for outside help. It was estimated that it could hold out no longer than a week. No wonder that in 2014 more Swedes favored NATO membership than opposed it. A 2014 poll indicated that only 6% of Swedish respondents trusted

their armed forces to defend the country. Upon Russia's invasion of Ukraine, a Novus poll conducted on 24–25 February 2022 found 41% in favor of NATO membership and 35% opposed. On 4 March 2022, a poll was released that showed 51% supporting NATO membership, the first time a poll has shown a majority supporting this position, and support has grown to an overwhelming amount since as the war progressed.

Sweden reconsidered its 200-year-old policy of neutrality, and concluded that the time had come to join the Alliance. NATO invited Sweden and Finland to join at its Madrid Summit in June 2022. On 5 July 2022, NATO signed the accession protocol for Sweden to join the alliance, which was quickly ratified by almost all member states by September, while Türkiye and Hungary delayed their domestic ratification; Türkiye over concerns about Sweden's support for Kurdish groups, while Hungary's leadership has not provided a clear reason for delays.

After 20 months of delay, on January 26, 2024, Turkish President Recep Erdogan has signed a decision of the Turkish parliament, approved on January 23, ratifying the protocol on Sweden's accession to the North Atlantic Alliance. Hungary is the last remaining NATO member to approve of Sweden's application, clearing the way for Sweden's official acceptance.

While it has not yet received the requisite unanimous ratification to be an official member, Sweden has been described as woven into the alliance in all but name. Whatever the outcome of its membership voting in Hungary, Sweden is already enlisted as a full-member participant of the "Steadfast Defender 2024" NATO maneuvers, the largest of its kind since the Cold War times.

In order not to be dependent upon other powers in wartime, Sweden produces about 80% of the weapons (and all the fighter aircraft) that its own armed forces need. In 1987 it unveiled its Gripen supersonic fighter, which is smaller, cheaper, and less in need of maintenance than its competitors. It was sold successfully abroad, including to the Swiss air force. To lower unit costs for its weapons and to earn foreign exchange, Swedish arms industries do sell abroad, despite widespread domestic opposition. It is the world's eighth-largest exporter of weapons. Arms constitute 2% of its exports. SAAB exports aircraft; Hagglunds, tanks; and Kockums, submarines. With Swedish defense spending inching downward, Bofors and other Swedish companies count on lucrative orders from other countries.

Sweden creates difficulties for itself by pretending that it sells arms only to countries that would be unlikely to use them and which do not violate human rights.

Sales to war zones are against the law. However, many of the 40 or so countries to which it sells arms do not meet those standards. By the turn of the century, Nordic arms companies were cooperating with each other more and more, coproducing, for example, ammunition and gunpowder and procuring jointly such big-ticket items as helicopters and submarines. This would have been unthinkable for neutral Sweden and Finland during the Cold War.

The election of Donald Trump to the US presidency at a time of heightened tensions related to Russian expansionism provided a new impetus for Nordic cooperation. President Trump's well-publicized criticism of NATO members contributing less than the 2% of GDP stipulated in the 2006 agreement was duly noted. Unique among the members, Iceland has no standing army and spends less than 0.3% of its GDP on its limited military services. To be sure, such countries as Norway (with its 1.55% contribution) may have more capable militaries than others, such as Greece, that did reach the 2% threshold. Yet the overall impression of Trump's May 2017 visit to NATO's headquarters was that the Europeans would have to step up their defense efforts. The Nordics, as well as their Baltic states brethren, reacted by initiating closer cooperation. The perception of a growing Russian threat further encourages the closing of the ranks among the Nordic states. While they are not pushovers individually, the defensive capabilities of the 25-million-people region are significantly higher if they act collectively.

Foreign Policies

Even if the five Nordic countries have different answers to questions related to defense, their foreign policies are similar in the sense that all are very active members in international organizations, especially the UN, and all but Iceland participate in UN peacekeeping operations. Norway provides more UN peacekeepers in proportion to its population than any other country. Each of the countries maintains a permanent quick-response standby force that can be placed at the disposal of the UN for deployment to world trouble spots.

A joint Nordic battalion operated in the Balkans to prevent war in North Macedonia. As did all Nordic peacekeepers in Bosnia and Herzegovina and Kosovo, it served under NATO command, even though then Sweden and Finland did not belong to that alliance. Sweden maintains a permanent delegation accredited to NATO headquarters in Brussels. In 2003 NATO established a Joint Warfare Center in Jatta in Stavanger, Norway, to help in the transformation of NATO's European forces.

All but Denmark participated in the EU-led peacekeeping force in North

Macedonia after the EU assumed command from NATO in 2003. Denmark sat it out because it had opted out of the EU's European Security and Defense Policy (ESDP), whose Headline Goal called for a 60,000-troop rapid-reaction force to be used when NATO and the US choose not to be involved in a crisis. Both Sweden and Finland made troops available to this EU force; Sweden offered 2,000 soldiers, including air and naval components. However, as then nonaligned, both resisted a mutual-defense clause in a new EU constitution that would have forced them to come to the aid of a partner under military attack. Since 2004 all five help Balkan countries modernize their military training and tactics.

All were active proponents of east-west detente and vocal opponents of South Africa's apartheid policy. In 1988 Sweden, which has a tradition of mediating between Arabs and Jews, played a crucial role in establishing a dialogue between the US and the Palestine Liberation Organization (PLO).

In 1993 Norway facilitated a landmark agreement between Israel and the PLO that paved the way to the beginnings of Palestinian autonomy in 1994. In 1999 Oslo again became the venue for two days of meetings between Israeli prime minister Ehud Barak, Palestinian leader Yasir Arafat, and Bill Clinton, who became the first US president to visit Norway. In 2014 Sweden became the first western European EU member to recognize Palestine. Norway had also hosted a historic cease-fire deal in 1996 between the Guatemalan government and rebel guerrillas. It subsequently played a mediator role in Myanmar. In 2000 its foreign minister was appointed to a fact-finding inquiry into the causes of the Palestinian-Israeli upheaval. In 2002 Norwegian government officials led the negotiations that resulted in a cease-fire and peace agreement in Sri Lanka. It also lent a hand in Sudan, and in Zimbabwe its monitors remained in place during the 2002 elections after the EU staff was thrown out. However, in 2002 it turned down a request by Chechen guerrillas to facilitate a peaceful end to a Moscow theater siege. In March 2008 the UN selected as its new envoy to Afghanistan a senior Norwegian diplomat, Kai Eide. In 2012–2015 Norway hosted talks in Oslo between Colombian officials and the rebel FARC movement aiming to end Latin America's oldest insurgency.

Following the devastating tsunami in Indonesia at Christmastime 2004, the Finnish government invited to Helsinki representatives of that country and of the rebellious Aceh Province for peace talks, mediated by former president Martti Ahtisaari, to find a solution to that deadly insurrection. In July 2005 they agreed to end their three-decade conflict.

All strive to maintain especially close relations with developing countries and are among the world's most generous donors to development aid, as measured by percentage of GDP. In 2015 Sweden, Norway, and Denmark were among the world's top four leaders (aid as percentage of GDP from 1% to .86%), with Finland number 7 (.53%). The UN goal is .7% of GDP, and the US, while the world's largest donor in total funding, gave .19%. In 2007 the OECD placed the Nordics at the top in terms of the effectiveness and impartiality of their relief efforts to crisis-affected nations. The Swedish government shifted its priorities to newly independent democracies in the Baltics and eastern Europe. It reduced aid to Vietnam and cut it to Cuba altogether.

Nordic Cooperation

A major emphasis of all their foreign policies is revealed by the fact that each has a minister for Nordic cooperation. The nerve center of this broad regional collaboration is the Nordic Council, which began its work in 1953. In all, it has 78 members elected by the national parliaments from among their ranks, and it is broken down into several standing committees, which submit proposals to the plenary sessions. Members of the various governments also take part in the discussions, but they do not have the right to vote. The Nordic Council has no sovereign authority; its decisions, which must be unanimous, are merely unbinding recommendations to the five governments. Critics charge that member governments ignore the council's advice unless they planned to do it anyway.

Nevertheless, the council does discuss many important pieces of legislation before they are passed by national parliaments. This has created a greater uniformity than is found in most other regions in a wide variety of laws dealing with such matters as marriage and child custody, contracts and commercial practices, copyright and patents, transportation, and maritime law. The council has a presidium with a standing secretariat in Stockholm, a secretariat for general affairs in Oslo, and one for cultural affairs in Copenhagen.

The five countries decided in 1954 to form a single labor market, in which a citizen of one member country can work in any other country without a work or residence permit and can travel within the region without a passport. In 1955 all agreed that citizens from other Nordic countries should receive the same pension, unemployment, and health and welfare benefits as each country's own citizens. The result is that almost a million persons have emigrated from one Nordic land to the other, and in Sweden 60% of all immigrants are from other Nordic countries.

The move toward greater unity received a setback in the late 1950s, when a Nordic Customs Union and a wider Nordic Economic Union failed to materialize. Nevertheless, these nations continued to tighten their links with each other. In 1971 a Nordic Council of Ministers was set up to provide a basis for closer practical collaboration among the five governments. In 1973 a treaty dealing with transport affairs went into effect, and for many years, a single airline, SAS, has been operated by private and public funds from Sweden, Norway, and Denmark. Finally, a Nordic Investment Bank, with its seat in Helsinki, was created in 1975 to finance investment and export projects of common Nordic interest.

The economic interests of the countries are by no means identical. As Iceland's former president Vigdís Finnbogadóttir, commented, they "are a family, not quintuplets." By 1995 only Norway and Iceland remained in EFTA (European Free Trade Association), which had been founded in Stockholm. The five have different approaches to Europe and its integration, although all abide by the EEA agreement with the EU, which involves free trade in everything but farm and fish products.

The transfer of sovereignty involved in EU membership challenges the strong national identity that each Nordic nation feels. Danish scholar Lykke Friis put it this way: "All Nordic countries are struggling to find a credible fit between their national identity and the EU. This fit is especially difficult because Nordic identity is about being better than Europe." An in-between status would be a Pan-Nordic Federation, recommended in a 2010 book by Swedish historian Gunnar Wetterberg. It would have 26 million citizens under a single monarch, Queen or King of Denmark. Such a federation would be the world's 12th-biggest economy; 42% of Nordic citizens favored it in a poll.

Scandinavian students at the College of Europe, Bruges

The Nordic Countries

In a host of international comparisons, Nordic countries regularly come out on top in terms of quality of life, child welfare, or competitiveness; all are the most generous donors of development assistance. Women are treated equally more than anywhere else. For instance, a planned soccer game between Muslim imams and Swedish priests had to be cancelled in 2007 because the Swedes could not accept their opponents' demand that women priests be kept off the field.

Transparency International's Corruption Perceptions Index places the Nordic countries at the top for lack of corruption. Sweden was ranked in 2012 as the best EU country for innovation, followed by Finland, Germany, and Denmark. In terms of global competitiveness, Finland and Sweden were ranked in 2014 at the top, right behind Switzerland and Singapore. Nordic productivity is 17% above the OECD average. In terms of prosperity in 2012, Norway, Denmark, and Sweden were the top three in the world, with Finland in seventh place. In a 2011 European Lifelong Learning Indicators (ELLI) Index, which measured cradle-to-grave learning in 23 countries, Denmark came out on top, followed by Sweden (second) and Finland (fourth). Finally, the Yale and Columbia Universities' 2016 Environmental Performance Index (EPI) listed Finland, Iceland, Sweden, and Denmark as the top four countries in the world. The Nordic countries are continuously among the world's leading countries in international rankings on prosperity, productivity, social equity, trust, and health.

Finns were the most enthusiastic about being in EU and were proud of being the only Nordic country to adopt the common currency, the euro. The success of the xenophobic anti-EU party True Finns in the 2011 and especially the 2015 elections may signal a change in this attitude. Denmark has the most nuanced attitude about the EU, to which it belongs. It has won a record four "opt-outs," including from the euro. In a 2000 referendum, Danes voted 53% to 47% to remain outside the eurozone. The Swedes joined the EU but are divided over whether it was a good idea; they have rejected the euro for now. The Norwegians voted twice to stay out of the EU, and only a small minority in Iceland wants to join.

Sweden had second thoughts about going through with a plan it made with Denmark to build a 16-kilometer (10-mile) tunnel and road-and-rail bridge over the strait from Malmö to Copenhagen. This is the realization of a centuries-old dream to link the Scandinavian Peninsula to mainland Europe. It enhances the growing sense among 700 million Europeans that they all belong on a single continent. The

Øresund (UHR-ah-sohnd) double-decker bridge, completed in 2000, is a world-class technological achievement and an admirable aesthetic success. The upper deck is a four-lane highway, and the lower level is for rail traffic. From the Swedish coast, it arches for 5 miles over windswept waves before descending to a 2.5-mile-long artificial island. Finally, it drops beneath the sea into a 2.3-mile tunnel at the Danish end. Drivers and passengers must then cross two other bridges linking Denmark's main islands to arrive at the northern tip of the European mainland.

This $2 billion project created a city region of 3.5 million people, which is now one of the fastest-growing regions in Europe. In the years since the bridge's completion, tens of billions of euros in investment flowed in, especially in the biotech and pharmaceutical fields. Encompassing a 60-mile radius, it produces half of Denmark's and a tenth of Sweden's combined GDP. Within that region there are a dozen Danish and Swedish universities, with 10,000 researchers and 120,000 students.

Long a depressed area, Malmö is now Sweden's fastest-growing city, in part because of the influx of foreigners. Crime

became a serious problem, as demonstrated in 2012 by a wave of execution-style shootings. A police spokesman admitted that they had never experienced anything like that before.

For years Denmark had stalled the plans until its project to build a bridge linking the island of Zealand to the Jutland Peninsula was underway. Although only a disappointing 9,000 cars carrying 14,000 commuters use the bridge each day, largely because of the steep expense (€62 round-trip, half for commuters), it does provide the kind of easy access across the border to facilitate smuggling. An estimated one-third of beer consumed in Sweden has been brought in from outside, and smuggling and unregulated work account for an estimated 5%–10% of Sweden's economy.

Swedish opponents openly expressed another concern: that the moral environment of Malmö could be undermined by Copenhagen's laxer policies on drugs, alcohol, and prostitution. A concrete focus of their fears is the "Free City of Christiania," founded by squatters in 1971, who took over a former army barracks on 80 acres near Copenhagen. Occupied by anarchists, hippies, drug pushers, and "down-and-outs," this

Freetown Christiania, Copenhagen

Source: Wikipedia

settlement became so dangerous that most Danes, the police, and municipal buses usually avoided it. In 1993 the government failed to persuade the Danish parliament to evict Christiania's "citizens." In 1989 the leftist experiment established its own liaison office with the Danish Ministry of Defense, which owns the site; provides water, power, and other services free of charge; and accepts Christiania as permanent. Two-thirds of the residents of this settlement live on public welfare.

In 2012 the state offered to sell the area to the residents for $14.5 million, a fraction of its commercial value. The dilemma was vthat most of its residents reject the very idea of land ownership. Creative financing through a new foundation and the sale of shares in Christiania got around the worst problems, but officials had to adjust to dealing with an anticapitalist group run by consensus democracy.

Although still seedy by Danish standards, Christiania had become somewhat bourgeois and gentrified by the 21st century. Its aging hippies and counterculture residents are less dangerous now. By 2004 it had become Copenhagen's second-most popular tourist attraction, with an eccentric assortment of cafes, clubs, restaurants, weird architecture, and open-air concerts. However, it remained Europe's largest and most visible cannabis market, with stalls along the streets. When Denmark's center-right government decided in 2004 to crack down on both the use and sale of illegal cannabis, police raided Christiania, seized assets, and arrested dozens of people.

Some of the same concerns may weigh on Danish and German leaders, who decided in 2007 that a 20-kilometer bridge linking the two countries from Rødby to Puttgarden over the Baltic Sea should be constructed and completed by 2018. This was one of the largest infrastructure projects ever untaken in Europe. As an alternative to the original plans of a bridge, the solution eventually chosen was an immersed tunnel comprising both a road and a rail link. A tunnel connection that is under construction across the Fehmarn Belt is Denmark's largest infrastructure project and the world's longest immersed tunnel. The Danish government is financing its construction. It is planned to be completed in 2029.

A problem that plagued all Scandinavian countries is a long-lasting motorbike-gang war between the Hell's Angels and Bandidos. Violence involving machine guns, bombs, and antitank missiles had by 1998 left 12 dead and more than 80 injured and had terrorized citizens everywhere. In an attempt to control such warfare, Denmark suspended the right of biker gangs to assemble and put accused offenders on trial. However, it erupted again in 2009, with Hells Angels and immigrant gangs in Copenhagen settling their turf grievances with guns. The worst violence occurred in the Norrebro District, which is largely Turkish and Pakistani. Leaders in all the countries have met to discuss how this threat to the public can be eliminated.

Economics and Welfarism

All five Nordic countries have highly productive economies and have experienced rapid economic growth since 1945. On any measure of societal health, they are found at the top. Among the keys to their success are good government, consensus, honesty, anticorruption, transparency, pragmatism, education, and toughmindedness. In all the five lands, economic prosperity depends greatly upon foreign trade in view of their small domestic markets. This means that all need the kind of industry and agriculture that are competitive. A 2008 BBC poll showed that the Nordics peoples had the most positive attitude toward globalization.

All have, in varying degrees, the general goal of economic egalitarianism (equality). All have developed elaborate social welfare systems, which many people outside the region greatly admire and which include largely free medical treatment, high unemployment benefits, and generous child allowances. These many benefits are coupled with a widely spread high standard of living. There is less economic inequality and poverty in the Nordic states than anywhere else in the world. The economic prosperity has helped create the high level of political harmony and consensus within the countries, and it is therefore an important ingredient in the overall political stability.

At the same time, these countries also presently face a common dilemma: Taxes have been raised to stratospheric levels in order to pay for the welfare states. The average tax bite is around 50%. Nevertheless, despite the difficulties in paying for them (except in oil-rich Norway), no determined attack against the welfare state could succeed because most citizens are unwilling to sacrifice the social services and security that have been created. Nordic prosperity challenges the conventional wisdom that high taxes and large safety nets undermine competitiveness.

The "Nordic model"—a large welfare state with coordinated wage negotiations, the world's most egalitarian wage distribution, and maintenance of high productivity—is being powerfully challenged by external and internal forces. Swedish ex-foreign minister Carl Bildt provides a tongue-in-cheek reminder that there is no single perfect "Nordic model." It would have to be a composite: "Finland's education, Estonia's progressive tax policy, Denmark's labor market, Iceland's entrepreneurship, Sweden's management of big companies and Norway's oil."

Kingdom of Sweden (Konungariket Sverige)

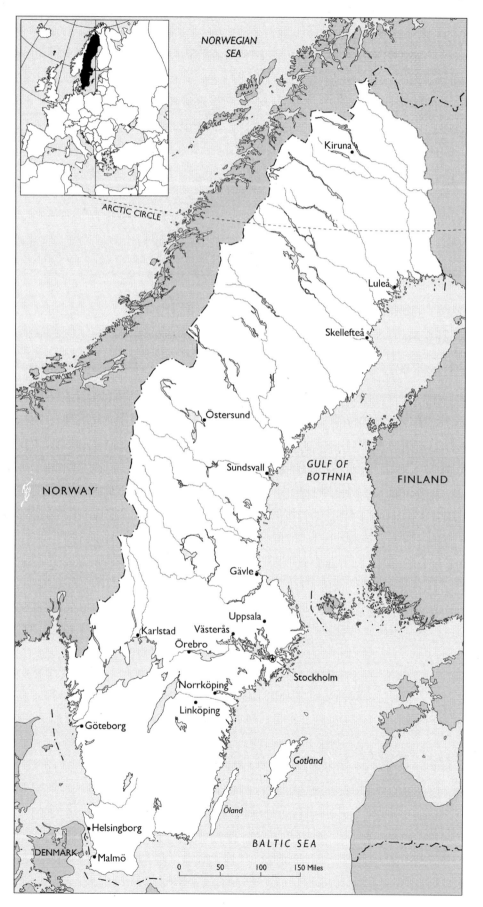

Area: 173,860 sq. mi. (450,295 sq. km), approx. 1,000 miles from north to south and 300 miles at its widest point.

Population: 10,565,000 (2023 estimate)

Capital City: Stockholm (pop. capital city 984,748, urban 2,121,000, metro 2,415,139; 2023 estimate)

Climate: Regardless to its northern latitude most of Sweden has a temperate climate with four distinct seasons and mild temperatures throughout the year. The northern regions have a subarctic climate with bitterly cold winters, while the central parts have a humid continental climate. The coastal south can be defined as having either a humid continental climate or an oceanic climate. In summers long hours of daylight extend from late spring through early autumn.

Neighboring Countries: Finland (east); Norway (west); Denmark (southwest); Germany, Poland (south across the Baltic Sea), Baltic states (southeast across the Baltic Sea).

Official Language: Swedish.

National minority languages: Sámi, Finnish, Meänkieli, Romani, Yiddish

Ethnic Background: Mostly Swedish with two minority indigenous groups (Finnish along the Finnish border, and about 15,000 of the Sami (Lapp) population scattered throughout the northern Swedish interior), and ca. 20% of a "foreign background."

Religion: 61.4% Christianity (55.2% Church of Sweden), 2.3% Islam, 0.3% other, 36.0% no religion. (2020)

Form of Government: Unitary parliamentary constitutional monarchy.

Chief of State: His Majesty King Carl XVI Gustaf (ascended the throne on September 19, 1973).

Head of Government: Ulf Kristersson, Prime Minister (since 2022).

National Flag: It consists of a yellow or gold Nordic cross on a field of light blue. The cross is horizontal extending

Sweden

to the edges, with the crossbar closer to the hoist than the fly. The Nordic cross design traditionally represents Christianity. According to an early legend, King Eric IX saw a golden cross in the sky as he landed in Finland during the First Swedish Crusade in 1157. He saw it as a sign from God and adopted the golden cross against a blue background as his banner. The exact age of the Swedish flag is not known, but blue and yellow have been used as Swedish colors at least since King Magnus III's royal coat of arms of 1275. Nevertheless, it is believed that the Swedish flag was created during the reign of King Charles VIII, who also introduced the coat of arms of Sweden in 1442, while the oldest visual presentations of a blue cloth with a yellow cross date from the early 16th century, during the reign of King Gustav I.

Public Holidays: June 6 (National Day of Sweden).

Currency: Swedish krona (SEK).

Main Exports: Machinery, motor vehicles, processed chemicals, wood pulp, paper products, finished iron and steel products, metal ores, telecommunications, and biotechnology.

Main Imports: Machinery, motor vehicles, petroleum and petroleum products, chemicals, foodstuffs, textile raw materials and fabrics, iron, and steel.

Major Trading Partners: Germany (10.2% of exports and 15.4% of imports), Norway (10.8% of exports and 12.3% of imports), Netherlands (4.8% of exports and 10.6% of imports), Finland (7.4% of exports and 4.6% of imports), Denmark (6.6% of exports and 6.4% of imports), United States (9.2% of export), China (3.6% of export and 6.0% of import), Poland (4.3% of imports). As of 2022.

The thought of post-war Sweden conjures many things: enviable prosperity, a dynamic industry producing well-designed products, assured future economic progress, absence of strikes and debt, and huge taxes that Swedes willingly pay to maintain them. one of the world's most advanced social welfare systems, the permanent rule of moderate and pragmatic parties, open arms to political refugees from all over the world and, finally, leadership in the sexual revolution.

Some of these things have changed by now, and the last point was always grossly exaggerated anyway. Sweden is still a country where a majority of the people relish social experimentation whenever it promises a more just and egalitarian society. It has done away with grades and programs for the mentally gifted in the lower classes; outlawed spankings in every institution of the society, including

the family; and introduced the use of first names between students and teachers (including most professors). It has done away with many titles and erased the distinction between the formal and informal words for "you" (a means for maintaining social distance, which virtually every other European language retains, except English). It has also extended post-natal maternity benefits to 14 months—12 for one parent and 2 for the other. The state pays up to 80% of his or her salary.

It remains a healthy, democratic political system that is totally immune from any internal shift toward authoritarian rule. Nevertheless, its political consensus is splitting a bit at a few seams. It is visibly prosperous, but it faces serious challenges to its economic health, as well as

to its way of life and its way of perceiving itself. At a time when many citizens of former communist countries' regimes look to the "Swedish model" of the welfare state as the most humane alternative to their former stultifying centralized autocratic systems, that very model has changed and grown weaker on its home turf.

Sweden is still the heart of the Nordic region and the keystone for the Nordic balance. It is the largest and most populous nation in the area. It had also been the richest for a long time, and it is accustomed to being regarded with a blend of expectation and envy. But now oil-rich Norway is reaping most of the envy, and for the first time ever, Sweden must approach its western neighbor as a needy suitor, not as a rich and slightly condescending patron. In

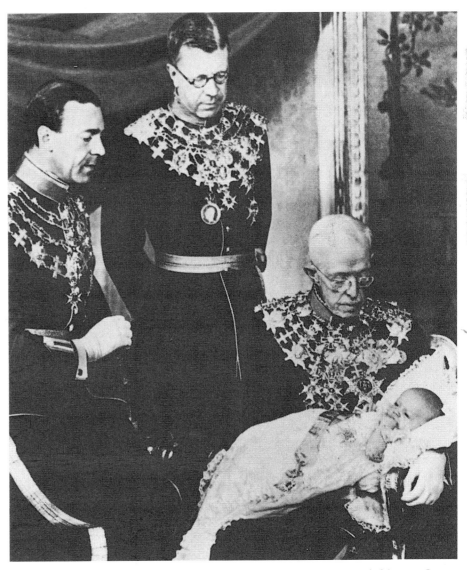

Four generations in a 1946 photograph: King Gustaf V (d. 1950, age 92), his son, Crown Prince Gustaf Adolf (who succeeded his father in 1950 as King Gustaf VI Adolf, d. 1973), his grandson, Prince Gustaf Adolf (who died in an air accident in January 1947), and his great-grandson, Sweden's present monarch, King Carl XVI Gustaf

Sweden

terms of GDP per capita, the Norwegians and Danes have surpassed the Swedes in wealth. Sweden has no oil resources. The poorer neighbors to the east, the Finns, have made considerable economic progress, and many of those Finns who had moved to Sweden to find a better economic life returned home.

Sweden is the third-largest country in the European Union. It is very sparsely populated, with 20.8 inhabitants per square kilometer, which is somewhat lower than in the US. Such overall figures are misleading because the Swedish population is distributed very unevenly. More than 90% live in the southern half of the country, and more than half live in the lower third. For many decades the northern people have migrated southward and from the countryside into the cities, although there are recent signs that this latter process may be reversing itself slightly. In 1880 only 10% of the people lived in towns, and even 100 years ago, Sweden was predominantly rural. During the second half of the 19th century, the move into the cities accelerated. By now about 83% live in cities or towns. About a third of the people live in the large urban areas of Stockholm (1,720,000), Göteborg (638,000), and Malmö (337,000).

Sweden has been an independent kingdom since 1523, and its relative isolation from the political and military storms that have swept the rest of Europe have created a firm national identity and unity, symbolized by the king. For most of its existence Sweden had a homogeneous population, and this was a key factor in the Swedes' ability to create such a sturdy social and political consensus. But this homogeneity has begun to change. This former country of emigrants, which once poured a fourth of its population into the US, has itself become a country of immigration. Immigrants and their children make up about 20% of a total population of 9.8 million; some 500,000 (nearly 5%) are Muslim. The proportion is higher in the ethnic ghettos of Stockholm, Göteborg, and Malmö.

If those with at least one parent born abroad are added, then more than a fourth of the population is at least partly of foreign descent. Their percentage is steadily rising since immigrants' birth rates are higher than Swedes', who until 2005 were in a state of negative population growth when the birth rate again began increasing. Also, by 2003 asylum seekers were entering the country at the rate of 40,000 per year. The Iraq war (2003—2011) prompted a couple million Iraqis to leave the country, and 80,000 ended up in Sweden, where they constitute the second-largest immigrant group, after Finns. In 2006 alone, more than 9,000 Iraqis applied for asylum, and 80% received refugee status; by 2009 that percentage had declined to less than a fourth.

Sweden always had a small Finnish-speaking minority in the north, numbering about 30,000. It also has had a Sámi (pronounced /sa:mi/ and sometimes still called "Lapp") minority, which now numbers about 20,000 and which has its own language and culture. The degree to which Sámi are integrated into Swedish society varies. The most traditional are the approximately 2,500 nomadic Sámi, whose livelihood is derived from raising reindeer. Sweden requires all Sámi children to attend the minimum nine years of school, although it permits the Sámi language (a Finno-Ugric language) to be used and Sámi culture, which has only a limited written literature, to be preserved. It even provides eight nomadic schools for the children who are constantly on the move, and there is a folk school at Jokkmokk, where Sámi of all ages can study their own culture. The state also broadcasts the news and special programs in the Sámi language.

Partly because of the rising concern in the world for the rights of minorities, a somewhat more aggressive consciousness has arisen among some Sámi, who maintain contact with Native American groups in North America. Some even raised a claim for possession of their people's native lands, but in 1981 the Swedish Supreme Court ruled that the Sámi can no longer claim possession of those lands, although they still have preferential hunting and fishing rights. The court also ruled that they could not interfere with energy projects or tourism in the mountainous Skattefjällen region of northern Sweden.

Since the 1945 Nordic agreement to allow free emigration within the area, Finns poured into Sweden. Finns in Sweden are not visible to the outsider, and they do not have the kinds of adjustment problems many other immigrants do. About 5.5% of the population in Finland speaks Swedish as the first language, and Finland has Swedish language newspapers, schools, universities, and a political party.

Stockholm, which was founded in the 13th century as a fortress to seal off the inland waterways from Baltic intruders, is the cultural, financial, and government center of Sweden. Unlike Copenhagen, Paris, or London, though, the Swedish capital does not overshadow the rest of Sweden, which is a decentralized country. Göteborg has Sweden's largest port and is in many ways as oriented toward such foreign cities as Oslo, Copenhagen, and London as it is toward Stockholm. Malmö is situated on the Øresund sound, directly across from Copenhagen, and its residents often cross a bridge to the Danish capital to do some of their shopping.

Approximately 15,000 years ago, Sweden was covered with ice, the movement of which cut deep scars into the land, leaving a long mountain chain along the Norwegian border. These mountains, which cover a fourth of the country, are the source of numerous rivers that flow eastward through the forests into the Gulf of Bothnia.

These rivers are sources of hydroelectric power, which provided the energy for Sweden's industrialization. They also offered rapid and inexpensive transportation for logs from the immense Swedish forests, which cover half the country's territory. Many of the indentations cut during the great ice age are now filled with almost 100 000 lakes, which occupy about 8% of the country's surface. Boats can travel all the way from Stockholm to Göteborg via lakes linked by rivers and the Gota Canal. Along the jagged coast of this country, which stretches 1,000 miles (1,600 km), are thousands of islands. The average width of the country is 250 miles (400 km).

As in Norway, all open land that is not cultivated or not part of a residence can be used by anyone for camping, hiking, skiing, or other outdoor recreational activities, regardless of who owns the land. Swedes are very proud of this allemansratten ("every man's rights"). The vast forests have long provided one of the three most valuable natural resources—wood. The other two are waterpower and mountains of Europe's highest grade of iron ore, found in the Bergslagen area in central Sweden and in the Skelleftea and Kiruna areas in the north. Kiruna is Sweden's most northerly town and sits on the world's largest underground iron ore seam. It accounts for almost 90% of Europe's iron ore production. In order that mining can continue, parts of the Arctic town began in 2012 to be moved two miles to the east. Hundreds of residential buildings have been torn down and rebuilt elsewhere.

Sweden also has sizable deposits of ferrous alloys, pyrites, fire clay, zinc, silver, lead, copper, and shale uranium. Its greatest poverty is in oil and coal, but with its people's proven ingenuity, it has been able to achieve almost unparalleled prosperity, even without "black gold." A heavy dose of this ingenuity was necessary to make Sweden basically self-sufficient in food, even though its soil is generally not good, its rainfall undependable, and its growing season short. Less than 10% of its land area is suitable for agriculture, but Swedish farmers, who now make up only 3% of the active population, apply a high level of mechanization and scientific farming techniques.

The climate is far milder than would be expected if one merely glanced at the globe. It is on the same latitude as

Sweden

Siberia and Alaska, and Stockholm is as far north as southern Greenland. Yet the Gulf Stream from the Caribbean is able to penetrate, bringing warm water that heats the air and produces a mild climate in the most populous half of Sweden.

The country has a varied landscape. The south, or Götaland, which includes the islands of Öland and Götaland off the eastern coast, is a region of fertile plains and rolling, verdant hills, dotted with clean, red and yellow barns and farmhouses, freshly painted and surrounded in summer by fields of yellow flowers. Here is the heart of Sweden's industry and agriculture and the home of half the Swedes. Central Sweden is called Svealand, from which was derived the name of the entire country, Sverige, or Svearike, which means "Kingdom of the Svear." This region contains the capital city as well as the old university town of Uppsala. It also has many farming communities and countless lakes. The northern half of the country, or Norrland, is a rugged, mountainous frontier area of wilderness, timber, and mining. In short, Sweden is a beautiful land of many scenic contrasts and of water everywhere.

RECENT POLITICAL HISTORY

Sweden's political system is known for being stable. For a half-century, Sweden had been governed by the Social Democratic Workers' Party (SAP), which now calls itself the Social Democrats (S). The election in 1976 of the first non-SAP

government since 1936 was a turning point. Swedes had decided that it was time to have a government that proposed a policy to stimulate the dynamism of the marketplace, increase productivity in the private sector by stimulating investment, and slow the growth of government. It was never a question of dismantling the social welfare net. No Scandinavian government has a mandate from its people to do that. The coalitions that ruled after 1976 shied away from truly decisive policies that would have been necessary to begin to solve the country's economic problems.

Olof Palme's SAP reaped the electoral rewards of this failure. Palme knew that, in the minds of many Swedish voters, his party was closely associated with the prosperity and full employment of the past. He also knew that his party's program was in harmony with the electorate's desire to maintain at all costs the social welfare system, which most Swedes have come to regard as permanent.

Palme stood at the zenith of his career when tragedy struck in 1986. Walking home unguarded with his wife late at night, he was killed by an unknown assassin's bullets. He was the first Swedish leader to be murdered since King Gustaf III, who was shot at a masked ball in 1792. The investigation that finally concluded in 2020 found that the murder was Stig Enstrom, an alcoholic graphic designer. Swedes mourned not only the loss of this talented, controversial leader but also the loss of Sweden's totally open society.

This tragedy repeated itself in 2003 when Foreign Minister Anna Lindh, one of Sweden's most popular politicians and an oft-mentioned future prime minister, was murdered in a department store in downtown Stockholm. The country was also deeply shaken by a hate crime directed against "dark-skinned" people when, in 2015, a 21-year-old racist extremist wearing a Darth Vader-like helmet used a sword to kill a teaching assistant and a student, also fatally stabbing a teacher and wounding another student at a school in Trollhättan. It was the deadliest school attack in Sweden's history.

These irrational acts challenged Swedes' sense of security and view of their country as exceptional, tolerant, and relatively free of crime, where only the king and prime minister have regular bodyguards.

Prime Ministers

Palme's personal deputy, Ingvar Carlsson, replaced him as prime minister and leader of the SAP. His state visit to the US in 1987, the first such trip in almost three decades, revealed how much the two countries' relations had improved since 1972, when Palme had compared the US bombing of Hanoi with Nazi Germany's extermination policy. That dubious statement prompted a mutual withdrawal of ambassadors for more than a year. Carlsson tried to be even-handed in his criticism of the US and Soviet Union. His successor in 1991, Carl Bildt, had always opposed Sweden's foreign-policy moralizing and its support for Vietnam during

View of Stockholm, with the royal palace (center-top)

27

Sweden

the war. After visiting US military cemeteries in Belgium, he wrote, "Swedes ought to take the time to go and see the row after row of the hundreds of white crosses." In 1994 Carlsson replaced Bildt as prime minister. In March 1996 Goran Persson assumed the prime ministership and ruled for a decade before handing the reins to conservative Fredrik Reinfeldt in September 2006. Reinfeldt's center-right government was reelected in 2010, with Bildt as its activist foreign minister. In September 2014, Stefan Löfven, leader of the Social Democrats, became prime minister. He led a coalition government between his own Social Democratic Party and the Green Party. Löfven was a soft-spoken but tough trade union leader who had never been a member of parliament. He had to resign in January 2021 after becoming the first Swedish Prime Minister to have a proposal rejected by the majority of the Riksdag. His colleague, Magdelena Andersson was appointed Prime Minister in November 2021 and formed a one-party minority government.

As of 2022, the prime minister of Sweden is Ulf Kristersson, the leader of the Moderate Party since October 2017. Kristersson has been a member of the Riksdag for Södermanland County since 2014 and for Stockholm County from 1991 to 2000.

GOVERNMENT AND POLITICS

As in other Scandinavian states, politics in Sweden is characterized by great stability, despite the existence of many political parties competing for power. It entered a democratic age without revolution, and violence is an element that has almost never raised its ugly head in Swedish politics until recently. This does not mean that there are no political conflicts or disagreements in the country's political life. It does mean that they are fought out verbally and in the democratic arena and with restraint and that they are almost invariably resolved by the Swedish talent for cool-headed, pragmatic negotiations and compromise.

The Swedish constitution consists of four separate documents (Basic Laws), unlike just one, as in the US. The first is the Act of Succession, which deals with the present royal family and which was amended, effective 1980, to permit the oldest child of the reigning monarch, not the oldest son, to succeed to the throne upon the death of the monarch. This meant that King Carl XVI Gustaf's son, who had been born crown prince, was moved behind his older sister, Victoria (b.1977), in the order of succession. Her daughter Estell is the next in line after her. The second document is the Fundamental Law on Freedom of Expression. The third is the Freedom of the Press Act of 1949. The most important document is the Instrument of Government, which went into effect on January 1, 1975, replacing the 1809 Instrument of Government. This change brought no radical reform, but it formally incorporated into the constitution the current governmental practices that had evolved since 1809.

This last document explicitly sanctions popular sovereignty, representative democracy and parliamentary government. Thus, while most other constitutionally governed countries have gradually developed actual political practices that are not clearly spelled out in a constitution, Sweden has tried to bring its constitution and actual political practices into harmony. In 1976 and 1979, parliament again passed laws amending the document in a way that strengthened the protection of human rights and fundamental freedoms. Thus, its existing observance of these rights and freedoms now has documentation.

Constitutional Monarchy

Sweden is a constitutional monarchy with a parliamentary form of government. As a result of the recent constitutional changes, the monarch does not have sweeping political powers on paper, as do other European monarchs. He is in theory and fact a symbolic figurehead who exerts no influence on politics and takes no part in it. A Swedish monarch never actually wears a crown, and he performs only purely ceremonial functions, such as opening the annual session of parliament each October and conferring four of the five Nobel Prizes. (The Norwegian government confers the Peace Prize.) Swedish chemist and inventor Alfred Nobel had donated the money for these prestigious prizes. He had made a fortune from his invention of dynamite, blasting gelatin, and smokeless explosives, which made the development of firearms and artillery possible.

The monarch does not formally sign government documents, and his former fictitious power to select the prime minister has been taken over by the speaker of the parliament. Also, the formal power of government now rests with the cabinet, not with the monarch. The Swedes have stripped their monarch of all his duties and powers and collect taxes from him as they would any other citizen. With an estimated net worth of about €38.5 million, he is by no means the wealthiest European monarch. The royal family receives approximately €9.7 million each year, around half of which is used to maintain castles and art treasures. All of his income is now subject to public scrutiny based on the country's transparency principle.

(Right to left) King Carl XVI Gustaf, Queen Silvia, Crown Princess Victoria, Prince Carl Philip, Princess Madeleine, and the king's aunt, the late Princess Lilian

Sweden's royal children—Madeleine, Crown Princess Victoria, and Carl Philip

This stripping of the monarch's formal powers does not mean that the Swedes are indifferent to their royal family. Opinion polls reveal that the king and his German-born queen, Silvia (neé Sommerlath), a commoner who was serving as a guide at the 1972 Munich Olympics when Carl met her, are by far the most popular public figures in Sweden. In fact, they are far more beloved and respected than are any of Sweden's present political leaders. Silvia, who still speaks with a noticeable German accent, is patron of over 60 charitable organizations.

The royal family strives to be very near to the people, sending their children to normal public schools and taking a great interest in such charities as those seeking to improve the lot of handicapped children. Without a doubt, their popularity is the best protection against the voices that are sometimes heard on the political left to abolish the monarchy altogether.

As the change in the constitution, effective since 1980, permits the oldest child, regardless of sex, to ascend to the throne, Crown Princess Victoria was preparing herself to be queen by studying history and political science at Yale University. In June 2010 she married a commoner, Daniel Westling, who is the founding owner of a small chain of Stockholm fitness clubs, where they met.

Parliament

Since 1971, Sweden has had a unicameral parliament (Riksdag). At one time, almost 90% of Swedes 18 years of age or over went to the polls to elect 349 members by proportional representation. For the election of 310 of the members, the country is divided into 28 constituencies, each of which chooses an average of 11 members. The remaining 39 are selected from national ballots in which all of the country constitutes a single constituency. A substitute deputy is selected simultaneously for each member so that there need not be a by-election if a deputy dies or resigns. In 2002, women captured 45% of the Riksdag seats and were awarded half of the cabinet posts.

Parliamentary elections are held at least every four years in September, although the prime minister can decide to call earlier ones. Such earlier balloting is very rare, and if it does take place, the newly chosen deputies merely serve out the remainder of the four-year parliamentary term. Many had found that three-year terms, in effect until 1994, were insufficient for a parliament; a government can act more decisively if it does not have to worry about elections so often. Therefore, parliamentary terms were lengthened to four years.

Sweden has a highly organized society. Each occupation group and such categories of citizens as consumers, members of cooperatives, environmentalists, women, tenants, and landlords have their own organizations which deal directly with the government. Before an important piece of legislation is introduced into the Riksdag, the government calls together a royal commission composed of members of that body (except communist members), experts from the concerned interest groups, and independent specialists to examine the proposals thoroughly and to develop,

if possible, a consensus behind the new laws. Representatives of the groups also belong to many administrative agencies. The participating organizations, therefore, are a part of the democratic system itself and not merely lobbyists.

Once the legislation is presented to the Riksdag, one of the 16 standing committees gives it another look, so that when a law is finally adopted, it usually enjoys a broad consensus. This process certainly helps to promote stability, but it has been severely criticized by some Swedes since the late 1960s. They charge that the process takes place behind closed doors and over the heads of most normal citizens and persons within the various occupations. This is mere "democracy at the top," they say. The parties have taken this criticism seriously and have developed some new proposals on the subjects of decentralization while continuing to practice the traditional method for achieving a consensus.

There is no institutional separation of power between the legislative and the executive branches in Sweden. Nevertheless, since the early part of the 19th century, Sweden has had a tradition controlling the governmental administration. The first form of guarantee against the abuse of power by judges, governmental officials, and civil servants is the requirement that all documents be made public (a principle Swedes call *Offentlighetsprincipen*), except in rare instances where secrets vital to the nation's welfare are concerned.

The second guarantee is the election by the Riksdag of ombudsmen, a specifically Swedish invention, who have the independent authority to act on their own initiative or on the basis of written complaints from individual citizens, newspapers, or other organizations. The justice ombudsman sees whether any public official, except a government minister, has acted illegally or improperly. If he finds evidence of misconduct, he can admonish the erring official or initiate corrective steps, although prosecutions are infrequent. If he finds that the laws are vague or faulty, he can recommend to the parliament a change in the law.

There are also other, more specialized ombudsmen. The press ombudsman deals with complaints about journalistic ethics. The antitrust ombudsman watches over the economy to see that competition is not stifled. The consumer ombudsman protects the consumer from unfair marketing methods, and the equality ombudsman primarily is responsible for ensuring that there is no discrimination against women on the job or in public life. It is scarcely surprising that a woman normally occupies the latter office. In 1999 an ombudsman for gays and lesbians was created. The ombudsmen can invoke a well-developed

Sweden

body of Swedish law, which is a synthesis of Roman and common law and which is interpreted by courts at three levels: Courts of the First Instance (Tingsratter), Appellate Courts (Hovratter), and a Supreme Court (Hogsta Domstolen).

In practice, the Riksdag is subordinate to the cabinet (Statsrad), usually composed of 18 to 21 ministers and led by the prime minister. Together they are called "the government" and must be able to win a majority in the Riksdag for their important policies. Beginning with the 2014 elections, a prime minister must actually win a vote of confidence in parliament rather than exercising power unless a majority called for his resignation. The government is collectively responsible for policy, but parliament can force individual cabinet members to resign. Of course, the prime minister can dismiss them. Cabinet members are normally leading politicians in the governing parties and had won seats in parliament, although their substitutes occupy their seats while they serve as ministers. Occasionally, specialists who are not professional politicians and who were not elected to parliament are included in the cabinet.

The Riksdag majority has the last word on whether a matter becomes law or not. That majority may choose to allow the people to express, through a referendum, their opinion on a particularly important subject, but the results of such a nationwide vote, which occurs very seldom, are not binding on the government. In 1979 the constitution was amended to allow another kind of referendum. If a third of the Riksdag deputies desire it, a binding referendum on a proposed constitutional amendment can be held at the same time as a general election.

Provincial Government

Sweden is a unitary, not a federal, state. But it does have provincial and local governments that have considerable responsibility. Each of the 24 provinces (län) is formally led by a governor (landshövding), who is appointed by the cabinet for a six-year term and who presides over a 14-member provincial administration (länsstyrelsen), which is appointed by an elected provincial council (landsting). As in the municipalities, the provinces have plural rather than single-person executives; such collective leadership encourages collaboration among all parties, and it therefore fosters nonpartisan, compromising, and practical leadership. The provinces lack the independence that the US states have, and since 1971 there is no upper house in the national parliament that would be in a position to guard provincial interests.

Local Government

There are 284 municipalities (kommun), each with an elected assembly. The kommun does not have the same measure of autonomy as does an American city and is largely occupied with administration on a day-to-day basis of services that have been mandated by the national government. The kommun's responsibilities extend to housing subsidies; roads; sewerage and water supply; elementary education; public assistance; health care; child welfare; and cultural, social, and athletic activities. They have the right to levy income and property taxes. They not only charge fees for some of the services they render, but they also receive subsidies from the national government for the services they are required to perform for it.

Absorption into the National Government

Provincial and local governments have been progressively transformed into administrative extensions of the central government. The provinces apply national policy and have primary responsibility for health care, hospital services, certain types of education, and vocational training. They have the right to impose an income tax to pay for their services. To make things even more complicated, there are also church councils at the local level, which are popularly elected and which look after church financial affairs.

Until the Church of Sweden was separated from the state in 2000, the church levied taxes, which about 90% of all Swedes chose to pay rather than leaving the church and lowering their tax burden. The state still collects membership fees for all registered religious organizations. The average Swede pays income taxes to nation, provincial, and municipal authorities. However, only a single tax return that covers all three must be filed.

Political Parties

As in other democracies, political parties are very much a part of Swedish government. The proportional representation electoral system produces a multiparty landscape, which is kept within manageable bounds by the requirement that no party can win seats in the Riksdag which does not win at least 4% of the vote nationwide or 12% of the vote in any one electoral district. Those parties who are able to win at least one seat receive state subsidies to cover a portion of their expenses.

There are several different ways of approaching the party scene. One is to see it as a multiparty system, with generally coherent and stable groups that are closely linked to specific occupation groups in the well-organized Swedish society. In a land

with no traditional language, ethnic, or confessional differences, it is understandable that the parties would form along occupational or class lines. These close ties, which most parties have, made it more difficult for them to broaden their bases and become mass-representation groups, which could single-handedly win a parliamentary majority. The one exception until 2006 was the Social Democratic Party (S), which by then had dominated Swedish politics for over a half-century, or 61 of the previous 74 years. Most parties now suffer from weakening voter loyalty.

Thus, Sweden has a stable, multiparty system that is divided into two roughly equal blocs. Since a hardline, antisocialist front never developed and since the major parties tend to be unideological and pragmatic, both blocs were always able to cooperate in the political middle. Most electoral shifts are among parties within each bloc, not between the two. Thus, electoral landslides are completely unknown.

The Social Democratic Party (S)

In 1989 S celebrated its 100th anniversary. Since the early 1930s, it ruled Sweden almost continually, with a three-month interruption in 1936. It won a majority five times. Sometimes it formed coalitions with the Center Party (1936–1939 and 1951–1957), but it tends to dislike coalitions and is happier to rule as a minority government with the tolerance of another party whenever it cannot win a majority. In 1976 it went into the opposition, returning to power after the 1982 elections. It reentered the opposition in 1991, but it came back to power in 1994. S's greatest strength is among the elderly, those living in small towns, and public-sector workers.

September 2006 interrupted S's rule for eight years. In the September 2018 elections, S captured 28.3% of the votes, down from 31.2%, its worst showing in a century. S won 100 seats but could no longer form a minority government with Stefan Löfven, a trade-union boss and ex-welder, as prime minister.

The historic secret of the S's success was its close ties with the Trade Union Federation (Landsorganisationen—LO), which links 25 unions and organizes about 90% of all Swedish workers. Sweden is a highly unionized country, and since the founding of the LO, most of its members must also belong to S. This is not merely formal membership; most Swedish workers vote for S in general elections. The LO supports S financially, organizationally, and through the trade-union press, such as the popular Aftonbladet, a tabloid newspaper whose circulation is by far the biggest. S revived its morning tabloid, Stockholms-Tidningen, which concentrates on local Stockholm news and on low-keyed presentations of the party's policies. The LO and S have a common committee during election years, and the LO chairman has a seat in the party presidium. S also has good relations with the Union of Employees (TCO), but its links with S are not nearly as close and its influence not so important as is the case of the LO.

S's party programs since 1897 have always contained some radical elements, such as presenting socialism as the long-range goal of the party, but these elements have been disregarded in practice. The program states that the "struggle for equality is directed against all kinds of class differences—economic, social and cultural." It declared that the existing freedoms and rights should be used to attain economic and social liberation and that economic democracy "should be an immediate goal."

The party supported socialist economic reforms, but it always took a gradualist approach to change and was willing to cooperate with other parties and with private enterprise. It left private property untouched and allowed Swedish companies to make high profits as a reward for financing full employment, a tight social welfare system, and an ever-increasing living standard for all groups within the society. In 1959 it changed its party program so that it would be in harmony with its moderate, pragmatic politics. The benefits for Sweden that flowed from this realistic approach were revealed in the country's undeniable prosperity.

The Communists and Greens

One party that advocates a leftist ideological course is the Left Party (V), which split from the SAP in 1917. It transformed itself into a "Eurocommunist" party in the 1960s by scrapping its advocacy of a "dictatorship of the proletariat." It also changed its name in 1967 in order to make itself more appealing to left-wing socialists and the SAP (now S). It cut its ties with the Soviet Union, a move that led some elements in the party to split off and form other communist groupings. None has mustered more than the feeblest support at election time nor has ever won a single seat in the Riksdag. V became a political home for a part of the "new left" in the 1970s, and it defines itself as "socialist-feminist" today. It now rejects any identification with communists.

V finds its major strength is in the industrial centers. It actively opposes EU membership, as well as austerity and cuts in the welfare budget. Until 2014 it had never been included in a Swedish governing coalition, although it was sometimes willing to support S's programs as the best

Göteborg, Sweden's second-largest city and Scandinavia's largest port

alternative to "bourgeois" governments. In 2018 it won 8% of the votes and 28 seats.

In 1988 the Greens had become the first new party to win seats since Sweden introduced universal and equal suffrage in 1917. It improved its position in 2010, forming a "red-green" alliance with the Social Democrats. In 2018 it captured 4.4% of the votes and 16 seats. They oppose the euro. Greens advocate strict environmental controls, the extinguishing of nuclear power, the transfer of politics from professional politicians to amateurs and laymen, and a clear distancing from the EU. When Reinfeldt sought to woo the Greens into his governing coalition, they made it clear that they could not support a government that "kicks sick people off health insurance, does not have a climate policy and wants to build ten new nuclear plants." The Greens were instrumental in introducing the welcoming approach to the 163,000 immigrants in 2015. Their leader, Asa Romson, was brought to tears when she had to announce the government's reversal of that policy in November, after considerable debate within her party.

The "Bourgeois" Parties

The second block of parties in Sweden is often called the "bourgeois" or "nonsocialist" bloc. The four largest conservative parties named themselves the "Alliance for Sweden." None of the parties in this group advocates a dismantling of the social welfare system, although all favor some correction of its excesses and abuses. They are not against collective action, which has deep roots in Sweden's heritage, but

they do lay more emphasis on individualism and the rights of private property than does S.

This is why all advocate greater decentralization as a barrier against excessively centralized authority and bureaucracy. They also call for lower taxes to stimulate and liberate individual initiative again, but they disagree about the precise form of such reductions. In foreign policy, their leaders tend to favor amicable relations with NATO.

The second-largest party after S is the Moderate Unity Party (M). It renamed itself "New Moderates" for the 2006 elections. M had changed its program and name in 1969 in order to reverse a constant loss of voters, but most Swedes still refer to it as the Right Party (from its pre-1969 name *Hogerpartiet*). It has always appealed more to the upper class, but it never was a reactionary party of the extreme right. Like other parties of the bloc, it had to adjust to Sweden's changing social structure and to extend its appeal into the urban areas, where it receives almost half of its votes. Its key supporters come from large and small businessmen, big farmers, the upper civil service, and young Swedes. It receives financial assistance from the Confederation of Employers (SAF) and from industry, as well as some sympathy from the union of academics and upper civil service (SACO/SR), but these forms of support are not nearly as significant for it as is LO support for S.

Many Swedish newspapers support the party, the most important being the respected Stockholm morning daily *Svenska Dagbladet*, a well-informed, low-keyed

Sweden

paper whose circulation is declining. This newspaper does retain its independence, and it does not hesitate to criticize M. The party has always had relatively strained relations with the other three parties in the "bourgeois" bloc. Its former leader, Ulf Adelsohn, summed up his party's position tartly by remarking that "things are pretty crazy if a man is taxed so much that he can't pay his rent, but the government is willing to pay him a rent subsidy to make up the difference." That kind of remark sounded like a serious threat to the welfare system and to the role of the state in the nation's economy. In a country in which the majority of voters derive their livelihood from public funds or employment, political assaults on the public sector and calls for a "change in the system," however logical they may be, are highly risky.

In 2006, Carl Bildt became foreign minister. He no longer used the word "neutral" to describe his country's foreign policy, and the center-right government he served in was sympathetic to closer links with NATO. It cooperated closely on airspace surveillance and intelligence exchange with its NATO neighbor, Norway. It provided training and equipment to the Baltic states, which are NATO members since 2004. It deployed 500 signals intelligence soldiers in northern Afghanistan, and it also sent fighter aircraft and other military assets to help NATO enforce a no-fly zone over Libya.

Bildt stepped down as party leader in 1999 and was replaced first by Bo Lundgren and then in 2004 by Fredrik Reinfeldt, who made the New Moderates more inclusive, including to gays. In fact, as prime minister he appointed the first black person—Burundi-born Nyamko Sabuni, a female model of integration—as minister for integration and equality—and the first openly gay ministers in the country's history. Reinfeldt edged the party toward the center without compromising its basic principles of individual freedom, free markets, and rule of law. He revitalized the party by ousting a third of its staff and hiring a young team of economists to draw up gentler plans that do not scare voters.

These became his alliance's platform, and they included tax cuts that included an end to the wealth tax. The latter accounted for only .3% of total revenues, but it drove rich Swedes, like IKEA founder Ingvar Kamprad and Bjorn Borg, out of the country. Sweden had already scrapped its estate tax. The government also sought to strengthen incentives to work. Although the official unemployment rate was low, Reinfeldt reminded Swedes that the more accurate figure was 15%–17% because of all the make-work and early-retirement schemes. Youth unemployment was 20%. The growing number of immigrants have

Former Prime Minister Stefan Löfven

severe difficulties finding work; only 51% of non-Europeans had jobs in 2013, compared with 84% of native Swedes. The conservative government implemented policies to boost employment, wean citizens off welfare benefits, and help them reenter the workforce. He persuaded voters that he aimed to refine rather than dismantle the welfare system.

Reinfeldt promised to sell off some of the government's stakes in the 55 companies the state owns. It began in 2007 with six companies, including the Scandinavian airlines SAS, the Nordea bank, Telia-Sonera communications company, and the stock market operator OMX. However, support for privatization dropped sharply, and the world financial market turmoil in 2008 prompted the government to delay the sell-offs.

In 2014 the conservative coalition had its worst result in modern times. M lost a third of its support, winning only 23%. Four years later M fell even farther, to 19.8% and 70 seats. This left the center-right parties with 143 seats and the center-left with 144.

The Center Party (C) also responded to the structural changes in Swedish society by changing its name in 1957 from the Farmer's Party. It now draws more votes from workers than from farmers, but its strength is still located largely outside the cities and mainly in southern Sweden. It receives about 70% of the farmers' votes, and farmers dominate its membership, leadership and parliamentary group. It also receives financial, organizational and political support from the Farmer's

Organization (LRF), with which it has an overlapping leadership. The Center has ruled with S in the past, and its goal of a "guided market economy" is still very compatible with the traditional economic policy of the SAP.

There has always been tension between the Center and M, and this tension was made worse within the government by the Center's antinuclear energy policy and by its strong ecological appeals, which from 1976 on were able to attract many protest votes. It now has a fragile and mixed electorate that merely intensifies its traditional difficulty in deciding, first, whether and with whom to form a coalition and, second, to what extent it should compete for votes at the expense of M or the Liberals. In 2018 it received 8.6% of the votes and 31 seats.

The third party in the nonsocialist alliance is the Liberal People's Party (FP), which has its main strength in the larger cities, especially Stockholm and Göteborg. Its voters are a very heterogeneous group, and unlike all other major parties, it is not backed by any large economic organization, although it does receive some financial support from the employer's organization, SAF. Traditionally it also has been supported by the nonconformist religions and by the anti-alcohol organizations. It does have a strong foothold in the press, especially the largest national morning newspaper, *Dagens Nyheter*, and the afternoon daily tabloid, *Expressen*, which had Scandinavia's largest circulation until it was overtaken by the Social Democratic *Aftonbladet*. The *Göteborgs' Posten* is liberal. None of these papers is directly connected with the party, though, and all criticize it freely.

For a while the FP successfully attracted nonsocialist voters by stressing the virtues of both a market economy and social responsibility through welfare policies. In

Carl Bildt, ex–foreign minister

Ulf Kristersson, Prime Minister
Source: *Wikipedia*

2018 it garnered 5.5% of the votes and 20 seats. The staid, God-fearing Christian Democrats won 6.3% of the votes and 22 seats in 2018.

The only genuine anti-immigration party was the Sweden Democrats, which was created in 1988. It seemed to come out of nowhere in 2010, doubling its votes in the 2014 elections to 13% and becoming the third-largest party. In 2018 it continued its meteoric rise to 17.5% of the votes and 62 seats. Its support comes mainly from young, working-class males. This untouchable party with neo-Nazi roots became the potential power broker, making it very difficult to form a majority. All mainstream parties agreed to make no deals with it or even to invite it to join the candidates' televised debate. It is in the opposition.

Led by Jimmie Akesson, who has worked hard to soften the party's image, Sweden Democrats tapped into the public's uneasiness about the way immigrants, especially Muslims, are changing Swedish society. It no longer calls for mass expulsions of Muslim immigrants, but it demands that the admission of foreigners be cut sharply by 90%. Between 2015 and 2019, it fell from 163,000 (1.6% of the population) to only 23,000. It calls Islam "un-Swedish" and the country's greatest danger. It advocates "Swedishness" against multiculturalism. It has moved the entire political spectrum to the right.

2022 Parliamentary Elections

In September 2022, the population of Sweden elected a new parliament. In the election, the Social Democratic Party became the largest party concerning the share of votes, but the center-right block (including the Moderate Party, the Christian Democrats and the Liberal Party), holding a two-seat lead over the left-wing bloc, formed a government afterward.

The dominant themes of the 2022 election campaign have been the issue of welfare reform, residential segregation, gang violence, the rising cost of living, the growing energy crisis, and the importance of the green transition. Also, the election took place following Sweden's decision to join NATO after over 200 years of military nonalignment, and the Covid-19 pandemic.

For the Social Democrats and the Moderate Party, the fight against segregation and gang violence were some of their key priorities. As a critical social problem, socially vulnerable housing developments on the outskirts of Swedish cities, mainly inhabited by immigrants and asylum seekers, have become associated with high levels of organized crime and gang violence. Thus, the far-right Sweden Democrats, who made significant gains in the 2018 general election standing on an anti-immigration ticket, again campaigned on a similar platform. They proposed some of the strictest immigration legislation possible within the EU's asylum and migration frameworks.

As to welfare reform, the Social Democrat's campaign was focused on "taking back democratic control of the welfare system"; the Moderate Party came forward with their plans to tackle dependence on state contributions; whilst the Sweden Democrats called for a 'Swedish welfare system for Swedish citizens,' arguing that migrants should not be entitled to support from the state until they are employed.

Magdelena Andersson's Social Democrats remain the largest party in the Riksdag. It has increased its number of seats from 100 to 107. The Swedish Democrats by gaining 11 seats, raising their total to 73, became the second-largest party. The Moderate Party came third with 68 seats, a decline of three.

Thus, despite winning the most seats, Magdalena Andersson announced that she would step down as prime minister, as the center-left block of parties her party was part of did not have enough seats to ensure a majority. The leader of the Moderate Party, Ulf Kristersson, was appointed Prime Minister.

ECONOMY

Sweden had entered the post-World War II era with its factories, cities and economic structure intact. This was a great advantage, especially since it had an ample supply of raw materials and was located close to western Europe, which had been ravished and partly destroyed by the war. It made full use of its advantages and soon had a highly productive and growing economy that created unimagined wealth and generosity.

Sweden has a market economy. One-third of the labor force is employed by the state. It is also very dependent upon exports, which account for half the country's GDP; 80% of its exports consist of industrial products. It must import heavily, especially oil. This reliance on foreign trade makes Sweden vulnerable to international economic conditions and prices.

The economy is not socialist, since most of the enterprises and means of production remain in private hands. This percentage had traditionally been about 95%, but it was lowered to 92% as a result of state takeovers under the non-S government between 1976 and 1982. In the 21st century, one family alone, the Wallenbergs, in their fifth generation as bankers and philanthropists, control about a third of the value of the companies listed on the Swedish stock exchange. Their holdings include such icons as Electrolux, Ericsson, Scania, ABB, and AstraZeneca. With their vast and diversified holdings, little happens in business without their involvement. About 10% of the workforce is employed by state-owned enterprises, which include the railroads, iron ore mining in Lapland, post and telephone services, and a large part of the domestic energy production, primarily hydroelectric. All are in the process of privatization. Sweden has a modern economy, with 78% of its workforce in the services sector, producing 73% of GDP, and 20% in industry, creating 25% of GDP.

It may seem ironic that the non-S coalition nationalized more Swedish industry in 4 years after 1976 than S had done in the previous 40. In the worst postwar economic crisis (1975–1977) the new government decided that some key ailing industries, especially steel production and shipbuilding sectors, could not be saved through increased state subsidies and mergers. Therefore, it boosted public spending and added more formerly private firms to the State Company (*Statsföretag*), which comprises the major part of the state-owned companies. The result was rapid wage inflation, a loss of international competitiveness, and gaping current accounts deficits.

After 1982, S returned some state-owned firms to private hands. The Bildt government carried this on in 1992 by launching the privatization of 35 such companies. S had returned to the noninterventionist rules of the "Swedish model." Subsidies to lame-duck industries were abolished, and ailing firms are allowed to die. In 2006, Reinfeldt's conservative government turned its attention to the 55

Sweden

state-owned companies, which employ 190,000 workers, and announced plans to begin privatizing 6 of them. Market forces decide which Swedish firms thrive or fail, and many industries, from telecommunications to airlines and banking, have been deregulated. Whatever financial assistance it gives is concentrated on research and development and on incentives for high-tech investment. Its overall investment in R & D is 4.3% of GDP, the world's highest, followed by Finland (3.5%) and the US (2.6%). Almost 60% of this is financed by private industry.

An impressive example of the growth of the knowledge sector and a new entrepreneurial culture is the expansion of Kista Science Park situated on a former waste site near Stockholm. Started by Ericsson and IBM in the early 1970s, it is now a sprawling complex with 600 technology companies and 27,000 workers. Even the Royal Institute of Technology and the Swedish Institute of Computer Science relocated there. Stockholm has become a breeding ground for Internet companies, and Sweden has more industrial robots per capita than any other country. Research and imagination help explain the country's continued development of modern products that sell well abroad.

S had always tended to leave the private character of the economy untouched, focusing instead on state influence over private industry and heavily taxing the profits. For S it was always more important for the state to be able to gather the eggs rather than to own the hen. What are some of the ways in which the state has influenced the economy and maintained the fabled "Swedish model"?

During its decades of rule, the priority of full employment was established so firmly that the other parties did not dare to challenge it. Unemployment had never risen above 3% since the 1930s, but it reached 6.9% in 2023; for young Swedes, that figure is a troubling 20% and 15% for migrants. It is somewhat higher among women and young people and much higher among immigrants. The actual total figure would be higher if the state did not "hide" unemployment through temporary work programs, broad retraining possibilities, early-retirement schemes, and students unable to find work. *The Financial Times* estimated in 2005 that as many as 1.6 million Swedes, or 30% of the potential workforce, were not working. The official retirement age is 67, but the average Swede retires at age 63.7. It has a higher female workplace participation (76.8% compared with 65.3% in the US) than most countries, thanks to excellent child care. Female university graduates outnumber males by six to four (57%).

Among the reasons for low unemployment formerly was an active policy of tackling unemployment, involving imaginative job retraining and other measures to make Swedish workers more mobile. It offers inducements to firms to locate in the north, where employment possibilities have always been limited. To add a stick to the carrot, generous unemployment benefits (about 80% of normal pay) are cut off if an unemployed worker refuses to accept either the training or the job he is offered. It was therefore better at reducing long-term unemployment. Even though employees are still protected from layoffs, the government allows companies to hire temporary workers who can be released at the firm's will. The result is a dramatic expansion of temporary employment companies. Fighting inflation, which stood at 1.7% in 2022, usually had a low priority. Yet, the fairly tight fiscal and monetary policy that the government pursues helps keep inflation low.

Sweden has a large public sector, high taxes, a generous welfare state, low wage differentials, and powerful labor unions. It has one of the world's highest living standards, and a 2007 UN report cited it as having the lowest incidence of poverty in the world. The 2004 UN Human Development Index ranked Sweden second only to Norway as the most attractive place in the world to live. Its vigorous private companies, such as Ericsson (which alone accounted for 8% of GDP in 2002), Volvo and SAAB (except for their automobile divisions, which were put up for sale by Ford and GM, respectively), Electrolux, ASEA, SKF, and Alfa-Laval, are world leaders in their main products. SAAB's car division was bought in 2000 by GM, which produced its cars in Germany before being put on the auction block in 2009. The Swedish government refused to buy it. As enterprise minister Maud Olofsson put it, "The Swedish state is not prepared to own car factories." SAAB sells Gripen fighter aircraft not only to the Swedish forces but also to the Czech Republic, Hungary, and South Africa. Many of these large companies are cutting their manufacturing workforce to remain competitive.

Its annual growth rate was 3.2% from 1998 to 2002. It temporarily plunged to –6.5% in the midst of the 2009 global downturn, but it bounced back to plus 2.9% in 2022. It did suffer in 2009–2010 as a result of the world recession. Its banks had lent the three Baltic states an equivalent of 18% of Sweden's GDP, so when those three economies contracted by over 10%, they dragged Swedish banks down with them. Fortunately, Sweden had learned a lot about rescuing desperately troubled banks in 1992, when the government temporarily

nationalized them, cleaned them up with a "bad bank," and then reprivatized them. Other countries, including the US, looked at this model in 2008–2010 in their efforts to save their banks.

Riksbank, the world's oldest central bank, maintains the krona, the currency the Swedes refuse to replace with the euro. The currency lost some 7 percent against the euro in 2016. The country enjoys negative interest rates, which led to an odd situation in which taxpayers found it advantageous to pay up as much tax as possible. Since the overpayments are guaranteed at least a 0.56% interest rate until they are refunded, the treasury was in effect offering a better rate than a bank. As a result, in 2016 the government's budget exhibited a $4.5 billion surplus from such overpayments alone.

Riksbank also launched a massive campaign to encourage citizens to bring their soon-to-be-invalid coins to the bank. This was no trifle, as some 1.4 billion coins worth $230 million remained in circulation just three months before they were all to become worthless at the end of June 2017. The bank even posted humorous "Wanted" posters for the old coins.

Sweden has a predominantly industrial and service economy, not an agricultural one. Its agricultural population has shrunk rapidly to 2% (producing 2% of GDP), but its modern farming methods have led to such increases in productivity that it can supply about 90% of the country's needs. EU entry has helped to keep food prices down.

Sweden is no longer the land of lumber-jacks; the number making a living from forestry has dramatically decreased in the past half-century. This is one reason for the shortage of employment opportunities in the north. The immense forests still can supply the raw material for the wood processing industry, which is competitive on world markets, despite the rather small size of the companies and the stiff competition from abroad, especially from North America. A fourth of all wood pulp and paper materials sold in the world is from Sweden. The export of other forms of raw materials has lost much of its former importance for the Swedish economy, although it still accounts for a seventh of total exports. And it was Sweden that led an adamant attempt in 2016 to ban the importation of American lobster from Maine into the EU once it discovered its growing population in Swedish waters, where it was competing with the European variety. Much to the relief of the Maine fishermen, whose catch dwarfs that of all of Europe, the attempt to prevent the "invasive species" from flooding the Swedish market failed.

It is a country with many large and multinational firms. The top 20 accounted for half of the country's total sales. Many of these giants, such as Electrolux, Volvo, and SAAB-Scania, export far more than they sell in Sweden. The large companies have also invested heavily abroad, especially in the US, Britain, France, and Germany, in order to get closer to their markets. In 1999 Volvo kept its profitable truck, construction equipment, and airplane and marine engine operations when Ford Motor Company acquired Volvo's passenger vehicle operation. In 2010 Ford sold the car known for its safety to Geely of China, which pledged to keep Volvo's production sites in Sweden and Belgium. At the same time, GM put loss-making SAAB on the auction block again and threatened to shut it down if no buyer could be found. Sweden's foreign subsidiaries employ more workers than do the home companies in Sweden. In 1996 the 25 largest Swedish companies had 75% of their employment, production, and sales abroad.

The best-known industry has traditionally been iron and steel. Sweden's iron ore is of high grade, and its steel production is also high. It has actually become a net importer of iron and steel products at present. Too much steel is produced in the world, and the steel industry everywhere is in dire need of restructuring. The state-owned mining company (LKAB) claims that it has discovered Europe's largest deposit of rare earth metals, located north of the Arctic Circle in the province of Lapland.

Machinery, automobiles, ships, armaments, metal processing, electronics (the fastest-growing Swedish industry), and other engineering products have a lion's share of Swedish production and exports. The weakest at the present time is shipbuilding, a traditional Scandinavian specialty. After the mid-1960s, Sweden had been building more ships than any country but Japan and was selling three-fourths of this production to foreigners. This reached a peak in 1976, but then it declined rapidly and never recovered. Nearly all shipbuilding wharves were closed. One of the few left is Kockums, owned since 2014 by Saab.

In a remarkable development, Sweden's telecommunications superpower Ericsson reported in 2016 the biggest drop in revenues in well over a decade, while its shares shrunk by some 50%. The company's failure to adjust to technology changes as well as its reluctance to reduce costs affected this poster child for new and dynamic sectors of Scandinavian economy that also includes Finland's Nokia. Ericsson announced plans to cut 3,000 jobs, or about a fifth of its Swedish workforce.

The innovation business also thrives in Sweden, helping incubate such popular services as Skype and Kazaa that made Niklas Zennstrom a billionaire. More recently, the world's largest music streaming company, Spotify, was established in Stockholm, where it is still headquartered. The company, however, signaled its frustration with the capital city's housing shortage and has already threatened that it might move elsewhere.

About 80% of Sweden's exports goes to the industrialized world, with Germany, Norway, the US, Denmark, UK, and Finland receiving almost half. Swedish companies want to be in the US market because of its size and so that they can absorb new trends in research and marketing. It buys most of its imports from Germany, Norway, Denmark, the Netherlands, and UK. Taken together, the other Nordic countries account for roughly a fifth of its foreign trade. Because the workforce is geared to the world market, speaks English, and is thoroughly computer literate (Sweden has one of the world's highest number per capita of computers), Sweden is one of the rich European countries that sees globalization as an opportunity, not a threat.

Those who believe that Sweden has a charmed economic existence received evidence of that in 2007. Two lady friends in the northern Swedish town of Överturingen were scouring the countryside in search of blueberries when they noticed something strange in the soil exposed by upended trees. They happened to have geologists' hammers and magnifying eyepieces with them. They dug for six hours and came upon what may be one of Europe's richest gold deposits. Sweden has some gold, but it has never been among the major gold-mining countries.

A different kind of gold-digging has led to a series of scandals since 2015, when many members of Sweden's business elite were accused of excesses, such as using corporate jets for flying their spouses, children, and even pets to hunting lodges, car races, or the Olympics. Cozy relationships among top executives sitting on various boards that mutually approved one another's pay were exposed, together with questionable bank operations overseas, revealed in the Panama Papers. Some of the most powerful businessmen in the country came under much public scrutiny in 2017 when their moose-hunting trips with politicians grabbed the headlines. Executive excesses are scorned, just as this generally egalitarian society has been experiencing the fastest rise of inequality among the most developed countries, according to the Organization for Economic Cooperation and Development (OECD). One major fallout from the scandals was the dismantling of the system of cross-shareholdings involving such major players as the holding company Industrivärden, Handelsbanken, and SCA.

European Union

The EU accounted for 56.9% of Sweden's exports and 67.3% of its imports in 2014. This offers the best explanation why Swedes voted 52.3% to 46.8% in 1994 to enter the EU in 1995. A united front of most of the country's business and political establishment supported entry. They argued that Sweden needed the EU to bolster its exports, keep companies from moving more jobs and investments abroad, improve its lagging international credit rating, and shore up its troubled economy. Farmers, environmentalists, and leftists, especially in rural areas in northern and central Sweden, led the opposition, arguing that Sweden's voice would be drowned out in the European cacophony.

Even after entry, opposition remained strong, especially to monetary union. The government held a referendum on the question in September 2003. All major parties, the business elite, and the media broadly favored the euro, with former communists, far-right, environmentalist Greens, and young Swedes against. Taking place only three days after the

Timber cutting

Sweden

popular foreign minister and spokesperson for the "yes" campaign, Anna Lindh, had been stabbed to death in a Stockholm department store, proponents expected a heavy sympathy vote in favor.

The results were a landslide defeat. With over 80% voting, 56% said "no" and only 42% said "yes." Voters under age 30 voted more heavily against it than any other age group. Swedes were persuaded by economics, not sentimentality. Sweden was performing better than in the eurozone. Its budget was balanced, its growth rate twice as high, and its unemployment rate much lower. Its economy has also benefited in the past from competitive devaluations of the krona against the dollar. There was much resentment about France's and Germany's disregard for their obligation under the euro rules to limit their budget deficits to 3% of GDP. This seemed to enable large countries to bend the rules to suit themselves while holding small ones to their commitments. Finally, the vote expressed the worry of many Swedes that European integration was creating too much centralization in Brussels.

Dissatisfaction over some other changes also played a role, such as the EU demand that Sweden liberalize its restriction on alcohol. This had been one of the cornerstones of Swedish social policy throughout the 20th century. It had to drop state monopolies on the import and wholesale distribution of spirits. Sweden is happy to be outside the eurozone until the euro turbulence quiets down. All parties support the kind of sound public finances that keep the krona stable. It is obligated to decide again on accepting the euro, but that will not occur in the near future.

Energy Dependence

Energy is one of Sweden's economic Achilles' heels. Like the other Nordic countries, which are sparsely populated and situated in a cold climate, its energy consumption per capita is among the highest in the world (but behind that of Norway, Canada, and the United States). It is very dependent upon OPEC countries, especially Saudi Arabia, for a particularly vital import: oil. Slightly over half of its energy needs must be covered by imports (down from 78% in 1973), especially by oil. Accounting for 15% of its overall needs, water power is its most important domestic source, providing half of its electricity generation; nuclear power produces the other half. Wood accounts for 2% of overall needs; nuclear power for about 15%; and coal, coke, wastes, and other domestic sources for 12%.

Efforts are being made to reduce reliance on oil. Sweden is continuing its effective conservation measures. Between 1976 and 1986, it halved its oil consumption in response to the "oil shock," despite a growing number of automobiles. It has begun to serve clusters of homes with heat produced centrally in nearby heat plants and also is increasing its use of imported coal, peat, its own wood, water power, and nuclear power (first introduced in the 1960s and 1970s). Sweden produces Europe's second-highest percentage of renewable energy as a proportion of its total energy needs (29.6% in 2007; EU average is 6.5%), after Latvia.

Sweden dived deeply into nuclear energy. S had developed plans during its last years in power before the 1976 election to build a total of 24 nuclear plants that could provide over half of all the country's energy. The Center Party placed the issue squarely in the political limelight during the 1976 election, and in power it refused to permit the fueling and starting up of the seventh and eighth plants. After two years of wrangling within the center coalition and countless demonstrations by the powerful environmentalist groups, the government collapsed on the issue.

When the nuclear accident occurred at Three Mile Island near Harrisburg, Pennsylvania, the government decided to put the issue of nuclear power to a referendum in 1980. The outcome of the referendum was a kind of compromise: Sweden would complete the construction of the 12 planned reactors, but it would shut down all nuclear plants by 2010. This defused the issue for a while. The Chernobyl accident in Ukraine in 1986 caused limited but highly publicized radioactive contamination in northern Sweden.

Sweden was on the horns of an energy dilemma. To buy more time, the government announced in 1991 that plans to abolish nuclear power would be postponed while energy-saving and pollution-free alternatives were sought. The country's 1997 energy policy allowed 10 reactors to operate longer than envisaged by the 1980 phase-out policy, but also resulted in the premature closure of a two-unit plant (1200 MWe). The Persson government (1996–2006) closed down 1 plant in 1999 and another in 2005, leaving only 10 plants running in 2006, producing 52% of the country's electricity. In 2006 one of them was temporarily shut down after its emergency systems were activated. The same thing happened again in 2008, when cracks in some control rods were discovered in the Oskarshamn 3 plant.

No adequate substitute sources have been found. That was why Prime Minister Reinfeldt announced in February 2009 a plan to reverse the 30-year ban on building new nuclear power plants.

In 2010, the Swedish parliament passed legislation allowing existing reactors to be replaced with new ones on existing sites.

The heat of the public debate over nuclear power in Sweden again reached meltdown levels, and it flared up in 2011, when six reactors in Japan were severely damaged by a tsunami and threatened to melt down.

In 2011 a formal application was made to build a permanent repository for high-level nuclear waste 500 meters below the surface in granite bedrock. In 2015 decisions were made to close four older reactors by 2020, removing 2.8 GWe net. And then, in 2016, the government announced a major change of direction, declaring its intention to build as many as 10 new reactors to replace old ones, including those 4 scheduled to close by the end of the decade. This compromise plan, reached by most mainstream parties, also qualified the plan to switch to renewable sources by 2040: It would not preclude keeping some nuclear plants after all. Furthermore, the utility companies were promised that a tax on nuclear power (that amounted to some $484 million in 2015) would be eliminated.

Sweden's energy problems will increase in the future, and Swedish heavy industry has argued that the country is not ready for a rapid switch to renewable energy, currently planned to be completed by 2040. The country's estimated uranium reserves of over 300,000 tons made it tempting to stick with this important source of domestic energy rather than to scramble to supply an even greater percentage of its total needs with expensive carbon imports. Sweden's nuclear power reactors already provide about 40% of its electricity.

In June 2023, the new Kristersson Cabinet established after the 2022 election voted to replace the national energy target from "100 percent renewable electricity production by 2040" to "100 percent fossil-free electricity production by 2040," a move seen as supporting and extending the ongoing use of nuclear power in the country.

Currently, there are three nuclear power plants in the country, with six reactors in operation. These NPPs are the Forsmark, Oskarshamn and Ringhals plants.

In November 2023 the government announced plans to construct two large-scale reactors by 2035 and the equivalent of 10 new reactors, including small modular reactors, by 2045.

The return to nuclear power facilitated the development of safer nuclear reactors. The Swedes, with their Process Inherent Ultimately Safe Reactor (PIUS), are pioneering in the newest nuclear technology and could turn a bitter necessity into a commercially profitable virtue. Sweden has an excellent record of nuclear safety.

Labor Unions

Since 1938, when an agreement between the employer organizations and trade unions was reached at Saltsjöbaden, relations between management and labor have, on the whole, been characterized by cooperation rather than by confrontation. All Swedes benefited from this. Every year or two, the highest representatives of the LO (Landsorganisationen), which represents 15 unions with 1.8 million members, and the SAF met to establish general wage guidelines, which were then normally observed down the line. The LO was able to insist upon the principle of "solidarity wages," which means equal pay for the same kind of work, regardless of the profitability of any specific firm. Thus, struggling firms could be strained even further by having to pay the same wages as the more successful companies.

The concept of "solidarity wages" is under attack by skilled workers' unions and employers. Also, the unions, to which 90% of the labor force belongs, carefully guard the pay differentials between certain categories of jobs. When these pay differentials are not observed, rare but serious nationwide strikes can break out. Centralized wage negotiations, abandoned in 1984, often brought stability and labor peace. The nonsocialist government proposed in 1991 to dismantle centralized wage bargaining (which has all but disappeared), de-regulating the labor market and lowering corporate wage bills. But Swedish unions resist the steep decline suffered by trade unions elsewhere by accepting necessary technological change. They traditionally are innovative, not reactive. They still run the country's unemployment benefits schemes.

National Debt

To pay for its imports, its budgetary deficits, and the foreign travel its prosperous citizens have come to love, Sweden went deeper and deeper into debt. High wage costs and tax rates deprived industries of investment funds they need to maintain their productivity. Any drop in productivity strikes at the very heart of Sweden's "middle way." That model, by which social welfare and income redistribution would be paid for by a robust private sector, now seems to work only in times of economic growth.

Sweden's high public consumption is vividly reflected in its comprehensive social welfare system, which some admirers contend make it the most just society in the world. Some observers have called it the perfect "postindustrial" society that has effectively solved its problems of production and can now concentrate on distributing economic and social benefits widely and justly. In other words, the consumption and distribution of wealth had allegedly replaced the production of it as the society's major problem. The resulting economic difficulties showed how the "postindustrial" situation is by no means static, if it ever existed at all, and that there are great dangers in focusing too much on consumption and losing sight of production. Welfare spending was significantly trimmed in the 1990s, bringing by 2013 the total national debt down to 42% of GDP (one of the lowest in the EU) and producing an annual budget deficit of only 2% of GDP in 2014.

Welfarism and Taxation

Swedes understandably do not wish to give up a welfare system that pays almost all doctors' bills and at least half of dental bills, which provides invalids with about 90% of their normal pay until age 65 and which pays the unemployed 80% of their former income. It provides five weeks of paid vacation time and allows the employee to save up his or her vacation time and take it all in one extended period. By 1995 the average workweek for a fulltime employee was 36 hours, one of the lowest in all Europe; the average time off work, for all reasons including vacation, is about 25%. Progress has been made toward gender equality, but women still earn less and are underrepresented on company boards.

Sick pay of 80% of normal earnings after the first day of illness (for which one receives nothing) encourage the average Swede to be officially absent from work for reasons of illness 25 days (more than a working month) per year. In the sparsely populated north, this sickness absenteeism rises to 70 days per year. Even though the average Swede smokes less, drinks less, weighs less, and lives longer than other Europeans, on any given workday, over 10% of the 5,6 million workforce (560,000) is absent due to illness. Such sickness costs Sweden roughly as much as it spends on defense, foreign aid, higher education, and research put together.

This welfare system is generous, but many Swedes agree that it is impossible to pay for. Costs of maintaining the system have expanded annually more rapidly than has economic growth. But as conservatives experienced in the 1994 elections, it was risky to reduce social programs that Swedes have grown to regard as their birthright. For more than 50 years, they had been taught that state and society were the same things and that the function of government was to attempt to solve all problems. The Bildt government's message was that "the state ought not to strive after doing what a free society can manage better or as well." It no longer saw a need for welfare services to be entirely under public management and control; private initiative enjoyed more encouragement. Even S, which built the welfare state, supported crisis measures to save Sweden's economy and currency. These included reducing housing subsidies, sickness benefits, and foreign aid; making employers and employees share health benefits and sickness insurance with the state; and raising gasoline and cigarette taxes.

Old-age pensions were changed to begin at age 67. Considering that the average Swede retires at 63.7 years of age, this requires an adjustment. The population is rapidly ageing: In 2008, 17% were over 65, and that will rise to an estimated 24% by 2040. About 93% of the elderly live at home. To secure the solvency of the system, Sweden radically restructured its basic taxpayer-funded retirement system and even permits a portion of the funds to be invested in the stock and bond market. It moved its pension system from defined benefits to defined contribution, meaning that what one receives in retirement varies according to how much one paid into the system. Thus, Swedes lost their guaranteed generous state pensions. Not surprisingly, the private pension market is booming.

Unlike Norway, Sweden has no oil revenues that can pay the difference. The national, regional, and local governments employ a third of the Swedish workforce (compared to the OECD average of one-fifth). Sweden has reduced public spending from 67% of GDP in 1993 to 49% in 2013. The bulk of government spending can only be paid for by direct and indirect taxes, which were over half (51.4% in 2005) of the average Swede's wages, the highest in the OECD.

Income taxes are steeply progressive. The top marginal rate in 2013 was 57%.

One of Sweden's many rivers—every fifth family owns a boat

Sweden

The tax code appeared unjust because rich Swedes learned how to use the complex system of deductions to lighten their burden. Estate taxes were abolished in 2005. Ex-finance minister Kjell-Olof Feldt called the system "rotten." The major parties agreed to simplify the income tax structure by introducing a differing rate structure: 34% for the average payer who earns under $43,000 per year and 57% for those earning more. Corporate tax was reduced from 50% to 22%. Many loopholes were eliminated. Taxes on capital gains were made more equitable with other forms of income. Swedes still pay a VAT of 25%.

The high tax level has had some negative consequences. It drove such wealthy Swedes as tennis star Bjorn Borg and skier Ingemar Stenmark into tax exile in Monaco. It drives some business out of the country. For example, Ericsson, a telecoms supplier, moved key corporate and production functions abroad; in 1999 it opened a big headquarters in London in order to help it recruit foreign managers who would refuse to settle in high-tax Sweden. It has encouraged tax evasion and "barter work," one of the most primitive forms of work whereby Swedes swap services with each other behind the backs of the tax officials. For instance, a carpenter builds a cabinet for a mechanic who repairs his car in return. It is estimated that such an "underground economy" combined with smuggling equals 5%–10% of GDP.

The tax system also discourages some Swedes from seeking promotions because most of the added pay would be collected by the state anyway. Working overtime is less attractive for the same reason. For example, in 1979 an employer offered his workers a bonus of $2,000 if they worked between Christmas and New Year, but it was turned down because taxes would make the bonus negligible. Also, a fourth of the total labor force now finds it more attractive to work half-time than full-time because of the tax structure.

The welfare system would not have some of these negative effects if the former Lutheran work ethic had remained intact. As late as the early 1970s, one's social status and self-esteem was still largely established by one's occupation and position. However, as in many other industrialized countries, many Swedes' drive to have individual success has weakened, and the importance attached to financial rewards and status has decreased. Fewer people obtain job satisfaction, partly because much work has become automated and routinized and partly because prosperity created leisure-time activities that became increasingly attractive. In other words, Swedes have fewer qualms about being absent from work.

The Reinfeldt government sought to crack down on welfare cheating by creating a fraud squad to investigate criminal misuse and passing legislation making it easier to prosecute cheaters. It also ended the previous practice of simply trusting without checking claims that are filed. A government-appointed commission concluded in 2007 that up to 6% of total social welfare payments result from fraud or abuse. Considering that 12% of the population are foreigners, many of whom cannot find work, an increasing number of Swedes believe the traditional welfare system is unsustainable. The government trimmed benefits to the point that the country no longer stands out for welfare excesses.

Finally, the social welfare system, which distributes 15% of GDP, has not evened out the differences in income, as many of its proponents had hoped, although these differences are certainly narrower than in most countries, including the US. The biggest gap faces non-European immigrants, who constitute 46% of the jobless and whose household incomes are 36% lower than native-born Swedes. Nor has the welfare system led to a diminution of crime, alcoholism, suicides, juvenile delinquency, vandalism, or other antisocial activities, as many of its supporters had argued that it would. In fact, crime has risen so much, especially in the cities, that Sweden became one of the first countries in the world to provide financial compensation to victims of violent crimes. Foreigners stand out: They constitute 26% of all prisoners and half of those serving more than five years.

CULTURE

The Equality Goal

Perhaps no nation in all of Europe has tried so hard to establish equality in so many segments of its society as have the Swedes. They have been willing to experiment, and their reforms are regarded with great interest from abroad. In many ways they have fallen short of this goal; there are still noticeable differences in wealth, income, and social status, and not all Swedes agree that every effort and policy designed to achieve the goal of equality has been a good one. Many of the policies are being criticized on the grounds that they are unrealistic or that they place limits on the ability of an individual to use his talents to the fullest and to reap the benefits of his own capacity and effort. Critics contend that the result is often mediocrity; omnipresent and suffocating bureaucracy; or, worse, a restriction of human freedom. But Swedes are a tolerant people with a strong pluralistic tradition. They debate these matters openly and do not try to hide the problems or the failures. Also, they have always had a pragmatic inclination and

are able to undo those reforms, which most might agree have created more problems than they have solved.

One distinction among people that has almost entirely disappeared involves the word "you." The person who speaks English uses the same word for all individuals he addresses, remnants of this lingual distinction having disappeared from English in the last century (the formal usage was "thee," "thou," and "thine"). But all other European languages have preserved different words for "you"—a formal one (in Swedish, *ni*) for persons whom one does not know well, whom one wants to keep at arm's length, or whom one wants to show particular respect, and an informal one (in Swedish, *du*) for friends, family, or often those beneath one's own social station (such as a maid or gardener). More than in any other European country, the formal *ni* has fallen into disuse, and almost everyone is simply addressed as *du*. The only exceptions are elderly persons, who cannot accept such a modern equalizing step in their last years, and the king and queen, whom only journalists dare to address in public as *du*.

By law boys and girls must be given the same opportunities in schools. A few pioneer schools seek to blur the gender line completely by avoiding the pronouns "he," "him," "she," and "her" altogether and simply calling the pupils "friends."

In addition to dropping the formal "you," they are also casting off many of the academic and occupational titles that used to adorn so many persons' names. Swedes were traditionally a very title-conscious people, with many persons attaching to their name a "Dr.," "Mr. Director," "Mr. Chief Postal Inspector," or, of course, a title of nobility in this monarchical country. The titles are less often in use now because they no longer fit easily into the egalitarian movement. Pupils do not call their teachers "Mr." or "Mrs.," and students at the universities seldom address their professors or instructors as "Professor" or "Doctor." It is also customary for students to address their lecturers or teachers by their first name.

The Family

More equality has seeped into the Swedish family, where few fathers are stern disciplinarians who are treated with a combination of love, respect, and fear by other members. With one of the world's highest female participation rates in the labor force, the patriarchal character of the Swedish family declined or disappeared, and the position of both sexes was equalized. Family members have a more relaxed, comradely relationship with each other, especially in urban, middle-class families.

Sweden

As in most advanced industrialized societies, the extended family no longer lives under one roof. The elderly are financially independent, since they receive at age 67 pensions that amount to two-thirds of their earlier working incomes and that are regularly adjusted for inflation. At present, 16% of Swedes receive old-age pensions. The state provides them with an array of social services if they are needed. These services include the cleaning of their apartments or bodies in order to keep hygienic standards high, delivery of complete meals, chauffeuring and even special subsidies to enable them to remain in their own homes as long as possible. When they need full care, they can move into state-operated homes for the elderly. This usually occurs at about age 80. This involves many Swedes, since the life expectancy is 79.7 for men and 83.7 for women.

Fewer and fewer persons are in the workforce to support them because the nation's population is growing only because of immigration. By 2003 the total fertility rate of Swedish women had fallen to 1.29 per woman, whereas the rate needed to match the number of people dying is 2.1. One baby in four being born is from an immigrant family. The modest annual population increase is almost entirely due to immigrants' high birth rate, but by 2006 Swedes' birth rate was again rising. Sweden has the lowest infant mortality rate in the world. Contrary to a popular misconception, it does not have Europe's highest suicide rate; even just within the EU, there are a dozen other countries with higher rates.

There are some persons who find drawbacks in the breakdown of the extended family under one roof, but the absence of the elderly from the homes of their children's families has undoubtedly brought greater freedom to most of those families and has eliminated an authority pattern which tended to bring more hierarchy and less equality into the family.

Not only the Swedish extended family has changed, but also the very institution of the family is undergoing radical alteration. By the end of the 1980s, the Swedish marriage rate had fallen to the lowest in the industrial world. Nonmarital cohabitation is now regarded legally and culturally as an accepted alternative rather than as a prelude to marriage. Two-thirds of all couples have lived together before marriage; among the young, the rate is close to 90%. Half the babies are born out of wedlock. The average ages for first marriages are 30 for men and 27 for women (vs. 25.5 and 23.3 in the US).

A growing number of Swedes are not marrying at all. In today's cohabitation environment, even the arrival of children is no longer a strong reason for marriage.

Swedish student at College of Europe, Bruges

Gone for the most part are engagement parties and elaborate weddings. Divorce is also reducing the number of families. Thus, an ever-larger percentage of Swedish families have only one parent.

In 1994 same-sex couples were granted the right to enter civil partnerships. Since 2004 they are allowed to adopt children or to have them by artificial insemination in Sweden. Most gay couples who opt for the latter go to Denmark for the procedure. In 2009 same-sex couples received the same right to marry as heterosexual couples. Individual churches retain the right to decide if they want to wed gay couples. There is an ombudsman for gay men and lesbians to ensure that their rights are respected.

In a country in which 70% of adult women have full- or part-time jobs (encouraged by the tax system, which taxes each partner separately), having children can cause strains. The state provides certain payments and allowances to families with children so that their living standards will not fall below those of families in which there are no children. These payments vary; the less the parents earn, the more such assistance they receive. When a child is born, both the mother and the father have the right to divide 14 months of almost fully paid vacation (80% of lost wages up to SKr24,562, or $3,425 per month) in order to care for the infant. An additional 90 days could be taken off for a token sum.

Even nonworking parents can receive a per-diem allowance for 14 months to care for the child. Or, they can put aside six months of this childcare vacation and use them at any other time for any reason until the child is eight years old. Mothers take 85% of all parental leave, although 85% of fathers take some parental leave. Both the father and the mother have the right to take up to 60 days paid sick leave per child, not only if they are ill, but also if their child is ill. Thus, while the law encourages both parents to work (an undeniable factor in national and personal prosperity), it has to provide benefits to enable them to perform the mother's traditional chores. Children are guaranteed a place in a full-time preschool costing no more than $150 per month. Family benefits are an expensive program, consuming 3.3% of GDP, the highest in the world, along with Denmark and France.

The child enjoys a legal protection against being spanked or hit by its parents: "A child may not be subjected to physical punishment or other injurious or humiliating treatment." Swedish children are very aware of the law, and there is considerable discussion among parents and children on how parents can discipline children without hitting them. In any event, the law reflects the extent to which the child's role in the modern Swedish family has changed.

The woman's role in the family has also changed; 60% work outside the home. The law protects her equality at the work place. A special equality ombudsman, who is usually a woman, is empowered to investigate complaints of discrimination. There are numerous visible signs of women's changed role in society. They can now perform sentry duty at the royal palace in Stockholm, a place where the head resident can be a woman now that the law of succession was changed. Sweden's UN Peacekeeping Forces include women. In 1999 the government proposed that the equality of women be recognized by subjecting them to military conscription. While the draft was abolished in 2010, it was reinstituted in 2017, and this time it includes women. The constitution forbids gender discrimination except in cases of military service or affirmative action. Since 1980 females are allowed to join the

Sweden

officer corps and constitute 2% of the total. They have entered the priesthood of the Swedish State Church. Women's wages in 2014 were 13.2 percent lower than men's. Despite specific quotas for female participation on major companies' boards, only 7% of companies listed on the Stockholm OMX Index have a female CEO, but that still gives Sweden the highest ranking in the world. Higher education remains a male fortress, with 75 percent of university professors being men.

Although the women's role as equals in family decision making is rather secure, they still have to do more of the housework than do men. The government-sponsored Equality Commission reported that in families where both partners had full-time jobs, 51% of the women worked 20 hours or more in the home, and 10% did more than 40 hours of work, compared with only 18% of the men, who did 20 hours or more and 2% who did more than 40 hours. As an expert said, "We are still a long way from achieving real equality in Sweden. In the home there is not a lot else we can do, except by keeping the debate alive." For a while, at least, men will continue to be able to take it a little easier at home than will women.

In 2016 the World Economic Forum ranked Sweden fourth in the world in terms of women's position in society, preceded by three other Nordic countries. More than 43% of Swedish parliament members are women, and an impressive 54% of the government ministers are female. Some of the paradoxes related to women's position in politics came to the fore with the "feminist government" created by the center-left coalition of Social Democrats and Greens that took power in 2014. And yet, when the Swedish governmental delegation went to Iran on a trade visit in 2017, its female members, including trade minister Ann Linde, who led the group, wore headscarves. This created quite a stir in Sweden, where violations of women's rights in Iran are widely condemned, and many expected the "feminist government" to make an opposite statement in this respect.

Thanks to vigorous public discussion of sexual violence, Swedish women have a strong consciousness of abuse. Laws protect them from a wide range of sexual assault and rape. Sweden has by far the EU's highest number of reported rapes.

Sexual Policy

The constitution protects freedom of expression, including adult pornography. While the publication and distribution of child pornography is banned by law, the fact that Swedes are unique in Europe in being permitted to own and view it prompted Queen Silvia to break with tradition and attack it in an outspoken television interview in 1996. Although most Swedes agree with her opinion, the audacity of a monarch to intervene in political debate was surprising.

The abortion law was liberalized in 1974 to permit abortions until the 18th week with no questions asked and until the 22nd week under certain circumstances, by permission from a health board.

Sweden has made the fight against the international trafficking of women a high-priority foreign policy issue. It is perhaps the only western country to pass a pilot law making the purchase, not the sale, of sexual services illegal. In other words, the prostitute is regarded as the victim, and it is not the prostitute but those who buy or organize the sexual services who break the law.

Education

Since the 1960s increasing stress has been placed upon achieving social equality and less on competition. The general idea is that all persons are born with talent and capabilities, but an unequal social environment creates the differences among human beings. The schools are seen as an important socializing agent to counteract the unequal environment in other parts of the society. Put in an oversimplified way, the schools should focus as much on social development as on learning.

Most children attend the basic school (grundskolan) for nine years. New teaching methods have been introduced, including group work; individualized curricula; and special activities, such as learning chess in the fourth grade. The issuing of grades is strictly limited in the first six years, and there are no final examinations during the first nine years.

After the nine compulsory years, about 80% continue for two or four years in an integrated high school called gymnasieskolan. This combines more than 20 different curricula under one roof. Some pupils take a more rigorous academic course, preparing one for university studies, while others take a more practical course, preparing one for a trade or commercial career.

Educational vouchers permit parents to send their kids to whatever school they choose. Parents may even take their vouchers to private schools. Private companies or voluntary groups may establish "free schools." Almost half of pupils choose not to go to their local schools. Over 10% of them under 16 and more than 20% of schoolchildren over age 16 attend these free schools. Two-thirds of these are run by private companies. They are funded by the state but are operated privately and permitted to select students according to their own criteria. Children attend free of charge, but the schools must meet national educational standards. Critics contend that these schools draw kids from middle-class families, leaving poorer children in badly performing public schools.

All pupils who finish a course of study at this integrated high school are eligible to apply for a place at one of the more than 30 state institutions of higher education, integrated in a single system of higher education (högskola). The major universities are in Uppsala, Lund, Stockholm, Göteborg Örebro, Växjö, and Umea. There are only a limited number of places in each field. Rather than distributing these places strictly on the basis of previous academic performance, a fourth of them are reserved for people over age 25 with four years of work experience or two years at the high school and knowledge of Swedish and English. The rest of the openings are given to those applicants with the best academic records. Women dominate the lecture halls in some fields: 60% of the university graduates are women. Most law and theology students are female, as are four-fifths of students enrolled in medical and diagnostic treatment programs. Men still predominate in departments of engineering, natural science and math, and business administration.

Many critics argue that the preferential treatment given to those who did not prepare for the university but who entered later in life creates at best an equality of mediocrity. They say that the academic standards have gone down considerably, that the university has become easier, and that the students cannot write well any more. There are almost no critics against the fact that there is no tuition at the universities and that most students receive loans to help finance their studies. The borrowers must pay back a sum to which intervening inflation has been added.

Nor is there any criticism against the well-developed system of adult education, which was created in the 19th century. These kinds of equal opportunity are seen to be good. But the kind of equality which subordinates academic talent and performance to class or social considerations and which thereby lowers the quality of scholarship has not been accepted. In general, there is something of a backlash forming against what many Swedes see as a lowering of standards and discipline in schools at all levels. Societies have been formed to press for changes in what they see as a trend toward mediocrity. Between 2000 and 2012, Sweden saw the most profound decline in learning among the most developed countries in the world, as measured by the Pisa tests. This adds to rising concerns over the trend toward privatization of public services, especially in education, where private schools, such as the English International School, successfully compete with public ones for the best students. However, it is too early to say what long-term effect this undercurrent of protest and dissatisfaction will have.

Ethnic Diversity

Further compounding educational (and economic) problems is Sweden's growing ethnic diversity. Unlike some other European nations, Sweden had no colonial possessions in the past several centuries that would have exposed its society to foreign influences. In the 1960s Sweden's booming industry was starved for labor, so immigrants were attracted to it from outside the Nordic area. But it never adopted a "guest worker" policy that foresaw immigrants returning to their countries once their jobs ended. The percentage of Nordics among the total foreign population in Sweden fell from about two-thirds in 1971 to less than half today.

The influx is greatly influenced by conflicts in the world. The crackdown and declaration of martial law in Poland at the end of 1981 brought many Poles to the country. A wave of "boat people" from Vietnam also drifted ashore.

After 2003 Iraqis became the second-largest immigrant group after Finns. By 2008 Iraqis numbered 80,000, a third of whom were unemployed. The governments of the two countries reached an agreement in 2008 allowing some of them to be returned home forcibly. The government altered the asylum requirements. Seekers had to prove that they were being singled out for persecution, and only one in five could do that (down from 80% earlier). Those denied entry could either accept a little money and a free plane ticket home, or they could be ejected by the police. In 2013 the requirements were eased for refugees from battle-torn Syria, who could reach Sweden. They were granted permanent residence with the right to bring their families. This influx pushed up the number of refugees to the highest level since the Balkan wars in the 1990s. By 2013 about 14% of Sweden's population were immigrants or asylum seekers.

Nordic immigrants can become citizens after only two years; for others the minimum is five, and there are inhibiting costs and complications. About 60% of the more than 1 million immigrants have acquired Swedish citizenship, but even non-Swedes with work and residence permits by law are treated on the basis of equality with native Swedes. This means that immigrants receive all welfare benefits for which they have contributed but little, that they are not forced to go home if they lose their jobs, and that they can even vote and stand for election in local and regional elections as long as they have been residents there for at least three years.

Government offices distribute information materials in 14 languages explaining residents' rights and duties, taxes, insurance, employment, and educational possibilities. The state also publishes an immigrant newspaper in six languages. Employers are required to provide foreigners with up to 240 hours of Swedish-language instruction on company time. In 2010 a new immigration policy took effect paying immigrants to attend full-time language classes, civic orientation courses, or job training for two years after they obtain residence permits. The chief aim is to get women into the labor market.

Schools are required to give auxiliary Swedish lessons to immigrant children for as many years as are necessary to make the child completely competent in the language. They must offer special instruction to an immigrant child in his own mother tongue for as long as the parents desire such instruction. For adults who desire it, the schools also arrange for home study of the non-Swedish native language. The basic principle is that the state should be committed to helping any person residing in the country to maintain his own language.

The extent to which Swedish officialdom has gone to accommodate immigrants is perhaps unparalleled in the entire world. Public opinion surveys also underscore the fact that, while there is widespread opposition to further immigration, there is still considerable toleration toward those immigrants who already are in Sweden. There had been no race riots as there had been in countries like France, Britain, and the US. But events in May

2013 showed that Sweden is not immune. Unprecedented rioting began after police fatally shot an elderly man wielding a knife. For several days and nights, bands mainly of young immigrants torched cars and buildings, first in Stockholm suburbs and then in a half-dozen other cities. The violence shook Swedes and shocked the world. Explanations for the hooliganism centered on youth unemployment (22%, higher for immigrants), widening income inequality, and tensions between immigrants and the native population. Benefiting politically from this mayhem is a rising vote-catching anti-immigration party called Sweden Democrats, who command about 15% in the polls, down from the high of 26% at the peak of the migrant crisis. Also gaining in popularity is the ultranationalist Sweden Democratic Youth party, whose chairperson, Jessica Ohlson, sees refugees as a cultural threat to the "Swedish tradition."

Many Swedes are having difficulties learning to live with the large number of foreigners within their midst, especially in the larger cities. By 2003, a tenth of the residents were non-Nordic. Assimilation of the one-fourth of the population that is either foreign-born or have a least one parent born abroad has not succeeded. Therefore, a new Integration Office reflects a changed government focus on ensuring that individuals in diverse groups have equal rights and opportunities and are not subjected to racism and discrimination.

This difficulty is made worse by the fact that the visible increase in non-European and southern European immigrants and asylum seekers has coincided with

The changing faces of Sweden

Sweden

a frightening rise in unemployment and crime. Immigrants, who most often but not always work at the dirtiest, noisiest, or most monotonous jobs, are increasingly confronting Swedish prejudice and anxiety about the changing ethnic composition of Swedish cities.

In some cities, such as Malmö, the immigrant population (either born abroad or having two foreign parents) had reached 37% by 2008 and will be a majority within a decade. In the suburb of Rosengård, it exceeded 90%, compared with the national average of 15%. Half and rising of the children in Malmö schools have at least one foreign-born parent. Malmö, one-fourth of whose population is Muslim, has become one of Europe's most racially divided cities, and there is little interaction between the communities. This is made worse by a Danish marriage law that forbids a foreign spouse under 24 from living in the country; to get around this, couples live in Malmö and commute to Copenhagen to work. A series of at least 30 grenade attacks in Malmö in 2015 exposed further problems, as possible gang warfare unsettled many residents, especially in the Rosengård area, often described as an immigrant ghetto. Poverty and overcrowding here are among the highest in Sweden.

In Europe today, any immigrant minority that approaches or exceeds 10% of the city's population usually spells trouble in one form or another. In 1989 a parliamentary commission of inquiry against racism and xenophobia judged the danger to have grown sufficiently that it recommended a law banning racist organizations. The extraordinary campaign to block the 2004 Olympic Games from coming to Stockholm demonstrated the problem. An extremist organization calling itself We Who Build Sweden asserted that it would "never allow a large number of niggers, Latinos and Eurotrash to come here, paid for by the Swedish taxpayer." Two bombs went off, and dozens of explosively racist threats were made. Partly because of this obnoxious campaign by a determined minority, Stockholm was not even among the top three contenders for the games.

The problem of rights violations does not stem only from extremist locals. Swedes were stunned in 2002 when a Kurdish father in the university town of Uppsala fatally shot his daughter in the head in the presence of her mother and younger sister for refusing an arranged marriage with a stranger from Türkiye. The victim had been an outspoken champion for second-generation immigrants seeking their way of life.

The killing called into question Sweden's capacity to integrate its growing ethnic minorities, which in 2011 included 450,000 Muslims. Authorities moved to close a

A nighttime scene of *The Nutcracker* performed at the Stockholm Opera

legal loophole that permitted foreign girls to marry at age 15, when others may wed only at 18. They also granted more money to crisis centers for young women trying to avoid arranged marriages or leave violent partners. Such incidents have lessened Swedes' readiness to allow foreigners to remain in the country: In the 1970s and 1980s, about 80% of applicants were permitted to stay, but that percentage had fallen to 40% in the 1990s.

A rude drawing by a cartoonist, Lars Vilks, published in 2007, along with Sweden's 500-troop deployment to Afghanistan, were seen as the motivation for a young man of Middle Eastern origin who blew himself up prematurely in a bustling Stockholm shopping district before Christmas 2010. He had a cache of explosives in his car that went off and more strapped to his stomach and in a backpack. There would have been mass casualties if the bombs had not ignited early, killing him and wounding two passersby. Carl Bildt stated the obvious: "We were extremely lucky."

Such suicide bombings were unprecedented in the country, and they threaten to shatter Sweden's self-image as a haven of peace and stability. A regrettable backlash was the more than a dozen arson attacks against mosques in 2014. In 2016, after more than 35,000 unaccompanied minors sought asylum in Sweden the previous year, Stockholm police prevented a mass attack by scores of masked men dressed in black who intended to rough up such young immigrants. The thugs turned out to be mostly soccer hooligans who, in a rare display of cooperation, gathered under the slogan, "It's enough now!" Afro-Swedes are particularly frequent targets of hate

crimes, but a number of Roma (Gypsy) migrants from Romania have been attacked and even doused with gasoline and set ablaze. As EU citizens, Romanians are free to move around throughout all member states. Their begging shocks the Swedes, however, as it used to be extremely rare in the prosperous and orderly country. Roma makeshift camps and squatting on private lands further aggravates tensions.

Swedes are very hospitable toward guests whom they invite in their homes, but as one observer, Richard F. Tomasson, wrote, "There is general agreement on the Swedes as stolid and stiff, shy or reserved, formal and conventional, inhibited—even dull, nonexpressive, more interested in things than in people." Even Olof Palme stated that "we're probably shy and reserved . . . and the humor of hell would have the humor of Sweden. We are distant and perhaps rather dull." Thanks to the influence of immigrants and the fact that Sweden is more open to Europe, that "distance" and "dullness" is changing, especially among the well-traveled youth.

This is still a country with much public decorum, and many Swedes are inclined to withdraw into quiet anonymity. The content of much of Sweden's contemporary literature and of many of its films is the problem that individuals have in establishing meaningful contacts and relationships with others. It is therefore not surprising that many immigrants perceive their official treatment as fair and generous, but on the personal level, such treatment is not always warm and friendly and is sometimes even aloof and hostile. Swedes see shyness as a positive trait and talkativeness as a negative one; they prefer being silent and alone. There is, of course, a positive side to

Swedish crime-writer superstar Henning Mankell

all this: They shun conflict and do not like to say things for the sake of teasing others. Half as many Swedes as Italians and Finns admit to losing their temper easily if they cannot get their way.

The growing Swedish anxiety has been reflected in much tighter regulations for newcomers. Almost no one coming from outside the Nordic area can now receive a work permit, and as a rule, only family members of immigrants already in Sweden are allowed to settle there. Authorities are making faster and stricter decisions on applications by political refugees and are immediately deporting those who are denied this status. Sweden, like most other wealthy European nations, began to close its open door. Syrians were granted special status, given the horror that befell their country.

It turns away people with unfounded claims to asylum. Nevertheless, 40,000 asylum seekers were arriving in Sweden each year by 2003, in part because other European countries had applied greater restrictions. It was estimated in 2005 that about 10,000 persons whose asylum had been rejected had simply gone underground in Sweden. In the face of furious demands from churches, parties, and immigration organizations that they be legalized, the government allowed such illegal residents to reapply for asylum. With EU enlargement in 2004, Sweden at first announced temporary restrictions on the free movement of workers from the eight new members from central Europe. But parliament decided that these measures were too restrictive, and Sweden became one of the few EU15 members to keep its doors open.

Swedish attitudes were severely tested during the 2015 migrant wave that swept Europe, with many migrants aiming specifically to reach the country. After some 80.000 asylum seekers entered Sweden in 2014, more than 160,000 asylum applications were received in 2015, with a huge, unprecedented number of unaccompanied minors. Sweden agreed to participate in the 2015 EU migrant relocation scheme of 160.000 people to be distributed from Italy and Greece among the other EU members; its share was up to 54,000. Blasting the east central European states that originally refused to participate—Hungary, Slovakia, Czech Republic, and Romania—Sweden's prime minister Löfven observed, "to say, 'this isn't my problem, we can't accept Muslims,'—no, I don't think this is part of our European values." Still, the large influx of young people was bound to put pressure on Swedish schools, while social services and law enforcement were put under tremendous stress, too. Löfven proposed a scheme through which all Swedish local government councils would be required to accept some refugees, while the government would provide assistance to help with the housing costs.

In the fall of 2015, 10,000 asylum seekers were arriving in Sweden every week. By November, Sweden reversed its open-door policy, reverting to the EU-mandated minimum. It introduced border checks and identity checks on all modes of transportation and restricted the right to bring families into Sweden. The country, proud of having taken in more refugees per capita than any other European country, had to acknowledge that it was no longer able to do this without jeopardizing vital social functions, such as health care and provision of housing.

By early 2016, it was announced that Sweden was rejecting 60,000 to 80,000 people who applied for asylum the previous year, and it was prepared for mass deportations to send people back to their country of origin, even by force if necessary. This plan also sent a message to potential asylum seekers that they would no longer be welcome in Sweden.

Sweden's vulnerability to ethnic and religious strife became apparent once again in April 2017, when an Uzbek migrant drove a beer delivery truck into a crowd on a pedestrian street in Stockholm, killing five people and injuring over a dozen. The attack followed the pattern of similar rampages in Nice, Berlin, and London. The perpetrator, who had jihadist links, had been denied asylum and went into hiding for a few months prior to the attack. Besides shaking the Swedish society, the case added fuel to the debate over the processing of migrants, since the killer had lived in the country for several years, having applied for asylum under apparently false pretenses.

Sweden is a generally tolerant and generous country and wants to remain a refuge for the politically oppressed. But it is not willing to be a land of unlimited opportunities for outsiders. Swedish idealism has its limits, especially in time of economic distress. Its legendary tolerance is starting to fray.

State Goals in Culture

Sweden has an ambitious cultural policy and devotes more than 1% of state expenditures to it. Anders Ehnmark, a journalist, explained why many Swedes think such an effort to support Swedish culture is necessary: "Sweden is a small country, with a low threshold of resistance to banality arriving from outside. For many years it has been a thoroughly Coca Colonialized country. American soap opera culture holds hegemony in the public mind." The Swedish parliament spelled

Sweden

out in 1974 the objectives in the state's cultural policy. In principle, cultural equality is considered to be just as important as economic and social equality. That means that any individual who so wishes should have the opportunity to develop whatever talents he possesses and to enjoy cultural experiences, regardless of geographic, educational, or other hindrances. This policy is underscored in practice by plentiful subsidies for cultural activities at all levels of government.

In order to aid authors, book publication is subsidized. Because the Swedish language is spoken by only about 10 million persons, the market is simply too small to make most books commercially viable. Also, in order to provide authors with a greater measure of economic security, the libraries pay the Swedish Author's Fund a small fee for every book that is lent out. These funds are used to pay the authors a guaranteed basic income, pension, or special scholarships. This is an effort to keep the Swedish literary tradition alive, which includes many fine writers.

In the second half of the 18th century, Carl Michael Bellman wrote poetry that could be sung. These songs describe the peculiarities and interests of the people of Stockholm in his day and give Swedes both entertainment and insight into their own past. He helped to establish a tradition of concentrating on the country's people and their folk culture, a characteristic of much Swedish literature before 1945.

The end of the 19th and the beginning of the 20th centuries were times of economic poverty and mass emigration, especially to the US. However, it was also a rich time for Swedish literature. Gustaf Fröding was a poet who wrote in the dialect of the common people and whose works were filled with folklore. Selma Lagerlöf was a romantic novelist who won a Nobel Prize. Perhaps the greatest literary figure in Swedish history, August Strindberg, produced dramatic works that were deadly serious, deeply psychological, invariably antifemale, and often downright depressing. His plays are still presented on stages throughout the world.

The 1930s were also times of economic crisis, and Ivar Lo-Johannsson, one of Sweden's best-loved authors, wrote several books, including *Good Night Earth*, about the landless peasants during these discouraging years. The 1940s were years of disillusionment among many Swedish intellectuals and writers, caused, at least in part, by the destructiveness of World War II and by the feelings of guilt and shame on the part of some Swedes at having been spared from this horrible conflict while other Europeans had suffered so much. This malaise was reflected in the works of such writers as Stig Dagerman and Karl Vennberg.

After the war, many writers tried to come to grips with the effects of a materialistic society on the individual, who can easily become alienated in an environment of cement and individual affluence. Other writers looked back at the Swedish past. Vilhelm Moberg produced a monumental series of books on Swedish emigrants to the US that included *Unto a Good Land*, *The Immigrants*, and *The Last Letter Home*, all of which have been translated into English. Moberg committed suicide in the late 1970s, but his literary description of Swedes in America was filmed by the Swedish director Jan Troell.

Another author, Astrid Lindgren, created unforgettable children's books with such figures as Pippi Longstocking. For decades they have helped children inside and outside Sweden to imagine the countryside, the people, the customs, and the spirit of Sweden's past.

Vastly different but similarly lucrative books are being written by crime-writer superstars Henning Mankell and Stieg Larsson. Mankell's 11 Inspector Kurt Wallander mysteries have been translated into 40 languages and have sold 30 million copies, in addition to having won many international prizes. In 2010, for the first time, one of his books reached the *New York Times* hardback best-seller list. His masterpiece Millennium trilogy, beginning with *The Girl with the Dragon Tattoo* and ending with *The Girl Who Kicked the Hornet's Nest*, with a fourth book reportedly in his computer, is a publishing sensation. By 2010 he had sold 6 million copies in the US, topping the bestseller lists, and by 2015 he had over 80 million copies in over 40 countries, nearly four times Sweden's entire population. Both probe the dark underside of Scandinavia's cradle-to-grave welfare societies.

In keeping with the country's objective to bring culture to as many people as possible, the state helps to finance theaters in many regions and has frequently subsidized independent theater troupes, which perform in the streets, in schools, or in factories and which help to bring theater to many groups of people, including children.

When one thinks of Swedish film, such performers as Greta Garbo and directors as Bo Widerberg, whose films focused on the industrial worker in modern society, come immediately to mind. The film giant Ingmar Bergman defined an entire genre of stark movies about the human condition. They included three titles that won Academy Awards as best foreign-language films: *The Virgin Spring* (1960) *Through a Glass Darkly* (1961) and his final film, *Fanny and Alexander* (1982). He also produced *The Seventh Seal*, *Wild Strawberries*, *The Silence* and *Persona*. He helped to make the 1960s a golden decade for Swedish filmdom. He passed away in 2007 at age 89.

To shore up this art form in Sweden, the state assumed more of the costs of production, and a 10% surcharge on all movie tickets flows to the Swedish Film Institute to help finance new films. Nevertheless, the industry remains in serious financial difficulties, and even the Swedes seem to show less and less interest in their own films. The average citizen goes to the movies only three times a year; 75% of all visits to the cinema are to see American films, whereas only 15% concern Swedish ones. The film, *Lilya 4-ever*, directed by Lukas Moodysson, won an Oscar nomination in 2002 as Best Foreign Language Film.

Performing Arts

Sweden's newest concert hall is named after Franz Berwald (1796–1868), Sweden's most famous composer of romantic music. The voice of another Swede, Jenny Lind, captured the ear of the musical world at the end of the 19th century. In the 1970s a versatile pop group called ABBA carried the Swedish banner throughout the world by entertaining millions of rock fans with their English-language songs, a feat repeated to a lesser extent in the 1980s and 1990s by Roxette and Ace of Base. With groups like ABBA, Sweden is one of the world's top three exporters of pop music. Since the late 1940s, the choreographer and ensemble director Birgit Cullberg has been the towering figure in Swedish ballet. As in theater and dance, the symphony orchestras in Stockholm and in the various regions receive generous and essential state financial assistance.

Artists

Swedish art gained an international reputation, especially through the works of Carl Larsson (1853—1915) and Anders Zorn (1860—1920). Larsson painted idealized and unproblematic scenes of middle-class daily life. Zorn was a pioneer in new art techniques and also painted many outstanding portraits, including ones of American president William Howard Taft and the steel magnate and philanthropist Andrew Carnegie. As elsewhere in the Nordic countries, modern, abstract art has been popular in 20th- century painting.

One of the eight cultural guidelines established by the Riksdag in 1974 was that commercialism was to be resisted in the country's culture. Nevertheless, Swedish art is a realm in which commercial and artistic objectives have blended to create well-designed objects for use in the home. They include furniture, textiles, glass, and porcelain, which are often in bright, fresh colors and are practical and beautiful. In Sweden, where skies are often gray and where the sun sometimes fails to shine for weeks, such objects in the home can have a particularly refreshing and therapeutic effect on the individual.

Sweden's neutrality cannot protect it from difficulties caused by the intrusion of politics in the arts. When the Israeli ambassador visited Stockholm's Museum of National Antiquities in 2004 and saw a work by an Israeli-born artist, Dror Feiler, which depicted a Palestinian suicide bomber in a sailboat floating on a pool of blood-red water, he threw a spotlight into the pool causing the exhibit to short-circuit. He was ejected from the museum.

Religion

Most Swedes (85%) consider themselves members of the Swedish (Lutheran) Church, the largest Lutheran denomination in Europe. An overwhelming majority of Swedes paid the optional church taxes (less than 1% of the average income) until they were abolished in 2000 with the separation of church and state. The state does collect membership fees for all faiths in addition to the Lutheran one. This makes sense in a country that has more than 200,000 Muslim residents, 160,000 Roman Catholics, 100,000 Orthodox Christians, and 16,000 Jews. Nevertheless, Sweden is a secular country, and only about 3% of Swedes attend church regularly. They generally attend only for special occasions, such as Advent, Christmas, Easter, baptisms, weddings, and funerals. The church faces a shortage of priests and has had difficulty organizing new parishes to keep up with the migration from rural to urban areas. In 1989 the church shed its legal obligation of recording all vital statistics,

Sweden

passing that function over to the Social Insurance Service. It retained its state financial support, though.

In 1995 the Lutheran Church agreed to a government-sponsored separation of church and state beginning in 2000; all political parties accepted this, and it went into effect as the new century was rung in. Before the change, the monarch had not been the head of the church, but he was required to belong to it; now he may be of any faith. The rights of the church are enshrined in the constitution under a law guaranteeing freedom of religious expression. Religion plays little role in politics, although the church does offer more than mere liturgy. Its preschools are crowded, and its youth movement is Sweden's largest youth organization. It has many summer camps and alternative programs, and it still attracts close to 70% of all teenagers for confirmation, providing it with a nine-month opportunity to influence a young person's thinking. Swedes in small towns tend to feel an attachment to the church building, which serves as a meeting hall, theater, nursery school, and finish line for ski races.

Religious veins can be tapped to win support for such policies as development aid to the third world or stricter controls on the use of alcohol. The latter movement gained momentum in the second half of the 19th century, when the Swedish nation seemed to be destroying itself through alcoholism and emigration. Legislation sought to control the use of spirits. Alcohol was rationed until 1955; the prices were kept very high in order to discourage its consumption. In 2005 it still had the EU's highest taxes on spirits. Official figures in 2002 suggest that this policy reduced intake. In the 19th century, the average adult Swede consumed 49 quarts of alcohol per year, compared with only 9.5 today.

Because these restrictions violate the EU's fair competition rules, they are being relaxed. Alcohol consumption has risen by 30% since EU entry in 1995 and reached by 2004 its highest level in a century. Wide-spread fears of the damaging effects on health and of alcohol-related crimes helped retain support for the state monopoly, Systembolaget, while most other monopolies are long gone. The state liquor stores still close at 7 p.m. on Fridays and 3 p.m. on Saturdays. However, in 2007 the European Court of Justice ruled that Sweden had no right to bar its citizens from importing alcohol from other EU states. Daily ferry services to Denmark, Germany, and the Baltic states allow enterprising Swedes to bring in about half the spirits consumed in their country. Taxes on alcohol are being reduced, so the price is falling. Experts say the previous strictures did little to change Sweden's

real problem: the tradition in Sweden and other Nordic countries to drink less often but to do so with the intention of getting drunk rather than to combine moderate drinking with eating, as is the practice in southern Europe.

Religious motives play almost no role in the popular campaign to stop smoking. The movement's slogan is "A Non-Smoking Generation"; English is used for the slogan because this language is quite fashionable today in Sweden, where it is learned by all schoolchildren. Most Swedes under age 45 usually speak English well.

The Media

Swedes buy more newspapers per capita than any other nation except Japan and Iceland. It has about 100 dailies and 85 weekly newspapers, with a total circulation of 4.5 million. The number of newspapers has declined in recent years, and in most localities, there is only one. Most have a definite political line; about three-fourths support the bourgeois parties, and only about a fifth back S. *Ny Dag* is the major communist paper and is published twice weekly. About a quarter of daily newspapers are distributed free. At the end of 2006, the world's oldest newspaper, *Post-Och Inrikes Tidningar*, published since 1645, stopped printing and now publishes only online. The print media's influence remains great. In 1997 a series in *Dagens Nyheter* broke the embarrassing story about Sweden's eugenics policy from 1934 to 1976. It was a shock to many Swedes and their admirers elsewhere to learn that at least 60,000 Swedish women were sterilized at the time because of their alleged mental defects. Moreover, the policy was passed in 1934 by the Social Democrats, largely credited with creating the foundations of Sweden's protective welfare state (and now again in power).

In the 1970s the Riksdag passed a series of laws designed to strengthen the economic base of the press and to ensure that there is a diversity of views. Except for the market leaders, all newspapers receive direct and indirect (tax breaks) subsidies, with the money distributed roughly equally between the socialist and nonsocialist press. Such state assistance appears not to make the recipients more docile, since subsidized papers are generally as outspoken about government policies as are those that are not. Those newspapers that appear in areas with few inhabitants receive especially significant financial support, and those newspapers that utilize the unified distribution system developed for magazine subscriptions also receive state assistance. The most popular evening newspapers are *Aftonbladet* and *Expressen*, while the major morning papers include *Dagens Nyheter* and *Svenska Dagbladet*.

Sveriges Radio AB is responsible for radio and television activities, which it coordinates through four independent subsidiaries: one for television (Sveriges Television—SVT), which operates two channels; one for national radio programs, which operates three stations; one for local radio; and one for educational radio and television programs. The pan-European satellite channels ended the state monopoly over the broadcast media and have changed public attitudes about Sweden's role in Europe. They add an international perspective to debates and contribute to greater diversity of opinions. Private industry, the press, and various popular movements own the stock in Sveriges Radio AB. In effect, though, it is state controlled, since the government appoints the director and half of the board of overseers. Also, its budget must be approved by parliament, which grants some subsidies and which determines the amount of the user's fee, which all persons who own radios or television must pay.

CURRENT ISSUES

In 1994, Swedes decided to join both NATO's Partnership for Peace and the EU. Lotta Forsman of the Foreign Ministry explained that "the collapse of the communist dictatorships in Eastern Europe has changed the military map and consequently the basis for Sweden's neutrality." Former defense minister Sten Tolgfors and other politicians argued that NATO was a natural source of Swedish security: "The Nordic countries cannot by themselves generate sufficient political and military weight." The army chiefs of Sweden, Norway, and Finland produced a report identifying 140 areas of possible military cooperation, including sharing airbases. This would save costs. In 2011, Sweden joined NATO efforts in both Afghanistan and in enforcing a no-fly zone over Libya. In 2020, it promised to send 150 commandos and helicopters to Mali to support France's fight against jihadists.

Popular support for NATO membership rose after Russia repeatedly violated Sweden's airspace, apparently perpetrated a cyberattack that closed the skies over the country, conducted a fake bombing raid on Stockholm (in 2013), and was suspected of penetrating Sweden's waters by a submarine. The country was humiliated when it could not scramble its fighter planes in time to intercept the Russian practice bombing raid against its capital city. No wonder that by 2018 43% of Swedes favored joining NATO and only 37% opposed it.

In 2016, it had signed a host nation support agreement, facilitating NATO's operation on its territory in case of a conflict in

Sweden

the region. Sweden has deepened military ties with America and its Nordic neighbors. It was increasing its armed forces to 90,000, and its draft was doubling in size to 8,000 a year. This was the largest military buildup in three quarters of a century.

Under prodding from the Baltic republics nervous over a possible looming attack from Russia, Sweden remilitarized its large island of Götaland in the middle of the Baltic Sea, placing a company of soldiers there. All five Nordic countries published a declaration that they would strengthen their defense cooperation, declaring that "Russia's conduct represents the gravest challenge to European security." Sweden plans to strengthen its defensive capabilities by investing an additional $717 million over five years, especially for antisubmarine equipment and the air force (previously downsized from 20 squadrons and over 400 planes to 4 divisions and fewer than 150 planes).

The strongest indication of Sweden's nervousness over the changing international situation is the 2017 decision to reintroduce military conscription, with 8,000 men and women drafted in 2021 to complement the voluntary system. To increase its capability, in 2017 the military requested $750 million in addition to the $5.2 billion already allocated. In June 2018 all volunteer soldiers were called up for the largest military exercise since 1975. It involved the largest-ever American force on Swedish soil. For the first time since 1961, the government wrote to all households, exhorting them to prepare for the worst. The aim is to hold on for three months, until help arrives.

Sweden was greatly unsettled by Russia's renewed pressure on Ukraine and the Baltics. It reconsidered its 200-year-old policy of neutrality and concluded after Russia's invasion of Ukraine in February 2022 that the time had come to join. NATO invited Finland and Sweden to join at its Madrid Summit in June 2022. Finland became a NATO member in April 2023, while Türkiye and Hungary delayed their domestic ratification for Sweden; Türkiye over concerns about its support for Kurdish groups, while Hungary's leadership did not provide clear reasons for its deferment. After 20 months of delay, on January 26, 2024, Turkish President Recep Erdogan signed a decision of the Turkish parliament ratifying the protocol on Sweden's accession to the North Atlantic Alliance. Hungary is the last remaining NATO member to approve of Sweden's application, clearing the way for Sweden's official acceptance.

Even though it has not yet received the requisite unanimous ratification to be an official member, Sweden has already been enlisted as a full-member participant of the "Steadfast Defender 2024" NATO maneuvers, the largest of its kind since the Cold War times.

Opposition to the European single currency will remain, and it could take many years before Sweden again seeks euro entry. It benefited from being outside the eurozone and able to devalue its krona to help it recover from the 2008 recession.

The 2018 elections left the Swedish politics in turmoil. The anti-immigrant Sweden Democrats deprived the two blocs of a majority. In July 2021 Stevan Löfven became the first Swedish prime minister to lose a no-confidence vote. He was replaced by the first female prime minister, Magdalena Andersson. Sweden was the last Nordic country to have a female prime minister. The September 2022 elections produced a three-party conservative coalition led by Prime Minister Ulf Kristersson. The Sweden Democrats placed second and therefore exercise considerable influence from outside the government.

Sweden's immigration and assimilation polices are increasingly challenged, with the previously welcoming approach abandoned in favor of protectionism. Sweden will continue to be tested in this regard, as the stark reality of trying to accommodate tens of thousands of asylum seekers overwhelms the affluent but not populous country. Integration will be a huge challenge, as foreigners are still 2.6 times less likely to have a job than are native-born Swedes.

Sweden has an economy that has transformed itself to meet the challenges of the 21st century. According to the 2016 IMD World Competitiveness rankings, it is the most competitive economy in the EU and is only behind Singapore, the US, Switzerland, and China globally. Its unemployment level (6.9% in 2023) is at one of the lowest rates since the financial collapse of 2008. Growth is 0.6%. Women's pay still lags 15% to 20% behind that of men. It remains a remarkably comfortable, steady, decent, peaceful, and generally egalitarian country.

Kingdom of Norway (Kongeriket Norge)

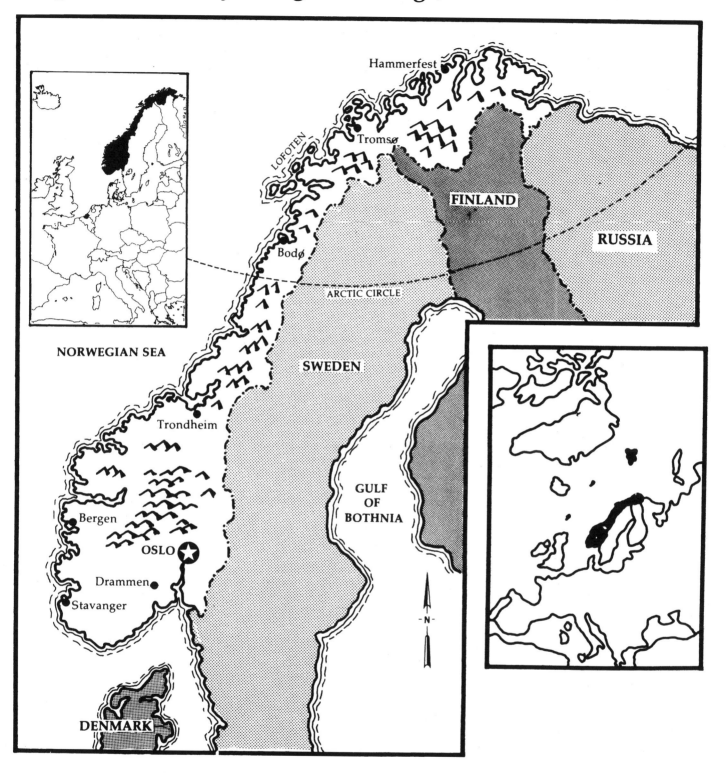

Norway

Source: *News of Norway*

Area: 148,729 sq. mi. (385,207 sq. km.).

Population: 5,488,984 (January 2023, Statistics Norway).

Capital City: Oslo (pop. 709,037 city, 1,064,235 urban, 1,588,457 metro; as of December 2022).

Climate: Depending on the geographical features, Norway has several types of climates. Parts of southeastern Norway have a humid continental climate, while the southern and western coasts and also the coast north to Bodø have an oceanic climate. The outer coast further north almost to North Cape have a subpolar oceanic climate. Farther inland in the south and at higher altitudes, and also in much of Northern Norway, the climate is subarctic to true arctic in Svalbard. Despite its northern latitude, Norway has a higher average temperature than expected, thanks to the flow of the warm Gulf Stream which keeps the climate temperate along the coast. Also, due to the geographical latitude, from the end of May to the end of July, the sun does not set completely so that a large part of Norway has up to 20 hours of daylight every day, while the territories near or north of the Arctic Circle have the appearance of the so-called "midnight sun." On the other hand, from the end of November to the end of January, almost all of Norway is in darkness.

Neighboring Countries: Sweden (east); Finland and Russia (northeast); Denmark (south, across the Skagerrak strait), UK (southeast, across the North Sea). Norway has an extensive coastline facing the North Atlantic Ocean and the Barents Sea.

Official Languages: Norwegian, Sámi (Lapp).

Recognized national Languages: Kven, Romani, Scandoromani; Norwegian Sign Language.

Ethnic Background: 81.5% Norwegian, 18.5% other (as of 2021).

Religion: Christianity (68% Church of Norway, 6.9% other Christian), 3.1% Islam, 0.8% other, 21.2% no religion (as of 2021).

Form of Government: Unitary parliamentary constitutional monarchy

Chief of State: His Majesty King Harald V, (since January 1991).

Head of Government: Jonas Gahr Støre, Prime Minister (since 2021), leader of the Labor Party.

National Flag: It consists of a red field crossed by blue Nordic cross bordered by thin white stripes. The cross is horizontal extending to the edges, with the crossbar closer to the hoist than the fly. This cross represents Christianity and is based on the tradition established by the other Nordic countries, Denmark and Sweden. The tricolor of red, white, and blue, traditionally denote freedom.

Public Holiday: May 17 (Constitution Day).

Currency: Norwegian krone (NOK).

Main Exports: Crude oil, natural gas, metals, machinery and transport,

49

Norway

food-stuffs, fish and fish products, pulp and paper, ships, chemicals.

Main Imports: Machinery and transport equipment, metals including iron and steel, chemicals, processed petroleum products, motor vehicles, textiles, foodstuffs.

Main Trading Partners: Germany (27.9% of exports and 11.4% of imports), UK (21.4% of exports and 4.3% of imports), Sweden (6.0% of exports and 12.6% of imports), Netherlands (6.4% of exports and 4.2% of imports), Denmark (2.4% of exports and 4.7% of imports), Belgium (7.6% of exports), France (9.4% of exports), China (12.3% of imports), US (6.1% of imports); as of 2022.

In many people's minds, Norway is a sparsely populated nation somewhere in the frozen north, with a tortured landscape filled with many majestic, snow-capped mountains, glaciers, isolated valleys, and a long coastline, which is dotted by small, quaint fishing villages and countless beautiful fjords. This image is certainly true, as far as it goes. This is a long, narrow country, with a 2,125-mile (3,200 km) coastline washed by the Arctic and Atlantic Oceans as well as the North Sea. It is the fifth-largest country in Europe and occupies 40% of the Scandinavian Peninsula.

Half of Norway and its waters is located north of the Arctic Circle. That is why it moved its joint armed forces headquarters northward to a nuclear-blast-proof tunnel system on a fjord near Bodø, just south of the Arctic Circle. Even the capital city

of Oslo in the south is on the same latitude as southern Alaska. This means that many Norwegians are able to experience the midnight sun in the summer, but they must go without much daylight in the winter. In the extreme north, it shares a 118-mile (196 km) border with Russia and a 430-mile (716 km) border with Finland. Flanked most of the distance by the Kjølen mountain range is a long, 972-mile (1,619 km) common border with Sweden, a friendly country to which Norway belonged until 1905.

Almost two-thirds of Norway is covered by mountains, although they do not give the country an Alpine character. Most of them are barren—without forests—in fact, only a fourth of the entire country lies below the timberline. One mountain range, the Dovrefjell, divides the country into a northern and southern part, whereas the Langfjell chain separates the eastern from the western part of the country. The Kjølen chain marks the country's eastern border. In the highlands there are countless cold, clear lakes and ponds, including the Hornindalsvatn, the deepest inland body of water in all of Europe. The rivers that originate in these mountains either flow gently in an easterly direction or precipitously into the sea. Its rivers provide Norway with a seemingly endless source of hydroelectric power, which was the basis for the country's industrialization.

Over a fifth of Norway is covered by forests, which supply wood, one of its most important raw materials, and 7% of its area is composed of 50,000 islands,

Crown Prince Haakon

only about 2,000 of which are inhabited. Lakes and rivers cover 5% of the territory, and only about 3% of the land is arable farmland, the lowest percentage in all of Europe. Despite its extreme northern latitude and the fact that 1.4% of its surface is covered by 1,700 glaciers, Because of the effects of global warming, by 2005 its glaciers had shrunk four years in a row at the fastest rate since 1900.

Norway has the lowest population density in all of Europe (except Iceland). It has 13 inhabitants per square kilometer, compared with 372 in the Netherlands, 225 in Britain, and 90 in France. Its population is also very unevenly distributed, with about half concentrated in the southeastern corner around Oslo and its fjord, with very few inhabitants in the northern part of the country. Four out of five live within 10 miles of the sea. Almost three-fourths of the country is uninhabitable.

There are many small villages, and a third of the population lives on the land or in towns with fewer than 2,000 inhabitants. Norway has no large cities, and only three have a population of over 100,000. Oslo, in which the government and much of the industry and cultural life are concentrated, has about a half-million residents; Bergen has about 215,000, and Trondheim about 135,000. A fourth city, Stavanger, with close to 90,000 people, has the headquarters for the state-owned oil company, StatoilHydro, and is the center for the petroleum extraction activities in the Norwegian sector of the North Sea.

The country's leaders have long recognized the danger that many Norwegians living in the large tracts of sparsely inhabited areas might move into the larger cities. For this reason, an important element

Princess Märtha Louise weds Norwegian author Ari Behn   Source: *News of Norway*

of the government's agricultural and industrial policy is to provide incentives for the people to remain in the less densely populated sections of the country. There is no possibility that Norwegians could settle these areas, since the natality rate declined to 1.88 in 2011; estimates are that there will be 1 million fewer Norwegians by 2050.

Norway was once an almost completely ethnically homogeneous country. There is an increasingly large number of foreign workers, some of whom came to Norway before the mid-1970s and who have either received Norwegian citizenship or are remaining with permanent residence permits. Except for those coming from other Nordic countries, no additional foreign workers are allowed to work in Norway. However, Norway has been an attractive goal for hundreds of thousands of immigrants and asylum seekers, although the country is no longer as hospitable toward newcomers as it once was. By 2003, the foreign-born made up approximately 7% of the total population.

Two ethnic minorities live in the northern part of the country. The largest are the 45,000 Sámi (formerly called Lapps) whose language and culture are completely different from those of the Norwegians. About two-thirds of all Sámi live in Norway, and the remaining one-third live in northern Sweden and Finland. Only about 10% of the Norwegian Sámi are now reindeer breeders who lead a nomadic existence and who cling most tenaciously to

Little Princess Ingrid Alexandra, likely to become Norway's only second female monarch

the traditional Sámi culture. The majority of Sámi now lead a settled existence.

The second minority is composed of about 7,000 descendants of a Baltic people who also entered Norway earlier via Finland. They are called kvener and have retained many of their original physical and cultural characteristics.

Norwegians call their country Norge, a word derived from the earlier name Nordvegr, "the Northern Way." The country is indeed on the northern extremity of Europe and appears on the map to be geographically isolated. But since the 19th century, it has been finely attuned to

developments in the rest of Europe and the world. As a nation facing westward and southward across three seas, it has developed a merchant marine that not only helps it maintain its links with the rest of the world but also helps other countries maintain links with each other. It does have weather-beaten fishermen, strapping lumberjacks, and ruddy-faced farmers, but these groups account for less than a tenth of the population.

Norwegians are proud of their athletes who won 26 medals in the 2014 Sochi Winter Olympics, third only to Russia (33) and the US (28). Norway balked at the cost of hosting the 2022 Winter Olympics. But the competitor who really put the country on the map was 22-year-old Magnus Carlsen. One of the youngest chess players to attain grandmaster rank when he was 13, he won the world championship title in 2013, becoming the first western European player in 76 years to do so. Norway also took pride in its two 2014 Nobel Prize winners in medicine: May-Britt and Edvard Moser. They are only the second couple to win in this category.

POLITICAL SYSTEM

Norway is a country in which there is a deep consensus supporting the democratic process and institutions. The individual's personal and civil rights are widely respected, and Norwegians are basically inclined to be very tolerant toward other viewpoints and manners of living. They enter into sharp debates with each other over political, economic, and social questions, but these debates are always kept within a framework in which recognized rules of the game are respected and observed. The result is a high degree of political stability.

The Monarchy

Norway is a constitutional monarchy with a parliamentary form of government; there is no aristocracy. Harald V was sworn in as king in 1991, coronations having been abolished in 1908. He is only the country's third monarch since independence in 1905. In 1937 he was the first Norwegian monarch to be born on native soil in 566 years. After the royal family fled occupied Norway (1940), Harald lived in the US with his sister and mother, the late Crown Princess Martha, wife of the late King Olav V. He attended two years of elementary school there. Martha lived in the White House for part of the time. The Norwegian-American community honored her in 2005 with a life-sized statue installed outside the ambassador's residence in Oslo.

After liberation in 1945, Harald continued his schooling in Norway, and he

Their Majesties King Harald V and Queen Sonja   Source: *News of Norway*

Norway

The late King Olav V opening the Norwegian parliament

pursued a military career; in 1977 he was promoted to general of the army and air force and admiral of the navy. His wife, Sonja, was the daughter of a Norwegian textile merchant. Harald's older sister could not succeed to the throne because of a law, now repealed, which favored male succession.

Since the new law of succession applies only to those born after 1990 (the year of the act), the current crown prince, Prince Haakon (born in 1973) is the heir apparent, not his older sister, Princess Martha Louise. Haakon graduated from the Norwegian Naval Academy and completed a bachelor's degree in political science from the University of California at Berkeley. He also studied law and political science at the University of Oslo. In 2000 he announced his entry into the training program for the foreign service. He married Mette-Marit Tjessem Høiby, a commoner, on August 25, 2001.

Princess Martha Louise married Norwegian writer Ari Behn. Cannons fired salutes, and flags were hoisted in April 2003, when she gave birth to a girl, Maud Angelica Behn. She was the first Norwegian royal baby in three decades, and she soon moved with her parents to New York. Only a year later, the crown prince and princess had a daughter, Ingrid Alexandra, who became third in line for the throne. She could become the first reigning queen in Norway since 1412.

The monarch performs mainly ceremonial functions, even though the constitution formally grants him considerable executive powers. Even decisions of the State Council (Statsrad), or cabinet, are denominated decisions of the "King-in-Council," although the king is seldom involved in their deliberations. Thus, the government merely acts in his name.

The king can play a role in facilitating the formation of a government when no party or coalition of parties receives a clear mandate in parliamentary elections. In times of extreme crisis, as was the case during World War II, the parliament can allow the king temporarily to perform the governmental and military functions, which are formally granted to him in the constitution. But no Norwegian king would dare attempt to do so under normal circumstances. The crisis during World War II also demonstrated the major function the monarch can perform: He serves as an important symbol of the nation's unity, and this can be extremely important, especially to a nation that did not become entirely independent until 1905. The king is the head of the state (Lutheran) church, and at least half of the cabinet members must also belong to that church. The royal castle in the middle of Oslo and the other properties used by the royals belong to the state, not to the royal family. They are lent to the monarch and are maintained by the taxpayers.

The king cannot be accused in a court of law for any misdeed. Since he is not permitted to make decisions in normal times, he is protected from making political mistakes. Kings are buried in the Trondheim cathedral, where the crown jewels are kept.

The Parliament

Real political power lies in the Norwegian people, represented by the 169 members of the parliament, called the Storting. Over a third of its members are women. Elections are held every four years, and all citizens 18 years of age or older are eligible to vote. The electoral system is a complicated form of proportional representation, which enables many political parties to function. This makes the creation of a workable coalition in the Storting difficult, despite a method of distributing seats that favors large and medium-sized parties. A party must win 4% of the votes nationwide in order to receive any seats at all. A newly elected Storting is obligated to serve the full four years, since the constitution forbids early elections. Even byelections are very rare, since vacated seats are filled by replacements who are elected at the same time as the deputies. Thus, substitutes are almost always available at all times.

The inability to call early elections forces the various party leaders to negotiate very seriously with each other in order to produce a government whose programs can win majorities in the Storting. No party has won an absolute majority since 1961, and from 1983 until 2005 there was not even a majority governing coalition. Therefore, the Norwegian talent for moderation and compromise, along with the basic political consensus in the country, has been essential for the maintenance of political stability.

Deputies are elected from 19 counties (fylker) in such a way that 38 representatives are elected from the northern counties, 49 from western and southern Norway, and 68 from eastern Norway (of which 15 are from Oslo). In order to try to prevent any domination by the large cities, the rural areas are represented by a slightly greater proportion of deputies than the urban areas.

Voters elect only one parliament, the Storting, but after each election, it is divided into two parts. One fourth of the members are assigned to the Lagting, or "upper house" or revising chamber, and the rest constitute the Odelsting, or "lower house." These two houses deliberate separately only when the Storting must deal with questions touching on the constitution, such as the rights and duties of citizens. However, most matters, including constitutional amendments, are discussed in joint plenary sessions. Once a majority in the Storting approves a piece of legislation, it automatically becomes law.

The Storting also has standing committees that correspond to the various government ministries and which perform most of the detailed work of the parliament. Unlike in the US, seniority plays very little role in the assignment of seats and chairmanships in the committees; party membership and special skills are the decisive factors.

The Storting has the responsibility of electing a special five-person committee representing parties from across the political spectrum that selects and awards the prestigious Nobel Peace Prize. As stipulated in the will (of 1895) of the Swedish-born inventor Alfred Nobel, the Prizes in physics, chemistry, physiology or medicine and literature are awarded in Stockholm (Sweden), while the Nobel Peace Prize is awarded in Oslo. Norway's selection in 2009 of American president Barak Obama, who had been in office less than a year, elicited much criticism throughout the world, as well as disbelief on the part of Obama himself. But 43% of Norwegians thought that the young American leader deserved the award. He donated the $1.4 million prize money to charity. In 2010 the committee selected the Chinese campaigner for human rights and democracy Liu Xiaobo, over China's strenuous objection. This decision provoked China to call off some high-level visits and to threaten a curtailment of Norway's long-standing trade and investment ties with Beijing.

The list of Nobel Prize laureates from Norway includes Bjørnstjerne Bjørnson (Literature, 1903), Knut Hamsun (Litera-

ture, 1920), Christian Lous Lange (Peace, 1921), Fridtjof Nansen (Peace, 1922), Sigrid Undset (Literature, 1928), Lars Onsager (Chemistry, 1968), Odd Hassel (Chemistry, 1969), Ragnar Frisch (Economics, 1969), Ivar Giaever (Physics, 1973), Trygve Haavelmo (Economics, 1989), Finn E. Kydland (Economics, 2004), Edvard Moser (Physiology or Medicine, 2014), May-Britt Moser (Physiology or Medicine, 2014), and Jon Fosse (Literature, 2023).

Storting deputies can be elected only if they represent parties; no independents can be elected, although one may leave his party after the election and retain his seat until the next election. As a rule, deputies vote with their parties, but they do have the right to vote against their parties. On some moral issues, such as abortion, the parties announce that deputies will be permitted to vote according to their consciences, although the party's position on such an issue would be well known. In order to encourage them to be conscious that they are supposed primarily to represent their constituents, not their parties, deputies are seated according to the alphabetical order of their counties, not according to their party affiliation, as is the custom in most European parliaments.

The Norwegian government is headed by a prime minister and a cabinet of at least seven ministers, the foreign minister being the highest in the hierarchy after the prime minister. The government meets in cabinet meetings at least once a week (usually on Fridays), although the various

members meet informally several times during the week.

The Judiciary

Norway has an independent judiciary, with courts at four levels. From the lowest to the highest, they are the Conciliation Councils (Forliksrådene), the local courts (Herredsrettene og byrettene), the courts of civil and criminal appeals (Lagmannsretten), and the Supreme Court of Justice (Høiesterett), composed of a chief Justice and 17 justices, of which only 5 sit for any one case. The framers of the 1814 constitution adopted the American innovation by granting the Supreme Court and the inferior courts the authority to declare as null and void any law they deem to be incompatible with the constitution. However, the Norwegian courts have exercised this right of judicial review very infrequently, preferring to leave it to the government and the Storting to make certain that the constitution is observed.

Constitutional Amendment and Referendums

The Storting also has the power to amend the 1814 constitution; all proposed amendments must be presented to the parliament, but in order to prevent the basic law from being changed too quickly or by a simple majority that might be available at any moment, any amendment must be approved by a two-thirds majority in a newly elected Storting.

There is no constitutional provision for a referendum. However, in a few instances,

The late King Olav V in his sailboat. He competed in the Olympics in 1964, 1968, and 1972.

Norway

the Storting has declared that nonbinding referendums could be held in order to give the people the opportunity to express an opinion about an important issue.

For instance, in 1972 a national referendum was held on the question of whether Norway should enter the EU. In this vote 53% said "no," and the government chose to honor this result and not to enter the EU. This rejection was due more than anything else to a general reaction by the periphery (rural) people against a move that, it was feared, could seriously affect the unique and traditional life and culture of the nation (see Culture). The EU was widely seen as a potential danger to Norwegian society. In 1992 the Storting voted both to accept EEA and, for the fourth time, to seek entry into the EU. But in a November 1994 referendum, 52% of the voters, citing many of the same arguments as in 1972, again voted EU membership down. This time prosperity and concerns for the structure of its economy tipped the balance.

In 2008 the governing and opposition parties agreed to amend the constitution in order to loosen the official ties between the government and the Lutheran Church, to which more than 80% of Norwegians formally belong. Some links remain, but the Lutheran faith is no longer the official state religion, and the government relinquishes to the church the right to appoint bishops. The monarch is still obligated to be Lutheran, but Lutheran parents are no longer legally required to raise their children as Lutherans. The state continues to provide funding for the church, but it is now required to give financial support to other faiths, as well as to atheist and agnostic communities.

As in other Scandinavian countries, the institution of the ombudsman guards citizens' rights. There is an ombudsman for consumer affairs who ensures fair advertising and marketing practices, a civil ombudsman who sees to it that the administration does not treat any citizen unjustly, and an ombudsman for the armed services who deals with grievances of military personnel. All are appointed by the Storting.

Regional and Local Government

It is not surprising that a country so spread out and cut up by mountains, fjords, lakes, rivers, and other natural barriers that make transportation within the country so difficult would have a lively tradition of local and regional government. There are about 50 municipalities (bykommuner) and about 400 rural communities (landkommuner), with their own councils elected every four years midway between the national elections. Non-Norwegians who have resided in the country for at least three years can vote in these local elections. The councils appoint

Source: *News of Norway*

a local government and a mayor, their authority extending to schools, churches, health care, social welfare, zoning and local construction, firefighting, traffic, and a host of other matters.

Norway is divided into 11 administrative regions, called counties (fylker) which until 1918 were known as Amt (pl. Ämter). There were 19 of them, but in 2017, the Solberg government decided to merge some of the counties to form larger ones, reducing the number of counties from 19 to 11, which was implemented on 1 January 2020. This caused popular opposition, and some called for the reform to be reversed. The Storting voted to partly undo the reform in June 2022, with Norway to have 15 counties from 1 January 2024.

The counties form the first-level administrative divisions of Norway and are further subdivided into 356 municipalities (kommune, pl. kommuner). Each of the counties is headed both by a governor appointed by the central government and to a lesser extent by their own elected bodies. The island territories of Svalbard and

Jan Mayen are outside the county division and ruled directly at the national level. The capital Oslo is both a county and a municipality.

The counties deal with tasks for which the national and local governments share responsibilities, such as hospital construction, public instruction, health care, and electricity supply. Each county has its own parliament, which is elected at the same time local elections are held. Although much political responsibility is assumed at the local and regional levels, it should not be overlooked that the nation's major political priorities are established by the central government in Oslo.

Overseas Territories

The government in Oslo rules over far-flung territories around the world. It has a large tract of land called Queen Maud Land on the continent of Antarctica, which could one day have great economic significance. It was a Norwegian explorer, Roald Amundsen, who in 1911 was the first man to reach the South Pole; he had also been

That sinking feeling

the first to navigate the Northwest Passage from 1903 to 1906. He was a disciple of Norway's first prominent polar explorer, Fridtjof Nansen. Norway also has two uninhabited islands near Antarctica: Peter I Island and Bouvet. Jan Mayen Island, situated between Greenland and Iceland, covers 380 square kilometers, with the Beeren Mountain with 7,400 feet (2,277 m) high. First discovered by the Dutch, Jan Mayen became Norwegian in 1930 and now serves as a meteorological station and as a post in the NATO early-warning system.

Closer to home is the Svalbard archipelago, lying halfway between the North Pole and the tip of the Scandinavian Peninsula. It is about 575 miles (959 km) by air from the northern Norwegian city of Tromsø, from which regular civilian air service commenced in 1975. The largest and only inhabited island is Spitsbergen. This rugged area, with mountains rising to 5,585 feet (1,717 m) and dangerous cliffs overlooking a landscape covered with ice and glaciers, exists in total darkness 112 days per year and in total daylight 127 days. Nearly two-thirds of Svalbard is covered by ice and provides an ideal habitat for polar bears, which outnumber humans two to one. By law, anybody going out of Longyearbyen, the capital, must carry a gun and know how to use it.

Spitsbergen's cold climate and remoteness make it an ideal place to store the seeds of almost 3 million different essential crops in the Svalbard Global Seed Vault, opened in February 2008. It is located 60 meters (almost 200 feet) below the permafrost and far away from potential intruders. The intention is to protect mankind's future food supply in the event of a nuclear, asteroid, or epidemic catastrophe. The "doomsday vault" would contain the means to restock the Earth's agriculture. The Norwegian government maintains the site at its own expense, assisted by private donations, including $6.5 million from the US.

Svalbard islands were first mentioned in Icelandic journals in the year 1194, and for centuries they were a meeting point for whaling crews from all over the world. At the beginning of the 20th century, they became economically significant because of their sizable coal deposits, which continue to be exploited today. Until 1920 the archipelago was a "no man's land" in international law, but in that year, a complicated treaty was worked out. The other great powers in the Arctic liked the idea that a small, seemingly harmless country like Norway would control the Spitsbergen Archipelago.

The treaty conferred on Norway sovereignty over the islands in 1925, while at the same time giving all nationals of the contracting parties the right to carry out maritime, industrial, mining, and commercial operations on the basis of absolute equality. It also explicitly prohibited the establishment of naval bases or fortifications on the islands, which could never be used "for warlike purposes." Norway was granted responsibility of ensuring adherence to this treaty. The only other country that showed any appreciable interest in Svalbard is Russia, which did not sign the 1920 treaty. The instrument granted the Russians predominance over 4 of the 40 islands, covering about 6% of the total land area. Norway's expansion into the Arctic temporarily went to its head. It occupied Greenland in the early 1930s, until the International Court of Justice ruled it illegal.

Only one Norwegian and one Russian company maintained permanent mining operations on the islands, even though both Norway and Russia lose money on them. In the mid-1990s, Russia extracted about 500,000 tons of coal a year, while Norway gets about 400,000. Almost certainly, the real reason for both countries' presence there is strategic. Each is scared of allowing the other to gain exclusive use of the harbors, which are so close to the sea lanes between Russia's northern ports and the Atlantic. It is no coincidence that the British used to call Spitsbergen an "Arctic Gibraltar."

The Russians have always had difficulty accepting the idea of Norwegian

Norway

sovereignty over the islands and have frequently challenged the scope of its authority. They have advanced the view that Norwegian regulations are subject to prior Russian agreement, a view that is wholly unacceptable to the Norwegians, who have established a hearing procedure for Russian citizens on Svalbard to air their grievances, and on the whole, the two nationalities on the islands get along rather well. But Oslo retains the right to make final decisions.

Russia also takes exception to Norway's position that the 1920 treaty deals only with the islands themselves and not to the waters around them. Norway, for which fishing is its third-largest export earner, has established a 200-mile fishing zone that gives it primary rights. It also has raised the claim that the Norwegian continental shelf includes Svalbard and that Norway therefore has the final authority over mining and drilling in those waters.

Until 2005 Norway did not dare begin any drilling operations in these waters until some kind of mutually acceptable agreement could be reached with Russia, which refused to accept the Norwegian position on how the Barents Sea should be divided between the two countries. The maritime boundary disputes extended much farther than the relatively short 118-mile land border with its powerful eastern neighbor. Both countries filed their claims with the UN Commission on the Limits of the Continental Shelf.

The fact that the geological indications for oil in the area are positive made the Russians impatient for a settlement. Norway's need for future oil and gas extraction prompted it in 2005 to begin boring test wells 230 kilometers north of Hammerfest after the government lifted the ban on drilling in the Barents Sea. Russia had already announced that it would begin prospecting in the Barents Sea, but drilling was to begin off the island of Novaya Zemlya, well outside the disputed area. Norway supplied some of the equipment for the Russian oil rigs and discussed with Russian officials the possibility of joint offshore projects in the Barents Sea outside the disputed waters.

Norway is intensely interested in the future development of the Arctic region. It calls the area the "High North" and pours money into it. It is Norway's main strategic priority. As the Arctic ice pack recedes, these waters become more open to increased shipping and the exploitation of offshore oil and gas reserves. Along with four other countries that border on the Arctic Ocean—Denmark, Canada, the United States, and Russia—it is determined to secure rights to the natural resources in the area. Competition is fierce, and the Russians raised the tension level

in 2007 by sending two minisubmarines to place a titanium national flag 14,000 feet below the ice at the North Pole. However, in May 2008, after a frenetic year of Arctic activity, the five countries met in Ilulissat, Greenland, and agreed to observe existing international laws, such as the Law of the Sea Treaty, to resolve their disputes in the Arctic.

In July 2011 the historic Treaty of Maritime Delimitation went into effect. Norway and Russia resolved their four-decade dispute over how to divide the Barents Sea and a portion of the Arctic Ocean into clear economic zones extending to the edge of Europe's northern continental shelf. The line they drew splits the disputed area approximately in half. It extends their 122-mile land border northward beyond all the islands in the Barents Sea and into the Arctic Ocean up to the continental shelf just short of 85 degrees latitude. They can explore for oil and gas in their respective zones. They will cooperate on developing arrangements for drilling and sharing revenues from hydrocarbon deposits that straddle the border. Because of its experience, Statoil, Norway's largest oil and gas company, agreed to help Russia's state gas company, Gazprom, to develop the huge offshore field called Shtokman. That project was suspended in 2012.

POLITICS AND POLITICAL PARTIES

There are two ways of looking at Norway's party system. One is to see it as a multiparty system, perpetuated by an electoral system of proportional representation that always favors the proliferation of parties. Such division was further stimulated by the bitter debate over entry into the EU. This emotional conflict hammered Norway at many of its social fault lines. It cracked some of the country's traditional parties wide open and created the conditions for some entirely new ones to spring up. In the 2013 elections, 21 parties threw their hats into the electoral ring. They included the People's List against Oil Drilling and the Christians. The Beer Unity Party decided not to run this time.

Another way of looking at the country's party system is that it is made up of two clusters of parties, one socialist, or at least social democratic, and the other nonsocialist. The votes of each cluster remain more or less equal from one election to the next, although there are noticeable, often dramatic shifts among the various parties within each cluster. However, these shifts are not such that a two-party system would be likely to develop. This existence of two rather firm blocks lends stability to the political system. Nevertheless, competition for votes within each cluster

Former prime minister and current NATO secretary-general Jens Stoltenberg

sometimes makes parties less willing to cooperate with each other than one might expect. Each must always think about the next election.

Parties are undergoing changes. Their total membership has declined by half since the early 1990s, thereby depriving leaders of a large recruitment base. Turnout is falling, especially in local elections; in the 2005 national elections, 77% cast ballots. The link between parties and social class has been broken as the middle class dominates the various channels of political participation. Finally, the fact that most governments are minority ones tends to diminish the importance of elections and raise the importance of post-election negotiations. Therefore, parties' accountability to the voters is weakened.

The Nonsocialist Parties

The Conservative Party (Høyre, or merely H) strongly supported Norway's entry into the EU and experienced dizzying growth during the 1970s, climbing to 50 seats in 1985. Led by Erna Solberg (nickname: Iron Erna) in the September 2013 elections, it won 26.8% of the votes (up from 17.2%) and 48 seats (a gain of 18). It tends to draw the votes of the better-educated and the better-paid, and since these groups grew in prosperous Norway, Høyre grew as well.

Høyre does not encompass the entire conservative spectrum. Its voters tend to be concentrated in the industrial, urban centers of the southeast, and it does not appeal to the populist, pro-prohibition Nynorsk, or religious movements, which are so strong in the periphery (see Culture). It is a modern, urban movement, which defines itself as a "conservative party of progress." It demands protection of individual rights and of private property. It is strongly oriented toward NATO, the US, and Europe.

In contrast to the other Norwegian parties, Høyre is not ridden with internal divisions, and ideological debates within the party are almost unknown. Like the Labor Party, Høyre is secular and supports economic growth and a high level of oil and gas extraction. It has basic differences with the other major conservative parties on a range of thorny subjects that include alcohol policy, abortion, environmental protection, and oil policy. The party emerged from the 2013 elections as the main governing party. Solberg radiates efficiency and was only the second female prime minister in Norway. She served as the 35th prime minister of Norway from 2013 to 2021. She formed a minority coalition government with the Progress Party, supported in parliament by the Christian Democrats and Liberals.

The Christian Democratic Party (KrF) is an observer member of the European People's Party (EPP). It currently holds three seats in the Parliament, having won 3.8% of the vote in the 2021 parliamentary election. The current leader of the party is Olaug Bollestad. The party, as its name indicates, it seeks to place Christian concerns in the political spotlight. It led a furious battle against the abortion law, which permits abortion on demand. It also appeals to many supporters of strong, antialcoholic legislation. Another policy it thinks is in harmony with the biblical spirit is a rise in Norway's development aid, which is already 1% of GDP. Even though Norwegians are overwhelmingly baptized Lutheran, the KrF's strong whiff of pietism and serious commitment to the values of the Bible has hampered it in attracting a considerably larger following in this largely secular country.

The hard core of KrF's votes mainly lives in the south and the west and is distrustful of the secular, cosmopolitan Høyre. The KrF is strong in the periphery and attracts about two-thirds of those who support the movement to elevate the social status of Nynorsk. The party is historically firmly opposed to EU entry. It stresses human rights, family values, higher welfare spending, and Norway's religious and cultural heritage.

Many politicians talk about values, but KrF puts its money where its mouth is. Noting that divorce ends half of marriages and is four times commoner than three decades ago, that a fourth of women aged 20 to 44 live with men to whom they are not married, and that 48% of children are born out of wedlock, the earlier KrF government instituted payments to a mother of 80% of her salary for 12 months or full pay for 10 months to stay home with her baby. Either parent can take the leave, although it is almost always the woman. When the

Former Prime Minister Erna Solberg

year is up, she or he may return to her job with at least the same pay as before.

Three-fourths of women work (over 80% of those with children), the highest percentage in the developed world, after Iceland. More than four-fifths of mothers with young children work. A mother also has the right to two hours off work each day to breastfeed her baby, either at home or in the office; 80% of women continue to breastfeed after six months. Each parent can take 10 days off work per year when their kids are ill. This approach appears to boost the birth rate, which at 1.8 children per woman is one of the highest in Europe. Men pitch in to do their share:

They perform an estimated 40% of household tasks, one of the highest rates in the world.

The earlier KrF government also unveiled a male equal rights program that allows for preferential treatment to men in industries like childcare, preschool and primary school teaching, and child welfare in order to provide male role models. Citing the need to strengthen the family, the KrF pushed through a law stopping larger shops from opening on Sunday. It adopted in 1999 a $57.7 million package to compensate Jewish families for some of the property that was plundered by the Nazis and to finance projects for the Jewish community.

The only conservative party to join the earlier governments in 2005 and 2009 is the Centre Party (Sp), now led by Trygve Slagsvold Vedum, who has served as Minister of Finance since 2021. It was earlier called the Farmers' Party; it did not change its name and move from an overtly anti-industrial position until 1959. Nevertheless, it is still wary of industrial growth, and like the KrF, it is a party of the periphery.

Like some elements within the KrF, the Centre adamantly opposed Norway's entry into the EU out of fear of the damage that membership might do to traditional Norwegian society. Also, like the KrF, it calls for a reduction in oil production, and it is hard-liner in its support of environmental protection. This issue also creates a kind of wedge between the conservative heart of the party and the younger

Bergen

Norway

members. The young wing is even more radical on environmental issues and is especially wary of any form of collaboration with the Conservative Party. It is in the opposition.

Seldom in contention as a member of the government was the Progress Party. But that changed after the 2013 elections, when it captured 29 seats (down 12) and 16.3% of the votes (down from 22.9%). This result was disappointing, but it was good enough to enter the Conservative minority government. This was the first time ever it was a governing party. Sharing ruling responsibility has cost it popularity in the polls. It is the last remaining protest party, which arose in the early 1970s, and it opposes the heavy tax burden and the growth of state control over the economy. Its early growth, especially in the Oslo area, reflected many Norwegians' opposition to the extremely high tax level in Norway, which siphons off close to half of the income that the average person earns. Its leader from 2006 to 2021 was Siv Jensen, formerly a young firebrand lady, who insisted that the government lower taxes but also spend more of the country's oil revenues to fix roads, shorten waiting lists for hospital treatment, and take better care of the elderly. Since 2021, the leader of the Progress Party is Sylvi Listhaug, who previously served in several cabinet positions under Prime Minister Erna Solberg.

The party portrays itself as the defender of the traditional welfare, health, and educational systems and generally the Norwegian way of life. It offers simple remedies for every problem and appeals to anti-immigrant sentiments. The party wins many votes by calling for limits on immigration, which is widely seen as a threat to Norwegian culture and identity.

The final nonsocialist party is the Liberal Venstre Party (V), often called the Liberals. This is Norway's oldest political party, but it was never tightly organized, and it split in 1973 over the EU issue. In fact, it was the chief victim of the EU battle, and it never recovered. Only that part of the party that opposed entry remained in parliament, and the entire debate drove the party to the left. It now defines itself as a "radical social-liberal party," and it presents itself as committed to environmental protection and more careful exploitation and utilization of Norway's natural resources. It currently holds eight seats in the Parliament, and was previously a part of Norway's government together with the Conservative Party and the Christian Democratic Party. Guri Melby has served as the party leader since 2020, and as Minister of Education from 2020 to 2021.

The Socialist Parties

The largest party is the Labor Party (A), a social-democratic party positioned on the center-left of the political spectrum. It is led by Jonas Gahr Støre who has served as the 36th and current Prime Minister of Norway since 2021. Støre has been Leader of the Labor Party since 2014. He served under Prime Minister Jens Stoltenberg as Minister of Foreign Affairs from 2005 to 2012 and as Minister of Health and Care Services from 2012 to 2013. He has been a Member of the Storting for Oslo since 2009.

From the 1930s the Labor Party has dominated Norway and has been the only party since then ever to win a parliamentary majority. Beginning as a democratic reform party, it took a temporary radical turn in the 1920s but then moderated its course again and now defines itself as a "socialist reform party." The pragmatic character of this group is such that one could hardly call it a true socialist party, even though its party program calls for the creation of a socialist society and the nationalization of large parts of the economy as long-range goals. In fact, its immediate goals are full employment and expansion of the social security net.

After World War II, the party broadened its base to include employees, small farmers, fishermen, and foresters, in addition to its traditional working-class base, which remains the backbone of the party. Geographically, the party is strongest in the north and in the Oslo area. In contrast to most social democratic parties in Europe, the Labor Party has never been wholly dominated by academically trained persons.

As in Sweden and Denmark, Labor sees itself as the political arm of the trade union movement, and it is formally linked to the Trade Union Confederation (LO) through interlocking leadership, collective membership, and organizational ties. The LO traditionally has two seats in the party's presidium, and representatives of the two parties sit in the LO directorate. Also, by tradition, the LO leader is given a Labor seat in the Storting, and the trade union apparatus is used at election time to support the party.

The Labor Party has been plagued by internal division. The youth wing of the party tends always to oppose the more pragmatic economic orientation of the middle-aged and older members. But the worst division arises from foreign policy disputes. There is an element in the party that never fully digested Norway's NATO role.

Polls indicate that support of NATO membership remains strong in Norway. During the 1991 Persian Gulf crisis, it sent a coast guard vessel and a supply and support ship to the gulf and a minesweeper to the Mediterranean, as well as financial assistance to countries affected by the crisis. In 1993 it dispatched 220 peacekeeping troops to North Macedonia as part of a UN trip wire to prevent the conflict in Bosnia from spreading. It also sent humanitarian aid to Bosnia. In 2001–2002 it sent special operations forces to Afghanistan.

It was the firm tie with NATO that convinced many Norwegians in 1994 that they did not need the EU for security. Nevertheless, Norway promised to assign 3,500 troops to the EU rapid-reaction force. It contributed forces to the EU's command of peacekeeping forces in North Macedonia in 2003. In Afghanistan its 400 soldiers are engaged in the stabilizing of Kabul through ISAF, and its special forces are involved in the US-led Operation Enduring Freedom, which combats al Qaeda terrorists. Because the UN had not sanctioned the war against Iraq in 2003, Norway could not lend its support to the actual fighting. It sent humanitarian aid and 164 troops to assist in the reconstruction of the country; all troops were withdrawn after the 2005 elections.

In 2000 Labor's former leader Jens Stoltenberg became Norway's youngest-ever prime minister. He was voted out of the prime minister's office in 2001, but he again attained that post in 2005.

Between 2005 and 2013, Labor returned to power after committing to a coalition agreement with other parties in order to form a majority government. It was the

Towing a concrete oil structure out from Stavanger

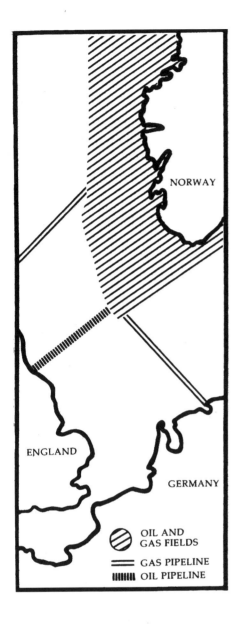

NORWAY

ENGLAND

GERMANY

⊘ OIL AND
GAS FIELDS

══ GAS PIPELINE

▥▥▥ OIL PIPELINE

senior partner of the governing red–green coalition from 2005 to 2013. It entered opposition again after losing nine seats in 2013. The party lost a further six seats in 2017, yielding the second-lowest number of seats since 1924. At the 2021 election, the party lost one seat but left-wing opposition gained a majority over the political right, with Støre becoming the prime minister and heading a minority government along with the Centre Party.

Stoltenberg's governing coalition was the first majority government in two decades, and 2009 was the first time in 16 years that a Norwegian government had won reelection.

Stoltenberg won again in 2009 because of his stewardship of the economy. Norway managed the recession better than any country in Europe, holding unemployment to 3%. Many voters still did not understand why the welfare system,

which for example provides full disability payments to alcoholics, seemed to have so many defects, kindergarten spaces so short, hospitals understaffed, taxes high, pensions barely adequate, and gasoline costs as high as elsewhere in Europe, despite the cushion provided by the "Oil Fund" (discussed below).

Stoltenberg promised lavish government spending, including for childcare, kindergarten spaces, free fruit for school pupils, and extended maternity and paternity leave. He pledged to stop tax cuts, and he used more of Norway's oil wealth to improve welfare programs. Even though it is a parliamentary rule that the government should not use more than 4% of the fund to cover a budget deficit in normal times, he used 7%. This insulated the economy from the global downturn. Stoltenberg's government heavily subsidized day care for any child and produced a law allowing same-sex marriages. However, Labor went into opposition after the 2013 elections, despite being the largest party in parliament. Voters wanted a change after eight years, and a report on the massacre of 77 people faulted the government for security lapses. Four of its parliamentary seats were won by survivors of that massacre. Stoltenberg became NATO secretary-general in September 2014, succeeding Anders Fogh Rasmussen.

The Labor Party requires that 40% of its candidates for public office be women, and 40% of the Storting's members since 1993 are women. By 2014, the prime minister and four out of seven leaders of the parties that received the most votes in 2013 are female. Gerd Kristiansen, the head of the LO union, and her counterpart on the employer side, Kristin Skogen Lund, are women, as are more than half the managers in the public sector. Thus, Norway has a higher percentage of women in top governing positions than any other nation in the world. However, in the private sector, only 6% of chief executives were female in 2013, although 41% of nonexecutive board members are women.

Progress is obvious. In 2003 no women were at the head of any of the country's large companies, and only 8.4% of corporate board and executive positions (compared with 12.4% in the US) were held by women. Legislation in 2002 changed that by forcing private companies to allot at least 40% of their boardroom seats to women, as was already the case in state-owned companies. Penalties began to be applied in 2008, but by that time the percentage of women on top boards already topped 40%, far above the Nordic average of 29%, the western European average of 9%, and America's 15% for the Fortune 500. Over 80% of Norwegian companies complied by the deadline. In unlisted

companies not subject to the law, fewer than 20% of board members are female. Some of the most talented ladies, known as "golden skirts," accepted as many as 35 directorships each, and this helped enable so many companies to reach the 40% target. However, only 6.4% of managers of listed companies are women. The government reported in 2016 that as many as 38% of all businesses in Norway employed only men (mostly in building, transportation, and storage), while 17 per-cent employed only women (especially in services and social care).

In July 2016, Norway became the first country in Europe, and second after Israel in the world, with mandatory peacetime military conscription for women. The former female defense minister Anne-Grete Stroem-Erichsen observed that "all citizens shall have the same rights and obligations, regardless of sex" and "in order to secure our operational capabilities in the future we need to recruit the best, and we need diversity. Therefore, we cannot limit our recruitment to the male half of the population." Only about 15% of draft-age people actually serve in the military, so not all women are drafted.

A further step was taken by introducing gender-neutral crosswalk signs. Pedestrians now watch for stick figures rather than little men in hats crossing a road.

The Socialist Left Party (SV) as a democratic socialist political party in Norway it is positioned on the left-wing of the political spectrum. It was founded in 1973, at first an electoral alliance of several socialist groupings (Communist Party of Norway, Socialist People's Party, Democratic Socialists—AIK) including elements from the Labor Party. In 1975, the coalition was turned into a unified political party.

Since March 2023, the SV is led by Kirsti Bergstø who previously served as one of the party's deputy leaders from 2017 to 2023.

SV had emerged from the political battle against EU entry and the European Economic Area membership. SV supports a strong public sector, stronger social welfare programs, environmentalism, and republicanism. Its program calls for a radical change of Norwegian society and places much emphasis on problems related to the environment, natural resources, feminism, and the third world. Until 1992 it opposed Labor's backing of NATO. Unlike Labor, its leaders are almost all from the intelligentsia.

In the 2005 Norwegian parliamentary election, SV became a governing party for the first time, participating in the red–green coalition with the Labor Party and the Centre Party. This partnership is something that had earlier been considered almost unthinkable due to differences

Norway

Jonas Gahr Støre, Prime Minister
Source: *Wikipedia*

of opinion on NATO, exploration in the Barents, and EU membership. Before that, it was frequently turned down by the Labor Party.

SV was reduced to the seventh-largest party following the 2013 Norwegian parliamentary election. It won 4.1% of the votes (down from 6.2%) and declined from 11 seats to 7, entering the opposition. It was its worst election on record, but it recovered in the 2017 and 2021 parliamentary elections, although it remained both times at the opposition.

The Green Party (MDG), described as center-left, represents green politics with social liberal features. It holds three seats in the Parliament (gaining 3.8% in the 2021 elections). It also has representation in municipal and county councils (gaining 4.1% in the 2023 elections).

MDG stands in a progressive tradition and also defines itself as an intersectional feminist party. It has gradually moved closer to liberal internationalism over time, allowing for the use of military force when it can promote peace and human rights. MDG supports Norwegian EU and NATO membership, while also advocating for a focus on arms control and peaceful conflict resolution. It is described as a party for "urban, liberal, moderately left-wing academics."

The Green Party maintains close ties to other Green parties, including the German and Swedish Greens. It is a member of the European Green Party and the Global Greens. Since 2022, it has been led by Arild Hermstad.

Communists receive very few votes and are politically insignificant. The former Beijing-oriented Red Electoral Alliance dissolved itself in 2007, and the Communist Party of Norway (NKP) led by Runa Evensen remained unrepresented in parliament, having won only about 1,000 votes in 2013.

In September 2021, Prime Minister Jonas Gahr Støre formed a center-left coalition government. It lacks a majority, but this is normal in Norway.

ECONOMY

Norway's geography has always greatly influenced the economic activity of its people. Its long coastline has made the country reliant on fish and, now, offshore oil. Facing westward, Norway has directed its trading activity toward other lands with access to the North Atlantic. Its mountains have enabled Norwegians to produce more hydroelectric power per capita than any other country and twice as much as the United States or Canada. Almost 99% of its electricity is hydro. This cheap, available electricity was the basis for Norway's industrialization, which gradually changed it from a country so poor at the end of the 19th century that 20,0 of its people chose to emigrate to the US each year into a nation with one of the highest standards of living in the world. The economic growth has been especially dramatic since World War II, a conflict that destroyed 20% of the national wealth, half of its merchant tonnage, 40% of its fishing fleet, and a third of its industry.

The small size of the Norwegian domestic market of some 5 million inhabitants has forced Norway to export many goods and services abroad in order to maintain its high standard of living and social welfare system. It must also import many raw materials to keep its industries operating, as well as many consumer goods to satisfy the rising demands of its prosperous people. Four-fifths of its exports now go to the EU countries, compared with less than half in 1974, while two-thirds of its imports come from those nations. As a member of the European Economic Area (EEA), Norway enjoys all of the EU's free-trade privileges, but it does not have a voice in EU decision making.

Its exports and imports represent more than 40% of its GDP, a higher figure than in many industrialized countries. This heavy dependence upon trade makes Norway particularly vulnerable to international economic fluctuations, though. Presently, 20% of the labor force works in manufacturing and related activities, producing 42% of GDP. The service industry employs 78% and produces 57% of GDP. Only 2.2% earn a living in agriculture, and 1% of GDP is generated in this sector.

Fjord water   Source: *News of Norway*

Hydroelectricity, Oil, and Gas

No other industrialized country has such an abundant supply of domestic energy for its inhabitants as does Norway. Its water-power is almost endlessly renewable, and it has developed only about half of its potential for hydroelectricity. Oslo has a well-developed recycling program. Half the city, including most of its schools, are heated by burning garbage; the process also produces extra electricity. Many northern European cities are following its example.

Its energy abundance saves it from that painful decision facing most other European countries: nuclear power. It neither has nuclear power plants nor plans to construct any. It has other riches of enormous immediate value right now: Oil and gas accounted for 17% of Norway's GDP and 30% of government revenues. Oil alone provided 76,000 jobs.

The shortage of qualified Norwegian-speaking oil workers has pushed average annual earnings to $180,300. This is due in part to a requirement that each be given four weeks off after two weeks of work. Foreign workers cannot be hired unless they can speak Norwegian on the rigs. Norway's workforce is 55% unionized.

As a result of an international agreement reached at the 1958 UN Law of the Sea Conference in Geneva, Norway received possession of a sector in the North Sea three times the size of its mainland. The offshore oil and gas resources in the North Sea are expected to be commercial throughout the 21st century. Less than a third of its estimated petroleum resources have been depleted. It exports most of the 2.8 million barrels it produces per day. However, its oil production has peaked. It increased until 2011 and then began a gradual decline to perhaps around 1.5 million barrels a day by 2014. Exploration is being conducted in the country's Arctic waters. Statoil, the largest company in the Nordic region, is searching for other sources in the Gulf of Mexico, Brazil, Africa, and onshore shale gas reserves. About 30% of its oil and gas resource base is in the US and Canada.

Drilling began in 1969, and in 1971 production started on the Ekofisk oil field in the southwest corner of the Norwegian sector. By the end of the decade, more fields had begun production, but in line with its policy of restraint, petroleum activities north of the 62nd parallel in the North Sea were delayed. One reason for this was the fact that two offshore disasters stung the nation. The first was in 1977 when a well in the Ekofisk field blew out of control, spilling thousands of tons of oil into the sea. The second occurred when a hotel platform capsized in 1980, killing 123.

This latter tragedy occurred on the first anniversary of the nuclear plant failure near Harrisburg, Pennsylvania, which had ignited a serious debate in all of Europe over nuclear power, even though the incident did not cause a single death. A month after a deadly explosion on BP's rig in the Gulf of Mexico in 2010, Statoil dodged a bullet when a major accident on one of its North Sea drilling platforms was averted by sheer luck. An official report found "serious deficiencies" in its offshore operations. It shut 50 wells in its Gullfaks oil field.

In 1980 drilling started north of the line, and production continues there slowly. The government wants to make sure that oil keeps flowing when the old offshore fields of Ekofisk, Frigg, and Statfjord become exhausted. It also wants the population north of the 62nd parallel to have the economic benefits of oil-related activities. Much of Norway's economic policy has always revolved around keeping citizens from leaving the sparsely populated parts of the country.

Norway's continental shelf contains around half of Europe's oil and gas resources. A gas platform named TROLL came on line in 1996, which doubled Norway's gas output and enabled it to provide 29% of European imports (half comes from Russia), including a third of Germany's and France's gas needs. By the turn of the century, Norway's enormous offshore gas reserves accounted for 15% of combined oil-and-gas income. Norway exports all of its gas to the EU through underwater pipelines directly from the North

Sea fields to a terminal at Emden, Germany. Its oil is delivered by underwater pipeline to Teesside, UK. Because of a deep underwater valley just off the Norwegian coast and the resulting precipitous rise of that coast, it is difficult to construct pipelines to the mainland. About 70% of its oil finds its way to Europe. On the world stage, it is the third-largest exporter of gas and the eighth-biggest exporter of oil.

Norway must cover about 85% of its own oil requirements through imports, which is why prices at the pump are the same as in the rest of Europe. But its oil needs remain relatively small, comprising only about 41% of its total energy consumption. About 2% is provided by coal, some of it from Svalbard. A whopping 57% is provided by hydroelectricity. With its electricity prices half those of oil, it is no wonder that Norway can afford to consume more electricity per capita than any other country in the world. For example, the average Norwegian heats his home with it and uses twice as much electrical power as the average American. In 2002 the average Norwegian used 25,240 kilowatt hours, compared with 6,050 in Germany, 4,080 in Greece, and 2,770 in Poland. It is also able to sell electricity to Sweden and Denmark.

At a time when Russia's energy shipments are becoming less certain, Norway is in a good position to fill European partners' need. In 2007 its two energy giants, Statoil and Norsk Hydro, merged to form StatoilHydro (62.9% state owned), the

country's largest company and one of the world's biggest offshore productive capacities. Almost all of increased production will go to Europe. But the formation of such a large company and the northward movement of extraction into the Barents Sea, north of the Arctic Circle, make for tricky negotiations with Russia.

The Russian state-controlled Gazprom chose StatoilHydro as one of its foreign partners to help develop its massive Shtokman gas field off Russia's north coast; this may prove to be the world's largest offshore gas reserve. This is especially true since 2011, when an agreement between Russia and Norway settling their maritime border dispute in the Barents Sea went into effect. Norway is already the first country to commence deliveries of gas from an offshore field inside the Arctic Circle: its Snehvit project.

Norwegians got a reminder in 2008 of the kind of hardball politics the Russian government is willing to play in order to get competitors' attention. It sent the aircraft carrier Admiral Kuznetsov, escorted by other ships and submarines, including at least one nuclear attack submarine, into the center of Norway's vast Gullfaks oil field, crowded with over 40 big oil platforms. There it conducted provocative aggressive air operations that grounded all offshore helicopter flights. An accidental crash into an oil rig would be a catastrophe. Norway had already suffered its second-worst oil spill ever a month earlier in its Statfjord oil field

Fishing boats

Norway

and was very worried about a repeat. Equally worrisome was a Russian mock-bombing run against Norway's northern command center at Bodø. Norway wants to cooperate with Russia, and it hopes to experience no further use of the Russian navy and air force to exert not-so-subtle pressure. This is a major reason Norway is increasing its defense cooperation with Finland and Sweden.

The Norwegian government restricted maximum extraction to 90 million tons of oil and gas annually (extraction is far below that figure). Norway wants to preserve its reserves as long as possible and feared that too-rapid exploitation could seriously disrupt Norwegian society and its economy. Norway is the only western European country to join the OPEC club of oil producers. Norwegians also debate whether their country should take advantage of global warming by drilling for more oil in "the High North" above the Arctic Circle while knowing that the consumption of that oil outside of Norway would accelerate climate change. A fresh controversy is the proposed drilling off the coast of the spectacular Lofoten and Vesteralen Islands in northern Norway, as well as Jan Mayen, promoted by the state-controlled Statoil company. Opponents indicated the ecological impacts, as well as the likelihood that, before the fields are operational, the world's demand for oil will likely be reduced by energy alternatives, rendering the enterprise useless. Bowing to the pressure from fishermen and environmentalists, in 2016 the government stopped its earlier plans for oil exploration. Stepping up the pressure, environmental groups Greenpeace and Nature and Youth used the 2015 Paris climate agreement to sue the government over its plans for drilling in the Barents Sea in the Arctic. Still, in 2017 Lundin Petroleum announced possibly one of the largest discoveries of oil in the same area, and the Norwegian Arctic is getting crowded with oil corporations flocking to newly opened fields.

On the surface, the official thinking in Norway is permeated by green considerations. Almost all of its electricity comes from hydropower, and it was the first country to capture carbon dioxide and store it underground. It was also one of the first lands to levy a carbon tax, and it has pledged to make the nation carbon neutral by 2030. However, for all the talk about *omstilling* (moving away from the fossil fuel-supported economy), it has a bad record of reducing greenhouse gas emissions: They have grown 15% since adoption of the carbon tax despite its ambitious target of being 30% below its 1990 emissions by 2020. Norway emits more than many other European countries. In 2017, Oslo decided to ban diesel cars from the center of the city, noting their contribution to exhaust emissions that make outdoor activity hazardous to children. The capital's location makes it prone to pollution trapping when the temperature in Oslo is lower than in the hills that surround it.

Oil and gas are very important for the country's economy. Through taxes and royalties, the state collects about 80% of the revenues from oil and gas production, and in 2006 it accounted for 36% of total central government revenue, compared with only 1% in 1975 and 5% in 1988. More than a third of overall investments is in the oil-and-gas sector. Improving technology steadily opens up previously inaccessible fields.

Norway was one of the biggest winners of Russia's invasion of Ukraine in 2022. It replaced Russia as Europe's largest supplier of gas and as a significant seller of oil and electricity.

Since World War II, Norway always centrally planned and steered the country's economy more than did most other western European countries. The goal always was to distribute income more evenly and to maintain full employment and stable prices. The state holds 37% by value of the Norwegian stock market. One in three workers is on the public payroll. It is no surprise that the Norwegian state took control of all phases of petroleum activity and sought to maintain its control through Statoil.

Although foreign companies continue to be active in exploration and drilling, their services are used only as the Norwegians decide they are needed. Such discrimination ran afoul of the EU competition policy, and Norway had to restructure its entire natural gas industry to satisfy EU authorities. Those foreign firms are preferred that invest money into mainland industries, including the ones that are related to petroleum activity, such as those involved in the production of petrochemicals or of platforms and other offshore equipment. This is particularly important because the weak link in the Norwegian economy is its mainland industry. Norway itself invests heavily abroad, and in 1996 this exceeded foreign investment in Norway for the first time. The bulk of its investments go to Sweden, France, and Ireland.

Statoil, which wants about a third of its output to come from international operations, is investing in operations in the Gulf of Mexico, where it is participating in many of the largest discoveries and projects. More than 100 Norwegian companies are located in Houston, Texas, employing around 6,000 Norwegians. This is the highest number of Norwegian expatriates outside of Scandinavia. Four out of five of these companies are in the energy sector. It is not surprising that the two countries' energy capitals—Stavanger and Houston—are sister cities that engage in many forms of cooperation.

Norway sets aside 80% of its oil earnings in the Government Pension Fund Global (formerly Petroleum Fund and generally referred to as the Oil Fund), a national nest egg that is invested in international equities in order to prevent inflation at home. It was valued at over $1.3 trillion in 2022 (an average of $185,000 per Norwegian). It is the world's largest sovereign wealth fund. It owns on average 1.5% of every listed company globally. According to law, the government can in normal times spend up to 4% of it each year to plug a budget deficit.

The largest retirement savings plan in Europe, it is an investment fund the country can use to spread oil wealth between generations. It is also there for a rainy day in the future. By 2030 pensions will account for 15% of GDP, and the fund would be able to pay about half of that. As one expert put it, "we will continue to receive our free lunch for many years after the oil itself has gone." Many Norwegians believe that some of it ought to be spent now. In 2016, with oil revenues plummeting due to the global price decline, Norway dipped into the fund for the first time. To fill the budget gap, $27.7 billion was withdrawn, or about $5,330 per citizen.

This "sovereign fund" sets the standard in the world for transparency and responsibility. It is invested in some 10.000 enterprises in 40 countries. One-third of the funds are in the United States. It is overseen by the finance ministry and managed by an arm of the Central Bank of Norway. A philosopher advises the bank on how to steer clear of morally questionable investments. For example, it divested its stock in Lockheed Martin because that firm produces cluster bombs and land mines and in Walmart because of its controversial labor practices. It increased its holdings in environmentally responsible companies in order to combat climate change. An ongoing debate is whether it should stop investing in fossil fuel companies. In 2016, Norway's parliament (rather than the fund's management) decided that the fund would divest from 52 companies reliant on coal production for more than 30% of revenues. The fund also increasingly focuses on corporate governance. For example, it launched a crackdown on excessive executive pay and has been more deeply involved in monitoring Volkswagen after the German automaker's corporate deception scandal.

Nonpetroleum Industries

Although Norway is a highly industrialized society, it remains within a nonindustrial landscape. This is because Norwegian industries tend to be rather small. Only a few hundred of the more than 14.000 companies have more than 200 employees, although those large companies employ about 40% of the workforce in manufacturing. Industries are 91% privately and largely Norwegian owned. They are geographically spread out and are often located in beautiful fjord or coastal districts, where they can be close to hydropower sources and ports.

Hydroelectric power provides more than 95% of the country's electricity. It is very important for industry in general, and especially for industries that produce chemicals, iron, steel and ferro-alloys, aluminum, and other metals. The latter are very power-consuming, and the approximately 30 companies in these sectors consume about a fourth of all electric power produced. Few other countries could supply such industries with cheap electricity to keep them alive. The largest of these electricity consumers by far is the primary production of aluminum for further processing into finished goods. In this sector Norway is the world's second-largest exporter after Canada, although all of Norway's bauxite must be imported. It is the largest producer of aluminum in Europe. Much of the other metal industry can be supplied either by domestic ores, which are generally of poor quality and are mined predominantly in the northern half of the country, or by importing the needed ores with money earned from exporting unneeded ores. In the northern mountains, new deposits of gold have been discovered in such massive sizes that they could influence the world price of this precious metal.

Iron ore resources can be mined for at least another century, and Norway has considerable deposits of titanium (used in paints), sulphur, pyrite, copper, zinc, lead, and nickel. The sad fact remains, however, that without state subsidies many of its metal-producing industries would fail. In order to maintain high employment, aluminum production is maintained at 90% capacity, although the industry loses money on every ton it produces. Other metal industries have been pared down to close to 50% capacity and are still losing money.

About the only industry that is not in trouble in Norway is the tourist business. Thanks to the beauty of its scenery and to the friendliness of its people, Norway normally attracts as many foreign tourists as its entire population. About 70% come from other Nordic countries. A major benefit of tourism is that it stimulates economic activity in the outlying regions, both in the mountains and along the coast. Tourism and the economy as a whole received a major boost in 1994, when the town of Lillehammer hosted the Winter Olympics.

Shipping

There are about 80 shipyards in Norway, most of them very small, although the industry is dominated by two large groups, Kvaerner and Aker. As orders for traditional ships declined, many companies converted to constructing offshore rigs and specialized ships. This adjustment has temporarily compensated for the loss of orders for regular ships, but many observers fear that even the market for specialized craft will soon be saturated. The state does subsidize this industry to keep it internationally competitive. But it stopped making new subsidy commitments to shipping companies in the 1980s, and it supported efforts to make the shipbuilding industry more efficient through rationalization.

Like Denmark, Norway has one of the world's largest merchant marine fleets. By 2007 it possessed 1,600 oceangoing merchant vessels, 5% of the world's fleet (down from 10% in 1967). About 60% fly the Norwegian national flag. Norwegians also own about a fifth of all ships used for offshore oil drilling. Well over 90% of these ships never dock at Norwegian ports, though. Oil tankers account for more than 60% of the total tonnage, and Norwegian shipping companies operate many oil-drilling platforms.

The deep-sea expertise Norwegian divers have acquired made Norway the logical provider of the Regalia seagoing platform and trained personnel to help rescue and then recover the bodies of 12 out of 118 Russian sailors trapped in the submarine Kursk in August 2000. Norwegians operate many of the cruise ships that circle the Caribbean Sea. Further, the world's largest passenger ship, *France*, was purchased by a Norwegian ship owner and rechristened *Norway*. Its fleet is very modern and is entirely privately owned. There are very few large shipping companies, and most are small or medium-sized. Maritime activities account for 11% of gross exports, making shipping the third largest export industry.

Norwegian Air Shuttle (ASA) is a Norwegian low-cost airline and Scandinavia's second-largest airline, behind Scandinavian Airlines. In 2012, it announced the purchase of 220 new Boeing and Airbus aircraft on its way to becoming Europe's third-largest low-cost airline. It had plans to expand to Asia and the United States. In 2020, it became a pandemic casualty, teetering on the brink of bankruptcy. After receiving bankruptcy protection aid from the Norwegian government, it has emerged with a much smaller fleet, terminated all of its long-haul flights, and focused on routes in Norway and around Europe. In 2023, Norwegian announced the acquisition of Widerøe, the largest regional carrier in Norway, and the acquisition was completed in January 2024.

Forestry and Agriculture

Norway's forests in the central and southern part of the country provide a good part of the raw materials for a wood-processing industry, although it does have to import some wood from Sweden. This industry traditionally exports 80% of its products, but heavy competition from its Nordic neighbors and Canada has also forced it to face fundamental reorganization. Much of the wooded area

Winners of the Award for Design and Excellence   Source: *News of Norway*

Norway

is owned by the farmers, many of whom derive supplemental income from forestry. Regardless of who owns the forests, they can, according to Norwegian law, be used by everybody for recreational purposes.

The country has not been self-sufficient in food for many decades, and Norway's agricultural production covers less than half of the people's food consumption. It is self-sufficient in dairy and meat products, but it must import 90% of its food grains. The problem, of course, is that only about 3% of the land can be used for farming, and the terrain is so rugged that the predominantly small farms make it difficult to combine them in a way which would permit large-scale and more efficient farming, although the state is making an effort to encourage this. Also, the northern climate means that the growing season is very short. The very best agricultural land is around the Oslo fjord, in the large valleys in the south-central region, and around Stavanger in the south and the Trøndelag area in central Norway.

The state's reserves have been open to Norwegian farmers for years, to the tune of $1.7 billion annually, in an effort to preserve the present pattern of settlement in the country. Every two years the government negotiates an agricultural agreement with both major farmers' organizations that fixes price levels, subsidies, and marketing rules. Many farmers could never hope to survive without such assistance. The state also controls the quantity and price of imported foodstuffs, allowing in only what is in short supply in Norway. This is done to protect Norwegian agriculture, and it is certainly one reason Norwegians were wary of joining the EU, which would prohibit such practices.

Fishing

Even Norway's most picturesque production, fishing, could hardly survive without state help. The number of fishermen has also declined in the past decades to a figure that is less than 1% of the country's total workforce. However, during the past decades, their catch doubled, mainly because of more efficient fishing and the declaration of a 200-mile economic zone along the Norwegian coast and around Jan Mayen and a separate fishery zone around Svalbard. Measured by quantity of catch, Norway is the second-leading fishing nation in Europe, behind Russia. Its fish farms are highly efficient, and it has the world's largest farmed salmon industry. Fishing accounts for 14% of non-petroleum exports and is still important because it supplies raw materials for the country's large fish-processing industry. Faced with a serious threat to its salmon farming industry from the proliferation of chemical-resistant parasites, Norwegians

turned to increasingly sophisticated methods, including huge futuristic enclosures intended to protect the fish until maturity.

Fishermen are strongly unionized and have well-developed cooperatives that buy the fish at fixed prices; they do not have to sell their catch by auction. Only 2% of the catches are sold fresh, and close to 80% is reduced to oil and meal, while about 10% is frozen and 8% is salted or dried. About 90% of the entire catch is ultimately exported. Norway suspended its commercial whaling after the 1987 season, but in 1993 it announced a resumption. Norway,

Iceland, and Japan are the last three countries in the world to hunt whales in violation of the 1993 ban by the International Whaling Commission. In 2006 Norway set its own catch quota for minke whales in the North Atlantic at 1,052, but it killed only 546 to November. In 2015, some 660 minke whales were killed, down from 729 in 2014. With the declining interest in whale meat at home and the difficulty with exporting the meat to Japan, whaling serves little economic purpose in Norway, but governmental subsidies help maintain the lifestyle and tradition for a small

The Scream by Edvard Munch

Edvard Munch by himself

Edvard Grieg

number of fishermen who seasonally turn to whaling.

In many coastal communities, especially in the north, these mainly small or medium-sized companies represent the only possible industrial element. Therefore, the state has long given subsidies to them to keep them alive and to keep persons in those communities from migrating south into the larger cities. This form of subsidy may make little sense from a purely economic point of view, but as in so many other instances in Norway, political objectives outweigh economic ones. In the north, the once-feared start-up of offshore oil operations north of the 62nd parallel is now more easily accepted as the only means of averting the Arctic region's depopulation and subsequent decline.

Economic Problems and European Union

Oslo has become one of the world's most expensive cities in which to live. Its prices are, on average, 29% higher than the average within the EU. Only Switzerland and Iceland, both non-EU members, have higher prices. Food costs a third more in Norway than in Sweden, which explains the vibrant cross-border trade in Sweden. This is a strong argument for joining the EU. Inflation disturbed the traditional labor peace and sparked strikes, which many are experiencing for the first time in their lives. It also drove up public spending. From where did the inflation come?

The extremely lucrative oil and gas activity brought lots of money into the country, which ended up more and more in the form of public spending rather than investment in private industry to raise productivity and to develop new technology. The oil operations also attracted much of the country's skilled labor and created a

very tight supply in the rest of the country. Despite appeals by the government, employees in the petroleum sector successfully forced the oil companies to pay everincreasing wages. To fill some of the labor shortages, 75,000 migrant laborers worked legally in Norway as of 2007, about 20,000 of whom are from the Nordic world. They made up 3% of the labor force.

As in all Nordic countries, the guidelines for wage settlements covering the entire country are established in summit meetings between the LO and the employers' associations every two years. Since these unified wage guidelines apply to all sectors of the economy, the unions (to which two-thirds of the labor force belong) have succeeded in insisting that all wages rise with those in the petroleum industry, regardless of whether a company in the non-oil sector is profitable or not. That is where both government subsidies and inflation come into the picture. The government pays much of the costs of higher wages in the form of subsidies.

In the 1980s the government created two-thirds of the new jobs. By 1995 public-sector employment had doubled since 1972, while industrial jobs had fallen by 100,000. Rising wage costs increase the price of products that Norwegian companies are trying to sell abroad. To make matters worse, Norway's sale of oil and gas greatly increased the strength of its currency, the krone (crown). Such a "hard" currency raises even more the actual prices of Norway's goods to foreign buyers. This caused Norway to lose some of its markets abroad.

No government could risk a dramatic rise in unemployment or a deep cut in the social welfare system. Any substantial dismantling of the social welfare system in a Scandinavian country could be fatal to any politician who would propose it, regardless of whether the system could be paid for or not. Unlike other Nordic countries, Norway can pay for its tightly woven social security net. It introduced a National Insurance Scheme in 1967, which by 1971

had replaced all private pension or insurance programs. It protects all citizens against sickness, unemployment, invalidism, and many other unforeseen calamities. At age 67 a person receives a pension which, for the average Norwegian, amounts to about two-thirds of the income he earned during his working years.

Employers' contributions pay 60% of the costs of the scheme; members', 20%; and appropriations from the central and local governments, the remaining 20%. As in other Scandinavian countries, welfare assistance is given as a right, not as an alm, and the objective is that neither personal calamity nor old age should endanger the living standard to which the citizen had become accustomed.

Things looked bright in the 21st century until the 2009 recession jolted the country. Real estate fell by 15% before beginning to rise again. There was no real estate crash,

Norway

since there were few mortgage-lending excesses. Banks remained generally healthy and prudent in their lending. The government set up two stimulus funds (one for banks and the other for business and industry) to try to mitigate the effects of the global crisis. Norway's annual economic growth in 2023 averaged 1.3%. Inflation in 2023 stood at 7%. Unemployment was an enviable 3.4% in 2023, among the lowest in Europe. It would be slightly higher if persons in training and employment programs were included, but essentially all Norwegians who want to work are employed. Per-capita GDP in 2010 was $85,390, the third-highest in the world, and it topped the Nordic nations. A study in 2009 found that Norwegians work the fewest hours of the citizens of any industrial democracy.

It is one of the few countries in Europe that is not reducing its welfare state. Its competitive position has improved because of productivity improvements following a shakedown of labor in manufacturing. It has made its tax system simpler to administer and understand. Although the real tax level stayed the same for the business sector, it reduced the highest marginal rate from 57.8% to 48.8%, and the middle class pays no more than 35.8%.

Its most important decision was whether to join the EU, to which it formally applied in 1992. In 1994 voters went to the polls, and 52.2% rejected EU membership. Its strong economy, low unemployment, and overall feeling of security allowed Norwegians an alternative to the EU. One explanation seemed to sum up the majority's attitude: "We know what we have, but we don't know what we'll get."

In many ways it enjoys most of the advantages of EU membership without most of the disadvantages. It is part of the internal market through the European Economic Area (EEA), which it joined in 1994 and which does not cover agriculture and fish. It had to restructure its natural-gas industry, accepts all the EU environmental and social legislation, and even makes as large a financial contribution to EU coffers as a comparable-sized EU member, such as Denmark or Finland. However, it does not have to adopt the euro; is not bound by the Common Foreign and Defense Policy (CFSP); does not pay into the wasteful Common Agriculture Policy (CAP) while subsidizing its own farmers more than would be allowed in the EU; and finally, does not have to abide by the EU's common fisheries policy, thereby maintaining its own 200-mile coastal exclusion zone, which remains well stocked with fish. Norway has agreed to pay €225 million to the EU over five years to help fund improvements in the 10 new countries that joined in 2004.

Norwegian Special Forces
Source: *News of Norway*

But it has no voice in EU decisions, being what former trade commissioner and now WTO president Pascal Lamy called "a fax democracy": It receives instructions and legislation from Brussels, but it has no input into the decisions. For example, in 2005 the EU slapped a 16% duty on Norwegian salmon, arguing that Norway "dumps" its salmon inside the EU at below the cost of production. Such rulings breed distrust toward Brussels, and the irritated minister of fisheries, Svein Ludvigsen, said, "If Norway was a member of the EU, this salmon issue would never be on the agenda." The matter was resolved by both sides accepting a minimum price for salmon sales.

Norway's public is still divided on the EU. Aware that four-fifths of Norway's exports are sold in the EU, industry supports membership. Many realize that the EU is expanding eastward and will soon encompass most of Europe; this makes it harder to stand outside. There is some desire to take part in the invigorated EU discussions concerning a European Security and Defense Policy (ESDP), for which Norway already provides troops. Belonging would help Norwegians shape the European decisions that ultimately affect them. Nevertheless, then-Prime Minister Jens Stoltenberg announced after the 2005 and 2009 elections that there would be no referendum on joining the EU during the lifetime of his government. Majority opinion in 2010 was against entry: 62.5%, the highest ever. The better the economic situation, the less support there is for joining. Wealthy Norwegians see no reason to belong, and the euro's problems are not encouraging. But the government still favors membership.

Norway is moving steadily closer to Europe whether its people are fully aware of it or not. Paradoxically, it was also frequently cited as a model by the British

proponents of the UK leaving the EU. It is Europe's top oil producer, and a third of its export revenue is derived from North Sea energy sources. It maintains its economic performance and energy production in a way that does not unduly pollute the environment. However, it dropped from 3rd place on the Environmental Performance Index in 2008 to 17th place in 2016, while its Scandinavian neighbors took the first 4 places.

Perhaps surprisingly, Norway's environmental credentials came under fire from critics accusing it of hypocrisy. On the one hand, the country's international efforts to curtail global warming are exemplary. In 2008, it gave $1 billion to Brazil to stop deforestation (making a huge impact on reducing its rate) and promised the same to Indonesia. In 2016, it pledged to ban clear-cutting of trees and not to buy such products as palm oil, timber, or beef obtained in ways that cause deforestation. Norway's sovereign wealth fund has a major economic impact on companies around the world, steering them toward environmental responsibility. Between 1996 and 2016, Norway's old-growth forest (over 160 years), essential to biodiversity, had grown from 1.3% of the country's territory to 2.4%, a paltry amount but a significant jump.

Norway also has the highest number of electric cars per capita in the world and is even discussing banning fossil fuel cars by 2025. There are numerous incentives to get an electric car, such as no sales taxes and no 25% VAT on purchases, low road tax, and free tolls, in addition to free city parking and permission to use bus lanes. Plus, electricity to recharge the batteries is free! The government's commitment to supporting the zero-emission car idea drew attention from other countries, and the electric cars' mass appeal in this frigid climate defies stereotypes about battery-run vehicles. In fact, electric car maker Tesla opened a salon in Tromsø, far north of the Arctic Circle.

On the other hand, the government stunned environmentalists by approving a plan to dump millions of tons of industrial mining waste into Forde Fjord (Førdefjorden) in southwestern Norway to facilitate the excavation of rutile for titanium dioxide (for tooth-whitening and paints) and to create some 170 jobs. Norway's carbon dioxide emissions are 23% higher than in 1990, and overall greenhouse gases are 2.4% higher, just when the Paris-New York climate accord commits its signatories to reduce global warming. Growth and development projects routinely trump environmental concerns, as does the preference for oil and fishing: Norway opened a new coal mine in Spitsbergen, new areas in the Barents Sea along Norway's maritime border with Russia have been opened for oil and gas exploration, and proposals to start drilling in the spectacular and environmentally sensitive Lofoten Islands keep coming from the industry and oil ministry alike. The licensees of exploration permits in the Barents Sea even enjoy a 78% tax break. And as if whaling itself were not controversial enough, Norwegian companies use leftover whale meat to feed fur farm animals that are then slaughtered. Animal and environmental protection groups are speaking out against these and other environmentally and morally questionable practices.

Norwegians are rich because of their oil, but they are confronted with the problem of how to use their wealth. All European countries have oil problems, but Norway has one of a different kind. The more they earn from oil, the more two different energy economies develop: one, a flourishing energy production in the high seas, and the other, a traditional mainland industry. They are still torn between wanting to keep their industry alive by avoiding a predominantly oil-based economy and wanting their standards of living to keep rising as a result of oil wealth.

The major parties know that oil revenues can bankroll the expanding welfare state and bureaucracy. For example, in 2003 the government announced plans to dip into the huge Government Pension Fund Global to cover its budget deficit, although a parliamentary rule allows no more than 4% of the fund to be used to cover a budget deficit. While former prime minister Stoltenberg tapped 7% of the fund's assets, the issue was not too contentious, since there was a budget surplus of 17.5% in 2008, falling to 0.2% in 2022. The state is free of debt.

Government subsidies can keep specific, weak industries alive and thereby fight unemployment. But such use of Norway's riches shelters its industry from change and real competition and robs it of the discipline that would be needed to make its mainland economy healthy again. The government subsidies that flow to industry are handouts to pay workers, not investments to improve production techniques. Thus, oil and gas help to freeze the status quo, while Norway's competitors gear up for the future. What will happen, though, when the oil and gas run out or if those two things lose much of their value due to future technological developments in the energy field? The Midas touch obviously creates problems, as well as opportunities.

CULTURE

Rural-Urban Traditional Distinctions

A major characteristic of Norwegian politics and society remains the contrast and tension between the periphery and the center. The center encompasses the leaders of the country's civil service, military, Lutheran Church, industry, and shipping in and around Oslo and the major cities. In this political and social center, one speaks a Norwegian dialect now called Bokmål (earlier Riksmål), whereas in the periphery most persons speak another dialect now called Nynorsk (which means "New Norwegian" and which was earlier called Landsmål). Both dialects have equal status in the state ad-ministration and schools, but the use of one dialect or the other reveals important social distinctions. Until the end of the 19th century, the only official dialect was Riksmål, which had been influenced by the Danish language during

the long period of Danish domination over Norway. Thus, it was the language of the more cosmopolitan and middle-upper-class city dwellers.

In the course of the 19th century, the dialect of Nynorsk was developed by a nationalist, Ivar Asen, from many diverse rural dialects that Asen judged to be untainted by Danish. Now spoken by only 12% of the population, Nynorsk was much closer to the speech used by the common people, who at that time lived mainly in rural areas of the south and west. Among these people, class distinctions were minimal, since most were fishermen or small, independent farmers who owned their own land. They were much more religious than their compatriots in the cities, and their respect for state authority was much weaker. They also spoke a dialect that was looked down upon by the city folk. The people in the periphery were much more supportive of movements calling for popular religious revival, the widened use of Nynorsk, and the prohibition of alcoholic beverages.

From 1917 until 1927, they were able to have all liquors and strong wines banned entirely, and they still are inclined to support politicians who call for tightened controls on alcoholic consumption. In the sparsely populated north, the contrast with the center was less pronounced, since the society there was more fragmented, with more prosperous trade families having a greater economic influence or control over the small farmers and fishermen. The tensions between the center and the periphery still influence Norwegian politics and parties today and were crucially important in the debate over possible Norwegian entry into the EU in 1972 and in 1994. But the mobilization of the periphery against the center has been replaced by a noticeable rebellion of the center against the periphery on many issues. For example, there has been a noticeable trend toward civil unions or long-term relationships rather than marriage, probably due to the high divorce rates that had persisted since World War II.

In 2008 parliament granted gay and lesbian couples the same right to marry, to adopt children, and to receive artificial insemination as heterosexual couples.

Norway is experiencing another form of tension: toward darker-skinned refugees and immigrants. Foreign-born and their children born in Norway constitute over 12% of the population of 4.9 million; almost half of them are Europeans, led by Poles and Swedes. They now constitute about a quarter (28%) of Oslo's population. This traditionally white nation had never regarded itself as a melting pot. The influx of as many as 16,000 such people every year has created a groundswell of

Sami with reindeer

Norway

unease. The Progress Party readily exploits hostility against them, especially towards the 3% who are Muslims.

Beginning on the east side of Oslo, a dingy area with about 130,000 immigrants, and now all over the capital, many frightened parents are taking their children out of their neighborhood schools because immigrant children constitute an overall majority in them. Parents fear that the quality of education is dropping. With the blue-collar class shrinking, immigrants now comprise the new lower class, and their numbers are rising, thanks largely to family reunification. They are divided among themselves on ethnic lines and are in constant demographic flux. They have gone to the bottom of a sort of minority hierarchy, with the Sámi at the top, favored because of their status in international law as an indigenous people and their own Sámi parliament. Immigration and integration have become emotional and controversial issues among established parties and organizations.

Male immigrants from Africa and the Middle East have been encouraged to attend courses intended to familiarize them with the Norwegian perspective on gender roles. Motivated by the incidence of sexual violence, the courses address some misconceptions they may have regarding promiscuity of women who dress in miniskirts, drink alcohol, or kiss in public, in addition to unacceptability of rape even within marriage.

In July 2011 a gunman who believed that Norway's tolerance of diversity, multiculturalism, and Islam were threatening the traditionally homogeneous Norwegian nation and its Christian values committed the worst atrocity in Norway's history. Disguised as a policeman, Anders Breivik first parked a van containing a half-ton of explosives outside the prime minister's office in downtown Oslo. The explosion could be heard seven kilometers (four miles) away, and eight people died.

He then proceeded by car and ferry to the island of Utøya, west of Oslo, which belongs to the ruling Labor Party's youth organization. Claiming to be a police officer, he called hundreds of Labor campers together and opened fire on them. When a SWAT team finally arrived, after a police helicopter could not get off the ground and two civilian boats had to be obtained, the gunman threw his weapons to the ground and surrendered. By that time there were 69 dead on the island making a total of 77 dead and many more wounded.

He had posted a 1,500-page manifesto on the Internet just hours before the attacks, writing that they were meant as a declaration of war on multiculturalism. In his mind, the future leaders of the Labor Party were tools of "Muslim colonization" of Europe. After showing no remorse and

telling the judge that he had acted to save the country, prosecutors ultimately declared him sane so that he is serving a 21-year prison sentence (the maximum under Norwegian law) with the possibility of indefinite extension rather than serving time in psychiatric care.

Norwegians were left with many questions, including the wisdom of their police being unarmed; an officer must have authorization from his chief to be issued a firearm. Hunting traditions in the Nordic countries mean that there is a high rate of gun ownership. More than 100,000 gathered in the streets to mourn the victims, and many more asked themselves whether their proverbial tolerance will survive. A government-commissioned report seriously rebuked the police and intelligence services for a litany of failings: They could have averted the bombing in Oslo. They responded too slowly to the shooting on the island, failed to mobilize helicopters, and ignored offers of boats from private individuals. Heads rolled, and the report had a devastating effect on the Stoltenberg government's popularity. In 2015, a much-publicized reopening of the island camp by 1,000 Labor Party youths was attended by Stoltenberg (later NATO secretary-general) and members of Norwegian parliament.

The case tested the Norwegian liberal approach to criminals again in 2016, when Breivik sued the government for violating his human rights by keeping him in solitary confinement and restricting his access to the Internet. He won, and the government was even ordered to pay his legal fees of about $40,000. This conclusion might seem astounding, considering the conditions of his confinement: a three-room suite with windows, equipped with a treadmill, a TV with DVD player, a fridge, and a Sony PlayStation. Unrepentant, Breivik gave a Nazi salute during the hearings.

The Arts

The two principal dialects of Norwegian, Bokmål and Nynorsk, are spoken by only 4.5 million persons, and in contrast to the Swedes, who allow English words to seep freely into their language, the Norwegians try very hard to prevent their language from being anglicized in any way, even though most Norwegians learn English in school. Despite the fact that so few people in the world speak the Norwegian language, Norway is a very active literary nation. It has the world's highest book sales per person, and book publishing is supported by sizable state subsidies. In 2012 a new translation of the Bible, called Bibel 2011, topped the best-seller lists week after week. One can read a digital version and one that has no verses or chapters and "reads like a novel."

Norway has four Nobel Prize winners in literature: Bjørnstjerne Bjørnson in 1903, Knut Hamsun in 1920, Sigrid Undset in 1928, and Jon Fosse in 2023. Hamsun is particularly perplexing because he had welcomed the brutal Nazi occupation of his own country. He gave his Nobel Prize to propaganda minister Josef Goebbels and flew to the Eagle Nest retreat to meet Hitler. He wrote an article for a collaborationist newspaper on May 7, 1945, glorifying Hitler, who had just committed suicide a few days earlier. Until his death at 92 in 1952, Hamsun was shunned and punished by his countrymen for his shocking betrayal. But his revered novels, like *Hunger*, *Pan*, and *Growth of the Soil*, are still on the nightstands and school reading lists of many Norwegians. The latest laureate, Jon Fosse, was honored for "his innovative plays and prose, which give voice to the unsayable," said the awarding body of the Swedish Academy.

The earliest Norwegian literature is Eddic poetry from the 9th or 10th centuries, and many fairy tales and folk poems survive from subsequent centuries. After the country's links with Denmark were broken in 1814, Henrik Wergeland won the reputation as the most significant Norwegian lyricist with his visionary romantic poetry. He ignited a literary renaissance in the country. Bjørnson was the first writer whose works became widely known beyond the country's borders; his earlier plays and short stories are infused with nationalist ideas and enthusiasm, but his later works are more characterized by modern realism. Also well received abroad were the plays of Henrik Ibsen, whose serious, penetrating works explore man's ethical and psychological dimensions. Ibsen, Bjørnson, and two other writers in the realist school, Jonas Lie and Alexander Kielland, are generally considered to be the most significant Norwegian authors, although Arne Garborg, Undset, and Hamsun should not be overlooked.

Just as the liberation from Denmark sparked a literary outburst, the emancipation from German occupation in 1945 had the same effect. For a while poetry and exciting narratives were produced, but Norwegian literature quickly moved from the optimistic enthusiasm of national emancipation to pessimism, intellectual indecision, fear, and powerlessness. Literature became more experimental. As Norway began its economic flowering and a wealthy consumer society developed, Norwegian literature turned to the alleged absurdity of society and the difficulties that individuals have in establishing their own identity and meaningful contacts with other persons in a cold, consumption-oriented society. Much Norwegian literature became thereby politicized, as authors pointed to a need for radical change.

A particular pride of contemporary Norwegian literature is Herbjørg Wassmo, who in 1987 won the Nordic Literature Prize for her 1986 novel *Hudløs himmel* (Sensitive Sky). She is the first Norwegian woman to win it. Her writings depict women's psyche, chiseled in drastic realism. She commands a sensitive, poetic language.

The society those authors criticized so mercilessly was, however, a very tolerant one, which not only bore criticism well but also which even chose to pay for such literary attacks against itself. As few Norwegian books could be financial successes on the tiny Norwegian market, the state created a cultural fund that purchased 1,000 copies of each work of Norwegian literature so that every public library could have a copy to circulate. The state also grants three-year scholarships to young authors in order to provide them with the financial wherewithal to work undisturbed.

An author who does not need the state's hand is Jostein Gaader, a high school philosophy teacher. His novel, *Sophie's World*, is a highly readable history of western thought told in a compelling mystery. After reaching the bestseller lists in Scandinavia and Germany, it was introduced to the American market in 1995. Also avidly read in the US is crime novelist Jo Nesbø, whose *Nemesis* was nominated for an Edgars Award and whose novel, *The Devil's Star*, appeared in English in 2010. Also riding this wave are Kjell Ola Dahl and Karin Fossum. Per Petterson's English translations, *Out*

Stealing Horses and *I Curse the River of Time*, have made the New York Times' best books of the year. Scandinavian literature is more popular than ever. One of the oddest works of the 21st century is *My Struggle* by Karl Ove Knausgaard. Meandering and devoid of plot, it is 3,770 pages of mental wanderings in 6 thick volumes. Its popularity is global.

The state and the municipalities also subsidize all cultural activities with a view to making culture largely decentralized and thereby available to as many persons as possible. It maintains six regional theaters, in addition to the National Theater in Oslo, the country's main stage, and the National Stage in Bergen. Oslo also has the Norwegian Theater, which presents plays only in Nynorsk, and the Oslo New Theater. Plays are also televised once a week so that Norwegians can have the chance to experience theater performances in every corner of the country.

State subsidies also keep the Norwegian film industry alive so that it can produce about 10 feature and 80 short films per year; most are aimed primarily at a Norwegian audience. These subsidies, amounting to $100 million in 2009, cover 45% of the production costs for black-and-white and 55% for color films. The state will also guarantee loans for up to 90% of the total production costs. All films shown in Norway must, however, be approved by a state film censor, a requirement that is highly controversial today.

Perhaps the internationally best-known Norwegian film figure is the actress Liv Ullmann, who often appears onstage in the US and in many films directed by

the Swede Ingmar Bergman, who died in 2007. Because of her fame and activism for the UN Children's Fund, she was named as the UN's first goodwill ambassador to various parts of the world, especially Africa. Bergman's and Ullmann's daughter, Linn Ullmann, who studied literature in the US from age 16 to 22 before returning to Oslo as a literary critic for the daily newspaper Dagbladet, won rave reviews in both countries for her debut novel in 1998, *Before You Sleep*.

Recommended in 1997 for an Oscar for best foreign film was Norway's The Other Side of Sunday, directed by Otto Nesheim. Set in 1959, it is a delightful portrayal of the maturing of a young girl who grows up in a pious family living in a rural part of Norway where almost everything was forbidden. Another Norwegian film won an Oscar nomination in 2002—Elling, based on Ingvar Ambjørnsen's novel *Blood Brothers*. At the Seattle International Film Festival, it was voted as the audience's favorite film out of 230 movies.

And 2008 was a banner year: 23 Norwegian films premiered, attracting 22.5% of moviegoers. Topping the list was the World War II drama Max Manus, based on a true story of the resistance hero. Close behind was The Kautokeino Rebellion, which chronicles a Sámi uprising in northern Norway in 1852, directed by a descendant of the rebellion, Nils Gaup. In 2012 Norway's most expensive feature film of all time ($15.5 million) opened—Kon-Tiki, based on Thor Heyerdahl's 1947 best-seller *The Kon-Tiki Expedition: By Raft Across the South Seas*. The movie featured the most special effects ever viewed in a Scandinavian production.

Norwegian art and music cross Norway's borders more easily, since they appeal to human senses and intellect without the restriction of language. The best-known composer was Edvard Grieg, who composed intimate, soothing romantic pieces. Another widely acclaimed composer, Johann Svendsen, produced symphonic music, which, like that of Grieg, drew inspiration from Norwegian folk music. The country has many active composers today, and there are four symphony orchestras in the major cities.

The Norwegian Opera was created under the directorship of the renowned singer Kirsten Flagstad in 1958 in order to provide a suitable setting for both opera and ballet. In 1994 the world heard one of Norway's most popular song artists, Sissel Kyrkjebø, open and close the Winter Olympics in Lillehammer. Many of her CDs and cassettes were released in the US. Also popular in America in the late 1990s were country music star Bjøro Håland and his band. A teen female duo, M2M (Marit Larsen and Marion Raven), won a

Norway

large following, not only at home, but also in Europe and the US. Maria Mena, an 18-year-old singer-songwriter from Oslo with a New Yorker father, toured America and snagged a top-15 spot on the singles chart in 2004. Higher-brow stars are opera singers Kjell Magnus Sandve and his wife, Kjersti Sandve.

The giant of Norwegian art is Edvard Munch, who is considered to be one of the fathers of expressionism around the turn of the 20th century. The product of a family with a history of insanity, he created paintings that scream at the viewer and reveal how some human beings can be alienated, desperately anxious, and torn inside. Unloved and misunderstood in the Norway of his time, he gained his fame in Germany. He moved back to his native country in 1909 and had an uneasy relationship with it until his death in 1944. Most of his works are displayed in the Munch Museum in Oslo, and other works of his are scattered among the 320 art museums and art collections throughout the country.

On the day the world's attention was focused on the opening of the Lillehammer Winter Olympics, his (and Norway's) most famous painting, *The Scream*, painted in 1893 and worth at least $75 million and of which there are four versions, was stolen from the National Gallery in Oslo by thieves who brazenly left a postcard reading, "Thanks for the poor security." Norwegians heaved a sigh of relief in May 1994, three months later, when the police recovered it undamaged in a sting operation. In 1996 four Norwegian men were sentenced to six years in prison.

However, the luck was not to last. In 2004, another version of *The Scream*, along with an additional Munch masterpiece from 1893–1894, *Madonna*, valued at $15 million and, like *The Scream*, uninsured, were violently ripped from the walls of Oslo's Munch Museum in a daytime raid while stunned visitors looked on. The paintings were whisked off in a waiting car. In February 2006 six suspects went to trial in Oslo for the theft. Three were

convicted and given sentences from four to eight years. The paintings were found in August only slightly damaged.

In March 2005 a watercolor called *Blue Dress* and two lithographs by Munch were pried with crowbars and stolen from the walls of an upscale restaurant of the Refsnes Hotel at Moss, south of Oslo. Police recovered the three works less than 24 hours later.

In May 2012 the only *Scream* that was privately owned was auctioned at Sotheby's in New York; its price was a record $119.9 million. The seller was a Norwegian businessman whose father, Thomas Olsen, was a friend, neighbor, and patron of Munch. He wanted to use the proceeds to build a cultural center at Nedre Raame, where Munch lived from 1910 until his death in 1944. The restored home and studio of Munch will be open to the public.

Norwegian artists have been leaders in the production of "monumental art," and as in the other Scandinavian countries, abstract art has become a dominant form. It also has produced recognized sculptors, such as Carl Nesjar, Odd Tandberg, Arnold Haukeland, and Nils Aas. The sculptor best known internationally, however, is Gustav Vigeland.

Education

At age seven, Norwegian children enter school, and for at least nine years they must attend an elementary school, which is financed and operated by the municipal governments. About 80% continue their education for an additional three years in schools that are operated and financed by the counties. A recent reform under an earlier Labor government combined in 1976 the separate tracks of secondary schools that had prepared young people for the university, for a trade, or for some other job which did not require a university education. The problem with such separate schools was that it was very difficult to change from one secondary school to another type; many critics also believed that such separate schools established

and hardened class differences within Norwegian society.

Therefore, comprehensive schools, similar to the American high schools, were created, which combined various tracks under one roof and which eased the difficulty of switching from one track to the other. Those who follow the college preparatory course in the new comprehensive schools usually qualify for entrance into one of the four state-funded universities in Oslo, Bergen, Trondheim, and Tromsø; into one of several specialized universities (which teach, for example, engineering, agriculture, architecture, business administration, physical education, or music); or one of seven regional teachers' colleges. Education is free at all levels, and needy students in the secondary schools can receive extra scholarships. Students at the universities or colleges receive both scholarships and loans that must be repaid within 10 to 15 years. As elsewhere in Europe, the universities are experiencing severe overcrowding.

As in all Scandinavian countries, Norwegian schools have been laboratories for experimentation, especially the kind that seeks to eliminate social differences. Many of these changes have not been well received, and one of the first things the earlier Conservative government changed was reevaluation of grades in schools, which had been deemphasized or done away with on the grounds that they were discriminatory and were hindrances to learning. The new administration also enhanced the financial basis of private schools and gave them more freedom to run themselves as they chose.

Norway hosts the European Wergeland Centre (EWC), a prestigious educational institution established by the Council of Europe and Norway in 2008. Its headquarters are in Oslo. It is governed by a board composed of representatives of the Council of Europe and Norway. Its Executive Director is Ana Perona-Fjeldstad.

EWC is a resource center on education for intercultural understanding, human

Educating for Democracy and Human Rights—EWC International Team

Source: EWC

rights and democratic citizenship. Its projects involve a wide range of stakeholders from policy, research and practice with activities ranging from training courses to participation in expert groups on policy development. EWC activities and services are free and open to all 46 member states of the Council of Europe.

EWC work builds on Council of Europe recommendations and policies, such as the Charter on Education for Democratic Citizenship and Human Rights Education, which was developed to ensure that the values of human rights, democracy and the rule of law are promoted in and through education. It also supports Norwegian priorities for multilateral cooperation, and contributes to international efforts towards reaching the UN sustainable development goals.

Aiming to build and sustain a culture of democracy and human rights through education by strengthening the capacity of individuals, educational institutions and educational systems, EWC has chosen to focus on five action areas: strengthening democratic competencies, promoting inclusive and democratic learning environments, providing teaching and learning resources, building partnerships and contributing to policy development in education.

The Media

Considering its small population, the Norwegian press offers both variety and a considerable number of individual publications—in all there are 161 daily newspapers. All are in private hands, although all receive state subsidies in one form or the other. Most generally support the political line of one party or the other without having formal ties to it. The largest newspapers are the independent to conservative Oslo dailies, *Aftenposten* and *Verdens Gang*, as well as the liberal dailies, *Dagbladet* from Oslo and the *Bergens Tidende* from Bergen. Favorite weekly magazines are *Allers, Hjemmet*, and *Norsk Ukeblad*, which are all family publications. The favorite monthlies are *Reader's Digest*, entitled *Det Beste* in Norwegian, and *Donald Duck Co.*, whose hero is very familiar to American and European readers. In 2016 the international organization, Reporters without Borders, rated the Norwegian press the world's third-freest after those of Finland and the Netherlands.

Local radio and TV stations compete with the state-owned Norwegian Broadcasting Company. Its activities are free of direct government control, although it is run by a council composed of representatives of the Storting, the public service, and certain public groups. The government also appoints the director. Financing comes from public funds, since no advertising is permitted (except on some foreign stations); radio and television must compete with one of the most beautiful natural settings for the people's attention. Norwegians are outdoors people, and they tend to spend their four weeks of paid vacation hiking, fishing, swimming, camping, and boating in the summer and cross-country skiing or skating in the winter. Prosperity has also enabled one out of six families to buy its own seaside cottage or mountain chalet. This is a striking proportion when one considers that 53% of the families own the houses or apartments in which they live.

The Native Population

One group that lives especially close to nature is the Sámi, about two-thirds of whom live in Norway's far north and about a third of whom live in the north of Finland and Sweden. It is believed that about 55,000 Sámis live in Norway. Isolated for centuries in the northern periphery of Scandinavia, they preserved their unique Finno-Ugric language, broken down into three broad dialects by region. Until after World War II, they were forbidden to use their language. Their exclusive identity with the Sámi culture is breaking down as most Sámi are being assimilated with the other Scandinavian cultures to one degree or another. They do not have facial features or skin color that distinguish them visually from other Norwegians.

The most tightly knit Sámi are the reindeer-raising nomads, who now constitute only a tenth of the total Sámi population. Each receives an annual subsidy of $14,400 from the central government. However, their grazing areas have been greatly reduced by fences erected along the Norwegian-Swedish border and by the construction of hydroelectric plants at the waterfalls in the north. The tundra in the northernmost province of Finn- mark may cover huge mineral deposits, and the central government wants the profits from mining to go into its own treasury. The Sámi, who are a minority in the north, are contesting this, as there are other irritating regulations from Oslo, such as new rules that only a veterinarian can castrate reindeer and that reindeer herds should be limited in size to prevent overgrazing.

The extension of the social welfare system to every corner of Norway has made practices of helping each other largely unnecessary, and therefore a part of the glue within the nomadic community has been destroyed. Of course, many Sámis want to become partially or wholly assimilated into the Norwegian culture, but an emotional debate is still taking place in Norway concerning the future of this minority within the larger society. Some Norwegians argue that the Sámis' standard of living should be elevated to the prevailing Norwegian level, while others argue that their cultural independence should be preserved at all costs, even though their culture scorns individual advancement and permits many social inequalities within its own society.

The Norwegian state does finance a Sámi school at Karasjok and elsewhere for those children whose parents want them to learn in the Sámi language. Other special schools and university courses are also provided, and they have their own largely symbolic government. It is certain that the most effective means for the survival of this unique minority is to preserve its language, and subsidized radio and TV programs are aired. There are also Sámi book publishers, newspapers (such as *Min Áigi—Our Times*—published twice weekly), and recordings of traditional Sámi chants. Nevertheless, the Sámi culture will continue to lose its grip on the lives of most of the group.

The lives of this faraway people were so vividly portrayed in the first Sámi film ever made, *Pathfinder*, that it won an Oscar nomination in 1988 for best foreign film. This film was half-financed by the Norwegian government and directed by a 32-year-old Sámi, Nils Gaup, under appalling conditions. It was shot above the Arctic Circle in temperatures which reached 40 degrees below 0 and when there were only two hours of daylight. Cameras had to be stored in a freezer to avoid condensation inside the mechanisms, and sound equipment had to be defrosted with electric hair dryers. The message was worth the extreme effort.

Through councils (called Siida) composed of representatives of the various families, the nomads regulate the use of grazing land. The councils also traditionally had the function of guiding the community and of arranging for the provision of food and other necessities for the socially weak within the group. In 1989 Sámis elected for the first time 39 representatives from 13 constituencies to their own Sámi People's Congress. It is elected every four years on the same day as the national parliament in Oslo. It convenes in the Finnmark town of Karasjok, where a park (named Sameland, or Sápmi in Sámi) offers visitors a poetic and magical trip through Sámi culture. The congress has advisory as well as decision-making powers in matters related to the Sámis.

At the third opening of this parliament in 1997, King Harald V publicly expressed regret to the Sámi people for the repression inflicted on them and their culture: "Today we must apologize for the injustice the Norwegian state once imposed on the Sámi people through policies of

Norway

Norwegianization." In 2002 the Sámi People's Congress demanded more self-government, although there is no consensus what that exactly means and for whom such a government would speak. Its electoral register contained only 10,000 names in 2002, and only two-thirds of them actually voted in the previous election.

A major issue was how to gain control of the Sámi region's natural resources. In 2003 the government in Oslo introduced the Finnmark Bill, which grants the Sámi no special rights in their homeland and gives the federal government control over the management of Finnmark's resources and lands.

The Sámi's growing political clout was on display when Norway's largest pension fund manager, KLP, announced in 2017 that it would withdraw its $68 million of investments from the companies behind the Dakota Access Pipeline in the US. The move was apparently reflecting a growing pressure from the Sámi, who acted in solidarity with the Native Americans protesting that the construction of the pipeline was in violation of their human rights.

CURRENT ISSUES

One of the most difficult and most critical political questions facing Norway today is how to find a healthy balance between the North Sea economy and that of the mainland, a balance that would protect traditional industry, environment, and society while providing a stable base for continued elevation in the standard of living and for maintenance of the social security net, which the country created for all citizens.

The country's large oil and gas revenues will continue to help it economically and will enable it to maintain its comprehensive social welfare net through the rest of the century. Russia, which exports many of the same things as Norway—oil, gas, timber—will continue to be a formidable competitor.

In general, the state of affairs in Norway is of the kind that most countries would be happy to have. Its democratic system functions well; its elites are accommodating and responsive; the citizens have a decent level of trust in government and enjoy channels for input in local government, organizations, schools, and the workplace; there is very little corruption and crime; the population is well educated; and the prosperity is widespread and visible, with an $1.3 trillion rainy day Government Pension Fund Global nest egg to fall back on.

Despite the brutal killing of 77 people in 2011, immigrants and minorities can count on the nation's tolerance. In fact, following the 2015 immigration crisis in Europe,

Norwegians actually protested against their government's plan to deport migrants with Russian visas back to Russia. This stemmed from an earlier influx of mostly Syrians who exploited a legal loophole to enter Norway far beyond the Arctic Circle through Storskog, the only border crossing from Russia. Since Russia did not allow anyone to cross on foot while Norway did not allow cars with undocumented passengers, some 5,500 people crossed the snowy border on bicycles. Entrepreneurial Russians sold bikes (even children's tricycles) to the migrants while local taxis brought them near the border, leaving the relatively short distance to be covered pedaling. The vehicles were immediately thrown into dumpsters as not meeting Norway's road safety regulations, and the Syrians were kept in a camp. Even though long, cold, and expensive, the Arctic route was actually far safer and cheaper than the sea crossings and cross-border smuggling at exorbitant prices in the Mediterranean. As Norway is part of the visa-free Schengen Area, migrants hoped they could move on to EU members states. In 2016 Norway's new immigration minister announced that all the recent entrants who did not have a transit visa would be sent back to Russia, which provoked popular protests because these people would then likely be deported back to Syria. Norway, protesters asserted, could afford to accept those migrants.

Norway will continue to have to pay attention to developments abroad as they affect the country. Partnering with UNICEF in the effort to provide access to the 2.8 million children without access to education, it gave $48 million of educational funds for Syria and its neighbors. It also increased its support to fight against ISIS by providing military training and operational support to Syrian rebels, sending $2.4 million for stabilization efforts in the region, and contributing $6 million for landmine detection and mapping. Terrorist plots to kidnap Norwegian diplomats and hold them hostage were foiled in late 2015, illustrating some of the pitfalls of the activist stance.

While Norway's credentials in addressing human rights are excellent, it does allow realism to trump idealism in some areas. It eagerly sought reestablishment of diplomatic relations with China after six years of frosty neglect when China took umbrage that the Norwegian Nobel Committee awarded the Nobel Peace Prize in 2010 to Chinese dissident Liu Xiaobo. So keen was Norway's government to please China that it refused to meet the exiled Tibetan leader Dalai Lama when he attended the Nobel ceremony in 2014. By the end of 2016, the Norwegians were

very happy to announce that the standoff was over. The price appears to be a possible 20-times increase in sales of salmon to China, where Norway was a near-monopolist before 2010. There is also a likely deal over a proposed Chinese research base on the Norwegian Arctic Archipelago of Svalbard, besides some oil opportunities for Statoil in China. Practical considerations also helped change Norway's approach to Russia. After more than two years of snubbing Russia over its annexation of Crimea, both countries revived cooperation in sharing data on Arctic oil and gas. As Norway plots its future course, it clearly is sensitive to its economic interests.

Norway's support of the US after September 11, 2001, was unconditional. Former defense minister Bjørn Tore Godal asserted, "the United States is Norway's most important ally." Norwegians all over the country observed a three-minute silence on September 14, and the government moved quickly to share intelligence with the US. When the war in Afghanistan began, Norway dispatched some of its best soldiers—Royal Marine Commandos and Army Special Operations Commandos—respected internationally for their expertise in winter warfare. These soldiers fought alongside American and other allied troops to flush out al Qaeda and Taliban fighters from their caves. It also sent mine-clearing specialists and armored vehicles, and it dispatched F-16 fighter jets in 2006.

Perhaps most touching to Americans was the fact that 16 Norwegian officers formed part of the AWACS crews that monitored US airspace during the 9/11 crisis. This was the first time since the American Revolutionary War that the US needed the protection of foreign troops on its own soil. The NATO connection became less predictable with the election of Donald Trump as US president. Like other Europeans, Norwegians scrutinized US policy direction following his inauguration. Former Prime Minister Solberg downplayed his criticism of NATO, agreeing that all members need to do their part in maintaining the organization. She observed, "I think the United States always will need some friends with the same types of values and their closest friends are in the NATO alliance." In 2018 Norway hosted NATO's Trident Juncture exercise involving 50,000 troops from all 29 member states and Finland and Sweden. Seven hundred US marines have been stationed in Norway since 2018.

Norway needs to address some economic issues partly overshadowed by its wealth. High level of bureaucratization related to its significant involvement in the economy ("state capitalism") and the very generous welfare state top the list. Norway spends twice the OECD average on early retirement and disability benefits; most people work 37 hours per week. However, with the drop of oil prices, Norway faces a choice of more stringent fiscal policies or continued largesse.

The public remains divided on the issue of joining the EU. One skeptic said, "it is no good telling people here that we should join the EU because other European countries want to do the same. We have to find strong Norwegian reasons why we should do so." Proponents could not argue that the country would be devastated economically if it stayed out; they made the same argument in 1972, but Norway prospered. It has benefitted by not using the common currency during the serious euro crisis. Norway is still a young country, only one century old in 2005, and it fiercely defends its independence and sovereignty. The United Kingdom's exit from the European Union—partly promoted by what the Britons thought was a cozy arrangement Norway had with the EU—is being carefully scrutinized for hints on whether changing the status from an insider to an outsider has any measurable benefits or disadvantages. After the official launching of "Brexit" in 2017, the UK has been insisting on finding its own way to interact with the EU rather than copying Norway. This may be inevitable rather than optional: For all the benefits of Norway's relations with the EU, the country is required to allow freedom of movement across borders, which was the primary trigger of the British decision to leave the EU. Therefore, Norway is unlikely to lose its position as the primary actor in the European Free Trade Association (EFTA) which gives it privileged access to the EU through the European Economic Area agreement. In the meantime, former Prime Minister Solberg expressed her hopes that the UK remains close to the European Union but added, "I fear a very hard Brexit."

As a supplier of energy, Norway is eminently attractive to Europe for its stability and reliability. Providing about 30% of imports of gas, it competes for the top spot with Russia, an increasingly problematic business partner. Yet, as Norway is about to expand massively its exploration of gas deposits above the Arctic Circle, it asks the EU to provide stronger evidence that this investment may be worthwhile, or else it may have to look for other takers. If the EU commits to gas as a long-term energy source, Norway will build hundreds of miles of pipeline to connect the Barents Sea gas fields to its existing network. Otherwise, liquefying the gas and shipping it off to other destinations remains the only viable option. Once again, even though ostensibly Norway can negotiate from a position of strength, ultimately its future depends on the European Union whose policy it cannot directly influence because of its chosen position outside of the organization. Norway dominated the 2018 Winter Olympics, winning 39 medals. World chess champion Magnus Carlsen decided not to defend his title after a ten-year reign at the top of the game.

Erna Solberg's minority government ruled until September 2021, when parliamentary elections were held. After eight years in office, Solberg made a bid for an unprecedented third term. She failed, and Labor leader Jonas Gahr Støre formed a center-left coalition government with the populist and anti-immigrant Centre Party. The government includes two survivors of the 2011 attacks. For the first time in 62 years, all five Nordic countries had a left-wing prime minister at the same time.

Kingdom of Denmark (Danmark)

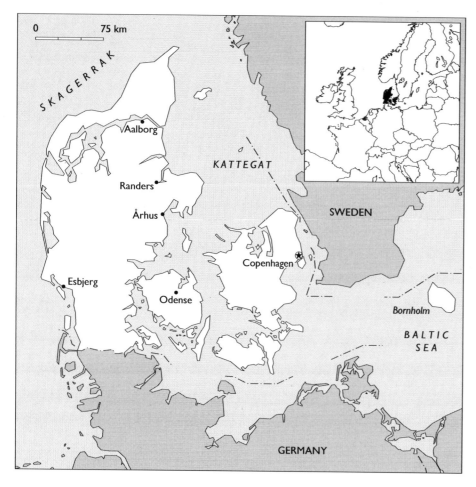

Area: 16,639 sq. mi. (43,094 sq. km.) including the Faroe Islands and Greenland.

Population: 5,935,619 (estimated, February 2023).

Capital City: Copenhagen (pop. city 660,842, urban 1,366,301, metro 2,135,634; as of 2022).

Climate: Denmark has a temperate oceanic climate, characterized by mild winters and cool summers. It has a relatively narrow annual temperature range with average temperatures in January of 1.5 °C (34.7 °F), and in August of 17.2 °C (63.0 °F). Autumn is the wettest season and spring the driest.

Neighboring Countries: Germany (south); Norway (north); Sweden (east and southeast).

Official Languages: Danish. Faroese and Greenlandic (Inuit) are the official languages of the Faroe Islands and Greenland.

Regional Language: German

Ethnic Background: 86.11% Danish, 13.89% other (as of 2020).

Religion: 75.8% Christianity (74.3% Lutheran/Church of Denmark, 1.5% other Christian), 4.4% Islam, 0.7% other, 19.1% no religion; (as of 2020).

Form of Government: Unitary parliamentary constitutional monarchy.

Chief of State: His Majesty King Frederik X (since January 14, 2024).

Head of Government: Mette Frederiksen, Prime Minister (since June 2019).

National Flag: It consists of a white Nordic cross on a red background. The cross represents Christianity. It extends to the edges of the flag and the vertical part of the cross is shifted to the hoist side. The Danes were the first to adopt the cross design, which now features on all of the Nordic flags. According to a legend, the Dannebrog ("Danish cloth") fell from the sky during the Battle of Lindanise (now Tallinn, Estonia), in 1219, and miraculously led to a Danish victory. The emblem of a white cross on a red field originates in the age of the Crusades. In the 12th century, it was used as war flag by the Holy Roman Empire, its red field symbolizing battle and its white cross suggesting the holy cause for which the battle was fought. A flag with a white-on-red cross has been used by the kings of Denmark since the 14th century, and it became popular as a national flag in the early 16th century. The flag holds the world record of being the oldest continuously used national flag, since 1625.

Public Holiday: June 5 (Danish Constitution Day- Grundlovsdag).

Currency: Danish krone (kr.; DKK).

Denmark

Main Exports: Machinery and transportation equipment, meat and dairy products, chemicals, energy, minerals, fuels, ships, pharmaceuticals, electronics, textiles, household furniture, toys, silverware, ceramics, plastics, clothing, and other goods notable for their creative modern design.

Main Imports: Industrial machinery, automobiles, grain and foodstuffs, chemicals, minerals, petroleum, textile raw fibers, yarns, metals, wood.

Main Trading Partners: Germany (14.3% of exports and 20.1% of imports), Sweden (8.5% of exports and 12.2% of imports), UK (4.0% of exports), Netherlands (5.5% of exports and 8.6% of imports), United States (4.7% of exports), Norway (5.6% of exports and 4.5% of imports), China (2.8% of exports and 8.4% of imports), Poland (3.5% of exports and 4.5% of imports), Italy (3.4% of imports). (2022)

A thousand years ago, the Danes were among the roving Vikings who terrorized most of Europe. Even after these marauders settled down, Denmark was a powerful country ready and willing to assert its domination over much of the Nordic area. Today the Danes are a peaceful and inventive people, who spend about 3% of their budget on defense. Characteristically, it was a Dane (Piet Hein) who thought of a way of constructing a super elliptical peace-negotiating table which can seat participants in such a way that all have a sense of prestige.

As in the other Nordic countries, there are more national flags displayed in Denmark than in any other Western European country, with perhaps the exception of Switzerland. Also, foreign flags can be displayed in Denmark only with special police permission and only as long as the Danish flag is displayed also. It is true that the Danes feel free to criticize their own state and society. But when any such discussion is over, most still remain firmly convinced that Denmark is by far the best place in the world to live.

Because the country is very poorly endowed with natural resources, Danes for centuries had to make a living primarily from agriculture and fishing, when they were not raiding various other lands during their medieval history. In this peninsula with its islands, there are still almost five pigs for every human, and Denmark remains one of the world's largest exporters of pork. Since 1945, though, Denmark has become an increasingly dynamic and innovative industrialized country, and its agricultural population has fallen from almost a fourth in 1945 to about 6% today. Danes have learned to make up for their lack of raw materials by know-how and ingenuity, and by the 1970s no more than a third of their exports were derived from agriculture.

Denmark is made up of the Jutland Peninsula that shares a 41-mile-long (68 km) border with Germany, which always exercised much cultural, economic, political, and military influence on Denmark. Since 1815 the only military actions directed against Denmark have originated from Germany, and Denmark's economy has always been considerably oriented toward its neighbor. In spite of World War II, Danes bear little hostility toward Germans, although a 2005 poll revealed that half (51%) of Danes said their relationship with Germans is influenced by the wartime occupation. But they do tend to view their southern neighbors as Canadians view the Americans: near, numerous, not intentionally threatening, but a bit too powerful economically and culturally.

Germany is Denmark's major creditor and customer today, and for Jutlanders, Hamburg is almost as important economically as is Copenhagen. There is a small German-speaking minority in the south of the country, approximately 30,000. On the other hand, the 50,000 Danes who live south of the border in Schleswig-Holstein (South Schleswig was lost to Prussia, then Germany, in the 19th century; most residents decided to stay with Germany in a 1920 referendum) have guaranteed representation in the state parliament there without having to win 5% of the votes. In 2012 their votes enabled the Danish minority's party, the South Schleswig Voters' Committee (SSW), not only to play a crucial role in determining the victors of the provincial elections, but also for the first time in any German state, an ethnic-minority party actually was included in a state government. Denmark finances 50 Danish schools, and most of the Danish students in Schleswig-Holstein go to university in Denmark. There are other cultural organizations and a daily bilingual newspaper, Flensborg Avis.

Denmark also includes 1,419 islands—443 of which have been named and of which 78 are inhabited, and no Dane lives further than 52 km (31 miles) from the sea. The numerous islands (including small bays and inlets) give the country a total coastline of 8,750 km (5,437 mi). This is equivalent to about one-sixth the way around the world at the equator, or the distance from Copenhagen to Mumbai, India. In fact, Denmark has more total coastline than India. Danes keep that coastline in their own hands. They won

The Danish royal family (left to right): Prince Joachim, Her Majesty Queen Margrethe II, Prince Henrik, Crown Prince Frederik
Photo by Klaus Møller

75

Denmark

Princess Mary with son Christian. His sister, Isabella, followed on April 21, 2007, and is the first girl to be born into the Danish royal family since 1946.

from the EU a permanent ban (derogation) on other EU citizens buying up coastal holiday homes; none of the new member states was granted this concession. With such a long coast, it is not a surprise that Denmark has always been a leading fishing and maritime shipping nation.

Close to a fourth of all Danes live in the capital city. In fact, few countries are so dominated by their capitals as is Denmark. Copenhagen is the governmental, administrative, economic, and cultural heart of the country. It has old streets and elegant buildings, a stately royal residence with colorfully dressed guards, and charming canals crisscrossing the city. It is also a vibrant, growing city that almost appears to be bursting at the seams. Copenhagen has a very active free port and a busy airport, which makes it one of the world's major transportations hubs. By opening in 1990 the first international air-link and ferry services to Latvia's capital city of Riga, it was reviving historical ties with other Baltic neighbors. As a small and highly prosperous nation with a very open society, this country is inescapably tied in with a heavily interdependent world and is vulnerable to all major political, military, and economic developments in Europe. Its people therefore know well that they could never hope to imitate the prince in Hans Christian Andersen's Danish fairy tale the "Swineherd," who "went back into his own country and locked the door behind him."

GOVERNMENT

Following the collapse of Nazi Germany, Denmark quickly reverted to its old pattern of leftist-socialist parliamentary government under its constitutional monarchy. Communists were never a major element and all but disappeared. The welfare state was gradually enlarged, as in other Nordic countries. A new constitution abolished the upper house of parliament in 1953, leaving a unicameral legislature. Government was predominantly by minority coalitions of the left.

Danish politics is characterized by a great measure of underlying stability despite a multiparty system, which makes it both impossible for a single party to win a parliamentary majority and difficult for a combination of parties to form a majority coalition. Such stability is due in large part to the Danes' tradition of tolerance and compromise and to the overall consensus about political aims and democratic means.

The Monarchy

Denmark has Europe's longest-standing monarchy, established in 985. In 1848 a peaceful revolution put an end to the absolute monarchy, and the constitution that was adopted the following year and which has been revised several times since is still valid. Today, the monarch continues to symbolize the unity of the nation. The last major revision of the constitution in 1953 permitted females to succeed to the throne if there was no male; this was supposed to be changed by the time Crown Prince Frederik and Princess Mary had children. This was rendered temporarily moot on October 15, 2005, when Mary gave birth to her first child, a son named Christian; a daughter, Isabella, was next. Royal twins, Vincent and Josephine, followed on January 8, 2011.

When King Frederick IX died in 1972, his daughter, Margrethe II, became queen. She is a hardworking and intelligent woman, the first now retired Danish monarch to give press conferences. As a queen, she was the most educated one in Europe, having studied law, social sciences, and archeology in Copenhagen, Arhus, Cambridge, the London School of Economics, and the Sorbonne in Paris. Using a pseudonym, she has translated French works, including Simone de Beauvoir, into Danish and has illustrated books, including those by Tolkien and Hans Christian Andersen. Despite an annual budget of about $3 million, as the queen she lived relatively modestly and was far less wealthy than the queens of Britain and Holland. In 2012 Danes celebrated her 40th anniversary on the throne; her popularity was at an all-time high.

In 1967, Queen Margrethe II married Count Henri de Laborde de Monpezat (France), named Prince Henrik of Denmark.

Queen Margrethe II did away with much of the court etiquette at Amalienborg Palace in the center of Copenhagen, as well as the clumsy addition to her royal title Queen of the Vends and Goths, Duchess of Slesvig-Holsten, Stormarn, Dithmarschen, Lauenburg, and Oldenburg. Like the Danish government, which in 1946 wisely accepted the permanency of the 1920 border between Denmark and Germany, even though the British gave it the chance to reopen the question, Margrethe fully accepted the loss of part of Schleswig to Germany. Unlike her father, she did not hesitate to travel to the lost province, where Danes vote in Schleswig-Holstein state and local elections and can determine which party would rule.

Mary and Frederik on their wedding day

Breaking with centuries of Danish royal tradition, Margrethe II announced her abdication as Queen of Denmark during her New Year's Eve address to the nation on 31 December 2023. Citing health issues, she ended her 52-year reign as Denmark's longest-serving monarch. Queen Margrethe's abdication was the first voluntary abdication of a Danish monarch since that of King Eric III in 1146.

She was succeeded by her elder son, King Frederik X (55), on January 14, 2024. King Frederik X is ruling alongside his Australian-born and hugely popular wife, Queen Mary. Frederik and Mary's eldest son Christian (now 18) has become crown prince and heir to the throne. Besides Crown Prince Christian, the royal couple has a daughter, Princess Isabella of Denmark.

King Frederik X was born on May 26, 1968 in Copenhagen. He is well prepared for his reign, having frequently represented his mother at official functions. While still a crown prince, after having driven a dog sled across Greenland for three months, he had a strip of land on that huge island named after him. On May 14, 2004, he married an Australian from the island of Tasmania, Mary Donaldson, a commoner whom he had met in a Sydney bar during the 2000 Olympic Games. He reportedly introduced himself to her as "Fred from Denmark." A professor's daughter, she has learned Danish well and is widely popular. She is the first Australian to be a queen in Europe.

Within months of the crown prince's wedding, Frederik's brother, Prince Joachim, and his wife, Alexandra, separated. Public opinion polls at the time of Frederik's marriage revealed that 82% of all Danes favored the monarchy. There is no republican movement. The royal family is divided on the ex-queen's decision to take away the titles of the children of Prince Joachim, sixth in line to the throne.

The Danish monarch's function is chiefly ceremonial. He does not attend cabinet meetings, and none of his acts is official without being countersigned by the responsible minister. He is so concerned to be perceived as being politically neutral that he does not even vote in Danish elections. His only political function is to oversee the formation of a government that can have its program accepted by a majority in parliament. This is, of course, a frequent and important task. But he always must accept the advice of the nation's parliamentary leaders. Since no Danish monarch is permitted to make an important political decision, the crown is kept safely out of the political fray; this insulation from political criticism helps to maintain the popularity of the royal family.

The Parliament

Real political authority originates from the popularly elected parliament, called the Folketing, which since 1953 has been unicameral. The Folketing, which meets in Christiansborg Palace, is composed of not more than 179 members, of which two each must come from Greenland and the Faroe Islands. For electoral purposes, Denmark is divided into 3 zones—Greater Copenhagen, Jutland and the islands—which are subdivided into 17 districts with a total of 103 constituencies. All Danes are eligible to vote if they are 18 years of age or older. The electoral system is complicated, with proportional representation enabling many parties to win seats in the Folketing, despite a requirement that a party must capture at least 2% of the total vote in order to gain any seats.

The fact that so many parties are represented in the parliament prevented any party from gaining a majority of seats during the entire 20th century and into the

21st. A majority coalition is a rarity. Most governments are now minority coalitions protected by a special provision that permits a new government to begin to rule without a parliamentary vote of confidence and to continue to rule until a majority can be mustered against it. Since the late 20th century, Danish parliaments normally survive the full four years for which they are elected.

Parliamentary sessions are quiet and most civilized. Applause and any form of interruption to show disapproval are strictly forbidden. At one time, members honored extraordinary oratory by quietly handing the person a 10 0re coin (a little more than 1 cent, now out of circulation). Members often meet together in coffee clubs to make many preliminary decisions and usually address each other by using the familiar form of the word "you." The formal word for "you" is now reserved for the queen and very old people or when writing an application letter.

The growth of government, especially of the welfare portion, has led to the strengthening of the prime minister and his cabinet, whose members are usually, but need not be, members of parliament. The cabinet introduces most bills. It would be a mistake, however, to underestimate the power of the ordinary membership. Because of the absence of steady and reliable majorities, governments must constantly count possible votes in the Folketing before making any decision. Further, one-third of the members can demand a referendum on any piece of legislation. This potent weapon is very seldom used, but it is a safeguard against possible disregard by the majority for the concerns of the minority. The constitution also requires a referendum in any case where Denmark agrees to transfer a portion of its sovereignty to an international body. Thus, in 1972, Danes were asked to approve their country's entry into the EC (now EU), and about two-thirds of them did so.

Since 1955 the Folketing has also had the power to appoint an ombudsman, who, with a staff of 12 full-time lawyers and 8 clerks, can process the claim of any citizen who thinks he has been treated unjustly by any government official or institution, except the legal courts. The ombudsman may also investigate a matter on his own initiative. He seldom uses his power to initiate legal action, but he frequently makes recommendations to ministries, and they are always acted upon. He can also recommend free legal aid to persons who wish to bring a case against an official, as long as the ombudsman believes that there are good grounds for such proceedings.

A second ombudsman, for consumer affairs, was created in 1975 with a staff of 22 to process complaints that goods or

King Frederick X
Source: *Wikipedia*

**Former PM and NATO secretary-general
Anders Fogh Rasmussen**

Denmark

Former Prime Minister Lars Lokke Rasmussen

Prime Minister Mette Frederiksen

Former prime minister Helle Thorning-Schmidt

services were sold through false advertising or unfair marketing methods. In most cases, solutions to these problems have been found through negotiation rather than through litigation. Whenever businesses are in doubt about the propriety of an advertising or marketing technique, they can request the advice of the ombudsman for consumer affairs in order to find out in advance what might be considered impermissible. Thus, in Denmark public and business officials alike must be aware that their practices could be investigated by one or the other ombudsman.

POLITICAL PARTIES AND GROUPS

Until well into the 1960s, parliamentary seats were distributed basically among four parties: the Social Democratic, the Radical-Liberal, the Liberal, and the Conservative. But the 1960s were in Denmark, as elsewhere in western Europe and North America, years of ferment. Taxes rose to pay for rapidly expanding social welfare programs. The number of employees in the changing Danish economy threatened the livelihood of some farmers and small merchants. Added to this there was a youth revolt that led many persons to ask fundamental questions about the increasingly comfortable technical and materialist society.

These developments gave rise to new parties on the left, while the uneasiness toward rising taxes and budgetary and balance of payment deficits led many Danes to support other unconventional parties. The explosion came in the 1973 elections, when five previously unrepresented parties got 36% of the vote, and their percentage has not sunk significantly since. The result is difficulty in producing a stable government.

In March 2007 Danes had a reminder of their tradition of nonconformism and tolerance for rebellion against the authorities when some of the worst riots in their history, lasting three nights, raged in Copenhagen. At issue was the clearing out, sale, and ultimate demolition of a building, called Youth House, which had been occupied by squatters since the 1980s. The young rioters engaged in running battles with the police, tore up cobblestones to throw at the authorities, and set dozens of cars and a school on fire. Even the famous but much-abused Little Mermaid was painted pink. The unrest erupted again in October 2007, leaving many Copenhagen residents weary of seeing their cars burned and their property defiled or smashed.

Danish voters are divided roughly evenly between left and right, but the sheer number of parties that win seats in the Folketing makes it difficult to maintain a governing coalition with a stable majority. Poul Schluter, the first Conservative prime minister since 1894, conceded on New Year's Day 1991, "One certainly can say we don't have Europe's strongest government!" Nevertheless, there is an underlying stability.

The Parties of the Left

From 1924 to 2001, the Social Democratic Party (S) was Denmark's most important party. It has always been a relatively un-ideological reform party with a working-class character and close ties to the labor union. In 1961 it eliminated all references to Marxism in its party program and began attracting more and more votes from public servants and employees. One result is that the party became quite heterogeneous, and the intraparty splits between its left and right wings inclined the major

trade union federation (LO) to become slightly cooler in its support of the party.

It faces difficulties as a working-class party in a country in which fewer and fewer people have blue-collar jobs. Also, it is split between leftists, who want to move leftward to compete with the Socialist People's Party, and those on the right, who wish to move back toward the center. In 2001, for the first time since 1924, it failed to emerge as the largest party. It became the major opposition party. In 2005 it suffered its worst electoral defeat in 32 years. In an attempt to resolve the internal split between left and right, the party held Denmark's first internal primary leadership election. Helle Thorning-Schmidt, a former member of the European Parliament, emerged as the winner, becoming the first woman to head the Social Democrats and in October 2011 to be prime minister at age 45. The Social Democrats won a close election in September 2011, with a turnout of 87.7%.

Thorning-Schmidt's government got off to a rocky start, facing criticism for her family's complicated tax arrangements. Her husband, Stephen Kinnock, son of the former British Labour Party leader Neil, works in London and was trying (successfully) to win a Labour seat. They met at the prestigious College of Europe in Bruges. By May 2013 her party's public support had fallen to just 14.4%, its lowest figure since 1898. The following year only 16% said she was an asset to her party. She got into a fight with teachers, who closed down the schools in April 2013. She alienated the left by pushing through a tax package with the center-right population that benefited some of the biggest earners at the expense of pensions and unemployment benefits. In January 2014 she brought her shaky coalition government to the brink of collapse by allowing Goldman Sachs to buy a 19% stake in the state utility, Dong Energy. Thousands protested in the streets, and one of the three coalition partners departed the government, leaving it with only 61 of 179 seats. Some Danes criticized as inappropriate the selfie she took of herself, Barack Obama, and David Cameron at Nelson Mandela's memorial service. It went viral and became a global sensation.

The Socialist People's Party (SF) was founded in 1959 by a former head of the Danish Communist Party (DKP) and originally was joined mostly by disaffected communists, who nevertheless advocated a more radical program than that of the Social Democrats. The DKP has practically disappeared. The SF is composed mainly of academics and pacifists, and about 60% of its members are employees and civil servants. Its major policies include unilateral disarmament, withdrawal from NATO, an atomic-free zone in Scandinavia, and increasingly close Nordic economic cooperation rather than Danish orientation toward the allegedly more capitalist EU.

Even limited cooperation with the Social Democrats in the past was too much for the SF's left wing, which broke away from it in 1967 and formed the Left Socialist Party. The latter reemerged under the banner of the Red-Green Alliance (0), which has a collective leadership.

One of the four traditional parties and one that is a regular coalition partner of the Social Democrats is the Social Liberal Party (B), founded in 1905 as the Radical Venstre Party (RV). It is composed of liberals who see themselves as being a little closer to the left than the other nonsocialist parties. They advocate the maintenance of an efficient private economy, as well as social reform without socialism. They used to vote with the conservatives on economic issues but with the left on foreign and defense policies. Although small, RV wielded power beyond its size since it often had the role of "kingmaker," determining which coalition will rule. Renamed the Social Liberal Party (B), under the leadership of Margrethe-Vestager, it joined the government. However, in 2015 it won less than half of that in votes (4.6%) and seats (8) and was relegated to opposition with the rest of the left. Leftist parties won the June 2019 elections and formed a minority government led by Prime Minister Matte Fredericksen. It commands 91 of 179 seats.

The Parties of the Center-Right

In recent years the parties of the center and the right have gained ground by promising to reduce taxes and to curb welfare spending. The Conservative People's Party (KF), founded in 1916, is a pragmatic party that defines itself as a party of the

Syrian-born Naser Khader enters parliament

political center. It is a staunch advocate of private property and free enterprise; a strong defense; and, since the onset of the energy crisis of 1973, of nuclear power. It draws its votes mainly from the middle class and self-employed. Following the 2001 elections it joined the center-right government. Its leader is Søren Pape Poulsen. In 2011 it fell badly, winning only 4.9% of the votes (down from 10.4%) and 8 seats (a loss of 10). In 2015, it slid further, receiving 4.2% of votes and six seats, which made it the smallest party in the Folketing. Søren Pape Poulsen, who had taken over the leadership the previous year, managed to double the party's seats to 12 in the 2019 election with 6.6% of the vote. But then, at the 2022 election KF gained only 5.5% of the votes, following an election campaign significantly influenced by affairs concerning Pape Poulsen's personal life.

The Liberal Venstre Party (V) was founded in 1870 and was traditionally a farmer's party; now it draws half its votes from cities and towns. It advocates a restriction of the government's activity in the economy, and since the 1970s, it has pressed for a reduction of public spending and private consumption in order to cope with the economic crises that have beset Denmark.

Its leader until April 2009 was Anders Fogh Rasmussen. At age 25 he had been

Denmark's youngest member of parliament. For more than two decades, he had been a right-wing ideologue and had written a book, *From Social State to Minimal State*, describing the welfare state as "developing a slave mentality in the people." But when he took over the party's leadership in 1998, he was aware that power is won through the political center, and he developed appealing positions on social affairs and the environment. He posed as a guardian of the welfare state and favored the euro and EU enlargement, although he wanted to get rid of the EU's wasteful Common Agricultural Policy and reduce Brussels's handouts to poorer regions. He is charismatic but was never known as a "man of the people." He has a serious air and is known for his sharp mind rather than great oratory. Following the landslide victory in 2001, he formed a center-right minority government. In 2007 he became the first Liberal leader ever to win a second and third consecutive term.

After only one year in office, Rasmussen's approval rating had soared to twothirds. He had avoided scandal. He kept his campaign promises to freeze taxes, cut foreign aid (.85% in 2014, the fourthhighest in the world), curb immigration, and pare down the civil service. Despite the global recession that struck Denmark in 2009, the economy is one of Europe's

Denmark

Protesting Danish cartoons

strongest, and its budget deficit was 1.8% in 2014. Voters viewed him as the best guarantor of their social system. They still regard free education, free health care, inexpensive childcare, and high-quality services for pensioners as their birthrights. But they are reluctant to pay for them with high taxes, currently the EU's second-highest after Sweden. They liked the tax cap, tax cuts, and reduction of duties on alcohol and cigarettes, as well as longer maternity leave and shorter hospital waiting lists. Although two-thirds of Danes had come to oppose the Iraq war by election day, the issue of Denmark's 501 troops there was largely absent during the campaign. Voters also seemed unconcerned about the international black eye the country has gotten because of its restrictions on immigration; most of them favor fewer foreigners.

His name was frequently mentioned as the possible first Danish secretary-general of NATO. Although he coyly denied that he desired such a high international position, that is exactly what he became from April 2009 until September 2014. He was succeeded at NATO by former Norwegian prime minister Jens Stoltenberg.

He was replaced as prime minister by the third Rasmussen in a row, all unrelated: Lars Lekke Rasmussen, the earlier health and finance minister. Affable and approachable, he had had much domestic political experience but little international exposure. Although it remained the largest party in parliament, it led the opposition. In the 2011 general elections, the party gained 26.7% of the vote and 47 seats, but was not able to form a government.

Instead, it led the opposition against the Social Democratic coalition.

The Liberals' fortunes changed in the 2015 general elections, when the party lost voter support gaining only 19.5% of the vote. The far-right Danish People's Party (DPP) which came in second did not want to cooperate with the Liberals, with whom it disagrees on the European Union, taxes, and social spending. This forced Rasmussen to create a one-party minority government that had only 34 seats in the 179-seat parliament and was only conditionally supported by the DPP. This government was short-lived. Another liberal party, the Liberal Alliance (L), led by Anders Samuelsen, captured 5% of the votes and 9 seats (a gain of 4) in 2011, further improving to 7.5% of votes and 13 seats in 2015. It immediately became clear that the future of Rasmussen's Liberal government depends on it being attuned to the wishes of the DPP, especially on immigration. In 2016 Løkke Rasmussen invited the Conservative People's Party and the Liberal Alliance to form a coalition government instead.

During the campaign of the 2019 general elections, Løkke Rasmussen opened up for the possibility of forming a government with the Social Democrats. That was seen as controversial, and Social Democratic leader Mette Frederiksen immediately declined the proposition.

Due to internal fighting in the party, Løkke Rasmussen and vice chairman

Kristian Jensen both resigned in August 2019. Political spokesman and former Minister for Environment and Food, Jakob Ellemann-Jensen was elected the party's next chairman in September 2019.

Following the 2022 general election, in which Venstre suffered its worst result since 1988, it joined a grand coalition government led by Social Democrat leader Mette Frederiksen. The coalition also comprised the Moderates, a Venstre splinter formed by former Prime Minister Lars Løkke Rasmussen.

The Danish People's Party (DF) was formed in 1995. Cofounded and directed for 17 years by Pia Kjaersgaard, it was later led by Kristian Thulesen Dahl. The party does very well at the polls with such slogans as "Denmark is for the Danes," a nationalistic twist on the traditional and inclusive "Denmark for the people." DF's campaign posters in 2001 portrayed a photo of a young blond girl and the slogan "When she retires, Denmark will have a Muslim majority." The DF also wins support because of its anti-European views. It got a huge boost in 2014 by winning 27% of Denmark's votes in European Parliament elections. In 2015, buoyed by the migrant crisis, it came back roaring in the parliamentary elections by winning 21.1% of the votes and 37 seats, becoming the second-largest party. It refused to join the government but agreed to support it in exchange for a considerable influence over the new government's policy.

"The situation is out of control"—Muslim fury over Danish cartoons (from Austria)

Because of its extremist views on immigration, DF had been excluded from center-right minority coalitions. A growing number of Danes, including in business circles, are embarrassed by its uncompromising hostility to immigrants. But DF is sometimes needed for its votes in parliament. For instance, DF support was required in 2002 for legislation to tighten immigration rules making it more difficult to seek asylum and receive welfare benefits and residence permits. By 2005, asylum applications had plunged by 75% in only three years' time, and the proportion of applicants granted asylum plummeted from 53% to only 10%. At election time in 2007, the number of immigrants granted asylum had been slashed by 80%. On average, every eight months during the decade after 2001, it prompted the government to tighten immigration rules. An important move was to reduce unemployment benefits to people who have not spent seven out of the previous eight years in the country. Almost 80% of those who were affected by this were immigrants. Here DF also appeals to the elderly, whose benefits it seeks to increase, in an unexpected similarity to Social Democrats.

In 2008 DF advocated that Islamic headscarves be banned for public employees. The government decided it had to support this, but it broadened the law to prohibit the wearing of all religious symbols by judges, be they Islamic, Christian, Jewish, or Sikh. Public opinion supported this, with 48% in favor and only 39% against it.

The 2007 election focused on the ideas of a new party on the center-right, formed only six months before the voting and calling itself the New Alliance, later Liberal Alliance. It was led by Naser Khader, a Palestinian immigrant and nonpracticing Muslim from Syria, who rose to prominence during the furious controversy about anti-Muslim cartoons in 2005. His was a voice of moderation, urging his fellow immigrants to put the values of their adopted country, such as freedom of speech, first. He supports a ban on wearing a burqa, calling it "oppression against women." He is charismatic, likeable, and clever. He advocates an end to so-called blokpolitik, which sees the party landscape sharply divided between right and left instead of the traditional governments clutching the center ground. The party won only 2.8% of the votes and five seats in 2007 and 5% and nine seats in 2011. As a center-right party, it supported the former conservative government on most important issues. It is fiercely opposed to the appeals of Kristian Thulesen Dahl's DF. Khader left the Alliance in favor of the Conservative People's Party but continued to assert that "the veto power must be taken away from the People's Party."

An early election was called for November 1, 2022. Voters returned Prime Minister Mette Fredriksen's center-left coalition to power. Her Social Democrats (SDP) captured 27.5% of the votes and collected together a narrow majority of one seat. Fourteen parties contested the election. Voters abandoned the traditional conservative and liberal parties in favor of new ones. Three seats were won by parties from Greenland and the Faroe Islands.

Immigration Problems

As could be predicted, the 2015 election and the height of the migrant crisis gave a disproportional influence to the Danish People's Party. The government tightened border controls, cut immigrant benefits in half, and soon announced that the migrants would be stripped of valuables to pay for their upkeep. The founder of the DF, Pia Kjaersgaard, once named "racist of the year" by a magazine in Sweden, became the parliamentary speaker. Clearly, Dahl and his party successfully exploit and fuel an explosive issue: growing discontent over a flood of refugees, particularly Somalis, Syrians, and other Muslims (Turks, Kurds, Pakistanis, Iranians, and Iraqis), into Denmark. By 2022 foreigners were 9% of the population. Unemployment among immigrants is high. They are blamed for exploiting the welfare system, crime, and harboring terrorists. By 2002 half were on welfare, a figure that rose to 90% among such ethnic minorities as Somalis. "Multiculturalism" is a politically charged word. The government set up a goal of "zero asylum-seekers."

In 1984 parliament introduced a law preventing border police from turning back people who claim political exile. As a result, the flood of refugees soared from several hundred in 1984 to 9,000 in 1985. By 1986 they were pouring in at a rate of 1.000 per week. This resulted in insulting graffiti on Danish walls and unpleasant racial incidents. One early sign of discontent was that, during the first nine months of 1986, some 15,000 Danes resigned from the Red Cross, the organization responsible for taking care of new arrivals. This dissatisfaction prompted parliament to amend the liberal asylum law.

By 2010 Denmark had approximately 450.000 immigrants and refugees from out-side the EU and Nordic region. Roughly 200.000 (3.5% of the population) were Muslim. They come chiefly from Türkiye, Pakistan, Morocco, and Bosnia and Herzegovina. The government tried to spread them out in the kingdom, but that failed. They remain concentrated, and 60% of them are unemployed. Denmark's

Denmark

inability to integrate them has exposed the ambiguity of Danish attitudes toward cultural diversity and the fragility of its famed social tolerance. A 1998 poll revealed that almost half of all Danes admitted to being "racist" or "fairly racist," the second-highest ratio in Europe (after Belgium) and the largest in the Nordic world. Polls a decade later confirmed that Danes remain solidly in favor of tight immigration controls.

The DF's party program states that Denmark "is not and never was a land of immigration," and it rejects any form of open borders. In 2000 it placed a controversial advertisement in a national newspaper showing a white homeless man, with the caption "When I become a Muslim, I'll have a home." This refers to the widespread opinion that immigrants jump to the front of the line for state housing and live off the country's generous welfare system.

The government has responded by introducing the strictest immigration laws in the EU. Family unification has been made more difficult. When a Danish court ruled in 1999 that a man of Turkish origin be expelled from Denmark, a gang of young immigrants and anarchists went on a rampage on Nørrebrogade, a major shopping thoroughfare in a district popularly known as "Mini-Mogadishu" because of the concentration of immigrants who live there. There was also a row over a decision by shop owners to prevent female employees from wearing the Muslim head-scarf while on duty. These controversies blow wind into the DF's sails.

Ex-prime minister Fogh Rasmussen found it politically expedient in his 2001 campaign to recognize the xenophobia that is in the air in Denmark by declaring, "we have to make stricter laws so that fewer foreigners come to Denmark." This policy helped him secure unprecedented electoral victories in 2001, 2005, and 2007. His government tightened legislation restricting family reunification, reduced welfare benefits for foreigners, and extended the waiting period for permanent residency from three to seven years. It reduced the country's acceptance rate of asylum seekers to 10%, the lowest in the Nordic region. Their numbers have diminished dramatically.

If a Dane and a non-Danish spouse want a residence permit, both partners must be 24 years or over, have a minimum annual income of $50,000, put up a deposit of 53,000 crowns (approximately $8,700) until the foreign spouse is able to get citizenship, not have drawn welfare benefits for the past 12 months, have their own apartment (meaning that they cannot sublet or live with parents), and be judged to have stronger ties to Denmark than to any other country. As of 2005 immigrants who seek a residence permit must first take a loyalty oath promising to fight terrorism. These requirements led about 1,000 couples to live on the Swedish side of the strait and ferry or commute across the bridge to work in Copenhagen.

Since 2013 immigrants are denied welfare if they have not learned Danish. The greatest concern is that immigrant women are marginalized in Denmark because they cannot speak the language. The minister of immigration stated bluntly, "We have closed our eyes and let them sit at home behind their curtains." A May 2008 poll showed how unwelcome many young Muslim students in Denmark feel: Two-thirds of the respondents were considering emigrating after graduation, mostly because of "the tone of the Danish debate about Muslims."

In 2005 the government announced plans to boost its antiterrorism security police by about 40%. A 2002 law forbids instigation of terrorism or offering advice to terrorists. Newer laws ban the financing of radical groups and give police the powers to eavesdrop on suspected radicals electronically. Suspected radicals are subject to close surveillance, and intelligence officers work closely with Danish universities to look out for suspicious activity and to monitor students from abroad.

In September 2006 police conducted a sting operation in Odense, the birthplace of Hans Christian Andersen. They found chemicals used to make bombs in several homes and arrested nine men, all Danish citizens and (except one) of immigrant origin. This created jitters in the entire country. Eight more Islamic militants, suspected of planning a bomb attack, were arrested a

A fish vendor in the olden days

year later. In 2008 two men who were secretly filmed mixing explosives were convicted of preparing a terrorist attack.

A 2005 poll found that 80% of Danes support new laws to battle terrorism and control immigration. That these laws contain restrictions on free speech is perhaps surprising for a nation famous for its toleration. But it is typical of Denmark that the public debate about how to balance individual freedoms with society's protections against terrorism is at the top of the political agenda.

In 2005 Denmark faced its worst international crisis since the World War II. For some time, a polemical war had been raging between anti-immigrant nationalists and fundamentalist Muslims among Denmark's 200,000 Muslim immigrants. Many Danes have come to view Islam as a threat to the survival of Danish culture.

In September 2005, a Danish newspaper, *Jyllands-Posten*, commissioned and printed a dozen cartoons portraying the Prophet Mohammad in an unflattering way. One of them showed bombs tangled in the prophet's headgear. In October Rasmussen declined to meet with 11 ambassadors from Muslim countries, who wanted to discuss the offensive drawings, and some subsequently withdrew their ambassadors. A February 2006 poll revealed that 58% of Danes believed that the problem was not the newspaper's action but that imams living in Denmark had exploited the situation for their own purposes.

By February 2006 the situation snowballed out of control. Danish products were (and to some extent still are) boycotted across the Muslim world and even in some European stores that were afraid of losing their Muslim customers. Denmark's embassies in Damascus and Lebanon were attacked and burned by angry mobs, and police in Afghanistan fired into a crowd trying to storm a Norwegian base. The Danish consulate-general in Dubai described what was happening as a "nightmare scenario": "I don't think anyone in their wildest imagination would have expected an escalation like what we have seen." More than 50 persons died in the demonstrations.

Some European newspapers fueled the flames by defiantly publishing the cartoons in solidarity with *Jyllands-Posten*, and the EU and US President George W. Bush publicly defended their ally's right of free speech. Its Nordic partners, especially Sweden and Norway (whose embassy in Syria was also burned), sought to distance themselves from the Danes, who were reeling from global protests and boycotts. In Denmark itself, the government, which refused to offer any apology for the publication, was riding high in the polls, and the popularity of the Danish People's

Party shot up from 13% to almost 18%. But the country had much work to do to win back its reputation and markets in the Islamic world. For two decades, Muslims had been forbidden to build mosques in Copenhagen, and there were no Muslim cemeteries. In 2009 the Copenhagen municipal council granted permission for the first mosque to be built; it opened its doors in 2013. It was funded by a sizable donation from the Qatari royal family and was constructed with private funds on a site purchased by the embassy of Iran.

A sensational best-selling book in Denmark entitled *Islamists and Naivists* equates Islamic fundamentalists with Nazis and Communists. The authors, Karen Jespersen and Ralf Pittelkow, wrote, "The reality is that nobody in Denmark bats an eye anymore when people talk about the threat that Islam poses to Danish values because this is viewed, however wrongly, as a fact of life." The work reflects the extent to which skepticism about Islam has become a part of the European political mainstream.

To facilitate assimilation in 2018, a law was passed requiring anybody taking Danish citizenship to shake hands at the ceremony. Another law banned full-face veils in public. A further law requires newly arrived asylum seekers to surrender valuables, like jewelry and gold, to help pay for their stay in Denmark. Objects of sentimental value, like wedding rings, are exempted.

Another former newspaper editor, Lars Hedegaard, is a fulminating anti-Islam polemicist who argues, "there is no such thing as moderate Islam." In 2013 an assassin shot at him at point-blank range but missed. It is significant that Muslim groups, though despising his ideas, defended his right to state them publicly. Hedegaard lives in a safe house under police protection.

In February 2008, when it was reported that the police had arrested three men suspected of plotting to murder one of the artists, 17 Danish newspapers decided to republish one of the offending cartoons to reiterate the principle of free speech. This sparked riots in the streets of Copenhagen, mainly in immigrant neighborhoods, where schools and cars were torched. Osama bin Laden denounced the publication and warned all Europeans of a strong reaction to come. The cartoon might have prompted a suicide bombing four months later outside the Danish embassy in Islamabad, Pakistan, which killed 8 people and wounded 20.

The artist who drew the most offensive of the dozen drawings, Kurt Westergaard, was forced to move nine times to escape assassins. In January 2010 a Somali fanatic broke into his home outside of Aarhus with an ax. He was prevented from

The Little Mermaid

completing his bloody mission only when Westergaard took refuge in a specially reinforced bathroom. He could communicate with the police, who arrived quickly and shot and wounded the assailant. Prime Minister Rasmussen called this outrage "an attack on our open society." The assailant was tried and found guilty in 2011. Even American citizens have been implicated in death threats against cartoonists and newspaper editors. Westergaard lived until 2021.

By 2011 at least six attempts to launch terrorist attacks against *Jyllands-Posten's* offices had been foiled by the police. One plan was simply to burst into the building and kill as many as possible. In June 2012 a court convicted four men of planning a terrorist attack against the newspaper's offices. They were sentenced to 12 years in prison.

Danes had a bloody reminder in February 2015 that the danger had not passed. A troubled Muslim boy born and raised in Denmark got a hold of a military weapon and sprayed bullets into a cafe where a free-speech discussion was taking place, killing film director Finn Norgaard. He then killed a guard at a synagogue before being gunned down by police. The young man had a long record of crime and had just been released from prison two weeks before his rampage.

In April 2009 the entire lamentable cartoon affair came back to haunt Fogh Rasmussen, whose last hurdle to becoming NATO secretary-general was the threatened veto of Türkiye, a Muslim country. Rasmussen and Denmark are perceived by many Muslims as insensitive to Islam, an important issue considering that NATO's biggest challenges at the time were Afghanistan and Pakistan. He had reformulated his earlier statement

about free speech, saying that it had to be balanced with a deep respect for personal religious convictions.

After the Turkish government again objected to his nomination at the NATO summit in Strasbourg, President Barack Obama took Turkish president Abdullah Gul aside for a half-hour chat. He then called Rasmussen into the back room, and the three leaders discussed privately. A phone call to Turkish prime minister Recep Erdogan was needed to break the deadlock, and Rasmussen was approved. This was a masterful diplomatic success by the new American president.

Provincial and Local Government

There are several other levels of government in Denmark. Since the 2005 reform, it is divided into five provinces, each led by elected provincial councils headed by a mayor (Amtsborgmester) elected by the council from among its own members. There are also about 150 primary municipalities led by elected municipal councils. Two other major areas under Danish jurisdiction have complete authority in domestic affairs, with only foreign and defense policy emanating from Copenhagen: Greenland and the Faroe Islands. Each is allowed to send two MPs to the Folketing.

Greenland

Greenland is at one point only 14.5 miles from Canada. In 2005 Denmark became embroiled with Canada over ownership of Hans Island, a patch of Arctic rock each country claims. The Danes even sent a war-ship to back up their sovereignty over the island. The two countries soon called a truce and agreed to disagree over its possession.

Greenland is the world's largest island and is 50 times the size of Denmark, 4

Denmark

times larger than France and about one-third the size of the US. Over 80% of its majestic but dangerous area lies under permanent ice and snow that continually breaks off into the ocean, forming many of the world's icebergs.

This is the earth's second-largest ice sheet after Antarctica and contains nearly 10% of the planet's frozen water. By 2000 it was melting on the margins at a rate of about 12 cubic miles per year. This shrinkage accounts for 7% of the world's sea-level rise. By one estimate, if all of Greenland's ice were to melt, the seas around the world would rise by 23 feet. While the ice in the higher elevation appears to be stable, the thinning of the ice is occurring around the coast. The dilution of the surrounding ocean with fresh water threatens to disrupt currents that keep Europe warm.

The melting is an economic blessing for the inhabitants. Greenland contains a tenth of the world's rare-earth metals, and the receding ice makes more metals accessible. It also makes the island more open to tourists. However, the left-green party (IA) that won the 2021 elections vowed to freeze the development of rare earth and oil.

The narrow coastal strip around much of the island (a strip that itself is eight times the size of Denmark) is tundra, on which trees cannot grow higher than knee level. Only 10% of Greenland's population of 57,000 is Danish. The rest are natives of Inuit (Eskimo) or mixed backgrounds, who speak an Inuit dialect, although they learn Danish in schools. Since 2009 Inuit (also called Greenlandic) is an official language along with Danish. Most live in the 120 or so towns or settlements located chiefly along the southwestern coast, the largest being the capital, Nuuk (formerly Godthaab). Nuuk is a modern city of 17,000 inhabitants with first-class Danish hotels and five-story apartment houses, which differ little from European dwellings, except that cod and seal skins often hang on lines from balconies along with jeans and fashionable Danish clothes.

Greenland (which the natives call Kalaallit Nunaat, or "Land of People") became a Danish colony in 1775 and was made an integral part of Denmark in 1953, but a new generation of Greenlanders wanted more direct control over their island's destiny. Denmark made it known that it would respect the people's wishes. In 1979, following a referendum in Greenland, the island was granted self-government as a "distinct community within the Kingdom of Denmark." The native population determines its own domestic affairs through a 21-member locally elected assembly called the Landsting and an executive called the Landsstyre. Denmark continues to determine foreign and defense matters and is represented in Greenland by the king's high commissioner.

The autonomy status does not affect the island's inclusion in NATO or the status of the Danish-American air bases at Soendre, Stroemfjord, and Narssarssuaq nor of the installation in Thule. A giant radar installation is located there roughly halfway along the shortest route between the US and Russia. Thule therefore plays a crucial role in the American early-warning system and in its missile-defense system. In 2003 both Denmark and Greenland agreed in principle to permit the upgrade of the radar, essential for tracking missiles.

Denmark deploys 300 soldiers in the Arctic and is improving its surveillance capabilities in Greenland and Faroe Islands to counter Russia's military build-up in the region.

In 1999 the Danish prime minister apologized to the native Inuit people for forcing them out of their homes in 1953 so that an American airbase could be expanded. For years they had demanded such an apology. But in 2003 the Danish Supreme Court rejected demands by Inuit hunters in Greenland for increased compensation for having been forced off their land in 1953. It also rejected the right of resettled people to return to the area around the air-base and to displace the Americans there. Danish and American officials were embarrassed in 2000 by new evidence that an unarmed hydrogen bomb onboard a crashing B-52 bomber in 1968 might still lie on the seabed in the frozen Baffin Bay off the Thule air base.

Greenlanders voted against remaining in the EU three years after receiving limited self-rule. It thereby became the first participant ever to leave the EU. In the first referendum over the membership in 1972, over 70% of the Greenlanders had voted against entry, but they were swamped by the Danish majority. Ten years later, after haggling with Brussels over fishing rights and with Danes over mining rights on the island, and after having achieved political autonomy and more self-confidence, the islanders decided to leave the EU, which had poured from $10 million to $20 million worth of investments into Greenland every year.

The 1983 electoral victory of the two parties that were committed to withdrawal from the EU—the socialist Forward Party and the leftist Inuit Movement—was the prelude for Greenland's final decision in 1985 to leave the EU. It entered partnership negotiations with the EU in 2005 centering on fishing rights. This is still Greenland's main source of domestic income. Denmark continues to send it costly subsidies, amounting to about $617 million per year ($10,000 per person, or over half of government revenues). However, it

Daily changing of the Royal Life Guard in Copenhagen

froze its annual subsidy when it granted Greenland home rule in 2009, and it will decrease the aid even farther in future years. It also sends thousands of technicians and advisers, without whom the island could not hope to survive in its present form. With economic and social modernization having only begun in the 1950s, Greenland is very dependent upon Danish expertise to build and operate housing units, hospitals (which have helped double average life expectancy since the 1950s), schools, power plants, and communication and transportation facilities. The last is particularly difficult because there are no trains or roads between towns and settlements.

The essential services that Danes perform should not, in the opinion of some islanders, give the Danes control over the island's economy and resources. The people live primarily from fishing and sealing, as well as from jobs in the public sector, and they raise sheep, lambs, and reindeer. Under the ice there are also such minerals as zinc, lead, and cryolite, which are already mined, as well as gold, rubies, diamonds, iron ore, uranium, nickel, molybdenum, and oil and gas, which may be extracted one day, mainly offshore.

After searching for decades, evidence of oil and gas was found off the west coast in 2010, and there are hopes of hydrocarbons off the east coast, as well. Experts talk of possibly the world's largest untapped hydrocarbon reserves. Oil has not yet been found in commercial quantities. Drilling can only take place in the summer months when the ice is melted, and there is little infrastructure. Environmentalist critics express concerns over drilling between Greenland and Canada, an area they call "iceberg alley," and Greenpeace ecowarriors try to disrupt operations. But most of the population supports such exploration in order to create jobs and wealth.

Melting ice provides rich potential for hydropower, which the native government hopes will one day supply 80% of electricity. With the Northwest Passage through Canada's north opening up, Greenland is well positioned to be a major shipping center. It is already enjoying booming tourism.

Data showing that Greenland's continental shelf is connected to a ridge under the Arctic Ocean is the basis for Denmark's claim to the North Pole. It is the first country to lay such claim, but others, such as Russia and Canada, rigorously reject it. The island helps Denmark exercise more influence in the world.

The compromise to which the Danes and Greenlanders agreed during the negotiations over autonomy was that each side would have a veto right over the exploitation and sale of Greenland's natural resources. Also, Greenland is granted half of any future proceeds from oil and minerals. This compromise was necessary, but it brought many disagreements.

In November 2008 over three-fourths of Greenlanders, with a strong sense of righting historical wrongs, voted in a referendum to loosen their ties with Denmark, and the home country accepted this. This went into effect on the national holiday, June 21, 2009. They took control of security, police, education, and justice affairs; made Inuit the official language; and took a larger percentage of future profits from minerals, including gold, diamonds, rubies and oil although much of this wealth is still inaccessible under ice. Denmark retained the last word on foreign and security matters. The then Prime Minister Kuupik Kleist promised that his country would act as an "equal partner" with Denmark. The Danish prime minister responded with a pledge that Greenland can choose full independence whenever it wants it. This was a remarkably amicable separation.

The people went to the polls in April 2018. It was won by the Siumut (Social Democratic) Party, and Kim Kielsen became prime minister.

Since April 23, 2021, the incumbent prime minister is Múte Bourup Egede, also of the Siumut party.

The attention should be paid to a protest party, Partii Inuit. Led by Nikku Olsen, it favors limiting the influence of foreigners, including Danes. Many Greenlanders fear the impact of a mining boom.

Full independence will not come quickly. Dominated by fishing, the economy cannot stand alone. Greenlanders and their Danish helpers must cope with many social problems that have emerged as a result of the extremely rapid movement of most natives from an isolated existence at the edge of civilization into modern life. This sudden change risks the collapse of the old way of life before a new one emerges.

The results are heavy unemployment among the young, venereal diseases, child abuse, and the familiar scourge of alcoholism. Today, 9 out of 10 crimes on the island stem from the latter, and any visitor sees its presence in Greenland almost everywhere he looks. The suicide rate is nearly 17 times as great as in 1960 and 4 times that of Denmark, which itself has one of the world's highest levels of suicide. Education and nutrition are bad. Social challenges to Danes and native islanders are very great and will require more than Danish subsidies to solve. Shedding light on these problems and on this rapidly modernizing world is a best-selling novel by the literary face of Greenland in the world: Niviaq Korneliussen's *Crimson*, set in Nuuk, is a fascinating window.

Greenland is of considerable strategic value. Former president Donald Trump's offer to purchase the gigantic island was immediately rejected.

The Faroe Islands

The Faroes, an archipelago of 18 islands in the North Atlantic between Norway, Scotland, and Iceland, have a rough and beautiful landscape of mountain peaks, high plateaus, valleys, and fjords. The 43,000 Faroese are descendants of the Norse settlers who came during the Viking era, and they still speak their own language, which is related to Icelandic and certain western Norwegian dialects. Of course, all Faroese also speak Danish.

These islands are not well suited to farming, but they are ideal for sheep and cattle grazing. Their waters were also full of fish, which provided work for a fourth of the labor force and comprised over 90% of the islanders' exports. Fish were the foundation for the islanders' economy until the industry collapsed due to overfishing. This dragged the rest of the islands' economy down with it. By 1994 unemployment had reached 20%, and about 9% of the population had been forced to emigrate. Only a series of emergency aid packages from Copenhagen staved off bankruptcy.

The islands have been self-governing within the Kingdom of Denmark since 1948. The ancient, locally elected parliament, the Logting, and the executive, the Landsstýri, are responsible for all matters except those involving foreign policy; defense; the police; the courts; and, until 2004, church policy and the "People's Church." The Faroese have their own flag, postage stamps and paper money. They do use Danish coins. Denmark pays for about a third of all public spending. Such support enabled the islanders to have a higher average income than the Danes themselves until the islands' economy turned sour in the 1990s.

The local inhabitants do not allow the Danes to make the most important economic decisions for them. They decided in 1974 not to be a part of the EU, fearing that the EU's fish policy might threaten that industry. They have also resisted all temptations either to permit the search for oil within their 200-mile economic zone or the establishment of what could be a lucrative tourist industry in the islands. They are in NATO, though, and have a small radar station. While the Faroese do not want to seal themselves off from the outside world, they do wish to avoid anything that could disturb their quiet island life, their cultural independence, or their native language. In a May 2001 referendum, they rejected independence from Denmark.

The islanders were thrust into the public eye in 2015 by the protesters from the Sea Shepherd Conservation Society who filmed a mass killing of 250 pilot whales in 24 hours, during the traditional "grindadrap" summer hunt. The sea mammals were rounded up into a cove and slaughtered with lances. Every year around 800 whales and dolphins are killed in this traditional way. The protesters decried the procedure and the alleged Danish government's complicity in the process.

ECONOMY

Denmark has long ceased being a primarily agricultural country, although its production in that sector is generally efficient and is an important component of its foreign trade. Denmark is now highly industrialized, even though it almost totally lacks raw materials, except salt and newly discovered North Sea oil and gas, which may eventually be capable of supplying up to a third of the country's energy needs. What the Danes lack in raw materials they must make up for in highly skilled labor and high-quality production. They must work with their brains, and they must have

Denmark

a sharp eye for niches in the world market that they could fill quickly and with a minimum of materials. This requires imagination and adaptability to customers' tastes, and these requirements are well suited to Danish ingenuity and the small size of Danish firms. In Denmark's modern economy, 78% of the work force is employed in services (producing 77% of GDP) and 20% in industry (creating 22% of GDP).

Danes specialize in finished goods and have moved in on highly specialized markets. For example, Denmark is the world's largest supplier of insulin for diabetics and of industrial enzymes. It also has a large share of the world market in marine diesel engines, hearing aids (especially those attached to eye glasses), and radio telephones. Danish furniture is known for quality, design, and flair. It produces Lego toys, which can be found in children's playrooms all over Europe and North America; 98% of its sales are abroad. By 2005 Lego was suffering losses due to the falling dollar, inexpensive Chinese toys, and modern kids' preferences for mobile phones and computers. Legoland Park outside Copenhagen continues to attract more than 1 million visitors a year and is Denmark's biggest tourist attraction. There are similar Legoland Parks in the UK, Germany, and the US.

Denmark also has become the world's largest exporter of a particularly familiar product throughout the world—beer. This is primarily because of the Carlsberg-Tuborg brewery group, which also has sizable operations in the US. Carlsberg patronizes the arts, grants scholarships, and owns such famous Danish brands Georg Jensen silver and Royal Copenhagen porcelain. In 2000 it sold one of the national jewels, Tivoli Gardens, to a consortium led by the Scandinavian Tobacco Corporation, which promised to improve the beloved park without disturbing its tranquil character. In 2005 an economic icon for Danes was sold to Nordic Telephone—TDC telecommunications, a former state-owned monopoly that dominated the home market.

As a highly prosperous nation with a small domestic market, Denmark is extremely dependent upon foreign trade. Indeed, it has one of the highest levels of foreign trade per inhabitant in the world. Industrial exports constitute from 35% to 40% of its total production, and few Danish farmers could hope to survive if the country's foreign agriculture markets were lost. Over two-thirds of its industrial exports go to other EU countries (mainly to Germany and Sweden). With such dependency upon exporting, it is no surprise that Denmark pursues a liberal (free) trade policy and chooses to remain in the EU, despite lingering opposition to membership.

After Sweden and Finland joined in 1995, and with enlargement deep into eastern Europe in 2004, a Danish exit from the EU seemed no longer to be a feasible option for a while.

In a September 2000 referendum, voters by 53% to 47% rejected the common currency, the euro. A disappointed then Foreign Minister Mogens Lykketoft noted ruefully, "there is a general animosity in Europe toward the EU bureaucrats issuing all these regulations, and that is particularly strong in Denmark. What we saw today was a political vote here, not an economic one." Danes feared that greater EU harmonization might have threatened their welfare state and maybe even their sense of national identity. The krone nevertheless remains tied to the euro (as it was linked to the German mark after 1982). Danes denied themselves the possibility of influencing EU policies regarding the new currency. Being outside the eurozone was especially significant during the first half of 2012, when Denmark had the EU presidency.

A 2008 poll revealed that 55% of voters favored adopting the euro, while only 38% opposed it. The Greek euro crisis changed that dramatically: In December 2011 only 24% favored the euro, and 60% regarded it as incapable of tackling the debt crisis. Danes have already gotten used to euros because they flow over the border from Germany and are widely accepted in restaurants and shops. The four opt-outs Denmark had won from the EU deal with the euro, defense, citizenship, and justice and home affairs.

Polls suggest that Danes are ready to join European defense efforts and scrap the other two opt-outs, which are fundamental powers for a sovereign state. It seems unnecessary, for example, for them to have to pull their soldiers out of a NATO operation when it becomes an EU one, as was the case in Bosnia. Many Danes are nervous about Russia and question the wisdom of their policy of not allowing foreign troops or nuclear weapons on their soil.

Danes, who are notoriously independent-minded on EU matters, are now among the most pro-European in the union; 66% agreed in 2007 that membership in the EU was a good thing. Torning-Schmidt made her first foreign trip as prime minister to Brussels, and she favored maximum cooperation with the EU. She supported the EU treaty dealing with defending the euro and promised to subject Denmark voluntarily to the same penalties and budget limits as the eurozone. She canceled her predecessor's plans to construct new customs-control facilities on Denmark's borders, which

would have violated the EU's Schengen Agreement. At the height of the migrant crisis in 2015, the new government of Lars Lokke Rasmussen expressed its outrage at Sweden's strengthening of border controls at crossings from Denmark, but it soon moved to enforcing various restrictions of its own.

Industry is overwhelmingly privately owned. The central or local government authorities operate only the postal service, gasworks, electricity generation, ports, certain transportation companies, and some other services belonging to the country's economic infrastructure. The state does not engage in industrial production, and it is seldom willing to subsidize lame-duck industries. Also, only about one-twelfth of its industry is foreign-owned, though there has been an increased interest from China to invest here. For example, in a 2017 deal, the Chinese carmaker Zhejiang Geely that owns Swedish Volvo became the largest shareholder of Denmark's Saxo Bank by buying about 30% of its shares. Firms are of small or medium size, with an average of 60 employees. Almost half employ less than 20. It is nevertheless true that most industrial exports stem from medium or large-sized firms, but Danes have never tried to build up gigantic industries, such as steel, automobile, or aircraft production. Anticipating the single EU market in 1992, mergers took place in basic Danish industries, like foodstuffs, sugar, and alcohol, that amounted to be the most far-reaching restructuring of Danish industry in a century. Finally, industry is geographically dispersed; there is no one concentrated industrial region.

Labor and Employers

Labor and employers are highly organized. The Confederation of Danish Employers (DA) represents 11 employer and manufacturer organizations. The National Organization of Trade Unions (LO) links 1,699 unions, which organize 80% of all wage earners, one of the highest percentages in the free world. DA and LO collectively negotiate wages and working hours every two years, and the government intervenes only if the two sides cannot agree. In that case, the Folketing legislates the final proposals presented by an impartial mediator. Strikes are forbidden while a valid agreement is still in force, and there are relatively few strikes.

One difference of opinion that exists between employers and the trade unions is the latter's wish to introduce what they call "economic democracy." There are already forms of employee participation in the firms' decision-making, but this does not extend to sharing profits. Supported by the Social Democratic and other leftist parties,

86

the LO maintains that the unions should be given a portion of the businesses' value, which the employees helped to create. There are many different proposals, but all call, in general, for 5% of all wages to be put into special funds under the control of the unions. These funds, provided by the employers, would be used to buy shares in industries, which would then be owned by the unions, not individuals, who would nevertheless derive some kind of financial benefit from this upon retirement.

Employers quickly noted that such a practice would enable the unions to gain quickly a controlling share in most industries, despite the fact that the Danish constitution would forbid this share to exceed 49%. The specter of the trade unions controlling the economy horrifies businessmen and others, but it delights some persons who think that such a measure would make Denmark a more just society. By the end of the 1980s, these funds were already cash-rich and were even being invested in a variety of ways, including agriculture. In 1990 the Conservative government initiated moves to restrict the unions' power to maintain closed shops and to pass on union dues to political parties, in effect to the Social Democrats.

The constitution guarantees Danes the right to work and to receive public assistance if they lose their work. Every year a fifth of workers lose their jobs, and 30% change employment. But most find a new job quickly, and the unemployment rate in 2023 was a low 2.8%. The secret is called "flexicurity," a Danish model that protects the worker, not the job. It is a blend of a flexible labor market, generous social security, and training and high benefits during bouts of unemployment. Since they can fire unneeded workers, Danish firms have a competitive advantage over their rivals. For two years (down from four), laid-off workers receive about 80% of their wages, an amount that is capped for high earners. They must take part in job-placement and retraining programs. This model is expensive and requires the world's highest tax level: The average tax rate is 53%. Not all countries would choose to imitate it.

Agriculture

The percentage of Danes engaged in agriculture and fisheries has fallen to only 2.3%. They produce a total of 1% of GDP, although the food industry provides between 12% and 18% of domestic employment. Two-thirds of farms have been merged or converted to other use since the World War II. About two-thirds of the land is still used for farming, almost entirely by single families, and nonfarmers are not allowed to own farmland. However, there are fears similar to those in the US that many family farms may fail. Favorable climate, good soil, and careful, but intensive land use result in the country's having two to three times as much farmland per inhabitant as do its more densely populated but less efficient EU partners—it maintains the highest productivity and export of farm produce per capita in all Europe.

Agriculture accounts for nearly 20% of its merchandise exports. This has helped Denmark produce three times as much food as its own citizens need, and it sells about 70% of its produce abroad; these sales account for about a third of its foreign currency earnings. EU countries purchase about two-thirds of its farm exports, which is an important reason Danes chose to join the EU in 1972. Americans, who have developed a taste for Danish cheese and canned hams, are the second-largest purchasers. In 2002 Danes were incensed by the EU decision that only Greek cheese can be labeled "feta" when three-quarters of the world's feta is produced outside of Greece, 25,000 tons of it in Denmark. The latter set an EU precedent in 2004 by publishing the names and amounts of EU cash received by its farmers. Embarrassingly, it turned out that Mariann Fischer Boel, the then EU's agriculture commissioner from Denmark, and her husband had received an annual EU farm subsidy of $100,000.

About 90% of the farmers' total income is derived from animal products and only 10% from grain. Denmark is home to 30 million pigs, its major livestock. Almost 80% of them are exported, primarily to Germany. It is one of the world's largest exporters of pork. Because of the growing size of pig farms, which cause strong, unpleasant odors over large distances, pork farmers are under attack from the tourism industry, environmentalists, and animal-welfare activists.

Farmers discovered that mink-raising can be quite profitable, and Denmark is the world's main supplier of these skins, mainly to Russia and China. When a mutated version of coronavirus appeared in 2020, the government ordered the culling of all the animals, only to discover that it lacked the legal authority to do so. Farmers have retained powerful clout through the Agricultural Council. The farmers themselves came under severe attack by ecologists, who claim agricultural methods and materials pollute the earth.

Shipping and Fishing

All Danes are surrounded by the sea and understandably have always been a seafaring people. Except for such "flag of convenience" states as Liberia, only Norway and Greece have more shipping tonnage per capita than does Denmark. Most of the fleet never docks in Danish ports, but 85% of all ships sailing Baltic waters have Copenhagen as their home port. Shipping provides close to a tenth of the country's total foreign currency earnings, ranking behind industry and agriculture but ahead of tourism and fishing.

Two of the world's largest shipping companies, A. P. Meller and the East Asiatic Company, are Danish. The crisis in world shipping has undeniably been felt in Denmark. A major reason for the decline in the competitiveness of Danish shipping is, without question, the wage levels.

Denmark is among the top 10 fishing nations in the world. An unusual feature among fishing nations is that company activity is almost unknown in Denmark. The captains own almost all fishing vessels; each ship's earnings entirely depend upon the catch, and the crews share in the distribution of profits. It is not surprising that there are no strikes in this sector. Vessels fish mainly in the North and Baltic Seas, but there is an important problem: Access to Norwegian, Swedish, or EU countries' waters has been restricted or eliminated. Danes face a general problem in these waters—there are too many fishermen chasing too few fish. The Danes' most important fish for use as food is cod. For industrial use, it is the sand eel. Their major buyers are the EU (especially Sweden), Switzerland, and the US. About 600 inland trout farms have sprung up, made possible sometimes by spring water and a cool climate. Faced with an unwelcome overabundance of invasive Pacific oysters along its coast, in 2017 Denmark went online to hawk the bounty to Chinese businesses. The enterprise raised much interest, aided by the involvement of Alibaba, one of the world's largest retailers, which had already agreed to help promote Danish products and tourist attractions.

Energy

Like most industrialized countries, Denmark underwent a major conversion in the 1950s and 1960s from coal to oil, and by 1972 its dependence on imported oil had swelled to 93% of its energy consumption. Thus, when the first oil crisis shook the world in 1973, Denmark was unprepared.

This was especially so since it had seemed to have obtained very little from the portion of the North Sea that had been carved out for it. Danes have so far resisted nuclear energy, but they have switched many power plants from oil to coal, with the goal of fueling at least 80% of them with coal. Power plants are also being geared to provide district heating (whereby heat is pumped into individual dwellings from a central plant) for about

Denmark

40% of households. About 30% are heated by gas, either in individual furnaces or from district heating systems. The country is self-sufficient in gas, but it has very little hydropower.

Despite its heavy use of hydrocarbons and abstention from atomic power, Denmark has been admirably successful in reducing its carbon dioxide emissions by almost 15% below its 1990 level. It has an effective carbon tax that requires polluters to pay for their environmental damage and then recycles the proceeds back to industry to subsidize research and environmental innovation.

It is fitting that Copenhagen was chosen as the host for the UN's summit on global warming in December 2009, which failed to achieve a global agreement. The country has a vital stake in slowing global warming. Its average elevation is only 31 meters (105 feet) above sea level. Nowhere in Denmark is more than 32 miles (51,5 km) from the ocean. Red flashing lights on walls around Copenhagen remind residents where the water would reach if sea levels raised by 7 meters (23.6 feet). Copenhagen has an ambitious goal of becoming the world's first carbon-neutral capital by 2025.

Finally, energy conservation measures help Danes continue to reduce their oil consumption. Wind energy supplies some 40% of Denmark's total power, the highest proportion in the world. The 80 offshore wind-mills near Esbjerg and Copenhagen harbor make up the world's largest wind farm. The country is an international powerhouse in this field. Its companies, of which Vestas is the biggest, control about half the industry worldwide and supply windmills, for example, to the New England coast. The Liberal government announced soon after taking power in 2015 that it would reduce funding for research into green energy sources from $55 million to $18 million. Nevertheless, Danes hope to expand their use of renewable energy sources from 17% in 2005 to 50% by 2020 and 84% by 2035. Of their waste, 42% is recycled, 54% is incinerated to generate heat and electricity (vs. 13% in the US), and only 4% (compared with 54% in the US) is buried in landfills.

Prosperity, Welfare Benefits, Taxation

Any visitor to the country can see that the average Dane lives a very prosperous life and that there is little visible poverty in the country. Average per-capita income is among the highest in the world. Almost 60% of households own the houses and apartments in which they live. The average Dane spends only a sixth of his income on housing and a fourth on food, drink, and tobacco.

Most Danes have supported the development of a comprehensive social welfare system, whose underlying philosophy is that a society should be judged by the way it treats its weakest members and that individuals are very seldom personally responsible for the social problems from which they might suffer. Therefore, the public should support any person unable to support himself. As a rule, these assistance funds come directly from tax revenues, not from insurance schemes to which the beneficiaries must contribute. Also, one qualifies for benefits merely by being a resident of Denmark, which means that foreigners can receive roughly the same benefits as can citizens. The fact that the state pays the cost of childbearing, funerals, and burials indicates that the country literally has a cradle-to-grave welfare system.

Danes work an average of 37.5 hours a week, have 4 weeks of paid vacation, receive 90% of their previous income for up to 3.5 years as well as retraining and relocation expenses in case of unemployment, and can claim a state pre-pension at age 60 (55 for widows), which pays 60% of the normal pension, and one is limited to only 200 hours of work per year. In 2005, half of all workers were taking advantage of this by retiring early at age 60. The government's decision to raise the retirement age from 60 to 65 (60 for military) was understandably unpopular, as is a subsequent decision to up it to 67.

Medical care is free (paid through taxes), and patients can choose their own doctor in their own town or area. If they go outside their town of residence, they cannot choose their doctor. Maternity benefits were raised beyond the earlier 14 weeks. Parents who have children under age 9 can get sabbaticals of up to 52 weeks per child and receive a weekly allowance worth $315. Over four decades of welfare legislation culminated in a comprehensive assistance act of 1976, which guarantees every resident in need economic aid, not merely to survive, but also to maintain the standard of living to which the person had become accustomed.

Many foreigners greatly admire such a complete welfare system, but the reverse side of the coin is one of the world's highest tax levels and the highest of any EU country. The income tax, which constitutes about two-thirds of all taxes, is heavily progressive, and even those with middle incomes feel the bite. The marginal personal income tax rate is 56%, and the minimum marginal rate is 43%. Corporate rates are 22%. Denmark also has the EU's highest taxes on many consumer goods; for instance, the VAT stands at 25%, the highest in the EU. Tax revenues in 2004 came to 49.6% of GDP, second in the world

only to Sweden's 50.7%. The Danish state spends 58% of GDP.

Many Danes have begun to wonder whether welfare assistance and other forms of government spending have gone too far. Unemployment pay is higher than the minimum wage, so many Danes prefer to collect the unemployment benefits than to go back to work by taking a low-paying job. To stem this trend, parliament passed a reform package in 1996 that declares that persons below the age of 25 are no longer permitted to collect full unemployment benefits. Demonstrating how far some people want to extend the welfare state, one prominent Social Democrat proposed in 1989 that the six-week maternity leave should be supplemented by a special leave to propagate (albeit only for those in jobs with a high risk of low fertility). These kinds of questions and abuses have fueled both tax evasion and tax revolts. High taxes on electronics, alcohol, and tobacco sent Danes (whose alcohol consumption is the second-highest in the Nordic world after Finland's) over the German border in droves to shop for these items. To prevent this and to lower the prices, the government significantly lowered taxes on alcohol and cigarettes in 2003.

In 2015 one-fourth of working-age Danes were drawing state transfer payments, such as student grants, sick or unemployment pay, or early-retirement entitlements. The costly welfare system has not rid Denmark of some seemingly intractable problems, including homeless who were usually alcoholics or drug addicts and who were entirely dependent on welfare payments for survival.

The desire for a high standard of living despite high tax levels has also contributed to the inclination of more and more women to work; 71% of Danish women between the ages of 16 and 66 have jobs, compared with 37% in 1950; this is the highest percentage of any nation after Sweden. Of members of parliament, 39% are female. In 2015 the World Economic Forum ranked Denmark number 14 in the world (rather far below the other Nordic countries that all ranked as the top 4) for gender opportunity. Only one in five children is cared for by a fulltime parent. One social by-product of the enormous increase in the number of working wives is that the fertility rate has declined to 1.73. That is intriguing, given that in 2017 nearly 40% of Danish women aged 15–39 declared that they would like to have three or more children, one of the highest percentages among the most developed countries. Denmark will increasingly be facing the demographic problem caused by growing numbers of older citizens being supported by a shrinking working population. Noting that the birth rate is the lowest in some 27 years, in 2014 a Danish travel agency advertised European vacations as a romantic opportunity to change this situation, under the slogan "Do it for Denmark!"

Economic Reform

Like many other people, Danes lived beyond their means. Only a partial sacrifice of the high standard of living could put the country's financial books back in order, and that is exactly what the government did from the early 1990s on. It made sweeping cuts throughout the economy, including the social welfare programs. It abolished the automatic indexing for wages and welfare benefits that tied them to inflation and imposed severe statutory limits on wage raises in both the public and private sectors. It also cut public borrowing and vowed to maintain the value of the currency. It consciously slowed down economic growth and placed a higher priority on combating inflation than on reducing unemployment.

The medicine worked and saved Denmark from the financial abyss. By 2023, it had inflation of 6%, economic growth of 6% and unemployment of 2.8%. It reduced the national debt to 36% of GDP, limited its annual budget deficit to 0.6% of GDP, improved exports, and maintained a current accounts surplus of 4.8% of GDP, one of the largest in the OECD in relation to size of economy. In 2017, it paid off its last loan denominated in foreign currency—for the first time in over 180 years. Denmark's financial institutions were also strengthened through mergers, and it escaped the serious problems facing banking in the other Nordic countries. In 2012 the World Economic Forum ranked Denmark 12th in the world in terms of global competitiveness, behind Finland, the U.S. and Sweden. In 2007 the same organization put Denmark in first place in terms of exploiting information technology; the US dropped to seventh. In 2013 The Economist magazine ranked Denmark fifth as the world's best place to do business, right behind the U.S.

Not everyone agrees: Citing restrictive regulations, Uber decided to withdraw from Denmark in April 2017. After courts declared that Uber is not a ride-sharing venue but really an illegal taxi service, the company was required to install expensive equipment, such as taxi meters and video cameras.

An ambitious austerity program is not easy for governing coalitions that have no majority in parliament and rule a nation long-accustomed to annual increases in real wages and welfare spending. But many Danes are encouraged that their country has begun to overcome the addiction to borrowing. Denmark has a culture and economy that are twice as likely to enable individuals to escape poverty than does the United States.

CULTURE

Literature

It is difficult for a small country with its own language to gain the world's attention to certain aspects of its culture. Although the Danish language is understood, albeit with some difficulty, by other Scandinavians, it cannot be understood at all by German and Dutch speakers, although all three languages are of Germanic origin. The geographically restricted reach of Danish has meant that most Danish literature remains unknown in the rest of the world, even though Denmark publishes more books per capita than any other nation in the world except Iceland.

The major exception is the literary giant Hans Christian Andersen (1805–1875), whose folktales filled with fantasies and down-to-earth moral insights have delighted children (and adults) for generations. The 200th anniversary of his birth was celebrated throughout the world in 2005 by appointing Hans Christian Andersen ambassadors. His mind has become a part of many persons' childhood: "The Princess and the Pea," "The Emperor's New Clothes," "The Steadfast Tin Soldier," and many other delightful tales.

Andersen's "The Little Mermaid" is memorialized by a 4-foot-tall, 385-pound statue created by Edvard Eriksen in 1913 in Copenhagen Harbor, which is one of the city's most beloved landmarks. In 1998 the maiden's statue was beheaded for the second time in 33 years. After three days a hooded figure dropped the head off at a television station, and police suspected that the culprits were to be found in the feminist protest milieu. In 2003 vandals blew her up, but officials repaired and returned her. She also lost an arm, which was later recovered and reattached.

In 2010 she was sent abroad to the Shanghai World Expo in China. This was the first time she had traveled, and she was sent by a secret route to foil any plots to "Shanghai" her. As the centerpiece of the Danish pavilion, her assignment was to help boost Danish trade and tourism. However, her voyage created an uproar: 6 out of 10 Danes thought she should stay home. The future of "mermaid diplomacy" is uncertain.

Andersen has by far the greatest international reputation of any Danish author, but Denmark has many other writers of which it can be proud. In the 18th century, Ludvig Holberg (1684—1754) wrote many comedies and a novel of fantasy, Niels Klim's Journey to the World Underground (1741),

The Little Mermaid, Copenhagen
Source: *Wikipedia*

which is a delightful plea for religious tolerance. A more intensive Christianity was presented in the lyrics of Johannes Ewald (1743–1781), especially *Ode to the Soul*.

In the 19th century, other Danish authors dealt with spiritual matters. Perhaps the most profound and the one with the greatest impact upon philosophical and theological thinking in the western world was Seren Kierkegaard (1813–1855), the father of existentialism. He attempted to get people to reflect on their own existence and to realize that human life is a problem and demands choices and self-creation.

N. F. S. Grundtvig (1783—1872) pointed to the spoken, live word as the key to a human and Christian community. He founded the current national state and Volk high schools. Frederik Paludan-Muller's novel *Adam Homo* (1842–49) is now translated and accessible to the English-reading audience. Another important Danish work, *Seven Gothic Tales*, appeared first in English in 1934 under the pen name of Isak Dinesen, a year before it was rewritten in Danish by its author, Karen Blixen. Her work deals with man's religious life, and she argues that man is a mere marionette of God and that he should simply live out the destiny to which God assigns him. Blixen is best known throughout the world for her book *Out of Africa*, later made into a hit film, an engaging portrayal of her two decades living and farming in Kenya. Peter Høeg (b.1957) more recently gave Danish literature a worldwide audience with his best-selling novel *Miss Smilla's Feeling for Snow* (1992).

Denmark

Crown Prince Frederik and Crown Princess Mary of Denmark

Several Danish writers won Nobel Prizes in Literature in the 20th century. They include Karl Gjellerup and Henrik Pontoppidan (1917), as well as Johannes V. Jensen (1944). Many Danes call Jensen's novel *Kangens Fald* (The Fall of the King) the Danish "book of the century."

Religion has played very little part in post-World War II Danish literature, with the notable exception of Martin A. Hansen's *The Liar*. Some authors, such as Thorkild Hansen in his three-volume biography of Knut Hamsun, have dealt with Denmark's experiences under Nazi domination. Others, such as Villy Sørensen, Niels I. Meyer, and K. Helveg Petersen, focus on the problems arising from the individual's life in a prosperous, materialistic society and offer moderate-left solutions to contemporary problems. Dea Trier Mørch, Elsa Gress, and Suzanne Bragger have produced sensitive literature focusing on women's roles in society. They also produced a satirical response by one of Denmark's most popular contemporary authors, Klaus Rifbjerg, in his 1978 novel *Dobbeltgænger* (The Double). Others, such as Peter Seeberg and Ole Sarvig, have written modern experimental novels, and Thorkild Bjørnvig, Marianne Larsen, and Henrik Nordbrandt, have written lyrical poetry that commands an attentive audience in Denmark today.

The 1930s brought three outstanding Danish playwrights to public acclaim. Kaj Munk (1898—1944) was a clergyman deeply influenced by Kierkegaard. He wrote about strong men who tried to accomplish great things but who were doomed to failure by man's inherent sinfulness. The German occupation force executed Munk for resistance activities. Carl Erik Soya (1896—1983) produced realistic drama, and Kjeld Abell (1901—1961) in his plays rebelled against the boredom and mediocrity of bourgeois society.

The Arts

It cannot be said that the Danes are passionate theater fans. A 1975 survey revealed that only 16% of the population ever attends a performance. Also, theater in Denmark is not commercially viable. The state provides a variety of subsidies to keep the 15 theaters in Copenhagen and 10 in the provinces alive. In general, the state gives financial support to most of the arts on the principle that it has a duty to provide an economic foundation for Danish culture without interfering with it. Artistic freedom is always to be respected. The Ministry of Cultural Affairs also supports efforts to bring traditional culture to Danes who have little education in order to try to close what some Danes see as a "cultural gap." It finances activity centers and events in working-class areas, but the efforts to expand cultural opportunities have not yet proven to be very successful. Such costly programs, as well as financial support for art and artists, are increasingly criticized by many Danes, who feel that tax money could be better spent for other more immediate economic needs.

The only theaters open during the summer months and comprehensible to non-Danish-speaking persons is the Pantomime Theater, which has a long tradition of artistic excellence. The Tivoli Gardens, in which this theater is located, is filled with amusements and cafes and is certainly one of the world's most famous and delightful parks.

A Dane, Carl T. H. Dreyer (1889—1968), was an early film pioneer, with such films as Jeanne d'Arc. No Danish filmmaker today would dare try to produce a film without state aid. Because of such aid, about 20 films a year are made, most of them focusing on everyday life in a very realistic way. Film directors Henning Carlsen (1927—2014) and Lars von Trier (b.1956) have international reputations. However, the latter's outrageous statements calling himself a Nazi and expressing understanding for Hitler make him controversial and a persona non grata at film festivals. Such directors as Henning Kristiansen, Morten Arnfred, Astrid Henning-Jensen, Anders Refn, Edward Fleming, Bille August, Hans Kristensen, and Jergen Leth create films for an avid Danish audience.

The towering figure in Danish music was Carl Nielsen (1865—1931), who gained a wide international public. Other composers, such as Per Nergard, Ib Nerholm, Hans Abrahamsen, Erik Norby, Bo Holten, and Poul Ruders, have also been creative and successful. Thanks to such American artists as Thad Jones, Copenhagen has become one of Europe's major jazz centers. Denmark is also a European ballet center. The Royal Danish Ballet's international fame was established in the 19th century by August Bournonville. It is housed in the Royal Theater in Copenhagen and has its own school, where talented youngsters from age 7 to 16 are trained. It has been particularly successful in producing great male dancers, such as Erik Bruhn, Peter Martins, and Peter Schaufuss.

At the forefront of Danish artistic achievement are the sculptor Bertel Thorvaldsen (1770—1844) and the painter C. W. Eckersberg (1783—1853). Thorvaldsen achieved an international breakthrough in Rome and came to be the most renowned sculptor of his day. Eckersberg also made his breakthrough abroad as a pupil of Jacques Louis David in Paris. From David he learned to observe nature very closely and to reproduce it honestly. His numerous paintings of the

Denmark

The Royal Danish Theatre, Copenhagen

Source: Wikipedia

Danish coasts, countryside, and prominent citizens of Copenhagen provide the modern viewer with a valuable look at 19th-century Denmark. He also taught at the Academy of Art, which had been founded in Copenhagen in 1754. There he was able to launch an entire school of Danish painters.

This included Christen Købke, often regarded as the country's greatest painter. Born in 1810 and the son of a master baker, he was a contemporary of Hans Christian Andersen. He preferred to paint Danish churches and the outskirts of Copenhagen, where town and country met. He died early in 1848, only 37 years of age.

In the 1940s daring Danish painters and sculptors, such as Richard Mortensen, Mogens Andersen and Robert Jacobsen, experimented in modern styles in nonfigurative art. Contemporary Danish artists, such as Jergen Haugen Serensen, Egon Fischer, Willy Orskov, Niels Strobek, Per Kirkeby, Stig Bragger, Paul Gernes, and Tonning Rasmussen, have continued the experimentalist tradition. This has had an important impact on industrial products and furniture, in which Danish design has been very innovative as well as commercially successful. World-class architects include Jørn Utzon (the Sydney Opera House) and Johan Otto von Spreckelsen (the Grand Arch at La Defense in Paris).

Religion

The focus of some of Denmark's greatest literature on religious subjects should not leave one with the impression that Danes are a deeply religious people today. They are not. A poll indicated that only 45% of the adults believe that there is a God. Even a Lutheran pastor declared in 2003, "There's no heavenly God, there's no eternal life, and there's no resurrection." In 2003 the government announced that it would begin allowing a group that worships Norse gods to conduct legally recognized marriages. Regular church attendance on Sundays had by 2003 fallen to 1%–3% of the population.

Danes are obviously not a people greatly concerned with religious questions and matters. A 1987 survey revealed that more Danes believe in reincarnation than in the Christian doctrine of the resurrection of the body and that there are more full-time teachers of new, non-Christian religions in Denmark than there are priests in the Evangelical Lutheran Established Church, which receives financial support from the government and which is called the People's Church, not the State Church. Anybody can opt out of paying the church tax, but around 12% of the church's income still comes from a direct state subsidy.

Nevertheless, the official church is so enmeshed in Danish society that 84% of all Danes belong to the church, although they are free to leave it. In fact, only one person in Denmark is required to belong: the reigning monarch, who is the head of the church. Working with the government's church minister, it is he, not the bishops or a synod, who decides about liturgy, ritual, Bible translations, and the outer appearance of the psalm book. More than half of the marriages take place in a church, and over 80% of Danish children are baptized; over 95% of Danes are buried at local churches. Danes admit that theirs is now a "four-wheeler religion": They come in a baby carriage to be baptized, are driven to the church in a fancy car to be married, and are transported in a hearse to their own funeral. The church is there when desired—sometimes Christmas, Easter, and for family needs.

A 1988 law granted same-sex couples the legal status of married couples, including inheritance, deductions, and alimony, but excluding the right to adopt children. This was the first such law in the world. The social event of 1989 was a group marriage of 10 gay couples in Copenhagen's city hall.

Education

All children are required to attend at least 9 years of school, from ages 7 to 16. All public education, which is administered and largely financed by local governments, is free from elementary school through the university. About 5% of the Danish children at the primary or lower secondary levels attend private schools. It is very easy to found a private school in Denmark, and the local government authorities ask very few questions about the proposed school's educational philosophies before granting the usual 70% state subsidy for nonpublic schools.

The egalitarian goal of many Danes is revealed by the facts that, during the first seven years of schooling, numerical grades and required tests cannot be given. Many Danes fear that lasting social distinctions among citizens could be created if younger children received such grades and tests. However, from the eighth grade on, voluntary examinations can be given to those pupils who want to enter institutions of higher education, and pupils also can be issued grades if the parents desire this to be done. Attempts by some left-wing politicians and educators to abolish all grades and examinations have not yet found a political majority.

After the seventh grade, about 30% of the pupils choose to pursue vocational studies, while the rest follow courses that lead to the grammar school (gymnasium

Denmark

or high school) and, after a three-year course, to university or higher technical studies. A grammar-school diploma automatically entitles a student to entry into a university without an entrance examination, although one's grades do help determine what one may study.

The oldest is Copenhagen University, established in 1479, and others are in Arhus, Odense, Roskilde, and Alborg. Separate colleges, such as the dental colleges of Copenhagen and Arhus, the Royal Danish Conservatory of Music, the Royal Danish College of Pharmacy, and the Royal Academy of Fine Arts, teach specialized subjects that are not normally taught at the Danish universities. As a sign of the times, there has been a shift in the subjects that students choose to study. In 1976 half of them chose liberal arts majors leading to teaching or civil service, while only a fifth of them selected majors targeting the private sector. By 1991 less than a fifth opted for majors relevant to the public sector, while more than 40% prepared for employment in business, computers, and engineering. Men are predominant in these fields, while most of the law and theology students and 80% of the medical students are women. Among the few professions in which women match or exceed their share of the general population are medicine and diplomacy; the foreign service makes sure that half of its new recruits are women.

The Media

Radio and television programming is the responsibility of Radio Denmark, a publicly owned corporation managed independently by 27 persons chosen by the Folketing. License fees finance all broadcasting, and in 1988 a second television channel became operational on which commercial advertising was permitted for the first time. This broke the state-run TV monopoly and improved the quality of the government-run station.

Many Danes still rely on the 55 daily newspapers, almost a dozen of which are published in Copenhagen, for much of their news. The most respected of the larger newspapers are *Politiken* and *Berlingske* (formerly *Berlingske Tidende*). The latter is one of Europe's oldest newspapers. It was the first European newspaper to publish the text of the American Declaration of Independence. It is a conservative and middle-class newspaper, which has come very close to bankruptcy in the past due in part to its employees' resistance to any measures of economic restraint. Many Danes wanted the latter to survive because it is the major nonsocialist voice in a predominantly left-oriented mass media landscape. It is now profitable.

Most Danish newspapers have severed their ties with political parties. The Social Democratic Party's *Aktuelt* and *Det Fri Aktuelt* folded. There are specialized newspapers, such as *Borsen* for businessmen and the fast-growing Information for the intellectual left. One non-Copenhagen newspaper has a national outlook and circulation: the slightly conservative *Jyllands-Posten*, published in Arhus.

CURRENT ISSUES

Denmark is much surer of itself now that its economy has become one of Europe's strongest. It enthusiastically endeavors to establish and tighten links with the Baltic states, especially Lithuania. It helped create a Danish-German-Polish corps, Multinational Corps Northeast, that has its headquarters in the Polish city of Szczecin along Germany's border. Prime Minister Fredericksen emphasized that "Denmark belongs in the heart of Europe, without any reservations. . . . We want a stronger US presence in Europe and in Denmark."

In 2009 it sent a naval vessel to the Indian Ocean to join allied efforts to prevent pirate attacks from Somalia; Danes are among the pirates' many victims. In 2012 one of its ships succeeded in rescuing 16 hijacked crew members and capturing 17 of the pirates. The previous year seven Danish citizens, including three children, were freed without violence after pirates had held them for seven months.

Denmark had been openly uneasy about the Maastricht Treaty. Referring to the EU, former Foreign Minister Niels Helveg Petersen said, "We are not ardent integrationists." In 1993 Danes nevertheless decided that their future belongs in the EU. In the previous year, a very narrow majority had rejected the Maastricht Agreement in a referendum, expressing concerns heard in other EU countries: Unelected bureaucrats in Brussels were concentrating too much power and acting with a heavy hand. Worse, they operated outside of democratic control and were rushing Europeans into greater unity by fiat.

After having negotiated four opt-outs from the EU, meaning that Denmark would not take part in the monetary union, common citizenship, cooperation in domestic and justice affairs, or defense, the government again took the question to the people, this time actively campaigning for a yes vote. Also, in the yes camp, there were virtually all of Denmark's political, economic, and media establishments. Although 57% of voters said yes, Denmark was left deeply divided. The June 2016

referendum in Great Britain where the majority of Britons opted to leave the European Union provoked immediate reactions among Euro skeptical parties that would like to hold a similar referendum in their countries. The Danish People's Party and the Red-Green Alliance demanded again a vote on Denmark's membership in the EU. A poll indicated that 42% of Danes wanted a public vote on the question, an increase from 37% just a few months earlier. Ex-Prime Minister Rasmussen reiterated that Denmark would remain in the EU; still, the issue will not go away. His party is the most pro-EU in Denmark, but the tighter border controls with Germany and Sweden challenge the very premise of border-free Schengen Area.

Brexit exposed Denmark's complex relationship with the EU as well as with the UK (whom Denmark followed to join the EU). Despite a long tradition of close economic ties to Great Britain, Denmark chose to support a hard line in the negotiations. The country's well-being depends greatly on trade, and allowing Britain to dilute the rules, standards, and the overall strength of the single market would be hugely detrimental to Denmark. The government also fears that soft terms of "divorce" for Britain could embolden the Danish Euroskeptics to present a "Dexit" as palatable. At the same time, Denmark is a cautious EU member with a number of opt-outs. Having rejected deeper justice cooperation within the EU, it quickly found its data-gathering capabilities hampered. In a truly convoluted arrangement reached in late 2016, several Danish officers are to sit in the Europol offices to receive their law enforcement agencies' requests for database searches. Then they are to talk face to face to the Europol official sitting next to them, who will perform the actual search. The *Financial Times* quoted a Danish scholar who commented, "It is very odd. But we are the odd man in the EU. It is a particularly Danish thing."

Both as an EU member and a country with sizable claims in the Arctic north of Greenland, Denmark finds itself at odds with Russian interests. In 2017 it proposed a new law that would allow it to consider not only environmental but also security and foreign policy concerns while approving underwater gas pipeline projects that cross Danish territorial waters, such as the Russian Gazprom's Nord Stream 2. Since the EU attempts to limit its dependence on Russian energy sources, the Danish initiative could provide it with a convenient way to derail such proposals. Denmark also snubbed Russia by rejecting its proposal for fast-track bilateral negotiations over delineating borders in the Arctic.

Danes prefer the much-slower process of multilateral determinations under the aegis of the UN. Both countries lay claim to the Lomonosov Ridge at the bottom of the Arctic Ocean all the way to the North Pole. Denmark has already spent some $50 million and more than a decade investigating and documenting its claim. The "scramble for the Arctic" will only be heating up as climate change exposes more and more of the region to resource exploitation.

On May 28, 1998, voters decided not to adopt the euro. But Denmark agreed to keep the krone in a band within 2.25% of the euro and follow the European Central Bank's interest rate moves. Thus, it is ready to join whenever its people choose to do so. The government held a referendum on the issue on September 28, 2000. It failed to pass by 53% to 47%. By 2012 support for adopting the euro had plummeted to a mere 24%, with 60% considering it incapable of coping with the European debt crisis.

The anti-immigrant stance taken by the Danish government created an international uproar in 2016, when the parliament passed a law requiring newly arriving asylum seekers to give up their valuables, including jewelry (though not wedding rings), to help cover the cost of keeping them in the country. No more than $1,450 may be kept. Even though the government insisted that it was only fair for the migrants to contribute to their upkeep, the move provoked immediate comparisons to Nazi confiscations of their victims' property. Family reunification rules for immigrants have been tightened. Some communities insist on serving pork in public schools, ostensibly to preserve national identity, while critics indicate that such moves are directed against Muslims. In general, the harsher treatment of migrants is intended to send a strong signal discouraging further arrivals from the Middle East and Africa. The issue will continue dividing Danes.

One person whose popularity is sky-high is Queen Margrethe, who celebrated her 45th anniversary as monarch in 2017. It helps that the Danes are the second-happiest people in the world after Norwegians, according to the 2017 UN World Happiness Report.

Republic of Iceland (Lýðveldið Ísland)

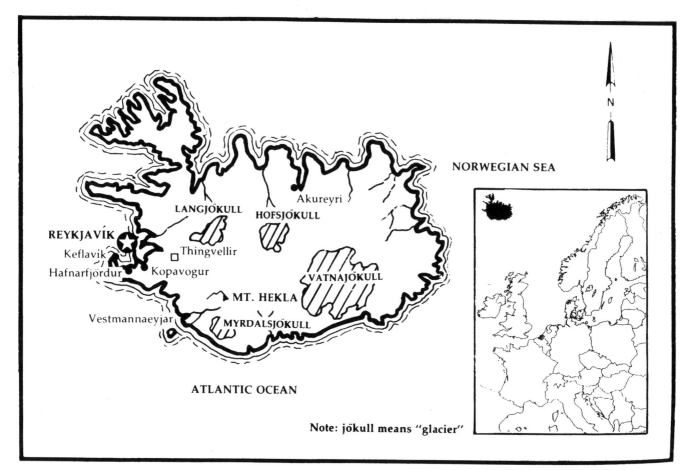

Note: jökull means "glacier"

Area: 39,817 sq. mi. (103,125 sq. km.).
Population: 399,189 (2024 census).
Capital City: Reykjavik (pop. 139,875 capital city and municipality, 247,590 metro). (2023 estimate). Over half (60%) of the country's population lives in Greater Reykjavik.
Climate: Considering its position, Iceland has the oceanic (or maritime) subarctic temperate climate. It varies between different parts of the island. The south coast is warmer, wetter, and windier than the north, while the Central Highlands are the coldest part of the country. The climate is affected by the confluence of two ocean currents: the warm Gulf Stream, from near the Equator, and the East Greenland Current which sometimes carries Arctic drift ice to Iceland's northern and eastern shores. But despite the proximity to the Arctic, its coasts remain ice-free through the winter. Temperature does not vary much throughout the country. The average January temperature is 31 °F (−0.5 °C), and the average July temperature is 51 °F (11 °C). The aurora borealis is often visible, especially in fall and early winter.
Neighboring Countries: Iceland lies alone in the North Atlantic, just touching the Arctic Circle, and is about 335 miles northwest of Scotland (UK) and approximately 425 miles from the coast of Norway. Greenland lies about 100 miles to the west.
Official Language: Icelandic (based on Old Norse).
Ethnic Background: 86% Icelandic, 6% Polish, 1% Lithuanian, 7% other (2021)
Religion: 72.4% Christianity (60.9% Church of Iceland; 11.5% other Christian); 1.5% Ásatrúarfélagið, 0.9% other, 25.2% no religion; (2022).
Form of Government: Unitary parliamentary republic.
Chief of State: Guðni Thorlacius Jóhannesson, President (since August 2016).
Head of Government: Katrín Jakobsdóttir, Prime Minister (since 2017).
National Flag: It consists of a blue field with the white-edged red Nordic cross that extends to the edges. The vertical part of the cross is shifted to the hoist side. The modern Icelandic flag dates from 1915, when a red cross was inserted into the white cross of the original flag. This cross represents Christianity. The colors reflect historical links with Norway, while the cross symbolizes close ties with the rest of the Nordic countries. The colors have no official symbolism but a popular modern interpretation is that they refer to the natural features of Iceland itself. Red is the fire produced by the island's volcanoes, white recalls the ice and snow that covers Iceland, and the blue is for the mountains of the island when looked at from the coast.
Public Holiday: June 17 (National Day; anniversary of the establishment of the republic).
Currency: Icelandic Króna (Krona, ISK)
Main Exports: Fish and fish products, animal products, aluminum.
Main Imports: Machinery, transport equipment, petroleum, food, textiles.

Main Trading Partners: Netherlands (37.5% of exports and 7.1% of imports), Norway (5.3% of exports and 12.3% of imports), United States (7.8% of exports and 6.3% of imports), Germany (6.5% of exports and 8.3% of imports), Denmark (6.0% of imports), China (9.4% of imports), Spain (4.3% of exports). United Kingdom (9.0% of exports and 3.9% of imports), France (6.4% of exports); (2022).

Hidden beneath the Myrdal Glacier is a treacherous volcanic fissure. When it erupts, the glacier melts instantly, changing from a benign sea of ice to a roaring wall of water racing across the flatland below it. In 1963 an underwater eruption off the southern coast resulted in the birth of a new island (named Surtsey), accompanied by exploding showers of hot lava, clouds of steam, and black smoke. These instances only help explain why Iceland is known as the battlefield of fire, ice, and steam.

Glaciers cover 12% of the country and its major ice cap is the world's third-largest. They provide an almost endless water supply for hydroelectricity. There are uncounted geysers and hot springs. The colors in Iceland's flag reflect these elements: red for fire, white for ice, and dark blue for the sea. Some 30 of its 130-odd volcanoes have erupted since the island's settlement in the late 9th century, and one-third of the world's lava production over the past half millennium has flowed in Iceland.

Icelanders were dramatically reminded of this in 1996, when a new volcano (subsequently named Loki after the Nordic god of fire) erupted under the Vatnajokull Glacier; the ice pack is the largest in Europe, measuring 1,800 feet in some places and covering 10% of the island's surface. It melted vast volumes of ice and formed a huge lake under the ice. Smashing through the ice, the volcano spewed black clouds five miles in the air and sent bursts of red lightning over the six-mile-long fissure. Then came a torrent of black sulphurous water, ice, and mud, at times five meters high, onto the deserted coastal plain 120 miles east of Reykjavik. Along its 20-kilometer-wide path to the sea, it destroyed roads, bridges, tunnels, and power and telephone lines.

In March and April 2010, the Atlantic world was once again reminded what an oversized influence tiny Iceland has on our lives. One of its least powerful volcanoes, Eyjafjallajökull (pronounceable only by Icelanders and mercifully shortened in the press to "E-15" for the eye-crossing number of letters), which had been quiet since 1821–1823, when it blew off and on for two years, erupted. It spit a plume of steam and ash about four miles

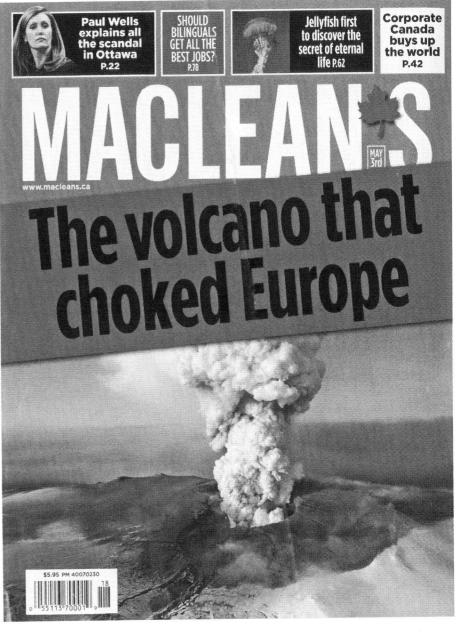

into the air. The cloud quickly covered most of Europe and North Africa. Since airplanes cannot fly through a volcano cloud without damaging their engines, air traffic largely stopped for five days as 100,000 flights were canceled. This cost the airlines over $3 billion at a time they could least afford it. The resulting chaos was a reminder of how interconnected we have become through the crisscrossing of airline routes and how Iceland's location is central in the Atlantic world. Because the volcano was located 75 miles southeast of Reykjavik and the winds were blowing southeast toward Europe, few Icelanders were affected by it, and their planes continued to fly. A year after the event, Grímsvötn erupted, and airlines

and air-traffic control experts conducted a simulation of a future eruption to determine if blanket bans on flights can give way to targeted bans.

The frightening thing is that other volcanoes, especially Katla, located only 16 miles away from E-15, pack a wallop 100 times more powerful. Katla is decades overdue to erupt. Even more intimidating is Öræfajökull, whose 1362 eruption was worse than Mount Vesuvius in 79 AD, and Laki, which covered Europe with poisonous gases in 1783 and reduced the island's population by a fifth to only 40,000. Iceland is a geological infant that is still in the state of formation.

Volcanic activity can be expected to increase in the coming decades. Iceland's

Iceland

Thingvellir—solemn and windswept, ancient site of democratic ideals

Bárðarbunga volcano erupted continuously for five months in 2015, producing a massive lava field and some small daily earthquakes.

Numerous earthquakes in 2021 were a concern. One expert said "Never before have so many in Iceland experienced so much seismic activity." Climate change creates more green earth for the country but also lifts pressures off the earth, which experts say could mean more volcanic eruptions in Iceland.

Although earthquakes are a frequent occurrence in Iceland due to the island's location, spanning the Mid-Atlantic Ridge between the Eurasian and North American tectonic plates, the 2021 swarm of tremors was noted for being more extensive than usual. Five identified volcanic eruptions have occurred in the Reykjanes Peninsula from 2021 to 2023.

Then, in October 2023, the ominous continuous tremors of the Reykjanes Peninsula began. This earthquake swarm was associated with a magmatic intrusion estimated to be up to 9.3 miles (15 kilometers) long that ran in a south-westerly direction, starting at Kálfellsheiði and following the line of the Sundhnúkur crater chain at a depth of around 800 meters (2,600 ft). The largest earthquakes originated under the Sundhnúkur craters but subsequently spread southwest under the town of Grindavík and into the sea. Grindavík is supposed to have been established on lava that erupted from Sundhnúkur around 2,350 years ago. It is one of six communities on the peninsula situated on or near an eruptive fissure. The frequency and intensity of the earthquakes dramatically increased on November 10, 2023, with 20,000 tremors recorded by that time, the largest of which exceeded magnitude 5.3, and large-scale subsidence in and around the town caused significant damage. On November 10, a state of emergency was declared, and an evacuation was ordered for Grindavík. This culminated in relocating nearly 4,000 residents, almost 1 percent of Iceland's population.

The first eruption started on the evening of December 18, 2023, at the Sundhnúkur crater chain north of Grindavík, with lava spewing from fissures. The intensity of the eruption and accompanying seismic activity decreased early on December 19, with lava seen spreading laterally from both sides of the newly opened fissures. The eruption was described as the largest in the Reykjanes Peninsula since the beginning of eruptive activity in 2021, with a lava fountain, up to 100 meters (330 ft) high, visible as far away as the capital Reykjavík, 26 miles (42 kilometers) away. The eruption ended on December 21. After a flight over the volcano, the Icelandic Meteorological Office said there was no lava erupting, but clarified that it was "too early to declare the eruption over."

Volcanic activity recurred on January 14, 2024, when two new fissure eruptions started north of Grindavík, with most of its lava steered away from the town by newly constructed protection barriers. A few hours later, a third fissure opened less than 100 meters (330 ft) from Grindavík inside the protection barriers, with its lava reaching and burning down three residential houses.

The Sundhnúkur volcanic eruptions remain an ongoing series of eruptions in the Reykjanes peninsula, with the town of Grindavík heavily damaged. President Guðni Th. Jóhannesson in his address following the January 14 eruption, said that "a daunting period of upheaval has begun on the Reykjanes peninsula," emphasizing the need to continue taking "actions that are within our power," while "hoping for as good an outcome as possible." He also advised citizens to "stand together and have compassion" for those displaced by the eruption. Prime Minister Katrín Jakobsdóttir saw the eruption as a "black day for all of Iceland," but added that "the sun will rise again," and expressed solidarity with those affected.

Geographic features

Iceland stands at the northern end of the Atlantic, guarding the boundary between that ocean and the Arctic. The Denmark Strait is to the west, the Greenland Sea to the north, and the Norwegian Sea to the east. The island is squarely on the "great circle" air routes between American, Scandinavian, and eastern European cities. The northernmost tip of Iceland touches the Arctic Circle.

The island is oval-shaped, with many peninsulas extending from the western and northern coasts. The maximum east-to-west distance is about 300 miles (480 km), and from north to south it extends about 200 miles (320 km).

Iceland is the result of thousands of lava flows and volcanic eruptions. Most of the island is plateau, typically 1,500 to 2,000 feet (457 to 610 m) in altitude, with volcanic peaks and high tablelands rising above it. Along the north and west coasts, steep cliffs border deep fjords, most of which have good natural harbors and from which broad valleys reach far inland. The largest plain is in the southwest and is Iceland's most fertile grassland.

Although the Polar Current chills the north coast, the Gulf Stream warms the south, bringing a surprisingly mild climate to a land on the doorstep of the Arctic. The average winter temperature is higher than that of New York City, although the almost-constant winds greatly intensify the chill factor.

When the first settlers arrived, the lower elevations were covered with forests, but they were cut for firewood and prevented from regrowing by sheep grazing and the cooler climate. Moss and grass cover many of these same areas today. Seals, walrus, and arctic foxes were the only native wild mammals, but humans introduced rats, mice, mink, and reindeer, deliberately or otherwise. Iceland's coastal waters were teeming with fish.

HISTORY

According to records created 259 years later, Iceland was discovered and settled by the Norsemen and some Celts during the Viking Age, between 870–930 AD. Most of the settlers came from Norway, but some came from other Nordic countries and from Norse Viking Age settlements in the British Isles. The 9th-century settlers noticed steam rising from the ground on a spot they called "Smokey Bay" or "Reykjavik." They came mostly from the coastal areas extending from Trøndelag to Agder in western Norway, especially the part known as Gulathing, today's Sogn Og Fjordane, Hordaland, and Rogaland, as well as from the ethnically mixed Viking colonies in Scotland and Ireland. Only the interior, which has always been largely uninhabitable, remained unsettled. The presence of the Celts probably explains the higher percentage of dark-haired people than in other Nordic countries.

Regardless of the original ethnic mix, the population soon became homogeneous. There was little additional immigration. In modern times there has been a steady increase in population because of the low death and high birth rates.

Icelanders continued their explorations beyond their home island in the 10th and 11th centuries. Erik the Red settled Greenland in 986. About 1000 his son, Leif Eriksson, who was born in Iceland, led the first proven expedition to the American continent, but attempts to settle "Vinland" failed.

At the foot of a great cliff and overlooking a broad lava plain, the Althingi (Alþingi), one of the oldest parliaments in the world, began its annual sessions in 930, 60 years after the arrival of the first settlers. Recently, a member of parliament suggested that, if the British insist on calling their country the "Mother of Parliaments," then Iceland should proclaim itself the "Grandmother of Parliaments." In 1000 that body decided that Icelanders would thereafter be Christians. Although the Althingi now meets in Reykjavik, the original location at Thingvellir is the most celebrated historical site in Iceland. Contacts with Norway remained strong through the first four centuries of Icelandic history. Around 1020 Iceland entered its first agreement with a foreign country: The Althingi and King Olav Haraldsson (St. Olav) reached an accord on reciprocal rights. The Icelanders' memory of their earlier independence outlasted centuries of foreign domination, famines, plagues, and natural catastrophes. Many of their legends and sagas hark back to the times when they were masters of their own fate.

Iceland was independent until it came under the control of Norway in 1262, then Denmark in 1380. When the Icelandic

Prime Minister Katrin Jakobsdottir

chieftains (the Godar) accepted the king of Norway as their sovereign under the "Old Covenant" in 1262–1264, Iceland became a part of the Norwegian realm. However, it retained its own parliament (Althingi), laws, and self-government

View of Reykjavík, where 60% of Icelanders live

Iceland

President Gudni Th. Jóhannesson

Iceland is a parliamentary democracy in which the most powerful political figure, the prime minister, must have a majority in the parliament, the Althingi. At least every 4 years, citizens at least 18 years of age elect 63 members of parliament by a system of proportional representation. In 1991 the upper house (Efri deild) was abolished, leaving only a unicameral lower house (Neðri deild). The prime minister is the head of government.

Political Parties

There is no majority party, and since the 1930s, successful government has depended on the formation of a coalition. There are six main political parties now represented in the Althingi. All of them have "open primaries" in which even non-members can have an influence on their leadership.

The Social Democratic Party (SDP) was the earliest party to call for Iceland to commence negotiations on entering the EU, but no other party supported this until later. In 1995, it was damaged by a split and formation of a breakaway leftist Awakening of the Nation (also called the People's Movement). The SDP had its own newspaper, *Althydubladid* (Alþýðublaðið, 1919—1998).

The Social Democratic Party was succeeded in 2000 by the Social Democratic Alliance founded in 2000 after a merger of four center-left political parties following a joint run by all parties in the 1999

in most internal matters. The kingdoms of Denmark and Norway (including Iceland) existed united in 1380. But Iceland continued to enjoy considerable self-government throughout the Middle Ages. The 15th century has been referred to as the "English Century" in Icelandic history due to the many contacts between the countries, including much trading and some skirmishing.

With the Reformation, enforced by the Danish crown in the 16th century, Danish royal power took firm hold, and the introduction of the trade monopoly in 1602 and absolutism in 1662 reduced Iceland, in effect, to the status of a Danish colony. The Althingi itself became increasingly powerless and was finally abolished in 1800. The trade monopoly, which meant that Icelanders received low prices for their products and paid high prices for the goods that they had to import on Danish ships, merely stimulated Icelandic resentment toward Copenhagen.

From 1835 to 1847, Jónas Hallgrímsson and other patriots edited the periodical *Fjölnir*. They advocated a return to the virtues of a golden past, the commonwealth of 930–1262, and the reestablishment of the Althingi, which occurred in 1843. In the middle of the 19th century, the Icelanders, led by long-standing Althingi president Jón Sigurðsson, continued this campaign finally to sever their ties with Denmark. The Danes were receptive to the idea of loosening their hold on Iceland, but their concessions seldom went far enough for the Icelanders.

Home rule was granted finally in 1904. During the World War I, Icelanders bolstered their self-confidence by being able to solve their own problems at home without Danish help. In December 1918 an agreement called the Act of Union between Iceland and Denmark granted the island full independence. It agreed to continue recognizing Denmark's king as the king of Iceland on the condition that

this arrangement be reexamined after 25 years. Until 1944 the state was called the Kingdom of Iceland.

When the 25 years had elapsed, Denmark was in no position to influence the Icelanders' decision to sever all royal ties between the two countries—it had been overrun by German troops in 1940. The British occupied Iceland that same year. In July 1941 the United States and Iceland concluded an agreement that provided for the stationing of American troops to protect the island. On June 17, 1944, following a referendum, the Republic of Iceland was proclaimed at Thingvellir, the venerated spot where the Althingi had been first assembled more than 1,000 years earlier. The US was the first country to recognize Icelandic independence.

A swimming pool in Reykjavík with thermal baths

Icelandic parliamentary election (the Social Democratic Party, the National Awakening, the People's Alliance and the Women's List).

The earlier conservative government of Geir Haarde collapsed in January 2009 in the midst of Iceland's worst economic disaster in history. The new government was led by Jóhanna Sigurðardóttir of the Social-Democratic Alliance. The daughter of a prominent labor leader, she had been an Icelandair flight attendant for 30 years and union organizer for its employees. She served as social affairs minister in several governments since 1987, strengthening the social welfare system and widening housing opportunities for the poor.

The April 2009 parliamentary elections were an opportunity for voters to take revenge on all politicians who had been tainted by the economic meltdown that laid Iceland low beginning in the fall of 2008. It brought a sharp swing to the left. The Social-Democratic Alliance was the big winner. In the campaign it had presented the European Union and the euro as Iceland's panacea and pledged to apply for EU membership within 18 months and to adopt the euro within 4 years.

The party, led by Arni Pall Amason, lost substantial support in the 2013 Icelandic parliamentary election, becoming the third largest in Alþingi. The Social Democrats were given only 12.85% (down 16.94%) of the votes and 9 seats (a decline of 11). The party, which was punished for the economic pain that was necessary for the country's recovery, moved into the opposition. The electoral collapse of the two ex-governing parties was the largest by any government since Iceland became a republic in 1944. In July 2009 parliament voted narrowly (33 to 28) in favor of seeking EU membership, but in 2013 plans for the EU were put on the back burner. Polls indicated that most Icelanders oppose entry. Electoral turnout is always high in Iceland: 85% in 2009 and 81.5% in April 2013.

The party nearly lost all its representatives at the 2016 Icelandic parliamentary election, where it polled 5.7%. In the 2017 Icelandic parliamentary election the party won 7 seats with 12.1% of the vote, but lost one of their seats and got 9.9% of the vote in the 2021 Icelandic parliamentary election.

The partner in the former governing coalition but now in opposition was the Left-Green Movement, also known by its short-form name Vinstri græn (VG). This eco-socialist political party, led by Katrin Jakobsdóttir, garnered 10.8% of the votes (down from 21.7%) and seven seats (a decline of four) in 2013. It is skeptical about entry into the EU for reasons widely shared in the country: that it would lose control of its exclusive fishing waters and of its other natural resources.

General Secretary Gorbachev and President Reagan in Reykjavík   White House photo by Terry Arthur

However, after the collapse of the coalition government and snap parliamentary elections in 2017, the party increased its seats in parliament to 11 and became the second-largest party, forming a three-party coalition with the Independence Party and Progressive Party. The party chair Katrín Jakobsdóttir became the 28th prime minister of Iceland. The party lost three seats in the 2021 parliamentary elections, but stayed in government. After the 2021 parliamentary election, it is the third largest party in the parliament, with 8 members of 63 in total. It is also the leading party in the new government which is, just like the previous one, a tri-party coalition of the Independence Party, the Progressive Party and the Left-Green Movement, also headed by Prime Minister Katrín Jakobsdóttir.

The Progressive Party (Icelandic: Framsóknarflokkurinn, FSF), is a slightly left-of-center party which has traditionally represented agrarian interests. It supports NATO, although it sought the removal of American troops from Iceland as soon as "conditions" permitted; they left in 2006. It opposed entry into the EU. In the recent past, its ex-leader Sigmundur Davíð Gunnlaugsson, who at age 38 was the country's youngest prime minister, had advocated union with Norway and the adoption of the Norwegian krone. It maintained a daily newspaper, *Timinn* (1917—1996), and it was the first Icelandic party to use TV advertising. For most of its history, the Progressive Party has governed with the Independence Party. Since November 30, 2017, the party has been a coalition partner in the Katrín Jakobsdóttir government.

The Independence Party (D) is a conservative political party in Iceland. It is currently the largest party in the Alþingi, with 17 seats. Since 2013, there have been three different coalition governments in Iceland, all of which have included the Independence Party. Every Independence Party leader has also, at some point, held the office of Prime Minister. The current chairman of the party is Bjarni Benediktsson, who served as prime minister of Iceland from January to November 2017. He has been the leader of the Icelandic Independence Party since 2009 and served as Minister of Finance and Economic Affairs from 2013 to 2017, a post he later retained under Katrín Jakobsdóttir and held until his resignation in October 2023. He is the current Minister for Foreign Affairs. The Independence Party was an undisputed loser in 2009 since it was in power as the economy disintegrated. It lost a third of its voters and suffered its worst result since the party's founding 80 years earlier. For the first time in 18 years, it was not in the government. Its then newly appointed leader, Bjarni Benediktsson, put on a brave face: "We lost this time, but we will win again later." He was right. In the April 2013 elections, the party garnered 26.7% of the votes (up 3%) and 19 seats (up 3). It was in the governing coalition enjoying a comfortable majority with the Progressives. The party's program is based on the market economy and membership in NATO, but it staunchly opposed joining the EU. The two governing parties promised to forgive or renegotiate mortgage loans and end austerity. A longstanding member of the International Democrat Union, in September 2023 the Independence Party obtained associate member status in the European People's Party.

Of the 15 parties that ran in the 2013 elections (up from 7 in 2009) 2 new parties did well. Bright Future, led by Guðmundur Steingrímsson, captured 8.25% of the votes and six seats. The Pirates, a party

Iceland

A fishing catch

expectations but still came in third with a respectable 14.5% (10 seats), behind the Left-Greens (15.9%, also 10 seats). The governmental majority was razor-thin and also included a new liberal Reform (or Revival) Party (10.5%, 7 seats), and the Bright Future Party (7.2%, 4 seats). The Progressives received a mere 11.5% (down from 24.4%) and lost 11 of the 19 seats they previously held. For all the prime minister's calls for "a strong government and no experiments," the future of the coalition was far from certain. Among other issues, the Independence Party's anti-EU stance clashes with the Reform Party's pronounced pro-EU preferences.

The poor showing of Social Democratic forces in the election helped usher in the creation of a new Socialist Party of Iceland, announced on May 1 (International Labor Day), 2017. It describes itself as "the party of wage earners and all those who suffer from want, invisibility and abjection."

The Bright Future party lost all of its Althing seats in the 2017 election. It did not present any lists in the 2021 parliamentary elections.

The September 2021 parliamentary elections were historic because women won almost 48% of the seats following a recount. The Conservatives (Independence Party) emerged as victors winning 24.39% of votes (16 seats). Following the elections, the Independence Party, the Progressive Party, and the Left-Green Movement of the ruling coalition government negotiated to continue cooperation. The coalition talks focused on energy and climate issues. They agreed to continue in office with Katrín Jakobsdóttir remaining Prime Minister.

The President

The president of the republic is the head of state and performs primarily ceremonial functions. However, he or she can play an important role in coordinating coalition talks after a parliamentary election. Presidents are elected directly for a four-year term, and there have been only five presidents since the establishment of the republic in 1944.

Ragnar Grímsson won his third term in June 2004 with almost 86% of the votes. Nevertheless, turnout was only 64%. This was 20% below that of the previous election, and more than a fifth of the ballots were cast blank. In January 2010 he revealed the reserve power a president has when he vetoed a law adopted by parliamentary vote the last day of 2009 requiring a $5.8 billion reimbursement to Britain and the Netherlands. This was only the second time in history an Icelandic president has withheld his signature from a law. This opened the way to the country's first referendum in March 2010. He is a political

calling for freer access to the Internet, better transparency in government, and more participatory democracy, got 5.1% of the votes and three seats.

The Pirates' fortunes improved after the political earthquake that brought about the resignation of Prime Minister Sigmundur Gunnlaugsson in April 2016 and his replacement by his Progressive Party's vice chairman, Sigurdur Ingi Johannsson. Sigmundur Gunnlaugsson was implicated in the Panama Papers scandal after he had set up a company in the British Virgin Islands with the help of Mossack Fonseca, the Panamanian law firm facilitating offshore investments that hid huge profits from the investors' tax authorities. Protesters accused him of a conflict of interest because the company held interests in failed Icelandic banks, over which he was to provide oversight. Because the rest of Icelanders were subject to tough financial controls, they were particularly irate at their prime minister. Thousands of people

took to the street, banging pots in demonstrations reminiscent of 2009 and demanding the prime minister's resignation. The whole affair strengthened the Pirates' standing before the fall 2016 elections.

The elections provided a jolt of excitement, partly because of a solid performance of the Pirates coupled with a poor showing of the Progressive Party and partly because in the scandal-charged atmosphere it took over two months to form a new government. Leader of the victorious Independent Party (29% of votes and 21 seats), Finance Minister Bjarni Benediktsson, had been listed in the Panama Papers as having had a stake in an offshore company, precisely the transgression that cost the previous prime minister his job. He managed to deflect the criticism, but it took four attempts to create a center-right coalition and only after two left-wing attempts had not succeeded. One of them was led by the Pirate Party that failed to meet the heightened maverick who is frequently in dispute with the government. But his popularity was again demonstrated in 2012, when he was reelected unopposed for a record fifth term. While he announced in early 2016 that he would not seek reelection in June, the political crisis stemming from the Panama Papers revelations and the resignation of Prime Minister Sigmundur Gunnlaugsson prompted him to change his mind in order to provide some continuity. However, once a number of viable candidates decided to run and his polling numbers turned out to be weak, he eventually opted to drop out of the race after all. His 20 years of presidency came to an end.

All candidates ran as independents. A history lecturer, Guðni Th. Jóhannesson won a plurality of 39.08% and became Iceland's sixth president on August 1, 2016. The results were announced on what happened to be Guðni's 48th birthday. The new president is opposed to Iceland joining the EU, has advanced degrees from prestigious British universities, and translated four Stephen King books into Icelandic. He promptly left for the Euro 2016 soccer match between England and Iceland's team, whose surprising success buoyed the nation. (It was also responsible for some 10% of the nation absent on election day because they all went to support their team in France.)

Local Government and the Judiciary

Iceland is a unitary state. For administrative purposes, it is divided into 23 rural districts. There are also 215 parishes and 14 incorporated towns. A subject of hot debate is the unceasing influx of rural Icelanders, especially the young, into the capital city of Reykjavik. About 70% of the total population lives in or around the capital.

The judiciary consists of district and lower magistrates appointed by the minister of justice. The Supreme Court, with eight permanent members, is the highest court in the land.

NATO and Defense

Although in 1918 the newly independent Iceland intended to follow a policy of "eternal neutrality," the tense world political situation in the late 1940s prompted it to join NATO. Polls indicate that about 80% of Icelanders are in favor of NATO membership; it has no army, navy or air force of its own, but it is an important member. It occupies a strategic position on the maritime and air routes between the northern seas and the North Atlantic sea-lanes so critical to NATO.

Its geo-economic significance is enhanced by the reality of global warming, which will open up the north to increased shipping as ice melts. It sits at the mouth of the Arctic

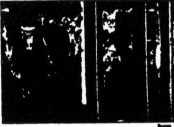

Ocean and is ideally located for the transshipment of cargoes to the Barents Sea or through the Northwest Passage in northern Canada to the Bering Sea. It has at least three potential deep fjord sites. Perhaps it is no accident that China maintains the largest embassy in Reykjavik.

As its contribution to the common defense, Iceland permitted the stationing of US forces on its territory at the NATO air base of Keflavik, located 30 miles (48 km) from the capital city. The size of that force continuously dwindled after the end of the Cold War. In 1993 the Americans announced the withdrawal of their F-15 interceptors and Orion P3Cs, and a year later, eight more F-15 fighters were brought home. When the Pentagon, citing Iceland's reduced importance as a strategic outpost, announced in 2003 a decision to withdraw its four remaining F-15s, along with five rescue helicopters and two refueling planes, the Icelandic government strongly objected. Iceland saw them as essential to its air defense and, more important, a symbol of America's commitment to defend the nation. Feelings were also bruised because Iceland's leaders were informed of the decision but not consulted about it.

In 2004 this Iceland Defense Force (IDF) numbered 1,658 US troops (of whom 960 were Navy, 650 Air Force, and 48 Marines). There were also 16 Dutch naval troops to man one P-3C surveillance airplane. In 2006 the Pentagon announced as a part of its worldwide base reductions and troop redeployment the final withdrawal of four Air Force fighter jets and a rescue helicopter squadron. More than 1,200 military personnel and 100 Defense Department civilian employees were brought home.

This move eliminated over 600 Icelandic employees' jobs. One idea in 2010 to bring those jobs back to the Keflavik area was to allow a Dutch-owned company to transfer a fleet of Russian-made fighter jets to the base for use by national air forces as mock enemy aircraft in combat training exercises.

After approving the plan, the government reversed itself in a matter of hours. Such equipment and troop reductions hurt the Icelandic economy since the US paid about $260 million in annual rent, which amounted to 8% of Iceland's total foreign earnings, and employed many local people. The Icelandic government was considering picking up the tab for the costs if the Americans remained. The redeployments leave the country with no military defenses, and this created understandable tension between the two allies.

While the IDF had the responsibility of defending Iceland from foreign attack, Icelanders are responsible for maintaining order at home. There are two groups of personnel who protect the cities. They do it well because there is less crime within the country than in the US. These forces are the unarmed 300-member police force and the 12-member Viking Squad. This squad is the Icelandic equivalent to the American Delta Force.

Its troops are heavily armed and well trained as antiterrorist commandos. Iceland also has a coast guard of 130 sailors operating 3 patrol craft.

The IDF had the mission to patrol the strategically important waters 140 nautical miles from its coasts. The American aircraft there included AWACS. Submarine-detection devices (SOSUS) under the water

Iceland

were maintained from the base. American forces have two radar stations in southern Iceland, and Icelandic civilians man two new radar stations in the north.

The Icelandic government long ago established several important limitations on the US base: There could be no nuclear weapons, even on US ships that enter Icelandic waters. In 1985 the Icelandic parliament declared the coast to be a "nuclear-free zone." Reports in 1985 that there may have been American contingency plans to deploy such weapons in time of crisis and that Marines who guard the base had manuals dealing with the handling of atomic weapons created some concern. Then-secretary of state George Shultz went to Iceland to assure the government that no measure of any kind would ever be taken without its permission. A second limitation was vague: The weaponry at the base had to be defensive, not offensive. When the two modern AWACS radar planes were introduced to the base, some critics feared that they could be used as command posts of an offensive war.

Until the late 1990s, the stationing of American soldiers in Iceland was a continuous bone of contention among the Icelanders. A vocal minority regarded their presence as a limitation of Icelandic sovereignty and openly advocated a termination of the bilateral agreement of 1951 providing for the American defense of Iceland. In 1973 the government of Ólafur Jóhannesson even considered closing the American-manned NATO base, but nothing came of the matter. Some Icelanders feared the cultural influence of American soldiers and dependents on Icelandic life, although this fear diminished as American force levels were scaled down.

In order not to irritate the sensitive and nationalistic Icelanders, the US maintained a low profile, although Americans were given considerable freedom of the country. American TV at the base was once available to Icelanders, but the opposition to it was such that cable TV was installed on the base. American radio could still be heard in Reykjavik, though. US forces and their families had to live within the military compound. Unless one of the spouses was an Icelander, soldiers could not leave the base in uniform or remain outside after midnight without special permission. All jobs that were not strictly military had to be given to Icelanders. Also, Iceland was perhaps the only country in the world in which the only banned alcoholic beverage was beer. Until this ban was finally lifted in 1989, American GIs had to be careful not to violate that unusual prohibition off base.

Instead of the usual military guards at base gates, there were Icelandic customs officials charged with protecting the country's stringent import restrictions. Americans could leave the base with no more than two packs of cigarettes, and one had to be open. Picnickers were not allowed to bring raw meat off base for barbecues and had to file a list of edible goods they took out of the installation.

Some Americans showed little understanding for the particular sensitivity of Icelanders. A land with only 320,000 inhabitants, with just over a half-century of independence but with a long tradition of relative isolation, is perhaps more inclined to overreact to outside influences that are not entirely wanted. Yet most Icelanders see no alternative to NATO membership and protection by allied forces. They would never dream of creating the kind of well-armed military units that would make foreign help unnecessary.

The Icelandic government has decided, however, to change its traditionally passive role within NATO. It has had very little military expertise and has therefore been unable to make competent assessments of the strategic situation as it affects Iceland. It has not sent representatives to the NATO Military Committee or Nuclear Planning Group, and the U.S. has always paid its required contributions to the NATO Infrastructure Fund. On April 1, 1985, it reorganized and upgraded its Defense Department of the Ministry of Foreign Affairs, which handles not only relations with the IDF but also with NATO headquarters and defense ministers. This reorganization, which is the greatest change in Iceland's military affairs since 1944, met with no public controversy.

By the end of the century, almost everybody favored the bilateral relationship. But the American flag was lowered for the last time at the US base on September 30, 2006, and the last US forces were withdrawn after 65 years of military presence on the island. This leaves Iceland with no military defenses and a coast guard of only 130 persons. The Americans promised to defend it as a NATO ally.

Foreign Relations

Since World War II, Iceland has established diplomatic relations with more than 76 countries. It was the first country in 1991 officially to recognize the independence of the Baltic states and was among the first to recognize the Yugoslav breakaway republics of Slovenia and Croatia. It sent a medical team to Bosnia, development aid to Africa, and food via the Red Cross to Russians around Murmansk. It has joined a number of international organizations. In 1946 it became a member of the UN. It is also a charter member of the Council of Europe, the OECD, and many of the institutions associated with the UN, such as the IMF. It joined EFTA (European

Free Trade Association) in 1970 and has had a free-trade agreement with the EU since 1972.

Iceland's geographic position has, for the most part, placed it out of the normal travel routes. This may change as the Northwest Passage through international waters in northern Canada opens up to shipping. In the recent past, there have been a few occasions when the world turned its eyes toward this island country. In 1973 then-presidents Nixon of the US and Pompidou of France met with Soviet leader Brezhnev to discuss world issues. Once again, in 1986, the leaders of the world's two most powerful countries came together in the Reykjavik summit. Ronald Reagan and Mikhail Gorbachev pushed diplomats aside and met face to face to discuss breathtaking visions of nuclear disarmament. In 1991 Iceland exercised some moral authority by supporting independence moves in the Baltic states within the USSR. It has contributed to peacekeeping operations in Afghanistan, where it took responsibility for air traffic control, and in 2003 it quietly approved of the US-UK war effort in Iraq and subsequently pledged nearly $4 million in humanitarian and reconstruction assistance to Iraq.

In 1972 Bobby Fischer defeated Boris Spassky in Reykjavik in the most celebrated chess match in history. While Spassky was advised between games by 35 Russian grand masters, Fischer had only his notebook. It was the first time since 1945 that a world champion was not from the Soviet Union. He gained such hero status in Iceland that parliament granted him citizenship and a passport in 2005 to protect him from deportation to the US. This allowed the eccentric chess genius to immigrate to Iceland, whose government refused to notify the US when he traveled abroad. Washington had issued a deportation order because Fischer had disobeyed international sanctions in 1992 by playing an exhibition rematch with Spassky in Yugoslavia, earning $3 million, while Serbia was engaged in a bloody war in Bosnia. This was his last public match. He passed away in Iceland in January 2008.

ECONOMY

Fishing and Agriculture

The most prominent characteristic of the Icelandic economy has always been its lop-sided dependence upon the fishing industry, one of the world's most efficient and profitable. Exports accounted for over half of its GDP, and 40% of its export earnings are from fish and fish processing, which provide a tenth of employment. It is heavily dependent upon cod, which accounts for 40% of fish exports. Its major fish markets are the EU, which takes about 60% of its fish and fish products, and the United States, which imposes almost no tariff duties on the fish. The importance of this single product has been so great that Iceland has a separate Ministry of Fisheries. Iceland has handled its marine resources adeptly and has prevented excessive overfishing.

In 1986 another segment of Iceland's fish industry was highlighted: Saboteurs from an environmentalist group Sea Shepherd Conservation Society, operating primarily out of the US and Canada, wrecked Iceland's only plant for processing whale oil and by-products and sank two of Iceland's four whaling ships. They charged that the country conducts illegal commercial whaling under the guise of scientific research. In 1992 Iceland left the International Whaling Commission and announced plans to resume commercial whaling. It rejoined in 2001 after concluding that it could best influence the whaling debate from within the organization. It resumed whale hunting, arguing that stocks of minke and fin whales in its coastal waters are robust enough to support it.

Whaling is economically unimportant for Iceland, but it remains a controversial issue. Icelandic fishermen contend that the protected whales compete with them for the decreasing fish stocks in their waters. Marine scientists analyzed the stomach contents of the whales scheduled for killing to determine how much fish minke whales eat. They estimate that the 43,000 whales living close to the island eat a total of 1 to 2 million tons of fish each year. A more precise figure would help Iceland manage its fish stocks better. In 2006 Iceland's authorities issued permits to catch 30 minke whales and 9 rarer fin whales on top of the 40 minkes already killed annually for "scientific purposes." In 2015 Iceland's largest whaling company, Hvalur HF, killed 155 fin whales, for a total of 706 since 2006. However, in 2016 it announced that no whales would be killed that year due to the difficulty in exporting the meat to Japan, where almost all the meat is sent. (Icelanders themselves do not eat meat from fin whales.)

The giant mammals have spawned a lucrative new industry in Iceland: whale watching. In 1949 only 100 tourists came to observe them, but by 2016 they attracted more than 200,000 tourists each year. This specialized tourism generates around $15 million annually and continues to grow.

The country so depends upon fishing that it was understandable for it to want to extend its fishing limit around its own coasts in order to reduce the fishing activities of other countries in these waters. It did so, first to 4 nautical miles in 1952, then to 12, 50, and finally 200 miles (350 km) in

Source: *NZZ am Sonntag*

1975. Each extension resulted in conflicts called "cod wars" with Britain, whose fishing fleets also worked in Icelandic waters.

In 1976 the third "cod war" flared up with particular intensity; Iceland sent coast guard gun boats against British trawlers, and warning shots were fired, boats were rammed, and trawler wires were cut. Britain responded by sending two naval frigates and surveillance flights in and over Iceland's self-declared waters. Iceland even temporarily broke diplomatic relations with London. Finally, an agreement was reached in the summer of 1976, when Britain accepted Iceland's conditions on cod fishing. Bilateral tensions remained, and not until 2006 did an Icelandic prime minister visit the UK.

Although the economy has become more diverse and less vulnerable, branching into tourism, manufacturing, and financial services, the fishing industry is still important. Iceland faced a dilemma since June 2010, when it became a formal candidate for membership in the EU. To qualify, it would have to participate in the EU's common fisheries policy, which sets national quotas. Icelanders hate this, and a poll in June 2010 revealed that 58% wanted the government to withdraw its application. When a couple of months later the EU and Norway attacked Iceland's decision to fish for mackerel in its own waters, it pressed ahead and brought in its bumper catch. Some spoke of a "mackerel war."

Agriculture is still important, although it provides employment for only 4% of the

workforce. Sheep-raising was formerly the nation's most important economic activity, and there are still some 800,000 sheep. In addition, there are over 50,000 cattle. Few grains are grown, although some can thrive in the climate. Geothermally heated greenhouses are a growing business, producing especially tomatoes, cucumbers, and flowers. Although the climate is too harsh for grapes, an increasingly popular (though expensive at $20 a bottle) wine, Kvöldsól (Midnight Sun), made of wild bilberries and crowberries picked in the summer, is made.

Energy and Living Standards

Much of the rest of Iceland's energy needs are derived from two renewable sources: hydroelectric and thermal, which generate five times what the country needs. Indeed, about 80% of its total energy and all of its electricity comes from such sources. That enables Icelanders to use twice as much electricity per capita as Americans and still not harm the economy or environment. As an island, its electrical power cannot be exported easily. Icelanders have learned to tap the hot lava and waters under their soil. Today, 99% of the home and hot water heating in Greater Reykjavik, where 60% of the country's population lives, comes from these sources. Four-fifths of all Icelandic homes are heated geothermally, with hot water being piped around towns and villages from nearby boreholes. Geothermal energy constitutes a fourth of electricity

Iceland

produced in the country, and almost all of the rest is renewable.

A pleasant by-product of hydro and geothermal energy is that these are "clean" and "green" sources. Therefore, Iceland is free of the air pollution and urban grime that are produced by fossil fuels. The country has established the goal of eliminating the use of fossil fuels entirely by perfecting hydrogen fuel cells, which produce energy by combining hydrogen with oxygen from the air. This would make Iceland the first nation in the world to derive all of its energy from clean, renewable sources. One pilot program involves three buses powered by such cells in the Reykjavik city transport system.

Industry now employs more people than agriculture and fishing combined. Some of it still processes fish or agricultural products. Machine and building industries are increasing in importance, but the country's almost total lack of wood and metals hampers the operations of such industries.

The state-owned power company, Landsvirkjun, sells only 17% of its electricity to households and local industry. The rest goes mainly to aluminum smelters owned by foreign companies. With about 90% of its energy potential unused, Iceland is well equipped to house such energy intensive industries as aluminum production. The Icelandic Aluminum Company, a wholly owned subsidiary of the Swiss firm Alusuisse, imports ore from abroad and processes it into finished metal. By 2016, aluminum and alloys constituted about 40% of Iceland's exports. International competition has not dampened hopes of expanding this industry.

Icelanders are divided. Environmentalists oppose the construction of hydropower to fuel the aluminum smelters, which require enormous amounts of electricity to operate. For example, to build the Kárahnjúkar Dam to block the Jökulsá á Dal River in 2006, 22 square miles of wilderness had to be flooded so that electricity for a new Alcoa Fjardaál smelter could be produced. The emotional issue of how to balance nature and development dominated the 2007 elections. Proponents argue that such economic activity is revitalizing the underpopulated east and providing jobs for 15% of the region's workforce. Polls indicate that a majority of Icelanders support it for that reason. Proponents also point out that Iceland has lots of clean energy and is therefore uniquely able to produce aluminum. To sweeten the pill, the government created the huge Vatnajökull National Park in 2007 to offset the wilderness lost to Kárahnjúkar.

An Italian company helped build a $2 billion hydroelectric system and aluminum smelter, completed by 2008. The world's largest aluminum company, Alcoa (American), also built a smelter. This was the largest single private-sector investment in Iceland's history.

Traditionally when fish catches and markets were good, the country experienced booms that encouraged the strong trade unions to demand higher wages. Indeed, Iceland loses far more working days to strikes per 1,000 employees than any other industrialized country in the world. When the economy turns sour, then Icelanders tend to continue living beyond their means. They did not want to give up their relatively high standard of living, which was generally on par with other Nordic countries. Before financial disaster struck, it had the world's fourth-highest per-capita GDP ($63,000 in 2007, ahead of the US with $45,600); by 2010 it had slipped to 26th place ($39,540). GDP in 2009 declined by 7% and another 1.6% in 2010, but it rose by 2% the next two years. The public debt ballooned from 29% of GDP in 2007 to 116% in 2010, but it had declined to 65.6% by 2013. That percentage ballooned if one included bank debts: 221%. Inflation peaked about 17%, but it had dropped to 4% by 2013.

Iceland GDP expanded 6.078 % YoY in Mar 2023. Icelanders no longer find themselves poorer. Tourism, energy, and IT businesses have replaced banks as the source of jobs and activity. The economy is visibly improving.

Almost 90% of all homes are owned by those who occupy them. This is perhaps the world's highest percentage of owner-occupied buildings, despite skyrocketing real estate prices, which doubled between 2004 and 2006. However, the economic crisis left many homeowners struggling to hang on to their dwellings. Real estate values plummeted, and many have mortgages denominated in foreign currencies. An estimated fourth of households are said to be on the brink of bankruptcy. Even in the best of times, the maintenance of prosperity is a challenge for a largely barren country of active volcanoes, lava fields, and glaciers, which must import almost everything it consumes.

After having experienced the highest inflation rate in Europe (12% in 2009, down to 4% in 2013), it abolished the indexing of wages (which tied them to the inflation rate) to help bring it under control. The continuing volatility of the krona was a major reason 7 out of 10 Icelanders said in a 2012 poll that they favored the adoption of another currency; they were split evenly between adopting the euro and the Canadian dollar. Tourism grew fast and more than doubled since 1990 to about 350,000 visitors a year by 2005, more than its own population. The collapse of the krona in 2008 stimulated foreign tourism even more. The boom in this sector helps provide some Icelanders with work. The tourist boom was brought to an abrupt standstill by the pandemic, starting in 2020. Unemployment fell from 10% in 2009 to ca 3.9% in 2023.

EU Membership and the Euro

In the 1990s interest in full EU membership came alive in all Nordic countries, which heavily depend on trade with Europe. Iceland was always the wariest of the EU, fearing that the sole prop for its economy—fishing—could be endangered. It has a 200-mile marine boundary and manages its fish stocks well. Through EEA (European Economic Area), Iceland is not isolated from the EU because it enjoys free trade in all things but fish and agriculture. There was growing interest in full EU membership, especially in the business community.

Iceland made a move in the direction of harmony with the EU by deregulating its banking industry to permit more competition; in 1990 its first privately owned bank, Íslandsbanki, came into existence. Shares in state banks and telecoms were sold to the private sector. The last two state banks and Iceland Telecom were put up for sale in 2001. The result for a while was that the economy steadily grew. Icelandic banks, led by the three largest (Glitnir, Kaupthing, and Landsbanki), aggressively supported a wave of Icelandic takeovers all over Europe, acquiring companies at an astonishing rate. They overexpanded into Scandinavia and the UK and opened branches in China. Iceland became a friendly place for financiers and was not subject to EU tax scrutiny. Corporate profits are taxed at only 18% (personal income at 36%), the third-lowest in the OECD, behind Ireland and Hungary. Some Icelanders were uneasy about the impact such huge economic changes had on the country. One observer argued, "The law of the jungle has been dominating our business life." This fear was justified.

Membership in the EEA provided an important impetus to liberalize the economy and temporarily blunted the debate on actually entering the EU. EEA membership enables Icelanders to live and work across the EU. Support for EU membership grew. Critics point out that Iceland must abide by many EU laws and regulations without having any input into them.

Polls in 2008 showed that 70% favored joining. One of the most convincing arguments in favor was currency stability. This was especially true in 2009, when the krona was worth about 40% less than in the previous year. No wonder the parliament voted 33 to 28 in July 2009 to begin accession negotiations immediately. One year later, after prolonged financial

Kristján Jóhannsson

turmoil and banking crisis, 58% opposed EU member-ship, and only a third favored it. Even 60% of the business community was against it. Bailouts of the euro and enforced austerity on small member states in 2010–2011 made the common currency seem like a trap, not a blessing. Hostility toward what was perceived as an uncaring Europe was focused on the EU. The European Commission's recommendation on February 24, 2010, to begin accession talks failed to change the majority opinion. Opposition parties exploited disputes with EU countries, especially Britain and the Netherlands, to stoke anti-EU sentiment. Icelanders' famous spirit of independence reasserted itself. By 2013 talks on joining had been largely suspended. After the 2016 parliamentary election, the center-right government announced that it would not be until the end of the parliament's term before a referendum on joining the EU might possibly be held.

One of the several explanations for why Iceland has not joined the European Union concerns the fishing—the importance of the fishing industry to Iceland's economy and the perception that EU membership (and its Common Fisheries Policy) will have an adverse effect on the fishing industry.

Kreppa: The Bottom Falls Out

The economy was ripe for a correction. But the credit crunch stemming from the US and infecting Europe in 2008 triggered a crisis in Iceland, even though Icelandic banks had not acquired the kind of mortgage-backed investments that shook up the American and European banking systems. The banks did build up an excessive level of foreign debt equivalent to 10 times

the tiny country's GDP. This overextension went far beyond the small depositor base at home and was a catastrophe waiting to happen. Standard and Poor reduced its credit rating to junk status, and investor confidence in the country fell sharply.

Since it must import almost everything, it has always had a huge current account deficit (the difference between the import and export of goods and services), that in 2008 amounted to 16% of GDP (down from 26% in 2006). In the spring of 2008, the krona lost almost 30% of its value compared with the euro, and the slide continued in the next year to 40%. Inflation ballooned to 12% in 2009, and the central bank had to raise interest rates to an astonishing 15.5% in order to curb such inflation and shore up the currency. Unemployment stood at 1.5% in 2006, but in 2009 it reached a shocking 9%.

Dangerous recession was in the air. Although Iceland has never defaulted on its debts, the Nordic central banks took the unprecedented step of setting up a €1.5-billion emergency fund for Iceland's central bank to use to save its banks. The government appealed to the banks to rein in their expansion plans, cut back acquisitions, and build a stronger deposit base.

In October 2008 the country's wealth engines, the banks, collapsed; 85% of the banking system became insolvent in a matter of days. They took the currency down with them. According to the International Monetary Fund (IMF), this was the largest banking failure in history relative to the economy's size. Panic spread. To avoid national bankruptcy, the government groveled abroad and borrowed about $11 billion: $2.1 billion from the IMF and $8 billion more from the Nordic and other countries. This amounts to about $33,000 for each of the island's residents. The government even considered borrowing $4 billion from the Russians, the first nation to offer Iceland help.

Icelanders will be increasingly wary of the success of high-flying businessmen and bankers who seem to build up financial empires overnight and then leave the island in financial turmoil. The three main commercial banks—Kaupthing, Glitnir, and Landsbanki—had been aggressively buying Scandinavian and British companies, and by 2006 Icelandic businesses employed more than 100,000 people abroad, 70% of them in Britain. Their assets were about 10 times the size of the country's economy. They have had to learn to restrain their expansionist impulses to conform more closely with the small domestic economy. The government seized them in October 2008, when they had accumulated more than $60 billion in overseas debt. It negotiated a deal to recapitalize them in July 2009

with an injection of $2.1 billion. They are new banks now. Control of two of them (Islandsbanki and New Kaupthing) was given to creditors. New Kaupthing became Arion Bank. New Landsbanki was more complicated. Capital controls restrict the movement of currency in and out of Iceland.

Public hostility toward bankers was strong. In 2012 the former heads of Kaupthing were charged with fraud and market manipulation, and more than 150 other business people were being investigated for white-collar crimes. Some faced trials, but only a handful were ever convicted. However, the crackdown continued. In 2013 four former Kaupthing executives, including the chairman and CEO, were sentenced to multiple-year prison terms. Litigation and foreign claims on the banks will continue for a long time.

Few Icelanders could believe how far and how fast their country had fallen. Their self-confidence was shattered, and thousands of them went into streets to join the only mass demonstrations to shake the country since the debate about NATO membership in 1949. In 2009 these brought down Geir Haarde's conservative Independence government, which was blamed for the mess. They became the first leader and government to lose power as a direct result of the global economic crisis. Haarde, who studied economics at Brandeis University and has an MA from SAIS at Johns Hopkins, and former prime minister and central bank governor Davíð Oddsson, along with other officials and regulators, were charged in an official April 2010 report with "extreme negligence" in the run-up to the crisis. A summary of the 2,300-page Truth Report was handed to the special prosecutor for use in a criminal investigation. A group of actors publicly read every word of the report aloud and around the clock from the stage of the Reykjavik City Theater; it took five days to finish.

In September 2010, by a narrow 33–30 vote, parliament indicted Haarde and ordered that a special constitutional court be set up to try him. He was the first politician in the world to be put on trial for his role in the 2008 financial crisis. He was charged with doing too little to protect the country from the banking crisis and for failing to keep his cabinet informed of the developments. This demonstrated how divided opinion is over the question of whether politicians should be legally accountable for economic crises. Could a single politician be held responsible for the complicated banking crash? Many people asked if this was fair. The action further poisoned the tense political environment, although anger softened as the economy slowly recovered.

Iceland

Haarde was found guilty of doing too little, but he was acquitted of three more serious charges. He thereby avoided a two-year jail sentence. Haarde called the court's judgment "absurd" and "laughable." He claimed his accusers were out to "settle scores" and were vindictive and "misapplying hindsight." He said, "Very few politicians criticized the growth of the banking system." Icelanders were generally disappointed about the trial, which produced no apologies or admissions of guilt. Nevertheless, voters put Haarde's Independence Party back into power in the April 2013 elections.

In 2009 the Sigurðardóttir government agreed to restructure or write off the $70 billion debt. A bare majority (33 to 30) in parliament agreed to pay Britain and the Netherlands about $5.4 billion for the money their governments had reimbursed to their own 400,000 depositors when Kaupthing's online bank, Icesave, went under. This amounted to half the country's annual GDP.

That was the last straw. In January 2010 President Grimsson cast only the second legislative veto in Iceland's history and ordered that the question be submitted to the country's first-ever referendum. Critics claimed this huge payment would penalize taxpayers for the recklessness of a private bank and that Icelanders would be saddled with higher taxes and budget cuts for decades in order to pay off the debt. It is not surprising that, in the March 2010 referendum, turnout was 63%, and more than 93% of voters rejected the plan. Only 1.6% approved.

This vote was nonbinding. But the fact that the prime minister and government had appealed to their countrymen not to vote in the referendum helped weaken their authority even further. This was just at a time when Iceland needed strong leadership to push through painful budget cuts. The government renegotiated more favorable terms with the two countries and again put the question to a referendum in April 2011: 60% rejected it a second time on the grounds that taxpayers should not have to bail out failed private banks. This outcome was in spite of a Dutch warning that EU entry could be disrupted by a no vote.

The matter went to the EFTA court, although the government claimed that at least 90% of the sum would be repaid out of Landsbanki's remaining assets. The court ruled that Iceland could not be forced to repay the British and Dutch governments. This was an important victory for Iceland, which refused to use taxpayer money to bail out foreign bondholders and depositors. The new government made it clear in 2013 that foreign creditors of the failed banks would have to take a big "haircut." Nevertheless, the UK and the Netherlands filed yet another lawsuit in 2014 seeking a sum two-thirds of Iceland's GDP. The prime minister told them to "forget it."

Iceland is slowly digging itself out of its economic morass. Its growth in 2012 was 2%, faster than the eurozone average. Fitch ratings restored its long-term foreign currency rating to investment grade. It has been relatively unaffected by the euro crisis afflicting Europe. It completed in August 2011 its three-year rescue program, supported by the IMF, which has heaped high praise on Iceland's recovery efforts. This is the basis for renewed access to international capital markets. Its banking sector shows evidence of recovery. A law caps mortgages at 110% of the property value, and the government promises an across-the-board mortgage write-down of 20% and tax relief for mortgage payments. This could be too expensive for the government to manage.

In March 2017 Iceland lifted the remaining capital controls imposed after the crisis. Despite a strong krona (at a nine-year high against the dollar), tourism remains robust, and so do the exports. The tourist boom likely contributes to Reykjavik's rapid rise in real estate and rental prices. Airbnb has been blamed for pushing room prices up so much that the young locals can ill afford to live in the capital city. Iceland is once again becoming an attractive investment destination, and the local banks are also becoming active internationally. Icelanders are nervous over a possible repeat of the collapse of 2008, though the economy is more diversified now.

Investments, Welfare, and Transport

In April 2013 China signed a free-trade treaty with Iceland to eliminate most tariffs. This was the first such agreement with a European country. Foreign investors are still attracted by Iceland's huge untapped reserves of hydroelectric and geothermal power. In 2011–2012 one of China's richest tycoons, Huang Nubo, made a bid to pay $9 billion to buy 300 square kilometers (118 square miles) of wilderness heathland to build an ecoresort in northern Iceland close to several of the country's most remarkable natural sites. This would have constituted .3% of Iceland's total land area. This prompted heated debate because it would violate rules restricting foreign land ownership. The government said no, but Huang countered with a request for a long-term lease.

Some, including the president, favored the project. But many others were baffled by such a bizarre plan to build a high-end resort, complete with a golf course, in such an isolated area. Many feared it could be a Trojan horse for Chinese strategic interests

Demonstrators protesting Iceland's financial collapse, 2009

Iceland

in and around Iceland, which is a member of NATO and is astride important shipping lanes through the Arctic as polar ice melts. Its ports could be stopping-off places. China also has its eye on Arctic and Icelandic energy resources. The controversy ended unexpectedly when a British billionaire and an advocate of fracking, Jim Ratcliffe, bought two-thirds of the estate in 2016. He promised that his only interest was in conservation, especially of the salmon population. The remaining portion is held by the Icelandic government and minor investors.

The welfare system remains generous though more modest than elsewhere in the Nordic world. Some reforms are bound to be unpopular, such as requiring contributions to pensions and the prospect of raising the official retirement age from

67 to 70. Bright spots in the economy are immense renewable energy resources, a well-educated skilled workforce, a work ethic that makes the 40-hour week almost unheard of, an open and transparent democracy, a predictable legal system, and a convenient mid-Atlantic location.

Iceland has a rather good transportation system for a country of its size compared to population. It has over 7,500 miles (12,343 km) of roads. Although efforts are being made to pave more roads, about 6,750 miles (10,893 km) are still dirt. The country has 4 major and about 50 minor ports and over 100 usable airfields.

Iceland's best-known transportation is a fleet of airplanes that transport passengers over the North Atlantic between Europe and North America. Operating outside of IATA regulations, Icelandair

(called Icelandic Airlines until its merger in 1973 with the country's other airline, Loftleidir) flies passengers for bargain prices. Skyrocketing fuel prices and fierce competition from the major commercial airlines and other cut-rate companies temporarily threw Icelandair's financial balance into the red. But it survives. A smaller airline, Eagle, also has some international routes. A highly successful upstart, WOW Air was founded in 2011, and its passenger capacity exceeded 1.5 million per year. It provided low-cost links to airports throughout Europe and now North America. WOW Air suddenly ceased operations in March 2019. The surge in fuel costs was mainly to blame for the airline's collapse. The WOW Air assets were acquired by United States-based holding company USAerospace Associates, which

The spectacular waterfall Godafoss in northern Iceland

107

Iceland

announced that it intended to relaunch the airline under the same brand. As of 2023, this had not happened.

CULTURE

Icelanders are proud of their Nordic heritage and in many respects are closer to their Viking forebears than any of the other Nordic countries. Their language (which has given the world such words as "saga" and "geyser") is so close to Old Norse that Icelanders can read the 13th- and 14th-century sagas in their original form. It was Icelanders who carried out the most dangerous Viking Sea voyages of all, those through Greenland and beyond to Newfoundland and Labrador. That heritage, combined with 680 years of rule by distant kings and their own isolation and hardships, has made Icelanders fiercely protective of their independence and their cultural purity. An American ambassador to the country, Marshall Brement, who translated and published Icelandic poetry, characterized Icelanders as "inward-looking, perhaps introverted. But above all, they are fiercely devoted to the preservation of their language and culture."

They create their own words for modern things: simi (telephone); ratsja (radar); rafmagn (electricity); tolva (computer). The latter is taken from two words meaning "number" (tol) and "female soothsayer" (volva). There are no dialects in Icelandic. Most of the Nordic literature of the Middle Ages and all of it which is truly world class came from Iceland. Much of our information about the Viking Age and later centuries in Scandinavia itself comes from those Icelandic writings. The people are fascinated with their own past, and there is scarcely a social conversation that does not touch on their history or genealogy. In fact, many families can trace their family trees back almost 30 generations; few peoples in the world are able to give such a complete picture of their heritage. The fact that two-thirds of all births in Iceland are now out of wedlock may make this more difficult in the future. Also possibly complicating such records is the fact that Icelanders almost exclusively use first names in referring to each other. They also keep the old Scandinavian tradition of using the father's first name as the basis for the child's last name rather than continuing with the same last name through generations. There is also a variation for each gender, so a son of Magnus Baldursson could be called Einar Magnusson, while a daughter's name could be Bjork Magnusdottir ("Magnus's daughter").

The vehicle for preserving their national identity and past is their literature, especially their sagas, which tell stories of their gods, heroes, and ancestors. Elves also play a role in Icelanders' imagination. Polls consistently show that a majority either believe in elves or are unwilling to rule out their existence. The 40-odd Icelandic sagas are a towering mixture of history, fiction, genealogy, and encyclopedias that are shrouded in mystery. While it is known that they were produced in 13th- and 14th-century Iceland, it is not known who wrote them. Ex-President Vigdfs, a former language teacher, asserted, "if we lose this identity, which is the language, a great treasure will be lost. We don't have anything from the past except the word."

This is why there was such an outpouring of joy in 1966, when the Danish decided to return the body of ancient writings collected by the Icelandic professor Arni Magnusson (1663–1730). The Danish decision prompted hundreds of Icelanders to assemble before the Danish Embassy in order to praise Denmark and at the same time to sing patriotic songs. When the writings arrived, the inhabitants streamed into the streets to celebrate.

After the sagas, Icelandic literature declined, not to revive until the 19th century. In the 19th and 20th centuries, there appeared a long line of fine poets and novelists. In 1955 an Icelander, Halldor Laxness, born on a farm in 1902, won the Nobel Prize for chronicling the life of modern Iceland. He also wrote Hollywood scripts. Among his most important works is *Independent People*, written in 1946. In 2005 Arnaldur Indriðason's *Silence of the Grave* won the British Crime Writers' Association Gold Dagger Award. Iceland was the featured country in the prestigious Frankfurt Book Fair in 2011. It displayed more new books than China had during its feature the year before. Iceland has an oversized market because the average citizen buys eight books per year. Such reading hunger is what kept alive the consciousness of being Icelandic during the time of Danish rule.

Icelanders are avid readers. They publish more books per capita than any other country, and 3 daily newspapers serve only 244,000 people. The largest, a morning edition called Morgunblaðið, has a circulation of more than 40,000. The other two are Fréttablaðið and DV. Three-fourths of the newspapers distributed daily are now free.

Iceland is the home of world-renowned tenor Kristjan Johannsson, who has performed in every major opera house, including Italy's La Scala, New York's Metropolitan Opera, the Vienna State Opera, the Royal Opera House, and Covent Garden.

Iceland occasionally produces such internationally acclaimed films as *When the Raven Flies* by the Icelandic director Hrafn Gunnlaugsson. This brutally authentic Viking film about violence and revenge captures both the mood of the Norsemen and bleak beauty of the Icelandic landscape.

An international celebrity, whom some tourist guidebooks call the most famous Icelander since Leif Ericson, is the pop star Björk Guðmundsdóttir, known simply as Björk. She won the best actress award at the Cannes film festival in 2000 for her role as a near-blind factory worker in the film *Dancer in the Dark*. She is a forceful political activist, arguing, for example, that Iceland's geothermal power facilities should remain publicly owned and not be sold into foreign hands. She led a movement to demand a referendum to prevent Magma Energy of Canada from making the largest foreign investment in Iceland since the banking crisis.

The country has no daytime TV. It has a state-run radio station. It also has a national television network (RUV), which aims to protect the national culture through higher Icelandic content. It charges a monthly fee that includes radio. It does not broadcast on Thursdays. The reason given is that this weekly blackout encourages more reading, chess-playing and spending time with the family. Network employees admit that the tradition also is designed to give them a day off each week. A live broadcast of President Reagan's arrival in October 1986 was the first time in two decades that Icelanders could watch TV on a Thursday evening.

Private radio and television stations are now permitted. A private TV network, the Icelandic Broadcasting Corporation (IBC), maintains two commercial channels that, for a monthly fee of 3,000 krona (about $30), compete with the state-backed Channel 1, which some critics call dull. They have at least one advantage: They broadcast on Thursdays. So does BSkyB (now Sky plc.), a satellite TV service beamed from London. It has no license to broadcast to Iceland; use of its output is therefore piracy. But by installing a satellite dish, Icelanders can receive its multichannel offering of entertainment, news, films, and sports. With hefty monthly fees of $75 to receive RUV and IBC, it is hardly surprising that many Icelanders choose to tune into Sky for free.

The Danes brought Lutheranism to the island, and the church is the official one. Ninety-five percent of the people profess to be Lutherans, although few attend church regularly. The state supports it, and the *Althing* must approve any change in its organization. There is religious freedom, and other churches are active in the major towns. There is a reemerging interest in Old Norse religions, especially Ásatrúarfélagið, which is now recognized as a formal religion and gathers some 3,000 adherents, or about 1% of the island's population. In 2015, in the wake of the Charlie Hebdo terrorist attacks in France, Iceland repealed its law that still banned blasphemy. This decision is not popular with the established church authorities but was a major political victory for the Pirate Party.

Education is compulsory between the ages of 7 and 16, and most pupils continue on. All students learn English and Danish. The University of Iceland, with 4,000 students, provides all of the higher education on the island and includes departments or schools of law, medicine, engineering, science, theology, philosophy, and economics; 8,000 study abroad each year, with America the most popular destination.

Given the bitter winters, it is remarkable that 90% return, keeping Iceland dynamic, modern, and open to new ideas. The country's literacy rate is 99%.

Special insurance is mandatory and covers old age, disability, maternity, sickness, and unemployment benefits. Some health costs are, however, paid by the individual. There is 1 physician for every 750 inhabitants. The 2017 World Happiness Report listed Iceland as the third-happiest country in the world, behind Norway and Denmark.

Iceland has Europe's highest fertility rate (2.0 children per woman), despite the fact that it also has the developed world's highest rate of female employment: 80%. However, their pay is 40% lower than that of the average man. Nevertheless, in 2013 the Swiss-based think tank World Economic Forum ranked Iceland first in the world (ahead of 17th-place US) in terms of gender opportunity.

The nation is experiencing a baby boom since the onset of the financial crisis of 2009. One theory is that, with unemployment at 9% just a few years ago, couples had more time to produce "Kreppa babies." Marriages are down by about 50%, as hard-pressed couples lack the funds to get married. Nevertheless, the record-setting bearing of children is praised as a sign of this hardy nation's optimism for the future.

Its population is so small and homogeneous, and such complete medical and family records have been maintained since the World War I, that it decided in 1999 to become the first country in the world to permit this information to be combined into a single linked computerized database. The aim was to create a genetic inventory that traces the likely chromosomal sites of the genes for a number of inherited diseases. A biotechnology company, deCODE Genetics, was set up to search these linked databases for clues into the nature of diseases.

By 2004 the project was in trouble because of concerns that it infringed on the privacy rights of Icelanders, even though 20,000 people chose to opt out. But 140,000 had already offered family records and blood samples, enough to keep the project going. When the devastating financial crisis hit the country, the company went bankrupt in 2010, even though its database made it one of the world's leading players in biotechnology. It emerged from bankruptcy, and in 2012 it was sold to biotechnology giant Amgen for $415 million. DeCODE, a privately held company, acquired a well-financed partner to continue its research, while Amgen gets cutting-edge findings.

In the meantime, a new search engine, Islandingabok (Book of Icelanders), offers the homogeneous Icelanders the possibility to check an online database of island genealogy to see if one is too closely related to a prospective suitor or lover. Its data go back 1,200 years and are derived from church records and other public and private sources.

Few moments of elation can rival the Icelanders' joy at qualifying for the Euro 2016 soccer tournament and then putting up an equal fight against much better ranked opponents, such as Portugal or Hungary, and besting Austria and especially England. Iceland was the smallest country to qualify, and almost 10% of the entire island's population showed up to matches in France. A rather petulant Portuguese player, Cristiano Ronaldo, inadvertently captured Iceland's mood after the tie with his team: "I thought they'd won the Euros the way they celebrated at the end. It was unbelievable." One of the first public acts of the new president-elect of Iceland, Guðni Thorlacius Jóhannesson, whose election was outshone by the tournament, was to attend Iceland's quarterfinals match against heavily favored France. Refusing to sit in the VIP box ("Why would I go in the VIP room and sip champagne when I can do that anywhere in the world?"), he opted for the stands with the fans, wearing his Iceland shirt.

CURRENT ISSUES

This resilient nation has much going for it. A Global Peace Index tests countries against 24 "peacefulness" criteria, including the crime rate and potential for terrorism within its borders; in 2011 Iceland was ranked first in the world. For nine years in a row, the World Economy Forum ranked it the globe's most gender-equal country. In 2018 it became the first country in the world to make it illegal to pay men more than women for the same work. The differential was 14% to 18% in 2018. Almost half the parliamentarians and 44% of boardroom executives are female. Women have been the nation's president 20 of the last 50 years. This is why there was such nationwide outrage when in 2018 a former prime minister and a foreign minister were recorded in a bar using sexist and obscene language about female colleagues.

In 2010 researchers at Yale and Columbia Universities ranked it first in the world in terms of environmental performance, with the US number 61. It was praised for its renewable energy sources and its green efforts. But the glory days were at an end for a few years.

Of concern to citizens in Atlantic countries, volcanic activity in this young geological island can be expected to continue for at least four decades. Besides Iceland's Bardarbunga volcano's fiery display in 2015, scientists worry about a potentially devastating eruption of Hekla that could happen "at any moment."

Icelanders' famous spirit of independence has reasserted itself, and a solid majority now opposes membership in the EU. One Icelandic sociologist put it this way: "Many people would not be able to tolerate a minister in Brussels deciding how many pounds of cod a fisherman was allowed to catch each year." Many EU laws already apply to Iceland. Membership talks were suspended.

It is not difficult to find reasons for optimism. The average age in Iceland is only 37, the birth rate is among the highest in the developed world and rising, the workforce is highly educated and trained, the economy is good again, and the pension funds are probably safe in the long run. There are abundant natural resources and energy. The stark beauty of this land exerts an undeniable pull. Iceland had 2.4 million visitors in 2017—seven times the entire population of the island. Surprising and pride inducing, Iceland became in 2018 the smallest country ever to qualify for the World Cup in soccer.

Thanks to its broad testing and contact tracing, Iceland remains the European champion in fighting the deadly coronavirus.

The next presidential elections in Iceland are scheduled to be held on June 1, 2024. The current President Guðni Th. Jóhannesson declared that he will not seek re-election in the upcoming elections.

Republic of Finland (Suomen tasavalta)

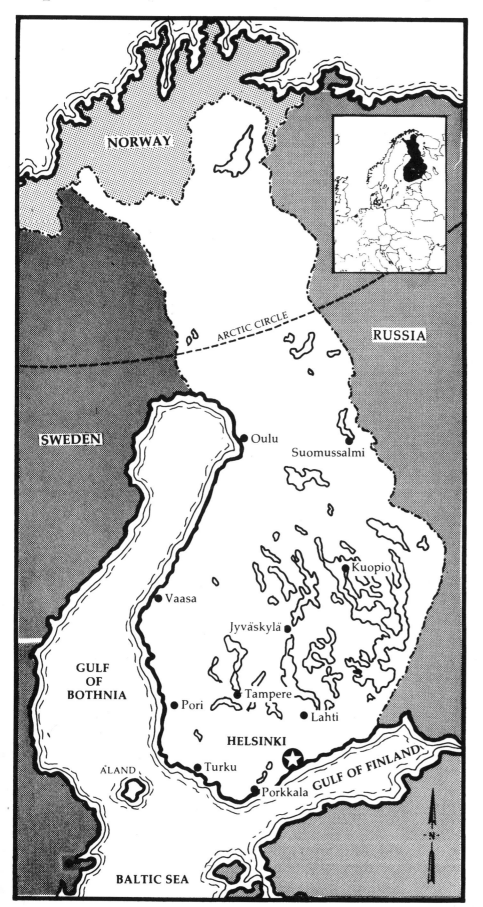

Area: 130,666 sq. mi. (338,424 sq. km.). (UN Statistics Division, October 2023)

Population: 5,614,571 (2023 estimate)

Capital City: Helsinki (pop. 673,011; urban 1,268,296; metro 1,576,438; as of 2023).

Climate: It is influenced by Finland's location at latitude from 60°N to 70°N, and has characteristics of both oceanic (or maritime) and continental subarctic or boreal climate. The Atlantic Ocean to the west and the Eurasian continent to the east interact and modify it. Although potentially subarctic it is comparatively mild because of moderating influence of the Gulf Stream, Baltic Sea, and more than 60,000 lakes. Summers are short, moderately warm and humid. Winter is the longest season. The part of Finland north of the Arctic Circle experiences extremely severe winters. The Aurora Borealis is common in Lapland.

Neighboring Countries: Russia (east); Norway (north); Sweden (west).

Official Languages: Finnish (92%), Swedish (5.5%).

Recognized regional language: Sámi (Lapp) dialects

Ethnic Background: Finns 91.5%, Others 8.5% (Finland-Swedes, Romani, Tatar and Sámi people).

Religion: Christianity (65.2% Evangelical Lutheran Church of Finland, 1.1% Orthodox Church of Finland), 1.7% other and 32.0% nonreligious. (2023).

Form of Government: Unitary parliamentary republic.

Chief of State: Alexander Stubb, President (since March 1, 2024).

Head of Government: Petteri Orpo, Prime Minister (since June 20, 2023).

National Flag: It consists of a sea-blue Nordic cross on a white field. The cross represents Christianity and closely connects with Sweden's and Finland's national flags. The flag was adopted after independence from Russia, but its design dates back to the 19th century. The blue color is said to represent the country's thousands of lakes and the sky, and white stands for the snow that covers the land in winter. This blue-white color combination has also been used over the centuries in various Finnish military, provincial, and town flags.

Public Holiday: December 6 (1917, Independence Day).

Currency: Euro (€; EUR).

Main Exports: High technology (especially electronics), paper and pulp products, machinery and metal products, iron and steel, timber, ships, clothing, and footwear.

Main Imports: Foodstuffs, petroleum, chemicals, cars, textile yarns, fabrics.

Main Trading Partners: Germany (11.7% of exports and 12.9% of imports), Sweden (10.7% of exports and 12.6% of imports), Netherlands (7.3% of exports and 5.1% of imports), US (9.5% of exports), UK (3.6% of exports), China (4.9% of exports and 9.2% of imports), Estonia (4.3% of exports and 3.7% of imports), Norway (6.9% of imports), Russia (6.8% of imports). (2022)

In the ancient past, Finland was regarded as a cold land of legendary witchcraft, far off Europe's beaten path. It was very thinly populated by a silent and complicated people, who spoke an extremely baffling language when they chose to speak at all. Now the country is dynamic and forward-looking and is very much in the mainstream of both western and eastern Europe.

With a land area about the size of Italy, but with less than one-tenth of the population, the Finns call their rugged and strikingly beautiful country the "land of lakes and marshes." Indeed, with 60,000 lakes, one-tenth of the country is under water. But outsiders would probably say "the land of forests, lakes, and marshes." The ever-present forests provide the country with its most valuable natural resource. They cover 70% of the surface area and are actually growing, not shrinking. Only Russia and Sweden have larger forested areas in Europe. An additional 22% is unforested peat land or marsh. Only 12% of the land area is used for cultivation, pasture, and urban settlement. Finland has few mountains.

This country is at the head of the Baltic Sea in the northeastern corner of western Europe and is the northernmost of the world's industrialized countries. Except for Norway's North Cape region, which touches Finland, the country extends farther north than any other mainland area of Europe. In fact, one-third is north of the Arctic Circle. It also extends farther east than any other western European country and shares an 800-mile (1,280 km) border with Russia. On the south it faces the Gulf of Finland, with Estonia beyond, and on the west, there are the Gulf of Bothnia and Sweden. With 130,000 square miles, Finland is the seventh-largest country in Europe, with only Russia, Ukraine, France, Spain, Sweden, and Germany being larger. There are some 20,000 coastal islands, most of which are in the southwestern archipelago, merging into the Aland Islands in the west. Finland extends about 700 miles (1,120 km) from north to south and 400 miles (640 km) east to west.

Glaciers miles thick completely covered Finland during the great ice ages. That is one explanation why the country is relatively flat, with thousands of lakes

filling the low spots. It also partly explains why much of the land, still recovering after the release 10,000 years ago from the unimaginable weight of the ice, is rising about 1 foot every 50 years. Where the Baltic is shallow, that uplift movement is giving Finland more land at the expense of the sea. The glaciers are the reason that the most common land type is moraine, a mixture of rocks and soil transported from other locations by the ice.

Finland has three major topographic regions, based on altitude. The uplands north of the Arctic Circle average 600 feet to 1,000 feet (183–305 meters) above sea level and include all the high points in Finland, the highest being 4,357 feet (1,328 meters). The coastal plain is less than 300 feet (91 meters) above sea level and extends inland from the Baltic 20 to 60 miles (32 to 96 km). The lake district fills the remainder of the country south of the Arctic Circle and is intermediate in altitude. The entire country averages about 500 feet (152 m) in altitude, only half of the average for Europe as a whole.

Although Finland lies between 60° and 70° North latitude, it has a much milder climate than most countries so far north. The Gulf Stream and the prevailing winds are welcome benefactors for the Finns, giving them a climatic advantage over southern Greenland, Canada's Northwest Territories, and most of Siberia, which lie in the same latitudes but which have much more severe weather. A better comparison is Alaska, also between 60° and 70° North and partly favored by warming ocean currents. The length of the day varies greatly, even in the south, which has 6 hours of sunlight daily in December and 19 hours in June. In northern Lapland, however, the sun never sets for 73 days in summer and never rises for 51 days in winter.

HISTORY

The Early Periods

When the Indo-European tribes pushed into the Baltic area about 4000 BC, they found people already there who are believed to be related to the present-day Finns. These early inhabitants probably had moved into the area soon after the continental ice sheet began to melt about 12,000 years ago. As the Indo-Europeans moved up the shores of the Baltic Sea, they pushed some Finns ahead of them. About 2000 BC and again at the beginning of the Christian era, waves of immigrants came to Finland from across the water to the south and land to the southeast and gradually pushed the Lapps, who had arrived earlier, into the northern portions of the country. All of these early Finnish tribes moved west from north and central Russia. Finnish is related to Estonian and to

A typical countryside panorama

Finland

the languages of isolated parts of northern Russia. It is also distantly related to modern Hungarian.

Scandinavian influence in Finland began during the era of great migrations, about 400 AD, and continues to the present. Christian missionaries first entered southwest Finland in the 10th century, and the Catholicized Finnish aristocracy developed close links with Poland. The king of Sweden and the bishop of Uppsala made a crusade into Finland 200 years later, establishing a foothold in the southwest, which was expanded in the following centuries to include all the northern shore of the Gulf of Finland. Swedes colonized the southwestern and southern coastal areas and the Aland islands, areas where Swedish language and culture is still very strong. The Swedes slowly annexed the remainder of Finland and ruled it as a Swedish province, though not as a colony, until 1808.

Following a successful Russian invasion, Finland was declared an autonomous Grand Duchy of Imperial Russia, a status that continued until 1917. During the 19th century, Finns were permitted to continue to practice the rudimentary representative government the Swedes had created. This early period of Russian rule saw very little effort at Russification. It actually gave the Finns a chance to overcome the heavy Swedish cultural and lingual influence and to assert their Finnishness while retaining those elements of Scandinavian traditions and values, such as the structure of society and the judicial system, which Finns found valuable. Not until the mid-19th century did the educated classes and the country's major newspapers begin to use the Finnish language. But in 1899 a Russification campaign began. The Finns were no longer permitted to practice the Swedish form of government, and Finland was required to provide troops for the Russian army. This provoked Finnish resistance to Russian rule, and in 1905 a general strike paralyzed the country.

In 1906 the Russian government, badly shaken by an unsuccessful revolution, agreed to a Parliament Act for Finland, providing for Finland's system of proportional representation voting and a single-chamber assembly. At the same time, Finnish women became the first in Europe to be permitted to vote. When the tsar renounced these concessions in 1910, Finns again mounted determined resistance. Such opposition to Russian domination made it logical after the outbreak of World War I in 1914 for Finnish nationalists to cooperate with the most powerful country opposed to Russia, namely Germany.

A Nation Is Born

The Russian Revolution occurred in early 1917. When Lenin's Bolsheviks

General Mannerheim

overthrew the Kerensky government in November 1917, the majority of Finns demanded full independence, and the Finnish parliament declared it on December 6, 1917. But the radical left was determined to unleash a revolution in order to establish a socialist state. Known at the time as Reds, they seized Helsinki and southern Finland in early 1918, causing the parliament to move north to the city of Vaasa.

Thus, Finland's independence was followed almost immediately by a civil war. Led by the former Finnish general in the tsarist army Gustav Mannerheim, Finnish government forces, known as Whites, won a decisive victory over the Reds at the city of Tampere early in April. Mannerheim's forces were later supported by a German division that landed on the southern coast and recaptured Helsinki early in the month. The rebellion was thus put to an end; Finnish society was able to remain western, not Soviet, but the costs of Finland's struggle for independence were enormous. Not only were 20,000 Finns killed, but also the nation was split into two hostile halves. Not until the Russians invaded the country two decades later was this wound healed.

In the struggle between monarchists and republicans, the former won a temporary victory. Two weeks before the end of World War I, the Finns chose a German to be their king, but the defeat of Germany made such a monarchy utterly unrealistic. Therefore, Finland adopted a democratic and republican constitution in 1919 that is still in effect.

Finland joined the League of Nations in December 1920. As the power of the league began to deteriorate in the 1930s, Finland

unsuccessfully attempted to ally itself with Sweden and other Scandinavian countries. Therefore, when the Soviet Union attacked Finland in November 1939, the Finns had no friends who would or could help.

The Red Army attacked on the ground in the east and southeast and by amphibious assaults across the Gulf of Finland. It threw almost 1 million men into the attack, who were opposed by about 300,000 Finns, 80% of whom were reservists. The Finns, regardless of their numerical inferiority, put up a fierce and effective defense, often fighting on skis. All the amphibious assaults were repulsed, as was the main Russian attack against the Finnish fortifications on the Karelian Isthmus.

Russian drives into Finland from the east proved to be disastrous. They came expecting an easy victory and were pitifully ill prepared. They were equipped neither with field tents nor with portable woodstoves. Finnish troops, attired in warm white winter clothing and familiar with the terrain and cold, cut the Russian columns into small pieces and destroyed them. The Russians were scarcely able to cope with the Finnish "invisible wall"— white-clad soldiers who appeared suddenly, fought fiercely, and then disappeared in the landscape of drifting snow. The Battle of Suomussalmi was the most dramatic example, with two Finnish divisions completely destroying two enemy ones, resulting in 27,500 Russians killed or frozen to death and 1,300 captured. The Finns lost only 900 men.

The British government sent two air squadrons and allowed its soldiers to leave its army to fight for Finland. As described in a well-known book in Finland,

The Help That Never Arrived, Britain and France were planning a large-scale military intervention when a Soviet breakthrough induced the Finns to make peace. The Soviet Union's overwhelming manpower eventually proved too much for the brave but outnumbered Finns. After three months they accepted the peace terms offered by the Soviets, which at the time were cooperating with Germany and which were reportedly nervous that the British might come to the aid of Finland via Norway and Sweden.

In the end, Finland had sustained 25,000 killed and 43,000 wounded, while Soviet casualties were 8 to 10 times as high.

One of the principal costs of the Winter War was the loss of most of the region of Karelia. The entire southeastern corner of Finland, containing 10% of the country's territory and people, went to the Russians in the peace settlement. Much of the Karelian population had to be resettled in the west. A further consequence of the war was that the Germans and many others concluded that the Red Army would be a pushover in any future conflict. This fatal misperception enticed the greedy Hitler to attack the Soviet Union only two years later.

When they did attack in mid-1941, Finland, desiring to regain the territory it had so recently lost, went to war on Germany's side. The Finns tried to keep relatively independent of Germany, however, and did maintain peaceful relations with the US throughout the war. They participated in the siege of Leningrad, but they apparently refused to help cut the rail lines linking the vital north Russian port of Murmansk and Moscow. It did take the opportunity to reconquer its lost territories and to seize eastern Karelia, which had always belonged to Russia, although it was populated by Finns. Sensing the way, the wind was blowing after the crushing German defeat at Stalingrad, the Finns began to explore ways to a separate peace in 1943, but they were not permitted to extricate themselves from the war so easily.

Things were, on the whole, very quiet on the Finnish front from late 1941 until the Allied landings along the coast of France in June 1944. At that time, the Soviet Union decided to launch another attack on Finland through the Karelian Isthmus. It directed some of the most concentrated artillery fire in history toward the Finnish positions, and the Finnish front cracked very quickly. It rapidly became clear that Finland could not withstand this furious Soviet onslaught, so it again sought material German help. Together, the two nations' forces brought the Soviet attack to a standstill.

However, General Mannerheim, who became president in the late summer of 1944, sued for peace with the Soviet Union. The latter placed very hard conditions on Finland. The most immediate demand was for Finns to expel the 220,000 German soldiers who had been stationed in northern Finland. The Germans nevertheless put up very stiff-necked resistance—during their retreat, they destroyed everything in their path, leaving Finns the postwar task of reconstructing the northern part of their country.

The September 1944 treaty with the Soviets forced it to accept the loss of the same areas as in 1940, and almost 400,000 Finnish refugees were set in motion once again. Further, Finland had to relinquish the area of Petsamo and to allow the Soviet Union to establish a naval base for 50 years on the Porkkala Peninsula, immediately southwest of Helsinki. It had to pay the Soviets heavy reparations (ultimately almost $445 million), which by 1952 it had paid in full. Finally, the Finns were required to reduce their army to its peacetime level within 2.5 months.

The strains of war had helped the Finnish people to draw together and to set aside some of the social and lingual differences that had continued to divide them since independence. Finland was fortunate in that it had been the only belligerent country in continental Europe that was not occupied during the war. But the Finns paid a very high price: About 2.2% of their population had been killed in action, and an equal number had been permanently maimed. They lost 12.5% of their territory and were forced to resettle 14% of their population.

Finally, they found themselves in a radically changed strategic situation. Germany had been totally defeated. The Soviet Union, with an 800-mile Finnish border, had emerged as the most powerful country in Europe and virtually the only great power in the Baltic area. Soviet troops had important base rights on Finnish territory within a few miles of Helsinki. Looking south, the Finns saw how the Soviet Union had simply annexed the Baltic states of Estonia, Latvia, and Lithuania in the course of the war. They were very aware that Finland was the only lost part of the pre-1914 Russian Empire that had not been reabsorbed by a revived Soviet Russia. Worse yet, Finland realized that there was not a single country in the world that would risk a war with the Soviets to keep Finland independent. What should a small, western-oriented country do in such a situation in order to maintain its national independence and its right to determine its own domestic political and economic order?

A Balancing Act

The Finns have always been noted for a quality known in Finnish as "sisu," variously translated as "perseverance, tenacity, steadiness, diligence, courage, or simply guts." This was a quality necessary for a people who always had to struggle to survive in a harsh natural environment. At the same time, they are a very realistic people whose main political problem since World War II has been one of foreign policy. Like other small countries that share borders with big powers, Finland did and now does have various options. It could disregard the security interests of its powerful neighbor and pay the price for that. Or it could recognize those security interests and see how it could adjust its policies to them without sacrificing its own national sovereignty. More and more Finns realized that the latter option was the only realistic one, and their leaders have long established the country's foreign policy on that foundation.

In order not to irritate the Soviet Union after World War II, Finland was forced to turn down all offers of Marshall Plan assistance from the United States. Moscow had viewed such aid with suspicion as a trick designed to undercut its influence and to establish an American predominance over Europe. Therefore, it forbade all of its newly developed client states in eastern Europe from accepting this aid. Finland's subsequent economic recovery and prosperity and the fact that it was the only European country fully to repay its war debts from both world wars are all the more astonishing when one remembers that it received no economic aid from the US.

A Finnish peace treaty with the Soviet Union came into force in 1947 that placed maximum limits on Finland's armed forces. This was followed in 1948 by a more important step, the signing of a Treaty of Friendship, Cooperation, and Mutual Assistance with its powerful neighbor. The Soviets had already entered into such treaties with the satellite states of eastern Europe, and so when it was announced in February 1948 that the Soviet Union had also invited Finland to work out a mutual-assistance pact, many Finns thought that the end of their independence was near.

Yet Finnish leaders acted quickly and skillfully. They politely rejected Stalin's offer to sign a treaty identical to the ones signed with Hungary and Romania, countries that had fought against the Soviets during the war. Instead, Finnish leaders drafted their own treaty, tailored to their own particular needs and circumstances. They drew on earlier proposals that the Russians had made to Finland in 1938 and 1939. Perhaps justifiably suspecting foul play in 1939, the Finns had rejected the Soviet proposals, and the Winter War had resulted.

The Soviet-Finnish Treaty

The Treaty of 1948 obligated Finland to defend itself in the case of an attack "with

Finland

the help, if necessary, of the Soviet Union or together with the Soviet Union." Such "assistance" would "be supplied as mutually agreed between the Parties." Article 2 adds that both countries "will consult together in case there is found to be a threat of the military aggression referred to in Article 1."

The decisive part of the treaty, as far as the Finns are concerned, is the preamble, in which "Finland's desire to remain outside the conflicting interests of the Great Powers" is recognized. This granted Finland a privilege not extended to the Soviet Union's eastern European satellites: the right to be neutral. It is certainly true that the Russians only chose to use this word in reference to Finland in 1970, and indeed, until the Soviet Union had withdrawn its troops from the Porkkala Peninsula in 1956, one could hardly speak of genuine neutrality. In large part, this Soviet decision stemmed from its buildup of adequate naval facilities on its own soil. It stemmed also from the changed strategic situation, which moved critical points from the waters south of Finland toward the Baltic area closer to Denmark and the straits leading to the North Sea, as well as toward the northern Norwegian and Bering Seas.

The Finns' basic assumption was that the Soviet Union did not want to conquer the entire world but that its policy was basically defensive and essentially oriented toward stability along its borders. Without question, the Soviets had in Finland a more stable and less threatening neighbor than anywhere along the entire huge Soviet border in Europe or Asia. From the standpoint of the Russians' self-interest, the treaty was also advantageous in that direct Soviet control of Finland, which no country in the world could prevent, would undoubtedly cause the neutral but extremely well-armed Sweden to join NATO and would eliminate Norway's policy of restricting NATO activity on its soil. Such an unpleasant event would immensely strengthen an enemy alliance by moving NATO several hundred miles closer to the Soviet Union and by strengthening the NATO presence in the Baltic Sea. Thus, like all good and lasting treaties, the 1948 one rested on a firm foundation of mutual interest.

For this reason, President Koivisto traveled to Moscow in 1983 to renew the treaty for another 20 years. It was not scheduled to expire until 1990, but the early renewal was an expression of the desire for continuity despite leadership changes in both countries. Immediately following the failure of the Soviet coup in August 1991, the Finns decided to renegotiate the treaty. Esko Aho was the first Finnish leader to question it. His government did not want it and the neutrality it imposes to be

Finnish soldiers—the "invisible wall"

obstacles to entry into the EU, which occurred in 1995.

In 1990 Finland unilaterally abandoned clauses of the treaty that limited the size of its military forces and relations with Germany. In 1992 Finland and Russia replaced the 1948 treaty altogether and forged independent Russia's first political treaty with a western country. Both nations committed themselves to respect the other's borders, to protect the other's citizens on their territories, and to renounce the use of force against each other. The treaty is valid for 10 years and renewable for 5-year periods unless annulled by either country.

Neutrality and Foreign Policy

Finland's foreign policy, which did not enjoy a widespread consensus even within the country until a generation had passed after World War II, depended upon almost constant Finnish reassurances to the Russians that it would never again present a threat to their security. J. K. Paasikivi, Finland's president from 1946 to 1956, devoted almost his entire effort to eradicating traditional anti-Russian views within Finland, lest they place Finland's security in danger. This policy, known as the "Paasikivi line" was reinforced and expanded by his successor, Urho Kekkonen. The "Kekkonen line" was based upon the realization that the worse east-west tensions are, the greater the ominous prospect that Finland would be obligated to support the Soviet Union. Therefore, Finland took a very active role in reducing such tensions.

For instance, it hosted the initial Strategic Arms Limitation Talks (SALT) between the US and the Soviet Union that resulted in a milestone agreement in 1972. Further, it actively organized, promoted, and hosted the Helsinki Conference on Security and Cooperation in Europe in 1975, which was attended by virtually all the highest political leaders in Europe. The "Helsinki Agreements" were a central element in all superpower and European dialogues.

Some observers in the West distrusted Finland's policy of bending over backward not to irritate the Soviet Union. In the late 1960s, the term "Finlandization" entered the international political vocabulary to refer to a condition in which a country is so frightened by Soviet power that it is no longer able to control its own foreign policy. It implied a loss of sovereignty and a kind of remote control of a country from Moscow. Finland's example was often presented as a warning to other western European nations, although the Finns never pretended that the relationship they maintained with the Soviet Union should be adopted by other nations. Finlandization was viewed as an ideal solution for eastern European countries, since the Soviet Union decided in 1989 to permit democratic revolutions there. During a highly symbolic visit to Helsinki in 1989, Gorbachev praised Finnish neutrality, stating that "for me, Soviet-Finnish relations are a model for relations between a big country and a little one."

Finland

Neutrality was a way of saying no to military cooperation with the Soviet Union. The rationale for this disappeared with the Soviet collapse. Finland's foreign policy was undergoing significant change. It no longer defined its approach in terms of neutrality but of nonalignment, since it was firmly anchored in the western family of nations. Initially it declined to enter NATO, a position supported by half of Finns, even though in 1994 it joined the Partnership for Peace. It believed that the kind of nonalignment best for Nordic regional security was backed up by growing cooperation with NATO, by a credible national defense, and by implicit collective security provided by the EU. Unlike Denmark it was willing to participate in a common EU defense arrangement, and a blueprint for this was adopted at the EU summit meeting in Helsinki in December 1999.

Finland's long-maintained military neutrality changed in February 2022 when Russia launched its full-scale invasion of Ukraine. The invasion shattered a long-standing sense of stability in northern Europe, leaving Finland, as well as Sweden, feeling vulnerable. Finland, supported by the overwhelming majority of Finns, embarked on an 11-month membership path to NATO. It officially joined the Western defensive alliance on April 4, 2023, becoming its 31st member. Its membership in NATO dramatically changed the security in Europe. It more than doubled the alliance's border with Russia.

Relations with the USSR and Russia

Finns bristled with anger when they heard the expression "Finlandization." The term implies indirect criticism of their earlier foreign policy. It was normally used by people who lacked deep knowledge of Finland and its history and who were referring to political situations that had nothing to do with Finland itself.

The Finns practiced careful self-censorship toward unpleasant actions of the Soviet Union. Finnish newspapers were expected to be discreet and wholly accurate when criticizing the Soviet Union, and such criticism could never be sensationalized. As one Finnish historian wrote, "The Finns deny themselves the luxury of making emotionally satisfying gestures." Another noted, "If we bow West, we present our bad sides to the East. We just can't afford to do that." Where self-censorship was practiced, former president Kekkonen openly appealed to the press to show "responsibility."

In 1986 a case of censorship involved a Finnish film entitled Born American, which depicts the imprisonment and harsh treatment of three Americans who cross the Soviet border. The Finnish government's response was to ban it because of its hostile portrayal of the Soviet Union. Such censorship did not determine Finns' personal attitudes toward their powerful neighbor. Opinion surveys in 1987 among high school pupils indicated that the USSR was viewed as an Orwellian society with no freedom and miserable living standards. However, two-thirds believed that the Soviet Union was not a threat to peace.

Finland's response to the Soviet Union's invasion of Afghanistan in 1979 was an example of restraint. This brutal venture was a severe shock to the Finns, especially since Moscow had often referred in official declarations to Finland and Afghanistan as "neighboring, nonaligned" countries with which it could entertain good relations. Although Finnish leaders publicly called on the Soviet Union kindly to withdraw its forces from Afghanistan, Finland, unlike most other nations of the world, abstained from condemning the invasion by vote in the United Nations. Further, in the aftermath of the Soviet Union's shooting down of a South Korean passenger jet with hundreds of persons aboard in mid-1983, the Koivisto government appealed to Finnish ground crews not to join an international boycott of flights in and out of the USSR. Finland avoided taking a stand whenever the interests of the great powers, including the United States, were in conflict. Thus, unlike some of the US allies, Finland almost never criticized American foreign policy in public.

Finland is always extremely sensitive to any development in northern Europe that might provoke a Russian reaction toward it. Finnish tempers flared in the spring of 1986, when the Soviet Union waited three days to inform the Finns officially about the Chernobyl nuclear disaster. Soviet leaders subsequently reached an agreement that such information would be exchanged immediately.

While western leaders could understand Finnish concerns in these matters, they had greater difficulty understanding Kekkonen's respectful allusions to Lenin, who had lived in Finland, had expressed sympathy and friendship toward the country, and had been the first leader to recognize Finland's independence. His visit to Lenin's birthplace and his willingness to stand with communist dignitaries on top of the Lenin Mausoleum in Moscow on the occasion of the 50th and 60th anniversaries of the Bolshevik Revolution were puzzling. After the failed August 1991 coup in the USSR, Tampere's Lenin Museum, which is independent of the Finnish government, offered to take Lenin's embalmed body if it were forced out of its Red Square Mausoleum. The museum's director said, "We always gave Lenin a hiding place when times were difficult in Russia."

The benefit of Finland's good relations with both superpowers was shown in 1990, when Mikhail Gorbachev, worried about the Baltic states' drive for independence, asked Koivisto to help. The latter informed President George H. W. Bush of the former Soviet leader's concerns. Only after president Koivisto's death in 2017 did the Finnish and Estonian people learn of a substantial financial assistance Finland was quietly funneling to its southern brethren in support of Estonia's independence from the USSR.

The turbulent events in the former Soviet Union in the 1990s created heightened anxiety in Finland, whose leaders feared that the gigantic multinational neighbor might head inexorably toward dissolution and catastrophe. Such a prospect fills most Finns with horror. It could drive hundreds of thousands of desperate and starved Russians across the 1,200-kilometer border with Finland.

Finnish uneasiness was heightened by the 1993 Russian parliamentary election campaign, in which ultranationalist candidate Vladimir Zhirinovsky spoke of reincorporating Finland into a new Russian empire and banishing Helsinki's Finnish residents to Lapland so that Russians could move into their apartments. In January 1994 the Russian ambassador in Helsinki sent a note to the Finnish Foreign Ministry complaining that the existence of two right-wing groups violated the 1947 Treaty of Paris, which bans fascist activity in Finland. Finns regard this treaty as obsolete and were incensed that Russian leaders would try to influence Finland's presidential election in this crude way.

Nevertheless, with Russian nationalism on the rise and with thousands of Russian troops deployed in the region of St. Petersburg, Finns wanted to avoid upsetting their giant neighbor. This is why President Martti Ahtisaari warned in 1995 against an eastward expansion of NATO, instead recommending opening the EU to central and eastern European membership. As the only EU state sharing a land border with Russia, Finland had a special interest in promoting what it calls a "northern dimension" of deeper cooperation with Russia. The idea was to assist Russia to settle down and prosper in the region with sympathetic and helpful Nordic states. When Finland assumed the rotating EU presidency in July 1999, it made improvement of relations with Russia one of its main themes. But in 1999 Finland's foreign minister, Tarja Halonen (who became president in 2000), openly criticized Russia's brutal military policies in the Caucasus, particularly in Chechnya and Ingushetia.

Finland

Worries about Russia increasingly directed Finns' attention toward western Europe, especially the EU. Many feared being isolated in a rapidly changing world.

As former Conservative Party leader Ilkka Suominen asked, "If the world changes from confrontation to more cooperation, then where does neutrality lie?" The government applied in 1992 for entry into the EU. In October 1994 57% of the voters accepted their country's entry into the EU. This historic event took what had been a western European bloc right up to the gates of Russia. Finland's Swedish-speaking Aland Islanders, who enjoy a self-governing status, initially voted not to follow Finland into the EU, but they changed their minds in 1994 and voted to go along with the rest of the Finns. Finland is the Nordic area's biggest enthusiast for the EU and is proud to be the first to adopt the euro.

Defense

The Finns tried to maintain sufficient military preparedness in order to be able to cope with any potential aggressors. Its military doctrine was based on self-reliance and territorial defense. It aimed to mobilize at short notice a well-equipped force of a half-million soldiers who could retain control of strategically important areas, and delay and wear down an attacker until it can concentrate the necessary force to defeat him in areas of Finland's own choosing.

Finland has compulsory military service for all males over 18 years; about 90% of all men serve. If males prefer to perform civilian service, they may do so but remain a few months longer. Since 1995 women may also volunteer, and 500 are in the active forces. They are trained for the same duties as men and have the same opportunities and responsibilities. There are 22,600 active-duty troops, of which the majority are conscripts. Finnish men must serve on active duty for 6 to 12 months. Most serve six months, but officers, noncommissioned officers, and certain technical specialists must remain for a year. A Finn is in the reserves until age 60. There are 16,000 soldiers in the army, 3,800 in the navy, 2,750 in the air force, and 2,750 paramilitaries; all are conscripts.

In wartime, it could mobilize 435,000 trained and equipped soldiers: 347,000 in the army; 35,000 in the air force; and 12,000 in the navy. Most serve in the southern part of the country, but efforts are now being made to shift more of the country's military capability northward into Lapland, where an eventual violation of Finnish territory would most likely occur. Finland's defense spending is 1.6% of GDP. Spending on 3,100 active and 22,000 reserve border troops and civil defense is included in other ministries' budgets. Finns show a strong affection for their military. Former prime minister Paavo Lipponen stated, "the army is the most popular institution in Finland."

Finnish troops are participants in UN peacekeeping missions, particularly in the Middle East. That this form of duty is not without risk was demonstrated in 1985, when 21 Finnish soldiers were captured in southern Lebanon and held for 8 days before being released by their Christian militia captors. The commander of the UN troops in southern Lebanon was a Finnish major-general. In 1995–1997 Finland dispatched a 450-man peacekeeping force to Bosnia to help enforce the Dayton Accords. In 1999 Finland provided forensic scientists to investigate massacres in Kosovo. In 2010 it had 407 troops in Kosovo and 165 in Afghanistan.

Former president Martti Ahtisaari was a key mediator with Russia and NATO in the search for a peaceful settlement of the Kosovo conflict. In 2006–2007, he again took the lead in guiding negotiations to find a formula for Kosovo's independence that would be acceptable to Serbia. Former prime minister Harri Holkeri, who was once president of the UN General Assembly, served 10 months as the UN administrator for Kosovo from July 2003. In 2000 Ahtisaari had helped secure Namibia's independence from South Africa. In 2005 he had brokered a truce between the Indonesian government and the tsunami-devastated Aceh Province. He directs the Crisis Management Initiative in Helsinki. For his brilliance as a negotiator and mediator, he was awarded the Nobel Peace Prize in October 2008.

Most Finns and all political parties still favor conscription. Polls in 2002 indicated that 80% were willing to defend their country "even if the prospects of survival are dim."

About a third of its military equipment is produced in Finland. It purchased arms from the Soviet Union (MIG jet fighters), Sweden (Draken interceptor aircraft), Britain (Hawker Siddeley jets), America (64 Hornet F-18C interceptors produced in Finland), and France. In 1992 it bought Russian tanks, artillery, and ammunition from the stockpiles of former East Germany. It sends its officers to the US, France, and Britain (and earlier, to the Soviet Union) for specialized training. Finland has assumed a special role in assisting the Estonian military. It sends advisers to Estonia, including instructors to the National Defense and Public Service Academy in Tallinn and Baltic Defense College in Tartu. It provides specialized training to some Estonian troops on its own soil. The Finns are backed by a well-deserved reputation for

Urho Kekkonen

fierce and imaginative defense on their own territory.

Finland was worried about a resurgent and assertive Russia, especially after it has committed itself to removing the landmines along its long common border by 2016. Russia's invasion of Ukraine in February 2022 upended decades of thinking about security. An angered then Prime Minister Sanna Marin explained: "Russia is not the neighbor it was . . . we have a very unpredictable, aggressive neighbor . . . we need to reevaluate our relations. . . . We have a very unpredictable, aggressive neighbor. . . We need to reevaluate our own relations. . . We should never have to be alone again." The solution was to join NATO. Finland has officially become its a member on April 4, 2023. Its entry was supported by the majority of NATO members, who believed that Finland's membership would enhance the alliance's strength in the Baltic area. Finland brings formidable capabilities in Arctic warfare, as well as Europe's largest artillery force. Its entry more than doubled Alliance's common border with Russia; it is now 832 miles (1340 km) longer.

GOVERNMENT

What the Finns gained from their particular brand of foreign policy was the privilege to have a domestic political and economic order far different from that which the Soviet Union required of its eastern European neighbors. Until March 1, 2000, Finland had the same constitution it had adopted in 1919. Unlike three of its Scandinavian neighbors—Norway, Sweden, and Denmark—Finland is a republic and the only country in Europe that never had a king or a homegrown aristocracy.

The President

At the time the 1919 constitution was written, supporters of a monarchy reached a compromise with advocates of a republic: The president would not be a mere figure-head who cuts ribbons and gives parties for foreign dignitaries. Instead, he or she would be the leading figure in the political system and would be required to sever all ties with a particular political party.

Finns elect their president directly by universal suffrage for a six-year term. When no candidate receives 50% of the votes on the first round, a runoff election between the top two candidates takes place three weeks later. Presidents must give up party affiliations when taking office.

In March 2000 the constitution was amended to reduce the president's powers. Finland essentially moved to parliamentarianism after strong presidential power. The prime minister is now clearly the most important political figure. Added authority was shifted to parliament, which decides who should represent Finland at international gatherings. Both the president and prime minister represent Finland in the EU's European Council, but that could change. The president continues to play a part in foreign affairs "in cooperation with" the government. He commands the armed forces, although declarations of war and important treaties require parliamentary approval. The government negotiates treaties.

He no longer has the right to dissolve parliament, to call new elections, to initiate and delay legislation, or to appoint the cabinet. He is obligated to work with the prime minister to achieve the government's goals. He still has the power of pardon and signs all laws approved by parliament. He formally appoints all bishops for the state-supported Lutheran and Orthodox Churches, all university professors, and the governors for Finland's five regions. The only exception is the predominantly Swedish-speaking island of Aland, which has been self-governing since 1921. Finland's 448 municipalities are administered by their own popularly elected municipal councils, which exercise the municipalities' power to collect taxes; maintain public order; and attend to education, culture, health, and social welfare.

The office of the presidency was once so powerful that some observers jokingly referred to Finland as the only real monarchy in Scandinavia. This seemed particularly appropriate because of the man who occupied the office from 1956 until 1981, Urho Kekkonen. Thanks to his own efforts, most Finns accepted his foreign policy views until the Cold War ended in the early 1990s. Because of Kekkonen's strong personality, the presidency grew even more powerful. This high office is rewarded by a special right to be exempted from taxes. The president's €126,000 annual salary is both gross and net income, and it remains the same until Parliament decides to amend it. Members of parliament earn €7,137 per month. The President's annual compensation is specified by law and remains the same until Parliament decides to amend it. Currently the President receives €126,000 per year.

In the 1982 presidential elections, a record 86% of Finns chose the popular Mauno Koivisto. His modesty and unpretentiousness contrasted strongly with Kekkonen's sometimes brash and almost authoritarian style. Further, he was a man who was far less inclined to intervene excessively in domestic politics. His presidency brought a gradual transfer of more responsibilities to the prime minister, cabinet, and parliament. Under his leadership, the Finnish political system began to resemble more closely that of the other Scandinavian countries, where the chief focus is on parliament, not on the head of state. Koivisto led his country through the application to the European Union and through the dissolution of the Soviet Union. Sadly, he lost his popularity over the perception of having been giving the cold shoulder to Estonians while they were aspiring to independence. Koivisto stayed largely silent on this subject until his death in 2017 at the age of 93. Only then did the public learn that, to avoid USSR's wrath, Finland quietly sent over $18 million to Estonia under the guise of cultural cooperation.

In 1994 Finns elected a new president, Martti Ahtisaari, a Social Democrat. A career diplomat and former UN under-secretary-general, he had never before run for public office. That fact proved to be his strength because he had not been associated with the economic disasters that had overtaken Finland. Actually, the president has very little constitutional power in the economic sphere; his or her power once lay in foreign policy, which was Ahtisaari's area of expertise.

His successor in 2000 was Tarja Halonen, who brought much political experience into the presidential palace. A former labor lawyer, she had been minister of foreign affairs, justice, social welfare, and health. As was every president since 1982, she was a Social Democrat, but her politics were farther to the left than any of her predecessors. She had a reputation as an anti-church, pro-gay feminist who has always struggled for the rights of minorities and the expansion of the welfare state. Because of her down-to-earth manner and consistent defense of women's rights, she was exceptionally popular and won the votes of many conservative women, especially in her hometown of Helsinki.

In 2006 she was reelected, defeating her Conservative rival Sauli Niinisto. The key issue was defense policy. After the Baltic states entered NATO in 2004, Finland and Sweden are the only remaining nonaligned countries left in Russia's northwestern border area. But only Finland has a long common border with Russia. With a sense that Moscow has become more aggressive in its foreign and economic policies, some Finns' wariness toward the eastern neighbor has grown.

Halonen argued that the EU offers Finland sufficient security against an external threat, whereas Niinisto spoke of a need to

Downtown Helsinki

Finland

President Sauli Niinistö

President Alexander Stubb
Source: *Wikipedia*

prepare for new challenges by embedding Finland more securely in the west, meaning NATO. Niinisto's strong electoral performance in 2018 indicated that opposition to NATO may be weakening. He was elected president in 2012 and again in 2018, capturing 62.7% of the votes. He is the first Conservative president since the 1950s and the first ever to be in the same party as the sitting prime minister. His appeal to voters was enhanced by his raising two young children after his wife was killed in an automobile accident. He also barely escaped death in the 2004 tsunami in the Indian Ocean. With a reputation for low-key competence, he is pragmatic and cautious, so there is no precipitous change in his NATO-friendly foreign and defense policies. In 2013, he proposed that his €160,000 a year salary be reduced to the 2006 level of €126,000 because, as he said, Finland's GDP had also decreased to the 2006 level. That change was implemented by the parliament.

The 2024 presidential elections were the first in Finland since it joined NATO in 2023 in response to the Russian invasion of Ukraine, ending decades of its neutrality in foreign policy. The outgoing president, Sauli Niinistö, the only Finnish president to have been elected with an outright majority in the first round of voting in his direct popular reelection in 2018, has enjoyed over 90 percent popularity ratings since 2021. However, he has rejected efforts by a citizen movement to allow him to run for a third term.

The 2024 presidential elections were the first in Finland since it joined NATO in 2023 in response to the Russian invasion of Ukraine, ending decades of its neutrality in foreign policy. The outgoing president, Sauli Niinistö, the only Finnish president to have been elected with an outright majority (62.7 percent) in the first round of

voting in his direct popular reelection in 2018, has enjoyed over 90 percent popularity ratings since 2021. However, he has rejected efforts by a citizen movement to be allowed to run for a third term.

The elections were held on January 28, 2024. As no candidate received a majority of votes, Alexander Stubb, former Prime Minister of Finland (2014–2015), and former Foreign Minister Pekka Haavisto, now independent candidate running with the endorsement of the Green League, contested in a runoff on February 11 with Stubb winning. Voters elected a President of the Republic for a six-year term.

Parliament

There are various reasons for the frequent parliamentary deadlocks. The 200-seat unicameral chamber, the Eduskunta (42% members are women, only exceeded in Sweden, with 44%) has many powers. They include the power to amend the constitution, to force cabinets to resign, and to approve legislation, which is not subject to judicial review. Its members are elected by a system of proportional representation. This kind of electoral system always permits a large number of parties to win seats in parliament. The greater the number of parties, the greater the difficulty of forming a stable governing coalition that can count on a parliamentary majority. Winning a vote on certain kinds of legislation, such as important or urgent economic measures, is particularly difficult. Such measures require majorities of two-thirds or even five-sixths of the members. This is a requirement that is unique to Finland and one that some leading political figures are determined to change.

At the present time, four big parties occupy most of the seats in the Eduskunta. None is a mass, catchall party that attracts voters from all social and occupational

groups. Therefore, there is no prospect of a parliamentary majority being won by any one party or even by the two left-wing or the two nonsocialist parties. This is especially true since the voting strength for all major parties has, on the whole, remained remarkably stable for the past 60 years. In practice, coalitions can be held together only if a minimum of three of the four largest parties participate in them. This confuses even Finnish voters; in 2011 a third of them could not name the four parties in the governing coalition.

Parties of the Left

The Social Democratic Party of Finland (SDP), led by Antti Lindtman, is the chief spokesman for organized labor and for lower-level employees. Although not a heavily ideological party, it is one of the most leftist members in the Socialist International. The party officially favors an expansion of the social welfare system. The latter objective is particularly difficult, however, because of the requirement for especially large parliamentary majorities to enact economic measures. Social Democratic prime ministers, who must always lead coalitions that include nonsocialist parties, have shown themselves to be pragmatists who are very willing to pursue a conservative economic policy if Finland's well-being seems to require it. Former party leader Sanna Marin has headed the center-left government from 2019 to 2023. At the age of 34, she was the youngest prime minister in Finnish history.

The other traditional leftist party was the Communist Party of Finland (SKP), a workers' party. In order to attract a larger following among intellectuals, youth, and others who favored a radical change of society, but who did not wish to belong to a rigidly structured communist party, the SKP operated within a broader united group called the People's Democratic League (SKDL). The SKP broke away from the SDP and declared itself a separate party in Moscow in 1918. It was banned from politics in the 1930s, and though legalized in 1944, the party spent the years from 1948, when it was widely suspected of having planned a coup d'etat, until 1966 in opposition. It remained organized along the Leninist lines of democratic centralism, requiring absolute obedience to the party line once the party had made a decision. The program dropped the Leninist concept of dictatorship of the proletariat, which granted a communist party, as the allegedly true representative of the people, the right to rule a country without free elections.

In the second half of the 1960s, an intraparty quarrel between an orthodox and a revisionist wing of the party erupted, and the chasm between them was opened

Finland

Former Prime Minister Juha Sipila

Prime Minister Sanna Marin

Parties of the Center and Right

The National Coalition Party (KOK, also called the Conservatives) founded in 1918, it is one of the "big three" parties that have dominated Finnish national politics for several decades, along with the Social Democratic Party of Finland and the Center Party. It is a conservative party that stresses the values of nation, private property and enterprise, religious principles, and restraint in expanding the social welfare system. It comes the closest of all Finnish parties to being a mass party, and it draws over 60% of its votes from skilled workers and employees. Led then by Jyrki Katainen, former finance minister, it maintained its leading position in the 2011 elections despite slipping to 20.4% of the votes (down from 22.3%) and 44 seats (six fewer). It formed a six-party coalition government, with Katainen as prime minister. He stepped down in 2014 to become the EC commissioner for jobs and growth. He was replaced by a member of the Swedish-speaking minority, Alex Stubb. Educated at Furman University, Sorbonne, and the College of Europe and with a doctorate from LSE, Stubb had already served as Finland's foreign, European, and trade minister. He is a strong proponent of European integration and globalization.

Although it supported the "Kekkonen line" in foreign policy, it was distrusted by the Soviet Union as being too nationalist, but it must be remembered that all Finnish parties are nationalist in the sense that their policies are oriented toward Finnish interests. It is open to NATO membership, but it does not push the issue due to popular opposition. The KOK's support for some of the government's legislation has been crucial in the past when the governing parties were unable to agree. Thus, the KOK has long been an essential feature of

wider when the Soviet Union invaded Czechoslovakia in August 1968. The more moderate, majority wing of the party embraced the idea of "Eurocommunism," or that branch of communism in democratic countries that is tailored not to the needs of the Soviet Union but to the needs of the home countries. Under chairman Avro Aalto, the leadership launched a new slogan: "Socialism with a Finnish face."

Backed by the Soviet Union, the orthodox wing, headed by Taisto Sinisalo, opposed this direction taken by the majority within the party. Therefore, Aalto's revisionist majority expelled the hardline faction of the party in 1985, leaving Finland with two communist parties, including the breakaway hardline faction called Democratic Alternative.

They joined forces under the banner Left Alliance (VAS), which under Paavo Arhinmäki's leadership won 8.1% of the votes (down .7%) and 14 seats (down 3) in 2011. Although the communists are often exasperatingly shifty partners who maneuver to avoid responsibility for unpopular programs, observers generally agree that their sharing of government responsibility has been good both for them and for Finland. In 2015, they lost 2 more seats (down to 12), with 7.2% of the popular vote. Under the leadership of Li Andersson, the party gained support in the 2017 municipal elections and the 2019 parliamentary election; in the latter, the party won 8.20% of the votes and 16 seats increasing its representation in the parliament for the first time since 1995. At the 2023 Finnish parliamentary election, the Alliance suffered a defeat, being reduced to 11 MPs (7.06% of the votes).

The Green League (VIHR) captured 7.3% of the votes (down 1.2%) and 10 seats (a loss of 5) in 2011. Environmental issues, particularly global warming and

nuclear power, played a leading role in the electoral campaign, as they did again in 2015, especially with the controversial planned nuclear power plant in Pyhajoki. This time the Greens, under the leadership of Ville Niinisto (the president's nephew), received 8.5% of votes and increased their share of seats to 15.

From 2015 to 2019, the party was in opposition providing severe criticism regarding the actions of the conservative Sipilä Cabinet, such as financial support for economically well-off companies, Fortum's purchase of Uniper, and the expedited process of constitution-changing surveillance laws.

In the 2023 parliamentary election, the Greens suffered a defeat, receiving only 7.03% of the vote (a decrease from 11.49% won in 2019) and 13 seats (a decrease of 7). Since June 2023, the party's leader and chairman has been Sofia Virta.

Finnish-designed products are known worldwide.

Finland

Finnish politics. Little separates the major rightist parties doctrinally. KOK party member Sauli Niinisto was elected president in 2012. In 2015, the party lost the leading position and a sixth of seats—down to 38 and 18.2% of popular vote. However, it was invited to join Juha Sipila's governing coalition, and Alex Stubb became the new finance minister. In June 2016, his leadership of the party was challenged, and Petteri Orpo became the new leader as well as Finland's finance minister. Petteri Orpo is currently serving as the prime minister of Finland. KOK became the largest party in Finland in the 2023 general election, winning 20.82% of the votes (48 seats), and it has been the lead party in the governing Orpo Cabinet since 20 June 2023.

The fourth and largest major party is the Center Party (KESK). It changed its name in 1965 from the Agrarian Union and attempted to expand its base to include more than the farmers. This effort was only partially successful, and although one-fourth of its voters are workers, about a third are farmers. Not surprisingly, its strength is in rural areas. It advocates protection of Finnish agricultural interests, private property, individual rights, and economic and governmental decentralization. It seeks to balance out the political left and right.

In 2003 and again in 2007, the Center Party narrowly emerged as the largest party. In 2011 it fell to fourth place, winning only 15.8% of the votes (down from 23%) and 36 seats (down by 16). Mari Kiviniemi relinquished her prime ministership, and the party moved onto the opposition benches.

The 2015 election brought the Center Party to power again when it won 21.1% of popular vote and gained additional 14 seats, for the total of 49. Its leader, Juha Sipila—a telecommunications and bioenergy multimillionaire and revivalist Lutheran—became prime minister. Expecting a tough fight ahead to jump-start the economy against labor unions' resistance, Sipila shunned the Social Democrats and created a three-party coalition with The Finns Party and the National Coalition Party.

The Center Party was again the biggest loser in the 2019 Finnish parliamentary election, winning 13.76% of the vote (down from 21.10%) thus losing 18 seats and going from largest party to fourth place. The party's support was even lower than in 2011. Due to the defeat, Sipilä consequently announced that he would continue as the chairman only until the Center Party's next convention. The party congress in September 2019 elected Katri Kulmuni minister of finance and the former minister of economic affairs to replace Sipila as the party's chair. On September 5, 2020, at the next party congress, Annika Saarikko was elected as the party leader

to replace Katri Kulmuni. At the 2023 parliamentary election, the Center Party won 11.30% of the vote (23 seats) and went into opposition.

A telling development involving the Center occurred in 2003, when it was led by a tough, no-nonsense farmer's daughter and lawyer from rural western Finland, Anneli Jaatteenmaki. Her party constructed a three-party governing coalition. For two months, she became the country's first female prime minister, and Finland became the first European democracy to have both a female president and prime minister. She accused then-prime minister Lipponen of having been too cozy with the Americans and having failed to take a firm enough stand against US-British policy on Iraq. However, she was accused of lying about the leak of Foreign Ministry documents used to blame Lipponen of compromising the country's neutrality by supporting the war against Saddam Hussein.

Since most Finns opposed the war, this played well to voters. However, Finns are even more insistent that their politicians tell the truth, and they were shocked. Transparency International cites Finland as one of the world's least corrupt countries. After denying that she had the documents, extracts from them showed up on her website, and a leak from inside her party revealed that she had the papers in her possession. The police interviewed Jaatteenmaki, and her government was paralyzed by a media frenzy. Although she admitted no wrongdoing, she concluded that the scandal made it impossible for her to remain as prime minister. After 63 days in office, she resigned in June 2003. A year later, in May 2004 she was tried on charges of illegally obtaining and leaking secret documents but was acquitted. The trial was broadcast on national TV and attracted record attention.

She was replaced as prime minister in June 2003 by ex-defense minister Matti Vanhanen of the Center Party. A teetotaling former journalist, he is a specialist on the EU. He was the country's most popular politician. With his unassuming manner and clean-cut good looks, he was named by a women's magazine as the sexiest man in Finland. His popularity was only burnished by a book, *The Prime Minister's Bride*, written by a former girlfriend, Susan Kuronen (who changed her last name to Ruusunen, Finnish for "Sleeping Beauty"), and published just before the March 2007 elections, exposing lurid details of their nine-month love life. Like a stoic Finn, he ignored it until after the election, when he sued the publisher for invading his privacy and won. Vanhanen left politics in 2011 to become CEO of the Finnish Family Firms Association.

Plenty of women remained in the government, including a former Miss Finland Tanja Karpela as culture minister. They must remain on guard while working in parliament. An internal report on sexual harassment, published in 2008, revealed that a third of female employees had received inappropriate comments from men, 15% had been subjected to improper advances, and 7% had received propositions for sex. In 40% of the cases, the advances or comments had been made by a member of parliament.

Over the years the Swedish People's Party of Finland (RKP) has declined steadily due to the decreasing percentage of Swedish-speaking voters to the present 5.5%. To counter this decline, the RKP disassociated itself in 1964 from its purely Swedish-language base and proclaimed a socially progressive national policy. Still, the great majority of its voters are found in the Swedish-speaking minority. In 2010, the party added the word Suomen ("of Finland") to its official Finnish name. Led by Stefan Wallin in 2011, it won 4.3% of the votes (down by .9%) and nine seats. In 2015, it received 4.9% of votes, without any change in the number of seats. It was left out from the ruling coalition. It became again a part of the ruling coalition after the parliamentary election in 2019 and 2023 winning 4.53% and 4.31% of the votes respectively, keeping the same number of seats.

The biggest electoral shock came from the antiestablishment populist the True Finns (Finnish: Perussuomalaiset, PS), a party founded in 1995 but in obscurity until 2011. Renamed The Finns and led by the jovial Timo Soini (SOY- knee), it catapulted to 19.1% of the votes (up from 4.1%) and 39 seats (up from a mere 5) at the 2011 parliamentary election. It was the only party entering parliament to gain seats. One of its greatest challenges is that it attracts only about 10% of women's votes. Soini is an effective, down-to-earth orator, who sells himself as a man of the people who understands the plight on the poor and working class. He played the anti-immigrant card, calling the country's 2.5% foreigners "parasites on taxpayers' money" and "gang rapists." Surprisingly, that he did not spare Finland's 5.5% native Swedish minority in his tirade.

Soini's party got its electoral breakthrough from the eurozone's sovereign debt crisis. Portugal requested about $110 billion from the EU 11 days before the Finnish election. Soini mercilessly criticized the notion that Finland should contribute to bailouts of profligate members. He liked to refer to the EU as "the heart of darkness," and he tapped into a growing feeling among some Finns that they are losing their national identity

Finland

and control of their destiny. He touched a nerve when he demanded that "the Finnish cow should be milked in Finland." Even though all the other major parties are pro-EU and proeuro, The Finns' success reverberates in Brussels and throughout the EU. A bailout requires unanimity of all members, and the Finnish parliament must approve any such expenditure. Soini vowed to block any bailout. He ruled out joining the government in 2011 because he refused to diminish his party's opposition to EU bailouts. This decision cleared the way for the National Coalition Party to form a broad six-party pro-EU government with the Social Democrats and some smaller parties. In 2012 Soini was trounced in the national presidential elections, placing a distant fourth.

The Finns did very well in the 2015 elections, gaining the second-largest share of seats (38), despite coming in third in terms of popular vote (17.7%). This time, they were helped by the growing anti-immigrant sentiment. In contrast to 2011, this time Timo Soini appeared eager to join the government, and indeed, The Finns did so, with Soini becoming Finland's foreign minister. Once in, he had to defend the government from the criticism from his own party, upset at its soft approach to immigration. His party's member of parliament publicly called for the destruction of "this nightmare called multiculturalism." Losing in public opinion polls and pressured to leave the coalition, the pragmatic Soini shot back, "When you are on the front line, you can't leave the machine gun, you can't leave the group. That is a very Finnish way. People vote for us to get things done, not just be the wise guy."

This accommodation did not work well for The Finns, as the party's popular appeal shrunk by early 2017 to 9% (from 17% at the last election). The party was involved in the labor-market reform that helped stabilize the economy, but its base felt disappointed. In June 2017, The Finns elected as their leader Jussi Halla-aho, an ardent anti-immigration advocate, together with a slate of nationalist hardliners. In 2012, Finland's Supreme Court found Jussi Halla-aho guilty of ethnic incitement and ordered him to pay a fine for having insulted Islam and Somali emigrants. Jussi Halla-aho vowed to push his party's Euroskeptic agenda and cooperate closely with the anti-immigration Sweden Democrats and Danish People's Party. His party's governmental partners acted to remove it from the government, but an imminent collapse was averted when, unexpectedly, The Finns split into two entities. Of their 38 members of parliament, 21 decided to leave and form their party, the more moderate Blue Reform, later renamed The Finnish Reform Movement. The group included foreign minister Timo Soini. In the words of one of the leaders, the politicians expected that "this decision will likely ruin our political careers . . . but we are determined to do this. . . Today we are not politicians, but we are doing this for the fatherland's sake."

Following this 2017 split, the defector group, Blue Reform, continued to support the government coalition, while the Finns Party went into opposition. The party, having been reduced to 17 seats after the split, increased its representation to 39 seats in the 2019 parliamentary election, while the breakaway Blue Reform failed to

Prime Minister Petteri Orpo
Source Wikipedia

win any seats. During the 2023 parliamentary election the Finns Party finished in second place and recorded their strongest result, 20% of the vote and 46 seats, since the party's founding.

Since 2020, further minor splits have occurred within the party, forming the Power Belongs to the People and Blue-and-Black Movement. In June 2021, Jussi Halla-aho announced that he would retire from his position as a party leader in August 2021. He was succeeded by MP Riikka Purra.

In April 2023, Petteri Orpo, National Coalition Party leader, announced his attention to form a governing coalition with the Finns Party, Swedish People's Party, and the Christian Democrats. In the Orpo Cabinet, The Finns have seven ministers out of 19. Their former party leader Jussi Halla-aho was elected Speaker of the Parliament of Finland. The Finns party's first minister of economy Vilhelm Junnila had to leave office after just ten days because of his past actions and potential connections to neo-Nazi organizations. His successor, Wille Rydman, was conspicuous for his racism. He had called Middle Easterners "monkeys" in private text messages.

From among the many parties, the parliament must put together a cabinet, called the Council of State (Valtioneuvosto), and appoint and dismiss the prime minister and up to 17 cabinet ministers. The latter need not be members of the parliament, but as a group must enjoy a majority in the legislature. Cabinets tend to be very short-lived, and the country had 60 governments before it had celebrated the 60th anniversary of its independence. There were 12 governments in the 1970s alone, and Finland now has about a dozen living

The euro comes to Finland.   Courtesy: Central Audiovisual Library, European Commission

Finland

ex-prime ministers. Yet, new governments are usually created by merely shuffling around a few cabinet seats.

Thus, there is somewhat more cabinet stability than meets the eye. The Center Party and the Social Democratic Party have been crucial participants in almost every government. Until 1995 the National Coalition was consistently excluded, and the major nonsocialist parties cannot assemble a majority in parliament. Of course, neither can the two leftist parties, so there is no alternative to the delicate broad coalitions that have become the rule.

ECONOMY

After World War II had ended, the Soviet Union handed the exhausted and defeated Finland a reparations bill that could only make the Finns shudder. They had to give the Russians a large part of their merchant marine and to deliver heavy industrial products—ships, metal, and engineering equipment—at prices that the Russians had established arbitrarily. This seemed like a terrible demand to make on a country that had always been primarily agricultural and whose industry was limited almost exclusively to wood products.

In the end, the Soviet demands proved to be a great blessing in disguise for the Finns. The sums to be paid were not impossible, and they were paid by 1952. But by having been forced to create a heavy industrial base and thereby to diversify its industry in order to pay the reparations, Finland established the very foundation for its present economic prosperity. The Finns have a habit of paying what they owe. They were the only Europeans to pay off all of their debts from both world wars. Finland experienced an extraordinary economic transformation in the second half of the 20th century. Shortly after the war, its gross domestic product (GDP) per capita was a third below that of Sweden, but today its high economic output per capita is similar to that of other Western European economies, such as Germany, Austria, and Sweden; 70% of its people worked the land, but now that latter figure is only 4%, producing 3% of GDP. Its modern economy employs 73% of the workforce in services, producing 71% of GDP, and 23% in industry, creating 26% of GDP. It is a mixed economy, which combines a free market with a Nordic welfare state model. In 2022, GDP in Finland amounted to over 269 billion euros.

Economic Links with Russia

Finland established significant trade patterns with the Soviet Union, which was until 1991 its most important single trading partner. Not only did the Soviet Union provide 90% of Finland's oil, half of its

electricity, and all of its natural gas, but also it was a guaranteed market for Finnish exports, even though this two-way trade declined somewhat in the 1980s, and both Finns and Soviets increased their trade with the west. As the USSR diversified its trade with the west under Mikhail Gorbachev after 1985, Finns began to worry about losing business and about their ability to compete. Nevertheless, when the average Finn thought of the Soviet Union, he thought perhaps as much of economic opportunity as of political danger. To some extent, this was still true three decades later, when the sanctions imposed on Russia in the wake of its meddling in Ukraine hurt Finland as much as Russia.

The Finnish shipbuilding industry was one of the greatest beneficiaries of the Soviet reparation demands. Finland had to replace its own fleet, and it then turned to production of ships for export. Until the 1990s sales to the Soviet Union accounted for more than 8% of Finland's total exports. The Soviet Union was particularly interested in Finnish-made ships suited for Arctic conditions, and more than 80% of the shipyards' orders came from that country. Russia was also an especially good customer in that it paid for these ships as soon as they left the slipway. Further specialties include high-technology shipping, such as liquid gas carriers, cable layers, and Arctic oilfield vessels. Most of the "love boats" cruising in the Caribbean, half of the world's icebreakers, and the drilling rigs used to bore a fourth of the offshore wells in the North Sea were constructed in Finland.

The Soviet Union was an avid buyer of products from its only immediate neighbor that had an advanced western economy and technology. It bought ships, machinery, paper, chemicals, and large quantities of food and drink, tobacco products, clothing and footwear. It also welcomed the large-scale production

projects that Finland conducted just over the Soviet border. These include the construction of a wood-processing complex at Paajarvi, the enlargement of a paper and pulp complex at Svetogorsk, and the largest of all—the Kostamus project, involving construction of an open-cast iron-ore-mining complex 30 miles (48 km) inside the Soviet Union. Such projects were far more attractive than similar Finnish projects in the Middle East because Finnish workers could return home on weekends, and the projects stimulated economic activity in the nearby northern and eastern parts of Finland, which badly needed economic stimulation.

The USSR gave Finnish firms contracts to build 50 villages deeper in the Soviet Union along the gas pipeline being constructed to transport natural gas from Siberia to western Europe. By 1991 Finnish companies had signed about 260 joint-venture agreements with the USSR, but only a handful went into operation.

Finland is one of the highest per-capita energy users of the world and has to worry particularly about its supplies. Its electrical consumption is third in Europe, behind Norway and Sweden. It is one of the richest countries in peat resources, and it does fire some power plants with this material. With no oil, gas, or coal of its own and with hydroelectric resources that do not come close to those of Sweden or Norway, it must import about two-thirds of its energy. Over a fourth (29%) of its energy is renewable, compared with the EU average of 6.4%. About half comes from Russia, including not only oil, electricity and all its gas but also nuclear fuel services.

In contrast to the Swedes, the Finns have not been paralyzed over the question of nuclear power. There is a powerful Green Movement that has to be persuaded. Two of Finland's four reactors are from the former USSR, and the fuel for its two Swedish-built ones is enriched in Russia. The

Finland

Russians also promised not only to provide nuclear fuel but also to dispose of much of the nuclear wastes, thereby largely freeing the Finns from that frightening problem. Nuclear power plants produce 28% of Finland's electricity and a seventh of all its energy. Again, Finns saw that the Soviet Union not only gave them headaches but aspirin, as well. Nevertheless, one reason for maintaining and expanding nuclear power is the fear of overdependence on Russia for energy supplies.

Finland is one of the few EU countries to expand its nuclear power after the Chernobyl accident in 1986 and the Fukushima disaster in 2011. A third of its electricity is now produced from nuclear power. Alternative sources of energy, such as solar or wind power, are of limited use due to the climate, and Finland is wary of dependence on foreign energy supplies. It constructed its fifth power plant, Olkiluoto 3, on the site of two existing safe and well-run reactors at Eurajoki on the western Bothnian coast. Financed privately and using cutting-edge technology, it was Finland's largest investment project to date whose construction began in 2005 and was due to be completed in 2009 but ran into massive cost overruns. The final cost ballooned from $3.4 billion to at least $9.6 billion. It was completed and its commercial operation began on May 1, 2023. Olkiluoto 3 is currently the most powerful nuclear power plant unit in Europe and the third most powerful globally.

The parliament approved the construction of two more nuclear plants that will allow the country to build its sixth and seventh nuclear facilities. In 2014 the government approved a further reactor constructed by the Russian state-owned Rosatom. However, Finland insisted that 60% of the cost of the Hanhikivi 1,200-megawatt reactor in Pyhajoki in western Finland should be covered by companies residing in the EU, Norway, Iceland, or

Finnish student (R) with a Norwegian (L) classmate at College of Europe, Warsaw

Switzerland. When one mysterious Croatian company, most likely financed by Moscow, was rejected by the regulators, the controversial project that strained relations with the EU (accusing Finland of placing Russian interests above those of the EU) was slowed down. Rosatom will own 34% of the plant and receive the same percentage of the power it generates, with the right to use or sell it. The power company Fennovoima announced in April 2021 that construction of the plant would begin in 2023 and commercial operation would start in 2029. In May 2022, because of the Russian invasion of Ukraine, Fennovoima terminated its contract with Rosatom to build the power plant.

Finland is at the forefront of nuclear waste disposal; an underground repository bunker for its highly radioactive waste is being built on the site. Its expansion of nuclear power is desirable, since it limits excessive energy reliance on Russia. Plans to build a cable between Finland and Sweden will make it easier for the latter to import electricity from Finnish nuclear plants.

After the arrival of perestroika in the USSR, the former certainties of trade with a reliable Soviet Union vanished. Finns no longer could be sure who on the Soviet side was making key business decisions, and they complained that they were no longer being paid on time. Because of violence and economic shortages in the USSR, Finnish workers were no longer eager to go there to work, even for short periods of time. The Soviets curbed oil and gas deliveries to Finland. Finns received a particularly rude shock in 1991, when the Soviet government ended the bilateral clearinghouse system based on semi-barter trade and replaced it with a normal trade arrangement financed through convertible currencies. This had a temporarily devastating effect on trade with the Soviet Union. Finnish exports to its neighbor dropped 34% in the first month alone to a level of 8% of Finland's total exports, a far cry from the 25% only two decades earlier. Overnight Finland was running a balance of payments deficit with the Soviet Union and was becoming far more dependent upon its markets in western Europe.

This turn of events plunged Finland into its deepest recession since 1945 and revealed a prominent Achilles' heel in the Finnish economy. In 1991 its GDP declined by 5% and its industrial production by 15%, and it faced record unemployment and bankruptcies. However, Finnish efforts to boost trade with Russia succeeded, rising by a third in 1994. By 2015 Russia accounted for only 9.7% of Finland's exports and 18.3% of its imports. Nevertheless, Finnish exports to Russia have grown by 25% per year in the 21st century. Half of its imports were oil and gas, and a growing percentage of its exports were luxury goods for newly rich Russians. Countries use Finland as a conduit to Russia for goods because the two countries' common border functions well.

Profiting from this burgeoning trade are the ports of Hamina and Kotka, located 36 and 66 kilometers, respectively, from the Russian border. These are the EU's most easterly ports and are becoming increasingly important hubs for lucrative Russian traffic. St. Petersburg's affluent bourgeoisie are welcome guests. Russian is replacing English as the first foreign language taught in local schools in those communities.

In 2012 Finland issued more than 1.2 million visas to Russians, a third of all visas issued to Russians in all Schengen area countries. This worried Finland's partners since the visitors to that country are then free to move throughout the borderless continent, bringing a lot of Russians to other Schengen member states. It is the responsibility of the country of entry to monitor and regulate the influx of outsiders to the area.

Other Sectors of Economy

Although only about 7% of its land can be used for agriculture, Finland was traditionally a farming country. But the percentage of Finns who earn a living from the land or from forestry has decreased steadily from almost 70% in 1880 to almost 50% on the eve of World War II to 36% in 1960 and to 14% by 1978. In 2015 farming employed only 4.1% of the population and contributed 3% of GDP.

Almost 90% of farms are still operated by families. They have grown in size by 44% since joining the EU in 1995 as farmers seek economy of scale. Because of the small size of most farms, the short growing season, and the bitter weather conditions in winter, productivity in agriculture is relatively low. Farm income has declined by 35% since accession to the EU because the country's high food prices fail to keep pace with rising production costs. Many farmers can survive only by engaging also in forestry, often in the wooded areas that they themselves own. Yet, Finland remains self-sufficient in all foodstuffs except fruits and vegetables and, if the harvest is bad, in grain. Dairy and meat products are in surplus and are therefore exported.

The rapid flight from the farms created serious economic and social problems for Finland. From the 1950s to the 1970s, many Finns either emigrated to other countries, especially to Sweden, or poured into the urban centers in the southern part of Finland. In the Economist of London, one observer described the development this way: "Finland is roughly a jug-shaped country.

Finland

Imagine the jug filled with the kind of liqueur that has tiny golden specks floating in it. Left alone, nearly all the Finns would, like those specks, drift slowly down to the bottom. Three out of five of them already live in the southernmost fifth of the country." The results of this southward drift were urban problems of tight and expensive housing; a proliferation of concrete suburbs; and, above all, unemployment.

Finland used to be called a country short on investment capital and long on labor, but many of its citizens who left to find work abroad, especially in Sweden, are returning home. Further, Finland has larger direct investments in other countries than foreign firms have in Finland. It has poured large sums of money into developing and diversifying the economic base in the northern four-fifths of the country. This is especially difficult given the transportation impediments caused by the great distances, sparse population, and cold climate. The only favorable transportation factor is the long water routes branching in many directions.

The main objective is not to make farming more attractive but to offer tax relief and other subsidies to businesses that locate there and train or retrain rural inhabitants. It does this primarily through the Regional Development Fund, shortened in Finnish to Finvera. Though state-owned, it refuses to rescue lame-duck industries. It encourages risk-taking, but it also demands profitability. The Finnish government promotes social, health, cultural, and educational services in the north and attempts to shift a portion of administration and decision-making away from the Helsinki area.

It looked to its neighbors, especially Sweden, for help; Sweden provided half the foreign capital invested in Finland. However, by the mid-1990s, Finland had become more of an equal economic partner with Sweden. Many foreign investments in Sweden are now of Finnish origin. The Nordic Investment Bank has helped to finance joint Finnish-Norwegian and Finnish-Swedish projects in the north of Finland.

Nokia (named after a town and river of that name in southwest Finland) is Finland's biggest high-tech company and was once the world's biggest producer of mobile phones, accounting for a third of the global market for mobile telephone handsets. It steadily lost ground due to stiff competition from companies like Samsung and Apple, accounting by 2013 for only 4% of the global mobile market. In 2014 it sold its handset division to Microsoft for $7.2 billion. When Microsoft subsequently slashed its handset business in half, thousands of Finns were laid off. Nokia now focuses on its profitable networking

technology, which enables telecom operators to run their wireless networks, and its map technology, which offers a global database of geographical information. This sale stirred up a lot of emotion, especially when it became known that Stephen Elop, the first non-Finn to manage the company, was getting a severance payment of over $25 million, which he refused to decline.

Although less than 1.5% of its global sales were in Finland, Nokia found an enthusiastic market in its very own neighborhood. Finland now has more mobile phones than fixed-line telephones: 92% of households have one or more cell phones, the highest percentage in the world. It is normal for seven-year-olds to begin using them.

Foreigners, primarily Americans, own about 90% of its shares, but Nokia's economic predominance in Finland was almost unique in the world. With $35 billion in annual sales, it was at one time the engine of the economy, accounting for 5% of GDP, a quarter of Finland's economic growth, two-thirds of the value of the stock market, nearly a fifth of Finland's total exports, up to 23% of all corporation tax, and as much as 30% of the country's R&D. Its earnings roughly equaled the total Finnish government budget. Only one of its nine plants worldwide is in Finland. About 22,000 of its 54,000 employees work in Finland, and another 20,000 Finns work for companies that depend on Nokia for contracts. A company located in the US comparable in size in proportion to the overall population would employ about 1 million persons.

Some Finns worry that their economy had become too dependent upon this one giant company. No wonder one Helsinki hotelier noted, "We pay more attention to the chief executive of Nokia than to the prime minister." However, due to poor leadership and complacency bred of success, compounded by an overconsensual culture that works against rapid change, Nokia missed the smartphone revolution, and its lead existed only in less sophisticated "feature phones." The firm uses English as its official language. The company announced in 2012 that a fifth of its workforce would be cut, many of them in Finland. More production has been shifted to Asia. HMD Global bought the handheld business back from Microsoft in 2016. In 2017, Finnish startup HMD launched a new Nokia smartphone line. More than half of the company's workforce are former Nokia employees, and its headquarters are located right next to Nokia's.

Finland is fortunate to have many valuable raw materials. The most plentiful, and luckily renewable, resource is wood—lots of it. Two-thirds of its forests are privately owned. This, together with

its paper products, accounts for a fifth of its exports and gross production. The wood and paper industry also provides employment for 19% of the work force. Although the financially strong US and Canadian paper mills meet half of western Europe's wood pulp needs, Finland's highly efficient paper plants still find their major market in western Europe. They are suffering from the shift away from printed newspapers and magazines toward online media. Finns must watch very carefully the less desirable by-product of paper mills: pollution.

About half of the iron ore needed for its domestic market is produced locally, and it has rich deposits of nonferrous metal, as well. It is one of Europe's leading producers of nickel and copper and also mines zinc, chromium, and cobalt and produces 10% of the world's vanadium. These generous mineral deposits, along with its forced diversification after 1945, have enabled Finland to build an efficient metal and engineering industry. This sector now produces 19% of exports and a fifth of the gross production. It also employs 34% of the labor force. Diversification has further spread to the chemical and textile sectors, which now produce 9% of exports and provide work for 19% of the labor force.

As might be expected, the economy is very export-oriented. More than a third of total production must be exported, and a quarter of total consumption must be met by imports. Of course, some industrial branches are even more dependent upon exportation than others. For instance, the forest industry exports 80%–90% of its production, the textile and clothing factories about 45%, and the metal and engineering industries about 40%. Overall 38% of GDP is generated by exports. This is an important reason Finland is very sensitive to any changes in the international trade or political climate and why it has a special minister for foreign trade. Its major market is western Europe; almost two-thirds of its trade turnover is with EU and EFTA countries. Germany, Sweden, and Netherlands are its major western European trading partners.

UK's and Denmark's entry into the EU made it advantageous for Finland to sign in 1973 an industrial free-trade agreement with the EU effective in 1977. Although it did not yet become a member of the EU's Common Agricultural Program, it enjoyed complete duty-free trade with the EU countries since 1984. The Commission approved Finland 's CAP Strategic Plan in August 2022, and its implementation started by stages during 2023. Its economic ties with the west were also facilitated by its associate membership in EFTA and its full membership in the WTO, the OECD, and the Nordic Council.

The sensitivity on the part of the Soviet Union had earlier dissuaded Finland from seeking EU membership. That changed in the 1990s. In 1992 the Finns formally applied, and in 1995 Finland joined the EU together with Sweden and Austria. A Finn, Jacob Soderman, became the EU's first ombudsman in 1995. The Finnish government regards membership as an essential economic and political anchor for the country in the post-Cold War era, especially given the economic problems at home and the instability in neighboring Russia. In 1999 it became the first Nordic country to adopt the euro.

Unlike in most other European countries, labor unions are gaining members and now represent 80% of the labor force. They are politicized and strongly support the SDP. Nevertheless, they usually have been willing to enter general income agreements with all governments and industries that are designed to keep the economy efficient and competitive. Finns' success also stems partly from a high degree of economic pragmatism. They used to view Sweden as their model, but much of their recent economic success was due to their willingness to deviate from that model.

Finns were concerned about unemployment, which had grown to 9% in 2014; however, the real figure would be as high as 15% if early retirement, training programs, and subsidized work were included. The problem remains, though, that job losses from low-tech plant closures almost match the number of new jobs created by high-tech successes. Finland has been hesitant to use public funds to shore up inefficient and unprofitable industries. Further, they have not avoided cutting public spending or taxes and introducing stringent monetary control and financial restraint to protect their overall economic health.

The Estonians are coming!

The May 2004 entry into the EU of Estonia, whose wages and corporate tax rates are far lower, caused unease. But Finland responded by cutting corporate taxes from 29% to 26% and by gradually lowering income taxes though the top end is still close to 50%. The wealth tax was abandoned in 2006. Every November 1, known as National Jealousy Day, every citizen's taxable income is published online.

The fact that a fifth of all alcohol consumed in Finland comes from Estonia compelled the Finns to reduce the price of alcohol by a third in order to compete. For two years it also required Estonians and other east Europeans to have work permits in order to stem the flow of cheap labor.

Finland in the early 21st century has one of Europe's steadiest economies, increasing an average of 3.4% per year from 1994 to 2005, a blazing 6% in 2006, 0.4% in 2015, and 2.6% in 2022, after a few disappointing years. According to international index rankings in 2012, Finland placed best in corruption perceptions, 3rd in global competitiveness, 4th in global innovation, 7th in prosperity, and 11th in ease of doing business. From 2005 on, the World Economic Forum (WEF) consistently ranked it at the top in competitiveness. The Economist in 2014 ranked its business environment eighth in the world. It does this while protecting its environment. Yale and Columbia Universities placed it as number 1 on their 2016 Environmental Performance Index; the US was in 26th place.

High technology and a research and development commitment of 3.5% of GDP (70% from the private sector) per year (compared with 4.3% for Sweden and 2.6% for the US) are among its secrets of success. Among the promoters of technology research in Finland is a national technology agency, called Tekes, which supports basic and applied research at universities and other research institutes (40%) and to businesses (60%); the Finnish National Fund for Research and Development; and the Finnish Academy of Science and Letters. In the 2015 Bloomberg Index of Innovative Countries, Finland came in 4th (out of 50 ranked), with particularly high scores for research and development, manufacturing, education, and research personnel.

Technology is so prevalent that students at the Helsinki University of Technology devised a computer program in 2005, called the Virtual Air Guitar Project. It enables literally anybody to create rock solos by simply wearing a pair of wired gloves and strumming an imaginary guitar, while a computer registers the hand movements and adds musical accompaniment to match the player's finger work precisely. Other Finnish computer geeks made their own full-length galactic animation film

that millions of viewers around the world downloaded for free. There is a thriving new gaming sector. It includes Rovio, which makes the wildly successful Angry Birds smartphone game that has already spawned a very popular movie and some theme parks. And when the British engineering group Rolls-Royce sought a place to locate its center for development of remote-control and autonomous ships, it chose Finland. The "intelligent ship" systems are intended to take control of navigation across fjords, with humans taking over only for maneuvers within harbors.

Another bright spot that confirms Finland's prowess in the world of consumer electronics is Supercell, the maker of such hit electronic games as Clash of Clans, Hay Day, and Clash Royale. With only 200 employees, in 2015 Supercell had revenues of $2.4 billion.

Finland maintains one of the highest levels of prosperity in the industrialized world. It is also one of the most inclusive societies, with economic inequality and a poverty rate among the world's lowest. It recovered well in 1991–1993 from its deepest recession since 1945, during which it suffered the worst decline of any western European country in recent times. Foreign trade by 2005 had doubled to 40% of GDP in only a decade and a half. Exports were booming, investment was high, growth was positive, and inflation was 1.5% in 2022. Total public debt was down to 50% of GDP in 2012, and the budget was in deficit by only 2.4% of GDP in 2022. Its earlier attempts to meet the convergence criteria for the EU common currency succeeded. They are only one of two original euro members that have always stayed within the EU's currency treaty limits. In 2012 Standard and Poor's left the country as one of only four triple-A-rated eurozone economies. The economy remains strong.

Finland did not escape the global recession that shook countries in 2009. In the first quarter of 2009, its economy contracted by 7.6%. This was the first time since 1993 that this had happened.

Despite their irritation, Finns contributed to the EU bailouts of Greece. But they are not willing to pay the debts of other states. This hard stance is a consequence of their tradition of national self-reliance. They suffered a severe banking crisis and recession from 1990 to 1993, and their country did not seek outside assistance. Their struggle to get out of the crisis laid the groundwork for strong recovery and reform. Finns believe the Mediterranean countries could do the same. A 2012 poll showed that 55% of Finns feel positive about EU membership, up from 37% a year earlier. Only 16% believed Finland should leave the euro, compared with 29% the previous year.

Finland

While the economy picked up briefly after the euro crisis, it then declined for three years and barely eked out a 0.4% growth in 2015, leading some to see Finland as the "sick man of Europe." This resulted from several factors, especially the fall of the giant Nokia that failed to capitalize on the smartphone wave, leading to the loss of thousands of jobs. In addition, wages continued to rise while productivity was falling, leading to noncompetitive labor costs. Worldwide demand for paper, an important export item, has been falling. Exports to Russia also fell by a third in 2015 due to EU sanctions and the economic crisis in that country resulting from low oil prices. It does not help that the population is aging, which means that the productive segment of the society is shrinking. Determined, the Finnish government seeks to apply the same medicine it helped force on Greece and other profligate eurozone countries: belt-tightening austerity.

In 2019 Finland ended its policy of granting unconditional pay for the unemployed. Among the goals is a new bargaining system that could lower labor costs. Also, on the table is cutting two paid public holidays, as well as reducing vacation time and pay for sick leave and overtime. Green leader Ville Niinisto criticized "the government's dictatorial package." Labor unions representing 2.2 million employees (nearly half of the country's population) immediately demurred and brought out their members on strike for the first time in decades. But former Prime Minister Sipila's government was determined to take on the unions that rejected earlier attempts at reforms. In March 2016 the largest union federation, SAK, conditionally approved a compromise plan that would lengthen annual working hours and allow for company-level wage negotiations.

The global COVID-19 economic recession, also known as the Great Lockdown, caused by the COVID-19 pandemic, began in most countries in the period February—April 2020. The economic situation in Finland during the crisis turned out to be less negative than the initial OECD prediction. By the end of 2020, the manufacturing sector had almost regained its confidence in production with the growth of business sales. The service sector, however, faced the effects of the pandemic longer due to mobility restrictions. On the other hand, the ICT industries in Finland had their momentum in both the manufacturing and service sectors and gained an advantage during this crisis. The Finnish government also managed the crisis well by effectively cushioning the shocks through, for example, adequate financial support for laid-off workers and companies in financial difficulties. Temporary changes in legislation also helped businesses survive the crisis. The OECD predicted a full economic recovery within two years.

Due to a decline in investments and household consumption, Finland's economy is in recession in 2023. Higher prices and interest rates are restricting growth in consumer spending. High-interest rates encourage households to save rather than spend. The weakness in the economy is widespread. Finland's GDP is predicted to decline by 0.5% in 2023 and by 0.2% in 2024. The slowing inflation and a downward turn in interest rates, combined with the moderately strong development of household incomes, will turn GDP into growth from the end of 2024.

CULTURE

For centuries Finnish culture was heavily dependent upon influences from abroad. Eastern Finland was always exposed to cultural trends from Russia, and Sweden was a conduit for such trends from the rest of Europe. Not until the 19th century did a specifically Finnish identity really awaken, and this was led by the elite's increased use of the Finnish language in literature, journalism, education, and politics.

Literature and Arts

A central figure in the break from the tradition of using Swedish was J. V. Snellman, a prominent university professor and statesman. Although of Swedish background himself, he was the first great author to write in Finnish. In 1835 the first part of Finland's greatest literary work, *the Kalevala*, was published. This monumental national epic by Elias Lonnrot presents traditional Finnish folk poems that tell of myths and legends. It gave

Former president Halonen celebrates her reelection.

a powerful boost to Finnish nationalism and to a yearning for independence. In 1870 another epic, *Seven Brothers*, was published by Aleksis Kivi, who portrayed the Finns of his time with great humor and realism but with very little romanticism. He established the standard for Finnish prose and drama and soon became universally recognized as Finland's national author.

Both of these epic works, *the Kalevala* and *Seven Brothers*, capture the importance that Finns attribute to common people and their identification of man's fate with mysterious, impersonal forces, often associated with forests and nature. This identification gives Finnish literature a sober, almost tragic, and often heroic tone. In most Finnish works, though, the reader senses an unmistakable national enthusiasm.

Since 1945 Finnish literature, as well as film, has reflected an intense national self-examination, with much social consciousness and criticism. It has been experimental and "modernist," with much use of loose imagery and collage. Finns have developed a particular passion for the spoken theater; it has more than 40 professional theaters and countless amateur ones, as well.

Domestic film products make up a quarter of all distributed films, up from 4% at the end of the 20th century. A few directors have an international reputation, such as Aki Kaurismaki and Aku Louhimies. The latter's film, *Frozen Land*, hardly puts his country's best foot forward; it is intended to remind the viewer of what a cold, dark, hopeless, and depressing country Finland is.

In 2007, at age 50, Kaurismaki announced his retirement with 22 other Finnish film producers when the government reneged on a promise to raise film subsidies by $1.6 million. They need the money. His 2006 film *Light in the Dusk* sold only 38,000 tickets at home, compared with 460,000 tickets sold for *Pirates of the Caribbean: At World's End*. Finns still prefer Hollywood fare.

Finland publishes more books per capita than any other nation in the world except Iceland. Because of the complexity of the Finnish language, much of its literature and drama remains untranslated and unknown outside of Finland. Other forms of cultural expression lend themselves better to international audiences. The music of Jean Sibelius (1865–1957), who drew much inspiration from *the Kalevala*, opened the way for a national romantic style and introduced Finnish music to a world audience. Finland trains more musicians per capita than any other country, and the Sibelius Academy in Helsinki is the country's highest institution for musical studies.

The Finnish opera receives particular support through the annual Savonlinna

Opera Festival, which draws large numbers of visitors from outside Finland and which presents important national works with high standards of international artistry.

The Metropolitan Opera of New York was so impressed with the quality of the Finnish National Opera that it invited the latter to perform in New York during the 1983 season. This was the first time the Met ever invited another opera company to perform in its own home. The Finns also have established a worldwide reputation for imaginative modern design in architecture, industrial arts, and city planning. In 2018 Helsinki was enriched by the opening of the Amos Rex Art Museum on Lasipalatsi Square. It was privately funded at a cost of $58 million.

Ninety percent of Finns belong to one of the two official Finnish churches, the main one being the Evangelic Lutheran Church. However, fewer than 5% attend church services outside the Christmas and Easter holidays. The two churches receive subsidies from taxes paid by registered members, but that income has dwindled so much that the Evangelic Lutheran Church had to dismiss a fourth of the people on its payroll.

Languages and Minorities

Finnish is a Finno-Ugric language related linguistically only to Estonian, Hungarian, and a couple dozen dialects spoken in isolated communities in Russia and the far north. Finnish and Estonian are very close, but the linguistic roots with Hungarian are meager. Philologists have identified only about 200 words that Finnish and either Estonian or Hungarian, on the other hand, have in common: 55 of them concern fishing, 15 deal with reindeer, and only 3 with commerce. One noted philologist came up with only one mutually comprehensible sentence: "The living fish swims in water." Finnish remains mysterious to the outsider. Finns keep it largely free of foreign words; they prefer inventing words, such as puhelin (telephone) or norsu (elephant), to borrowing them. They can make up words to be more precise. Finnish has no masculine or feminine, so they do not say "he" or "she." They have no articles ("a" or "the"). Unlike the Estonians, they have resisted modernizing their spelling, so their words seem bafflingly long.

The percentage of citizens whose primary language is Swedish has declined in the last century from 15% to about 5.5%, although both remain official languages. There are no longer serious social differences or tensions between the two language groups. In fact, aside from language, very little distinguishes the two groups from each other. Swedish-speaking Finns are still granted a great measure of cultural autonomy. There are 41 Swedish high schools in 31 cities and a Swedish university in Turku. Most Swedish speakers now also speak Finnish but not vice versa. Despite the fact that all Finnish children learn some Swedish in school, but few are able to speak it well. Most Finnish school children (91.7%) choose to learn English as their first foreign language, whereas 7.7% choose to learn Swedish as their first foreign language. Only a tiny percentage of pupils ever enroll in Russian-language courses.

Finland is probably the only state outside of the Vatican that has enough residents who understand classical Latin to justify a weekly radio program in the language. Every Friday before the evening news, five to six short news stories are reported in Latin. Many educated Finns learned it in school and consider it to be one of the country's most important links to western culture. One university professor even sings Elvis Presley songs in Latin: "Tenere me ama" ("Love me Tender") or "Ursus Taddeus" ("Teddy Bear").

There is a third population group in Finland, which has a culture and Finno-Ugric language of its own: Sámi, also known as Lapps, a short but strong people toughened by a hard life. They should not be confused with Laplanders, anyone who lives in the north (Lapland), the majority of whom are not Sámi. Their origins remain obscure, but scholars believe they were Finland's first inhabitants. Finland has only about 3,800 Sámi; there are far more in Norway (40,000) and Sweden (17,000). To the disappointment of tourists, they no longer wear their colorful blue, red, yellow, and white costumes except on festive occasions; they are mostly settled and make their living chiefly from timbering, farming, and tourism.

A fourth category of residents is immigrants and refugees. Finland still maintains a tightly restrictive refugee policy, insisting on evidence of political, religious, or racial persecution. Amnesty International had criticized Finland for returning Soviet seekers of asylum. Laws and regulations also discourage immigrants, who comprised 2.3% of the total population in 2008. Of its 108,346 foreign-born residents in 2005, Russians, Estonians, and Swedes represented 43%, and fewer than 25,000 (23%) came from nonwhite countries and were visible minorities. Its net immigration is only about 10,000 per year. It has the EU's lowest percentage of immigrants. This explains why it is the only major European country that has not generated a strong far-right party.

Still, the large influx of Somali refugees in the 1990s generated a sizable diaspora, as family reunification and a word of mouth encouraging new immigrants swelled the ranks to 16,000 by 2015 (from merely 49 in 1990). The Somalis remain poorly integrated, there are very few mixed marriages, and the immigrant children of all back-grounds tend to struggle at school, scoring significantly lower on educational tests.

Because of its low birth rate, Finland wants to attract more immigrants, and it is seeking ways to find the right kind and to make them welcome. The country's image as being cold (both in its people and climate), its remote location, its difficult language, its lack of established foreign communities, and its sky-high costs and taxes are not alluring. For centuries Finnish identity has been based on ethnic homogeneity, so the natives are not overtly welcoming. The government provides free Finnish lessons and help with job retraining. Nevertheless, an estimated quarter of foreigners are unemployed.

The migrant crisis of 2015–2016 affected Finland less than some other European countries, especially its neighbor Sweden. Still, there have been disquieting signs. As nearly 15,000 migrants from Iraq (and some 32,000 overall) entered Finland in 2015, in September a bus transporting refugee families with small children to a converted army barracks was attacked by nationalists with rocks, flares, and smoke bombs. Protesters also threw rocks at Red Cross workers. One demonstrator was dressed in a KKK-style white robe while waiving the Finnish flag. Others created a "human wall" near the Tornio border crossing from Sweden, from where most newcomers arrived, and in another city, a man threw a Molotov cocktail at an emergency shelter for migrants. The coalition government, including The Finns, condemned the violence. However, the party exploited the anti-immigrant sentiment, and its member of parliament condemned "Sipila's noble-minded gesture [that] was like a Christmas gift for human traffickers and refugees." In Tampere, far-right vigilant patrols clad in black leather and calling themselves the Soldiers of Odin walk the streets to "protect" the city from some 1,200 Syrian and Iraqi asylum seekers. The group's branches sprang up in two dozen Finnish cities.

Finns are culturally closest to their kin 50 miles across the Gulf of Finland in Estonia. They are from the same ethnic stock and can understand each other's language, with a bit of effort. The Estonians have much more practice since they have watched Finnish television for years, thereby making them the former Soviet citizens best informed about the outside world and most familiar with western problems, pornography, and advertising. In fact, their favorite Finn was a jovial TV character who did commercials for

Finland

sausages and meat, reminding them of how prosperous life could be with a capitalist economic system.

In the Gorbachev era, Finns' interest in Estonia increased. Finnish farmers sent shiploads of used farming equipment to Estonia to help in the agricultural reform, and Finnish paper was donated for use in greater book publication. Finnish and Estonian firms have established numerous joint ventures. By 1994 half of the foreign-owned businesses had Finnish partners, and 13 of 22 commitments made by the government financing corporation Finnfund were to Estonia. In characteristic fashion, the Finnish government had kept its distance from the enthusiasm toward Estonia, not wishing to appear to be undermining Soviet rule there. Finland had recognized de facto Soviet annexation of the Baltics in 1940. But in 1991 it joined other nations in recognizing the newly independent Baltic states.

Finns arrive in Tallinn by the ferry load to cash in on low prices in Estonian stores and bars. Some Finnish tourists' free-spending and heavy-drinking behavior has given Finns a bad reputation in Estonian eyes. Very few Finns behave that way at home. They are ingrained with modesty and find it difficult to self-promote in this consensus-driven society. It is sometimes said only half-jokingly that "anger in Finland is a bigger taboo than sex." It is normal to see people in restaurants eating in silence. Many consider silence to be a sign of wisdom and good manners, not boredom.

There is a Finnish-speaking minority in Estonia and in the St. Petersburg (Russia) area called Ingrians. About 30,000 of them have emigrated to Finland. They are among the most popular immigrants in Finland, but their integration is not easy. Those from Russia often no longer speak Finnish and are indistinguishable from Russians, who are much less liked. Russian immigrants complain that they are discriminated against on-the-job market and that the media view them all as gangsters, spies, or prostitutes.

Looking east, Finns also see Slavicized brethren in Karelia, who after the collapse of the USSR are pressing for greater independence from Moscow or, in some cases, outright annexation by Finland; 8,000 Finns from there have already moved to Finland. But not wanting to assume a huge economic burden, Finland wants neither a further influx nor any talk of annexation. Of the 716,000 people who live in Karelia, only about 80,000 are Finno-Ugric-speaking Karelians, of which only 18,000 (2.3%) are Finns and 6,000 (.8%) Veps, another ethnicity related to Finns. Thus, Finns and their relatives represent less than 15% of the population; most of the rest (73.6%) is Russian.

To discourage more emigration to Finland, whose wage level was 100 times as high as that in Russia in 1993, Finnish organizations are founding schools in Karelia and supplying books in Finno-Ugric languages. Also, Finnish companies have two-thirds of the 120 joint ventures there. In general, unlike in the rest of Scandinavia, immigration to Finland is almost unknown, and there are few resident aliens.

The Media

Finnish-Swedish bilingualism is practiced in the mass media. The Finnish Broadcasting Company (YLE), a state-owned organization, operates or supervises all radio and television broadcasting. It has no radio advertising, and two of its television channels have none. It broadcasts Swedish TV programs in western and southern Finland, and there are Swedish-language radio stations. A Sámi radio station broadcasts in Lapland, and Radio Finland transmits in various European languages. Domestic production accounts for 57% of all programs, and 54% of foreign programs are from Europe and 29% from the US. Foreign programs are transmitted in the original language with subtitles. The Finnish Broadcasting Company gets the large part of its revenues from license fees. There is a privately owned MTV Ltd. (having nothing to do with American MTV), which finances its operations through advertising. There are also private local radio stations (most owned by newspapers and publishers), cable TV companies, and a few local TV stations.

More than 200 Finnish-language and more than 20 Swedish-language newspapers are privately owned. In the decade following independence, Finnish newspapers were mainly tied to political parties, but now more and more are independent of parties. The *Helsingin Sanomat* has become by far the largest in circulation, followed by *Ilta-Sanomat, Aamulehti, Turun Sanomat,* and *Maaseudun Tulevaisuus.* In 2016, the international organization Reporters without Borders placed Finland 1st in the world in terms of press freedom; the US was 41st. Thus, it was particularly jarring to the Finns that their prime minister would be seen as interfering with media freedom. Upset by accusations of potential corruption, in December 2016 Juha Sipila fired what he later described as an "emotional" email to a journalist of a state broadcaster YLE. "My respect for YLE is now exactly zero, which of course does not differ from yours for me. So now we're even," stated the prime minister, only to find himself on the defensive over accusations of applying undue pressure on the media. While he quickly attempted to backpedal, the affair greatly upset his compatriots, who compared him to autocratic rulers abroad.

Education

All Finnish children must attend nine years of school starting age seven. At age 16 they are divided up between academic and vocational streams. They have completed the transition to nontracked comprehensive schools at the secondary level. The goal in establishing such unified schools, similar in some ways to American schools, was to equalize educational opportunities. After completing the comprehensive school, about half of the pupils enter a three-year senior secondary school that prepares them for a matriculation examination and access to the universities. There are no private schools or universities. Only 5% drop out at age 16. The rest continue their education or enter vocational programs.

The country's largest university is the University of Helsinki, with approximately 20,000 students. To create a new, innovative, world-class university, three universities in the metropolitan area were merged: the Helsinki University of Technology, the Helsinki School of Economics, and the University of Art and Design. It is following the example of Oulu University, which was the country's first integrated multidisciplinary university, combining a traditional university, a technical university, and a business school. There are further universities at Jyvaskyla, and Tampere, as well as Swedish-language universities in Turku and Vaasa. Lapland University in Rovaniemi on the Arctic Circle teaches in Finnish.

Because of the flood of students to the universities and polytechnic schools today, many applicants used to be turned away, but they are now able to accommodate 70% of high school graduates. Those who are admitted receive free (tax-paid) tuition and a monthly stipend for the full 55 months (6 years) of study. To attract more foreign students, several universities offer degree programs in English. The best ones are among the most selective in Europe. Most universities are independent of the state.

In the 1990s Finland adopted an Arena 2000 project that hooked up all Helsinki schools to the Internet. In a cold country like Finland, people are able to meet by Internet when they cannot go physically from one place to the other. By 2013 Finland had more Internet subscribers per 1,000 inhabitants than the US.

International PISA comparisons of 65 countries, administered every 3 years and sponsored by the OECD, ranked Finnish schools among the world's very best: first in science, second in reading, and fourth in math. Finns slipped in later years and are being increasingly overtaken by Asian pupils, especially in math. One OECD education expert estimated that Finnish pupils on average were more than 1 school year ahead of American 15-year-olds, thanks in part to the "highly effective way of recruiting, training and supporting teachers."

The quality and social standing of teachers are key to this success, despite the facts that they are not better paid than their counterparts elsewhere and that class sizes approach 30. Average teacher's pay in 2013 was about $3,600 per month, compared to $3,320 for a nurse and $5,650 for a physician (or $3,470 for a wood grinder). That they are among the most respected professions (only physicians are seen as more desirable as partners) helps persuade some of the best university students to go into teaching; there are 10 applicants for every place at the university that trains teachers. Teacher training is more selective than admission to medical or law school.

Pupils do not enter school until age seven, with preschool available through age six. Homework and testing are postponed until pupils are well into their teens. Teachers are free to design their own curricula and develop their own tests. All must learn at least two foreign languages: Swedish by law and usually English by choice. The successes tend to cover up the problems: There is a high dropout rate, and youth unemployment is high.

A sign that all is not well in this country with the world's best schools were three tragic shooting events in 2007 at Jokela High School in Tuusula, in 2008 at a trade college in Kauhajoki, western Finland, and in 2013 in Oulu. Finland ranks 16th in the world in per-capita gun ownership. Then-prime minister Vanhanen called for stricter gun controls, and a law was passed in 2011 to allow pistol licenses only after two years of documented shooting hobby, with the minimum age of 20.

Social Welfare

There is an extensive social welfare system, as sweeping as that in neighboring Sweden. Finland's social welfare is certainly expensive: One-fifth of the national budget is devoted to it, and it is one reason the average Finn spends over a third of his or her income in taxes. The people receive generous unemployment benefits and pensions. Medical care is not totally free. Finns must pay for the first visit to a doctor, but they are free thereafter for the rest of the year. They do not pay for many medicines, and hospital care is usually not more than $10 per day in public institutions. The economic crisis in the 1990s adversely affected the welfare system. There have been cuts in social benefits and public health care.

Its universal and generally good health care system costs the country 9.7% of its GDP, compared with 17.1% in the US, which cannot finance universal care. The

ban on smoking in bars and restaurants makes Finns even healthier.

Finns have average life expectancies in western Europe (78.3 years for men, 83.8 for women in 2015). Some observers attribute this to a predominantly meat and dairy diet that lacks sufficient vegetables. It confronts—as do many nations—a continuing problem of excessive alcohol consumption. One of the first things independent Finland did was to attempt to prohibit the drinking of alcohol. Prohibition was in effect from 1919 until 1932, but as in the US, its only effect was that of creating a new and prosperous occupation: bootlegging. Alcohol consumption, including binge drinking, doubled in the first decade of the 21st century. This has made the substance the number 1 killer in Finland.

Finland's birth rate of 1.8 in 2014 is below the replacement rate of 2.1. One group of parliamentarians found the situation so desperate in 2008 that they proposed a law to give Finns an additional week off work in order to go on a "love vacation." The sponsors explained that this would help stressed-out Finns revive passion and reduce their high divorce rate. At the same time, 2017 data indicate that Finland is one developed country with the largest percent of women aged 15–39 who would prefer to have three or more children. Some 45% of Finnish women expressed this preference, more than twice the number in Germany or Italy.

The percentage of the population over age 64 will jump from 17% in 2010 to 27% in 2035. By 2030 there may be only 100 employed workers for every 75 children and pensioners. This is due only partly to a very liberal abortion law. But it puts a squeeze on the economy and pension system as fewer workers will support an aging population. Finland expected to have the EU's oldest population by 2017. The average Finn retires at age 61.7. However, a 2005 reform phased out early retirement, raised the minimum pension age to 63, and created incentives to keep working until age 68.

Sports and Relaxation

One will hardly find a Finn who does not engage in the favorite national sport: cross-country skiing. The loggers' paths through the pine forests are ideal for skiers. When the snow melts, then Finland's long-distance runners attract the world's attention and have done so since the legendary Paavo Nurmi. "The Flying Finn" won six gold medals in the 1924 Paris Olympics. In the 1970s Lasse Viren carried the banner by becoming the first person ever to win gold medals in the 5,000- and 10,000-meter runs in two successive Olympics. At the 2014 Sochi Winter Olympics,

Finnish athletes won only five medals. But their men's hockey team had the satisfaction of defeating both the Americans and the Russians.

Americans blink their eyes in disbelief to see Finns playing Pesapallo, a very popular modified form of American baseball, although the players dress like race drivers. Golf is increasingly popular. Most Finns dream of spending part of their year at a country cottage, preferably on one of the many lakes. A fourth of the population owns one and uses it in both summer and winter. There in solitude they enjoy spiritual renewal and such pleasures as sauna bathing.

One pleasure that bears an expensive price tag in Finland is speeding on public roads. Traffic fines are based partly on an offender's income. When in 2004 a wealthy heir to a local sausage factory was clocked at 50 miles per hour in a 25-mile per-hour zone in downtown Helsinki, he was given a €170,000 ($221,000) fine. Even Nokia's president had to shell out €35,000 for running a red light. Finnish drivers, such as Tommi Makinen and Marcus Gronholm, won 14 World Rally Championships, the largest number of any country. Perhaps not surprisingly, two of the country's candidates for the European Parliament in 2004 were race car drivers.

Probably the most widely known Finnish tradition is the sauna, one of the few Finnish words that have become part of the international vocabulary. Of the 5.4 million Finns, 1.5 million own saunas. Many Finns build them in their basements or in little wooden sheds outside their houses, and there is now one sauna for every five Finns. After sitting in temperatures from 180°F to 210°F (80°C to 100°C), they jump into ice-cold water or take a roll in the snow. They claim that there is nothing better for a person's health or frame of mind.

A sauna bath is also a meeting point for friends or business associates. In fact, the cabinet even conducted a working session once a week in the sauna. If former president Kekkonen had particular difficulty getting the various political leaders to agree on a policy, he merely took them into the sauna, where problems could be ironed out in a more relaxed style. This is no longer possible since the late 1980s because women are now in the cabinet. In Finland, men and women who are not in the same family or are not close friends traditionally do not steam together. In 1992 former defense minister Elizabeth Rehn ended the practice of conducting national security debates in the sauna once and for all by declaring, "I believe in making decisions when I am fully clothed, and not when I'm naked. That way I have my notebooks in my hand, and everybody

Finland

knows what has been decided!" Helsinki's first female mayor, Eeva-Riita Siitonen, a modern former TV announcer, ex-president Tarja Halonen, and ex-prime minister Anneli Jaatteenmaki no doubt agree.

CURRENT ISSUES

In many ways, Finland found itself in an uncomfortable place. Its economic performance is in obvious need of repair, as its economy has been compared to some struggling Mediterranean eurozone members that Finns are used to dress down.

The worrying rumblings of Russian expansionism in Ukraine and in the Baltic region continue to unsettle the Finns, who not only share a border with Russia at 832 miles, longer than that of all other EU members combined, but who also never forgot the painful lessons of history of interactions with its eastern neighbor. Even with the sanctions against Russia, it remained Finland's fifth-largest export partner.

The immigrant problem continues to split the country. In 2016 Finland announced its plans to expel 20,000 asylum seekers, or about two-thirds of the 32,000 who entered during the previous year. This rate of rejection is not unusual; either way, about 12,000 people will become new residents in need of accommodations and assimilation. Some 4,000 asylum seekers withdrew their applications, and many decided to return to the more familiar conditions in Iraq and other countries in the region. Those who stayed are likely to grapple with the same disadvantages for ethnically different immigrants that the earlier waves of newcomers experienced.

With Russian planes provocatively buzzing NATO ships in the Baltic Sea, and with Estonia's large Russian population seen as a potential excuse for Moscow's intervention in the region, Finns increasingly saw NATO as a welcome security umbrella. Within a few days of Russia's invasion of Ukraine in February 2022, parliament voted to join NATO. A major two-week Arctic Challenge Exercise (ACE) was hosted by Finland, Norway, and Sweden, bringing together around 3,000 soldiers from 29 May to 9 June 2023. This now regular Nordic large-force, live-fly field training exercise is focused on joint and combined air operations of NATO Allies and other Partners throughout the Arctic region. The aim is to train units in planning, command and control, and orchestration of air operations.

Finland remains one of the strongest advocates of free trade in the developed world. Even as opposition to the Transatlantic Trade and Investment Partnership (TTIP) with the United States grew in many European countries in 2016, Finland continued to support it. While hopes for the deal appeared moribund with the election of Donald Trump, Finland urges both the US and China to avoid a trade war. With a small domestic market and much interest in exports to other countries, Finland stands to suffer should economic nationalism prevail in relations among the major players.

While the euro crisis precipitated Finland's economic woes, there are no serious attempts to change the currency. The electoral success of The Finns, however, indicates that many Finns think that too much power has been transferred to Brussels. An example important to the locals is a regulation from the faraway European capital ordering member states to protect wolves and other endangered predators. The 7,000 reindeer herders in northern Finland protest having to watch the growing wolf population decimate their herds relentlessly while having to get a permit to kill the well-fed predators. Even former president Halonen asked an interviewer from the Financial Times: "Do you really think that in Brussels they know how many wolves we should have?" Still, there is little appetite for leaving the European Union. Even after he left the government and lost his party's leadership in 2016, former prime minister Alexander Stubb tweeted eloquently in fewer than 140 characters, "The EU was not set up to take us to heaven but to save us from hell." Finns proudly celebrated their country's centennial in 2017.

Finland will continue to have one of Europe's lowest coronavirus infection rates. Several factors play a role. Its focus on preparedness is a result of the country's collective experience during the 1939–41 Winter War. Finns tend to keep a distance from each other, the country has a low population density, and Finns trust the authorities.

The Finns are doing something right—it is the happiest country in the world, according to the World Happiness Report 2023. This is the sixth year in a row that Finland has been named the happiest country on Earth.

The Baltic Republics

Due to their shared histories, as well as frequent geographical and cultural similarities, there is necessarily some repetition from one entry to the other.

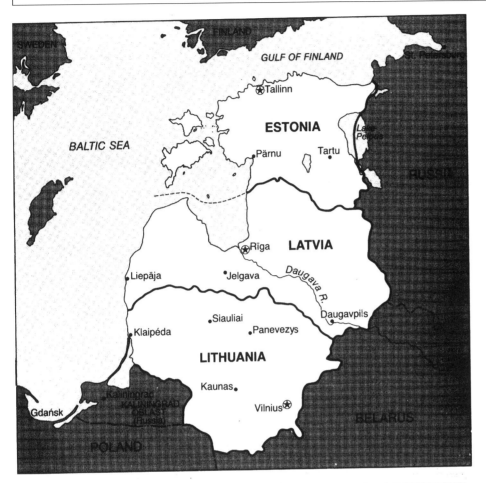

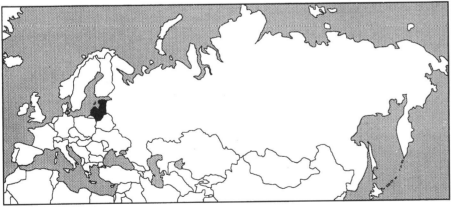

capriciously changed borders. All three Baltic states were left to deal with the residual problems.

The three republics of Estonia, Latvia, and Lithuania are located along the eastern shores of the Baltic Sea. Finland lies to the north, separated from Estonia by the Gulf of Finland, while Sweden lies to the west, across the Baltic Sea. Estonia, the most northern of the three republics, borders on Russia to the east, though the two countries are physically separated along most of the border by a series of lakes that stretch from just north of Pskov to the Baltic Sea. Tallinn, the capital, major port, and largest city, lies on the Gulf of Finland, 50 miles across from Helsinki, the capital of Finland. Estonia has 1,000 islands off its coast, while Latvia and Lithuania have none. Latvia, to the south of Estonia, shares borders with Belarus and Russia on the east. Its capital, Riga—located on the Gulf of Riga at the mouth of the Daugava (Western Dvina) River—is its largest city and best port.

Lithuania, the most southern of the three republics, borders on the Kaliningrad enclave of the Russian Republic to the south and the Republic of Belarus on the east. Its shoreline, only 99 kilometers long, is relatively narrow, and it has only one good port, the city of Klaipeda. Vilnius and Kaunas, its two major cities, lie considerably inland, Kaunas along the upper reaches of the Nemunas (Niemen) River and Vilnius on the Neris River, a tributary of the Nemunas. Vilnius, the current capital and the ancient capital of the Grand Principality of Lithuania, lies quite close to the current border of Belarus and was actually part of Poland between the First and World War IIs.

The entire Baltic coastal area is a plain with occasional higher elevations, particularly as one moves away from the sea, but the highest of these elevations are never more than about 900 feet in height. Nevertheless, they are the reason a number of small rivers flow through the Baltic republics and into the Baltic Sea. The shoreline itself consists mostly of low dunes running along the beaches. There are plenty of sandy beaches, but the water is extremely shallow for a good distance into the sea, making swimming difficult. Pine forests, which predominate throughout the Baltic coastal area, often come down almost to the shore.

It is these pines that help to explain amber, the symbol of the Baltic. Fifty million years ago, the Baltic Sea was a vast marshland covered by pine trees. The resin oozed

The disintegration of the Soviet Union in 1991 enabled the Baltic states to be the first Soviet republics to regain independence. All three faced myriad challenges: They were severed from their traditional markets, introduced new currencies, established from scratch their own military forces, negotiated the departure of former Soviet troops and started cleaning up the environmental damage they had caused,

adopted new constitutions and sets of laws, and organized their first democratic elections in a half-century.

This dramatic turn in history did not automatically eradicate the legacies of an overbearing Soviet Empire. In order to maintain control over a sprawling multinational state and promote its own socialist industrialization, the Kremlin had intentionally mixed peoples and

Baltic Republics

out of the pine trunks and dripped into the silt of the marsh, where it eventually hardened and then petrified over succeeding millennia. Today, amber is often found along the shore, washed up by the sea.

Most of the area was originally a combination of marsh and forest, and even today farms give the appearance of having been cut out of the forest. Small lakes are very common, with an estimated 3,000 in Lithuania alone. Soils, which are usually gray, are relatively poor, and most farming is dairy farming. One arm of the Gulf Stream reaches into the Baltic, making the climate milder than it would otherwise be. Summers tend to be cool, with frequent light rains. Winters are cold and damp.

Languages

The Estonian language belongs to the Finno-Ugric branch of the Ural-Altaic family, though it contains words taken from Swedish, German, and Russian. It is closely related to Finnish. Because most Estonians watched Finnish Television during Soviet time, they understand Finnish much more easily than Finns understand Estonian. The Estonians, along with the Finns, are the remnants of tribes that once lightly peopled much of the northern two-thirds of what is today European Russia. Although still existing in a couple dozen small pockets in Russia, particularly in the Karelian Peninsula, most were absorbed into the larger Slavic population over the centuries.

The Lithuanian and Latvian languages belong to the Letto-Lithuanian family of Indo-European languages. Lithuanian was heavily influenced by Polish, however, while Latvian shows influences from Swedish, German, and Russian, the tongues of peoples who once controlled the country. Although Latvian and Lithuanian are related to each other, the three Baltic languages are mutually incomprehensible.

HISTORY

Balts have occupied this same area for over 2,000 years. The first historical reference is in Tacitus's *Germania*, where he praises the Lithuanians for their talents in farming. The Baltic area had some contact with the civilizations to the south because of amber, which is found along the Baltic coast and became the basis for a trade route that came into existence as early as the second millennium BC. The decline of the Roman Empire turned this area once more into a backwater, however, and nothing more was heard for several centuries.

The next historical reference dates from the 7th century, when Viking raiders swept down out of Scandinavia and launched a series of raids along the coast and up the rivers. These invasions, continuing for the next 200 years, eventually resulted in some Viking settlements along the rivers.

Most of the Baltic Sea area was under the control of the Vikings at this time, but their main interest was on expansion of the trade route across Russia down to Constantinople. Accordingly, they only levied an annual tribute on the Baltic peoples and otherwise left them alone.

On the periphery, the Baltic peoples all remained pagan, even as their neighbors to the west and the south embraced Christianity. That led, at the beginning of the 13th century, to a Christianizing effort by German missionaries. These first were peaceful, and a bishopric was actually established at Riga in 1201. This peaceful penetration was soon followed by an invasion of crusading knights, the most significant being the Knights of the Sword and the Order of Teutonic Knights. The Teutonic Knights conquered present-day Latvia in 1225. Gradually, the area of Estonia was also brought under the control of the Knights of the Sword, who subsequently turned it over to the Order of Teutonic Knights. The Latvians and Estonians were made serfs and converted to Christianity, but they managed to retain many of their customs and their own languages.

Meanwhile the Lithuanians, who up to this time had been organized into separate tribes, formed a federation. Gediminas (1316–1341) founded the Gediminid dynasty and laid the basis of the Grand Duchy of Lithuania. During his lifetime, Gediminas extended his conquests southward, fighting both Russians and Tatars until his kingdom extended from the Baltic to the Black Sea. He thus freed the western part of Kievan Rus from the control of the Tatars, including the city of Kiev itself.

Modern Nordic solidarity. Estonian (l) and Swedish (r) students at the College of Europe.

Gediminas was slain in 1341 while once again attempting to drive back the Teutonic Knights. His grandson, Jogaila (Jagiello), married Hedwige (Jadwiga), queen of Poland. Jagiello, having converted to Roman Catholicism, took over as ruler of Poland and turned over the Grand Duchy of Lithuania to his cousin, Vytautas. Christianity was adopted in 1387. Vytautas died without an heir in 1430, however, so the crown reverted back to the Jogaila line. From that time, the Grand Duchy of Lithuania was increasingly tied to Poland until, in 1569, the two kingdoms were merged in the Union of Lublin. In its heyday in the 16th century, the Grand Duchy of Lithuania was a huge multiconfessional empire, extending all the way to the Black Sea, with six legal languages, including Hebrew and Armenian.

Lithuania continued to have its own laws and army. But the upper classes became increasingly polonized, and most of them became Roman Catholic. Polish replaced Russian as the language of administration in the 16th century.

In 1772, 1793, and 1795, Poland-Lithuania was partitioned among its neighbors. As a result, Russia obtained the Ukrainian and White Russian territories plus all of Lithuania proper up to the Nemunas River. Russia obtained the remaining Lithuanian territories in 1815.

The spread of the Protestant Reformation in the 16th century led to the creation of the two secular states of Courland and Livonia and the dissolution of the Teutonic Knights in 1560. The former knights converted to Lutheranism and became a secular nobility. Their Estonian and Latvian serfs were also converted at this same time.

Courland and Livonia became takeover targets of their neighbors. The Russian tsar, Ivan the Terrible, wanted to gain control of ports along the Baltic and launched his Livonian War in 1558. He was successful in the beginning, but when the Teutonic Knights collapsed in 1560, Poland stepped in and stole his conquests, annexing Livonia and Courland to Poland-Lithuania. At the beginning of the 17th century, the Swedish king, Gustavus Adolphus, intervened and seized most of Livonia in 1626. The Swedish territory, which included most of modern-day Estonia, was given a relatively liberal regime. The privileges of the German nobility—the so-called Baltic barons—were curtailed somewhat, and a university was established at Dorpat (now Tartu). It was also as a result of Swedish rule that the Lutheran Church continued as the established church in Estonia.

At the end of the 17th century, Peter the Great came to the throne in Russia and launched his Great Northern War against Sweden in 1700. The war lasted until 1721, but Riga fell to Russia in 1710 and

Tallinn (Revel) soon afterward. Russia obtained Livonia and Estonia by the Peace of Nystadt. Courland gradually became a Russian protectorate during the 18th century and was formally annexed in 1795.

The Baltics under Russian Rule

Peter the Great allowed his new Baltic subjects to retain their own laws and the autonomous status they had enjoyed under the Swedes. There was no attempt to intro-duce Russian institutions or to encourage the spread of the Orthodox religion. Peter's second wife, Catherine, was actually a Baltic peasant girl whom he took as a mistress during the Baltic campaign and later married. It was the German-speaking nobility who benefited most from this autonomy; the Letts and Estonians were still mainly serfs. There were some economic benefits to the area, however; in the 18th century, Riga became Russia's second major port after St. Petersburg, a position it would continue to hold in the 19th century.

A major change occurred at the beginning of the 19th century when Alexander I became tsar. He detested serfdom and as early as 1803 issued a decree permitting the voluntary emancipation of the serfs. Later in his reign, Alexander abolished serfdom in the Baltic provinces, in Estonia in 1816, Courland in 1817, and Livonia in 1819. In Lithuania, which was under a separate administration, serfdom continued. It was abolished there in 1861 as part of the general serf emancipation throughout the Russian Empire.

In the Baltic provinces, the short-term consequences of emancipation were mainly negative. The Baltic serfs were freed without land. Having no alternate means of employment, they found themselves working as day laborers for the same large landowners who had been their masters before emancipation. But the long-term consequences were both positive and far-reaching. The presence of free labor made Estonia and Latvia logical places to locate manufacturing plants when foreign capital began pouring into Russia after Alexander II launched his great reforms in the 1850s.

Russian rule also had its negative aspects in the 19th century. In Lithuania, in particular, the Russian government resented the role of the Roman Catholic Church and actively fostered the spread of the Orthodox Church in this area. It did not help that Lithuania participated, along with Poland, in the uprisings of 1830 and 1863. The University of Vilnius was closed down after the 1830 uprising, and the Russian language was introduced in all schools. After the 1863 uprising, land ownership was limited to adherents of the Orthodox faith.

Lachemaa National Park, Estonia

Perhaps the greatest sustained effort at Russification came during the reign of Alexander III (1881–1894). Alexander, a Slavophile and strong adherent of Russian Orthodoxy, extended previous Russification efforts to the areas of Estonia and Latvia and even applied them to the previously exempt German-speaking upper classes.

The industrialization process, begun by Alexander II, was continued by his son, Alexander III. One result was the creation of both an urban working class and a middle class, including professionals and intellectuals, in the Baltic provinces. All this provided the basis for the beginning of Estonian and Latvian national movements.

In Lithuania, a similar development occurred, though on the basis of a different class, the peasant landholders who emerged as a result of serf emancipation in 1861. Many of these peasant proprietors sent their sons off to be educated in Russian universities, and they came back as doctors, lawyers, teachers, and engineers. This led to the creation of the first specifically Lithuanian nationalist movement in the 1890s.

By 1905, illegal nationalist political parties existed in Estonia, Latvia, and Lithuania and took an active part in the Revolution of 1905. The Lithuanians were perhaps the best organized, having suffered longer from repression, but similar activities were carried in all three areas. A provisional revolutionary government was established in Riga, and two separate congresses met in Vilnius in December 1905. With the collapse of the revolution, widespread arrests were carried out, but government repression only succeeded in forcing the more prominent nationalist leaders to emigrate, while the nationalist movements themselves went underground.

Baltic Republics

The beginning of World War I provided a new opportunity for the nationalists. Although the majority of the Baltic peoples loyally supported the war effort in the beginning, the subsequent course of the war brought disaffection here, as it did in other parts of the Russian Empire. After March 1917, the Baltic nationalists backed the democratic aspirations of the first Russian Revolution of 1917 but began pressing for their own governments. The Bolshevik Revolution of November 1917 further alienated the Baltic peoples because the vast majority favored the creation of democratic states.

Creation of the New Baltic Governments

Developments in the Baltic provinces followed a fairly similar pattern after March 1917, although the fact that almost all of Lithuania and the southern half of Latvia were occupied by German troops obviously made for differences. The most important factor between March and November 1917 was the attitude of the Russian provisional government. Although not sympathetic to independence movements, it authorized establishment of an autonomous Estonian government in April 1917, which led to elections for an Estonian National Council in July. Konstantin Pats, leader of the Farmers' Union, was installed as president of the National Council on July 14.

Lettish delegates to the Russian Duma had organized a Latvian Refugees' Committee even before the March revolution. After March 1917, they began urging the provisional government to establish an autonomous administrative district for the part of Latvia still under Russian control. Local elections were held in the north, but the German occupation in the south militated against any further developments at this time.

The situation in Lithuania was even worse because almost the entire country was under occupation. Nevertheless, Lithuanian deputies to the Duma organized a Lithuanian National Council in Petrograd and began to demand political autonomy from the provisional government.

The Bolshevik seizure of power in November 1917 proved to be a turning point. The national movements rejected Bolshevism and tried to break away from the new communist government. The Bolsheviks, in turn, rejected the national movements and tried to suppress them.

A Latvian National Council, established after the November revolution, declared Latvian autonomy on November 16 and called for election of a constituent assembly to form a Latvian government. The Estonian government proclaimed its independence on November 28 and also called for elections to a constituent assembly.

The Bolsheviks not only refused to recognize the Latvian National Council; they also abolished the local government bodies set up by the provisional government. In Estonia, they arrested President Pats and dispersed the National Council. The Bolsheviks did permit elections to a new constituent assembly, but when the parties of the old government won a majority of the seats in January 1918, the Bolsheviks moved to suppress the winners. A civil war broke out and lasted about a month before German troops moved into Estonia, and the Bolsheviks were forced to flee. The Lithuanian National Council, split between radicals and moderates, did not take a specific stand against the Bolsheviks, but they moved to suppress the Lithuanian National Council anyway.

The Bolsheviks soon lost control of the Baltic provinces, first because of advances of the German army, and then through agreement to the Treaty of Brest-Litovsk. The Bolsheviks had wanted to retain the Baltic provinces, but one of the results of the Bolshevik seizure of power in 1917 was disintegration of the Russian army. Unable to stop the German advance, the new communist government signed the Treaty of Brest-Litovsk with Imperial Germany in March 1918, thereby giving up all claims to the Baltic provinces. The entire Baltic coastal area was at this time occupied by the German army. Baltic nationalists now faced the threat of annexation by Germany and again found themselves suppressed and their leaders imprisoned. The collapse of the German Empire in November 1918 put an end to that. But as the German armies began to pull out, the Bolsheviks poured back in, and the Baltic peoples had to fight another round with the Bolsheviks in order to establish their independence.

The armistice called for the German army to begin evacuating the Baltic provinces, a process that eventually stretched over several months. In the meantime, the nationalist leaders began organizing independent governments. Estonia, which had had an operating government once before, began reconstituting itself immediately after the armistice. The Estonian National Council met on November 20; President Pats was released from prison soon afterward. The new government began operating on February 24, 1919. Two months later Pats was replaced by Otto Strandman, a member of the leftist Workers' Party. A few months later, Strandman gave way to Jaan Tõnisson, the leader of the People's Party, who served until 1920.

Governments had to be created in Latvia and Lithuania, but the nationalist leaders had been active for some time and so were well known. An All-Latvian Council of State met at Riga on November 18, 1918, formed a provisional government and

appointed a president and prime minister. Kārlis Ulmanis, leader of the Peasants' League, became the first president. He held this office until 1920.

In Lithuania, a provisional government was also set up in November. A National Assembly met in Kaunas in January 1919, and the first Lithuanian president was elected on April 4. Even as they were organizing their governments, the nationalists found themselves again under attack as Bolshevik armies reopened the war following the German surrender. By February 1919, Latvia had been completely overrun, and most of Lithuania was under occupation by Bolshevik forces. Estonia, which had begun to form its own army, was a little luckier. It managed to drive the Bolsheviks back to the border.

The situation in Latvia was more complicated. A Latvian army was created and began driving back the Bolsheviks, with some assistance from German army units still in the country. Once they had regained control of most of the country, however, the German army supported a coup d'etat against the Latvian government, installing a new one controlled by Baltic Germans. The Estonian and Latvian armies first joined to drive out the Bolsheviks, then turned on the puppet Baltic German government and overthrew it. The Latvian government was reinstated on July 7, 1919. Riga, the Latvian capital, came under attack again by German forces in October but managed to hold out. Meanwhile, part of Latvia was still held by Bolshevik forces until they were driven out in January 1920.

The Bolsheviks had invaded the new Estonian state in March 1919 to take power in northeast Estonia. However, the Estonians defeated them in January 1920 and signed with Soviet Russia the Treaty of Tartu on February 2, 1920, which drew the border along the military front lines and recognized Estonia's independence, sovereignty, and neutrality "forever." It represented a major victory over Bolshevik Russia and was one of the few military victories in Estonian history. Similar treaties recognizing Baltic independence were signed with Lithuania on July 12 and with Latvia on August 11, 1920, several months after the last Bolshevik forces had finally been withdrawn from the Baltic area. International recognition soon followed, and all three states were admitted to the League of Nations in 1922.

Reoccupation and Sovietization

Like other European countries, the Soviet Union peered anxiously at a restless and expansive Germany, and it sought to protect itself. On August 23, 1939, the USSR and Germany signed a nonaggression pact that contained a secret protocol dividing Europe into spheres of influence; Finland,

Baltic Republics

Baltic Area – 15th to Early 18th Centuries

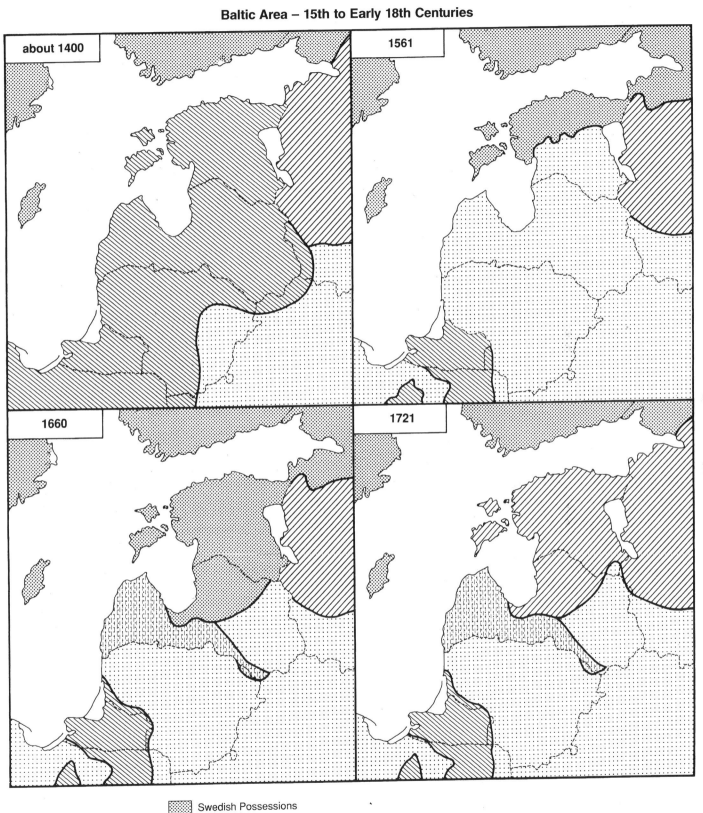

about 1400   1561   1660   1721

Swedish Possessions

Teutonic Order (about 1400) / Prussia (1561, 1660 and 1721)

Republic of Novgorod (about 1400) / Muscovy (1561) / Russia (1660 and 1721)

Lithuania (about 1400) / Poland-Lithuania (1561, 1660 and 1721)

Duchy of Courland: Dependency of Poland-Lithuania (1660 and 1721)

Baltic Republics

Mindaugas

Estonia, Latvia, and (one month later) Lithuania were assigned to the Soviet Union.

This freed Moscow's hand to attack Finland in November 1939 and ultimately force it to make territorial concessions while remaining independent. It also enabled Stalin to issue an ultimatum to the Baltic states in 1939 and again in 1940 to accept Soviet troops on their soil. It then demanded governments loyal to the Soviet Union. With a small number of their own troops surrounded on their own territory by superior numbers of Soviet army troops, and noting that 25,000 Finns had died in the unsuccessful effort to thwart a Soviet invasion, they did not dare resist.

Believing he could temporarily stave off disaster for the Estonian nation until the frightening political situation improved, President Pats signed a document accepting Stalin's demands. He and most other Estonian leaders were then deported to the Soviet Union. The new Moscow-controlled government, aided by local Estonian communists (numbering only 133 in the entire country) staged elections to parliament, during which no mention of any impending annexation by the Soviet Union was made. Only communist-dominated organizations were allowed to nominate candidates. Deputies obedient to the communists won 92.8% of the votes. The new parliament formally asked to join the Soviet Union on July 22, 1940, and was accepted on August 6, 1940. The other Baltic states were led through the same procedure and met the same fate in August 1940.

Russia today adamantly denies that the Soviet Union had ever "occupied" the Baltic states and that their joining was involuntary, despite some admitted pressure at the time. In May 2005 the Russian ambassador to the European Union asserted: "One cannot use the term 'occupation' to describe those historical events. At that time the troop deployment took place on an agreed basis and with the clearly expressed agreement of the existing authorities in the Baltic republics."

Although a very different regime rules in Russia since the collapse of the Soviet Union, the United Nations acknowledged the Russian Federation as the successor to the USSR. Therefore, Russia is cautious about renouncing what was done under communist rule. It fears that concessions could open Pandora's box of claims against it and provide a precedent for other newly independent republics and even nations within the present borders of Russia, such as Chechnya. It has never apologized for the Soviet Union's actions in 1940 or subsequent crimes, even though the Baltic states demand such an apology. Nor has it ever hinted that the occupation might have been illegal. The fact that the Balts accepted their fate without armed resistance in 1940 lends some credibility to the Russians' interpretation. Interrupted only by German occupation from 1941 to 1944, the Baltic states spent the next half century as disgruntled but relatively prosperous republics of the Soviet Union.

Independence

Encouraged by Mikhail Gorbachev's reform proposals, which permitted more free discussion and toleration than ever in Soviet history, the Baltic states seized the opportunity first to enlarge their self-determination within the Soviet Union and then to gain complete independence.

In 1988 popular fronts, composed of both Gorbachev communists and non-Communist democrats and nationalists, were formed, first in Estonia, and then in Latvia and Lithuania. On August 23, 1989, the 50th anniversary of the German-Soviet nonaggression pact, 2 million Estonians, Latvians, and Lithuanians formed a human chain from Tallinn to Vilnius to dramatize their demand for freedom. With large and articulate exile groups, especially in the US, the three peoples were able to mobilize considerable international sympathy and diplomatic support for their aspirations. This was especially facilitated by the fact that all western democracies, except Sweden and briefly Australia, had refused to recognize the Soviet Union's annexation of the Baltics in 1940.

Lithuania became the first Soviet republic to declare its independence on March 11, 1990, followed by Estonia on March 30 and Latvia on May 5, 1990. On May 12 the heads of all three countries signed the Declaration of Concord and Cooperation reestablishing the 1934 Council of the Baltic states.

Gorbachev indignantly rejected these demands for independence and even ordered that Interior Ministry troops use force against dissidents in the streets of Vilnius on January 13, 1991, killing 15. A week later six persons were killed in Riga, and the threat of violence also hung over Estonia. Russian president Boris Yeltsin supported the Balts' calls for freedom, and Gorbachev ultimately joined him in agreeing to sign a

On the way to church, Estonia (19th century)

136

Baltic Republics

Courtesy: George Skudos

Germany on May 9, 1945. The entire affair reopened old wounds. The presidents of Estonia and Lithuania boycotted the ceremony, refusing to celebrate their countries' own occupation. The Latvian president agreed to go, but she stated that, while victory over Hitler meant freedom for many, "for others it meant slavery, it meant occupation, it meant subjugation and it meant Stalinist terror." All three were revolted by Vladimir Putin's statements that the collapse of the Soviet Union was "the greatest geopolitical catastrophe of the 20th century" and that the 1939 Molotov-Ribbentrop pact had been a measure to enhance Russia's security. In light of Moscow's policy of intimidation toward the Baltics, in 2008 all three avidly supported Ukraine's and Georgia's bid to join NATO.

Putin was irritated by ex-president George W. Bush's decision to "bookend" his own trip to Moscow by visiting Riga beforehand and Georgia afterward. In Latvia on May 7, 2005, Bush, met all three Baltic presidents and received Latvia's highest medal, the Three-Star Order. He repeatedly spoke of the earlier "occupation," while acknowledging that the US and Britain shared some blame for the division of Europe and the annexation because they had caved to Stalin at the February 1945 Yalta conference. Recognizing Russian sensitivities, he gently urged all three countries to respect the rights of their Russian minorities. In 2008 the US granted all three visa-free travel. It is galling to Russians that they need visas to enter the three Baltic states.

The fact that the three Baltic states did not act like a unified bloc was a reminder of how different they are. Ex-president Vīke-Freiberga of Latvia put it like this: "Don't expect us to dance out onstage in a line like the little swans in Swan Lake." She noted that their accession to NATO and the EU had diminished their need for cooperation. EU membership means that they have to compete over benefits from Brussels.

Like most countries in central Europe, all three Baltic states were nervous about President Barack Obama's talk of pushing the "restart" button with Russia. Russian references to a "sphere of privileged interests" in former Soviet states do not sound good in their ears, even though Obama rejected such a notion. An open letter in July 2009 signed by former Baltic presidents and ministers, among other central European leaders, warned that "all is not well either in our region or in the transatlantic relationship? . . . NATO today seems weaker than when we joined," and "Russia is back as a revisionist power pursuing a nineteenth-century agenda with twenty-first-century tactics and methods." The Russian attack on Georgia in August 2008 terrified all three republics, especially

new union treaty on August 19, 1991. This treaty, along with the prospects of Baltic independence, triggered the Moscow coup attempt against Gorbachev on that day. The insurrection's failure after only three days prompted most countries in the world to recognize the Baltic states' independence.

The Nordic countries and the European Community (EC, after 1994 called the European Union—EU) were first, followed by the United States on September 2 and the postcoup Soviet government on September 6, 1991. On September 17, 1991, the Baltic republics, which had belonged to the League of Nations, were admitted to the United Nations. With strong western support, all three Baltic states negotiated the withdrawal of Russian troops from their territories—by August 1993 for Lithuania and by August 1994 for Estonia and Latvia.

All three states entered NATO in April 2004. Their three top commanders form the Baltic Military Committee, which meets twice a year to review their NATO requirements and joint defense projects. In an important speech in Warsaw in June 2001, President George W. Bush had given the signal by saying, "all of Europe's new democracies, from the Baltic to the Black Sea and all that lie between, should have the same chance for security and freedom."

Before then it had been assumed that Russia would never have permitted Baltic participation in NATO, but much had changed. Russia's past threats and bluster had been counterproductive by merely underscoring the Baltic states' need for protection from an overbearing neighbor. Finally, there was little Russia could do to stop NATO enlargement into the Baltics. Lithuania's president Valdas Adamkus made it unmistakably clear why the Balts wanted to join: "Accepting Lithuania into NATO is a signal to Russia that never will Lithuania be taken over by Russia again. This is a formal declaration to Russia politically that we are free, and declaring ourselves free forever."

At NATO's Prague summit in November 2002, that signal was given, and all three Baltic states were formally invited to join, which they did in April 2004. Nevertheless, the warnings did not go away. A senior Russian general warned NATO in March 2004 against deploying weapons and aircraft close to the Russian border. The NATO secretary-general responded by assuring the Balts that "it will be NATO airspace, and NATO airspace will be policed." Some NATO nations rotate in providing air cover for the Baltics.

Even before joining NATO, the three states had acquired an advanced radar system, called Baltnet, which looks deep into Russia. The Russians have tried to test the alliance's decisiveness by their planes flying over NATO airspace without filing flight plans or communicating with ground control.

The three states responded differently in 2005 to Russia's invitation to attend the 60th anniversary of the victory over Nazi

137

Baltic Republics

Russia's public declaration that it had intervened militarily to protect the rights of Russian citizens. It reverberates, especially since it prompted no clear and determined western response from the NATO allies. Then Estonia's then-president Toomas Hendrik Ilves noted, "What we have seen is a complete paradigm shift in the security architecture of Europe. Everything we have done has been based on the assumption that Russia won't engage in aggression. . . That premise is no longer operable." To calm Balts' nerves, the American government scheduled in 2011 its largest military exercise in the Baltics. The US deployed 18 F-15 fighter aircraft to Lithuania and Poland, joining other NATO allies in policing Baltic airspace.

The Russia's 2014 invasion and annexation of Crimea, which belonged to Ukraine, and its meddling in southeast Ukraine proved Baltic warnings to be correct that Russia still has aggressive intentions. It was unnerving that President Putin reasserted his country's right to protect Russian speakers in the former Soviet Empire. Two-thirds of Russians in Latvia approved of this blatant violation of international law. It reminded many Balts of 1940, when rigged elections and manipulated requests to be annexed by the Soviet Union ended the three countries' freedom. Lithuanian ex-president Dalia Grybauskaitė exclaimed, "Thanks be to God, we are NATO members. . . First it's Ukraine, Moldova will be next and finally it can reach the Baltic states and Poland." Only Estonia had met the NATO goal of spending 2% of GDP on defense, but Latvia and Lithuania immediately pledged to more than double their defense budgets. Realistically, though, that combined increase would amount to no more than the equivalent of three sophisticated fighter jets. The three called on NATO to send more troops as either permanent or rotational forces and to increase its naval presence in the Baltic Sea. The US sent additional fighter jets to Šiauliai Air Base in Lithuania and to Poland to police the skies and publicly repeated its NATO commitment to stand by fellow members. Estonia requested even more jets at its Amari airfield.

A Russian law outlawing any identification of Nazism with Soviet communism criminalizes the Baltic states. Perhaps worst, opinion polls in many European NATO countries reveal that a majority of citizens oppose the use of their national armies to defend east European and Baltic nations from a Russian attack. Only in Britain and France did more people support defending the Baltic states than oppose it. NATO foreign ministers met in Tallinn in April 2010. Then-secretary of state Hillary Clinton assured the leaders of all three Baltic states of America's commitment to defend them and that "we believe there is no sphere of influence, no veto power that Russia or any country has over any country in Europe concerning membership in NATO."

In his September 2014 visit to Estonia, President Barack Obama insisted that defending Tallinn, Riga, or Vilnius was "just as important as the defense of Berlin or Paris or London." The US pushed its NATO partners to agree to develop military contingency plans to defend the Baltic allies. NATO responded in January 2010 by expanding an article 5 defense plan for Poland to the Baltic states. That broadened strategy, which commits NATO to defend the Baltics, is in place and called "Eagle Guardian." In 2014 it began constructing a rapid-reaction brigade for use in the Baltics and central Europe.

NATO commanders share Baltic worries that Russia can concentrate awesome combat power in the region on short notice. They bolstered forces there to a total of 4,530 rotating soldiers near the Russian border in four battle groups led by Germany in Lithuania, Britain and Estonia, Canada in Latvia, and the US in Poland. An additional task force of 5,000 troops can be deployed in a week.

In May 2015 Estonia staged the biggest military exercise in the nation's history, as its 13,000 soldiers were joined by another 1,000 NATO troops from the US and Europe. It was prompted by fears of Russian aggression. In November 2018 all three countries took part in Trident Juncture, the alliance's largest military exercise since the Cold War. All remain resolutely pro-American, even though they are wary of Donald Trump's commitment.

Economies

The Baltic states have been the most successful former Soviet republics in transforming their economies from socialism to market economies. They had always been the most prosperous republics within the Soviet Union and the most enthusiastic practitioners of Gorbachev's perestroika, so they were well poised to reform their economies when the opportunity came in 1991. They were the first to introduce their own currencies; to free prices, wages and trade, to reduce government subsidies and inflation; and to sell off state enterprises. The visitor now finds increasing signs of prosperity everywhere.

This change has not been experienced at equal rates, and the diminution of many citizens' living standards, especially of those on fixed incomes, cannot be ignored. High inflation in the early post-communist years, affecting such essentials as rent, heat, food, and day care and such free-time activities as cultural entertainment, caused many persons grudgingly to change their lives and, at times, reflect on the ways things were materially better in the old regime.

Young and well-educated persons, along with some well-placed former communist elites who could benefit from privatization, are doing well. Elderly persons, large families, and single women are struggling. The social welfare net that most western European democracies have built up over the past few decades does not yet exist, mainly because their states cannot afford it and, in the case of Estonia and Latvia, because their constitutions mandate balanced budgets.

The global recession hit the Baltic states very hard, shaving 17% off Estonia's GDP in 2009, a stunning 24% off Latvia's, and 15% off Lithuania's. This downturn began two years earlier, when reckless credit and real estate bubbles began popping. It took several years to return to the stability and growth they had experienced. All pulled out of the recession but at different speeds and great economic suffering.

At the beginning of the 21st century, the Baltic states enjoyed the fastest economic growth rates in Europe. That was again the case in 2013, although their small size prevents them from being an economic model for much larger EU partners. Estonia's grew by an average of 8% annually from 2000 to 2007 and 11.4% in 2006 alone. No wonder they were called the "Baltic tigers." This was the result of good luck and good policies.

They are stable, business-friendly, inexpensive, and close to rich markets. They have free-trade agreements with each other. Unemployment was low in all three, although it climbed with the recession. A thriving shadow economy and the fact that by 2007 several hundred thousands of young Balts had found work in the UK and Ireland and later in Sweden and Finland meant that real unemployment was even lower. But this migration created serious labor shortages. On May 1, 2011, all temporary barriers preventing workers in EU states from moving freely to another EU state to find work were lifted.

Such rapid growth and westward migration created problems. Every country worries about a brain drain of its educated youth. Remittances drive up inflation, including for housing, whose prices rose in Estonia by 28% in 2005 alone and at a rate of 10% to 15% annually from 1999 to 2007. Tallinn especially became a magnet for foreigners eager to speculate on property, particularly in the medieval old town. Soaring lending fueled this rise in property prices until they fell sharply in 2008. Annual wage growth of 20% (30% in Latvia) was good news for the employed, but it exceeded productivity increases and added to inflation. All three countries have a long way to go to catch up with western Europe. The richest, Estonia (at $28,140 per capita GDP-PPP in 2014) and Lithuania ($27,686) are three-quarters the EU average, and Latvia ($23,548) is at two-thirds—all a clear improvement over the starting point. The overheated economies cooled sharply. With high inflation and sky-high current account deficits (23% of GDP in Latvia, 16% in Estonia, and 13% in Lithuania in 2008), hopes of qualifying for the euro before 2014 were dashed for all but Estonia. On January 1, 2011, it became the first ex-Soviet republic to adopt the euro. Latvia followed on January 1, 2014, and Lithuania on January 1, 2015.

They produce a variety of goods that western consumers want to buy, from cars, ships, and clothing to medicines and beer. They have dramatically shifted their trade from the ex-Soviet Union toward the prosperous west, especially the Baltic Sea area, with some 70 million consumers. For example, between 1991 and 2015, Estonia's foreign trade with Russia had declined from 95% of total trade to about 10%. About three-fourths of its trade is now with the EU, a figure that grew after 10 new countries, including the Baltic states, entered the EU in May 2004.

Many Balts are anxious about Russian political and economic interference. Baltic trade with Russia remains important, even as all three struggle to minimize their energy dependence on Russia. They are scrambling to prevent their major power industries from being gobbled up by much larger Russian energy companies, which seek to increase their control over pipelines and the supply and distribution of natural gas and electricity. For example, Gazprom owns 37% of Estonia's Eesti Gaas, 34% of Latvia's Latvijas Gaze, and 34% of Lithuania's Lietuvos Dujos. Lukoil gasoline stations are all over the Baltics. All three are heavily dependent on Russian natural gas.

The Baltics face such common problems as trying to minimize pollution in the Baltic Sea, a particularly sensitive body of water because of its shallowness, its semi enclosure, and its brackish waters that are renewed only every 30 years. The Baltic Sea had been used as a weapons dump for the Soviet, American, and British militaries after the World War II; entire German ships full of captured weapons, including bombs, blistering agents, nerve gas, and 14 chemical agents, were scuttled. These toxic substances are returning from the depths to haunt fishermen and the littoral states. Pointing to this danger, Estonia became the first Baltic Sea country to reject a request by the Russo-German company Nord Stream to lay a gas pipeline in its waters on the sea floor between Russia and Germany; the pipeline nevertheless went into service in 2011. Latvia and Lithuania are building a "power bridge" to Sweden.

The Baltics are making relatively good progress toward establishing rule of law, including established and impartial commercial law. Among 166 countries ranked in the 2016 Economic Freedom Index, Estonia was 9th, Lithuania 13th and Latvia 36th. All are experiencing organized crime and high crime rates in general. Lithuania has one, the world's highest suicide rates; they are also high in Latvia and Estonia. But these problems are far below the level found in the Commonwealth of Independent States (CIS). In 2012 by a parliamentary vote of 91 to 0, Estonia became the last EU country to criminalize human trafficking.

A whiff of corruption hangs over the privatization program, which is largely finished. Such corruption exists in the political and economy sectors in all three, although Estonia is less corrupt than some western European countries, and all are making progress in reducing it. In 2015 Transparency International ranked Estonia 23rd among 168 countries in terms of corruption, Lithuania 32nd, and Latvia 40th. Indeed, one reason they were all invited to join the EU was that they were judged to have the cleanest public administrations in the former communist world.

EU membership brings challenges. Latvia and Lithuania have three times the proportion of farmers and one-third of the EU's average agricultural productivity. They are creeping up in the UN human-development ranking: Estonia 30th, Lithuania 37th, and Latvia 46th in 2014. Estonia topped Freedom House's 2010 rankings of ex-communist political systems. All three benefitted by creating a parliamentary rather than a presidential system; every ex-communist country with a strong president became an autocracy. Their proportional representation electoral systems ensure that minority parties have a presence and a voice in parliament.

EU membership does not in itself bring wealth. The Economist estimated that it could take more than a half-century for them to draw level with the earlier EU members. But it will certainly bring all three more stability and security, trade and investment, freedom of movement for their citizens, and the opportunity to act as bridges between east and west.

Newspapers from Estonia, Latvia, and Lithuania. *Diena* folded in 2009.

Republic of Estonia (Eesti Vabariik)

The 15th-century City Hall, Tallinn

Courtesy: NOVOSTI

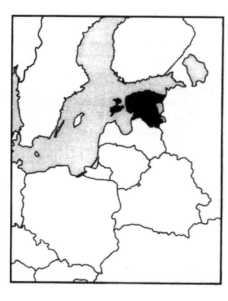

Area: 17,505 sq. mi. (45,339 sq. km).
Population: 1,365,884 (2023 estimate)
Capital City: Tallinn (pop. 453,864, urban area 614,561). (2023 estimate).
Climate: It is both maritime and continental, temperate with cool summers and cold winters, fairly moderated by an arm of the Gulf Stream that reaches into the Baltic. The northern and western coastal areas tend to be milder than the country's inland regions, while the eastern and southeastern regions tend to have a continental climate. The country has four seasons of near-equal length. The warmest month is July with temperatures range from 17.8 °C (64.0 °F) on the Baltic islands to 18.4 °C (65.1 °F) inland, and the coldest is February with temperatures range from –1.4 °C (29.5 °F) on the Baltic islands to –5.3 °C (22.5 °F) inland.

Neighboring Countries: Russia (east); Latvia (south). Finland (north, across the Gulf of Finland), Sweden (west, across the Baltic Sea).
Official Language: Estonian.
National Minority Language: Russian.
Ethnic Background: 67.8% Estonians, 22.5% Russians, 9.0% other (Ukrainian, Belarusian, Finn), 0.7% unspecified. (2023)
Religion: 26.7% Christianity (Lutheran, Eastern Orthodox), 2.2% other, 12.7% undeclared, 58.4% no religion. (2021)
Form of Government: Unitary parliamentary republic.
Chief of State: Alar Karis, President (since January 2021)
Head of Government: Kaja Kallas, Prime Minister (since January 2021)
National Flag: It is a tricolor featuring three equal horizontal bands of blue (top), black (middle), and white (bottom). Popular symbolic interpretation says that the blue is for the blue sky above the native land, the black for attachment to the soil of the homeland as well as the fate of Estonians—for centuries black with worries, and white for purity, hard work, and commitment.

140

Former President Kersti Kaljulaid

Public Holiday: February 24 (Independence Day).

Currency: Euro (€; EUR) (since January 1, 2011).

Main Exports: machinery and equipment, wood, textile, metal and metal products, and processed foodstuff.

Main Imports: machinery and equipment, vehicles and transport equipment, and chemicals.

Main Trading Partners: Finland (14.6% of export and 16.9% of import), Latvia (14.1% of export and 9.6% of import), Sweden (9.2% of export and 6.9% of import), Lithuania (6.1% of export and 10,2% of import), Germany (5.7% of export and 9.9% of import), Russia (7.2% of import), United States (5,5% of export). (2022)

Political Status: Estonia was conquered by German and Danish knights in the 13th century. It came under Swedish control in the 17th century. Peter the Great annexed it in 1710, and it remained part of the Russian Empire until 1918. Independent state, 1918–1940. Annexed to the Soviet Union by Stalin in 1940; declared its independence in August 1991. (See chapter on The Baltic Republics)

ESTONIA SINCE WORLD WAR I

Independent Estonia, 1918–1940

Estonia had elected a constituent assembly charged with drawing up a constitution for the country in April 1919. The left dominated the assembly, so the constitution that was eventually produced was what might be called "radical liberal" in orientation. Approved by the assembly in June 1920, it went into effect on December

21, 1920. All power was vested in a single-body legislature of 100 members called the Riigikogu. This was a modified parliamentary system. The "commission of the legislature" was essentially a cabinet, while the presiding officer, called the Riigivanem (senior statesman), performed the functions of a premier. There was no separate head of state, however, so the senior statesman performed all ceremonial functions, as well. Another unusual feature of the constitution is that it provided for popular participation in decision making by means of the referendum and the initiative.

A survey taken in 1922 gives a good picture of the country. The total population was 1,107,300, with Estonians making up 87.6% of the total. Another 8.2% of the population spoke Russian, while 1.7% spoke German. Estonia was thus the most homogeneous of the Baltic states at this time, and its minorities enjoyed full citizenship rights. It was also religiously homogeneous, with 78.3% of the population declaring themselves to be Protestant and another 19% professing Eastern Orthodoxy. And it was rural, with 58.5% of the population earning their living from agriculture.

In 1918 two-thirds of the rural population had owned no land whatsoever but, instead, supported themselves by working as day laborers for the large estates that made up 58% of the land. Land reform legislation, passed in October 1919, expropriated nearly all the estates and distributed the land to the landless rural laborers. An additional 56,000 small holdings were created. This undoubtedly made political sense, since Baltic Germans owned a majority of the estates. But the plots turned out to be too little, so that a majority of the new owners were unable to survive without extensive governmental assistance. The eventual solution was to organize the small holders into cooperative societies, which were able to buy modern machinery that could be used on several farms.

An economic crisis began in 1929 and then turned into what the Americans called the Great Depression. Estonia was heavily dependent on agricultural exports, and the sharp drop in the international price of these products led to great distress in Estonia, particularly in the countryside. As in many other European countries, the Depression placed unbearable burdens on democracy.

It was at this time that a new political grouping, the Association of Estonian Freedom Fighters, began to grow in significance and power. It had been organized in 1929 as a veterans' organization espousing patriotism, nationalism, and anticommunism. By 1932 it was beginning to show increasing tendencies toward

antiparliamentarianism and antiliberalism. The Freedom Fighters, organized into paramilitary organizations, wore gray-green shirts, with black and white armbands bearing a hand grasping a sword and the dates 1918–1920.

Their most important demand was for the creation of a separate executive power that would be independent of the legislature. The Freedom Fighters' proposal for constitutional reform was submitted to referendum in October 1933 and passed. This constitutional change created the office of president of the republic, to be popularly elected for a term of five years. It also vested executive power in the president rather than the legislature. The president could appoint and dismiss governments, declare states of emergency, and dissolve the legislature. The revised constitution went into effect on January 24, 1934, and elections were set to fill the new presidency. Among the candidates was General Andreas Larka, president of the Freedom Fighters. Another candidate was Konstantin Pats, then serving as premier. The Freedom Fighters swept urban local elections at the beginning of 1934, and it appeared that their man would win the presidency, as well.

Pats decided to take preemptive action by pulling off his own coup before

Early Estonia: outdoor museum in Tallinn

Estonia

elections could occur. He therefore gave the commander-in-chief of the army special powers to maintain law and order and then banned the Freedom Fighters as a "threat to the security of the state." He also banned all political assemblies. The Estonian legislature met, approved Pats's emergency legislation, then was dismissed. Pats issued a decree postponing presidential elections indefinitely. The legislature met for a short time in September 1934, but it was dissolved when it did not prove to be completely pliant. Pats continued to rule by decree. In February 1935, another decree dissolved the political parties. In their stead, a number of "corporations" representing various interest groups were formed to represent the interests of the people.

In February 1936 Pats began moving to legitimatize his authoritarian regime by submitting a referendum to the people asking them to approve calling a constituent assembly. This passed, and the assembly met in February 1937 to ratify a new constitution drafted by the Pats government. This constitution, which went into effect on January 1, 1938, provided for a strong presidency to be elected by a special electoral chamber, not by popular vote. The new parliament also consisted now of two chambers, with the upper chamber partially appointed by the president. The electoral chamber met in April 1938 and confirmed Pats in office.

A small oppositional group was permitted to exist in the lower body of the legislature, but it held only 7 out of 80 seats. This was the structure that was still in operation in 1939, when Stalin entered a pact with Hitler putting the Baltic states in the Soviet sphere of influence.

World War II

Hitler launched his invasion of Poland on September 1, 1939, and Soviet troops entered to occupy the eastern third of Poland on September 17. On September 19, the Estonian government was informed that the Soviet fleet had extended its defense perimeter to include the Estonian coastline. Six days later, the Soviet Foreign Ministry presented the Estonian government with a treaty for a military alliance between the two countries, which included the establishment of Soviet bases in Estonia. Left with no alternative, the Estonian government signed the agreement. On September 28 the first Soviet troops entered Estonia.

Nothing happened for several months, probably because the Soviet Union was tied down in its "winter war" with Finland. The 25,000 Finnish deaths in that war convinced Estonia's leaders that resistance to the Soviet Union was futile. Once that was resolved, the Soviet Union turned its attention back to the Baltic states. Toward the end of May 1940, the Soviet Foreign Ministry accused all three states of violating the 1939 mutual-assistance pacts with the Soviet Union. Then all three were pressured into installing popular-front governments. These did not last long, however. In July all political parties other than the Communist Party were banned, and most noncommunists were dismissed from office.

This was followed by waves of arrests in all three countries, and Pats was deported to the Soviet Union. In one night alone, on June 14, 1941, 10,000 Estonians were deported to Siberia. With only communists, organized as the Working People's League, permitted to stand for office, new

elections were held on July 14. The newly elected legislatures met on July 21. Their only piece of business was to vote to join the Soviet Union, which they did by acclamation. The following month, the USSR Supreme Soviet acceded to their request.

They thus became Soviet socialist republics. This created the myth that the Baltic states had voluntarily joined the Soviet Union, a position the Russian government continues to maintain.

Germany's invasion of the Soviet Union beginning on June 22, 1941, temporarily reversed this situation. German troops overran and occupied the three Baltic republics later in 1941. Such occupation lasted until 1944. Because of the mass arrests, the deportations to the Soviet Union, the drafting of 33,000 conscripts into the Red Army, the collectivization of farmland, and the scorched-earth withdrawal policy ordered by the Soviets, many people initially welcomed the German soldiers as liberators.

Many remember having more to eat and less fear of arrest under German rule, despite the activities of the German secret police. Whereas the Soviet occupiers immediately destroyed Estonian national symbols, the Germans did not forbid them. The Estonian flag could be flown, subject to some controls, and Estonian soldiers could wear it on their uniforms. In general, the Germans left the impression that Estonians could have some self-government after the war, whereas the Soviets left no doubt who would remain in complete charge. Many Estonians were drafted into the German army and fought against the Red Army. For that reason, many Russians referred to Estonians for decades as "fascists."

With the German retreat, the Baltic republics once again fell under Soviet control. A fifth of the Estonian population either fled to the west or was deported to Siberia. After the end of the war in 1945, guerrilla fighters, known as Forest Brothers because they fled to the woods from where they conducted their "war of the woods," continued to oppose Soviet control in the three republics for a decade. They hoped in vain to receive help from the west. The movements got no outside assistance, and they were eventually suppressed.

The Soviet Era

Many changes occurred in the three republics over the next 45 years. Soviet policy was to integrate the republics so thoroughly that there would be no question of their ever leaving the union. To that end, the Soviet government first carried out policies of nationalization and collectivization. Next it sought to bind the Baltic republics to the rest of the Soviet Union economically by locating branch

Tallinn's harbor in Soviet times

Courtesy: NOVOSTI

factories of Soviet industry in the three republics. Such factories received most or all of their raw materials from other parts of the Soviet Union and delivered most of their finished products to customers in the other republics.

After becoming part of the Soviet Union, Estonia's demography began to change dramatically. By the time Soviet rule ended in 1991, 2.3 million Russians were left behind in the Baltics, over a half-million in Estonia alone. Estonians had constituted 97% of the country's population in 1945 (after Russia had incorporated predominantly Russian-speaking areas in eastern Estonia totaling 5% of its territory). As a result of Moscow's policy of moving and mixing nationalities, Estonians constituted only 72% in 1953, 64.7% in 1979, and 61.5% in 1989. By 1996 this had risen to 64.2% due to Russian out-migration after independence, leaving an ethnic mix of 28.7% Russians, 2.7% Ukrainians, 1.5% Belarussians, 1% Finns, and 1.9% other nationalities. In 2001, 46% of Tallinn's population was Russian speaking. Massive inward migration of Russians seeking employment in industry, mining, and the civil service and preferences in housing, combined with outward deportation of native Estonians in 1941 and again from 1944 to 1949 (totaling at least a fifth of the native population), had dramatically changed the demographic mix. In the opinion of many Estonians, this threatened their national survival.

Among non-Estonians resettled in the republic were employees of the Soviet government, particularly its security agencies and military. Many were part of projects to develop Estonia's lignite and brown coalfields and branches of the Soviet military-industrial complex in the Narva area. As a result, the population in northeastern areas, such as Narva, was eventually more than 95% non-Estonian. More than one-third have Russian citizenship.

This program of economic integration was accompanied by a program of "Soviet Russification," aimed at transforming the cultures of the three republics. All students received Russian-language training in the schools, plus general indoctrination lectures on the nature of Soviet culture. In addition, there was a systematic effort made to settle non-Baltic nationals in the republics. When a new factory was built, most of the workers would be transferred there from elsewhere in the Soviet Union. They were given priority in the assignment of scarce housing, a practice that greatly irritated native Estonians. The heavy industrialization carried out after 1945 meant that the standard of living in Estonia was above that of any part of the Soviet Union. However, the polluting effects of Soviet industries cast an unhealthy gray and dull

Celebrating Independence Day beside the parliament in Tallinn   Courtesy: NOVOSTI

shadow over Estonia. Combined with the unaesthetic Soviet-style buildings that were thrown up and the general dilapidation that accompanies all communist life, Estonians and the other Balts remain surrounded by reminders of the undesirable Soviet legacy.

Estonia Regains Its Independence

The Estonian people accommodated themselves to Soviet rule, but they were never happy with it. When, therefore, Gorbachev launched his programs of glasnost (openness) and perestroika (restructuring) after coming to power in 1985, Estonians were the first to take advantage of them.

In enunciating his policy of glasnost, Gorbachev called on the Soviet peoples to speak out against negative tendencies in the society and to support his reforms. This became a manifesto that led to the creation of thousands of "unofficial" organizations all over the Soviet Union. Formed originally in support of Gorbachev's policy of reform, many of them soon began to push their own agendas. For Estonians, his policies were a welcome breath of fresh air, and they were among the first to throw their enthusiastic support to him. At the same time, and almost from the beginning, the Estonian people used glasnost for their own purposes.

The first unofficial Baltic organization was the Estonian Heritage Society (EHS), founded in December 1987. Ostensibly aimed at preserving the national heritage and environment, the EHS very quickly became a vehicle for Estonian nationalism. It stressed Estonian history; it honored

Estonian heroes killed while fighting for Estonian independence; and it resurrected the old Estonian blue-black-white flag. Opposed by the government at first, its programs proved to be so popular that the Estonian communist leaders eventually endorsed some of its positions. For example, the presidium of the Estonian Supreme Soviet legalized the prerevolutionary flag in June 1988.

An organization destined to play a much larger role than the EHS was the Popular Front of Estonia (PFE), first suggested in April 1988 by Edgar Savisaar, a sociologist and planning official. Many reform communists threw their support to the idea so that the PFE quickly won preliminary approval both from the Estonian Communist Party Central Committee and the Estonian Soviet government. This gave the PFE access to the public media, and it rapidly began to build up public support.

This led to a split in the Estonian Communist Party. Karl Vaino, party secretary since 1978, began to fear the challenge presented by the PFE and sought to limit its influence. Reformers within the party challenged him, however. Moscow sided with the reformers, and Vaino Valjas replaced Karl Vaino.

Valjas officially addressed the first congress of the PFE, held in October 1988, and expressed his support for the goals of the PFE. With 22% of the delegates also belonging to the Estonian Communist Party, it appeared that the PFE was merely a popular arm of the party. That was misleading, however. Although communists made up a significant percentage of the

Estonia

Estonian cadets

membership, it was overwhelmingly reform communists who joined the PFE. Increasingly, the PFE was used to allow reform communists to take control of the Estonian Communist Party and the Estonian government. For example, Savisaar, head of the PFE, was appointed deputy chairman of the Estonian Council of Ministers and head of the State Planning Committee.

Another Estonian unofficial organization was the Estonian National Independence Party (ENIP), established in August 1988. Political parties other than the Communist Party were illegal at this time, so in the beginning, the government gave the ENIP a hard time. It was undoubtedly the existence of the ENIP that helps explain the significant communist support for the PFE. Other unofficial organizations that were formed in 1988–1989 were the Estonian Green Movement, the Estonian Council of Churches, and a Rural Movement. In addition, the Social Democratic Party was revived in 1989, and a Christian Democrat movement came into being.

Meanwhile, there was a further split in the Estonian Communist Party. Faced with a choice between nationalism and communism, more and more Estonian communists opted for nationalism. Valjas tried to control this tendency by specifically catering to it. He reduced the size of the Central Committee, purging mainly non-Estonians, and he carried out a similar purge of the Estonian Supreme Soviet, increasing the number of Estonians to two-thirds of the membership. In January 1989 the government declared Estonian to be the state language and required knowledge of it for recruitment to certain government and professional posts.

The goals of the Popular Front of Estonia were also shifting during this period. The original emphasis had been on breaking the control of the "centralized administrative-bureaucratic system" and establishing the right of Estonians to decide their own affairs without outside interference. This had been symbolized by the call for sovereignty. Increasingly, however, the argument was made that these goals could not be achieved without political pluralism and that this was not possible without a break from the communist system. For people who accepted this argument, independence became the necessary goal.

The elections to the USSR Congress of People's Deputies in March 1989 gave the PFE the chance to test its strength, although the results were somewhat obscured by the fact that many PFE-endorsed candidates were also members of the Communist Party. Nevertheless, PFE candidates swept the slate, winning 18 out of 21 contested seats.

A new test came in February 1990, when republic elections were scheduled. The Popular Front of Estonia adopted a platform in October 1989 calling for sovereignty and independence. Thus, the PFE went on record for the first time as publicly favoring independence.

Responding to these developments, the Communist Party of Estonia began moving in the same direction. In February 1990, then Prime Minister Indrek Toome, a former head of ideology for the CPE, founded the Free Estonia Group as his vehicle for reelection. He ran on a platform of experience and competence. Arnold Rüütel, president of the Supreme Soviet, also maneuvered to assure his reelection. As presiding officer for the Full Assembly of People's Deputies—a meeting of deputies at the local, republic, and union levels of government—he steered through a resolution declaring that Estonia's independence should be restored on the basis of the 1920 Tartu Treaty with Soviet Russia.

Thus, Rüütel was also on record as supporting Estonian independence.

Reform communists who had endorsed Estonian independence did well in the February 1990 elections. But it was the candidates endorsed by the Popular Front of Estonia who made the best showing, winning a clear majority of the seats. When the new Supreme Soviet met at the end of March, it first passed a resolution declaring that it did "not recognize the legality of state authority of the USSR on the territory of Estonia." The next day, it elected Edgar Savisaar, head of the Popular Front of Estonia, as the new prime minister. Since he had resigned his membership in the Communist Party some months earlier, he became the first non-communist to be elected head of Estonia's government since 1940.

Savisaar's government now began taking on many of the trappings of independence. Postage stamps were issued and plans were announced to issue an Estonian currency, the kroon. The government also launched a campaign aimed at privatizing service industries and state distribution networks. In addition, the Estonian Supreme Soviet passed a law prohibiting the drafting of Estonian youths into the Soviet military.

On May 8, 1990, Estonia became the third Baltic republic to declare its independence. Six days later, Gorbachev issued a decree invalidating the declaration. Vadim Bakatin, Soviet minister of the interior, ordered troops into Estonia to enforce the decree. However, Prime Minister Savisaar telephoned Bakatin and got the order reversed. Bakatin later signed an order guaranteeing the Estonian government control over law enforcement in Estonia. His leniency was probably an important reason he was later dismissed as interior minister and replaced by a hardliner, Boris K. Pugo, one of the plotters of the August 1991 coup. Estonia was to remain in a state of suspended animation for another year before its independence would be recognized.

Periodically, Gorbachev condemned Baltic demands for independence and continued to insist that the Baltic states could only obtain their independence by complying with legislation passed by the Supreme Soviet on the issue. This was out of the question for the Baltic states since their legal position was that they were reasserting an independence that, under international law, had never been lost. Meanwhile, the Communist Party of Estonia, which had voted the previous March to separate from the Communist Party of the Soviet Union, carried through its break in September 1990. One more connection was thus severed.

During the fall of 1990, Gorbachev sought to enforce a more hardline position.

Estonia

This lasted until May 1991, when it finally became clear to him that his policy had alienated reform-minded individuals without producing anything positive. Moreover, he now began to realize that he could not achieve a new union treaty without reaching an accommodation with reformers. This included accepting a major transfer of power and authority to the individual republics. Negotiations for a new union treaty went on during the summer, and it was due to be signed on August 17, 1991.

Hard liners opposed to the new union treaty launched their coup d'etat against Gorbachev on August 16. The failure of that coup finally broke the logjam on recognition. Estonia and Latvia declared their independence while the coup was still in progress. After it had failed, most of the world rushed to extend recognition to all three Baltic republics. The postcoup Soviet government granted its own recognition in September.

Estonia as a Sovereign State

Edgar Savisaar remained as prime minister of an independent Estonia for approximately five months. In January 1992 he came increasingly under attack for the state of the economy. The parliament approved his request to impose a state of emergency to deal with the economic situation. However, criticism of him continued, and he resigned.

Tiit Vahi was selected as the new prime minister of a government of experts. Individuals entering the cabinet dropped their party membership while in the cabinet. One of his first acts was to repeal the state of emergency and to promise to work closely with parliament. He said that he expected to remain in office only about six months. His political agenda included a new constitution and a new law on Estonian citizenship, to be followed by new elections to the parliament. The Supreme Council approved the new citizenship law on February 26, 1992.

In April 1992, another law restructured the government by replacing the Supreme Council by the Riigikogu, a single-chamber assembly consisting of 101 members. The same law created a president of the republic to replace the chairman of the Supreme Council. The new constitution was submitted to a referendum in June 1992. The question of denying citizenship to individuals who had moved to Estonia after 1940 was also included on the ballot. Both measures were approved overwhelmingly. The new legislative elections that took place in September were therefore limited almost exclusively to ethnic Estonians.

That helps explain why the right-wing Pro Patria "Isamaa"/ERSP Bloc became the dominant group in the new legislature. The new prime minister, Mart Laar,

Former president Lennart Meri

headed a coalition government made up of the Pro Patria electoral alliance, which controlled 51 out of the 101 seats in the Riigikogu. The elections also included a popular vote to fill the office of president of the republic. Arnold Rüütel, who had steered Estonia to independence as head of the Estonian Communist Party, actually came in first with 43% of the vote. Because he failed to win an absolute majority, however, the Riigikogu elected the new president. Their choice was Lennart Meri, candidate of the Pro Patria "Isamaa" Bloc, even though he came in a poor second in September with only 29% of the vote.

Meri was a former foreign minister and ambassador to Finland. The son of a diplomat, he was educated in Berlin and Paris and speaks a half-dozen languages fluently. His family was among those deported to Siberia in 1941. They were permitted to return to Estonia in 1946. An ironic reminder of that dark past was given in 2007, when President Meri's 88-year-old cousin, Arnold Meri, a highly decorated Soviet soldier, was charged with genocide for assisting in the deportation of hundreds of Estonians to Soviet camps in 1949.

During the Soviet time, Meri had a varied and distinguished career as a translator, writer, and filmmaker. He was best known for his histories of Estonians and other Finno-Ugric peoples. He had a reputation for his bluntness. Once, when he was in the White House with other Baltic presidents, President George H. W. Bush asked him if he liked to fish. Meri answered by reaching for an indelible pen, circling Estonia on an expensive electronic map, and saying that the biggest fish can be caught there. At another occasion he was asked to speak

to a group of Russian leaders. Speaking in perfect Russian, he began his remarks by saying, "I hate Russia!" There was a hush in the startled audience. Then he continued, "The Russia of Lenin. But I love the Russia of Pushkin [Russia's beloved 19th-century poet]." In 2001 he was replaced as president by Arnold Rüütel. Meri passed away in 2006 and will be remembered as a uniquely erudite and amiable but blunt statesman who firmly stood against Russia at a critical time and ably steered his country toward partnership with the west.

Even though the government of Mart Laar had a right-wing orientation, it was outflanked on the right by the Eesti Kodanik (Estonian Citizens). This was a rightist-nationalist movement headed by Jüri Toomepuu, a US citizen and retired US Army colonel, who repeatedly attacked the government for being too lenient toward residents who are not ethnic Estonians.

Citizenship Laws

Estonian independence in August 1991 did not automatically eradicate the legacies of the Soviet Empire. All three Baltic states were left to deal with important residual problems: Who belongs to the restored sovereign states, and who does not? Concretely, who should be granted citizenship? Can a democracy deny full rights to a sizable minority who were living and working in the country at the time of independence?

For Estonia the question of citizenship became vital. It faced the prospect of continued heavy Russian influence on most aspects of policy if all residents

Ex–prime minister Mart Laar

145

Estonia

were granted automatic citizenship (called the "zero option") or dual citizenship, as Russian speakers and Russia demanded. Thus, it refused to grant either.

Estonians see this not only as a question of control over their nation's affairs but also as a matter of principle: In the Estonian view, the majority of Russians had been permitted to settle in Estonia in order to implement a Soviet policy of occupation after it had forcibly annexed Estonia in 1940. On what basis could occupiers and their descendants expect to be recognized as citizens? For example, Germans who had been part of the occupation forces in various European countries during the World War II would not have been permitted to claim citizenship rights there merely because they were residing in the country at the time when Hitler's Reich collapsed. Why should Russians be permitted to claim that right today? A 1949 Geneva convention declared that the settlement of occupied territory under the aegis of a military occupation regime is impermissible.

Russia adamantly denies that the Soviet Union had ever occupied the Baltic states and that their joining the USSR was involuntary, despite some admitted pressure at the time. It regards the Estonians' acceptance of their situation without armed resistance and the signing by a democratically elected president of the agreement ratifying the changes as justifying the Russian interpretation. Therefore, Moscow's political leaders have never apologized for the Soviet Union's actions in or after 1940.

Nor have they ever hinted that the occupation might have been illegal. They remember the effect their admission had in 1989 that there had been secret protocols to the Molotov-Ribbentrop Treaty consigning the Baltic states to Soviet rule. This public confession galvanized the Baltic independence movements and accelerated their achievement of freedom.

A majority of Russians in Estonia agree with the position that the country had voluntarily joined the Soviet Union and had never been annexed. They do not regard themselves as occupiers or colonialists, even though they did enjoy certain advantages during Soviet rule in terms of housing, employment and education. Most had moved within their own country, the Soviet Union, in order to seek a better economic standard of living, and many of their children were born in Estonia. They do not consider it fair to blame them for any injustices that were committed by the discredited and now-abolished Soviet Union.

Many Russian speakers find themselves in a dilemma. For them, return to Russia or any other former Soviet republic, where there is considerable economic and political turmoil, is unthinkable because their jobs, residences, friends, and relatives are in Estonia. Their roots in the rest of the former USSR have been broken after decades of residency in the Baltics. Most want to stay: A 1995 poll revealed that only 1% was willing to leave Estonia, although a third is keeping open the option of repatriating.

Estonians based their citizenship laws on the notion of legal continuity of their prewar republic. They insisted that severe restrictions be introduced. They granted citizenship automatically to pre-1940 residents and their descendants. In Estonia a sixth of the Russians qualified on this basis; subsequent naturalization raised this to over a third by 1998.

Confronting criticism that Russian speakers were being made permanent non-citizens, Estonia opened citizenship to all persons who met certain criteria, including residency in Estonia for two years and the willingness to take a loyalty oath to the Estonian Republic. Applicants must demonstrate competence (though not fluency) in Estonian, a difficult language unrelated to Russian. Applicants for Estonian citizenship must answer questions in Estonian about the constitution and political system, and they are permitted to look up the answers in the text of the constitution (which is written in Estonian). In 2003 the Supreme Court ruled that the 7,000 Soviet veterans and their dependents living in Estonia may receive permanent residency permits, but the parliament's Constitutional Committee vowed to ignore this ruling.

All peoples show a special interest in how their countrymen are treated abroad. Russia is no different, and its leaders were incensed by Estonia's citizenship laws. They pointed to the Agreement on the Bases of Interstate Relations of January 12, 1991, signed by Boris Yeltsin and Estonian leaders. Article 3 obligated Estonia to offer citizenship to any Russians wanting to be Estonian citizens and living in Estonia on that date. Since this was signed eight months before Estonia became independent, at a time when it was not yet clear that Estonia could become a separate state and when the citizenship issue was still largely irrelevant, the new leaders of a free Estonia decided not to implement it. Russia believes that Estonia's reneging on a formal, signed agreement created the conditions for subsequent bad relations between the two countries.

Estonians claim that their citizenship law does not discriminate on formal ethnic grounds. However, since the immediate effect was the disenfranchisement of most ethnic Russian residents, many Russians, as well as some persons in the international community, see it that way. Few Russians can meet the language requirement without major effort. In 1989, when Estonian was declared to be the only official language of Estonia, only 13% of Russians in Estonia had a good command of the local language. The others had seen no need to learn Estonian because Balts were expected to speak Russian well if they wanted to work or study, and most

Estonian and Russian students mingling at their professor's home in Tallinn

did so. There was an outcry after independence in 1991 that the new language restrictions were "unfair" and "human rights violations."

Estonians reply that the rights of those who do not speak Estonian are greater than in some other small nations, such as Quebec Province in Canada, which fear absorption and destruction of their cultures. They face no restrictions on using their language at the workplace, although it is an advantage to speak Estonian, and the defense forces and many categories in the civil service are blocked to noncitizens.

Parents are free to send their children to Russian-language schools, and almost half the public schools in Tallinn are such. Parliament rejected a law in 2003 that would have required Russian-language secondary schools to switch to Estonian in 2007. But current rules require those schools to teach 60% of their subjects in Estonian in the upper grades. They have in effect become bilingual schools. Inspectors from the National Language Inspectorate drop by the schools to chat with teachers, who can be fined or disciplined if they are not competent in Estonian. In 2008 about a third of the teachers in the Russian-language schools failed. Amnesty International criticized these tactics as heavy-handed.

Estonian authorities point out that the success rate of those who take the Estonian exam is high. After the test's standards were raised in 1995, over 80% still passed it, and about 93% succeeded in the constitution and citizenship exam. To raise these figures even further, a new category of teacher was introduced. The "teacher of the state language" received special training in Estonian-language teaching and twice the pay of other teachers. This is open to any nationality, including Russians. Finally, when certain aspects of the Estonian citizenship create special difficulties and tension, authorities have demonstrated a willingness to be flexible and to make the requirements more feasible. Deadlines are routinely extended. But success over time is undeniable. By 2007 the percentage of Russians speaking Estonian had climbed from 15% in 1991 to 40%; among 18- to 24-year-olds, it is nearly 60%.

Critics counter that such success statistics are deceiving since only persons confident of passing are willing to pay the $25–$40 fee and take the all-day exam. Also, in areas where the population is overwhelmingly Russian, such as Narva, the success rate is only 60%. Many Russian speakers complain of a lack of state funds for language classes, poor instructional materials, absence of clear guidelines for what needs to be learned for the language test, mystifying application procedures, needless delays, unfriendly and unhelpful Estonian officials, and generally an unspoken conspiracy to make it as difficult as possible to acquire Estonian citizenship.

Article 50 of the Estonian constitution states that, where more than half of the permanent residents in a locality are members of an ethnic minority, such as in the overwhelmingly Russian-speaking northeast of Estonia, they have a right to deal with the state and local authorities in their own language. Legal resident aliens in Estonia are permitted to vote in local elections. Although all candidates must be citizens, they are not required to speak Estonian. State radio and television are broadcast in Russian, as well as Estonian. There are Russian-language theaters and a wide variety of Russian newspapers and magazines available. Many university courses are taught in Russian, and almost all examinations at Estonian universities may be written in Russian if the student prefers.

Russian nationals residing in Estonia resent several aspects of the citizenship policy as demeaning and unfair: being ascribed the status of aliens, with the implicit risk of deportation even though they do not feel like aliens, having lived much or all of their lives in Estonia; the necessity to choose between two nationalities (either Estonian or Russian) or accept an alien's passport; the need to take formal steps to secure residency permits even though they may have lived all their lives in Estonia; and, of course, the need to learn the Estonian language, spoken by only a little over 1 million people in the entire world.

The Estonian government argues that its citizenship laws, adopted by elected parliaments, are reasonable by western standards. While a fifth of the adult population in Estonia is disenfranchised in national elections, other democratic countries, such as Luxembourg and Switzerland, have similar percentages of resident aliens. It claims that its policies toward minorities have been more successful in easing ethnic tensions than in most former communist states. Unlike such ex-Soviet republics as Moldova and Georgia, Estonia (and Latvia and Lithuania) has experienced no ethnic violence. Like the other Baltic states, it has maintained a democratic regime in an ethnically diverse society by applying a rule of law. This has helped it gain international support.

International organizations have issued mixed reviews of Estonia's citizenship law, in part in response to Russia's energetic efforts to have Estonia condemned for human rights violations. In April 1992 the Human Rights Watch Helsinki published a policy guideline for all former Soviet republics supporting the granting of citizenship to all legal residents at the time of independence. It recognized that international law gives great freedom to sovereign states in setting citizenship requirements. Nevertheless, it found that Estonia's citizenship law, based on the principle (called jus sanguinis, "blood law") that one is considered a citizen of a country if his forefathers were also citizens of that country, seemed to violate several international conventions.

Both Russia and Estonia have used international organizations to internationalize their bilateral problems rather than to cooperate in finding solutions. They first aired their differences at the Conference (later Organization) for Security and Cooperation in Europe (CSCE, now OSCE). At Russia's initiative, the CSCE appointed a high commissioner to monitor human rights developments in the Baltics; in December 1992 the Estonian government invited a CSCE mission to come to Tallinn to evaluate its citizenship laws.

That mission became permanent in February 1993. It proposed the formation of a presidential roundtable, an advisory body composed of five members of parliament, five persons from the Russian Representative Assembly, and five representatives from the Estonian Union of Peoples, an umbrella group for diverse minorities. This roundtable has functioned effectively. In December 1995 it recommended a relaxation of the language and citizenship laws to help the non-Estonian population integrate. The OSCE published a report in late 1995 concluding, "one could not speak of a consistent pattern of human rights violations in Estonia."

Undeterred, Russia took its grievance to the United Nations, distributing a memorandum on human rights violations in the Baltics. President Yeltsin personally called on the secretary-general to look into the matter. In 1995 the UN Committee on Human Rights issued a report criticizing Estonia's citizenship and naturalization policies. Russia also raised the issue in the Council of the Baltic Sea States (CBSS); in May 1995 the CBSS authorized a commissioner to monitor Russian speakers' civil rights in the Baltic states.

Russian president Boris Yeltsin charged in 1993 that Estonia's citizenship law was an act of "ethnic cleansing and the imposition of an Estonian version of apartheid" (terms first used by one of the leaders of Estonia's independence movement, Edgar Savisaar, who opposed the strict citizenship law). Estonian officials counter that every person is free to choose his own citizenship. Article 49 of the Estonian constitution declares, "every person shall have the right to preserve his or her ethnic identity"; no one is forced to integrate or to learn Estonian. At the same time, citizenship is open to every person, regardless of nationality, who is not an active-duty

Estonia

member of foreign armed forces, who had not worked in such Soviet intelligence and security organizations as the KGB, and who goes through the proper procedures and learns a modicum of Estonian; there is no ethnic requirement for citizenship.

Whatever one's citizenship, residents of Estonia are permitted to criticize the government and its policies openly, organize rallies, or form organizations. Since 1995 deputies of the Russian coalition of three political parties, Our Home is Estonia, voted into parliament by the one-third of Russian speakers who are citizens, represents Russian-language citizens of Estonia in parliament and serves as a voice for Russian residents' concerns. In close parliamentary votes, such as the election of the Estonian president in August 1996, the votes of six Russian deputies can be decisive. These heterogeneous Russian parties usually support the ruling coalitions.

The absence of political prisoners and martyrs gives a hollow ring to charges from Russia of "human rights violations," "genocide," and "fascism" (a particularly favorite tag for Estonians, stemming from the German occupation from 1941–1944 and the fact that many Estonians had served in the German army). The result is that Russians with diverse and moderate views have come to the forefront as spokespersons for the immigrant community. Talk of rebellion and "fifth columns" has subsided. Although Russian speakers and Estonians lead largely separate lives in Estonia, they bear little hatred or deep aversion toward each other.

Resentments both in Russia and in the Baltics stemming from citizenship laws adversely affect bilateral relations. Former Russian president Boris Yeltsin warned, "If the Russian-speaking population expresses the natural desire to protect itself from crude discrimination, Russia will not be able to remain in the position of an indifferent onlooker." Russia denied it normal trade status, temporarily cut off all gas shipments to Estonia, and doubled its customs charges on imports from Estonia. Russian propaganda attempted to portray Estonia to the international community as a rogue state. Most important, in order to protest Estonia's citizenship laws, Russia protracted the signing of a border treaty satisfactory to Estonia. It thereby burdened Estonia's efforts to join the EU and NATO.

In 1995 the government sped up the process of issuing residence permits and gray noncitizen passports (citizens carry blue ones) to replace old Soviet passports that many ethnic Russians carried. These new passports guarantee that noncitizens, whose numbers are down to about 100,000, may return to Estonia after visiting their relatives in Russia. Russian

Former Prime Minister Jüri Ratas

president Vladimir Putin's call to Russians residing in Estonia to return to Russia permanently fell on deaf ears.

In response to EU concerns about Estonia's treatment of non-Estonian nationals expressed when it issued its 1997 invitation for Estonia to join fast-track negotiations for membership, the government announced an amendment to the citizenship law. It grants citizenship to all children born in Estonia of noncitizens if the parents had been residents for at least five years. Finally passed in December 1998, the amendment also stipulated that the children's parents must apply on their behalf and be themselves stateless. This does not apply to those who have already chosen to accept Russian citizenship. Estimates vary on how many of them are in Estonia: The Estonian government says about 120,000, but its Russian counterpart puts the number at about 147,000.

The amended law went into effect in July 1999 and opened Estonian citizenship to approximately 3,500 children. In spite of the small numbers involved, the EU hailed the action as "a forward-looking approach which promotes the stability of Estonian society and is consistent with the principles and aims of the European Union." The Estonian government actively encourages noncitizens to make the effort to acquire citizenship. In order to present role models and to show that the effort can pay off, it sponsored a television series involving interviews with Russian speakers who became citizens. In 2023 there are still approximately 64,000 stateless persons in Estonia, making the country's stateless population the world's 10th largest.

POLITICAL SYSTEM

Estonia is a multiparty, parliamentary democracy that has enjoyed political stability since 1991. It established the kind of institutional and legal conditions that place it within the western political model. It developed a multiparty system in which democratic procedures are respected. Despite frequent changes of coalitions and cabinets, it has maintained underlying political stability while demonstrating that power can be transferred peacefully from one coalition government to another. In contrast to Latvia and Lithuania, parties of former communists have been unable to win power in Estonia.

It proceeded rapidly to establish a democratic regime and to hold its first free elections since the 1930s. An Estonian constitutional assembly with a wide popular and political base and led by the democratic nationalist segment of the independence movement prepared a new constitution. Remembering the autocratic government that emerged in the tumultuous 1930s, the majority rejected the former 1938 constitution, with its strong executive, and adopted instead a parliamentary rather than a presidential system. The new constitution and a law denying automatic citizenship to non-Estonians who had moved to the country after 1940 were submitted to a referendum on June 28, 1992, three months before the first parliamentary elections. They were accepted overwhelmingly.

The President

The president is elected for a four-year term indirectly by parliament. An exception was made for the first post-Soviet presidential election, when citizens cast the first round of votes. An amendment to have the president elected by the Riigikogu stipulated that a candidate needed a two-thirds majority to win. It also created an electoral college to take over, should no candidate be able to obtain the required 68 votes. Following this procedure in 1996, the Riigikogu deadlocked between Meri and Rüütel. President Meri stood for reelection and was opposed by Rüütel. Neither was able to command the necessary 68 parliamentary votes to become elected. The matter was then referred to the electoral college, which reelected Meri by a vote of 196 to 126.

The prestige of the only president in the 1990s, Lennart Meri, was so great that the presidency gained a level of importance and authority that the drafters had not intended. A multilingual philologist and specialist in Finno-Ugric languages, he was the son of a prewar diplomat. He and his family had been deported to Siberia from 1941–1946, an experience that helped him decide never to join the Soviet Communist Party. He was foreign minister and ambassador to Finland before winning the presidency.

Estonia

The constitution barred Meri from seeking a third term in 2001. Arnold Rüütel, an earlier leader in Estonia's drive for independence, edged out Toomas Savi, to become president. As in 1996, the parliament was unable to decide on a candidate, so an assembly of 101 members of parliament and 266 local government delegates met to vote in the new president. In 2003 the government endorsed a constitutional reform for the president to be elected directly by the people, but it had not been enacted in time for the September 2006 presidential election.

Toomas Hendrich Ilves narrowly beat out Rüütel. Born in Sweden in 1953, his family moved to Leonia, New Jersey, when he was three. He lived in the United States for 23 years and got a degree in psychology and literature at Columbia University. He became a commentator for the Estonian service of Radio Free Europe in Munich until 1993. When Estonia won its independence, he renounced his American citizenship and returned to Estonia. He was its first ambassador in Washington and served as foreign minister from 1996 to 1998 and again from 1999 to 2000. During this time, he led the negotiations for entry into the EU and NATO. He later became deputy chair of the European Parliament's Foreign Affairs Committee. He left government service in order to engage in electoral politics. He is one of his country's few senior politicians with firsthand experience in Brussels and the US.

Ilves had to step down at the end of his second term in 2016, and the election of his successor proved to be a complicated affair. When no candidate won the required two-thirds majority in the parliament, the electoral college was convened and failed to create a required absolute majority, upon which the process returned to the Riigikogu. Finally, a compromise was reached, and the parliamentarians elected Kersti Kaljulaid, then Estonia's member of the European Court of Auditors, as the fifth president of the country. A self-described liberal-conservative, she became the first woman and, at 46, the youngest person to ever serve in this position. She served as the president of Estonia between 2016 and 2021. She was succeeded by Alar Karis, a molecular geneticist, developmental biologist, civil servant, and politician who has served since October 11, 2021, as the sixth president of Estonia.

The Parliament and Government

The political heart of Estonia is a unicameral 101-seat Riigikogu, elected by proportional representation every four years. In order to limit the number of parties in parliament and thereby increase the chances that stable governments can be formed, a party must win at least 5% of

President Alar Karis
Source: *Wikipedia*

the total votes cast to be represented in the Riigikogu. The politician who can assemble a majority coalition in this parliament becomes prime minister, the most important political figure. The prime minister presides over the cabinet and oversees day-to-day operations as head of government. Although formally appointed by the president, he must be approved by, and maintain the support of, a majority in the Riigikogu in order to remain in office. The prime minister's cabinet must also be approved by the legislature made up of numerous political parties. Since no one party ever controls a majority of the seats, governments are always coalitions.

Only Estonian citizens can vote in national elections, but noncitizens who are legal residents are permitted to vote in local elections. Although only citizens can stand as candidates, noncitizens can have an input into that level of government closest to them. This is important, especially in areas with large Russian-speaking populations, such as the northeast around Narva, and in the capital city of Tallinn, where 46% of the residents are not native Estonians. It led to a change in the leadership of the Tallinn City Council after a Russian-oriented party, the People's Trust, won four seats on the council in 1999. The nationalist-oriented parties of the Estonian ruling coalition had wished to oust the Center Party-dominated city government, but it lacked a majority. It got its majority by negotiating a coalition agreement with the People's Trust.

Perhaps no country in the world has gone as far into "e-government" as Estonia. The buzz words are "faster, more effective, more transparent, and more favorable." Every Tuesday the prime minister

meets with his 13-member cabinet. Each follows the agenda on a flat-screen monitor. No papers and pens are used (at a savings of €200,000 each year). All items for discussion and necessary documents are on computer for study in advance. Votes are done by mouse click. Ministers who are abroad can vote through their laptop computers. Like all public documents, all cabinet decisions are put on the Internet. All draft legislation is publicized online so that citizens can read them, express their opinions, and offer suggestions. An estimated 5% of all ideas citizens express through this channel find their way into legislation.

Government services are offered to citizens 24 hours a day via computer so that they can avoid bureaucratic hassles. Since government offices are linked by Internet to each other, quicker action is possible. Parliament approved Internet voting for the October 2005 Tallinn local elections and the 2007 parliamentary elections. Voters only need an official electronic ID card, which 1 million residents already had by 2005.

Parliamentary Elections

Estonian prime ministers always face the difficulty of holding shifting party coalitions together. Mart Laar, chairman of the Pro Patria Bloc and prime minister in 1992–1995, assumed power in 1999. He abolished the corporate tax and introduced an across-the-board 26% flat tax for companies and individuals (later 21% and 20% in 2015). The constitution requires a balanced budget.

Laar's government, the longest-serving in Estonia's post-Soviet history, collapsed in 2002. He was replaced by Reform's leader, Siim Kallas, who became prime minister in a minority government with the Center Party. He pursued the major

Former prime minister Andrus Ansip

149

Estonia

objectives of the previous government, namely to steer Estonia into NATO (successful in April 2004) and the EU (entry in May 2004). In August 2004 he became Estonia's first EU commissioner (for administrative reform) and one of the five vice presidents of the European Commission.

After the elections of March 2003, the Center Party got the most votes, but it could not form a government. That was done by a newcomer, Res Publica, a conservative, business-oriented party that campaigned on an anticorruption and anticrime platform. It was led by 36-year-old Juhan Parts, former chief state auditor, who became prime minister.

In April 2005 Parts stepped down after parliament had expressed no confidence in his justice minister over proposed anticorruption measures. He was replaced as prime minister by Reform Party leader Andrus Ansip, former manager, banker, mayor of Tartu, and economics minister in Parts's government. He had once joined the Communist Party.

In March 2007, Ansip's Reform Party emerged as the largest party, winning 27.8% of the votes and 31 seats. This was a rare case of a government being reelected in central Europe; in fact, he was the first Estonian prime minister to be returned to office since independence in 1991. The Union of Pro Patria and Res Publica (which merged in 2006) captured 17.9% of the votes and 19 seats.

In the March 2011 elections, Ansip and his Reform Party did it again, emerging as the leading party with 28.6% of the votes (up from 27.8%) and 33 seats (up 2). Voters rewarded him for ably steering the economy through crisis. They like his unpretentious style and his ambition to make Estonia one of the EU's five wealthiest countries in 15 years. Ansip remained in the prime ministerial chair until March 2014, when he resigned to improve his Reform Party's chances of winning the general election in March 2015. He was the EU's longest-serving head of government. He was replaced by the EU's youngest prime minister, 34-year-old Taavi Rõivas. Pro Patria and Res Publica, led by Mart Laar, climbed to 20.5% of the votes (up from 17.9%) and 23 seats (up 4). The center-right parties enjoyed a decisive victory.

On the left, the Center Party captured 24.8% and 27 seats. Its leader, Edgar Savisaar, was hurt by his approval of Russia's annexation of Crimea and by the Russian military maneuvers on the Estonian border just days before the election. Three other parties cleared the 5% hurdle: the Free Party (8.7% and 8 seats), the Conservative People's Party (8.1% and 7 seats), and Pro Patria and Res Publica, the biggest loser with 13.7% and 14 seats.

Prime Minister Kaja Kallas
Source: *Wikipedia*

In November 2016 the ruling coalition split over a proposed vote of no confidence. Prime Minister Rõivas refused to step down, but his cabinet lost the subsequent vote of confidence. A new coalition was formed by the Center Party, Social Democrats, and the Pro Patria and Res Publica Union, led by the Center's leader, Jüri Ratas.

In the May 2019 elections, the far-right Conservative People's Party (EKRE) captured 19 seats and entered the governing coalition. Jüri Ratas's Estonian Center Party won a second term as leader.

The March 5, 2023, parliamentary elections produced a resounding victory for Prime Minister Kaja Kallas's Reform Party. It captured 31% of the votes and 37 seats. The populist EKRE won 16% and 17 seats. The Center Party got 15% and 16 seats.

Of importance is the number of exiles who returned to play significant political, military, and economic roles. However, Balts who lived in comfortable western exile during the Soviet times sometimes experience resentment. They must learn to be tactful in offering more efficient foreign ways of doing things. In Estonia the top vote-getter in early parliamentary elections was an American, Juri Toomepuu. A loser in the first presidential election was an American political scientist, Rein Taagepera, who was founding dean of Tartu University's School of Social Sciences. Estonia's first defense minister was Hein Rebas, a Swedish reserve officer. A retired American colonel, Alexander Einseln, commanded Estonia's defense forces.

Foreign and Defense Policy

The US government, having always refused to recognize the 1940 incorporation of the Baltic governments into the USSR, was an early and enthusiastic supporter of their efforts to regain their independence. One example of just how far the US government was willing to go in that regard relates to Aleksander Einseln (1931—2017), recruited by the Estonian government to head the newly created Estonian Defense Forces. An Estonian native who had fled with his family to America in 1944, Einseln was a former tank commander and Vietnam veteran who retired from the US Army as a colonel. Not wanting to jeopardize either his US citizenship or his army pension, he requested permission from the US Army to accept the assignment. Since there was initially no approval from the US authorities, there were various problems. This went so far that, in addition to Einseln's pension from his service in the US armed forces, his US citizenship was also at stake. These difficulties were eventually overcome.

Einseln became involved in domestic Estonian politics and after arguments with the then Defense Minister Andrus Öövel, he was forced to ask to be released from his army duties in December 1995. In 2015 his Reform Party captured 27.7% of votes and 30 seats. His Social Democratic partners won 15% of the votes and 15 seats.

Estonia became a member of the World Trade Organization in 1999 after the parliament had ratified the accession protocol by a vote of 48 to 7. A number of opposition political parties abstained during the vote on the grounds that the terms of admission were against Estonia's national interests.

Estonia has relations with 170 countries and has worked especially hard to establish close and friendly relations with Scandinavia, and it was involved in intensive negotiations to become a member of the European Union, which occurred for all three Baltic states in May 2004. Estonia's early invitation was well merited. It has been consistently in the vanguard in reforming its economy since 1991. It has also been the recipient of the largest amount of foreign investment of any of the Baltic states. In fact, Estonia is Europe's largest recipient per capita of foreign investment. With a turnout of 63.4% in September 2003, 66.9% voted yes and only 33.1% no in the referendum approving membership. No political party opposed it, and a common refrain to the one-third that opposed it was, "A no to the EU is a yes to Russia." Then-prime minister Juhan Parts exclaimed, "Spring has arrived in Estonia; we're back in Europe!" Foreign Minister Kristiina Ojuland asserted, "This decision will guarantee the future of Estonia."

Estonia joined NATO in April 2004, along with the other two Baltic nations. Estonians do not discuss NATO with Russia

Estonia

on the grounds that every state has the right to choose its own security arrangements. As a NATO member, Estonia needs a very different kind of military than the one it has. Its troops would have to be mobile and useful for peacekeeping missions rather than being a citizen's army with secret arms dumps in forests waiting to fight a territorial war on its own soil.

It has 4,750 active forces, including 1,310 conscripts, who serve terms of 8 months (11 for officers, NCOs, some specialists, navy, and border guards). There are about 25,000 reservists, 10,766 of whom are in 15 Estonian Defense League (Kaitseliit) units. Of the active forces, approximately 4,200 (including 2,000 conscripts) are in the army, 300 in the navy (with 5 ships), and 250 in the air force (with 7 aircraft). It has 2,600 border guards, including 170 conscripts. As in all Baltic states, women are permitted to serve in the armed forces.

NATO is advising all new members to shift their forces from territorial defense based on conscripts to a professional army with mobile units trained for NATO operations. The government expressed support in 2003 for the Defense Ministry's plan to reduce the number of conscripts by 50% and to raise the number of professional troops. It also committed the country to preparing troops for NATO's rapid-response force by 2006. However, there is resistance among parties and the military to eliminating conscription altogether.

In 2002 it had 46 peacekeepers in Bosnia, and in March 2003, it deployed 120 peacekeepers to Kosovo for six months, replacing a Latvian unit that had served there since September 2002. In August 2004 it sent 95 peacekeepers back to Kosovo, again replacing a Latvian unit. It also dispatched a mine-clearance team and a canine unit to Afghanistan in August 2002 to enhance security around airfields used by American forces. They stayed one year, but its 12-member mission was extended to March 2005. In 2010 it had 150 soldiers in Afghanistan.

Estonia supported the US-British war effort in Iraq in March 2003. Then-prime minister Siim Kallas emphasized the importance of the US for Baltic security by stating, "I do not want war. But I believe we must pick a side. And I believe it is the side where the United States is." Aware that many Estonians did not agree with his policy, he continued, with a potentially threatening Russia in mind: "Isn't it absurd to imagine that hiding behind the wardrobe and wagging a reproaching finger at America would better ensure our defense from Stalin Jr. than being an outright and public friend and ally of the United States?" After hostilities ended, Estonia dispatched 55 soldiers for peacekeeping duties in Iraq, and in 2004 it sent a

Christmas with the Angelstok family in Tallinn

32-member Estpla-8 infantry platoon and a 13-member CT-2 cargo team. By 2010 it had no soldiers deployed in Iraq.

It was on America's side at the 2008 NATO summit in Bucharest when it supported membership for Ukraine and Georgia against Russia's vehement objections. President Toomas Ilves argued, "The main reason for saying no is a Russian veto, and that's the most dangerous thing about all of this." The US compensates Estonia for some of the expenses and upon entry into NATO unblocked its military aid to all three Baltic states.

Estonia's allies rate its British-trained intelligence service as one of eastern Europe's best; it has an ironclad rule not to spy on politicians. It was good intelligence work that led to the arrest in 2008 of Herman Simm, a former KGB colonel before becoming security chief in the Estonia defense ministry. He sold 3,000 top-secret NATO and EU documents to Russia's SVR Foreign Intelligence Service for about $131,000. This made him the most damaging spy in NATO history. The Kremlin denied any involvement in the case.

Russia got even in September 2014, two days after President Obama reiterated US security assurances to the Baltic states. A well-armed squad of Russian security operatives crossed into Estonia and kidnapped an Estonian intelligence officer. He was sentenced to 15 years for espionage, but within a year, he was swapped for a former Estonian security official serving a 16-year sentence for spying for Moscow. After a high-profile diplomatic game, in which President lives urged citizens to wear yellow ribbons and international pressure was put on Moscow, a Cold War-style exchange of agents on a bridge resolved the issue that greatly unnerved the Estonians.

Border and Other Disputes with Russia

Border disputes belong to the most complicated and serious international conflicts

in which any country can be involved. Agreements concerning them are especially important because they are of such long duration. Two friendly countries, such as Estonia and Latvia, who do not threaten each other and who genuinely want good neighborly relations, can solve their border disputes relatively easily, after dealing with technical issues and sorting out conflicting economic interests. It is very different with negotiations between a small, proud country that possesses few power resources and a long memory of domination by the negotiating partner and a large power that has controlled or strongly influenced the small country for two and a half centuries. Such negotiations are highly political and emotional. They go to the core of each country's definition of themselves and of their security needs. They are affected by each nation's attempts to come to grips with the past and to adjust to the present.

A small country like Estonia has few borders to fix. Russia has them all around it. The rapid unraveling of the USSR, which enabled Estonia and the other Baltic states to become independent in August 1991, left numerous border uncertainties throughout the former empire. They extend from the most contentious (the Kurile Islands claimed by Japan) and run along the long-disputed Chinese frontier, past the new central Asian and Caucasian republics, the Ukraine, and even inside the Russian Federation itself, where a few ethnic minorities, such as the Chechens, are determined to carve out their own sovereign states. Thus, compromises in any one set of border negotiations could be invoked as precedents in countless other talks.

It made no sense to discuss borders while all were ruled from Moscow. Internal borders within the highly centralized Soviet Union were largely irrelevant. But frontier disputes now affect the neighbors' foreign relations and are charged with

Estonia

symbolism and emotions, especially in Estonia. Few issues are more important for sovereign states than their borders. Most consider their inviolability to be vital interests, for which they would be willing to go to war.

In 1945 Estonia lost territory to Russia, but it could do nothing to prevent it. Estonia's losses east of the Narva River and in the southeast Petseri District amounted to 5% of its total land area. Independence in 1991 raised the question of where the permanent border should be drawn. On September 12, 1991, Estonia declared the border changes forced on it in 1945 to be invalid. Specifically, it argued that its border along the Narva River in the northeast corner of the country and in the southeast corner of Estonia, south of Lake Peipus, be moved eastward to where it was before 1945. Also, the frontier running through Lake Peipus before 1945 should be recognized.

Estonia realizes that it does not have the power to restore the old border. It is also nervous about accepting back more than 2,0 square kilometers of territory now inhabited almost entirely by Russians. The Estonians repeatedly suggested that it was prepared to renounce this territory if Russia recognized the Tartu Peace Treaty, an important 1920 agreement with Russia. That is, it would accept Moscow's redrawing of the border in 1945 in exchange for an important Russian political concession that would legitimize

Estonia's restrictive citizenship law. In November 1995 the Estonian government announced that it would treat the current demarcation line as the de facto state border. This ignited a storm of criticism from Estonian nationalists.

Negotiating Estonia's maritime borders was easier than dealing with land borders because negotiators are drawing new lines, and there exists much international law that can be applied. By October 1996 the major differences over Estonia's maritime border with Russia had been resolved. An agreement between the two countries was reached, and Finland, which had to agree to any lines drawn in the Gulf of Finland, approved. But Russian negotiators announced that no sea agreement would be signed until the thornier land negotiations are completed. It is on the land border between the two countries that a settlement is especially urgent for Estonia. But despite the fact that only a few minor issues remained unresolved, the talks are at an impasse.

Estonia knew that the EU and NATO were hesitant to accept it as a member as long as it had an outstanding border dispute with a powerful country like Russia. Neither of these international organizations ever officially stated this, but representatives offered unmistakable hints. NATO Deputy Secretary for Political Issues Gebhardt von Moltke said in Tallinn that "Estonia's outstanding border issue with Russia would have to be solved

peacefully . . . before membership would be possible." The EU communicated the same message in May 1996.

The US had communicated that it would like to see the two countries develop good neighborly relations. This was made most explicit on January 16, 1998, when the American president endorsed in principle the Baltic states' desire to join the Atlantic Alliance by signing with the three Baltic presidents a Charter of Partnership. Though not a guarantee of future NATO membership or of American protection, it put on record Washington's "real, profound and enduring interest" in Baltic security and the conviction that the three new democracies have as much right to join NATO as do the three ex-communist countries that were invited in 1997 to enter: Poland, Hungary, and the Czech Republic.

The overriding desire to join first the EU and then NATO made it clear to the Estonian government that a change in its negotiating strategy toward Russia was essential. Estonia was ready not only to concede territory lost to Russia after minor border adjustments were made but also to back away from its insistence that Russia accept the validity of the Tartu Treaty "for even a half an hour."

A reexamination of the international legal aspects of the border treaty led Estonian officials to conclude that there was no longer any need to tie the issue of continuity assured by the Tartu Treaty to the signing of a border agreement. An announcement from the EU in 1997 that Estonia is a front-rank contender for admission, successful negotiations to establish visa-free travel with the Nordic countries, and the absence of any serious international objections to Estonia's citizenship laws outside of Russia indicated that almost no countries questioned the continuity of Estonia's statehood or its sovereignty. Thus, there was no need to underscore this fact by insisting that Russia recognize this in the context of the border treaty. In effect, it would have meant that it was Russia's right to decide whether Estonia was a sovereign state that could make its own laws, including those regarding citizenship.

Therefore, with most of the technical border questions and all the general questions already solved, Estonia accepted an agreement with Russia on November 7, 1996. The text made no mention of the Tartu Treaty, and it placed the border where Moscow had fixed it by unilateral decree in 1945. However, in January 1997 then-Russian foreign minister (later prime minister) Yevgeny Primakov announced that Russia would not sign the agreement until the two countries could hold bilateral talks aimed at changing certain pieces of Estonia's domestic legislation. This no doubt included the citizenship law, which the OSCE, the UN, and the Council of Europe had basically approved.

Estonia and Russian negotiators met three times during 1997 to finalize the border maps to accompany the border treaty. But Russia insisted that the November 1996 agreement be reopened, adding, for example, a clause concerning the point where Estonia, Latvia, and Russia touch each other. It haggled for an hour and a half over the color of the folder for a treaty. It contested the names of places on the maps, insisting, for example, that Pskov not appear in its Estonian spelling, Pihkva. Tallinn concluded that these stalling tactics revealed that Russia lacks the political will to implement the treaty. There are also political dangers for Russia's leaders. A treaty with Lithuania in November 1997 ignited controversy in the Duma, and they do not want to risk that again.

By 1998 bilateral relations with Russia had improved. The two governments reached a gentlemen's agreement that the OSCE must be the channel for all citizenship questions; Estonia no longer accepts advice on these matters directly from Russia. Having gone through the door to western integration, Estonians themselves are not in as much of a hurry to sign a border treaty with Russia. President Toomas Hendrik Ilves said to the Estonian parliament on February 12, 1998, "The government is awaiting the settling of this issue calmly since 1997 proved that Estonia can achieve its foreign policy goals, regardless of whether it has or does not have a border agreement with the Russian Federation."

The EU, which Estonia entered in May 2004, provided $77 million to help it secure its border with Russia, as required by the EU's Schengen Agreement, which all three Baltic states entered in December 2007. The EU has always regarded Estonia's and Latvia's border treaties with Russia as purely bilateral matters and has given little diplomatic assistance, despite the fact

that those borders are its only nondemarcated external borders. On May 18, 2005, the foreign ministers of both Russia and Estonia signed a treaty governing their sea and land borders. All parties in the Estonian parliament ratified the treaty after adding a preamble referring to the founding of the Estonian Republic in 1918 and to the Treaty of Tartu. Russia refused to ratify the treaty and withdrew its signature.

In February 2014 negotiators agreed to a Russo-Estonian border treaty that confirms the status quo and makes a few commonsense adjustments. Reference to the 1920 Tartu Peace Treaty remained a bone of contention, and both sides had to yield a bit on this. Some vocal nationalist Estonians were outraged by the outcome. Both sides face the challenge of getting this treaty accepted by their respective parliaments at a time of high tension over the Russian invasion and annexation of the Crimea. The Russians had once before aborted the treaty at this stage.

In April and May 2007, relations between the two countries reached their lowest point since independence. The newly elected government decided to move a Soviet war monument, known as the Bronze Soldier, along with about a dozen nearby graves of unknown soldiers, from the center of Tallinn to a military cemetery outside of town. Designed six decades earlier by an Estonian sculptor using an Estonian model, the statue meant totally different things to resident Russians and Estonians. The former saw it a memorial to the wartime sacrifice to defeat Nazi Germany. The latter saw it as a symbol of the hated occupation after 1944; some Estonians even dubbed it the "tomb of the unknown rapist." However, fearing violence and perceiving political motivation only two weeks before parliamentary elections, 49% of Estonian respondents said in an Eesti Paevaleht poll at the time that they opposed the movement of the Bronze Soldier, while only 37% favored it.

Estonian bank lures customers

The relocation, which the Russian government called a "sacrilege" and "blasphemy," sparked the worst riots Estonia had seen since becoming free. Ethnic Russians attacked the Academy of Arts and the main theater, and they looted businesses. One man was stabbed to death, and a dozen police officers and 44 protesters were injured. A youth group close to President Putin, Nashi, attacked and besieged the Estonian embassy in Moscow. This was an action that, along with Russia's generally aggressive behavior, prompted US, NATO, and EU protests and unified Estonia's allies in support of it. Estonia later retaliated against Nashi by barring its young members from entering Estonia. By putting them on an immigration blacklist, Tallinn prevented them from traveling elsewhere in Europe because of Schengen restrictions.

Russia discontinued passenger train service between St. Petersburg and Tallinn, banned heavy trucks from using the main bridge across the border at Ivangorod, and terminated gas and oil shipments to Estonia. Estonia is not dependent upon energy

Estonia

Grease opens in Tallinn

from Russia, and only about 8% of its foreign trade is with Russia. Moscow lifted all these measures after the crisis dissipated.

Then ex-president George W. Bush invited President Ilves to the White House in a show of support. Suspecting political motives on the part of the prime minister, who was facing a close reelection at the time, Ilves, like Tallinn's mayor Edgar Savisaar had opposed the moving of the memorial.

In November 2006 Bush had been the first sitting American president to visit Estonia. Current Prime Minister Kaja Kallas became one of the most high-profile leaders from the NATO states that border Russia. This ensures Estonia punches above its weight in international politics. She calls for permanent NATO bases and more US troops on Baltic soil. Estonia is the biggest military donor to Ukraine relative to its GDP.

ECONOMY

Estonia was hit very hard by the global recession that began in 2008. It took a couple years to work its way out of the hole it was in and become again the acknowledged tiger among the Baltic states, and indeed among all 23 countries emerging from communism. Its GDP declined a depressing 14.1% in 2009 before bouncing back to 3.2% in 2023. At 9.9% in 2013 (down from 19% in 2009), unemployment is the next target. But ex-prime minister Ansip was the only Baltic head of government to have remained in power as the boom turn to bust and back.

It resumed positive growth in its GDP in 1995. It was the first former Soviet republic to introduce its own currency, the kroon, which it tied to the German mark until the euro came into being in 2002. To keep its money stable, it created a currency board, which takes monetary policy largely out of the state's hands. Upon entry into the EU in May 2004, it pledged to adopt the common currency as soon as possible. It already permitted the use of euros within Estonia if both parties agreed to the transaction. It joined the EU's exchange-rate mechanism (ERM2) in 2004, and it had the privilege of designing its future euro coins. It adopted the euro in January 2011. Estonia is a model of financial virtue and the paragon of flexibility and pain-for-gain austerity. In 2012 its public debt was only 6.7% of GDP, the lowest in the EU, and its budget deficit a mere 1.3% of GDP. Its currency was stable throughout the recession, and its wages and prices remained flexible. It did not have to rescue failed banks because Estonia's are all foreign-owned.

The structure of its economy reveals how modern it is. Sixty-four percent of the workforce is employed in the services industry, producing 67% of GDP. Industry employs 31% and produces 29% of GDP. Estonia reduced its inflation rate from a dizzying 1,000% in 1992 to 9.5% in 2023 due to fast economic growth and a fixed exchange rate. As in the other ex-Soviet-bloc countries, the rising price for Russian energy drives up inflation, since they use power less efficiently than in western Europe. Wages grew faster than productivity. Although the gap between rich and poor has increased, it is obvious especially in the cities that prosperity has reached a large part of the population.

Its economy grew by 7% every year throughout the 1990s and by about 6% annually after a slump in 2003; in 2007 it shot up 11.5%, which some analysts saw as a sign of dangerous overheating. By 2008 economic growth and property prices had declined sharply. Tallinn had become a magnet throughout Europe for property speculators, driving values up by 10% to 15% annually for eight years in a row. Property values doubled between 2004 and 2007. Apartments in the city's medieval old town had shot up to €5,000 ($7,500) per square meter. Real estate prices plummeted in the subsequent recession and are only slowly recovering.

Estonian law requires governments to maintain a balanced budget and to deposit the surplus into a currency-stabilization reserve fund. In 2005 it had an astounding state net asset of 6% of GDP rather than a national debt. This nest-egg enabled it to weather the recession better and to hold its debt down.

It quickly privatized the bulk of its economy and did it in a way that prevented oligarchs from gaining control of large parts of industry. It began immediately to dismantle the command economy inherited from the Soviet Union, setting up a privatization agency modeled on Germany's trust agency (Treuhand) in 1992. By the end of 1994, privatization was 90% complete. Rejecting tariffs and bailouts, cutting off subsidies to industry, and allowing wages to rise freely stabilized the value of the Estonian kroon and gave a great spurt to both foreign investment and exports.

As a result, new stores, restaurants, and other service enterprises sprouted, while foreign investment, particularly from Scandinavia, led to additional jobs in private industry, replacing the ones lost in the crumbling state enterprises. Retail shops have all been privatized. The number of foreign companies opening headquarters has ballooned. By 2006 a third of Estonia's total economy was wholly or partly owned by foreigners, who produce half its exports. Three-fourths of those investment funds come from Finland and Sweden. By the end of the 20th century, three-fourths of its GDP was generated by the private sector, including privatized businesses and startups, so its privatizing agency could be closed at the end of 2000. Railways, ports, and energy utilities were placed on the auction block and sold.

New factories had been built during the Soviet era. Constructed on the Soviet model, many have had to sharply cut their labor forces in order to become even marginally competitive. Therefore, the Estonian government's policy of privatization affected these factories the most. This is particularly true with regard to the area of Narva, located in the northeastern part of Estonia. Narva is inhabited almost entirely by Russians, the result of the fact that the Soviet government decided in the 1960s to build a branch of its industrial-military complex there.

In spite of the numerous factories built in the 1960s and 1970s to serve as suppliers of the Soviet arms industry, Estonia's largest industry is still that of primary extraction, the production of oil from oil shale. Two other major industries are the manufacturing of mineral fertilizers and shipbuilding. It also has consumer industries, such as textiles, and medium industry, such as electrical and mechanical equipment. Most of the rest of its industry is concerned with the processing of forest products (timber, wood pulp for paper manufacturing, peat) or food processing. Fishing is another major industry.

Among the former communist countries, Estonia enjoys the highest foreign direct investment (FDI) per head and the highest credit rating. Its per-capita FDI in 2004 was €115.7, compared with €47.8 in Latvia and €54.7 in Lithuania. It is appealing to investors, among other reasons, because of its flat tax rate of 21% for both personal and corporate income (down to 20% in 2015), its lack of tariffs and general openness, and its habit of treating foreigners and Estonians alike in business. Eight other eastern European countries, including Latvia, Lithuania, and Russia, followed the Estonian lead on the flat tax. Only 3.6% of total tax revenues fall directly on corporations.

A country that is three-fourths urban, it is on its way to becoming a predominantly information-based service economy, with native Estonians constituting the minority of the workforce in industry. Despite severe financial limitations, its university system produces a high-tech work force. But Estonia spends less than 1% of its GDP on research and development.

Estonians use the Internet more than any other post-Soviet country and twice as much as do French and Italians. Some speak of "e-stonia." The state provides countrywide WiFi free. This is an addiction it has in common with its most important trading partner and source of investment, Finland, a country with which it shares close and unique linguistic and cultural ties. Over half of all Estonian bank customers manage their money online. In a new parking system, 25,000 use their mobile phones (of which there are 89 per 100 people) to pay for parking. Since Tallinn became the first European city to offer free public transportation starting in 2013, there is no need to park. A third of voters cast their ballots online, and 98% of taxpayers file their annual returns online. It takes about an hour to file, and refunds are paid within 48 hours. Estonia is the European programming base for Skype, owned by eBay. Former prime minister Andrus Ansip became the European Commission's vice president in charge of Europe's digital future.

This growing use of the Internet also exposes a worrisome vulnerability. This was seen in April and May 2007 in the aftermath of an emotional dispute with Russia over moving a Soviet war monument out of the center of Tallinn. For three weeks a flood of unwanted data and hits on its computer systems came pouring in mainly from Russia. It quickly clogged the websites of the government, businesses and newspapers. NATO, the EU, and the US sent experts to try to help deal with this Internet near-shutdown and electronic blockade. Some saw this as the first real war in cyberspace, and it raised questions about whether NATO's collective defense commitment applies to such cyber

harassment. In 2008 the US announced that it would sponsor an Estonian institute to work on computer defenses and international security. It is home to NATO's Center of Excellence for Cyber-Defense. In 2014 NATO staged the world's longest digital war game in Estonia.

Giant Finnish firms, such as the state oil company Neste; department store chains, such as Stockmans; and hundreds of medium and small-size businesses find Estonia a congenial place to do business. About 500 Finnish companies, including Nokia, operate in Estonia, employing 22,000 Estonians. Sweden is also an important nearby partner. Swedish banks control most of Estonia's banking system. Estonia's producing and exporting of mobile-phone kits for its largest exporter, Ericsson, boosts its economic performance.

Despite a host of political problems between them, Russia still plays a significant role, though much reduced from 1991, when 90% of Estonia's exports went into the Soviet economy; by 2015 that figure was 21% to Russia. However, Russia's exports to Estonia include some of the energy Estonia needs and all of its natural gas. This directly affects inflation. Its trade patterns look westward. About 80% of Estonia's GDP is generated by foreign trade, and it was rising by 25% per year. The bulk of its trade (66.3% of exports and 77.4% of imports) is with EU countries.

Determined to minimize its economic dependence on Russia, Estonia relies far less on its eastern neighbor for energy than do Latvia and Lithuania. It buys more from the west and continues to extract oil from shale, which is an infamous polluter but which still is its largest industry, ahead of mineral fertilizers, shipbuilding, and the processing of forest products. It is the only country in the world to exploit oil

shale deposits. Its desire to protect its oil shale industry, which supplies 90% of its energy needs, delayed its closing of the energy chapter with the EU. However, it is Estonia's major resource. It is also a main employment source for Russian speakers concentrated in the northeast, which already has the country's highest rate of unemployment.

Estonia has no nuclear power plants. To give both Germany and Russia a stake in its prosperity and stability, it granted Russia's Gazprom and Germany's giant Ruhrgas partial ownership in its gas industry, a move that slightly warmed Estonia's chilly relations with Russia. Estonia is struggling to keep its state-owned electricity company, Eesti Energia, alive and out of Russian hands. Since 40% of its sales go to 500 industrial clients, it is vulnerable to losing those clients through price wars. To reduce its energy dependence, it derives 18% of its energy from renewable sources, hoping to raise that further.

Agricultural land occupies 37.4% of Estonia's surface, forests 48.7%, swamp and wetlands 7.4%, water 4.6%, and artificial surfaces 1.9%. Five percent of the workforce is engaged directly in farming, and they produce 4% of the country's GDP. This is one sector in which privatization has been slow. Nationalist pressure postponed the free sale of land. By 2000 most agricultural land was individually owned.

Estonia wins rave reviews from private business and bank people, as well as from such international governmental organizations (IGOs) as the London-based European Bank for Reconstruction and Development (EBRD) and the EU. Because of its economic progress and democratic political stability, it entered the EU in May 2004 and adopted the euro in 2011. Foreign businesses consider Estonia the

Estonians at Old Town Days Festival, Tallinn

Estonia

least corrupt of all former communist countries, and investment is pouring in, especially into Tallinn. Ironically because it has virtually no trade barriers, its belonging to the EU actually raised them. While the financial crisis affected Estonia's credit ratings greatly, by 2016 it regained its footing and improved the ratings to above their precrisis peak.

CULTURE

Estonia's culture is very much associated with its historic cities, the most important of which are Tallinn (the capital), Tartu, and Narva. Tallinn, historically known as Reval or Revel, was first mentioned in written sources in 1154 and has played an important role in Estonian history ever since. The town's fortress was built by King Waldemar II of Denmark beginning in 1219 on the site of an earlier fortress. The city became a member of the Hanseatic League in 1284 and a major trading center. Over the centuries, it belonged to the Danes; the Teutonic Knights; the Swedes; and, from 1710 onward, Russia.

The old city was surrounded by a wall, about two-thirds of which still stands. Half of the guard towers and some of the gates also remain. Medieval buildings include the Dom Castle and the Long Hermann Watch-tower. The oldest of the churches is the Domkirk (cathedral, originally called Toomkirik in Estonian), which dates from 1232. Other churches of interest are St. Nicholas, built in the 14th century; St. Olaf's, built in the 15th century, with a late-Gothic spire from the 16th century; and the Bremer Chapel of St. Mary, built in the 16th century. Most Estonians are nominally Lutherans, but there are also many Russian and Estonian Orthodox churches, including a Russian Orthodox cathedral, St. Alexander Nevsky's in Tallinn, built in 1902–1904. In 2003 President Rüütel gave the visiting patriarch of Moscow and All Russia Aleksii II, who had been born in Estonia, the highest state award, the Terra Mariana Cross, 1st Class. Aleksii passed away in 2008.

Other cultural treasures include the Town Hall, built in 1402–1404 on the site of an earlier one-floor building dating back to the beginning of the 14th century, and the Blackheads' Club, which dates from the 14th century. The Academy of Sciences, established in 1946; Estonian State Opera House; numerous Estonian-language theaters; and the Russian-language Russian Drama Theater are located in Tallinn. The capital city also has an art institute and conservatoire, founded in 1919, and two universities. The country boasts dozens of institutions of varying quality that offer competitively priced, multilingual courses.

Tartu, known historically as Dorpat, was founded in 1030 by Grand Prince Yaroslav of Kievan Rus. Then called Yurem, it was built at the site of an earlier Estonian settlement, Tarpatu. Yuriev was conquered by the Teutonic Knights in 1212, and it later became the seat of the Livonian bishops. The Germans gave it the name of Dorpat. Fought over numerous times throughout the centuries, it passed back under Russian control in 1710, when Peter the Great took it from Sweden. The modern name dates from the first period of Estonian independence following World War I.

Tartu, also a member of the Hanseatic League, was a major trading center; its chief claim to fame is its university, founded in 1632 by King Gustav II of Sweden. Transferred for a time to the city of Parnu during the 18th century, it was returned to Tartu in 1802. Today Tartu University, Estonia's most prestigious, has 7 faculties and 15,000 students. The university library, once housed in the Cathedral of Peter and Paul, contains over 2 million volumes. The cathedral, in ruins in 1802 when it was reconstructed as a library, is probably the oldest building in Tartu. Most of the other university buildings date from the 19th century.

Although the ancient Estonians had an oral literature, very little of that survived the centuries of domination by other cultures. The roots of modern Estonian culture can be traced to the formation of the University of Tartu in 1632 because that marked the beginning of a small educated

Estonian elite. The first book of Estonian grammar appeared in 1637, followed by an Estonian translation of the Bible in 1739.

Little more happened until the 19th century, when an attempt was made to revive a folklorist tradition. Many songs, sayings, and fairy tales were eventually collected, most strongly reminiscent of Finnish folklorist survivals. Somewhat later, Friedrich Reinhold Kreutzwald used many of these oral works to create an epic he called *Kalevipoeg* (The Son of Kalev). It was published by the Estonian Learned Society in 1857–1861. This nascent Estonian literature slowly replaced German culture, which was preeminent in Estonia for centuries. Many Estonians today have German names, a reminder of earlier times when a people that traditionally had no last names was given them by a Germanic upper class.

Kreutzwald's epic marked the beginning of an Estonian national literature, exemplified by the appearance of such poets as Lydia Koidula, Friedrich Kuhlbars and Jacob Tamm; such novelists as Eduard Vilde Juhan Liiv; and Ernst Scrgava; and the playwright August Kitzberg. Estonian writers worked under a great handicap, however, for the Russian government enforced a censorship down to 1905 that attempted to suppress themes that might encourage Estonian nationalism.

The Revolution of 1905 forced a number of writers to flee abroad. But the constitutional regime established in 1906 led to the abolition of most censorship and the appearance of a vigorous Estonian press. It also marked the birth of a new literary movement called Young Estonia, whose chief representative was the poet Gustav Suits. Suits, who had fled to Finland in 1905, continued to live abroad until after the Russian Revolution of 1917. He eventually became a professor of Estonian literature at Tartu University.

The greatest novelist of the first republic (1920–1940) was Anton Hansen Tammsaare, whose most important work, *Truth and Justice*, is about rural life. Another figure from this period was Friebert Tuglas, a writer of short stories and novels. Suits and Tuglas, along with Ernst Enno and the poet Marie Under, became the dominant figures in Estonian literature during the period of independence down to 1940. Tuglas, a member of the Social Democratic Party prior to 1917, succeeded Suits as professor of Estonian literature at Tartu in 1944, after Estonia had come under Soviet domination. However, Tuglas made no literary contribution after that time except for a travelogue, *The First Trip Abroad*, which appeared in 1945, and a volume of musings called *Thoughts and Moods*, published in 1960.

Alexander Nevsky Cathedral, Tallinn

A number of Estonian writers made their way abroad during World War II. These included Marie Under, Karl Rumor, Artur Adson, and August Gailit. These and other writers kept Estonian literature alive as emigre literature, even as the Soviet occupation regime was imprisoning such figures as Hugo Raudsepp, Estonia's greatest playwright, and exiling others, such as the poet Heiti Talvik and former president Lennart Meri, to Siberia. Most of these figures are too well integrated into their new environments to resettle in Estonia, but their influence on the new generation of emerging Estonian writers is likely to be great.

During the communist era, Jaan Kross, who has been a frequent nominee for the Nobel Prize in Literature, wrote allegorical short stories (e.g., *Conspiracy and Other Stories*) and historical novels, such as *Between the Three Plagues* and *The Czar's Madman*. Alexander Solzhenitsyn wrote large parts of his epic on Stalinist crimes, *The Gulag Archipelago*, in the Estonian winter resort Otepaa. Tõnu Õnnepalu became famous after independence in 1991 through such novels as *Border State*, which deal with non-national subjects and always with homosexuality.

The nation has produced well-known artists, such as the late-medieval painter Michel Sittow, the 19th-century exponent of the Estonian national awakening Johann Koler, and the 20th-century bohemian artist Eduard Wiiralt, who spent most of his life abroad. Johannes Paasuke is regarded as the father of Estonian cinema and produced the country's first full-length film in 1924. Probably the best-known Estonian work is the cloak-and-dagger film set in the 16th century Viimne Reliikvia (The Last Relic). Priit Parn initiated a school of animated film producers.

The collapse of communism and the Soviet Union enable Estonian culture and language to thrive and develop again. Polite formulations and expressions reentered their vocabulary after having fallen into disuse during foreign rule. Even treasured traditions, such as celebrating Christmas publicly, are again possible. During the Soviet era, December 25 and the Orthodox Christmas Day were normal workdays, and Estonians had to pull their window shades and celebrate in the privacy of their families.

Estonia has again become itself. The Museum of Occupations and the Fight for Freedom opened in 2003. It chronicles the trauma the nation endured during the war and the half-century of Soviet rule that followed. A long line of old suitcases honors the thousands who had disappeared into Soviet gulags. In 2007, Estonia's Jewish community of 3,000 opened its first synagogue, located in Tallinn, since the Holocaust.

There is probably no other country in the world in which music and politics are more closely linked. As is true of all of the Baltic states, folk songs had for centuries been a means for the people to express their national culture and identity. During Soviet rule huge song festivals were the only legal way for large numbers of Estonians to gather and to express their national feeling. Indeed, Estonia's movement to become independent is often referred to as the "singing revolution." Its choral music remains excellent. Other forms of music are also popular. Arvo Pärt, who was born in 1935 and spent many years in Berlin, is one of the most frequently performed composers in the world. In the 1970s he was a symbol of musical dissent in Estonia. He achieved world fame with large-scale religious works. This is especially remarkable given the fact that Estonia is a very secular nation; only 29% indicated in the 2000 census that they are followers of a particular faith.

Conductor Neeme Järvi has lived in the United States since the 1980s. Nevertheless, he tirelessly promotes Estonian classical and contemporary music, and his repertoire always includes Estonian pieces. Tanel Padar and Dave Benton (a native of Aruba living in Estonia) won the 2001 Eurovision song contest with their soul song spiced with a touch of hip-hop, "Everybody." In 2004 the country put its best face forward when supermodel Carmen Kass ran unsuccessfully for a seat in the European Parliament.

Estonians are optimistic about their future. It is reflected in the dramatic rise in the Estonian birth rate. This is crucial for a nation whose birth rate had fallen to only 1.2 children per woman and whose divorce rate is one of the world's highest, with two-thirds of marriages breaking up. Estonia has the EU's highest out-of-wedlock birthrate at 59%. In 2014 same-sex partnerships were legalized for the first time in a former Soviet republic. They grant almost the same rights as married couples.

The government made population increase a priority. It introduced one of the world's most generous state-funded maternity leaves: Mothers (or fathers) receive as much as 15 months leave at full pay. Nonworking mothers get $200 per month, known as the "mother's salary." But greater economic stability and membership in the EU have also strengthened parents' willingness to bring children into the world.

A less encouraging development is the shockingly high HIV epidemic. Estonia (together with Latvia) has the highest adult prevalence rate in the EU, 0.7%; this is more than three times the EU average. Fewer than half are intravenous drug users, and officials fear it could get worse through unprotected sex. Due to excessive drinking, other unhealthy habits, and a run-down health-care system, the life expectancy of Estonian men has fallen to 69.8 years, the shortest within the EU. The average woman can expect to live to age 80.

The murder rate has dropped by 70% since 1995, and robbery and car theft has fallen almost as far. Even during the recession, crime continued to decline.

The sport in which Estonia is a true superpower is "wife-carrying," invented in Finland. A man has to carry his wife or partner over a rough 253-meter obstacle course that includes two timber hurdles and a chest-high water pool. The Estonians devised the winning "Estonian carry" upside-down position, which permits the man to run and use his arms freely during the race. In 2007 Estonians ran off with the title for the 10th year in a row. One of the contestants revealed their secret: "Estonians win because they have thin and beautiful women."

CURRENT ISSUES

All three Baltic states entered the 21st century with some major challenges left to be faced. For the sake of their prosperity and security, all three successfully sought economic and military integration with the west. Estonians voted two to one in favor of EU entry, and in 2004 Estonia joined both NATO and the EU. Their need for the security that western integration provides stems from the long-standing Russian claim to predominance over the nations on its periphery. All must remain on guard to ensure that they do not lose all or part of their sovereignty. That would be the case if Russia were able to restrict their ability to make their own decisions, such as on joining a military alliance. All three Baltic states constantly remind their EU and NATO partners to be wary of a resurgent Russia. This appeared appropriate after Russia attacked Georgia in August 2008, Ukraine's Crimean Peninsula in March 2014, and northeastern Ukraine in February 2022, justifying its actions as protecting the rights of Russian speakers.

Estonia is one of only four NATO members to meet the 2% target for increasing their defense spending. Estonia, like its Baltic neighbors, is fearful of a possible reversal of America's commitment to the defense of each member of NATO. Estonia's military leaders have already called for Patriot missiles to be deployed to

Estonia

protect their country. They were delighted in 2017 to welcome 800 British troops to be stationed in Estonia together with French, Danish, and American soldiers as part of NATO's biggest deployment to the region.

Estonia is a small state with a well-educated population. In 2019, Estonian pupils were the highest achievers among OACO countries in the PISA tests. In May 2013 it became the 41st nation in space. Its EST-Cube satellite monitors solar winds.

Its long-term prospects are bright. With its economy developing briskly, its greatest remaining problem is how to deal with the large Slavic minorities that make up almost a third of its population and much of the industrial workforce. Like Latvia, Estonia faces both foreign and domestic political problems that are sometimes in conflict with each other. To preserve its language and culture and to survive as a nation, it chose to restrict its citizenship and create strong motivation for members of ethnic minorities to recognize the Estonian character of the restored republic.

In 2015, Estonia launched a new TV channel created to reach out to Russian viewers. The sense of bitterness among the Russians persists, as they complain over discrimination in hiring, salaries, and education.

While pursuing its policies, Estonia must always calculate Russia's response and adjust it to what Moscow would be willing to tolerate. How Estonia resolves this problem will strongly influence not only its own domestic tranquility but also its relations with its eastern neighbor. Tension is always present and has already prompted the world's first cyberwar. Russian fighter planes have also been intercepted in Estonian air space.

Estonia was among the countries hit particularly hard when Russia banned EU products in retaliation for EU-imposed sanctions over its interference in Ukraine. In February 2015 and again in October 2018, both NATO and Russia engaged in high-visibility maneuvers on both sides of the Russian-Estonian border.

All three Baltic republics celebrated the 100th year of independence in 2018. Flags were hoisted everywhere. People were encouraged to wear clothing in national colors. The three states are in the process of important change. A new globally minded generation born in the 1980s and 1990s is coming of age. With no memory of the Soviet Union, young people from both language communities are more interested in the future than the grudges of the past. They are more open to each other.

Republic of Latvia (Latvijas Republika)

Dressed for a festival on a street in Riga

Courtesy: NOVOSTI

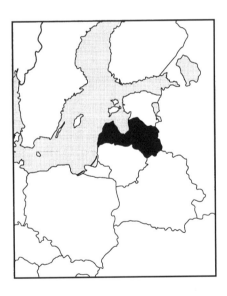

President Egils Levits

Area: 24,938 sq. mi. (64,589 sq. km).
Population: 1,842,226 (2022 estimate)
Capital City: Riga (pop. 609,489 capital city; 920,643 urban; 870,000 metro). (2023).
Climate: It is humid continental and oceanic (maritime). Coastal regions have a more maritime climate with cooler summers and milder winters, while eastern parts are characterized by a more continental climate with warmer summers and harsher winters. Latvia has four distinct seasons of near-equal length. The weather in spring and autumn is fairly mild weather. The temperature variations are little as the territory of Latvia is relatively small. Winters have average temperatures of −6 °C (21 °F), and summers have average temperatures of around 19 °C (66 °F).

Neighboring Countries: Estonia (north), Russia (east), Belarus (southeast), and Lithuania (south).
Official Language: Latvian (Recognized languages: Livonian, Latgalian).
Recognized Minority Language: Russian.
Ethnic Background: 63.0% Latvians, 24.2% Russians, other 12.8 (includes Belarusians, Ukrainians, Poles, Lithuanians, Roma, Jews, unspecified)
Religion: 64% Christianity (36% Lutheran, 17% Roman Catholicism, 9% Orthodox, 2% other Christian), 1% others, 35% no religion. (2018)

Form of Government: Unitary parliamentary republic.
Chief of State: Edgars Rinkēvičs, President (since July 2023).
Head of Government: Evika Siliņa, Prime Minister (since September 2023).
National flag: It is the traditional red-white-red flag. The Latvian flag was officially adopted in 1921, but it was already in use as early as the 13th century and is among the oldest flags in the world. Its carmine red color is sometimes described as symbolizing

Latvia

the readiness of the Latvians to give the blood from their hearts for freedom and their willingness to defend their sovereignty. An alternative interpretation comes from a legend recorded in the medieval Rhymed Chronicle of Livonia (Livländische Reimchronik, 1180—1343), which recounts the story of a Latgalian leader who was wounded in battle, and sheet he was laid on were stained by his blood with only the center stripe of the sheet being left unstained. During the next battle the bloodstained sheet was used as a flag. The legend has it that this time the Latgalian warriors were successful and drove the enemy away. Ever since Latgalian tribes have used these colors.

National Holiday: November 18 (Independence Day).

Currency: Euro (€) (EUR) (since January 1, 2014).

Main Exports: wood and wood products, refined petroleum, wheat, metals, foodstuffs, medicaments. and textiles.

Main Imports: machinery, oil, foodstuffs, and chemical products.

Main Trading Partners: Lithuania (18.3% of exports and 24.2% of imports), Estonia (11.7%% of exports and 10.2% of imports), Germany (6.6% of exports and 9.4% of imports), Russia (5.6% of exports and 6.8% of imports), Poland (9.4% of imports), Finland (5.8% of imports), Sweden (5.1% of exports). (2022)

Political Status: The Latvian lands were part of the territory governed by the Teutonic Knights from the 13th to the 16th centuries. They were subsequently ruled by Poland, then Sweden. Peter the Great annexed Riga in 1710; the remainder of the country fell to Russian rule in the 18th century. With the collapse of the Russian Empire, Latvia declared its independence in 1918. Occupied by Soviet forces in June 1940, it was annexed by Stalin in August 1940; it declared its independence May 4, 1990.

Latvian national identity has been shaped by the desire to be liberated from foreign domination and to protect the small nation's language and culture from absorption. Like the other Baltic states, it experienced a succession of foreign masters—Danes, Germans, Swedes, Poles, and Russians. During the Great Northern War, which began in 1700, Russian tsar Peter the Great conquered Riga and what is now Estonia in 1710. Estonia and Livonia (a state consisting of what is now southern Estonia and northern Latvia) officially became a part of the Russian Empire in the 1721 Treaty of Nystad and remained so for more than two centuries.

Latvians had passed down innumerable folk songs, legends and fairy tales. Many were recorded in written form in the 19th century, when the consciousness of Latvian nationhood solidified. The concept of the Latvian nation sprang not from the reality of an independent political state but from its national culture. There were Latvian fraternities and student organizations at the Universities of Tartu (in Estonia) and St. Petersburg (in Russia). Toward the end of the century, a national organization, Jaunā Strāva, thrived; one of its later members was Janis Rainis, Latvia's most famous poet.

For most of this time, the tsars supported those reforms that enabled Latvians and other Balts to develop their national cultures. This ended in 1881, when Alexander III came to power. Sensing a danger from their national revival, he tried to stop it. He ordered a policy of Russification. Russian was declared the official language and the medium of instruction, and the Russian Orthodox religion was imposed. This strict Russification program was terminated after the 1905 Russian Revolution. This was a great emotional event for Latvians, who began struggling against German landlords and the Russian police. Their nationalism grew progressively stronger in the 20th century.

The World War I created the conditions for Latvian independence; it was the first time the Latvian national flag was raised. Latvian rifle regiments were formed to fight against the Germans, and many were killed in 1915, when the front line ran right through Latvia. When the Bolshevik Revolution occurred in 1917, many Latvians supported the new Soviet government, hoping thereby to win their freedom. On November 18, 1918, Latvia declared its independence, but it had to continue to fight against German troops and the Red Army in order to secure it. Russia signed a treaty recognizing it on August 11, 1920. However, this lasted only two decades.

Latvia after World War I

Latvia's history as an independent state after World War I bears many similarities to that of Estonia. That is not surprising, since the two countries were alike in many respects. The next decade and a half witnessed political instability, as many different political parties and such extreme nationalist organizations as Pērkonkrusts (outlawed by the government) struggled for control.

Like Estonia, Latvia created a 100-member single-chamber parliament (called the Saeima) based on proportional representation. Latvia's use of this electoral system made it more difficult to form stable governments, since it increased the number of political groups competing for seats. In the 1931 elections, for example, 27 different political groupings won representation in the legislature. Twelve of the groups managed to elect only a single member. At the other end, only two groups had more than 10 members.

The Latvian constitution, approved in February 1922, provided for the election of a president of the republic to a fixed five-year term. The president, who was made commander-in-chief of the military, was also authorized to issue decrees when parliament was not in session, subject to parliamentary confirmation when it reconvened. The first president of the republic elected, under terms of the new constitution was Jānis Čakste. A lawyer and early nationalist leader, he had headed the Latvian delegation to the Paris Peace Talks.

Latvia's population at this time was approximately 1.9 million, with Latvians making up about 75% of the population. The largest single minority was Russian, which comprised about 7.8%. Another 8.1% were other Slavs, mainly White Russians and Poles. Other minorities included Jews (5.2%), Baltic Germans, and Lithuanians.

Like Estonia, Latvia had an agrarian-based economy, with two-thirds of the population supporting themselves through agriculture. One difference is that Latvia had significantly more industry, particularly in and around the city of Riga. The majority of the population was Protestant (57.2%), but there were significant Russian Orthodox (13%) and Roman Catholic (22.6%) populations.

Latvia also began its independent existence with a land reform that expropriated the old landed estates and provided for their distribution to landless peasants. As a result of the reform, small holders who had obtained their land at this time held 22.2% of the total. In general, Latvia had better luck with its land reform than Estonia, and food production, particularly of beef and dairy cattle, continued to grow through the 1920s and 1930s.

Latvia's Move toward Authoritarianism

The inability to reach consensus was made worse by the world economic depression that began in 1929. It led to a growth of antiparliamentarianism in Latvia, mainly led by right-wing, nationalist forces. The Nationalist Association, then a small and relatively insignificant right-wing party, proposed giving additional political powers to the president of the republic. A number of fascist or semi fascist groupings also emerged at this time advocating anticommunist, antisocialist, anti-Jewish, and antiforeign policies. The Latvian government outlawed most of these, but the mainline political parties began to take a more nationalist and antiforeign stance, as well.

Kārlis Ulmanis, leader of the Peasants' League and one of the founders of modern Latvia, having served as first provisional president from 1918 to 1920, could not get sufficient support from among the other members of the legislature, however, so his constitutional proposals were tabled at this time. On March 16, 1934, he was made premier. Claiming that he had discovered a communist plot to overthrow the government, Ulmanis declared a state of emergency, suspended the parliament, banned party political activities, and outlawed the Thunder Cross Association, a fascist organization. Two months later, Ulmanis organized a separate government committee to take on certain functions of the parliament, that is, to handle matters that would normally require legislation. President Alberts Kviesis gave his approval to this new arrangement in June.

Most Latvians quietly accepted this new authoritarian regime, apparently convinced by Ulmanis's argument that he needed the additional powers to defend Latvian democracy. Two years later, Kviesis's term came to an end. When he stepped down, Ulmanis took his place. Since Ulmanis continued to hold the office of premier, the effect was to merge the two offices from this point onward. In 1934 Prime Minister Kārlis Ulmanis, supported by the army and the paramilitary organization Aizsargi, dissolved parliament and ruled without it.

The Soviet Union Annexes Latvia, 1940

The authoritarian direction of the Latvian government after 1934 weakened it internationally, especially insofar as the western democracies were concerned. When the leaders of Nazi Germany and the Soviet Union negotiated a "nonaggression" pact in August 1939, their stipulation that Latvia fell within the Soviet sphere of influence caused less of a reaction than it might otherwise have done. Following this pact, the Soviet Union tightened its hold on the Baltic states.

Hitler launched his invasion of Poland on September 1, and Soviet troops entered to occupy the eastern third of Poland on September 17. With Poland settled, Stalin moved to bring the remaining areas of the Soviet sphere of influence under his control. In September 1939 Latvia was forced to accept Soviet troops in Liepaja and Ventspils numbering more than Latvia's own army. Latvia was compelled to sign a mutual-assistance pact with the Soviet Union on October 5, 1939.

Nothing happened for several months, probably because the Soviet Union was tied down in its Winter War with Finland. Once that was resolved, the Soviet Union turned its attention back to the Baltic states. In May 1940, the Soviet Foreign Ministry accused the Latvian government of violating the 1939 mutual-assistance pact signed with the Soviet Union. Almost immediately thereafter, the Latvian government was forced to resign, and a popular front government was installed in its place.

This government remained in power for just a little over a month. It came to an end in July, when the Communist Party was made the sole legal party. Most noncommunists were dismissed from office, and a considerable number of them were arrested. New elections were then held on July 14, with only communists permitted to stand for office. The freshly rigged legislature met on July 21. Its only piece of business was to vote on a resolution asking to join the Soviet Union. With all noncommunist voices having been suppressed, it was passed by acclamation. The following month, the USSR Supreme Soviet acceded to the communist request made by their Latvian comrades. Latvia thus became a Soviet socialist republic. Russia continues to insist that all three had voluntarily joined the USSR. From August 1940 to June 1941, the communist government nationalized the land, then launched a program of "land reform," whereby larger estates were turned into state farms, while smaller parcels were distributed to landless laborers.

Germany's invasion of the Soviet Union beginning on June 22, 1941, temporarily reversed this situation because German troops overran and occupied Latvia later in 1941. Latvia remained under German occupation until 1944. During the German occupation from 1941 to 1944, Latvians fought on both sides. Although most Latvians who wore German Wehrmacht uniforms were conscripts who served in normal military units, some became members of the SS. During the 1990s a few hundred of them marched through Riga every year on March 16 to commemorate their fallen comrades. Such displays were forbidden in 2000, and a few Latvians face trial in Latvian courts for alleged war crimes. At the same time, Latvia began at the turn of the century to bring to trial a handful of Soviet military veterans accused of wartime atrocities against Latvians.

Latvian folk dancer   Courtesy: NOVOSTI

161

Latvia

Soviet Rule

With the German retreat in 1944, Latvia once again fell under Soviet occupation. A guerrilla movement known as the Forest Brothers arose to oppose Soviet control after the end of the war in 1945, but such efforts were ineffectual. Latvia got no outside assistance, and the opposition was eventually suppressed. The Baltic states spent the next half-century as disgruntled but relatively prosperous republics of the Soviet Union.

Many changes occurred in Latvia over the next 45 years. Soviet policy was to integrate the Baltic republics so thoroughly that there would be no question of their ever leaving the union. To that end, the reestablished Latvian communist government reinstated its 1941 nationalization decree, then carried through a general collectivization of agriculture. Meanwhile, the Soviet government sought to bind Latvia and the other two Baltic republics to the rest of the Soviet Union economically by locating branch factories of Soviet industry in the three republics. The first factories in the 1950s emphasized primary extraction, but a much larger range of factories was built there in the 1960s and 1970s. Such factories received most or all of their raw materials from other parts of the Soviet Union and delivered most of their finished products to customers in the other republics. This economic integration was so successful that Latvia and the other two Baltic republics became more integrated into the Soviet economy than any other area of the Soviet Union.

Economic integration was accompanied by a program of Soviet Russification, aimed at transforming the cultures of the Baltic republics. All students received Russian-language training in the schools, plus general indoctrination lectures on the nature of Soviet culture. In addition, a systematic effort was made to settle non-Baltic nationals in the republics. When a new factory was built, most of the workers would be transferred there from elsewhere in the Soviet Union, and scarce housing was allotted to them.

The effects of this policy can be seen by examining the figures of the 1989 Soviet census. Ethnic Latvians made up only 52% of the population of the republic. They had become a minority in the country's seven largest cities. Latvians had nearly become a minority in their own country. These overall figures also masked the fact that, in certain industrial regions near the border, Latvians had become a tiny minority. In many urban areas, including the capital city Riga, it was more common to hear Russian spoken than Latvian. Russians also tended to monopolize many types of jobs, particularly in management and in parts of government. Everywhere,

the Russian way of doing things became dominant. On the positive side, the heavy industrialization carried out after 1945 meant that the standard of living in Latvia and Estonia was above that of any other part of the Soviet Union.

Latvia Regains Its Independence

The Latvian people accommodated themselves to Soviet rule, but they could not forget their brief period of independence between the wars. When Gorbachev launched his programs of glasnost (openness) and perestroika (restructuring) after coming to power in 1985, Latvians were therefore among the first to take advantage of them. Latvians seized the opportunity first to enlarge their self-determination within the Soviet Union and then to gain complete independence. In 1988 a "people's front," composed of both Gorbachev communists and noncommunist democrats and nationalists, was formed. In the late 1980s, nationalist fervor was fanned by the conference of Latvian writers. On August 23, 1989, 2 million Estonians, Latvians and Lithuanians formed a human chain from Tallinn to Vilnius to dramatize their demand for freedom.

With large and articulate exile groups, especially in the US, Latvia and the other two Baltic nations were able to mobilize considerable international sympathy and diplomatic support for their aspirations. This was especially facilitated by the fact that all western democracies, except Sweden and briefly Australia, had refused to recognize the Soviet Union's annexation of the Baltics in 1940.

In enunciating his policy of glasnost, Gorbachev called on the Soviet peoples to speak out against negative tendencies in the society and to support his reforms. This became a manifesto that led to the creation of thousands of "unofficial" organizations all over the Soviet Union. Formed originally in support of his policy of reform, many of them soon began to push their own agendas.

Latvians were among the early supporters of Gorbachev's policies of glasnost and perestroika, and Latvian unofficial organizations also sprang up, taking advantage of the new atmosphere. One of the first such organizations was Renaissance and Renewal, a religious rights organization. The Popular Front of Latvia (PFL), organized in October 1988, incorporated many of these earlier unofficial organizations into its overall structure. The leader of the PFL was Dainis Īvāns, a journalist.

Within a year its membership had grown to 250,000, about 85% of whom were Latvians. This provided an important contrast with the Latvian Communist Party, which had a membership of 184,000, only 39.7% of whom were Latvians.

Latvian student reading this book

The ethnic issue was a greater one in Latvia than in either of the other two Baltic republics because of the larger percentage of non-Latvians in the republic. Conservatives were particularly disturbed by what the front represented and managed to get the PFL decertified in January 1989. This did not stop the front from continuing to operate, however. In the March 1989 elections to the USSR Congress of People's Deputies, front-supported candidates won three-fourths of the seats.

Like Estonia, Latvia had a political party specifically committed to independence, the Latvian National Independence Movement (LNIM). Labeled an extremist organization, it nevertheless exercised influence on the PFL. Under the prodding of the LNIM, the Popular Front of Latvia went on record in June 1989 as favoring "Latvia's independent statehood."

Russians and other non-Latvians had become very concerned about Latvian nationalism, and there were rising fears of ethnic strife. The Popular Front of Latvia sought to alleviate these anxieties by advocating equal rights for all persons living in Latvia, regardless of nationality or other affiliation. The front specifically supported the right of other nationalities either to receive instruction in their own language in the public schools or to set up their own schools. It also advocated political pluralism. This defused a lot of the opposition and helped to win additional support for independence from among the non-Latvian sections of the population.

The Latvian Communist Party, which had more Russians than Latvians among its membership, proved to be the most conservative of the Baltic communist parties. However, even it came under pressure from its Latvian members to take a more nationalistic stance. In September

Latvia

1989 Jānis Vagris, the first secretary, endorsed the concept of a sovereign Latvia, including republican economic autonomy.

The overlap between the Latvian Communist Party and the Popular Front of Latvia can be seen in the list of delegates to the second congress of the PFL, held in October 1989—24% of the delegates were members of the Latvian Communist Party, while 45 out of 100 of the members of the steering committee were LCP members. They obviously represented members of the reform wing of the party, however, for the congress not only endorsed Latvian independence and creation of a multiparty political system but also called upon the Latvian Supreme Soviet to declare illegal Latvia's 1940 incorporation into the Soviet Union.

New elections to the Latvian Supreme Soviet were scheduled to take place in March 1990. Hoping to coopt the nationalism issue, the communist members of the old Supreme Soviet adopted a declaration on February 15 endorsing an independent Latvia. That statement proved to be too weak for the new delegates elected in March. On May 4, the new Supreme Soviet proclaimed Latvian independence with a transition period before implementation. Although the declaration got 138 positive votes, 57 deputies refused to participate in the vote, claiming that the declaration was unconstitutional. Most of the delegates abstaining had been elected by the large non-Latvian element within the population. On May 12 the heads of all three

Baltic countries signed the Declaration of Concord and Cooperation reestablishing the 1934 Council of the Baltic States.

On May 14 Gorbachev issued a decree invalidating Latvia's declaration of independence. The Soviet military also became involved in the issue when it began dropping leaflets on Riga, accusing the Latvian government of counterrevolution. The next day, several hundred Soviet army troops, accompanied by cadets from an officers' training school in Riga, joined a protest march against Latvian independence. By June 1990, however, the Soviet government had begun ignoring the situation in Latvia, even as it began easing off on its pressure on Lithuania and Estonia. The negative international reaction to the Soviet moves in the Baltic was clearly a factor in this change of policy.

Gorbachev indignantly rejected continuing demands for independence and even ordered that Special Force Units of the USSR Ministry of Interior (OMON) use force against dissidents in the streets of Vilnius, Lithuania, on January 13, 1991, killing 15. Latvians from all over the country came to the capital to defend their democratically elected parliament. Nevertheless, on January 21, 1991, OMON troops killed six persons in Riga.

Coup in Moscow and Latvian Freedom
In May 1991, Gorbachev threatened the new union treaty for the USSR, which he wanted to get negotiated and signed

Enjoying their work: chimney sweeps, Riga Courtesy: NOVOSTI

over the summer. He began a rapprochement with Boris Yeltsin, which led to nine of the republics agreeing to sign a new union treaty on August 17. This became the signal for conservative hard-liners to organize a coup with the aim of overthrowing Gorbachev and reasserting centralized control.

The August 1991 coup failed, but even as it was going on, the Latvian government again declared its independence. The postcoup Soviet government temporized for two weeks, but it soon found the number of states granting recognition to Latvia and the other Baltic republics to be irresistible. In early September, it, too, recognized the independence of the Baltic republics. On September 17, 1991, the Baltic states, which had belonged to the League of Nations, were admitted to the United Nations.

Numerous exiles returned to the country to play important political, military, and economic roles. The United States' first ambassador to Latvia was of Latvian heritage. Gunārs Meierovics was a leader in what was then one of the country's most successful parties, Latvia's Way. It was wiped out in the 2002 elections.

A major preoccupation of the Latvian government for several years after that time was the continuing presence of ex-Soviet troops in the republic, plus the problem of an extremely large non-Latvian population. These troops were originally under the jurisdiction of the Commonwealth of Independent States (CIS), but the Russian government assumed responsibility for Russian troops stationed in the ex-Soviet republics in the summer of 1992 after establishing its own Ministry of Defense. Subsequent negotiations between the Latvian and Russian governments elicited a Russian promise to have all troops out of Latvia by the summer of 1993; however, President Yeltsin rescinded this agreement in September 1992 after the

Canal boat in Riga Photo by Tscharner deGraffenried

163

Latvia

Latvian government stripped non-Latvians of citizenship.

Demography and Citizenship

The Latvian government had taken this action because it was under pressure from nationalists within its ranks concerned with the extremely large non-Latvian element in the population. Latvia has a small population: ca 2 million, 800,000 of whom live in Riga. It seems odd that in 2010 there were 16% more women than men in Latvia. In part this can be explained by differing life expectancy (66.6 years for men and 77.5 for women), men's inclination to emigrate to find work, heavier drinking habits, and the fact that men are four times more likely than women to commit suicide.

In 1934, ethnic Latvians had constituted 75.5% of the country's population. Russians were the largest minority in Latvia (12%), and they enjoyed citizenship, language guarantees, their own schools, and cultural autonomy. After being bullied into the Soviet Union in 1940, Latvia's demography changed. Indeed, when Soviet rule ended in 1991, 2.3 million Russians were left behind in all the Baltic states, with the lion's share in Latvia.

Russia and Russians living in Latvia demanded automatic citizenship ("zero option," adopted by most former Soviet republics). In Latvia the non-Latvian population had reached almost half by 1991 and an astonishing 63% in the capital city of Riga (and a majority in the six next-largest cities). By 2005, 57.7% of the country's residents were Latvian, 29.6% Russian, 4.1% Belarussian, 2.7% Ukrainian, 2.5% Polish, and 1.4% Lithuanian. Massive inward migration of Russians and outward deportation of native Latvians had dramatically changed the demographic mix and threatened its national survival.

According to Latvia's post-independence citizenship law, automatic citizenship could be claimed only by persons who were Latvian citizens—or their direct descendants—prior to Latvia's incorporation into the Soviet Union in 1940. This rendered about 48% of the population of the republic "stateless." These regulations were subsequently incorporated into a new electoral law passed in October 1992. Under the terms of this new law, non-Latvians needed to establish competency, though not fluency, in the Latvian language and permanent residence in the republic for at least 16 years extending back into the Soviet era in order to qualify for naturalization. An important exception was ex-Soviet military and security personnel and their families stationed in the country. Their 16 years of residency requirement did not begin until after independence.

Latvia's parliament

In December 1992, the government announced the first partial results of a citizen registration that it had begun carrying out. About 67% of the inhabitants of the republic had been registered by that time. Of those registered, 1,339,530 were classified as Latvian citizens, while an additional 452,378 persons were classified as noncitizens. However, the government also announced that 405,124 of these noncitizens—or 89.5%—had expressed a desire to become citizens.

Latvia subsequently reduced the minimum permanent residence requirement to five years. According to figures published in 1995, 40% of the nonethnic Latvian population had passed Latvian-language and -history tests and qualified as citizens. Nevertheless, more than one-quarter of Latvia's adult population remains without the franchise. In 1998, 53% of Latvians voting in a referendum approved of giving automatic citizenship to all children born in Latvia since 1991. Adopted by elected parliaments, the citizenship laws appear reasonable by western standards. Latvia's policies toward minorities have been more successful in easing ethnic tensions than in most post-communist states. International organizations, such

as the UN and Council of Europe, have also generally accepted the laws despite Russia's energetic efforts to have Latvia condemned for human rights violations. In 2001 the OSCE declared that its language and citizenship rules meet European standards but that the government could do more to ease the naturalization process, such as lowering the $50 fee and offering Latvian-language classes.

Devising citizenship policies that are both acceptable to Latvians and tolerable for Russians is the most persistent political problem in relations with Russia and the one that elicits the most visceral resistance from Moscow. For Latvia the question of citizenship is of vital importance. With a large Russian-speaking minority, it faced the prospect of continued heavy Russian influence on most aspects of policy if all residents were granted either automatic or dual citizenship. Thus, it rejected these options.

This was not only a question of control over Latvia's affairs. It was also a matter of principle: In the Latvian view, the majority of Russians had been permitted to settle in Latvia in order to implement Moscow's policy of occupation after it had forcibly annexed the two lands in 1940. On what

Former president Vaira Vike-Freiberga

Prime Minister Krišjānis Kariņš

basis could occupiers and their descendants expect to be recognized as citizens? Russia adamantly denies that the Soviet Union had ever occupied Latvia and that its joining was involuntary, despite some admitted pressure at the time. It has never apologized for the Soviet Union's actions in 1940 or subsequent crimes. Nor has it ever hinted that the occupation might have been illegal. The fact that Latvians accepted their fate without armed resistance in 1940 lends some credibility to the Russians' interpretation.

Determined to remain masters in their own house, Latvians based their citizenship laws on the notion of legal continuity of their prewar republics. They imposed severe restrictions, granting citizenship automatically to pre-1940 residents and their descendants. Subsequent naturalization raised this by 1998 to about 40% in Latvia. Confronting criticism that Russian speakers were being made permanent noncitizens, Latvia opened citizenship to all persons who met certain criteria. They include the willingness to take a loyalty oath and a language test. Few Russians can meet the language requirements without major effort. In 1989, only 22% had a good command of the local language. The others had seen no need to learn the language because Balts were expected to speak Russian well, and most did so. There was an outcry after independence in 1991 that the new language restrictions were "unfair" and "human rights violations." Latvia's citizenship laws do not discriminate on formal ethnic grounds, but since the immediate effect was the disenfranchisement of most ethnic Russian residents, many saw it that way.

A 1998 law in Latvia called for the phasing in over a decade of Latvian as the sole language of instruction in public schools. By 2014 there were no purely Russian-language schools. The Saeima (parliament)

passed a new language law in 1999 that mandated the use of Latvian in most aspects of public life and in areas of the private sector, such as first aid and public safety. Ex-president Vīke-Freiberga vetoed an earlier version of the law after the US government and the EU criticized it. However, she signed a watered-down version after it had received the approval of the OSCE and the Council of Europe.

The Russian government remained critical of the new legislation, which went into effect on September 1, 2000. Its anger was again provoked in 2004 by a law that reduces the use of the Russian language in secondary schools. It requires that at least 60% of teaching at minority schools be in Latvian beginning in 2004 with the 10th grade. Latvian education experts traveled to Moscow to explain the new law and provide assurances that Russian is not being banished from the schools. Thousands of ethnic Russians rallied in the streets of Riga to protest it, shouting "Hands off our schools!" The most radical antireform organization (Shtab) called on students to boycott classes until the law is abolished. Some Shtab organizers even went on a hunger strike. The government organized a concert with the popular Russian rock band Mummy Troll in Riga's old town to siphon off support for the protests. The OSCE high commissioner on national minorities judged the law reforming minority education to be "necessary." In a February 2012 referendum, citizens rejected overwhelmingly by 75% a proposal to adopt Russian as a second official language. Turnout was over 70%. It must be remembered that 290,000 non-Latvians (mainly Russian speakers) who do not have citizenship were barred from voting. About a third of the ethnic Russians are classed as "noncitizens." They are pre-dominantly older persons, and they are issued passports

that allow them to travel in Russia and the EU countries.

Nevertheless, the rights of those who do not speak the local language are greater than in some other small nations, like Quebec Province in Canada, that fear absorption and destruction of their cultures. Parents are free to send their children to bilingual Russian-Latvian-language schools. Russians face no restrictions on using their language at the workplace. It is an advantage to speak Latvian, and the defense forces and many categories in the civil service are blocked to noncitizens. State radio and television are broadcast in Russian. There are Russian-language theaters and a wide variety of Russian newspapers and magazines available. Many university courses are taught in Russian, and most examinations at Latvian universities may be written in Russian if the student prefers.

The Latvian position on citizenship is grounded in notions of citizenship widely held in the rest of the world. Like most countries, they chose *jus sanguinis* as the principle for conferring citizenship: descent from an individual of a particular nationality. Every child with at least one parent who is a Latvian citizen has the right, by birth, to citizenship. Thus, Latvia offers citizenship to anybody who follows certain procedures and learns the local language and demonstrates a basic knowledge of its political system.

This latter requirement points to a deeper aspect of genuine citizenship: It should involve more than merely endowing an individual by law with certain rights and the expectation that he or she will perform certain duties. In the fuller sense, a citizen is a person who feels a moral commitment and loyalty to the state and who is willing to put aside some aspects of self-interest in favor of the interests of the community at large. In ancient Greece and Rome, this was called "civic virtue." Alexis de Tocqueville wrote that good citizenship needs to be underpinned by "habits of the heart." Latvia wants citizens whose primary loyalty is to Latvia (where 71% were Latvian citizens in 1996), not to any other state. By 2012 there were about 290,000 noncitizens, or nearly 20% of the population.

Russian leaders are incensed by these laws. Complaints from some of the 25 million Russians living in the newly independent former Soviet republics do not fall on deaf ears in Moscow, where a wide assortment of political leaders and groups are ready to exploit them for their own purposes. Although Russian speakers lead largely separate lives in Latvia, they bear little hatred or deep aversion toward Baltic nationals. According to a 1995 poll, two-thirds (63%) of Russians living in Latvia found relations with the

Latvia

**Former prime minister
Valdis Dombrovskis**

majority nationality to be good; only 37% found that minorities were being "badly treated." One in three marriages is mixed. Clearly ethnic tensions are not only far below the threshold of violence, but also, they are diminishing as non-Latvians are adjusting to the eased requirements established in the citizenship laws.

POLITICAL SYSTEM

Like the other Baltic republics, Latvia has established the kind of institutional and legal conditions that place it within the western political model. It has a multiparty system in which democratic procedures are respected. Despite frequent changes of coalitions and cabinets and a series of embarrassing political scandals, Latvia has maintained underlying political stability while demonstrating that power can be transferred peacefully from one coalition government to another. Former communists have been able to win power since Latvian independence, but they relinquished it when they no longer had the voters' support.

With some alterations, Latvia readopted on July 6, 1993, its 1922 constitution, which calls for a stronger president than in Estonia. He or she is elected to a three-year term by the unicameral legislature, the Saeima. Its 100 members serve three years and are elected by proportional representation in five constituencies. Parties must win at least 5% of the votes to obtain seats. Unlike in Estonia, noncitizens are not permitted to vote in national or local elections. As of 2012, initiatives that are backed by 10,000 signatures of citizens 16 years or older must be taken up by parliament. They can be gathered online, making Latvia a leader of European efforts to shift some forms of political participation to the Internet.

President

Perhaps the most famous returned exile is Vaira Vīķe-Freiberga, whom parliament elected as president of the republic after President Guntis Ulmanis's second term had ended a month earlier. She was sworn in on July 8, 1999. At age seven she had fled Latvia before the advancing Red Army. A linguist and psychologist by training, she became a psychology professor at Montreal University. While in exile she had lobbied the Canadian government never to recognize the Soviet annexation of the Baltic states and had organized the emigre effort to scan thousands of Latvian folk songs into a computer database. One of the reasons she is so admired is that she is steeped in Latvian folklore.

After retiring from teaching, she returned to Latvia in 1998, became the head of the Latvian Institute, relinquished her Canadian citizenship, and became one of eastern Europe's first female heads of state. One of her first acts as president was to send back to parliament a new language law she deemed too harsh because it would have required that private commercial transactions be in Latvian. A tenacious and energetic political leader, her overwhelming reelection in June 2003 underscored the fact that she was Latvia's most popular politician ever.

Because of the two-term limit, she had to step down in July 2007. She was succeeded by Valdis Zatlers, an orthopedic surgeon with little political experience. He was not reelected by parliament in July 2011 because he used his presidential powers to

President Edgars Rinkēvičs
Source: *Wikipedia*

call for new elections after parliament refused to lift the immunity of a deputy and blocked a corruption probe. On his last day in office, he signed an order calling for a referendum to dissolve parliament, which Zatlers maintained was in the pockets of three powerful tycoons who were mixing business and politics. His proposal was backed by 95% of the voters with a 45% turnout. This unique act cost him the presidency. Irate parliamentarians elected ex-banker Andris Bērziņš to replace him. Raimonds Vējonis, a member of the Latvian Green Party, part of the Union of Greens and Farmers, served as the 9th President of Latvia from 2015 to 2019. Egils Levits, lawyer, political scientist and jurist, served as the tenth president of Latvia from 2019 to 2023. He was succeeded by Edgars Rinkēvičs, a Latvian politician serving as the 11th and current president of Latvia since July 2023. Rinkēvičs previously served as the minister of foreign affairs of Latvia from 2011 to 2023, as head of the

Latvian school chorus breaks out in song in Siena, Italy

Chancery of the President of Latvia, and as state secretary of the Ministry of Defense.

Prime Minister and Parliament

Executive power is exercised by the prime minister and his cabinet, who govern on the basis of majority support in the legislature. Because of the extremely fragmented nature of the Saeima—100 members divided among more than a half-dozen political parties or blocs, plus a dozen or more independents—it has often been impossible to form a majority-backed coalition government.

In 2002, an entirely new party emerged as the winner, Einars Repše's New Era. He formed a center-right coalition that endorsed a generous maternity leave law that grants mothers (or fathers) monthly subsidies up to her (or his) salary to care for a child. With 33,000 annual deaths and only 20,000 births, Latvia faces a severely low birth rate. Repše lamented, "The Latvian nation is dying out, there will be no one to work soon." The population has shrunk from 2.38 million in 2000 to 1.93 million in 2019. Emigration has made the problem worse.

He resigned in 2004 and was replaced by the amiable Indulis Emsis of the Greens, which in Latvia are conservatively oriented. He became Europe's first Green prime minister, but he resigned after only eight months when parliament rejected his budget. Emsis was replaced as prime minister by Aigars Kalvitis of the center-right People's Party. His four-party coalition was the country's 13th government in 14 years. In October 2006 it became the first Latvian governing coalition to be reelected since independence.

In March 2009, the 37-year-old Valdis Dombrovskis was sworn in as prime minister. He was Europe's youngest head of government. He is a physicist by training and former finance minister and member of the European Parliament for the ERA Party. He showed great courage in introducing the kind of painful austerity measures needed to secure EU and IMF help in overcoming Latvia's worst economic crisis since independence.

It is difficult for any democratic government to win support for brutal spending and wage and budget cuts and tax increases, but that is exactly what Dombrovskis did. He defied what diplomatic observers often say about Latvia: that it is not as politically mature as the other two Baltic states because of the strength of business oligarchs, deep Russian economic interests, growing Russian political influence, and the tense social divisions between ethnic Latvians and the 30% of the population with Russian roots.

Dombrovskis unexpectedly resigned in November 2013 in the wake of Latvia's worst peacetime disaster since independence. The roof over the Maxima supermarket in Riga collapsed, killing 54 and injuring dozens. Some Latvians believed it exemplified the corruption in the state and the government's lack of concern for the citizens' daily concerns. The prime minister felt he shared some of the blame for that and stepped down.

He was named EU commissioner for the euro, becoming the chief budget enforcer. He was replaced as prime minister by mathematician and former agriculture minister Laimdota Straujuma. She did not belong to any party but joined Unity the day before taking office. She led her party to victory in the October 2014 elections, winning 22% of the votes and 23 seats. Her center-right coalition captured 61 of 100 seats.

Consigned to the opposition was Union of Greens and Farmers, led by Raimonds Vējonis. It garnered only 20% of the votes (down from 19.7%) and 21 seats. The main opposition was Harmony Center, which won 23% of the votes and 24 seats. This was the second time a pro-Russian party emerged as the country's largest. A center-left party founded in 2005, it is supported chiefly by ethnic Russians and had contacts with Vladimir Putin's party in Russia. But it attempts to broaden its appeal to ethnic Latvians hard hit by plunging wages and soaring unemployment and fed up with the established parties. It supports membership in NATO and the EU. Since it refuses to admit publicly that Latvia had been occupied during the Soviet era, it is not an acceptable coalition partner for other parties. However, youngish party leader Nils Ušakovs, a former newspaper editor and TV personality, says he is "not allergic" to calling the period of Soviet rule "occupation" as long as persons who migrated to Latvia at that time are not called "occupiers." It rules the Riga municipal government with Ušakovs as mayor.

Harmony emerged as the largest party in the October 2018 elections, capturing 20% of the vote, down from 23% in 2014. Placing second was a new antiestablishment party, Who Owns the State? (KPV LV), led by flamboyant ex-actor Artuss

Prime Minister Evika Siliņa
Source: *Wikipedia*

Kaimiņš. It won 14.1%. An anticorruption newcomer, New Conservative, was third, with 13.6%. Māris Kučinskis remained in office after weeks of coalition negotiations. He was later replaced as prime minister by Krišjānis Kariņš of the New Unity Party.

In the 2015 presidential election, the alliance's then-leader Raimonds Vējonis became President of Latvia and subsequently resigned his leadership of the alliance. In January 2016, after the resignation of Prime Minister Laimdota Straujuma, Liepāja Party member Māris Kučinskis became the head of government. After the 2018 Latvian parliamentary election, ZZS lost ten seats and ultimately in 2019 became a part of the opposition to the Kariņš cabinet. It stayed in opposition until 2023, when it became part of Evika Siliņa cabinet.

Foreign and Defense Policy

Since 1991, three ideas have guided Latvia's foreign policy—building Baltic solidarity, reorienting the economy toward the west, and protecting Latvian sovereignty from Russia. The Latvian government has had to spend a great deal of its time on its relations with Russia. In theory, Latvia would like to have good relations with Russia, and it sees the necessity of a continuing, if diminished, economic relationship, as well. The large number of ethnic Russians in the country is a major concern, and the Latvian government's decision rendering them "stateless" had an extremely negative effect on its relations with Russia. In 2015 there were 290,000 such noncitizens, 17.5% of the total population. They possess permanent residency and work permits. Latvia's language law mandating the use of the Latvian language in most facets of public life, passed in 1999, was also denounced in Russia, so the problem continues.

Latvia

In 2004 the law lapsed that had banned former Soviet secret police from public office and sensitive jobs, such as in the judicial system. In 2006 parliament passed a bill to publish the names of almost 4,500 persons suspected of having been Soviet secret police informants.

One way of punishing Latvia for both the language laws and trials was not to sign a border agreement. Russia had planned to sign such a treaty with Latvia on May 10, 2005. However, it postponed this indefinitely when the Latvian government issued a declaration saying that such a border treaty did not mean that it had given up other issues, such as compensation for former gulag inmates or holding Stalin and Hitler equally responsible for causing the World War II. Vīķe-Freiberga demanded that Russia "express its regret" for its "subjugation" of eastern and central Europe. In March 2007 the two countries finally signed a treaty demarcating their border, but the Russian Duma (parliament) delayed ratification.

When the European Union decided in 2000 to open membership negotiations with Latvia and Lithuania, Vīķe-Freiberga commented that "Latvia has left behind for good the post-Soviet period and has become a democratic and open European state." She proclaimed that "justice has been done" when Latvia was invited in 2002 to join. It entered in May 2004, after 72% of voters turned out for a referendum in September 2003 and voted 67% to 32% in favor of entry. The country's government and business community strongly supported entry. Latvia's constitution requires such a double majority (of turnout and of approval) for a measure to pass in a referendum. The largest daily newspaper, *Diena* (which collapsed in 2009), ran a banner headline: "Latvia returns to Europe!" In May 2008, polls showed 72% popular approval of the EU, and parliament approved the quasi-constitutional Lisbon Treaty.

With strong western support, all three Baltic states negotiated the withdrawal of Soviet troops from their territories. Since August 1994 Latvians are undisputed guardians of their own nation. Feeling insecure and knowing that no western power would defend them militarily without a formal guarantee, Latvia and the other Baltic states made it known that they wished to enter NATO. Latvia's trade has already shifted from about 80% to the other Soviet republics to 90% toward the west. Latvians regard NATO as the only alliance capable of thwarting any future Russian expansionist temptations or attempts to restore "spheres of influence." It joined in April 2004. The importance of the NATO decision at its Prague summit in November 2002 was underscored by

A charming street in Riga

Photo by Tscharner deGraffenried

Vīķe-Freiberga: "Latvia lost its independence for a very long time and knows the meaning of independence and the loss of it, knows the meaning of security, and the loss of it."

Prompted by Russia's unprovoked invasion of Ukraine in February 2022, the Latvian-American President Egils Levits called on Baltic leaders to "stop being a political midget" and grant Ukraine candidate status to the EU. For years, Latvia warned the EU about the threat posed by Russia.

NATO membership required changes in Latvia's armed forces. It has 5,745 active forces. Women may serve. There are 11,034

paramilitary forces that include 551 full-time national guard and 10,483 part-time. Its army numbers 1,058, its navy 587 (and 12 ships, including coastal patrol craft), and its air force 319 (with 24 aircraft). A joint staff has 3,202 soldiers. Most of its forces are geared for territorial defense, but the government decided in 2003 to shift to a volunteer army and to end conscription. The resulting military is better trained and more able to carry out NATO missions outside of Latvia.

Latvia once sent 97 peacekeepers to Bosnia, and it had 11 soldiers in Kosovo. The Latvian government supported the 2003 American-British war in Iraq, although the majority of Latvians opposed it. After the end of initial hostilities, the government authorized the deployment of 125 soldiers to help stabilize Iraq. It dispatched a 36-troop unit to Kirkuk in northern Iraq to serve under Polish command. The US provided assistance to these forces before they were withdrawn. Latvia deployed 175 soldiers in Afghanistan.

In 2008 Latvia entered a bilateral agreement with the US that led to mutual visa-free travel.

ECONOMY

Latvia, the most industrialized of the Baltic states, lags behind Estonia in terms of overall economic success and foreign investment, and its privatization program had greater problems. On the positive side are the Baltic states' best port (Riga, which increased its tonnage by 20% in 2003) and a corporate income tax rate of only 15%. On the negative side there was a catastrophic downturn of the economy in 2008 and 2009 caused by the global credit squeeze and recession. It had seen a 30% annual increase in wages (bad for businesses but good for the people) and a current accounts deficit of almost 23% of GDP.

The economic statistics in the midst of its worst recession since independence were depressing: The budget deficit soared to 9.2%. This would be a disaster for a country that aspires to adopt the euro. It adamantly refused to devalue its currency, choosing instead the stronger medicine of deep cuts in public spending and wages. A third of civil servants were laid off. Salaries of public-sector employees were cut up to 50%, pensions were reduced by 10%, and

Riga university student

hospital budgets were lowered by 40%. GDP fell by 18% in 2009 (24% since the recession began), the worst performance in the EU. Imports and exports fell by more than 40%, a magnitude rarely seen in peacetime. Its credit rating was downgraded to junk before being raised again in 2010 in recognition of the country's bold efforts. The government's painful austerity program, introduced as a condition to gain IMF and EU support, sparked the worst

riots since independence in the streets of Riga in January 2009. Its government became the second in Europe (after Iceland) to fall because of the global recession.

Its official unemployment rate was 19.7% in 2010, double the EU average; it drifted down to 14.3% in 2013. Its population shrank by 7.6% between 2007 and 2012, as many young Latvians found work in the UK, Ireland, and Nordic countries. Because of the underground economy, the real jobless rate is perhaps somewhat lower. Real estate values drastically declined with the rest of the economy. Housing prices were down two-thirds from their peak, and the banks were hesitant to lend. Its national debt climbed from 9% of GDP to 40% in 2013.

Amid the crisis, the government fought fiercely to prevent a devaluation of the lat, which was pegged to the euro. It did so through drastic public- and private-sector salary cuts and a reduction of public spending. Since almost 90% of Latvians' borrowings are in euros, such devaluation would have been a disaster.

Its euro coins include the freedom monument, the national coat of arms, and the same picture of a Latvian girl that had been on the interwar Ls5 coins. Latvia adopted the euro on January 1, 2014. Public opinion was against it until almost to the end because of fear of losing some sovereignty and having to support other euro countries financially.

Latvia's economic recovery is so dramatic that the EU and advocates of austerity else-where in Europe regard it as a model; others argue that its austere economic policy could only succeed in such a small country. In 2014 its growth rate of 4% was the EU's fastest. Nevertheless, Latvians still feel the pain and the negative social effects of one of history's worst depressions. Latvia has among Europe's highest rates of suicide and traffic deaths caused by drunk driving, and crime is high.

Latvia has a modern economic structure: 68% of the workforce is employed in the services sector and produces 74% of GDP. Industry employs 23% of the workforce and produces 22% of GDP. Its major industries include machinery, metalworking, electrical equipment, light industry, agricultural equipment, chemicals, and pharmaceuticals. Forestry products and extractive industry are also important, including timber, paper, peat, limestone, dolomite, and clay. Riga, a major center for industry, manufactures consumer goods like radios and other electrical appliances, cars and trucks, and agricultural equipment. Light industry, including food processing and woodworking, is also important.

Only 8.4% of the workforce remains in agriculture, producing 4% of GDP. Agriculture no longer has the significance in

Old-town Riga

Latvia

the economy that it formerly had. But Latvia still has an important dairy industry whose exports have been redirected to the west since 1991.

The government used its decree-issuing authority to carry through a general denationalization of domestic retail trade in 1992. In 2004 foreign direct investment per capita was €47.8, the lowest in the Baltics. It did not help that by 2005 Latvia had 13 different prime ministers in 14 years. The top investors are Sweden and Germany tied for first, followed by Denmark and the United States.

The government has worked at establishing ties with the Scandinavian countries. After implementing a comprehensive policy of privatization, foreign private investment has begun to grow, much of it coming from its Nordic neighbors.

In 1995, the economy suffered a setback when about one-third of the country's 67 commercial banks collapsed. Although Latvia has a well-run central bank, Riga became a significant offshore financial center for Russians seeking a safe home for their money. About half (49%) of deposits in Latvian banks are from the former Soviet Union. One Latvian bank (Parex, which was rescued through nationalization in 2008 to prevent a bank crisis) even ran an advertisement on Russian TV showing a dollar bill and the words, "We are closer than America." Many influential banks have uncomfortably close links with Russia. Parex's two Russian founders were able to acquire Latvian citizenship without having to pass the normal Latvian language exam. A large part of Latvia's banking assets is owned by foreign banks, especially ones from Scandinavia.

Swedish banks were hurt by the recession in Latvia. But Latvia accounts for less than 5% of Sweden's largest lender in the region, Swedbank. Despite losses, no foreign bank pulled out.

Latvia's trade has shifted from about 80% to the other Soviet republics to 90% toward the west, particularly the EU (63.5% of exports and 78% of imports). It moved more slowly than Estonia to redirect its trade from Russia, which provides 10% of Latvia's imports, largely energy. One reason is that the majority of the population in the major cities plus most workers in industry are non-Latvian, usually Russian.

The main northern route for Russia's oil exports ran through Latvia to the main oil port of Ventspils. This has supported a powerful commercial group in Latvia that favors close ties with Russia rather than with the EU. Russia's leverage was demonstrated in 2003 when it stopped pumping oil to Ventspils. Some Latvians saw this as a move to gain complete control over the port. The Latvian government wants the port to serve as a key connection between Russia and an enlarged EU. Like other new EU members, Latvia fears Russian domination of its energy supplies; it depends on Russia for 60% of its oil and 100% of its gas. Russian energy groups supply more than three-fourths of eastern Europeans' oil and gas, compared with only one-fourth of that needed by western Europeans. They prefer buyers in the west if possible.

In April 2017 Latvia opened up its gas market, hoping for greater independence from Russia. However, Russia's exclusive rights to deliver gas to a major Latvian provider is guaranteed through 2030, and Russian Gazprom owns a third of shares in both major companies. Latvia also seeks greater regional energy connections with its Baltic neighbors through Balticconnector and liquefied natural gas (LNG) terminals to receive gas from other countries.

Latvia is highly committed to green politics. It is second in Europe behind Sweden in the production of renewable energy. Almost half of the electricity used in the country is provided by renewable energy sources. Latvia hopes to raise this since it must import more than 40% of its energy. The Energy Ministry forecasts that its total energy consumption will increase by 3.7% between 2020 and 2030.

Latvia has other problems it must tackle. Its dismal Soviet-era hospitals must be modernized. Its poor rural areas must be developed. Corruption is an issue, and the respected Berlin-based organization Transparency International ranked Latvia as the most corrupt country among the Baltic states. Still, it is ranked 40th best out of 167 countries worldwide. This is a clear improvement over the years when US ambassador Catherine Todd Baily warned that Latvia was in danger of becoming "a playground of a few individuals where they go to line their own pockets and those of their friends."

CULTURE

Latvian belongs to the Baltic family of Indo-European languages. It is closely related to Lithuanian but contains words taken from Swedish, German, and Russian, the languages of peoples who controlled the country at various times in the past.

Latvian culture was historically the culture of the peasantry, the upper classes being mainly German. The same was also true of the cities, for that was where the German and Jewish merchants and tradesmen lived. Thus, a great deal of Latvia's historical culture is not Latvian at all, though as Latvians became educated and entered the middle class in the 19th century, they tended to adopt elements of that earlier culture. Modern Latvian culture is no longer a peasant culture, and it is, in fact, mainly an urban culture.

Approximately a third of the population lives in the city of Riga, Latvia's capital, its chief port and its largest industrial center. In the 12th century, German merchants of the Hanseatic League began trading with Latvian tribes living along the Daugava (Western Dvina) River. In 1201, Bishop Albert of Bremen, who had been given the title of bishop of Livonia by the pope and dispatched to the area accompanied by the Teutonic Knights, built a fortress along the right bank of the river. Bishop Albert also founded his own militant Order of the Brethren of the Sword, and he used it to spread Christianity among the Latvians.

A town grew up around the fortress, and Riga quickly became a major center for trade. It joined the Hanseatic League in 1282. But Bishop Albert's religious order controlled the city until the Reformation. Riga became an independent merchant city-state in 1561, but it was soon taken over by the Polish king. It passed back and forth between Poland and Sweden until 1710, when Peter the Great captured it, and it became part of the Russian Empire.

Riga remained mainly a city of foreigners until the late 19th century. Today it is not only the political and cultural center of the republic but the industrial center, as well. Riga University, founded in 1861, is now called Riga Technical University. The country's main university is the University of Latvia in Riga, with a large student body. There are numerous colleges and technical schools, as well. The Latvian Academy of Sciences and its 14 affiliated research institutes are also located here. The city has an opera and ballet theater, numerous other theaters for plays, and four concert halls. It is therefore the center for higher Latvian culture. In 2014, Riga was named the European capital of culture, a special opportunity to highlight its achievements in this regard.

The city itself is full of historic buildings, including guildhalls, medieval warehouses, and private residences dating back as far as the 14th century. One of the oldest buildings is the Riga Castle itself, headquarters of the Livonian Order in Riga, which dates from 1330. There are also many churches, a few of which are from this same period, though most of them were at least partially rebuilt in subsequent centuries. The oldest of these is the Dome Cathedral, a brick church consecrated in 1211. For centuries the seat of the archbishop of Livonia and Prussia, it has been rebuilt or remodeled many times and shows evidence of many architectural styles, stretching from the Romanesque

to the Baroque. The Reformation reached Riga in the middle of the 16th century and the Domkirk became a Lutheran Church at that time. Today it is a museum. The city also has many operating churches representing various denominations: Roman Catholic; Russian Orthodox; Baptist; and, of course, Lutheran. There is also one remaining synagogue.

Latvia has a strong folklorist tradition, but because most Latvians lived in the countryside, the bulk of the early collections of Latvian folktales was made by German residents in the cities. Most were translated into German before being published. Written literature by Latvian writers first appeared in the 19th century as the number of educated Latvians began to grow. The man usually given credit for laying the foundation stones for a Latvian literature was Juris Neikens, a 19th century author of numerous short stories. A contemporary, Juris Alunāns, was the first Latvian poet, but he helped to start a school of poetry, represented by Krišjānis Barons, Fricis Brīvzemnieks, and Atis Kronvalds. Another 19th-century figure, Ādolfs Alunāns, is considered to be the father of Latvian drama. The novel was given Latvian form by two brothers, Reinis and Matiss Kaudzites, who jointly wrote *The Times of Land-Surveyors*, published in 1879.

Two novelists of the early 20th century were Augusts Deglavs, author of *Riga*, a three-volume work published between 1912 and 1921, and Jēkabs Janševskis, author of *The Native Land*, a six-volume work published in 1924–1925. Realism is represented by the dramas and short stories of Rudolfs Blaumanis and the poems of Vilis Plūdonis. Romanticism is represented by the dramas of Janis Rainis, whose greatest work, written in 1905, is an epic tragedy dealing with early Latvian history entitled *Fire and Night*. Rainis was also a social reformer who spent several years in tsarist prisons before 1905. He participated in the 1905 revolution and subsequently had to escape to Switzerland, where he lived until 1920. *Fire and Night* became the basis for an opera written in 1921 by the composer Jānis Mediņš.

Literary figures of the period of Latvian independence include the novelist Janis Akuraters, the poets Karlis Skalbe and Edvarts Virza, the short-story-writer Jānis Ezeriņš, and the novelist Jānis Jaunsudrabiņš. Jaunsudrabiņš is unusual in that he also made a reputation for himself as a painter.

Some good writers of the Soviet period managed to make their way abroad. They include the playwright Mārtiņš Zīverts; the essayist and novelist Zenta Mauriņa; and the novelists Anšlavs Eglītis, Ģirts Salnais, and Antons Rupainis.

CURRENT ISSUES

Latvia is a small state with a well-educated and disciplined population. This has helped make the transition to a market economy more successful than in any of the other Ex Soviet republics, except Estonia. However, it has two problems for which it has found no solution: a fragmented electorate that has often meant that there was no majority for any specific action and a large non-Latvian population that threatens the political stability. The two problems are interrelated because part of the political fragmentation results from disagreements over how to treat the non-Latvian population. Both problems will diminish as more and more non-Latvians acquire citizenship and learn Latvian.

Its long-term prospects are bright. In the first quarter of 2017, Latvia had the fourth-fastest economic growth among EU member states.

Latvia's greatest remaining problem is how to deal with the large Slavic minorities that make up a third of its population and much of the industrial workforce. Like Estonia, Latvia faces both foreign and domestic political problems that are sometimes in conflict with each other. To preserve its language and culture and to survive as a nation, it has chosen to restrict its citizenship and create strong motivation for members of ethnic minorities to recognize the Latvian character of the restored republic. Progress has been made: Most Russian speakers have become citizens and can vote. In a 2011 referendum, citizens rejected a proposal to make Russian a second official language. The percentage of people citing Russian as their primary language shrunk from 40.5% in 1994 to 29.8% in 2016. That is despite a recent inflow of Russian immigrants attracted

Latvia

by free-press opportunities offered by the Riga-based Internet portal Meduza, highly critical of the Kremlin.

To keep its NATO spending commitment of 2% of GDP, the government picks "guns over health care," according to the country's health-care and social-care worker union, who protested in 2015. Latvia has the worst access to health care and some of the lowest health workers' wages in the EU.

An existential crisis also emerges due to the demographics and emigration: Latvia's population is shrinking, partly due to low birth rates and partly due to the massive exodus of mostly young and enterprising people to other EU countries. In 2010, annual emigration rate reached nearly 40,000 in this country of 1.96 million. The United Kingdom's decision to leave the European Union sent shockwaves through Latvia since the remittances sent back by Latvian workers in the UK constitute more than 5% of the country's GDP. Since then, net migration to the UK from Latvia diminished significantly. Still, many academic programs find it difficult to survive. Some streets in Riga are depopulated, and employers hurt for well-qualified workers. The government even created a post of the ambassador for the diaspora, whose job it is to lure Latvians back from often menial but well-paid jobs abroad. An alternative—to encourage immigration—proves very controversial. It has threatened to declare a state of emergency and build a fence to stem the flow of migrants from Belarus.

As elsewhere in the EU, Latvia struggles with plans to accommodate migrants from the Middle East and Africa. It originally rejected the EU's quotas and reluctantly agreed to take in 250 people over the course of two years. Even this number seems high to some, worried about the further threat to Latvia's ethnic makeup.

Some major challenges must be faced. For the sake of their prosperity and security, Latvians sought economic and military integration with the west. Their need for the security that such integration provides stems from the long-standing Russian claim to predominance over the nations on its periphery. The economic fallout from sanctions against Russia affected Latvia's growth rates. Latvians must remain on guard to ensure that they do not lose all or part of their sovereignty. Both the EU and NATO offer Latvia some reassurance for the future. In June 2017, 450 Canadian soldiers arrived there to join military personnel from Albania, Italy, Poland, Slovenia, and Spain as part of NATO's enhanced Forward Presence (EFP) Battlegroup Latvia. The deployment of some 1,140 troops is intended to bolster NATO members in the region and to provide deterrence against a possible Russian threat.

The October 2022 elections produced a center-right coalition led by the party of Prime Minister Krišjānis Kariņš. Russia's war in Ukraine dominates political debate.

Republic of Lithuania (Lietuvos Respublika)

Wedding day at Trakai Castle

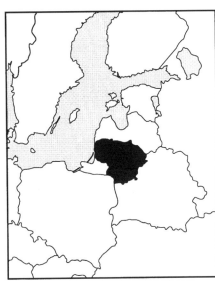

Area: 25,200 sq. mi. (65,300 sq. km).

Population: 2,867,725 (2023 estimate)

Capital City: Vilnius (pop. 593,436, July 2023 estimate).

Climate: It is a temperate climate with both oceanic (maritime) and continental influences. It is oceanic in a narrow coastal zone and humid continental farther east. Average temperatures range from about −5 °C (20°F) in January, the coldest month, to 17 °C (61 °F) in July, the warmest month. On the coastal zone they range from−2.5 °C (27.5 °F) in January to 16 °C (61 °F) in July. Winters can be very cold with the extremes of −34 °C (−29 °F) in coastal areas and −43 °C (−45 °F) in the east of Lithuania.

Neighboring Countries: Latvia (north), Belarus (southeast), Poland (southwest), Russia (Kaliningrad exclave; west).

Official Language: Lithuanian.

Other Languages: Polish, Russian. Belarusian, Ukrainian, Yiddish.

Lithuania

Ethnic Background: 83.6% Lithuanian, 6.4% Polish, 5.1% Russian, 1.7% Belarusian, 1.6% Ukrainian, 1.6% other. (2023)

Religion: Christianity (74.2% Roman Catholic, 5.2% other Christian), 20,6 others (other religion, no religion, unidentified). (2021)

Form of Government: Unitary semi-presidential republic.

Chief of State: Gitanas Nausėda, President of the Republic (July 2019).

Head of Government: Ingrida Šimonytė, Prime Minister (since December 2020).

National Flag: It is a horizontal triband of yellow, green and red. The flag was adopted in 1918 during Lithuania's period of independence from 1918 to 1940, and again re-adopted in 1988. The choice of colors was only determined by the national tradition. These three colors were frequently used in folk weavings and in traditional dress.

National Holiday: February 16 (Independence Day).

Currency: Euro €) (EUR) (since January 1, 2015).

Main Exports: refined petroleum, foodstuffs, machinery, textiles, and transport equipment.

Main Imports: crude petroleum, machinery, foodstuffs, chemical products, and metals.

Main Trading Partners: Russia (6.19%of exports and 5.14% of imports), Germany (7.94% of exports and 11.6% of imports), Latvia (12.8% of exports and 7.88% of imports), Poland (9.05% of exports and 11.6% of imports), US (5.3% of exports and 7.47% of imports), Sweden (4.12% of exports and 5.23% of imports), Netherlands (5.43% of exports and 4.5%of imports), Estonia (5.72% of exports), UK (3.49% of exports), Belarus (3.23% of exports), Norway (4.76% of imports), Saudi Arabia (4.05% of imports), China (3.78% of imports). (2022)

Political Status: An independent principality in the 13th century. A dynastic union with Poland in 1385 led to an increasing closeness between the two countries, until they were merged in 1569. Lithuania became part of the Russian Empire in the 18th century and remained so until 1918. It was an independent state 1918–1940, annexed to the Soviet Union in 1940, declared its independence again in March 1990, and took control of its borders on August 26, 1991.

LITHUANIA SINCE WORLD WAR I

Independent Lithuania, 1919–1939

For centuries Lithuanians dreamed of again being masters in their own house. The cataclysm that shook and reordered

Europe from 1914 to 1918 provided that long-awaited opportunity. Elections to the Lithuanian Constituent Assembly took place in April 1920. A new constitution went into effect August 1, 1922, which created a parliamentary system with a single-body legislature, called the Seimas. It also created a ceremonial president of the republic, elected for a five-year term. Aleksandras Stulginskis (1885—1969) became the first president under the new constitution.

Lithuania was overwhelmingly rural at this time, with 79% of the population earning their living from agriculture. It was also relatively backward; according to the 1923 census, approximately a third of the population was illiterate. There was no individual agriculture among the peasants since their holdings were organized into communes similar to the mirs of Russia and farmed in common. The large estates were mainly in the hands of either Poles or Russians, though the Poles were mainly descendants of individuals of Lithuanian extraction who had been polonized in the 16th to 18th centuries, when the Polish monarchy and Polish culture dominated the united Poland-Lithuania.

A 1922 land reform program expropriated the land of Russian estate owners

Source: *The Economist*

Former President Dalia Grybauskaite

and limited the size of other estates to 375 acres. These lands were subsequently redistributed to peasant smallholders. The land reform also provided for the breakup of the peasant communes and the distribution of the land to the peasants to create private farms. Turning the peasants into individual farmers brought increased prosperity to the countryside. But the plots of land carved out from the large estates were so small that these peasant smallholders had great difficulty making a go of it. In the 1930s, many either sold or abandoned their land and then sought employment in the cities or emigrated.

Lithuania was the most densely populated of the three Baltic states. With 2,035,121 in 1923, it also had the largest population of the three. Its people were mixed ethnically, with approximately 80% speaking Lithuanian. Jews were the single largest minority (7.6%), followed by Poles (3.2%), Russians (2.5%), and Germans (1.4%). There were also a few White Russians and Latvians. Religiously, Lithuania was rather homogeneous, with 85.7% professing Roman Catholicism. The remainder was either Jewish or Protestant.

Lithuania's Border Disputes

Lithuania's chief problem in the period of the 1920s was in securing acceptable international borders. Although there were a number of border disputes, its most significant problem by far was the city of Vilnius, the historic capital of Lithuania. Some of the leaders associated with the new Polish state, including Joseph Pilsudski (1867—1935)—sometimes called the father of modern Poland—had strong ties to the Vilnius area. Pilsudski was a descendant of a polonized Lithuanian noble family and had been born in Vilnius. When the Lithuanian leadership opted for a separate, independent Lithuania, Pilsudski decided that the Vilnius area ought to be part of Poland. His real aim was to recreate the old Polish-Lithuanian Commonwealth.

The background of the dispute is extremely complicated. The original Lithuanian proclamation of independence had been made in the city of Vilnius, but the newly proclaimed Lithuanian government was forced to abandon that city in January 1919 as Bolshevik forces approached. They fled to Kaunas, which became the provisional capital. The Bolsheviks were forced out in April 1919 by Polish forces, who then occupied the city. In the summer of 1920, the Bolsheviks launched a counteroffensive, driving the Poles back.

Soviet Russia and Lithuania signed a peace treaty on July 12, under which the Bolsheviks recognized Lithuanian independence. Three days later, they offered to restore Vilnius to Lithuania if it would ally itself with Soviet Russia against Poland. This required Lithuania to grant Soviet troops transit rights during their invasion of Poland. In the process, they occupied Vilnius. The Soviet invasion force continued westward toward Warsaw and was only stopped by a major battle at the Vistula River in August. As the Soviet forces retreated, they turned Vilnius over to the Lithuanian government, which took possession of the city on August 26, proclaiming it once again the national capital.

Meanwhile the Polish forces pressed farther and farther eastward. They hoped to fulfill Pilsudski's dream of restoring the ancient borders of Poland-Lithuania. Since the Polish government was desirous of Allied support against Soviet Russia, it gave in to Allied pressure to end its border dispute with Lithuania. On October 7 Poland signed the Treaty of Suwalki, providing a demarcation line between both countries that stopped short of Vilnius. The treaty did not mention Vilnius or its future status, leading to opposing interpretations.

Two days later, a Polish unit under General Lucjan Żeligowski broke away from the main Polish force and advanced into Lithuania, apparently acting under secret instructions from Pilsudski. Vilnius was quickly occupied. General Żeligowski then moved farther into Lithuania, apparently intending to conquer the entire country. Lithuanian troops counterattacked, however, and General Żeligowski was forced to withdraw to Vilnius.

The Polish government disavowed Żeligowski, but that was only for international consumption. Żeligowski, acting on orders from Pilsudski, proceeded to create a Central Lithuanian Republic,

supposedly independent of both Poland and Lithuania. All attempts to solve the matter diplomatically failed. Then General Żeligowski arranged for rigged elections to take place in January 1922, which were won by pro-Polish candidates. The puppet legislature voted for union with Poland.

The Polish Sejm proceeded to annex the Vilnius area. The Allied ambassadors accepted the annexation, thereby recognizing the existing line as the final frontier. Refusing to accept the annexation, Lithuania broke diplomatic relations with Poland. These were not resumed until 1938. In the case of Vilnius, Lithuania waited a long time to achieve an acceptable international frontier. Lithuania got Vilnius back in 1940, but Poland did not officially relinquish it until 1994.

These memories still put a chill in relations between Poland and Lithuania. The latter is the only country outside of Poland that offers Polish-language education from elementary through high school. But it requires that more subjects be taught in Lithuanian. It also does not permit local Poles to use unique Polish letters, such as Ę, in their official documents. The Polish foreign minister, Radek Sikorski, refused to visit Lithuania until that policy was changed. Poland accuses Lithuania of dragging its feet on restoring prewar property and breaking its promises on language rights. It is an unequal dispute, since big Poland is 12 times larger and can afford to ignore Lithuania, but Lithuania and its Baltic allies cannot ignore Poland. Vilnius sees Warsaw as arrogant and interfering.

The second boundary question was with regard to Memel, located on the Lithuanian coast a short distance from the mouth of the Nemunas, Lithuania's largest river. Memel had been part of Prussia since the 18th century, but it was taken from Germany at the Treaty of Versailles. The Allies had intended that Memel go to a reconstituted Poland-Lithuania. Although Lithuania's decision to seek its own independence ended that possibility,

Ornamental cats   Courtesy: NOVOSTI

the Allies, refusing to recognize Lithuanian independence because of its border dispute with Poland over Vilnius, could not bring themselves to turn Memel over to Lithuania. Instead, Memel was placed under French military administration, and the matter was put on hold.

Memel itself (now Klaipeda) was a town of only about 20,000, most of whose citizens were German nationals. Lithuania's interest in the city was that it needed a seaport, and Memel was the only good one along the entire Lithuanian coast. Its interest in Vilnius was much greater, however, so it did nothing until it had become clear that the international community had recognized Poland's annexation of Vilnius.

With nothing further to lose, the Lithuanian government decided to seize Memel by force. On January 7, 1923, days after the French had begun their own occupation of the German Ruhr area, Lithuania sent troops accompanied by a large number of "volunteers" to invade and occupy Memel. The Lithuanians lost 20 men, while 2 Frenchmen and a German policeman were killed. With the French tied down in Germany and the German and Soviet governments supporting Lithuania, the Allies decided that nothing could be done and agreed, in February 1923, to transfer Memel to Lithuanian sovereignty.

Thus, in this dispute, Lithuania got both the desired seaport and international recognition of its acquisition. The government immediately gave the Lithuanian name of Klaipeda to the city and the region and established it as an autonomous province with its own government. With all of Lithuania as its hinterland, it flourished in subsequent years, although it continued to have a significant German population. That would become a diplomatic issue between Germany and Lithuania after Hitler came to power in 1933.

Lithuania's Move Away from Democracy

The May 1926 elections resulted in a political transformation when the Christian Democrats, who had dominated every government up to this time, were defeated. A new coalition government under the premiership of Mykolas Sleževičius now took power, composed of the Social Democrats and the Peasant Populists. One month later, in June 1926, the coalition's candidate, Dr. Kazys Grinius, a prominent leader of the Peasant Populists, was installed as president.

Among the changes introduced by the new government was a different attitude toward the Soviet Union. This was symbolized by a nonaggression pact, which the two countries signed in September 1926. The Christian Democrats and the Nationalists had opposed an agreement with the Soviet Union from the beginning,

Lithuania

and they began planning a counterstroke. On the night of December 16, with the support of the army, they carried out their coup d'etat against the government. Entering the parliament building accompanied by a group of officers, they seized control. Then they dismissed the cabinet, adjourned the session of parliament, and deposed the president. Antanas Smetona, leader of the Nationalists and first president in 1919–1920, was reappointed.

The coup having succeeded, the left decided to cooperate to save what they could of Lithuanian democracy. Grinius submitted his resignation as president, and Sleževičius resigned as premier. The parliament met and elected Antanas Smetona as president. The coup had thereby been legalized. One of Smetona's first acts was to name Augustinas Voldemaras, a prominent Nationalist, as the new premier. Voldemaras formed a cabinet composed of Christian Democrats, Nationalists, and members of parties of the center.

The Social Democrats and Peasant Populists continued to control a majority in the legislature, however. When, after a period of cooperation, they challenged the government in April 1927, the latter dissolved the legislature. Smetona ruled for approximately a year by decree, then proclaimed a new constitution in May 1928, which formalized the new structure. From that time onward, Smetona and his premier, Augustinas Voldemaras, ruled the country by decree. Lithuania was thus the first of the Baltic countries to abandon democracy and replace it with a form of authoritarianism.

The Lithuanian Authoritarian Regime

Lithuania differed from its two Baltic neighbors in that its authoritarian regime involved two figures, Smetona and Voldemaras, and because some political organizations continued to operate. The Nationalist Party was the most significant of the political groups at this time, although Voldemaras created a semi fascist group, Iron Wolf. It was forced out in September 1929 after he came under clerical criticism and became the target of a failed assassination attempt by three Lithuanian students. Juozas Tūbelis, President Smetona's brother-in-law, succeeded him as premier. Tūbelis remained premier until 1939.

In 1934, spurred on by worsening economic conditions, a number of military officers attempted a coup to restore Voldemaras to power. When it failed, he was arrested and sentenced to several years in prison. Released in 1938, he left the country and settled in southern France.

There were also numerous peasant revolts in 1934 that were put down by force. Believing that the revolts were the result of political agitation, Smetona banned all

The old part of Vilnius, the Lithuanian capital

Courtesy: NOVOSTI

political parties other than the Nationalists. The government permitted the election of a new legislature in 1935, but this was largely meaningless since the government nominated all electoral candidates. A new constitution was also approved in 1936. In essence, it legalized the authoritarian presidency that had existed since 1926. In one innovation, Smetona was henceforth to be addressed as Tautos Vados, or "Leader of the People."

Lithuania under Soviet Rule, 1939–1991

Although the Lithuanian people had failed in some respects with regard to

domestic policies, their greatest mistake was in foreign policy. Perhaps nothing they could have done would have made any difference, but they were at odds with almost all of their neighbors and had no friends. Thus, when Nazi Germany and the Soviet Union got together to negotiate their "nonaggression" pact in August 1939, Lithuania was among their victims. Dividing eastern Europe into spheres of influence, the original agreement assigned Estonia and Latvia to the Soviet Union, while Lithuania fell within the German sphere of influence. However, a protocol signed on September 23, 1939, reversed

Vytautas Landsbergis

this. Lithuania was placed within the Soviet sphere of influence, while Nazi Germany got an extra piece of Poland.

Hitler launched his invasion of Poland on September 1, and Soviet troops entered to occupy the eastern third of Poland on September 17. In October all three Baltic states were forced to sign mutual-assistance pacts with the Soviet Union. As an aside, Lithuania was the only one to get anything out of the agreements. The Soviet Union transferred the city of Vilnius and surrounding area, which it had just taken from Poland, to Lithuania.

Nothing happened for several months, probably because the Soviet Union was tied down in its Winter War with Finland. Once that was resolved, the Soviet Union turned its attention back to the Baltic states. Toward the end of May 1940, the Soviet Foreign Ministry accused Lithuania of violating the 1939 mutual-assistance pact. Then, on June 14, Soviet foreign minister Molotov demanded the arrest of the Lithuanian interior and security ministers and the creation of a new Lithuanian government capable of supporting the 1939 treaty. In addition, Molotov demanded that Soviet troops be authorized to enter the country and to occupy "the most important centers."

Lithuania had no choice but to give in to the Soviet request. After the Red Army had entered the country, Molotov demanded the right to name a new premier. A popular front government was now established. The Social Democrats and Peasant Populists were given ministerial seats, but the communists controlled all the important ministries.

The popular front government had a remarkably short life. In July, all political parties other than the Communist Party were banned, and most noncommunists were dismissed from office. This was followed by a wave of arrests. With only communists, organized as the Working People's League, standing for office, new elections were held on July 14, 1940. The newly "elected" legislature met on July 21. Its only piece of business was to vote on whether to join the Soviet Union, which it did by acclamation. The following month, the USSR Supreme Soviet "acceded" to this request. Lithuania thus became a Soviet socialist republic.

The new communist government immediately began to implement general Soviet policies. A government decree nationalized all of the land. Larger estates were taken over directly and turned into state farms, but there was also a promise of land to landless laborers. Smaller farmers were permitted to retain up to 75 acres, though technically they did not own it any longer. Nationalist elements now began to organize opposition to the new policies. In retaliation, the communists began rounding up oppositional elements and deporting them to Siberia.

Germany's invasion of the Soviet Union beginning on June 22, 1941, reversed this situation, after German troops overran and occupied Lithuania later in 1941. It remained under German occupation until 1944. With the German retreat, however, Lithuania once again fell under Soviet control. The murder of the city's Jewish population by the Nazis and Stalin's deportation of most Poles meant that Vilnius lost 90% of its population during World War II. In all, 160,000 Jews, 95%, perished, some of them at the hands of the virulent anti-Semitic Lithuanian Activist Front. Thousands of Jews died in pogroms even before the Nazi death machine was ready. In 2011 parliament voted to pay $53 million in compensation for the Nazi seizure of property during the war. The money is paid into a special fund to support social, cultural, and education projects for the 4,000 or so surviving Lithuanian Jews, down from 220,000 before the war. The Museum of Genocide Victims honors the dead. An anticommunist resistance movement arose, often consisting of individuals who had been active in guerrilla actions against the Germans.

By the summer of 1945, this movement had approximately 50,000 members and was operating throughout Lithuania. Units functioned mainly in rural parts of the country, with their encampments in the middle of a forest. Guerrilla units would move out to attack centers of communist control while, back at the encampment, others worked to organize popular resistance. The reconstituted Lithuanian communist government countered the resistance movement by creating its own People's Defenders, although the main struggle against the guerrillas was carried out by the NKVD (secret police). This war between the Lithuanian resistance and the NKVD went on until 1947. Such efforts were ineffectual. Lithuania got no outside assistance, and the resistance movement was eventually suppressed.

Many changes occurred in Lithuania over the following 35 years. Soviet policy was to integrate the Baltic republics so thoroughly into the Soviet system that there would be no question of their ever leaving the union. To that end, the Soviet government first carried out policies of nationalization and collectivization. Next, it sought to bind the republics to the rest of the Soviet Union economically by locating branch factories of Soviet industry there. Such factories received most or all of their raw materials from other parts of the Soviet Union and delivered most of their finished products to customers in the other republics.

Economic integration was accompanied by a program of Soviet Russification, aimed at transforming the cultures of the three republics. All students received Russian-language training in the schools, plus general indoctrination lectures on the nature of Soviet culture.

It was Estonia and Latvia that became the chief victims of this policy, however. According to the figures of the 1989 Soviet census, Lithuania was still 80% ethnic Lithuanian. By comparison, ethnic Estonians by this time made up only 61.5% of the population of the republic, while in Latvia the figure was only 52%. On the positive side, the heavy industrialization carried out after 1945 meant that the standard of living in the three Baltic republics was above that of any part of the Soviet Union.

Lithuania Moves toward Independence

The Lithuanian people were a little slower to get organized than the Estonians and Latvians, but once organized they proved to be even more determined to split with Moscow than either Estonia or Latvia. Sąjūdis, the Lithuanian Popular Front, traces its origins to a commission established by the Lithuanian Academy of Sciences on May 23, 1988, to propose changes to the Lithuanian constitution to accommodate Gorbachev's policies of glasnost, perestroika, and democratization. The commission brought together party and nonparty intellectuals and professionals who, in turn, decided that the times demanded something more. On June 3, they created an "initiative group," which subsequently took the name of Sąjūdis.

Over the summer of 1988, Sąjūdis organized mass meetings and demonstrations

Lithuania

on such issues as the 1939 Molotov-Ribbentrop Pact, the status of the Lithuanian language, and the possibility of some form of economic autonomy. From the beginning, the animating spirit behind Sajūdis was a nonparty intellectual, the musicologist Vytautas Landsbergis. Sajūdis held its founding congress in October 1988. A resolution was passed calling on the republic's government to issue an assertion of Lithuanian sovereignty.

Algirdas Brazauskas, who had just been appointed first secretary of the Lithuanian Communist Party, was one of the invited speakers at the congress. He supported the measure initially but was then forced to reverse himself on orders from Moscow. The Lithuanian Communist Party lost much of its credibility as a result, as can be seen by looking at the results of the March 1989 elections to the USSR Congress of People's Deputies.

Sajūdis candidates won 36 out of 42 seats to the congress and might have won even more had they not deliberately refrained from challenging certain top communists, including First Secretary Brazauskas, who was liked personally, in spite of his having toed Moscow's line on the sovereignty issue. In fact, there was an overlap in the electoral positions of Sajūdis and the Lithuanian Communist Party, for the latter advocated economic autonomy, pluralism of opinions, democracy, and glasnost.

The Lithuanian Communist Party came under tremendous pressure after it had lost to Sajūdis in the spring elections. In an attempt to create nationalist credentials, the party began in mid-1989 discussing a split with the Communist Party of the Soviet Union. Another indication of the way opinion within the party was evolving came on August 22, 1989, when a commission of the Lithuanian Supreme Soviet, at that time still controlled by communists, voted to condemn the 1940 Soviet annexation of Lithuania and to declare it invalid. The party's formal split with Moscow came in December, at the Lithuanian Communist Party Congress. It became the first republic party to split with the CPSU.

Even so, the Lithuanian Communist Party still found itself following along in Sajūdis's wake. On August 23, 1989, the governing council of Sajūdis voted unanimously that Lithuania should "take the peaceful course to becoming an independent democratic republic once again." In December 1989 Brazauskas, going further than he had ever gone before, could only bring himself to advocate a "sovereign Lithuanian state in a new union of free republics." Even that position caused a split in the Lithuanian Communist Party, when a faction claiming to represent one-fourth of the membership broke away and reaffirmed its ties with Moscow.

If you don't help Lithuania, who will? Be socially active!

It was against this background that elections were held to elect a new Lithuanian Supreme Soviet. The elections took place on February 24, 1990, with runoff elections on March 10. The Sajūdis slate, which included reform communists, as well as representatives of the newly legalized Christian Democrat, Social Democrat, and Green Parties, won an overwhelming majority.

The newly installed parliament elected its chairman of the presidium Vytautas Landsbergis, head of Sajūdis and a noncommunist. Lithuania had its first noncommunist government since 1940. On March 11, 1990, the Lithuanian Supreme Soviet adopted a declaration of Lithuanian independence.

The Soviet Union not only did not recognize Lithuanian independence, but it also organized a partial economic boycott against the republic. Orders went out to all state enterprises in the republic to obey only orders from Moscow. There was public discussion about presenting Lithuania with a bill for Soviet capital investments over the years—estimated at 21 billion P—payable in hard currency. There were also Soviet military maneuvers held in March

1990 in and around the city of Vilnius, though Gorbachev claimed at the same time that force would not be used except to prevent bloodshed.

The Lithuanian response to the Soviet demand for indemnities was to raise counterclaims for goods and services extracted from the republic, environmental damage, and for the tens of thousands of Lithuanians killed by Soviet officials over the years. The rhetoric escalated still further in April, when Gorbachev threatened to reduce sharply the flow of gas and oil to Lithuania if it did not immediately retract its declaration of independence. The Lithuanian government offered to discuss the question of the effective date of independence but not the question of independence itself. Oil shipments to Lithuania's sole refinery were then cut off, and reductions were made in the delivery of other raw materials.

Meanwhile, Lithuania got some support of sorts when the Estonian and Latvian governments joined Lithuania in issuing their own declarations of independence, though the declarations were not to take force immediately. In addition, the United States threatened to withhold most-favored-nation trading status from the Soviet Union if it blockaded Lithuania. As a result, after some further threats, the Soviet Union lifted its partial embargo on Lithuania.

Things remained quiet for several months, but Moscow hard-liners made a new move against Lithuania in January 1991. Gorbachev claimed no advance knowledge when USSR Ministry of Interior troops seized a television tower in Vilnius, but he did not repudiate the action.

The issue of Baltic independence was one of the issues that precipitated the coup against Gorbachev in August 1991. Its failure led most of the world to extend recognition to the Baltic states and led the postcoup Soviet government to extend its own recognition in September 1991. Lithuania was admitted to the United Nations in October 1991.

Sovereign Lithuania

In a surprise, the electorate gave Sajūdis, the party of Landsbergis, only about 22% of the vote in the first parliamentary elections in 1992. The winner was the Democratic Labor Party, the successor party to the Lithuanian Communist Party, led by Algirdas Brazauskas. It got over 40% of the vote and a majority of the seats in the Seimas. This result was reaffirmed in the subsequent presidential elections that were won by Brazauskas, who then took office in February 1993. He succeeded the first post-Soviet prime minister, Kazimira Prunskienė.

It would be misleading simply to say that the communists returned to power

Lithuania

Presidential palace, Vilnius

in Lithuania in 1992. In fact, Brazauskas is a nationalist first and foremost. It was he who was responsible for the Lithuanian Communist Party's split with Moscow in 1990 and its subsequent support for Lithuanian independence. Moreover, when Brazauskas founded the Democratic Labor Party after independence, many communists became politically inactive, with the result that only about 5%–10% of its membership in 1992 were formerly members of the Lithuanian Communist Party.

It was not politics but economics that was responsible for Brazauskas's victory. By 1992, the economy was in relatively poor shape, with salaries frozen and many people being paid up to three months late. Moreover, Lithuania had been forced to cut its imports of oil and gas beginning in July 1992, after Russia began charging world prices payable in hard currency for exports to areas outside the ruble zone. By October Lithuania did not have sufficient fuel to heat most buildings. As one commentator explained the vote, "the simple people know only that before it was warm, and now it is cold."

After his victory, Brazauskas asked, "Can you imagine how a person receiving a small salary can survive, with world prices coming down upon their heads? A government has to reply to the people's cries." His win did not bring about a change in direction, although it did involve a change in style. In an attempt to cushion the transition to private enterprise, for example, the government made a point of working out its policies in close consultation with factory managers. This slowed the process somewhat, but it did not reverse it.

The newly independent Lithuanian government initially concentrated mainly on domestic problems, although it also pressed for the removal of Soviet troops from Lithuania as soon as possible. That presented a particular problem as long as the troops remained under the aegis of the Commonwealth of Independent States

(CIS). The Russian government set up its own Ministry of Defense in the summer of 1992 and subsequently negotiated an agreement with Lithuania for the removal of the troops as soon as possible.

There were approximately 20,500 troops in Lithuania at this time. Some small token force withdrawals began in September 1992, and Russia promised that all would be out by sometime in 1993. President Boris Yeltsin suspended the troop withdrawals in October, asserting a "profound concern" over the treatment of ethnic Russians in the Baltic republics. Since Lithuania, unlike the Estonians and Latvians, had extended citizenship to all persons who were resident prior to mid-1990, it is not immediately clear why Lithuania was included in the decree. Moscow wanted guarantees concerning the pensions and status of retired Russian military personnel living in Lithuania. In any case, new negotiations with Russia led to the evacuation of the last Russian troops from Lithuania in the summer of 1993.

National Minorities

Lithuania has also had some problems with minorities within the country, mainly Poles and Russians. District governments in and around Vilnius where Poles were in a majority were suspended, apparently because the Poles elected communists to office. In spite of nationalist demands to the contrary, the government eventually ended up extending citizenship rights to its minorities. Around 80% of the population is ethnic Lithuanian. Only about 7% of the residents are Russian, living mainly in cities.

Through its acquisition of Vilnius and the surrounding area in 1940, Lithuania acquired a sizable minority of Poles. Although most were deported, they are still the largest minority, numbering about 260,000 or a little over 7% of the total, and they reside principally in Vilnius and in the rural southeast. The republic's Soviet leaders had skillfully prevented a large

influx of Russian speakers. This had been made easier by the fact that Lithuania was not as industrially developed as Estonia and Latvia. This condition enabled independent Lithuania to grant almost universal citizenship to all residents in 1991 without risking a loss of control over the nation's destiny. This was the kind of automatic citizenship ("zero option") adopted by most former Soviet republics and demanded by Russia in Estonia and Latvia, where the demographic situation is dramatically different.

POLITICAL SYSTEM

Lithuania completed its transition from the earlier communistic system in October 1992, when the Lithuanian people approved a new constitution in a national referendum. It is now a multiparty, parliamentary democracy. The constitution calls for a semi presidential system. Although the president formally oversees both foreign and domestic policy, in fact the president takes the lead in foreign policy, and the prime minister conducts domestic policy. He or she may issue decrees, declare a state of emergency, and return laws passed by the single-chamber legislature, the Seimas, for reconsideration. Next in order of importance is the chairman of the 141-member Seimas. Its deputies are elected for terms of four years; 71 are elected by direct vote and 70 by proportional representation. Second-round runoffs take place in constituencies where no candidate wins a majority the first round. The president appoints the prime minister, who must retain the support of a majority in parliament and who is responsible for day-to-day operations, as well as maintaining diplomatic relations with foreign countries and international organizations.

The President

The president of the republic is the highest official of the state. Popularly elected for a term of five years, he represents the country internationally and provides general political leadership domestically. He appoints and dismisses state officials. He may issue decrees under certain circumstances, and only he may declare a state of national emergency. Laws passed by the Seimas may either be approved and published or returned with remarks for reconsideration.

In 1998 a former senior official of the US Environmental Protection Agency, Valdas Adamkus, was elected president. In the runoff election, he narrowly defeated the son of a KGB colonel, Arturas Paulauskas, who had the endorsement of the sitting president, Algirdas Brazauskas. Adamkus, who was 71 when first elected, had spent most of his life in the United States

Lithuania

as an emigre. Because of that background, he had to fight a lawsuit to get on the ballot. His emigre past was an important issue in the election. In the end, the Lithuanian people, forced to choose between an outsider and Paulauskas, opted for the outsider. They hoped that Adamkus would be able to lead Lithuania westward and that his know-how and international connections would firmly root their future in the west. In his words, "I want to see Lithuania as a democratic country so that the younger generation will grow up under western cultural influence." The primary function of a Lithuanian president is to represent the country abroad, and he spoke excellent English and German and knew American ways.

The Lithuanian constitution gives the president only a limited domestic role, but Adamkus got around this limitation after his election by building a working relationship with the parties of the government coalition. By 2003 he seemed tired and was often ill. Ineffective at home and surrounded by a weak team, he appeared to be increasingly out of touch. Nevertheless, he sought reelection as the favorite. But twice, former prime minister and Vilnius mayor Rolandas Paksas conducted a well-organized and well-financed campaign hammering at the country's corruption, poverty, and bad government. Paksas did well in rural areas, which have not shared equally in Lithuania's increasing prosperity. Fascinating voters by such stunts as flying his own plane under a Kaunas bridge, he scored an upset victory, winning 54.9% of the votes to 45.1% for Adamkus. Turnout was 52%.

Paksas's presidency was engulfed by scandals and lasted only 15 months. In April 2004 he became the first European leader to be impeached and removed from office. He was accused of improperly restoring Lithuanian citizenship to a Russian businessman and crony with connections to organized crime, Yuri Borisov, who had financed his campaign with a $400,000 contribution. The State Security Department reported that Paksas had leaked classified information by tipping Borisov off that Lithuanian authorities were investigating him and tapping his phone. In a brazen move, Paksas even hired Borisov as a presidential adviser while the impeachment proceedings were going on. Quickly realizing the stupidity of that act, he reversed his decision within hours.

The Constitutional Court ruled that he had "grossly violated" the law. By the required three-fifths majority, parliament voted narrowly to convict him of improperly granting citizenship and influencing a privatization deal. Prime Minister Brazauskas, most politicians, the Roman Catholic Church, and 60% of the people favored

Prime Minister Ingrida Šimonytė

his removal. To the end Paksas denied the charges, portraying himself as the victim of a corrupt system and accusing his opponents of exacting political revenge for his unexpected victory a year earlier.

Although embarrassed, many Lithuanians viewed the way with which the scandal was dealt to be evidence of how strong the country's democracy has become. The turmoil it caused at the very time that the country was entering NATO and the EU also revealed the undercurrent of fear about Russia's meddling in Lithuanian affairs and the determination to finalize its break with Moscow. Given the country's past, this is a very sensitive issue.

Since Lithuania has no vice president, Parliamentary Speaker Arturas Paulauskas became interim president until elections could be held in June 2004. In the two electoral rounds, five candidates vied for the presidency. The chief election commission refused to register Paksas as a candidate. The election was marred a few days before the voting by police raids on the offices of four parties supporting Adamkus. They were undertaken by the Special Investigation Service, headed by Paksas sympathizers. The action was so frightening that the mayor of Vilnius, who backed Adamkus in the election, took temporary refuge in Poland for fear of arrest.

The frontrunner emerged from the second round as the victor—former president Valdas Adamkus, who in 2003 had been appointed as a goodwill ambassador for UNESCO. With 52.5%, he defeated Kazimira Prunskiene, the leader of the populist Peasants' Party and first post-Soviet prime minister, who had the backing of the still-popular Paksas.

In May 2009 Dalia Grybauskaite was elected president by a landslide, with 68% of the votes. In 2014 she became the first president to be reelected. Voters liked

President Gitanas Nausėda
Source: *Wikipedia*

her condemnation of Russia's aggression in Ukraine and call for increasing NATO forces in Lithuania. She was supported by Foreign Minister Linas Linkevičius, who proclaimed, "We cannot trust a single word of the Russian leadership." Born in Vilnius in 1956, she studied political economy in Leningrad, working at a fur factory to pay her way. A tough politician with a black belt in karate earned while she was a diplomat in Washington, she is a former finance minister who speaks four languages. The five preceding years, she had served as the EU's budget commissioner, where she acquired a reputation as hardworking, incisive, and successful. Her nickname is "Iron Lady." Perhaps because of her EU experience, she does not share the fervent Atlanticism one finds among most Lithuanian politicians. She ran as an independent candidate. She is very popular and quite stubborn when she has to be.

Although her powers on paper were relatively limited, she had a powerful personal mandate and dared to use it. There were limits, though. A controversial law she inherited bans the "promotion" of gay rights through education to the young. Her predecessor had vetoed it, but parliament overrode that action. Although she opposed the ban, she was unable to overturn it. She was succeeded as president by Gitanas Nausėda. He is an economist and banker who is serving as the ninth and current president of Lithuania since 2019.

Parliament and Prime Minister

The Seimas is a single-body legislature with a total of 141 members elected for a period of four years. Under Lithuania's voting system, 71 of the seats are filled by direct vote; the remaining 70 seats are awarded on a proportional basis, each political party being assigned seats on the basis of its share of the popular vote. A

Lithuania

A modern Lithuanian take on the "fraternal kiss" of Leonid Brezhnev and Erich Honecker: Presidents Putin and Trump "make everything great again." The mural was painted over by vandals in August 2016.
Photo by Logan Hancock

party must receive at least 5% of the votes to gain parliamentary seats. The Seimas has the power to amend the constitution, enact laws, control the activities of the government, approve the budget, appoint and dismiss chairs of the state institutions, and settle other issues pertaining to state power. Its chairman is one of the republic's top three political figures.

As the constitutionally designated head of government, the prime minister and his cabinet are responsible for the day-to-day operations of government. He is also charged with implementing laws and resolutions of the Seimas and decrees issued by the president of the republic. He maintains diplomatic relations with foreign countries and international organizations.

Formally appointed by the president, the prime minister must be confirmed by the Seimas and must retain the support of a majority of that body to remain in office. Thus, among his other functions, the prime minister must maintain a close working relationship with the Seimas. Ministers are appointed and dismissed by the president of the republic upon the recommendation of the prime minister.

The October 2012 parliamentary elections pitted Algirdas Butkevičius's Social Democrats against the conservative Homeland Union, led by then-prime minister Andrius Kubilius. The latter had done a good job despite the worst recession since independence. He countered the steep recession by reining in public spending and trying to ease tension with the country's neighbors. To deal with the crisis, he had cut public spending by 30%, slashed pensions by 11%, taken a personal pay cut of 45%, and raised taxes.

The medicine worked, with the economy growing by 3.6% and unemployment declining to 13.1% in 2013. But the elections came too early for angry voters to see the benefits of austerity. Although Kubilius had led the first-ever Lithuanian government to serve a full four-year term, his government was thrown out. His Homeland Union captured 33 seats (a loss of 12) and 15% of the votes (down 4.6%). Its partner, the Liberal Movement, won 10 seats (down 1) and 8.57% of the votes. Both parties are in the opposition.

The Social Democrats came out on top, winning 38 of the 141 seats (a gain of 13) based on 18.4% of the votes (up 6.6%). Its leader, Algirdas Butkevičius, became prime minister in December 2012. With a doctorate in economics, fluency in Russian and English, and considerable experience in party and government, he is well qualified.

His logical coalition partner in the leftist government was the Labor Party, led by a controversial leader, Viktor Uspaskich. It made dramatic gains, winning 29 seats (up 19) and 19.8% (up 11.8%). A Russian-born entrepreneur who had lived two decades in Lithuania, Uspaskich made a fortune importing gas from Russia in the 1990s. Because he owns a pickling factory, he acquired the nickname of "Mr. Gerkin." A populist with considerable charisma, he and his Labor Party attracted votes from disgruntled Lithuanians who were not among the winners of the transition from communism: pensioners, farmers, unemployed, and others with gripes against the government and the free-market economy.

He campaigned against corruption (a third of Lithuanians admitted in a 2004 poll to having paid a bribe within the past year) and for sharply increased pensions and living standards for poorer people. Ironically his party was supported by more multimillionaires than any other party or bloc.

One editorial summed up his campaigns: "promise, promise, promise." Because his party was alleged to have bought votes, President Grybauskaite took the unprecedented step of refusing for a few weeks to allow a governing coalition to include the Labor Party. This was supported by a large majority of voters, but she ultimately relented.

Two other parties joined the ruling coalition. The Order and Justice Party garnered 11 seats (down 4) and 7.3% of the votes. For the first time, a small party representing the Polish minority, AWPL, surpassed the 5% electoral threshold and received some proportional representation seats, increasing its usual two to three seats to eight. Its leader, Waldemar Tomaszewski, is trying to broaden his appeal by reaching out also to ethnic Russians, which is controversial, as Lithuania is warry of Russia's influence. The new government also announced plans to "reset" relations with Russia, to "build cooperation with Russia on European values." However, it quickly caused rancor with Latvia and Estonia, announcing that it does not intend to build a nuclear power plant at Lithuanian town of Visaginas, which would have supplied power to all three Baltic countries.

The 2016 parliamentary elections revealed a significant and unexpected shift in Lithuanian politics. For one, weak economic performance, massive emigration, and a controversial labor law hurt the parties in the government. That was also the year of political earthquakes—from the Brexit vote to the election of Donald Trump in the US. Similarly, Lithuanian voters went against the political establishment, especially by abandoning the Social Democrats, who saw their 40 parliamentary seats reduced to 17 (and received 15.04% of votes). The surprise winners were the Lithuanian Farmers and Greens Union (LVZS), who jumped from a mere 1 seat and 4.05% votes to a whopping 54 seats (22.45%). Led by a wealthy agribusiness owner, Ramūnas Karbauskis, the

Lithuania

party had to modify its English name, which earlier had been rendered as Peasants and Greens Union, leading to unintended associations. Homeland Union gained a slightly higher proportion of votes (22.63%) but only 31 seats, down by 2 from the previous election. Liberal Movement won 14 seats (9.45%), the Electoral Action of Poles (AWPL) retained its 8 seats (5.72%), and Order and Justice also won 8 seats (5.55%). The Labor Party was nearly obliterated, as it won only one district and did not clear the 5% threshold, being shut out of the parliament. The LVZS formed a government in coalition with Social Democrats. This government was soon replaced by a fragile governing alliance led by Prime Minister Ingrida Šimonytė.

The last parliamentary elections were held in Lithuania on October 11 and 25, 2020. Homeland Union—Christian Democrats once again received a plurality of votes, similar to the prior elections, and won 24.86% of votes (50 seats). Farmers and Greens Union gained 18.07% of votes (32 seats). The Labor Party saw a rebound at the national level from its disappointing performance in 2016, gaining 10 seats overall and obtaining nearly 9.77 % of the popular vote. The Social Democratic Party lost a further four seats, achieving 9.58 % of votes (13 seats), its worst seat result since 1992, and its worst vote result since 1996. Freedom Party saw success gaining 9.45 % of votes (11 seats), and Liberal Movement gained 7.04 of votes (13 seats). The Electoral Action of Poles failed to pass the 5% threshold for national list seats for the first time since 2008.

All parties involved in the pre-election coalition, including the Lithuanian Farmers and Greens Union, Social Democratic Labor Party, and Electoral Action of Poles in Lithuania—Christian Families Alliance, lost seats compared to what they held prior, with the Farmers and Greens losing over 40% of their prior seats. Overall, the Homeland Union—Lithuanian Christian Democrats, the Liberal Movement, and the Freedom Party got the most support from the cities. Turnout was roughly 47% in the first and 39% in the second round.

As no party or electoral coalition won a majority of seats (71), a coalition had to be formed. On October 15, after the first round, the leaders of the Homeland Union—Christian Democrats, the Liberal Movement, and the Freedom Party announced a joint declaration, which stated that they nominate Ingrida Šimonytė as their joint candidate to be Prime Minister of Lithuania. On November 9, a formal coalition agreement was announced between the three parties mentioned above. Viktorija Čmilytė-Nielsen of the Liberal Movement was elected as Speaker of the Seimas.

Mass is celebrated in Kaunas.

Courtesy: NOVOSTI

On November 24, Ingrida Šimonytė was appointed president.

Next parliamentary elections are scheduled to be held in Lithuania by October 6, 2024, with a second round two weeks thereafter.

Foreign and Defense Policy

Former president Brazauskas managed to annoy Russia when he announced in 1994 in a television address that the Lithuanian government had submitted a formal request for membership in NATO. Lithuania was the first Baltic republic to do so. Moscow was especially sensitive to Lithuania's entry into NATO because its only land bridge linking Russia proper and its troops in Kaliningrad runs through Lithuania. Therefore, its reaction was swift and negative, with a spokesman for President Yeltsin warning that any moves to expand NATO could "trigger military-political destabilization in the region."

Foreign policy did not change significantly under President Adamkus, who took office in 1998. He favored better relations with Russia and all of Lithuania's neighbors. Lithuania was warming up especially to one of its oldest rivals, Poland, although their relations were testy. In June

1997 it forged a "strategic partnership" with Warsaw. It also created with Poland a joint battalion called LITPOLBAT that is interoperable with NATO. In 2010 NATO decided to expand its defense plan for Poland to cover the Baltic states, as well. In case of a Russian attack, Polish soldiers would be expected to defend Lithuania.

In July 1998 Lithuania hosted 5,000 soldiers at maneuvers on its territory. The participants included units from the United States, Denmark, Norway, Germany, and all other Baltic states, with Russians, Ukrainians, and Belarusians present as observers. Its then deputy defense minister Povilas Malakasuskas underscored the goal of all these cooperative efforts: "to make Baltic membership in NATO a logical inevitability."

Backed by the lobbying activities of more than 700,000 Lithuanians living in the US, these diplomatic and military efforts succeeded. Lithuania joined the alliance in April 2004. All parties supported membership, and some leaders rejoiced that NATO membership enabled the country to deal with Russia from a position of strength. A NATO meeting in Vilnius in April 2005 to coordinate policy toward Lithuania's volatile neighbor, Belarus, demonstrated how

Founded in 1570—Vilnius University Library, with over 4 million volumes
Courtesy: *NOVOSTI*

dramatically Europe had changed since the end of the Cold War.

In preparation for NATO membership, Lithuania began raising its defense budget to reach 2% of GDP in 2004. However, by 2014 its military expenditures had fallen to less than half that. By 2022, its defense spending had climbed to 2.5% of GDP. Its forces are small, numbering only 7,950 active forces, plus 3,000 to 3,500 conscripts.

Women are permitted to serve in uniform. It has a total of 4,400 reservists, plus 14,600 paramilitary that include coast and border guards. Its special forces have reaped particular praise from NATO. The navy has 470 sailors and 14 ships. The air force numbers 950 troops and 16 aircraft. It has 5,000 border guards and 540 coast guards. To adapt to NATO requirements, the structure of the armed forces is being reformed. Lithuania had suspended its military draft in 2009, but it reintroduced it in 2015 for five years as a response to Russia's aggressive actions. It affects men from age 19 to 26.

In 2004, Armed Forces Commander Major General Jonas Kronkaitis, who had served in Vietnam as a young American officer, was replaced by Brigadier General Valdas Tutkus, who, along with 5,000 other Lithuanian soldiers, had fought in Afghanistan as a Soviet officer.

Lithuania deployed 37 peacekeepers in Kosovo and 250 in Afghanistan. It had 53 infantrymen in southern Iraq in a Danish battalion and 45 in the international division in Iraq commanded by Poland. It maintained a provincial reconstruction team in central Afghanistan and 14 soldiers in Iraq. It purchased 60 shoulder-launched Stinger missiles from the US to defend major installations like nuclear power plants from terrorist attacks. ABC News reported that Lithuania, along with Poland and Romania, hosted a secret CIA prison. The government spokesman denied any knowledge of the jails or having approved of them.

As Lithuania entered NATO in 2004, tensions with Russia heated up. All three Baltic states expelled Russian diplomats accused of spying on NATO activities. Within days of its enlargement, NATO dispatched four Belgian F-16 jets, supported by 100 Belgian, Danish, and Norwegian troops, to Siauliai Air Force Base outside of Vilnius. It had also sent an AWACS electronics plane in February on a demonstration flight to Rumbula Airfield in Latvia and then to Šiauliai. The F-16s' assignment was to police the skies over the Baltic states and to underscore the new border being drawn between Russia and Europe. One hundred Germans in the NATO Baltic Air Policing unit operate six F-4F Phantom II jets out of Lithuania. Additional jets were sent to Šiauliai during the 2014–2015 Ukraine crisis, including 10 American F-15 fighter planes. Pledging to raise its defense spending from just 0.8% of GDP, the government decided to create its own 2,500-soldier rapid-reaction force "to buy some time until NATO can get here." A small NATO "forward presence" of 1,200 German and other troops was stationed inland.

Although Russia had grudgingly accepted NATO's eastward enlargement, its leaders were furious about the deployments and denounced them. Russian politician Vladimir Zhirinovsky even warned that the Baltic capitals would be the first bombing targets on Russia's list if there were ever a confrontation with the US. The largest Russian TV channel in Lithuania, ORT, which is under direct Kremlin control, aired a show on August 31, 2004, questioning the historical grounds of Lithuania's independence. It specifically accused Lithuanians of collaborating with the Nazi regime. In 2005 the Russian ambassador in Vilnius called Lithuania a "nation of scandal-mongers," where "everyone is dirty." In 2014 Moscow spoke about reopening criminal investigations against Lithuanians who refused to serve in the Soviet army after Lithuania's independence in 1990.

Two weeks after the Lithuanian government outlawed the display of Soviet symbols, Russian hackers attacked about 300 Lithuanian websites, including those of government agencies, political parties, and businesses. They littered them with Soviet symbols like hammers and sickles and five-pointed stars, as well as anti-Lithuanian slogans and profanities. It is this kind of rough behavior that prompts Lithuania to take a tough line when the EU talks about improving ties with Russia.

Such bellicose and insulting talk merely enhances the Balts' comfort and pride in joining the Atlantic alliance. Some even compared the welcomed roar of the F-16s' engines to the rumble of Soviet tanks that rolled into Vilnius in January 1990. Colonel Edvardas Mažeikis, Siauliai base commander, said it this way: "For us, history is close. We are in a very dangerous place. All through our history, war has passed through here, from Napoleon to the Nazis to the Soviets. Lithuania is a very good place for tanks. That's why collective security is so important to us."

Adamkus placed a greater emphasis on Lithuania's joining the EU, a position also endorsed by his predecessors and successor in the presidency. Formal entry occurred in May 2004, following a successful referendum in May 2003, when Lithuania became the first former Soviet republic to vote itself into the EU. Virtually every party supported EU entry.

In the second half of 2013, Lithuania became the first ex-Soviet republic to assume the rotating EU presidency. To ensure that his cabinet team could represent the country well on the European stage, Prime Minister Butkevičius required each minister to be fluent in English, French, or German. It was in this capacity that Lithuania hosted the EU summit in November 2013 that offered six former Soviet states trade and association agreements. The crisis in Ukraine and the subsequent annexation of Crimea by Russia in March 2014 grew

Lithuania

out of President Vladmir Putin's rejection of this link with the west. In January 2014 Lithuania began a two-year term on the UN Security Council.

In order to polish the country's international image as a prelude to admission to the EU, the Lithuanian parliament passed a law in 2000 enabling trials of former Nazi collaborators to take place even if the individual is too old and weak to attend the proceedings, as long as the charges are for genocide and war crimes. During the German occupation of the Baltic states from 1941 to 1944, some Balts had participated in the eradication of 99% of the 300,000 Jews who lived in the three republics; of Lithuania's prewar Jewish population of 235,000, only 9,000 remain.

Kaliningrad

Lithuania has no land disputes with its neighbors (Belarus, Poland, and the Russian exclave of Kaliningrad). Its major dispute with Russia was Russian transit rights for its military forces in Kaliningrad. Earlier post-Soviet Lithuanian foreign policy had tended to be confrontational toward Russia. This was partly because of the continuing presence of Russian troops after Lithuania reestablished its independence in 1991. With the election of President Brazauskas in 1993, there was a significant change in foreign policy. During the campaign, he had pledged himself to work for a closer working relationship with Russia, particularly in the economic area, and in general he succeeded. He also managed to negotiate an agreement with Russia, whereby it agreed to remove the last of its troops by September 1993. Lithuania was thus the first of the Baltic republics to be totally free of Russian troops.

It refused to grant Russia a corridor for transporting Russian troops to and from Kaliningrad. However, it accepted an informal agreement in 1991 to allow Russian troops to cross Lithuania by rail only, with a maximum of 180 soldiers on any one train and their weapons in a separate car. Lithuanian soldiers could inspect these rail transports to ensure that these stipulations are being followed. This agreement was renewed on a year- by-year basis until 2003.

Lithuania's invitation in 2002 to join the EU necessitated a new transit agreement for the 950,000 Russians living in the Kaliningrad exclave who want to travel to Russia through Lithuania. Russian president Vladimir Putin had warned of a new "Berlin Wall" around Russian citizens. Since July 2003 they can receive a "facilitated-transit document" (STD), which is basically a simplified multiple-entry visa valid for three years. It costs only €5. Visa holders can travel through Lithuania either by train or by automobile, and they

have 24 hours to complete their transit. The Lithuanian government opened a second consulate within the Kaliningrad oblast in the city of Sovetsk to deal primarily with Russians living in the eastern part of the exclave. To circumvent the visa requirement, many more Russians fly to and from Kaliningrad.

Both countries are studying the possibility of a high-speed, nonstop train link connecting Kaliningrad and the Russian mainland. The travel compromise was linked to the Russian Duma's ratification in May 2003 of the Lithuania-Russia border treaty that had been signed in October 1997. This included the land border, the exclusive economic zone, and the continental shelf in the Baltic Sea.

The Kaliningrad region depends upon Lithuania and Poland to provide for many of the daily needs of its residents. They are the chief foreign investors, and foodstuffs, clothing, furniture, and other consumer goods from these two countries are prominent in stores; 80% of its electricity comes from Lithuania. Russia worries about the exclave becoming an energy island without power, as Lithuania and the other Baltic states integrate their power grids with Sweden and the rest of Europe. It is therefore building a nuclear power plant only 6 miles (10 km) inside the Kaliningrad region and is financing another one in Belarus, only 25 miles upriver from Vilnius. Lithuanians are furious about being squeezed in between two atomic plants, and they are concerned about the reactors' safety.

Lithuania's communist leader, Antanas Sniečkus, had wisely refused an offer made in the 1950s by Soviet party chief Nikita Khrushchev that Lithuania takes control of the Kaliningrad region. Sniečkus feared that his republic would invite the same problems with a large Russian minority that were mounting in Latvia and Estonia. Nevertheless, having lived within the USSR for a half-century, Lithuanians are particularly familiar with Soviet behavior and mentality and can collaborate with Kaliningraders even more effectively than can Poles. Nevertheless, Lithuanian public opinion was incensed in November 2008, when Moscow threatened to deploy missiles in Kaliningrad; it made good on that threat by 2016.

ECONOMY

Until it cooled down in 2008, the Lithuanian economy had been growing at a blistering pace: by 9.7% in 2003, 7% in 2004–2005, and 8% in 2006–2007. In 2010 it was .4%, after having fallen to –14.8% the year before. In 2023, growth was –0.3%. Lithuania felt the full force of the global economic downturn. It was particularly hard

hit because sales to its largest export partner, Russia, were reduced by half in 2009. The economy contracted by 22% in 2009. Lithuania's growth was stunted at least in part due to a massive outflow of people to other EU members, including many young and energetic potential contributors to its economy. Because 1 million Lithuanians emigrated after 1990, more than 10% of the country's working-age population live in another EU country.

Its currency, the litas, was also under severe attack. However, the government was determined to keep it pegged to the euro and to continue its bid to adopt the European currency by middecade. Unemployment leapt to 13% in 2012, while corporate taxes were raised from 15% to 20% and the VAT from 18% to 21%. The budget deficit ballooned to 9.5% in 2010. The real estate bubble burst, leaving many Lithuanians holding mortgages denominated in foreign currencies for property worth far less than earlier. The country faced several painful years as it tried to regain competitiveness.

But the economy is rebounding. The growth rate in 2021 was a hardy 3.8%, among the best in the EU. Unemployment was heading downward in 2015 to 9%. By 2018 the economy was doing well. Living standards rose from half the EU average in 2014 to three-quarters.

Lithuania is the least industrialized of the Baltic republics. However, the fact that 66% of its workforce is in the services sector, which produces 68% of the GDP, indicates that it has an increasingly modern economy. Industry, including mining, employs 25% of the people and produces 28% of GDP. It is clearly no longer a predominantly agricultural country: Agricultural employment has fallen to 9% of the workforce, creating 4% of the GDP.

Most of Lithuania's industry is located in or near its major cities. Kaunas, Lithuania's second-largest city, has metal and woodworking industries, as well as light and food industries. Kleipeda, Lithuania's third-largest city and its major seaport, is the largest ice-free port in the Baltic area and a major hub for trade between Scandinavia, western Europe, and eastern Europe. It is home to a large deep-sea fishing fleet, and it has one of the largest shipyards in the Baltic. The main local industry is fish processing. The town also has a pulp and paper mill, a woodworking factory, and textile mills, plus a large plant that manufactures radios and telephones. In addition, it is a traditional center for the working of amber. Vilnius, Lithuania's largest city and its capital, is a center for computer manufacturing, machine tools, electric meters, drills, farm machinery, building materials, and food processing.

There is also a small amount of industry located in smaller towns.

Forestry products are another source of income for persons residing in the countryside. With approximately 25% of the land covered by trees, Lithuania produces both timber and pulpwood, and wood is its main export. There are also considerable deposits of peat, plus materials used in construction, such as limestone, chalk, dolomite, clays, and gravel, whose exploitation provides additional jobs in the countryside.

Before 1991 about 55% of Lithuania's exports went to other parts of the Soviet Union. Negotiations with Russia and some of the other republics extended those arrangements. But post-independence Lithuanian governments have been committed to reorienting Lithuania's trade more toward the West. Currently 60.5% of its exports and 57.6% of its imports go to and come from the EU. Many farmers receive agricultural subsidies from the EU. Lithuania joined the World Trade Organization (WTO) in 2001, with the US leading the WTO accession negotiations.

Approximately one-third of the republic's industrial workers work in engineering or metal-working factories created during the Soviet period. Built to serve customers located mainly in the other republics, they were particularly hard-pressed in the first three or so years of independence, but they are doing much better today.

In 1993, Lithuania began issuing its own permanent currency, the litas, to replace the talon, an interim coupon issued after independence. Immediately upon entering the EU in May 2004, its government announced that it would move quickly to join the eurozone. Prime Minister Butkevičius swore he would resign if his

Lithuanian student reading this book

country did not adopt the euro in January 2015, which it did.

The government began a program of general privatization, which was largely implemented by the end of 1996. In 1998 it completed one of the biggest privatizations in eastern Europe, selling off 60% of Telekomas, the country's fixed-line telecoms monopoly. At the end of the century, it confidently turned its privatization efforts to shipping and ship repair, oil refining, gasoline station networks, and television and radio.

Investment is pouring into the port of Klaipeda, a free economic zone catering to much of the former Soviet Union. From 1995 to 1999, its cumulative foreign direct investment doubled every year, with the US as the leading source. In 2004 it attracted €55 of foreign direct investment (FDI) per capita, less than half what Estonia received but slightly more than Latvia. Unemployment was declining due to the approximately 450,000 Lithuanians (a tenth of the population) who had left to work abroad. This is a worrisome brain drain that has caused labor shortages in certain sectors of the economy.

A major impediment to entry into the EU had been the Soviet-era Ignalina nuclear power plant, which once supplied 80% of the country's electricity. With promises of EU financial support, Lithuania shut down the first plant in 2004. It pledged to decommission by the end of 2009 the safer and more modern second reactor, which produced three-fourths of the country's electricity and provided enough to export to neighboring countries. Polls indicated that 70% of the population would have liked to postpone the shutdown. In a 2009 referendum, 90% voted for such delay, but the low turnout invalidated the result. Therefore a few hours before midnight on New Year's Eve 2009, the reactor was shut down.

This loss of its main electricity source came at a bad time. It drove electricity prices up by 30%. It also meant that Lithuania is now a net importer rather than exporter of energy. It became totally dependent upon Russian gas and oil. Ex-prime minister Kubilius warned that this made Lithuania "very sensitive to anything that happens on Russia's borders."

To minimize that risk, Lithuania negotiated with the other two Baltic states and Poland to construct a modern 3,200-megawatt nuclear power station at the Ignalina site. Difficult technical and ownership issues must be worked out. Vilnius complicated the talks by passing a law in 2006 calling for Lithuania to have a 34% share in the plant and each of the other three only 22% apiece. The new plant would start producing electricity in 2018 at the earliest. In 2012 the government caused consternation in Latvia and Lithuania by

announcing that it had no intention of building a nuclear power plant in Visaginas in eastern Lithuania, which could have supplied power to all three Baltic states. Cooperation on the station came to a halt.

It also began in 2010 to construct a new undersea cable between Sweden and the Baltic states to draw energy from the Swedish grid by 2016. The cable, NordBalt, was officially inaugurated on December 14, 2015. However, due to a fire near the Nybro substation, test transmission with a capacity of 30 MW started only on February 1, 2016. A similar power cable is planned with Poland. The Polish-Lithuanian Harmony Link power interconnection will be built on land and will run alongside the European standard-gauge railway Rail Baltica. Lithuania has set an ambition to increase the generation of electricity from renewable sources to 70% of total domestic electricity consumption by 2030 and 100% by 2045 and is currently planning to advance the targets even further.

Lithuania's largest oil refinery, ORLEN Lietuva in Mažeikiai, dominates the country's gasoline supply and contributes a tenth of its GDP. The 2006 sale of control of it to a Polish company, PKN Orlen, was an effort to protect its largest industrial enterprise from the Russians. Russia promptly closed the sole pipeline that supplies the refinery in order to force the Lithuanians to reconsider the sale. It was never reopened. The only thing the country could do in retaliation was to veto EU negotiations with Moscow in 2007.

Ex-president Adamkus suggested only half seriously that the only Russian railroad supplying Kaliningrad runs through Lithuania and could perhaps be shut for what the Lithuanian media termed "political repairs." That did not happen. But it became necessary for Mažeikiai to bring in more expensive crude oil by ship. In order to try to reduce its dependency on Russia, Lithuania agreed to form a consortium with Ukraine, Poland, Georgia, and Azerbaijan to extend the Odessa-Brody pipeline through Ukraine as far as Gdansk in Poland. It is uncertain whether the extension will ever be built.

Oil had become a key symbol of the country's independence since the Soviets had shut off its pipeline to Mažeikiai in 1990 after Lithuania became free. With this memory in mind, the Lithuanian state invested $300 million to construct a Baltic Sea tanker terminal in order to have an alternative to Russian crude oil. Lithuania showed in 2004 that it feared dependency even on smaller Estonia by resisting efforts of Eesti Energia, the state-owned electricity company, to buy in 10 years all or part of Lithuania's electricity-distribution industry. Part of Lithuania's electrical infrastructure is controlled from Russia.

Lithuania

In an attempt to break Gazprom's stranglehold on the natural gas Lithuania needs, a South Korean ship anchored in the port of Klaipeda was leased, with an option to buy in. It can process deliveries of liquefied natural gas into fuel. The vessel is appropriately named Independence. This ship can process half of the country's needs from friendly countries like Norway. This blunts Russia's energy weapon. President Grybauskaite proclaimed that "we are now an energy-secure state." Gazprom charges Lithuania 30% more for gas than it does the average European customer, an issue the EU has been pressuring Gazprom to address. The country has no natural gas storage capacity and very few hydropower resources. Unlike Estonia, it does not use oil shale.

In 2022, Lithuania became the first EU country to cut off Russian gas supplies completely, followed by Estonia and Latvia.

In 2015, Lithuania, Poland, and the EU signed a trilateral agreement on financing a gas link between Poland and Lithuania, GIPL. Later that year, the LitPol electricity link was launched, allowing 1,000 megawatt transfers from the European synchronous grid. Lithuania is also considering linking with Sweden's electrical grid.

Russia's sanctions against EU agribusiness, combined with the massive decline in Russian demand due to lower oil prices, reduced Lithuania's growth to around 2.5% in 2015 (from 2.9% in 2014). Some exports collapsed completely, including especially dairy products that Russia banned. As a result, milk prices collapsed in Lithuania, prompting angry protests by farmers, who demand the government's intervention.

CULTURE

Lithuanian belongs to the Letto-Lithuanian family of Indo-European languages. It is often cited as the oldest Indo-European language still spoken and maintains many of its ancient characteristics. It is closely related to Latvian and contains some influences from the Polish language. Lithuanians, mentioned in Tacitus's *Germania* as excellent farmers, have occupied the southern shores of the Baltic for over 2,000 years. A dynastic union with Poland in the 14th century brought a polonization of the Lithuanian upper classes. Russian influence began in the 18th century, when Lithuania became part of the Russian Empire.

Lithuanian culture was essentially a rural, peasant one until the end of the 19th century. After that, it developed an urban culture, based on the rising professional and middle classes, though the population of most Lithuanian cities remained largely non-Lithuanian until the latter part of the 20th century. Vilnius, the capital and largest city, continues to have a large Polish population. It was, in fact, part of Poland until 1939 and only became Lithuanian shortly before Lithuania itself was incorporated into the Soviet Union. In one sense, then, Kaunas, the second city and the capital of Lithuania during the interwar period, is more Lithuanian than Vilnius.

Vilnius has Gediminas Castle, the fortress-residence of the Grand Dukes of Lithuania, the Gothic Church of St. Anne that dates from the 14th century, the university building in the oldest part of the city, and the "Medininku vartai" ("The Gates of the Dawn"), all that is left of the nine gates in the former wall that surrounded the city when it was the capital of the Grand Duchy. There are also some houses that date from the 15th to the 17th centuries. But the city became polonized after the union with Poland in 1569. Vilnius University, the republic's greatest center of learning, was originally founded in 1579, but the Russian government closed it in 1832. When it reopened in 1919, Vilnius was part of Poland, so a new school, the University of Lithuania, was located in Kaunas until after World War II. Vilnius is home to the Lithuanian State Opera and Ballet Company and to

numerous drama theaters, as well as the republic's main philharmonic orchestra.

Kaunas also has its own philharmonic orchestra and numerous theaters, though it lacks an opera and ballet company. It has numerous churches and museums. There are five institutes of higher education in the city, including a medical college. Another is Kaunas's Technological University, founded in 1951 after the university was shifted to Vilnius. A number of scientific research institutes are situated in Kaunas.

The foundation of Hungarian-born American billionaire George Soros has expended $65 million in Lithuania to support research, scholarships, book translations, school texts, and such social actions as fighting AIDS and drug addiction. Nevertheless, in 2005 the maverick Labor Party began to attack him through the leading tabloid, *Respublika*, as an evil foreign meddler involved in "financial schemes and networks." Many of the best-known intellectuals published an open letter demanding that the tabloid cease its "destructive attacks."

Literature

Although the Lithuanian people had a strong oral folklorist tradition, a written literature was rather late in developing. In fact, the first book published in the Lithuanian language was a religious text, *Katekizmas* (Catechism) of Mikalojus Dauksa, which appeared in 1595. The religious controversy associated with the Reformation led to the translation of the *Bible* into Lithuanian in 1590. As a result of the triumph of Catholicism in Poland-Lithuania, it was never published but remained in manuscript form in the library of Königsberg University (now in Kaliningrad in Russia). The Jesuits, who were primarily responsible for the triumph of Catholicism, did produce several publications in Lithuanian, including a catechism, a collection of sermons, and a dictionary, the latter published in 1629.

The first example of secular literature in the Lithuanian language, a translation of 10 of Aesop's fables, appeared in 1706. The first Lithuanian author, the poet Kristijonas Donelaitis, lived in the 18th century, though his epic poem, *The Seasons*, circulated only in manuscript form during his lifetime and was not published until 1818. Donelaitis was a Protestant pastor in the town of Tolminkiemis, and parts of his poem appear to be paraphrases of his sermons. Yet the poem also presents a realistic portrayal of the life of the peasants, at that time still struggling serfs. The German poet Goethe, who was familiar with the poem, compared Donelaitis to Homer.

A second poet, Antanas Baranauskas, who lived and wrote in the 19th century, had a background similar to that of Donelaitis in that he also followed a religious avocation and in later life became the Catholic bishop in Seinai (Sejny). Baranauskas wrote his poems during his youth before being ordained as a priest. His most important poem, written during summer vacations at home in 1858–1859, was "The Forest of Anyksciai." Baranauskas projects a mystic oneness with nature that is almost pagan in its orientation:

Forest and peasant knew no discord,
Grew up together, aged in accord.
To the Lithuanian, caveman of yore,
The forest gave a strong wooden door;
And since he never would hew the wood,
Till aged it fell, the dry trees still stood.

Lithuania became a part of the Russian Empire at the end of the 18th century, along with parts of eastern Poland. At that time, there was no separate Lithuanian nationalism, but Lithuanians supported Polish attempts—in 1831 and again in 1863—to throw off the Russian yoke. As a result, the Russian government attempted to stamp out Polish-Lithuanian nationalism by Russifying the people and the culture. The University of Vilnius was closed after the 1831 uprising; then the Latin alphabet was replaced by the Cyrillic alphabet following the 1863 upheaval. These efforts to stamp out the local culture were unsuccessful.

Lithuanian political and cultural leaders arranged to have Lithuanian-language books and newspapers published in East Prussia, then smuggled them across the border. The first Lithuanian-language newspaper, Auszra (The Dawn), began publishing in Tilset (now Sovetsk) in 1883. In addition, increasing numbers of Lithuanians entered universities either in Russia or abroad and subsequently added their literary output to the stream. Jonas Maciulis Maironis studied at Kiev and St. Petersburg and later became a professor and a priest. His collection, *The Voices of Spring*, published in 1895, glorified the Lithuanian countryside. He also wrote ballads and satires and even a drama in verse, *The Death of Kestutis*, which was not published until 1921. Another dramatist, Vilius Storasta, who wrote under the name of Vydunas, produced *The Shadow of Ancestors* in 1908, *The Eternal Flame* in 1912, and *Bells of the Sea* in 1914. A fourth play, *The World on Fire*, appeared in 1928.

Vincas Krėvė-Mickevičius, another playwright, produced his first dramas before World War I, but his most important plays appeared in independent Lithuania. They include *Skirgaila* (1922), *On the Roads of Destiny* (1926), *The Death of Mindaugas*

(1930), and *The Son-in-Law* (1939). Kreve served for a short time as minister of foreign affairs in the Soviet-dominated government in 1940, then went into hiding before fleeing abroad. In 1947, he became a member of the faculty of the University of Pennsylvania and remained there until his death in 1954.

The second major figure of the period of Lithuanian independence was Vincas Mykolaitis, who wrote under the nom de plume of Putinas. Extremely versatile, Putinas, who was also an ordained priest, produced poetry, novels, and plays. His two best novels are probably the autobiographical trilogy *In the Shadow of Altars* and *The Crisis*, both written in the 1930s. Putinas, who died in 1967, continued to write after the Soviet occupation of the country in 1940, but these works, favorable to the new regime, are lesser works.

There is also a corpus of writings done by Lithuanians in emigration. Antanas Vaičiulaitis taught at several American universities after World War II, then joined the Voice of America. His books include three volumes of short stories, legends, and myths. Jurgis Gliauda, who also made his way to America after World War II, is the author of *House upon the Sand* (1951), *Ora pro nobis* (1952), and *The Sonata of Icarus*. Other writers in emigration include Nelė Mazalaitė, Alfonsas Sesplaukis, Henrikas Radauskas, and Stepas Zobarskas. The oldest continuously published Lithuanian newspaper, Draugas (Friend), is published in Chicago, where 100,000 still identify themselves as Lithuanian.

Vilnius became home to the European Humanities University (EHU). It had been founded in Minsk, Belarus, after the collapse of the Soviet Union to promote western-style teaching of philosophy, history and other humanities. After the Belarus government shut it down in 2004, it moved across the border. It now serves as a haven of free inquiry for some 1,500 mostly Belarusian students, about half of them online.

A worrisome development in Lithuania is its suicide and murder rate that is the fourth highest in the world and the highest in the EU. 28.2 per 100,000 people for both sexes, 51 for males, and 8.4 for females. Also, Lithuania's drug overdose mortality rate is more than double the EU average, with 44.4 cases per million compared to the EU average of 19.2. Lithuania is one of the biggest producers of methamphetamine in Europe; this drug is the most common culprit in the death cases.

CURRENT ISSUES

Like the other two Baltic states, Lithuania entered the 21st century with some

Lithuania

major challenges. For the sake of its prosperity and security, it sought economic and military integration with the west. It joined NATO in April 2004. Its need for the security that such integration might provide stems from the long-standing Russian claim to predominance over the nations on its periphery.

Lithuania's greater ethnic unity and the strong unifying role of the Roman Catholic Church help stabilize the country. It has shown that it can have many peaceful changes of government. The government pursued austerity policies to bring the country out of the deep recession. Their measures are working after several painful years. In 2021, the economy grew by 3.9%, one of the highest in Europe, and unemployment shrank to 9% in 2015. Government debt is among the lowest in the EU, and its budget deficit has fallen to 2.7% of GDP.

Adoption of the euro in 2015 has benefited Lithuania's economy. Within a year, it strengthened the real estate market and put housing construction at an all-time high. Real wages grew by 5%, as did retail trade, and domestic consumption is rapidly rising. It helped improve business and consumer confidence. Now, according to Foreign Policy magazine's baseline profitability index 2015, Lithuania, together with Estonia, were ranked the second-best place to invest in Europe, after Poland. In a welcome reversal, more Lithuanians returned home than left the country in 2017.

Britain's exit from the European Union is not welcomed in Lithuania, and the future treatment of Lithuanians residing in the UK remains a great concern and a sore spot.

When in 2017, as the country was preparing for the centenary celebration of declaring its independence on February 16, 1918, the nation's spirits were lifted upon a discovery of its long-lost declaration of independence. With the declaration discovered in German archives, Ex President Grybauskaite exclaimed, "We now have the best gift, the best monument to our centenary."

Like its fellow Baltic countries, Lithuania has become one of the most outspoken defenders of liberal democracy and dissidents. To protest China's deplorable treatment of its Uyghur minority, it allowed a Taiwanese trade office to open in 2021. China's leaders were furious. They imposed on Lithuania the most sweeping sanctions any country has faced for upsetting Beijing. Only 1% of Lithuania's exports are to China, and China has little investment in Lithuania.

The country's long-term goals—raising a low birth rate, lowering emigration, and strengthening ties with NATO and the EU—remain.

Kaliningrad Oblast (Russia) (Калининградская область)

University where philosopher Immanuel Kant taught

Country: Kaliningrad Oblast is a semi-exclave; the westernmost federal district of the Russian Federation.

Area: 5,840 sq. mi. (15,125 sq. km.)

Population: 1,029,966 (2021 census)

Administrative center: Kaliningrad (pop. 498,260). (2021 census)

Climate: It is a temperate climate gradually transitioning from oceanic (maritime) to humid continental depending on distance from the Baltic Sea. It has very mild winters, above freezing, and cool summers.

Source: *The Economist*

Neighboring countries: Lithuania (northeast), Poland (south).

Official language: Russian

Other languages: German

Ethnic Background: 78.6% Russians, 1.2% Ukrainians, 1.1% Belarusians, 0.8% Armenians, 0.4% Lithuanians, 0.4% Germans, 17.5 Others (Tatars, Uzbeks, Azeris, Poles, Tajiks, others and unidentified). (2021 census)

Religion: Christianity (30.9% Russian Orthodox, 0.5% Other Orthodox, 1% Catholic, 1.7% Other Christian). 10.3% Other and undeclared, 34% Spiritual but not religious, 21.6% Atheism. (2012)

Form of Government: The top permanent executive authority, formed by the Governor of the Kaliningrad Region.

Governor: Anton Alikhanov (since September 2017)

Public Holiday: February 23 (Defender of the Fatherland Day)

National Flag: It consists of three horizontal stripes—red, yellow and dark blue. The upper red stripe has in the canton a silver-and-black stylized medieval castle with open gates and the monogram of Empress Elizabeth Petrovna (under which reign parts of the region were shortly under Russian control during the Seven Years' War). A thin (1/3 of the upper strip) yellow stripe is in the middle and a dark blue stripe of the same size as the red one is at the bottom. There is no an official statement what the colors stand for. Nevertheless, there were informal interpretation in the Russian press that the silver fortress with open gates stands for hospitality, the dark blue color for the Baltic Sea and tranquility, the yellow for the wealth of amber and the red for active man principle. Other interpretations hold that the red stands for the belligerent past of Prussia, the Red Army, the Hanseatic League, or the historical connections with Brandenburg and Poland. It was only in 2006 that the law about the flag and the coat of arms went into effect. Before that Kaliningrad Region had no flag.

Currency: Ruble (RUB)

Main Exports: food products and agricultural raw materials, mineral products and metals.

Main Imports: machinery, equipment and vehicles (48.6%), foodstuffs and agricultural raw materials.

Main Trading Partners: Belarus (20,4 of exports and 5,42 of imports), Germany (3,22 of exports and 5,57 of imports), Egypt (18,7 of exports), Norway (14,2 of exports), Algeria (9,94 of exports), Lithuania (5,81 of exports), Netherlands (4,67 of exports), Finland (2,95 of exports), Poland (2,8 of exports), South Korea (27,6 of imports), China (9,73 of imports), Paraguay (6,54 of imports), Brazil (8,15 of imports), Slovakia (6,37 of imports), US (5,62 of imports), Argentina (2,53 of imports). (2021, 2022)

The Kaliningrad oblast (Russian region) is the northern half of the former East Prussia; the southern rest went to Poland after World War II. Renamed in 1946 after a former president of the USSR, Mikhail Kalinin, who never set foot in the area, it contains the earlier German city of Königsberg, founded in 1255 as a fortress of the Teutonic Knights. It joined the Hanseatic League in 1340, and in 1457 it became the seat of the Teutonic Order's grand master after the knights had lost Marienburg to Poland. From 1525 until the union of Brandenburg and Prussia in 1618, it was the residence of the dukes of Prussia, and in 1701 it became the coronation city of the Prussian kings. It was there that the philosophical giant, Immanuel Kant, had lived and worked from 1724 to 1804.

In World War II, it was the scene of determined German defense against the Red Army that was driving westward to conquer Germany. The furious warfare left the city devastated, and the Soviet Union

Abandoned and unfinished House of Soviets, Communist Party building.

Kaliningrad (Russia)

made no effort to rebuild Königsberg in its former style. It demolished the ruins of the old castle. On its site Soviet officials began to construct a municipal city and Communist Party administration building, the House of Soviets, that is still empty.

Before the war the city was admired for its architecture, wealth, and culture. East Prussia was a breadbasket for all of Germany. After the war, all 1.2 million German citizens were expelled, and the region became a Soviet garrison and deployment area for the Soviet naval, land, and missile forces. It was closed to outsiders from 1948 to 1992. Some of its skilled labor force produced or serviced advanced weapons systems during the communist era. A fifth of its workforce is still paid by the military.

The number of soldiers has dramatically diminished to 24,000 (US estimate) or 40,000 (Polish estimate), roughly a tenth of the 1991 strength. A Soviet space mission control center was located there. While Moscow still has 66 Lenin statues standing, only one remains in Kaliningrad—on Victory Square, earlier Hansa Square, renamed Hitler Square in 1933. Its agriculture declined so far that the oblast must import food to support its residents.

The Post-Soviet Era

After the Baltic states gained their independence in 1991 and the Soviet Union collapsed a year later, Kaliningrad became a Russian exclave that continues to belong to the Russian Federation. But it is separated from the rest of Russia by independent Lithuania and Belarus. This 65-km Suwalki Gap is one of NATO's most vulnerable points. If Russia seized this Polish-Lithuanian border strip, the Baltics would be cut off from NATO. This heavily militarized enclave is home to Russia's Baltic fleet. It can launch missiles, including nuclear Iskander ballistic missiles. It has threatened to end the region's non-nuclear status. Its over 1 million people increasingly call themselves "Euro-Russians" and travel to nearby Warsaw (280 kilometers away in Poland) and Vilnius (195 kilometers away in Lithuania) much more often than to St. Petersburg or Moscow. One survey in 2002 found that 80% of its youth under age 25 had traveled in western Europe (including Poland), while only 15% had been in other parts of Russia.

Although Lithuania has no land dispute with Russia over Kaliningrad, a sensitive issue existed concerning Russian transit rights for its military forces in Kaliningrad. An informal agreement was reached in 1991 to allow Russian troops to cross Lithuania by rail only, with a maximum of 180 soldiers on any one train and their weapons in a separate car. Lithuanian soldiers can inspect these rail transports to ensure

that these stipulations are being followed. This agreement is renewed on a year-by-year basis. The trickiest place to defend in all of NATO is a choke point called Suwalki Gap, the 40-mile Lithuanian-Polish corridor between Kaliningrad and Russia-friendly Belarus. It is the Balts' only land link to the rest of Europe, and the single rail line is the Russian gauge. Currently, Rail Baltica is a new high-speed railway under construction that will run through the Suwałki Gap to connect Warsaw and the three Baltic capitals with each other. This EU-funded project, first envisioned in the 1990s, is scheduled to be completed by 2030. Crucially, this Rail Baltica is being built in Standard, not Russian Gauge, which will make it the only major railway of Standard Gauge in the Baltic States.

When Lithuania joined the EU in May 2004, a new transit agreement was needed for the 950,000 Russians living in the Kaliningrad exclave who want to travel to Russia through Lithuania. Russian president Vladimir Putin had warned of a new "Berlin Wall" around Russian citizens. He called the issue a "litmus test" for Russia-EU relations and warned of a "blue curtain," referring to the color of the EU flag.

Neither Poland nor Lithuania would hear of "corridors" across their territory. In the words of former Polish president Aleksander Kwasniewski, "talk about corridors takes us back in history to the start of World War II, which began with demands from Hitler's Germany to enjoy free access to Danzig across Poland." The EU had never made any exceptions to its requirement for a strict visa regime toward nonmembers, and it clearly did not relish the idea of having a criminal haven located inside the EU, with no control over its borders.

An agreement was reached. Since July 2003 Kaliningrad residents can receive a "facilitated-transit document" at the cost of €5, which is basically a simplified multiple-entry visa valid for three years. Visa holders can travel through Lithuania either by train or by automobile, and they have 24 hours to complete their transit. Those residents wanting to travel elsewhere, including to Lithuania or Poland, must pay €35, present a work ID or invitation, and wait 10 days to receive their visa. The Lithuanian government opened a second consulate within the Kaliningrad oblast in the city of Sovetsk to deal primarily with Russians living in the eastern part of the region.

To circumvent the visa requirement, many more Russians fly to and from Kaliningrad; nine daily flights connect it with Moscow. The government has modernized Khrabrovo Airport and constructed one of the most modern air traffic control

systems in the hope of making the airport a hub for air travel between Europe and Russia. Both countries are studying the possibility of a high-speed, nonstop train link connecting Kaliningrad and the Russian mainland. The travel compromise was linked to the Russian Duma's ratification in May 2003 of the Lithuania-Russia border treaty that had been signed in October 1997. This included the land border, the exclusive economic zone, and the continental shelf in the Baltic Sea.

Kaliningrad's strategic importance for Moscow was enhanced by Russia's weakened position in the Baltic area and by the fact that Kaliningrad is Russia's only warmwater port in the Baltic Sea. It remains home to the Russian Baltic fleet. Russia hopes to find a way someday of transforming the region into a trade window open both to the west and the east. Russia has already begun building a terminal at Baltisk (formerly Pillau) for large cruise boats traveling to St. Petersburg, Scandinavia, and Germany. Some routes of the old "Reich Road One," called "Berlinka," have been improved and incorporated into a major inter-state highway connection to the Via Baltica. The road that leads to Poland has also improved.

Moscow worries about the fact that the exclave is located about 250 miles from the rest of Russia and borders on Poland, which was admitted to NATO in 1999, and Lithuania, which entered in 2004. Many in Russia, especially in the military and security agencies, regard Kaliningrad as a precious war trophy and military bastion that must be protected from outside interference. That is why it teems with nuclear-capable missiles and other weaponry.

Relations with Germany

From 5,000 to 15,000 of the approximately 2 million Russians of German heritage (Volksdeutsche) remaining in Russia were permitted to resettle after 1990 in Kaliningrad. From 60% to 70% of these Germans later emigrated to Germany. The exclave has 950,000 residents, 435,000 of whom live in the city of Kaliningrad. The overwhelming majority (80%) is Russian; the rest come from various parts of the former Soviet Union. By 1994 there were also as many as 100,000 military forces, many left there after the Soviet Army withdrew from Poland, the Baltic states, and eastern Germany. At the time of the Two-Plus-Four Agreement, which unified Germany in 1990, Germany unmistakably emphasized that it makes no territorial claims to Kaliningrad.

In fact, about the only German involvement today is the brisk trade of German tourists. Approximately 40% of the 100,000 tourists who visit annually are German. In

Kaliningrad (Russia)

2004 the direct rail connection with Berlin, the Königsberg Express, was restored after three years of inactivity. Since 2007 the rail ferry Vilnius provides the first nonstop ship connection from Sassnitz-Mukran in Germany to Kaliningrad's Baltijsk port.

It is a reassuring signal to Russia that Germany shows little political interest in and makes no claims to Kaliningrad. Former Russian president Boris Yeltsin had felt it necessary to declare during an election visit to the exclave in 1996 that the "Kaliningrad Oblast is Russian soil. Nobody should have any doubts about that." Germany has supported multilateral European efforts to stimulate economic development and the creation of a special economic zone. It created a "German-Russian House" in 1997 to help coordinate cultural and economic exchanges. In 2001 1,000 Russians were learning German there, and 600 were getting training in manual trades.

Germany's request to establish a German consulate was refused until 2004. In 2002 Russia permitted the first western country to open a consulate: Sweden. This was followed by two Lithuanian consulates in Kaliningrad and Sovetsk. By 2005 Denmark and Poland had opened consulates, with more to follow. Moscow jealously guards its own authority to establish taxes and approve joint ventures. It even requires all outgoing mail to be processed first in Moscow.

Political Situation

No foreign government makes any claim to the territory, and there is no internal support for separation from Russia. Germany renounced any demands in the 1990 treaty of German reunification, and Poland has also signed treaties with both Russia and Germany abjuring any territorial claims against either country. A few right-wing Lithuanian politicians still contend that parts of Kaliningrad, roughly those parts between the Pregel and Nemunas Rivers, should belong to Lithuania, but their views carry little weight. This was obvious when the country signed border treaties with Russia in 1991 and 1997 and an agreement of cooperation in 1999. The Lithuanian government is aware that its country received a significant portion of East Prussia after World War II, namely the former Memel (with the port city of Klaipeda). Any suggestion that Lithuania should have part of Kaliningrad would be answered by Russian claims against present Lithuanian territory.

Washington's position since the 1945 Potsdam Conference is that the Soviet Union earlier and Russia today possess only administrative, not de jure, control of the region and that the question of its status remains to be decided. However, wishing to integrate Russia into the Euro-Atlantic community, the US government has shown no inclination to press this interpretation. It adopts a low-profile approach as an unassertive supporter, not leader, of western efforts to help the exclave.

Vladimir Putin asserted, "Kaliningrad will always remain Russian. This soil has become particularly near and dear to Russia." In 2005 he appointed a former tax minister and entrepreneur, Georgi Boos, as governor with orders to "organize the area like a German enterprise: everything must be effective." With Putin's backing, the energetic Boos made the exclave one of the most dynamic regions in Russia. The cathedral was restored, a Russian-Orthodox church was constructed, and a commitment was made to rebuild the royal castle, dynamited in 1969, at a cost of €100 million.

However, the falling standard of living, economic crisis, cut in subsidies, excessive bureaucracy, higher taxes, and autocratic rule by appointed governors and officials raised tensions to a breaking point in December 2009 and January 2010. An estimated 10,000 citizens, bearing buttons and signs reading "Putin resign" and "No Boos" poured twice into a central square to demand Boos's resignation. This forced the disliked governor to hold serious talks with opposition leaders for the first time. In a rare move, the Kremlin denied Boos a second term because he lacked public support. An opposition editor noted with regret, "There is the will to change something, but not the means to change anything. That is the problem. We have no say in anything."

Economy

The region has the potential for economic growth. Its people have the highest standard of living in Russia. It has a well-educated workforce, a deepwater harbor that is Russia's only warmwater port (although its deepest part remains off-limits for commercial trade), over 90% of the world's amber, rich farmland, modest crude oil reserves, and an industrial infrastructure that produces ships, machinery, food products, processed fish, and wood. However, despite the highest per-capital level of foreign direct investment in Russia, many investors are scared away by endemic corruption, powerful organized crime, a drug epidemic out of control, and Russia's highest HIV/AIDS infection rate.

Up to 70% of its GDP is generated by medium- and small-sized enterprises. There are over 2,000 joint ventures in Kaliningrad—400 Lithuanian, 360 German, and also American. Gas-guzzling Hummers are assembled in the region, as are KIA, BMW, and General Motors vehicles for the Russian market. The Chinese state company, Chery, which acquired Volvo from Ford in 2010, began its car assembly in the Kaliningrad factory in 2006.

Unemployment averages 10%–15% but it is over 50% in some areas. At least 10% of Kaliningrad's population works in the black market, which makes any statistics suspect. Because of the boom, however, these percentages are falling. Per capita GDP is more than one-third below the Russian average and even much farther below that of its neighbors. The average monthly pay is less than €250 ($310), but 4 in 10 live below the poverty line of $100 per month. Surprisingly, 1 in 3 residents owns a car, compared with 1 in 10 in the rest of Russia. Kaliningrad has Russia's highest crime rate; 2,000 homeless children survive from petty crime. The disastrously low level of health is shown by the fact that life expectancy for men is only 59, one of the lowest in the world; for women it is 71 years.

Until Poland and Lithuania joined the EU, citizens of Kaliningrad enjoyed visa-free travel there and were permitted to import goods duty-free that they could then resell in Russia. Thousands eked out a living by crossing the border with sacks full of cut-rate cigarettes, black-market CDs, and other wares to sell to their relatively prosperous neighbors. That had to stop once Poland and Lithuania were EU states.

Statue of Immanuel Kant at Kaliningrad University

Kaliningrad (Russia)

At least half of its commerce is transit trade to and from the Russian mainland, and its travel agreement with Lithuania in 2003 did not hinder that. This mixture of legal trade and smuggling has been a crucial benefit for the local economy. It is estimated that the underground economy accounts for 40%–60% of Kaliningrad's total trade. However, with Poland (its leading trading partner) and Lithuania in the European Union, the open borders slammed shut, and the exclave could become even poorer and more isolated than it is now.

The annexation of Crimea by Russia and consequent sanctions further complicated the lives of the locals. Russia retaliated by placing a ban on EU food imports, which affected people in Kaliningrad because of their reliance on EU imports.

A few months after the 2022 Russian invasion of Ukraine, Lithuania started implementing EU sanctions, which blocked about 50% of the goods being imported into Kaliningrad by rail. Food, medicine, and passenger travel were exempted. Russia protested against the sanctions and announced it would increase shipments by sea.

Located so far away from the rest of the Russian Federation, it must depend on its immediate neighbors, Lithuania and Poland, to provide for many of the daily needs of its over a million residents. They are the chief foreign investors, and foodstuffs, clothing, furniture, and other consumer goods from these two countries are prominent in stores; 80% of its electricity came from Lithuania until the Ignalina nuclear power plant was shut down in 2009. To prevent it from becoming an "energy island" without power, while Lithuania and the other Baltic states integrate their power grids with Sweden and the rest of Europe, Russia launched two new coal and gas powered power plants in 2018. The Pregolsky gas-powered plant was launched in 2019. With a capacity of 455.2 megawatts, it is the largest of five power plants Russia hopes will make Kaliningrad self-sufficient. Starting from 2025, the power system of the Kaliningrad oblast will switch to isolated operation due to withdrawal of the Baltic states from the common energy supply of IPS/UPS.

As a politically effective and economically profitable solution for Kaliningrad's gas independence, a floating vessel was built in the Far East, from where it was later shipped to Kaliningrad. In January 2019, Russian President Vladimir Putin visited Kaliningrad to take part in the launch of the "Marshal Vasilevsky" tanker that had come from Singapore in mid-December. Its total construction cost exceeded 300 million dollars. While visiting the Baltic exclave, Putin announced that gas supplies to the region could no longer be blocked by neighboring Lithuania. The terminal's overall capacity is expected to fully satisfy local demand.

This troublesome exclave needs outside help to prevent it from exporting its many problems to its neighbors and to deal with economic decline worse than in the rest of Russia. However, the worst economic problems are homegrown: the persistence of Soviet-era practices, corruption, and the Russian Duma's failure to pass laws to meet the concerns of foreign investors about the security of their ventures. All of these helped foil attempts to create a free economic zone (FEZ) in the oblast and put an end to any talk of it becoming a "gateway." But a "special economic zone" involving a preferential customs and tax regime was put in place and boosted the local economy. Still, Kaliningrad lost this special status on April 1, 2016, so it is now cut off from duty-free trade with EU member states. This affected over 700 local companies employing a quarter of the local workforce, with a direct impact on about one-third of the local population. Besides what has been described as "epic" levels of corruption and bribery, the local economy suffers from low productivity (5–20% of the German productivity levels), lack of qualified labor force, and low levels of foreign direct investment. EU sanctions cut off European bank loans for development there. In a telling twist, in 2016 the mayor of Yastarny placed an ad offering the small coastal city's town hall for sale as the only way to pay for municipal services.

The region's future remains uncertain. It depends on general developments in Russia proper. As Russia was shifting its focus to another outside region, Crimea, Kaliningrad residents worried that the special attention and funding that Russia used to give them may be switched to that area instead. Additionally, Russia focuses its attention on waging war it started with the invasion of Ukraine in February 2022. One shining gift to the exclave was an expensive new stadium used in the 2018 soccer World Cup hosted by Russia. With four new hotels, many hope for a boost in tourism.

CULTURE

In July 2005 the city celebrated its 750th anniversary, and this seems to have prodded Moscow to take a greater interest in it. Past attempts to polish up the city were only partially successful, although some streets were repaved, sidewalks improved, and concrete facades covered or painted. The German weekly news magazine *Der Spiegel* financed the digging out of the remaining walls of the razed castle, which became a sort of outdoor museum. There are now plans to rebuild it. Kaliningrad University was renovated and renamed Immanuel Kant University. In 2016, Russian state authorities demanded that Kaliningrad restore a decrepit 14th-century Teutonic Knights castle in Bagrationovsk (German: Preufiisch Eylau). The imposing structure was abandoned to squatters and graffiti artists and later partly destroyed in a fire when hopes for converting it into a hotel failed for lack of investors.

CURRENT ISSUES

Given the continued influence of nationalist voices in Russian domestic politics and Russia's concerns about NATO enlargement, it is unlikely that Kaliningrad's military status will change. Indeed, this very fact added urgency to the Polish and Baltic desire to join the Atlantic alliance. These concerns were greatly enhanced in late 2016, when the Russian government confirmed that it had deployed Iskander-M cruise missiles in Kaliningrad. With a maximum range of up to 440 miles and capable of carrying both conventional and nuclear payloads, they could carry out precise strikes against the three Baltic states and Poland and possibly even Berlin. Russia had used these missiles during its war against Georgia in 2008. It already had shorter-range Tochka missiles, as well as antiaircraft and antiship missiles in Kaliningrad. After NATO proceeded with ballistic missile defense in Romania, Poland, and Lithuania in 2016, Russia threatened to arm the Iskanders with nuclear warheads. Russia insists that the missiles cannot be removed from Kaliningrad while NATO missiles are still present in Europe.

The US demanded that Russia allow flights to pass through Kaliningrad's airspace for monitoring its military. Poland built six 50-meter-high watchtowers at Kaliningrad's border for round-the-clock surveillance. In 2017 Lithuania started building an 80-mile (130 km) fence along the border with Kaliningrad. The 6.5-foot-high fence would not be able to withstand a military attack but is intended to prevent smuggling as well as infiltration by military units.

Kaliningrad oblast finds itself increasingly isolated amid Russia's war in Ukraine as neighboring countries restrict its residents' movement and NATO adds new members.

Federal Republic of Germany (Bundesrepublik Deutschland)

DENMARK

NORTH SEA

BALTIC SEA

RUGEN

Kiel

SCHLESWIG-HOLSTEIN

Rostock

Wismar

MECKLENBURG-WESTERN POMERANIA

Lübeck

Hamburg

Schwerin

HAMBURG

Bremerhaven

Weser

Elbe

BREMEN

Bremen

POLAND

NETHERLANDS

LOWER SAXONY

BRANDENBURG

Hanover

Brandenburg

Berlin

Potsdam

Braunschweig

SAXONY-ANHALT

Munster

Dessau

Cottbus

NORTH RHINE-WESTPHALIA

Weser

Göttingen

Halle

Elbe

Dortmund

Leipzig

Meissen

Görlitz

Essen

Dresden

Düsseldorf

Weimar

SAXONY

Cologne (Köln)

Gotha

Jena

Chemnitz

Eisenach

Erfurt

Gera

Zwickau

Bonn

THURINGIA

Aachen

Rhein

Plauen

BELGIUM

HESSE

CZECH REP.

Frankfurt am Main

RHINELAND-PALATINATE

Wiesbaden

Mainz

LUX.

Main

Trier

Nürnberg

Kaiserslautern

BAVARIA

SAAR

Heidelberg

Regensburg

Saarbrücken

Karlsruhe

FRANCE

Stuttgart

Danube

BADEN-WÜRTTEMBERG

Ulm

Augsburg

Munich (München)

AUSTRIA

Freiburg

0   25   50   75 km

SWITZERLAND

Germany

Midnight, October 2–3, 1990: Unification, as throngs converge on Berlin's Brandenburg Gate, which for over 40 years symbolically divided east from west of the restored capital city of Germany

Area: 357,592 sq km (138,066 sq mi)

Population: 85,887,000 (2023 estimate)

Capital City: Berlin (official capital by parliamentary vote in June 1991, following German unification on October 3, 1990; pop. 3,850,809; urban 4,890,363, 2021 estimate).

Climate: It is temperate, ranging from oceanic (maritime) in the north and west to continental in the east and southeast. Winters range from the cold in the Southern Alps to cool, while summers can vary from hot and dry to cool and rainy. Westerly winds prevailing in the northern regions bring in moist air from the North Sea, moderating the temperature and increasing precipitation. The southeast regions have more extreme temperatures.

Neighboring Countries: France, Luxembourg, Belgium, the Netherlands (west); Denmark (north); Poland, the Czech Republic (east); Austria, Switzerland (south).

Official Language: German.

Other Languages: Recognized native minority languages are Danish, Low German, Low Rhenish, Sorbian, Romani, North Frisian and Saterland Frisian; The most used immigrant languages are Turkish, Arabic, Kurdish, Polish, Greek, Serbian, Croatian, Bulgarian and other Balkan languages, as well as Russian.

Ethnic Background: German 91.5%, Turkish 2.4%, other 6.1% (mainly Greek, Italian, Polish, Russian, Serb, Croat, Spanish).

Germany

Religion: Christianity (Protestant-Evangelical Lutheran, Roman Catholicism), Islam.

Form of Government: Federal parliamentary republic.

Chief of State: Frank-Walter Steinmeier, President (since March 2017, reelected February 2022).

Head of Government: Olaf Scholz, Chancellor (since December 2021).

National Flag: It is a tricolor design consisting of three equal horizontal bands of black at the top, red in the center, and gold at the bottom. Black, red, and gold are the national colors of Germany. In the period of German unification, after the wars of liberation in 1815, the colors were attributed to the black uniforms with red piping and golden buttons worn by the Lützow Volunteer Corps, which had taken part in the fight against Napoleon. The flag itself was first seen in 1848 in the German Confederation. It has come to symbolize democracy and the modern German state, and it is recognized as the country's official flag. However, the three colors have particular meanings for the modern National Flag of Germany. Black is said to symbolize the dignity and determination of the German people. Red is said to symbolize bravery, strength, and valor. The color of gold historically represents wealth, power, and prestige.

Public Holiday: October 3 (Day of German Unity).

Currency: Euro (€) (EUR)

Main Exports: Transport equipment (including automobiles), chemicals, machinery, telecoms technology, electrical devices, fuels, packaged medicaments, some food products and wine.

Main Imports: cars, motor vehicles; parts and accessories, packaged medicaments, crude petroleum. The imports fall into remarkably similar categories as exports but in addition they include raw materials and semifinished products for industry.

The top imports of Germany are cars ($71.1B), Vaccines, blood, antisera, toxins and cultures ($41.6B), motor vehicles; parts and accessories (8701 to 8705) ($41.1B), packaged medicaments ($32.3B), and crude petroleum ($29.2B), importing mostly from China ($134B), Netherlands ($129B), Poland ($89.4B), Italy ($78.4B), and France ($74.1B).

Main Trading Partners: Netherlands (6.7% of exports and 7.6% of imports), France (7.4% of exports and 5.2% of imports), UK (7.9% of exports and 4.8% of imports), US (6.9% of exports and 6.0 of imports), China (7.5% of exports and 11.8% of imports), Belgium (4.0% of imports), Italy (5.5% of exports and 5.4% of imports), Austria (5.0% of exports and 4.3% of imports).

Few people of the world have such a rich and varied past as do the Germans. Without German science, theology, philosophy, music, literature, and the other arts, western civilization would have been left with gaping holes. But Germans have known times of shame and destitution so deep and dark that many could not be sure that the sun would ever shine again.

German history is one of religious, class, and territorial division. Austria's foreign minister, Prince Klemens von Metternich, said in the early 1800s that Italy was merely a geographical conception, but he could have said exactly the same about Germany. For many centuries there existed the fiction of a unified, almost universal German Empire stretching from the North Sea to Sicily. Yet, until 1871 Germany was, in fact, a highly fractured scene of independent and rival kingdoms, principalities, ecclesiastical states, and independent cities. Even though most of their subjects spoke one of hundreds of German dialects, few considered themselves Germans; rather they felt themselves to be Saxons, Bavarians, Prussians, Rhinelanders, or Frankfurters.

When political unity finally came in 1871, many Germans were left outside the new German Empire, such as the German-speaking Swiss and Austrians. This unity lasted only three-quarters of a century and ended in disgrace and destruction. Not until the Berlin Wall came tumbling down on November 9, 1989, did reunification become possible; on October 3, 1990, Germany became one country again, and that date is now celebrated as the national holiday.

Germany is populated by a dynamic, talented, and imaginative people who for centuries have defied definition. Two thousand years ago, the Roman historian Tacitus called the Germanic tribes (which later migrated to most other parts of western and eastern Europe) warlike, but until the 20th century, the Germans brought war to other nations far less frequently than did others. Germans, though, were deeply involved in tragic wars in the 20th century.

Nowadays Germany is a country in which pacifist sentiment is perhaps stronger than in any other European or North American country. Surveys in 2000 also showed that Germans had the lowest level of national pride of any European nation except the Slovaks. They rarely sing the national anthem, probably because only half of all western Germans and less than a quarter of those in eastern Germany can recite even its first line. One young German noted with pleasure and with some exaggeration that "Europeans have always wanted a pacifist Germany; well, now they have one!" Indeed, a major source of American irritation toward Germany after World War II was the unwillingness of many Germans to defend themselves.

The French-Swiss writer Madame de Staël described the Germans almost 200 years ago as a pacific, poetic, and romantic people, but Germans also acquired a reputation for diligence and order. German

Germany's highways

195

Germany

Crop fields in a medieval pattern radiate from a Bavarian village.

Jon Markham Morrow

politics has often been described as romantic and irrational. But it was a German statesman (Bismarck) with whom one most directly associates the term "realpolitik," which describes a carefully measured, rational policy based on a realistic assessment of a nation's interests and means. The Germans' Road to democracy was very bumpy, and they have made several wrong turns. But today Germany is one of the world's most stable and tolerant democracies, about which former chancellor Willy Brandt could say in the early 1970s, "Germans can again be proud of their country."

Germans are still, to a degree, haunted by their history. No people today try so hard to come to grips with its own past, and almost no one is more critical of Germany and its past than is the German himself. But the Germans' critical eye to their own past has brought some undeniable benefits to the present. It has helped to harden both the democratic consensus in Germany and the determination to bend over backward to respect and protect human rights and dignity.

Cliches are never more than half-truths, but those relating to Germans are much more in need of revision than those about most other peoples. Germany is a country in the process of rapid change, in part because of industrialization familiar to Americans and other western Europeans, and in part because of a lingering reaction to their own experience under Hitler, a

dictator almost universally regarded outside and inside Germany as the most evil and brutal individual in recorded history. One can witness change in Germans' attitudes on politics, social problems, religion, and work and in almost all German societal institutions, including the family and the schools. The process of integrating the former German Democratic Republic (GDR), which had been ruled by a communist dictatorship for 40 years, is altering Germany even further. In short, Germany is a country that one must approach with a fresh and open mind.

The People and Place

Germans are the largest nationality in Europe west of Russia, where more than 1.5 million ethnic Germans still live. The FRG has over 85 million inhabitants after absorbing 17 million East Germans. Germany is a very densely populated country, with 611 inhabitants per square mile. The only European countries where the people live more closely together are the Netherlands and Belgium. The FRG's population is unevenly dispersed, though. The most thickly settled part is the Ruhr-Rhine area around Dusseldorf, Cologne (Koln), Dortmund, and Essen (a conglomeration of cities and heavy industry often called "Ruhr City").

Other large urban concentrations are the Rhine-Main area around Frankfurt, the Rhine-Neckar area around Mannheim, and Ludwigshafen, the Swabian industrial concentration around Stuttgart, as well as

the cities of Berlin, Leipzig, Dresden, Bremen, Hamburg, Hanover, Nuremberg and Munich. There are, however, very thinly settled areas in the Northern German Plain, the Eifel Mountain region, the Upper Palatinate, the Bavarian Forest, and the peripheral areas adjacent to the earlier border with the GDR. Those latter areas on both sides of the former dividing line are experiencing rapid growth in unified Germany as they become the new heartland.

The FRG, like other countries, has experienced a rapid flight from farms into cities and towns; the rural population dropped from 23% in 1950 to less than 5% today. But about half of all Germans live in towns or villages of less than 20,000 inhabitants. Unlike such countries as France, Britain, Italy, or Denmark, no single German city dominates the political, cultural, and economic life of the entire country, although Berlin may gradually assume this position in the 21st century.

For centuries Germany has been called the "land of the middle" because it occupies the heart of Europe. This is a major reason other European powers have often sought to keep Germany divided and weak. It has no natural frontiers, and the North German Plain, which is interspersed with hills, has always been and remains an ideal invasion route. Only the Alpine foothills in the southeast offer uninviting terrain for invading commanders. Because the altitude rises from the North Sea to the Alps, most of Germany's rivers, which provide the country with an excellent inland waterway system, flow north and empty into the North Sea via the Rhine, Ems, Weser, and Elbe Rivers. The only exception is the Danube, which flows southeast toward the Black Sea.

The FRG is ribboned by highly modern superhighways traveled by millions of private automobiles with no speed limit on most. Its modern cities in the west show few signs of urban blight, and cities in the east are overcoming their four decades of mindless and tasteless urban renewal or neglect. It is an economic giant in the world and now operates in European politics with far more confidence, effectiveness, and respect than almost any other nation dreamed would be possible after Germany's total collapse in 1945.

The FRG has even become a less tense and far more pleasant place to live. With high incomes in the west, a short work-week, lots of vacation, and a commitment to quality of life, Germans have become world-champion travelers abroad. When they stay home, they enjoy "free-time centers," which have proliferated everywhere. Their cities contain museums, concert halls, and pedestrian zones filled with sidewalk cafes, street-shows, and pleasant street life. They enjoy their comfortable lives with a spontaneity that invites a much closer look at this modern country.

HISTORY

Roman Penetration

Around 2,400 years ago, Germanic tribes, which were of Indo-European extraction, began entering from the north and east of what is now Germany and displacing or mingling with the Celtic peoples whom they found there. These tribes were, however, not the only people to be attracted by the soil, rivers, and strategic importance of this area in the heart of Europe. In 58 BC Julius Caesar led a Roman army that defeated the Germanic tribes in Alsace and in other Germanic areas west of the Rhine River. A good cultural observer as well as a good commander, Caesar wrote the earliest description of the tribes that he had just defeated and thereby sparked the interest and imagination of other Romans, who later came to colonize or develop the area.

The Romans extended their frontier eastward toward the Elbe River in 9 BC, but this expansion survived only two-decades. A German chieftain, Arminius (later known to Germans as Hermann), in 9 AD led an army that practically decimated the Roman occupation forces during a furious battle in storm and rain in the Teutoburg Forest, which is said to be located southeast of the present-day city of Bielefeld. The remnants of the Roman forces withdrew westward and southward

Roman-built Porta Nigra in Trier

again beyond the Danube and Rhine Rivers. Thenceforth, the Romans remained behind their heavily garrisoned frontier stretching from Cologne (Colonia) to Bonn (Bonna) to Augsburg (Augusta Vindelicorum) and all the way to Vienna (Vindobona). Here the Romans built beautiful cities, such as Regensburg (Castra Regina) and Trier (Augusta Treverum), with their stone structures, warm air heating underneath their floors, aqueducts, baths, coliseums, and even running water in some villas and public buildings.

They introduced advanced Roman agricultural methods; a money economy; and Roman law, administration, and culture. Trier even served temporarily as a seat of the Roman emperor, especially for Constantine the Great from 306 to 312 AD. What is now known about the Germanic tribes at that time came from such Romans as Tacitus, who in his book *Germania* describes the tribes' legends, customs, appearance, morals, and political and economic systems. His characterization of these tribesmen as particularly warlike helped launch a cliche about Germans that is by no means an inherent trait nor is valid today.

In the latter half of the 2nd century AD, Germanic tribes began hammering away at the Roman front and, attracted by stories of great wealth in the Italian Peninsula itself, actually invaded the heartland of what had become a decadent Roman Empire in the 5th century, causing it to collapse in the west. For centuries the Roman cities were left largely to decay, and much of the legal, administrative, and cultural advancements of the past were forgotten. Yet the Romans left their traces in the grammatical structure and some words of the German language, in the German concept of law, and in the cities that after the

first Crusade in 1095 began to gain significance in Germany again.

Some historians have dated the beginning of German history at 9 AD, when Arminius defeated the Romans at Teutoburg, but the various German tribes he led against the Romans certainly felt no common identity among themselves as Germans. There can hardly be a German history without a German people and some kind of German state. It is a mistake to identify Germany with the various tribes that began to enter what is presently Germany before the arrival of the Romans and with those such as the East and West Goths, Vandals, Burgundians, and Langobards, which swept into the area during the great migrations before and after Roman supremacy. Those migrations almost completely changed the racial makeup of Europe from the 2nd through the 5th centuries AD. The German nation was formed only very gradually over many centuries through the conquest and integration of a great number of Germanic tribes. Of course, some, such as the Angles, some Saxons, the Danes, the Swedes, and the Norwegians, never became a part of the German nation. Others were initially conquered, particularly by the larger tribes—the Friesians, Franks, Swabians, Bavarians, Saxons, and Thuringers—and ultimately grew into a community larger than any single tribe.

It is highly doubtful that a German nation would ever have emerged if a Carolinian Empire had not taken shape after the Roman rule had effectively ended. This far-flung empire, composed 80% of Germanic peoples and encompassing those speaking Latin-based languages in the west, reached its peak under Charlemagne (Charles the Great), who ascended the throne in 768 AD.

Germany

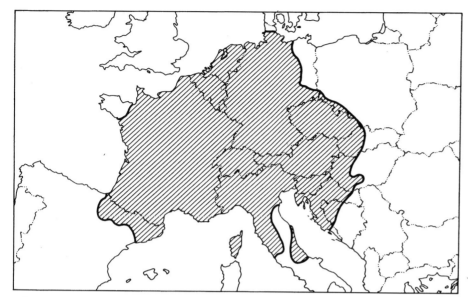

Charlemagne's empire in 814

During his rule the empire extended from northwestern Europe south to Rome and from Hungary to northern Spain. Charlemagne was a leader of extraordinary personal qualities who spent half of his time in the saddle holding his vast territory together. His empire survived only a few years after his death in 814. It was divided in 817 into Kingdoms of East and West Franconia and Lorraine. After bitter and complicated inheritance quarrels, two realms faced each other along roughly the same line as the present border between Germany and France. By 843 this border had become more or less fixed, and in 925 it became firmly established. Only in the east could subsequent German expansion take place.

Although Charlemagne's huge empire had been considerably reduced after his death, he had created the indispensable foundation for the formation of a German nation and a German consciousness. There were no other geographic, racial, cultural, or strictly linguistic factors that could have pulled Germany together without Charlemagne's political and military acumen. During his reign some persons began to refer to the tongues spoken in the eastern part of the empire as "Deutsch" (Doich)—German, a word derived from "Diutisk," meaning "common" or "popular." In the following three centuries, more and more inhabitants of what is now Germany developed a consciousness of being German.

The eastern Franconian realm in 919 became the German Empire. "Empire," however, is a somewhat misleading word, since it connotes a centralized, unified power. In Germany there was a strong degree of unity, but until almost the end of the 19th century, rule was by a multitude of heads of local states and independent cities. However, by the 11th century, these states and cities had become the most powerful in Europe and were able to claim the title "Roman Empire." In the 13th century, this was dignified to the title "Holy Roman Empire" and, in the 15th century, "Holy Roman Empire of the German Nation." The reach and power of this empire expanded and contracted, but it always retained certain organizational features: The highest nobility (usually called "electors") actually elected an emperor.

Although this position was not hereditary, as was the case with other European monarchies, there was a dynastic element in that, with very few exceptions, the new emperor had to be a blood relative of his predecessor. There was no capital city; he moved around continually, ruling from wherever he happened to be. He usually resided in various bishoprics or in a collection of buildings known as a Pfalz. As one can now see in the charming medieval city of Goslar in the Harz Mountains, the Pfalz contained a royal residence; buildings and stables for the emperor's retinue; at least one church or chapel; and surrounding farms, mines, and businesses from which the emperor could derive his income. Since no taxes were levied, he was compelled to finance his activities from the various imperial estates throughout the empire. Finally, the major and minor nobility met infrequently in an imperial diet called the Reichstag. This was a body whose work cannot be compared to a modern democratic parliament but one that displayed how much the emperor depended upon the lesser noblemen if he wanted to conduct a war, increase his revenues, or the like.

Germany always has been a mixture of central and regional power, of unity and disunity. There were endless struggles over who should lead in the empire, and the emperor's actual power was never assured, even after he had been elected. He had to maintain a powerful army and forge delicate alliances among the rival dukes in the realm and powerful archbishops who ruled such important cities as Mainz, Cologne, and Trier. This is why German provinces and cities became much more important in Germany than in other countries.

During the 8th and 9th centuries, the Hungarians posed a constant threat to the German Empire. The fortresses Romans built had long since fallen into ruin. To cope with this threat, the German kings and emperors erected fortresses around the imperial estates, royal and ducal palaces, abbeys, and cities with the treasured right to maintain a marketplace. Erfurt, Meissen, Merseburg, Frankfurt, Ulm, Gosler, and Aachen originated from fortified royal estates and palaces, and Augsburg, Passau, Strasbourg, Trier, Worms, Cologne, Mainz, and Speyer originated from fortified abbeys and monasteries. Martin Luther's characterization of God as "a mighty fortress" specifically refers to the safety found in these walled cities. The Hungarians were decisively defeated in 955 and were rooted out of what is now Austria, thereby permitting Bavarian settlers to pour into this "East March" (whence the German name for Austria: Osterreich).

The Zenith of the Empire

The German emperors focused their attention far beyond what is now the German-speaking world, particularly on Italy. In 962 the Saxon king Otto I was crowned emperor by the pope in St. Peter's Cathedral in Rome, a tradition which was to last over 500 years. This unique privilege, which was bestowed on no other ruler, entitled the German monarch to be called "emperor." It also gave the German Empire a universalistic claim to rule over the entire western world as the protector of Christianity. This claim never became reality.

The special relationship established between the emperors and popes proved to be of questionable value for both. German emperors became embroiled in Italian and papal affairs for more than three centuries, a costly diversion from the more important task of creating a unified Germany. Emperors became active in papal selections and on occasion succeeded in driving popes right out of Rome. At the same time, popes often connived with Germany's enemies and bitterly fought against emperors' attempts to gain control of the Catholic Church within Germany.

A showdown between the two occurred in 1077, when Emperor Heinrich

Germany

IV replaced Pope Gregor VII when the latter refused to permit Heinrich to appoint bishops and other high church officials in Germany. Gregor struck back by taking away Heinrich's imperial crown, releasing all of Heinrich's subjects from their loyalty to the emperor, and excommunicating Heinrich. The latter soon realized how much he had overreached his power and authority and felt compelled to go to the fortress of Canossa, where the pope had sought protection. Dressed in the simple garb of a penitent, Heinrich pleaded three days for forgiveness. Then with outstretched arms, he threw himself at the pope's feet, who had no alternative but to forgive him. Heinrich's act of prostration at the feet of the pope was a turning point in German history. Soon thereafter, a revengeful Heinrich drove Pope Gregor into exile and lonely death in southern Italy. For centuries the German emperors could always count the popes among their enemies, even though they continued to influence their election until about 1250.

The perennial activity of the emperors in Italy tended seriously to weaken their ability to contend with the domestic challenges to their authority. One of the few exceptions to this was Emperor Friedrich I of the Swabian dynasty of Staufen, which from 1138 ruled Germany for about a century. Known as Barbarossa because of his red beard, Friedrich was a strong monarch from the moment he ascended the throne in 1152 at the age of 30. He was a handsome and imposing man, intelligent and well-educated. A highly charismatic figure who attracted loyalty and devotion

The *Bamberg Knight,* one of the 13th century's finest examples of statuary

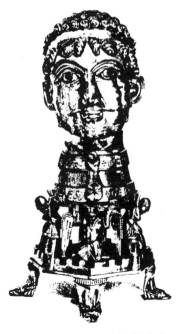

Romanesque Friedrich I

like a magnet, he was a model knight whose martial skills he continued to display by participating in tournaments until age 60. Despite a determined challenge within Germany by the Saxon duke, his aims were clear: supremacy in northern and central Italy without suppressing the Italian cities' freedoms and continued influence over the papacy without directly controlling Rome. He wanted to crown his reign with a triumphant crusade, but after forging a mighty army and guiding it toward the Holy Land, he drowned in a river in Saleph in Asia Minor.

After his death bards circulated a legend throughout Germany that the red-bearded emperor was not really dead but instead had sunk into a magic slumber within the mountain of Kyffhauser, sitting on an ivory throne, his head resting on a

marble table. He would leave Kyffhauser only when his land signaled that it needed his help; if, however, all was in order, ravens would fly around the mountain, and Barbarossa would return to his sleep for another 100 years. Those ravens are still circling the mountain.

The Decline of "the Empire"

The German emperors' attention had become so fixed on Italy that the last Staufen emperor, Friedrich II, an erudite and farsighted ruler, tried to rule the enormous empire from Sicily. Yet, by the time he died in 1250 and his successor, Conradino, had been executed in 1268, the German emperors could hardly pretend anymore to control large areas outside Germany. They had lost much of their power and influence within Germany, as

199

Germany

well. Due largely to the emperors' obsession with crusades and Italian campaigns rather than with consolidating and increasing their power within Germany itself, a process of erosion of their power set in, which left some free cities, several hundred German noblemen, and the church largely free of imperial control.

By 1268 no one could speak any longer of a powerful and supreme emperor over all of Germany. He could not call on the princes to support him in wartime without their approval; there was no common foreign policy, nor was there an imperial army. The only imperial laws that had any chance of being obeyed were those that had been approved by all three segments of the Reichstag—the "electors," the other princes, and the cities—which the emperor convened infrequently in Worms, Frankfurt, Regensburg, Augsburg, or some other important city in southern Germany.

From the 13th century on, the parts of the empire predominated over the whole; the regions over the empire; the princes, kings, and high clergy over the emperor. The absence of any strong, centralizing power in Germany prevented for six centuries the development of a unified German nation, as the French and English had been able to do. For six centuries German politics was largely characterized by conflict between ruling houses. After 1438 the

imperial crown practically became the sole possession of the House of Habsburg, and Austria gradually became the predominant German-speaking territory and one of the most powerful countries in Europe.

The Rise and Fall of "City Power"

By the end of the 14th century, the population of Germany had risen from less than 1 million in 500 AD to 13–15 million, despite the great plague, which had reduced the European population by about a third. Most Germans lived on the land or in villages, and many were tied to the ground they worked and were compelled to deliver a considerable part of their produce to large landowners. Cities had begun to sprout up everywhere by the 10th century, primarily to provide protection. They also provided peasants with a place of refuge from the bondage that was widespread in the countryside.

The Crusades also had provided a mighty stimulation for cities, whose prosperity was often reflected in the mighty cathedrals that were built. Ulm built one, for instance, which could hold two and a half times as many people as lived in the city. Tradesmen and craftsmen in the cities began to develop guilds to protect their economic existence and to maintain a good reputation by assuring that quality work was done. These guilds also sometimes

forcefully challenged the elite, patrician rule of the cities.

The power and influence of German cities was greatest when they joined together in leagues. The most important league was that of the Hansa cities. In 1241 Lubeck and Hamburg forged an alliance in order to protect the land and sea lanes between them from robbers, and gradually more and more cities along the North and Baltic Sea coasts and even deep within the interior of Germany, Poland, the Baltic area, and Scandinavia joined. By the time the Hansa League had reached its height in the first half of the 15th century, it embraced such cities as Cologne, Brunswick, Bremen, Wismar, Rostock, Danzig, Konigsberg, Breslau, and Cracow, and the League had large trading colonies in London, Bruges, Gotland, and Novgorod. Seldom did the Hansa cities conduct traditional military warfare; they preferred the far more effective trade war. Not until the end of the 15th century was the Hansa League's dominance over the North and Baltic Seas area broken.

By the 15th century, Germany had become a comparatively rich part of Europe, but like today, its economic strength far outstripped its political influence. Although they remained far smaller than the leading cities in southern and western Europe, German cities had very much to do with such prosperity. The wars that were to ravage Germany in the 17th century, and especially the shift of the trade routes westward following the discovery of America, brought about the decay of the great German cities. This stagnation tended to clip the wings of the middle classes, which cities produce and strengthen, and therefore tended to stifle the development of democracy in Germany. It also left Germany primarily an agricultural country until the middle of the 19th century.

Intellectual Awakening

The 15th and the early 16th centuries were ones of intellectual awakening. This discovery of man and the world was the focus of humanism, which has remained controversial to this day and age, and the Renaissance. The latter was an Italian creation of the 14th and 15th centuries and for Europe signaled an important turning point. It meant an inclination on the part of a few to question all previous religious, scholarly, scientific, and political authority that had placed limitations on man. It was a time when Leonardo da Vinci showed that natural science must be based on exact observation and experimentation, when Christopher Columbus dared to cross the ocean to disprove previous theories about the shape of the earth, when a Florentine political figure named Niccolo Machiavelli ripped the

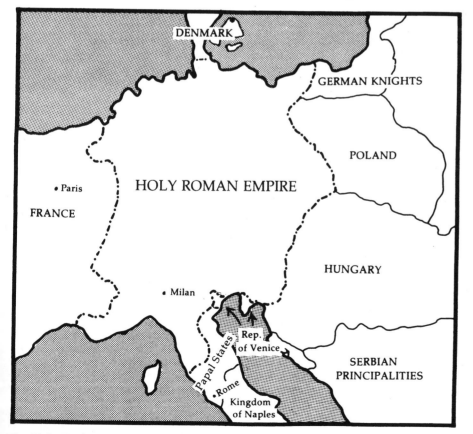

The Holy Roman Empire, mid-14th century

idealized cloth from politics to show it in its raw, nonethical reality.

Germans were very much a part of this burst of discovery. Nikolaus Kopernicus, a clergyman from Frauenburg in Prussia, showed that the Earth was not the center of the universe and was merely one of the many bodies in a much larger planetary system. Martin Behaim constructed the first globe of the earth. Peter Henlein produced the first pocket watch. Berthold Schwarz discovered shooting powder quite by accident and thereby revolutionized warfare. An ingenious goldsmith from Mainz, Johannes Gutenberg, developed the first printing press using movable type, which was a prerequisite for taking the written word out of the libraries of the rich, the noble, and the clergy and into the reach of the masses. In art, Albrecht Durer, Hans Holbein, and Mathias Grunewald achieved deserved recognition throughout the civilized world. Universities sprouted up all over Germany in this time of inquiry and became important centers of research and learning to the present day.

In this time of serious questioning, it is not surprising that the practices and teachings of the Roman Catholic Church were also examined by critical minds. The master of all humanists was Erasmus of Rotterdam (1465–1536), who lived a part of his life in Germany and has amused the educated world with his *Praise of Folly*, in which he pointed to the grotesque difference between what men profess in this world and what they actually do. He also challenged the theologians to reexamine the New Testament in light of "the original sources." He criticized the abuses, pomp, and ceremony of·the church and demanded a rational basis for the Catholic faith and a return to the "simple, pure Christ." He never broke with the Catholic Church nor joined forces with those who later did, but he helped establish the theological foundation from which a Catholic monk in the provincial town of Wittenberg launched a powerful attack that shook the church to its very roots.

Martin Luther

Martin Luther was the son of a minister from Thuringia who was able to save enough money to send his gifted but brooding son to the University of Erfurt to study law. Luther was reportedly shocked by a sudden flash of light and decided instead to become a monk, pastor, and professor in Wittenberg. In 1511 he left for a long-awaited voyage to Rome as a firm believer, but he returned to Germany with his faith in the church badly shaken. His anger and frustration built up as the Roman pontificate devised a method for raising its own revenues by selling to Catholics forgiveness for their sins.

Martin Luther

In countries with strong central rulers, such papal financial maneuvers could be resisted, but until 1517 the church's agents needed not fear resistance in the weak and fragmented Germany. When a papal representative knocked on Martin Luther's door to present the scheme one day, the glowing kettle boiled over. On October 31, 1517, he published his "95 Theses" branding the Catholic Church as an insult to God and challenging it to an open debate over fundamental theological issues. It is not certain that he tacked this highly explosive writing on the cathedral door at Wittenberg. What is certain, however, is that the Vatican was never the same after this angry monk rolled his weighty stone in its direction.

The church decided to enter into a three-year debate with Luther, but this merely stimulated the interest that curious and critical Europeans paid to the stream of speeches and writings that poured from Luther's mouth and hand. When the pope

finally decided to silence this troublesome monk, it was too late. Martin Luther merely burned the papal bull (writing) in public and defiantly proceeded to the Reichstag in Worms. There he presented his views on April 18, 1521, to Emperor Charles V and to the leading German nobles, clergy, and bourgeoisie in Germany. Luther held firmly to his views and asserted, "as long as I am not contradicted by the Holy Scripture or by clear reasoning, I will recant nothing since it is difficult and dangerous to act against one's conscience."

In order to protect this renegade with an enormous following in Germany, sympathizers captured him during his journey back to Wittenberg and took him to the Wartburg fortress outside of Eisenach. There he lived for a year under the assumed name of "Junker Jorg" far away from the furious controversies of the day. In 1522 he completed a German translation of the New Testament. This was not the first translation of the Bible into

Germany

German; over 170 handwritten ones in the same language had appeared in the Middle Ages, and since the invention of the movable type printing press, there had been 14 previous High German (northern Germany) translations. But Luther, the scholar, was able to penetrate deeply into the Greek and "Vulgata" texts and produce a translation, which, as he himself said, forced the prophets and apostles to speak a comprehensible German. Only such a text could enable the Christian to read and understand the Bible on his own, without the guidance or interpretation of the church. In 1534 he published his final translation of both the New and Old Testaments, which found its way into enthusiastic hands all over Germany. In this way, Luther's German became the standardized High German spoken by the educated in every corner of Germany. Although a multitude of dialects continue to be spoken in Germany, Luther gave a land that was fractured into many tiny splinters a common language, which is essential for any collection of people hoping to be called a nation.

His call for a liberation from the theological confines of Rome unleashed demands for change and other forms of liberation that seriously shook the social structure of Germany. In all of these conflicts, the ultimate victors were the German princes.

There was a rebellion of knights in 1522 led by Franz von Sickingen, about whose origins we shall read later. Compared with the growing bourgeoisie (middle-upper class), which was becoming more and more prosperous in the cities, the economic importance of that portion of the lower nobility that had also been knighted (barons, etc.) was steadily declining. Also, armored knights on horseback had become militarily obsolete since Swiss infantry armed with halberds (a wide-shaped axe on a long pole) had learned to decimate their opponents with relative ease. Because of this, Swiss foot soldiers, not knights, became the treasured military mercenaries in half of Europe. The knights had lost most of their income and all justification for existing. Their rebellion was a desperate attempt to turn the clock back in Germany, but the princes crushed it. The status of knighthood was thereby eliminated once and for all as a power factor in Europe.

Although the princes became powerful, the people also became more assertive. In 1524–1525 an idealistic priest, Thomas Muntzer, led a futile revolt of poor artisans and day workers against the princes in order to establish a "Christendom of the poor." A far more serious convulsion occurred when thousands of German peasants, primarily in the southern part of Germany, revolted. This was the largest and most forceful revolution in the history of a people who have manifested very little attraction to revolutionary causes. Almost four centuries later, the professional Russian revolutionary, Vladimir Ilyich Lenin, remarked scornfully that if would-be German revolutionaries wished to storm a train station, they would first buy a ticket before setting foot on the platform.

Revolt

The peasants revolted against the remnants of serfdom that still bound many of them to the higher nobility. The nobles tended to despise all simple people who worked the land as persons without rights. The peasants resented the steady increase in payments and workdays owed to the lords, and they demanded protection for fishing and hunting rights, as well as a return to community use of much of the grazing and watering facilities the lords had simply appropriated for themselves. They demanded a reestablishment of earlier institutions, which had granted them some self-rule, and they insisted on a return to "the earlier justice," to German law, rather than Roman law. The lords preferred the latter because it denied peasants any freedom whatsoever.

Those who joined this revolt found in Luther's words, about the "freedom of a Christian man," a divine justification for their goals and actions. Initially, Luther sympathized with the peasants' demands and encouraged the lords to take their pleas seriously. But when the bands of rebels began to attack fortresses and churches and to dispatch with bloody swiftness those who wielded earthly authority, Luther became furious and lashed out against those whom he accused of turning Germany into a battlefield.

When it came to "things belonging to Caesar," Luther did not hesitate to decide in favor of order and princely authority. His reaction to this social revolution and its ultimate cruel suppression had serious consequences for Germany. Peasants remained poor, despised, unfree, and without political influence for almost 300 years, until reforms in the wake of the French Revolution finally eliminated the formal chains that had been placed on them. Perhaps more important, Luther's stand left a legacy of freedom in Germany, which was interpreted only as inner, purely mental freedom but not political freedom. Thus, this man who had led the charge against the limits placed on man through Catholic theology actually justified external obedience to the princes and thereby strengthened the hierarchical political order within Germany. This helped to retard the victory of democracy within Germany until the middle of the 20th century. It even allowed some Germans who strongly disapproved of National Socialism (Nazism) after 1933 to remain within a brutal dictatorship, but nevertheless to persuade themselves that they could embark upon an "internal emigration."

The new Protestant faith spread quickly throughout northern Germany and

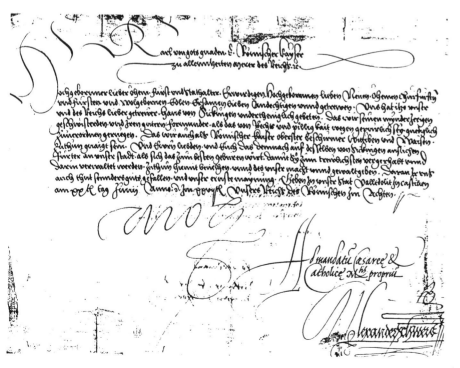

Document signed in 1529 by Charles ("Carolus") V, the Holy Roman emperor

Germany

Scandinavia. By 1555 about four-fifths of all Germans had embraced the new belief. In that year the Peace of Augsburg was reached, which recognized that the Protestant faith had an equal status with the Catholic and that each territorial prince and free city would decide which faith all residents under their control should practice. *Cuius regio, eius religio* ("whoever rules chooses the religion") was the formula for a kind of religious freedom that was restricted to the rulers. Those subjects who could not accept their rulers' preference had to move to another territory or city, and thousands of Germans did just that. Thus, the religious division of Germany was sealed for centuries.

The Time of Troubles

The Peace of Augsburg did not permanently settle the religious question in Germany. A Catholic counterreformation, set in motion in Rome and supported by the Habsburg emperors, heated tensions between German Protestants and Catholics, who formed a Protestant Union and Catholic League in 1608 and 1609, respectively. All that was needed was a spark in Bohemia to ignite an almost indescribably destructive Thirty Years' War on German soil that ravaged this weak and divided land from 1618 until 1648.

In the early years of the war, the Catholic states, particularly Austria and Bavaria, won brilliant victories, penetrating northern Germany to the Baltic Sea and reconverting by the edge of the sword many Germans to Catholicism. Catholic successes stemmed largely from strong internal friction within the Protestant camp between Lutherans and Calvinists and from extraordinarily capable generals, Tilly and the dashing and overly ambitious Wallenstein.

These initial successes under Habsburg leadership prompted other European powers to enter the war. It was soon obvious that this war was not even primarily a religious struggle for the souls of Germans. Fearing Habsburg control over a strategically important part of the Baltic Sea, and noting suspiciously a Habsburg alliance with Catholic Poland, the Danish king, Christian IV, and then the Swedish king, Gustavus Adolphus, took over leadership of the Protestant cause. They received financial support from England and Holland. More importantly, the Swedish king was able to receive aid from Catholic France, which was always determined to prevent the Habsburgs from growing too strong, especially when in control of Spain as well as Austria.

Thus, Germany was crisscrossed by marauding foreign armies that lived off the land in a manner summarized by Wallenstein, "The war must feed the war." No

Contemporary drawings of the Thirty Years' War

door, wall, or fortress could protect the civilian population from the armies that cut wide swaths through the countryside and cities, followed by hordes of often disease-ridden camp followers, and leaving a trail of wreckage, ashes, and corpses behind them. Ironically, some of the powerful, comforting, and assertive Lutheran hymns were written during this devastation. An example of how arbitrary such destruction could be was Rothenburg ob der Tauber, today one of Germany's most beautifully intact medieval cities. Field Marshal Tilly offered in 1631 to spare the town and its leaders only if one of the city councilmen could drink about a gallon of wine in one

draw. The elderly mayor stepped forward and accomplished this incredible feat, thereby saving his city and colleagues.

The Treaty of Westphalia

Who won this 30-year nightmare? A quick glance at the Treaty of Westphalia in 1648 gives the answer. Sweden took control of the city of Wismar; the Dukedom of Bremen-Verden (except the city of Bremen); the islands of Rugen, Usedom, and Wollin; and part of Pomerania, thereby depriving Germany of the outlets to the sea via the Elbe, Weser, and Oder Rivers. France got most of Alsace and the cities of Metz, Toul, Verdun, Breisach, and the Rhine and

Germany

achieved protector status over 10 German imperial cities. Germany's western border, which had existed since the 9th century, was thus fundamentally altered. Switzerland and the Netherlands were granted full independence from Germany.

The German princes' official right to determine the religious beliefs of all of their subjects was withdrawn, at least in theory. But the German princes were granted full sovereignty within their own territories, including the right to make treaties with foreign powers. The proviso that these treaties could not be directed against the emperor or the empire remained valid only on paper. Germany was left with almost 2,000 sovereign states, such as the large territories of Brandenburg, Austria, Saxony, and Bavaria; 83 free and imperial cities (including Hamburg and Frankfurt am Main); and countless ecclesiastical and other small units, some of which included as few as about 2,000 inhabitants. The map of Germany now looked more than ever before like the face of a child with measles. At a time when centralizing, centripetal forces were at work in England and France, centrifugal forces were prevailing in Germany,

throwing it farther and farther away from national unity. There could no longer be any serious talk of "imperial politics."

Germany was left breathless, devastated, and demoralized from the plunder and destruction. In some areas, such as Württemberg, the Palatinate, Thuringia, and Mecklenburg, two-thirds of the inhabitants had been eradicated, and overall losses in Germany ranged from a third to a half of the total population. The total population dropped from about 20 million to 10–14 million. Thus, Germany, which at the beginning of the 17th century had the largest number of inhabitants in all of Europe, fell behind that of France for the next century and a half and behind that of Russia to the present day. It was more than a century before it reached its pre-1618 level. In addition to human deaths, 1,600 cities and 18,000 villages had been totally demolished, and livestock, farmland, and the rest of the economic infrastructure had been left in shambles. In comparative·terms, the destruction to Germany was far greater in 1648 than in 1945. Only an atomic war could produce comparable damage today.

Alien Forces Move In; Germans Leave for America

It is not surprising that the Turkish Ottomans and the French took advantage of Germany's plight to try to enrich themselves further. While Prince Eugene of Savoy was able to stop the Turkish invasion at the gates of Vienna in 1683, the French were far more successful under King Louis XIV to acquire what Cardinal Richelieu called *une entree en Allemagne* ("a gateway into Germany"). In several campaigns France snatched about 600 cities, villages, and fortresses in Alsace. It took Strasbourg and a large tract of territory between Alsace and Lake Geneva, and its decision to "burn the Palatinate" left such lasting traces as the ruins of Heidelberg Castle.

One of the many consequences of the seemingly perpetual war and religious strife in this era was that many beleaguered sects, such as the Mennonites, Quakers, and Dunkers, decided to seek their peace and happiness in the New World. There they could escape the political and religious hierarchy, as well as the earthly corruption into·which the European nobility had apparently fallen. The first German immigrants to America tended to settle in New York, Maryland, and Virginia, but in 1681 William Penn established the first religiously free state in Pennsylvania. The German exodus to Pennsylvania began with 13 Mennonite families from Krefeld in Westphalia, who landed in Philadelphia on October 6, 1683, a day still celebrated in some parts of the United States as "German Day." They created Germantown on the outskirts of Philadelphia. They were followed by the Moravians, so-called because they came from the Habsburg province of Moravia, and the Amish (erroneously called Pennsylvania Dutch) from the area of Bern, Switzerland, who have retained to this day most aspects of a lifestyle characteristic of pious Germans in the 17th century, including the Bern dialect of German.

Not all Germans found in America the "quiet, honest, and God-fearing life" of which they had dreamed, but their reports back to Germany helped open the floodgates for further waves of refugees from religious persecution in the 18th century. One Protestant group from the area of Brunswick set sail in 1707 for New York, but unfavorable winds forced them to land in Philadelphia. They decided to settle in New Jersey, which in 1733 became the home of an immigrant named Johann Peter Rockefeller, who founded what later became one of the richest families in the world. By 1776 there were more than 250,000 Germans living in the 13 colonies. Germany's religious quarrels were America's gain.

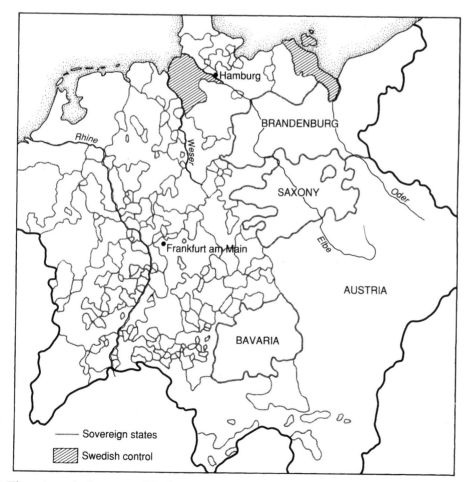

Sovereign states

Swedish control

The extremely fragmented Holy Roman Empire after the Treaty of Westphalia: 1648

Germany

It was at this time that one of the most durable legends in Germany was born. To this day many German pupils learn in school that, in the early years of the American republic, a vote was taken in Congress to determine which language the nation should officially adopt, and German lost by only one vote. That deciding vote was supposedly cast by the Speaker of the House of Representatives Frederick Augustus Conrad Muehlenberg, himself a German immigrant.

The fact is that no such vote was ever taken, either in Congress or in the Pennsylvania legislature (1828 according to another myth) or any other state legislature. The misunderstanding stemmed from a petition presented to Congress in January 1794 by a group of Germans from Virginia demanding that laws be translated into German for the benefit of the large German population. The appropriate committee rejected the proposal by a vote of 42 to 41. As speaker, Muehlenberg abstained, but he proclaimed afterward, "The sooner Germans become Americans, the better."

Even though German was never to be the leading language in America, the Germans introduced many words into the American vocabulary: angst, blitz, dachshund, delicatessen, flak, frankfurter, glitz, hamburger, hinterland, kaput, kindergarten, kitsch, leitmotiv, pretzel, realpolitik, rucksack, sauerkraut, schadenfreude, wunderkind, zeitgeist, and zigzag, among many others.

Movement to the Northeast

By the middle of the 17th century, the Germans had been reduced largely to mere spectators and objects of European politics. However, the next 50 years saw this situation change; a highly dynamic state arose on the sandy soil in the eastern part of the empire, which forced its way into the ranks of world powers by sheer force of will, hard work, and discipline: Prussia.

Before the 12th century, Germany had consisted of two basic parts: a Romanized Germany west of the Rhine and south of the Danube and a Germanic territory east and north. After the 12th century, a third part began to take shape: in the Slavic and Baltic east, which came to include Mecklenburg, Brandenburg, Pomerania, Upper Silesia, and East Prussia. This development involved the often-violent conquest of Slavs and Balts and the partial absorption of these peoples. With the conquest and colonization of the east, the empire's center of gravity slowly began to move eastward.

The motives of those Germans moving east were by no means nationalistic but rather materialistic and idealistic. German farmers sought land and more independence from their earlier masters; noblemen wanted to open new ground

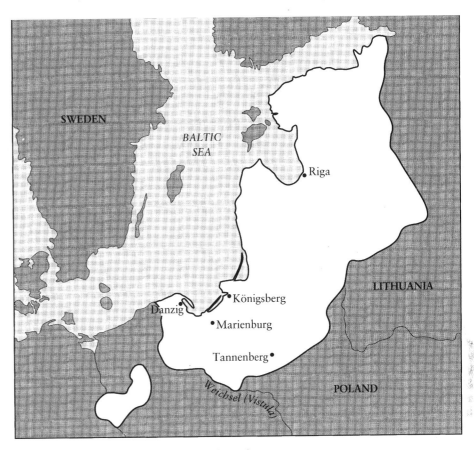

The German Order of Knights at its pinnacle

and to gain income from it; skilled craftsmen and businessmen sought new opportunities and markets. However, none of these desires could have been fulfilled if another powerful motive had not been at work as well: the Christianizing of "heathen" peoples.

Medieval Knights

The Crusades that began at the end of the 11th century sparked the imagination of a class of persons that had begun to emerge before the 10th century: the knights. Warfare had been revolutionized in such a way that foot soldiers were replaced by well-armed knights who often fought on horseback. Therefore, the high nobility required knights to live in their vicinity or in fortresses or estates that the lords placed at their disposal. Most of the knights in the earlier days were not of noble birth, so they attempted to make up for their humble status by developing certain virtues, such as bravery, courage, loyalty, and consistency. The highest virtue was moderation in every situation but battle.

One of Friedrich Barbarossa's sons founded a German Order of Knights in 1198, whose mission at first was to care for pilgrims and crusaders in the Holy Lands. It soon joined the active military struggles against the Islamic disbelievers who had

laid an allegedly unjust claim to the Holy City of Jerusalem. The order took in both knights, priests, and other brothers who could perform useful services, and its uniform was a white cloak with a black cross on it. Their rules were as strict as those in a monastic order. Since they saw themselves as fully dedicated to the service of Christ, they did not marry. They were also forbidden to own property and swore to maintain absolute loyalty and personal poverty.

The Rise of Prussia

Less than a quarter-century after the order was founded, its sights were cast in an entirely different geographic direction. A Polish duke, Conrad of Masovia, asked for the order's help in 1226 to assist in crushing a hardy tribe of "heathens" called Prussians. This was a Baltic people related to the Lithuanians and Latvians and regarded by Germans and Poles alike as barbarians. They had no written language, but they had strange customs, such as polygamy and placing unwanted babies out to die. The conquest and Christianizing of such a tribe received the blessing of the pope and the approval of the Holy Roman emperor. With such encouragement and advancement under the call of "Death to Disbelievers," this conquest was bound to be a cruel one.

Germany

The German Order crossed the Vistula River in 1231 in order to engage the Prussians. Not until 1283 was the bloody job completed and the entire territory from the Vistula to the farthest border of East Prussia (that portion of Prussia east of the Vistula estuary) brought under the order's control. The struggle had devastated much of the land and almost completely eradicated the Prussian tribe. The remnants were converted to Christianity upon the threat of death and were ultimately absorbed by the German conquerors. Their language disappeared completely, and all that remained of them was the name "Prussia," by which the territory came to be known and which became the official name of the state in 1701.

It created a holy republic over the land, and in 1309 the order's supreme master, who was elected by the other knights, moved his seat from Venice to the fortress of Marienburg in Prussia (now in Poland). From there commands were issued to fortresses and cities throughout the entire area. It became a German-led, rigidly organized land administered by the knights, who, since they were forbidden to own property, possess wealth, or marry, were more like ascetic civil servants than feudal lords. They directed the systematic colonization of the land and were responsible for the establishment or further development of more than 1,000 villages and 100 cities, including the major ones, Danzig (now Gdansk in Poland), Elbing (Elblag), and Königsberg (now Kaliningrad in Russia). Until well into the 15th century, the history of Prussia is the history of colonization, and in some areas, this was more violent than in others.

Germans, Slavs, and Balts lived side by side, although in most places Germans occupied the key political and economic positions. The nobility and bourgeoisie were predominantly German, but the agricultural population was mixed. This condition continued more or less to exist until Hitler and Stalin launched massive exterminations and expulsions in the 20th century to homogenize the ethnic composition in these areas.

The German Order of Knights reached its pinnacle in the 14th century, but its hold over the area was broken in the 15th century. Poles and Lithuanians attacked Prussia in 1410 and delivered the knights a crushing defeat in the woods of Tannenberg (Grunwald). This was the first major military defeat the order had ever suffered, and sensing the way the wind was blowing, many German noblemen sided with the Poles. Only Marienburg remained unconquered, but new battles eventually drove the order out of all the area except East Prussia, which in 1466

became a tributary of Poland. The order was compelled to swear loyalty to Poland.

One area in the German east that had resisted domination by the Poles was the elector principality of Brandenburg, a relatively insignificant, poor, and backward territory on the periphery of the German Empire and ruled by a dynasty from southern Germany, the Hohenzollerns. Brandenburg and East Prussia had become linked in 1525. Taking advantage of the severe turmoil caused by the Reformation, the last supreme master of the German Order, Albrecht von Brandenburg-Ansbach from the family of Hohenzollern, simply assumed in 1525 the earthly title of Duke of Prussia, and in 1660 the last ties that bound East Prussia to Poland were severed.

The Hohenzollern dynasty, which had made its residence in Berlin and whose heartland remained Brandenburg, was able to gain control of West Prussia, Pomerania, and Silesia, and ultimately it acquired huge chunks of territory in the Rhineland and Westphalia, as well. From a poor land known derisively as "the sandbox of the empire" with no raw materials and a population of little over 1 million persons grew a huge and powerful kingdom ultimately embracing about two-thirds of all Germans and serving as the foundation for the first truly unified German Empire in 1871.

Perhaps more than any other European state, Prussia did not evolve but was made by the human hand. A series of extraordinarily able rulers in the 17th and 18th centuries enabled Prussia to rise like a meteor to the ranks of the major European powers. From 1640 to 1688, Friedrich Wilhelm, "the Great Elector," laid the cornerstone for a powerful Prussia. He had spent three years in the Netherlands during his youth, and there he had been deeply influenced by the Calvinist dynamism and sense of obligation. He married a woman from the ruling House of Orange. From the Thirty Years' War, he had drawn the lesson that his state needed to enhance its military prowess. He said, "Alliances are good, but one's own power is even better; one can more safely depend on that." He therefore enlarged the Prussian army from 3,000 to 30,000 soldiers.

Friedrich Wilhelm also established an oft-forgotten Prussian tradition which lasted for a century and a half and which was both humanitarian and strengthened Prussia. When the French king invalidated the Edict of Nantes in 1685, which had granted considerable religious and civil liberty to the Huguenots (French Protestants), Friedrich Wilhelm responded with the Edict of Potsdam, opening the Prussian gates to the religiously persecuted. More than 20,000 French Huguenots, most of them skilled craftsmen and businessmen,

poured into Prussia, and by 1700 one out of three residents of Berlin was French. Far from attempting to Germanize these newcomers, foreigners were permitted to retain their own language and customs.

The Huguenots built their own schools and churches and powerfully contributed to the arts and to the vibrant economic life of Prussia. Many of the area's greatest names until the present day are of French origin. More than 20,000 Protestants from Salzburg fled the Counter-Reformation, and in the course of the 18th century, there was a steady stream of emigrants and religious refugees to Prussia: Mennonites, Scottish Presbyterians, Jews, and sometimes Catholics. In some ways Prussia in the 18th century was to the persecuted of Europe what America was in the 19th century: a religiously tolerant land that offered enormous opportunities

Prussia Becomes a Center of Culture

Friedrich I ascended to the throne in 1688. He was a well-educated and cultured man who maintained a glittering but excessively extravagant court. He established another Prussian tradition that is also frequently overlooked today: He established Prussia, especially Berlin, as a leading home for science and the arts. He founded the Academies of Art and Science, and he ordered the building of many edifices, such as the Charlotteburg Palace, which changed the face of Berlin from that of a peripheral and provincial town to that of one of the most dignified cities in Europe. He also achieved through patient and skillful diplomacy an important political goal: In 1701 he won the emperor's approval for the Prussian elector to bear the title of "king." This was a considerable boost for the prestige of a still-poor country on the outskirts of the German Empire.

The Soldier King

When Friedrich Wilhelm I (so numbered because the earlier Friedrich Wilhelm had not been a king) was crowned in 1713, Prussia gained a ruler who was capable but greatly different from his predecessor. What one now most often associates with Prussia was largely due to the new king's influence: the spirit of Spartan simplicity and the conscientious fulfillment of one's obligations to the state, which was to be ruled by the king alone but for the good of the subjects. As he told his son, "The dear Lord placed you on the throne, not in order to be lazy, but in order to work and to rule his lands well." He discarded the luxurious court life his father had conducted to compete with the glittering courts of France and Austria and introduced an austere court. He also created a first-rate civil service staffed by duty-conscious, highly respected, but poorly paid officials.

His popular name, "the Soldier King," indicates where his primary attention was paid. Although during his entire reign he led his country into only one short war, he poured four-fifths of all state income into the army, whose size he doubled to 70,000 men. The stunningly rapid growth of the Prussian army in size and importance prompted the Frenchman Mirabeau to remark shortly after the death of Friedrich Wilhelm I, "Other states possess an army; Prussia is an army that possesses a state!"

Located in the middle of Europe with a conglomeration of often-unconnected territories and no natural frontiers and a relatively small population, Prussia had to have a strong army to maintain itself in the kind of international setting that prevailed at that time. One could argue the Prussian army was disproportionately large in relation to the country's population and financial strength. But it must be remembered that the new army was still considerably smaller than those of Austria, France, and Russia and that "militarism" was by no means restricted to Prussia during this "Age of Absolutism." Further, the Prussian army never "possessed" the state, as Mirabeau charged. It was the most disciplined army in the world and never made the slightest attempt to rule the state.

The army was, without a doubt, first rate. Thomas Carlyle once wrote that Prussia had a shorter sword than Austria, France, and Russia but that it could draw it out of the sheath much more quickly. It was open to the newest military technology. Also, the Prussian army became more and more a national army and less and less a mercenary army. Prussia was one of the first countries in the world to learn that its own citizens serve better than the troops of a foreign country. Its discipline and well-planned supply system was also a blessing for the civilian population in those areas where the army operated. In an age of undisciplined armies that "lived off the land," the civilian population was constantly subjected to plunder, murder, and rape. Civilians seldom needed to fear such horrors from the new Prussian army.

Friedrich Wilhelm I was interested solely in establishing the best-organized, most modern, and most efficient state and military in the world. Unlike his father and his son, he was utterly disinterested in art and education. This brought him into violent conflict with his son. The father was a stern ruler who was wholly absorbed in enhancing his state's power. In 1758 his son, who in 1740 had become King Friedrich II, wrote this about his father: "Books, flutes, writings—if he could ever get his hands on them, they were thrown into the fireplace, and the burning of my books was always accompanied by several blows or by very emphatic rebukes."

Voltaire's room at Sans Souci

Friedrich the Great

The son was a sensitive, highly intelligent humanist who composed flute concertos, which are still played in concerts, and who preferred all his life to use the French language. He even wrote thoroughly respectable poetry and essays in French. Most of his writings, which now fill 25 volumes, are in French rather than German, which he never learned to write without numerous mistakes. He was a close friend of the French philosopher and satirist Voltaire, whom he invited for prolonged visits to Berlin and Potsdam. In general, the young Friedrich was open to all the cultural, philosophical, and liberal political ideas of his day. He was an enlightened man with a strong sense of taste, as his favorite residence in Potsdam, Sans Souci (French for "carefree"), manifested his nature. He despised the absolutist government of his father, even if it was aimed for the good of the people. Once, at age 18, he even tried to flee his father's kingdom with a close friend, but they were caught and delivered back to an irate parent and placed in prison.

What should his father have done? Have the heir to the throne and his friend both hanged for treason? Disregard the law of the land and forgive both for a treasonous act? The father's solution: He had the friend executed for treason right in front of Friedrich's eyes. This paradoxical mixture

Germany

of strict justice, mercy and reason of state has troubled many people ever since.

Finally, at the age of 28, Friedrich II ascended to the throne in 1740. The young king's reaction to this event was characteristic: "How I abhor this job to which the blind coincidence of birth has condemned me!" Many persons saw in the new king the first philosopher to ascend a throne since the Roman emperor Marcus Aurelius. Friedrich announced, "any man who seeks the truth and loves it, must be treasured in any human society." Within the first week of his rule, he abolished torture in all cases but high treason. Throughout his 48-year reign, he demanded of every subject a strict performance of his duty. But he was always inclined to permit anything else that did not directly hurt the interests of the state. This tolerance was applied not only to religious practices and intellectual and artistic pursuits but to personal behavior, as well.

After Friedrich became king, he for all practical purposes put his flute away forever. Before he had been crowned, he had referred to a military uniform as "a gown of death," but afterward he was scarcely ever seen wearing anything else. His transformation from a sensitive humanist to "the first servant of the state," as he later called himself, is one of the intriguing mysteries of history. Few would have ever guessed in 1740 that he would become known as Friedrich the Great as a result of his leadership.

As king he had become a lonesome figure with a tortured soul, inwardly unhappy but restlessly active, working 18 hours per day. He was always unkempt and ungrounded, and he loved nobody and was loved by nobody. He had especially troubled relations with women and preferred the company of men in his beloved Sans Souci palace in Potsdam. Against his will he was pressured by his family to marry Elisabeth Christine von Braunschweig. He relented, but after about three years, he packed her off to a separate palace and saw her only a few times the rest of his life. It need not be said that their marriage was childless.

The first half of his reign was a time of almost constant war, which at times seemed to threaten his country's very existence but which in the end elevated Prussia to the rank of a great European power. The newly crowned king had just published an elegant attack on Machiavelli's immorality and duplicity in politics; within weeks Friedrich unleashed an unprovoked and unjustified attack on Austrian-owned Silesia. Certainly, he was no more unscrupulous than most other rulers of the time, but in this and in almost all other wars during his reign, justice happened to be on the side of his enemies.

Friedrich later said that he had started what was known as "The War of the Austrian Succession" because "the satisfaction of seeing my name in the newspapers and later in history had seduced me." However, one should not take very seriously such remarks made by such a cynic as Friedrich. What really motivated him was a unique opportunity: In the same year he had become king (1740), a young and politically inexperienced woman, Maria-Theresia, had ascended the Austrian throne. He calculated that she would not have known how to respond to such a brazen act on Prussia's part. There were few Austrian troops in Silesia, so the venture promised to be a military cakewalk.

Perhaps surprisingly, the young Austrian empress rejected Friedrich's ultimatum to withdraw from the province, so the latter unleashed his troops in late 1740. The two armies clashed in furious battle at Mollwitz, and things looked so hopeless for the Prussians that the young ruler actually fled from the battlefield, an offense normally punishable by death. But he was saved by a Prussian victory later that day. Ultimately, two campaigns were necessary to secure Prussian domination of Silesia, and by also taking a substantial portion of land from the Poles, Friedrich was able to unite East and West Prussia into a single territory.

Friedrich tried to justify his action in 1743: "I hope those who will later judge me . . . will be able to differentiate in me the philosopher from the prince, the honorable man from the politician. I must confess that whoever is dragged into the mess (Getriebe) of high-level European politics finds it very difficult to preserve his own

Friedrich the Great

Germany

character frankly and honestly." He wrote that the art of politics appears in many ways "as the opposite of private morality. However, it is the morality of the princes, who . . . do only that which promises to be to their advantage." The prince had no alternative to "following the practice which authorizes deceit and the abuse of power."

His qualms were not such that he could resist the temptation in 1756 to swoop into Saxony and thereby to become embroiled in the Seven Years' War with Austria, which lasted until 1763. Friedrich's troops met with initial success. He published Maria-Theresia's secret plans that were found in the Saxon state archives, which the Prussian troops had captured. These plans showed that the Austrian empress was by no means above duplicity when her state's interests were at stake.

This war provided clear examples of the extent to which the fate of whole nations depended at that time upon the personal preferences and whims of their absolutist rulers. When the Russian tsarina Elizabeth, the daughter of Tsar Peter the Great, was informed that Friedrich had cracked a joke about her at the dinner table in Sans Souci, she exploded with rage and joined Austria, France, Bavaria, and Saxony in a war against Prussia. Her decision almost dashed Friedrich's kingdom to its destruction. Soon the Russians were at the gates of Königsberg, the French were approaching the Elbe, and the Austrians reentered Silesia. Friedrich tirelessly led his almost

hopelessly outnumbered troops from one edge of his kingdom to the other, meeting first one enemy and then another. He was imaginative and bold, and his administration in Potsdam, which his predecessors had built up, worked like a perfectly constructed and oiled machine.

Though he received money from England, which as usual was very interested in weakening France, the Prussians stood alone against all the great European continental powers. Friedrich's army had lost almost all of its artillery by late 1760. Berlin had fallen to the enemy, and England had stopped sending money to a ruler so near to defeat. But in early 1762, a wonder occurred when Tsarina Elizabeth died. Her successor was Peter III, a glowing admirer of Friedrich the Great. He not only left the enemy coalition, but he also entered into an alliance with Prussia, thereby saving that country from certain defeat. Peter III was assassinated a year later, and his wife, who was later called Catherine the Great, quickly withdrew Russia from the war entirely. But by that time, Austria was physically and financially exhausted and had to sue for peace in 1763.

Peace for 23 Years

In the Peace of Hubertusburg, the situation seemed to revert to that which it had been prior to the start of the conflict, with Prussia retaining Silesia and East Prussia and with Saxon independence being reestablished. But in reality, this was a

great triumph for Prussia. By maintaining itself successfully against three great powers in Europe, it won recognition as a great power in its own right. Prussia also learned that good relations with Russia were absolutely essential, and until 1890 such relations remained a primary goal of every Prussian leader.

After the war's end, Prussia under Friedrich the Great enjoyed 23 years of peace. Prussia was able, however, to continue to enlarge itself by participating in the partition of Poland with Russia and Austria. Seeing that Russia was perfectly willing to intervene militarily in Poland in order to prevent any strengthening of the Polish state, Friedrich suggested the first partition in 1772. Maria-Theresia had serious qualms about such a dastardly act of political immorality, and Friedrich gleefully reported later, "she wept, but she took." In 1793 and 1795, these three powers partitioned Poland again, creating a potentially dangerous domestic political situation within Prussia by rendering the Poles a majority of all inhabitants within the borders of Prussia.

Friedrich II was one of the most brilliant military leaders of all time. It has been said that one of Adolf Hitler's favorite films was one about Friedrich the Great. It can only be considered unfortunate that one obvious lesson Hitler learned from the Hohenzollern ruler's almost miraculous victory in 1763, despite overwhelming material and manpower superiority of

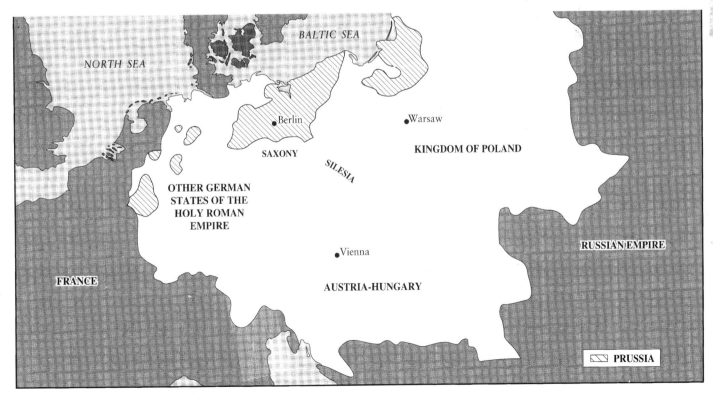

Middle Europe in 1740, when Maria Theresia (22) became empress of Austria, and Friedrich the Great (28), king of Prussia

Germany

the enemy coalition and crushing military defeats, was that an iron will and bitter determination not to surrender can ultimately carry the day. His tragic attempt to repeat Friedrich's feat almost two centuries later brought scarcely describable death and misery to Germany, its people, and its neighbors.

Friedrich II was called "the Great" during his own lifetime. This was not only because of his wars and his successful, if sometimes morally questionable, foreign policy, but also because of his reforms, his intellectual and cultural achievements as a young man, and the kind of state he helped to create. The Prussian state was feared by its neighbors because it was militarily strong and prepared and because of its qualities as a state. It had an uncorrupted administration, an independent judiciary, and a state of law (Rechtsstaat) in which there was more legal equality for all citizens than could be found in most other European states at the time. Journalists could write relatively freely, although Friedrich did have a newspaperman beaten who once wrote uncomplimentary things about the king.

Prussia's tolerance toward all religions was considered in Europe to be a very bad example during most of the 17th and 18th centuries. It was also very tolerant toward the different nationalities within its own borders and toward enlightened learning of all kinds. By the standards of the 18th century, which are those that should be used to judge the state ruled by Friedrich the Great, Prussia was a modern and enlightened state. It was certainly no democracy, but enlightenment in politics at first meant basing the affairs of state on reason. Such manifested itself in Europe initially in the form of absolutism, and France under Cardinal Richelieu was an early model. Not until the French Revolution, when a brand of enlightenment which stresses human rights and popular sovereignty and when the call of "liberty, equality, and fraternity" caught fire in Europe (outside Holland and England), was Prussia challenged by a state and by ideas that were clearly more modern than its own. Indeed, after Friedrich's death in 1786, the newly risen Prussia had only two more decades before it crumbled in the face of Napoleon's France.

The years 1789 to 1815 were for the German states years of unrest, of war, but also of almost unparalleled genius, talent, and productivity in literature and philosophy. It was a time of openness to new ideas, including political ones.

Admiration of America

The American Revolution had sparked the imagination of many literate Germans. The Americans were celebrated as the "Hellenes of our time," who, by challenging the exclusive rule of the "breed of the nobility," had shown feudal Europe the way to "sweet equality." The greatest German poet of all time was Johann Wolfgang von Goethe, who along with Friedrich Schiller was the greatest exponent of both the impetuous Storm and Stress (a literary age when writers rebelled against the restraints of classicism and the enlightenment) and of the restrained Classical period in German literature during the second half of the 18th and early part of the 19th centuries. Goethe wrote in *Poetry and Truth* that the youthful United States was "a magnificent country," "a magnet for the eyes of the whole world." He wrote, "America, your lot is fairer than ours."

In 1781 Friedrich Klopstock wrote a hymn to the new nation entitled "The Present War." It said, inter alia, "You are the rose dawn of a great new day . . . that will last for centuries." Two years later an anonymous poet gave expression to the popular feeling: "The nations of all Europe will respond with echoes of this holy victory."

While many Germans were inspired by the American ideas and events, it was the French Revolution in 1789 that brought the spark of democratic revolution to Europe. Prussia had been a state well-ordered from above; France was now a nation whose most powerful inspiration came from below—from the people. Revolutionary France was able to fuse ideals, whose force had already been put into practice in America, with national power to an extent that no country on the continent of Europe could resist. The French Revolution was a declaration of war against the old Europe. To underscore this, French revolutionary leaders promised in the early years of the revolution to help any people that rose up against despotic rulers, and Napoleon's Grand Army later carried the message through the heart of Europe and all the way to was compelled to join France and Russia in the Peace of Tilset. This peace treaty permitted Prussia to continue existing as a state, but it lost half its territory, including all Prussian lands west of the Elbe, and Moscow.

Napoleon—Admired and Despised

Some leading Germans greeted Napoleon and the French Revolution. The philosopher Friedrich Hegel called this mighty convulsion "the end of history," while his compatriot Immanuel Kant admired the idealism of the French masses, as did Friedrich Schiller, whose admiration, like that of many others, diminished when the guillotine began doing its grisly work. Goethe went to meet Napoleon in Erfurt, where the masses and princes greeted the Frenchman with such flattery and servility that Talleyrand wrote disgustedly, "They kiss the hand which could destroy them today or tomorrow." In Germany, Napoleonic power was recognized and, for one reason or another, respected. Wherever it was not, Napoleon sent his armies, and by 1807 all German states had been compelled one by one to make peace with France.

French domination over most of Germany brought an enormous territorial reshuffling at the expense of the smaller territories, which he eliminated. He abolished all religious rule over sovereign territories, gave the medium-sized states more territory, and elevated Bavaria and Wurttemberg to kingdoms. In 1806 he grouped 16 medium-sized states, including Bavaria, Wurttemberg, and Baden, into a Rhenish League, with one of Napoleon's brothers as the monarch, all under French protection. They were obligated to supply 64,000 troops to Napoleon, who assumed control over their armies. All were compelled to declare their exit from the German Empire, which thereby lost a third of its territory. This, combined with Napoleon's defeat of the Austrians and Russians at the battle of Austerlitz, 60 miles (100 km) north of Vienna in 1806, spelled the end of the German Empire, which had existed for almost 1,000 years, although it had been weak and very divided. Shortly thereafter, Emperor Franz II cast off the German imperial crown, and the Holy Roman Empire of the Germans came to an end.

Napoleon's objective was clear: He wished to create states in Germany that were strong enough to support France but too weak to constitute a threat to it. The French occupiers were loved nowhere in Germany, and French rule was absolute, in the sense that all orders came from above. Yet it was in some respects very progressive and liberal. Everyone was equal before the law, class privileges were reduced or abolished, schools were taken over by the state, the legal systems were simplified, and the churches' active hand in politics was reduced or eliminated. This liberal influence was most lasting in the Rhineland, where it henceforth always outweighed the absolutist tradition.

Prussia had made peace with Napoleon in 1795. This gave it a decade without war but also permitted Napoleon a free hand in Germany. When Prussia finally had to act against France, it stood alone. At first Napoleon had been friendly toward Prussia in order to keep it out of any coalition directed against France. There was no need for such friendliness once Austria had been defeated, so Napoleon simply marched his troops through Prussia. When the Prussian king, Friedrich Wilhelm III, protested this, Napoleon unleashed his armies against Prussia, delivering humiliating defeats in the Battles of Saalfeld, Jena, Auerstadt, and Friedland.

Napoleon on campaign

At the end of October 1806, Napoleon led his troops into Berlin, where he declared his continental blockade against England. He also helped himself, as he did in every land he dominated, to art treasures, including the four horses on top of the Brandenburg Gate, and shipped them off to Paris. In the summer of 1807, Prussia was compelled to provide France with money and troops. In short order, Prussia had been reduced to an insignificant country completely in the hands of Napoleon.

Partial Reform

After this devastating defeat, the Prussian king declared that the Prussian state must replace through intellectual and cultural strength what it had lost in material strength. He knew that Prussia had to reform and modernize itself, so he appointed such men as Karl vom und zu Stein, Karl August von Hardenberg, Neidhart von Gneisenau, Gerhard von Scharnhorst, and Wilhelm von Humboldt to make all Prussian citizens, in von Gneisenau's words, "free, noble and independent so that they believe that they are part of the whole."

Prussia now experienced a burst of reform activity, brought to a head by the misery of defeat. The overall strength of that country seemed to indicate the strength of the new ideas coming out of France. The social, political, military, and educational reforms were not sufficiently democratic in the modern sense, and some of them were undone after 1815. But they were without a doubt step in the right direction, and they aroused much enthusiasm throughout Germany at the time.

Serfdom was abolished, although the serfs were obliged to pay for their emancipation by incurring debts or by ceding much of land they had tilled to the former landowners. Thus, many Junker (aristocratic landholder) estates actually grew larger, and many former serfs became landless agricultural workers whose lot in life had improved very little, especially since the landowners still maintained control over police and the lower-level judiciary within their districts. Still, it was an important turning point which allowed peasants to win back much of what they had lost in 1525. Noblemen were allowed to practice bourgeois professions, such as law and commerce, and the bourgeoisie was permitted to acquire former knightly estates. Also, Jews were granted social and economic equality, though they still did not gain equal political rights.

The cities were given a greater measure of self-rule in that public officials were to be elected by all property owners. Right into the 20th century, local government in Prussia was admired throughout Europe, even though it stood in sharp contrast to the semi absolutism in the countryside.

General von Scharnhorst wrote in 1798, "we will not be able to win battles until we learn like the Jacobins to awaken the community spirit." The model was the new French army, and the goal was to create an army motivated by patriotic spirit. All degrading punishments were abolished. Universal military service was introduced "to unify the army and the nation," and foreigners were no longer permitted to serve. Ability was to become the sole criterion for advancement, so the officer ranks were opened up more to non-noblemen. The change was slow, but the percentage of commoners in the officer corps rose from 7% in 1806 to 21% by 1848.

The farsighted minister of culture, Wilhelm von Humboldt, introduced educational reforms aimed at opening up the

Germany

system to the talented from all classes. Elementary schools were created for all, and humanistic high schools (each called a Gymnasium) were created for those destined to rise to higher positions. In 1810 the University of Berlin was created. This was the first university in Germany to combine free research and teaching, and it was permitted to administer itself in order to guarantee it continuing freedom.

From 1807 until 1812, the Germans experienced a peace that was really more like a slow preparation for war. In 1812 the great part of Napoleon's Grand Army, which at the time included some 30.000 Bavarians, 30,000 Austrians, and 20.000 Prussians, froze in the snows of Russia. German statesmen stuck their wet political fingers in the air and began to make secret preparations for a change of alliances. Napoleon feared that the worst was ahead of him. In mid-1813 he called the Austrian chancellor Metternich to his headquarters in Dresden and announced that he "would not withdraw from a single inch of territory. . . I was brought up on the battlefield, and a man like me worries little about the lives of a million persons." Metternich asked icily why he said such a thing behind closed doors instead of announcing it from one end of France to the other. Napoleon replied, "It may cost me my throne, but I will bury the world underneath its rubble." Just 132 years later, another defeated dictator who had brought war and destruction to all of

Europe would say the very same thing from an underground bunker in Berlin.

Within four months after his meeting with Metternich, Napoleon's hold on Germany, Italy, and Spain had been broken. Napoleon suffered a crushing defeat in late 1813 at the Battle of the Nations near Leipzig, a battle that brought a scarcely believable carnage: 70,000 Frenchmen and 52,000 allies lost their lives. On March 31, 1814, the Russian tsar and the Prussian king marched into Paris at the head of their troops. The following year an English army under Wellington and a Prussian army under Generals Blucher and Gneisenau played the key roles in defeating Napoleon once and for all at Waterloo.

Napoleon's occupation of Germany was not a total disaster—he left the German nation far less fragmented than it had been before—about 300 German states, cities and territories had been joined into 50, and the Vienna Congress would reduce that number even further. This paved the way for a united and aggressive Germany in the future. The French also brought a valuable reform impulse.

As in 1918 and 1919, it was most unfortunate that democratic ideas had been brought into Germany by the troops of an alien occupation power. The French Revolution therefore ultimately created in the minds of many influential Germans considerable enmity toward France and toward democratic ideas. Initially, some leading Germans greeted this momentous

event, and in Mainz a revolutionary republic inspired by France was established briefly. However, the excesses of the Revolution became increasingly visible, and it progressed from civil war within France to an international struggle for power, largely on German soil. These excesses led some important Germans, such as Goethe and Schiller, to reject revolution as a valid means of change, and it therefore strengthened the traditional German allergy toward revolution. The bloody excesses in France also led many to doubt that the French Revolution was in fact a step in the direction of eliminating political tyranny and social injustice.

The French occupation of Germany also spawned German nationalism by enabling persons in all parts of Germany to put aside some of their local patriotism and to struggle side by side to rid Germany of a foreign power. From then on, German nationalism became an increasingly important factor. Since no unified German state yet existed, German nationalism took on an idealistic and romantic character.

Also, since it was born in reaction to a conqueror who seemed to understand how to achieve French national interests under the cover of high-sounding calls for "liberty, equality, and fraternity," German nationalism and the struggle against alien rule became linked in the minds of far too many Germans with resistance against the ideals of the French Revolution, known in Germany as the "ideas of 1789."

This unfortunate link helped conservative rulers throughout Germany to water down or undo reforms Napoleon had introduced or promised before 1815. It also established in many German minds a strong resistance, which lasted until at least 1945, to the ideas of democracy, equality, civil rights, popular sovereignty, mass participation in politics, and representative government legitimized by the consent of the governed.

The Congress of Vienna

The statesmen at the Congress of Vienna were tired of revolution and were interested in restoring much of which had existed a quarter-century earlier. None wanted a unified Germany, and none wanted the dissolution of his own state. Their chief objective was to protect Europe from a renewal of the kinds of shocks and challenges that had come out of France. None talked of popular sovereignty, but all spoke of legitimate monarchy. In the end, Prussia gave up some land to a newly created Kingdom of Poland but received the northern part of Saxony, Swedish Pomerania, and the island of Rugen, as well as territory in the Rhineland and Westphalia. These new territories were separated from

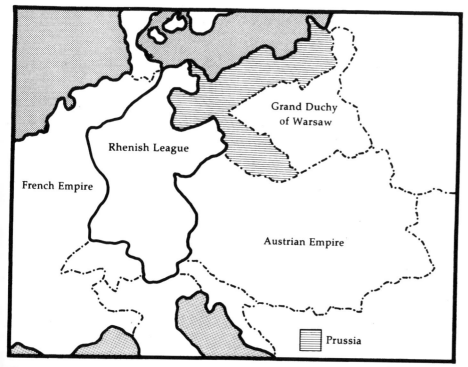

The Rhenish League, or *Confederation of the Rhine*

the rest of Prussia by Hanover, Brunswick, and Hesse-Cassel, but they placed it along a common border with France. Its job was one that was earlier performed by Austria—to prevent France, whose 1789 borders remained practically unchanged, from threatening central Europe. As a result of the settlement, Prussia grew into Germany, while Austria grew out of Germany toward northern Italy and the Balkans. The mineral resources in Upper Silesia and the Rhineland provided Prussia with the potential to become the greatest industrial power in Germany and ultimately in Europe.

The Congress of Vienna had, as we saw, no interest in a unified Germany, but it did create a German Confederation to replace the old empire that had died a quiet death almost a decade earlier. The confederation was a loose association of 35 sovereign German principalities (including the five kingdoms of Prussia, Hanover, Bavaria, Wurttemberg, and Saxony) and 4 free cities. Its sole institution was a federal parliament (Bundestag) in Frankfurt, whose chairman was always an Austrian and whose delegates were not elected but were appointed by the member states. In other words, it was a diplomatic organization, not a real parliament. It was dominated by Austria and Prussia, whose main goal by now was to prevent all change. They were not alone.

The violent events that had shaken Europe in the past quarter-century had left many Germans and non-Germans alike longing for peace, order, and authority. All members of the confederation pledged, however, to introduce constitutions, which, if they were observed, would always place limits on rulers. Such constitutions never saw the light of day in most German states until more than three decades later. This included Prussia and Austria, where absolutism was quickly restored and which joined with Russia in a "Holy Alliance" in 1815 to suppress signs of revolution anywhere in Europe. Only in southern Germany were constitutions introduced that established monarchies and brought more citizens into political life. The most shining example was Baden, where the first signs of parliamentary democracy in Germany became visible.

Conservatism and Obedience

After 1815 there was an ultraconservative reaction led by the governments of Prussia and Austria, a development that sorely disappointed many Germans, especially the youth. Many had hoped during the wars of liberation from French domination that Germany would become democratic and united. Indeed, they believed that the despotic power of the individual German sovereigns could be

broken by creating a unified Germany. Until the 1860s the aims of unity and freedom went hand in hand. Nowhere were these hopes stronger than at the universities, where idealistic students formed highly politicized fraternities under the banner of "honor, freedom, fatherland." The fraternity members dressed in clothing fashionable in Germany in much earlier days, and their colors were black, red, and gold, which had been the colors of volunteers during the wars of liberation and which thereafter became the symbolic colors of republicanism in Germany. They are Germany's colors today.

The fraternity at the University of Jena sponsored in 1817 a mass assembly at Wartburg Castle for persons from all over Germany on the 4th anniversary of the Battle of Leipzig and the 300th anniversary of Luther's Reformation. Thousands came, and passionate speeches were given calling for individual liberty, constitutional government, and German unity. Reactionary policies of the leading German states were criticized. At the end of this nationalistic rally, the father of the popular gymnastic associations, Friedrich Ludwig Jahn, organized a particularly unfortunate ceremony which was repeated 116 years later in Berlin: Not only the symbols of authority, such as a pigtail and a Prussian corporal's cane, but also "un-German" books were thrown into a huge bonfire.

Among the books thrown to the flames were those of a playwright, August von Kotzebue. Two years later a deranged and

fanatical theology student assassinated him, calling him a "traitor of youth." This senseless act was just what the leaders of most German states needed to declare the Carlsbad Acts in 1819. They called for rigid censorship, prohibition of any political activity directed against the authoritarian order in most states, the outlawing of fraternities (which continued to operate underground), and close scrutiny and supervision of the universities. The Prussian king dismissed all his reformist ministers, and Prussia and Austria remained the centers of conservative reaction.

Romanticism

For the next three decades, Germans were intellectually as divided as ever. This era has been called the Biedermeier period: a time of relative peace and security in which the bulk of Germans passively did not look very far beyond their family and village lives. This view of life is well-portrayed by the paintings of Carl Spitzweg and the operas of Albert Lortzing. Another artistic and philosophical movement, romanticism, emerged at roughly the same time. Romanticism stressed feelings and was a reaction against the rationality of the enlightenment. The romantic sought to break all barriers, including those of reason, and sought refuge in the past, in nature, in art, or in fantasy. He was drawn to legends and fairy tales, especially following publication by Jacob and Wilhelm Grimm of German fairy tales in the years 1812–1814 and of legends a few years later.

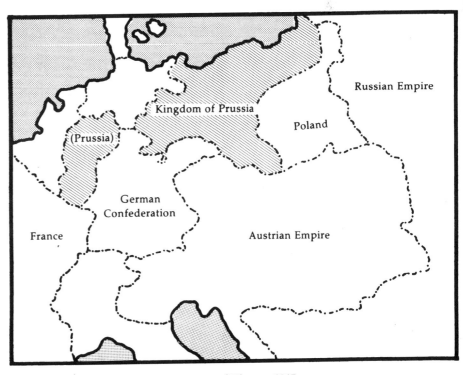

Prussia and Austria after the Congress of Vienna, 1815

Germany

Caspar David Friedrich's *Two Men Gazing at the Moon* (1819)

Romanticism in art was best portrayed by the painter Caspar David Friedrich, whose superb landscape paintings showed the links between man and nature; in literature by the Schlegel brothers, E. T. A. Hoffmann, Clemens Brentano, Ludwig Tieck, Joseph von Eichendorff, and Eduard Mörike; and in music by Franz Schubert and Carl Maria von Weber. At first romanticism was not political. But by the end of the 19th century, it had seeped into the political thinking of many Germans and lent their views an often unrealistic and immoderate air.

A third and expressly political trend was liberalism, that longing for the previously promised but largely undelivered constitutional government and individual freedom. The uprising in Paris in 1830 spread to cities all over Germany and forced the introduction of constitutions in Brunswick, Hanover, Hesse-Cassel, and Saxony. There were further uprisings in 1832.

Queen Victoria ascended the British throne in 1837, which nominally included the Hanover crown. The linkage had been established in 1713 when the Hanover monarch George became king of England. Tradition, however, forbade women from ruling Hanover. The new Hanoverian king abolished the constitution, an act publicly opposed by seven prominent professors at the University of Gottingen, including the Grimm brothers. When the seven were promptly dismissed and given three days

to leave the kingdom, loud voices of protest were heard throughout Germany.

It was in reaction to the reestablishment of authoritarian rule in a politically fragmented Germany that gave rise in the early 1830s to the Young Germany movement, to which a number of German writers belonged, most notably Heinrich Heine and Ludwig Börne. These young writers were convinced that literary figures should become politically active and socially critical. Their influence was so feared by the authorities that the German Confederation forbade their writings in 1835, and their leading exponents were driven into exile, particularly to Paris.

Like most German intellectuals of their time, these writers saw German nationalism and liberalism as goals that went hand in hand. It was in this spirit that Hoffman von Fallersleben wrote a song, "Deutschland, Deutschland uber alles," ("Germany, Germany above All Others") in the 1840s. The melody had earlier been written by Austrian Joseph Haydn and was a well-known hymn in Protestant churches. This song, which became the national anthem for a united Germany in 1871 and whose third verse is Germany's anthem today, is often misunderstood as having been a call for German domination over the whole world. In fact, it was directed against the disunity of Germany. It was a call for placing the goal of a united and democratic Germany above all provincial loyalties

and above all inclinations to find happiness in one's own private corner. The final verse sums up the song's message: "Unity and Law and Freedom for the German Fatherland." It was assumed that all these goals were inseparably linked.

A final powerful intellectual force at the time was the Berlin philosopher Friedrich Hegel, whose almost encyclopedic work gave rise to at least two contradictory traditions: one supporting authoritarian rule and one supporting revolution. In some of his writings, Hegel describes the state as an organism that is not a mere instrument in the hands of the citizens, but which grows and has needs of its own. Such growth, he argues, is completely rational; in fact, he maintains that reason reaches its highest perfection in the state. Which state had reached the highest existing perfection? The Prussian state, he answers. A state's power reflects the rationality of the state. "What is rational is actual and what is actual is rational," he writes. The life of the individual human being has meaning only within the state, he argues. Authoritarian rulers could not have been more pleased with a philosophical doctrine than with this one.

However, Hegel also developed a doctrine called the dialectic, which involves the clash of opposites and the development of something entirely new. Hegel meant the clash of ideas, but one of his bright German PhD students, Karl Marx, converted this concept of clashing ideas to one of clashing economic forces. The explosive implications of this theory became clear very soon. Marx, who was born in Trier, the son of a Prussian customs official, and who married a woman of minor nobility, was forced to flee Germany in 1843 because of the biting social and political criticism that he wrote in his Cologne newspaper, Rheinische Zeitung. In his London exile, he wrote in 1848 the *Communist Manifesto*, which predicts a violent revolution as a result of which the working (proletarian) class would replace the capitalist overlords who owned the land and factories. This powerful tract ends with the words "Proletarians of the world, rise up; you have nothing to lose but your chains!" Such a rising never came in England or in Germany, but Marxism became a far more significant intellectual and political doctrine in Germany than in the United States.

Closer to Unity

The German Customs Union was established in 1834 by all German states except Austria, Hanover, Mecklenburg, Oldenburg, Holstein, and the Hansa cities. This farsighted move, which created a unified inland market, not only became the cornerstone for a united Germany 37 years later, but it also became an important model years later for the EC. The German Customs Union greatly stimulated the industrialization of Germany, whose population at the time was three-fourths agricultural. At the same time, it diminished the position within Germany of Austria and enhanced the economic predominance of Prussia.

The authoritarian German princes seemed to be firmly in their saddles when they were severely shaken in 1848 by a spark of revolution, which had started in Sicily and southern Italy and which, as usual, arrived in Germany via France. But the rebels' objectives in Germany and France were different. What many Germans wanted was unity and freedom, things that had already been realized in whole or in part in France a half-century earlier. As a student in Bonn, Carl Schurz, wrote in his memoirs, "The word democracy was on all tongues and many thought it a matter of course that, if the princes should try to withhold from the people the rights and liberties demanded, force would take the place of mere petition."

Few Germans wanted a revolution as in France in 1789, but many wanted the traditional authorities to approve of more freedom for the people and of a constitutional monarchy that would include the principle of popular sovereignty. What specific demands were made became clear very quickly. In frightened response to the spontaneous demonstrations and assemblies in the first week of March 1848, many princes granted freedom of press and assembly, the creation of citizen's militias, jury trials, reform of the electoral system, and collaboration in constructing a federal German state.

In Prussia, King Friedrich Wilhelm IV waited a little too long to make concessions. Not until he had been informed that Metternich had been driven out of Austria did he decide to grant Prussia a constitution and support the move toward a united Germany. An unfortunate incident in the square before the royal palace, where nervous troops fired a volley of shots into a crowd that had presumably assembled to applaud the king's concessions, touched off a rampage of violence in Berlin that was not to be duplicated until the end of World War I. The Prussian troops, which had not engaged in combat since the Battle of Waterloo, were baffled and quickly demoralized by fighting street battles against snipers, who fought from rooftops and from behind barricades and who disappeared into side streets and alleys when regular troops closed in on them.

After one day of such fighting, the army was compelled to withdraw from the city,

Courtesy: *Irmgard M. Baylor*

but the king valiantly chose to stay with his "dear Berliners." He was thus a sort of captive of the revolutionaries and was forced to call together bourgeois and intellectual groups to discuss reforms. He later looked back with regret on that humiliating time: "We were on our bellies then." It seemed that the death knell for the loosely organized group of mainly authoritarian states called Germany had been rung, but time would reveal that the princes had just temporarily lost their nerve. By the end of March 1848, all German states, including Austria and Prussia, had concluded that there was no alternative to allowing representatives to be elected by universal manhood suffrage to a national parliament to draft a liberal constitution for a German federation. This first German national parliament convened on May 18 in the Paul's Church in Frankfurt on the Main.

The Parliament of the Professors

This has often been called the "parliament of the professors" because of the fact that an overwhelming number of delegates were professors, lawyers, or university-educated civil servants who had little practical experience in politics and in typical German scholarly fashion spent weeks on end discussing abstract notions of law, freedom, and the state. The delegates had good intentions and produced an admirable document called the Fundamental Rights of the German People. However, they were unable to unite on the question of parliamentary control of royal power. Gradually, their slow, deliberate, and discursive work was overtaken by events outside the Paul's Church. The demands for reform were not quite strong enough to realize themselves. The resulting frustration led to outbursts of violence in Vienna, Frankfurt, Berlin, and elsewhere that discredited the entire reformist movement in more and more Germans' eyes.

The reestablishment of firm monarchical control in Vienna stimulated a longing for order. Suspicions among the states and the classes began to reassert themselves. Nowhere was this more evident than in Prussia, where the king soon began resisting any diminution of his power. The king's disposition was strengthened by a renewal of mob violence in Berlin in June 1848, in which weapons in the state armory were seized and distributed among the rebels. This violence frightened the middle-class citizens and played into the hands of the king.

He ordered the troops back into their Berlin barracks in November, an order that ignited more resistance and that could be carried out only by force. But this order ended the revolutionary activity in Prussia. Friedrich Wilhelm caught many of his critics off guard by decreeing a constitution. Revised in 1850, this document provided formal safeguards for Prussian subjects' liberties and established a bicameral legislature that was clearly designed to prevent truly innovative action by more

Germany

radical elements. The upper house was composed mainly of the nobility and the lower house was elected in a complicated way based on the amount of taxes the citizens paid; two-thirds of the seats were thereby elected by 15% of the population, which paid two-thirds of the total taxes. This strange electoral system remained a thorn in the side of the Prussian working class and liberal reformers until it was finally abolished in 1918. Despite its many shortcomings, though, this constitution was a step away from absolute government and toward constitutional, parliamentary government in Prussia.

After entirely too much debate, the Frankfurt parliament made two fundamental decisions: First, the majority recommended a "small German" solution to German unity, with close links to Austria rather than a "large German" solution under the Habsburgs of Austria. It was decided that it would be nonsense to establish a German nation-state that would include Milan, Venice, Budapest, Prague, and Krakow. Second, it offered the German imperial crown to the Prussian king in 1849.

Friedrich Wilhelm IV brusquely rejected this gift with the words "If the thousand-year-old crown of the German nation, unused now for 42 years, is again to be given away, it is I and my likes who will give it!" No doubt, it was not his idea of monarchy

to see it based on the sovereignty of the people and offered by lawyers and professors who had been elected by the people. It is possible that he would have accepted it from other princes. But the king was aware that accepting such a crown might very well have meant war with Austria, which, as later events showed, was not prepared to accept German unity under Prussian domination without a fight. He could also not forget his heritage nor muster enthusiasm for a new state in which the Prussian identity might ultimately disappear.

His rejection of the crown sealed the fate of the revolution. Nevertheless, for the rest of the year he continued to send diplomatic feelers to some other German princes to explore the chances of establishing a form of German unity more to his liking, but these came to nothing. More successful was his troops' suppression of the last acts of rebellion in Saxony in 1849, where they restored the Saxon king to the throne, and during the summer in Baden and the Rhineland-Palatinate, where they crushed a ragtag "people's army" of intellectuals, poets, and professional and amateur revolutionaries. That last victory enabled the king of Wurttemberg to disband the Frankfurt parliament, which had dwindled to about 100 die-hards who had fled to Stuttgart. His comment: "Against democrats only soldiers will do. Adieu!"

Migration to America

As was the case after Hitler jolted Germany with his brutal intolerance after 1933, America greatly profited from the events that had shaken Germany in 1848–1849. Revolutionaries and sympathizers fled by the thousands to the United States, which had been one of the few countries in the world to send a message of encouragement to the Frankfurt Parliament. These German exiles brought their ideals and their zeal with them, and many of them spoke out elegantly against slavery, streamed into the new Republican Party, and fought mainly on the side of the North during the Civil War. Frederick Hecker organized an all-German regiment for Lincoln; the young Graf (Count) Ferdinand von Zeppelin made his first ascent in a balloon in America and acted as an aerial observer for the North in the Civil War.

The former leaders of the Baden Revolutionary Army, Franz Siegel and Carl Schurz, fought for the North. Major General Siegel led an army in the Battle of New Market on May 15, 1864, against Confederate units that included the Virginia Military Institute corps of cadets. Partly because of the young cadets' legendary bravery, Siegel's forces were badly beaten. Schurz was a particularly towering figure among the "1848ers." He campaigned for Lincoln in the 1860 election, was named by

19th-century Hamburg

the winner as ambassador to Madrid, but resigned this post later in order to return to America to command a division in the Union Army.

Under President Rutherford B. Hayes, he was secretary of the interior and introduced civil service reform and advocated the integration of the Indians into American society. New Yorkers today can stroll in the Carl Schurz Park on East End Ave and 86th Street. In the 19th and early 20th centuries, 86th Street from Lexington to Second Avenue was popularly known as "Sauerkraut Boulevard" and the "German Broadway." It was during the Civil War that the cartoonist Thomas Nast, who had emigrated from Landau to New York in 1846 and later to Morristown, NJ, drew the rotund, red-nosed Santa Claus who became firmly anchored in the American imagination. He was also responsible for many other American caricatures: the Democratic Party's donkey, the GOP's elephant, and Uncle Sam.

The end of the American Civil War stimulated even greater numbers of Germans to seek a better life in America. In the years between 1866 and 1896, Germans were the largest immigrant group to go to America, reaching a peak of a half-million in 1882, or more than two-thirds of all immigrants in that year. In fact, Germans led in overall immigration between 1820 and 1920, and in 1907 alone, 1.3 million Germans arrived in the United States. Most settled in the quadrangle of New York-Minneapolis-St. Louis-Baltimore, where they established German communities with their own schools, newspapers, churches, hospitals, and clubs. They also opened breweries and beer gardens.

Their habit of engaging in more pleasant Sunday activities, such as sponsoring band contests, festivals, or simply walking with the family or chatting in a beer garden, contributed to lightening the Sunday severity found all too often in 19th-century America. In the 21st century, some 49 million Americans (17% of the total population) consider themselves to be of German descent. There are actually more, since many Americans identified themselves as "western European" and "northern European" in the 2000 census rather than specifying countries. Americans of German descent are the largest ethnic group in 23 US states, ranging from Alaska to Florida. In Wisconsin and the Dakotas, they constitute more than 40% of the populations. Unlike Poles, Italians, or Irish, they are not a cohesive group influencing political life.

The history of these German Americans is traced by the German American Heritage Museum, which opened its doors in Washington, DC, in March 2010. One learns, for example, that the forebears of Elvis Presley immigrated to America in 1710 under the name Pressler. Also, the inventor of blue jeans, Levi Strauss, hailed from Germany. The museum was funded mainly by an umbrella group of many contemporary German American fraternal and social clubs.

Prussian Power Emerges

The 1848 revolution was over. It has often been said that the Germans' main problem was that they had never had a successful revolution. Of course, as the case of England demonstrates, revolutions are not absolutely essential in the establishment of democratic government, as long as reform is possible. However, Germany was to experience too little reform in years to come. Many liberals who had participated in the "March Revolution" became very self-critical after its failure and became convinced that they had to adjust their political objectives much more to the prevailing political conditions. They thus became more open to ideas associated with Otto von Bismarck, who had become the Prussian minister-president a few years later: Realpolitik (politics that recognize the hard facts of the world) and the inclination to tone down the demand for freedom if the possibility of national unity is at stake.

During the two decades following the events of 1848–1849, Prussia not only steadily increased its industrial base and power, but it also moved aggressively to establish the preconditions for German unity under Prussian domination. One step was the submission by the new king, Wilhelm I, of a bill to reorganize and double the size of the army, a measure hotly opposed by a majority in Prussia's lower house. The majority did grant a large sum to strengthen the existing army units, but when Wilhelm simply used this money to finance his desired reorganization, the parliament refused to grant any more funds until the king canceled his unauthorized

army reform. The result was such a serious deadlock and tension that the king reportedly considered resigning. Only a person of extraordinary skill could lead Prussia out of this crisis. That man was soon found: Bismarck.

Bismarck's background and reputation seemed to be just what a conservative king like Wilhelm I would have wanted. An East Elbian aristocrat, his disdain for scholarly things and his youthful love for beer-swilling and disorderly conduct had caused him to be banished from the city limits of Göttingen, where he had been sent for an unsuccessful year of university study. Yet, since 1850 he had gained much diplomatic experience, first as the Prussian representative to the parliament of the German Confederation in Frankfurt, then as an envoy in St. Petersburg and Paris. These assignments helped him to broaden his scope beyond Prussia and to conclude that Prussia should become the heart of a unified Germany without Austria.

Already in 1856, he had written, "Germany is clearly too small for us both. . . In the not-too-distant future we shall have to fight for our existence against Austria . . . since the course of events in Germany has no other solution."

Appointed Prussian minister-president in 1862, Bismarck was unsuccessful in persuading parliament to accept the king's plans for reforming the army. For a while he simply ignored parliament, but he knew that he could not continue to do so forever. Thus, he decided to initiate a bold foreign policy, which would capture the imagination of nationalists and liberals alike and which would ultimately achieve German unity. The success of this policy won the admiration of many of his countrymen for generations to come.

Bismarck's first years as chancellor of Prussia were ones of armament and war. In 1864, 1866, and 1870, he conducted short but significant wars against Denmark, Austria, and France. The war conducted by both Prussia and Austria against Denmark in 1864 over Danish control of the predominantly German-populated territories of Schleswig and Holstein gave Prussian commanders useful battlefield experience. The Prussian victory at Düppel in Jutland in Jutland also stimulated patriotic feeling in Prussia and in other German states. It weakened liberal opposition to the army reform bill and inclined more and more Germans to look to Prussia for leadership.

It is hardly surprising that the joint administration of Schleswig-Holstein agreed upon by the Prussian and Austrian victors did not go well. Friction was inevitable, and Bismarck was very astute in exploiting it to force a showdown with Austria, which would never have peacefully

C. Schurz

Carl Schurz

Germany

Kaiser Wilhelm I

acquiesced to his designs for German unity. In mid-1866 Bismarck ordered Prussian troops to occupy Holstein, and after declaring the German Confederation dissolved, he declared war on Austria. It lasted only seven weeks. With new breech-loading rifles, which had just been used so successfully in the American Civil War, and with the capacity to move their troops to the battlefield on new railroads, the far-better-prepared Prussians were able to deliver a stinging defeat to the Austrian and Saxon armies at the Battle of Königgrätz. This victory eliminated Austria from the soon-to-be unified Germany.

North German Confederation

In mid-1867 a North German Confederation composed of 22 German states north of the Main River came into existence, with the king of Prussia as its president. Bismarck's very moderate treatment

Otto von Bismarck

of the defeated Austrian Empire enabled Prussia to gain in Austria a trustworthy ally for a half-century. When in 1870 Prussia launched its final war to establish German unity, Austria did not support that last active opponent to a united Germany—France.

With increasing nervousness, the French looked east across the Rhine, where Bismarck had created momentum toward German unity. Feverish French diplomatic activity in the south German states and Austria failed to create determined opposition to Prussia. The crisis erupted in mid-year, when the Prussian government announced that Prince Leopold of the House of Hohenzollern had accepted the Spanish throne, which had been vacant since 1868. As Bismarck well knew, the French would never tolerate a Hohenzollern on the Spanish throne, since they would then face a hostile dynasty on their eastern and southwestern borders. The French ambassador to Prussia, Benedetti, persuaded Wilhelm I at the spa Bad Ems that it would be a good idea to withdraw Leopold's candidacy.

Wilhelm politely refused to assure the French diplomat that the Hohenzollern candidacy would not be renewed in the future. The king wired his description of the talks to Bismarck, who then published the telegram after intentionally shortening it in such a way that Wilhelm's reply to Benedetti seemed far more abrupt and impolite than it actually had been. The French were infuriated by this "Ems Telegram," and in an atmosphere of inflamed emotion, the French government declared war on Prussia on July 19.

The Birth of the German Empire

To French surprise, the south German states immediately joined the Prussians in the war. Never known for indecision, the Prussians struck quickly and fatally. Smashing through Lorraine, the Prussian army cut Paris off from the two main French armies and delivered a devastating blow to the French at Sedan on the Belgian border. By January 1871, all resistance ended. A humiliated France looked on as the German Empire was proclaimed in the Hall of Mirrors in the Palace of Versailles on January 18, 1871. For the first time in history, there was a united Germany. The Prussian king became Kaiser Wilhelm I.

Bismarck was probably mistaken in acquiescing to pressures from the kaiser (Caesar—i.e., "emperor"), Prussian military leaders, and others by imposing a harsh peace on a prostrate France. Germany annexed Alsace and most of Lorraine, with their advanced industry and rich iron deposits. Also, France was required to pay a very large indemnity and to allow German occupation troops to remain in France until the sum was paid.

For the next half-century, French policy would revolve around undoing these terrible losses, and the pigeons that German leaders had turned loose in 1871 would in 1919 come back to roost with a vengeance.

These limited wars were models of the primacy of political over military objectives. Military actions ceased the moment Bismarck's political objectives were achieved. Faced with demands to crush entire armies or to humiliate defeated enemies by way of triumphant marches through their capitals, Bismarck always insisted that the business at hand was the conduct of Prussian or German politics, not an attempt to administer "justice" or to humiliate or destroy great powers. Bismarck strove after 1871 to protect what Germany had gained. Above all, he guarded Germany's most vital interest, the European center. He did not allow Germany's attention to be dangerously diverted by numerous colonial adventures. He once said, pointing to a map of Europe, "Here is Russia, and here is France, and here we are in the middle. That is my map of Africa."

To ensure Germany's protection, Bismarck built up one of the most complicated and delicate alliance systems ever known in peacetime. He saw Germany threatened from two sides and sought to eliminate this threat by preventing the French and Russians from forming a coalition against Germany. He accomplished this by maintaining friendly relations with Britain; by isolating France diplomatically; and by establishing a Dual Alliance with Austria in 1879 and the Reinsurance Treaty among Austria, Russia, and Germany in 1887. The latter obligated Germany to stand by whichever partner was attacked by the other, thereby discouraging potential aggression from either Austria or Russia. Bismarck did not regard this treaty as incompatible with the Dual Alliance with Austria because in neither agreement was Germany obligated to aid any aggressor. Of course, one factor gave Bismarck great flexibility: He alone could determine guilt for any outbreak of hostilities, and this decision would always have been in accordance with German national interests.

Of course, the legacy Bismarck left Germany was not all positive. His alliance system was exceedingly complicated, and he failed to train successors to continue the policy. His followers, who wished to simplify the alliance system, did not renew the Reinsurance Treaty in 1894. Also, his style of Realpolitik demanded great skill, the sober and unimpassioned recognition of the limits of power, the exercise of moderation, and the respect of other nations' vital interests. His successors often imperfectly understood his policies, and they tended to remember the gestures of his statecraft and not its substance.

Bismarckian Realpolitik, if understood only in fragments, could be a dangerous inheritance for any nation.

The legacy that Bismarck left German domestic politics was also by no means entirely positive. The German Empire had the outward appearance of being democratic. However, while some other European countries, such as England and France, were in the process of becoming more democratic in practice, Germany was not. It remained a country in which the most important decisions were made by people who were not elected and not directly subject to popular or parliamentary control. Bismarck's skill as a politician prevented a process of democratic reform from gaining any momentum.

The chancellor, like many of his countrymen, felt uncomfortable about political and cultural pluralism in Germany. This was especially revealed in laws Bismarck introduced to limit the influence of the Catholic Church and the Social Democratic Party of Germany (SPD). His campaign against the Catholic Church, called the Cultural Struggle, was similar to campaigns conducted in many European countries in the 19th century to limit the church's influence over education and other social affairs. Bismarck also resented the growth of the Catholic Center Party and suspected that the Vatican was trying to stir up opposition to the imperial government among the Polish minority within Germany and among the other Catholic countries in Europe. A series of laws whittling away at the church's privileges was passed starting in 1873, but these laws unleashed such an outcry among Catholics and Protestants alike that Bismarck was forced to repeal most of them by 1881.

The leader was also unable to view German socialists as loyal citizens because of their Marxist revolutionary program and their talk of internationalism. He blamed the socialists for two unsuccessful assassination attempts against the kaiser in 1877, and in October of the following year, he succeeded in persuading parliament to pass an Anti-Socialist Law forbidding all associations that aimed to subvert the existing order or that showed "socialist tendencies." This law forced the SPD to operate underground, crippled the growing labor unions, deprived socialists of the customary protection of the law, and drove many of them into exile abroad. Like the laws against the Catholic Church, these antisocialist laws also backfired and actually stimulated an increase in the membership and overall strength of the SPD.

At the same time, Bismarck linked these repressive measures with progressive social welfare laws to help the needy and working classes. The first social insurance laws were introduced in 1881, and in 1883

Germania, **overlooking the Rhine Valley, commemorates the unification of 1871.**
Courtesy: Jon Markham Morrow

there came a Sickness Insurance Law, one-third of the premiums for which were to be paid by the employers and an accident insurance financed entirely by the employer; finally, in 1889 old-age disability insurance financed by employees, employers, and the government was introduced. These laws were far in advance of those of any other nation and were the model for the National Insurance Act of 1911 in Britain; not until the 1930s were such programs introduced in the United States by the federal government. Even today, Germans are proud of their social welfare legislation.

Industrialization and Urbanization

Some Germans hoped for an era of liberal reform when Wilhelm I died in 1888. But his son, Friedrich III, who was known to favor such reforms, died of throat cancer only 99 days after his coronation, and a young, inexperienced, and impetuous Wilhelm II became kaiser. The new ruler hoped to become popular by canceling the Anti-Socialist Law, introducing some domestic reforms, and conducting an energetic German foreign and colonial policy. Noting that Bismarck had wholly different ideas, he fired the Iron Chancellor in 1890. He was then free to take the lead over a people who were enthusiastic about the prospects for Germany's future. The kaiser, who was rather intelligent and superficially interested in many different things but who was unable to focus his attention on anything very long, was boastful about Germany's power. He also had a way, as one of his biographers noted, of approaching every matter with an open mouth. Although in actual crises

Germany

the young kaiser tended to be cautious, he seemed to many non-Germans to represent a restless country with more power than it could use well.

German unification and rapid economic and population growth had given Germany a strong hand to assert its claims in the world. By the end of the 19th century, the extremely rapid industrialization and urbanization had transformed Germany into one of the world's foremost industrial, trading, banking, and urbanized countries. All western countries experienced difficulties in adjusting to the social consequences of industrialization. However, the suddenness of German economic and population growth had no equal in Europe.

Between 1816 and 1913, Germany's population almost tripled from 25 million to 67 million, and more and more Germans moved into the cities. In 1830, four-fifths of the population lived outside of towns and engaged in agriculture, but in 1895 barely one-fifth did so. Berlin's population alone

grew from three-quarters of a million in 1870 to over 2 million in 1910. The increasingly urbanized people were hard at work making Germany the most economically powerful country in Europe.

With Alsace-Lorraine, Germany became the leading producer of iron and steel. It almost quadrupled its domestic rail net between 1871 and 1914, and it built one of the world's largest merchant marine fleets. Its industries were very diversified, ranging from armaments producers, such as Krupp, and electrical plants, such as those of Siemens, Halske, and the General Electric Company (AEG), to chemical industries, such as Bayer, Agfa, and I. G. Farben. Overall German industrial production had already surpassed that of the French in the 1870s, caught up with that of Britain in 1900, and had overtaken it by 1910, when only the United States outproduced Germany.

Imperial Germany also exploded with artistic and scholarly creativity. Its

universities and research laboratories became places where the most imaginative thinking in the world was being done. For instance, Wilhelm Konrad Roentgen discovered X-rays; Max Planck, the quantum theory; and Albert Einstein, the theory of relativity. Robert Koch did groundbreaking research on tuberculosis, cholera, and sleeping sickness; Paul Ehrlich, on syphilis; and Rudolph Virchow, on pathology. The work of such great professors as Theodor Mommsen and Heinrich von Treitschke in history; Wilhelm Dilthey in philosophy; Ferdinand Tonnies, Georg Simmel, and Max Weber in sociology; and Adolf Wagner, Lujo Brentano; and Werner Sombart in economics is still admired today.

Berlin also gained a reputation as an exciting cultural center. Johannes Brahms and Richard Strauss composed their music there. The sympathetic Prussian social critic Theodor Fontane wrote his novels, focusing on the Prussia that he loved but that he saw in decline. Also, after the

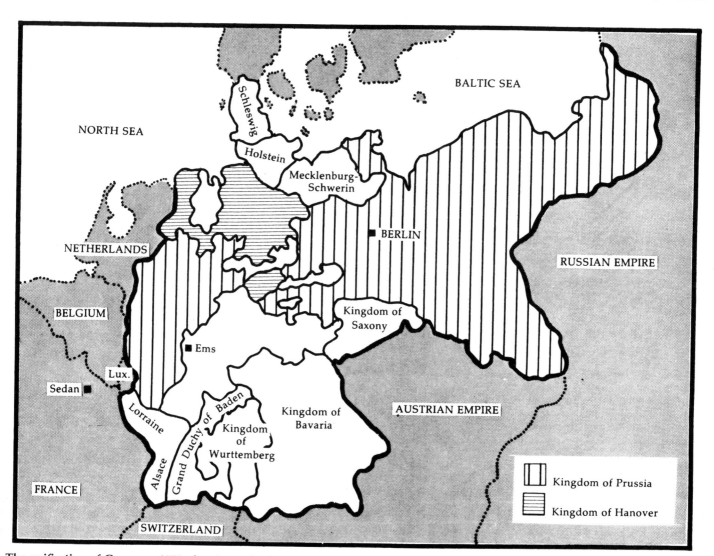

The unification of Germany, 1871, showing only the major states and areas

220

Germany

Capt. Alfred Thayer Mahan

opening of Die Freie Buhne (The Free Stage), such talented playwrights as Gerhard Hauptmann and Frank Wedekind were able to introduce a new element of criticism and expressionism into the German theater. Unlike France then and today, Germany's culture and scholarship was not concentrated in the nation's capital but was also distributed among such cities as Hamburg, Cologne, Leipzig, Munich, and Frankfurt on the Main. Despite the cultural creativity of the time, many educated Germans were gripped with a kind of cultural pessimism. They looked around themselves and saw what they considered to be excessive materialism and consumerism, values they viewed as British and American. German spirit was in decline, they lamented, and many agreed with the philosopher Friedrich Nietzsche, who in 1888 claimed, "German spirit: for the past 18 years a contradiction in terms."

Social Division, Foreign Adventurism, and Nationalism

Industrial and population growth changed the face and character of German society. The German Empire, which had become united territorially in 1871, became increasingly divided socially. Expressed in an oversimplified way, German society became more and more polarized. A class-conscious, somewhat doctrinaire, and fairly well-organized proletariat confronted a ruling class that was, in the main, stubbornly conservative. Nationalism grew to be very strong in Germany, but it could never overcome the extreme antagonisms that arose out of this split in German society.

The robust and assertive foreign policy on which Wilhelm II embarked in the 1890s, when Germany enjoyed relatively good relations with the other major countries in the world, led Germany by 1914 into a diplomatic situation in which it felt encircled and distrusted. By building a powerful navy, pursuing colonial ambitions in Africa, and frequently brandishing the sword, Germany's rulers created more problems than they were able to solve.

Bismarck had kept the German Empire within the limits its geographic position in the middle of Europe imposed upon it. He had avoided colonial adventures, which would only have antagonized the other European powers, especially Britain. However, supported by German public opinion, his successors changed this, and by the turn of the century, the German flag flew in Africa (Cameroons, South-West Africa, and Tanganyika), and there was a tiny foothold in China and a smattering of Pacific islands (named, ironically, the Bismarck Archipelago). In 2021, President Steinmeier apologized for colonialist crimes committed a century ago in southern Africa.

In order to try to protect this usually unprofitable empire, Germany decided to build a battle fleet that would enable it to conduct a major naval war against the great powers. Kaiser Wilhelm II announced in 1898, "Our future lies on the water." This decision was a major factor in the deterioration of good relations between Britain and Germany. A German navy that challenged Britain, which, as an island, was completely dependent upon open sea-lanes, was bound to be destabilizing and to drive the English into the arms of Germany's potential enemies.

Undoubtedly the chief influence on German naval thinking was Captain A. T. Mahan of the United States Navy. In *The Influence of Sea Power on History*, he argues that mastery of the oceans is identical with world domination and that any strong land power fighting against an amphibious master that also has land forces is destined to lose. Mahan visited Germany in 1893 and was received like a hero. He was invited to dine aboard the kaiser's yacht. The ruler wrote in 1894 to a friend, "I am just now not reading but devouring Captain Mahan's book and am trying to learn it by heart. . . It is on board all my ships and constantly quoted by my captains and officers."

What worried the British and the French was that Germany was willing to use its new navy. In mid-1911 Wilhelm sent a gunboat to Morocco's Atlantic port of Agadir in response to France's dispatching a military mission to Fez. France's action was a clear violation of the 1906 agreements of Algeciras, but the German overreaction to this move caused other Europeans to overlook this point. German bellicosity concerned Europe more than a questionable French interpretation of a treaty. Thereafter, German political calculation had always to include the possibility of a war with Britain, which was now firmly on the side of the Entente (France and Russia).

The German chancellor's chief foreign policy advisor, Kurt Riezler, who later emigrated to the US, viewed with concern the kind of nationalism that was gripping his countrymen. He wrote in 1913 that too many Germans exaggerated the "power of force." Due to their craving for international recognition, they lacked political sense, judgment, and goal orientation. Their nationalism showed "the manners of a young dog" and was laden with "envy and resentments," both of which were poor advisors for an "upstart" who did not know how to "let things ripen." The most vocal spokesman for this kind of impatient nationalism was the Pan-German Union, about which Chancellor Bethmann-Hollweg declared in 1912 almost in despair, "Politics cannot be made with these idiots!"

World War I

Long before June 28, 1914, the day on which the Austrian archduke Franz Ferdinand was assassinated in Bosnia, there

Mata Hari, executed German spy, 1917

221

Germany

had been much dissatisfaction in the capitals of Europe. The preceding decade had produced numerous crises that could have served to ignite a war. However, in order for a crisis actually to lead to war, several powers must conclude that they are in a favorable position to gain from such a conflict. That feeling of confidence prevailed in many European capitals in July and August 1914.

Within six weeks after the assassination of the archduke, all of Europe's major nations were locked into a war that was to last four years and that far exceeded all previous wars in terms of casualties and destruction. Of course, no European leaders had contemplated, let alone wanted, the kind of war that actually came in August 1914. In the minds of most statesmen at the time, war was a relatively violent action lasting a month or six weeks and conducted as a part of intricate diplomatic games. The memory of the Napoleonic wars having faded, they had not yet had the opportunity to observe the consequences of wars that unlocked powerful emotions stemming from nationalism and democracy. They also vastly underestimated the capacity of countries in possession of modern industry and technology to conduct theretofore inconceivably destructive wars for long periods against one another.

There was general shock and indignation in all of Europe when Archduke Franz Ferdinand's assassination was announced. On July 5 and 6, Germany granted its ally, Austria-Hungary, a free hand to deal with the matter, and Russia (and indirectly France) gave the Serbians a similarly free hand. Only in the final days of the crisis did the German chancellor desperately try to regain control of the situation. Subsequent events revealed that a tighter German rein on Austrian policy would have served German interests better. However, in the eyes of German leaders, there appeared to be no alternative to their policy of allowing Austria to deal harshly with Serbia at this time.

On July 28 Austria-Hungary declared war on Serbia, and two days later, Russia made the critical decision to order general mobilization, thus indicating its unwillingness to allow the Austrian-Serbian war to remain localized. German leaders had for a long time made it clear that they perceived a Russian general mobilization to be a direct potential threat to Germany itself. When Russia refused to withdraw its call to arms, Germany sent a last warning to both Russia and France, but when the German note remained unanswered by August 1, Germany declared war on Russia. It did not immediately declare war on France, but France mobilized its army anyway on August 1. With Russia, Germany,

The combatants in World War I, 1915–1918

and France carrying out general military buildups, a European war had become unavoidable. When Germany violated Belgian territory in order to gain easier access to France, Britain also entered the war, thereby transforming the European war, which Germany probably would have won, into a world war.

All of the European powers shared the responsibility for the outbreak of World War I. Some, such as Austria-Hungary and Serbia, bore the greatest responsibility. Germany, Russia, and France must be blamed for not having sufficiently restrained their respective allies and thereby having allowed a local Balkan dispute (where there had already been two wars in 1912 and 1913) to ignite a world war. Without doubt, Britain bears the least responsibility for the war that came. Nevertheless, crowds of people in all belligerent countries greeted the outbreak of war with a gaiety that is usually reserved for carnival time. Two million German, more than 1 million French, 1 million British, 1 million

Austrian, a half-million Italian, and countless Russian soldiers were to perish in the four-year bloodletting that followed. The war also destroyed the old Europe, and what could be pieced back together collapsed a mere two decades later.

Almost immediately after the start of hostilities, German troops knifed through Belgium and into France according to a carefully laid Schlieffen Plan, but by mid-September at the Battle of the Marne, they had been stopped in their tracks before reaching Paris. For four years two opposing armies faced each other in trenches stretching from the English Channel to the Swiss border and protected by mazes of barbed wire, machine-gun nests, mortar, and heavy artillery batteries. Chemical warfare (gas) was also introduced during the grisly conflict. Occasionally massive attacks were launched against the opposing trenches that sometimes brought infinitesimal gains and always huge human losses. For instance, in the inconclusive Battle of the Somme in 1916,

General von Hindenburg, Kaiser Wilhelm II, General Ludendorff

the Germans lost 650,000 men, and the Allies, 614,000.

It was a different story in the east, where warfare was highly mobile and brought huge gains and losses of territory. After an initial Russian advance into East Prussia, German forces scored stunning victories against the Russians at Tannenberg and the Masurian Lakes. Out of these victories the legend was born of military genius and invincibility that surrounded the victorious Generals Paul von Hindenburg and Erich Ludendorff for the remainder of the war. By 1916 their authority over military and political questions alike exceeded even that of the kaiser and the chancellor.

The German successes in the east enabled their armies to march right into the heart of Russia. Still, the badly shaken tsarist empire managed to put up stiff resistance. It became clear to the Germans that the two-front war was a vice that could eventually crush Germany. This became especially apparent when the United States entered the war on the Allied side in the spring of 1917. President Woodrow Wilson had been determined to keep the Americans out of the war, but the Germans made several blunders that drew the United States into the conflict. A high official in the Foreign Office, Arthur Zimmermann, sent a telegram to the Mexican government promising territorial rewards north of the Mexican border if it would support Germany in the war. This telegram was intercepted by the Americans and understandably antagonized American leaders and public opinion.

The most serious German mistakes involved its naval warfare against neutral shipping. By the spring of 1915, German surface ships had been swept from all of the major seas except the North and Baltic Seas. It had been built up with so much fanfare and political sacrifice. But because of the ever-tightening British blockade of the North Sea and English Channel outlets, the bulk of the German navy remained bottled up in Germany's northern ports. This blockade also brought increasing hunger and deprivation to the German population and gradually led German leaders to use submarines to strike at Allied shipping. Submarines were regarded as a particularly hideous weapon at the time, since they torpedoed ships without warning and without any capacity to help survivors. A particular outcry had gone up in the United States when a large passenger liner, the Lusitania, was torpedoed off the coast of Ireland in mid-1915, with a loss of 1,198 lives, including 139 Americans. The indignation in America was such that the Germans promised not to repeat such attacks.

For a while German submarine activity died down, but by early 1917, Generals von Hindenburg and Ludendorff, backed by their immense popularity, forced the adoption of unrestricted submarine warfare on the unwilling chancellor. The head of the German admiralty misjudged the ultimate effect of America's entry into the war to be "exactly zero"; in any case, it was widely believed that Britain would be forced to its knees before Americans

would arrive. Although the first American divisions did not arrive in France until almost a year later, the immediate boost to Allied morale and the military contribution American soldiers made in the final months of the war were decisive in the defeat of Germany.

Ending the War on the Eastern Front

American entry into the war made it essential that the Germans eliminate the eastern front. Because the weapon of war had not worked entirely, they selected another weapon—that of revolution. On March 15, 1917, the Russian tsar abdicated, but to the Germans' surprise, the new government decided to continue the war. Therefore, German leaders decided to transport a group of Russian revolutionaries from their exile in Switzerland through Germany to Scandinavia, from where they could return to Russia. This group was composed of Marxists who were known to favor Russian withdrawal from the war and included most predominantly Vladimir Ilyich Lenin. The Germans incorrectly figured that Lenin would be an ideal marionette for Germany, since he and his faction-ridden Bolshevik Party would presumably be unable to hold power more than a few weeks without German support.

Neither the Germans nor Lenin had any concern for each other's interests. As Leon Trotsky wrote in his memoirs, "In the case of Lenin's trip two opposite plans crossed at a definite point, and this point was a sealed [rail] car." The train, which departed from Zurich with 32 Russian

Germany

revolutionaries, had such high traffic priority that the German crown prince's own train was kept on a side track in Halle for two hours until Lenin's train had passed. The group arrived at Petrograd's (now St. Petersburg) Finland Train Station on April 16 and was greeted by thousands of supporters. It cannot be doubted that the transport and subsequent German financial assistance was vital to the Bolsheviks before their seizure of power in Petrograd on November 7, 1917.

Lenin did indeed announce Russia's withdrawal from the war, but the Germans imposed an extremely harsh peace treaty upon the new Bolshevik leadership at the Russian border town of Brest-Litovsk in early 1918. The Soviets, as the Bolsheviks had come to be called, were forced to relinquish huge chunks of territory from the Russian Empire. This treaty,

along with the reparations demanded of Russia in August, set a most unfortunate precedent. It merely stimulated the Entente's will to resist and reinforced the enemy's moral self-confidence to impose on the Germans nine months later a peace no less dreadful than this one. That moral self-confidence was also strengthened by a weakness Germany demonstrated during both world wars—its lack of moderation. Without such moderation, no negotiated settlement was possible, only a dictated one. German occupation authorities after 1871 tended to mistreat or try to "Germanize" conquered nations, which could have been potential allies. The highest German diplomat in Russia in the summer of 1918 made a bitter comment about his own people: "Never was a Volk more capable of conquering the world and more incapable of ruling it!"

Collapse of the War Effort

Early in 1918 Hamburg, Leipzig, Cologne, Munich, and the heavily industrialized Ruhr area had experienced serious strikes, and in Berlin 200,000 munitions workers struck. Hunger was causing the home front to collapse—the average rations for German civilians had been cut to only 1,000 calories per day. The tensions were greatly increased by a worsening of the military situation. Large numbers of fresh American troops began arriving in France in the spring of 1918. Germany's last great offensive was launched on March 21, 1918, but the exhausted German troops were unable to cope with the Allied counteroffensive, which began on July 10. On August 8, known to Germans then as Black Friday, British infantry broke through the German lines at Amiens and threw the German troops in France into a mass retreat. On August 14, Ludendorff was forced to admit that the war could not be won militarily, and on September 29, he communicated to Supreme Headquarters that "the present condition of our army demands an immediate cease-fire in order to avoid catastrophe." On October 3, von Hindenburg told the chancellor that "under these circumstances it is necessary to break off the fight in order to spare the German people and its allies' needless victims."

Despite such calls of desperation at the time, these men and many others had the audacity to claim later that it had been the civilian leadership, especially those who had founded the new republic, who had "stabbed Germany in the back" by losing nerve and suing for peace at a time when Germany's armies had allegedly not been defeated in the field. This legend placed an unbearably heavy burden on Germany's postwar democratic leadership.

Its armies retreating, its allies crumbling, its people starving, Germany sent a delegation to seek peace with the Entente. It met French marshal Foch at Compiegne in a railcar Hitler used to conduct the French surrender ceremonies almost 22 years later. There the French marshal delivered nonnegotiable conditions which Germany could take or leave: The 34 articles included the withdrawal of the German army from France, Alsace-Lorraine, and Belgium to the Rhine; Entente occupation of the left bank of the Rhine; and delivery to the Entente of all German submarines and heavy military and transport materials. The disheartened Germans had no alternative but to accept. The war officially ended on November 11, 1918.

Collapse of the Empire and Birth of the Republic

Even before the cease-fire could be signed, the German Empire ceased to exist.

Labor unrest in Germany's Ruhr area

Germany

Kaiser Wilhelm simply could not bring himself to abdicate, as the victors had demanded, so Chancellor Max von Baden simply announced the kaiser's abdication on November 9. A short time later, the Social Democrat Philip Scheidemann was informed that German communists were about to declare a republic, so he rushed to the window of the Reichstag building and announced, "The emperor has abdicated. . . Long live the German Republic!"

The new Social Democratic chancellor, Friedrich Ebert, made no secret of the fact that his emphasis would be on creating order and a parliamentary-democratic political structure in the badly shaken country. But no sooner had the republic been declared than demands began to be made for a second, more radical revolution. The Polish revolutionary theorist and activist Rosa Luxemburg remarked sarcastically, "Oh how German this German Revolution is! How proper, how pedantic, how lacking in verve and grandeur."

It was not long before some groups chose to use force against Ebert's government, and Germans witnessed significant events that threatened the republic in its infancy. In late 1918 the Communist Party of Germany (KPD) was formed, and on the same day, the Steel Helmet League, a right-wing paramilitary organization of disenchanted war veterans, was created. The fatal split in German society, which would paralyze and ultimately destroy the republic, continued to widen. The regime clearly found itself in a crisis from which it would never be able to extricate itself.

The communists made two unsuccessful violent attempts to seize power in Berlin. More than 1,000 lives were lost in defeating the first attempt, January 6–12, 1919. The second erupted during the first two weeks of March 1919 and caused 2,000 deaths and considerable destruction to the city of Berlin. The government crushed a leftist uprising in Munich in May 1919 with such brutality that many observers accused the new republican government of being "blind in the right eye." That later right-wing strikes against the republic were not suppressed with equal brutality stemmed from the fact that the postwar German army of only 100,000 soldiers (Reichswehr) and the Free Corps troops, which were hastily assembled to cope with the crises, were, on the whole, antirepublican and far more sympathetic to the right; they were never successfully transformed into reliable instruments of the Weimar Republic.

The government found itself in the predicament of having no alternative to the use of troops to restore and maintain order who were, in the main, unruly, disillusioned freebooters who had become far too accustomed to violence during a war that had severely shaken their sense of values and proportion. Such troops were extremely difficult to control, and the blemish of partiality toward the right was placed on the new republic itself.

The Weimar Republic and a Disastrous "Peace" Treaty

In the spring of 1919, delegates to a national assembly met in Weimar, a city chosen because it lay outside the storm of revolution that raged in Berlin and because of its association with the humanists Goethe and Schiller, who had lived and worked there. This assembly, whose venue gave the new republic its name, had three tasks: to form a government of Germany, to sign a peace treaty, and to draft a new constitution. It legitimized the "Weimar Coalition," composed of the SPD and Center and German Democratic Parties, which had ruled Germany since the November revolution of 1918. However, the necessity of fulfilling the second, highly unpopular task of signing a peace treaty caused this coalition of the republic's supporters to lose its parliamentary majority in 1920, which it never regained.

The first major problem with the Versailles Treaty was the manner in which it was written. In contrast to all previous peace settlements in Europe, the vanquished (in this case, the Germans) were not included in the negotiations. If the Germans had been included, perhaps they would have felt some responsibility for the treaty, but as it was, it represented a dictated peace toward which the Germans never felt any moral obligation to subscribe to its terms. The settlement had a strong whiff of "victor's justice."

Prior to American entry into the conflict, President Woodrow Wilson had proposed a "peace without victory" and later issued a written document containing "Fourteen Points" as a basis for European peace that contained very lofty language. The Germans later accepted the text, but it faded into the background at Versailles as French prime minister Georges Clemenceau ("the Old Tiger") virtually dictated the terms of what turned out to be an attempt at revenge. Little did he know that he was helping to sow the seeds of disaster, particularly in the mind of a wounded Austrian corporal, Adolf Hitler.

The Germans could hardly believe their eyes when the terms were forwarded to Berlin in mid-May 1919, with the warning that nonacceptance would result in an immediate resumption of hostilities. They had expected to lose all territory conquered during the war, as well as Alsace-Lorraine, but they also lost a tenth of their prewar population and an eighth of their territory. Danzig was to become the Free City of Danzig under the League of Nations' supervision, the province of Posen (Poznan) was ceded to Poland (from which it had been taken in late 18th century), and a narrow corridor was cut through West Prussia to connect Poland to the Baltic Sea. Worse, the coal-rich Saar region was placed under League of Nations and French control for 15 years.

This, combined with the loss of practically all its merchant marine fleet, made it far more difficult for Germany to pay the shockingly high reparations demanded of it. The Rhineland was occupied by Allied soldiers and was to be demilitarized permanently. Germany's high seas fleet was to be turned over to the Allies, a requirement that prompted the Germans to scuttle all their naval ships, which had been interned at Scapa Flow in the

The colossal Reichstag, Berlin

Germany

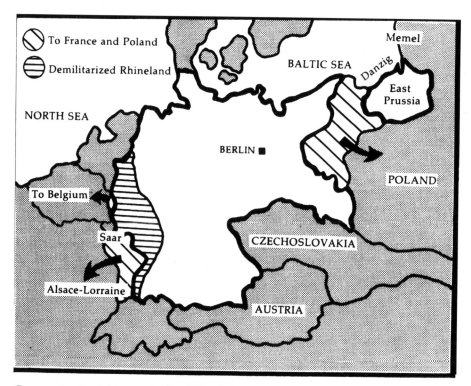

German territorial losses to the Allies following World War I

Orkney Islands north of Scotland in mid-1919. The future German army was to be restricted to 100,000 career officers and men with no military aircraft, tanks, or other offensive weapons.

Perhaps worst of all, article 231 of the "treaty" placed sole responsibility for the outbreak and therefore for all destruction of the war on the shoulders of Germany and its allies. This article had been written by a young American diplomat, John Foster Dulles, as a compromise to the French, who had wanted to annex the Rhineland and to have even higher reparation payments from Germany. But Dulles had to admit later, "it was the revulsion of the German people from this article of the Treaty which, above all else, laid the foundation for the Germany of Hitler."

At the time of the treaty, Adolf Hitler was only beginning to emerge from the political shadows. Born in Austria, he drew around himself a growing circle of enthusiastic admirers. Soon he helped found an energetic and antidemocratic party, the National Socialist Workers' Party of Germany (NSDAP), abbreviated "Nazi." Although he had little formal education, Hitler was a fiery speaker, capable of stirring his listeners with haranguing, emotional tirades. For the next quarter-century, he never ceased to rail against the weak Weimar government and the wickedness of the Versailles Treaty.

The document actually made a mockery of many of Woodrow Wilson's Fourteen Points, such as "open covenants openly arrived at," freedom of the seas, the "impartial adjustment of all colonial claims," and of course the self-determination of nations. The victors permitted this latter right only where people wanted to detach themselves from Germany, such as in northern Schleswig and part of Upper Silesia. Wherever an area's population

**Goethe and Schiller Monument
in Weimar**

clearly wanted to join Germany, such as Austria or northern Bohemia, no referendum was permitted. Such hypocrisy stimulated within Germany cynicism toward both the treaty and toward any German government that would sign it. Of course, Germany's harsh policy toward a collapsing Russia at Brest-Litovsk had provided a disastrous precedent. Nevertheless, Germany's shortsightedness in 1918 could not reasonably be invoked to justify an equally shortsighted Allied policy a year later.

As Chancellor Scheidemann said to the national assembly in 1919, "Which hand would not wither up which put itself and us into these bonds?" The treaty was a millstone around the neck of the new republic. It not only helped create a deep division in German society, but it also seriously hampered the normalization of Germany's relations with the outside world. It could only be maintained by force, but the United States quickly withdrew from Europe's military affairs, and Britain and France gradually lost the will to enforce it energetically. One day a spellbinding demagogue would be able to untie the "fetters of Versailles" right before the eyes of a weary and lethargic Europe and reap much applause within Germany for this.

An Attempt at Democracy, Runaway Inflation, and Anarchy

It was unfortunate that national humiliation coincided with the birth of the first democracy in Germany. When at last it had adopted the political organization extolled by the victorious allies, it had become an international outcast. The new German constitution reflected the democratic spirit of the "Weimar constitution." The delegates sought to accomplish what the delegates of the Frankfurt assembly had tried to do in 1848: to combine liberty with national unity and strength. It guaranteed basic individual rights and created a strong lower house of parliament (Reichstag) that had the right to initiate legislation. It also maintained certain traditional German political institutions, such as a federal form and a strong presidency elected every seven years (as a republican substitute for a strong kaiser).

The Weimar constitution did include several weaknesses. In order to give parliamentary representation to as many different groups as possible, it established the proportional representation electoral system. The unfortunate result was that not only antirepublican splinter groups, such as the Nazi Party, could publicize their causes in parliament, but also the large number of parties that could win parliamentary seats made the formation of a majority almost impossible. The result was predictable: parliamentary instability and ultimately paralysis.

A second weakness was the provision for initiatives and referendums. While such instruments of direct democracy often appear progressive, they can frequently be manipulated by enemies of the democratic order, as Hitler did after 1933. The third mistake was the inclusion of emergency powers in article 48, which could be invoked in the event that "public order and safety be seriously disturbed or threatened." As we shall see, this article was later used to circumvent parliament and thereby to undermine the democratic intentions of the framers. This constitution on the whole was an admirable document, but the German nation was too divided on fundamental political values to be able to live by it.

The Weimar Republic experienced continuous crisis. The population had been impoverished by the long war and postwar chaos. The republic saw no other way of keeping up its reparations payments than to borrow money abroad and to produce new money as fast as it could be turned out by the printing presses. The devastating result was inflation. At the beginning of 1922 the German mark was worth only one-fiftieth of its prewar value; one year later it was worth one ten-thousandth. In 1914 the US dollar had been worth 4.2 marks; in 1923 it was worth 25 billion marks.

The hero in Erich Remarque's novel *Three Comrades* gave an idea of what this meant in personal terms: "In 1923 I was advertising chief of a rubber factory. . . I had a monthly salary of 200 billion marks. We were paid twice a day, and then everybody had half an hour's leave so that he could rush to the stores and buy something before the next quotation of the dollar came out, at which time the money would lose half its value." There finally was a currency reform in 1923 in which one new mark (Rentenmark) was equal to a trillion old marks. But this dizzying inflation had already had the effect of a second revolution in Germany. It had financially wiped out millions of Germans and had spread fear and cynicism throughout the land, which merely weakened the republic further.

The republic was continuously battered from the left and the right. During the night of March 12–13, 1920, Free Corps troops marched on Berlin, singing military songs and flying the black-red-white flag of imperial Germany. On their helmets was a popular Free Corps symbol: the swastika, the distorted cross that was also the Nazis' chief symbol. The troops faced no armed resistance since the majority of generals in Berlin refused to allow their soldiers to fire on former comrades from the front. The leader of the coup d'etat was Wolfgang Kapp, who had been brought up in the United States. He installed himself as chancellor and forced the government to flee the city. A general strike called by the government before departing was observed by socialist labor unions, radical leftist militants, shopkeepers, and the government ministries. Factories, schools, banks, and stores were closed; streetcars and buses ceased running; and water, electricity, and gas were shut off. This resistance finally forced Kapp and his supporters to flee Berlin only five days later. Almost immediately after the Kapp effort, the communists staged disorders in Berlin, Münster, and the Ruhr area, especially Dusseldorf.

Former finance minister Matthias Erzberger, who had signed the Versailles Treaty, was gunned down in the Black Forest in 1921 by a right-wing squad, and the following year, Foreign Minister Walter Rathenau was felled by assassins' bullets. The next day, Chancellor Joseph Wirth declared in the Reichstag, where Rathenau's body lay in state, "The enemy is on the right!" He was correct. Although the radical left tried to destroy the republic, the right did present a greater danger, primarily because it was so well placed in the civil service, the judicial system, and the army.

Stagnation and Loss of the Ruhr

The year 1923 saw the suppression of a Nazi-attempted coup in Munich and of communist disorders in Hamburg, Saxony, and Thuringia. It also saw the French military occupation of the Ruhr area, Germany's industrial heartland. The German government temporarily suspended all reparations payments and called upon Rhinelanders to practice passive resistance by refusing all cooperation with the French, but this form of retaliation merely meant more hunger and inflation for Germans. The French action was partially a reaction to Germany's signing the Rapallo Pact with the Soviet Union in 1922, calling for a normalization of political and trade relations between the two countries. The two armies began to maintain secret contacts with each other, and German officers began training in Russia with weapons

Rampant inflation in the Weimar Republic's darkest days: 1,000 marks is hastily overprinted to make it worth 1 million . . . then 1-billion-mark note!

Germany

Caricaturist George Grosz catches the cynical attitude of the times as he satirizes the wealthy in the badly divided, economically hard-pressed Weimar Republic: (left) "The Landlord" and (right) "View of Tauentzienstrasse," which depicts a blindman, a prostitute, and a corrupt capitalist.

that the Versailles Treaty forbade: tanks, airplanes, and submarines. The Soviet Union was also an international outcast at the time and was seeking some support against the western Allies.

That the storm over the Ruhr finally blew over was the work of the man who became chancellor for a few months in August 1923 and who served as foreign minister until his untimely death in October 1929—Gustav Stresemann. Before and during World War I, he had been a fervent nationalist who had strongly advocated German expansion. But he was one of those persons who had learned from Germany's past and who had concluded that its future was best served by cooperating with the west, not by fighting it. Like Konrad Adenauer after World War II, he helped to restore Germany's position in the world without having much military power at his disposal. However, unlike Adenauer's policy, Stresemann's foreign policy failed to win much domestic support and legitimacy for the Weimar Republic.

The Golden Twenties:
Satisfaction and Dissatisfaction

Stresemann ended passive resistance in the Ruhr, and he set out to reach an

international agreement that would enable Germany to pay its reparations. In 1924 the American banker Charles Dawes led a committee of experts that drew up a plan to regulate German reparations payments and to channel foreign credit into Germany to stimulate its recovery. This plan set the stage for a remarkable increase in German living standards and wages in the second half of the 1920s. The results were so promising that five years later the Young Plan, also of American origin, sought even further economic stimulation by scaling down the payments scheduled in the Dawes Plan.

The overall result was that more than 25 billion marks worth of foreign capital was poured into Germany, mainly from the United States. This inflow of capital actually exceeded the outflow of reparations payments from Germany. Thus, in the long run, the payments did not have as adverse an economic effect on Germany as agitators constantly charged.

Stresemann also reached out to France. In the Locarno Treaty of 1925, Germany agreed to recognize the permanence of its borders with France and Belgium, to foreswear (with France and Belgium) the use of force against each other except in

self-defense, to submit any disputes to arbitration or conciliation, and finally to enter the League of Nations, which Germany did in 1926. Although Germany did not recognize the permanency of its eastern borders, it agreed to seek their modification only by peaceful means. It underscored this commitment by signing in 1926 a pact of friendship, the Berlin Treaty, with the Soviet Union. The foreign minister's main focus remained on the west, though. His cooperation with the British and French leaders created considerable enthusiasm in Europe and greatly cooled tensions for the rest of the decade, which, because of its increasing prosperity, optimism, and cooperation, was known as "the golden twenties."

The second half of the 1920s was also a time of relative political stability, thanks not only to Stresemann's influence but also to another event—the election in April 1925 of Field Marshal von Hindenburg, the "Wooden Titan" and "Hero of Tannenberg," as president of the republic. At the time, many democrats threw up their hands in despair that such a man, who was mentally embedded in the imperial past, could become the highest political leader in Germany. But he actually took seriously his pledge to defend the Weimar constitution, and with this war hero in the presidential palace as a kind of substitute monarch, many German conservatives began for the first time to accept the legitimacy of the republic and to tone down their attacks against it.

This was also a period of extraordinary cultural achievement, although the roots of "Weimar culture" no doubt were planted during imperial Germany. It was a time in which the Mann brothers, Thomas and Heinrich; Gerhard Hauptmann; Bertold Brecht; Kurt Tucholsky; Erich Kastner; Oskar Kokoschka; and Gottfried Benn were reaching huge audiences and were producing works that in some ways supported the new political order.

Still, many writers continued to capture the attention of those whose ideals had been crushed by the fall of the empire and the loss of the war and who could not view civilian life in the new democratic republic as a satisfactory replacement. Erich Remarque's novel *The Road Back* portrays a disillusioned returning soldier, who asks, "what are we doing here? Look about you: look how flat and comfortless it all is. We are a burden to ourselves and others. Our ideals are bankrupt, our dreams are kaputt, and we wander around in this world of rotten opportunists and speculators like Don Quixotes in a foreign land." Such feelings were intensified by the immensely popular battlefront novels by such authors as Ernst Junger, Werner Beumelburg and Edwin Erich Dwinger, which call for a return to heroic virtues.

Some of Germany's most respected academic minds, such as Martin Heidegger and Carl Schmitt, focused on the shortcomings of liberalism and democracy. Also, many antiliberals were able to sooth their consciences by reading such bestsellers as Oswald Spengler's *The Decline of the West*, which decries the republic and the alleged death of culture in the materialist west, and Arthur Moeller van der Bruck's *The Third Reich*, which calls for a new and better political and social order.

For the first time in its history, Germany had a city that was not only the political but also the cultural and intellectual center of the country. In fact, Berlin in the 1920s equaled or even surpassed Paris as the cultural center of Europe. Painters, writers, dramatists, and filmmakers from all over Europe found Berlin to be the most stimulating place to work and live, and entertainers like Marlene Dietrich and American-born Josephine Baker found wildly enthusiastic audiences there. However, some Germans were repelled by the experimentalism in art, sexuality, and living styles that were taking place in Berlin and rejected the city as a center of decadence. In fact, one of the first things to be swept out of Germany when the Nazis came to power was the Weimar culture.

Two things brought the "golden years of the twenties" to an end. First, Stresemann died of a stroke in late 1929. He had been the only leader who had made parliamentary government work acceptably well, had brought about compromise between labor and capital, and had enabled Germany to take an equal place among the nations of the world. His death was an untimely tragedy for a nation entering a grave crisis, for he was perhaps the only leader who could have successfully competed with Hitler for control of Germany's destiny. Only 10 days after his death came the second blow to the republic—The American stock market collapsed, and overnight the chief source of credit for Germany dried up. Germany was thrown into a fatal economic crisis.

By 1930 the Weimar Republic was practically dead, although it limped on for another three years. Dr. Heinrich Bruning became chancellor and attempted to master the economic crisis by reducing government spending rather than by trying to stimulate the economy through decisive government economic programs. This policy earned him the name "hunger chancellor." He had no parliamentary majority. The SPD sometimes supported him begrudgingly in the absence of any acceptable alternative, but Bruning was compelled to resort to the emergency powers granted in article 48 of the Weimar constitution, which had been designed originally to enable the president to "restore public safety and order" in times of crisis.

Article 48 was never intended to enable a president or chancellor to rule for long periods of time semi-independently of the parliament, as all chancellors did during the imperial time and which all did again after March 1930. When the Reichstag voted its no confidence for the government for this violation of the constitution, Bruning dissolved parliament and called for new elections for September 1930. He disregarded all warnings that elections in the middle of such an economic depression and widespread unemployment could only benefit the extremist parties of the left and right. After all, unemployment had risen from 1.37 million in 1929 to 3.15 million in 1930. Such warnings were absolutely correct.

The Communist Party increased its number of seats in parliament from 54 to 77, and the Nazi Party grew from 12 members to 107, thereby becoming the second-largest party after the SPD. The Nazis were thereafter in a position to hammer away at the republic through parliamentary obstruction. Unemployment continued to rise to over 6 million in 1932, while production by 1932 had fallen to barely half the 1929 level. Such economic desperation and governmental paralysis gave a man with a small, socially unpolished minority of followers but with great demagogical skill the power to sway the frightened masses—the chance he had waited for a decade.

Throughout the 1920s the Nazi Party had great difficulty gaining political momentum and a significant following. It had first taken shape in the confusion and frustration following the end of World War I and had aimed its appeal toward the disillusioned and impoverished, first in Austria and shortly afterward in Germany. Its official name indicated the wide spectrum of groups it tried to encompass: National Socialist German Workers' Party. Throughout its entire existence, it was not a party that aimed to serve one particular class, as the Communist, Social Democratic, or Conservative Parties tried to do. Instead, the Nazi Party was one that attracted the social scrap of all classes. This is why it was and is difficult to put a political label on the party or movement. It was not exactly conservative because it attacked the capitalist economic system and the status quo, and as a rule, German business leaders did not support the party financially or

President von Hindenburg's signature (actual size)

Germany

Adolf Hitler leaves a Nazi party meeting.

otherwise until after it had actually come into power in 1933.

In a famous speech before the Industrial Club in Dusseldorf in 1932, Adolf Hitler made it unmistakably clear that he considered German business leaders to bear a heavy share of the blame for the 1918 disaster and that business interests would never achieve primacy over political interests in the soon-to-be Third Reich. He always kept this promise. Hitler sought many social changes. In many ways he advocated and introduced a revolution (called by many a "conservative revolution") against bourgeois and industrialized society. National Socialist policy and aims were not leftist, either. They were blatantly nationalist, a fact that attracted many conservative supporters who abhorred his means of gaining power. Also, he openly attacked the Communist Party and Social Democrats as unnational and, in the case of the communists, as handmaidens of the Soviet Union. He detested liberalism, democracy, and the Weimar Republic, aversions he of course shared with the communists.

An Early Attempt in Bavaria

Hitler made an almost comical attempt to seize power in Bavaria in 1923 by having his followers "arrest" government leaders in the Munich Burgerbrau beer hall (now razed). He had hoped this brazen act would set in motion events that would result in the crash of the Weimar Republic. Instead, he was arrested, and there was a highly publicized trial that gave this well-practiced demagogue the opportunity to capture the attention of all of Germany and to articulate his attack against the Weimar Republic. He was sent to Landsberg prison for a five-year sentence, although in the end he served less than one year. While in prison he produced his rambling, often raving, book *Mein Kampf* (My Struggle), put into writing by his loyal follower, Rudolf Hess.

Hitler's unsuccessful "beer hall putsch" and his imprisonment convinced him that he must try to gain power by means of the ballot box. While in prison, he told a friend, "It will be necessary to pursue a new policy. Instead of working to achieve power by an armed coup, we shall have to hold our noses and enter the Reichstag against the Catholic and Marxist deputies. If outvoting them takes longer than out-shooting them, at least the result will be guaranteed by their own constitution. Any lawful process is slow. . . Sooner or later we shall have a majority—and after that, Germany."

Ten years later he accomplished his goal, but it is mistaken to argue that Hitler came to power entirely legally. When the critical elections came in 1930–1933, he unleashed his two private armies, the Sturmabteilung (Storm Division—SA) and Schutzstaffel (Protective Troop—SS), to break up other parties' rallies and meetings, to beat up opponents in the streets, to terrorize those who manifested an inclination to vote for another party, and to make other kinds of unnerving demonstrations, such as throwing up blockades around Berlin at election time. No person with democratic convictions and a rudimentary knowledge of the Weimar constitution could call such tactics legal.

Party Organization

In the 1920s Hitler set about the reorganization of his party from top to bottom. He divided all of Germany into districts, each called a Gau and led by a hard-core Nazi called a Gauleiter. These districts were subdivided into circles (each called a Kreis) and groups. Such units were also created for Austria, Danzig, the Saarland, and the Sudetenland, which at the time were not even a part of Germany but which gave a clue as to what Hitler had in mind for the future. At the top of this party organization was the leader (Fuhrer), Hitler himself. Such rule from the top was called the "leadership principle." Until he committed suicide in 1945, Hitler's leadership within the party was only once seriously challenged by a group of military officers who sensed that Germany was committing suicide under the Fuhrer during the waning days of World War II. Indeed, it is inconceivable that the party would have been so successful without Hitler's powerful will and his ability to coordinate a diverse collection of ambitious Nazis.

Throughout most of the 1920s, the Nazi Party found members and votes primarily among fanatical, nationalistic patriots; anti-Semites; and social misfits fascinated by militarism. They had a psychological need for rabble-rousing rhetoric that was well supplied by party rallies and a daily reading of the party's newspaper, the Volkischer Beobachter (People's Observer). But the party was getting nowhere fast, with 32 parliamentary seats in 1924 and only 12 in 1928. However, after the economic disasters of 1929 and 1930, more and more Germans began to look to the former corporal from Austria, who had gained German citizenship through the back door of Bavarian citizenship only shortly before becoming chancellor of all Germany in 1933. As the novelist Erich Kastner wrote, "people ran after the pied pipers down into the abyss."

When Bruning was dismissed as chancellor in May 1932 because of his inability to muster a parliamentary majority, the senile octogenarian von Hindenburg and three intriguers—Hitler, General Kurt von Schleicher, and Baron Franz von Papen—dominated German politics. The latter had been the German military attaché in Washington during the first part of World War I who later was expelled from the US for spying. In the twilight of the Weimar Republic, many Germans had the impression that there were only two alternatives—the conservatives, with their established position in the army, coupled with the civil and diplomatic service on the one hand, and Hitler, who stood at the head of a dynamic mass movement on the other. It turned out that Hitler, who had a much clearer idea of what he wanted than did his political opponents, had the clear advantage.

He was no democrat, but he was a populist, whose power was based on the masses, not upon the country's elites. It is true that Hitler was in some political trouble: In the parliamentary elections of November 1932, his party had lost 2 million votes. In this last free election in prewar Germany, two out of three Germans voted against Hitler, and most of those who voted for him in that election had not voted for all that he was to do in the following 13 years. Hitler refused to participate in any coalition in which he was not chancellor, and von Hindenburg wearily tried every conceivable conservative combination to prevent the chancellorship from going to Hitler, whom he personally despised. But all efforts were to no avail. Von Papen finally persuaded the aged

"Trains to Life – Trains to Death" memorial in Berlin: a few Jewish children traveled to safety in Britain, many more to death camps

president that he, von Papen, could control the upstart Hitler. So, on January 30, 1933, von Hindenburg, backed to the wall, appointed Hitler chancellor in a cabinet containing only three Nazis.

Political responsibility usually moves radicals and ideologues to more practical viewpoints, a historical fact that must have quieted von Hindenburg's worries at the time. In any case, Hitler came to power by miscalculation rather than by overwhelming popular demand. His ascension to power in Germany was neither inevitable nor a culmination of 1,000 years of German history as he asserted; such an evaluation honored Hitler far too greatly. In some unsteady situations, such as in 1933, power is like a ripe piece of fruit waiting to be picked by that person who is most ready to act decisively. On January 30, 1933, in Germany, that person was Adolf Hitler.

Hitler Seizes Total Power

For a few weeks, Hitler had to be cautious because he had no parliamentary majority, by coalition or otherwise, and because von Hindenburg, who was still very cool toward him, had not given him permission to exercise emergency powers. But an incident during the night of February 27, 1933, gave Hitler the chance to throw off most of the restraints on his power and to fire the *coup de grace* into the drooping head of the Weimar Republic. In that night the Reichstag was gutted by fire. Controversy still surrounds this incident, but it is probable that the Nazis themselves set the fire. Hitler acted "quickly as lightning" (which along with "ice cold" was one of his favorite expressions). He declared that this had been an act of communist violence and won von Hindenburg's formal approval the next day to suspend constitutional guarantees for individual and civil liberties.

During the first four weeks of Hitler's chancellorship, the courts had dared to reject many of the high-handed methods employed by Hermann Göring's Prussian police force to victimize the Nazis' political opponents. That was no longer possible because Hitler now wielded emergency powers and thereby had the ability to terrorize Germans through instruments of the state. His storm troopers were able to race through the streets arresting socialists, communists, and liberal party leaders; taking sledgehammers to newspaper presses; breaking up all opposition political meetings and terrorizing the entire nation. Neither von Hindenburg nor the German army resisted these moves.

In this atmosphere of violence and intimidation, the last election of the Weimar Republic was held on March 5, 1933, in which the Nazis were still unable to

receive more than 44% of the popular vote. Yet, by scaring and arresting enough members of parliament, Hitler was able to manipulate a majority in the Reichstag in favor of the so-called Enabling Act, which in effect suspended parliament's power and made Hitler the sole leader of Germany. Only the SPD dared to vote against this. Only a few more steps were necessary to give him full dictatorial power.

Anti-Semitism and Repression

Hitler and his party proceeded to enforce a so-called Gleichschaltung, an untranslatable German word meaning the destruction or restructuring of all independent groups or institutions so that none could exist without supporting Nazi rule. In March and April 1933, he abolished the federal organization of Germany, and for the first time in its history, Germany became entirely centralized, with governors (*Reichsstatthalter*) carrying out Hitler 's policy in the various regions. By June all independent labor unions had been outlawed, and a Labor Front was created under the leadership of the invariably intoxicated Robert Ley, with the task of keeping labor under firm control. By July all political parties except the Nazi Party had been abolished, and concentration camps were established, where alleged enemies of the state could be "concentrated" and controlled.

By October all communications media, including film, were brought under Nazi control, and all newspaper editors were required to be Aryans (non-Jewish members of an ancient race to which, according to Nazi doctrine, Germans belonged). They could not even be married to Jews. This was only one of a steadily growing number of measures directed against Jews within Germany, who, according to Nazi ideology, were social parasites who weakened the German nation—this despite the fact that 12,000 Jewish soldiers had died fighting for Germany in World War I. Some of them had been awarded the Iron Cross. Many Jews, including brilliant intellectuals and scientists, began to flee Germany during the ensuing years. One of them was Albert Einstein, who came to the United States. These anti-Jewish measures reached a prewar crescendo in the night of November 9–10, 1938, when hundreds of Jewish homes, stores, and synagogues were systematically damaged and plundered. The amount of broken glass this senseless and criminal rampage left gave the event the name of *Kristallnacht* ("Crystal Night"). Although many Germans were sickened by this incident, none dared to resist.

This event increased the tempo of the stampede of Jews from Germany, which started in 1933, when all non-Aryans and

Germany

people who were "no longer prepared to intercede at all times for the National Socialist state" were excluded from civil service and ultimately from posts in the universities. Many young Germans had streamed into the Nazi student organization and assumed the right to control the lectures and writings of their professors for "un-German" or other politically revealing utterances. Youthful idealism can sometimes have a beneficial effect in politics, but it can also be disastrous. In 1933–1934 an estimated 1,684 scholars, including 1,145 professors, were dismissed from the universities. At the Universities of Berlin and Frankfurt am Main, about a third of the faculty was fired, and in all of Germany, the size of the student body fell by about one-third, due largely to the inclusion of Nazi Party membership in the admission procedure.

This policy of *Gleichschaltung* issued an almost fatal blow to the cultural and intellectual preeminence of Germany. But there was one country that benefited enormously from this self-defeating and shortsighted policy: the United States. Before the outbreak of war, approximately 200,000 Germans, half of whom were Jewish, had fled to the US. American immigration quota restrictions, which had been tightened during the economic depression of the 1930s, were such that a large portion of the German refugees to the United States were intellectual or cultural leaders who could find sponsors more easily. They were attracted by such universities as the New School for Social Research in New York, Princeton University, and the University of Chicago or to such magnetic cultural centers as Hollywood or New York City.

Even an abbreviated list of these refugees gives an idea of the enormous loss to Germany—in addition to scientists Albert Einstein and Edward Teller, in literature practically the entire Mann family (Thomas, Heinrich, Klaus, Erika, and Golo), Bertold Brecht, Stefan Zweig, Carl Zuckmayer, Alfred Doblin, Leon Feuchtwanger, and Erich Maria Remarque. In film there were Fritz Lang, Marlene Dietrich, and Otto Preminger; in theater, Max Reinhardt; in music, Arnold Schonberg and Kurt Weil; in art, Georg Grosz and Max Ernst; in architecture, Walter Gropius and Ludwig Mies van der Rohe; in publishing, Frederick Praeger and Kurt Wolff; and in scholarship, Paul Tillich, Erich Fromm, Hans Morgenthau, Theodor Adorno, Ernst Bloch, Leo Strauss, Erich Voegelin, Hannah Arendt, Ernst Cassirer, and Kurt Riezler. By 1938 the New York columnist Dorothy Thompson could claim with justification that "practically everyone whom the world considers to be representative of German culture before 1933 is now a refugee." Of course, some stayed in the United States only until Hitler was defeated, but most stayed for good.

"Night of the Long Knives"

In the dark hours of June 30, 1934, known as the "night of the long knives," Hitler had hundreds of potential challengers to his authority within his own party murdered, especially the SA leadership, including Ernst Rohm. While his assassination squads were at work, he also eliminated many prominent non-Nazis, such as von Schleicher and some of von Papen's closest aides, as well as leading authors, lawyers, civil servants, Catholic politicians, and harmless citizens who at some time had caused irritation to one or the other Nazi bosses. Von Papen and Bruning escaped by the skin of their teeth, the latter eventually landing in a professorial chair at Harvard. These cold-blooded acts were enough to intimidate most resistance to Hitler within or without the Nazi Party until his death in 1945.

The senile von Hindenburg died August 2, 1934, and Hitler simply combined the offices of president and chancellor and declared himself the absolute Fuhrer of party and state. He then required that the nation give retroactive approval of this unconstitutional act in a plebiscite, a favorite maneuver of dictators whereby one may vote "yes" or "no" under the watchful eyes of party henchmen. Despite intimidation measures, 5 million Germans voted "no" to this act. Hitler then proceeded to require all officers and soldiers to take an oath of allegiance, not to Germany, but to him alone. Many German officers had grave misgivings about taking such an oath. But Hitler's shrewd treatment of the army gradually eliminated it as an immediate threat to his power, although high-ranking officers would later prove to be his most daring, though ill-fated, foes.

The Third Reich

By fall 1934, Hitler stood as the undisputed leader of a dictatorial state he called the "Third Reich." This name was used to remind Germans that he had created anew a Germany worthy of the two earlier German Empires—the one created by Heinrich I in 919 and the one formed by Bismarck in 1871. His path to power had been washed by blood and strewn with corpses. Many of his subjects had been driven through fear to passivity. Yet in 1939 he could claim with justification that he ruled a people that generally supported him. How was this possible? In the first half of his 12-year rule, he was able to achieve certain things that many Germans and non-Germans alike regarded as little less than miraculous. His accomplishments confused and disarmed his opponents, who in 1933 were still the majority within Germany. But their numbers had dwindled considerably by 1938, even if most of them did not actually become Nazis.

Before 1933 Hitler had shown himself to be an excellent organizer and hypnotic speaker, but few Germans expected him actually to succeed in conducting the complex affairs of state. Before he came to power, he remained largely in the realm of fuzzy generalities. For example, he made no concrete suggestions on how to combat the problem of unemployment. He also seemed to reveal his cards very quickly after coming to power, inflicting a heavy dose of terror on the German people. Indeed, that his rule always rested in part on terror indicated that the whole German people never entirely embraced National Socialism. But terror gradually declined and remained at a level just sufficient to keep the population in a state of fear without driving them into desperate resistance. His orchestration of terror within Germany and his skillful use of his own undeniable charisma were psychological masterpieces.

In retrospect, some professionals have diagnosed Hitler as clinically paranoid. Continuously tense and expectant, he was sensitive and suspicious. He had no close relationship with anyone, not even with his mistress, Eva Braun, whom he finally married moments before committing suicide. Untrusting, he always felt that his failures resulted from the enmity or failure of others, even those close to him. He was able, however, to maintain his conduct within nominally acceptable bounds and to many people could appear to be no more than a "crank." They could also rationalize their support for him not in terms of infatuation with a charismatic demagogue but rather of cool-headed appreciation for some of his tangible accomplishments.

Initial Successes

What were his specific accomplishments? By far his most important and popular was his dealing with the economic crisis. In early 1933 there were more than 6 million Germans out of work; by 1936 Germany achieved full employment without creating inflation. Germans had been put to work building an admirable network of superhighways known as Autobahnen, as well as other public works.

Industries were given tax relief, and the government's financial leaders, especially Dr. Schacht, channeled investments to desperately needy economic sectors and successfully manipulated government funds and the money supply so that the economy would not be choked for lack of money. Hitler also revitalized the arms industry in Germany. This provided an important stimulus for the economy, but it

Germany

should be noted that most of Germany's unemployed found jobs in civilian industries, not in arms industries. In the three years after Hitler had assumed power in Germany, the country's GNP and national income had doubled, and Germans had begun to enjoy a modest prosperity.

Within Germany the mood had changed from one of hopelessness to one of confidence in the future. Of course, it should never be overlooked that by 1939 many Germans had become soldiers and approximately 300,000 were in concentration camps. Hitler's economic performance was so successful that many persons in and out of Germany gained the impression that this man could indeed perform "wonders." Others in countries all over Europe began to see totalitarianism and cooperation with and imitation of Germany as attractive.

A second accomplishment was that he accelerated a process begun several decades earlier in Germany, namely the breaking down of class differences. The Nazis were officially in favor of this Volksgemeinschaft. They did not speak of a "classless society," as do communists, but of "community." This latter term had become very attractive to many Germans who were sick and tired of conflict and who wanted to see central authority established in Germany. "Community" as interpreted by the Nazis required a high degree of social mobilization of youths, women, farmers, and other groups. In fact, Germans were expected to become so active in politically dominated groups that they could not possibly go their own way and be individually free. Still, in the Third Reich there was much upward and downward mobility, mixing of classes and open opportunity for the talented (so long as they were not Jewish or openly critical of the new political order).

It would be wrong to argue that Hitler eliminated class conflict entirely. Despite the rapid economic recovery, the problems between capital and labor, big and small business, or industry and agriculture were not solved. But there was less social inequality in Germany during the Third Reich than there had been before, and both East and West Germany greatly profited from and continued this process after 1945.

A third accomplishment that won the admiration of many of his countrymen was Hitler's rapid rearmament of Germany. In January 1933 Germany had a 100,000-man army without an air force and modern weapons. By 1938 it had a conscript army and was the strongest military power in Europe. Hitler also made the significant decision, against the advice of many military experts, to integrate armored units with other combat forces. This

Autographed portrait of the *Führer*

Courtesy: David W. Staton

later proved quite successful in overrunning most of western Europe. The military buildup may have been a curse for the rest of Europe, but many Germans approved it. They saw it as a means for revising the despised Versailles Treaty.

A fourth accomplishment was a string of almost stunning diplomatic and military victories. Until 1942 Hitler had always been a master of recognizing when houses of cards were about ready to collapse and then of acting decisively while others wavered. He had the instinct of a buzzard that told him when to swoop in on that which had been already dying. He had seen when the Weimar Republic

had reached the end of its road, and Hitler merely gave it the coup de grace. He also could see that the international system that had emerged from Versailles was collapsing. At that conference, one of the four pre-1914 great European powers, Austria-Hungary, had been destroyed, and another, Russia, had been excluded from the victorious coalition. The United States refused to help enforce the treaty, so only Britain and France remained to hold the dictated settlement together. In the course of the 1920s, Britain grew tired of its role and began to seek a policy of moderation and accommodation toward Germany. French leaders did not favor such a policy

Germany

of appeasement, but France had become so weakened by pacifism and political division from within that it could no longer oppose Germany energetically.

Hitler violated the Locarno Treaty in 1936 and remilitarized the Rhineland. In March 1938 Germany swallowed up Austria in the face of virtually no opposition from it or any other country. Six months later, Germany obtained French and British approval at a conference in Munich for Germany's absorption of the Sudetenland, the predominantly German speaking western part of Czechoslovakia. Hitler's appetite was whetted, so in 1939 he declared Bohemia (capital: Prague) and Moravia to be German protectorates and occupied the Memel area. He had marched his troops a long way while the rest of Europe slept, but when his troops entered Prague, Britain woke up and resigned itself to the bitter fact that it would have to prepare for war against Germany. France reluctantly agreed.

The Start of World War II

By the spring of 1939, Britain and France had already allowed Germany to become the dominant power in Europe. Hitler's crucial mistake was that he cast this enormous accomplishment away by leading Germany into war. After 1938 he had no further diplomatic victories. From 1939 to 1941, he led Germany to dazzling successes, but all were of a military nature. With relative ease his newly created army (Wehrmacht) rolled over part of Poland, Denmark, Norway, Holland, Belgium, Luxembourg, Yugoslavia, and Greece.

The most astonishing victory, in the eyes of the world, was the victory over France.

Most German generals shuddered at the thought of attacking France, remembering the failure of the 1914 advance and the four-year war of attrition, which had sapped Germany's strength and will. But Hitler had great faith in the tank warfare tactics developed by General Heinz Guderian and in the brilliant strategic plan devised by General Friedrich Erich von Manstein. He also recognized the most important factor—France was simply unwilling to fight a war.

In six weeks, Germany had rolled into France via a flank attack around its famed Maginot line of supposedly impregnable fortresses. The amount of French military activity is vividly evident even to this day. If one inspects the war memorials in the towns and cities of France, the names of those who perished in World War I outnumbers by 10, 20, and even 30 to 1 the names of those victims of World War II.

By the summer of 1940, Germany controlled Europe from the Arctic Circle to the Pyrenees and from the Atlantic Ocean to the Soviet Union. If Hitler had made a generous peace offer to France, he might have destroyed Britain's and other countries' will to resist, but Hitler never thought of such a possibility. He could not grant a magnanimous peace because, as he himself later wrote, the victory of the stronger always involved "the destruction of the weaker or his unconditional subservience." He had a knack for seeing the weakness in his enemies, but he was unable to build anything lasting. Also, because he considered himself to be infallible and irreplaceable, he insisted on doing everything quickly; he could not plant anything that required time to grow.

Based upon his writings and actions, one can say with reasonable certainty that Hitler sought to establish German hegemony in Europe and direct domination over the Soviet Union, which, along with the older European powers' overseas colonies, would occupy the bottom of Hitler's power pyramid. Above them would be the rest of the European countries, divided into Germanic lands bordering on Germany; servant peoples, such as the Poles; and satellites and quasi-independent states. On top would be an all-powerful Germany. This German-dominated order would place Hitler in a good position later to struggle against America and Japan for world domination. That he did not accomplish this stunning goal was due in large measure to serious mistakes he himself made after such stunning successes.

The Beginning of the End

In 1940 he launched an aerial attack against Britain, which left rubble piles throughout the kingdom but which also inspired heroic British action in what Prime Minister Winston Churchill called Britain's "finest hour." While still involved in this furious struggle, violating the treaty whereby Germany and Russia had split up Poland between them, Hitler unleashed his armies against the Soviet Union in mid-1941, against the advice of his generals, thereby creating a two-front war that had been such a nightmare for Germany during World War I. The attack was launched too late, so in a repeat of Napoleon's humiliation, "Mother Winter" saved the weaker Russians. Cold weather and snow closed in on the German troops, many of

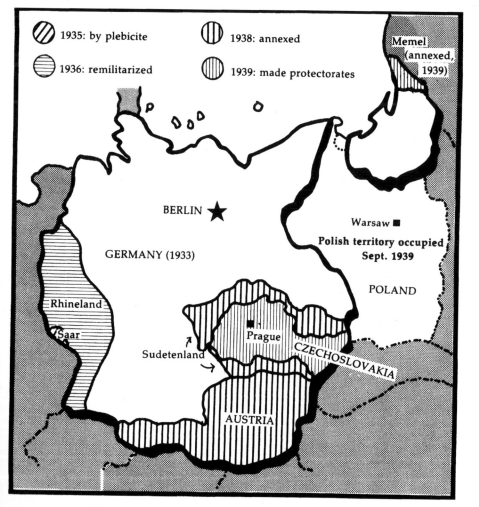

German expansion, 1935–1939

German officers examine a captured Polish banner.

whom had not been issued proper winter equipment. After initial victories against an enemy Hitler had grossly underestimated, the German advance slowed to a freeze. Hitler saw his dreams of grandeur buried under Russian snow and ice.

In the midst of this truly desperate situation, Hitler compounded his difficulties even further. On December 7, 1941, Japan attacked the US fleet at Pearl Harbor in Hawaii, and the US responded by declaring war on Japan but not on Germany. Germany had no treaty obligation with Japan, but inexplicably and without conferring with anyone, Hitler declared war against the US. Germany had no military means for conducting military operations against the Americans, but this step decisively tipped the scales in favor of his opponents and ultimately sealed Germany's defeat. Thereafter, he had no idea how to extricate Germany from ruin. For example, he could not follow up on General Erwin Rommel's victories in North Africa in the summer of 1942, and of course, he excluded the very idea of a political settlement. His only order was "Hold at all costs!" In 1942 Germany began losing territory in the east, especially after a disastrous defeat at Stalingrad in early 1943.

After 1941 Hitler withdrew more and more from public view and spent most of his time in military headquarters. Since his first goal—to dominate Europe—was slipping out of reach, he turned toward a second goal—the eradication of the Jews. He began astonishing the world with crimes the extent of which the world had hitherto not known and the extent of which would only be discovered at the end of the war. Earlier and contemporary dictators or would-be world conquerors such as Alexander the Great, Napoleon, and Stalin, had caused thousands or millions of deaths. But whether one agreed with them or not, they usually had political or military motives for their brutality. In contrast, Hitler's mass murder of the Jews worked against his political and military objectives. This campaign was not only morally repugnant, but it also sapped further the strength of a weakening Germany.

The "Final Solution"

From the time he first began making public speeches, Hitler left no doubt that he was intensely anti-Semitic. He put this in writing in *Mein Kampf* and underscored it with anti-Jewish legislation after coming to power in 1933. On January 30, 1939, the sixth anniversary of his acquisition of power, he spoke publicly of "eradicating the Jewish race in Europe." This actually was another manifestation of his paranoia. His delusion was that the Jews were responsible for Germany's failure in World War I and were a threat to his current ambitions for Germany. Sometimes, a paranoid's delusions are directed against one person, but Hitler's were directed toward millions.

In mid-1941 Hitler began having Polish and Russian Jews rounded up and shot beside mass graves. At the Wannsee Conference at the outskirts of Berlin on January 20, 1942, the decision was made to extend this policy to Jews in Germany and other occupied countries, as well. Special extermination camps were constructed in Treblinka, Sobibor, Maidanek (Lublin), Belzec, Chelan (Kulmhof), and Auschwitz for this grisly purpose.

By the spring of 1942, the "final solution," which caused the needless death of about 6 million innocent people by 1945, was in full swing. This policy was pursued with such single-minded determination that the German war effort itself was greatly hampered. Manpower badly needed at the front or in domestic industries was either sent to extermination camps as victims of this policy or to SS units or other special military units (called Einsatzgruppen) as executors of this policy. Railroad rolling stock was diverted and rail lines were clogged. Also, this policy of murder prompted the western Allies to declare as a major war aim the "punishment of those persons responsible for these crimes"; the Soviet Union proclaimed the same in November 1943. This new war aim made any kind of compromise peace with Germany unthinkable and prompted Hitler's enemies to demand Germany's "unconditional surrender."

The Jewish Museum in Berlin documents this lamentable tale—of 560,000 German Jews before the war, 276,000 emigrated to safety; 25,000 in mixed marriages with non-Jews survived; 8,500 escaped over the German border; 10,000 went

Germany

Hitler addresses a Nazi rally.

into hiding, of which only 1,500 survived; 200,000 were deported from Germany and occupied countries and perished. After the war, 50,000 German Jews were homeless. They were joined by 150,000 Jews from eastern Europe, who poured into the American occupation zone. Most ultimately emigrated.

How much did the German people know about this ghastly policy at the time? Certainly, all Germans of a sound mind knew that their country had adopted an official policy of discrimination against Jews, and all had been informed that their government was "resettling" Jews in the east. However, for a variety of reasons, the regime did not reveal to the German population details about the policy. The most important reason, no doubt, was that Hitler did not trust his own people and suspected that they would not approve. He surely had to have noted that most Germans had supported neither the nationwide boycott of Jewish businesses in 1933 nor the "Crystal Night" of 1938, which actually produced more pity for Jews, shame and irritation (but no more than that) among non-Nazis than anything else.

Further, in mid-1941 Hitler had to suspend a policy he had introduced publicly in 1939 to eliminate 70,000 to 80,000 patients in convalescent and nursing homes, 10,000 to 20,000 sick and invalids in concentration camps within Germany, all Jewish patients in mental hospitals, and about 3,000 children between the ages of 3 and 13 in orphanages and special schools for the handicapped. One of the major reasons for the suspension was the increasing unrest within the German population and the active opposition of the churches.

Hitler spared the Jews no misery, but he was careful not to allow most Germans to know for sure what was happening to the Jews. The exterminations were conducted in eastern Europe, outside Germany, and careful precautions were taken not to enable unauthorized persons to witness what was happening within the camps. He even took the special measure, whenever possible, of sending German Jews first to large ghettos such as Theresienstadt in Bohemia, where they were able to write postcards back to Germany for a while before being transported to death camps.

Of course, rumors about what was really happening filtered into Germany, but the absence of confirmation enabled anyone to reject the rumors or to remain in doubt if he or she chose to do so. Most Germans did just that, as did most non-Germans in the other occupied areas, for that matter. In Germany and in other occupied areas, there were persons who took risks by hiding or helping Jews. But nowhere was there the kind of mass uprising that would have been necessary to put an end to that shameful policy. In fact, only the military power of Hitler's enemies brought the Third Reich to its knees.

Other Genocide

Hitler's policy of liquidating people whom he considered to be *Untermensch* ("subhuman") was, of course, not restricted to the Jews. Only about a fifth of the 25,000 Roma (Gypsies) living in Germany in 1939 survived by 1945, and estimates of the total number of European Gypsies murdered at Hitler's order range up to a half-million. In October 1939 German leaders began a five-year campaign

to destroy the entire Polish elite and culture. Polish priests, professors, journalists, businessmen, and earlier political leaders were systematically liquidated. When one considers that the Soviet Union conducted a similar policy against the Poles in those areas under its domination, most dramatically in the Katyn Forest in 1940, when Soviet forces murdered some 22,000 Polish officers and elites and dumped them into mass graves, it is almost miraculous that Poland was able to survive the war as a nation. In the end, Poland had lost about 6 million countrymen, about half of whom were Jews and not more than 300,000 of whom had fallen in battle.

The German treatment of the Russians and of subject peoples under Russian control was even worse than that of the Poles. German policy in the Soviet Union revealed the extent to which Hitler's racial theories thwarted Germany's national interests. Many peripheral peoples in the Soviet Union who had never joined with it voluntarily greeted invading German soldiers more like liberators than conquerors. A farsighted German policy to transform these people into allies might have been successful and extremely beneficial to Germany.

Instead, Russians and non-Russians alike were treated with the same brutality. The German army was involved in the actions directed against the civilian population in the Soviet Union. The Germans especially mistreated Soviet prisoners of war. According to German military records, by May 1, 1944, the Germans had captured more than 5 million Russian soldiers, mostly in 1941. However, at that time, fewer than 2 million remained alive. Almost a half-million had been executed, 67,000 had fled, and almost 3 million had died in the camps, mostly of hunger. German mistreatment of the Soviet population helped Stalin to unify the population in the war effort against the Germans. The many acts of brutality committed later by Soviet soldiers in occupied Germany, as well as the strong distrust that the Soviet Union showed toward Germany after 1945, must be seen against this background, although nothing can excuse the bestial acts committed by these two peoples against each other.

Minimal Internal Resistance

There were, of course, some symbolic acts of resistance to Nazi rule within Germany. In early 1943 two young Christians in the Catholic youth organization, Hans and Sophie Scholl, brother and sister, passed out flyers on the streets of Munich for a few minutes calling Hitler a tyrant and demanding acts of sabotage in the arms factories before they were whisked away and promptly executed.

Germany

The most serious opposition to Hitler came from within the German army, supported by a unique coalition of aristocrats, civil servants, trade unionists, and clergymen from both churches. The German military traditionally had considered itself superior to Nazis, whom it tended to regard as uneducated, rowdy troublemakers. On July 20, 1944, this coalition made a bold attempt to assassinate Hitler, but the bomb placed under the table during a meeting in Hitler's eastern headquarters miraculously failed to harm the Fuhrer seriously when it exploded; it had been placed there by Colonel Claus Schenk von Stauffenberg, a decorated war hero who had lost an arm and an eye in battle. Assuming that the Nazi leader was dead, the plotters moved to take control of the major governmental and military command centers in Berlin. However, Hitler quickly went on the air to announce that he was alive, and he ordered that the plotters be arrested. Within hours the leaders were executed. Hitler suffered nerve damage to an arm and appeared shaken by the incident.

The assassins were without question prompted to act by information they had of Hitler's grisly extermination policies. When asked about his motive before the People's Court following the attempt, Count Yorck von Wartenburg said, "I thought about the many crimes," before he was shouted down by the hated Chief Justice Roland Freisler. But there were other motives, as well. Germany was entangled in a war it could not win, and there was no attempt on the part of Germany's leaders to reach a political settlement. It was characteristic that after the July 20 plot Hitler ordered mass arrests of more than 5,000 former cabinet ministers, mayors, parliamentarians, and civil servants (including such important postwar figures as Konrad Adenauer and Kurt Schumacher), whom the enemy coalition could have viewed as a possible alternative to the Third Reich. For Hitler, the only conceivable alternatives were Germany's holding on under his own leadership or facing total destruction.

The Allies Close In

By the fall of 1944, enemy armies were advancing on Germany from the east and west, and more and more Germans saw the hopelessness of the situation and began to regard conquest by the western Allies as liberation. But Hitler did not share this secret war aim of many Germans. He had personally assumed command of the German forces. He had unleashed a torrent of powerful rockets on London and its suburbs using technology only recently developed. These attacks by what he called his "wonder weapons" merely served to

YOU ARE LEAVING THE AMERICAN SECTOR
ВЫ ВЫЕЗЖАЕТЕ ИЗ АМЕРИКАНСКОГО СЕКТОРА
VOUS SORTEZ DU SECTEUR AMÉRICAIN
SIE VERLASSEN DEN AMERIKANISCHEN SEKTOR
US ARMY

Divided Berlin

harden even more the determination of the British and their American ally.

Disregarding warnings from military advisers that the Red Army was poised for a massive strike from the east, Hitler ordered his last military offensive against the western Allies in the Belgian Ardennes Forest in late 1944. The element of surprise and extremely bad weather that kept Allied aircraft grounded for a few days helped the Germans to gain initial success and to stop the western powers' advance on Germany in its tracks. However, once American and British air power could be brought into the action, the German offensive was stopped, and by the first week of January, the German forces were being decimated or rolled back.

As some of Hitler's generals had warned, the Red Army crashed through the German line in the east and in one violent movement pushed from the Vistula to the Oder Rivers. Hitler had nothing left to stop the Russian advance.

In the first half of February 1945, President Roosevelt, Prime Minister Churchill, and General Secretary Stalin met in Yalta in the Crimea area to discuss the postwar control of Germany and to divide Germany into zones of occupation. The lines they drew were heavily influenced by the calculations of where exactly the Allied armies would be in Germany at the end of the war. At the time, it appeared that Russian troops would be somewhat farther within Germany than was actually the case when hostilities ceased. However, based on the decisions made at Yalta, US troops had later to be pulled back from Saxony and Thuringia, which were within the designated Soviet zone. Also, the

collapse of cooperation among the four Allies after the war left the temporary line drawn between the Soviet zone of occupation and the zones of the western Allies as the dividing line between East and West Germany until 1990.

Seeing enemy armies advancing within his own country's territory and with no hope for stopping them, any rational and responsible leader with a concern for his own people would have done anything to salvage whatever would be necessary for his people's survival. Hitler was not such a leader. In late 1941 he had made a chilling statement to the Danish and Croatian foreign ministers: "If ever the German Volk is no longer sufficiently strong and willing to sacrifice its own blood for its existence, then it should fade away and be destroyed by another, stronger power. . . . In that situation, I will lose no tears for the German people."

The Collapse

On March 18 and 19, 1945, he gave two orders that demonstrated he had not changed his mind and he now thought it was time to carry through with the end of Germany. He ordered all Germans in areas threatened by the invasion forces in the west to leave their homes and set out on what could only have been a death march eastward. The following day he gave the so-called Nero order: "to destroy all military, transport, communications, industrial and supply facilities as well as anything of value within the Reich that could be used by the enemy for continuing its struggle either immediately or in the foreseeable time." When Albert Speer, his trusted confidant and munitions minister, objected to this policy,

237

Germany

In Germany . . . desolation

Courtesy: The Marshall Library, Lexington, VA

which would have completely eliminated the Germans' ability to survive after defeat, Hitler answered "ice-coldly," "If the war is lost, then the people will be lost also. . . In that case the people will have shown itself as the weaker, and the future would belong solely to the strengthened Eastern people. Whoever survives this struggle would be the inferior ones anyway since the superior ones have already fallen."

Hitler himself chose not to be among the survivors. On April 30, 1945, a few hours before his underground bunker in Berlin was captured by Soviet troops, he stuck a pistol in his mouth and pulled the trigger. Speer and others did their best to prevent these orders from being carried out. But the important effect of these orders was that many Germans, at least in the western part of Germany, viewed the enemy occupation of Germany as liberation. While the occupation forces expected to find a nation of fanatic Nazis, they found instead a shell-shocked, seriously disillusioned people. They had been more thoroughly "denazified" by Hitler's treatment of Germany in the closing months of the war than the carefully planned denazification and reeducation program would ever have been able to accomplish. The occupation powers interpreted Germans' passivity and willingness to cooperate as typical German servility. Instead, it was a reflection of the extent to which Germans felt themselves to have been deceived and betrayed by Hitler.

The Early Postwar Period

Hitler had unwittingly strengthened the chances for democracy to succeed after

he had left the stage. But what kind of Germany did Hitler leave behind? Seven million Germans had perished; 1 in 10 Germans died, and 3 out of 10 German soldiers did not survive. Only the Russians suffered greater human casualties as a result of the war. Germany lost a fourth of its territory, and what remained was divided into two German states.

Not since the Thirty Years' War from 1618 to 1648 had the Germans suffered so much destruction or loss of life. Not a single great German city survived the war undamaged by saturation bombing by the western Allies and, later, artillery shells. One-fifth of the nation's housing was destroyed, and in the larger cities, the situation was genuinely desperate. Only 47% of the buildings in Hamburg were left standing, and most others were severely damaged. In the commercial city of Frankfurt, only about a fourth of the houses survived, and in Nuremberg, where Hitler had held some of his most impressive party congresses and rallies, only about one-tenth of the dwellings remained unscathed. Shocked and hungry Germans without shelter were cramped in houses and apartments belonging to others, in hotels, in makeshift structures, or even in former bomb shelters. Everywhere were mountains of rubble with narrow paths cut through them to enable pedestrians, carts, and vehicles to pass. Bridges, viaducts, water mains, and power lines were cut. All bridges over the Rhine, Weser, and Main Rivers had been destroyed, and these three key waterways were closed to shipping. Power facilities, even if left intact or repaired, were often unable to function

for lack of coal. Home heating was almost nonexistent for all but the occupation forces, and often the only warmth the Germans could get was at warming stations in certain places in the city, where they could go for a few minutes a day.

The German population had suffered frightful losses in the war, which for the first time since 1814 had been fought in the heart of Germany. Over 2 million German soldiers had been killed in action, 2.5 million had been taken prisoner, over 1.5 million were missing, and at least an equal number had been crippled by the war. Civilian deaths and injury were in the hundreds of thousands, and far more than 1 million German children had been orphaned.

There was very little food, especially in the Soviet and French sectors, where occupation troops and authorities were compelled to "live off the land." Prewar Germany had never been self-sufficient in food, and during the Weimar Republic, it had to import about 20% of its needs. Because of the economic disruption and the loss of extensive agricultural areas in the east, this figure rose to 50% in the three western zones after the war. In those zones, the official target in the immediate postwar years was a mere 1,550 calories per day, but in the heavily populated British zone in 1946, the actual rations sank to 600 to 1,000 calories per day. Malnutrition was especially harmful to the young. Hamburg reported 10,000 cases of hunger edema (abdominal swelling), and in towns and cities in Hesse, 90% of the children developed rickets. The mortality rate for infants and young children rose to 154 per 1,000 in the Ruhr area and 160 in Berlin.

For most Germans, finding the next meal was immensely more important than the political future of their country. The defeated country had suffered economic collapse. For a couple of years, the Allied occupation powers restricted production, delayed recovery, and decentralized or dismantled industrial plants in order to reduce the power of industrial leaders or to provide reparations to some of the victorious Allies, particularly the Soviet Union, which transported whole factories to mother Russia. As a result of this economic turmoil, the great majority of the population had become pauperized. Many were reduced to selling or swapping their most treasured heirlooms for a pittance in order to obtain food or other necessities, often on the thriving black market and at exorbitant prices. In some cases, honorable women actually had to resort to prostitution among the occupying forces in order to provide food for their families and relatives. Former president Herbert Hoover reported in February 1947 that the situation in western Germany was worse than in any other

Germany

part of Europe. He told President Truman bluntly, "You can have vengeance, or peace, but you can't have both."

Migration from the East

The available food, housing, and jobs had to serve not only the prewar residents of the three western zones but also the flood of refugees who poured in from the east. Million of Germans were expelled from southern European countries or from former German lands east of the Oder and Neisse Rivers, which now form the border between Germany and Poland. These lands in 1938 had amounted to about 44,000 square miles (70,400 sq. km, or 24% of Germany's entire land area), and they had supplied a large part of Germany's food and coal. Most of these areas became a part of Poland to compensate Poles for their lands the Soviet Union had seized. Germany officially relinquished these lands to Poland within weeks after it regained its unity and full sovereignty in 1990. The rest (a part of East Prussia, including the city of Königsberg, now Kaliningrad) was absorbed by the Soviet Union.

These expulsions of ethnic Germans from eastern Europe reached a height in the winter of 1945–1946. Those affected were often given 24 hours' notice and were able to take with them only 50 to 60 pounds of baggage apiece. Other Germans fled the Soviet occupation zone in order to escape the kind of authoritarian political order that was being established there. These refugees placed severe strains on the western occupation authorities and on the previous residents, who were required to share their meager incomes with the often highly unwelcome newcomers in order to distribute the nation's material burdens more fairly. By the time the Berlin Wall was erected beginning August 13, 1961, approximately 12 million refugees had poured into West Germany.

Adding to the refugee problem was that of the displaced persons (DPs), whom the Nazis had brought to Germany to perform forced labor. They numbered about 6.5 million persons by the end of the war, and about 2 million of them refused to return to their homelands in the Soviet Union or in the Baltic states, which had been annexed by the USSR. They were fed and clothed largely by the US through the UN Relief and Rehabilitation Administration, but they often occupied jobs and housing that were denied to Germans.

The German people were largely disgraced and demoralized. Hitler had greatly changed German society, having reduced or eliminated permanently the power and influence that, for example, noblemen, military officers, or large Prussian landowners had wielded earlier. Unlike 1918, the collapse of the Third Reich

A demoralized population

Courtesy: The Marshall Library, Lexington, VA

eliminated the nation's entire political elite. Germany's highest surviving Nazi leaders were placed on trial in Nuremberg from November 1945 until October 1946, and most were given either death sentences or long prison terms in Spandau Prison in West Berlin. Only one prisoner, Rudolf Hess, remained there. Blind and crippled, he died in August 1987 at age 93, and the prison was razed.

The controversial denazification programs of the occupation powers required that those Germans who had held positions of obvious authority or influence under the Nazis be jailed, fined, or demoted. Others, such as civil servants, teachers, journalists, or industrial leaders, most of whom had no choice about joining the Nazi Party, were temporarily removed from their jobs. In the end, all of the elites under the previous regime had been deprived of their status, except church leaders. *Mein Kampf* was not allowed to be published, although unofficial copies could later be obtained on the Internet. (Its copyright ended in 2015, and a heavily annotated two-volume edition was published in 2016 amid much controversy.) It is questionable that most of the denazification measures were necessary at all. Defeat and utter destruction under the leadership of Hitler had been the best antidote to Nazism. Although it took several more years to convince many Germans that even the general idea of National Socialism had been wrong, their approval of the concrete form Nazism had taken had disappeared almost completely by the end of the war.

The German army was completely disbanded, and when the Federal Armed Forces were created in 1956, the military's influence and prestige in political and social life had been almost entirely eliminated. The various classes had not been eradicated, but they had been brought more closely together during the Third Reich and the aftermath of the war. Germans now mingled more easily with one another. Although an end to hostilities brought no political revolution or social upheaval, as had been the case in 1918, the quiet social and political revolution that culminated in 1945 was much more far-reaching than that of 1918.

Germans were now divided territorially, but they were no longer so divided domestically. The old conservatives had been discredited, and the romanticism of war, assertiveness in the world, and ideas about German national unique superiority had been extinguished. Ideologies had little appeal anymore, and most Germans had become convinced that a flight from the much debunked "bourgeois values," including especially parliamentary democracy within a rule of law, solves no problems and can bring immense suffering to human beings. Many Germans emerged from the war politically apathetic, but important changes in their political attitudes had occurred which would augur well for a new German democracy.

Collapse of Allied Cooperation

The Soviet Union and Poland annexed large chunks of German territory in the east, and Germany was reduced to about

239

Germany

three-fourths its prewar size. What remained of Germany was divided into four occupation zones: the Soviet zone was former East Germany; the British zone was in the north; the French zone was in the southwest, and the American zone was in Bavaria, Hesse, and the port of Bremerhaven in the north. Berlin was also divided into four sectors. Full power was in the hands of the four Allied commanders, who bore enormous burdens in bringing order to the chaos, feeding the population, reestablishing a tolerable economic situation, and creating political conditions that would make the return of National Socialism impossible.

The Allies tried to work together, and the United States even pulled its troops out of Saxony and Thuringia in July 1945 in order to honor its agreement on occupation zones established at Yalta in February 1945. Also in July, the leaders of the three major Allies—the Soviet Union, the United States, and Great Britain—met at Potsdam, outside of Berlin, to discuss Germany's future. France had not taken part in the Yalta Conference and, to the ire of General de Gaulle, was not invited to the Potsdam meeting.

There were many disagreements on details, but the three basically agreed that Germany should be denazified; that the Oder-Neisse frontier would temporarily be the border between Germany and Poland; that Germans in Hungary, Czechoslovakia, and Poland would be transferred to Germany; that Germany would be required to pay reparations as long as these payments would "leave enough resources to enable the German people to subsist without external assistance"; that "during the period of occupation Germany shall be treated as a single economic unit"; that the German political structure would be decentralized; and, finally, that German political life should be reconstructed on a democratic basis.

It soon became obvious that Allied cooperation was impossible, given the differing definitions of such terms as "democratic" and the four victors' greatly different security and political objectives in Europe. The Allies' disharmony was West Germany's opportunity that permitted it to rise so quickly from the ashes of defeat. Talks involving the political and economic future of Germany stalled, and American soldiers became impatient to go home. At the end of 1945, there were spontaneous GI (US armed forces) demonstrations in Paris and Frankfurt which left no doubt in the minds of American leaders that the large part of the 3 million US soldiers in Europe had to be demobilized very quickly. GIs were sent back to the US at a stunningly fast rate; clearly a long occupation of Germany was not in American plans. Nor was a permanent feeding and economic subsidy of a part of the German people among those aims. Despite the agreements at Potsdam, Germany was not operating as an economic unit. It had become increasingly clear to US leaders that the resulting prolongation of German poverty and economic stagnation would not only greatly harm Germany's neighbors, who were traditionally dependent upon trade with Germany, but also would perhaps make it vulnerable to communist appeals.

The Beginning of Political Activity

The excessive political indoctrination and activity during Hitler's rule had Germany after World War II extinguished political interest in the minds of most Germans by the spring of 1945. Most Germans' thoughts were directed toward food, warmth, and privacy, and this fact helped divert their attention from both a horrible past and the very uncertain politics of the present. Still, political activity began to bubble from below, on the municipal and Land (state) levels and always under the surveillance and supervision of the occupation authorities. The future direction of German politics was far from clear. German communists had high hopes, and a number of right-wing parties began to take shape. Antidemocratic attitudes among some Germans also persisted for a while. But there was also a democratic movement, which gathered steam and which was especially encouraged by the three western occupation powers. The memories of National Socialist crimes prompted many thoughtful Germans to reintroduce morality and religious principles into politics and to construct a new political order around basic human rights and democracy.

American leaders soon became convinced that US policy should shed all its punitive aspects and shift toward wholehearted support of the democratic potential in Germany. President Roosevelt's treasury secretary, Henry Morgenthau, had advocated the former aspects. He had wished to change Germany forcefully from an industrialized nation back to an agrarian society. His proposals had never become official US policy, but elements of it had been incorporated in the official American occupation guideline, JCS 1067. However, US secretary of state James Byrnes announced in Stuttgart on September 6, 1946, a significant change in US policy. In the opera house of that bombed-out city, he aimed to quiet German fears by assuring them that "as long as an occupation force is required in Germany the army of the United States will be part of that occupation force." He went on to propose a greater measure of German self-government and, as a first step, the merging of the American and British zones. A British observer commented on the dramatic effect of this speech, "At the time they were spoken these were bold words and they

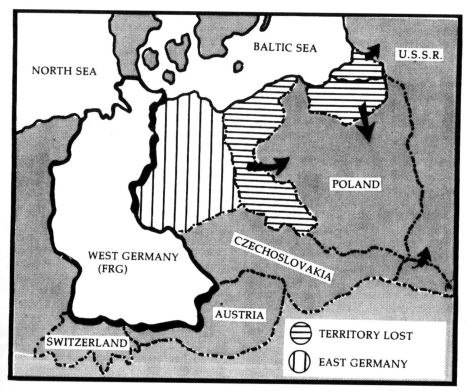

Germany after World War II

240

came to the millions of Germans who had heard or read them as the first glimmer of dawn after a long, dark night. Their moral impact was incalculable."

One month later the Berliners revealed in their first municipal elections how receptive they were to a democratic direction. Despite the Soviet presence in East Berlin and the Soviets' open support of their German communist creation, the Socialist Unity Party of Germany (SED), which ruled the GDR, communists received less than one-fifth of the votes. The Soviets and East German communists quickly saw that they dared not agree to any settlement of the German question that involved free elections.

Secretary of state and ex-army chief of Staff George C. Marshall foresaw that Europe would economically stagnate for an unnecessarily long period of time unless massive American aid were poured into the war-ravaged countries. The generous American offer, known as the Marshall Plan, even included the Soviet Union and what were slowly developing into its satellite states it had occupied militarily.

The year 1947 saw the end of any possibility that the four victorious Allies could work together in harmony and good faith. The failure of the Foreign Ministers Conference in Moscow in April, the refusal of the Soviet Union to allow itself or those countries under its domination to accept Marshall Plan assistance, the breakdown in June of a meeting of all German Land government chiefs in Munich, and the founding in October of the Cominform in Moscow, calculated to coordinate a communist propaganda offensive against the "imperialism of the United States and its western Allies," all reflected a degeneration of east-west relations.

The year 1948 brought no improvement. In February the British and Americans created a sort of economic government, which was joined in the summer by the French zone (except the Saar, which was not reunited with Germany until 1957 following a plebiscite). This union, at first called Bizonia, tightened the links that had already emerged between the two zones. This new body brought together leading German political figures, who began discussing future German government and thereby established an early foundation for the FRG.

Leaders of Bizonia elaborated the future guiding West German economic principle of the "social market economy." This combined a free-market approach (which helped West Germany rapidly to become prosperous in contrast to its counterpart in East Germany) with a commitment to the social welfare of its citizens, which was crucial for social peace within Germany and, more important, for democracy. Bizonia

The Berlin airlift

A/P Wide World Photo

also used the Marshall Plan assistance to improve its citizens' well-being. In July 1947 representatives of 16 European countries receiving Marshall Plan aid had declared in Paris, "the German economy should be integrated into the economy of Europe in such a way as to contribute to a raising of the general standard of life." It is, of course, possible that with this measure the other nations sought through economic means to ensure that Germany could not again become an aggressive political enemy.

In the next few years, West Germans received almost $4 billion in money and supplies from the Marshall Plan. This not only enabled West Germans to rebuild their industrial plants with the most modern tooling, but it also established the foundation for west European cooperation, which the plan required and which culminated in the European Community (EC), now called EU. It also introduced a long-range liberalization of European trade and payments, which has been a key to the economic prosperity of many European nations.

Further Economic Progress

West German economic recovery also got important support from a bracing currency reform in mid-1948, through which a new *Deutschmark* replaced the increasingly worthless Reichsmark. Every German started at the same point, with only DM 40 in his pocket. This reform was followed by a scrapping of all rationing and price controls—a bold move widely criticized at the time but one that the chairman of the Bizonal Economic Council, Professor Ludwig Erhard, and the US occupation governor, General Lucius Clay, considered essential.

They proved to be right. Suddenly goods reappeared in the stores and markets. One witnessed a disappearance of the black market, whose more treasured items had come from the US military post exchanges (PXs). For a while Germans had a de facto "cigarette economy," in which American cigarettes, not old German Reichsmarks, were the country's actual currency. After several years many Germans could actually begin smoking cigarettes again rather than hoarding them as a money substitute. The economic improvement was so dramatic that in 1949 Erhard's party could enter the first West German elections with the convincing slogan "Es geht wieder!" ("It's working again!").

The Cold War Begins— The Berlin Blockade

The Cold War, which resulted from the severe differences between the Soviet Union and the western Allies, ultimately helped to seal Germany's division, but it also offered the three western zones the chance to regain a large part of German sovereignty. The sense that the western Allies and the West Germans had important common objectives was stimulated by the communist seizure of power in February 1948 in Czechoslovakia, although the country had functioned since 1945 as a parliamentary democracy.

Especially revealing was the blockade of all road and rail routes to West Berlin from June 1948 until May 1949. This was in response to increasing political and economic unity among the three western zones, most visible in the currency reform. No doubt the Soviets expected that the western Allies could be forced

Germany

to relinquish their rights in Berlin and to abandon the city.

The American reaction was to organize an aerial supply line between the western zones and the besieged city. This seemingly impossible task (which even included transporting coal) sparked American, British, and West German imagination and admiration. Several hundred American and British aircraft carried up to 12,000 tons of supplies to Berlin each day. The success of this heroic operation, combined with the effect of adverse world opinion, forced the Soviets to lift the blockade. Although more than three-quarters of the freight was carried on American planes, the action claimed more British lives (39) than American (32). The operation was the first time the western Allies signaled in no uncertain terms that they would resist the

The Air Bridge Monument in Berlin which commemorates the land blockade of the city in 1948–1949

Soviet takeover of the eastern part of Europe. For Germany it signaled a shift from being a defeated and distrusted enemy to being an inseparable friend and ally of the western partners. It further cemented West German-American solidarity. A Berlin city referendum in May 2008 failed to save Tempelhof Airport, where most of the flights landed. This monument was closed at the end of that year, and Berlin shifted its air operations in 2011 to a refurbished Berlin-Brandenburg International Airport at Schönefeld, southeast of Berlin.

The Federal Republic of Germany— Konrad Adenauer

From the winter of 1948–1949 on, the great majority of West Germans would accept no foreign policy that did not merit the confidence of the US, whose protection over Berlin and West Germany were considered indispensable.

The disagreements among the four occupation powers reached such a low state that the three western Allies decided in the summer of 1948 to permit German leaders in their three zones to write a constitution and to found a West German state. The Constituent Assembly met in Bonn under the chairmanship of the elderly former mayor of Cologne, Konrad Adenauer, and under the watchful eyes of the three occupational authorities. Things were finally settled in May 1949, almost four years to the day since the capitulation of the Third Reich.

What was created was seen to be strictly "for a transitional period." The document was called a Basic Law, not a constitution, a word that might connote something more permanent. The founders wrote into the preamble that they had acted also on behalf of those Germans living under Soviet occupation and that "the entire German people is called upon to accomplish, by free self-determination, the unity and freedom of Germany." Thus, West German leaders imposed upon themselves the obligation to bring the two parts of Germany back together, even though that goal seemed to be slipping farther and farther into the distant future.

On August 14, 1949, most of the eligible voters in West Germany went to the polls to elect their first parliamentary representatives. Adenauer's Christian Democratic Union (CDU), along with the Bavarian Christian Social Union (CSU), captured 31% of the votes, and the SPD, 29.2%. Several other parties also won seats, and Adenauer was able to patch together a coalition government with only a one-vote majority, his own vote. Adenauer was to serve as West German chancellor until 1963, longer than the entire Weimar Republic had existed. The voters saw this shrewd politician as a comforting

father-figure (Der Alte—"The Old One"), who took a firmer control of West German politics than any other chancellor since. As a confident (some say authoritarian) ruler, he was able to place his imprint on the young democracy. The Soviet Union responded to the creation of the Federal Republic of Germany by converting its occupation zone into the German Democratic Republic (GDR), ruled by the communist-led SED.

The FRG's new capital was not established in a major West German city such as Frankfurt on the Main. That might have appeared as a permanent capital city for a state that was expressly intended to be provisional. Instead, the sleepy Rhenish university town of Bonn was selected as the "temporary" seat of government, and an architecturally unattractive former teacher's college became the new Parliament and governmental center. Until late 1987, West Germany's capital remained the least impressive governmental seat in all of Europe. Some liked to call it "the federal village." The new government ordered that the gutted Reichstag building, located a few meters within the Western sector of Berlin, be reconstructed so that it could again serve as the capitol of a "soon to be" reunified Germany. Work on the renovation was finally completed in the 1970s.

NATO Is Created

The Cold War froze the division of Germany, but it also provided West Germany the opportunities its crafty first chancellor knew how to exploit for the benefit of his country and his party. There were intense fears in western Europe and North America that the Soviet Union sought direct or indirect domination over all of Europe. This fear led to the establishment of the North Atlantic Treaty Organization (NATO) on April 4, 1949, several months before the creation of the FRG. When NATO planners began working on plans for defending western Europe, it was quickly apparent that the western Allies and smaller western European countries alone could not provide the necessary forces. This was especially true since the United States had no intention at that time of permanently maintaining large numbers of American troops in Europe. Western European defense was conceivable only with the help of Germany. In the fall of 1949, the US general staff drafted a plan for the inclusion of German troops in NATO.

Adenauer listened very carefully to the message coming from western capitals: "No NATO without Germany; no Germany without NATO." He reflected on his country's three principal goals and the best way it could achieve them: (1) West Germans, painfully viewing the plight of their countrymen in East Germany, wanted

Germany

protection from Soviet domination; (2) they wanted political and economic recovery from the ashes of disgrace, to regain much of their national sovereignty, to create jobs, to rebuild their cities, to share in international trade and thereby to acquire material prosperity, and to be respected as equals in the western world, whose values they shared; (3) finally, they wanted their country to be reunified within the German borders of 1937.

The chancellor decided to strike a bargain with the NATO countries. On November 11, 1949, the 31st anniversary of the cease-fire ending World War I, Adenauer announced in an interview with the French newspaper *L'Est Republicain* that "if a common Supreme Command could be created, the Federal Republic would be willing at an appropriate time to integrate itself into a European defense system." He presented this decision to his own people as the "politics of necessity," and he stated the issue very simply: "We are faced with a choice between slavery and freedom. We choose freedom." In the years to come, Adenauer was successful in getting an important political advantage for each increase in German activity or responsibility in NATO. He helped to establish the United States as the permanent guarantor of West German security and to counteract the goal that many American leaders had well into the 1950s of withdrawing US troops from western Europe. He set a course that was never fundamentally changed by his successors in the chancellor's office until the end of the Cold War.

There was, however, a problem with Adenauer's bargain with the west, which the opposition Social Democrats simply could not get out of their minds: How would this integration with the west, especially the military part of it, affect the goal of German reunification, a goal that most Germans at that time wanted very much and that was an obligation placed on all West German governments by the framers of the Basic Law? Social Democrats strongly sensed at the time that, by seeking to achieve the goals of security and recovery through political, economic, and military integration with the west, the FRG was greatly reducing the chances that the Soviet Union would permit the reunification of Germany.

Social Democratic Opposition to NATO

The SPD's order of priorities was almost the complete reverse of Adenauer's. Throughout the 1950s, reunification was its top priority. The party was not in principle opposed to reconciliation and integration with the west, nor was it ever opposed to a military defense for Germany. It believed that the military and economic commitments the FRG had assumed in

order to achieve Adenauer's goals would reduce or eliminate the chances that the pieces of Germany would find their way back together again. With the FRG integrated economically in western Europe, with NATO and Soviet troops facing each other along the Elbe River, and with each part of a divided Germany serving as an essential element in the European balance of power, the Soviet Union would be far less inclined to withdraw its troops from East Germany. This would especially be the case if a reunified Germany were free to join NATO, as Adenauer always insisted it should be. The SPD feared that the military balance in Europe would require a perpetually divided Germany and therefore showed much greater willingness than the Adenauer government to examine closely Soviet proposals for reunification and to assume that the Soviets were acting at least partly in good faith.

Adenauer continued to argue that his policy was not hostile to the aim of German reunification. He, like the Social Democrats, aimed toward German reunification "in peace and freedom." He argued that in return for the FRG's entering the western Alliance, the three western powers had formally committed themselves to seek German reunification. He also cast an eye on the west's greater industrial capability to arm itself quickly, on the high degree of western political and economic integration in the future, and on the prospects of

unrest in eastern Europe, which would be directed against the Soviet Union's tight and self-serving grip on its satellites.

He therefore predicted that in time the balance of power would shift in favor of the west, and this shift would make possible negotiations "on the basis of strength" with the Soviet Union. He argued that the Soviets held the key to reunification and would ultimately be compelled to settle the German question on western terms. This latter element of Adenauer's reunification policy was, as the SPD correctly foresaw, an illusion. With the Soviet Union's acquisition of nuclear weapons, there could be no serious talk of rolling back what Churchill had so aptly named "the Iron Curtain" through demonstrations of military strength.

Adenauer was right in his assessment of what West Germans wanted most and of the enormous advantages for his disgraced and impoverished country, which western European unity, crowned by the creation of the Common Market (EC) in 1957, offered: The FRG would be an equal member of such a community. It would derive all of the economic benefits the trade and pooling of raw materials would bring. Although it appeared to be grounded on the desire of many Germans for reunification, the position of the SPD actually caused an erosion of the SPD's domestic political position within the FRG. Social Democrats had to watch with dismay and bitterness

Konrad Adenauer (r) with SPD leader Kurt Schumacher (l) and Carlo Schmid (m)

243

Germany

how Adenauer's party grew progressively stronger while the SPD stagnated.

Political Tensions of the 1950s

The domestic battle over the crucial foreign and security policy decisions made in the 1950s was so intense and emotional that it is almost a wonder that the young democracy survived them. The issues were serious ones related to the future of Germany and the German nation. These bitter controversies of the 1950s never completely disappeared.

German rearmament was a truly explosive issue that dominated West German politics until the FRG's formal entry into NATO in 1955. From the point of view of the western Allies and the Adenauer government, the major problem was how to place international controls on West German troops. The FRG's future allies, who had fought against Germany only five years earlier, wanted security from West Germany, as well as security for it. Well aware of these fears, which he found entirely justified, and desiring German integration and equal status with the west, Adenauer also stubbornly refused to consider establishing an independent German national army. In an effort to solve this problem, the French had presented the Pleven Plan in 1950, calling for the establishment of a European Defense Community (EDC). West German military units would be completely fused with a larger European army, and no German generals would command German corps. The FRG would technically not have NATO status, but it would be included de facto since the EDC itself would belong to NATO.

The link between the FRG's entry into the EDC and the regaining of West German sovereignty was clear from the very beginning. In 1951 the FRG was permitted to establish a Ministry for Foreign Affairs and to establish diplomatic relations with other states. Also, the Deutschland Vertrag (German Treaty, also known as the Bonn Conventions) was drafted and was to be signed together with the EDC Treaty. The Bonn Conventions provided for the abolition of the occupation statute and of the Allied High Commission, which formally ruled Germany, and prepared the way for West German sovereignty, with certain restrictions.

The issue of a German military role became acute again when in 1954 the French National Assembly rejected the EDC, which an earlier French foreign minister had proposed. Surprisingly quickly, however, the foreign ministers of Great Britain, Canada, and the US met with the prospective members of the EDC to discuss alternatives. In October these powers signed the Paris Treaties calling for the direct entry of the FRG into NATO, an end to Germany's occupation status, and the restoration of full German sovereignty. The three western powers retained their authority on matters relating to German reunification, Berlin, and a final German peace treaty. In late 1955 Adenauer traveled to the Soviet Union to establish full diplomatic relations with that victor and to negotiate a trade treaty and the release of the last German prisoners of war remaining in Soviet hands.

The West German debate over foreign policy remained very polarized. In January 1956, less than a year after the FRG had become a full member of NATO, the first 1,000 volunteer soldiers entered the Federal Army (*Bundeswehr*), whose creation the SPD had opposed. There was a powerful pacifist strain within the SPD that opposed all forms of German rearmament. This element was a part of an emotional mass movement known by the slogan "ohne mich" ("without me"). Because of the recent memories and the direct experience that Germans had with the war, the "ohne mich" movement enjoyed widespread support among the general population. For instance, one opinion survey in 1955 revealed that, while 40% of the respondents were in favor of a West German army, 45% were opposed. Among those respondents identifying with the SPD, only 21% were in favor of the Federal Army and 71% were opposed. Opinion polls also indicated that West Germans were not happy about the stationing of American nuclear weapons on German soil or about the Federal Army's acquisition of dual-capacity weapons that could fire or deliver nuclear warheads.

Minimal SPD Gains at the Polls; Continued German Division

The SPD went into the federal parliamentary elections of September 15, 1957, confident that it could make significant gains, but the results stunned the Social Democrats and probably Adenauer, as well. The SPD vote did rise from 29% to 32%, but this rise was partially due to the fact that the Communist Party of Germany (KPD) had been ruled unconstitutional a year earlier and was therefore not permitted to participate in the election. However, the CDU/CSU vote rose from 44% to over 50%, and it gained an absolute majority in the Bundestag, the only time this has ever happened since the founding of the FRG. The election was widely interpreted as approval of Adenauer's foreign and economic policies.

This election disaster, plus another Berlin crisis in 1958, convinced the SPD to change its foreign policy tack and to

American, German, Polish, and Czech soldiers in NATO maneuver in Poland

Germany

support Adenauer's policy of rearmament and integration with the west. Although there were quarrels between the parties occasionally, by the time of Adenauer's retirement in 1963, a foreign policy consensus had taken shape in the FRG that continued to exist throughout the 1960s.

With the FRG firmly planted in the western alliance, West German leaders began to look eastward to see how they could improve West Germany's relations with the Soviet Union and its satellites. The construction of the Berlin Wall in August 1961 had made it clear that the two Germanys would not be reunified for a long time. Before August 1961 East and West Berliners could pass freely from one part of the city to the other. But the ugly wall, which cut right through Germany's largest city, destroyed the last hope of national unity.

From the very beginning, West Germany's foreign policy was heavily influenced by the fact that Germany was a divided nation in the middle of Europe. After 1955 the FRG did not pursue a determined policy of German reunification, preferring instead to focus on Western economic and military integration, while preventing the legitimization of the status quo in central Europe.

Once the signals for a relaxation of tensions between east and west began to be given by France and the US, culminating in such agreements with the Soviet Union as the Nuclear Test Ban Treaty in 1963, German foreign minister Gerhard Schröder began in the early 1960s a "policy of movement." This involved a loosening of the Hallstein Doctrine, which had forbidden West German diplomatic contact with any country except the Soviet Union that officially recognized East Germany. The FRG established trade missions in Warsaw, Budapest, Sofia, and Bucharest. This policy was an important beginning, but it did not go far enough. The FRG neither discarded the Hallstein Doctrine altogether nor recognized the Oder-Neisse border between the GDR and Poland. Worst of all, it still aimed to isolate the GDR diplomatically.

The FRG had always worked closely with East German officials on practical, day-to-day questions, especially involving economic matters. For instance, the FRG insisted as a condition for its entry into the EU that trade between the two Germanys be conducted as if there were only one Germany. Such free trade was enormously beneficial for the GDR, providing it with an open entry to the EU and serving as a basis for the relatively high economic prosperity in the GDR as compared with other eastern European countries. Yet, top-level political contacts were studiously avoided.

In 1966 the FRG's two largest parties formed a Grand Coalition, with Kurt

From the Main River Bridge, the *Franconia* statue ignores the castle of Würzburg.
Photo by Jon Markham Morrow

Georg Kiesinger of the CDU as chancellor. Although the parliamentary system was operating very smoothly and although the war damage and mass poverty had given way to visible prosperity, the major parties' leaders saw economic troubles ahead. The SPD also wanted to participate in such a coalition government in order to demonstrate that it also was capable of ruling the FRG.

The Grand Coalition stimulated considerable domestic opposition, especially in 1968, when its majority in the Bundestag passed a series of constitutional amendments and laws granting the government certain emergency powers in times of crisis. Although it argued that any truly sovereign state had to be able to take special measures in times of emergency to defend the democratic order, many West Germans pointed out that similar emergency laws had been misused during the Weimar Republic to undermine democracy. This controversial issue, combined with doubts about

American policy in Vietnam, sent thousands of mainly young Germans into the streets. They employed confrontation tactics, which they had learned from the civil rights and antiwar movements in the US, even using the American terms for these tactics, such as "sit-in" and "go-in." They called themselves the "extra parliamentary opposition" (APO), which they claimed was necessary since the opposition within parliament had sunk to a negligible 5%.

Far less controversial in the eyes of young Germans was the Grand Coalition's policy of seeking improved relations with the east. This received a particular push from foreign minister Willy Brandt and the crafty Minister for all-German affairs, Herbert Wehner, both of the SPD. The Kiesinger government took steps toward overcoming the impasse in German reunification. It announced that it was prepared to accept the East German regime as a de facto government, and it even exchanged letters for the first time with East German

245

Germany

leaders on a semiofficial basis. It established a trade mission in Prague in 1967, and its diplomatic recognition of Romania in 1967 and Yugoslavia in 1968 indicated that the Hallstein Doctrine was in fact dead, even if not wiped off the books.

The Brandt Government

In 1969 the SPD and Free Democratic Party (FDP) won a razor-thin victory in parliamentary elections, and Willy Brandt became chancellor. The new government had no intention to change the FRG's policy toward the west, but it was determined to conduct a dynamic and innovative policy toward the east. Fundamentally, the Brandt government decided to overturn two decades of West German foreign policy and to recognize the territorial status quo in Europe, including the division of Germany. The word "reunification" was dropped from the government's terminology.

The first dramatic step in August 1970 was a German-Soviet Treaty in which both states renounced the use of force in Europe. West Germany also declared that it had no territorial claims against any country and that the borders of all European states are inviolable, including the Oder-Neisse line

and the border between East and West Germany. This treaty was the first West German recognition of East Germany's international legitimacy. Brandt was no doubt correct in commenting that in actual fact "nothing is lost with this treaty that was not gambled away long ago."

The second step was a German-Polish Treaty in late 1970, containing basically the same points as in the German-Soviet Treaty but underscoring the acceptance of the Oder-Neisse frontier. The treaty also provided for normal diplomatic relations, and in a separate accord, Poland agreed to exit permits for some ethnic Germans living in Poland. To demonstrate his sincerity in introducing a new era of Polish-German relations, Brandt dropped to his knees in reverence before a monument in Warsaw honoring the Polish Jewish victims who were killed or mistreated by Germany during World War II. The Poles have never forgotten this electrifying gesture.

A third step, not involving the FRG directly but strongly encouraged by it, was the Four-Power Agreement on Berlin in 1971. The FRG had linked its ratification of the German-Soviet Treaty with a successful resolution of the Berlin problem. Brandt reasoned that, if the FRG was

willing to recognize the status quo in Europe, the Soviet Union should be willing to recognize the status quo in Berlin. The Four-Power Agreement contained a Western Powers' acknowledgment that west Berlin was not a constituent part of the FRG and the Soviet Union's recognition that there were ties between the FRG and West Berlin. Further, the FRG would perform consular services for West Berliners and represent them in international organizations and conferences. The Soviet Union also promised that transit traffic to and from West Berlin from the FRG would proceed unimpeded. That was deemed necessary since the East German government had frequently hampered access to the city it surrounded in order to place pressure on the Bonn government. The Soviet Union admitted that West Berlin was neither located on the territory of the GDR nor was it an entity entirely separate from the FRG.

The last significant step was the Basic Treaty between the two Germanys themselves. Bonn knew that it could not bypass East Berlin despite the fact that the East German regime was defensive, rigid, and determined to exact a very high price for any concession. After many months of frustrating negotiations, an agreement was signed in late 1972 and ratified in mid-1973. It normalized the access between the FRG and West Berlin and made it possible for West Berliners to visit both East Berlin and the GDR. By signing the Basic Treaty, the FRG publicly accepted the GDR as a legitimate state and agreed to deal with it as an equal. Yet, Bonn continued to insist that there was only one German nation (even if there were two German states) and that the GDR would not be treated like any other foreign country. To underscore this, the FRG maintained a permanent liaison mission in East Berlin, not an embassy, and Bonn's dealings with the GDR were conducted by the chancellor's office, the Ministry of All-German Affairs, or a special office in the Interior Ministry but not by the foreign office. The official relations between the two Germanys improved as a result of the Basic Treaty. But the two countries' relationships remained ambiguous and tense, charged with conflict and suspicion.

A major scandal occurred in 1974, when it was revealed that one of Brandt's chief aides, Gunter Guillaume, was an East German spy who not only had access to top secret information but also was privy to knowledge of Brandt's intimate private life, which was reported to be spicy. This embarrassing revelation and intraparty criticism against Brandt's leadership led to his resignation from the office of chancellor in May. Helmut Schmidt took his place. This was during a time of global

Willy Brandt as mayor of West Berlin hosting President John F. Kennedy

economic difficulties associated with tremendously increased oil prices. The energy crisis and the resultant economic problems began increasingly to replace the eastern policy focus of the government. Although Schmidt signed the Helsinki Accords at the Conference on Security and Cooperation in Europe (CSCE) in 1975, his attention became more directed toward the west and away from the east. His goal was to maintain what had already been achieved and to preserve or reestablish the economic health and military security of western Europe.

Plagued by continual dissension within the SPD and recurrent coalition crises with the FDP, the Schmidt government collapsed in 1982, when the Free Democrats switched partners and enabled the CDU, led by Helmut Kohl, to take power. The following year, voters confirmed this Wende (change) by giving the new CDU/CSU-FDP coalition government a solid endorsement in the Bundestag elections. The Kohl government set about tackling the problems of u-employment and the emotionally charged deployment of American Pershing and cruise missiles on German soil.

The Schmidt government had agreed to do the latter in the 1979 NATO Twin-track decision, which was designed to counter a renewed Soviet nuclear missile threat. At the same time, the Kohl government pursued the policy of detente with the GDR and the USSR with as much vigor as had the SPD while in power. Like most West German leaders, Kohl no longer believed that German reunification could be achieved in the present era. In 1987 he stated in Moscow that he personally would never live to see the day when the two Germanys would become one country. Like virtually everybody else, he was caught completely by surprise as the GDR collapsed before his unbelieving eyes, and the elusive German unity fell into his lap.

History of the German Democratic Republic (GDR)—East Germany

At first the Soviet Military Administration governed the Soviet zone of Germany. But the Soviet authorities had long-range plans for Germany that involved reeducating the people and eventually winning them over to communism. German communists who had spent the Nazi years in the Soviet Union were brought back; put in charge of local governments; and given control over the press, radio, and book publishing. Their instructions were to educate the people in antifascism and to gain their cooperation for Soviet occupiers. On April 30, 1945, Walter Ulbricht returned from the USSR in a Soviet aircraft and in June announced the reestablishment of the Communist Party of Germany (KPD). It combined with the CDU, SPD, and Liberal Democrats to form an "Antifascist Democratic Bloc," which was soon dominated by the KPD. The Soviets had expected that the communists' long record of antifascism would make the KPD popular among workers, but the latter clearly preferred the SPD. In April 1946 this prompted the forcible uniting of the two parties into a Socialist Unity Party (SED), with Ulbricht as general secretary. The other parties declined in significance until they were little more than a facade.

In 1948 work on a new constitution began, and on October 7, 1949, the GDR came into being. Industry was nationalized and agriculture was collectivized,

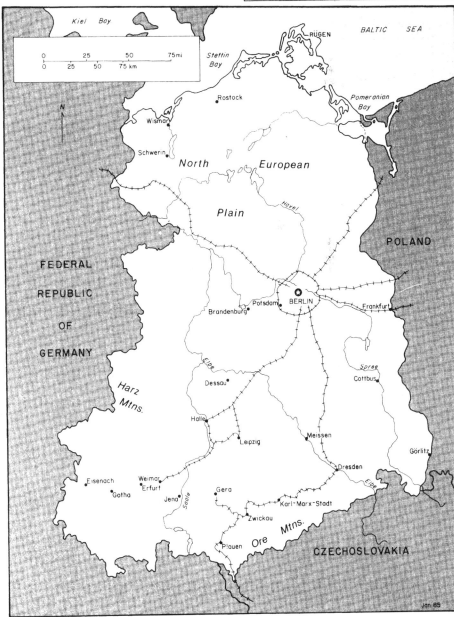

The GDR before German reunification

247

Germany

creating a state-controlled economy. SED domination was tightened through a pervasive state police (Stasi) that spied on the citizenry and stifled dissent in every form. On May 26, 1952, the border between the two Germanys was sealed by barbed wire, minefields, watchtowers, and free-fire zones.

Revolt and Suppression

Stalin's death in March 1953 and the gradual rise of a new Soviet leadership undermined the positions of all orthodox leaders in eastern Europe. Although he was Stalinist from the beginning, Ulbricht managed to hold on to power until 1971. He faced occasional challenges to his leadership. Almost immediately after Stalin's death, the Politburo disregarded Ulbricht's will and adopted a New Course, which moved toward greater political and economic pluralism. Enraged by onerous reparations to the USSR, higher production quotas, and the lack of personal freedom, workers revolted on June 17, 1953. But Soviet forces brutally put down the insurrection. Until German unification in 1990, this date was commemorated in the FRG as the Day of German Unity. The revolt may have saved Ulbricht's career; the Soviets now backed him against the moderates, who found themselves removed from their positions of authority.

On January 29, 1956, the GDR joined hands militarily with the Soviet Union by creating a National People's Army (NVA) and joining the Warsaw Pact. In 1956 Soviet leader Nikita Khrushchev delivered a dramatic speech attacking the Stalinist heritage. This message emboldened communist intellectuals in the GDR who wanted to make the SED more responsive to the people and to create a more popular, humane form of socialism. Their chief

spokesman, Wolfgang Harich, was arrested and sentenced to 10 years. Other reformers were branded as "revisionists" and forced to retreat.

Ulbricht met his most serious political challenge on August 13, 1961, when, backed by the Soviets, he authorized the sudden construction of a wall between West and East Berlin, where hundreds of thousands of East Germans had continued to flee. This sealed the last escape route and forced East Germans to come to terms with their plight and their government; there was no longer any alternative. This was the only historical instance in the world that a wall was erected to keep an entire people confined rather than to keep enemies out. The constant drain on manpower, particularly skilled persons, had been an important economic reason for the wall. Despite the devastating blow it delivered to the international prestige of this socialist state, which presented itself as the model for Germany's future, it led to greater prosperity in the GDR after 1961 and helped provide East Germans with the highest standard of living within the Soviet Empire.

Ten years later the Soviet Union concluded that its interests required closer relations between the two Germanys. When Ulbricht opposed this, he was replaced in 1971 by Erich Honecker, a roofer who had grown up in the Saarland. In 1935 he was jailed by the Nazis and spent 10 years in a Berlin prison. After the war he became chairman of the communist Free German Youth. Following political training in Moscow, he oversaw the military and security services. He had opposed any form of "revisionism" and was totally loyal to the Soviet Union. He strongly supported the erection of the Berlin Wall and was deemed responsible in 1990 with the

Happier times: a decorated fragment of the former Berlin Wall

orders to shoot to kill along the dividing line between East and West Germany.

About 350 persons were killed trying to cross the border. For this he was charged with manslaughter in the newly united Germany. To rescue him from German justice and the embarrassment he might cause the USSR by his testimony, Soviet leaders first protected him in a military hospital outside of Berlin and then whisked him off to the USSR in March 1991, violating German sovereignty in the process. When the Soviet Union itself ceased to exist at the end of 1991, he was told he would have to leave. He took refuge in the Chilean embassy. On July 29, 1992, he was forced to return to Germany to face charges of manslaughter, corruption, and breach of trust. East German bosses are the only leaders in the ex-Soviet Empire to face justice in western courts. His trial began in November, but in January 1993, he was proclaimed terminally ill and was released. He immediately joined his family in Chile, where he died a year later.

When Mikhail Gorbachev launched his reformist policy of perestroika in 1985, Honecker and other members of the SED leadership resisted introducing it in the GDR on the grounds that the East German economy had already been reformed in the 1970s and was allegedly working well. Their rejection of a market economy was ideologically motivated. They argued that, if the GDR adopted a market economy, then little or nothing would distinguish it from the FRG; consequently, there would be no further justification for the GDR to exist as a separate state. They also resisted introducing more freedom in the political realm and even prevented the distribution

A "freedom train" to the west, October 5, 1989

Germany

of some free-thinking Soviet newspapers, such as the *Moscow News*. It was extremely embarrassing for a party that had been so servile to the Soviet Union to be in a position of having to resist its leadership. The SED found itself in a fatal dilemma from which it could never extricate itself.

Collapse of the GDR

In 1989 one of the most dramatic postwar developments began taking place before the very eyes of a stunned world public—German reunification. In early summer a human hemorrhaging westward commenced, as East German vacationers began crossing the newly opened border between Hungary and Austria. Budapest informed the irate East German leaders that the human rights agreements accepted at the Helsinki Conference in 1975 superseded earlier bilateral treaties preventing the free movement of peoples. The next avenue of escape was through Czechoslovakia. After thousands had taken refuge at the West German embassy in Prague, "freedom trains" took East Germans through the GDR into the west. The stampede grew when Czechoslovakia opened its western borders.

Under enormous stress, the GDR celebrated its 40th and final anniversary on October 7, 1989. The SED's slogan for the event was "Ever Forward—Never Backward!" The prediction was accurate, but the communist chiefs were badly mistaken about which direction was forward. The honored guest was Gorbachev himself, who at that time was the most popular political figure in Germany. However, rather than lend his prestige to the struggling East German leaders, he made it known that they would have to pay a high price if they did not learn the lessons of history and adopt timely reforms. He informed them that they could not expect the support of Soviet troops in the GDR to prop up their rule against the people. Without Soviet military backing, communist rule could survive nowhere in Germany.

This was a very important message in a country in which public demonstrations had been going on for some time. An umbrella opposition group, New Forum, had come into existence a few weeks earlier, and huge demonstrations had spread to all major East German cities. Things came to a head on October 9 in Leipzig. Honecker reportedly issued an order to security forces to put down the demonstration by any means. Communist leaders in Leipzig, fearing a massacre such as had occurred in China the previous June, decided to prevent such a bloodbath in their city. With Kurt Masur, director of Leipzig's Gewandhaus Orchestra, as spokesman and joined by Protestant Church leaders, they issued an appeal for calm. They coupled this with

Young Germans on the wall: November 9, 1989. Sign attached to the wall: "Cement Demolition Technique"

a call for nonviolence and "a free exchange of opinions about the continuation of socialism in our country." Such a dialogue would occur "not only in the Leipzig area, but with our national government." On October 18 Honecker was ousted from power and replaced by Egon Krenz.

The End

The Berlin Wall came tumbling down on November 9. It is ironic that a wall constructed in 1961 to keep East Germans in was opened in 1989 for the same reason. Within minutes millions of East Germans began pouring over the border. Germans, who for decades had suppressed displays of national feeling, experienced a deeply emotional outpouring. While millions sat in front of their televisions and wept, Berliners danced together on top of the wall, embraced each other on the streets, and chiseled away at the ugly barrier. When word arrived at the Bundestag, many members, including some Greens, stood up and spontaneously sang the third verse of the national anthem, which stresses "unity and justice and freedom." The rest of Europe looked on with mixed feelings, uneasily remembering a frightening German past but stirred by the sight of people casting off their shackles and demanding freedom and self-determination.

Krenz proved to be only an interim figure. Unable to put an end to either the demonstrations or the continued emigration to the west, he promised "free, democratic and secret elections"; a move toward a market economy; separation of party and state; freedom of assembly; and a new

law on broadcasting and press freedom. He also appointed as prime minister Hans Modrow from Dresden, one of the very few East German communists who was personally popular.

Krenz could not save his party or himself. He and the other members of the East German Politburo resigned on December 3. Five days later, a special SED party congress met and installed Gregor Gysi, a lawyer who had made a name for himself by defending dissidents and the opposition New Forum. Upon accepting the leadership, Gysi admitted that a complete break with Stalinism and a new form of socialism was needed and that the SED was responsible for plunging the GDR into crisis. Feeling betrayed, 700,000 of the 2.3 million party members quit within two months the party, which renamed itself the Party of Democratic Socialism (PDS) in an attempt to escape the impending doom.

There was an outpouring of disgust and rage among East Germans as massive corruption on the part of their former leaders was revealed. They had enriched themselves while in office. Television broadcast images of the "proletarian" leaders' luxury compound in Wandlitz, estates with as many as 22 staff members, hunting lodges, deer parks, well-stocked wine cellars, and satellite dishes for better reception of western broadcasts. Their living standards had been totally removed from the meager everyday existence of normal GDR citizens long fed on exhortations for austerity. Even worse were revelations of shady financial dealings totaling millions of marks, involving illegal arms sales to

249

Germany

Third World countries and foreign currency maneuvers, the profits of which ended up in personal Swiss bank accounts. One rank-and-file SED member said, "We did not expect this of communists and their creed of equality."

At the last moment, Honecker was whisked out of Germany on a Soviet military plane, an act that the Kremlin admitted was a "technical violation of German sovereignty." The FRG tolerated the incident with little more than bland diplomatic protests because it did not want to antagonize the declining superpower. An American diplomat put it this way: "The Soviets have done things that are not nice, but the Germans have their eye on the ball, and the ball is a timely troop withdrawal. The German interest is to smooth over any bumps." The arrest of the GDR's former premier, Willi Stoph, Defense Minister Heinz Kessler (who was planning to flee to the USSR) and two other SED leaders was ordered.

Reunification

Suddenly German reunification was back on Europe's and the superpowers' agenda, and developments toward it raced faster than any government's ability to react. The rapid collapse of communist rule left a political vacuum in the GDR. Demonstrators in East German streets unfurled banners pronouncing "Germany—One Fatherland!" Aware of his constitutional mandate to seek German unity and wishing to calm the waters and head off right- and left-wing extremists, Kohl announced on November 28 a 10-step plan for reunification, which included humanitarian assistance to refugees, freer travel between the two Germanys, massive economic aid

contingent on free elections in the GDR, and ultimately reunification if that was the will of the German people, especially of East Germans. He applied no timetable. To reassure his NATO and EU allies, he stressed that any reunified Germany would be embedded in the western community of nations and NATO. To those who feared for stability in Europe, which until then had been guaranteed by a divided Germany, he asserted, "freedom does not cause instability." West Germans no longer needed to sacrifice unity for freedom, as they had done since 1949.

In March 1990 the last communist government, led by Modrow, collapsed. East Germans had conducted the only successful revolution in German history, and it was a bloodless one. The pace of the reunification movement quickened with the first free elections in East German history on March 18, 1990. The surprise victor was the conservative coalition, "Alliance for Germany," led by the CDU-East, which won 48% of the vote by promising prosperity and union with the FRG. The SPD-East was a distant second. The communists, running under a new name—PDS—won only 16% and sank temporarily into irrelevance. As in 1949, Germans turned to the CDU as the party of prosperity and assured democracy. A "grand coalition" of conservatives and SPD formed a government and entered negotiations with the Kohl government to overcome the political, economic, and military obstacles to "One United Germany."

The train was speeding toward unity, and the best the Bonn government could do was to make it an orderly, legal process. There was no time for a transition, no pause to "study the problems." A

breathless Kohl saw a unique opportunity and had announced in February, "We are jumping with a single leap!" He waved aside Social Democrats' call for a more deliberate process and the demand of many intellectuals for a "better" East Germany treading a "third path" between capitalism and socialism.

The next steps toward unity on October 3, 1990, were taken with dizzying rapidity. On July 1 the West German mark was introduced in the GDR in a currency reform without precedence on such a large scale. In a stunning diplomatic breakthrough, Kohl went to the Soviet Union July 14–16 to get Gorbachev's assurances that he would not stand in the way of German unity and that a united Germany could decide "freely and by itself if, and in which alliance, it desires membership"; in other words, Germany would not have to leave NATO in order to be united. Returning to Moscow on September 12, Bonn's leaders joined GDR minister president Lothar de Maiziere and the foreign ministers of the four Allied powers to sign the "two plus four" treaty granting full sovereignty to Germany and suspending the four powers' rights. The Conference on Security and Cooperation in Europe (CSCE) endorsed the agreement in New York on October 1. It went into effect at midnight on October 2, when a "Liberty Bell" the US had given Berlin four decades earlier rang in unity.

Unity left much unsettled business for a part of Germany in which the economy had to be privatized and in which the secret police, Stasi, supported by 85,000 officers and over a half million informants, had penetrated every niche of GDR society and maintained files on six million persons. This frightening phenomenon was portrayed in film director Florian Henckel von Donnersmarck's international hit *The Lives of Others*, which won an Oscar in 2007 as Best Foreign-Language Film. It is a gripping tale of a Stasi officer who begins to doubt his work as a spy and ends up protecting his victims.

Germans were left to wrestle with the problem of what to do with such files, which had been assembled with complete disregard for the individual's privacy. They hold many of the keys to rooting out and punishing those persons who suppressed citizens' freedom, but their misuse could again endanger that freedom. They shed light on the GDR's extensive contacts with and training of terrorist organizations, the sheltering of fugitive West German Red Army Faction killers, and the staging of anti-Semitic attacks in the FRG to discredit Bonn. They also helped Bonn uncover spies who had infiltrated the FRG more thoroughly than had ever been imagined. Still, after the 2009 federal elections, the Bundestag had as members

Discussions on German reunification, Bonn, May 5, 1990

Germany

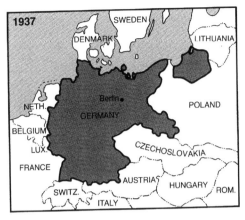

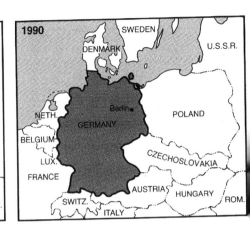

more former Stasi agents than human rights activists. Roughly 17,000 former Stasi informants work openly in the nation's bureaucracy. Considering that Stasi employed more than 90,000 agents and 200,000 "unofficial collaborators" constituting 1 out of 50 GDR citizens, this is not surprising. Most found good jobs after the collapse of the GDR, including in the west's spy service. They made sure their old comrades were well taken care of.

One set of files the German government did not receive is that containing identities, code names, and other vital data of thousands of Stasi foreign agents, most of whom worked in West Germany. The CIA spirited them away after the fall of the Berlin Wall. Until 1999 it refused to turn them over to the Germans, saying that the archives would expose many friendly agents still operating in the west to retaliation by their victims. This became an emotional test case for the German government, which considers the files to be its property, as it seeks to reassert the full sovereignty of a reunited Germany and establish a more equitable partnership with Washington. Most of the files were returned; only those relating to foreigners who worked for the Stasi in the US, Europe, the Middle East, Africa, and elsewhere were not given back.

Not wishing to announce open season for witch hunts but wanting to protect the rights of citizens, the government decided in 1991 to allow individuals access to their own files while threatening journalists with three-year jail terms if they published information from them without permission. Joachim Gauck, former director of the agency that investigated the Stasi files (and later president of Germany), admitted, "Charges, accusations. The memories, the pain and sadness, the failures—that will last very long. We must face it. We must show ourselves that injustice, and especially injustice in high places, does not pay." He was followed as director of the Stasi documentary authority by Marianne Birthler and in 2011 by Roland Jahn, a former victim of Stasi terror.

This prompted charges of press muzzling by civil liberty advocates, who called the decision the most serious effort at limiting freedom of the press since the Hitler era and a repetition of earlier times in the FRG, when many prominent Nazis were permitted to resume their careers after 1945 without a review of their histories in well-kept Nazi records. Other former GDR citizens had to confront their own troubled past. The legendary former head of East Germany's foreign intelligence service, Markus Wolf, returned to Germany from exile in the Soviet Union and was released on $30,000 bail, a paltry sum for a man who was paid at least that much for interviews with the sensation-hungry western press. When his treason trial began in 1993, he asked, "What country am I supposed to have betrayed?"

Because such cases had the hint of retroactive justice, since the defendants were fairly operating under the laws of their country at the time, the Constitutional Court ruled in 1995 that former East German spy masters like Wolf cannot be prosecuted for conducting Cold War espionage against the west. His conviction was overturned, but he was tried and convicted again in 1997 on charges of kidnapping three Germans on both sides of the Berlin Wall 30 years earlier. His sentence was suspended. In 1998 he was jailed once more for refusing to identify a western informer during a spy trial. Again, he was freed quickly. In 2006 he died in Berlin, age 83.

Amnesty applies neither to East German agents caught in the west (although the court urged mercy in such cases), to West Germans who committed treason by spying for the GDR, nor to former East German spies accused of such offenses as kidnapping or bribery, crimes condemned by the GDR's own laws. Thus, prosecution continues.

In 1996 appeals by the GDR's former defense minister, Heinz Kessler, his aide, and top party boss Hans Albrecht, convicted for killing people attempting to escape across the wall, were denied. By 1997, more than

30 former GDR officials and border guards had been convicted of shootings. In August 1997, for the first time, former members of the GDR political elite were held accountable for deaths along the border. Its last leader, Egon Krenz, and his codefendants, Guenter Schabowski and Guenter Kleiber, were convicted of manslaughter. Krenz was sentenced to 6.5 years in prison and was released in 2003 after only 4 years. The other two received three-year jail terms. Krenz defiantly shouted, "The political persecution is revenge for the fact that East Germany existed!"

The prelude for the first free all-German elections in almost six decades, scheduled December 2, 1990, were state elections in the five newly recreated Lander in the east; on October 14 the CDU won in four of them. Therefore, few observers were surprised to see the CDU/FDP coalition win a resounding victory in December and Kohl reap the electoral reward for presiding over the mending of Germany's division.

Columbia University historian Fritz Stern noted that "Germany had been given something uncommon: another chance. The century ended as it began, with a major German lead in Europe based on economic clout, technological advance, and human efficiency and performance . . . [but] under much more favorable circumstances than in the pre-1914 age of rough-hewn nationalism." Prussia has not been recreated, despite the reburial of Frederick the Great at his beloved Sans Souci Palace in Potsdam outside Berlin and the return of the Prussian eagle and iron cross to the newly restored statue of the victory goddess atop the Brandenburg Gate in 1991.

Kohl and Foreign Minister Hans-Dietrich Genscher knew that, while no European country wanted to thwart German unity, there was uneasiness about the possibility that an economically powerful Germany, 43% larger than before and more populous than any country west of Russia, would dominate Europe. Most European leaders were too polite to express these fears publicly—not British prime

Germany

Former chancellor Kohl addresses the opening session of the Bundestag of a united Germany, December 22, 1990.

minister Margaret Thatcher and French president Francois Mitterrand. Thatcher bluntly told Soviet leader Gorbachev two months before the wall fell that "we do not want a united Germany." Her own foreign office disagreed with her. In January 1990 Mitterrand expressed his fear that reunification would turn Germans into the "bad" people who once dominated Europe. He thought this would require a Russian-British-French alliance to counter it. It was astonishing after a half-century of partnership how quickly both leaders fell back into antiquated 19th-century thinking. Both were dramatically wrong in their judgment. Mitterrand settled his nerves by persuading Chancellor Kohl to trade the German mark for the euro, thereby binding Germany more tightly to its European allies.

To minimize these fears, Germany signed landmark treaties with the USSR and Poland. On November 9 it signed a friendship treaty with the Soviet Union that amounted to the closest links the Soviets had with any major western nation. It contains a section affirming that both nations "will refrain from any threat or use of force which is directed against the territorial integrity or political independence of the other side." Neither country would aid an aggressor against the other. Bonn insists that this agreement, ratified in the USSR in March 1991, was aimed at forging a new relationship with the USSR in a way consistent with Germany's obligation to NATO, which is a defensive alliance.

The ink was hardly dry when Germany signed a treaty with Poland on November

14, 1990, fixing their mutual border along the Oder-Neisse line. The former German land to the east of this demarcation constituted a third of Poland's territory.

Genscher stated bluntly, "We Germans are aware that the treaty does not surrender anything that was not lost long ago as the result of a criminal war and a criminal system." But he also admitted that settling this last major dispute of the war hurt: "For those who have lost their homelands, who suffered expulsion [after 1945], it is an especially painful one."

POLITICAL SYSTEM

In 1949 West Germany's founders called their new constitution a Basic Law in order

The 16 states (*Länder*) of the FRG

to emphasize that it would apply only temporarily until reunification. But in 1990 the newly formed eastern German states chose to be absorbed by the FRG through article 23, which was then scrapped to assure neighboring countries that no other former German territories could enter the FRG that way. Thus, the Basic Law became, in effect, a permanent constitution. It reflects several objectives that the founders hoped to achieve: individual freedom, political democracy, stability (to prevent a repetition of the Weimar experience), built-in safeguards against the emergence of another dictatorship, and links with some aspects of the German political tradition.

In contrast to the US Constitution, which has a Bill of Rights attached at the end, the Germans placed in the first 20 articles of the Basic Law guarantees for unalienable rights and liberties and the protection of life. Also, in contrast with the US document, the Basic Law explicitly grants Germans, who had never experienced a successful democratic revolution, the right of revolution. Article 20 reads in part, "all Germans shall have the right to resist any person or persons seeking to abolish the constitutional order, should no other remedy be possible."

A Powerful Court

To underscore its commitment to the principles in this document, the founders, with the full support of the American occupation authorities, created the Constitutional Court, which would have the power of judicial review and therefore would be the final arbiter in constitutional questions. With two chambers located in Karlsruhe, where founders thought it could remain freer from political influences, the court reviews legislation, adjudicates disputes between the national and Land (state) political institutions, rules on questions concerning individual rights, and can even ban groups or parties if it believes that their activities are not in harmony with the principles of the Basic Law. For instance, in the mid-1950s, it banned the neo-Nazi Socialist Reich Party and the Communist Party for this reason.

The court has a clearly political character, as the selection of the justices reveals—half of the 16 justices are chosen by the lower house of parliament, and half are selected by the upper house (in order that state interests are not overlooked). Each serves one 12-year term. The parties nominate candidates. For example, on March 5, 2010, the SPD nominee, Andreas Vosskuhle, a 46-year-old law professor, was elected president of the Federal Constitutional Court. The FDP's nominee, Andreas Paulus, was elected on the same day as a justice on the court.

Because of its powerful effect on the law, it is often called the "third chamber of the legislature." Like the US Supreme Court, it can judge laws or parts of laws to be unconstitutional, but it had done so only in 611 cases in 60 years. Unlike the US court, it seeks consensus and seldom writes dissenting opinions. Any citizen may bring a constitutional case, and about 6,000 do that each year. The court is administratively independent and cannot be impeached by the parliament.

It has not been afraid to lock horns with the government. For example, it struck down Chancellor Adenauer's attempt in the mid-1950s to create a second television channel under national control because this would have clearly violated the states' constitutional jurisdiction over mass communications media. In 1983 it decided to postpone the national census on the grounds that the questions the state intended to ask would have violated the citizens' right of privacy. The next census was not conducted until 2011, when the EU required all member states to collect data that includes profession, household size, family status, and housing. In 1995 it struck down Bavaria's requirements for schools to hang crucifixes in every classroom, and it prevented the punishment of pacifists caught shouting the slogan, "Soldiers are murderers." The first female chief justice, Jutta Limbach, faced further parliamentary criticism for agreeing to rule on parliament's power to restrict political asylum, as it did in 1993.

The court sometimes upholds the government's policies, as it did in 1993, when it ruled that the Maastricht Treaty for European unity and the FRG's participation in UN-sponsored peacekeeping operations outside of Europe are not unconstitutional. In July 2009 it gave the green light for the EU Lisbon Treaty, but it concluded that Germany's sovereignty could be endangered by some parts of the treaty. It had ruled only one month earlier that the parliament should pass a new law giving itself more authority over EU decisions. It made clear that there are limits to the powers the German parliament can turn over to the EU. The European Parliament is not a proper legislature, and the EU is not a democratic state. The court ruled out some forms of participation, such as the establishment of a single EU military command. It has thus shown itself as a vigorous protector of national sovereignty and limiter of the EU's powers. In September 2011 it ruled that the consent of the parliamentary budget committee was needed for extending credit guarantees. The new limitations made Chancellor Merkel more careful about contributing money to eurozone loan packages for financially distressed Greece.

All parties in disputes before this powerful court, including the national government, have always complied with its decisions. Almost 80% of citizens trust the court, while less than half have faith in the federal government and parliament.

State Government
More than any other state in Europe, with the exception of Bosnia and Herzegovina, Switzerland, and Belgium, Germany has decentralized and fragmented political power. Such decentralization is traditional in Germany, which consists of what had been a myriad of states and free cities. The only experience with highly centralized government—the Third Reich and the GDR—left a bad taste in Germans' mouths. The FRG is now broken down into 16 states (each called a *Land*). Most of these states were newly created after 1945, and the five in the former GDR, plus a unified city of Berlin, were recreated in 1990. In May 1996 Eastern German voters rejected unequivocally an effort by all major parties, except the PDS, and the governments of Brandenburg and Berlin to merge these two states.

The massive influx of refugees into the western occupation zones did much to break down the formerly strong regionalism of the various areas of Germany. But Bavaria has retained its own unique character, visually, culturally, and politically, more than any other state. It proudly calls itself the "Free State of Bavaria" and, curiously, has never formally ratified the Basic Law, although it has abided by it since 1949. The eastern German states also have different political cultures.

Each state has its own government, and it is free to choose the form it prefers. The state constitutions differ considerably in some respects, but they all call for forms of parliamentary government. A government, led by a minister president, is

chosen by a unicameral parliament, called a Landtag, elected by proportional representation. State issues play the dominant role in such state elections, but since the early 1960s, these elections, which are seldom held at the same time as national elections, have increasingly become indicators or bellwethers for citizens' approval of national policies or leaders. Therefore, national leaders lend their active support in local campaigns, an important reason the voter turnout is very high by American standards, averaging about 70% since the early 1950s.

In accord with German tradition and to prevent a single leader or group of leaders in the central government from gathering all strings of power, the founders granted specific exclusive power to the states: education at all levels (although the national government does contribute to the financing of universities, and it is responsible for constructing all school buildings), law enforcement and internal security (although the central government does maintain an Office for the Protection of the Constitution, roughly equivalent to the FBI in the US, and a Federal Criminal Office, which maintains data that is useful to the state police authorities), the administration of justice, and mass communications and media. Only in the areas of defense and foreign policy is the national government largely free of the state governments. As in the US, all powers not expressly granted to the national government belong to the states. In 2004–2005 all 16 minister presidents accepted the need to reform the federal structure, but they failed to agree on the powers they should cede to the central government, especially regarding education.

States used their powers over regional broadcasting to resist a unified national satellite television policy. State leaders travel around the globe and conduct their

Germany

Sie haben 2 Stimmen

	X		X	
hier 1 Stimme für die Wahl **eines/einer Wahlkreis-** **abgeordneten** **Erststimme**			**hier 1 Stimme** für die Wahl **einer Landesliste (Partei)** – maßgebende Stimme für die Verteilung der Sitze insgesamt auf die einzelnen Parteien – **Zweitstimme**	

1	Reinhardt, Erika Hausfrau S-Wangen Ludwig-Blum-Straße 5	CDU	Christlich Demokratische Union Deutschlands	○
2	Conradi, Peter Bundestagsabgeordneter, Architekt Ostfildern 4 im Haurer 1	SPD	Sozial- demokratische Partei Deutschlands	○
3	Kiesswetter, Ekkehard Rechtsanwalt S-Ost Plettenbergstraße 14	FDP/ DVP	Freie Demo- kratische Partei/ Demokratische Volkspartei	○
4	Rühle, Heidemarie-Rose Hausfrau S-Süd Römerstraße 13	GRÜNE	DIE GRUNEN	○

○	**CDU**	Christlich Demokratische Union Deutschlands Dr. Wolfgang Schäuble, Matthias Wissmann Dr. Lutz Stavenhagen, Anton Pfeifer, Udo Ehrbar	1
○	**SPD**	Sozialdemokratische Partei Deutschlands Dr. Herta Däubler-Gmelin, Harald Schäfer, Hans Martin Bury, Wolfgang Roth, Dr. Liesel Hartenstein	2
○	**FDP/ DVP**	Freie Demokratische Partei/ Demokratische Volkspartei Dr. Helmut Haussmann, Georg Gallus, Martin Gruner, Dr. Wolfgang Weng, Dr. Olaf Feldmann	3
○	**GRÜNE**	DIE GRÜNEN Christa Vennegerts, Oswald Metzger, Ursula Eid-Simon, Dr. Thilo Weichert, Monika Knoche	4
○	**LIGA**	CHRISTLICHE LIGA Die Partei für das Leben Karl Simpfendörfer, Bettina Schega, Ewald Jaksch, Wilhelma Schmidts, Marion Gotthardt	5
○	**CM**	CHRISTLICHE MITTE Anny Stark, Peter Bella, Michael Platt, Erna Schönstein, Werner Keller	6
		DIE GRAUEN Initiiert vom Senioren-Schutz- Bund „Graue Panther" e.V.	7

"You have 2 votes"

own foreign policy to a degree. Some have even opened offices in Brussels to influence EU policy and seek financial favors. The upper house (*Bundesrat*), which the states control, has been used to force the federal government to consult with them on any foreign policy deals that affect them. The states wield great powers in Brussels, particularly over budget contributions and the ability to block the European Commission from imposing antitrust (competition) and industrial policy on the states. All these trends underscore the fact that regional politics is more significant in the FRG than in any other European country. Almost all important political figures in federal politics rose from a strong base in the states.

Two factors prevent the states from being as individualistic as American ones: legal uniformity and shared taxation. German law, which was decisively influenced by Roman law and by the Napoleonic Code, was codified in the last three decades of the 19th century. Since the 1950s the criminal code has been in the process of revision. The point is that German law is the same in every state. In general, the national government wields the most legislative power, while the state governments have most of the administrative power. The staffs of most federal ministries are relatively small. Indeed, if one excludes the employees of the Federal Railways and the Federal Postal Service

(both of them privatized), only about 10% of public employees work for the national government, whereas roughly a third work for local governments, and over half work for the states.

The states finance and set operating rules for local governments in the communities (*Gemeinden*). Local government differs from state to state, but all communities have an elected council (*Stadtrat* or *Gemeinderat*). Also, each county (*Kreis*) has an elected council (*Kreistag*) led by an executive officer (*Landrat*).

Germany's decentralization has its positive and negative consequences. On the one hand, the great number of decision makers and the necessity for consensus are mighty barriers to tyrannical government. On the other hand, it makes reform exceedingly difficult. The levels of government are so intertwined that they often block each other. The 16 *Länder* have as many elections, and on average there is a *Land* election every three months. This fact enables the opposition in Berlin to gain control of the upper house of parliament, the Bundesrat, and thereby to block reform. Anticipating approaching *Land* elections, a federal government is inhibited in introducing radical reform. Finally, the largest political parties themselves are organized federally with powerful regional leaders. This makes it hard for central leaders to impose changes.

Parliament—the Second House

The states' interests are also guaranteed by their legislative role at the federal level. The second house of parliament, the Bundesrat, is composed of delegates from the state governments and, like all upper houses in federal states, exists primarily to protect states' rights. Seats in the Bundesrat are apportioned on the basis of each land's population; each of the most populous states (including North Rhine-Westphalia, Bavaria, Baden-Wurttemberg, and Lower Saxony) receives five seats; each of the medium-sized states (such as Hesse, the Rhineland-Palatinate, Schleswig-Holstein, and the five new Lander in the east) receive four; and each of the three smaller

Reichstag and Brandenburg Gate

states (Hamburg, Bremen and the Saar) receive three. The Lander send specific delegates depending upon the subjects being discussed; sometimes they are administrators, and other times they are leading politicians, including the minister presidents. Delegates are always bound by instructions from the state governments, and each delegation must cast all of its votes for or against a matter.

The Bundesrat can initiate legislation, and it must approve all legislation relating to the states' constitutional or administrative responsibilities. Also, it must approve any legislation affecting state boundaries, national emergencies, and constitutional amendments. Presently, about 60% of all legislation falls within the Bundesrat's veto power. In many cases, party lines do not decisively affect votes in this body. For instance, smaller or poorer states often have more in common than do larger or wealthier ones, regardless of which parties rule in the state capitals.

Parliament—the Lower House

The lower house of parliament (Bundestag) is the most important chamber. It is normally composed of 598 members elected at least every four years by Germans 18 years of age or older. The 2017 federal election created 709 seats in the Bundestag. This was raised to 735 seats in 2021. The electoral system is a complicated mixture of proportional representation and single-member districts. Half of the members are elected by plurality vote (more votes than any other single candidate) in over 299 constituencies with an average size of approximately 250,000 residents.

The other half is elected by proportional representation from Land party lists. Each voter casts two ballots, one for the constituency candidate and one for his preferred party. The party vote is the more important because it determines the percentage of total seats in the Bundestag each party will receive.

A further complication is the concept of "overhang votes." If a party wins more seats in the "first vote" than it would be entitled to under strict proportional representation, it keeps the extra seats, and the size of the Bundestag expands accordingly. Thus, after the 2021 elections, the Bundestag was enlarged to 735 seats. In 2008 the Constitutional Court had ruled that these extra seats were unconstitutional and that the Bundestag would have to change the law. Even though this still has not happened, an intraparty agreement was reached that provides for the addition of seats for parties whose proportional allocation would otherwise be affected by other parties' overhang seats. So, in the end, the Bundestag achieves proportional representation (PR).

The new chancellor's office in Berlin, dubbed the "washing machine"

In the 2021 elections women won 35% of the seats. A third of all representatives were new. The average age was 47.5 years, making it the youngest Bundestag ever.

With German unity, Berlin became the official capital, but that did not automatically mean that the seat of government would be transferred to Berlin. Faced with the daunting costs of integrating and modernizing the bankrupt economy of the GDR, many shirked from the price tag of moving all their operations to Berlin. A massive move severely affected the economic livelihood of Bonn and its suburbs. There were also political considerations. Some western German politicians did not want to transfer the capital from Bonn, which is located close to Brussels and other EU centers, to a faraway city with a reputation for past militarism and present rebelliousness and a thriving counterculture. Also, until 1994 Berlin was surrounded by a large number of Soviet troops, who could possibly have intimidated the German government if relations between the two countries were to become strained.

On June 20, 1991, in one of the longest (12 hours) and most emotional debates ever held in the Bundestag, a narrow majority (338–320) voted to make Berlin the seat of government. Younger legislators tended to favor Bonn, whereas those old enough to remember the earlier Berlin and its grandeur, such as Kohl and Brandt, favored Berlin. The outcome was a powerful message of reconciliation to Eastern Germans. But the latter played a decisive role in the vote—whereas narrow majorities in both the two largest parties, the CDU/

CSU and SPD, voted for Bonn, it was the 25 members from the small East German parties, the PDS and Alliance 90, who tipped the scales for Berlin.

Seven ministries, including agriculture and, temporarily, defense, remained in Bonn and maintain offices in Berlin. But the rest, along with at least 20,000 government workers, were transferred to Berlin in 1999. Some 140 embassies had to move, along with countless organizations, such as lobby groups and industry representatives, who must be close to the center of power. By 2009 one found 8,732 officials working in Bonn, while 8,931 were based in Berlin. The additional cost for maintaining two capitals covers 751 tons of official mail that is shipped back and forth annually and 132,000 plane tickets booked for shuttles.

Confounding expectations, Bonn not only survived the change, but it also is thriving after remaking itself into an international R&D campus and convention center for everything from research into alternative energy and medical science to a locale for UN offices. It has created 12,000 jobs since the move, and 1 in 10 jobs in its environs is now in health care. It used to be called a sleepy bureaucrats' town, but now it is a living, growing city.

On April 19, 1999, former chancellor Gerhard Schröder spoke at the inaugural session of the newly renovated Reichstag building, with its massive glass dome that symbolizes, in his words, "the openness and the transparency of our democratic politics." He emphasized that "equating *Reichstag* with *Reich* makes no sense," given the strong and stable democracy in

Germany

Former chancellor Helmut Kohl

today's FRG. But exactly what to call the new capitol, if not *Reichstag*, consumed months of debate. Finally, the all-party Council of Elders declared a solution that satisfied no one: *Deutscher Bundestag— Plenarbereich Reichstagsgebaude* (German Federal Assembly—Plenary Area, Imperial Assembly Building). Modern glass structures to accommodate the members of parliament and their staffs were constructed adjacent to the *Reichstag*.

For the first time in German history, the parliament in 1949 was granted exclusive control over the country's government and bureaucracy, and it has supervisory power over the military. It elects a military ombudsman, who is unique in the world. He or she has access to all military facilities at all times and can speak with any armed forces member. Even the highest-ranking officers cannot block access. Although most legislation originates with the government, the Bundestag must debate and approve all. Debates in the Bundestag plenum are conducted in a very free and relaxed atmosphere. They are punctuated with humorous or pointed quips, boisterous interruptions, laughter, applause, and desk pounding.

Major debates are televised in order to bring the activity of the parliament closer to the attention of the citizens. The Bundestag combines the role of a debating parliament, such as the British House of Commons, with that of a working parliament, such as the US Congress. Most of the work is actually done in the 19 standing committees, which, though not as powerful as US congressional and senatorial committees, thoroughly examine and amend legislation.

Parliamentarians also increasingly use their investigatory and information-gathering powers quite effectively to perform their function of being a responsible critic of the government. They insist on having full details of negotiations with the EU before giving the government a green light. This kind of assertiveness is new in a chamber that automatically endorsed most decisions the government took in Brussels. An interesting feature is that seats and chairmanships in the committees are distributed according to party strength in the Bundestag itself. Thus, the opposition party will occupy many committee chairmanships and by tradition will always occupy that of the finance committee.

The Bundestag's function as a "working parliament" is enhanced by the fact that almost half of its members are civil servants, who, in contrast with US civil servants, are freed from their normal jobs while serving in political positions and can return to the civil service at any time. Even their promotions and pay raises are continued while they are in political office. Civil servants are represented in the Bundestag at a rate 10 times higher than their proportion in the larger population, and workers, farmers, housewives, and those in business and professional occupations are greatly underrepresented. A third of Bundestag members are women. The number of Muslims has risen to eight.

The FRG is a parliamentary system, and the most important of the functions of the Bundestag is to choose a government. A majority chooses the chancellor, the most powerful political figure in the FRG, from among its own members, and he/she then chooses His/her cabinet, most of whom have seats in the Bundestag and who are then directly responsible to the chancellor, not to the Bundestag. The chancellor is always responsible to the lower house. However, in order to prevent the continuous cabinet instability that plagued the Weimar Republic, he/she can be voted out of office only if a majority is immediately able to choose a replacement. This requirement for a "constructive vote of no-confidence," which has been attempted very infrequently, ensures that Germany will always have a government.

Ex-chancellor Schröder's decision in May 2005 to call federal elections a year early was constitutionally questionable. To prevent the instability that had plagued the Weimar Republic, Germany's founding fathers made it hard to dissolve parliament and call early elections. Only if there is no majority in the Bundestag behind the chancellor can it be done. Since Schröder had a majority, albeit a narrow one, he had to engineer his own defeat in a no-confidence vote on July 1, 2005, by persuading some of his supporters to defect to the opposition.

The federal president has the power to refuse early elections if he thinks there is no need for them. Then-president Horst Köhler decided to permit them, but parties or MPs can challenge his decision in the Constitutional Court. This was done, but in an August 2005 ruling, the court gave chancellors broad latitude in deciding when to cut parliamentary mandates short. It argued that the erosion of the Bundestag's confidence in the chancellor "cannot be established in a court of law." The judges thereby opened the path for more frequent votes of confidence to bring about early elections. If after an election no chancellor candidate wins the majority of votes in the Bundestag after three

Former Chancellor Angela Merkel: a new beginning

Germany

rounds of voting, as seemed possible in November 2005, the president can decide whether to allow a minority government or to call new Bundestag elections. The 2005 elections reminded Germans that the presidency is a more powerful office than they had realized.

The chancellor's office (*Bundeskanzleramt*)—the equivalent of the US executive office of the president, has a staff of about 500 in 6 departments. It is located in a new and modern structure with much glass (dubbed by Berliners as the "washing machine") opposite the Reichstag building in Berlin. The chancellor directs the work of all governmental ministries, which answer to him. Since Konrad Adenauer, chancellors have been very powerful figures, whose popularity almost always runs ahead of that of their own party or challengers. Some observers have even called the FRG a "chancellor's democracy."

The President

The federal chief of state is the president. Remembering how the powerful Weimar presidency had overshadowed and, to a certain extent, undermined parliament, the founders decided to grant the president largely ceremonial powers, such as formally naming the chancellor and his cabinet, signing all laws, and appointing and dismissing national civil servants and federal judges. In each case, however, he merely carries out the will of the government or parliament. He could possibly be an important mediator and conciliator in the event of a parliamentary crisis, but that has not yet occurred in the FRG. The president has a villa in Bonn, but he resides in Dahlem (western Berlin) and works in Bellevue Palace in central Berlin.

Former president Richard von Weizsacker (1920—2015) was a patriarchal Christian Democrat whose style and substance earned him almost universal respect by transforming the presidency into a post of real authority. He used the office to describe broadly the direction in which he believed the FRG should go. He spoke out at carefully chosen moments on the meaning of Germany's past, the potential dangers of nuclear power, the importance of trade unions in the society, the significance of German unity, and the need to move the seat of government to Berlin. Weizsacker strengthened the nature of the presidency as a kind of conscience of the nation. He showed that the president's power lies in his use of the bully pulpit. A president's success is thereby measured in large part by the quality of his speeches. His successor in May 1994 was also a Christian Democrat, Roman Herzog (1934—2017), former president of the Constitutional Court. Herzog was followed in May 1999 by Social Democrat Johannes

President Frank-Walter Steinmeier

Rau (1931—2006), popular ex-minister president of the FRG's largest Land, North Rhine-Westphalia.

In May 2004 and 2009, Horst Köhler (1943–), former head of the International Monetary Fund (IMF) and Christian Democrat, was elected. He provided a respected economic voice at a time of national economic uncertainty. However, it was his economic focus that caused him to resign in May 2010. Köhler unleashed a barrage of criticism when he said in a radio interview in Afghanistan that Germany, as "an export-oriented nation," might sometimes need to "defend our interests, for example open trade routes." Critics interpreted his message to be that German soldiers are sent abroad to secure German economic interests. That was not what he meant. He had made repeated efforts to encourage Germany to conduct a debate about its global role. This was the first time a president quit his post.

The regional chiefs of the ruling CDU replaced Köhler with an active and experienced politician, Christian Wulff (1959–), minister president of Lower Saxony. He was narrowly elected in June 2010. The opposition Social Democrats and Greens nominated the popular human rights activist and former commissioner for the Stasi records Joachim Gauck (1940–).

For the second time in only a year and a half, the president had to resign in January 2012 over a scandal involving a shady loan. The president made a mistake in calling the country's largest tabloid daily, Bild, and threatening the editor with "war" if he published the story. He apologized two days later, but the damage was done. After prosecutors demanded that his immunity be lifted, Wulff stepped down. In 2014 Wulff was acquitted of all charges of corruption.

He was replaced in March 2012 by Gauck, who was supported by all major parties except the Left Party, which

nominated Nazi hunter Beate Klarsfeld. Gauck had crossed swords with some of its communist members while investigating files. He is the first president who did not belong to a political party. Although they are not political allies, Gauck and Merkel have some things in common: Both grew up in eastern Germany and entered politics at the time of reunification in 1990. Like Merkel's father, Gauck is a Lutheran pastor. One of Gauck's major tasks was to restore respect and trust in the presidency, and he was quite successful in this regard. In June 2016, he announced that he would not be seeking reelection because, at 76, he wasn't sure he would have "the adequate amount of energy and vitality that is required."

The candidate who was certain to win the 2017 election by the Federal Assembly because he was supported by both partners in the grand coalition was Frank-Walter Steinmeier (1956–). The former Social Democratic candidate for chancellor and the current foreign minister, Steinmeier has spent much of his life in politics. He led SPD to a humiliating electoral loss but later earned respect for his conduct of foreign policy, especially in seeking solutions to the crisis in Ukraine. However, he was also seen as more (perhaps too) conciliatory toward Russia than Chancellor Merkel was, with an implication that his approach was driven more by Germany's business interests than by moral considerations. He earned similar criticism for refusing to meet the Tibetan leader Dalai Lama so as not to upset China.

Germany's presidents exercise moral rather than political power. Even before his election, Steinmeier set the course for his future approach to the then-US presidential candidate Donald Trump by describing him as a "hate preacher" and lumping him together with those who "make politics with fear," such as the Alternative for Germany (AfD) party or the pro-Brexit campaigners in the UK.

In order to prevent the president from claiming a superior role based upon a popular mandate upon direct election by all the people, the founders decided to have the president selected every five years by a Federal Assembly (*Bundesversammlung*) composed of all members of the Bundestag and an equal number of delegates from the various *Land* parliaments. In fact, no national political figure is elected directly by all voters.

The founders also distrusted elements of direct democracy (such as initiatives, referendums, or plebiscites) at the national level. They did not wish to create a useful tool for a popular demagogue like Hitler who could undermine the authority and responsibility of parliament, the very heart of democracy. Although the Basic

Germany

Law does not explicitly forbid them at the national level, the *Bundestag* never enacted laws to permit them to take place.

Since reunification in 1990, they are possible in all states and municipalities and are conducted with increasing frequency; almost 300 are held at the local level each year. For example, almost every power project must suffer a referendum, as do some private-sector investments. Schleswig-Holstein sponsored a referendum that rejected the German spelling reform, although the state legislature overturned the result. Bavarian voters abolished their state senate in 1998. Advocates of direct democracy argue that this mechanism has become necessary since membership in parties and trust in politicians are falling. A 2008 poll indicated that 80% of respondents want referenda at the national level.

Political Parties

A crucial point is that a person can be elected to the Bundestag only as a member of a political party. In the past, Germans had regarded parties with distrust. They allegedly divided the body politic, and their logrolling and pursuit of particularistic interests had an undignified and illicit air in the eyes of the average German. This condescension before 1945 had greatly weakened the prestige of parliament and therefore of democracy. Also, so many parties had seats in the Weimar parliament that it was almost impossible to construct a stable and lasting majority.

Therefore, the Basic Law (in contrast to the US Constitution) granted political parties official recognition and status, as well as the responsibility to organize the country's political life. Also, the Basic Law requires any party to receive a minimum of 5% of the votes cast nationwide (unless it can win three seats directly) in order to receive any seats in the Bundestag. In the first election in 1949, many parties cleared this hurdle, but since 1953 only seven parties have been able to accomplish this. But seven is a crowd when it comes to forming stable coalition governments. Electoral arithmetic makes the classic governments of center-left or center-right almost impossible. The only alternative to a grand coalition (known as GroKo) of the two largest parties is an agreement among three parties to rule together. Given the differences among the parties, this is very difficult. The parties are increasingly incapable of delivering working coalitions. It is a recipe for policy paralysis. The big-tent "people's parties" that have dominated German politics since 1949—the CDU/CSU and the SPD—are in steady decline. The 2021 elections were the first in which the two largest parties did not win a combined majority of the votes.

The Bundestag is made up of parliamentary parties (each called a *Fraktion*) that practice a high degree of party discipline; almost 9 out of 10 votes are straight party votes. Many observers have called the FRG a "party state," and they are largely correct.

Since 1959 the major political parties have received increasing amounts of financial subsidies from the national treasury. Direct corporate donations account for only 5% of party revenues, donations by individuals for 15%, and state financing and membership fees for the bulk.

The Christian Democrats and Christian Socials

The largest party in the grand coalition following the 2005 and 2013 elections was the CDU, which is linked in parliament and in federal elections with its Bavarian sister party, the CSU. The CDU / CSU is the first successful political party in German history that did not rest on a single confessional or class base. It is a union of diverse groups who, after the Nazi catastrophe, wanted to put Christian principles back into political life and to take ideological rigidity out of it. They wished to give Germany a new moral, democratic, and socially just beginning. Adenauer's economics minister, Ludwig Erhard, introduced a brand of capitalism with a social conscience (called the "social market economy") that brought not only prosperity but also a broad net of social assistance for the uprooted, the hungry, the unemployed, the old, and the sick.

Germans are very proud and protective of their generous social legislation, and the creation of the FRG's modern social net is primarily the work of the CDU/CSU; the SPD-FDP coalition only tightened this net in a few places during the 1970s. It is thus a democratic, reform-oriented party, which attracts votes primarily from Catholics, independent business people, white-collar employees, and civil servants. It would not be considered a conservative party in the US political sense, even though it does win the votes of most conservatives in Germany. However, this does not weaken or embarrass the CDU/CSU, since almost all conservatives in the FRG, in contrast to the Weimar Republic, support the democratic system. For years the party grappled with the problem of how to put aside the internal struggles within its talented and experienced leadership in order to present a picture of unity.

Catholic Bavaria is the FRG's most conservative state, and the CSU is therefore also conservative. The CSU, which especially appeals to Catholics, rural and small city dwellers, craftsmen, small business groups, and increasingly those in the service industries, until 2018 easily won *Land* elections in Bavaria (though not in Munich, the state capital). Its support sank to 37%. Its leader was Edmund Stoiber, who was chosen as the combined CDU/CSU chancellor candidate in the 2002 Bundestag elections. He lost, thereby continuing the tradition that no Bavarian can become federal chancellor. In 2007 he stepped down. When in the 2008 state election the CSU lost its absolute majority in Bavaria for the first time in 46 years, he was replaced by Horst Seehofer. Many of their supporters were lost to a new party of CSU rebels that focused on local issues, the *Freie Wahler* (Free Voters), who took a tenth of the vote. The CSU had lost its aura of invincibility.

The political and economic success of Kohl, the first German chancellor to have been too young to have played any role in Nazi Germany, helped restore in many citizens an interest and pride in being German. Kohl and his party believed that Germans have atoned enough for the nation's past sins. Former president Weizsäcker occasionally deflated such self-satisfaction by reminding Germans of the seamier side of their past, while encouraging them to be proud of what they have accomplished since 1945. Kohl frequently spoke of the "Fatherland" and the *Heimat* ("Homeland"). He also encouraged displays of patriotism and the frequent playing of the national anthem, the third verse of the *"Deutschlandlied"* ("Germany Song," often mistakenly called *"Deutschland, Deutschland uber Alles"*).

Before Germany's dramatic move toward unity, it appeared that Kohl's party, which was ridden with dissatisfaction about what appeared to be a bumbling chancellor, was heading for defeat in the December 2, 1990, federal elections. However, Kohl instinctively knew that, faced with the challenges of melding two Germanys into one, German voters would choose that leader who was decisive and exuded confidence that future problems could be solved. Therefore, the union parties adopted the slogans, "Yes to Germany, yes to the future!" At each of its election rallies, a campaign song was sung in English: "Feel the power, touch the future, reach the heart!"

The first all-German election in 58 years was a plebiscite on unity, after the fact. Those parties that had seized the opportunity to bring it about were handsomely rewarded, and those that seemed petty and afraid and that cast doubt on unity were punished. With voter participation falling to a new low of 77.8% (74% in the east), the governing CDU-CSU-FDP coalition won 55% of the votes. It actually performed better in the east than in the West. The CDU/CSU captured 44% of the votes and 319 seats. It won big in the former GDR,

Germany

where few Catholics live. Half of East German workers voted CDU, and it was the preferred party for young voters in both parts of Germany.

The CDU's standing in the east was troubled after the election by the cabinet resignation of the GDR's last minister president, Lothar de Maiziere (1940–). As a lawyer and high lay official in the East German Protestant Church, he was shown to have maintained contacts with Stasi from 1981 to 1988. He maintained credibly that these were necessary for his efforts to defend his clients and church. He was cleared of allegations that he had actually spied for Stasi, but he was forced to relinquish his party vice-chairmanship to another eastern German, Angela Merkel (1954–), who became the party's general secretary in 1998. Other leaders of the old eastern CDU, one of the bloc parties that had cooperated with the communists, were gradually forced out of their posts.

The CDU / CSU won a narrow victory in October 1994. By 1998 Kohl surpassed his political hero, Konrad Adenauer, to become the longest-serving chancellor in the 20th century: 16 years. Both had sought to bring Germany greatness, not through military strength and Realpolitik, but by making it liberal, democratic, trusted, and prosperous. In some ways Adenauer's job was more difficult. He had led a defeated, despised, divided, and impoverished country that was occupied and partly ruled by foreign troops. His compromises prompted critics to call him "chancellor of the allies." By contrast, Kohl led a Germany that was unified, rich, and powerful, with a mature democracy and the third-largest economy in the world. He almost completed Adenauer's dream of "a free and united Germany in a free and united Europe."

No one could deny Germany's strength under Kohl. But by working closely with Germany's European allies, especially France, as well as with the US and by pressing for a unified Europe more vigorously than anybody else, he helped solve the perennial problem that had vexed European statesmen for years—how to make Germany strong without terrifying the rest of Europe.

By September 1998, voters had grown tired of Kohl, who had not been able to solve Germany's main problem: unemployment. For the first time in the FRG's history, they voted to throw out an incumbent chancellor and to remove from power all the parties in the ruling coalition. Kohl was gracious in defeat, took full responsibility for the fiasco, and announced that he was stepping down.

He was replaced as party leader by Wolfgang Schäuble (1942–), later finance minister and Bundestag president, who was almost killed by an assassin's bullets in 1990 and who is confined to a wheelchair. His tenure was cut short by a scandal that came crashing down on the CDU. Kohl confessed to accepting $1 million in illegal campaign funds. The press was filled with lurid reports of corruption, party slush funds, secret bank accounts, and bribes by shady international arms dealers. Kohl made matters worse by refusing to reveal the names of donors, claiming that he had given his "word of honor" to keep them confidential. He also ordered the destruction of a huge number of key documents and two-thirds of his government's chancellery computer files. Not only public opinion and voters but also the party itself turned on the formerly unassailable leader. Schäuble admitted that the CDU was in "the worst crisis of its history."

The first party notable to dare call for an end of the Kohl era was Angela Merkel. He never forgave her for this, and she prevented him from being named subsequently as the honorary party chairman because of his historic achievements. However, on his 80th birthday in 2010, she said, "You will go into the 20th-century history books as a great statesman." On his death in June 2017, she declared, "Helmut Kohl's efforts brought about the two greatest achievements in German politics of recent decades—German reunification and European unity. . . Helmut Kohl understood that the two things were inseparable." The same day, the European Commission president Jean-Claude Juncker described Kohl as "the very essence of Europe" and ordered flags at EU institutions to be flown at half-mast.

Merkel is a Lutheran pastor's daughter and East German doctor of physics who had entered politics in 1990 in order to fight for democracy in the former GDR. A quick learner and a good administrator who is unpretentious and shows courage, integrity, and coolness under fire, she was the only easterner to survive an entire decade near the top of the CDU. Her asset was that she was a female Ossi who was free of the unsavory cronyism and backroom dealing that had tarnished the party elite. At the 2000 party congress, she was endorsed as leader by a resounding 90% of delegates. However, in 2002 her party decided that CSU leader Stoiber had the better chance of leading the CDU/CSU to victory in the September 22 elections, so it chose to back him as chancellor candidate instead of Merkel. She became the party's parliamentary leader.

Merkel reestablished her grip on the party and began to recast herself as a radical reformer. Because of her courage to advocate fundamental change, willingness to take risks, and ability to become leader against the will of the party establishment, she was often compared with Margaret Thatcher. She finds this comparison tiresome because she is not a radical reformer. The CDU/CSU won only four more seats than the SPD in the federal elections on September 18, 2005, but they were enough to make her chancellor, the Federal Republic's eighth, over a grand coalition with the SPD. She is many firsts: the first female, East German and Russian-speaking chancellor; the youngest German chancellor ever (age 51 in 2005); a Protestant leader of a predominantly Catholic party. She is a childless remarried divorcee, a fact that cost her among traditional Catholic CDU and CSU voters. She had made the decision to conduct a "gender-neutral" campaign and was rewarded by only 35% of women votes nationwide. Most Germans voted for change but not the root-and-branch kind.

Her first four years in office were a foreign and domestic policy success. In late 2009 Forbes magazine called her the "most powerful woman in the world." She was seen as having steered Germany relatively safely through the greatest global economic storm in seven decades. She persuaded voters that the superiority of Germany's postwar model of consensus,

For peace, against blind obedience

259

Germany

Guido Westerwelle, ex–foreign minister

wealth, wage discipline, and a social market had been demonstrated.

Entering the September 2017 federal elections, the CDU/CSU was certain to win more seats than any other party. The big question was whether its favorite coalition party, the FDP, would do well enough that they could together form a majority government with the Greens. With a turnout of 76.2%, the CDU/CSU captured a disappointing 32.9% of the votes and 246 seats, a loss of 65. Since this was shy of an absolute majority, the CDU/CSU ultimately had to enter a grand coalition with the SPD after six months of difficult negotiations. This was a personal fourth victory for Chancellor Merkel. The campaign revolved around the explosive issue of immigration, which has been sharply cut back her popularity and voters' trust in her. Her youth supporters wore black shirts that said "Stay cool, and choose the chancellor." In all, 11 ethnic Turks won seats. The results of the 2017 election expanded the size of the Bundestag to 709 seats. Women occupy 40% of cabinet seats and 30% of parliamentary seats, down from 36%.

In the new seven-party political constellation, the large parties (CDU/CSU and SPD) are steadily getting smaller. Their combined vote in 2017 was only 53.5%, a far cry from 91.2% in 1976 and around 80% thereafter. It is the small parties that are getting bigger. The 2009 and 2013 elections were the first with the participation of a generation that knew of the fall of the Berlin Wall only from hearsay.

The refugee crisis visibly affected the union when Horst Seehofer, the prime minister of Bavaria and the leader of the CSU, demanded in 2016 that no more than 200,000 migrants be allowed into Germany, roundly criticizing his coalition

partner, Angela Merkel, for a far more permissive approach to the refugee influx. The Bavarian party has always been the more conservative one in the CDU-CSU partnership, and it served an important role by attracting rightwing voters. Yet, it must tread carefully so as not to weaken the CDU, without which it would fade into political irrelevance. Disastrous electoral defeats in Bavaria and Hesse prompted an increasingly unpopular Merkel to step down as party leader in December 2018 but to remain as chancellor until the 2021 federal elections.

In the 2021 elections the party fell to 24.1% of the votes and 197 seats. This was the worst result in its 76-year history, and it entered the opposition.

The FDP—"Liberals"

For a long time, the FDP (called the "Liberals" or "Free Democrats") was the only small party to survive in the Bundestag. It had never received more than 13% of the vote, and at times it danced dangerously close to the 5% line. Yet the FDP played a role in German politics far out of proportion to its size or voter strength. Only once (in 1957) has a single party ever won an absolute majority of seats in the Bundestag. Thus, German governments must almost always be coalitions of at least two parties, and for a long time, the FDP was the linchpin for almost every governmental coalition. This changed after the Bundestag had to accommodate five parties; ruling coalitions must sometimes have three.

The FDP sees itself as the heir to the traditional German liberal movement, which was always composed of two strains: a strong nationalist commitment and the protection of individual rights through minimizing state intervention in the economy and society. In the early 1970s, the

nationalist strain largely left the party, so throughout the 1970s, the FDP could be more comfortable in the center-moderate left coalition with the SPD. From 1969 to 1982, the FDP was in the governing coalition with the SPD. However, it is economically more conservative than the SPD. The FDP attracts most of its votes from the middle class, mainly in urban areas. It always wins many strategic second votes from Christian Democrats or Christian Socials who want to boost it over the 5% hurdle in order to be a coalition partner in the government.

When it sensed a conservative wind blowing, it decided in 1982 to change partners, thereby enabling the Christian Democrats to rule. The FDP was widely criticized for the way in which it brought the Schmidt government tumbling down. Thousands of its members and some of its parliamentarians left the party in protest.

The buzzards seemed to be circling in the lead-up to the 1998 elections, but its dynamic party secretary general, Guido Westerwelle, succeeded in scaring some of them away. This experienced survival party arose from the dead. But for the first time in almost three decades, the FDP found itself neither in the government nor in possession of the foreign minister's post. That did not change in 2002. It had its best result ever in the 2009 federal elections, and it emerged as the junior partner of Chancellor Merkel's CDU/CSU. The party was ecstatic, but disaster loomed on the horizon.

Its coalition government with Merkel got off to a bad start in 2009 with lots of public bickering. That cost the FDP and Westerwelle popularity. Germany did win a two-year seat on the UN Security Council, but that feat was engineered by the country's talented UN ambassador, Peter Wittig. In May 2014 he assumed the post of ambassador to the United States.

Something had to be done to stop the FDP's loss of popularity. Westerwelle relinquished his posts as deputy chancellor and head of the FDP. He retained his position as foreign minister. Replacing him was former health minister Philipp Rösler, who moved into the cabinet post of economics minister. A 36-year-old physician born in Vietnam, he was the first Asian to occupy such high office in Germany. The change of leaders did not turn its fortunes around. On federal election day in 2013, it fell below the 5% threshold for the first time since the war: It won only 4.8% of the votes, down from 14.6% in 2009. The CDU/CSU attracted 2.1 million of the 3.8 million lost by the FDP. Its entire senior leadership resigned, and it faced a major rebuilding task to regain political relevance.

By the 2017 election, the FDP got recharged, mostly through the efforts of its new leader, Christian Lindner. He was bolstered by his stance on immigration policy that was stricter and less welcoming that those of the CDU or SPD. The apparent weakness of the SPD at the national level offered the Free Democrats a chance to once again play the oversized role of kingmakers for one of the main parties at the national level. It tripled its votes to 10.7% and 80 seats. It chose to join the opposition. This changed in 2021, when the FDP captured 11.5% of the votes and 92 seats. It joined the coalition government, and Lindner became finance minister.

The Social Democrats

The SPD is a traditional working-class party that is the only one in the FRG having had a continuous existence since before the German Empire. In the Weimar Republic, it was one of the regime's staunchest supporters, and during the Third Reich, its leaders either found themselves in concentration camps or went into exile. After the war it fully expected to become Germany's governing party because of its former opposition to the Nazis, but its leaders badly misread the voters' minds. West Germans, gripped by poverty, were less interested in the SPD's socialist solutions than they were in the prosperity its opponents promised and actually produced. Also, Social Democrats' focus on strong national policy directed against all four occupation powers and especially aimed toward German reunification proved to be far less appealing than Adenauer's policy of winning West German sovereignty, international respect, and military security through military and economic integration with the west.

In order to break out of the "one-third ghetto" (winning only a third of the votes) within the electorate and in order to attract more Catholic and middle-class voters, the SPD changed its program at the party congress in Bad Godesberg in 1959. It cast off the Marxist ballast in its party program and made the basic decision not fundamentally to challenge the capitalist order but instead to seek to correct its flaws through social reform. The following year the party's chief strategist, Herbert Wehner, announced in the Bundestag that the SPD would accept Adenauer's foreign policy of integration with the west.

Having become in theory as well as in fact a mass social reform party anchored in the democratic west and with a new young chancellor candidate, Willy Brandt, who remained the party's chairman until 1987, the party began attracting increasing numbers of middle-class voters. These included gains among civil servants, white-collar employees in industry and the service sector, and especially youth; these groups soon gained a far greater share of the party's leadership positions than workers. This opening of the party to the middle class was crucial to the SPD's gaining power in 1969, but it also converted the SPD into a broad-spectrum party whose main problem became that of unifying such diverse groups behind a common leadership.

In 1990 the SPD picked as its chancellor candidate its biggest vote-getting provincial politician, Oskar Lafontaine, ex-minister president of the Saarland and one of the party's most outspoken leftists. He belonged to a new generation of politicians who did not directly experience Nazism or the onset of the Cold War. His political outlook was significantly shaped by the student rebellion of the 1960s, and his politics are postindustrial, postmaterialist "new politics" emphasizing environmental issues. He was brought up in a divided Germany and showed no emotions toward the idea of a united country, to which he derisively referred as a "provisional entity" until the nation-state became superfluous. He hated words like "fatherland," and on the occasion of Germany's unity at midnight October 2 to 3, 1990, he alone among political leaders refused to sing the national anthem. He was unable to notice, let alone tap, the emotions released by the opening of the Berlin Wall. This antagonized many of his party comrades, including former chancellors Brandt and Schmidt.

In his campaign, during which he was almost killed when a deranged woman slit his throat with a butcher knife hidden in a bouquet, he harped on the problems and costs associated with unification and was perceived as a prophet of doom. His message was depressing, and his leftist themes did not interest German voters in 1990, especially those in East Germany, who wanted prosperity within the FRG. *Die Zeit* called him "the wrong man at the wrong time," and the electoral disaster proved this. The SPD dropped to 33.5% of the vote and 239 seats. Its 24.3% in the east, which had been the party's electoral fortress before Hitler's takeover, was shocking. It got the votes of only a fourth of East German workers.

Having led the SPD back into the "one-third ghetto" from which it had worked so long to escape, Lafontaine left his party to rebuild itself. Rhineland-Palatinate minister president Rudolf Scharping assumed leadership. He was the first national party leader in Germany to be selected by means of a poll of 870,000 party members throughout the country. He was a moderate, hard-working, but uncharismatic leader. Voters ignored his calls for change in the 1994 federal elections, although the SPD was able to increase its votes to 36.4% (37.6% in the west and 31.9% in the

Former chancellor Gerhard Schröder

east) and seats to 252. In the aftermath Social Democrats began bickering among themselves, and many blamed the party's deep malaise and plunging popularity on Scharping's vacillating policies and weak leadership. In 1995 Oskar Lafontaine replaced him as party leader.

Lafontaine was a traditional left-wing politician who enjoyed enthusiastic support by many of the party's rank-and-file. But another Social Democrat was showing himself to be a more promising vote-getter in general elections, and this became very important for a party that had lost four straight Bundestag elections in 16 years. When Lower Saxony's minister-president, Gerhard Schröder (1944–), won an impressive re-election victory in March 1998, the SPD turned to him as chancellor candidate, while Lafontaine continued as chairman of a party that had historically been prone to self-destructive divisiveness.

Schröder came from humble origins, the son of a widowed cleaning lady. Born in 1944, he is the first chancellor with no memory of the war. As a student he was a Marxist who took part in the student rebellion and became chairman of the Young Socialists, the SPD's youth organization. However, being ambitious and a skilled political tactician, he saw that his dreams could be fulfilled only in a "new center." Despite an insecure private life (four wives) and criticism that he lacked deeply rooted convictions and vision, he made full use of his extraordinary speaking abilities, his telegenic good looks, and his pragmatic bent. He had forged close ties with Germany's business community. In the 1998 *Bundestag* elections, Schröder

Germany

led the SPD to a decisive victory, capturing 40.9% of the votes and 298 seats. For the first time in FRG history, the combined parties of the left won both a majority of votes and of seats in the lower house.

Many observers, including Schröder himself, had expected a grand coalition of SPD and CDU / CSU to rule Germany after the elections. But the SPD's dramatic gains and the conservatives' shocking loss of 8% of its votes enabled the Social Democrats to form a coalition with the Greens that enjoyed a 21-seat majority. That coalition turned out to be divided during its first one-half year. Traditionalists (led by Lafontaine, who took the post as finance minister), advocated antibusiness neo-Keynesian policies. They clashed with modernists (led by Schröder), who wanted to work with business to overcome unemployment. Schröder seemed not to be in full control.

This perception was strengthened by serious conflicts with his Green partners, who pushed hard for a quick timetable for phasing out Germany's nuclear power. In March 1999 the boil was lanced. Lafontaine resigned all of his political posts and seat in the *Bundestag* and reemerged six years later as an effective populist coleader of the ex-communist Left Party. Schröder assumed the chairmanship of the SPD and set about to establish order.

In the 2002 elections, it seemed almost certain that he and his party would be soundly defeated because he had failed to lower unemployment. But he pulled out

"The first time—Close your eyes when kissing. Open them when voting," the Left.

a card never before played in elections in the federal republic since the war–he openly criticized US policy, declaring that Germany would not support Washington's "adventures" in Iraq and that "the German way" leads in a different direction. He apparently believed that the transatlantic relationship was sufficiently strong to survive a few weeks of campaign effrontery against the US. Worse was an alleged statement by his justice minister comparing President Bush's approach to Iraq with Hitler's tactics. Schröder called Bush to apologize for this outrage, but the furious American president refused to take the call. A diplomatic ice age followed. Still, given the fact that 80% of Germans, including three-fourths of conservative voters, opposed warfare against Iraq, these opportunistic declarations, along with an unexpectedly strong performance by his Green partners, provided Schröder and his party with just enough votes to win. ·

One thing about the 2002 election was very American—for the first time, the chief rivals squared off in nationally televised debates. It was a setting that well suited the silver-tongued, telegenic Schröder. This practice has been followed in subsequent elections.

Halfway into his second term, Schröder had become one of the most unloved chancellors in FRG history. The grassroots discontent stemmed from his Agenda 2010 reform program, approved in 2004, which called for adjustments in the social welfare system by reducing pensions, weakening job protection laws, and introducing copayments for state health care. It did not challenge the basic need for generous social protection. Nevertheless, leftist and trade union critics saw it as a betrayal of social democratic principles. Voters welcome the abstract notion of reforms, but they tend to oppose any specific measures. A frightening exodus of members from the party (180,000) prompted Schröder to recognize his failure as party chief.

When the SPD was trounced in a May 2005 election in Germany's largest *Land*, North Rhine-Westphalia, Schröder had had enough. Without consulting with his party or his Green coalition allies, he called for *Bundestag* elections a year early. His party was furious, and a widening rift opened up between Schröder and his SPD.

All signs pointed to a crushing SPD defeat in September 2005, but Schröder again proved to be a tireless and resourceful campaigner. *Der Spiegel* called him a "testosterone bomb." In a way he campaigned as an old-style leftist against his own reforms and railed against "Anglo-Saxon liberalism" (the free market). He succeeded in making his party seem like the protector of Germany's social achievements. He

emerged from the TV debate with Angela Merkel as the clear favorite in the polls to be chancellor.

Given preelection predictions that the party might get little more than a quarter of the votes, the SPD's final result was almost sensational: 34.2% of the votes and 222 seats, only 4 fewer than the CDU/ CSU. This was the first time in FRG history that a government had been voted out of power but no alternative government was elected to take its place. Nevertheless, in his euphoria on election night, Schröder went over the top. In the so-called Elephant Round of the top party leaders on TV, he condescendingly told Merkel not to be provincial and that she could not expect him to recommend that his party enter a coalition with her as chancellor. He claimed that the voters' message was that he should remain chancellor. This insensitive behavior was widely criticized and helped undermine his leadership. He underestimated Merkel's ability to maintain her party's backing and to prevent him or anybody else from taking her place in the top job, despite her poor electoral performance.

After a few weeks, he realized that he had to go. He decided to earn big money on companies' boards of directors, including the Russian-German pipeline consortium led by Gazprom. Only 10 days before the elections, he had signed a controversial deal with President Vladimir Putin to ship gas to Germany via an undersea Baltic pipeline that bypassed and therefore infuriated Poland and Ukraine. This "North Stream" pipeline began delivering Russian oil in 2011. A second one doubled capacity by 2013. His €1 million annual salary with Gazprom so soon after leaving office stirred up a firestorm of criticism.

He left the SPD in turmoil. A new generation of leaders moved into the leadership positions of both large parties. Those who had come of age during the social tumult of the 1960s, like Schröder, were giving way to younger, potentially more pragmatic, and less ideological leaders who entered politics after the collapse of the Berlin Wall in 1989.

His chief of staff, Frank-Walter Steinmeier (1956–), became foreign minister (and federal president in 2017). He was the first vice chancellor not to have a parliamentary seat. He positioned himself as the party's chancellor candidate for the 2009 federal elections.

Witnessing the creation of a strengthened unified opposition Left Party, SPD leaders were unsure whether they should shun the new party, ally with it, or shift leftward to undercut it. One wing in the party, led by chancellor candidate Steinmeier and Peer Steinbrück, wanted to depart from the proletarian party image and adjust to a "new center." Temporary party leader Kurt Beck and left-wing leader Andrea Nahles (1970–) wanted to win back lost voters on the left. Others, including Beck, abandoned the party's categorical ban on alliances between the SPD and the neo communist Left Party. The furor over this U-turn threatened to tear the party apart. No one could keep the peace between the feuding wings.

The polls were not kind to the party as it entered the September 2009 federal elections. Once Europe's most successful and influential center-left party, the SPD struggled to find a new path between Merkel's pragmatic center and the Left Party's hard-left course. With Steinmeier as chancellor candidate, the party suffered its worst defeat in almost 80 years, plummeting to 23% of the votes (a loss of a breathtaking 11.2%) and only 146 seats, down 75. The party was in disarray, and there was nowhere for it to go except into opposition.

The question in the air was not when the party would get back on its feet but whether it would survive as the main leftist political force. It was time for a new generation of leaders. With Peer Steinbrück as chancellor candidate in the September 2013 federal elections, the party suffered its second-lowest result ever, winning only 25.7% of the votes (up by 2.7%) and 193 seats (a gain of 47). After the longest coalition talks in history, lasting almost three months, the SPD entered a renewed grand coalition with Merkel. In an online vote by the SPD's 475,000 members, 78% took part, and three-fourths of them approved the 185-page coalition agreement.

During 2017 several momentous changes affected the SPD. Martin Schulz (1955–), the two-term president of the European Parliament, decided to return to German politics after 22 years in the EP. He promptly became the leader of the SPD, as well as its candidate for chancellor in the 2017 elections. This temporarily boosted the party's public opinion support, and the media announced a "Schulz effect." However, within a few months the new star lost his halo.

The 2017 federal elections were a disaster for the SPD. It fell to 20.5% of the votes (a loss of 5.1%) and 153 seats (a loss of 40). This was its worst result in postwar history. Its participation in a grand coalition had eroded its socialist identity. But a desperate Merkel invited it back into the government under favorable terms for the SPD. It took six months to complete the coalition, which only continued the party's dangerous slide in popularity. The party made a dramatic comeback in 2021, winning 25.7% of the votes and 206 seats. Party leader Olaf Scholz (1958–), a popular former finance minister and Hamburg mayor, became chancellor.

**Guido Westerwelle,
Olaf Scholz, Chancellor**
Source: *Wikipedia*

The Left Party

The Party of Democratic Socialism (PDS), renamed the Left (*Die Linke*) in 2007, is a credible electoral and parliamentary political force, especially in the former East Germany but now also in the west. It is burdened by its own history, being the heir to the SED, which misruled the GDR for 40 years. Antipathy against the party was kept alive by continuing revelations about financial scandals and outrageous Stasi activities, such as its harboring and training former West German terrorists in the GDR. Prosecutors issued arrest warrants for former top East German leaders for ordering that persons attempting to escape from the GDR be killed. From 1961 to 1989 about 350 lost their lives.

Some view it as representative of the interests of former SED members, who make up a majority of its membership. Of its 72,000 members, about half are eastern Germans over age 65. It capitalizes on the problems felt in the east—disappointment, insecurity, unemployment, comparatively lower wages, and the view that East Germany has been taken over by arrogant West Germans and their uncaring capitalist economic system. It receives many protest votes against the established national parties, which seem to focus their attention mainly on the west. At the same time, it has successfully broadened its demagogic appeal in western Germany by playing on anxieties about globalization, wealth distribution, welfare cuts, and job losses. It calls for a shorter workweek, restoration of full welfare benefits, a minimum wage, a "wealth tax," and "wealth for all." It opposes Germany's deployment in

Katja Kipping, the Left cochair

Afghanistan and elsewhere, favors closer ties with Cuba and Venezuela, and takes a critical stance toward the United States.

The Left's appeal is no longer restricted to the eastern parts of reunified Germany and Berlin. It casts itself as a party that has purged itself of Stalinism but not of socialism. In most of its federal electoral campaigns, its leader was the only media star in a very mixed bag of socialists. Gregor Gysi (1948–) is a witty, brilliant East Berlin lawyer who, being Jewish, is a rarity in modern German politics. He had made a name for himself by defending dissidents in the GDR. He tried to give the party a modern, fresh image, and his followers wore buttons in 1990 reading in English "Take it easy Gysi!" He filled halls whenever he appeared in the west, and the visitors were predominantly young people who liked his unconventional and open style and refusal to speak in communist "functionary's Chinese."

For the 1990 federal elections, it formed a "Left List/PDS," of which it was the senior partner. This alliance garnered only .3% of the votes in the west and 11.1% in the east, for a total of 2.4% nationwide. For this election only, the 5% hurdle was waived for new parties, so the PDS was given 17 seats in the Bundestag. Gysi won a directly elected seat in East Berlin's Hellersdorf-Marzahn, a very unusual feat for a candidate from a small party.

The party's momentum continued in 1994. It captured 19.8% of easterners' votes (but only .9% among westerners). More important, by capturing four of the five directly elected seats in its stronghold of

Germany

German soldier in Kabul, Afghanistan

eastern Berlin, it benefited from an almost forgotten route around the 5% clause into the Bundestag—to give regional parties the possibility of gaining a significant parliamentary presence, the founders decided that any party that can win at least three direct mandates should receive a number of seats proportional to its overall percentage of votes. Thus, the PDS, which won 4.4% nationwide, was awarded 30 Bundestag seats in 1994.

This was a very colorful mixture of representatives, which included nine westerners, about half women, a lesbian activist, the great-grandson of Otto von Bismarck, an author of steamy short stories, and several nonparty members. One was Stefan Heym (1913—2001), a former Jewish émigré to the US. He fought as an American soldier against Germany and then settled in the GDR in 1952 to become one of its most acclaimed novelists.

In 1998 the party continued its climb by winning 5.1% of the votes, almost all in the east. Although it again won four direct seats in eastern Berlin, this is the first time that it cleared the 5% hurdle and would have entered the *Bundestag* anyway. It gained 5 seats for a total of 35.

In January 2002 the PDS entered the mainstream of reunified German politics by joining the Berlin city government headed by Social Democrat mayor Klaus Wowereit (1973–). In the 2002 federal elections, it lost its star vote-getting leader, Gregor Gysi, who resigned over a trivial

air-miles scandal. It saw its share of votes in eastern Germany fall from 22% to only 16.9%. In the west it got a paltry 1%, adding up to only 4% nationwide, well below the 5% threshold. What was especially devastating was that it won only two direct seats. Thus, it had only two seats in the Bundestag. The PDS's political influence seemed to be on a downward slide.

The party is determined not to be branded as a social democratic party but rather as Germany's only true socialist party. In a report on threats to the constitution, the federal security service categorized it in 2009 as having "extremist aspirations." It keeps its eye on parts of it, such as its "Communist Platform."

The PDS entered the 2005 elections as the part of a left-wing ticket with the western-based Electoral Alternative Labor and Social Justice Party (WASG). The team called itself Leftists in the west and Leftists-PDS in the east, and it was co-led by populists Gysi and Oscar Lafontaine. The latter was the populist unifier, who tied together very different followers in the east and west. The strongholds are in the east, where a core of the people remains uncomfortable with the free market. Its followers there are more pragmatic and are interested in sharing in rule. Western followers tend to like more radical Marxist models and prefer protest to responsibility. What brought them together was dislike of Schröder and "neoliberal" (free-market) thinking. With a base in both

eastern and western Germany (something the PDS lacked) and with star power at the top, it was able to attract disgruntled leftists in the east and west and to clear the 5% hurdle needed to win parliamentary seats.

The alliance's hatred of the former SPD- Green government's reforms and its message of preventing any diminution of the welfare state resonated with voters. It captured 8.7% of the votes and 54 seats. In the east it got 25.4%, an increase of 8.5%, and in the west, it shot up to 4.9% of the votes, an impressive 3.8% more than in 2002. A fourth of Germany's unemployed voted for it. It was clearly a successful electoral alliance.

The two parts formally merged to form the Left in 2007. Whether this combination of power-conscious ex-communists, who have an effective grassroots organization in the east, and idealistic western trade unionists and disappointed Social Democrats, who formed an ad hoc milieu party (WASG) in the west, can ever become a permanent fixture in German politics is uncertain. However, their prospects look much brighter after winning legislative seats in west German states; by 2012 it had seats in 13 state legislatures and helped govern in 3 eastern states. These results stunned the mainstream parties and shook the entire political system. The Left became the largest opposition party on the federal level, winning the support of one out of seven Germans. Its gains were mainly at the expense of the SPD.

Since no other party will form a coalition with it at the federal level, it practices total opposition. Such parties thrive in opposition. The Left strengthens a trend within the Bundestag that power is now divided among seven national parties, making coalition building trickier.

It slipped in the 2013 elections, although it overtook the Greens to become the third-largest party in the Bundestag. It won 8.6% of the votes and 64 seats. Its upward climb continued in the 2017 federal elections. It captured 9.2% of the votes and 69 seats.

The party was divided over what its relations with the SPD should be. It had served as a union partner under the SPD in eastern *Land* governments. But in Thuringia it became the senior member of a "red-red" coalition in November 2014. In the 2021 elections it fell to 4.9% of the votes and 39 seats. It no longer constitutes a serious opposition force in parliament.

Greens

The Greens were the first new party in over 25 years to find its way into the federal parliament. Their presence affected not only the ability to form stable governments but also the tone and style of parliamentary government. The key to their earlier success was their focus on

Germany's foreign office in Berlin

environmental problems, which most Germans view as very important. This is why all parties turned their attention to this issue and robbed the Greens of their monopoly on it. Ecological problems are particularly acute in eastern Germany, where the former communist rulers showed appalling disregard for the environment.

In their early days, the Greens showed their ability to mobilize hundreds of thousands of persons for mass demonstrations against the federal government's defense policy or against a state government's plans to build a nuclear power or reprocessing plant or to expand the Frankfurt Airport. Some feared that it could threaten the democratic regime. In the past, mass movements had weakened and ultimately destroyed the Weimar Republic. For this reason, the founders of the FRG created a purely parliamentary democracy rather than one in which a plebiscite is possible.

In 1990 their eternal infighting, rejection of German unity, absence of a positive program, and ambivalence toward taking responsibility in government caught up with them. Grossly misreading the popular mood supporting unity, western Greens adopted the slogan "Everybody talks about Germany; we talk about the weather!" Failing to unite their parties for the Bundestag elections, western German Greens received only 4.8% of the votes in the west and were therefore ejected from parliament, to their shock and dismay. An election coalition of eastern German Greens and Alliance 90, a collection of eastern German grassroots groups that organized the 1989 revolution, won 6% of the votes in the east (1.2% nationwide) and eight seats under the special election law that applied only to the 1990 elections.

The party was split between realists (Realos), who favored accepting government posts to achieve the party's goals, and the fundamentalists (*Fundis*), who argued that the party had tarnished its image by ceasing to be an exclusively opposition force and by entering an "arrangement with capitalism." In 1991 the inevitable occurred: The *Fundis* broke away from the Greens and formed their own Ecological Left/Alternative List, which vowed to concentrate on strengthening nonparliamentary opposition, but it became politically irrelevant. This split made the Realos more respectable in the eyes of some voters. In 1993 the eastern and western parties merged, calling themselves Alliance 90/Greens, or Greens for short. They staged a political comeback in 1994, winning 7.3% of the votes and 49 seats. In 1998 the party dipped slightly to 6.7% of the votes and 47 seats. But this was sufficient to enable the Greens to enter the federal government for the first time.

Its leader at the time, Joschka Fischer (1948–), a school dropout and activist who once gave his profession as "street-revolutionary," became foreign minister. He is a brilliant and humorous speaker with great political skill in forging unity in a party that was created to oppose party discipline and establishment politics. He proved himself to be a reliable partner to Gerhard Schröder, even though his party was forceful in pressing on the SPD its ideas concerning ecological taxes and a rapid shutdown of Germany's 19 nuclear power plants.

Fischer's greatest challenge was to reconcile the Greens' antiestablishment roots with a yearning to prove that they are capable of serving as responsible ruling partners. He labored to keep his party unified behind the NATO bombing of Yugoslavia to stop ethnic cleansing in Kosovo. He argued that Germany had emerged from World War II with two firm convictions: "never again war" and "never again Auschwitz." Recognizing the contradiction, he reasoned that, in order to prevent crimes against humanity, Germany must sometimes be prepared to put aside its pacifism, which runs deep in German society and especially in the Green Party.

Not all of his party comrades agreed. In a raucous special party conference called in May 1999 to discuss a bombing halt in Kosovo, Fischer was pelted so hard by

Germany

**Former leader of the Greens
Joschka Fischer**

red paint that he suffered a perforated eardrum. A human chain tried to block delegates' entry into the hall, and posters depicted Fischer and Schröder with Hitler-style mustaches. Stink bombs were set off in the arena, fights for control of the microphone broke out, and one man strolled naked in front of the dais to mock the leaders' efforts to maintain some decorum. Fischer was decried as a "warmonger."

In the 2002 elections, the Greens ran on little else than Fischer's popularity. He was an effective foreign minister, and he tried hard to maintain good ties with the United States when it was not popular in Germany to do so. Although he and Schröder actually campaigned together, a first in German elections and a practice that was not repeated in 2005, he was more careful in his language about Iraq and the partnership with the United States. The Greens' votes in 2002 leaped by 30% to 8.6% and 55 seats. As usual, the Greens performed better in the west.

The Greens entered the September 2005 elections uncertain of its future role in federal politics. The party did well, winning 8.1% of the votes overall and 51 seats. It was no longer an overwhelmingly western party, winning 5.1% of the votes in the east (up .4%) compared with 8.8% in the west (down .6%). It entered the opposition. This was particularly satisfying to the Fundis in the party. Fischer vacated his Bundestag seat and accepted a visiting professorship at Princeton University.

Leading the party into the 2009 federal elections were Claudia Roth (1955–) and the first German party chairman with an immigrant background Cem Özdemir (1965–), a Realo. His Turkish parents had come as guest workers. Because of his youth (early 40s) and good looks, some party members called him the "Green Obama."

By 2011 its popularity had soared to about 20% nationally. It performed very well in *Land* elections and was leaving the other small parties behind. In the past, the Greens were almost always on the political left. However, many of its voters have become well-to-do city dwellers with lots of education. For them, coalitions with the CDU/CSU or FDP are no longer unthinkable. Its anticapitalist wing has largely disappeared. They entered the 2013 federal elections riding high, with polls showing that the party could win a fifth of the votes. Its electoral collapse was a shock. It won only 8.4% of the votes (down by 2.3%) and 63 seats, a loss of 5. The party leaders were swept out.

The Greens have become an establishment party and no longer appeal to voters outside the political mainstream who feel unrepresented and dissatisfied with the established parties. It has become a sensible center-left alternative to the SPD. It is centrist on economic issues and leftist on social issues, such as the environment, feminism, and immigration. That is why it appeals to young and female voters. It has reenergized the left.

The Greens gained ground in the 2017 elections, winning 8.9% of the votes (up by .5%) and 67 seats, a gain of 4. They offered to form a governing coalition with Merkel and the FDP, but the Free Democrats rejected that possibility. The Greens have become the third-largest party behind the CDU and SPD. In 2021 they won 14.8% of the votes and 118 seats. They entered the governing coalition. This means that the government will make environmental protection a high priority.

Cem Özdemir, Green cochair

Right-Wing Parties

The biggest surprise in the 2013 federal elections was the lightning rise of the Alternative for Germany (AfD) Party, which had been created only in April, five months before the election. It came within a whisker of winning seats in the Bundestag, capturing 4.7% of the votes. Party cofounder Bernd Lucke (1962–), a Hamburg University economics professor, swore that the party was not "right-wing." It advocates a decentralized, less bureaucratic European Union. It favors the dissolution of the eurozone and retention of the common currency only by fiscally responsible countries, such as Germany. It also called for more direct democracy with Swiss-style plebiscites, prohibiting same-sex marriage, curbs on immigration, and pension guarantees. The years 2014–2015 brought impressive electoral success—it won 7% of the European Parliament votes, 9.8% in Saxony, 10.6% in Thuringia, 12.2% in Brandenburg, and 7.4% in Hamburg, entering state parliaments for the first time.

In the summer of 2015, Lucke and his liberal-conservative antieuro group were ousted from the party by a faction supporting another cofounder, Frauke Petry (1975–), a chemist and a mother of four who was a dynamic leader not afraid to steer AfD far toward the right. The focus of AfD narrowed accordingly—it started talking almost exclusively about refugee issues.

By May 2017, AfD won seats in 13 of Germany's 16 state parliaments. In Saxony-Anhalt in the east, it came in second, with 24.2% of votes, or nearly as much as the third and fourth parties (SPD and the Left) combined. An unusual coalition of the CDU, SPD, and the Greens had to be hastily created to keep the Alternative out of the state's government. As the refugee crisis abated by mid-2017, the party lost some of its appeal. However, it remained in a good position to clear the 5% threshold during the parliamentary elections in September of that year, therefore becoming the first right-wing party in post-World War II Germany to enter the Bundestag. It succeeded dramatically, capturing 12.6% of the votes (up by 7.9%) and 92 seats. It won 25% in the east.

In 2021 the AfD received 10.3% of the votes and 82 seats. It remained in the opposition. Voters resisted the voices of nationalism and populism.

There is little doubt that AfD's popularity reflects the growing uneasiness over the massive wave of migrants entering Germany. Petry caused an uproar with a comment that German border guards "must prevent illegal border crossings and even use firearms if necessary." At its congress in April and May 2016, the party

Germany

stunned Germany by capturing 9.2% of the votes and 10 seats for the state parliament in its electoral fortress of Saxony. In the 2009 state elections, it retained eight seats.

Every February 13 it mobilizes 6,000 demonstrators in Dresden to protest the terrible bombing of that city in 1945, which it describes as a "bombing Holocaust." Its deputies in the Saxon parliament walked out of the chamber during a ceremony to honor the victims of Auschwitz, saying they would only honor German war victims. The intelligence service considers the party to be "racist, anti-Semitic, and revisionist," aiming to destroy democracy in order to create a Fourth Reich. Nevertheless, one voter in four in Saxony considers it to be a "normal" party. It worries about the large number of its voters who are migrating to the AfD.

It has found a fertile recruiting ground—the unorganized young skinheads and neo-Nazis linked to a wave of far-right violence. About half of those violent crimes occur in the east, the only part of Germany where the NDP thrives. It has modernized its strategy by no longer seeking merely to defend the Third Reich. It has broadened its appeal to resist global capitalism and to oppose Türkiye's entry into the EU and labor-market reforms. It has also sprung beyond the skinhead scene to find a place in the world of youth music.

In 1992 the government outlawed six neo-Nazi groups, including German Alternative, which was involved in antiforeigner violence. In 1995 it banned the small, militant Free German Workers' Party. The German cabinet asked the Constitutional Court in 2000 to ban the NPD. However, that effort failed in 2003, when the Constitutional Court refused to hear the case because the government had cited as evidence inflammatory statements and writings by party members who turned out to be paid informants of state security services. A 2005 poll revealed that 73% of Germans supported a ban on the NPD. In 2009 the German Youth Faithful to the Homeland was banned for spreading Nazi propaganda to young people after two other far-right organizations had been banned the year before.

The scores of right-wing nationalist and neo-Nazi groups do not follow one leader. But they are better organized, more dangerous, and in closer contact with each other than most Germans had thought they were. Their effect on Germany's international image can be devastating despite their electoral impotence. That is a major reason the federal government introduced legislation in 2005 banning far-right demonstrations at Holocaust memorial sites and at the commemorations of the end of World War II.

East German Trabant atop a remnant of the Berlin Wall

adopted an anti-Muslim platform, calling for a ban on minarets, calls to prayer, and burqas and directly contradicting former president Wulff's and Angela Merkel's statements by declaring that "Islam is not part of Germany." Josef Schuster, president of the Central Council of Jews in Germany, accused AfD of attacking Judaism and violating the constitution. It routinely attacks the press and questions the principles of liberal democracy. In 2019 it became the first party in postwar history to come under surveillance of the country's intelligence agency as a threat to democracy.

Its popularity is surging. It enjoys particularly strong support among men and appeals to the same segment of the population as Pegida (Patriotic Europeans against the Islamization of the West), an adamantly anti-Islamic movement based in Dresden.

Almost all Pegida supporters vote AfD. Some 25,000 took to the streets in early 2015. Continuous demonstrations led to clashes of supporters and opponents of the movement that erupt especially in eastern states. Pegida's coleader Lutz Bachman (1973–) temporarily stepped down after he posed on social media dressed as Hitler. He later went on trial in Dresden on charges of incitement. At the time some polls indicated that as many as 60% of Germans thought that Islam does not belong in their country.

Germany has witnessed a strengthening of parties on the far right, a development that causes anxiety in both the FRG and abroad. They range from illegal neo-Nazi groups to legal parties that feed on myriad dissatisfactions, including hostility toward immigrants, tight housing, high unemployment, globalization, and rising crime. Some Germans bemoan what they see as a breakdown in law and order caused by the leftist alternative subculture. The domestic intelligence service estimated in 2008 that there are 4,400 neo-Nazis in Germany.

The Republicans claim to be a nationalist, not a neo-Nazi party. But in 1992 the government ordered intelligence surveillance of it to determine if it is antidemocratic. It found a warm reception in western Berlin, where more than 10% of the population is foreign. The Turks living there constitute the largest Turkish community outside of Türkiye. The Republicans call for repatriation of foreign workers in stages and for tough measures to stem the flow of asylum seekers into the FRG, noting, "a multiracial society is a red flag to our party." Its image has been tarnished by unpopular skinhead violence against foreigners, including the American national sledding team in the eastern German city of Oberhof. The Republicans' .2% showing in the 2013 Bundestag elections demonstrated its electoral irrelevance.

The same cannot always be said of the National Democratic Party of Germany (NPD), Germany's oldest neo-Nazi party and a refuge for unreconstructed Nazis. It is more conservative than the Republicans and won 1.3% of the votes in the 2013 federal elections and no Bundestag seats. Its headquarters are in eastern Berlin, and the party has 6,000 members. In 2004 it

Germany

The Constitutional Court determined that the right to assembly does not apply to groups glorifying Hitler's regime.

In 2011 the suicide of two bank robbers about to be captured by the police in the eastern German city of Eisenach led to the solving of a hate-filled killing spree from 2000 to 2006 of eight Turkish men, one Greek man, and one German policewoman. The murder weapons and much more evidence, including a propaganda video and a hit list containing 88 names, were found in the charred remains of an apartment in Zwickau occupied by a group calling itself the Nationalist Socialist Underground. Police authorities admitted that they had mishandled the case and estimated that 25,000 belong to far-right groups, of which 9,500 could be violent. They figured that at least 137 people, mostly foreigners, had been killed by right-wing extremists since unification in 1990. This is far more than the victims of radical leftist or Islamic groups on which the police have focused. Members of the Bundestag stood in mourning silence, and Chancellor Merkel apologized to the families, calling the killings "an attack on our country."

German authorities struggle to contain the wave of right-wing activism and banned at last nine such groups between 2012 and early 2016, often seizing their weapons and neo-Nazi paraphernalia, and closing one related web portal. Nevertheless, many more remain active and even conduct violent attacks, such as the bombings of refugee shelters in Freital near Dresden.

In May 2016 a right-wing publisher announced its plan to publish Adolf Hitler's *Mein Kampf*. Unlike the scholarly yet still controversial annotated edition issued earlier that year, Der Schelm (Rogue) Publishing declared that its version would be "an unabridged edition without the good

guy comments." The Bavarian government, which up to 2015 owned the copyright to the book and used it to prevent the book's reissue in Germany, threatened to use Germany's antisedition laws because of its potential for racial incitement.

The serious threat posed by a radical far-right group was demonstrated in December 2022. The "Reich Citizens" hatched a plan to storm the Bundestag and overthrow the democratic government. The ringleader, a minor nobleman—Heinrich XIII Prince Reuss—was to be installed as the new head of state. He was among 25 members arrested. The group numbers 21,000.

A Past That Is Not Past

The American novelist William Faulkner once wrote, "the past is never dead. It is not even past." This is certainly true for Germany today. More than a half-century after World War II ended, the government had to decide on a Holocaust memorial in the heart of Berlin close to the Brandenburg Gate. After much emotional debate, it was agreed that there would be a toned-down memorial with a wall-shaped library containing 1 million books, and a research center for scholars. Designed by New York-based architect Peter Eisenman, the memorial is an undulating field of 2,711 concrete slabs the size of two football fields.

Before the memorial could be completed, controversy erupted again. It was learned that the material to be used as an antigraffiti coating on the 2,751 concrete slabs to prevent swastikas or other neo-Nazi slogans from being spray-painted on them was produced by a German chemical company, Degussa, which had once owned the firm (Degasch) that had produced the Zyklon B gas used to murder Jews in the concentration camps. After much soul-searching discussion, the product was approved. The memorial opened to the public on May 10, 2005. It is a red flag to

neo-Nazis, and only federal law prohibiting right-wing demonstrations near Holocaust memorials keeps them away.

The Schröder government had to confront the multibillion-dollar demands to compensate foreign laborers who had been forced to work for German companies during the war. A settlement was finally reached in 2000, whereby Germany would create a special foundation that will pay up to $5 billion to nearly 1 million forced laborers. Each receives payments of between $2,500 and $7,500.

In 1999, a chastened Chancellor Schröder reflected on whether his generation has a different attitude about the Holocaust: "No. This event will always influence the way German politicians think and act. Even if one says there is no such thing as collective guilt, it is still our task to see to it that people remember what happened because by remembering we can assure it will not happen again." Such remembering remains part of Germany's future. In a mutual act of reconciliation, Schröder joined other leaders in Normandy in June 2004 to commemorate the 60th anniversary of the D-Day invasion. A 2005 poll revealed that 80% of Germans now see May 8, 1945, as a day of liberation, not of surrender.

In 2008 additional memorials were dedicated in Berlin that honor others in the broad spectrum of victims. In January ground was broken on the long-delayed Topography of Terror center at the site of the former Gestapo and SS headquarters; it is now completed. April 2008 saw the unveiling of a memorial and documentation center concerning Germans forcibly expelled from central and eastern Europe after World War II. This had antagonized numerous countries, especially Poland, which argued that this was an attempt to rewrite history and mitigate German war crimes.

However, Germany was still prosecuting perpetrators of war crimes in 2010. In March a former SS soldier, Heinrich Boere, was convicted of killing three Dutch resistance fighters. Court proceedings also began in November 2009 against 89-year-old John Demjanjuk, charged with aiding in the murder of 27,900 Jews. He was a former Red Army soldier captured by the Germans and recruited for concentration camp duty. After the war he fled to America and worked as an auto worker before being extradited to Germany in May 2009. Because of the age of the defendants, these may be the last such trials. One German newspaper called the men "fragile, doddering and deaf."

In May 2008, a memorial dedicated to gay men and lesbians persecuted and killed during Nazi rule and located on the edge of the Tiergarten near the Jewish memorial was inaugurated. It features a concrete slab with a window that shows clips

Holocaust Memorial in Berlin

Germany

of men kissing and women kissing alternating every two years. Klaus Wowereit, Berlin mayor (2001–2014), who is gay, attended the ceremony. Only one month earlier, the former Kochstrasse was renamed Rudi-Dutschke- Strasse (street) after the leftist student leader in the 1968 student rebellion who was assassinated.

The FRG: A Stable Democracy

The significance of problems facing the established political parties in the wake of unification should not be exaggerated. The FRG has weathered many serious problems in the past—moral, political, and economic regeneration after 1945; a student rebellion in the late 1960s; urban terrorism; fundamental political changes, such as the Eastern Treaties; and the economic shocks of the 1970s.

The democratic order of the FRG has over the years earned and received a reservoir of goodwill from its citizens to help it survive serious crises. This springs not from the actual constitutional structures but from Germans' political attitudes. That is, it depends on the political culture—those political ways of thinking that provide the basis for a workable political system. The FRG has become more than a fair-weather democracy that would collapse quickly if confronted with a crisis.

One sometimes heard of radical criticism of "bourgeois society" and of the allegedly "pseudo democratic" and "illegitimate" political order. Such criticism was very audible and was also scribbled on the walls. Yet, there was and is no "legitimacy crisis" in Germany. During its entire existence as a state, it has not faced a single truly serious challenge to its legitimacy; this stands in stark contrast to the Weimar Republic, which was born into such a crisis and never extricated itself from it. It made remarkable strides to win the approval and support of its citizens.

Sensible observation of Germany, combined with an examination of relevant public opinion surveys, indicates that the German political culture had changed considerably since 1945 and that it is a stable and democratic country with a politically interested, informed, involved and tolerant citizenry. Immediately after the war, after excessive political mobilization and propaganda under Hitler, Germans tended to withdraw from public affairs and to seek refuge in private and family circles. Now Germans still appreciate that comfort zone but are no less active in public or political affairs than their counterparts in such older democracies as the US and the Netherlands. In terms of voting, they are even more active than those counterparts. Germany has been accurately described as a country that has a strong and activist civil society and a relatively weak

German soldiers arriving in Mogadishu, 1993

Courtesy: *German Information Center, New York*

state. More and more direct democracy, involving referenda and citizen initiatives, is practiced on the state and local levels.

A few facts help demonstrate Germans' overall satisfaction with their regime, at least in the western part. In 1951, 90% of all adult West Germans believed that Germany had been better off during an earlier German regime, and a third even favored restoration of the Hohenzollern monarchy. By 1976, however, 90% thought they were better off under the present scheme, and almost no one wanted the restoration of the monarchy. This was due to many western citizens' positive experience under democracy. Their country has had a high level of accomplishment. Prosperity and the expanded social welfare system smoothed class conflicts and allowed all groups in the society more benefits from the system and a greater opportunity to advance.

Germany is a functioning democracy in which only a small percentage of Germans are asking whether it should remain a democracy. In a 2007 Spiegel poll, only among eastern Germans over the age of 35 was there a majority that admitted to being "little" or "not at all" satisfied with the way democracy is practiced in Germany today. The criticism that Germans have become very materialistic is certainly valid. But while materialism might be rejected in principle (but seldom in practice) by some leftists and intellectuals, it has no doubt

made Germany far more governable and respected as a political democracy.

FOREIGN AND DEFENSE POLICY

The FRG became more independent and critical of the US, and it is more willing to side with its European allies on some issues. It is less restrained by the embarrassing German past and has been confronted with a diminution of Russian, French, and British power in Europe. Also, Washington was absorbed during the 1960s and early 1970s with Vietnam and a new relationship with the Soviet Union and the People's Republic of China. The FRG increasingly shouldered political responsibilities and exercised diplomatic flexibility throughout the world. Because of its past, the FRG prefers a low-key, quieter diplomacy, which would be least likely to arouse fear or envy in other countries. For the first time in its history, Germany has clearly defined borders not disputed by any nation. It has neither destabilizing minorities abroad nor any claims to former German territories. The cliche that the FRG was an "economic giant and a political dwarf" is outdated.

In his first policy statement in the all- German Bundestag, ex-chancellor Kohl pledged that "there is no comfortable niche in international politics for us Germans, and we must not shirk our responsibility." The united nation would,

269

Germany

he promised, not be a "restless Reich." A new Germany in a new kind of Europe has emerged, and it is realistic that the continent's largest and richest democracy bears more responsibility in a world. This is not a role Germany seeks but one that is thrust upon it.

The new Germany displayed its willingness to use its new political clout in 1991, when it muscled its EU partners to recognize the independence of the Yugoslav republics of Slovenia and Croatia, despite serious misgivings in London, Paris, Washington, and the UN. It was especially noteworthy that Bonn did not even reply to a formal US request to withhold such recognition. Uncomfortable with bad feelings that unilateral action caused, Germany was careful to get allied backing before recognizing North Macedonia in 1993, a move Greece bitterly opposed.

Germany and the First Gulf War, 1991

Germany dealt clumsily with its first test as a strengthened power. When fighting broke out in the Persian Gulf on January 17, 1991, it took a week for the government to show solidarity with its allies. The fear that Germany would be dragged into the war by joining a defense of Türkiye, one of Germany's NATO allies, prompted the government to insist that it would not become involved. No other ally had disputed Türkiye's right to be defended by the full force of NATO.

While it was paralyzed, opponents of the war efforts took over in the streets and denounced the US and Iraq both as aggressors. "Say no!" and "No blood for oil," read the posters. The mayor of tiny Pfedelbach in the Black Forest was forced to withdraw his invitation to General Norman Schwarzkopf to visit the town from where his ancestors came when angry antiwar residents branded the war hero as a "mass murderer." An exasperated finance minister, Theo Waigel, exclaimed, "Again and again we see a misconceived pacifism which does not restore peace but puts up with the aggressor!" The *Frankfurter Allgemeine Zeitung* agreed: "What distinguishes the Germans from other peoples is not that they fear war, but that they fear war more than they love freedom." Polls a few days after hostilities commenced revealed that four out of five Germans indeed agreed with the allies' war effort and were critical of the anti-American rallies, but three out of four opposed German participation in the war.

After regaining its composure, the Kohl government acted decisively by criticizing the "one-eyed" protestors, cracking down on firms breaking its arms export laws, and sending emissaries to Israel. It agreed to deliver weapons, including Patriot missiles, to the Jewish state, violating Germany's long-standing policy of not sending weapons into "areas of tension."

The German government went even farther, crossing some important thresholds: It dispatched 1,000 soldiers to Türkiye, equipped with 18 fighter aircraft and Roland and Hawk missiles, to protect NATO airbases. This was the first time since World War II that German military forces had been sent abroad in response to a threat of war. It also sent 2,200 naval forces with minesweepers and frigates to the eastern Mediterranean and offered more than $11 billion to aid the allies. It served as the hub of the resupply effort; provided doctors for allied military hospitals in Germany, freeing allied doctors to serve in the gulf; and gave precision-guided weapons and vehicles to its allies for use there. It gave the US Army alone 1.000 vehicles, including Czech-made tank transporters, which former East German soldiers had to instruct the Americans how to use.

Arguing after the conclusion of hostilities for the need to render humanitarian aid to the war's victims and to open up the Persian Gulf to free trade, Germany sent 2.000 troops and airlifted assets to Iran to help Kurdish refugees, as well as minesweepers to the gulf to help clear out Iraqi mines. Although these measures met with almost no protest in the FRG, it emerged from the crisis damaged by the charges that it had shown ingratitude for the diplomatic help it had received to achieve unification and had let its allies down in time of emergency.

The Right to Deploy Abroad

Kohl's intention to amend the constitution to allow Germany to join in international coalitions was successfully blocked by the SPD; it refused to allow *Bundeswehr* troops to participate in anything more than UN peacekeeping forces. Germany seeks a permanent seat on the UN Security Council, not for itself, but for the EU. In 1992 it sent three spotter aircraft and a naval destroyer to help enforce the UN sanctions against Serbia and Montenegro, and it sent a *Bundeswehr* unit with a UN mission to Cambodia, where Germans suffered their first fatality since joining peacekeeping operations. In 1993 it assisted in the American airlift of humanitarian aid to Bosnia. That same year the Constitutional Court ruled in a landmark decision that it was not unconstitutional for German airmen to serve in AWACS reconnaissance planes supporting NATO enforcement of a no-fly zone over Bosnia. They became the first *Bundeswehr* soldiers to take part in a potential combat mission since 1945.

In 1993 the FRG dispatched 1,700 troops to join the UN effort in Somalia; these were the first German soldiers to serve in Africa since General Rommel's *Afrikakorps* in World War II. In 1994 the Constitutional Court ruled that German troops may join military ventures abroad as long as they are acting under the aegis of the United Nations or another international group (such as NATO) to which Germany belongs and provided that a majority in the lower house of parliament approves. In 1995 the FRG dispatched 14 Tornado fighter jets for duty over Bosnia. This was the first German combat unit deployed since 1945. It also sent peacekeeping forces to help implement the Bosnian peace agreement later in the year. Each of these "out-of-area" operations was subjected to intense and emotional debate within Germany. But when the government agreed to commit 3,000 troops, including armored infantry, to the 30,000-soldier Stabilization Force in Bosnia in 1997, almost no one in Germany raised any objection. The Social Democrats and Greens, then in the opposition, backed the plan.

Germany is cautiously but steadily overcoming its postwar aversion to the use of military force. From 1990 to 2015 it conducted 44 military deployments overseas. In 2019 it had 3,500 soldiers engaged in 11 foreign deployments, including Mali and Afghanistan. Its 650 troops in Lithuania serve as a "trip-wire" force. With the Balkans as a testing ground, the *Bundeswehr*'s emergence as an international intervention force helped to diminish Germany's subordinate role within NATO. When the alliance launched an air war against Yugoslavia in the spring of 1999 to stop brutal ethnic cleansing in Kosovo, Germany was a full participant. It sent eight combat aircraft and a warship, and it dispatched several thousand troops to neighboring North Macedonia, where in 2002 it had 586 peacekeepers deployed. This was the first time since World War II that Germany engaged in warfare against a sovereign state.

In former chancellor Schröder's words, "we are trying to contain the ongoing human catastrophe—to stop the killings and deportations. . . NATO has to win this military conflict." It assigned 6,000 troops to KFOR (down to 2,500 in 2011), which helped maintain the peace in Kosovo. The total of 44,000 soldiers from 35 different nations were commanded in 1999–2000 by German general Klaus Reinhardt, a scholarly man with a doctorate in history who completed some of his military education in the United States.

According to opinion polls, most Germans agreed with the military action in Kosovo. One survey even suggested that a stunning 90% of young Germans aged 18 to 24 supported NATO. But there was a clear split between western Germans and those in the east: 64% in the west back the bombing, compared with only 40% in the east. The PDS was the only major political party that opposed the war. The war over Kosovo helped Germans, who emerged from the Third Reich with a powerful aversion to any use of force, to cross a large and significant psychological boundary.

Only less than a decade earlier, former SPD leader Oskar Lafontaine had said in reference to the Persian Gulf War that requesting Germans to take part in any military action was "like offering brandy chocolates to a reformed alcoholic." But Volkmar Schultz, a member of the Bundestag's foreign relations committee, said that that was over: "We have reached the end of the postwar period in German history. We cannot automatically run away from military action. Since 11 September most of the political class in Germany accepts this as an unavoidable fact."

There are limits. Any hint that Germany's troops are fighting to support the country's economic interests is unacceptable to a population so ambivalent about war. This imprecision prompted the resignation in May 2010 of President Horst Köhler. It took courage for former defense minister zu Guttenberg to call the conflict in Afghanistan a "war" and the German soldiers fighting there "heroes."

At one of the many public demonstrations in Germany supporting the United States in its hour of crisis, President Johannes Rau (1931—2006) said, "No one knows better than the people here in Berlin what America has done for freedom and democracy in Germany. Therefore, we say to all Americans from Berlin: America does not stand alone." The first person ever convicted of aiding the September 11 hijackers was convicted in a German court.

Germany's willingness to support a military effort on the other side of the globe in Afghanistan in 2001–2002 was a sensation, but it followed a steady development since 1994 to shed the country's postwar psychological and constitutional inhibitions about using military force for anything but territorial defense. After cliff-hanging negotiations and threats within his governing SPD-Green coalition and supported by 59% of the German population, Schröder committed 3,900 troops to the war effort. It sent three transport planes to Incerlik Air Force Base in Türkiye to support operations in Afghanistan, as well as 2 frigates and escort vessels with up to 1,800 sailors to patrol the waters off the east coast of Africa. Berlin offered up to 800 soldiers to operate Fuchs armored vehicles equipped to check soil for nuclear, chemical, and biological contamination; 250 troops for evacuating wounded; 500 troops for air and ground transport; and 92 of its total of 1,000 special forces (KSK).

German soldiers fought in Afghanistan, even though they were not deployed in the more dangerous southern part. It removed some of the troops' limitations. As of 2014, 54 soldiers had been killed, among the lowest casualties in NATO. In 2003 Germany and the Netherlands assumed command of all peacekeepers in Kabul. In 2007 the German government dispatched six Tornado reconnaissance jets to Afghanistan to provide support for NATO and for its own troops there (retained in 2014 at 3,100). It repeatedly extended its commitment, although about two-thirds of public opinion had swung against the mission. Withdrawal began in 2011. Some soldiers stayed to train Afghan forces. Only the Left Party demanded an immediate withdrawal. By the time Germany exited from Afghanistan in 2021, 150,000 *Bundeswehr* troops had served there.

Germany also deployed 126 soldiers in Termes, Uzbekistan, from which it supplies its men and women in Afghanistan. After the US was expelled from Uzbekistan in 2005, the future of that base became uncertain. Berlin ordered about 1,500 naval forces to the Horn of Africa and the coast off Kenya. In 2011 it had sent 1,400 naval forces to defend against piracy off the Somali coast; 350 remained by 2014. Its soldiers train Somali troops in Uganda, and it has small contingents in Congo, Djibouti, and Kenya. It also deployed 880, many of them naval forces, to Lebanon to try to stabilize that country after a brief war in the summer of 2006; by 2011 those had been reduced to 300. It has had 800 troops in Kosovo, 900 in Bosnia and Herzegovina, 50 in Darfur, and 700 in the Mediterranean as part of NATO's Active Endeavour. It contributes to the air defense of the Turkish border with Syria. It broke a long-standing taboo against sending arms into conflict zones by providing weapons to Iraqi Kurds. Its largest overseas deployment was in Mali. Its troops head a NATO "tripwire" force in Lithuania.

By 2014 it had approximately 5,000 soldiers deployed on foreign peacekeeping and antiterror missions. Ex-President Gauck criticized Germans who "use Germany's past guilt as a shield for laziness or a desire to disengage from the world." Some want to make the German army more active abroad, although 62% of her countrymen oppose that. It is severely hampered by a dangerously low defense budget (1.3% of GDP), which has caused the maintenance of much of its weaponry to be neglected. Since 2015 its defense budget has risen.

In addition to these military assets, Germany granted generous humanitarian aid, including $28 million for the American victims of the terrorist attacks donated by individuals and corporations in Germany. Finally, Germany hosted a UN-sponsored political summit in 2001 in the famous Petersberg Hotel overlooking Bonn, which

German protest against war in Afghanistan

brought together representatives of the many Afghan factions to discuss the formation of a post-Taliban regime and government. The German government played an active and supportive role in helping achieve an agreement. For instance, then-foreign minister Joschka Fischer phoned the leader in Kabul temporarily recognized by the UN, Burhanuddin Rabbani, who was dragging his heals, to remind him that the billions of dollars in promised international aid to Afghanistan would not be released until a broad-based government were in place.

The years 2009–2010 brought rude reminders that German soldiers were engaging in warfare, not merely serving as peacekeepers and development personnel in Afghanistan. Just days before the 2009 federal elections, a German commander called in airstrikes against Taliban forces, only to learn later that many of civilians had also perished. The bombing was especially delicate since it was the deadliest action by German troops since World War II. Because of the way he handled the incident, Defense Minister Franz Josef Jung was forced to resign. His replacement, Karl-Theodor zu Guttenberg, then fired the most senior general, Wolfgang

Germany

Schneiderhan. Chancellor Merkel called this regrettable occurrence "a combat mission," and the government properly calls its activity in Afghanistan "war."

The War in Iraq

The 2003 Anglo-American war in Iraq showed to what extent Germany, under Chancellor Schröder, had begun to assert itself more in foreign affairs. Some German politicians and diplomats were appalled by the strident tone and style of his diplomacy over Iraq, although many were convinced that he had been right to stand up to the US on this matter. In 2010 official documents revealed that, on a visit to Washington on January 31, 2002, over a year before the outbreak of war, President Bush had told Schröder of his intention to topple Saddam Hussein. The chancellor's reply was that, if he intended to do that, he should carry it out as quickly and decisively as possible. Never did the US ask that German troops be sent to Iraq.

Schröder's later refusal to participate in any war and to sign up to any UN resolution that permitted military action was also supported by an overwhelming percentage of his countrymen. Polls at the time revealed that, while 90% of German respondents thought the United States would continue to be an important partner, three-fourths believed that the US has "too much power," and over half went so far as to consider it a greater threat to world peace than even Saddam Hussein's Iraq or North Korea. Schröder himself said his firm policy was part of his country's

"coming of age," its "emancipation." For the first time, it dared oppose the US on a really important issue.

Germany, which began a two-year stint on the UN Security Council in January 2003, teamed with France, which saw an opportunity to limit US power and influence in Europe, to lead the resistance to the war. They both quickly discovered that although most Europeans on the street agreed with their opposition to war in Iraq, their attempt to unify European governments behind their lead backfired and actually divided Europe. Official support of the transatlantic link remained very strong, especially in the new democracies in eastern and central Europe. A majority of European governments did not appreciate what they saw as a Franco-German attempt to isolate the US in the name of Europe.

Germany nevertheless provided the United States with more indirect support than most other allies. It assigned 2,500 of its soldiers to special security duties guarding US bases in Germany, thereby freeing about 5,000 American soldiers. German armed forces helped the US ready and move its armored units out to Emden and Bremerhaven for shipment to Iraq. The US military was granted unlimited use of installations and of Germany's airspace in order to support allied forces in Iraq and the Persian Gulf area. Germany dispatched a chemical and biological detection unit to Kuwait, sent troops to operate Patriot missile batteries in Türkiye, and permitted its soldiers to serve in AWACS aircraft missions north of the war zone to protect Türkiye. In 2004 it offered a hand to the struggling Iraq by writing off about 80% of that country's debt to Germany; this amounted to $5 billion. In 2005 it also expanded to about 250 the number of Iraqi security forces it trains in the United Arab Emirates (UAE). It also agreed to send €70 million in assistance.

In the aftermath of the 2003 Iraq war, Germany and France joined with Belgium and Luxembourg to create a joint rapid-reaction unit built on the existing 5.000-strong French-German brigade, which has never been used. The four said they would set up a multinational head-quarters and a separate military center in Belgium to command and plan EU military operations when NATO is not involved. They invited other European nations to join their effort, but sensing that its real purpose was indeed to weaken the transatlantic alliance, none did. The four found themselves isolated in Europe, and they abandoned the plan. However, in June 2004 Britain joined with France and Germany to create the EU's first planning cell and to speed up the creation of effective rapid-reaction

"No blood for Hussein and Bush"—2003

units. Based in Brussels, the planning cell was used by the EU to back up its takeover from NATO of the 12.000-stron mission in Bosnia in 2004.

Franco-German Collaboration

In January 2013 the two neighbors, Germany and France, who are each other's most important trading partners, celebrated the 50th anniversary of the Treaty on German-French Cooperation. The 40th was remembered in grand style. President Jacques Chirac and Schröder met at the Elysee Palace, and 603 German parliamentarians joined 577 counterparts in the palace of Versailles. The next day, the two leaders met in Berlin. In their Elysee Declaration, the two leaders agreed to increase the frequency of their special meetings to every six weeks; to appoint in each other's capital a "secretary-general for Franco-German cooperation" who would coordinate, prepare, and follow up their common European policies; to dispatch the relevant minister to the other country's cabinet meetings when discussing a subject of interest to the other; and to propose common Franco-German legislation to each other's parliaments. They hope that such integration at the top, along with partner relationships between cities and combined military units, will help warm their citizens' hearts toward the other.

France made an important gesture to Germany by inviting Schröder to the 60th anniversary of the D-Day invasion in June 2004. He was the first German leader to attend the celebration, and he interpreted the invitation as a sign that, "the postwar period is finally over" and that as a "tested democracy, we can now be accepted by the former Allies as a full-fledged partner whose foundations lie in the same fundamental values." At the same time, he felt obligated to say, "We Germans know that we unleashed this heinous war. We recognize the responsibility our history has laid upon us, and we take it seriously." Remembering that his own father was killed four months after D-Day, he noted that the German people also suffered in the war.

On November 11, 2009, Merkel became the first German leader to commemorate on French soil Armistice Day ending World War I. She was invited to the Arc de Triomphe in Paris for a full military ceremony, where she publicly held hands with French president Nicholas Sarkozy. She said in her speech, "When there is antagonism between us, everybody loses. When we are united, everybody wins." Sarkozy called for "an ever-closer association of French and German policies." He well

understood that the special relationship between the two countries had traditionally multiplied French influence in Europe and the world. A deepening of their relationship could make Europe "one of the principal players of the 21st century," as he told his ambassadors. Merkel was more cautious of such grandiose statements.

The reality is that French and Germans are not particularly attracted toward each other. One can see that in the choice of languages schoolchildren take. Fewer than 1 million French secondary pupils learn German; 9% learn German as a first foreign language and 14% as a second. Only 5% of German children are still learning French in their final year. Nevertheless, polls in both countries indicate that the strengthened Franco-German relationship rests on popular approval.

However, as transatlantic tensions cooled down in 2004, more and more German foreign policy specialists had second thoughts about the notion that France and Germany should be a counterweight to the US. Germany had always sought to prevent France from transforming the EU into an instrument of French policy against the US. German foreign policy swung back to its traditional position of equidistance between France and America, of being a counterweight to the French dream of being a "counterweight" to the United States. Many German analysts began again to

regard close Franco-German relations as necessary but not sufficient for an effective foreign policy.

French president Sarkozy seemed to agree, writing in his autobiography, "If the Franco-German understanding is still necessary, it is not a strong enough motor for Europe today." For the partnership to work well, there have to be good personal and working relationships at the top, and that is lacking. Sarkozy and Merkel were known to get on each other's nerves. They had different temperaments and leadership styles. Sarkozy was impulsive and wanted the credit for actions that he often took unilaterally and without consultation. The physicist Merkel weighed arguments and assembled allies before deciding. The Germans' main rules were "no surprises" and "nobody wins" in the Franco-German relationship. Sarkozy played by different rules. As a French diplomat put it, "Franco-German co-operation is hard work. We are very different. There is nothing natural to it and yet it works."

The continent-wide debate on a new EU constitutional treaty in 2005 revealed that the two partners were going in different directions. While the Bundestag ratified the constitution on May 28, French voters turned it down a day later. Thoughtful Germans realize that, in the enlarged EU of 28 states, Franco-German agreement is no longer sufficient to determine EU

Germany

SM
B Gemäldegalerie
Staatliche Museen
zu Berlin

Poesie des Augenblicks

Meisterwerke der französischen
Genremalerei im Zeitalter von
Watteau Chardin Fragonard

French painting visits Germany

policy and move the union ahead. France is not in a position to lead, and because of its history, Germany must be careful about stepping forward as Europe's leader. But there can be little doubt that on economic issues Germany now dominates.

The euro crisis over Greek debts exposed a wide rift in the two countries' economic philosophies. Germany wanted strict rules on budget deficits with tough penalties. The crisis, one of the most serious in EU history, highlighted Germany's changing attitude toward the EU. It no longer thought automatically that what was good for the EU was good for Germany. Its government asserted its national interests more forcefully, as France and Britain have always done.

This signaled a subtle shift in the balance of power toward Germany and away from France. It is based on Germany's economic superiority. Germany tends to get what it demands in the EU. Nothing is decided or gets done without its agreement. This preponderance is by default, not by choice; Germany is strong chiefly because the rest of the EU is weak. The euro crisis strengthened Germany's position even further. Nevertheless, it is still important for it to come to a common policy with France before EU summits. This perception of equality protects Germany from being accused of unilateralism, dictating to its allies, or trying to dominate Europe. French approval strengthens its initiatives. There is the usual paradox—When the two governments disagree, allies complain of paralysis in Europe; when they agree, they protest against unwanted diktats. In any case, France remains Germany's chief trading partner.

Without changing its position toward the Iraq war, Germany restored normal relations with the US. It also renewed its call for its own permanent seat on the UN Security Council. The US does not support this bid, focusing instead on more major reform of the UN and its Security Council. Most Germans want the UN to play a role as sole provider of legitimacy for the use of force. But that requires, in their opinion, that the Security Council be reformed to reflect the momentous global transformations after the end of the Cold War, including the weight of a unified Germany.

By supporting French policy over Iraq so strongly in 2003, Germany temporarily diminished its influence in eastern Europe. Like most new members of NATO from the east, Poland tended to look to the US as the key guarantor of its security. Berlin turned down Poland's invitation in 2003 to contribute troops to serve under its command in postwar Iraq. Polish-German reconciliation has been very important for post-Cold War Europe. Four hundred city partnerships have been established, twice as many as between Germany and the US. Germany was the most important sponsor for Poland's entry into the EU in 2004, although half of the Germans opposed Polish membership. They feared the competition from Polish workers. Poland now looks to Germany as the natural leader in Europe and fears German inactivity more than its activity. As the US reorients its foreign policy toward Asia and away from Europe, the former Atlanticist loyalties are weakening.

The German government resented strong and critical Polish positions within the EU on such matters as the EU constitution. At the same time, Poles no longer universally regard Germany as a model. A climate of mistrust reentered Polish-German relations for a few years. It was fueled by differences over the Iraq war and former chancellor Schröder's special relationship with Russia. A Polish scholar noted, "Always at the moment when Berlin and Moscow get too close, we have been threatened." Donald Tusk was elected Polish prime minister in 2007 on a promise to mend ties with Poland's neighbors, especially Germany, and he largely succeeded. Immediately after German reunification in 1990, 85% of Poles regarded Germany as a threat; 20 years later, that had fallen to a fifth. With the resounding electoral victory of the nationalistic Law and Justice (PiS) Party in Poland in 2015, elements of mistrust returned to the dialogue.

The first foreign visit of Emmanuel Macron a day after his inauguration as French president in 2017 was to Berlin. There was much mutual goodwill as both countries pledged to cooperate on strengthening the European Union and the eurozone. In the face of a growing number of challenges, the Franco-German alliance is likely to remain the core of the European project, even if other countries choose a slower path. Macron's clearly pro-EU orientation reassured Angela Merkel, and his defeat of the anti-immigrant and nationalistic Marine LePen revealed limits of the populist Euro skeptical wave unleashed by the Brexit. Both countries also pledged increased cooperation between their largest companies so as to jumpstart the eurozone economy.

US as an Ally

The US relationship has always been and remains very important for the FRG; indeed, no ally supported German unification more resolutely than did the US. Like most Europeans, Germans are generally mystified by the American political system. The US is a large, highly decentralized country whose national powers are separated and distributed to competing and sometimes almost hostile institutions in the nation's capital. Such separation of powers is particularly significant in foreign policy because it often makes it impossible for a president to produce that which he had promised foreign leaders. The American political system enables unknown persons of various professional backgrounds to rise to the highest national political offices through a painfully long and complicated electoral system largely unfathomable in Europe. Because of the parliamentary system in the FRG, aspirants for the highest offices must enter politics at an early age and deal with a wide variety of political problems while they slowly work their way to the top.

In stark contrast, the unique American selection system permits a person to arrive in the White House who had pursued a nonpolitical career and who might have little political experience. This is why many Germans are so shocked to see that a former peanut farmer or actor or businessman could almost suddenly appear in the White House. Since Europeans focus almost exclusively on American national politics, they are often unaware of presidents' prior political activity at the state or local levels. Americans must remember that the image of the US and its leaders is in itself an important factor in European politics.

Germans are particularly troubled by the fact that a newly elected president may have notably little experience in foreign affairs. Already during the 2016 presidential campaign in the United States, Germans expressed mixed feelings about the Republican Party candidate, Donald Trump. Even in the tidy village of Kallstadt, from

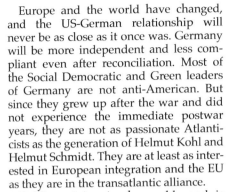

ZWÖLF SONDERSEITEN ZUM SIEG VON BARACK OBAMA

die tageszeitung

Gute Wahl

Wer Obama gewählt hat +++ Die Megaparty der Demokraten +++ Die Niederlage der Republikaner +++ Finanzkrise, Irakkrieg, Energiewende: was Obama verändern kann +++ Bewegende Bilder einer historischen Nacht +++ Glückwünsche weltweit +++ Das Ende einer düsteren Epoche +++ Kann Obama das gespaltene Land einen ?   SEITEN 2–11, 21

Dienstagabend in Chicago: Familie Obama, die neuen Bewohner des Weißen Houses, bedankt sich bei ihren Anhängern für die Unterstützung FOTO: TIMOTHY A. CLARY/AFP

taz muss sein   Wir sind Obama   KOMMENTAR VON BERND PICKERT ■ verboten ■

Good choice

where his ancestors known as the Drumpfs came to America, some residents expressed a fairly typical sentiment: "We're of two minds about Trump. On the one hand, it's great to see someone with Kallstadt roots become such a business tycoon in America. It's the American dream. But on the other hand, it's hard to be proud of anyone who makes such statements against Muslims, immigrants and women." After President Trump's first European tour in 2017, the Bild daily commented, "Rowdy behavior and bluster—Trump's first visit to NATO causes consternation among observers and NATO leaders alike."

After the 2003 Iraq war, Germany moved to salvage what Schröder called the "vital

friendship" between Germany and the US. The chancellor said he regretted his "exaggerated remarks" during the 2002 election campaign. He rejected being forced into a "senseless choice" between its two key allies, the US and France, and argued that the debate over creating a "multipolar world" (France's term for a checked America) is counterproductive. Ex-foreign minister Fischer called the transatlantic relationship "indispensable." Germany and France both supported US-British resolutions in the UN for the reconstruction of Iraq. Fischer argued that the debate over Iraq was always a matter of tactics, not goals, and that it is in Germany's interest for the US to succeed there.

Europe and the world have changed, and the US-German relationship will never be as close as it once was. Germany will be more independent and less compliant even after reconciliation. Most of the Social Democratic and Green leaders of Germany are not anti-American. But since they grew up after the war and did not experience the immediate postwar years, they are not as passionate Atlanticists as the generation of Helmut Kohl and Helmut Schmidt. They are at least as interested in European integration and the EU as they are in the transatlantic alliance.

Public opinion is changeable and is strongly influenced by the popularity or unpopularity of incumbent American presidents. In a 2004 poll, 90.4% of Germans thought good transatlantic relations were important, although 71% considered that the US selfishly and inconsiderately defends its own interests. In the tense aftermath of the Iraq war in 2003, only 45% considered strong American leadership in world affairs to be desirable, versus 68% a year earlier. Nevertheless, a large majority still believed that Europe and America should cooperate, not compete, with each other.

The extent to which public opinion is influenced by who sits in the White House was demonstrated by the election of Barack Obama in November 2008. During his campaign he had traveled to Berlin in July and attracted a crowd of 200,000 wildly enthusiastic admirers. German newspapers greeted the electoral result with headlines like "The world celebrates Obama," "Good Choice!" and "Germany congratulates the new US president. Yes, we can be friends!" In his April 2009 trip to attend the NATO summit in Baden Baden and Strasbourg, he had an electrifying effect on crowds in the streets and in a town meeting. He was obviously far more popular than any of the European leaders, including Merkel. In polls at the time, 89% of German respondents said that with him the US was again on the right path, and 76% wished Germany had politicians like him. France remained the Germans' most trusted friend in the view of 87%, but the US had risen dramatically to second place, with 78%, followed by Britain with 71%. In 2009, 56% of western Europeans believed US leadership was desirable (44% in central and eastern Europe); 63% of western Europeans saw America in a positive light (53% in the east).

Perhaps because Chancellor Merkel has such a different personality from the charismatic president and because so many Germans asked, "Why don't we have a German Obama?" she had a strained and stiff relationship with him, even though they shared the same cerebral style. It

Germany

was the opposition Social Democrats who saw him as a natural ally. Nevertheless, Obama saw a German-led Europe as America's most effective foreign partner, and he frequently pleaded with her to prevent Greece's problems from affecting world markets.

In 2013 the image of America and President Obama was seriously tarnished by the National Security Agency's (NSA) electronic spying on German citizens, including the mobile phone of Chancellor Markel. Some Germans compared these illegal practices to those of the Stasi. In a July 2013 speech in Berlin, Obama explained that these measures were counterterrorist and that the results were shared with German intelligence. However, nobody could consider Merkel a terrorist. She and many Germans felt betrayed by their most important ally. Things got even worse when it was revealed that a German intelligence operative had passed secrets to the CIA. In response the CIA's Berlin station chief was expelled. This is a rare move among allies.

A broad consensus on foreign policy remained under Chancellor Angela Merkel's grand coalition of CDU/CSU-SPD, despite differences on Turkish membership in the EU. Germans are still committed multilateralists in spite of their growing predominance in the EU. They cherish the thought of being a "civilian power," believing most conflicts can be settled by diplomacy. But it has become easier for them to press for their national interests. They are not totally averse to power politics when it seems unavoidable and when its allies are involved. The American allies like this. They greet an outward-looking Germany that is less conflicted about its influence in the world. By contrast, Europeans look to Germany for leadership in some things, but they prefer that it be tempered by Germany's postwar restraint.

As in previous governments, the main lines of foreign policy were made in the chancellor's office, not the Foreign Ministry. Merkel practiced a different style in foreign affairs, seeking to pursue German interests without alienating allies, including the US. She was more Atlanticist and pro-British than Schröder, and she wanted to be both Atlanticist and European.

On November 3, 2009, a reelected Merkel gave one of the best speeches of her life before a joint session of the US Congress. Not since Konrad Adenauer a half-century earlier had a German chancellor been granted this high honor, and he spoke only before the House of Representatives. In an emotional speech, she thanked US presidents from Kennedy to George H. W. Bush for standing by the FRG during the Cold War: "We know how much we owe you and we will—I will—never forget this." In June 2011 President Obama presented her with

the Medal of Freedom, America's highest civilian honor.

In May 2017 Obama—by now the former president—visited Berlin to a thunderous applause of tens of thousands of Germans and a very cordial meeting with then Chancellor Merkel, whom he addressed as "one of my favorite partners." Merkel reciprocated, and the meeting became "more like a love-in than a talkfest," according to a journalist. The atmosphere reflected much nostalgia for a period of warm relations, as contrasted to the changed approach when Donald Trump was elected as US president. Merkel's pragmatic take on the transatlantic partnership has already been challenged by Trump's personal snubs (when he ignored her invitation to a handshake) and nearly all foreign policy initiatives, from the support for Brexit to withdrawal from the Paris Accord to anti-free-trade policies and closing of the borders. Stung by President Trump's lambasting of US allies at the NATO summit in May 2017 and his description of Germany as "very bad" on trade, Merkel uncharacteristically proceeded to warn publicly that "the times when we could completely rely on others are, to an extent, over . . . we Europeans must really take our fate into our own hands."

The relationship between Germany and the U.S. has significantly improved since Joseph R. Biden became U.S. president. On October 6, 2023, President Byden and German President Frank-Walter Steinmeier met at the White House to mark the occasion of German-American Day, celebrating the strength of their bilateral relationship as NATO Allies and close partners. The holiday celebrates German-American heritage and commemorates the founding of Germantown, Pennsylvania, in 1683. President Biden emphasized this in his address: "On this day—340 years after the first German settlement was founded on American shores—let us celebrate the incredible legacy of generations of German Americans and the unbreakable bonds of friendship between our two countries." He urged "all Americans to celebrate the rich and varied history of German Americans and remember the many contributions they have made to our Nation."

The two presidents exchanged views on strengthening democratic resilience, respect for human rights, and the importance of transparent and accountable government at home and abroad. They also discussed their countries' ongoing efforts to provide Ukraine with security, economic, and humanitarian assistance.

Armed Forces

In 2015 the Federal Armed Forces (*Bundeswehr*) celebrated its 60th anniversary. Unification and the collapse of

the Soviet Empire in central Europe profoundly affected the size and the mission of the *Bundeswehr*. Since 1991 the military's budget has been cut by 15%; by 2014 the FRG was spending only 1.3% of its GDP (compared with 3.8% in the US) on defense. More than half of its defense budget goes to salaries and benefits for personnel, a third of whom are civilians. Only 13% is spent on new equipment, and existing equipment is inadequately maintained. Its military capability is dwarfed by that of France and the UK, which together account for 70% of the EU's military R&D and 60% of its deployable forces. Nevertheless, Germany remains the largest NATO land army in Europe and also contains a formidable air force and a small navy that operates in the North and Baltic Seas. Almost all German soldiers are assigned to NATO, the supreme commander of which is always an American general.

Soon after unification, the *Bundeswehr* began a unique effort of merging two formerly hostile armies into one. About 25,000 professional East German soldiers who were judged to be reliable defenders of Germany's democratic order became a part of a combined force that, in compliance with an agreement made with the Soviet Union in July 1990, numbered 332,800 troops, 73,450 of whom were draftees. The agreement specified that no West German units were to be deployed on former GDR territory until Russia had withdrawn its 375,000 troops by August 31, 1994, and that no foreign troops and nuclear weapons would ever be stationed there. On September 8, 1994, the last Allied soldiers departed from Berlin, leaving the city free of foreign troops for the first time since 1945.

In 2011, before the most dramatic military reform since the mid-1950s, the *Bundeswehr* had a total of 250,613 active forces. The army had a strength of 163,962, including 112,0 conscripts. The navy had 24,407, including 3,720 naval aviation, 4,950 draftees, and 490 women. The air force numbered 62,244, with almost 12,000 conscripts and 950 women. Germany had a reserve force of 161,812. Officer and NCO reservists serve until age 60; other males, until age 45. All these numbers steadily declined as Germany reshaped its military for new kinds of threats. By 2011 the number of *Bundeswehr* installations had fallen by 105 to a total of about 450 distributed throughout the country, so that every region had a stake in the country's military. Total armed forces numbered 178,900, of which 11.9% were women. They numbered 21,310, and they served in all branches and specialties.

In 2004 all major groups across the political spectrum supported a change in strategy from a focus on territorial defense

Newspaper headline: "How Great Is the Danger for Our Soldiers?"

aimed at Soviet and Warsaw Pact forces to overseas interventions and peacekeeping with lighter, more mobile forces. This change was in line with shifts occurring in US, NATO, and EU security doctrines. The country remained committed to only multinational operations with a clear international mandate.

The biggest obstacle to fundamental military reform was the draft. Germany had retained its conscript army until 2011 on the principle that it was a vital link between the military and society. The founders of the *Bundeswehr* feared the creation of a "state within a state," as was the case during the Weimar Republic. This rationale became less compelling after 60 years of stable democracy. The reasons for retaining the draft had more to do with maintaining the health- and elderly-care system at minimal expense. Many worked in these sectors of the economy, which are bound to suffer without them.

Males in both parts of Germany were required to perform six months of military service, lowered from nine months in order to maximize the number of young men who can be drafted. If a man was judged to be a conscientious objector, he had to perform 13 months of alternative civilian duty. In 2010, 90,555 (20% of those of draft age) reported for civilian duty, while 68,304 (15%) were drafted for military service; two-thirds (65%) did no service at all.

As more and more of its NATO allies abolished conscription and created professional armies, and as the shrinking *Bundeswehr* inducted progressively fewer

young males, making the system more and more unfair, more voices were raised to advocate a professional army, such as those the US, UK, and France have. In a 2007 opinion poll, two-thirds of Greens and Left supporters favored the abolition of conscription, an opinion shared at the time by only 37% of the CDU, 49% of SPD, and 45% of FDP. Taken as a whole, 48% of respondents favored scrapping against 48% who did not. However, by 2010 all parties supported it.

In 2010 the government proposed a dramatic military reform. The reforms included the suspension of conscription by July 2011 (ending completely in 2012); the constitutionally mandated national service would be retained and could be brought back at any time if a law to that effect were adopted. From 5,000 to 15,000 "volunteer draftees" can choose to perform from 6 to 23 months of service. The overall force level would be reduced from 250,000 to 170,000 professional and long-term volunteers, plus the short-term volunteers totaling no more than 183,000 soldiers. Deployable forces abroad would be doubled to 14,000. The military's civilian staff would be reduced from 76,000 in 2012 to 55,000,

The driving force behind the change was then-defense minister Karl-Theodor zu Guttenberg. By appointing her loyalists, Thomas de Maiziere and Ursula von der Leyen, as defense ministers, Chancellor Merkel signaled that her government would throw all its weight behind these far-reaching reforms.

The result is a professional army with greater expeditionary capacity, thereby enabling Germany to bear a larger burden in international operations. NATO looks approvingly on these long-overdue changes. Of course, social changes will be needed, such as getting young men and women to do a year of social work, replacing the earlier 90,000 conscientious objectors. Already overcrowded universities must be ready for many more males to enter a year earlier.

The armed forces are no longer among the least respected German institutions. A 2008 survey revealed that 89% of the population supports the German army, although some would describe Germans' relationship with their armed force as one of "friendly indifference." In a 2013 poll, 32% of respondents answered that the army enjoys a high image in the society, 47% said "so so," and only 19% believed its image was low. It is important that the armed forces are always presented to the public as lightly armed providers of humanitarian assistance. In April 2009 a surprising 84% had a positive view of NATO. Asked what institutions they most trusted, respondents listed the military third (after police and the Constitutional Court), ahead of churches, parliament, and government and far in front of political parties. Nevertheless, a 2007 poll found that only 42% of Germans were proud of the *Bundeswehr*'s achievements, compared with 87% of Americans.

Thanks to this renewal of trust in the nation's soldiers, the country was able to award in July 2009 the first medals for bravery since World War II. They were received by four veterans of the Afghanistan War, who saved civilians and wounded comrades after an attack. The new *Bundeswehr* Cross has the shape of the original Iron Cross, but it is gold rather than black.

After intense domestic debates, Germans by and large have come to accept military deterrence as a means to maintain peace. But until the war over Kosovo in 1999, few could accept the notion that the actual use of force is ever justified. There was little room in their minds for a concept of the "just war." This is partly a result of West Germany's efforts for decades to drive home the lessons of two world wars that militarism is wrong and war never pays. This black-and-white message is taught in the schools, propagated in the public media, and expressed on public monuments. Everywhere are "peace museums."

Because of his persuasive justification for military intervention in Bosnia and Kosovo, ex-foreign minister Fischer played an important role in weakening Germany's traditional postwar pacifism. But Germany's

Germany

NATO allies should never assume that Germans' caution and hesitancy toward using military force have disappeared.

Another aspect of military service is also being rethought and debated: the role of females. Among the NATO countries, only Germany and Italy had not permitted women to bear arms. They were traditionally permitted only to serve in the *Bundeswehr*'s medical and musical corps. But in 2000 the European Court of Justice in Luxembourg ruled in favor of a German woman who claimed that Germany's constitutional ban against women in the military amounted to unlawful sexual discrimination. It upheld a complaint by Tanja Kreil, an electrical engineer, whom the Defense Ministry rejected as a weapons technician. The court left open the question of "where sex constitutes a determining factor for access to certain special combat units." This refers to the appropriateness of women serving in elite commando regiments specializing in hand-to-hand combat or on one of Germany's 14 submarines. The armed forces now include 18,500 women, 10% of the total; the goal is 15%. There is an ongoing debate on how to treat them equally with male soldiers and how to make service in the *Bundeswehr* compatible with a stable family life.

As of May 2023, the *Bundeswehr* had a strength of 181,672 active-duty military personnel and 81,612 civilians, placing it among the 30 major military forces in the world, and making it the second largest in the European Union behind France. For 2024, Germany is ranked 19 of 145 out of the countries considered for the annual GlobalFirepower (GFP) review.

Germany's Strategic Situation

NATO strategy has been reexamined in a fundamental way to adapt to the post-Cold War era in which the Warsaw Pact has ceased to exist. It was discovered in 1993 just how threatening and prepared that pact had been. Documents found in the former GDR revealed that East German and Soviet planners had drawn up detailed and regularly updated plans for a military invasion of West Germany. They had already made street signs for western cities (renaming such streets as Dusseldorf's Konigsallee "Karl Marx Allee"), printed money for their occupation government, built equipment to run broad-gauged Russian trains on western tracks, stocked more ammunition for the 160,000-man National People's Army than was possessed by the half-million-man *Bundeswehr*, and made-up medals for officers who performed well in the conquest.

Germany's strategic situation dramatically changed in the 1990s. Its eastern flank used to confront directly the Warsaw Pact countries, with no buffer against

a heavily armed, suspicious, and unpredictable Soviet Union. Now a larger Germany faces an unthreatening group of eastern European democracies that desperately wanted to become NATO and EU partners; in 2004 seven of them joined NATO, and eight, the EU.

To respond to a wide range of threats in the 21st century, Germany has integrated some of its units into multinational divisions and corps within NATO: A Dutch-German corps under alternate command has been formed. British, German, and Belgian troops constitute a lightly equipped multinational rapid-reaction force with an airmobile brigade. A corps has been created with headquarters along Germany's eastern border in Szczecin, Poland, that comprises Polish, German, and Danish troops. This unit was modeled on the French-German Eurocorps in Strasbourg, France, created in 1992. A US combat division serves in a German-led corps, while a German division is part of a US-led corps. Like all these joint units, it can be used to defend member states, serve in peacekeeping missions, or operate under EU aegis.

For a long time, the "German problem" had both an interior and exterior dimension. The inner problem, the failure of

democracy, was solved long ago. However, the exterior one still existed—what role should Germany play in the European system of states, given the inability of other European powers to form a counterweight to the power of a reunified Germany in the heart of Europe? Many doubt that France could play that role. Since 1945 it was the United States that provided that counterweight. Any weakening of Germany's Atlantic ties could have stirred renewed fears of a Germany unbound in Europe.

American forces permanently stationed in Germany had shrunk by 2021 to about 34,500. This is a massive reduction from 213,000 when the Berlin Wall fell in 1989. Before he left office, President Trump announced that a further 9,500 would be withdrawn. No European country, including Germany, wants the total withdrawal of American troops. No major German political party, except the Left Party, has campaigned for the withdrawal of US soldiers. Berlin still contributes $1 billion per year to support US bases. In addition to the US soldiers, Germany also hosts 22,400 British troops (lowered to 17,400 in 2019 and subsequently withdrawn entirely); 2,800 French (who will also be withdrawn completely); 300 Dutch; and 287 Canadian.

The US is conducting a complex worldwide shift in its overseas bases to be closer to potential crisis areas; to "deter forward" is the motto. This change affected American troop levels in Germany. Two heavy divisions (the 1st Infantry and the 1st Armored), as well as selected V Corps and US Army Europe units, moved back to the US. Half of the installations in the country was closed or downsized, including such important training grounds as Baumholder, which hosted 12,000 US soldiers. In 2005, it shut down Rhein-Main Air Base, adjacent to Frankfurt Airport. In 2007 it reverted 11 bases in southern Germany, especially in and around Wurzburg. That left 62 American bases in Germany, over half of the total US military installations in Europe. Some of its F-16 fighter jets were to be reassigned from Spangdahlem Air Base to Türkiye.

The plan for the divisions was to be replaced by a much smaller light combat brigade, and other units to be rotated in and out for exercises and deployments. It would retain a few key facilities, such as Ramstein Airbase and its nearby military hospital in Landstuhl. Many of its units would be rotated on six-month unaccompanied assignments to such countries as Poland, Bulgaria, and Romania, which are closer to the Balkans, the Middle East, and Central Asia and where military stocks could be prepositioned. The Pentagon insisted that this future redeployment has nothing to do with tensions with Germany or its antiwar stance toward Iraq.

While insisting that "the Alliance and the presence of US troops in Europe remains indispensable for our security," the German government believes that a common European foreign policy must, in the long run, include a common security and defense policy in some form. Europeans are discussing a distinct European Security and Defense Policy (ESDP), which has barely gotten off the ground. Karsten Voigt, formerly in charge of US policy in the Foreign Ministry, stated, "you cannot ask about a European identity if Germans don't take part." A consensus exists in the EU that such an identity is necessary while preserving NATO in one form or the other. Americans have often called on Europeans to bear a greater responsibility for their own defense but not in competition with NATO. Nevertheless, the US government came to accept ESDP as a necessary European contribution to the common defense.

NATO still retains a diminished role for nuclear weapons. Traditionally, FRG governments have always supported a NATO defense strategy that calls for the use of nuclear weapons in the event that an enemy attack cannot be stopped by means of conventional arms. Since the FRG refuses to possess nuclear, chemical, or biological weapons (although it does possess multipurpose weapons capable of delivering nuclear warheads), it must rely on its allies, particularly the US, to provide the kind of nuclear deterrence that might be necessary to dissuade a potential aggressor from either attacking the FRG in the first place or from continuing such an attack.

To underscore its determination to defend the FRG, the US maintains a drastically reduced number of nuclear weapons (about 20 free-fall bombs in Buchel) in the western part of the FRG. They would be delivered by German fighter-bombers and German pilots. Another 200 or so are stored in the BENELUX countries, Italy, Norway, and Türkiye. Even the presence of such a small number of bombs is a matter of controversy in German public debate. When a Pentagon report published in 2008 found that security standards at most nuclear weapons sites in Europe fell short of requirements, critics called on the US to remove all its nuclear weapons stored in Germany. However, in late 2015 an expansion of the Buchel Air Base was announced, with Germany expected to cover one-fifth of the estimated cost of $154 million.

Polls consistently show that a clear majority of Germans opposes the nuclear presence. The CDU/CSU are the only parties that want to keep the bombs, but Türkiye and the central European NATO partners want them as a deterrent to Russia. Despite President Obama's rhetoric about nuclear nonproliferation, the US government rules out removing the weapons

European ambivalence toward US
Copyright 1987 by Herblock in the *Washington Post*

unless Russia agrees to reductions in its own arsenal. Former secretary of state Hillary Clinton made that clear in 2010: "As a nuclear alliance, sharing nuclear risks and responsibilities widely is fundamental."

Three days after Russia invaded Ukraine on February 24, 2022, Chancellor Scholz gave a speech to the Bundestag considered to be a "turning point" in German security policy—spend 2% of GDP on military, put military in constitution, reduce dependency on Russian energy, send weapons to conflict zones, and "defend every square meter of NATO territory." Polls indicated that 78% of Germans supported this.

ECONOMY

The FRG deserves its reputation as an economic giant. It is the world's third-largest exporter of goods, after China and the United States, and 40% of its GDP is generated by exports. It has the largest economy in Europe, 30% of the eurozone's GDP, and a quarter of its exports and is economically the most important member of the EU, one-fifth of whose budget is paid by Germany. Its economic activity is guided by the principle of the social market economy. This means that, while it does not permit unrestrained economic competition whatever the social costs, it does openly advocate and support a liberal (free) world trade.

It is the world's fourth-largest economy. Because of its dependence upon global export markets, it was inescapable

that it would be severely shaken by the world economic downturn that began in the fall of 2008. Germany was in the midst of its worst economic recession since World War II. By the middle of the year, GDP had contracted by 6.9%, compared with 4.8% in the eurozone as a whole and 2.5% in the US. Unemployment had risen to 3.2% (13.3% in the east). Its budget deficit was 2.1%.

The government devised a couple of stimulus packages worth €64 billion ($90 billion), a €500 billion ($700 billion) bank rescue, and a wildly popular "cash for clunker" bonus to drivers who scrapped old cars to buy new ones. By providing firms with subsidies to keep workers on the payrolls, even if on short shifts, the federal government helped ensure that those trained workers would be immediately available when the economic upturn came. Germany worked its way out of its lamentable situation, which it shared with all its allies and trading partners.

Integrating Eastern Germany's Economy

Germany's unification in 1990 presented the FRG with difficulties and challenges. In a way, the problems were even greater than when the FRG had to rebuild a devastated land after 1945. During the 12-year Nazi regime, Germany had maintained the institutional infrastructure of a market economy, private property, a private-sector legal code, and an administrative sector that understood the market system. East Germans could not fall back on such continuity in 1990. During 40 years of communist rule, the economy was continuously plundered, first by the Soviet occupiers in the form of war reparations, and then by the SED, who let the country's capital stock, housing, transportation network, communications systems, and environment degenerate. Enterprises had no resources of their own for investment; profits were sent to the central government, which was stingy in returning money for modernization. The economy was planned from the top, and the country was isolated economically from the capitalist world. Trade of generally shoddy goods was on a state-to-state basis and directed primarily toward the GDR's communist partners in eastern Europe and the Soviet Union. This "command economy" created hopeless bottlenecks and shortfalls and robbed individuals and firms of the opportunity to apply their own initiative and creativity to improve their economic situation. Only 5% of the workforce worked independently in repair shops, small stores, and restaurants. Citizens were nurtured to be passive, obeying the leaders at the top in return for a guaranteed job and income, which was the highest in the communist world.

Germany

"We calculate fairly" opposing euro price rises

Thus, when West Germans woke up from the initial euphoria of unification, they found an economy in the east in which roughly half of the workforce in the average company was unproductive, a majority of the companies were uncompetitive in the world market, a third of the country's production had traditionally been exported to countries in the east which could no longer pay for poorly made and overpriced East German goods, most of the property used for industry and farming had been taken out of private hands, environmental neglect had reached crisis proportions, and citizens had huge pent-up consumer expectations they hoped would be gratified immediately. Perhaps worst of all, citizens had forgotten over the past four decades how a market system, a private company, and a western legal system operate.

It was in this setting that Chancellor Kohl, who like most German politicians genuinely underestimated the economic difficulties involved with the unparalleled merger of two so different economic systems and who wanted to win the first all-German federal elections, announced that "no one will be worse off" after unity. Such unjustified optimism rapidly instilled disappointment, pessimism, cynicism, fear, deep unrest, and rage among East Germans when they soon experienced the worst economic collapse in Germany since the Great Depression of 1929–1933. Within a month after unification, East German industrial output and employment (including short-time work) had fallen by more than a third and was getting steadily worse.

Why did this collapse occur? On July 1, 1990, the western *Deutschmark*, one of the world's hardest currencies, was introduced in the GDR at an exchange rate of one to one, even though experts estimated the eastern mark to have only a quarter of a western mark's value. The Kohl

The euro arrives

government regarded this as a political necessity to keep the momentum of unity going, but it made no economic sense. East Germany's former communist trading partners could no longer buy its goods, so a third of its customers disappeared. These markets could not be replaced in the west because of the low quality of eastern products. The problem was further aggravated by the fact that East Germans themselves wanted to buy higher-quality western goods, rather than goods produced in their own part of Germany. Thus, demand for their products declined even further, while western Germany's economy boomed because of the huge demand in the east.

Production costs rose because pay was in a more valuable currency, while output

was going down. At the same time, wages also rose as East Germans desired to have the same pay level as their countrymen in the west. Within a year of monetary union, wages had risen 50% to 80% in many eastern firms, and East Germans' pay had risen to about half of that in the west and was steadily going up. These rises occurred despite drastic cuts in productivity; therefore, eastern companies' competitive advantage from cheap labor was destroyed. Run-down East German companies that had to pay employees at West German wage levels could not produce goods at prices that people are willing to pay. By mid-1991 fewer than 1 in 10 companies in the east was economically viable. Unless productivity increased, the higher wages climbed, and more employees had to be laid off to meet the payroll. But to increase productivity enough to pay high wages, companies needed to be dramatically modernized. That is, they desperately needed investment, but this was perhaps the greatest disappointment.

It was expected that western companies would invest heavily in the east and thereby cushion the shock of transition to a capitalist economy, but several factors held them back: First is precisely the fact that most eastern enterprises were not economically viable. Investors do not want to buy companies that lose money and have antiquated equipment, bloated work-forces, unrealistically high wage levels compared with productivity, and environmental liabilities that could bankrupt an investor. East German firms were so careless in polluting the air, soil, and water that the cleanup costs could be prohibitive. Legal changes were necessary to relieve new owners of the responsibility for a firm's past pollution. East German factories used high-polluting energy

Germany's largest banking center: Frankfurt/Main

**Worker in the electrical industry:
Siemens in Berlin**

sources, such as brown coal with a high sulfur content, which have to be replaced with cleaner fuels at high costs. In many cases it would be cheaper to create new companies rather than to take over problem-ridden old ones.

A second problem was a complicated jumble of property claims resulting from earlier expropriations by the Nazis, the Soviets, and the SED. Property taken and redistributed by the Soviets between 1945 and 1949 (called at the time "Junker Land") is not to be returned to former owners, in contrast to that confiscated before and after, with some qualifications. In 2005 the European Court of Human Rights in Strasbourg confirmed that families of expropriated landowners between 1945 and 1949 have no right to compensation beyond the financial indemnity offered by the Kohl government at the time of reunification. More than 1 million claims to such property were filed, but the litigation is complicated and time-consuming. This is especially true, since local and *Land* government administrations were understaffed and practically bankrupt and since many East German judges were removed because of their earlier collaboration with the communist state.

Investors are fearful of time-and cost-consuming litigation involving property claims, and they are therefore inclined to wait until such problems are sorted out before sending in their money. Realizing the difficulty, the federal government,

working together with the eastern *Land* governments, finally agreed that property could be sold to investors rather than returned to prior owners (who would be compensated) if this were necessary to create jobs. The government wanted to protect jobs not only in order to quiet fears and unrest in the east but also in order to prevent a massive migration of East Germans into the west. Most wanted to remain in eastern Germany, but in 1991 an estimated 10,000 persons a month, often those with dynamism and badly needed skills, were moving westward; several hundred thousand more commuted up to eight hours per day to work in the west. By 2000 most property claims had been settled.

A further problem in stimulating economic activity is that East Germans were understandably mystified by the intricate complexity of West German laws and regulations that have been introduced into the east. Anxious East Germans who suddenly had to live under totally different and unfamiliar rules were buying hastily published paperbacks with titles like *Your Rights as a Tenant, Your Rights as an Employee, and How to Deal with the Tax System*. Few knew how a capitalist business works and how to start one up; they lacked management and financial know-how and were unprepared to dive into a free-market system.

Leipzig's mayor spoke of "a whole society far more complicated than any of us realized—everything here is new." Investors, as well as ordinary East Germans, were dismayed to see that management in struggling East German firms, at least below the top level, was still largely the same as during the communist era. There were doubts about not only how much such managers know about a capitalist system but also how much they believed in it. Although they may be well educated and experienced, their presence is a psychological blow to those East Germans who had dreamed of starting anew.

Finally, the infrastructure needed for modern business was antiquated: a 1920s vintage telephone and communications system, an absence of modern and pleasant office space, a road network that has barely been maintained since Hitler's time, and a largely non-computer-literate workforce.

In 1992 East Germans earned half as much as West Germans in an economy with about 40% of the real output per worker. Per household the easterners had half as many cars (to say nothing about the low quality of East German automobiles), deep freezers, and color televisions, 7% as many telephones, and a seventh as many automatic washing machines. In 1991 the average East German household had financial assets valued at DM20,000 versus

DM100,000 in the west. The Bundesbank noted, "the financial situation of the population in the new federal states is similar to the situation in Western Germany in the early 1970s."

They had only 27 square meters of living space per inhabitant (compared with 35.5 in the cramped West) in decrepit housing, 40% of which was built before World War I. Although about 42% of East German housing was privately owned before 1989, the bad effects of rent control and centralized allocation were visible. The poor condition of housing was the price East Germans had to pay for having to spend only 3% of their disposable income on it. Toxic pollution and poor medical delivery kept East Germans' life expectancy lower than in the west: 69 years for men and 75 years for women, compared with 70 and 77 years in the west respectively.

To help guide the transition from an unproductive socialist economy to a modern capitalist one, a Trust Agency (*Treuhand*) holding company was established. With a staff of 3,000 by mid-1991, its job after unity was to try to privatize at reasonable prices and as quickly as possible the huge empire of former East German state assets, consisting of more than 8,000 companies, 60% of the forests, and 35% of the farmland. It also had to divide up state assets among the various levels of government, distribute liquidity cash, supervise the restructuring of companies not yet fit for sale, and prevent the creation of monopolies.

No agency could accomplish such a massive task easily. It assumed from the start that a third of the companies could be privatized quickly, another third only after considerable restructuring, and a final third would have to go under. Some flagship East German companies were allowed to fail when the right kind of buyers could not be found, such as the Interflug airline and the Wartburg automobile manufacturer.

The Trust Agency's work went painfully slowly. By 1993 nearly 9,500 companies had been sold (95% to West German companies), and 435 had been closed. When large street demonstrations took place in the spring of 1991, the Trust Agency was instructed to shift its emphasis to making companies viable that were not ready for sale while still officially aiming to transfer ownership of the East German economy to private hands. This amounted to massive infusions from the federal treasury, including from a German Unity Fund, to keep the companies afloat and to save jobs.

This assistance could not prevent the Trust Agency, which in 1995 was broken down into smaller agencies, from becoming a scapegoat for the downturn in the eastern economy and for capitalism's slow

Germany

start. Amid mounting protests against unemployment and soaring costs for rent, energy, and transportation, its chairman, Detlev Rohwedder, was assassinated in his Dusseldorf home. His violent death eliminated the last hopes that the merger of two unequal parts into one harmonious whole could be done without upheaval.

In the meantime, the federal government sought ways to speed up the recovery. This was an unaccustomed challenge because West Germany had created its economic prosperity and strength by slow, steady, balanced growth, not by quick action, as is being demanded for the east, which produced only 10% of the FRG's GDP. From 1991 to 2014, the west transferred $3 trillion to the east, a sum equivalent to 4% of GDP annually. Those cash transfers continue in the 21st century in the amount of €80 billion ($104 billion) per year. They were scheduled to end in 2019. This cash infusion provides buying power to eastern Germans and replaces the decrepit communist infrastructure. Almost half of East Germans live on state benefits. Although the jobs of about 850,000 eastern workers depend on the transfers, they have failed to generate more work in the east and have left the eastern German economy unable to function without subsidies. In some ways it merely papers over the cracks of unification.

Germany's commitments caused the federal government deficit temporarily to balloon to 7% of GDP (a flagrant violation of the EU's stability pact). This prompted embarrassing EU warnings that Germany was over the 3% limit, which could have triggered stiff fines of billions of euros for having violated the euro's guidelines if the law had been strictly applied. It was not, mainly because several other key EU countries, including France, ignored their obligations. Many Germans had forgotten this when they criticized Greece for running up a high budget deficit.

Because the German savings ratio is high, the federal government can draw on those large domestic savings to help finance the budget if necessary without borrowing abroad. By 2012 the German national debt had risen to 80% of GDP, up from 47.3% a decade earlier and higher than that of many European countries.

Healthy economic growth enabled Germany to lower its unemployment to under 3 million, the lowest in two decades. The rate had declined by 2019 to an overall average of 3.3%; among immigrants the rate is 15%. It remains almost twice as high (9.7%) in the east, and it is even worse in the northern part of the east. Although youth unemployment, at under 8%, is a third of the European average, two-thirds of them have no permanent job, working instead on "fixed-term contracts," which make it

easier to lay them off. A tight money policy by the European Central Bank in Frankfurt held inflation to 1.7% in 2019.

Berlin is the only European capital poorer than the nation it rules. Its overall unemployment rate in 2011 was 14%, almost twice the national average. Its economy is lifeless, and it staggers under a debt of $64 billion. It has Germany's highest rate of residents on welfare—18.6%, and it receives $4 billion in subsidies annually. The capital city's boom is in tourism. During 2008 it lured 7.9 million tourists, breaking its own record for the fifth consecutive year. Prices are a major reason, with hotels less than half the price compared with London or Paris.

Whereas Berlin once had a population of 4.5 million, that had by 2010 declined to 3.4 million. The fact that since unification 4.3 million easterners went west to find work, and only 2.6 million westerners took their place spelled trouble. If that trend had continued, the east's population between the ages of 15 and 64 could have been cut in half by 2050. That westward migration has largely ended.

There are encouraging signs: 300,000 new (mainly small) businesses created since 1990 survived. The fact that five-sixths of eastern industrial firms, which cover a third of all industrial workers in the east, opted out of the practice of nationwide wage accords has meant that the workforce there can protect some jobs by adjusting wages and working hours to what their companies can pay. By 2012 half of West German workers were covered by nation-wide contracts, down from two-thirds decade earlier. Much red tape has been slashed. Thus, easterners are showing the kind of adaptability that all nations must have in order to thrive in the globalized economy. This and subsidies helped induce 1,700 foreign firms to invest in the east during the 1990s.

Few large companies have moved their head offices to Berlin; Sony and Coca Cola are exceptions. In the east as a whole, there are hardly any major company headquarters, and successful eastern firms have tended to move their head offices west. Noteworthy exceptions are Jenoptik in Jena and DHL in Leipzig. The consequence is that eastern cities lack a business elite, which means less spending and philanthropy. Nevertheless, the east's infrastructure has improved immeasurably.

The telecommunications network is better than that in the west. The east now has the world's most modern, efficient, and clean brown-coal-fueled power stations. The government subsidizes new coal plants, even though few of them have the capability of capturing carbon emissions. Much of the former pollution has disappeared. Roads are much improved,

universities are being modernized, and crumbling city centers are being restored. On their outskirts are new factories, exhibition complexes, and high-tech research centers. More than 750,000 new homes were built in the last seven years of the 1990s, and over 40% of easterners own their own homes, compared with a national average of 58%. Car ownership has trebled since 1989. Per-capita GDP remains at 67% of western Germany's.

Although average gross wages are 20% lower than in the west (10% lower for public-sector workers, who have to work 90 minutes longer per week than their western counterparts), and living standards are a third lower, progress has been made since unification. Life expectancy and the birth rate have reached western levels. Real wages and pensions have almost doubled. Net household income has grown to 90% of that in the west, and productivity has jumped from 41% to 76% of western levels. Labor costs are 62% of the western German level, but they are still four times higher than in the neighboring countries to the east. More than three-quarters of all industrial plants have been replaced since 1990.

In general, economic prospects in the east are best in the southern part of the region, encompassing the federal states of Thuringia and Saxony and located below the so-called White Wurst Line (named for the southern part of Germany where white sausage is eaten) extending 220 kilometers from Erfurt to Leipzig, Zwickau, Chemnitz, and Dresden. A similar north-south divide exists in the west: Greater prosperity is found south of the line extending from Cottbus, on the Polish border, to Aachen in the west. Of 31 self-sustaining industrial clusters in the east, 23 are in Saxony and Thuringia. They have more manufacturing jobs than many states in the west. East Germany is peppered with areas of growth, with Dresden having reached western level. The area is also earning a new nickname as "Silicon Saxony" for its leading role in research and production of electric and hybrid cars. Auto manufacturers, such as Volkswagen, Daimler, and BMW, push there for developing competitors to American Tesla. The region also has the largest deposit of lithium in Europe, the major component of batteries.

The decade of the 1990s witnessed major deindustrialization in the east—30% of jobs disappeared, and 80% of its workers had to learn a new profession. But the vast majority of easterners are far better off materially than they were in the GDR. In a 2000 poll, 60% admitted that their lives had improved over the preceding decade, but two-thirds complained that they still did not feel "totally at home" in unified Germany.

Perhaps most distressing is easterners' attitude toward democracy. Asked in a 2003 Eurobarometer survey whether they were "satisfied with the functioning democracy in Germany," 66% of westerners answered yes, but the percentage of easterners answering in the affirmative fell from 38% in 2000 to 32% three years later. (In 2007, 56% of eastern Germans over age 35 and 46% of those aged 14 to 24 were dissatisfied with democracy, as it is now practiced.) Fewer than half of Eastern Germans (49%) thought democracy was the "best form of government for Germany" (compared with 80% in the west). A telling 76% (compared with 52% in the west) agreed that "socialism is a good idea that was poorly implemented." In 2007, 57% of central easterners and 45% of westerners agreed with that statement. Westerns' reaction to these views is growing animosity.

A 2004 Forsa Institute poll showed 24% of western Germans wanting the Berlin Wall back. Three years later two-thirds of eastern German respondents said they remembered the GDR positively. Angela Merkel spoke of the tendency by westerners to reduce the old GDR to the dictatorship and secret police. "No one's life, even in a dictatorship, is completely formed by that dictatorship." Everybody still had some good experiences and fond memories, and no one wants to abandon all those aspects of their lives all at once. However only 18% still dreamed of its return; 71% did not want the communist regime back. More encouragingly, 2009 polls showed that 91% of easterners and 85% of westerners support reunification. Four out of five eastern German 14–19-year-olds no longer see themselves as "Ossi" or "Wessi." Nevertheless, only one out of four (27%) easterners believe that all Germans have become "one nation." The gulf is revealed most visibly in the way they vote.

Taxation and Federalism

The federal government and the *Länder* try to coordinate their policies through such advisory bodies as the *Konjunkturrat* (economic council) and *Finanzplanungsrat* (finance planning council). But the central government cannot order the Lander to follow its policy, largely because it has no monopoly on taxing power. According to the Basic Law, the living standards in all states must be uniform; this became a very problematic requirement after unification in 1990, which linked a prosperous west with a pauperized east.

In 2000 and 2003, the government won parliamentary approval for the most dramatic tax reform in a half-century. The top rate of corporate tax was cut from 52% to 38.7% to 25%. The top income tax rate was reduced from 51% to 42% by 2005.

The bottom rate was lowered from 23% to 15%. The capital gains tax on the sale of company cross-holdings, theretofore 50%, was abolished. Since German banks and insurance companies held some of the largest shares of industrial companies, the latter measure provided a strong incentive for long-overdue corporate restructuring. Banks got their costs under control by selling off much of their real estate portfolios and nonperforming loans. The business and trade union communities greeted this historic reform.

Whereas in the US prior to World War II the states were virtually financially independent, in the FRG the question has revolved around how to divide common tax revenues. The financial relations between the national government and the states are extremely complicated, but it involves roughly the following: federal payments to poorer states, the sharing of common tax revenues, payments by richer states (such as Hesse and Baden-Wurttemberg) to poorer ones (such as Schleswig-Holstein and the new *Länder* in the east), intergovernmental grants and subsidies, and federal payments to states for administrative services rendered.

Individual and corporate income taxes, the biggest source of revenue, is divided in a way that the national government gets 40%, the states get 40%, and the cities get 20%. Thus, there is no need for a German citizen to file two different income tax returns. The states receive 44% of the second-biggest source, the value-added tax, which rose from 16% to 19% in 2007. This tax means what its title literally says; thus, if, for example, parts from several companies are used to make an automobile, a tax is imposed on the value added to the parts after they have been assembled to manufacture the car. The federal government gets all taxes on gasoline and alcohol, the Lander all car taxes, and the cities all property taxes.

In all, the central government receives about 55% of all taxes but makes less than 45% of all expenditures, including national defense. The states, on the other hand, spend more than they receive, and the federal government must make up the difference. No one is entirely satisfied with the present tax system, but as yet no one has found an acceptable alternative to the continuous haggling over the distribution of revenues. In 1986 the Constitutional Court demanded a fairer equalization of payments between richer and poorer states. In 1990 the controversy flared again, as cash-strapped new *Länder* in the east clamored for a full share of the pie. Some politicians in both parts advocated tax breaks for eastern Germans during the difficult transition. In any case, the system of redistributing tax resources has not succeeded

Käthe Kollwitz with young Germans in Prenzlauer Berg, Berlin

Germany

in evening out the economic gaps between rich and poor lands.

In the federal government a "dynamic tension" often exists between the separate ministries of Economics and of Finance. They receive expert advice from the FRG's five leading economic research institutes and from the government's own council of economic advisers, known as the "five wise men." To help maintain stability are two government banks. The *Kreditanstalt fur Wiederaufbau* (Loan Corporation for Reconstruction) was founded in 1948 to channel Marshall Plan funds and now helps finance German trade, foreign aid, and domestic investment. Owned 80% by the central government and 20% by the *Länder*, it receives funds from both the budget and the capital market to help provide long-term investment capital on favorable terms for small and medium-size companies, environmental protection, such hard-hit sectors as shipbuilding, and regional development.

The powerful and prestigious *Bundesbank* (Federal Bank), located in Frankfurt, as are most German banks, was one of the world's most independent central banks. Since the introduction of the euro on January 1, 2002, it has lost much of its power to the European Central Bank, located across town and operating with a much smaller staff (600 vs. 2,600). The *Bundesbank* is no more influential now than the other 18 central banks in the eurozone.

The *Bundesbank* was charged with issuing bank notes and defending the currency's value against inflation. Remembering how political manipulation helped cause the hyperinflation in the 1920s, the FRG's founders ensured that the new central bank would be impervious to government pressure. All presidents of the *Land* central banks are on its council, as well as up to 10 directors appointed for eight-year terms upon recommendation by the federal government. Also located in Frankfurt is the *Deutsche Borse*, which runs Germany's stock markets.

The Government's Role in the Economy

Before unification in 1990, FRG governments were more hesitant than many other western European governments to intervene directly in the economy and to protect or prop up lame-duck industries. The state participated in the ownership and management of some public services, such as the telephone, rail, and airline systems. Federal and state governments have given financial assistance to service, aerospace, computer, automotive, and energy-related industries. The bulk of subsidies was paid to service industries, especially transport. The average farmer also receives handsome subsidies.

The central government also moved to dismantle many of the controls and regulations that were characteristic of the traditional postwar German economy. It also fulfilled its promise to sell off a large part of its shares in private industry. The FRG had sold its stakes in such groups as Veba (energy), Volkswagen (although a fifth is still owned by the *Land* of Lower Saxony, from which it receives subsidies), Viag (metals and chemicals), and Salzgitter (steel and engineering).

The state sold its 53% stake in Lufthansa and its 66% stake in the Rhine-Main-Danube waterway authority, which in 1992 completed the last canal, opening a maritime link between the Atlantic Ocean and the Black Sea. The Federal Railway (*Bundesbahn*), minus the rail network, was sold into private hands. Even the interstate highways (*Autobahnen*) are heading for the auction block; since 2004 tolls have been levied on truck traffic. A plan to levy tolls on foreign cars (for $99.13 a year on average) was blocked by the European Commission in 2015 as discriminatory. Direct state aid to failing sectors in the west was significant in the coal, shipbuilding, and electrical industries. Polls in 2008 revealed that Germans were skeptical of privatization—77% thought the states should take large equity stakes in energy companies; almost two-thirds thought financial institutions should be partly nationalized, and another 60% thought that Lufthansa, the postal service, and the railways should be state-owned.

The states are also involved in such pragmatic (not ideologically inspired) intervention. For example, Bavaria offered BMW money not to create a new plant in Austria. Baden-Wurttemberg also offered Daimler-Benz, the country's biggest company, funds to keep a new plant within the state. In fact, Baden-Wurttemberg devotes one-tenth of its budget to science and research facilities to enable its companies to stay ahead in technology. These subsidies can create conflict with EU authorities, as was seen in 1996, when the government of Saxony insisted on providing assistance to Volkswagen plants, despite objections that they violated EU guidelines. But without subsidies eastern states are unable to attract large investments.

Natural Resources and Energy

The economy suffers from several important handicaps. Except for modest deposits of iron ore, natural gas, and especially hard coal in the Ruhr and Saar regions and brown coal in the foothills of the Harz mountains, near Cologne, and in the east, the FRG is poor in natural resources. In general, it must import raw materials and export finished goods. Since raw

materials are usually priced on the international market in US dollars, the FRG's strong currency, the euro, lowers its bill for imported materials.

In no sector is the FRG's dependence upon imports as critical as in energy, especially oil, which accounts for 35.6% of Germany's needs. It has succeeded in reducing its dependence on oil imported from the Persian Gulf; its main supplier is Russia, from which it gets 35% of its oil and 55% of its gas. Some 90% of its natural gas, which provides 10.5% of its electricity, must be imported. Germany hopes to end its dependence on Russian energy by 2024.

The only significant domestic energy source is coal, from which 37% of its total energy and almost half of its electricity was once derived. It accounted for about 28% of the west's energy needs and a far higher percentage of the east's. However, German coal had to be subsidized since its extraction costs were higher than the costs of importing foreign coal. In 2007 the government decided gradually to eliminate all subsidies by 2018 for the hard-coal mines in the west. The eight mines (seven of them in the Ruhr) were shut down, and the 32,000 remaining miners were retired early or given other jobs. The last piece of black carbon was coaled in 2018. Brown-coal production continues in the east.

Germany deserves a lot of credit for putting renewable energy among its priorities and even for inventing the term that improbably tends to be used without translation in other countries—Energiewende, or energy transition. Through generous subsidies and an innovative incentive program that allows individual households to sell extra energy to the grid, Germany outshines most countries far more endowed in abundant sunshine. Daimler already offers home power-storage systems and is planning an expansion into the US, in competition with Elon Musk's Tesla. Recognizing the economic advantages of the shift, the two largest utility companies in the country, Eon and RWE, decided in 2016 to split themselves by separating their fossil fuel business from the more profitable renewable-power operations. Taken together, renewable forms of energy, including hydroelectric power, account for 2% of total energy consumption and an impressive 33% of electricity in 2016, an eight-fold increase since 1990. Germany is the world's biggest producer of solar power, which provides nearly 7% of its electricity, and it is a world leader in wind power (14.4% of electricity generation in 2016). Its renewables are growing faster than in almost any other EU country. However, it is uncertain whether Germany can achieve its goals of renewable sources providing 55–60% of electricity by 2035.

Although conservation measures have had some success, total energy consumption continues to rise. The government had once planned to cope with this through nuclear power, which in the 21st century accounts for 15.4% of the country's electricity. Germany had 17 nuclear power plants in 2010, but the number fell to six by 2022. Earlier plans to increase them were stopped in their tracks by the intense domestic protest against the construction of nuclear power plants and of facilities for the reprocessing and storage of nuclear wastes. By 1991 the FRG government had shut down all Soviet-designed reactors in the east because they failed to meet safety standards. At Greifswald a meltdown almost occurred in the mid-1970s.

Germany's large and powerful anti-nuclear lobby regularly targets shipments of nuclear fuel or waste with massive, sometimes violent protests. The former SPD-Green government pledged to shut down Germany's remaining plants, but the two parties differed on timing and tactics, with the SPD wanting a longer phase-out period done with the collaboration of industry. Germany has contracts to use French reprocessing facilities and temporarily store wastes at the power stations. It also has nuclear commitments with Britain. Thus, a quick shutdown of nuclear generation would create difficulties not only with allies but also with the industry within German itself. Also, it is not clear how the one-fourth of electricity produced by atomic plants would be recouped by other means.

Opposition to nuclear power soared in March 2011, when a Japanese atomic plant faced meltdown as a result of a double blow of severe earthquakes and tsunami. There was mass revulsion against nuclear power. Merkel quickly announced that seven of Germany's nuclear plants that went into operation before 1980 would be closed immediately. The remaining reactors would be phased out until all six were shut down. This suspended her government's earlier decision to keep older plants operating an additional 12 years. Because of energy shortfalls caused by the war in Ukraine, the government ordered the last three remaining nuclear power plants to stay open temporarily. The EU also decided to test all 143 plants in its 28 countries. The consequences are that Germany is more dependent on natural gas from Russia and must burn more of the dirtiest fossil fuel (coal, especially lignite).

The inability to ensure nuclear power generation well into the future and to develop alternative sources rapidly, despite the fact that many government research subsidies are devoted to energy-related projects, prevents the FRG from improving the structural weaknesses of its energy

Atomic power? No thanks!
The Greens

position. It remains the highest per-capita importer of energy and food of any major industrialized country.

Foreign Trade and Investments

Foreign trade remains the essential pillar of Germany's prosperity. It is the world's third-leading exporter after China and the US, with 10.4% of the world market share, even though it has only 1% of the world's population. Its exports account for over half of its manufacturing jobs; 40% of its GDP is derived from exports, a fact that makes the FRG very sensitive to world economic climates. Its trade with central Europe doubled in value in the decade following the end of communism and now far outstrips that with the United States. More than 2,000 American firms have invested in Germany.

Export success has provided the FRG with enormous amounts of investment capital, much of which is invested in the US. Of the $300 billion German foreign investments in 1999, nearly 60% was in the US, compared with 19% in Great Britain, 9% in Italy, and 5% in France. In the 1990s there was a surge of foreign investment by German companies. By 1999 Germany had twice as much capital invested abroad as foreign companies had invested in Germany.

Auto manufacturers employ one in seven of all German workers. To avoid high production costs, German automakers are cutting jobs and shifting production abroad. BMW built a factory in South Carolina. Daimler-Benz, which laid off thousands of workers, had a training

program in "southern American English" before opening its plant in Alabama. In 1998 it entered a super merger with Chrysler to create the world's third-biggest automaker after General Motors and Ford (both of which have major operations in Germany). The venture collapsed by 2007, when Chrysler was sold. Volkswagen, which purchased the Rolls Royce factory (while BMW acquired the famous RR brand name), is producing in the Czech Republic and Mexico.

An estimated 1 million Americans work for more than 3,000 German-owned subsidiaries. Many may not even know it: A & P is owned by Tengelmann; Budd Car Co. by ThyssenKrupp; Scientific American, Henry Holt, St. Martin's Press, and Farrar, Strauss and Giroux by Holtzbrinck publishing company in Stuttgart; Chicago's Spiegel mail-order house by Otto Versand of Hamburg; Clorox and Loctite by Dusseldorf's Henkel; Allis-Chalmers' agricultural equipment division by Klockner of Duisburg; Celanese by Hoechst in Frankfurt (which also acquired Marion Merrell Dow, Cargill Hybrid Seeds of Minneapolis, and French Rousel-Uclaf pharmaceutical). Bertelsmann, which already owned Bantam, Doubleday, Dell, RCA, and Arista Records, seven American magazines (including *McCall's*, *Family Circle*, *Parents*, and *Fitness*), and half of Barnes and Noble Internet bookselling service, bought Random House to become the world's largest publisher of English-language books. Siemens, the Munich-based electronics conglomerate, the majority of whose employees work abroad, owns Westinghouse's nonnuclear power plant operations. Two German discount grocers and retailers, Aldi and Lidl, started expanding in the US. Aldi decided to invest more than $3 billion to boost the 650 stores it already has there to more than 2,000 by the end of 2018. Lidl started in 2017 with 20 stores on the East Coast, with plans for a further 80 in 2018. It hopes to spice up its discount offerings with such premium extras as supermodel Heidi Klum's fashion collection.

Global integration has brought an unexpected negative by-product to German companies. As Swiss banks discovered, expansion into the US market makes foreign companies vulnerable to suits filed in American courts. In 1999 more than two dozen class-action lawsuits were filed against German companies that had used slave labor (90% of whom were not Jewish) and had reaped profits from the Holocaust during World War II. Deutsche Bank admitted that it had financed the building of Auschwitz, and marquee names like Daimler-Benz, Volkswagen, and Siemens were called to the dock.

A year later the Schröder government reached a settlement that created a special

Germany

foundation that would pay up to $5 billion to the millions of survivors. Each would receive from $2,500 to $7,500. The deal fell short of full corporate immunity, but it called for the American government to urge courts to dismiss all class-action cases and to advise plaintiffs to seek financial redress through the foundation. A cap on attorney payments was set at $50 million. Not only German but also American, British, and other European companies are being pursued. Their subsidiaries in Germany also allegedly used slave labor. They include GM, Ford, Chase Manhattan Bank, and J. P. Morgan.

The FRG has undeniable economic assets. It is located in the middle of Europe and has an excellent net of road, rail, water, and air connections that tie it to all the world's major markets. It continues to enjoy a tradition of efficiency and quality production and service. When after World War I the victors wanted to place the loser's goods at a disadvantage, they required the words "Made in Germany" to be stamped in English on all German products. However, this measure boomeranged: German goods and services were of such high quality that purchasers did not avoid but instead sought goods with those words stamped on them. To such quality must be added a well-educated and well-trained workforce and excellent English-language skills.

Today, Germany is the third-largest exporter in the world after China and the United States. In 2016, its trade surplus was $282.7 billion, and the US trade deficit with Germany was nearly $65 billion. This prompted complaints from President Donald Trump, who threatened in 2017 to impose a 35% tariff on German auto imports. However, many German cars are built in the United States rather than being imported. For example, BMW's South Carolina plant builds more than 400,000 cars a year. Many of them are then exported from the US, therefore *lowering* the trade deficit.

Labor, Unions, Employers' Organizations

The supply and cost of labor is a problem for Germany. For years, the FRG had a shortage of labor and even brought in "guest workers" from southern Europe and Türkiye, now numbering about 4.5 million. While a majority of these guest workers remain indispensable for many sectors of the economy in which few Germans care to work, they do present the FRG with immense and potentially explosive problems of social integration that will tax German ingenuity and tolerance for years to come.

Also, labor costs exceed those in the US and are among the highest in Europe. Employees receive a 13th months' pay at Christmas time. At 35 hours (42 in the east), Germany had one of the world's shortest workweeks, but it is easing upward again as workers sacrifice to save their jobs. The actual work week in 2009 was 41.2 hours (EU average: 38.6 hours). The average American worker works longer hours (1,900 versus 1,557 in western Germany each year), 25% more hours in a year's time, and receives 12 days of paid vacation versus 6 weeks and 13 to 16 holidays for the German. Social benefits applied to each American job are half as high as in the FRG, where they add 80% to basic wage costs.

In the past, productivity was raised to match rising labor costs, but the country's ability to do this in the future is clouded. It has a higher percentage of its workforce in industrial production (28%, producing 28% of GDP) than in most EU countries, but its products are mainly the high-end and high-quality kind that do not face much competition from low-wage economies. Its service sector has grown to 70% of the workforce, who produce 71% of GDP.

The FRG has a highly skilled labor force and, equally important, a high degree of labor peace, despite restlessness among frightened eastern German workers faced with unemployment and retraining, and despite periodic tensions between employers' and employees' groups, which are called "social partners." Both vigorously represent their members' interests, but since the early postwar period, when these groups cooperated closely to help the FRG recover from the war, they have both assumed that they share responsibility for the economy as a whole. The success of this partnership is seen in the fact that strikes are relatively few. From 1992 to 2001, Germany lost only 9 working days a year per 1,000 workers to strikes, versus 22 in Britain and 48 in the US. Also wage contracts increased wages above the inflation rate but not so high that inflation would be seriously stimulated. The latter fact has helped produce and protect Germans' prosperity.

After unification, East German unions merged with those in the west. The structure of labor unions (to which about a third of all workers and employees belong) helps to ensure a great measure of labor peace. The 17 major individual trade unions each follow the principle of "one union, one industry." For example, instead of metal workers in the entire country being organized by many different and competing unions, any one of which can paralyze an industry through a strike, all metal workers who wish to join a union join only one labor-negotiating partner, not with many. All 17 unions then belong to the German Trade Union Federation (DGB) that, like all individual trade unions, is independent of political parties and religious denominations. The DGB helps to coordinate trade union goals and activities and is listened to very carefully by all German governments on labor matters. In addition to the DGB, there are a few other trade union organizations, such as the Union of Salaried Employees (DAG) and the German Civil Servants' Federation (DBB). By law the latter is forbidden to enter collective bargaining and to call strikes.

Unions are on the defensive. To save jobs from being shipped abroad, they have become more pragmatic and flexible. They are composed largely of blue-collar workers in a white-collar world and are harder to organize. They are not attracting enough young Germans, and they were weakened by the recession and downsizing of companies' workforces. Union membership has fallen from about 30% of the labor force in 1991 to 20% in 2004; by 2008 it had lost 44% of its members since 1991. In the east, it has halved since 1990. Although their power is eroding, unions retain some influence, especially when the Social Democrats rule. After the 2002 federal elections, three-quarters of their deputies in parliament were themselves unionists. The unions could not prevent the earlier Schröder government from introducing its Agenda 2010 reforms, but they supported its being watered down a few years later by raising unemployment benefits for older workers.

Firms may choose to opt out of collective bargaining if their works councils agree, and 56% of eastern workers are outside of it, compared with 35% in the west. On the other side of the fence are several hundred employer organizations, many of which are part of a larger umbrella organization called the Confederation of German Employers' Associations (BDA), which coordinates fundamental employer interests.

Another institution that helps to ensure labor peace is co-determination (*Mitbestimmung*). In all but the smallest firms (those with fewer than five employees), all workers, including foreigners, 18 years or older can elect representatives to a works council, which has many rights, especially in social welfare and personnel matters. Workers in large companies also send representatives to the supervisory councils that are the control organs for the companies' management.

The exact composition of these supervisory councils has been and remains a hotly debated issue since the 1950s because of its implications for policy making within the various industrial units. Workers elect half of the members in the large mining and steel companies and slightly less than half in other large companies. Despite the many disagreements, co-determination did provide a far larger scope for worker participation in decisions made in German firms than in most other countries, including the US. It gave labor more responsibility in the firms' policies and served as an important stabilizing element in the economy and society.

They are beginning to be seen as a relic and an impediment in a global economy. Critics say they have too much power and block firms from making the kinds of decisions necessary to maintain competitiveness. Worker participation has turned into self-serving union bureaucracy.

Agriculture

A final economic advantage is a fairly efficient agriculture in the west, which was able to produce about three-fourths of western Germany's food needs. This is remarkable when one considers that before the war the western part of Germany was predominantly industrial, whereas the eastern part was the country's agricultural breadbasket. The main crops are flour and feed grains, potatoes, sugar beets, vegetables, fruits, and wine, and most farmers also raise livestock, mostly cattle. Government-sponsored land-consolidation schemes have raised the number of large and medium-sized farms considerably, although small farms still predominate in the west. Cooperatives, which link together about three-fourths of the western farms, strengthen small farmers' competitiveness. Western German farmers exercise impressive political clout; they have been able to prevent the government from accepting in GATT negotiations freer trade in agriculture, which the Americans especially demand.

Agriculture was collectivized in East Germany in 1958, creating large collective farms and fields. Many former owners retained titles to their land, but it was nonnegotiable and therefore worthless to them. In the GDR, 12% of the workforce was engaged in agriculture, compared with only 5% in West Germany. In 2015 only 1.5% of the nation's workforce was employed in agriculture, and they produced a minuscule 1% of GDP. Farmers in the east enjoyed certain privileges, compared with their countrymen in industry: They escaped the worst pollution, many had their own homes and private plots, they were heavily subsidized, and they enjoyed the time off and sick leave that private farmers in the west do not have. Despite the large scale of their farms, East German farmers produced only 40% as much per capita as their West German counterparts, although they had made the GDR self-sufficient in food. Like everybody else in the east, farmers had to undergo a tortured transition to other jobs or to a forgotten form of private agriculture.

Perhaps its most famous consumable product is beer, whose purity has been preserved by the 1512 *Reinheitsgebot* (purity law). Germans shun mass-produced beers, calling it "dish water." The four largest brewers in the world have less than a fifth of the German market. The 1,300 local breweries dominate. Although the country remains the world's fifth-biggest beer market and by far the largest in Europe, Germans are drinking less and less of it. In 1991 the average German downed 142 liters, but by 2014 that had fallen below 105 liters, less than that consumed by Czechs and Austrians. Habits are changing. Drinking beer at lunchtime, to say nothing of on the job, is now frowned upon. Wine is preferred by upscale Germans. Still, no self-respecting "beer tourism" guide could fail to list a number of locations in Germany, including Frankonia, where, in the words of one smitten reviewer, "God and brewing go hand in hand."

Present Economic Challenges

The greatest challenge the country faced was the worst economic downturn since the war. The danger that a disappearance of economic success could threaten democratic values applies more or less to all countries. But in the case of Germany, it applies to a greater extent. Germany's first real experiment with democracy during the interwar years was rocked from the beginning by staggering economic problems, and the Weimar Republic finally fell in January 1933, in part because an economic depression had left more than 6 million Germans out of work. The FRG was able to win and maintain legitimacy in the eyes of its own citizens largely through its almost-stunning economic accomplishments.

It wrestles the daunting challenge of absorbing a once-bankrupt, unproductive socialist economy in its eastern Lander, whose people had been deprived of prosperity for four decades. It proved to be more difficult than expected to stimulate western investment in the east in order to create jobs and raise the standard of living.

Some question whether Germany can remain a competitive producer in the world economy. Its labor costs are among the world's highest. It benefits from its proximity to former communist countries to the east, with their cheaper labor and well-educated workforces. Its firms are good at outsourcing. Its working year is one of the shortest, its productivity below its peers in America and Japan, and its social spending enormous. Among Germans 55 to 64 years of age, only 38% were still employed in 2005. The Merkel government realizes that this cannot be sustained. It is estimated that, if nothing changes, the government would need 80% of the state budget in 2050 just to support

the state pension system. Therefore, the retirement age was raised to 67 for Germans born after 1970. The call for some economic "rethinking" is being echoed by some and vehemently rejected by others, who regard the status quo as a birthright, regardless of global economic realities.

Despite the problems, Germans are unlikely to alter their economic system in a fundamental way. Asked what the fundamental purpose of an economy is, most would answer "for social stability," while most Americans believe it exists to raise the living standards of persons willing to work hard and imaginatively. Few Germans want the social consequences of America's emphasis on efficiency and individual economic freedom, especially after the debilitating 2009 recession. They are willing to pay the necessary taxes to enable the government to alleviate the pain that capitalism can create.

Under Merkel's leadership, the economy was changing more quickly than at any time since the "economic miracle" of the 1950s. Its corporations have taken the lead in restructuring, trimming down their workforces, and cutting unit costs in order to remain competitive and profitable. More than 30% of the nation's workforce now has temporary or part-time jobs, and this gives firms more flexibility. During the recession the government provided subsidies that enabled firms to cut working hours instead of firing employees. Thus, the companies had the personnel they needed when the economy improved.

The euro crisis that began in Greece in 2010 forced Germany to be the largest contributor to two bailout packages to prevent Greece's debt problems from infecting the rest of Europe. Two-thirds of German public opinion was against these bailouts, seeing no reason German taxpayers should pay for other nations' financial mismanagement. *Bild* proclaimed in its headline, "Once Again We Are the Idiots of Europe." Another headline read, "Greeks Want Our Money." In 2010 *Bild* expressed the widespread fear that the European Union was turning into a "transfer union": "Will we finally have to pay for all of Europe?" The left-leaning prestigious *Spiegel* even called for an abolition of the euro.

The prevailing view was that Germans had saved and sacrificed, while the Greeks had lived beyond their means. Why should Germans, in effect, extend their welfare state to the Mediterranean? Further, postwar German democracy had won the citizens' consent by offering thrift and monetary stability within a context of consensual capitalism. This was based on the folk memory of hyperinflation wiping out life savings after each world war.

This time, there was little sense of solidarity with Europe. It seemed like

Germany

The relaxed atmosphere . . .

Germans were being forced to choose between economic stability and European integration. Critics in Brussels talked of German selfishness and nationalism. But after much hesitation, the Merkel government saw no alternative to joining the effort; the EU's economy is too integrated for one member to go it alone. After all, Germany benefits greatly from the euro. Almost half its exports are to other euro countries, and they produce 15% of Germany's GDP.

It is true that the debt crisis compelled the 19 eurozone countries to pool a greater degree of their economic sovereignty than any had thought possible. Merkel called for "more Europe, not less Europe" and offered sweeping proposals, but she struggles to balance the requirements for European solidarity with Germany's ideas of responsible behavior. That is why she called on countries using the euro to practice Germany's brand of wage restraint and fiscal discipline. Some pine for the old *Deutschmark*: 45% of respondents said in a 2010 Stern poll that the euro had brought more disadvantages than benefits, whereas only 33% said the opposite.

By 2022 its economy was stronger than it had been a decade and a half earlier. It grew by an impressive 4.2% in 2022, the fastest rate since unification. Its 3.2% unemployment (higher in the east) is low, and inflation stood at 1.5%. Its budget surplus was 2.1% of GDP. Job losses to offshoring slowed, and one German company returned to Germany in 2010 for every three that went abroad. Many companies are abandoning China.

The German automotive industry has been facing numerous challenges, most of them of its own making. In late 2015 Volkswagen admitted to equipping up to 11 million diesel cars with test-cheating software that allowed them to fool instruments measuring emissions. Top executives at VW and Porsche were investigated over alleged market manipulations. In 2017 the diesel emission cheating investigation reached also Daimler, with

suspicion of "fraud and criminal advertising." Volkswagen argued that, while the devices were indeed illegal in the US, the European regulations allowed their presence. The cost of the US imbroglio could be up to $26 billion. In Europe, VW agreed to provide a de facto two-year additional warranty to vehicle owners. In turn, a top trade union representative at VW was investigated over his allegedly excessive salary of up to $836,000 per year.

CULTURE

One German Culture?

Germany is politically and legally unified, but the two sides have not yet formed a harmonious blend, and the resentments that separate west from east are deep. For decades Germans on each side of the wall had assumed that they were basically the same, speaking the same language, reading the same literature, and sharing the same historical and cultural traditions. They thought they knew and understood each other, but they were wrong. Germans are not psychologically unified, and so far,

a sense of national solidarity is lacking to complete the unification process. Ostpolitik expert Egon Bahr remarked at the time of unity, "We Germans got married in a hurry and enjoyed it. Now we must get to know each other. Normally it is the other way around, but, then, what is normal in Germany?" Foreign Minister Genscher liked to tell the joke about the Ossi (East German) saying that "We are one people!" to which the Wessi (West German) replies, "So are we!"

Many West Germans believe they have inherited an unknown, problem-ridden country populated by German-speaking strangers. East Germans, in turn, are still baffled by the new Germany of which they are now a part and had expected more sympathy from westerners than they have gotten. They are stunned to see how little remains of the society in which they grew up; West German laws and traditions are so much the norm that many easterners agree with psychologist Margit Venner: "This is not unification, it's an annexation!" Former president von Weizsacker always said it best: "We cannot deny how much still divides us . . . The form of unity has been determined—now we must give it substance."

Visually the two parts look like each other. The east has undergone a facelift. Facades of shops have been freshly painted, and city streets refurbished. Stores are bountifully stocked with consumer goods, and western firms, banks, and gasoline stations are opening branches everywhere. But anyone visiting both parts of Germany hears an earful about the other and quickly realizes that misunderstandings abound. Ossis are allegedly petty bourgeois, narrowminded, provincial, and ungrateful, despite their outstretched palms, and want all the benefits of capitalism now, despite the fact that they are lazy (a questionable

. . . in German schools

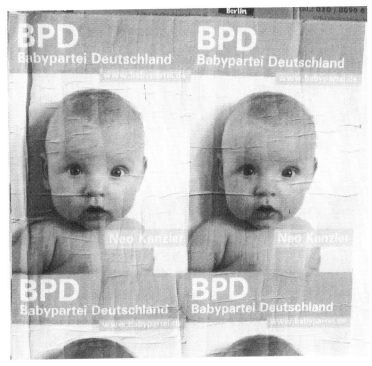

Baby Party of Germany

impression given the fact that eastern Germans created 300,000 new businesses in the first seven months of unity). By contrast, Wessis are seen to be rich snobs, arrogant, inconsiderate, insensitive, egotistical, distrustful, and less kind toward children. Many eastern Germans suffer from an inferiority complex in comparison to western Germans, whom they find to be more decisive, independent, more open to the world, more confident, and more able to achieve and to master problems.

In a 2004 study of the German cities with the highest quality of life (based on prosperity, employment, communal finances, etc.), Munich came out on top. Not a single eastern city, not even Berlin, placed in the top 10. However, there are clear indications that easterners' quality of life has been enhanced. They live on average six years longer than before 1989.

A 2007 *Spiegel* poll revealed that eastern Germans are generally satisfied with their new Germany. Asked if they considered themselves "losers" after unification, only 20% aged 35 to 50 and 15% of those between 14 and 24 answered "yes." The mood has gradually improved. In 2010, for the first time, a narrow majority of Germans (48%) thought the two halves were growing together, as opposed to 47% who disagreed; 57% of western Germans and 57% of eastern Germans found unification "a cause for joy." Prejudices remain, though: 69% of easterners regarded their western German countrymen as "arrogant," and 54% thought they were "out

for the money." Over 40% said their differences outweighed their similarities.

Asked in 2007 if they would rather live in the east if the wall were put back up, 37% of the older group and 35% of the younger group answered in the affirmative. However, these figures reflect the fact that a minority would prefer to live at home regardless of the regime under which they would have to live. What they miss most from the GDR is social security, the school system, and protection from criminality.

However, one should not dwell exclusively on the differences. Eastern and western Germans voted in much the same way in 1990, although voting habits have diverged since then. Many polls revealed similar opinions after unification: Both prize the same thing: high income. A total of 71% of Germans see the environment as the top priority, with 82% of eastern Germans and 87% of westerners favoring increased spending in that area. Both sides reject any suggestion of increased spending on the military, although rising crime, drug use, violence against foreigners, and soccer hooliganism prompt 40% of eastern Germans but only 22% of westerners to desire more respect for state authority, and 65% and 25%, respectively, want greater police presence.

Two-thirds of Germans in both parts were "proud to be German," although western Germans had a greater sense of being European than did their eastern countrymen, who had been kept largely isolated. They generally agree who their

favorite nationalities are: French, Americans, and Austrians, although the easterners put the Austrians ahead of the Americans. They also dislike the same peoples—Poles, Turks, and Gypsies—although eastern Germans' antipathy is somewhat stronger. Asked what country should be the new Germany's model, 40% said Switzerland because of its "wealth and independence," and 29% said Sweden; only 6%, 8%, and 2%, respectively, cited the US, France, and Britain as their models.

One reality that grates on easterners is their underrepresentation in the country's elite and the top jobs. Merkel's cabinet in 2011 contained no easterners but herself. There were no generals, even though about half the soldiers serving in Afghanistan were from the east. There were no police commanders, no Constitutional Court judges, and no leading newspaper editors.

Family Structure and Life

German society was already in a process of change when two different German societies were grafted together in 1990. For the third time since 1933, Germans in the east must adjust to a very different kind of society. From an earlier German society characterized by authoritarian behavior and institutions and by great social and economic differences among citizens has emerged in the west a predominantly middle-class society with widespread prosperity and with more opportunities, education, and upward social mobility. Some of these changes are clearly reflected in important social institutions.

Particularly since World War II, the authoritarian family structure has given way to a more relaxed family organization. This breakdown actually started during the Third Reich, when children were mobilized in activities outside the family and were even encouraged to report on their parents' opinions and behavior, if they veered from Nazi ideology. One now sees more and more permissiveness in the contemporary German family, and it is also fashionable in some middle- and upper-middle-class families for children to call their parents by their first names.

The combined effects of weaker religious beliefs, the former practice of favoring single mothers in the distribution of apartments, and the fact that 91% of women in the east worked, compared with only 51% in the west contributed in East Germany to considerable family differences compared with the west. In the preunification GDR, 32% of children were born out of wedlock, compared with 9% in the west. The divorce rate was a third higher in the east. Among the thousands of legal and social issues that had to be resolved before unification, very few were so controversial that no agreement was possible.

Germany

The most celebrated example was abortion, and the GDR's law permitting legal abortion on demand within three months was left in place there, while the west's more restricted Paragraph 218 applied in the old FRG. Polls after unification revealed that 57% of eastern Germans favored legal abortion on demand, compared with only 28% in the west. In 1995 a single law came into effect: Abortions are illegal, but a woman who has one anyway will not be prosecuted, provided that the abortion takes place during the first 12 weeks of pregnancy and she attends compulsory counseling geared to "the protection of unborn life." Abortions on medical grounds and in the event of rape are legal and are paid by the national health system.

A decade and a half after unification, there still are two societies. Easterners have lower incomes and higher unemployment. Westerners still dominate business and government. Immigration into western Germany, especially by the well-educated and creatively talented, continues unabated. Combined with a drastically low birth rate, the eastern population is becoming dramatically elderly. Even east-west personal unions are rare. In Berlin only slightly more than 2% of marriages are between partners from different parts of the city. It is believed that there are more mixed romantic relationships than friendships because friendships are based on similarities and love on opposites.

The Education System

One sees very few traces of the former stern discipline in the schools. The school environment is relaxed, and pupils' relations with their teachers are often close and warm. Discussion and the free expression of opinion are generally encouraged, and discipline and orderliness are far less evident than in most American schools. Americans' most probable reaction when visiting a German school is that it is considerably more permissive than the schools to which they are accustomed.

Reforms since the late 1960s have attempted to open up the school system in the west to permit more working- and lower-class children better educational opportunities, as had already been done in the east. The unspoken model for some of these reforms has been the American school system, which has always been more oriented toward providing an equal education opportunity for all rather than producing an academic elite. Since education is a state responsibility, there is considerable diversity in the school systems within the FRG. Roughly half of the children between the ages of three and six attend kindergartens, which are not a part of the state school system and for which fees are normally charged.

All children at age seven enter unified primary schools (*Grundschule*), which they attend for four years (six in Hamburg, Bremen, and Berlin). After this, children enter one of three different kinds of higher schools. About 30% (compared with two-thirds in 1969) complete a five-year short-course secondary school (*Hauptschule*) until age 15. This used to be followed by three years of part-time vocational school combined with on-the-job training. But fewer and fewer *Hauptschule* pupils can become such apprentices (called *Azubis*—trainees) that lead to a marketable skill. In an intermediate school (*Realschule*), another 30% (compared with about 22% in 1969) complete a course lasting six years, leading to a graduation certificate (*mittlere Reife*), which permits persons to enter certain advanced technical schools and the medium levels of business and administration. Some continue on for a "limited" *Abitur* (called a *Fachabitur*), which then allows university-level study in a limited number of subjects.

The third kind of school, the *Gymnasium*, offers a more academically demanding nine-year course (although an increasing number of states are eliminating grade 13), aiming toward a diploma acquired by over half of pupils in 2015. It is called the *Abitur*, which entitles one to enter the universities; 55% attend a variety of universities, compared with 6% in 1950 and fewer than 15% in 1969.

Critics argue that such a tracked system merely hardens class distinctions within the society by favoring the children of civil servants, salaried employees, and the independently employed. In contrast to workers, these groups traditionally encourage their children to enter the more academically demanding schools and to make financial sacrifices by entering their future jobs much later in life. There is no doubt that class background heavily influences educational results. A child whose parents went to the university is four times as likely to attend a *Gymnasium*.

In credential-conscious Germany the secondary school children attend, the exams they pass, and the degree they obtain classify them for life. However, one can argue that, because German secondary schools have only a 7% dropout rate (one-third for Turkish immigrants), compared with about 25% in the US and 45% in the UK, and therefore prepares young Germans better for the workforce, the school system actually narrows social and economic differences more effectively than do the US and UK. Nevertheless, certain reforms have been introduced that are praised by some and severely criticized by others.

First, some pupils in advanced classes are given state financial support in order to reduce the monetary burdens for poorer families, which longer schooling entails. Second, a "second educational path" was introduced for those pupils who later conclude that they made the wrong decision at age 11 concerning what higher school they should attend. This path involves demanding evening courses for three to six years, but these pupils with determination can receive *Realschule* or *Gymnasium* certificates and gain access to higher-educational institutions.

A third reform was the creation in some cities of "comprehensive schools" (*Gesamtschulen*). Like the American high school, the comprehensive school combines all pupils under one roof but nevertheless permits certain interior tracking for pupils with different interests and objectives. These schools were never widely accepted. Fourth, a far greater percentage of students has been allowed to attend the formerly elite *Gymnasium*, which is the essential way station toward the universities and well-paid, prestigious professions.

Elementary schools teach the new simplified spelling and grammar rules finally agreed upon in 1996, after 15 years of discussion, by the culture and education chiefs from all German-speaking countries. The 212 spelling and punctuation rules were dropped, and the peculiar "s-z" character was replaced by a double "s." The official dictionary of the German language, the *Duden*, has been revised accordingly. Confusion has reigned ever since.

Not surprisingly, this reform unleashed furious criticism in the land of Goethe and Schiller. Hundreds of writers, journalists, and publishers signed petitions against it, and the German Academy for Language and Poetry called on teachers, editors, publishers, and writers to ignore the new rules

TOUCH THE FUTURE!

CDU

DIE JUNGEN IN DER UNION

altogether. That fury simply will not die. In 2000 one of Germany's most prestigious newspapers, the *Frankfurter Allgemeine Zeitung (FAZ)*, decided to ignore the reforms officially introduced in 1999. Scholars and writers, such as Günter Grass, praised the paper, and some polls indicated that most Germans reject the changes. In 2004 *Der Spiegel, the Suddeutsche Zeitung,* and *Bild* joined the bandwagon by returning to the old way of spelling.

While the education system has been considerably opened up, criticism against it still abounds. Some argue that the reforms have left too many traditional elements in place. Others counter that the reforms have greatly lowered education standards. With western Germany's earlier economic success in mind, some foreign observers focus on four strengths of the German school system. First, secondary school pupils are educated according to their aptitudes. Second, they avoid overspecialization. They must show competence in at least 10 subjects before graduation and must achieve a minimum standard, judged by authorities from outside each school, in the core subjects of mathematics, science, German, and, for all but the least able, a foreign language. Third, teachers are treated as members of the professional middle class, with high social status, the best pay in the world, tenure as civil servants, and a short school day from 8 a.m. to 1 p.m. More and more schools have pupils in class until later in the afternoon.

Fourth, future workers are given career training. Three-fourths of all graduates (most of whom are not going to the university) spend at least three years in a rigorous apprenticeship working for a fourth of the normal pay under the guidance of a qualified "master." At the same time, they go a day or two a week to vocational schools to learn the theory of their chosen trade. They cannot get a good job until they have served their time as apprentices and have passed a practical and theoretical examination. In the 21st century, there are too few apprenticeships to meet the demand, especially in the east. But as more young Germans choose to attend university, fewer are seeking apprenticeships.

East German schools always tried to narrow social differences by merging tracks within the old German educational system and giving pupils a "polytechnic" education: one that brings all pupils into the working world for practical experience. Unfortunately, those schools also included heavy doses of propaganda in their curricula. Therefore, after unification in 1990 a shakedown began. Many schools were renamed so that their original names replaced their communist-inspired ones. Former textbooks were discarded and

German students at the College of Europe, Bruges

replaced by ones from the west. Courses on communist ideology were dropped, and the approach in civics and history courses was altered. Former teachers who belonged to the SED had to fill out questionnaires and survive a screening process to continue teaching.

When Russian was made an elective rather than a required course, 90% of the pupils dropped it and picked up English instead. East Germans had never liked Russian, and very few ever mastered it, despite the years they were compelled to study it. Studies in 1990 showed that their competence in English equaled that of Russian, even though their exposure to English in school had been scant. Of course, thousands of teachers of Russian had to be hurriedly retrained to teach English. A study of schools in both parts of Germany a few weeks after unification revealed astonishing similarities in kids' attitudes and cast doubt on the effect of intense communist propaganda over 40 years. In both parts of Germany, children wanted an "interesting job," safe from economic ups and downs, and with maximum free time; both preferred free enterprise and believed that pay should be linked to performance; they were not interested in political activism; and English was their foreign language of choice.

The extremely rapid increase in pupils who finish the *Gymnasium* has led to serious overcrowding at the universities. With the military draft ending in 2011, the problem became even worse, as many more young men go straight to the university.

For instance, the University of Munich has an official capacity of 25,000, but 50,500 are enrolled. At the Free University of Berlin, 35,000 students occupy 29,000 places. No wonder a quarter of all students (half in the social sciences) give up before graduation.

Although more than 20 new universities have been built in the west since the mid-1960s, students have great problems receiving admission to the programs and universities of their choice. Budget cuts prevented the universities from expanding their staff to cope with the high numbers of students. Many students are highly dissatisfied with the lack of sufficient facilities and staff. This problem is exacerbated by the fact that the average student now spends 13 semesters at the university before taking final examinations, thereby strengthening the *ewiger Student* (eternal student) image.

The university system, designed by Wilhelm von Humboldt in the early 19th century, is not suited to an era of mass education. There is much justification for the students' complaints of declining higher education due to sharp spending cuts (from 1.32% of GDP in 1977 to only .92% in 1997), a doubling of university enrollment (to more than 1.8 million in 1998) in the same period, overcrowded classes in poorly maintained university buildings, understocked libraries and computer centers, and unconcerned professors who in some institutions are outnumbered by as many as 600 students to 1. The ratio of faculty to students is almost four times better in the US and Britain than in Germany.

In an attempt to deal with some of these problems, a three-year degree similar to the American bachelor's was introduced as an alternative to the generally six-year Diplom (diploma), which Germans claim is higher than the American or British equivalent. This was part of a Europe-wide decision, called the Bologna process, by 29 science ministers in 1999 to introduce the Anglo-American system of separating bachelor's from master's degrees. By 2009 most of the old diploma curricula had been changed.

Professors hired since January 2002 receive less pay than their older colleagues, but they are entitled to performance-linked bonuses to encourage them to do better. In 2004 the Schröder government launched an "innovation offensive" to try to improve the quality of research and learning. Discussion focused on how to develop the kind of "elite universities" one finds in the US. This is difficult to do in a country like Germany with a tradition of state funding and control. Fund raising and high tuition are anathema, as is the notion that all universities would not be equal in prestige and support. The government decided in 2004 to provide added funding for the

Germany

Overcrowded German universities, Munich Technical University

country's 10 leading universities and research centers.

With the looming prospect of unemployment even if they complete their studies, students reject talk of paying tuition or shortening their study time. The states, which are responsible for education, complain that they lack the money to solve the problems. They call on the federal government to help, but it claims to have empty pockets because of the weak economy and the costs of unification. In 2005 the Constitutional Court ruled that universities are allowed to charge tuition, but such fees were so controversial that all state institutions dropped them. Only 4% of western students chose to move east to study. There are 300,000 foreign students at German universities. In part because of all these problems, only 6 German universities are among the top 100 in the Shanghai rankings; Munich is the highest, in 55th place.

In order to offer an alternative to the crowded universities, the first private German universities were founded in Witten/Herdecke, Koblenz, and Ingolstadt. Modeled largely after American private colleges, 44 of them had been founded by 2004, but the future of these private universities remains uncertain. They attract 6% of the student population. An extension of Touro College from New York opened its doors in western Berlin. It is the first Jewish-affiliated college in Germany, and about half of its students are Jewish.

Until well into the 1970s, an economically booming FRG, with expanding

industries and financially strong and generous state treasuries, could absorb almost all university graduates. In 1974–1975, for example, 85% of university graduates were given public-service jobs. Today, the restricted job market that awaits students after they finish their studies exacerbates their uneasiness.

Religion

About 90% of Germans belong to Lutheran Protestant or Catholic churches, divided roughly equally in the western part of the FRG, although they are not evenly dispersed throughout the country. In general, the north is predominantly Protestant, whereas the south and the Rhineland are predominantly Catholic. The east was traditionally solidly Protestant; only 6% of eastern Germans are Catholic, compared with 43% in the west. Thus, a united Germany became more Protestant. The churches' hold over the school system has long since been severed, and there are few denominational schools left. Religious instruction is, however, offered in the schools on a voluntary basis and in separate classes for Protestants and Catholics.

Beginning in 2010 Muslim pupils are required to attend Islamic religious education as a regular subject, taught in German by teachers educated at German universities. The federal government also announced that it would finance Islamic studies at three public universities (Osnabrück, Münster, and Tübingen). They will train religion teachers, prayer leaders and imams (clergymen) so that they would

be more familiar with and sympathetic to western values.

There is no clean separation of church and state in the FRG as in the US. The opening words of the Basic Law remind Germans of their "responsibility before God and mankind," and two-thirds of respondents in a 2000 poll favored keeping God in their constitution. Politicians take oaths invoking God, although they are free to delete such references, as did Gerhard Schröder and half of his cabinet in 1998. Crosses are hung in all but 12 of Bavaria's 40,000 classrooms. Both major churches, and since 2002 the Central Council of German Jews, receive funding from a church tax (a tax surcharge of 8%–9%, depending on the *Land*) that the state collects with the income tax. This amounted to $10.2 billion in 2010. The state also pays the salaries of all bishops and archbishops, though not of priests, and about three-fourths of the teaching costs in church schools. Since German Jews were granted equal standing with Protestants and Roman Catholics, there is increased state financing for Jewish schools and other institutions.

A person may be excused from paying the tax if he officially leaves the church of which he is a member. Such a step used to bring a person social or professional handicap. A doctor or a kindergarten teacher could be denied employment at a church-related hospital or kindergarten because he had formally left his church. But this is the exception today. More than 100,000 people are formally leaving the churches each year.

There are differences in religious beliefs between Germans in the two halves of the country. Only 7% of eastern Germans say they believe in life after death, compared with half of western Germans. Two-thirds of eastern Germans were either never baptized or left the church, compared with only 7% in the west. While most western German children go through religious confirmation ceremonies, eastern Germans had a secular "youth dedication" (*Jugendweihe*) ceremony. As a part of the eastern nostalgia wave in the 21st century, the "youth dedication" has returned for about half of the young people (80% in some areas), albeit in deideologized form.

About two-thirds pay the tax, which provides the churches with two-thirds of their income. The state also finances churches directly. With that income the churches run one hospital in three, as well as many daycare centers and schools. They are Germany's second-largest employers after the government.

By the 21st century, the proportion of Catholics who attend church regularly had fallen to 14%, less than half as many as 25 years ago. Among Protestants, it had shrunk to only 4%. Attitudes sometimes change when it is time for a baptism, wedding, or funeral or when children are being raised. However, the number of church weddings and baptisms had also declined by a third in both faiths over the last three decades of the 20th century. From 2008 couples who have a church wedding no longer have to undergo a second civil ceremony afterward.

The churches were the only institutions to survive the Third Reich practically unscathed, although the Lutheran Church admitted in 2000 that it had used forced laborers during the Nazi era. It agreed to pay $5 million to a compensation fund. The Catholic Church said that only two of its communities had used such labor in cemeteries and that it had no plans to pay into the fund. The churches have contributed significantly to establishing a moderate and compromising political culture. Mindful of the horrors of Hitler's rule, Germans still retain the Christian foundations of their society.

However, questions remain concerning the extent to which they should actively enter the political arena. The Protestant Church was very visible in the "peace movement" in both parts of Germany. It was particularly important in the east, where the communists had officially encouraged atheism but where churches were tolerated if they did not meddle in politics. Protestants could not agree with the latter stipulation, and their church became a sanctuary for growing oppositional groups in the 1980s; because of this, young people took a new interest in it. In the GDR it opposed the militarization of society through military education in the schools. It advocated a right of conscientious objection that did not exist in the GDR. Under the banner of "Swords to Plowshares," it opposed all countries' arms buildups.

It brought into the limelight the GDR's first massive, organized opposition to the regime by protecting it and providing it with meeting rooms and a podium for all persons interested in a critical dialogue. It supported civil courage to question the regime and urged dissidents to remain in the GDR to build a better country. It made bold and articulate demands for freedom. Perhaps most important, it succeeded in keeping the revolution against the SED regime nonviolent. The Leipzig demonstrations every Monday, which broke the back of the regime in the fall of 1989, always began in the Nikolai Church with a "peaceful God's service." It was there on the critical date, October 9, that the call for nonviolence, penned by symphony conductor Kurt Masur and five others, including clergymen, was proclaimed. In the noncommunist government that ruled the last half-year of the GDR's existence, Protestant clergymen were the largest single professional group.

Catholic bishops and priests, especially in Bavaria, have not been above trying occasionally to influence the voting of their parishioners through messages from the pulpit. Yet the strength of religion as an influencing factor in politics and society has declined greatly. It has little bearing on voting. Only about a third of the Catholics and a tenth of the Protestants in the west attend church regularly, and most of those who do have become largely secularized. In April 2005 Cardinal Joseph Ratzinger from Bavaria was selected to be the new Pope, Benedict XVI. Many German Catholics rejoiced, even though his doctrinal views are far more conservative than mainstream Catholic opinion in Germany. In 2013 he became the first pope in almost six centuries to step down voluntarily. He was replaced by Pope Francis.

That rejoicing has become much more muted, as hundreds of previously unreported cases of sexual and physical abuse are coming to light in Catholic institutions all over Germany. One of the most conservative Catholic leaders, Bishop Walter Mixa, resigned amid allegations he routinely flogged kids decades ago. Corporal punishment in Germany was banned in the 1970s. Over 200 former pupils of a prestigious Jesuit secondary school in Berlin, the Canisius-Kolleg, phoned a hotline to report prior abuse. The statute of limitations bars prosecution for abuse that occurred decades ago. But this has embroiled the pope, since he had been an archbishop in Germany while some of these offenses took place.

Thousands of Catholics are leaving the church. The diocese in Freiburg lost more than 5,300 parishioners in March 2010 alone, and 56% of German Catholics say they have lost all confidence in the church. To shore up the German church, Benedict XVI made his first official state visit to Germany in September 2011. He became the first pope to speak before an elected German parliament, and he celebrated Mass for more than 60,000 followers in the Olympic Stadium, where the 1936 games had been held. Benedict's successor, Pope Francis, demands simplicity and modesty. He demoted Germany's

Students in a multi-racial Germany

Germany

youngest bishop, Franz-Peter Tebartz van Elst, for shocking extravagance—$7.43 million for his new house; his bathtub alone ran €15,000 ($20,500). Such scandals seriously hurt the churches.

Before the Third Reich, there were about 600.000 Jews living in Germany. At the war's end, there were 1,500 who survived in hiding, 9,000 were alive in concentration camps, and 15,000 survived by marrying non-Jews. There are now more than 200.000 Jews, 20,000 of them in Berlin. This constitutes Europe's third-largest Jewish population, after France and Britain, and the fast-growing. In Berlin there are seven synagogues, Jewish preschools and a high school, cemeteries, social service agencies, and retirement homes. There are 89 synagogues in the entire country. As a further sign of the renaissance of Germany's Jewish community, its largest synagogue, with space for 1,200 persons, reopened in Berlin in 2007. It had not been fully destroyed in the November 9, 1938, Crystal Night anti-Jewish rampage because it was located in a courtyard surrounded by the houses inhabited by non-Jewish Berliners. The Nazi arsonists were afraid to completely torch the synagogue for fear of burning the houses, too. In 2002 Germany passed Israel as the leading destination for Jewish immigrants from the former Soviet Union, over 19,000 in a single year. Over time twice as many Jews from the former Soviet Union settled in Germany than in Israel. This prompted the government to limit the entry of such Jews from 2006 on. About half have joined an established Jewish community, and three-fourths depended upon welfare assistance.

They come because Germany offers them citizenship and automatic government benefits. They face challenges in integrating. Many do not speak German; many are near or past retirement age; and most of their academic degrees are not recognized. There are other complications: Rabbis do not recognize as many as 30% of them as Jews because their mothers were not Jewish. When the head of the Central Council of Jews requested the government to remove "improper Jews" from the applicants, the Foreign Ministry refused, vowing that never again would Germans determine who is a Jew.

There are anti-Semitic graffiti and street attacks. Most are committed by Muslim youths. However, the commander of the elite special-forces army unit was dismissed in 2003 for publicly agreeing with remarks made by CDU member of the Bundestag Martin Hohmann, who argued that if Germans were a "race of perpetrators" because of the Holocaust, so, too, were the Jews because of their role in terror associated with the Russian revolution.

The people of Berlin stand by you.

In memory of September 11, 2001

Our hearts are with the victims and their families.

We feel solidary with all Americans in this dark hour.

We in Berlin will never forget what you have done for us.

You were there when we needed you.

And now we will be there for you when you need us.

Detlef W. Prinz, PrinzMedien Berlin
Klaus Groth, President and CEO of the Groth Group
Peter Dussmann, Chairman of the Board of Dussmann AG
Dr. Eric Schweitzer, Member of the Board of ALBA AG
Theodor Baltz, President and CEO of MedienKontor Berlin
Rafael Roth, President and CEO of Kurf rstendamm Karr e
Dr. Volker Hassemer and Dr. Wolfram von Fritsch, Partners for Berlin
Dr. Thomas Guth, Chairman of the Board of Dr. Joachim Schmidt AG & Co.
Dr. J rg Franke and Holger Timm, Chairmen of the Board of Berliner Effektengesellschaft AG

Former central bank board member Thilo Sarrazin was also sharply criticized in 2010 for writing about a "Jewish gene" in a best-selling book dealing with immigrants. Such talk of Jewish genetics crossed a line in postwar Germany, and Sarrazin expressed regret for mentioning it. Polls in 2005 revealed that 80% of German respondents are "angry" about how Israel treats Palestinians. An astonishing 50% even share the view that what Israel is doing to Palestinians today is "in principle" nothing else than what the Nazis did to the Jews during the Third Reich.

In an effort to prevent the two countries from drifting apart, Chancellor Merkel, who was very popular in Israel, took eight members of her cabinet to Israel for a joint session with the Israeli cabinet in 2008. In a highly symbolic gesture, she became the first postwar German leader ever to be invited to speak before the Israeli parliament.

She said that "for me, Israel's security will never be open to negotiation. . . Whoever threatens Israel also threatens us." During the debate over Resolution 67/19, upgrading Palestine to observer state status in the United Nations in 2012,

Germany

A Turkish grocer in Hamburg

Courtesy: German Information Center

German is the most widely spoken native language in the EU and is the language of almost a fifth of all books worldwide. However, by the 21st century, only 1% of the world's published scientific works are written in German. Thus, German scholars publish their work in English if they wish to be read outside of Germany. More and more university classes are taught in English, theses and dissertations are being written in English, and colleagues at German-based research centers increasingly communicate with each other in English.

American slang has mightily invaded the German language, and young people, businessmen, and scholars seldom express themselves for long without using some English words. But, unlike many French, most Germans do not seem to be distressed by this lingual invasion.

The *Financial Times* quoted the deputy editor of the daily *Die Welt*, who discovered that one could write German articles while using hardly any German words: "Unser Way of Life im Media Business ist hart, da muss man ein tougher Kerl sein. Morgens Warm-up und Stretching, dann ein Teller Corn Flakes und ein Soft Drink oder Darjeeling Tea, dann in das Office—und schon Brunch mit den Top-Leuten, meeting zum Thema: Sollen wir die Zeitung pushen mit Snob Appeal oder auf Low Profile achten? Ich habe den Managern ganz cool und businesslike mein Papier presentiert: Wir mussen News powern und erst dann den Akzent auf Layout und Design legen, auf der Front Page die Headline mehr aufjazzen und die Deadline beachten. Fur jede Story brauchen wir ein starkes Lead. Der Cartoon muss gut plaziert sein. Das

Germany abstained, certainly reflecting its unwillingness to act against the interests of Israel.

There are 3.2 million Muslims (about 4% of the total population). The 2.5 million of Turkish origin (120,000 in Berlin) are the largest. There are sizable communities from former Yugoslavia, Iran, and Iraq. They worship in mosques all over the country. Until students of Islamic studies in German universities begin to graduate, virtually all imams (religious leaders) active in Germany will continue to be foreigners, some holding short-term visas. In an attempt to defuse tensions, the German government supported the creation of a Central Council of Muslims to represent the interests of Muslims in the country. The Constitutional Court ruled twice in 2003 that a Muslim teacher in Stuttgart and shop assistants could not be fired for wearing head-scarves to work. Nevertheless, three Lander, including Baden-Wurttemberg, passed laws in 2004 banning teachers from wearing Muslim head-scarves in state schools.

Attitudes toward America

German Americans are America's largest single ethnic group, numbering 46 million. Perhaps nothing is more noticeable for visitors to the FRG than the attachment of Germans, especially youth, to anything that is American (except in politics). On the radio one hears far less German music than American and British. For young singers, sales outside of Germany were more important than nationalist urges. Even the CDU's 1990 electoral campaign was sung in English: "Feel the power, touch the future, reach the heart!" However, by 2005 German-language groups

had made a comeback, capturing 49% of music sales.

There is seldom an evening in which an American television show cannot be seen. Jeans, T-shirts, and jogging shoes are worn by young Germans, who crowd into such fast-food chains as McDonald's and Burger King, which one finds in every city of any size. An estimated 85,000 Germans, inspired by Karl May's novels, belong to American Indian clubs. A "powwow" in Essen attracted 6,000 Germans in 1994. They came with native garb and paint on their faces, calling themselves names like "Old Powderface."

295

Germany

Editorial muss Glamour und Style haben, unsere Top Priority bleibt: Action und Service!" Using English terms in advertising gives the impression that one is livelier, younger, and more modern. Using them in everyday speech can be a status symbol and give a person a chance to show off his education.

The business community has accepted terms like "service center," "flat rate," and "fax" with no problem, although a survey revealed that 85% of Germans did not understand one company's slogan, "Be inspired." Sometimes companies go too far in adopting English. For example, a cell phone is called a "handy." The first time they hear it, Anglo-Saxons invariably have to ask what that is. The Internet has brought many terms that have stuck, such as "log in," "scan," "Google," and "Twitter."

Even Americans have adopted some German words that they mix with English, such as "love fests," "music fests," and "spin meister." "Ersatz" is used to describe a negative substitute. Some German words fail when introduced into English. For instance, the VW ad about its cars' "Fahrvergnugen" (pleasure to drive) was riding high until a wise-guy added a "t" in the middle.

Many German protest movements, such as those against war, for women's and minorities' rights, and in favor of environmental protection, are largely based on American examples. Yet, despite the undeniable and seemingly irresistible attraction which many Germans have toward aspects of American culture, there is anti-Americanism in the FRG. Traditionally it was only among the militant leftist circles that it would come blatantly to the surface. Anti-American sentiments were largely silent among a part of the politicized youth and left-leaning intellectuals. That has changed. The extreme right now also embraces anti-Americanism. Anti-Americanism is associated with criticism against certain American policies, such as high military budgets, seeming disregard for international institutions and law, the death penalty, the availability of handguns, apparent indifference to global warming, or the Iraq war. Those policies are also criticized in the US, so anti-Americanism should not be seen in terms of a general aversion against the US or its people.

Criticism of America is sometimes a general way of expressing anticapitalist, antigrowth attitudes. It can involve cultural rejection of globalization, "Anglo-Saxon liberalism" (free-market economics), and a scientific and technical civilization the US seems to represent. It is also an outgrowth of a conflict between generations. On the one hand is an older generation in the west which admired American democracy and prosperity and which has never forgotten

the Marshall Plan and the US defense of West Berlin in the late 1940s and 1950s. One TV journalist said at the time of unification, "We had help from the Americans, who had thought carefully about what should become of Germany, and this enabled us to make something of ourselves." Helmut Kohl frequently told campaign audiences in the east that, if the Americans had occupied them, their lives would have been as democratic and prosperous as in the west.

On the other hand, a younger generation grew up amid material prosperity and talk of detente. Their political consciousness was shaped at a time when the shock waves of severe racial tension in American cities, the Vietnam War, and Watergate were being felt outside the US. In East Germany much propaganda had been directed against America, but polls reveal little anti-Americanism there.

Much of the anti-Americanism is rooted in protest against the prevailing culture of the westernized Germany. It has been linked with longings, observable in other western European countries and the US, as well, to drop out of a highly competitive, urbanized society oriented toward comfort, economic prosperity, and individual success and to adopt alternative forms of living, which are poorly defined. More recently it has involved escaping the fierce economic competition globalization has created. Thus, anti-Americanism is less a political call to arms against the US than it is a code word for a change of values among a part of German younger people that embodies a conflict among several cultures within the FRG itself.

Of course, emotional disagreements on international events and the unpopularity of an American president can color attitudes, at least temporarily. That was the case in the aftermath of the US-British war against Iraq in March-April 2003, which was extremely unpopular in Germany and elsewhere in Europe. In a Pew Global Attitudes poll in May, only 45% of Germans expressed a favorable view of America, and 75% of those who disapproved cited as the reason personal animosity toward former American president George W. Bush, who was unusually unpopular in Europe. In 2007 only 19% said they had confidence in him. Almost 60% of respondents said they wanted looser ties with the United States. In 2005, only a third expressed gratitude for the help the US had given Germany after World War II. The highly critical films and books of US filmmaker Michael Moore sold well in mainstream German society, and conspiracy theories flourished. A national poll in 2005 revealed that one of five Germans (one-fourth of the young) believed that the CIA was behind the September 11, 2001, attacks.

How rapidly such negative attitudes can change was shown after Barack Obama became president in January 2009. By April 89% of Germans believed that with Obama the US was "again on the right path," three-fourths "wished they had politicians like him in Germany," and 63% saw America in a positive light again.

One frequently hears negative cliches in Germany about Americans: that they always chew gum, are fat and loud, generally dress tastelessly (in loud colors), and are fanatic joggers and sports addicts. Some Germans find that many Americans are shallow, unilingual, uncultured, slightly naive, and politically uninformed about the rest of the world, even though Americans seem to have an almost missionary desire to spread the American way of life. Yet, opinion polls reveal different, more positive descriptions of Americans: that they have a good business sense, and are individualistic, energetic, patriotic, progressive, and technically talented. Less than a fifth of all Germans consider Americans to be ill-mannered or ruthless, and only 4% consider them to be insecure.

Americans and Germans mingle rather well with each other although there are differences between them. Like some other European nationalities, Germans tend to be more private than Americans. They often do not know their neighbors and are more apt to put fences around their houses to ensure their privacy. They also observe certain social conventions that somewhat slow down the development of intimate social contact.

For instance, the German language has two different words for "you." Germans say "Sie" if they want to keep formal and at a distance and "Du" if they want to be more familiar. The English equivalent of a formal "you," "Thee," fell into disuse years ago, even among small religious sects that had retained it. In Germany, colleagues who have worked with each other for years might still address each other as "Herr" (Mr.) or "Frau" (Mrs.). "Fraulein" (Miss) has fallen into disuse because there is no male counterpart, and there is no German equivalent to "Ms."

However, the usage of "Du" and "Sie" has changed over time. For example, everybody of student age says "Du" to each other. Employees at some relatively egalitarian companies, such as IKEA, or in left-wing parties use "Du," whereas law firms, banks, and the government bureaucracy prefer "Sie." It was big news when the two top politicians in the governing center-right coalition, Angela Merkel and Guido Westerwelle, agreed to say "Du" to each other.

Europeans, including Germans, are uncomfortable about answering such personal questions when one first meets as where one works, for whom one voted, or how one acquired a certain painting or piece of furniture in his abode, questions the Americans generally feel free to ask in order to open a conversation. This is not to say that Germans do not form firm friendships. They certainly do, even if it takes longer to do so. But while Germans seem to like the more relaxed American manner, they do generally recognize and mildly criticize the superficial aspect of Americans' personal interaction. Unlike most Americans, Germans tend not to call other people by their first names and to use casual expressions like "drop by sometime," unless they really mean it and wish to give an unmistakable signal of friendliness to a person.

Foreigners

The FRG was highly successful after 1945 in absorbing and integrating more than 14 million German refugees and expellees from East Germany and the former eastern territories. Now Germany is faced with the very difficult problem of integrating racially and culturally diverse groups of non-Germans.

Because of Germany's economic prosperity, political tolerance, liberal asylum laws, and constitutional guarantee of asylum "for persons persecuted on political grounds," it has become a magnet for refugees, although it does not accept as high a percentage of immigrants per capita as does the US. Also, in the 1950s and 1960s, West Germany recruited southern Europeans and a large number of Turks in order to overcome severe labor shortages in low-paying jobs. Together with about 120,000 foreigners in eastern Germany, foreigners then number over 7 million, or approximately 8.8% of the population (12.7% of the working-age population); these figures were down because over a million took German citizenship from 2000 to 2005 and are no longer considered foreigners. All but 3% live in the west. People with a "migrant background" constituted more than a quarter of the population.

In 2005 the largest group was Turks (2.5 million), followed by 1 million from the former Yugoslavia, Italians (558,000), Greeks (346,000), and Poles (286,000). Their numbers were rising because of their usually higher birth rate and because members of their families were arriving from their countries of origin to join them. One-fourth of all newborns had a foreign parent. Approximately 15 million residents had an immigrant background—they included 11 out of the 23 players on Germany's 2010 World Cup soccer squad. By midcentury half the population will have non-German origins.

Most foreigners intend to stay in the FRG forever. Relatively few of them accepted governmental bonuses to return

to their countries. Of the children born in Germany in 2008, 38% have an immigrant background. In cities with more than 200,000 inhabitants, 45% of children under age 15 have such a background. Although an estimated 20% of foreigners were born in Germany, few were granted citizenship. For example, of the 2.75 million Turks in Germany in 2008, about a fourth (700,000) were German citizens; among the total immigrant population, 950,000 have acquired citizenship. Turks are especially hesitant to give up their Turkish citizenship because they would become ineligible for inheritances in Türkiye. By 2008, however, more Turks were leaving Germany than entering, attracted by Türkiye's growing political stability and economic success.

The federal government vowed to change Germany's citizenship law. After a furious debate that focused especially on initial plans to permit dual citizenship, parliament accepted an amended law in 1999 that nevertheless represents a landmark overhaul of the 1913 citizenship law. It cuts the link between German blood ties and nationality. Beginning in 2000, children born in Germany to foreign parents were granted German citizenship if at least one parent has lived legally in Germany for eight years or longer. These children can hold dual citizenship until age 23, when they must renounce their foreign citizenship if they choose to retain their German one. However, they may keep both passports if they can show that they had grown up in Germany for at least eight years. No naturalized citizens may hold dual citizenship. In gratitude for this law, about 95% of Turkish German citizens voted SPD until 2013, when 31% voted for Chancellor Merkel's party. In 2013, 11 politicians of Turkish ethnicity won seats in the Bundestag. By 2021, that rose to 18. Merkel's coalition government sought

to grant citizenship to all Turks born and raised in Germany.

Immigrants are especially concentrated in certain large industrial cities, where they sometimes constitute a majority in poorer sections of the cities and serve as convenient scapegoats for certain alarming urban ills, most notably rising crime. For example, foreigners constitute a quarter of Frankfurt's residents. Unemployment rates for them are double the national average and rise to 43% in Berlin; 40% of their youth have acquired no vocational qualifications; among Turkish men, that figure is almost three-fourths. About 40% live below the poverty line. A third of young children come from immigrant families. Although most Germans are disgusted by antiforeigner violence, most believe that the number of foreign residents has become too high.

Glasnost in the Soviet Union seriously affected emigration. In 1989 alone, 377,000 ethnic Germans from eastern Europe (especially Poland) and the USSR joined 344.000 Germans from the GDR and the steady stream of non-German refugees into the FRG. This was the largest wave of ethnic Germans entering the FRG since 1949, and the influx continued in 1995, when 218.000 entered. The sudden outpouring temporarily swamped the procedures in funds. All competed for limited accommodation and employment and, as polls and city elections show, are testing Germans' patience. About 2 million Germans remain in the former Soviet Union. Many of these also wish to emigrate, even though it is not easy for them to adjust to working and living in a less protective state like the FRG.

Ethnic Germans from eastern European countries enjoy an open-door immigration policy, and 700,000 ethnic Germans from outside of Germany poured into the country in the year following the collapse of the Berlin Wall; many could speak no German. By 1997 the numbers of both asylum seekers and German resettlers had declined dramatically. In 2002 Germany received 91,416; this was about 7,000 fewer than the year before.

There is one group, numbering 60,000 (40,000 in Saxony and 20,000 in Brandenburg), that speaks a Slavic language but is not foreign—the Sorbs. They have lived in eastern Germany since the 6th century. Their unique language and customs are legally protected. The extent of their successful integration was demonstrated in May 2008, when Stanislaw Tillich, a Sorb, was sworn in as Saxony's minister president. He finished his oath of office by repeating the words "So help me God" in both German and Sorb.

Turks display a greater resistance to social integration than do other nationalities.

Germany

This was not helped by Turkish prime minister Recep Erdoğan 's visit to Germany in February 2008. He urged them to remain aloof from German society, arguing that assimilation is a "crime against humanity." Turkish children should be able to learn in Turkish-language schools and at a Turkish-language university on German soil. Many Turks responded positively to this message, but he quickly wore out his welcome in other quarters. He came back in 2010 and advised Turks to teach their children Turkish first and then German and not to assimilate but rather to "integrate."

The hesitancy to become an integrated part of German society creates particular problems in the schools, where the percentage of foreigners in classes sometimes rises to over 50%. Thus, Germans must tackle the problem of bilingualism in the schools, of resultant lowered standards in the classrooms, and of an increasing inclination on the part of German parents to avoid sending their children to schools in which there is a high percentage of foreign children enrolled. This is an extremely delicate problem for a country that tries very hard to be tolerant, compassionate, and just. By the mid-1990s, many Turks had ascended to the middle class. Germany's Turks own 90,000 businesses, employing half a million people. 15,000 study at universities, and Turks have become lawyers and software experts. One is a member of the Bundestag as a representative of the

federal Green Party, Cem Özdemir. He currently serves as Federal Minister of Food and Agriculture since 2021. Prior to that he was the first person from an immigrant background to became a party chairman. In 2010 Aygul Ozkan became the first Turkish German to be appointed as a member of a *Land* government. However, if they have a Turkish-sounding name, they still face discrimination in housing and hiring.

Fears that the FRG might become swamped by foreigners persist, as the Pegida marches demonstrated. The federal and *Land* governments have found it necessary to warn against xenophobia, which is strongest in the east, although only about 2% of the population there is foreign. The GDR was a far more isolated society, so its people had far less contact with outsiders. Also, the communist regime in the GDR had never accepted responsibility for the crimes of World War II, so its citizens had not grown up with the same feeling of guilt toward wrongs done to other peoples, such as the Jews, as people in western Germany had been. About 100,000 guest workers had been sent there from communist countries like Angola, Cuba, Vietnam, and Mozambique, and many refused to return to their homelands when the GDR collapsed. It is noteworthy that xenophobia in the east is stronger among young people than among older, whereas the opposite is true in the west.

The former general secretary of the CDU Laurenz Meyer made an unfortunate remark in 2000 that enflamed passions: "France has a predominantly French culture, Italy the Italian. Why shouldn't we have the German defining culture [*Leitkultur*] in our homeland?" German feelings on the subject of foreigners are ambiguous. A 2010 poll revealed that a third of respondents believed that "too many foreigners" are living in Germany, that foreigners come "to abuse the welfare state," and that foreigners should be sent home "in a limited job market." A majority were in favor of "sharply restricting" Muslim religious practice. Asked in 2006 if they were "very" or "somewhat" concerned by the rise of Islamic extremism, 82% answered "yes," compared with 77% in Britain and 76% in France. In 2016 43% of Germans declared that the Muslim community posed a "threat" to national identity, and almost half saw it as excessively influential and visible." Sixty percent thought that Muslims had not assimilated into society because they refuse to adapt to local customs and values. Following the massive influx of some 1.1 million refugees into Germany, the University of Leipzig's survey in 2016 found that half of all Germans (up from 43% in 2014) feel like "foreigners in their own country" because there were too many Muslims in Germany. Some 40%

Europe attracts me!

wanted Muslims to be prevented from immigrating to Germany.

The social atmosphere heated up in 2010 with the publication of a best-selling book by an SPD board member of the central bank, Thilo Sarrazin, *Germany Does Away with Itself*. In this diatribe, he argued that generous social benefits attracted many Muslim immigrants, who are genetically inferior and inbred, dumb down German society, and refuse to integrate. They bear too many children, compared with Germany's educated classes, and they undermine Germany's future and doom it to decline. Sarrazin lost his job, but he touched a nerve and prompted some politicians to depart from political correctness. Bavarian minister president Horst Seehofer publicly stated that "we do not need any more migrants from other cultural centers." Even Chancellor Merkel entered the fray by asserting that Germany's attempt to create a multicultural society has "utterly failed." But she said at the same time that Islam "is part of Germany."

Many Germans blamed the untenable situation partly on article 16 of the Basic Law, which granted political asylum to all who claim it. It had been inspired by the fact that many German anti-Nazis had

Cats playing in Stuttgart

been saved during the Hitler era because they found asylum in democratic countries and by the fact that thousands of Jews perished because other countries had turned them away.

Germany receives many asylum seekers. In 2003, for the first time, more foreigners asked for asylum in Britain than in Germany, whose number was about 50,000. By 2007 that number had fallen to 19,000, the lowest in 30 years. However, the numbers were up the next year, due mostly to an increase in Iraqi applicants. Only about 1% of the Iraqis are granted asylum, but about a third are given refugee status, meaning that they can remain temporarily. In general, only a small minority of applicants is granted permanent sanctuary. One political result is that the right-wing parties continue to be demolished at the polls. Like many other EU countries, Germany had, in effect, adopted a zero-immigration policy. The year 2008 saw the lowest number of immigrants obtaining German citizenship since unification in 1990.

This created serious long-term problems for Germany, which needs new immigrants each year to fill out its shrinking labor ranks. German society is aging and in need of a large young cohort. The percentage of people of working age (20–65) is predicted to fall from 61% to 54% by 2030. The birth rate had fallen to only 1.4 children per woman. In 1960 German women bore 1.3 million children but only 680,000 in 2005. The average first-time mother is almost 30. By 2050, Germany's population could fall from the present 83,3 million (2024) to only 65 million; today it is falling by ca100,000 each year. To help working mothers manage work and newborns and to encourage middle-class and well-educated women to bear more children without abandoning their careers, "parents' pay" linked to their salaries is granted for 14 months; either parent can take up to 12 months off. Means of assisting unmarried couples and single mothers have also been devised. They still face problems with the schools, which are oriented around the stay-at-home mom. School is usually out at 1 p.m., and provisions have to be made to care for the kids the rest of the day. Only one in five children under three can get a place in a daycare facility (only 9% in the west).

About half of university-educated females have no children, and 51.1% of university graduates are female. Nevertheless, in 2010, only 69.7% of women worked (more in the east), up 6% since 1990. However, of women aged 25–49, more work part time (39%) than full time (34%). Few make it to the top: Only 9.5% of the board seats and 5% of senior management positions in the biggest companies are occupied by women. The wage gap is 23%, among the widest in the EU.

Mothers may return to their jobs after three years, but they often find that they have lost ground to men, who earn one-quarter more in full-time employment than women. Few top jobs in business are held by women. Every third woman with a job works part time, which is a serious career killer. *The Financial Times* of London estimated in 2005 that, in terms of promotion equality in the workplace and work-life balance, German women are a decade behind the rest of Europe and at least 15 years behind the US.

Concerns about mass immigration are an important reason two-thirds also opposed the eastward expansion of the EU. Their fears that they would lose their jobs to a flood of immigrants from the east prompted the government to negotiate a seven-year transition period before the labor market would be open to citizens of the new member states. The sentiment was so strong that politicians, most of whom supported EU enlargement, feared tackling it head on. Former chancellor Kohl had spoken for many when he declared, "Germany is not a country of immigration." Former chancellor Merkel did admit that Germany had become such a land. But to enable potential immigrants to integrate better, a new law in 2007 requires spouses from non-EU countries to acquire a basic knowledge of the German language before they are permitted to join their partners in Germany. Turks especially felt offended by this requirement.

In 2004 Germany adopted its first-ever immigration law. Proponents argued that the country needed to attract educated specialists to keep the economy competitive and stimulate excellence in research. Former chancellor Helmut Schmidt said in a 2004 interview, "There is almost no area where Germany stands out with its achievements." The law is a compromise that reflects the view that immigrants are risks and recognizes the widespread fear of opening the borders to political and religious militants. Although it makes it easier for skilled workers to come, it rejected a point system that would have permitted highly qualified foreigners to enter without an employment contract. Only those with a contract in hand may come. Employers must also continue to demonstrate that no German citizen can do the job that is being filled. It contains a long list of antiterrorist and antiextremist measures and gives the government greater leeway in arresting and deporting undesirable foreigners. Thus, although for the first time Germany has defined itself as an immigrant society, it remains difficult for foreigners to work or settle in Germany.

Germany participates in the EU Blue Card scheme. Similar to the Green Card in the US, the program offers up to four years

of residency (that can be extended) if the applicant has a job contract with a salary of at least €38,688 per year. A university degree is required, and people with specialized skills, such as mathematicians, scientists, engineers, doctors, and IT-skilled workers, are particularly welcome.

According to the Central Register of Foreign Nationals from 1990 to 2022, approximately 13.38 million foreigners lived in Germany in 2022. The share of foreigners was around 15 percent.

The Media

Germans are relatively well informed. Roughly three-fourths of all adults read at least one of the wide range of daily newspapers, although Germans under age 30 are less likely to read a daily than those over 40. The total number of independent dailies has declined. Most are regional papers; 76% of German readers buy a local paper rather than a national one. More and more newspapers and magazines have become concentrated in publication groups, and the majority of dailies are no longer editorially independent.

The largest such group is that controlled by Axel Springer, who produces about 25% of the total national output of daily newspapers. This includes the most widely read daily, *the Bild* (literally "Picture"), a sensationalist mixture of conservative politics, crime, sex, and gossip and read by more than a fourth of all adults. With a circulation of about 2 million, it is the world's largest-selling newspaper outside of Asia. Even this boulevard newspaper shares Germans' postwar restraint. When the German and English soccer teams faced each other in the semifinals of the European championships in 1996, British tabloids displayed headlines like "Watch Out Krauts!" "Achtung! Surrender," and "Filthy Hun!" German papers refused to respond in kind, and the Germans went on to win the cup.

The Springer enterprise also publishes one of the four informed, serious, nationally distributed elite newspapers, *Die Welt* (circulation 188,000). The others are the best-selling among quality newspapers (with a circulation of 370,000 in 2015), slightly left of center *Suddeutsche Zeitung* (published in Munich), the next-best-selling moderately conservative *Frankfurter Allgemeine Zeitung* (circulation 264,000 daily copies), and the outspoken left-liberal *Frankfurter Rundschau*. The authoritative *Handelsblatt* is the German counterpart to *the Wall Street Journal*, and Britain's *Financial Times* has a German-language edition. The lively *Taz* aims at an alternative audience. Most are having to shed staff, reduce pages, switch to tabloid formats (such as *the Berliner*), or be sold to other owners (e.g., *the Suddeutsche Zeitung*) in order to survive.

Germany

The political party press no longer plays a significant role as it did in the empire and Weimar Republic days. The CSU puts out its weekly *Bayernkurier*. Also, the Left Party continues to publish the daily *Neues Deutschland*, which has changed greatly from its dogmatic SED days; it reports news more objectively and is free to criticize some Left policies. All other newspapers in the GDR had been censored and controlled at least indirectly by the communists. In 1991 they were put on the auction block, and all but 2 of the 15 East German dailies were sold; the Trust Agency intervened to ensure that they did not all fall into the hands of the four major media magnates.

West German publishers bought the East German regional papers and gave them a new look. But none of West Germany's newspapers caught on in the east; only one-eighth of the total circulation is western. *Berliner Zeitung*, *Freie Presse* (Chemnitz), *Sachsische Zeitung* (Dresden), *Mitteldeutsche Zeitung* (Halle), and *Volksstimme* (Magdeburg) are widely read.

There are widely read weeklies. The highly influential *Der Spiegel*, with 5.9 million readers and 830,000 copies sold weekly in 2015, originally modeled itself after America's *Time*. Now it is far more opinionated, investigative, critical, and crusading in its reporting. In the words of the Economist, it "has probably done more to raise German blood pressure over the years than any other single publication." Its website has overwhelmed all rivals. Its staff controls the magazine and in 2008 dismissed its long-serving editor, Stefan Aust. Stern, with 735,000 copies and declining, is also investigative (some would say "muckraking"); since 1983 it has sported a black eye for publishing faked Hitler diaries, for which it had paid a fortune. *Die Zeit* is intelligent and politically moderate.

Public radio and television are administered by nonprofit public corporations that are financed chiefly by monthly fees paid by those who own televisions or radios and by limited advertising. There are nine regional radio-TV corporations, which combine to form the Association of Public Broadcasting Corporations (ARD) in the federal republic. The ARD sponsors the first TV channel, televised nationally, and the third channel, televised regionally. It also encompasses the two radio corporations, the *Deutschlandfunk* (Germany Radio), which broadcasts within all of Europe in German and 14 other languages, and the *Deutsche Welle* (German Wave), which transmits on short- and medium-wave all over the world in more than 30 languages. *Deutsche Welle* also has a televised version in German, English, and other languages.

A second German television channel, based in Mainz, transmits nationwide on the second TV channel. In order to ensure

that the radio and TV corporations remain politically independent, their legal basis is in state laws, and they are overseen by broadcasting councils composed of representatives of all important political, ideological, social, and religious groups. Although they are duty-bound not to favor any particular political party, their programming and the appointments to their councils and management do sometimes become subject to controversies among the parties.

Since the 1980s ARD's and ZDF's ratings have dropped significantly as private TV channels capture a larger and larger share of the audience. A growing number of adults watch a private all-news channel (N-TV) similar to CNN, and Phoenix, which is equivalent to C-Span. Private TV provides a lucrative market for US companies; of the foreign programs purchased by German networks, most are American.

Artistic Traditions and Theater

Germany has a glittering cultural tradition, but Nazi rule drove its cultural elite abroad, especially to the US. Germany has never regained its earlier preeminence. It can still claim a reputation for music, however. It has 72 orchestras and music theaters in the west, generously subsidized by the states or cities. Some are highly regarded internationally, such as the Berliner Philharmonik, the Sinfonie-Orchester of Munich, the Stuttgarter Kammerorchester, the Bach-Orchester of Munich, and the Berlin Amati-Ensemble.

Many foreign musicians, such as Ingrid Bjoner, Evelyn Lear, Jess Thomas, Tomas Stewart, and, it should not be forgotten, the Beatles, received their first significant stage experience in the FRG. Since the 1980s Anglo-Saxon musicals, especially those composed by Sir Andrew Lloyd Weber, have become popular. For example, by 1995 three of his shows had run for eight years in specially rebuilt theaters: *Starlight Express* in Bochum and *Cats* and *Phantom of the Opera* in Hamburg. *Cats* and *Dance of the Vampires* played to full audiences in Stuttgart in 2002. Major cities in the GDR also enjoy an excellent quality of performing arts.

In painting and sculpture, no postwar German artists have been able to establish a distinguishing German style that is internationally recognized as such. The FRG does have many artists who produce recognized works in styles coming from abroad. This is particularly visible in pop-art and hyperrealism, movements that emanated from the US.

The country is also filled with richly stocked art museums that show how many treasures the nation produced in the past. Sometimes new troves are found. In 2010 workers digging a new metro line near Berlin's Alexanderplatz unearthed many bronze and ceramic sculptures by such artists as Marg Moll and Otto Baum that had been stored in the burned-down Nazi propaganda ministry. They were part of the 5,000 works by such artists as Ernst Ludwig Kirchner, Paul Klee, and Max Ernst branded by Joseph Goebbels as "degenerate art" and confiscated from private collections and museums. Many are now admired in Berlin's Neues Museum and other museums.

In 2013 a spectacular collection of 1,406 works of art, valued an estimated €1 billion ($1.37 billion), were discovered in the Munich apartment of a reclusive 80-year-old, Cornelius Gurlitt. They included many "degenerate art" paintings. Sixty more works were found in his second home in Austria. His father, Hildebrand, had been one of only four traders allowed by the Nazis to deal in such art. In 2014 he returned about 300 of the paintings that had clearly been stolen from Jews. The sensation created by this discovery helped inspire an exhibit of "degenerate art" at New York's Neue Galerie in 2014. Fans thronged to this jewel of a museum to see it.

Gurlitt died in 2014, but he had named the Kunstmuseum Bern in Switzerland as his sole heir. It accepted the collection, but it stipulated that pieces suspected of being looted by the Nazis would remain in Germany until researchers could identify

their owners. It accepted those paintings the Nazis seized from museums as "degenerate art."

In literature, German writers after 1945 strove to make a clean break from the past. In their writings they tried to come to grips with their nation's experiences under dictatorship, in war, and in postwar misery. In the 1950s and 1960s, though, new themes emerged which focused on the materialism and egotism of a prosperous society. Many German writers became unmistakably political in their writings and, in a few cases, in their public involvement. The best known of such writers in the west are Heinrich Böll and Günter Grass, a Nobel Prize winner in 1999. Böll, who in 1972 became the sixth German to win the Nobel Prize in literature, wrote with grace and simplicity. He was an avowed moralist, who was in the forefront of the "peace movement."

Grass's German is full, rich, and imaginative, and through his fantasy characters, he bitterly criticized the shortcomings of his society. He was a staunch if often critical supporter of the SPD. He campaigned actively for the party and even wrote about his electoral activities in a book, *From the Diary of a Snail*. He was a man who relentlessly impressed upon his countrymen the moral necessity of not evading the memory of the Third Reich. It therefore came as a shock when he admitted in *Peeling the Onion* late in life that, as a 17-year-old boy, he himself had been a passionate Nazi and had even served in the Waffen-SS. His unit had the unusual assignment of trying to rescue Hitler from his Berlin bunker. He

**Günter Grass at
Stanford University in 1989**
Depicted by the author

ended up in an American POW camp disliking his victorious and well-fed captors.

In 2009 Herta Müller won the Nobel Prize in literature. She was largely unknown both abroad and outside of literary circles in Germany itself. Born in 1953, she grew up in a German-speaking city in the Banat region of Romania, where her thoughts and ideals collided with the rigid communist regime. She immigrated to Berlin in 1987. Her novels deal with the challenges of living in a dictatorship. Among her four novels translated into English are *The Land of Green Plums* and *The Appointment*. Her last book in 2009, published just before she received the prize, is a masterpiece about life in Soviet labor camps—*Everything I Own I Carry with Me*.

Much of contemporary western German literature is characterized by anxiety, malaise, self-doubt, and social criticism. The German public had also been receptive to another kind of critical literature, namely that coming from eastern Germany, where some of Germany's best postwar writing originated. GDR authors, like Stefan Heym, Christa Wolf, Ulrich Plenzdorf, and Jurek Becker (1937—1997), were widely published in the west. They were popular enough to disregard the simplicity of "socialist realism" and to criticize certain characteristics of the SED state. Wolf, who died in 2011, was criticized for withholding some of her criticism of the regime until after the GDR's fall, when she published *Was Bleibt* (What Remains), written 10 years earlier, describing how she had been watched by the secret police.

German theater survives because of massive state subsidies. They totaled €8.2 billion in 2003—45% from the localities, 43% from the states, and 12% from the federal government. That comes to €99 per capita. Ticket sales yield only about 15% of theaters' income. About half of western Germany's 370 theaters are privately owned. While many persons argue that state support enables more artistic guidance rather than commercial ambitions,

Germany

government cuts are hitting the arts hard. In 1993 two of Berlin's most famous theaters, the Schiller and the Schlosspark, were closed. Several dramatists have won international recognition, such as Heinar Kipphardt, Franz Xaver Kroetz, Martin Walser, and Peter Weiss. Rolf Hochhuth's play, *The Representative*, dealing with Pope Pius XII's attitude toward Hitler's extermination of the Jews, stirred up much impassioned discussion after the war; this gives an idea of how Germans searched their souls to understand their recent past.

The works of several East German authors, such as Peter Hacks and Ulrich Plenzdorf, were played with much success on western stages. East Germany had succeeded in maintaining a high standard of theater. Bertolt Brecht had returned there after wartime exile in the US and provided an important impetus to it. After 1989 eastern German theater has been able to become more experimental.

Until the mid-1960s it appeared that the German reputation in film, established before the war by such directors as Fritz Lang, Ernst Lubitsch, F. W. Murnau, G. W. Pabst, and Leni Riefenstahl (who died in 2003 at age 101) would be lost forever. The first two decades of postwar productions were mainly provincial, unproblematic entertainment films, which could be summed up in one German word: Schmalz (corniness). The need to compete with television for viewers helped keep the level of films low. Between 1956 and 1976, the annual production of German films and the number of cinemas dropped by 50%. Even today, about a fourth of all films shown in the FRG come from the US and a fifth from Italy and France.

Partly because of the 1968 Film Promotion Measures Act and a Film Promotion Agency (FFA), which channels state subsidies to producers of feature, documentary, short, and youth films, a wave of creative filmmaking, known as "the young German film," emerged in the 1960s. Federal funds, including its start-up loans, combine with a host of regional funds to dispense more than €200 million ($280 million) each year. A federal fund created in 2007 provides about €60 million ($84 million) more.

German directors in this wave have succeeded in winning international recognition. They include Alexander Kluge, Volker Schlöndorff, Johannes Schaaf, the late Rainer Werner Fassbinder, Hans-Jürgen Syberburg, Bernhard Sinkel, Margarethe von Trotte, and two directors who particularly like to place their films in American settings, Werner Herzog and Wim Winders. However, since they often fail to attract sufficiently large audiences, the federal government decided to curtail funding for heavily experimental and purely artistic films after 1983.

Merkel and Westerwelle, poor victors, no money for good deeds

A refreshing exception to social criticism in film is Doris Dorrie, a self-assured young director. She went to the US to become an actress, but instead she studied film and theater in California and New York. In her box-office success *Manner* (Men), the characters laugh about themselves and each other, and their laughter is contagious for the audience. She reflects the waning ideological inclinations of contemporary Germans: "I grew up with pop concerts, not with political discussions. The fact that I do not deal with big political themes is directly linked to that."

Some German producers learned to thrive on the American market, such as Wolfgang Peterson, who did *The Perfect Storm*, and Roland Emmerich, who produced the ultimate American flag-waving film *The Patriot*. In 2003 a film directed by Caroline Links, *Nowhere in Africa*, won an Oscar for best foreign-language film. This came 24 years after Volker Schlöndorff's film, *Tin Drum*, won the same award.

A banner year for German film was 2003, when two blockbusters hit German theaters. *Good Bye, Lenin!* is a bittersweet comedy of a young man who recreates the former GDR in the bedroom of his sick mother. She had gone into a coma just before the Berlin Wall fell and would die of shock to know that her socialist paradise no longer existed. The fond memories of the GDR delight audiences, especially in the east. Directed by Wolfgang Becker, it grossed $40 million in one year and dominated the European Film Awards.

Germans had a different emotional experience in 2003 when they saw *The Miracle of Bern*, directed by Sönke Wortmann. It retells the story of Germany's come-from-behind victory in the soccer World Cup in

1954. The victory had unleashed a tremendous wave of emotion in a Germany still recovering from defeat and devastation. It was the first time in decades that Germans were recognized in the world for nonaggressive achievement. It was a "feel-good" film with the message that one can feel proud of Germany and also sympathize with the millions of Germans who suffered during and after the war.

The same cannot be said about the 2004–2005 international hit *Downfall*, a troubling film by Oliver Hirschbiegel portraying a humanized Hitler in his Berlin bunker during the last five days of his life. Some Germans and Americans argued that it was inappropriate to show Hitler as a human being, who was polite and considerate toward his female staff and willing to kiss his mistress Eva Braun on the lips.

Another good year for cinema was 2007, when Florian Henckel von Donnersmarck's film *The Lives of Others* won the Oscar for best foreign-language film. It is about a Stasi officer who oversteps his orders and covers up for his victims. Von Donnersmarck's next movie, in 2010, was the exact opposite, an expensive Hollywood film *The Tourist*. In 2010 Michael Haneke's *The White Ribbon* won the Palme d'Or at Cannes and an Oscar nomination for best foreign-language film. This stark black-and-white film explores the culture and society out of which national socialism grew.

East Germany's film industry was centered in the DEFA film production studios in Potsdam-Babelsberg (using the oldest large-scale film studio in the world). Founded in 1946, it was the site of the entire GDR film industry and included a college

Goethe's reminder: "The country that does not protect strangers will soon go under." Photo by Logan Hancock

for film and TV and an agency for film exports and imports. Before 1989 it had annually produced about 20 feature films, 25 TV films, 170 documentaries, and many animated films. In 1992 Volker Schlöndorff stepped in to rescue the Babelsberg studio, acting as its business manager and attracting investors. By 1996 it had again become one of the world's most advanced film facilities, producing more than one feature film a month, as well as soap operas and TV dramas.

Some movies with international stars were made there. They included Matt Damon in *The Bourne Supremacy*; Tom Cruise, who played Hitler's hapless assassin Claus Schenk von Stauffenberg in *Valkyrie*; and Clive Owen and Naomi Watts in *The International*.

A controversial German TV series about five friends drawn into World War II was made in 2014 into feature film entitled *Generation War*. Shown in more than 80 countries, it portrays a young German generation subjected to systematic indoctrination and gradual brutalization. Critics detected a message of German victimhood. It was particularly condemned in Poland.

GERMANY IN EUROPE

In many ways, Germany is at the crossroads, and its current policies are likely to shape the future of the country in dramatic ways similar to the reunification process or the aftermath of World War II. Facing growing challenges and international demands, the Germans are searching their souls and taking on some taboos. The massive migration of refugees, primarily from the Middle East and Africa, created unprecedented demands but also opportunities, exposing some fissures within the society while also allowing Germany to redefine itself. In the process, Germany is searching for its new place in Europe, especially as Brexit provoked a massive reshaping of the continent. Germany will also have to play the crucial role in the European response to challenges from Russia.

The influx of 1.3 million refugees thrusted Angela Merkel into the global spotlight like few other events. Her steadfast conviction that "we can manage that" stood in sharp contrast to reactions throughout the European Union, earning her much goodwill and admiration. Germans initially responded with enthusiasm, and the images of common citizens opening their arms and houses to foreigners in need provided a striking counterpoint to far more hostile actions in Hungary or North Macedonia. Yet, the welcome did not last long, as two events in particular turned the tide of public opinion. In November 2015 ISIS terrorists killed 130

people in a coordinated series of attacks in Paris. Later, on New Year's Eve in Cologne, Hamburg, and other German cities, gangs of young North Africans harassed and sexually assaulted as many as 1,000 women. Even though the Paris terrorists were EU citizens and only some perpetrators of the Cologne attacks were recent asylum seekers, the wave of indignation against Angela Merkel's open-door policy brought out thousands of protesters into the streets. The protesters captured public imagination with posters proclaiming (in English) "RAPEfugees not welcome" and featuring a black hand reaching between white legs, a controversial image originally published on the cover of *Suddeutsche Zeitung*, one of Germany's most respected liberal publications. Merkel's popularity suffered greatly, and challenges kept mounting. Not the least of them was the terrorist attack in December 2016, when a jihadi extremist drove a heavily loaded truck into a crowd of Christmas shoppers in Berlin. The perpetrator was a Tunisian national whose application for asylum had been rejected and who pledged allegiance to ISIS. The attack left 12 people dead and 56 injured.

Germany has changed the way it looks. A majority of Frankfurt residents have an immigrant background, including three-quarters of children under age six. The newcomers need housing, schools, and jobs, not to mention ways to assimilate into their new cultural surroundings. A teachers' association estimated that an additional 25,000 teachers were needed, and some feared a lowering of standards in the German educational system. College-age refugees stand to lose years of education, as they lack school records and German-language skills, which prompted the creation of a transitional online Kiron University, sponsored by donations. Language remains a serious barrier to most (an important reason for the rapidly growing popularity of German as a second language in the Middle East), and some nationalities are further hampered by high illiteracy rates or the inability to read the Latin alphabet. A disproportionate percentage of refugees end up on Germany's generous unemployment rolls.

However, the overall economic impact of the migrant influx is likely to be positive. The estimated $4.5 billion in 2015 and as much as $11 billion in 2016 that Germany had to spend on accommodating the refugees has been likened by *the Economist* to a stimulus package of sorts. Indeed, Germany's solid economic performance at the federal and state levels still allows it to be generous, and the additional spending may actually increase the growth rate. Labor shortages in the industry can be alleviated, too. The refugees also fill a crucial demographic niche in the rapidly aging country that badly needs

Germany

overall rejuvenation, as well as young workers to help pay for the benefits of the older generation. Germany is once again calling out for foreign labor.

Some estimates predicted the population of Germany to shrink by 20 million by 2060, with eastern and rural regions affected the most. Here the refugees provide more than a glimmer of hope, since many are directed to settle in old industrial towns in former East Germany, now partly depopulated because the old companies have been boarded up and many young people have moved west. Some such locations can no longer support schools, banks, or libraries, so the new residents may help resurrect them. For example, Merseburg in Saxony-Anhalt accepted some 2,800 refugees, who swelled the quiet city's population of 36,000.

Such instances create new social challenges since, rather than being scattered throughout the country, large concentrations of foreigners are clustered together, making assimilation more difficult. They also make for easy targets for the propaganda and assaults by right-wing groups. At its time Merkel's government could ill afford to ignore the rumbling on the far right just as its neighbors, Poland and Austria, have been shifting in that direction.

Despite the refugee upheaval and the associated rise in right-wing parties and movements, Germany remains an economic powerhouse and easily the biggest economy in Europe. In 2022, the unemployment rate was 3.2%. According to the Boston Consulting Group's Sustainable Economic Development Assessment for 2015, its greater investment in education and infrastructure results in higher economic well-being than that of the United States. Remarkably, sportswear maker Adidas announced that, in a reversal of the usual direction of outsourcing, it is bringing

manufacturing back to Germany after 20 years of production in Asia. The new shoe line will be produced entirely by robots.

Acts of international terrorism, Russia's growing assertiveness, and thousands of refugees knocking on Europe's door force the usually inward-looking Germans to re-evaluate their position in the world. Only two decades ago, even sending peacekeeping troops to Bosnia was extremely controversial, as was bombing Serbia a few years later. In 2011, Germany preferred to abstain from a UN Security Council vote that authorized "all necessary measures" to protect civilians in Libya. Chastised for years for contributing little to maintaining global security from which it was benefiting, Germany is moving with more self-assurance now. Merkel's tough stance on the Greek bailout confirmed to the rest of Europe who really calls the shots in the European Union and signaled Germany's readiness to hold its partners to its own standards. While Germany had volunteered to anchor itself in the EU in order to be constrained by the institution, it is now steering the European colossus.

Former Chancellor Merkel, unlike most of her predecessors, boldly confronted Russia and led the efforts to contain Putin's ambitions in Ukraine and beyond. In this she was often ahead of her own compatriots, who supported sanctions on Russia only reluctantly and who were not in favor of any military action in the region. This may be changing, too. Having seen its military forces gradually trimmed from 585,000 in 1990 to 179,000 in 2019, Germany announced plans to increase its military budget by 6% over five years and to boost its troop level to 184,000 by 2023. Public- opinion polls indicate an increase of support for such plans—from only 15% in 2009 to 45% in 2016. More than at any time since World

War II, Germans seem ready to defend the postwar order and the prosperity and peace it brought. Before the EU-imposed sanctions related to Moscow's intervention in Ukraine, Russia accounted for 4% of German trade; with sanctions in place, this number shrunk to 2.4%.

Besides the military, other extended security measures include large handouts to countries surrounding Syria, with the calculation that it is cheaper to prevent new refugees from reaching Europe than having to accommodate them and face potential problems within the EU's borders. Germany was a crucial mover of the deal between the EU and Türkiye, signed on November 29, 2015, that gave the EU a huge if morally questionable respite. Türkiye agreed to stem the tide of refugees passing through it on their way to Greece and the rest of the European Union and to accept those rejected for asylum. In exchange, Türkiye's moribund membership application to the EU was restarted, and visa-free travel was promised, with additional substantial resources offered to Türkiye to help manage the refugees in that country. This was a radical change for then Chancellor Merkel, who had opposed Türkiye's EU bid and criticized the human rights record of Recep Erdoğan, now the increasingly autocratic president of Türkiye. Then a German satirist decided to test the limits of free speech in his country by declaiming on television a highly offensive poem ridiculing Erdoğan, to which both the Turkish president and his government responded by demanding that Germany enforce the outmoded paragraph 103 of its penal code, providing penalties for insulting foreign heads of state.

Among much political outcry, Angela Merkel overrode her coalition partners' objections, and the government approved criminal prosecution in the case. SPD, as well as some opposition parties, accused Merkel of trading freedom of speech for the convenient refugee deal with Türkiye. However, after Erdoğan's crackdown on his opponents in the aftermath of the July 2016 abortive coup in Türkiye, the EU again hardened its approach. Germany granted political asylum to several hundred Turkish diplomats and military officers threatened with persecution by Erdoğan. In response, Türkiye blocked a delegation of German parliamentarians from visiting German troops stationed at the Incirlik Air Base near the Syrian border. The 260 troops were engaged in reconnaissance and refueling flights while fighting against ISIS. Germany would need to move the troops to Jordan, a far less convenient location and not a NATO member. Türkiye was also angered by a number of German municipalities that prevented governmental officials from Türkiye from

Body language: Barack Obama and Angela Merkel

Germany

campaigning among the Turkish population in Germany in favor of constitutional changes giving Erdoğan substantial new powers. He compared those moves to "Nazi practices." Despite the tensions, EU's refugee agreement with Türkiye remains in place.

For all the criticism, at the 2017 parliamentary election, Merkel's position remained solid, both because of her achievements and because there seemed to be no viable alternative to her. She remained Germany's most trusted politician and Germans nicknamed her "Mutti" (Mom). In 2015, Time magazine declared her the person of the year "for asking more of her country than most politicians would dare, for standing firm against tyranny as well as expedience, and for providing steadfast moral leadership in a world where it is in short supply." Various rankings listed her among the most influential politicians in the world, and some even called her an "indispensable leader in Europe."

Merkel dealt with the US in a way that she could say no without alienating it. For example, she publicly criticized American detention policy at Guantanamo Bay while on an official visit to Washington. She also called NSA spying in Germany "unacceptable." In her first government declaration, she appealed, "Let the battles of the past lie. Those battles have been fought." She maintained a rather stiff but constructive and later even warm relationship with the American president, Barack Obama. Facing change in the White House after the 2016 presidential elections, Germans needed to acknowledge the American preoccupation with China rather than with Europe and the demands that Germany and other Europeans should shoulder more burdens for common defense.

Germany is the third-largest exporter in the world, and its trade surplus in 2016 was $282.7 billion. Germany reacted with outrage in June 2017 when the US Senate approved a bill imposing new sanctions on Russia that could penalize foreign companies for providing material support to Russia in building gas or oil pipelines. German companies working on or benefiting from the Nord Stream 2 project would be likely to suffer, and German officials publicly warned of a possible retaliation. In the process, the allies' unity on the sanctions themselves was damaged. In an unguarded—or perhaps calculated—moment, Angela Merkel dropped a bomb when she declared that "the times when we could fully rely on others are, to a certain extent, over."

At the same time, Merkel fully understood the importance of the transatlantic connection that has been one of the cornerstones of Germany's policy since World War II. Before the July 2017 G20 summit in Hamburg, then US secretary of defense Mattis and German defense minister von der Leyen reaffirmed the bond between their countries.

The reinvigorated Franco-German axis may be the European Union's best hope after the earth-shaking reverberations of Brexit and the populist challenges to the European project. Tellingly, one fallout from the Brexit negotiations is the sizeable increase in support for the European Union among Germans. In 2017, the Pew Research Center found that 68% of them had a favorable opinion of the EU, up from just 50% a year earlier. Germans also noted with some glee that the number of German citizenship applications from Great Britain nearly quadrupled in 2016 from 2015.

CURRENT ISSUES

More than 25 years after reunification, Germany has yet to see its society unified—despite all the early enthusiasm and willingness to sew the two parts together, stiches are still visible, and economic disparities create new wounds. And yet, Germany is a very different country now than it was in 1990—increasingly confident and not afraid to tell others what to do, a model in green thinking, and an inspiration to other victims of totalitarianism. It ranks at the top of BBC surveys of the most popular countries in the world and boasts one of the fastest-growing Jewish communities worldwide. It joined the military operations against ISIS and sent thousands of soldiers to Afghanistan (more than 50 were killed there). Defying persistent stereotypes and attempts to detect "national traits" that supposedly make them naturally prone to authoritarianism, Germans are one of the success stories in post-World War II Europe. They are solidly democratic and seemingly able to deal with occasional extremist setbacks; they are financially secure and innovative, with a generous welfare system that is an envy of others. It is also a magnet to others, which is creating its own challenges, still to be solved. One way or another, it is probably safe to say that never in their history have Germans been simultaneously so free, so peaceful, so prosperous, and so admired in the world as today. In a 2018 Pew survey in 134 countries on global leadership, 41% of respondents ranked Germany as the top-rated global power, well ahead of the United States.

Chancellor Merkel's humane decision in 2015 to allow over 1 million refugees into the country cost her dearly. Germany was ready for change. She had served as chancellor for 16 years, only two weeks short of Helmut Kohl's record. The September 2021 elections were the first in the postwar period in which an incumbent chancellor did not stand for reelection. However, she left with an 80% approval rating, while her Christian Democratic Union is in historic decline. Many Germans will see her successor, Olaf Scholz, as a pale shadow of her leadership.

However, he shares Merkel's air of serenity and competence. A successful employment lawyer in his native Hamburg, where he had been mayor, he has displayed skillful leadership in dealing with his country's support for Ukraine's valiant struggle to be free of Russia's domination. It took only two months after the 2021 elections to put together a rare three-party "traffic light" coalition, so named after the colors of the parties that make it up. Germany is a strong, rich, democratic country that has a bright future.

Body language: Donald Trump and Angela Merkel

Republic of Austria (Republik Österreich)

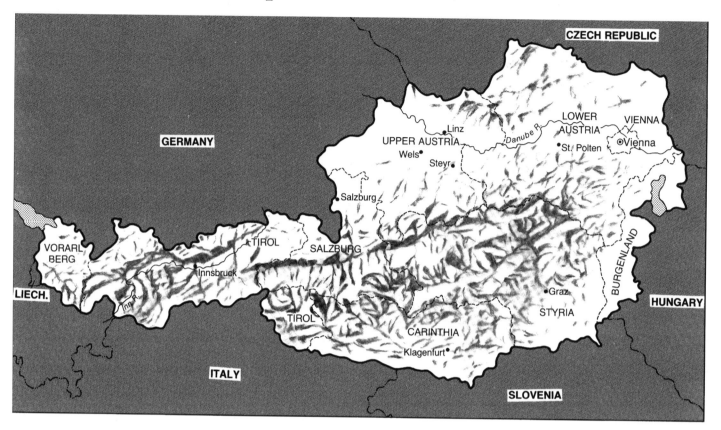

Area: 32,383 sq. mi. (83,871 sq. km).
Population: 9,050,000 (2023 estimate)
Capital City: Vienna (pop. 2,002,821 urban; 2,890,577 metro)
Climate: As nearly three-quarters of the country dominated by the Alps, the Alpine climate is predominant in the west. In the east, in the Pannonian Plain and along the Danube valley, the climate is continental with less rain than in the Alpine areas. The temperatures range from about −11°–0° C (12°–32° F) in January to about 2°–20° C (36°–68° F) in July, depending on the region.
Neighboring Countries: Czech Republic and Germany (north); Switzerland and Liechtenstein (west); Italy and Slovenia (south); Hungary and Slovak Republic (east).
Official Language: German.
Other Languages: Official regional languages—Hungarian, Slovene, Burgenland Croatian
Ethnic Background: 75.6% Austrians, 24.4% other
Religion: 64.1% Christianity (55.2% Roman Catholic, 5.1% Orthodox, 3.8% other Christian), 8.3% Islam, 1.2% other, 26.4% no religion (2021 estimate).
Form of Government: Federal parliamentary republic
Chief of State: Alexander Van der Bellen, President (since January 2017).
Head of Government: Karl Nehammer, Chancellor (since December 2021).
National Flag: It is a horizontal triband of red, white, and red. The Austrian flag is considered to be of the oldest national symbols still in use by a modern country. It originated from the arms of the Babenberg dynasty and its first recorded use was in the 13th century. The legend has it that the flag was devised by Duke Leopold V of Austria as a consequence of his fighting during the Third Crusade. After a fierce battle, his white surcoat was completely drenched in blood. When he removed his belt, the cloth beneath remained unstained, revealing the combination of red-white-red. He was so impressed by the sight that he adopted the colors and scheme as his banner. Unlike other flags, such as the black-and-yellow one of the Habsburgs, the red-white-red flag was from very early on associated, not with a reigning family or monarch but with the country itself. In addition to serving as the flag of Austria, it was adopted as the naval ensign and flag of the Grand Duchy of Tuscany in the 18th and Duchy of Modena and Reggio in the 19th century, which were then ruled by cadet branches of the House of Habsburg. As a state emblem, the Austrian flag has the national symbol, a double-headed, black eagle centered in the white band.
Public Holiday: October 26 (Austrian National Day).
Currency: Euro (€) (EUR).
Main Exports: Machinery and transport equipment, consumer goods, chemicals, food, drink and tobacco, paper products.
Main Imports: Machinery and transport equipment, consumer goods, chemicals, raw materials, food, drink and tobacco.
Main Trading Partners: Germany (29.9% of exports and 32.2% of imports), United States (6.7% of exports and 4.1% of imports), Italy (6.8% of exports and 6.1% of imports), China (8.1% of imports), Switzerland (5.1% of exports and 4.7% of imports), France (4.2% of exports), Czech Republic (4.6% of imports), Hungary (4.0 of exports).

Austria is a landlocked Alpine country. Three-fourths of its territory, particularly in the west and south, is covered by some of the most majestic mountains in the world. It is but a small piece of the huge, multinational Austro-Hungarian Empire that collapsed in 1918. It was always a hub for north-south European traffic, and the Danube River, which flows from southern Germany through northern Austria and Vienna, through eastern Europe, and empties into the Black Sea, has always been an important transportation link between eastern and western Europe.

About three-fourths of Austria is embedded geographically within what has been known since World War II as eastern Europe; this fact made the former Soviet Union particularly interested in Austrian neutrality. It also has made Austria a natural meeting place for leaders of eastern and western Europe, as well as a land of refuge for several hundred thousand eastern Europeans since 1945.

Austria is a country of truly extraordinary natural beauty. Its snow-capped peaks overlook lush, green valleys; countless streams and lakes; and picturesque mountain villages. Austria is filled with architectural reminders of its imperial past. Everywhere one sees elaborately decorated baroque churches; imposing castles and palaces; and large, serene monasteries and cloisters. Every major city, especially Vienna, has rich museums and elegant theaters that keep alive the artistic tradition of the country. Also, more than a dozen musical festivals take place in Austria every year, the most famous being in Salzburg. These testify to a creative musical past almost unparalleled in the entire world.

The visitor is greeted by a people who are relaxed, friendly, hospitable, and strongly traditional, especially outside the capital city of Vienna, where about one-sixth of the country's population lives. Almost 9 out of 10 of its people are Roman Catholic, and 99% speak dialects of German that have a distinctive and pleasant musical ring to them. There are three small language minorities in Carinthia, where 20,000 Slovenes live along the border of Slovenia, and in the Burgenland, along the southeastern border, where 25,000 Croatians and some Hungarians live. Small Czech and Slovak minorities have also survived in Vienna. There are about 750,000 foreigners in the country, 9% of the total population. Many are from former Yugoslavia and Türkiye.

In some ways Austria is strikingly similar to neighboring Switzerland. Both are naturally beautiful and economically prosperous countries. Despite a high degree of cultural diversity, both are politically stable democracies. Both are federal states, although Austrian politics are more centralized than is the case in Switzerland. Both pursued neutralist foreign policies. Yet there are also undeniable differences. Whereas centuries ago the Swiss established a secure national identity, Austrians until recently lacked a clear consensus on what it actually meant to be an Austrian. Also, in Switzerland a stable democracy was able to evolve slowly and was therefore able gradually to gain the backing of the overwhelming majority of its citizens. By contrast, Austria remained a highly stratified and traditional country until well into the 20th century and has confronted an almost-traumatic change of its political, social, and economic practices and values.

HISTORY

The Early Period

Historical evidence indicates that what is now Austria has been settled since the late Ice Age, almost 3,000 years ago. Indications of earlier human presence are uncertain. Between 35 and 15 BC, the Romans conquered the Celtic inhabitants and divided the area among three Roman provinces. The new masters gave the region many of the same benefits they bestowed on other lands: Roman law and administration, a well-developed network of good roads, aqueducts, and new forms of agriculture, including wine making. They founded most of Austria's cities, such as Vienna, Salzburg, and Linz, and between 150 and 350 AD, they introduced Christianity.

When the Roman Empire began to crumble, the area that is now Austria became vulnerable to invasions by Germanic, Hun, and other tribes, which brought much destruction to the area from the 5th through the 8th centuries. Not until Charlemagne established a bulwark in the extreme eastern part of his huge empire in 799 did the area become relatively stable and secure. He called this area his East March (frontier); its present name in German, Österreich, reflects the area's earlier role. From 799 on, Austria's destiny was very closely tied to that of the rest of the Germanic world.

Part of the Holy Roman Empire and Habsburg Rule

Austria became a part of the Holy Roman Empire in 962, and a few years later the House of Babenberg began its 270-year reign over the country. The Babenbergs gradually moved their capital eastward and, in the 12th century, finally established it in the Hofburg (literally, the "court fortress") in Vienna. The last Babenberg ruler fell in 1246 in one of the countless struggles against the Hungarians.

Count Rudolf of a family from the "Habichtsburg" in the Aargau area of Switzerland was selected Holy Roman emperor in 1273. This Habsburg family ruled Austria for the next 600 years, and under its leadership, Austria rose to be one of the grandest powers of all of Europe. This extremely rapid growth inevitably changed European

Young Maria Theresia

Mature Maria Theresia

Austria

A salon in the Schönbrunn Palace

politics drastically. The Habsburg genius was to be able to expand its empire more by wise marriages than by war. By the 16th century, they had acquired an empire over which the sun never set. Flanders and Burgundy had been gained through a marriage with Mary of Burgundy. In 1516 Spain came under Habsburg rule, and in 1521 two Habsburg brothers saw a need to divide administratively the last empire between themselves. This was not the end of growth; in 1526 Bohemia and Hungary were unified with Austria. Most of Latin America, except Brazil, came under Habsburg rule, as did the Netherlands, the rest of Belgium, Naples, Sardinia, Sicily, and a few provinces in eastern France. This huge empire was geographically divided, with major centers as diverse as Vienna, Brussels, Zaragoza, and Naples; it had no unifying elements, except the ruling House of Habsburg.

Defense against the Turks

Austria was often forced to perform its duty of defending Europe from the east. In 1529 and 1683, the Turks actually reached the gates of Vienna and besieged the city. Both times the Austrians pushed them back, the second time with the help of Poland's Jan III Sobieski and his "winged hussars" in one of the largest cavalry charges in history. Led by a foreign prince, Eugene of Savoy, a grand nephew of the French cardinal Mazarin, the imperial forces drove the Turks out of Hungary, thereby stemming once and for all the Turkish tide westward. An influential national hero, Eugene ordered the construction of one of Vienna's most beautiful palaces, Belvedere, which served as his summer residence. His winter palace is now the office of the Austrian minister of finance. His time was an era of the

Baroque, a style which reached its zenith in Vienna and Salzburg and which can still be admired everywhere in Austria.

Maria Theresia

The Austrian Empire had become the envy of other rising European states, which looked for a chance to snatch attractive chunks of its holdings. When the Austrian Emperor Karl VI died in 1740, one rising power moved particularly swiftly—Prussia. In both Prussia and Austria, two young monarchs ascended to the thrones in 1740. They dominated much of the European scene for the next four decades and converted Germany into a loose bundle of many states with two dominant powers.

In Prussia, a philosophically inclined 28-year-old Friedrich II was crowned king. Later known as Friedrich the Great, he had composed chamber music and written books condemning war and immorality in politics. In Austria a 22-year-old woman who had shown great interest in the arts but virtually none in politics became empress—Maria Theresia. Preferring to reside in the more gracious Schönbrunn Palace rather than the Hofburg, she became a devoted wife and the mother of 16 children to whom she gave as much love and concern as any mother could.

She presented herself to her people as a happy, sincere, pious, philanthropic, and folksy ruler, and she was loved and respected by almost all of her subjects. Yet she was a courageous and hardworking ruler who had a knack for choosing able advisers and was stubbornly determined to defend her empire and the Catholic faith. Calling her the "first and supreme mother of her lands," the Austrians under her leadership tenaciously fought Friedrich in three wars and were forced in the Treaty of Hubertusburg in 1763 to concede

the province of Silesia to Prussia, which had risen to the status of a major European power as a result of the wars. She had moral qualms about taking advantage of some of the diplomatic opportunities that offered themselves, such as participating in the partition of Poland, but for reasons of state, she did it anyway. It is no wonder that Friedrich the Great referred to her as "the only man among my opponents."

During her reign Vienna bloomed. Today both the works of Haydn and Mozart, as well as the streets in the city that boasts palaces, fountains, and statues, attest to the greatness of her era. Vienna became the cultural center of the German speaking world. It also became the sole center for administering the far-flung Austrian Empire, and Austrian politics still reflects the high degree of centralization that Maria Theresia intensified. She was absolutely opposed to religious toleration and attempts to reform her empire "from below." She herself introduced lasting reforms, though. She separated the judiciary from the administration, abolished torture, established elementary schools, and removed the universities from church control.

Her son, Josef II, a liberal ruler, accelerated the reform process after her death in 1780 by eliminating all traces of serfdom and by granting his subjects the right to choose their preferred religion. Habsburg rule at this time was conscientious and, in some respects farsighted, but it nevertheless was "enlightened absolutism." The principles of democracy and equality were greatly distrusted and persistently opposed, which is one reason Austria was unable to resist the tide set in motion by the French Revolution in 1789.

Napoleon

When Napoleon created in 1806 a "Confederation of the Rhine" dependent upon France, Kaiser Franz (the title derived from "caesar" meaning "emperor") renounced the crown of the "Holy Roman Empire of the German Nation," and that long moribund entity ceased to exist entirely. Napoleon's Grand Army crushed the Austrian forces in 1809 at Wagram, and the French emperor was able to dictate a humiliating "Peace of Schönbrunn" from the once-beloved residence of Maria Theresia. Austria had its revenge after the bulk of Napoleon's experienced troops had frozen to death in the bitterly cold snows of Russia. An Austrian general, Prince Karl Schwarzenberg, commanded the victorious allied forces at the Battle of the Nations against Napoleon near Leipzig in 1813.

The Congress of Vienna and the "Holy Alliance"

An Austrian foreign minister, Prince Klemens von Metternich, was a Rhinelander who led Austria from collaboration with Napoleon to an alliance with his enemies and therefore ensured victory. He was able in 1814 to assemble 6 emperors and kings, 11 princes, and 90 accredited envoys at the Congress of Vienna for eight months in order to reconstruct Europe after the fall of Napoleon. The flood of political figures and their entourages provided many Viennese the splendid opportunity to rent out their houses at exorbitant prices and to escape to the countryside to count their windfall profits.

Those foreign notables who could not afford the high prices either slept in the city's beautiful parks or in or under their carriages. Most envoys spent their time in cafes, at balls, at receptions, or at tournaments trying to amuse themselves, while the major powers, Britain, Austria, Prussia, Russia and, surprisingly, the loser—France—were deciding Europe's fate behind closed doors. In the final settlement, Austria's hold over peoples in eastern and southern Europe was recognized. The Austrian monarch thus continued to rule over a multinational empire led by Germans and composed of Czechs, Slovaks, Poles, Hungarians, Italians, Croatians, Slovenes, Serbs, and others.

Austria's attention now more than ever had to be directed away from the German world. Still, it was determined to compete with Prussia for dominance within Germany. Prussia had been granted German lands in the Rhine and Palatinate areas in order to help keep a potentially revengeful France from springing beyond its borders. This arrangement, which led Prussia into the heart of Germany and Austria out of it, ultimately helped Prussia to defeat Austria in the struggle for control of Germany.

Emerging from the Vienna Congress was a "Holy Alliance," which was dedicated

Maximilian I of Mexico
Source: *Austrian Information*

to preventing further reform within Europe. Britain left this pact almost as soon as it had been created, but Russia, Austria, and Prussia remained. All three ultimately paid very dearly for their determination to dig in their heels and to ignore the signs of the times.

The spirit of the "Holy Alliance" matched Austria's mood very well. It had a conservative elite, who ruled over a very hierarchically organized society. The nobility owned most of the land and provided the bulk of the army officers, diplomats, and upper civil servants. Most of the peasants were poor and powerless, while the bourgeoisie scrambled for whatever authority or titles they could obtain. To this day, Austrians probably remain the most title-conscious people in Europe. Fortunate are those who can attach a "Herr Doktor" or a "Frau Professor Doktor" to his or her name—and female spouses are permitted to borrow their

partner's titles. Others use such titles as "Herr Engineer (or Businessman) with Diploma," "Herr Government Counselor," or "Herr Chief Postal Official."

Prince Metternich took the task of opposing change as seriously as did Kaiser Franz, who proclaimed in 1831, "I won't have any innovations!" The press was heavily censored, and mail was opened and read by government agents. Spies were sent into university lectures, and school authorities were obligated to report any sentiments that might be considered subversive. Students were forbidden from studying in foreign universities, and until 1848 all reading materials used in schools or universities required government approval.

Revolutionary Stirrings

Given the repression of individual freedoms and of the right of national minorities to manage a part of their own affairs, it is not surprising that the wave of revolution in 1848 also shook the Austrian state. A Hungarian nationalist, Louis Kossuth, and others demanded constitutional government for Hungary, but Kossuth admitted that this would be impossible as long as "a corrupting puff of wind that benumbs our senses and paralyzes the flight of our spirit comes to us from the charnel house of the cabinet of Vienna." Fighting soon broke out in Vienna, where a flabbergasted kaiser asked, when told that rebels were taking to the streets, "But are they allowed to do that?" The rebels had momentary success, until they became hopelessly disunited over the objectives that should be sought.

The Habsburgs were forced to dismiss Metternich, and the incompetent kaiser abdicated in favor of his 18-year-old nephew, Franz Josef, a serious and hardworking monarch who ascended the throne with

The Young Franz Josef

Seat of the Congress of Vienna (Foreign Ministry until 2005)

Austria

Archduke Franz Ferdinand and Emperor Franz Joseph

the words "Farewell youth!" and who ruled for the next 68 years. His younger brother, Ferdinand Maximilian, ruled as Emperor Maximilian I of Mexico from 1864 until 1867, when he was executed by firing squad. A constitution, albeit authoritarian in character, was accepted, and Austria sent representatives to the Frankfurt Assembly, which sought unsuccessfully to draft a liberal constitution for all German speaking people. Ultimately the revolution failed in Austria, as it did almost everywhere else in Europe. Nevertheless, it had badly shaken the empire and revealed deep dissatisfaction with a form of government that was not democratic and did not recognize the rights of subject nationalities. Yet, once the revolutionary storm had blown over, the new ruler showed how little he had learned by enforcing a policy characterized by absolutism and tight centralization.

Competition and Partnership with Prussia

In 1866 Austria suffered a crushing defeat at the hands of the Prussian army at the Battle of Koniggratz. With new breech-loading rifles, which had been used so successfully in the American Civil War, and the capacity to move their troops to the battlefield on new railroads, the Prussians were far better prepared than the Austrians, whose wealth had been spent to construct the stately Ringstrasse in the center of Vienna rather than to modernize their army. This defeat finally wiped away any Austrian dreams of dominating or sharing power over all of Germany and cleared the way for a "small German"

unification clustered around Prussia and excluding Austria.

For more than a century, the dualism within Germany pitting Austria and Prussia against one another had powerfully influenced the European constellation of nations. That dualism was destroyed, and the relationship between the two states became one of partnership. The Prussian chancellor, Otto von Bismarck, refused his generals' request for permission to make a victory march straight through the heart of Vienna in order to humiliate Prussia's longtime rival. Bismarck remarked that it was not his aim to humiliate or judge but rather to serve Prussia's interests. Prussia needed a trustworthy ally, and for the next half-century, Austria played that role. For instance, in 1870 Austria did not try to prevent Prussia's unification of Germany by supporting the French in the Franco-Prussian War of 1870.

Continuing Nationalities Problems

The new German Empire, which was proclaimed in the Hall of Mirrors at the Palace of Versailles in January 1871, had acquired an ally that would become increasingly weakened by its nationalities problem. The 19th century saw the birth of nationalist movements all over Europe. A multinational state like Austria had to swim against the current of the age and could survive only by introducing timely reforms to satisfy the aspirations of national minorities. Austria was never able to do this.

The German-speaking minority of the Austro-Hungarian Empire was able to reach a compromise with the Hungarians in 1867 as a direct consequence of the

Crown Prince Rudolf

defeat at Koniggratz. The Habsburg Empire was converted into a dual monarchy, composed of two independent and equal states, with the Austrian emperor serving also as the Hungarian king. Military, diplomatic, and imperial financial affairs were handled in Vienna, but Hungary had its own parliament, cabinet, civil service, and administrative system. While this settlement did increase the efficiency of governmental operations within the empire, it stimulated yearnings for independence or autonomy on the part of the empire's other nationalities, especially the Czechs. From time to time, there was

Balkan students visit archduke's assassination site, Sarajevo, 2004

talk in the empire of federal reforms that might extend the same privileges to all subject peoples, but these always foundered on the rocks of Hungarian and Austrian intransigence.

Despite a short-lived liberal era in the late 1860s and 1870s, the last decades before World War I displayed growing tension within and along the borders of the Austro-Hungarian Empire. As elsewhere, these were decades of rapid industrialization that not only increased the country's wealth but also gave birth to a powerful working-class movement and to a Socialist Party that demanded better pay and working conditions. Although the socialists were moderate in their aims and methods, they were bitterly opposed by conservatives, who saw in them a mortal threat to the state.

The steady collapse of the Turkish Empire and growing Russian interest in Balkan affairs (clothed in idealistic terms of pan-Slavism) seriously threatened the very existence of Austria-Hungary, which sought to preserve the status quo at all costs. In 1912 the Balkan states had fought against Türkiye in order to enlarge themselves at Türkiye's expense, and in 1913 the same Balkan states fought each other over the booty. To Austria's chagrin, the chief winner in both was the rising and highly ambitious Serbia, which began to serve as an attractive model for the southern Slavs within the Austro-Hungarian Empire. Also, in 1913 a high military official, Col. Alfred Redl, was revealed to

Austrian chancellor Dollfuss ("Mini-Metternich")

have been a spy for the Russians for over 10 years. This shocking revelation shook Austrians' confidence in their own governmental structure and weakened its international reputation.

World War I

Thus, the Austrians tended to overreact when one of the most important events in world history occurred on June 28, 1914, a Serbian holiday commemorating the assassination of the Turkish sultan in 1389 by a Serbian patriot. A Bosnian Serb student, Gavrilo Princip, murdered Austrian archduke Franz Ferdinand and his wife in Sarajevo, now Bosnia's capital. The archduke had become successor to the throne after the kaiser's only son, Rudolf, had become entangled in an extramarital love affair and killed himself and his mistress in 1889.

The shots of Sarajevo sounded the end of an almost 50-year absence of major wars among European great powers. Austria held Serbia responsible for this act and, ultimately backed by Germany, made unacceptable demands upon Serbia. All over Europe, alliances were invoked, threats were made, and "blank checks" and ultimatums were issued. In the end, all major powers had painted themselves into a corner with their many commitments and could not get out. By the first week of August, Europe was locked into a war that lasted four long years and far exceeded all previous wars in terms of casualties and destruction. Shortly before his death in 1897, Bismarck had correctly predicted, "one day the great European War will come out of some damned foolish thing in the Balkans."

During World War I, Austria-Hungary primarily sought to retain some control

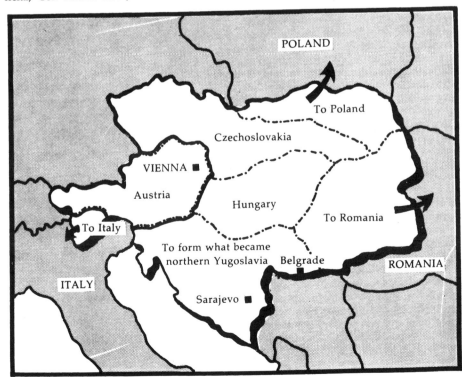

Austria-Hungary until 1918, showing the nations carved from its borders

Austria

Germany's Hitler enters Vienna, 1938

over the Balkans. As Germany's military power ebbed, Austria became increasingly bewildered and confused. Proportionately, Austria-Hungary's losses of men were greater than those of Germany—1.2 million killed and 3.6 million wounded.

By the fall of 1918, the various non-German nationalities within this empire had begun to mount opposition movements. An exhausted Austria simply ceased to fight in the face of such resistance and the quite imminent and predictable collapse of Germany in the fall of 1918. Another casualty of the war was the mind of wounded Austrian corporal Adolf Schickelgruber, a reject of the prestigious Austrian Academy of Art in Vienna. This mind was further inflamed by the Germanic defeat as he fumed in prison. It would come into full bloom in just 15 years, when he would become master of Germany, using the name Adolf Hitler.

On November 11, 1918, Kaiser Karl abdicated. He had ascended to the throne upon the death of Franz Josef in 1916. The next day the Austrian republic was proclaimed. Karl's son, Otto von Habsburg, was only six at the time. In 1922 he became head of the House of Habsburg. He detested the Nazis and as a student in Berlin irritated Hitler by refusing to meet him. At the invitation of President Franklin D. Roosevelt, Otto spent the World War II years in America. He lived and worked most of his life on the German side of the border. Not until later in life was he allowed to enter Austria freely. He did not regret the demise of the Austrian monarchy. He passed on his passion for pan-Europe to his seven children—One (Gabriela, princess imperial and archduchess of Austria) became Georgia's ambassador to Germany in 2010. Her younger sister (Walpurga) was a leading conservative Swedish politician, while their brother Georg was ambassador-at-large for Hungary. Another

brother had a seat in the European Parliament. Otto died July 4, 2011, at age 98. European royals gathered in Vienna for his funeral while huge crowds in Vienna watched the traditional funeral procession.

In 1920 a democratic constitution was put into effect. The new republic, at one-eighth the size of the former empire, was only the small German part. The Treaties of Trianon (with Hungary) and St. Germain distributed the rest of the territory to Romania, Poland, and Italy or were used to construct the new states of Hungary, Czechoslovakia, and Yugoslavia.

In the process, Austria lost 4 million of its German-speaking population to Hungary, Poland, Czechoslovakia, Yugoslavia, and Italy. It also lost access to the sea. Proportionately, it lost much more territory than Germany. Such fragmentation destroyed the Austrian economy. This was the worst possible atmosphere for an untried democracy, and for the next two decades, Austria was unable to regain its balance. In desperation, many Austrians demanded in 1920 a referendum to join the newly formed German republic to the north, but the victorious powers vetoed such a combination, fearing that it would strengthen Germany.

Hopeless Internal Division

From the start, Austria was hopelessly divided into two hostile camps, represented politically by socialists, whose strength was in Vienna, and the Christian Social Party, which was strongest in rural areas. These camps not only created such social institutions as sports clubs, reading circles, and youth groups, which isolated their members from those in the other camp, but they also created large and well-armed paramilitary units. The socialists had their *Schutzbund* (Protective League), and the opposing *Heimwehr* (Home Guard)

had become so heavily armed by 1933 that it reportedly had tanks and howitzers and enough material to equip 500,000 men for a military campaign of moderate length.

Inflation, unemployment, and working-class and rural poverty eroded the sympathy and patience for a formally democratic state, which could be kept alive during the 1920s only by loans from the League of Nations. The worldwide economic depression that shook Europe so violently in the early 1930s eliminated whatever shreds of stability were left in Austria and opened the door widely to political extremism.

Through that door stepped an authoritarian Chancellor Engelbert Dollfuss, a diminutive man of 4 feet 11 inches, who reportedly liked his nickname of "Mini-Metternich." A shrewd and competent politician who had been a lawyer and university lecturer in economics, he strongly opposed socialism and any talk of Austrian union with Germany. He sought to convert Austria into a corporatist state (one in which all citizens belong to highly organized groups bound together by the political leaders in order to achieve the state's goals) on the model of, by then, fascist Italy.

In 1933 he dissolved parliament, and in early 1934, he ordered the arrest of political opponents, especially socialists, liberals, and trade union leaders. He even commanded that artillery fire be directed against workers' tenements in Vienna and that ruthless methods be used to suppress any resistance within the working-class districts. The socialists were crushed in street fighting. He promulgated a constitution that allowed him to rule Austria as a dictator, but his time was very short. In July the Austrian Nazis attempted an unsuccessful coup d'etat in Vienna. They were able to seize the chancellery for only a few hours, during which time they murdered Dollfuss.

"Union" with Germany

His replacement, Kurt von Schuschnigg, tried to retain Austrian independence, but he soon discovered that he had very little

Kurt von Schuschnigg

support. The socialists and trade unions had been crushed, and the middle classes liked more and more the idea of a union with the increasingly dynamic Germany. When Adolf Hitler, Nazi leader of Germany, decided that the time had come for Austria to become a part of Germany, there was little which Schuschnigg could do. Under orders from Berlin, the pro-Nazi Austrian interior minister, Arthur von Seyss-Inquart, assumed Schuschnigg's functions and called upon the German Reich to save Austria from alleged communist chaos. On the night of March 11, 1938, two days before a scheduled national referendum to determine whether Austria should become an integral part of Germany (which the unifiers were expected to lose), German troops entered Austria. The referendum was immediately called off. Two days later it became a province of the German Third Reich.

By the time that Hitler greeted the cheering crowds at the Heldenplatz in Vienna, 70,000 Austrians had already been put into jails or concentration camps. Schuschnigg was interned in various concentration camps until American troops liberated him in 1945. He emigrated to the United States and was a professor of law and politics at Saint Louis University from 1948 to 1967. He called these the best years of his life.

This *Anschluss* ("joining") of the two countries lasted seven years, a time of almost-continuous war, destruction, and suffering for the Austrian people. Loss of Austrian lives during the war, although not as severe as in World War I, nevertheless was substantial. Altogether 6% of the population, almost 400,000 Austrians, including 65,000 Jews, perished during the Nazi period. Of course, Austrians were both victims of and participants in the Nazi terror. In 1945 more than a half-million Austrians were members of the Nazi Party, a higher proportion of the population than in Germany. Also, about a fourth of the convicted Nazi war criminals were Austrian. On the other hand, Austria had, in fact, been occupied against its people's will in 1938 and had been forced to fight alongside the Germans. Beginning in 1944 the victorious Allies emphasized that Austria would be treated as a victim of Nazism; they did this to encourage Austrians to surrender. After the war, many Austrians gladly accepted this interpretation of occupation along with the collective absolution it offered.

Memories of this war experience helped to convince almost all Austrians that they had a destiny that could not be linked directly to Germany. In prisons, concentration camps, and resistance groups, many Austrians who had earlier professed widely different political views learned to know and admire each other. This helped create a sense of tolerance and determination to work out political differences peacefully. Also, the need to rebuild the country after the war helped Austrians to put aside their ideological differences and to work together for the good of all Austria.

Thus, out of the ashes of destruction, a strong commitment to democracy was born. Also, the looting for which some Soviet soldiers were responsible in the post-World War II period horrified and alienated most Austrians. This antipathy helped prevent the communists from winning the active support of the Austrian people and thereby from accomplishing the Soviet goal of quickly consolidating power in Austria and then of legitimizing this power through controlled national elections.

The Postwar Occupation Years

The four principal victors divided Austria into four occupation zones—the Russians occupied the eastern part of the country surrounding Vienna; the Americans occupied the north-central part, which included Salzburg; and the British occupied the southern and the French the western portions of the country. In mid-1946 restrictions on interzonal traffic and trade were lifted. The inner city of Vienna itself was declared an international zone and placed under four-power occupation, a fortuitous factor that made it more difficult for any one power to coerce the Austrian government.

The Allies declared that Austria had been illegally occupied by Germany in 1938 and had been "liberated" in 1945. Therefore, on May 1, 1945, Austria's constitution of 1920, as amended in 1929, and all laws passed prior to March 5, 1933 (the date chancellor Dollfuss took power) went into effect. Unlike Germany, Austria was permitted to have its own civilian government from the very beginning, so Allied control was always indirect rather than direct, as was the case in Germany. In 1948 Nazis who had been purged or sentenced to death after the war were granted amnesty.

At first, political conditions in Austria seemed to be just to the Soviets' liking. There was no strong and popular noncommunist partisan group to liquidate (as was the case in Poland), nor (or so it seemed at the time) was there a strong noncommunist political party that had to be intimidated into submission. Despite the fact that the communist cadres, who had spent the war years in Moscow, were generally unknown and distrusted by most Austrians, they were aggressive and confident that they could control the political future of Austria. They thought their opposition to Hitler had increased their popularity and that the presence of Soviet troops could enhance their political status and influence.

The Soviet occupiers looked for a leader of a multiparty Austrian government that, they hoped, would be dominated by their compliant Austrian comrades. They thought that they had found just the right man—Karl Renner, a popular and highly respected socialist who had been the first chancellor of the earlier Austrian Republic. Because he had hesitatingly supported the *Anschluss* in 1938, the Soviets assumed that he could be blackmailed, if necessary. Best of all, they assumed his old age would rob him of the stamina to deal with detailed problems of governing, and this would make him more amenable to compromise with the communists.

Renner skillfully and tactfully proceeded to dash the Soviet hopes. He formed a three-party government composed of the Communist Party, the Socialist Party of Austria (SPO), and the old Christian Socialist Party, now purified of its former authoritarian ideas and renamed the Austrian People's Party (ÖVP), which shared executive and administrative positions. The Ministries of Interior, which controlled all police and security forces, and of Education, Public Information, and Worship were given to communists, but Renner devised an ingenious way of minimizing the potential dangers of having such important ministries guided by communists.

He proposed that two undersecretaries be appointed to each ministry so that all three governing parties would be represented at the top of each ministry. The communists were delighted because they thought that this arrangement would enable them to exercise influence in every ministry. The real result, though, was general inefficiency and deadlock in most departments. If any undersecretary

Dr. Karl Renner

Austria

vetoed a matter, it was sent to the cabinet for consideration. To get the cumbersome 35-member body to act quickly on matters of importance, he established the policy of serving wine and food to the cabinet members after each session. Because normal rations in Vienna in 1945 were a near starvation 400 to 800 calories, the meals that followed the meetings were often of greater importance to the participants than the business at hand.

Renner held the most controversial matters until the end, so that the cabinet could reach an agreement very quickly and with a minimum of controversy. Further, after June 28, 1946, the Soviet authorities could no longer unilaterally reverse the decisions of the Austrian government. Austrian legislation was submitted to the Allied Control Council (ACC) for approval, but if a majority of the Allied commanders did not disapprove it within 31 days, the legislation automatically became law. The significance of this was that the Austrian government could continue to function even when the Allied powers were in disagreement. As was clear by 1947, an unfortunate single vote arrangement doomed the ACC in Germany to impotence.

In the fall of 1945, the Allied powers agreed to permit elections for the newly established Austrian parliament to be held in November. Austrian communists confidently assured the Soviets that they could gain 25% to 30% of the votes, but Russian and Austrian communists were stunned by the results: the ÖVP received 49.8% of the votes, the SPO 44.6%, and the communists a mere 5.42%, which gave them only four seats in parliament. The Soviets had clearly misread the political temper in Austria, and the election was one of the most important events in

postwar Austrian history. It brought to a halt the communist hopes to gain control of the country.

Until 1966 the ÖVP and the SPO ruled Austria together in a *Proporzsystem* (proportional system), whereby cabinet and administrative posts and many other jobs, down to janitorial positions, were distributed to leaders and members of the two parties according to their electoral strength. This system allowed the two largest to work together as a team rather than have to join with extremist parties. It also enabled the government to defend the country's interests against the Allied occupation forces and to combat attempts to destroy or pervert democracy in Austria.

After the election disaster, the Soviet Union had no consistent and clearly defined aims for Austria except economic exploitation. The Soviets originally had demanded that Austria pay it reparations because Austrian soldiers had served in the German army and had participated in the destruction of the Soviet Union. The other three Allies refused this, pointing out that this would be inconsistent with their agreement that Austria was to be treated as a liberated country. Therefore, the Soviets demanded and were granted the right to administer the many economic assets the German government had acquired in the Soviet zone in Austria.

In 1946 it assumed ownership of the Danube Steamship Company, which had come into German ownership after *Anschluss*. Through the Soviet Petroleum Administration (SMV), the Russians controlled most of Austria's petroleum reserves. The Administration of Soviet Property in Austria (USIA) operated 420 confiscated industries and agricultural

holdings by 1955 and employed about 10% of industrially employed Austrians.

Fearing further Soviet expropriations, which in the end would leave very few industries and resources in eastern Austria for the Austrians themselves, the Renner government dropped all ideological reservations and began in 1946 to nationalize the nation's three largest banks and all heavy industry, including all principal mines; the largest steel, iron, and aluminum plants; most petroleum facilities; the main electrical plants; the automotive, locomotive, and shipbuilding industries; and the Danube Steamship Company. In 1947 they nationalized the power industries. The Russians, who controlled about 60% of these nationalized industries, were greatly angered and simply refused to recognize the Austrian legislation. In return, the Austrians refused to recognize most of the Soviet holdings. In the years that followed, the Austrian government nationalized the railroads; civil aviation; public utilities; radio and television; and the salt, tobacco, liquor, and match monopolies.

By the early 1950s, Austria had established a stable domestic political order, and Marshall Plan aid from the US helped to create the conditions for the rapid reconstruction of the country and for the gradual return of prosperity. From 1945 to 1947, the US financed 88% of Austrian imports and 57% in 1948. In the time period from July 1948 to June 1949, Marshall Plan aid alone accounted for 14% of the Austrian national income, a far higher percentage than in any other European country. In the early days, the Marshall Plan provided 88% of the foodstuffs and 73% of the coal. In 1961 the United States transferred to the Austrian government all the loans (counterpart funds) that had accumulated through Marshall Plan assistance ($11.2 billion by then).

However, the country was still occupied and divided, and it was therefore not yet sovereign. Austria was caught in the great power tensions that had replaced the unified Allied effort to crush Hitler. Austrian foreign minister Leopold Figl said before parliament in 1952, "The Austrian people know that it is not because of technical or objective matters that the treaty is being held up: it is purely power political considerations to which justice must give way."

Within the first decade after occupation of Austria, more than 300 meetings of the Allied deputy foreign ministers had been held to discuss a settlement in Austria, but the results were always the same. Suddenly, in February 1955, an important break in the stalemate came when Soviet foreign minister Molotov announced that the Soviet Union would consider signing a state treaty with Austria. The following

The Austrian Parliament

Austria

month it called on Austria to send representatives to Moscow to discuss the matter. When a rather skeptical Austrian delegation, which included the state secretary for foreign affairs and Bruno Kreisky (who later served as chancellor of Austria), got off the plane in Moscow and was greeted by all the major Soviet leaders, it was clear that something good was about to happen. Kreisky whispered into Vice Chancellor Scharf's ear, "If they receive us with such pomp and circumstance, they cannot send us home without pomp and circumstance."

The talks went extremely well, and the concluding "Moscow Memorandum" outlined the major provisions for the subsequent treaty. First, Austria was to adhere to a policy of neutrality on the Swiss model. Second, occupation forces would be withdrawn from Austria by the end of 1955. Third, all Soviet economic holdings in the country would be returned, for which Austria would pay over $152 million and ship 1 million tons of oil to the Soviet Union each year for 10 years. The western Allies accepted this settlement very quickly, since its terms were far more favorable than they had ever sought. On May 15, 1955, the Allied foreign ministers Molotov, McMillan, Dulles, and Pinay and Austrian foreign minister Figl signed the Austrian State Treaty in the Belvedere Palace.

Full Sovereignty Again

Austrian surprise and joy at this formal ending of Austria's occupation status was indescribable. In the west, reactions were a mixture of perplexity, pleasure, and uneasiness. Why, after 10 years of delay, did the Soviets leave Austria? There are many reasons, but the main one is probably that the Soviet Union wanted to make a final attempt to prevent West Germany from entering NATO, whose founding in 1949 Soviet leaders had been unable to prevent. Many Germans desperately wanted to see their country reunified, and by dangling before their eyes an attractive example of what a low price must be paid for national unity and a withdrawal of foreign troops, the Soviet Union hoped to persuade them to remain neutral and to work out a form of German national unity acceptable to the Soviet Union.

The *New York Times* noted, "The Kremlin is producing a little miracle play for the benefit of the Germans, not the Austrians." However, neither the western Allies nor a majority in the West German parliament could overlook the fact that the stakes in Austria were not nearly as high as in Germany. Austria is a small country with little influence on that balance of power that had prevented the Soviet Union from seriously considering attacking western Europe. By contrast, Germany was the key

Austrian troops marching past the Hofburg imperial palace

to maintaining that balance of power. This fact made many West Germans highly skeptical that the Soviet Union would be as willing to tolerate for long an independent and neutral Germany as it would an independent and neutral Austria.

POLITICAL SYSTEM

Military Limitations

As a fully sovereign state, Austria spelled out the precise status of its neutrality in a constitutional amendment enacted on October 26, 1955, now the country's national holiday. The amendment explicitly forbade Austria from entering any military alliances or permitting any foreign troops to be stationed on Austrian soil. It also pledged to use all the means at its disposal to maintain and defend its neutrality.

Austria formed no military links with the Soviet Union, but it has its own armed forces, which the treaty severely limited in size. All services are combined in the army of 27,200 active-duty soldiers, of which 13,600 (including 6,900 conscripts) are ground troops. There are 2,300 in the air force, of which 900 are conscripts. Conscripts must serve 8 months after turning 17. They must participate in 30 days of refresher training (60–90 days for officers and NCOs) within 8 years after discharge. There is a 72-hour reserve force numbering 195,000, backed up in an emergency by 990,000 reservists with training but no commitment. Officers, NCOs, and specialists remain in the reserves until age 65, others until age 50.

In 2005 the Defense Ministry announced sweeping changes: 37% of its bases, barracks, and other property would be closed and sold, numbering 51 out of 140 properties. In addition to cutting costs, the army would be streamlined and gradually converted into a reduced all-volunteer force.

Conscription has been reduced to six months as a step toward a professional army. The idea was to build a smaller streamlined professional force that could take part in European operations engaged in conflict prevention; 21 EU countries have already done that. However, voters had other ideas in a January 2013 referendum. Almost 60% rejected any change to compulsory military service. Many Austrians fondly remember draftees shoveling snow in villages buried by avalanches or lifting sandbags to protect towns from flooding. They also asked who would replace the many conscientious objectors who substitute their military service by working in social services agencies.

The Austrian military is forbidden by the treaty to possess guns that fire farther than 30 kilometers or to possess nuclear or special weapons, including missiles. Although it is not forbidden to have an air force capable of protecting its own airspace, NATO and Warsaw Pact aircraft violated that airspace for more than three decades. As its army commander noted, the country's defense "stops ten meters above the ground." In 2000, for the first time in Austrian history, it decided to purchase American aviation equipment—nine Sikorsky S70 Black Hawk helicopters.

To improve its air defense, Austria ordered 18 Eurofighter Typhoons to replace its antiquated Draken planes starting in 2007. This was an extremely controversial decision that the Social Democrats, supported by the Green and Freedom Parties, vowed to cancel on the grounds that they are too expensive and are unnecessary for a neutral country. Even military personnel in other branches argued that the money was needed for other defense purposes. Austria allots only .8% of its GDP to defense; in fact, it spends more of its national budget on opera than on

315

Austria

The Vienna Opera House

its military. But cancellation of the contract was too costly, and the People's Party made the acquisition a condition for entering the Grand Coalition. In 2017, the ministry of defense launched a probe into alleged corruption linked to that sale, insisting that some $200 million in costs were illegally included in the price. Airbus, which was part of the Eurofighter consortium, fought back, insisting that the government was trying to score "cheap political points" ahead of the election.

Even with an improved air-defense capability, it is still doubtful that Austrian troops could defend their country against a well-equipped and determined attacker, in contrast to the Swiss military, which would probably be able to do that. It may not need to: Except for Liechtenstein and Switzerland to the west, Austria is surrounded by NATO countries.

Foreign Policy

Austria's chief foreign policy goals are to preserve its independence and to promote peace and stability in the community of states. This called for a form of neutrality that Austria terms "active." Austrians interpreted theirs as military, not political, neutrality. From the beginning Austria rejected Swiss practices by seeking to join certain international political organizations. In December 1955 it joined the United Nations, and the following year, it entered the European Council (which does not deal with military questions).

Over the years, about 60,000 Austrians have participated in more than 50 UN peacekeeping missions in the Congo, Cyprus, and the Middle East, especially on the Golan Heights between Israel and Syria. Since joining the EU in 1995, Austria has participated in practically all international missions in the Balkans. In 1997 it sent soldiers to Albania to help stabilize that country, which had temporarily fallen into chaos. In 2010 alone there were 462 Austrian soldiers serving in Kosovo, 99 in Bosnia, and 378 in Syria, including the Golan Heights. By 2011 it had 1,700 military police and civilians serving in peacekeeping missions. Austria's commitment to the UN was particularly conspicuous while Kurt Waldheim served as UN secretary general from 1972 to 1982. It was elected three times to serve two-year non-permanent appointments on the UN Security Council: 1973–1974, 1991–1992 and 2008–2010.

The policy of neutrality placed no muzzle on either politicians or private citizens. As Foreign Minister Leopold Gratz stated in 1984, "Our neutrality binds the State, but not the individual and not the press, and not our thinking. So, we never left any doubt as to which political system we adhere to." Also, that neutrality did not necessarily prevent Austria from considering sanctions against other countries.

Austria also had no problems entering purely economic organizations. Its association with the EU, with whose members three-fourths of its trade is conducted, was

problematic because of the EU's stated goal of political unity. The Soviet Union objected to Austria's full membership. In the early 1990s, Austria formally applied for full EU membership, and in 1994 two-thirds of Austrians voted for it in a referendum. The EU required Austria to give assurances that its neutrality would not stand in the way of a common foreign and security policy. The entry of Poland, the Czech Republic, and Hungary into NATO in 1999, followed in 2004 by seven other central European countries, affects Austria's security deliberations.

Although public opinion remains opposed, the People's Party supports NATO entry, which is unlikely to occur soon. Along with many Austrians, it argues that neutrality no longer makes sense after joining the EU, which has developed a security and defense policy with which Austria cooperates. Austria contributes to the EU's small ad hoc battle groups, and in the Balkans, Austrian soldiers even serve under NATO command. However, more than 70% of the public still support neutrality, which in the country's security doctrine is defined as "nonaligned."

Austrians remember the humiliating EU sanctions against it in 2000. This is one reason it is among the most Euroskeptic in the club. In the July 2007 Eurobarometer poll, only 36% of Austrians agreed that their country's membership was a good thing, and just 44% said it had benefited from joining, against 43% who maintained it had not. Only the UK registers lower approval. The EU is strongly supported in the business community, and it is extremely unlikely that the people would ever vote to leave the club, despite their disenchantment. Opposition to Turkish entry is intense.

Former chancellor Wolfgang Schüssel strongly urged his countrymen to rejoin western institutions: "European enlargement provides us with a huge opportunity. It marks the return of *Mitteleuropa* and puts Austria back at the heart of Europe. Hungary, Slovenia, Croatia, the Czech Republic, bits of Poland, have long been part of our economic and cultural area. We want to build on that to coordinate ideas and interests in a region of more than 40 million people." Austria has clearly benefited more from this opening to the east than any other country among the older EU members. Its trade and investment have boomed, and its stake is less in manufacturing than it was earlier and more in financial services and property.

Ex-foreign minister Benita Ferrero-Waldner of the Freedom Party, later the EU's commissioner for external affairs, agreed, stating in 2000, "It has become obvious that since Austria joined the European Union in 1995, the participation in

European security structures has become more important to Austria than the preservation of its traditional policy of neutrality. The reasons for Austria's declaration of neutrality in 1955 have always been that by doing so, Austria's independence and security would be best served. Today these goals are best served by a full integration of Austria into a European and Euro-Atlantic security structure."

Austria joined the Partnership for Peace (PfP) in order to strengthen its ties with NATO. The country would provide a convenient land bridge to NATO peacekeeping forces in the Balkans. During the war in Iraq in March-April 2003, Austria did not allow American troops or airplanes to cross its territory because the action had not been authorized by a UN mandate.

Standing outside all military alliances, Austria provides for its own security by making a contribution to peace in the world. At least since the Congress of Vienna in 1814–1815, Austria has been the location for important international meetings. It sees itself as especially qualified for the role of a "bridge builder" between east and west. President Kennedy and Soviet party chief Nikita Khrushchev met in Vienna in the early 1960s. From 1970 to 1972, most of the meetings between American and Soviet negotiators to work out the SALT I Treaty were held in Vienna, and President Carter and Soviet president Leonid Brezhnev signed the Salt II Treaty there in 1979. After 1989 NATO and Warsaw Pact nations conducted Conventional Forces in Europe (CFE) negotiations in Vienna, aimed at achieving reductions of conventional weapons in Europe. The CSCE decided in 1990 to create a conflict-prevention center in Vienna.

Austrians see themselves in a totally new situation. Before 1989 they were in a kind of cul-de-sac, surrounded on three sides by the communist bloc; now that dead end has been transformed into an intersection with a bustling thoroughfare opening into the east. One Austrian diplomat put it this way: "We used to be on the eastern fringe of Western Europe; now we are in the center of Europe again."

Austria and Hungary liberalized their border relations when, in 1989, Hungary dismantled the electronically monitored fences and watchtowers along the Austro-Hungarian border. This played a central role in the westward exodus of East Germans. This opportunity to render a dramatic humanitarian gesture strengthened its application to the EU by demonstrating that it is a useful and trusted western country with excellent connections in eastern Europe. It also helped form the *Pentagonale*, joined by Italy, Hungary, Czechoslovakia, and Yugoslavia, to foster a project-centered approach to issues of

international affairs, such as the environment, where more progress can be made through regional negotiations.

Involved in more than 8,000 joint ventures with its eastern neighbors (4,000 in Hungary alone), Austria became more deeply integrated with eastern Europe. For example, three of its major banks—Raiffeisen, Bank Austria Creditanstalt, and Erste Bank—possess more than a fourth of the 62% of eastern European banking assets owned by foreign banks. This large stake makes Austrian banks particularly vulnerable to the kind of unrest experienced in Ukraine.

Austria finds itself besieged by cheap imports and immigrants from the east. Therefore, it introduced protective measures against sensitive imports and, for the first time in decades, halted the flow of immigrants. Austria sets aside public funds amounting to 0.32% of its GDP for aid to developing countries.

Vienna is the location for many permanent international organizations. For instance, the headquarters for the Organization of Petroleum Exporting Countries (OPEC) is located there, as is that of the Organization for Security and Cooperation in Europe (OSCE). The city is one of the three major centers for activities of the UN. Austria built, at its own expense, a huge and ultramodern Vienna International Center, which it rents to the UN for a symbolic sum less than $1 per year. This "UN on the Danube" houses the International Atomic Energy Agency, the UN Industrial Development Organization (UNIDO), the UN Relief and Works Agency for Palestine Refugees, most UN offices dealing with drug traffic and abuse, the UN Commission on International Trade Law, and many others.

Along with the embassy staffs, these organizations raise the total number of diplomats and their families living in Vienna to 20,000. Such a large international community provides excellent cover for the estimated 2,500 spies from as many as 80 countries who continue since the end of the Cold War to operate out of Vienna. In July 2010 the largest exchange of Russian (10) and American (4) spies since 1986 took place at Vienna's airport. Espionage is punishable by three years in prison but only if the spy does damage to Austria.

In 2005 the Foreign Ministry moved from its cramped quarters across from the Hofburg and five other locations into splendid new offices under one roof in the heart of the government district on Minoritenplatz. In 2007 the name was changed to Federal Ministry of European and International Affairs, and in 2014 it was renamed Federal Ministry for Europe, Integration, and Foreign Affairs. At 27, its former head, Sebastian Kurz, became the youngest foreign minister in the EU in 2013.

In sharp contrast to Switzerland, Austria never believed that its neutrality should prevent its political leaders from speaking out publicly on important international questions. For instance, Austria always sharply condemned the Soviet Union's disrespect for human rights and its use of military force in eastern Europe and in Afghanistan.

Territorial Losses and Claims

In addition, Austria's neutral stance did not prevent it from defending its own territorial claims, which it found entirely legitimate. After the end of hostilities in 1945, Yugoslavia again raised its claim to part of the Austrian province of Carinthia and underscored this by occupying the province. However, the British, in whose zone the province was located, ordered the Yugoslav forces out of the area. After the split between Yugoslavia and the Soviet Union in 1948, there was no major power that continued to support the Yugoslav claim. Therefore, in 1955 it recognized Austria's possession of the region in exchange for some promises to make cultural concessions to the Croatian minority located there.

Austria was less successful in gaining control of the largely German-speaking and traditional Austrian area of South Tyrol, which the Treaty of Saint Germain had awarded to Italy in 1919. For more than two decades, Austria unsuccessfully demanded that the South Tyrolians be permitted to determine in a referendum whether they wished to belong to Austria or Italy. After World War II, none of the victorious Allies supported Austria's claims. Therefore, it was forced to enter long negotiations with the Italian government to achieve the highest possible cultural autonomy for German-speaking residents of the area of Bozen, which the Italians combined with the overwhelmingly Italian-speaking region of Trentino.

These talks were periodically marred by bombings in South Tyrol by German speaking Tyrolians, who favored annexation by Austria. Finally, in 1969 an agreement was reached, whereby the language rights of the South Tyrolians would be respected, and certain governmental responsibilities would be transferred to Bozen, which would become autonomous. Also, low-income housing, public-service jobs, funds for kindergartens and schools, and many other subsidies are distributed on a proportional basis depending on the size of the respective population groups. The formula has been German, 60%; Italian, 30%; and Ladiner (a small minority isolated in two valleys, speaking a Latin-based language and related to the Romansch minority in southeast Switzerland), 10%. Though falling short

Austria

Presidential palace flying EU and Austrian flags

of their original demands, South Tyrolians approved this solution in a referendum, and Austria pledged to relinquish all of its claims over the area as soon as the language rights were fully realized. Although some South Tyrolians assert that Italy has not yet fulfilled its promises, the problem is resolved. Still, Freedom Party's leader Heinz-Christian Strache hinted at his party's interest in inviting South Tyrolians to rejoin their Austrian kin.

The Emergence of Stable Democracy

Austria is an economically prosperous and stable democracy with a federal form to help accommodate diversity and a consensus approach to political and economic problems, which helps guarantee political and labor peace. This contrasts almost completely with Austria before 1918; numerous ethnic minorities demanding independence, a militant working class demanding a world socialist revolution, rampant anti-Semitism (which helped produce both Hitler's anti-Jewish ravings and Theodor Herzl's Zionist dream of a Jewish homeland), anticapitalism, anticommunism, and anticlericalism all dangerously blended to generate constant tension, hatred, and violence.

In contrast to Switzerland, whose democratic system has evolved slowly over centuries, Austria has undergone radical changes in political and social values and practices. German-speaking Austrians often had no clear national identity. Did they belong to the German nation or to a separate Austrian nationality? In a poll taken in 1956, 46% indicated that they belonged to the German nation, but in 1991, three-fourths said that an Austrian nationality already exists, with only 5% rejecting

Austrian nationhood. This explains why there was unease in Vienna in 1990, when the German government adopted plans to include Austria in the new German History Museum in Berlin. The polls reflect an important change, but one former US ambassador still asserted that "there is no Austrian. . . The Austrians are the creoles of Europe. Look at the Vienna telephone book. It's like a final exam in Germanic and Slavic pronunciations."

During the first republic after 1918, far too few Austrians held firm democratic values. Most had formed their political views under the authoritarian empire, and many were outright antagonistic and scornful toward democracy. In addition, there was a weak liberal tradition. The chief enemy of the socialist and Catholic subcultures (called *Lager*) was liberalism, which stressed individual rights and free economic activity largely uncontrolled by the state. Finally, common experiences during and immediately after World War II had a great effect on the minds of many Austrians, in that extremist politics of the left and right were discredited. Of course, the basic subcultures did not immediately disappear after 1945, but most Austrians strongly supported their government, which sought to rid the country of foreign occupation and to establish a democratic Austria. They shared a widespread determination not to allow the country to devour itself as it once had.

Overcoming the National Socialist Past

A shadow hung over the 1986 presidential election. Former UN secretary-general Kurt Waldheim was haunted by revelations that he had served on the staff of a German general who had been executed

in 1947 for war crimes in the Balkans area. His election was not a vote for Nazism or anti-Semitism. Austrians had grown tired of 16 years of Socialist rule, which had been marked by political scandals, wasteful bureaucracy, money-losing nationalized industries, and ineffective economic policies. Therefore, voters elected the first conservative president since 1945.

Indeed, Waldheim's past increasingly made him unable to perform his largely ceremonial duties. In his first year in office, he became known to some as the "prisoner of the Vienna Hofburg." He could not receive foreign heads of state. The most stinging rebuke came from the United States.

In 1987 Waldheim was put on the "watch list" after the Justice Department concluded that there was evidence that he had "assisted or otherwise participated in the persecution of persons because of race, religion, national origin or political opinion." This was the first time the US had declared a friendly country's head of state an undesirable alien barred from entry. Not a single other western government invited Waldheim. In spite of reassurances, many Austrians viewed the action as an insult to their nation; popular reaction within Austria was intense and negative at the time. The exact nature of the charges was made public in early 1994, and Waldheim was found to have aided and participated in the Nazi efforts directed against Jews and foreign nationals. Other inquiries produced no conclusive evidence that he had actually had a hand in war crimes, but they cast doubt on his claim not to have known what was happening. He died in 2007 at the age of 88.

More and more Austrians agree that their country must "come to grips" with its past. An ominous reminder was given in 1991, when a Gallup poll conducted for the American Jewish Committee revealed that 39% of Austrian respondents held the view that "Jews have caused much harm in the course of history"; 31% preferred not to have Jews for neighbors, but even higher percentages were averse to living near Poles, Slovenes, Croats, Serbs, and Turks. Of the approximately 200,000 Jews who had lived in Austria in the 1930s, more than half emigrated before the 1938 annexation by Germany, and 65,000 perished. The total now is only about 7,000, many of whom are recent arrivals from the former Soviet Union.

Unlike the Germans, the Austrians have never engaged in a cathartic debate about their Nazi past, hiding behind the comfortable official interpretation that they had been Hitler's first victims. For the first time in 1991, Chancellor Franz Vranitzky acknowledged that many Austrians had supported Hitler and had taken a hand in

318

his crimes; he apologized for the atrocities Austrians had committed. In 1993 he became the first chancellor to visit Israel, where he acknowledged that Austrians had been not only victims but also "willing servants of Nazism."

Textbooks were subsequently changed to emphasize the complicity of many Austrians in Nazi crimes and the fact that Austria was not merely a victim of Hitler. Vienna's mayor decreed that the film *Schindler's List* be required viewing for all schoolchildren. In November 2005, British revisionist historian David Irving found out the hard way that it is against the law to deny the Holocaust. Austria had issued an arrest warrant against him in 1989 for denying the existence of gas chambers. While on his way to Vienna to give a lecture, Irving was arrested. In February 2006 he was sentenced to three years in prison, even though he had pleaded guilty and said that he now accepted that the mass murder of Jews had taken place. In December 2006 he was released to serve the remainder of his term on probation, and he was deported to Britain.

In 1995 parliament voted for the first time to pay compensation to 30,000 victims of Nazi persecution. In 1996 the government finally agreed to abide by the terms of the 1955 Austrian State Treaty, which obligated it to return to the Jewish owners or heirs those art pieces that had been confiscated by the Nazis. In a gesture of atonement, it handed over 8,000 items to the Federation of Jewish Communities in Austria, which auctioned them for more than $14.5 million, donating the proceeds to Holocaust victims. After two paintings by Egon Schiele, which Austria had lent for a show in New York, were seized because of suspicions that they had belonged to Holocaust victims, Culture Minister Elisabeth Gehrer ordered that, once prior ownership is certified, all art confiscated by the Nazis would be returned to their rightful owners. In 1998 parliament unanimously approved this decision, which may ultimately strip more than 100 masterpieces from Vienna's leading museums.

The issue became more complicated in 2004, when the US Supreme Court ruled that an 88-year-old Jewish refugee in California, Maria Altmann, could seek to recover $328 million worth of art, especially five paintings by Gustav Klimt, which the Nazis had looted from her family after the German annexation of Austria in 1938, along with a priceless porcelain collection and the family's sugar refinery. An earlier settlement negotiated with the US government had made payoffs contingent on the dismissal of all World War II-era lawsuits in American courts. Thus, Altmann's case postponed by a year the payment of $210

The Spanish Riding Academy with its world-famous Lipizzaner stallions being put through their paces

million in compensation to more than 2,000 claimants.

Finally, in January 2006 an Austrian arbitration court ruled that the paintings should be returned to Altmann. Austrian art lovers waited in line for hours at the Austrian Gallery to get one last look at the paintings before they were shipped to their rightful owner in America. This was the largest return, in monetary terms, of art looted by the Nazis.

Viktor Klima, the first Austrian chancellor born after the Second World War, emphasized in 1997 that his government is committed to confronting and studying the Nazi past; "it must teach us." The Judenplatz Holocaust Memorial was unveiled in 2000 in Vienna. Critics had decried the structure, which they likened to a "concrete bunker" located close to the spot where hundreds of Jews had committed suicide in the midst of an anti-Semitic pogrom in 1420. In 2003 the Wiesenthal Center in Vienna cited Austria as having done the least to pursue war criminals, relative to the number probably inside its territory. In 2018 Austria celebrated its 100th birthday and a new House of Austrian History

was opened to help Austrians understand their past.

Government Structure—The President

Austria has a parliamentary form of government. The head of state is a president, who is elected directly for a six-year term, with one reelection possible and with all citizens of voting age required to vote. The presidency is largely a ceremonial post. Austrians want in a president a moral authority who represents the country well internationally and who acts as a moderating influence at home. However, the office would potentially have significant power in times of political instability.

In the 1992 and 1998 presidential elections, Thomas Klestil of the conservative Austrian People's Party won. A former ambassador to Washington and number 2 in the Foreign Ministry, he quickly succeeded in reestablishing ties with countries that had boycotted Austria and in enabling his country to assume a higher profile in international affairs.

He died the day before he was succeeded in July 2004 by Heinz Fischer, who had served as speaker or deputy speaker

Austria

of parliament since 1990. A seasoned moderate politician known for his adeptness in mediating partisan bickering, Fischer was the first Social Democrat to be president in two decades. Winning 52.3% of the vote, he defeated Benita Ferrero-Waldner of the People's Party, who became the EU commissioner for external affairs.

In April 2010 Fischer was reelected by a landslide, winning 80% of the votes. His opponent was a right-wing firebrand, Barbara Rosenkranz of the Freedom Party. Wife of a fundraiser for imprisoned neo-Nazis, she is nicknamed the "Reich Mother" because of her presumed Nazi sympathies (she also is an actual mother of 10 children). She suggested that all anti-Nazi laws be scrapped and that denial of the Holocaust be made legal. She captured only 15% of the votes.

By the end of his presidency, Fischer raised quite a few eyebrows by hosting President Vladimir Putin in Vienna in 2014 just a few months after Russia's takeover of Crimea. He defended Austria's "much more relaxed" approach toward Moscow as stemming from Vienna's tradition of neutrality and reminded his critics of his country's culpability in the invasion of Russia during World War II.

The election of April and May 2016 stirred up a lot of emotions and even international concern when the candidate of the Freedom Party, Norbert Hofer, convincingly won the first round by getting 35.1% of votes. Much to the surprise of the main parties, the SPO and the ÖVP, their candidates gained some 11% each and failed even to qualify for the next round. Instead, the second-largest vote getter, at 21.3%, was Alexander Van der Bellen, a former Green Party leader running as an independent. Another independent, Irmgard Griss, came in third. This was a powerful rebuke to establishment parties (Hofer gained more than three times the number of votes either of them received). The runoff campaign got heated at times, with Van der Bellen calling his opponent "a populist right-wing, pan-Germanic fraternity member," while Hofer called him a "fascist green dictator."

Among much uncertainty, the second round of elections hinged on some 700,000 mail-in ballots. In the end, Van den Bellen prevailed by just over 30,000 votes, 50.35% to 49.65%, really a neck-and-neck finish in the race that could have installed a right-wing president in the country still uneasy about its Nazi past. The fact that half of Austrians were willing to vote for the FPÖ reveals a significant shift in the fortunes of that party.

Alexander Van der Bellen, aged 72 and nicknamed Sascha, is an economics professor of Russian Estonian descent who presented himself as a "child of refugees who

President Alexander Van der Bellen

has received a lot from Austria." While he did not formally run on the Green Party ticket, the party supported him. His main electorate were the urbanites, women, and the educated—his rival Norbert Hofer taunted him by claiming, "you have the glitterati, but I have the people." A strong supporter of the European Union, gay rights, and protection of minorities in general, Van der Bellen promised to try to mend the fissures within Austria's badly split society. However, he also vowed not to swear in the leader of the FPÖ Strache as a chancellor, should that party prevail in the 2018 parliamentary election. In turn, Strache brought to Austria's constitutional court a 150-page formal complaint of "massive violations of the law" during the election.

In a shocking and unprecedented (at the federal level) decision on July 1, 2016, the court annulled the second round of the election due to irregularities pertaining especially to the pivotal mail-in vote. There was no evidence of vote rigging, but some formal procedures had not been followed, affecting possibly over 70,000 votes. With the razor-thin margin of victory, this was seen as necessitating a rerun of the second round, scheduled for the fall of 2016. Announced just a week before Alexander Van der Bellen was supposed to be sworn in, the decision threw the political system into much confusion. Adding to the complexity of the situation was the provision that, in the absence of a president, a trio of the three presidents of the National Assembly take on his duties—and one of them is Norbert Hofer! Since in the meantime the British voters opted to leave the European Union and Hofer and his party called for a similar referendum for Austria, the

repeated runoff would occur in different circumstances than the election in May. Furthermore, the election of Donald Trump to the US presidency provided another variable, as populists throughout Europe took courage at this development.

The saga continued when the rerun, scheduled for October 2016, had to be postponed due to an embarrassing discovery that postal voting envelopes had faulty glue, making tampering possible. In the end the election on December 4, 2016, resulted in a convincing victory for Alexander Van der Bellen (53.8% of votes) over Norbert Hofer (46.2%). The electoral turmoil shook the society's trust in the working of its democratic institutions. And yet in the end, the election did not bring a far-right populist to the presidency of Austria, a possibility considered with much trepidation throughout Europe. Van der Bellen won re-election in the 2022 presidential election on October 9, 2022 with 56.2% of the votes.

Parliament and Parties

In normal times, the most powerful political figure is the federal chancellor, who must control a majority in the National Council, by far the more powerful chamber in the bicameral legislature. By means of a complicated proportional representation electoral system in 25 districts, 183 members are elected. In 2007 the voting age was lowered to 16 and the term extended to 5 years. Despite this proportional representation system, which in other countries usually enables a large number of parties to win seats in the parliament, only five Austrian parties have been able to win any seats at all.

The SPO, which renamed itself in 1991 the Social Democratic Party of Austria, is the country's second-largest party. It ruled alone from 1970 until 1983 and in coalition with the Austrian People's Party (ÖVP) after 2006. Its socialist appeals have been increasingly moderated, and it has become a pragmatic, reform-oriented party. Some of its members are still attracted to Marxist doctrine, but its program stresses that it welcomes all supporters who embrace the party's ideals as a result of religious, philosophic, humanistic, or Marxist analysis. The party is openly anticommunist and was often critical of the former Soviet Union. It refuses any form of political cooperation with the Communist Party of Austria (KPO), which has sunk to political insignificance. The SPO's strength is found mainly in urban and industrial areas, especially in Vienna. The SPO dominates the trade union movement and attracts the votes of most workers.

In the September 2013 federal elections, the two main parties reached their lowest points in history, barely amassing between them half the votes cast (50.8%, down from 78% in 2002). Both parties are having trouble attracting young voters. At the same time, two far-right parties enjoyed their greatest success ever. The SPO fell, but it emerged as the largest party. It was overtaken in the October 2017 snap election by the ÖVP, which won 31.5% of the votes.

The politically adroit Greens are led by Werner Kogler. Their message is well suited to prosperous times. Their voters are predominantly well off, middle class, and younger than supporters of other parties. In their egalitarian manner, they distribute their seats equally among men and women. One of their top candidates, Alev Korun, became the first member of parliament of Turkish origin in 2008. The Greens are the only party that favors Türkiye's entry into the EU. They are in opposition.

The Austrian People's Party (ÖVP) was founded in 1945 by the antifascist elements of the former Christian Social Party. The Catholic Church now abstains from direct political activity, but the ÖVP, which does not view itself as a specifically Catholic party, can usually count on the support of most practicing Catholic lay organizations. The party is also successful in gaining the votes of farmers, independent merchants and industrialists, lawyers and doctors, and generally the middle class. The ÖVP's program favors a social market economy and private property, but it also supports social welfare and workers' participation in the management of companies.

In the 2013 elections, it tumbled to its worst performance ever. Party leaders feared being overtaken by the far-right Freedom Party, which with 26% had surged past the two parties in 2015 polls and nearly won the presidency in 2016.

In an October 2017 snap election, the ÖVP, led by a new 31-year-old Sebastian Kurz, the youngest democratic leader in Europe and a former diplomat, emerged as the largest party. He is modest, a good listener, and the darling of Europe's conservatives. The ÖVP formed a coalition with the FPÖ and was sworn into office in December 2017. Six out of 10 ministries were given to the FPÖ. Kurz adopted some of the FPÖ's policies in his campaign, such as a ban on burqas, reduced welfare benefits for migrants, harder borders, and a tougher defense of national identity. He explained, "Those who do not put clear limits on migration will soon start to feel like strangers in their own land." Its stance on immigration is one of the toughest in Europe.

Kurz's success did not last. In 2021 he stood down amid a scandal involving his use of taxpayer money to bribe the media to give his party favorable coverage. He was replaced by Alexander Schallenberg, who resigned after two months.

Taking his place was Interior Minister Karl Nehammer.

The ÖVP and the SPO had ruled together until 1966. During this time, they devised a "proportional system," which called for the fair distribution of governmental and administrative posts to members of the two major parties. For instance, state secretaries who belonged to the opposite party often aided cabinet members. The Transport Ministry, with its patronage in the railways and highways, was a fiefdom of the SPO, while the Ministries of Agriculture and Defense were in the ÖVP's domain. Even jobs with the EU in Brussels were allocated according to this outdated practice. This system rested on a fundamental consensus about the nature of the democratic regime. It also encouraged Austrians to join parties so that they can be considered for these jobs. At 15% of the adult population, such membership is among the highest in the west.

Nevertheless, there is a widespread feeling that the "proportional system" has outgrown its usefulness and that it has encouraged corruption and inefficiency, since jobs are distributed on the basis of political affiliation rather than competence. Among its absurdities is the fact that the Austrian Airlines (sold in 2009 to Lufthansa) and the Vienna Airport each had two presidents. It is already being phased out in the many state industries that have been privatized, and overall fewer jobs are handed out. But it has not disappeared and remains strong in banking. A growing number of voters think it should be abolished in the civil service. Jörg Haider (1950–2008), the long-time FPÖ leader, hammered relentlessly and successfully against this outdated system of patronage. After his Freedom Party's stunning success in the 1994 elections, he boasted that "we have finally succeeded in putting postwar Austria behind us."

A new centrist party, NEÖS ("New Austria") did well in its first election. Led by Matthias Strolz, it captured 4.96% of the votes and nine seats. It is in the opposition.

Another neophyte party, Team Stronach, managed to garner 5.73% of the votes and 11 seats, although its own high expectations of becoming the king maker for the future governing coalition were frustrated. An antiestablishment party, it does not even call itself a party. It is led by an 80-year-old billionaire who emigrated to Canada in the 1950s as a penniless 22-year-old. Frank Stronach made a fortune in the auto parts business. He is a magnet for protest votes. A free-spending populist, he taps into the antiparty, antiestablishment, antieuro feelings that are widespread. It is not anti-immigrant. In the run-up to the elections, he refused any pact with established parties. His tool for maintaining control is money. He provided his party with €23 million (€13 million of which are loans that he can call at any time). The party descended into damaging bickering after the elections and was unfit for a governing role.

The phenomenon of the Freedom Party of Austria (FPÖ) deserves extended discussion, since it has been generating much controversy and nervousness internationally. The near-victory of its candidate for presidency in May 2016 focused new attention on the party.

The Freedom Party of Austria rose dramatically, winning an astonishing 26.9% and 52 seats in 1999, mainly at the expense of the ÖVP. This was one of the greatest electoral successes in recent years by a far-right party in western Europe. Particularly potent were Haider's fulminations against EU eastward enlargement and the massive influx of central Europeans that could unleash. All Austrian politicians conceded more politely and privately that fears of being swamped made enlargement a hard

Austria

Poster in Vienna of the FPÖ's Susanne Riess-Passer; we have done it!

sell domestically. The three neighbors, the Czech Republic, Hungary, and Slovenia, have a combined population nearly three times larger than Austria's. The government estimated that 5 million foreign workers lived within commuting distance of the main Austrian cities.

The FPÖ's main objective was to prevent the formation of a dominant, completely two-party system. Haider, who assumed leadership of the party in 1986, had branded the earlier grand coalitions as a "marriage of elephants." He was a fiery orator and a charismatic crowd pleaser, who called for a more nationalistic policy and denounced corruption, privilege, and the influx of immigrants. Haider also appealed to young Austrians who were fed up with politics being dominated by the two big parties and who wanted change.

In 1989 he was chosen as minister president of Carinthia, a post he held until 1991, when provincial legislators voted him out for daring to compliment the Nazis by saying that "they had a sound employment policy in the Third Reich." In 1995 he again harmed his party by making sympathetic remarks to Waffen SS veterans. No wonder it was said that many ex-Nazis were attracted to the FPÖ. Right-wing politicians must walk a fine line when speaking about the Nazis, since the law prohibits the Nazi Party, praise of its ideology, and attacks on Jews.

The government felt obliged to respond to Haider's calls for stricter controls on immigration by doing just that in 1993. It introduced some of Europe's toughest immigration laws. In 2003 plans were announced for even tougher asylum rules that would make it easier for the government to deport rejected seekers and restrict even further who could be entitled to claim refugee status. One of the FPÖ's

election posters read, "Don't let Vienna turn into Chicago!" Its more recent version is, "Vienna mustn't become Istanbul."

The influx of immigrants, including 60,000 from Bosnia alone in 1992, brought the number of foreigners living in Austria to over 1 million, or 11.4% of the total population by 2013; 16% are foreign-born, and 3% were born to a migrant family. Few immigrants are Muslim, and only 3.3% are Turkish. In Vienna 38% of residents are first- or second-generation immigrants. They experienced none of the violence that afflicted Germany, but the issue was propelled to the top of Austria's political agenda.

If immigrants are from a non-EU country and cannot speak German, they must take German-language lessons, paying half the costs. If they cannot pass a language examination after four years, their residency permits are supposed to be withdrawn. But that happens only in about one-tenth of the cases. Welfare assistance for asylum

Jörg Haider

seekers from places no longer deemed as a zone of conflict, such as Kosovo, was reduced. It was made easier for family members to join immigrants already settled in Austria, but in 2005 the waiting period to get citizenship was raised to at least 6 years for refugees or 10 years of "legal and uninterrupted" stay for others.

Like all but three of its EU partners (UK, Ireland, and Sweden), when enlargement took place in May 2004, Austria declared a transition of up to seven years before workers from the new central European member states could gain access to Austria's labor market. The country's labor shortage soon forced it to drop many of those restrictions. However, central Europeans could come as students, tourists, or retirees, and they had the right to establish a business or be self-employed. Many Austrians regard east-to-west migration as a problem, and public hostility to immigration is strong. But given the country's low birth rate, it will accept such migrants in the medium and long term to fill gaps in the labor force. Also, many of the immigrants from neighboring countries are well educated, speak fair German, and are willing to adapt to Austrian society. This is not the case for most of the new wave of migrants from the Middle East and Africa that started entering Austria in 2015.

Austrian politics had received a powerful jolt when the Freedom Party was invited to enter the ÖPV governing coalition in 2000. Before it was sworn in, the new government issued the fullest acknowledgment of Austria's complicity in Nazi crimes ever made by a postwar Austrian government. In power it did nothing to suggest that either democracy or minority rights were at risk in Austria.

Although Haider did not join the cabinet, there was an international uproar within the EU, supported by the US and Israel. All other EU members and the Czech Republic individually decided to ostracize Austria in their bilateral relations, even though Vienna had broken no EU rules. In an attempt to soften international hostility to Austria, Haider formally stepped down as party leader in March 2000, and Susanne Riess-Passer took his place. This did not defuse the crisis. But EU countries became increasingly embarrassed about the precedent they had set and the effect their sanctions had on Austrians. Polls in 2000 showed that 9 out of 10 Austrians of all political stripes opposed the EU's measures.

To get out of the corner into which it had painted itself, the EU asked the European Court of Human Rights to appoint a panel of "three wise men," led by former Finnish president Martti Ahtisaari to investigate. In September 2000 they completed their inquiry and called the sanctions "counterproductive." They concluded that the Austrian government's respect for the rights of minorities, refugees, and immigrants is not inferior to that of other EU states and that its standards are often higher. They did find that the Freedom Party is a "right-wing populist party with radical elements" that exploited racist sentiments during election campaigns. An incensed Haider retorted, "Unlike in Germany and other European countries, asylum seekers' homes are not burned in Austria, and there are no neo-Nazi marches."

The People's Party-Freedom Party coalition chalked up some accomplishments. It pushed through laws to do away with the Proporz system, which had given the two largest parties an equal share of the patronage spoils. It introduced constitutional changes to give minorities more strongly guaranteed rights. It negotiated compensation for victims of the Nazi period in Austria. Tuition was introduced for students in its underfunded and overcrowded universities, something the SPÖ has vowed to rescind.

Perhaps its greatest accomplishment was that it was able to force a reform of the pensions system through parliament in 2003. It raised the retirement age, reduced the pay-as-you-go pensions for future retirees by 10% for those over age 35, and eventually abolished the separate and more generous pensions for public employers. The issue had threatened to blow the federal budget apart in a few years. With a declining working-age population, the country faces a future pension crisis, as Austrians tend to retire before the official age of 65 for men and 60 for women. Nevertheless, in 2009 *Forbes* magazine ranked Austria as the best place in the world for retirement because of its standard of living, good medical care, and beautiful cities and landscape. Mercer Consulting consistently ranks Vienna as the world's most livable city because of its excellent public transport, low crime, and unbeatable cultural offering. It is one of the few major cities in the world that possesses an infrastructure for more inhabitants than it now has.

Unable to negotiate a coalition with the Social Democrats after three months, chancellor Wolfgang Schüssel turned again to the Freedom Party, which entered the new government in 2003 to secure a nine-seat majority. This time it was very much under the thumb of the victorious People's Party rather than being the more or less equal member earlier.

Haider decided to purge some of the party's most hard-core right-wingers, drop his nationalism, and create in April 2005 a new party devoid of ideology—the Alliance for Austria's Future (BZÖ). He sought to moderate his anti-immigration rhetoric, but his message was still aimed against excessive foreign presence, immigration,

"loss of identity," bureaucrats in Brussels, globalization, and Türkiye's EU entry, which only 10% of Austrians supported. Most grassroots activists remained with the old party, however.

Feeding on the massive discontent due to the global recession, both the Freedom Party and the newer Alliance for Austria's Future achieved spectacular results in the 2008 elections, coming to within a whisker of the SPO if their votes were combined.

Haider was fatally injured in an automobile crash in 2008 at age 58. He was intoxicated and driving more than twice the speed limit (142 kilometers, or 88 miles, per hour in a 70-kilometer, or 42- mile, zone), when he struck a concrete divider and rolled several times. His death unleashed an outpouring of shock, emotion, and grief seldom witnessed in Austria. Even most of those who opposed him mourned the passing of one of Austria's most colorful postwar political leaders.

One of Haider's legacies is his part in putting an end to the proportional system and the resulting dominance of the two largest parties. But more important is the way that he articulated Austrians' confusion about their past. They could recognize in him their own mixture of defiance and repentance, victimhood and guilt, and the struggle to expel old ghosts.

Under its new chairman, Heinz-Christian Strache, the FPÖ won votes from both large parties. But Strache's most spectacular feat in 2008 was to win the votes of over 44% of voters age 16 to 19 and more than a third among those under 30. This was especially important since the voting age dropped to 16 for the first time. It was "cool" to vote for him. He also attracted many blue-collar voters. In a 2010 poll, only 8% of respondents indicated they would like to see him as chancellor, but a year later, his support level was 26%.

In 2013, the FPÖ won 20.5% of the votes, up from 17.5%, and 40 seats, up from 34. No other far-right party in Europe enjoys such wide support, and the Freedom Party has almost caught up with the two traditionally dominant parties. This reflects the fact that antiforeigner sentiments are more pronounced in Austria than in any other EU country. Taken together, protest parties won over 30% of the votes.

Strache is a dental technician by training and a sports fanatic by nature. His direct and approachable populism struck a chord with much of the electorate. He styles himself as a man of the people. He rails against Brussels, immigration, and foreign competition, which he blames for the ongoing economic crisis. He advocates creating a ministry for the deportation of immigrants. He distanced the party's rhetoric from Nazism and racism. He eased out one of the party's candidates,

Viennese housing designed by artist Hundertwasser

who had said that the EU was in danger of becoming a "conglomerate of niggers" (*Negerkonglomerat*). Considering the astonishing results of the 2016 presidential election, in which Freedom Party candidate Norbert Hofer won the first round and lost only by a fraction in the second round, it became possible for the party could join a governing coalition.

Unexpectedly, the FPÖ was handed a chance to solidify its popularity much sooner than the regular election, scheduled for 2018. Instead, when the leader of the center-right People's Party, Reinhold Mitterlehner, resigned in 2017 over disagreements with the grand coalition partner, Social Democrats, an early election was called for October 2017. ÖVP promptly elected a new leader, the young and dynamic foreign minister Sebastian Kurz. The Freedom Party became the indispensable coalition partner, despite the lingering memories of EU's snubbing of the previous government in 2000 that had included the FPÖ. Kurz positioned himself as an alternative to the FPÖ with his tough approach to immigration. Thus, whether with or without the Freedom Party in the government, Austrian policy has already shifted in the direction preferred by that party. The 2017 "antiburqa" law and the requirements of an "integration contract" for immigrants to teach them local values have obviously been influenced by the far-right populists.

The FPÖ's star is falling. In the October 2020 Vienna (where 1.9 million of the

Austria

Former Chancellor Sebastian Kurz

Chancellor Karl Nehammer
Source: *Wikipedia*

country's 8.8 million citizens live) city elections, it collapsed to a mere 9% of the votes. This enabled Kurz's ÖVP to form a groundbreaking governing coalition with the Greens.

Chancellor Sebastian Kurz had to resign in October 2021, bowing to growing pressure over a bombshell corruption probe that has rocked the country's political establishment to its core. He was accused of allegedly making false statements to a parliamentary inquiry in 2020, regarding his role in the setting up of a holding company, OeBAG, which administers the state's role in some companies,

and the appointment of his former confidant Thomas Schmid to its leadership.

After Kurz announced his resignation, Alexander Schallenberg was proposed by the ÖVP to replace him as Chancellor of Austria. Schallenberg was sworn in on 11 October 2021, but he resigned after less than two months in office and returned to the position of Minister of Foreign Affairs.

Following the resignations of Sebastian Kurz and Alexander Schallenberg, Karl Nehammer, of the same party (ÖVP), assumed the chancellorship on December 6, 2021. Nehammer is both a party leader and Chancellor.

A Federal State

Austria is a federal state composed of nine provinces: Vienna, Salzburg, Vorarlberg, Carinthia, Upper Austria, Lower Austria, Burgenland, Styria, and Tyrol. Each province (called a *Land*) has a popularly elected legislature, which elects a governor and members who serve four- to six-year terms in the 58-member Federal Council, the upper house of the Austrian parliament. The number of seats allotted to each province depends upon its population. The smallest receives at least 3 seats, whereas the largest may receive no more than 12. Unlike the US Senate, the Federal Council has far fewer powers than the lower house. It may only review and delay legislation, and it has the right to veto only the annual budget.

The provinces are not as powerful as states in the US, since most government authority, including police power, rests with the central government. The provincial governments do have certain authority over welfare matters and local government, and strong provincial loyalties

persist. However, in general, Austria, despite its federal structure, is highly centralized politically. This condition prompted citizens in one province, Vorarlberg (which after World War I attempted to join the Swiss Confederation), to vote in a provincial referendum in 1980 for negotiation with the federal government to achieve more say over political decisions affecting its citizens, such as taxes and the allocation of funds.

Other Government Elements

The Austrian constitution provides for a Constitutional Court, whose members are appointed by a number of federal institutions and leaders. This court has the task of reviewing all cases involving constitutional questions and of deciding on jurisdictional conflicts between the various levels of governments.

The constitution also calls for the election of chambers financed by taxes and representing various segments of the economy, especially the Chambers of Agriculture, of Labor, and of Commerce. These have the right to present advisory opinions on government bills and actions affecting their particular interests. Such chambers are no doubt holdovers from the former corporate state. However, they do play an important role in bringing diverse interest groups into the governing process, and they contribute to establishing a political consensus that helps to maintain stability.

Thus, they reflect the nature of democracy in Austria today, which aims to reduce conflict and to promote compromise in a land that historically was tragically torn. The process of compromise places much responsibility on the shoulders of political and economic elites, who must tie together various groups in the Austrian society.

This is one rationale for the rule of proportionality, by which offices are distributed among members of both major parties. The Austrian system would be fundamentally changed if one party or group would take all of the spoils on the grounds that it won more votes in the last election. Of course, electoral campaigns are hotly fought and are filled with exaggerated rhetoric about how disastrous it would be if the other party won.

However, between elections the parties and economic groups cooperate with each other. To make this cooperation work effectively, political leaders must enjoy much freedom from their constituents or supporting subcultures. Some critics argue that this fact somewhat weakens popular control over the elites and weakens political participation of lower levels. Also, young protesters maintain that their actions are in part directed against a political system that leaves far too little room

Announcement of special exhibition in Kunsthaus Vienna

for young people to determine their own future. But the democratic experiment in Austria has been so successful since 1945 that very few voices demand a fundamental change of the political system.

ECONOMY

Austria is the fourth-richest country in the EU by purchasing-power parity. It has basically a free-enterprise economy in which the market determines what is produced and at what price. Economic competition exists and is encouraged, although it was traditionally not as highly valued as in the US. After 1945 it had a higher percentage of the economy under government ownership than any other country in western Europe. Almost two-thirds of all corporate capital belonged to the public sector, and a quarter of the entire labor force worked in nationalized industries or in industries controlled by nationalized banks. These were permitted to operate largely independently of government control and accounted for about one-fifth of the country's GDP and one-third of its total exports. However, large-scale privatization has changed all this.

The largest trade union, the centralized Austrian Trade Union Federation (ÖGB), represents about one-third of all wage and salary earners, somewhat above the European average. It has been steadily losing members, but almost the entire workforce is covered by collective-bargaining agreements. The idea of "social partnership," whereby government, employers, and employees cooperate over pay and economic policy, remains strong. The former Schüssel government from 2000 to 2007 weakened it by legislating reforms on matters the ÖGB thought were its prerogative, such as pensions and health care. The ÖGB is a nonpartisan, moderate, labor organization that aims not toward revolution but toward securing good pay and working conditions for its members. No doubt, memories of bitter social tensions in the past and the small size of the country help enable such cooperation to work.

There are other important results of close cooperation among labor, management, and government. Strikes are almost unknown in Austria. Statistically, the average Austrian worker strikes a few seconds per year, compared with 192 minutes in the US, 215 in Britain, and 553.5 in Italy. Second, Austria had the lowest unemployment in Europe (5% in 2023) and inflation (9% in 2023). Employers are traditionally hesitant to lay off workers, a fact that helps maintain labor peace but which sometimes hurts the financial situation of particular firms. However, the labor market is less rigid than in Germany.

Some restructuring in traditional branches is necessary. The public debt stood at 75% of GDP in 2012, and the budget deficit was 5.7% in 2023. GDP growth was 4.7% in 2022. The government worked the budget down through pay freezes to the public sector; cuts in welfare; reductions in subsidies to state-owned firms, railways, and farms; and possible reform of the pension system that allows early retirement at age 59. Overall, a third of the workforce in state-run industries was cut.

Ex-chancellor Vranitzky announced plans to privatize many state companies: "In Austria, the shelter that the state has given to almost everyone—employee as well as entrepreneur—has led to a situation in which a lot of people think not what they can do to solve a problem but what the state can do. This needs to change. Once people have sniffed the fresh air of self-initiative, it will change." Shares were sold from the country's largest oil and gas company, the largest utility, and Austrian Airlines (sold to Lufthansa in 2009). The principle is to reduce the state's shareholdings and to remove day-to-day political interference in management.

The pope is coming [to Austria].

But there are limits. When the government proposed in 2003 the sale of one-third of the Voestalpine steel group, there was an outcry. It had been founded by the Nazis in 1938 under the name of Hermann-Göring-Werke in Linz. After the war it was the flagship of state-owned industry and a fief of the Socialist Party and trade unions. The government had to promise that the firm would not be split up or sold to foreigners. Because the Schüssel government decided there was not enough domestic capital to buy such companies as Telekom Austria or the state-owned postal service, privatization was put on ice. To make small savings, 300 of the 1,640 post office branches were closed in 2005, and up to half the postal service was for sale in 2006.

A third reason for labor peace is that the real earnings of workers and employees have steadily increased. High labor costs affected Austria's trading position. Although wages are roughly on a par with those in Germany, the cost of fringe benefits, including payments for the very generous social security system, add about 80% to wage costs, as opposed to about 60% in Germany. Since 2000, unit labor costs have been reduced. The states' claim on the national tax income, in the form of taxes and other payments, now exceeds 40%.

Austria lowered its corporate tax to 25% (22% including allowances) in 2005. This is well below the EU average of 40%, and it attracts investment and helps keep businesses from moving to low-tax western European neighbors. This hurts nearby Bavaria most, which is losing investment

Horst Hiemer · Jörg Gudzuhn · Johanna Schall · Gudrun Ritter **DIE DREIGROSCHENOPER**
Bertold Brecht's *Three Penny Opera* announced in Vienna

325

Austria

to Austria. However, the corporate rate is high when compared with the flat-tax regimes in central and eastern Europe. The overall tax burden, at 43% of GDP, is some seven points higher than the EU average. With the top individual tax rate of 50% on incomes over €60,000 per year, its personal taxes are among the highest in the EU. Austria is most immediately concerned by Slovakia, which has become a foreign-investment hotspot. Industrial and prime office rents in the capital city of Bratislava are already higher than Vienna. Many Slovaks are buying up housing on the Austrian side of the border because it is much cheaper than in and around the Slovak capital. Bratislava Airport could help service Vienna, with high-speed rail connections.

Austria is fortunate to have some important natural resources: gas, brown coal (peat), iron ore, zinc, aluminum, magnetite, lignite, copper, timber, and others. These can be traded or used in their own diversified industries, which produce iron and steel, chemicals, capital equipment, and consumer goods.

Exports account for 53% of Austria's GDP, up from 38% in 1990. About three-fourths of its trade is with the EU, which it formally joined on January 1, 1995. Germany is by far Austria's most important trading partner, with 30.79% of exports and 41.9% of imports. Unification greatly stimulated its sales to the FRG.

Austria likes to see itself as a bridge between east and west, and its trade with Russia and central Europe grew rapidly. By 2009 its exports there amounted to 19.6% of Austria's total, and its imports 14.4%. Trade with the east was helping keep Austria's economy a step ahead of its

neighbors, even though it remains far less than with the old EU-15. But such large economic and banking exposure to the eastern countries can be a real risk in times of economic distress, such as 2009–2010. Proportionally Austria is the most vulnerable country dealing with the east, especially at a time of Russian aggression. Its loans to eastern Europe total three-fourths of its GDP, followed by Sweden (30%) and Greece (19%).

The US accounts for only 4% of the nation's foreign trade. One Austrian product that has become visible in American convenience stores is the high-energy drink Red Bull, whose sales in dollar terms have overtaken Diet Coke and Diet Pepsi. General Motors is the single largest investor of any foreign company in Austria.

As in most other European countries, maintaining sufficient energy supplies is a major problem. Because of its mountain water, it is able to supply about two-thirds of its electrical power through hydroelectricity. Over the entire year, Austria is actually a net exporter of this kind of power, but in the winter, when there is little water, it must import electricity. Petroleum is used for 39% of energy needs. Its oil reserves are becoming rapidly depleted, so Austria must now import almost 90% of its petroleum, thus sometimes throwing its balance of payments into deficit. It needs natural gas for 22% of its energy. It imports 80% of its natural gas from Russia. Reserves are also declining, thus requiring Austria to import about 60% of its needs, largely from Russia, which supplies 71% of its gas imports, and eastern Europe.

In 2009 it signed a transit agreement joining the EU-endorsed Nabucco pipeline

project intended to bring gas from the Caspian Sea via Türkiye, circumventing Russia. A year later it signed a pipeline deal with Russia allowing the latter's South Stream project to penetrate farther into the EU. Both efforts remain years away from realization.

Coal constitutes 8% of its energy needs, and Austria must import about 80% of it. Overall net imports account for about two-thirds of its energy, up from 63% in 1974. About a fourth is supplied by Russia. Thanks in part to its plentiful hydropower, Austria gains 31% of its energy from renewable sources; 43.5% of that renewable energy comes from hydropower.

It was intended that nuclear energy would be able to supplant the country's needs, and a nuclear power station was built at Zwentendorf near Vienna, which could have supplied 11%–15% of the country's electrical needs. However, in a 1978 referendum, a narrow majority voted against putting the power station into actual operation. Leaders of both industry and labor want to activate the plant, but the nation's political leaders and public opinion remain divided on the question. The nuclear disaster and subsequent discharge of radiation at Chernobyl in the former Soviet Union has increased the anti-nuclear-power sentiment within the country. Austria intensely opposes Czech nuclear power stations, especially the one in Temelin, 40 miles (60 km) from the border, as well as Czech plans to expand its atomic generation and sell electricity to Germany. The Austrian government entered a treaty with the Czechs guaranteeing better safety measures at the plant.

Some of Austria's international economic successes are not readily visible due to self-imposed attempts by companies not to be associated specifically with Austria. Thus, few consumers of Red Bull drinks or Swarovski crystals realize that these are Austrian companies because of the intentionally cosmopolitan marketing intended to have a broad international appeal. Others, like the soft-drink manufacturer Almdudler, attempt to include the country's folklore into their commercial image, betting on the attractiveness of the dirndl dresses and lederhosen.

The pictures of scenic mountain landscapes; Alpine villages; stately baroque cities; and singing, yodeling, and waltzing Austrians, dressed either in ballroom finery or in leather pants and Alpine hats, thoroughly enjoying life, have always attracted millions of tourists each year. Austrians have the highest per-capita income from tourism, which produces 9% of its GDP, in all of Europe, and without this source, the Austrian economy would likely collapse. Tourist receipts can no longer balance the trade deficit as they once

Austrians were gripped by the eight-year captivity of this young girl in 2006.

could, but they keep such a deficit within bearable limits. As in Switzerland, it also helps retard the flight from rural to urban areas and stimulates businesses outside the major industrial areas that support the tourist industry. The economic drawbacks of tourism are that it is seasonal and very heavily dependent upon German, Dutch, and British economic prosperity. Germans account for about three-fourths of the overnight stays and the Dutch for about 10%, with a growing number of eastern European and American visitors.

Austria's roads and ecology are also sensitive to the increasing number of trucks and cars that traverse the country and leave their exhaust fumes behind. As east-west traffic grows, the problem becomes doubly serious. The government failed to renegotiate an agreement with EU partners to limit heavy trucks. Limits and high fees on truck traffic in Switzerland redirects much of it onto Austrian roads.

Only 5% of Austria's workforce is engaged in farming and forestry, and they produce 2% of GDP. By contrast, 26% of employment and 29% of GDP are derived from industry, and 69% work in the services sector and produce 69% of GDP. Farms are predominantly small or medium-sized, family-owned, often fragmented, and located in the northern and eastern part of the country. Mountains cover three-fourths of the country, and half of its farms are located in mountain regions. Generous subsidies from Vienna and the EU help make them viable. Austrian farmers can still supply about 90% of the country's food needs. Some items, such as cheese and beef, can be exported.

It has the highest share of organic farming in Europe, accounting for 19.4% of agricultural area and 16.2% of farms in the country. About 46% of Austria is covered by forests, which also provide the country with a valuable natural resource—timber.

CULTURE

Austria is traditionally an overwhelmingly Catholic country, but the faith is rapidly losing its grip on the people. In 1900 91.6% claimed to belong to the Roman Catholic Church; by 2007 that had fallen to barely 70% overall and less than 50% in Vienna. Only 13% attend weekly Mass (17% among those claiming to be Catholic). The number paying the state-administered church tax of about $400 per year is also declining. Pedophilia and pornography scandals among priests have taken their toll. For example, Cardinal Hans Hermann Groër of Vienna was removed from office in the 1990s for molesting boys, but until his death in 2003, he never confessed or faced trial. Thousands of shocked Austrian Catholics left the church because of this scandal.

A majority of the population favors abolishing the celibacy of priests, and 49% say they do not take to heart what the pope says about marriage, sex, and birth control. A fifth of the churches no longer have a priest of their own, and the number of priests since 1990 has fallen from 5,100 to 4,262 in 2007; only 31 new priests were inducted in 2006.

To address this issue, a dissident priest movement, Call to Disobedience, led since 2006 by Fr. Helmut Schüller and claiming

support from some 70% of Austrian Catholics, challenges the church by promoting the abolishment of priest celibacy and the introduction of female priests. This approach was decried in strong terms by former Pope Benedict XVI, who traveled to Austria in September 2007. However, he was met by widespread indifference. In a poll at the time, 82% said the visit meant nothing or very little to them; among those under age 30, this figure was 96%.

Since 1912 Islam is considered an official religion, thanks to the minority policy of the Austro-Hungarian Empire. However, fear of fundamentalist Islam today has created tense populist opposition to the construction of mosques and minarets within the country. In October 2017 a new law came into effect outlawing in public places the burqa (full-face Islamic veil) or other clothing concealing the face. Extremist materials are banned, and immigrants must undergo a 12-month "integration program," including courses in "values."

Despite its small size, Austria is a land with an enormously rich scholarly and cultural heritage. Europe's oldest remaining German-speaking university was founded in Vienna in 1365. During the empire it became famous the world over for learning and research, especially in medicine, as exemplified by pioneering work in antiseptic and brain surgery of Theodor Billroth and Theodor Meynert.

There are 12 universities and 6 art academies. The universities have no tuition, while the others charge low tuition for citizens of Austria or of countries in the developing world. As in many European countries, the school system is tracked horizontally into general education, trade or commercial, and basic education courses. The first two can provide access to the universities; the ticket is the *Matura*, or high-school diploma. In 2005 the European Court of Justice ruled that German applicants who wish to get around admissions quotas at home cannot be excluded from the overcrowded and underfunded Austrian universities. Traditionally Austrian students can study whatever they want without restrictions on majors. This has led to an explosion of enrollments. For example, the University of Vienna (UniVie) had 93,000 students in 2016; about two-thirds of foreign students are from Germany. In overcrowded subjects like political science or psychology, student-faculty ratio can be 200:1. Lecture halls fill up long before the classes begin. Graduation rate is only about 30%. In QS ranking of best universities, UniVie's ranking slipped from 87th a decade ago to 153rd. However, admission to the country's four medical universities has become highly selective.

As elsewhere in the EU, the universities have undergone reforms. Shorter BA

UNABHÄNGIGE TAGESZEITUNG FÜR ÖSTERREICH | GEGRÜNDET 1848
Montag, 6. 2. 2006 | www.diepresse.com | Mo 06 / Nr. 17.397 / 1.20 Euro

Die Presse

Allein gegen alle
Irans IAEA-Botschafter
Soltanieh im Interview Seite 2

Die besten Aktien der vergangenen Woche	ATX ▼	Dow Jones ▼	Eurostoxx 50 ▲	DAX ▼	FT-SE 100 ▼	Nikkei-225 ▲	Tec-Dax ▲
	Raiffeisen Internat. + 9,52 %	Honeywell – 3,76 %	Endesa + 5,65 %	Continental AG + 5,72 %	Centrica + 7,81%	Toho Zinc + 20,44 %	Solarworld AG + 27,32 %

ÖBB-Streikbrecher siegt
OGH gibt dienstbereitem
Eisenbahner Recht. Seite 7

Quoten-Echo in Salzburg
Mozarteum will inländische
Studenten bevorzugen. S. 8

SMS gegen Diebe
Wiener Warnsystem wird
ausgeweitet. Seite 9

„Die Lage ist außer Kontrolle"

▶ BRENNENDE BOTSCHAFTEN. *Gewaltsame Angriffe auf skandinavische Vertretungen.*

▶ ESKALATION IM KARIKATURENSTREIT. *Westen mahnt eindringlich zur Zurückhaltung.*

Austria

curricula have been set up, and modest fees have been introduced in some institutions, such as the technical colleges (*Fachhochschulen*), in an attempt to reduce the 40% dropout rate. There is disagreement on whether university education should be free and how restrictive admission should be. Only 18% of the working population has higher-education qualifications, substantially below the 25% OECD average. In order to promote high-level scientific study, the government created an Institute of Science and Technology (IST Austria), located in Klosterneuburg on the outskirts of Vienna. It is modeled on elite American universities and offers only PhD programs.

One can scarcely think about classical music without thinking of Austria. The first opera performance north of the Alps took place in Salzburg, and in Vienna opera and orchestra music thrived. Joseph Haydn, Wolfgang Amadeus Mozart, a child prodigy from Salzburg; and Ludwig van Beethoven, who chose Vienna as his second home, helped give Vienna the reputation as the music capital of the world, especially toward the end of the 18th century.

In the 19th century, Viennese-born Franz Schubert became one of the forerunners of the musical romantic movement. Twice a year, in early and late summer, the "Schubertiade" festival is held in the tiny village of Schwarzenberg in western Vorarlberg. Anton Bruckner, Johannes Brahms, and Hugo Wolf produced their musical treasures. Richard Strauss's opera *Der Rosenkavalier*, whose words were written by Hugo von Hofmannsthal, premiered in Vienna in 1911. Light comedy became a particular Austrian specialty, with such masters as Johann Strauss, Karl Millocker ("The Beggar Student"), and Franz Lehar ("The Merry Widow").

One has many reminders of Austria's musical past. There are many traditional musical festivals in the nine provinces and Vienna. Especially well known is the festival in Salzburg, where many of the best conductors and musicians in the world assemble.

One musical show that is not a part of the country's past is *The Sound of Music*. It had never been produced at an Austrian theater until March 2005, when it began playing in German to sellout and enthusiastic audiences at the venerable Volksoper.

For decades it was believed that Austrians would resent a light American-style comedy set in the period when Hitler took over their country. Even the 1965 block-buster film version starring Julie Andrews and Christopher Plummer never became popular in Austria. There are, expectedly, some dour music critics who are not amused by Hollywood's version of Austria. One critic for the newspaper *Kurier* even complained that the song

"Edelweiss" is "an insult to Austrian musical creation." Contrary to popular beliefs, the song was neither a traditional tune nor the Austrian national anthem. The main political parties agreed in 2011 to change the lyrics of the actual national anthem to include a reference to women: "Home of great daughters, sons."

Kaiser Maximilian I founded the Vienna Boys' Choir in 1498 to sing in daily masses and occasionally at the royal table. Some of its notable members were Haydn and Schubert. Since 1950 the boys, organized in 4 choirs of 24, have made many foreign tours and have become musical ambassadors for Austria.

Austria also has a rich literary heritage. In the 12th and 13th centuries, the chivalrous and court poetry of Walther von der Vogelweide (1170—1230) was admired throughout the German-speaking world, and he remains one of the greatest writers of middle (high medieval) German. The greatest German medieval epic poem, the *Niebelungenlied* (about 1200 AD) was partly set in the Danube area. In the 18th and early 19th centuries, Franz Grillparzer was an especially important Austrian literary figure, and Adalbert Stifter's novel, *Indian Summer*, written in the 19th century, is one of the greatest novels in German literature.

Around the close of the 19th century, Vienna experienced a burst of artistic creativity. This time, known as the fin de siècle, was one in which Austria was experiencing social and political disintegration, a condition that created a fertile breeding ground for all that was new and for artists who wished to break with their past. So new and different were the young artistic products that one spoke of "Young Vienna."

"Viennese schools" developed in psychology, art, and music and reached their full maturity by the outbreak of World War I. One poet described the city at that time as "the little world in which the big one holds its tryouts." Salons and cafes became lively places where intellectuals, professionals, and businessmen met and discussed the issues of the day.

Sigmund Freud gave psychology a new direction he elaborated in his monumental work *The Interpretation of Dreams*. Having moved man's sexual urges to the center of man's subconsciousness and behavior, he influenced the way humans view themselves and their motives as did few thinkers in history. Sigmund Freud Private University (SFU) opened its doors in 2005 in Vienna to train students in psychotherapy and psychology.

A contemporary of Freud, Konrad Lorenz, analyzed animal behavior to look for important clues to that of human beings. In art, the work of Gustav Klimt, Franz von Stuck, and Kolo Moser was so unique that it was referred to as the "Vienna Secession."

In music, Vienna became a rich terrain for the experiments of Gustav Mahler (who was allowed only one premiere in Vienna), Franz Schmidt, Alban Berg, and Arnold Schönberg. The last dispensed with traditional tonality and was perhaps the greatest musical revolutionary of the 20th century. His concerts often unleashed cries of "garbage!" and conspicuous rushes to the exits! The work of these experimentalists no doubt was partly a protest against the values of their society and was not very well received in their time.

In literature, Hugo von Hofmannsthal and Arthur Schnitzler appear as the very mirror of Vienna in their day. The first wrote mystical novels and a comedy in 1921, *The Difficult One*, which vividly portrays the Austria that collapsed in 1918. Schnitzler's works, with their mixture of irony and sentimentality, were entertaining, but they also reflected the influence of Freud and contained effective attacks on the social ills of the day. Psychological insights into the human soul were also particularly revealing in the fascinating biographies of Stefan Zweig.

At the same time, Prague became an important German literary center within the Austrian Empire. Franz Kafka was a lonely figure who described man entrapped in a bureaucratic world. Rainer Maria Rilke, a master of German lyrical poetry, and Franz Werfel were also products of that intellectual crossroads between the Germanic and Slavic worlds.

World War I represented a true collapse with which the writers Joseph Roth and especially Robert Musil, in his fascinating portrait of Austria in *The Man without Qualities*, tried to come to grips. In art, Austria showed its independence. It remained practically untouched by impressionism but was deeply touched by expressionism and surrealism, as was shown by the works of Oskar Kokoschka and Alfred Kubin. The interwar years also produced one of the world's greatest movie directors: Billy Wilder.

The end of World War II signaled a new beginning for Austrian artists and writers. Among them were young artists from the Vienna Academy of Fine Arts, who introduced Fantastic Realism, which combines religious and esoteric symbolism with psychoanalysis. One of its founders, Franz Janschka, taught art at Bryn Mawr College in Philadelphia for over 30 years. A new Museum of Fantastic Realism was opened in Vienna's Palais Pallfy in January 2011.

Many young and highly experimental authors, such as Gernot Wolfgruber, Franz Innerhofer, Peter Henisch, and especially Peter Handke, attracted serious attention. Handke's works are within the spirit of the antitheater, which aims to break from the restraints of the traditional stage and to

Gustav Klimt, The Kiss (1907–1908)

Source: Wikipedia

shock and teach the viewer. Some of Austria's talented authors and novelists chose to live and work in Germany. The 2004 Nobel Prize in literature was awarded to Austrian novelist and playwright Elfriede Jelinek, who is especially known for her autobiographical novel *The Piano Teacher*. Now, as earlier, Austria provides a fertile home for traditional as well as avantgarde artistic movements.

Austrian film directors like Billy Wilder, Fred Zinnemann, and Otto Preminger

were Hollywood greats. The country still produces some internationally acclaimed films. An example, *38*, directed by Wolfgang Glueck, depicts a Jewish writer who searches desperately for a hiding place in Austria after the German invasion in 1938. *38* was nominated for best foreign-language film at the 1987 Academy Awards.

The 2008 best foreign-language film was won by an Austrian film, The *Counterfeiters*, directed by Stefan Ruzowitzky. Based on a true story described in a 2007 book

by Adolf Burger, *The Devil's Workshop*, the film focuses on 140 Jewish prisoners in Sachsenhausen concentration camp who were forced by the Nazis to forge foreign currencies, stamps, and documents. Burger was one of those prisoners who survived. The 2012 best foreign language film award went to *Amour*, directed by Austrian Michael Haneke. In 2010 Viennese stage star Christoph Waltz won an Oscar for best supporting actor for his role portraying the cultured multilingual "Jew

329

Austria

Hunter" SS Colonel Hans Landa in the *Inglourious Basterds*. The film is based on a true story. In 2012, he won the same award again for his role in *Django Unchained*.

With EU membership, Austria is unable to maintain the state broadcasting monopoly through the Austrian Broadcasting Corporation (ÖRF). Besides ÖRF's two television programs, about half of Austrian households can watch German channels through cable television. Private radio stations were permitted in 1994.

German newspaper concerns have purchased large stakes in some of Austria's largest publishing groups, and many newspapers depend on German money. Its quality newspaper market is led by the lively *Der Standard*, which was launched by the Axel Springer Group in 1988. The second-largest daily is *Kurier*, which owns several important magazines and is itself partly owned by the German *Westdeutsche Allgemeine Zeitung*. They are followed by the stodgier *Die Presse* and the *Salzburger Nachrichten*. The powerful *Neue Kronen-Zeitung* dominates the tabloid market. Most papers backed by political parties have folded.

CURRENT ISSUES

The wave of migrants from the Middle East and Africa that created a crisis situation throughout Europe in 2015 affected Austria greatly, too. At first, the then Chancellor Faymann government followed former German Chancellor Angela Merkel's approach by offering a hearty welcome to the migrants. A network of nongovernmental organizations and thousands of volunteers sprang into action to provide food, shelter, clothes, and medical attention. The world was shocked to hear in August of the death of 71 migrants asphyxiated after being locked up in a truck and abandoned by a Bulgarian human-trafficking gang. Another group of 80 barely survived a similar event the following day. However, the supportive attitude changed when a flood of over 1 million people entered the country at a rate of 7,000 to 10,000 per day, overwhelming social and security services. Most of the migrants soon left on their way to Germany, Sweden, and other destinations, but some 90,000 remained to request asylum in Austria, a sizeable number in a country of 8.7 million inhabitants.

While it earlier criticized Hungary for building fences along its borders, by late 2015 at that time Austrian foreign minister and later chancellor Sebastian Kurz urged EU to strengthen its external borders and stop "indirectly running a people-smugglers' promotion program." In 2016 Austria declared that it would accept only 37,500 asylum seekers for the year and would only allow 3,200 a day to enter the country and only 80 to actually apply for asylum at the border. The move angered countries on the migrant route from the south, since they feared that they would now be saddled with the task of handling masses of frustrated people prevented from going north. To indicate its displeasure, irate Greece even recalled its ambassador from Austria. Some critics blame immigrants for the worrisome uptick in terrorist violence. In November 2020, a jihadist went on a gun and knife rampage in central Vienna, killing 4 and wounding 23. It condemned Russia's war against Ukraine, although Chancellor Nehammer was the first Western leader to visit President Putin. Austria took in 66,000 Ukrainian refugees.

As Türkiye agreed to stem the flow of migrants entering Greece from its territory, the central Mediterranean route through Italy regained huge popularity, prompting Austria in April 2016 to build an 800-foot fence at the Brenner Pass in the Alps. Both the Italian and EU authorities expressed opposition to the move as possibly violating passport-free traveling rules within the Schengen area, as well as being likely to create another massive squalid squatting camp on the border. However, Austria clearly does not trust the Italians' willingness or ability to screen out and process potential refugees according to the Dublin Regulation rather than letting them pass on their way to the north. Clearly, despite the special deal the EU reached with Türkiye in exchange for reopening its membership application process, the refugee issue will continue to affect Austrian politics. In fact, in December 2016 Austria was the only holdout insisting that the EU formally "freeze" Türkiye's membership bid in the wake of President Recep Tayyip Erdoğan's crackdown on opponents after a failed military coup. The other 27 EU members preferred not to ignite a row with Türkiye and to use a more oblique language, but no agreement was reached.

Perhaps the most striking impact was the dramatic rise of the Freedom Party of Austria. Not unlike Poland and Germany, Austria has experienced an increase in support for right-wing political parties in the wake of the refugee crisis. The FPÖ—a party founded in the 1950s by some neo-Nazis—had been faring quite well until it fell to only 9% in Vienna city elections.

This portended a few developments. For one, it was clear that about half of Austrians were ready to see a right-wing president of their country. The position itself may be largely ceremonial, but in times of political crisis, the president can matter far more, for example, by dissolving the parliament and forcing new elections or by blocking EU trade agreements. Secondly, FPÖ supporters are sure to have plenty to fret about, as the influx of immigrants further exposes societal fissures and prejudices.

The Freedom Party undermined the established two-party consensus by forcing the SPÖ and the ÖVP to alter their courses so as to accommodate the disgruntled voters willing to support the FPÖ. The antiestablishment mood was laid bare when neither of the presidential candidates from the two main parties made it to the second round. The grand coalition was losing voters' support. It collapsed in 2017 before it had a chance to adjust its course in the necessary direction, starting with reducing bureaucracy and cronyism, reforming the educational system, and facing such economic weaknesses as some of the EU's highest taxes and health-care costs, plus overly generous early retirement and pensions. One way or another, the country where grand coalitions of mainstream parties have governed for 53 of the past 72 years may need to adjust to less consensual politics.

The integration of 90,000 new immigrants remains a formidable challenge. However, economic prosperity, which has resulted from social peace, active cooperation of all economic groups, low defense budgets (0.8% of GDP), and relatively productive industries, will be maintained. Austria's 5.7% unemployment in 2023 is among the lowest in the EU. Its banks, which are heavily exposed to central Europe and Italy, have weathered the eurozone storm rather well, though they are vulnerable to turmoil on EU's eastern border. The policy of neutrality is being changed to become compatible with Austria's membership in the EU. NATO membership is unlikely anytime soon.

Austria's public opinion still seems more skeptical toward the EU than in most other member states, and hostility toward Turkish entry and Greek bailouts is strong. But there is little likelihood that voters would choose to leave the EU. The European Union and the euro were important supports in dealing with the global economic crisis that caused its GDP growth to plummet to –3.5% in 2009 before rising by 1.2% in 2023, and its budget deficit was 6.2% in 2022. Overcoming the deep economic recession was a challenge, but the worst is over. Austria started making some painful but necessary economic and political adjustments that made the country one of the EU's best economic performers. With its traditional consensus politics under assault, it needs to seek further reforms to weather the current challenges.

Republic of Poland (Rzeczpospolita Polska)

A glimpse of the interior of the royal castle, Warsaw

Courtesy: Embassy of Poland

Area: 120,733 sq. mi. (312,696 sq. km).

Population: 38,036,118 (2022 census); 37,546,000 (2023 estimate)

Capital City: Warsaw (pop. 1,863,056 capital city and county)

Climate: It is highly variable with a transitional character between oceanic (maritime) type in the northwest and continental type in the southeast. The mountainous southern edges are situated within an alpine climate. Summers are warm, with an average temperature of around 20 °C (68.0 °F) in July, and moderately cold winters with an average temperature of −1 °C (30.2 °F) in December.

Neighboring Countries: Ukraine, Belarus (east); Lithuania (northeast); Russia—Kaliningrad Enclave (north); Czech Republic, Slovakia (south); Germany (west).

Official Language: Polish.

Other Languages: Belarusian, Ukrainian, German.

Ethnic Background: Polish 98%, German 0.2%, Ukrainian 0.1%, other / undeclared 1.7%.

Religion: Christianity 72.2% (Roman Catholicism 71.3%, other Christian 0.9%), other 0.4%, no religion 6.9%, unidentified 20.5%.

Form of Government: Unitary parliamentary republic.

Chief of State: Andrzej Duda, President (since August 2015).

Head of Government: Donald Tusk, Prime Minister (since December 2023).

National Flag: It features two horizontal bands of equal width, the upper one white and the lower one red. The two colors, white and red, were officially adopted as national colors in 1831. They were associated with Poland since the Middle Ages and were emphasized on royal banners. They are of heraldic origin. They derive from the colors of the coats of arms of the two constituent nations of the Polish–Lithuanian Commonwealth—the White Eagle of Poland, and the Pursuer of the Grand Duchy of Lithuania, a white knight riding a white horse, both on a red shield. The national flag was officially adopted in 1919. A variant of the flag with the national coat of arms set in the middle of the white band is legally and traditionally reserved for official use abroad and at sea. Since 2004, May 2nd has been celebrated as Polish Flag Day.

Public Holidays: May 3 (Constitution Day. Marking of the day in 1791 when Poland adopted the first democratic constitution in Europe); November 11 (Independence Day. The anniversary of regaining independence after World War I in 1918).

331

Poland

Currency: Zloty (PLN).
Main Exports: Machinery, metals, textiles and clothing, coal, and food.
Main Imports: Machinery, chemicals, and fuels.
Main Trading Partners: Germany (27.8% of exports and 20.2% of imports), UK (4.9% of exports), Czech Republic (6.6% of exports and 3.1% of imports), France (5.7% of exports), Russia (3.8% of imports), Netherlands (4.6% of exports and 3.4% of imports), Italy (4.6% of exports and 4.6% of imports), China (14.8% of imports), US (3.0% of exports and 4.3 of imports). (2022)

"Only two trains leave from the historic station at which Poland is standing. One is the European Express. The other is the Trans-Siberian Railway." These words by a spokeswoman for the opposition Modern Party were uttered at a huge anti-government rally in Warsaw in 2016, but they encapsulate the dilemmas Poles have faced throughout more than 1,000 years of their history. A mostly Roman Catholic people whose hearts and minds have always pointed westward, Poles paid a heavy historical price for living between Europe's two largest nations, Russia and Germany, with an expansive Austro-Hungarian Empire to the south until 1918. Unlike such countries as the United States or Britain, they seldom had the tranquility and luxury to determine their own place in the world and to manage their own affairs. That changed dramatically in 1989 with the end of communism in Poland and again in 1991 with the collapse of their eastern nemesis, the Soviet Union. Poles have not only regained their sovereignty, but they also find that the world around them has totally changed.

Poland is shaped in an uneven square as a result of the boundary changes that occurred after World War II. The land is mostly a flat plain that rises to mountainous heights only along the southern border, where the Sudeten and Carpathian ranges are found. Several Tatra Mountain peaks exceed 7,000 feet in elevation within Poland. The soil is not very rich, and for this reason, agricultural yields are rather modest, except in relatively small areas of black soil and wind-driven topsoil found in the center and south of the country. Europe's fifth-largest country, Poland is located at the crossroads of the continent,

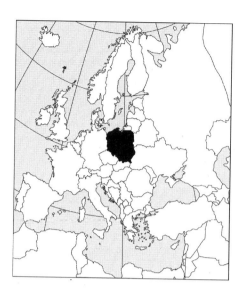

halfway between Brussels and Moscow or Stockholm and Athens.

The climate reflects the middle position of Poland between western Europe, with its moist oceanic climate, and eastern Europe with a dry, continental climate. The summers are warm and permit the cultivation of fairly good crops, except during the years when there is not enough rain.

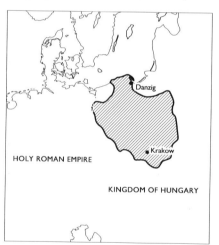

Shifting borders: c. 1150 . . .

and c. 1350

332

Poland

The winters, on the other hand, can be bitterly cold.

Poland had significant Ukrainian, Belarussian, Jewish, and German minorities prior to World War II. Today, as a result of events associated with that war, Poland is ethnically and religiously homogeneous. Almost every citizen is both an ethnic Pole and a Roman Catholic.

Political Status: Independent kingdom from the 10th century; joined with Lithuania in the 14th century; decline in power in the 17th century, leading to partitions of Poland by Russia, Prussia, and Austria at the end of the 18th century; independent from 1918 until German conquest in 1939; People's Republic within the Soviet sphere 1944–1989.

HISTORY

The Early Polish Kingdoms

Poland officially celebrated its millennium—1,000 years of existence as a state—in 1966. This date, observed with much pomp by the communist government, is actually the 1,000th anniversary of the introduction of Christianity into the area in 966.

The Piast ruling dynasty was named after its semilegendary founder, Piast, who brought together under his leadership a number of Slavic tribes living in the area between the Vistula and Oder Rivers. The most important of these were the Polanie, which means "inhabitants of the plains" in Polish. It is from the name of this tribe that the name Polska ("Poland" in English) is derived. Prince Mieszko I adopted Roman Catholicism in 966, and it thereafter became the religion of the country, as well.

Mieszko I's adoption of Christianity may have been genuine, but it was also a wise political move. A thousand years ago, it was an insurance policy against the continued pressure of German rulers who justified their incursions into Polish lands as a movement to convert the pagans.

The fact that Poland adopted Christianity in its western form has been of great and lasting influence in Polish history. With Roman Catholicism came the Roman alphabet, to which were added letters designed to render some specific Slavic sounds. In contrast, the Russians and other eastern and southern subbranches of the Slav family adopted the Cyrillic script, which is based on the Greek alphabet.

Because of the split between the Roman Catholic and the Eastern Orthodox Churches, Poles later came to think of themselves as an outpost and frontier of Catholicism and western culture. The Russians, being orthodox ("correct") Christians, viewed the Poles as "intruding Roman heretics." A mixture of political rivalries and conflicting spiritual values resulted in a lasting hostility between the two leading Slav nations.

The consequences of this split did not fully appear for several centuries. Prior to that, the Polish state, linked in a dynastic union with the much larger Grand Duchy of Lithuania from the 15th century onward, was one of the most important European realms. The land that would later become known as Russia did not free itself from the long period of Tatar rule until toward the end of the 15th century. It did not emerge as a regional power until the 16th century.

The early history of Poland was marked by the struggle to create a stable national state while fending off incursions by German princes from the west and contesting with "Russian" princes for territory and power in the east. In addition, Polish kings sometimes had to block early Bohemian (Czech) rulers who claimed some of the areas held by the Polish crown.

One of the early Piast rulers occupied Kiev (now the Ukrainian capital) briefly, while another ruler, Boleslaw the Brave, extended his control toward the Black Sea. Important trade routes were brought under Polish control during this period. However, these successes were undermined by a method of inheritance called the appanage system, whereby the territory of a ruling prince was divided among all his sons. While destroying the unity of the kingdom, this led to endless clashes among brothers and cousins for the position of leadership. The same kind of inheritance system prevailed after 1054 in the early "Russian" state of Kiev, with similar results. The contenders were forced to rely on combinations of fighting men and on alliances with the higher clergy for support. This was paid for by land grants or by delegations of political power to the landed gentry (szlachta). The political power of the gentry thus grew, and this hampered the growth of a strong, centralized monarchy. It also led later to a concept of liberty, almost bordering on anarchy, thus making orderly government practically impossible.

The most famous—or infamous—example of this development in later centuries was the concept of the liberum veto, which was never used from 1505 to 1648. By 1795, however, it brought the state down. By speaking the words *veto nie pozwalam*—"I do not allow," *a single member* of the national assembly could block legislation and force the assembly to be dissolved. In practice, these obstructive votes of minor gentry could be controlled or purchased by powerful magnates or even by agents of foreign powers meddling in Poland's affairs. Although praised as a "democratic system," the constitutional freedoms and privileges were actually extended almost exclusively to the gentry, which was about 10% of the population. The city dwellers enjoyed some rights, but the peasants were reduced to serfdom. This oppressive system continued with little change during the existence of the Polish-Lithuanian "commonwealth."

The unity of the state was restored in the 14th century under Wladyslaw Lokietek, father of Casimir (Kazimierz) the Great, who strengthened the state. The cities now expanded as German artisans and Jewish traders moved eastward under official encouragement. Culture advanced. Jagiellonian University in Krakow was established in 1364. It later became a distinguished seat of learning and the alma mater of the astronomer Copernicus.

In spite of Casimir's wisdom and great contributions to government, law, and

Shrine to the Virgin Mary, Czestochowa

333

culture, his rule was characterized by a loss of Polish territories in the west and southwest. The province of Silesia was ceded to semi-Germanized Czech rulers, while the Teutonic Knights, a militarized German religious order, was allowed to extend its control over areas adjacent to the Baltic Sea. Poland expanded eastward, setting the stage for future clashes with the Russian state once it had freed itself from Tatar domination. For a while, however, it seemed that the Polish state was safely launched on a course of greatness, with its power embracing territory from the Baltic to the Black Seas.

The Jagiellonians

Casimir the Great was the last of the Piast dynasty because he had no male heir. The throne passed to his nephew, Louis of Anjou, who was also the king of Hungary, and then to the latter's daughter, Jadwiga. A new era in the history of Poland opened when she married the grand duke of Lithuania, Jagiello (Jogaila), who converted to Roman Catholicism upon his marriage. He turned the grand duchy over to his cousin, Vytautas, and became king of Poland in 1386, founding a dynasty that lasted until 1572.

However, Vytautas also died without an heir in 1430, so the Grand Duchy of Lithuania reverted back to the line of Jagiello. It

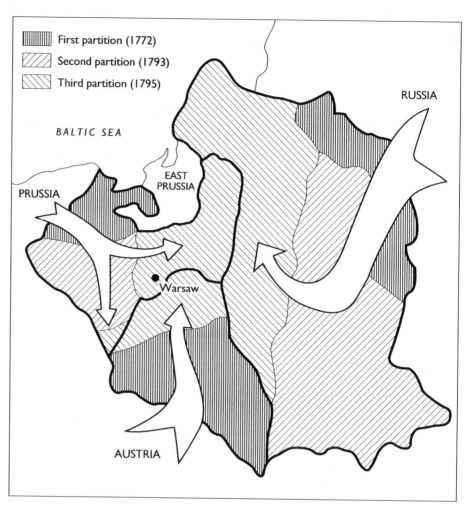

Poland: a land devoured

became increasingly tied to Poland until, in 1569, the two kingdoms were merged in the Union of Lublin.

One of the reasons for the union of Poland and Lithuania was joint defense against the Teutonic Knights along the Baltic Sea. Although Polish forces soundly defeated the knights at Tannenberg (Grunwald) in 1410 and forced them to acknowledge the authority of the Polish king, they were never fully brought under Polish control. Thus when, with the advent of the Reformation in the 16th century, the knights dissolved their religious order—becoming eventually the nucleus of the kingdom of Prussia—they became a standing menace to Poland's access to the sea. The Reformation also resulted in a widespread adoption of Protestantism in Poland. But this was reversed by the new order of Jesuits, which essentially won Poland back for Roman Catholicism during the Counter-Reformation.

Decline and Fall

The previously loose organization of Poland-Lithuania was transformed in

1569 into a more centralized state. However, soon thereafter, with the end of the Jagiellonians, the process of decline began. Until a final collapse at the end of the 18th century, there was a succession of elected kings, most of whom were foreign.

One of these monarchs, Sigismund III of the Swedish royal house of Vasa, involved Poland in the "Time of Troubles" that raged in Russia following the death of Ivan Grozny ("the Terrible"). Polish troops occupied Moscow in 1610 and used false pretenders to the Russian throne to advance Polish policy. These attempts to profit from Russia's weakness were unsuccessful, but they created lasting resentment and distrust.

The rest of the 17th century was one of much misery for Poland. It was during this period, for example, that Poland lost most of Ukraine. Part of the territories of the Grand Duchy of Lithuania, which had been united under the Polish crown in 1569, this area was occupied mostly by Cossacks, nearly all of whom were Russian Orthodox. Intent on separating them from Russia in the 17th century, Poland

Poland

alienated them by trying to force them all into a new "Uniate" Church that recognized the authority of Rome. An economic factor was also present: In addition to encouraging Polish noblemen to settle in the area and to polonize the Ukrainian nobles there, the Polish crown had issued decrees that would have turned the mass of Ukrainian peasants into serfs.

Bogdan Khmelnitsky, whose own lands had been taken over by a Polish nobleman, now became a leader for Ukrainian autonomy. Elected Hetman (chief) of the Zaporozhian Cossacks, Khmelnitsky launched an uprising in 1648 that cleared much of the Ukraine of Polish forces. However, a defeat by Poland convinced him that the Cossacks were not strong enough to achieve victory on their own. Believing that a Polish victory would mean the end of the Orthodox Church in Ukraine, Khmelnitsky sought Russian help to win independence for Ukraine. After helping the Ukrainians, however, Russia later controlled them.

Russia accepted the Cossack offer in 1653. War broke out the following year between Poland and Russia. A year later Sweden took advantage of the situation to invade Poland. But it was too large for Sweden to control. It had almost destroyed Poland before the Swedish forces were stopped near a shrine to the Virgin Mary at Czestochowa. Tradition credits the rescue of the country to the miraculous intervention of the Virgin Mary.

The war between Russia and Poland had been "put on hold" during the Swedish invasion, but when the Swedes had been driven out, that war started again. It ended in the Truce of Andrusovo, signed in 1667. Under its terms Russia obtained all of Ukraine east of the Dnieper River and was permitted to occupy the city of Kiev for two years. Russia never gave back Kiev, however, and the terms of the truce were made permanent by a treaty of peace signed in 1686.

Poland's decline was briefly interrupted during the reign of Jan Sobieski, a native Polish ruler who led a Polish army to Vienna in 1683 to help lift the siege of that city by the Ottoman Turks. Although this victory bolstered the self-image of the Poles as a strong Christian power, the image was misleading.

After Sobieski's death, the Poles turned to a foreign ruler, Augustus, king of Saxony, and offered him the Polish crown. King Augustus II (his Polish title) offered the young Peter the Great an alliance against Sweden, suggesting that Charles XII, the new young Swedish king, would be unable to defend the extensive territories along the Baltic Sea that his grandfather had seized in the 17th century. The result was the Great Northern War that began in 1700.

Augustus was wrong about Charles XII, although that young ruler made a mistake in concluding, after the Battle of Narva, that Poland, not Russia, was the real enemy. Charles XII spent the next seven years waging a war against Poland, eventually defeating Augustus II and forcing him to abdicate as king of Poland. He then placed his own candidate on the throne. Augustus II was reinstated as king of Poland after Peter the Great's defeat of Charles XII at Poltava in 1709.

This marked the real end of Polish independent action, if not formal independence. From this time onward, foreign powers would dictate who sat on the Polish throne. The last king of Poland was Stanislaw August Poniatowski, a former favorite of Catherine the Great, empress of Russia. He was a man of great culture and charm, but he possessed only limited talents for governing a country in a state of disintegration.

Partitions of Poland were carried out in 1772, 1793, and 1795 by neighboring Russia, Prussia, and Austria. They first diminished, then finally ended, the independent existence of the once-glorious commonwealth. Before the final partition, there were still occasional expressions of Polish patriotism. Casimir Pulaski, the youthful leader of one such movement, eventually left Poland for the United States and died while fighting the English in America's War of Independence. Another Pole, Tadeusz Kosciuszko, led an unsuccessful uprising in Poland after fighting in the American

Revolutionary War. There was also a final effort to reform the political structure that resulted in a proposed constitution, regarded with reverence even today as the May 3 Constitution (1791), although it was never actually put into effect.

"Not Yet Lost"

After the collapse of the old commonwealth, the struggle for the revival of Poland was continued mainly by trying to interest foreign powers in sponsoring restoration of an independent Poland. Poles also flocked to various armies fighting or preparing to fight one or the other partitioner. Many were attracted by the high-sounding slogans of the French Revolution. This led many to enlist in a Polish legion created by Napoleon in the Italian province of Lombardy. Their official song began with the words "Poland is not yet lost as long as we live." It became the national anthem in later years and still is today. Napoleon actually had little concern for the cause of Polish independence, although he was glad to see Poles join his armies. He did create a symbolic "Polish" state in 1807—the Duchy of Warsaw—which collapsed with the defeat of his forces in the historic battles of 1812.

At the Congress of Vienna, Alexander I of Russia demanded that the historic Polish lands be brought together to form a new kingdom of Poland, with himself as head of state. Adam Czartoryski, a Pole who was one of Alexander's advisers, had actually suggested the idea. Neither Austria nor

Signing the German-Soviet Pact (August 23, 1939), which divided Poland between them. L. to r.: Germany's Ribbentrop with Stalin and Molotov

Poland

Prussia was eager to give up Polish territories obtained as a result of the partitions, but they eventually agreed to Alexander's demands. The kingdom of Poland thus came into existence in 1815 as a separate possession of the Russian emperor. Alexander took the title of king of Poland and not only granted the Poles a constitution but also set up a separate Polish government and army. He then named his brother, the Russian grand duke Constantine, as regent and actual ruler of Poland.

Although Constantine's wife was Polish and he ruled by all accounts both competently and fairly, many Poles were dissatisfied with this arrangement which, after all, implied Russian domination, even if indirect. They therefore rebelled in 1830 and attempted to expel the Russians. The attempt failed, and Nicholas I, who had in the meantime become tsar, punished the Poles by abolishing the constitution and making Poland an administrative unit within the Russian Empire. In spite of another unsuccessful Polish uprising in 1863, it remained part of Russia until World War I.

Throughout the 19th century, there were many expressions of sympathy for the cause of an independent Poland, especially whenever spectacular but unsuccessful uprisings occurred, such as in 1830 and 1863. But there was no occasion for outside intervention in "the Polish Problem" until the First World War. That war, which ended with the defeat of Germany, the collapse of the Austro-Hungarian Empire, and the weakening of Russia through revolution and civil war, finally led to the rebirth of Poland as an independent state. Among those who advocated it even prior to the end of the war was President Woodrow Wilson, who made the argument that "statesmen everywhere are agreed" that an independent Poland was necessary as part of a reconstituted Europe.

Poland after World War I

Poland was officially reborn on November 11, 1918, but it enjoyed an independent existence for a little more than 20 years. The Treaty of Versailles, signed in June 1919, granted Poland access to the Baltic Sea through a narrow corridor that separated East Prussia from the main body of Germany. In addition, the city of Danzig (Gdansk), which had been designated as Poland's port, was organized as a free city with a League of Nations high commissioner. Although permitted internal self-government, its foreign relations were placed under Polish control. This clumsy arrangement was necessitated by the fact that the League of Nations did not want to put this largely German-speaking city under Polish rule but believed that it had to provide Poland with a port. Hitler's demand for Danzig's

return to Germany was later used to "justify" the Nazi invasion of Poland.

The reborn Polish state consisted of provinces that had been under the foreign rule of three different countries for over a century. There was much wartime destruction. Immediately following the end of the war, Poles experienced widespread hunger, alleviated to some extent by an American relief program. Politically, the nation was badly divided, with a number of groups and parties competing for power. In addition, the country was still largely agricultural, and its rapidly growing population made the economic situation even more difficult.

From 1918 to 1920, Poland fought six border wars—against Germany, Czechoslovakia, Lithuania, western Ukraine, and Bolshevik Russia. The latter war was significant for all of Europe, in that it prevented the Bolsheviks from linking up with communists in Germany. It thereby helped foil the communist revolution there and kept the Bolsheviks out of the heart of Europe. The Bolsheviks viewed Poland as the "red bridge" to Europe. Poles saw the struggle as a crucial test of whether the Bolsheviks could rebuild the tsarist empire and whether the bordering countries could resist Russian imperialism disguised as socialism. The fighting lasted two years. Led by Marshal Jozef Pilsudski, a former socialist who had fought on the side of Germany and Austria in World War I, the Poles struck in the east and took

Warsaw, 1945 and today

most of Lithuania and Belarusia and entered Ukraine. The Bolsheviks drove them out of Ukraine in June 1920 and within six weeks were at the gates of Warsaw. But in August the Polish army delivered a devastating blow to the invaders, decimating three Soviet armies. Admitting his mistake in believing the Poles would welcome the Red Army, Lenin sued for peace. Before the fighting ended, Poland took Vilnius from Lithuania in October 1920. In March 1921 the Treaty of Riga drew the line between Poland and the Soviet republics, established diplomatic relations between Poland and the USSR, and completed Poland's struggle for acceptable borders.

One of the first prime ministers, the world-famous pianist Ignacy Paderewski, left the country after a few months, disgusted with the constant political squabbles. Pilsudski, the provisional chief of state, temporarily retired from politics during this period, as well. He was persuaded to return to power in May 1926, however, to rescue the country from disaster due to the political bickering. From that time until the end in 1939, the country was governed first by Pilsudski, who died in 1935, and then by his associates, especially a group known as "the colonels."

Parliamentary government was never fully abolished, but the system was "streamlined." Political parties were permitted to continue in existence, but only the candidates who had the approval of the administration could be elected to the parliament (Sejm, pronounced as "same").

During this period domestic affairs were dominated by continuing problems concerning the economy and ethnic minorities with doubtful loyalties to Poland. The Nazis later recruited many Germans, while the Ukrainians had their own strong revolutionary movement with a terrorist wing.

In addition, some young alienated Poles joined the illegal Communist Party, then an elite party. But filling the prisons with these disaffected youngsters only turned the jails into "prison universities," where the inmates received thorough indoctrination from fellow prisoners, sometimes deliberately planted there by the party.

The fear of communism and the bitter relations with Soviet Russia, against which Poland had waged a war in 1919–1920, forced Poland to maintain a large army. Aware of their dangerous location between Germany and the Soviet Union, the Poles tried to maneuver between the two powerful neighbors. Although they signed a nonaggression agreement with Hitler in January 1934, they refused to enter into a closer, anti-Soviet association with the Nazis. In the end, neither the Germans nor the Soviets had any reason to side with the Poles against the other. Poland also alienated western public opinion by

participating in the division of Czechoslovakia, which occurred following the Munich Conference in 1938.

Poland during World War II

Undeterred by a guarantee of territorial integrity the government of Great Britain gave to Poland, Hitler made a series of brash demands on Poland during the summer of 1939 that were rejected by the Polish foreign minister. Then, on August 23, 1939, Hitler signed a nonaggression pact with the Soviet Union. The secret portions of the pact provided for a new partition of Poland. The Soviet Union received the eastern part of the country, with its heavily non-Polish population. Poland's poorly equipped force proved unable to resist the massive attack launched by Hitler in September 1939.

The heroic but futile Polish resistance to the German armies ended in mid-September 1939. Soviet troops marched into eastern Poland on September 17 and stopped along an agreed-upon boundary, called the Ribbentrop-Molotov Line, named after the German and Soviet foreign ministers. The Polish government had, by this time,

already fled the country, making its way first to Romania, then to France, where it set up a Polish government-in-exile. It finally moved to London in May 1940 after Hitler's invasion of France. The partitioning powers energetically tried to wipe out all traces of an independent Poland between September 1939 and June 22, 1941, when the short-lived cooperation between Hitler and Stalin came to an end with Hitler's invasion of the Soviet Union. A large part of Poland was directly incorporated into the Greater German Reich. The remainder was formed into a "general government" under a Nazi governor, Hans Frank.

A systematic policy of exterminating Poland's political and intellectual leaders reflected a Nazi plan to make the Poles a source of manual labor, working for the benefit of the "master race." Separately, Jews were driven into ghettos, then later shipped off to death camps and gas chambers. When only 60,000 were left in the Warsaw ghetto, Jewish fighters rose up in April 1943 and valiantly battled against German soldiers for almost a month. There was no chance of military success,

Poland

Warsaw uprising: Listening for instructions

and the uprising was crushed. The same happened in the second Polish insurrection that broke out in Warsaw on August 1, 1944. The last survivor of the 1943 ghetto uprising, then-23-year-old Marek Edelman, said, "Humanity has decided that it is more beautiful to die with a gun in your hand than without." He passed away in 2009 at age 87.

One brave woman, Irena Sendler, was awarded Poland's highest honor, the White Eagle, in 2003 for having organized an elaborate and dangerous scheme that rescued more Jewish children from the ghetto than the Jewish workers Oscar Schindler had been able to save. She died in 2008 at age 98.

Many Polish families protected Jews. Of the more than 26,100 rescuers worldwide honored by Israel's Yad Vashem memorial as the Righteous among Nations, over 6,600 are Polish. But in at least one case, it was Poles themselves who perpetrated the crime. In a shocking book, *Neighbors*, published in 2000, Princeton historian Jan T. Gross details how in July 1941 Polish townsmen beat, clubbed, and drowned 100 Jews in the small town of Jedwabne; then they forced 1,500 more into a barn, doused it with gasoline, and set it ablaze. This chilling incident was the inspiration for a film directed by Wladyslaw Pasikowski in 2012, *Aftermath*, shown all over Poland. It ignited a furious debate over how to deal with the dark side of Poland's past. The same reaction greeted a subsequent book in 2013 by Ottawa University historian Jan Grabowski, *Hunt for the Jews: Betrayal and Murder in German-Occupied Poland*. He described how Polish

"blue police" participated in and often initiated the hunt for Jews who had gone into hiding.

To postwar Poles, who for 60 years had been taught that their people had been heroic victims, never collaborators, in Nazi atrocities, this was a shattering revelation for which ex-president Aleksander Kwasniewski publicly apologized in 2001. In 2008 Gross published a second book, *Fear: Anti-Semitism in Poland after Auschwitz*, which recounts how some returning Jewish concentration camp survivors were killed by Poles who had occupied their property. An opinion poll taken in 2008 concluded that 36% of Poles still had a negative view of Jews and 46% had negative views of Muslims. At the outbreak of the war, 3.3 million Jews lived in Poland; this was Europe's largest Jewish community. In the 2011 census, 7,508 Poles identified themselves as Jews. Estimates of the true number range upward to 30,000.

To help explain the complex history of Polish Jews, a new POLIN Museum was opened in April 2013 in Warsaw on the 70th anniversary of the ghetto uprising. Along with many American donors, Poland's richest man, Jan Kulczyk, contributed $6.4 million. In 2016, the museum received the prestigious European Museum of the Year Award. Foreign and domestic foundations also help resurrect elements of Jewish culture by establishing cultural associations or restoring the Jewish quarter of Kazimierz in Krakow, depopulated during the Holocaust.

An independent Poland continued to exist in the form of its government-in-exile in England. Many thousands of Poland's fighting men managed to make their way west in 1939 and formed military detachments pledged to fight side by side with the western Allies. Polish airmen, in particular, distinguished themselves during the Battle of Britain, the massive German air assault on England in August-September 1940. They fought anywhere the British fought, including in Narvik, Tobruk, and elsewhere in North Africa.

The position of the Poles was complicated by the fact that, while the west was allied with the USSR in their joint struggle against Nazi Germany, the Poles saw the Soviet Union as an enemy, as well, since it had obtained extensive Polish territories as a result of the Nazi-Soviet nonaggression pact of 1939. After Hitler launched his invasion of the Soviet Union in June 1941, the British attempted to mediate the breech. They managed to persuade the Polish government-in-exile to sign an agreement restoring relations between the USSR and Poland.

As a result, the Soviet Union permitted the formation of a number of Polish fighting units from among prisoners taken by the Soviet Union in 1939 and from among the many Polish citizens who had sought refuge in the Soviet Union. Because of the serious rifts between the Polish forces and the Soviet leadership, the troops, commanded by General Wladyslaw Anders, were placed under British command and trained in Palestine. Later, they served gallantly in

First Secretary Wladyslaw Gomulka (left) chats with Chairman of the Council of State Aleksander Zawadzki AP/Wide World Photo

338

Italy, especially at Monte Cassino, where they were the first Allied soldiers to enter the ruins of the famed monastery.

The Soviet Union had always insisted that it intended to retain the territories obtained as a result of the Nazi-Soviet non-aggression pact. As Soviet war fortunes began to improve, it showed increasing dissatisfaction with the insistence of the Polish government-in-exile on regaining the prewar frontiers of Poland in the east.

The break between the USSR and the Polish government-in-exile occurred in 1943, when the Germans announced the discovery of a mass grave of 21,768 Polish officers in the Katyn Forest, near Smolensk, Russia. Each had been murdered in April-May 1940 by a bullet to the back of the head. Since many were only reservists serving in wartime, the victims included the military, political, intellectual, medical, scientific, legal, and business creme of Polish society. The Soviets had slaughtered them and blamed the crime on the Germans. General Wladyslaw Sikorski, the Polish prime-minister-in-exile, asked for an impartial inquiry by the International Red Cross. Claiming its total innocence, the Soviet Union accused Sikorski of helping Nazi propaganda and severed all ties to the Polish government-in-exile. He died in a 1943 air accident, and one theory holds that Stalin ordered his killing. His body was exhumed in 2008 to try to determine the cause of his death, but no evidence of foul play was discovered.

In the Soviet Union, a Union of Polish Patriots now emerged as spokesman for the Poles. A Polish "army" was formed as an auxiliary of the Soviet troops. These communist-led organizations became the nucleus of the Lublin Committee, which was installed July 22, 1944, as the new government of Poland after the Red Army had reached what the Soviet Union was willing to recognize as Polish territory.

On August 1, 1944, when the Soviet army had moved to the eastern bank of the Vistula River and it looked like the Germans were withdrawing from Warsaw, the underground loyal to the London leadership staged an uprising, assuming that the Allies would help them. The Polish fighters hoped to obtain control of the city before the Red Army captured it, thereby making it impossible for Stalin to ignore Poland's lawful authorities. That proved to be naive.

At the last moment, Hitler issued orders for his troops to make a stand, and the Warsaw uprising was brutally crushed after 63 days, leaving 200,000 persons dead (including many of the country's intellectuals and leaders) and 80% of the city destroyed. The Red Army made no attempt to cross the Vistula and come to the aid of the Poles. Stalin called the fighters a "band

of criminals" and made airlifts impossible by refusing to allow British and American planes to refuel in the Soviet Union. The Soviets later arrested some of those who had escaped through the sewer system.

The official Soviet explanation was that the Red Army had run out of steam after a successful push over the summer, and it needed time to pause and regroup before pushing on westward. The failed uprising added another lasting element of bitterness and resentment to the relations between the two countries. Stalin was, in fact, extremely suspicious of any Poles not under his control. At one point, 16 leaders of the pro-London underground were lured into the open, supposedly for the purpose of negotiation with the Soviets. Instead, they were unceremoniously arrested and imprisoned. The psychological and physical magnitude of the catastrophe is almost unimaginable. In August 2004, on the 60th anniversary of the uprising, a museum commemorating it was opened in Warsaw.

Following the Yalta Agreement of February 1945, the US and Great Britain "derecognized" the government-in-exile. This was after the Soviet Union had agreed to add a few noncommunist leaders to the communist government in Warsaw and to create a government of "national unity." The most prominent noncommunist addition was Stanislaw Mikolajczyk, leader of the Peasant Party.

Stalin's vague promises of "free and unfettered elections" made at Yalta offered little protection to noncommunist groups that tried to resume their political activities after the war. The fiction of "national unity" died as soon as the onset of the Cold War ended the illusion of postwar accord between east and west. Mikolajczyk had to flee the country in 1947.

From "People's Democracy" to "People's Republic"

Poland lost 16% of its population in the war, about half of them Jews. On average, 30,000 people were killed each day. Postwar Poland is, in many respects, an almost entirely new country. It is located about 185 miles farther to the west than it had been in 1939. At the expense of Germany, it gained a 325-mile-long coast on the Baltic Sea. This is a large coastline when compared to the narrow corridor of the interwar period. What had been East Prussia prior to the war was divided between Poland and the Soviet Union. It eliminated what many Poles viewed as a "dagger pointed at the heart of Poland." The former German city of Königsberg became the heart of the present Russian exclave of Kaliningrad (see separate chapter). The frontier with Germany was substantially shortened. The "recovered" lands taken

Edward Gierek

from Germany are economically more valuable than those surrendered to the USSR.

Another basic change was in the demographic composition. Instead of having a population more than 30% ethnically non-Polish, the country today is inhabited by almost 39 million people, only about 2.3% of whom are ethnic minorities. Most of the Ukrainians and Belarusians who had lived in Poland were annexed into the Soviet Union. Half of Belarus belonged to Poland before the Second World War, and a half-million Poles still live in Belarus. From 200,000 to 300,000 Ukrainians are left in the western part of Poland, where they had been forcibly resettled in 1945. In northern Poland about 200,000–300,000 Belarusians still live. Around 20,000 Lithuanians, 20,000 Slovaks, 3,000 Czechs, and 13,000–15,000 Russians live within Poland's borders. All the above minorities are well integrated into Polish society.

That does not apply to the heterogeneous collection of 23,000–25,000 Roma (Gypsies) who live in Poland. One also sees increasing numbers of Vietnamese and Armenians, who have crossed the border and settled. The Germans had exterminated the bulk of the more than 3 million Jews. This meant that half of the victims of the Holocaust were Poles. The majority of Jews who managed to survive chose to leave the country, but not more than 30,000 remain. Only in the 21st century are Jews beginning to return to Poland. Most Germans were expelled, and only an estimated 300,000–500,000 presently well-integrated Germans remain, mainly in Opole. Thus, Poland is more Polish and more Roman Catholic than it had been for many centuries.

Until mid-1947, during the period of "national unity," the official claim was that the system established in Poland was to be

Poland

different from both the capitalist model of the west and the communist one of the Soviet Union. This claim could not survive the beginning of the Cold War, however. While the United States proclaimed a policy of "containment" of communism, the USSR sponsored creation of the Communist Information Bureau (Cominform) at a conference held in western Poland in 1947. Under the circumstances, Moscow compelled Poland to reject an offer of Marshall Plan aid extended by the US. Soon thereafter, the rift between Stalin and Marshal Tito of Yugoslavia led the Soviet Union to exert even more pressure to hold the line elsewhere in central and eastern Europe. In one country after another, communist leaders identified with the "national" road to socialism were removed from office, jailed, and sometimes executed.

For a variety of reasons, events in Poland did not lead to such extreme measures against leaders accused of "nationalist deviationism," but there were drastic changes. Wladyslaw Gomulka, who had been active in the pro-Soviet underground during the years of German occupation and who presided over the absorption of the territories "recovered" from Germany, was removed from office at this time and eventually imprisoned. Never tried, he was able to reemerge as a leader in 1956.

Communist domination over all aspects of social life and Soviet direction of Polish internal affairs were substantially strengthened in the late 1940s. Political parties that had kept their prewar names were brought under communist control. Some of the pre-1945 noncommunist leaders were induced to merge either with the communists or with the communist-front groups. Thus, the Polish Socialist Party (PPS) was merged with the communists, who had been using the name Polish Workers Party, to form the Polish United Workers Party. It is important to note that the word "communist" had such a negative ring in the ears of most Poles that the ruling party never dared call itself by that name.

In spite of all of the changes in the wartime and early postwar period, the communists could not compete for the support of the workers against the traditional Polish Socialist Party. It was merged out of existence, largely with the help of one of its younger leaders, Jozef Cyrankiewicz. He was rewarded with the job of premier from 1947–1953 and 1955–1970; he was later appointed chairman of the Council of State (1970–1972). The Peasant Faction, which had retained a large following under its prewar leadership, was forced to combine with a communist-front group to form the United Peasant Party. Independent social organizations were also herded together into "united" groups controlled by the communists.

The high point of Soviet meddling in Polish affairs was reached when Konstantin Rokossowski, a Soviet army marshal, was made commander-in-chief of Poland's armed forces, minister of defense, and a deputy premier in the government. Important positions in the army were given to Russian officers, not all of whom could claim, as he did, to be of Polish descent. Economic transformation was reflected in stepped-up industrialization plans and an almost-complete elimination of private enterprise in industry and commerce. There was also an attempt to shift land ownership from individual peasant holdings to a form of collectivized farms. However, in comparison with other countries of the area, the results of collectivization remained limited. Throughout the entire period of communism, agriculture in Poland remained the least collectivized of the communist-governed states, with the exception of Yugoslavia. Only about 15% of the land was removed from private ownership.

After 1947, increasing pressure was brought to bear on the Catholic Church, directed principally against its educational efforts. Church schools were secularized, church lands were confiscated, and restrictions were placed on religious activities. This pressure reached its peak in 1953, when Cardinal Wyszynski was placed under house arrest in a monastery and forbidden to carry out his functions as primate of Poland. However, the confiscation of church lands and the general persecution probably had an effect opposite to that intended. The fact that the church was no longer a landowner probably increased its prestige among the rural population. The general persecution mainly served to increase its hold over the masses, which always remained remarkably strong.

The Catholic University of Lublin and the Theological Academy in Warsaw topped the Catholic educational system. The communists looked upon the church as a rival organization that competed for the allegiance of the people. No efforts were spared to make the position of the church difficult. At the same time, the regime had great respect for the traditional power of the church in Poland. This protected the church from an all-out frontal assault. This also produced some anomalies as when, for example, the communist leadership publicized its endorsement of Cardinal Wyszynski in the 1956 elections, even though it had kept him under house arrest since 1953.

The Polish Struggle of October 1956

Following the death of Josef Stalin in 1953, the Polish government launched a "new course," which involved some relaxation of the old Stalinist norms. Workers

were little affected, but there was a reduction in taxes for the peasantry and a slowdown in the process of collectivization. Intellectuals found they could be a little more critical in their comments about Polish life. Then an event occurred that had widespread repercussions.

Jozef Swiatlo, a high-ranking official in the Polish secret police, fled westward soon after Stalin's death. In 1954 Radio Free Europe in Munich began a series of broadcasts of Swiatlo's memoirs. His well-documented disclosures of the terrorist activities of the UB, the political police organization, became widely known in Poland and led to the abolition of the Ministry of Public Security. This was followed later by the arrest of some leading secret police officials.

Several economic reforms were also introduced, especially with regard to labor discipline. Critical voices began to be heard, first among writers and students, and then among the rank-and-file membership of the party. In the realm of communist political theory, "revisionist" views came to the fore, accompanied by a tendency to question some of the most basic tenets of Marxism-Leninism. Students and recent graduates began to organize discussion clubs in which pointed questions embarrassing to the government were raised in lengthy debates.

Poland was thus in a state of political turmoil when Soviet Communist Party chief Nikita Khrushchev made his famous "secret" speech at the 20th party congress in 1956, denouncing the evil deeds of Stalin. As luck would have it, Boleslaw Bierut, first secretary of the communist Polish United Workers Party, died in Moscow two weeks after Khrushchev's speech. He was succeeded by Edward Ochab, a shrewd politician who recognized the need for reform. Władysław Gomulka was placed under house arrest in a villa on the outskirts of Warsaw that served as a secret police prison. It was mild incarceration, in the sense that he was not tortured. He was freed in 1955.

A wave of strikes by industrial workers broke out in June 1956, accompanied by clashes between workers and troops in Poznan. The regime tried at first to blame the outbreaks on "capitalist provocation." But it soon came to the conclusion that the entire structure of communist rule might crumble unless there was a dramatic change of direction in government.

The logical choice to accomplish this was Gomulka, who, because of his insistence on a "Polish road to socialism," had become a symbol of independence from the Soviet Union. He was thought likely to satisfy the "revisionist" elements within the party, as well as the masses of workers and ordinary citizens.

Poland

However, his reputation as a revisionist worried part of the Soviet hierarchy. As preparations were going on to elect Gomulka to the position of first secretary of the party in October 1956, a delegation of top Soviet leaders suddenly appeared in Warsaw. Rumors began to fly that Soviet troops were on the march toward the Polish capital.

In the end, Khrushchev and his comrades were reassured about continued Polish-Soviet ties and possibly impressed by the resolute stand of factory workers. They agreed to Gomulka's election as party secretary and departed. The Soviet delegation also grudgingly accepted other changes in the Polish communist leadership, including the removal of Marshal Rokossowsky, a visible symbol of Soviet interference in Polish internal affairs.

The Aftermath of Turmoil

A tragic clash such as occurred about the same time in Hungary was avoided. As for Gomulka, many considered him to be a liberal who favored popular control of government because of the role he played during the "spring in October." Actually, he was a rather austere, conservative communist with a political sense for what could be done in Poland and with the Polish people. This kept him in power in Poland until 1970. However, as the "thaw" of 1956 passed into history, many of the more visionary hopes of the intellectuals were disappointed.

Nevertheless, the Polish regime continued to differ from those in neighboring communist-ruled countries. There was a reversal of the trend toward collectivization of agriculture. For example, there was a massive abandonment of even the token collectivization that had occurred after Gomulka returned to power.

So-called agricultural circles were about the only form of cooperative organization in the farmlands. Their main function was the joint purchase and use of farm machinery. This was a far cry from the practice of totally controlling agricultural production through a system of collective farms. Gomulka decided that the Polish peasant had to be left to discover for himself the blessings of socialism rather than be forced into it.

In other branches of the national economy, especially in industry, Gomulka saw less room for noncommunist management. Workers councils, organized during the 1956 upheaval, were later discouraged, and industry was once again managed in a centralized manner. There were, however, some attempts to make central planning of the economy less rigid. For a number of reasons, industry continued to suffer from serious shortcomings. Various emergency measures occasionally resulted in

unemployment and a halt in the movement of people from the overcrowded countryside to the cities. In commerce, a degree of private enterprise was permitted, although it was overburdened by state controls and taxation. Individual craftsmen were also permitted to work alone or in small groups.

In the cultural sphere, there was a tremendous outburst of creative activity after 1956. The rigid rules of "socialist realism" were relaxed, and it became possible to experiment with new and nonconformist forms of artistic expression. Access to the western press and literature was relatively free, and travel permits to areas outside the communist bloc were issued more generously than elsewhere in central Europe.

In political life, an effort was also made to create a real function for the Sejm (parliament). The habit of debating proposed legislation in committee and attempts critically to evaluate the efficiency of government changed the legislature from a rubber stamp completely controlled by communist leaders to a reasonably authentic voice of some parts of public opinion. Polls and other studies of public attitudes also came into use. Polish sociologists point with pride to the fact that, under their influence, a revised interest in the social sciences spread to other nations of central Europe and to the Soviet Union.

In 1964, the relatively tolerant Khrushchev was dismissed from office, and his successors began to retighten control. These Soviet events were mirrored in Poland, where the "spring" of 1956 was followed by a new freeze. Although the people continued in various ways to have

"little freedoms," a sense of disappointment and distrust characterized the attitude of intellectuals, who had high hopes of basic changes under Gomulka.

The Events of 1968–1970

Dissatisfaction with the regime came into the open in early 1968, when students and intellectuals clashed with the police. The reason for the conflict was the suppression of a theatrical performance of a work by Poland's greatest poet, Adam Mickiewicz. His 19th-century work *Dziady* (Forefathers) contained anti-Russian themes that audiences lustily applauded. There also was dissatisfaction with the official attitude of the government. Following the lead of the Soviet Union, it came out in support of the Arabs in their conflict with Israel. This policy enabled one of the groups within the leadership, the so-called Partisans led by the ambitious General Mieczyslaw Moczar, to open an attack on "Zionist" elements, supposed to be in the government and the party.

These charges appealed to a deeply rooted anti-Semitism in Poland. Although married to a Jewish woman, Gomulka decided to go along with what turned out to be a massive purge of Jews within the government, universities, and cultural organizations. Many had to leave the country, renouncing their Polish citizenship and leaving most of their belongings, because they could not make a living in Poland. Thus, the once-flourishing Jewish community, reduced by Hitler's destruction and postwar emigration from over 3 million to less than 30,000, almost 3 to exist.

December 1980, Lech Walesa with supporters

Poland

Gomulka's political maneuvering and his obedience to the Soviet Union, demonstrated by his support for the invasion of Czechoslovakia in 1968, saved him temporarily from political defeat. In spite of pressure from Moczar and his Partisans, Gomulka was reelected party leader in 1968. He was supported by Edward Gierek, boss since 1957 of the party organization in the important mining and industrial province of Upper Silesia. But Gomulka (aptly described as a "spent force" by one observer) could no longer control the conflicting trends within the party leadership. Moreover, the differences that arose reflected not only the direction of leadership but also the generation gap between old-timers, such as Gomulka, and younger, better-educated, technically minded elements demanding a share of power.

Gomulka's final downfall came after an apparently spontaneous outbreak of protests by workers expressing dissatisfaction over increased food prices on the eve of the Christmas holidays in 1970. In the party, a coalition of competing factions agreed to dismiss Gomulka and replace him as first secretary with Edward Gierek.

The Gierek Era, 1970–1980

Under the leadership of the initially popular Edward Gierek, an ex-miner, Poland embarked on an ambitious plan of rapid industrialization and economic growth. It was financed by heavy borrowing of capital from the Soviet Union, as well as from a number of western governments,

General Wojciech Jaruzelski

international financial institutions, and private banks.

The results seemed impressive until about the mid-1970s. The gross national product increased substantially during these years, and there was a striking improvement in the standard of living. Several factors brought this economic "miracle" to an end. The immediate cause was a dramatic change for the worse in the international economy. A second factor was the widespread graft and mismanagement within the government. But the most important, long-range reason was that Poland was borrowing money from abroad to finance domestic consumption. None of the new plants financed by the loans produced any significant amount of goods for export. Thus, Poland lacked the necessary hard-currency reserves to pay back the loans when they became due.

To service its foreign debt, therefore, Poland had to resort to increased exports of food products, thereby cutting into the supply of food for domestic consumption. While workers' wages had increased, less and less was available to buy. In 1976 an attempt to raise prices on basic food articles led to the outbreak of strikes, as well as looting and attacks on Communist Party headquarters in many localities. The decision to cancel price increases barely 24 hours after they had been announced undermined the prestige of the government and the ruling party.

In addition, governmental attempts to prosecute workers who had incited strikes led to the creation of KOR, an organization for the defense of arrested and dismissed workers. In 1977 another organization, called Movement of Defense of Human and Civil Rights (ROPCIO), came into being.

Gierek expressed a desire to "improve communication with the working masses" and sought a further normalization of relations with the Roman Catholic Church. Several antichurch measures were dropped, permission was given to construct churches in the new industrial towns, and the church's debts to the state were cancelled.

The election of a Polish pope in 1978 added another factor to this development. The election of Karol Wojtyla, archbishop of Krakow—who took the name of John Paul II—brought an outburst of national pride that extended even to many members of the Communist Party. Gierek himself sent a message of congratulations to Rome, and negotiations began immediately for a papal visit to Poland. This occurred in June 1979 and included a nationally televised meeting between the pope, Gierek, and other party and state leaders.

Gierek was more successful in his relations with the Catholic Church than he was in his second goal of improving

Pope John Paul II

communication with the masses. When he took over as party leader, he promised that workers would be consulted, that intellectuals would be heard, and that the party could not possibly regulate everything. The political thaw did not last long, however. By 1973, censorship had been fully restored, and it was soon clear that the party was instituting through a further centralization in the name of reform instead of reducing its intervention in national life.

Moreover, the party was granting its own members special pay and privileges that set them off from and aroused the hatred of the masses while claiming to be the "leading political force in society in constructing socialism." Isolated and filled with bureaucrats, the party became more and more a hollow shell, determined to stonewall just about anything.

Strikers and Dissidents

Dissatisfaction with the communist system had been simmering in Poland for a number of years. It resulted in the emergence of various political and intellectual dissident groups, ranging from barely legal to illegal organizations. While claiming a belief in the basic tenets of communism, some advocated reform of the system and removal of those who mismanaged it. Others, on the extreme right, advocated abandonment or overthrow of the system.

Illegal publications, study circles, and "flying universities," often holding classes in church buildings, proliferated. The decisive change came when the small intellectual groups identified themselves

Poland

Polish troops at Tomb of Unknown Soldiers, Warsaw

with the plight of the workers, who had resorted to strikes to protest oppressive conditions in the factories and the undercutting of their living standards by hikes in the price of food. The most prominent of those groups was KOR, the Workers' Defense Committee.

Opposition in Poland derived substantial support from the outspoken position of the Catholic Church under the leadership of Cardinal Wyszynski, who died in 1981. The election of a Pole as pope was also a source of moral support. Nevertheless, it was the spectacular collapse of the economy after a decade of what looked like successful development that set off Poland's crisis in 1980–1981.

Facing a rapidly deteriorating economic situation and a foreign debt that had grown to $28 billion, the government tried to appease both workers and political dissidents by promises of improvements that could not be kept. Matters came to a head when thousands of workers in the Gdansk shipyard went on strike and occupied the premises of the enterprise.

Confrontation, Confusion, and Clumsiness

Under the leadership of Lech Wałęsa, an unemployed electrician who emerged from nowhere to a position of prominence, workers insisted that the government send a negotiator to deal with the *Twenty-one Demands* posted by the workers' strike committee. The main point of the demands

was permission to establish independent trade unions in competition with the party-controlled official trade-union organization. When the government accepted this demand, a new institution, Solidarity, was born. It claimed a membership of 10 million workers. Soon, an extension of the protest movement to the countryside resulted in the creation of a rural branch of Solidarity, as well. Whether intended or not, this ultimately set into motion a confrontation of Polish workers, supported by the Roman Catholic Church, intellectuals, and students, with the communist leadership and the Soviet Union.

What followed in Poland was a drastic shake-up of the party-state leadership. Gierek and his close associates were ousted, and the relatively unknown Stanislaw Kania was named party leader. The post of chairman of the council of ministers (prime minister) was assumed by General Wojciech Jaruzelski, a career military officer who was already defense minister and therefore head of the Polish armed forces.

For a while, negotiations involving the communist government, the independent Solidarity movement, and the Catholic Church raised the hope that Poland might enter a new phase of its history. This would have involved a rather unusual triangular arrangement between the discredited communist authorities (with the Soviets in the background), the independent trade-union movement, and the church (led until 2004 by Cardinal Wyszynski's successor, Cardinal Jozef Glemp, who died in 2013). However, a worker movement independent of the Polish United Workers Party was, by its very existence, a challenge to the communist claim to be the party of the workers. It soon became clear that an independent Solidarity was unacceptable both to significant elements in the PUWP and to the Soviet leadership. The true picture was visible in October 1981, when Kania resigned as party secretary and was replaced by Jaruzelski, who added this party post to his other jobs.

During previous periods of unrest, the armed forces had not been used to restore order. On December 13, 1981, however, General Jaruzelski declared martial law throughout the country and ordered the military to begin a roundup of trade-union activists and dissident intellectuals. Thousands were detained, including Lech Wałęsa and most of the other Solidarity leaders. A curfew was enforced throughout the country, and telephone communications between cities were restricted.

The government also sought to discredit Solidarity by attempting to show that the trade union was not merely seeking an improvement in the economic situation, as it claimed, but that it also was interested in either sharing political power with the

Father Popieluszko

communists or taking it away from them. Secret tapes made by the security police at a national conference of Solidarity in the city of Radom had Wałęsa and others stating that the time had come for "confrontation" with the government rather than "compromise." The tapes were probably altered.

In late 1982 Solidarity and the discredited old official labor unions were banned, and new official trade unions replaced them. According to the government, the new official unions had a membership of about 7 million, of which 60% were former members of Solidarity. Since that figure represented slightly less than half of the total labor force, it was obvious that, although Solidarity had been banned, it was by no means dead.

After being held in custody for several months, Wałęsa was eventually released without any charges being filed against him. His receipt of the Nobel Prize for peace also strengthened his hand. As a result, he was permitted to continue to speak out publicly. However, the government closely monitored his actions, and he was continuously under the threat of harassment or worse. A 1984 amnesty resulted in the release of 652 Solidarity detainees, though a few were rearrested after meeting with Wałęsa. They, too, were subsequently released but remained subject to government harassment when they attempted to speak out publicly. The final amnesty that freed all detainees was declared in September 1986. During this time, American labor unions were giving Solidarity important assistance, such as providing outlawed printing equipment.

There were those within the leadership of the PUWP who opposed the independent

343

Poland

A church courtyard's fence displays a banned sign.

Solidarity movement. However, the decisive factor that led the Polish government to declare martial law and ban the movement was the strong pressure the Soviets were exerting at this time. Jaruzelski later maintained publicly that he had imposed martial law to prevent an invasion by the Soviet Union, and he defended this decision the rest of his life. Subsequently published documentation revealed that Moscow's leaders had, in fact, agonized over whether to crush Solidarity, but they had been dissuaded by their own military, who argued, "The Polish armed forces are battle-ready and patriotic. They will not fire on their own people." One Kremlin leader, Mikhail Suslov, warned that military intervention "will mean a catastrophe."

Notes of conversations between Jaruzelski and the commander of the Warsaw Pact, Marshal Viktor Kulikov, published in late 2009, revealed that the Polish commander had asked the Soviets for help in gaining control over Solidarity. He reportedly said that if demonstrations "sweep through the whole country, then you [the Soviet Union] will have to help us. We won't be able to deal with a crowd in the millions." This would seem to undermine his later assurances that he was acting only in Polish national interest to stop a Soviet

invasion. By the time martial law ended in 1983, nearly 100 people had died, tens of thousands were arrested without charge, and about 10,000 were confined in internment camps.

The Roman Catholic Church

A major concern of the Soviet leadership under Leonid Brezhnev was the still important position of the Roman Catholic Church in Polish life. At least up to 1985, the Polish government was under pressure from the Soviets to reduce the influence of the church. The government was divided on the issue, with moderates arguing the value of cooperation with the church and hard-liners arguing the danger of such an accommodation. The Soviets' concern appears to have increased after Karol Wojtyla, archbishop of Krakow, was elected pope in October 1978. It is for this reason that many scholars accepted the argument that there had been a connection between the Soviet KGB (secret police) and a subsequent attempt on John Paul II's life while he was officiating at a ceremony in St. Peter's Square in Rome.

While the internal struggle was still going on, three members of the Polish security police, acting under orders of their superior officer, a colonel, brutally murdered

Father Jerzy Popieluszko, a priest. He had become a target because he was an ardent and public supporter of Solidarity. Eleven days after he had been reported missing, his body was found, weighted, at the bottom of a reservoir. An autopsy showed that he could have been beaten to death before being thrown into the water, although that was never proved. The cause of death was not established in the trial, and he could have still been alive when he was thrown into the reservoir.

This grisly act forced General Jaruzelski's hand. Disassociating himself and his regime completely from the killing, he ordered that the four implicated individuals be put on public trial, and extensive but selective television and radio coverage was permitted nationwide. All four were convicted and received long prison sentences. In addition, their superior in the Ministry of the Interior was fired. Jaruzelski himself took the further step of assuming direct responsibility for the police and the internal security forces, replacing two members of the party secretariat who had formerly been in charge of those activities.

In spite of Jaruzelski's actions, church and state relations reached a new low. They were charged with emotion arising out of the revelations during the trial of the dirty war the security police waged against the church. Responding to these emotions, Cardinal Glemp began to take a more militant line, and Jaruzelski answered in kind. Speaking in a 1985 press interview about differences with the church, the general was quoted as saying somewhat defensively, "In Poland the church has a vast, favorable opportunity to carry out its priestly mission. Regrettably, certain priests abuse this freedom to stage unlawful acts. We talk about it openly."

Church-state relations began to improve again in 1986. They climaxed in January 1987, when General Jaruzelski paid a state visit to Italy and was received by Pope John Paul II. A Vatican spokesman described the 70-minute private talk as "earnest, clear and profound." Symbolically, Jaruzelski's daughter Monika, who accompanied him, was given a rosary and took another home to her mother. Equally symbolically, he invited the pope to visit Poland. The most important visit had taken place in 1979, followed by return trips in 1983 and then June 1987. According to press reports at the time, Jaruzelski also promised to grant the church full legal status, a move that would allow the church's youth organization and its various professional bodies to operate publicly. However, nothing was done to put this into effect before the papal visit in June.

Whenever the pontiff arrived, the fireworks began. Solidarity banners appeared everywhere he went. Crowds ultimately numbering into the millions attended the many masses he said, cheering him with wild enthusiasm. At each mass or appearance, he praised Solidarity with warm enthusiasm in order to show his disapproval of the government. Jaruzelski was unable to silence him. In 1987 the pope kissed the tomb of Father Popieluszko, reviving all of the old emotions surrounding his death. Upon his departure, the general appeared at the airport to say relatively harsh words to the highly respected pope. Usually "unflappable," Jaruzelski had been visibly disturbed and was shaking with undisguised anger. The damage had been done.

Although Jaruzelski had not gotten what he wanted from the pope's 1987 visit, he was evidently impressed by the response of the Polish people to the pope. From this he concluded that some accommodation with the church was necessary if he wanted to reconcile the Polish people to continued communist rule. As a result, the government began permitting the church to enlarge its area of activities and to become, in the words of one Pole associated with the movement, "the most interesting independent intellectual and social center in Poland."

As in East Germany, the church became a refuge for dissident artists. In September 1987 Wroclaw's large Gothic Church of the Holy Cross arranged an exhibit of the works of 151 artists from all over Poland under the title "National Biennial of Young Artists." The government permitted the exhibit, even though many of the 423 works of art on display had secular themes and, according to Polish law, could not legally be exhibited inside a church.

The church was also permitted to expand its educational role. Church schools teaching secular subjects were established throughout the country, and the Catholic University in Lublin added faculties in law, economics, psychology, and sociology. In addition, the church established publishing facilities, where it began printing its own textbooks. Many of the activities originally sponsored by Solidarity were thus given new life under the patronage of the church.

In January 2007 the widely held view that the church had acted as a courageous opponent of communism was badly shaken. Warsaw's new archbishop, Stanislaw Wielgus, announced just minutes before he was to be formally installed that he was resigning over disclosures that he had cooperated with the secret police during the communist era. Dozens of priests were then revealed as collaborators.

The Regime Loosens Up

Jaruzelski did not want the church to be the sole intellectual alternative, and he accordingly moved to grant more freedom

Wilanow Palace in Warsaw, the summer residence of Polish kings
Courtesy: Embassy of Poland

generally. This led the government to give approval to *Res Publica*, a privately owned magazine, to begin publishing in July 1987. Although allowed only 25,000 copies, it was important as the first of Poland's many underground magazines to achieve legal status.

An even more important move came in January 1988, when the government stopped jamming the broadcasts of Voice of America, Radio Free Europe, and the Polish-language broadcasts of the BBC. Although Jaruzelski made the final decision himself, it was reportedly on the advice of Mieczyslaw Rakowski. The latter was then deputy chairman of the council of ministers. Before joining the government he had for 24 years been the editor of *Polityka*. That was the most readable official publication in the Soviet bloc and is still today the best and most important political weekly newsmagazine in Poland.

All of this provided background for Jaruzelski's greatest gamble—his attempt to implement an economic reform that had much in common with what Gorbachev was trying to do in the Soviet Union. To obtain public backing, Jaruzelski submitted the plan to a referendum in November 1987. The three-year program contained such elements as increased private enterprise and a decentralization that was supposed to cut the number of government jobs by a quarter. It also included a cut in subsidies that would have brought an immediate, significant increase in prices. Whether for that reason or because they simply did not trust the communists, voters rejected the reform.

Stung by its defeat, the government decided to begin implementing the reform anyway, although more slowly than originally planned. The first price rises went into effect at the beginning of 1988, with food, rent, and fuel increasing by an average of 45%. It was the official party unions that first protested, and this led to a strike among transport workers in the city of

Bydgoszcz. The government granted a 60% pay increase to the transport workers. In the meantime, the strike began spreading to other parts of Poland. Among those joining the strike were the workers at the Lenin Shipyard in Gdansk.

The August 1988 strike now became explicitly political. This was the birthplace of Solidarity, and Lech Wałęsa once again emerged as a local leader. Occupying the Lenin Shipyard and refusing to leave, the Gdansk workers demanded that, in addition to a pay increase, Solidarity activists dismissed in 1981 should be reinstated in their jobs. The government agreed to a wage increase, but it refused to bargain over the political issue. It soon became clear that this was not to be a replay of 1980–1981. There was no national groundswell of support for the Gdansk workers. After eight days they ended their strike in return for a government promise to open a political dialogue with Solidarity.

The government had won a victory of sorts but not one of much value. For its economic reform to have any chance of success, it had to have the active support of the workers, and this it did not have. A public opinion poll taken in early 1988 indicated that only 7% of those polled believed that the economic reform had any chance of success.

That is not surprising. After all, the political leadership had been pursuing a program of economic reform since 1980, all without tangible results. This bred a sense of pessimism exemplified by the comment of one Polish journalist in July 1988 that Poland had already been through reform, "and it did not work."

Inflation, already high, grew worse as the summer progressed and there were increasing shortages of all kinds of consumer goods. Later a new and different wave of strikes swept across Poland, spreading for the first time to the Silesian coalfields. Because coal exports were one of Poland's major sources of hard-currency earnings,

Poland

the government had always gone out of its way to keep the miners happy. But even they had seen their standard of living drop in the preceding months, and they were now demanding action.

In a final irony, it was the official trade unions, not the outlawed Solidarity, that declared a lack of confidence in the government and demanded that it resign. The government stepped down in September 1988, and Jaruzelski appointed Mieczyslaw Rakowski as the new chairman of the council of ministers (prime minister).

Determined to break the political-economic deadlock, Rakowski introduced a new phrase into the communist lexicon—the "constructive opposition"—and offered four cabinet seats to Solidarity supporters. He also called for roundtable negotiations with the opposition. But what he offered was the chance to participate in the economic reform; there were to be no political reforms. Solidarity was not to be legalized. In fact, Solidarity supporters were urged to repudiate their leadership, since "it is impossible to compromise with Wałęsa." Under the circumstances, no one in the opposition was willing to join the government, and the proposed roundtable negotiations never got started.

Rakowski was left with the alternative of either dealing with Wałęsa or of somehow discrediting him. The party decided to assign that task to Alfred Miodowicz, leader of the official trade unions and a member of the party Politburo. Miodowicz challenged Wałęsa to a television debate, which took place in November. With 70% of the nation watching, it was Wałęsa who came across as the statesmanlike leader. This point was conceded even in the USSR.

Reporting on the debate, *Komsomolskaya Pravda* wrote that some of Wałęsa's "recent speeches have been distinguished by a certain political balance and reasonableness. It would also be possible to agree with a number of his assertions made directly during the debate." The party next tried to coopt Wałęsa personally by offering to make him a deputy prime minister. But he held out for formal negotiations and "laws, rights, positions offered by law, not by privilege."

By December 1988 it had become clear that all of Rakowski's efforts to push through economic reform while ignoring Solidarity had been a failure, as were the party's efforts to discredit Wałęsa. Yet conservatives in the top leadership of the party continued to oppose any compromise with the opposition.

To clear the way, General Jaruzelski called a Central Committee meeting just before Christmas. Six hard-liners were removed from the Politburo, and eight persons were added. This was followed by

a second two-day meeting of the Central Committee in January 1989, which ended with a communique supporting the legalization of Solidarity. Even at this meeting, conservatives attacked the leadership decision to deal with Wałęsa. But Jaruzelski pushed through the decision against their opposition. Among those who opposed the decision was Alfred Miodowicz.

Roundtable Discussions with Solidarity

Roundtable negotiations between the government and Solidarity opened on February 6, 1989. Once the two sides began talking, they quickly carried their discussions beyond the question of the legalization of Solidarity and began to put together a historic compromise. As Tadeusz Mazowiecki, a leading Solidarity negotiator, commented, "both the communists and we crossed the Rubicon. It's really surprising how far things went."

In addition to legalizing Solidarity, an agreement in April called for creation of a Senate as a second legislative body, all of whose members were chosen by popular election in June. New elections to the Sejm, the old legislative body and now again the lower house of the parliament, also took place at the same time. In the latter case, however, the communists and their allies were guaranteed 65% of the seats, with the remaining 35% to be freely contested. To provide executive authority and to act as a counterweight to a more powerful legislature, the post of president was also created, to be chosen by the newly elected legislature.

Most of those in leading positions in the Solidarity movement decided to stand for

Smart young Poles in Brussels

either the Sejm or the Senate. Wałęsa declined, saying that he did not want to compromise his credentials as a trade unionist. He did, however, create a Citizens' Committee of approximately 100 opposition figures who over management of the campaign for the opposition. He actively campaigned for Solidarity candidates.

In the June elections, the Polish United Workers' Party suffered a crushing defeat. Solidarity took 99 out of 100 seats in the Senate, plus all of the open seats in the Sejm. In addition, most of the top communist leadership, running unopposed for Sejm seats, was rejected because they failed to get 50% of the valid votes.

The newly elected legislature agreed to install Jaruzelski as president. But the failure of the communists at the polls meant that they were unable to form a government. Their allies, the United Peasants' Party and the Democratic Party, refused to support the PUWP candidate for chairman of the council of ministers (prime minister) and opened discussions with Solidarity. This led Lech Wałęsa to propose a Solidarity-led coalition government that would include representatives of the PUWP. Tadeusz Mazowiecki, Lech Wałęsa's handpicked candidate, was installed as prime minister at the end of August.

Poland's First Postwar Noncommunist Government

In December 1989, the legislature made several changes in the constitution. The adjective "People's" was dropped from the official name of the country, making it is once again the Republic of Poland. All references to socialism and the leading role of the People's United Workers' Party were also deleted.

On January 1, 1990, the government instituted its plan to bring about Poland's transition to a free-market economy. Prices were freed, subsidies to industry were canceled, the currency was set free to float, and the draft budget showed a surplus. The plan, named after Leszek Balcerowicz (later president of the Polish National Bank), produced hardships throughout the society, but it also began the process of transforming the economy. Unemployment rose as inefficient state industries lost their subsidies and had to begin laying off employees in order to cut their costs. However, individual Poles began establishing thousands of small businesses, and small amounts of foreign investment began to pour into the country. For the year, foreign investment was estimated at $100 million.

As the year progressed, however, a split became evident in the Solidarity ranks. In particular, Wałęsa began publicly attacking specific policies of the Mazowiecki government. His first target was the program of economic reform, which, he argued, was being implemented in a way that made it harder on the Polish people than it needed to be. His main objection was that the government was not moving fast enough in clearing communists out of key positions. Poland was, by this time, the only country in central or eastern Europe other than Albania that still had a communist as head of state. Communists also held 45% of the seats in the Sejm, though the results of the June 1990 local elections suggested they would not be able to retain most of those seats in a genuinely free election.

When Wałęsa first raised the issue of his becoming president, many of his supporters in Solidarity tried to dissuade him from running. He backed down at first, then changed his mind, and declared his candidacy on September 17. Two days later General Jaruzelski, sensing the direction of political winds in Poland, agreed to step down because of his "concern to prevent undesirable public sentiment" and to "promote democracy."

Parliament modified the office of the presidency, setting a five-year term of office and specifying that the president was to be elected by popular vote. The election was set for November 25. Prime Minister Mazowiecki then announced that he would stand for the presidency himself.

Perhaps Mazowiecki had his falling out with Wałęsa because he feared that Wałęsa as president would repudiate his economic program. Or perhaps it was related to the fact that Mazowiecki was a university graduate and had a reputation as a learned theorist, while Wałęsa had only a trade-school education and a background as a shipyard electrician. Adam Michnik, editor of the Solidarity-founded newspaper *Gazeta Wyborcza* (Electoral Gazette), accused Wałęsa of having dictatorial tendencies. In any case, Mazowiecki's candidacy represented the end of Solidarity as the unifying umbrella organization of the noncommunist forces.

Though still the head of Solidarity, Wałęsa did not attempt to use it in his presidential campaign. His supporters were formed as the Center Alliance. Mazowiecki's political organization was supported by another group known under the acronym ROAD. Later in the campaign, a third candidate emerged, based on his promise to bring western business know-how to Poland. This was Stanislaw Tyminski, a Pole who had emigrated to Canada and whose qualification was that he was a successful businessman.

The only one to attack the government's economic reform program, Tyminski edged Mazowiecki out for second place, taking 23% of the vote to Mazowiecki's 18%. Wałęsa came in first, with about 40%.

Chairman Lech Walesa addresses Congress, November 1990.

Since he did not get a majority, there had to be a second round of voting on December 9. This time, Wałęsa got an overwhelming 75% of the vote and was sworn in as president on December 21, 1990. Mazowiecki had submitted his resignation as prime minister after his defeat in the first round of voting. Wałęsa asked him to continue to serve until new parliamentary elections. He refused but remained on in a caretaker capacity. Wałęsa offered the position to several people, including Leszek Balcerowicz, finance minister in the Mazowiecki government. Balcerowicz declined, saying he wanted to stay on as finance minister. Wałęsa eventually offered the position to Jan Krzysztof Bielecki.

Before becoming prime minister, Bielecki was leader of a small-free-enterprise political party in the parliament, the Liberal-Democratic Congress, and head of a consulting company. From Gdansk, he had also been involved in the Solidarity underground. The Liberal-Democratic Congress was strongly committed to the development of private enterprise in Poland, and Wałęsa's selection of Bielecki was seen as his way of underscoring his commitment to Poland's program of economic reform.

Wałęsa was also anxious that new elections to the Sejm take place as soon as possible in order to remove the influence of the communist deputies still sitting there. Under the compact negotiated with the communists in 1989, new elections were not required until 1993. In March 1991, Wałęsa urged the legislature to ignore the 1989 deal. "I am convinced that Poland today

needs instant elections," he told the legislature. "One has to put an end to growing disillusion and mistrust of political institutions, including Parliament." Parliament did schedule a debate on Wałęsa's appeal, but it ultimately decided to postpone new elections until October 1991.

Before the elections occurred, however, the Sejm passed a new electoral law that instituted an extreme form of proportional representation in an apparent attempt to protect as many seats as possible held by the communists and their allies. President Wałęsa vetoed the legislation on the basis that it would produce a too-fragmented legislature. However, the communists and their allies, with control of 65% of the seats, passed it over his veto.

The election results were what Wałęsa predicted. Twenty-nine parties won seats in the Sejm, with the largest of the parties winning only 12.2% of the vote. The Democratic Left Alliance—the renamed communists—came in second with 12.1% of the vote, while their ally, the Peasant Party, got 8.9%. Creating a coalition government that could count on a stable majority in the Sejm was no easy task, and it was not accomplished until the end of December. Wałęsa even offered to lead a government of national unity himself, but there was no significant support for that idea. A string of shaky, short-lived coalition governments followed.

A new electoral law in 1993 sought to reduce the number of political parties in the Sejm. While retaining the principle of proportional representation, the law specified that individual parties would need 5% of the vote to enter parliament; coalitions would need 8%. It was expected that the new law would reduce the number of parties represented in parliament from 29 to fewer than 6. It accomplished this.

Subsequent elections were not always friendly to reformers. There was clearly a backlash against the pain of reform. As one commentator put it, "forty years of communism had ingrained expectations of social security that the new parties failed to provide." A major theme of the left during the campaign was that the post-communist governments had used all the state's resources to support capitalism and ignored the needs of workers, peasants, and pensioners.

Another factor was the matter of social policy, particularly the role of the Catholic Church. Post-communist governments had instituted religious classes in school; negotiated a concordat with the Vatican; and, after considerable arm-twisting by the Catholic hierarchy, passed a rigorous abortion law that largely reflected the church's position on the issue. Considering that only 45% of all Poles are practicing Roman Catholics and far fewer than that accept the

Poland

church's moral mandates on such matters as divorce, birth control, and in vitro fertilization, it is not surprising that not a single political party with a specific religious orientation made it into the parliament in 1993. After the fall of communism, there was a backlash against what was viewed as excessive involvement in politics on the part of the Roman Catholic Church.

POLITICAL SYSTEM

After nine years of effort, the parliament was finally able to agree to a new constitution, and it was approved by the Polish people in a referendum in May 1997. It clearly spells out the relations between the parliament, the president, and the government, eliminating previous ambiguities. It also provides for an independent judicial review of laws. The preamble invokes God as the "source of truth, justice, goodness and beauty." The body of the constitution provides guarantees for religious instruction in public schools and grants the Catholic Church autonomy from the state. Although some right-wing politicians attacked the document, Poland's Catholic primate, Jozef Cardinal Glemp, said, "many people accept this compromise constitution, regarding it as historically important."

Poland is a presidential-parliamentary system. The president has some powers in certain areas, but the government itself is run by the prime minister, who in turn is responsible to the Sejm. Any government must be able to receive a majority of the votes in the Sejm in order to assume power. Once installed, a government is difficult to unseat. It can be done only by a "constructive vote of no-confidence": First a majority must vote against the government; then it must immediately vote in favor of a new one. That is difficult in a multiparty system like Poland's.

The prime minister must have the confidence of a majority in the Sejm. He is the political leader of the country and is in charge of the government. He has overlapping responsibilities with the president in the area of foreign affairs and the military.

The legislature consists of two bodies, an upper house called the Senate, which was created in 1989, and a lower house, called the Sejm. The term of office is four years. Of the two houses, the Sejm is more powerful. The Senate has the right to review legislation and propose amendments, but the Sejm decides the final version of any legislation.

The Senate has 100 members. Until 2011 all were elected by their regional constituents in 40 districts. The new electoral method is the "single-member constituency" winner-take-all system. This favors the larger parties and limits the number of parties that win seats. In 2015 two parties won all but five seats.

Ex-Deputy Prime Minister Beata Szydło

The Sejm has 460 deputies, all of whom run in 41 electoral districts and are elected under a complex system of proportional representation. Under a 1993 law, individual parties need 5% of the vote to enter the Sejm, while a bloc needs 8%. In 2011 only five parties and coalitions cleared these hurdles. As an exception, the German and all other ethnic minorities are exempt from the 5% rule. The reason for this rule is to limit the number of parties in parliament and thereby make coalition governments more manageable and stable. A new requirement that went into effect in 2011 is that at least 35% of the candidates on party lists must be women. The ruling party in that year, Civic Platform, had the highest percentage of females in parliament—35.8%. Since 2002 the governmental heads at the provincial (wojewodztwo), district (powiat), and commune (gmina) levels are elected through direct popular vote.

Given Poland's uncomfortable communist past, parliament passed a law in 1998 requiring all Poles seeking high office, as well as high-level civil servants and judges, to declare publicly whether they ever worked with the secret police during the communist era. If a candidate admits to such earlier activity, he or she is permitted to stand for election, and the voters can decide whether to punish the offender by not voting for him. If a candidate lies about his past, he can be banned from politics for 10 years. In the 2000 presidential elections, both the winner, Aleksander Kwasniewski, and the trounced Lech Wałęsa were cleared of charges of spying for the communist secret police because

The late president Lech Kaczynski (right) with his twin Jaroslaw, PiS leader and ex–prime minister

Poland

of lack of evidence. This allowed both of them to run for the presidency. (Documents discovered in 2016 seem to indicate that Wałęsa did collaborate with police in the early 1970s, before his involvement in Solidarity. Wałęsa continues to challenge the authenticity of these documents.)

Presidential Elections

The president is directly elected every five years at a different time than parliamentary elections. If, as is usually the case, no single candidate receives a majority of votes, then a second round of elections is held two weeks later between the top two contenders. He is titular commander-in-chief of the military and also has general responsibility for the police and foreign and defense policy. Thus, he can influence military deployments and relations with other countries. He can veto laws, and a three-fifths majority in parliament is required to override that veto. There is no vice president. If a president dies, as happened on April 10, 2010, then the speaker of the lower house of parliament, the Sejm, assumes the role of acting president and calls a new presidential election within 60 days.

The president formally appoints the prime minister and the members of the council of ministers (cabinet). He also has the right to dissolve parliament in certain limited circumstances; an example would be if a submitted budget were not approved within three months. The president is supposed to use his veto power sparingly.

In the 1995 presidential elections, Aleksander Kwasniewski, of the ex-communist Democratic Left Alliance (SLD), defeated Wałęsa in a runoff election with 52% of the vote. Always more pragmatic than ideological, he publicly apologized in the early 1990s for the "injustice and misdeeds" of communism. The reasons for his victory hinged partly on Wałęsa's unpopularity after five years in office. Inevitably, Wałęsa was associated with the pain of that time, even though the powers of the presidency are quite limited.

Kwasniewski was reelected in 2000 with 54% of the votes in the first round, miles ahead of his 12 other challengers. Under the Polish system, all candidates enjoy equal and free television time, regardless of their standing in the polls or performance in prior elections. He is credited with keeping Poland united on the long road to EU entry in May 2004.

In October 2005 Lech Kaczynski of the Law and Justice (PiS) party and Donald Tusk of Civic Platform (PO) vied to be Kwasniewski's successor. Tusk was the favorite, but Kaczynski overtook him by convincing older and poorer voters that he would protect the social welfare system,

Kaczynski twins as child movie stars

which had eroded in the 16 years since the fall of communism. He also promised to preserve Catholic values, such as maintaining the ban on abortion and same-sex marriage. In the second round, he won 54% of the votes to Tusk's 46%.

Lech Kaczynski and his twin brother, Jaroslaw, who is leader of PiS, offered social conservatism, religious nostalgia, protection of the poor, and assertion of Poland's national interests. Born to a famous resistance fighter 56 years earlier, they won national fame in 1962 as sweet-faced 12-year-old child stars in a hit film, *The Two Who Stole the Moon*. Both served as advisers to Solidarity and its leader, Wałęsa, and Lech Kaczynski, who had studied law, was jailed by the communist authorities under martial law in the 1980s.

Ideological and personal differences between the Kaczynskis and Tusk exacerbated a tussle over the relative importance and power of the two top executive positions: the president and prime minister. These tensions contributed to a tragedy that decimated the Polish government.

Second Katyn Tragedy

On April 10, 2010, President Lech Kaczynski boarded a military aircraft with his wife, six out of the seven top military commanders, the deputy foreign and defense ministers, the head of the Polish Central Bank, high-ranking party leaders, and many other Polish notables—96 in all. The passenger list reflected not only the

country's political and military leadership, but it also included personalities who had left their stamp on Polish history, such as Ryszard Kaczorowski, the last president of the London-based government-in-exile during the Second World War, and Anna Walentynowicz, the activist at the Gdansk shipyard whose dismissal in 1980 triggered the strike that led to the formation of Solidarity and the end of communism. President Kaczynski had a conciliatory speech in his pocket for Russian ears.

Their destination was the site of the Katyn Forest massacre on the outskirts of the Russian city Smolensk. Seventy years

Bronislaw Komorowski, former president of Poland

Poland

President Andrzej Duda: "I am very grateful to those who put their trust in me. Thank you very much."

earlier, 21,768 of Poland's military, political, and intellectual elite were murdered by order of Soviet dictator Joseph Stalin. His intention was to decapitate Polish society permanently. Kaczynski had wanted to share in the victims' memory, but he had not been invited with Prime Minister Donald Tusk to a commemoration held at the site a few days earlier. At that time, Russian prime minister Vladimir Putin had spoken openly about the horror of the crimes and how both Poles and Russians had been victims of Stalin's inhumane system. He embraced the Polish prime minister and joined him in laying wreaths at the Polish officers' graves, kneeling in commemoration.

Kaczynski's plane was 90 minutes behind schedule. When it arrived over Smolensk, the airport was buried in a thick fog. Russian air traffic controllers and the onboard instruments gave the pilots 16 warnings not to try to land but to divert to another airfield. Determined that the dignitaries would not miss the ceremony, the pilots put the plane down, despite frantic warnings to "pull up, pull up!" About a kilometer (two-thirds of a mile) from the runway, the plane ran into trees and broke apart. All people onboard perished. There was no proof of rumors that the president had ordered the pilots to land.

The shock and pain that Poles felt were immense, and all were united in grief and disbelief. When the bodies were returned home to Warsaw, Polish flags with black ribbons of mourning were flying everywhere. Church bells rang. TV stations broadcast somber music. Thousands gathered in front of the presidential palace, lighting candles and placing flowers. Boy and girl scouts kept order. At noon, the entire country and all traffic came to a halt

for two minutes, as sirens sounded to remember the dead.

The impact of the calamity was magnified by the fact that it had occurred at the very spot where so many Poles had been sacrificed 70 years before. But this time no one could speak of a decapitation of the Polish state. The speaker of the Sejm, Bronislaw Komorowski, immediately stepped into his role as acting president and set about arranging for a new presidential election. Empty posts were filled calmly. The military commanders were

Modern police car in rural Poland

seamlessly succeeded by their next in command. Members of parliament were automatically replaced by the next-highest vote winners from the same party in the last election. Political parties moved the next-in-line personnel up to fill newly vacant positions. Never for one moment were there any doubts about the stability of the country. Normality reigned. The political and military institutions functioned exactly as they were supposed to.

The feeling of national unity was shaken a few days later by an unexpected decision to bury the deceased president and his wife below the Wawel royal cathedral in Krakow, where Pope John Paul II had once been archbishop. This is the burial site for Poland's kings, poets, and national heroes, such as Tadeusz Kosciuszko, Jozef Pilsudski, and Wladyslaw Sikorski. No president had been buried there, and few Poles would ever regard Lech Kaczynski as a hero. His approval rating was below 30% just before he died, and he was expected to lose his bid for reelection in 2010. In the end he was buried with the heroes.

One foreign policy by-product of the tragedy was the display of sympathy by Russian leaders, especially Prime Minister Putin, who embraced his Polish counterpart at the site of the carnage. Polish leaders hailed the compassionate and empathetic Russian response. Putin personally oversaw the investigation. He also allowed the sobering Oscar-nominated film by Andrzej Wajda, *Katyn*, which depicts graphically the mass murder that had occurred, to be aired twice on Russian prime-time television. Wajda's own father was among the victims of the wartime massacre. Russian president Dmitry Medvedev brought flowers to the Polish embassy in Moscow and told the Polish people, "All Russians share your grief and mourning." Russia continues to refuse categorically to pay compensation for the Katyn murders. A poll taken in Russia after the crash indicated that only 19% considered Stalin's secret police to have been responsible for the crime. But in November 2010, the Russian parliament (Duma) approved a statement holding Stalin responsible for the mass killings.

Tensions quickly reappeared over the crash. It prompted some Polish theories that the accident was a group assassination by the Russians. These conspiracy theories keep popping up. In 2012 an erroneous newspaper article reported that traces of explosives had been found in the wreckage; it was quickly dismissed. Russia's 2011 report on the disaster placed all of the blame on the Polish pilots, who were allegedly poorly prepared, disregarded traffic control warnings not to land in the dense fog, and under the influence of intoxicated commanders to land anyway.

There is no evidence that the president or any other official ordered the pilot to land. The report disregarded Polish concerns that the Russian air traffic controllers might have given the incorrect flight paths and altitudes. Prime Minister Tusk found the investigation "incomplete," and opposition politicians accused the government of gullibly accepting the Russian report. The Polish government ordered its own investigation and did find some fault in the Russian air control. However, it blamed the accident chiefly on the bad training of Polish pilots and a disregard for air traffic procedures. As a result, the defense minister resigned, and 3 generals and 10 other officers were sacked. The air force regiment in charge of VIP flights was disbanded. There was a dispute about the wording on the plaques affixed at the site. The Poles were incensed that the Russian one made no mention of the reason the Polish delegation was flying to the region.

There is intense disagreement in Poland about what exactly caused the disaster. Conspiracy theories thrive. Director Antoni Krauze stirred things up with his 2014 film *Smolensk*. It suggests a cover-up. A more objective film that stuck close to the facts of the investigations was produced and aired by National Geographic, *Death of a President*. PiS politicians called this documentary "scandalous." In May 2016 Antoni Macierewicz, the defense minister in the PiS government and one of the strongest proponents of conspiracy theory, declared that the plane crash was an act

of "terrorism" and that Lech Kaczynski's criticism of Russia led to a "reaction that caused death to the entire Polish elite."

More Presidential Politics

After Lech Kaczynski's death, the speaker of the Sejm, Bronislaw Komorowski, assumed the role of acting president and represented the Civic Forum in the presidential campaign that followed. An aristocrat, former dissident, and promoter of pro-EU policies, he had been the favorite until Jaroslaw Kaczynski, former prime minister for the PiS, entered the race.

It is not surprising that Jaroslaw enjoyed considerable sympathy in a campaign that was more about emotions than substance. While Komorowski was wooden and uncomfortable in public, Kaczynski reminded voters that the economy had been strong during his twin's years in office. Komorowski came out only 5.1% ahead after the first round on June 20. He and Jaroslaw Kaczynski entered the second round on July 4, neck and neck. Komorowski emerged as the victor, winning 53%.

The year 2015 provided a number of earthshaking surprises and changes in Poland's politics. For one, defying the expectations that the country's strong economic performance would favor PO, in the presidential elections in May, Poles elected a lawyer and little-known European Parliament member, Andrzej Duda, selected by Jaroslaw Kaczynski to run on the ticket of Law and Justice. Having received slightly more votes than the incumbent Bronislaw Komorowski during the first round, Duda prevailed in the runoff round, when he garnered 51.55% of the votes over Komorowski's 48.45%. The election portended trouble for Civic Platform before the upcoming parliamentary elections in the fall. Duda benefited from support by many youngsters critical of the "establishment" (he won some 60% of the under-30 vote), as well as the conservative elderly. In a powerful signal that the country's impressive growth since 2008 had not been equally distributed, his support stemmed mostly from the poorer eastern regions and rural areas, while all more affluent regions in western Poland and most urbanites preferred Komorowski. Duda's public image as a youthful, energetic, and modern pragmatist helped sway some moderate voters otherwise wary of what another stint with Law and Justice might mean for the country. Still, he had openly presented himself as a political and spiritual heir to the late president Lech Kaczynski, so the results signaled Poland's political shift to the right and a possible change of its domestic and foreign policies.

Duda was reelected in July 2020 by the narrowest of margins against the popular

**Former Prime Minister
Mateusz Morawiecki**

mayor of Warsaw, Rafal Trzaskowski, 51% to 49%. To win, Duda stirred up hatred of gay people, liberals, and Jews. He advocated a tightening of abortion rules, which touched off massive demonstrations.

Parliamentary Elections

In the October 2015 parliamentary elections, the two largest political parties, Law and Justice (PiS) and Civic Platform (PO), dominated again, with 60% of the votes between them. This continues the general polarization of Polish politics, though at a lower level than the 70% in 2011.

PiS, headed by Jaroslaw Kaczynski, and PO, previously led by Donald Tusk and now by Grzegorz Schetyna, are divided both by personality conflicts and by policy issues. This was true despite the fact that both stem from the anticommunist Solidarity movement and both emphasize the importance of the Catholic Church. PO is economically free-market and probusiness. PiS advocates protectionism and state intervention, added welfare spending, and controls on foreign investment. Both are socially conservative, but PiS has a strongly pro-Catholic stance, opposing the legalization of abortion.

PiS wishes to end the tradition of compromise between ex-communists and opposition. It talked of creating a "Fourth Republic" to get away entirely from the corrupt "Third Republic," created after 1989. In government before 2007, it created a high-powered anticorruption body to investigate questionable privatization deals and crony-infested state bureaucracy. It sought to purge ex-communists from public life and to clean up the intelligence services; it dissolved the Military Intelligence Service (WSI).

In 2006 it ordered prosecutors to file charges against the last communist leader, General Jaruzelski, for imposing martial law in 1981. In September 2008 he went on trial with six other octogenarian officers and party officials on charges of being

Poland

part of a "criminal conspiracy." This was the first time Poland had sought to hold its former communist leaders responsible for imposing martial law. Because of delaying actions on the part of the infirm and aged defendants, a verdict was unlikely. In 2011 Jaruzelski was found medically unfit to stand trial, and he died in May 2014. In 2012 the interior minister at the time, Czeslaw Kiszczak, was given a two-year suspended sentence (he died in 2015). The Institute of National Remembrance in Warsaw opened thousands of files to citizens for investigation. In 2012 1 million Poles filled cinemas to see a film by Antoni Krauze, *Black Thursday*, which explores the gunning down by government troops of dozens of protesters in Gdynia and other cities on the Baltic coast in 1970.

There have been disagreements over foreign policy. Although both are pro-American, the PiS has often taken an assertive, nationalist, patriotic, and populist stance, including toward the EU, Germany, and Russia. Just months before the 2011 elections, Kaczynski was complaining that Poland was a "Russo-German condominium." It is a Euroskeptic party, whereas PO is pro-EU.

They also have different electorates. Civic Platform's support tends to be overwhelmingly in the dynamic, more affluent, western parts of Poland; in large cities; and among younger and better-educated Poles (including two out of five students). It attracts the globalized elite who want Poland to be respected in Europe and have one of the continent's most competitive economies. It is the party of

Poles who clearly benefitted from the collapse of the old regime.

Law and Justice is a populist party that does well in poorer, rural parts of society, especially in eastern and central Poland and among older, more devoutly Catholic voters. Its success reflects the anger of those who consider themselves to be losers in the transition. The difference in the bases of the two parties is between a more modern, liberal Poland that is well integrated in Europe and the world and a more nationalistic and fundamentalist Catholic Poland that focuses on its own interests.

The Civic Platform (PO) emerged the winner of the 2007 and 2011 elections. This by itself was a sign of greater stability in the political arena: For the first time since the collapse of the communist state in 1989, a government served its entire four-year term and was reelected. In 2011 PO captured 207 of the 460 seats (down from 209) with 39.2% of the votes (down from 41.4%). Donald Tusk's success derived from his personal charm; his sharp tactical sense; the glow of Poland's economic success; and his refusal to preach bold reform, blood, sacrifice, and patriotism to the voters. He was tapped for a top job at the EU, European Council president. In July 2021, Tusk returned to domestic politics and again assumed the leadership of Civic Platform. At the time, only 23% of Poles believed he could become prime minister again, which would happen in two years. He faced opposition from the new Poland 2050.

Tusk was replaced as prime minister in September 2014 by Ewa Kopacz, a chain-smoking doctor and former health

minister. She was the second female government leader after Hanna Suchocka. PO's governing partner, the Polish Peasants' Party (PSL), led by Deputy Prime Minister Waldemar Pawlak, received 8.4% of the votes (down from 8.9%) and 28 seats (down from 31). This gave the ruling coalition 235 seats.

In the opposition, Law and Justice (PiS) won 29.9% of the votes (down from 32.2%) and 157 seats (down from 166). Kaczynski toned down his polarizing views and populist rants during the campaign and adopted a softer, statesman-like demeanor. He also treated attendees at his rallies to a bevy of attractive ladies, hinting at a more modern outlook. He led a good campaign but failed to translate into a political victory the personal and national tragedy of the air crash that claimed the life of his twin brother. The Democratic Left Alliance, led by Gregorz Napieralski, fell badly to 8.2% of the votes (down from 13.2%) and 27 seats (a loss of 26). As always, the German Minority, led by Ryszard Galla, is exempted from the 5% threshold and was granted two seats, winning one outright in Opole.

The greatest surprise in the 2011 elections was the sensational success of a party that had broken off from Civic Platform: Palikot's Movement, named after its leader, Janusz Palikot. It came out of nowhere to win 10% of the votes and 40 seats. Palikot was a philosophy student who made a fortune in the vodka business before becoming a maverick politician. He aimed his new leftist party at a growing niche in Polish politics: those who are generally pro-European in outlook; socially tolerant, especially toward gay people; and increasingly skeptical of the Catholic Church's privileged position in the schools and in society in general. More and more Poles are drifting away from the church and seeking a secular state more in line with western Europe. Many young people are attracted by this appeal.

The party rejected a political tradition of tiptoeing around the powerful church and is the first party to face seriously the problems of the gay community. Among its deputies are the first trans member of any European national legislature, Anna Grodzka, and the first openly gay Polish member of parliament, Robert Biedron. Lech Wałęsa provoked outrage when he remarked that gay people have no right to serve in parliament, but if they do, they should sit in the back or "behind a wall." Palikot's Movement sought the removal of the cross that hangs in the parliament the introduction of same-sex marriage or civil unions and abortion on demand. For the 2015 elections, the renamed Your Movement joined the left-wing coalition.

Polish peacekeeper in Bosnia flanked by US troops

Poland

The surprising outcome of the presidential election of 2015 indicated that Civic Platform had underestimated the growing perception that it got too comfortable with its position, combined with the impact of the replacement of its leader, Donald Tusk, with the less charismatic or effective Ewa Kopacz. Accusations of corruption abounded, even as Transparency International ranked Poland in 2015 as 30th of 168 countries in the world and 14th in the European Union, ahead of all former communist countries except Estonia.

PiS's chances for success in the parliamentary elections in October 2015 appeared to grow as the summer and fall unfolded, bringing the government more external challenges, as well as some self-inflicted wounds. Under tremendous pressure from the EU seeking to relocate 120.000 refugees, Poland agreed to accept some 5,000 people in addition to the 2.000 already accepted earlier. This stirred up a lot of emotions, and the opposition harnessed the rising resentment toward foreign newcomers. Two weeks before the elections, Law and Justice leader Kaczynski warned publicly that the refugees might bring with them "various parasites, protozoa that... may be dangerous here." Such comments raised many eyebrows but seemed to resonate well with the party's supporters and many uncommitted voters.

The governing Civic Platform had an additional problem on its hands: the continuing fallout from the wiretapping scandal of 2014 that compromised several prominent politicians. In June 2015 Prime Minister Kopacz announced the resignation of several senior PO officials, including six ministers of her government and the speaker of the Sejm, former foreign minister Radoslaw Sikorski. Kopacz apologized to PO voters for "the many difficult moments" and hoped the move would redirect public attention toward electoral platforms and away from scandals. Still, the rivals would not let the issue die. And to increase its appeal, Law and Justice announced that its candidate for prime minister would be Beata Szydlo, a capable though largely unknown campaign organizer. This created an extremely rare situation in Europe—that the main candidates of both major parties were women. (The election got even more remarkable when the left-wing coalition also ran a female candidate.) Sensing that his own candidacy would have been controversial, Jaroslaw Kaczynski opted for the role of a kingmaker pulling strings from behind the scenes. Furthermore, even though President Duda had to relinquish formally his membership in PiS once in office, his respectable image and performance was also helping the party.

In the end it was not so much the victory of Law and Justice in the election of October 25, 2015, that was surprising but rather its scale. With 37.58% of popular vote, PiS became the first party in post-communist Poland to win an outright majority of seats in the Sejm (235 seats, or 51%); it also won a majority in the Senate (61). Civic Platform won 24.09% of votes and obtained 138 seats in the Sejm (30%) and 34 seats in the Senate. The shift to the right was accentuated by the demise of the United Left coalition of the Democratic Left Alliance

Rare antiwar poster during 2003 Iraq war

(SLD), Polish Socialist Party, Labor United, Your Movement, and the Greens. With 7.55% of votes, the coalition failed to clear the 8% threshold and was completely shut out of the parliament.

The elections also confirmed a recent trend toward personalized political parties centered around an individual. While Janusz Palikot's movement failed to repeat its 2011 success, two new entities performed quite well and together gathered over 16% of popular vote. One, Kukiz'15, was a movement created after Pawel Kukiz, a rock-musician-turned-activist, came in a surprising third in the presidential elections, gathering 21% of votes. His movement demanded the introduction of single-mandate electoral districts and a presidential system in Poland. It received 8.81% of votes, and with 42 seats, it became the third-largest party in the Sejm. Another new movement was the Modern of Ryszard Petru, later styled as .Modern (.Nowoczesna) or simply .N. This classical liberal party created by an economist, Ryszard Petru, received 7.6% of votes and 28 seats in the Sejm (it later gained an additional deputy who left Kukiz'15). The new Sejm is rounded off by the mostly rural Polish People's Party (5.13%, 16 seats, and 1 seat in the Senate) and a single representative of the German minority. Four independents won seats in the Senate. Barely half (51%) of Poles bothered to go to the polls, though that dismal turnout was still better than the 49% in 2011.

The new government wasted little time in implementing its agenda, including institutional reforms. It removed political opponents from state companies and

Polish and American Special Forces during the Iraq war, 2003

Poland

Jagiellonian University, Krakow

governmental agencies, including heads of intelligence; it tightened control of public media and even raided at night a NATO-related center to replace its leadership. A number of legislative sessions extended well into the night, keeping the process out of prime viewing time and accumulating thousands of dollars' worth of staff overtime.

A serious crisis emerged when the government blocked the appointment of 5 judges of the 15-member Constitutional Tribunal, Poland's highest court deciding the constitutionality of laws, and instead appointed its own judges. The tribunal itself declared the move unconstitutional, but this decision could not be binding until its official publication—and that was prevented by the government. On December 28, 2015, a law was signed requiring the court to pass its rulings by a two-thirds majority with at least 13 judges present, thus making it more difficult for the court to block any new legislation passed by the PiS-controlled parliament. The law drew international and domestic condemnation, including an unprecedented intervention from President Obama, who offered his subtle though public criticism during the NATO summit in Warsaw, in front of President Duda.

The government's policies provoked mass protests in the country, bringing tens of thousands of marchers into the streets. The most prominent force organizing such demonstrations is the Committee for the Defense of Democracy (Komitet Obrony Demokracji—KOD). It protests what it sees as the violation of the constitution, takeover of public institutions by PiS,

and the rejection of "European values" as promoted by the EU. Demonstrators carry copies of the constitution wrapped in black ribbons and wave Polish and EU flags. Counterdemonstrations by supporters of the government wave Polish flags only.

Another flood of street protest was incited by a church-supported proposal for a ban on abortion, discussed later. PiS continues to pursue its traditional social agenda—it announced that it would stop state funding for in vitro fertilization (IVF) while also sharply increasing public spending, including a new family benefit paid for each child, though not to single mothers. It also raised the specter of a communist and foreign infiltration of Poland's public institutions and of the alleged conspiracy behind the 2010 airplane crash that killed President Kaczynski and scores of Polish officials. Its wholesale replacement of many executives in state-owned companies gained widespread attention when PiS appointed a manager with little horse-breeding experience to run the most elite and world-renowned stud farm in Janow Podlaski—and within two months two horses belonging to the wife of the Rolling Stones' drummer died there. A new civil service law eliminated competitions for senior jobs, indicating that loyalty may trump competence.

The frenetic pace of the legislative work and administrative changes stems from the lessons Law and Justice drew from their previous short stint in power in 2003–2005, as well as from the playbook of Hungary's right-wing prime minister Viktor Orbán. In turn, Hungary announced

that it would veto any sanctions against Poland the European Union might be considering. When Orbán came for a surprise six-hour consultation to Niedzica in southern Poland, there was little doubt who the power behind the throne in Poland is. He met not with Poland's president or prime minister but with Jaroslaw Kaczynski.

A political crisis erupted in December 2016, with opposition deputies occupying the parliament podium to protest the government's restrictions on media presence in the building. In turn, the ruling PiS party moved to another room and voted in the 2017 budget by a show of hands, in an unconstitutional procedure. The opposition continued to occupy the chamber throughout the winter break, even though heating and power got turned off. The stand-off, related more broadly to the "illiberal democracy" course adopted by the Polish government in the mold of Hungary, delayed opening of the parliament. Finally, by mid-January 2017, the Civic Platform announced it was suspending the blockade in exchange for Law and Justice's dropping of the media restrictions. In the meantime, a new sore point arose when the Senate passed the budget bill, even though its lower-house version was only adopted by the government's party. As it happens, decisions on legality of the law would be up to the Constitutional Tribunal, temporarily controlled by the government. All this drama was augmented by street protests by supporters of each side.

The PiS government continued its attacks on the courts, the media, and civil society organizations as the 2019 parliamentary elections drew nearer. For the first time, the EU warned Warsaw of disciplinary sanctions if the illiberal trend continued. Fearing a showdown with Brussels, the government reversed its purge of the Supreme Court and reinstated the dismissed judges. This marked a striking change in tone and policy. Poles clearly want to remain a part of democratic Europe. To improve its image abroad, a moderate finance expert, Mateusz Morawiecki, was appointed prime minister. He was a banker, but he lacks a political base. In a poll only 14% knew who he was. A third of the cabinet was fired.

Nevertheless, President Duda signed legislation in 2018 criminalizing any reference to "Polish death camps" or Poles' complicity in the Holocaust. This would cover up the anti-Jewish pogroms before and after World War II.

In the October 2019 parliamentary elections, the ruling Law and Justice Party retained its majority in the Sejm, but it narrowly lost control of the less-powerful Senate. The government has clashed repeatedly with the EU since its highest court

Poland

Female Polish students with Slovenian classmate at College of Europe, Warsaw

ruled in October 2021 that within Poland, national law takes precedence over EU law. Warsaw resents EU demands "with a gun to our head." Brussels regards Poland as the EU's most rebellious member.

The results of the 2023 parliamentary elections and the re-election of Donald Tusk as prime minister might bring about a change in that reputation.

The 2023 Polish parliamentary election took place on October 15th. There were 29,532,595 voters registered for the elections, including over 600,000 who applied to vote abroad. The historic high turnout of 74.4% (21,966,891) was the highest in contested elections and the highest since the fall of communism in 1989, beating with an increase of 12% the previous record set in 2019. At the polling stations, a referendum was also voted on with four questions concerning the government's economic and immigration policy.

The elections took place in a highly polarized atmosphere and were regarded by many as critical to Poland's democratic future. The campaign was seen by the observation mission as "highly confrontational and often negative, with candidates repeatedly using intolerant, misogynistic and discriminatory language, including anti-migrant narratives from some parties that were at times xenophobic."

In the lead-up to the elections, Donald Tusk led the Civic Coalition political alliance in opposition to the ruling right-wing Law and Justice Party (PiS). During his campaign, Tusk advocated for enhanced LGBT rights.

The United Right alliance won a plurality of seats but fell short of a Sejm majority. Tusk's Civic Coalition finished as the second-largest bloc in the Sejm and in combination with two other opposition parties, Third Way and New Left, took 54% of the vote, winning enough seats to allow them to take power and form a majority coalition government.

In the Senate also, the opposition electoral alliance Senate Pact 2023 won a majority of seats.

After the election, in November, the Civic Coalition, the New Left, the Polish People's Party, and Poland 2050 officially signed an agreement to support Tusk as their candidate for prime minister.

President Andrzej Duda nominated PiS incumbent Mateusz Morawiecki for another term as prime minister. However, it was evident that Morawiecki would not be able to get the support needed to remain in office, as PiS and its allies were 40 seats short of a majority. With that in mind, Tusk publicly announced the agreement before the new Sejm convened to show that he and the opposition were ready to govern. Morawiecki's cabinet was sworn in on November 27, but on December 11, he lost the necessary support in the Sejm with 190 votes for and 266 against. According to the constitution, if the candidate for prime minister does not receive a vote of confidence within two weeks of taking the oath, the Sejm has the right to designate its candidate, and the president has to appoint the person so nominated. The four parties that signed the agreement had the required number of votes, so the Sejm later proposed Tusk as its candidate for prime minister. He was elected with 248 votes for and 201 against. Tusk's cabinet was sworn in on December 13, 2023.

Foreign Policy

Just as postwar Germany discarded its earlier *Schaukelpolitik* (policy of swinging back and forth) between east and west and planted its roots firmly in the west, Poland has also rejected such "to and fro." It is fixed politically where it always was culturally and emotionally—to the west. This is captured in the saying that the Poles, have "always considered that east is east

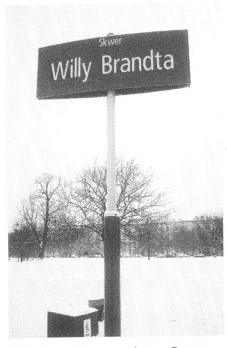

Willy Brandt Square, where a German chancellor knelt to honor ghetto victims

Incumbent Prime Minister Donald Tusk
Source: *Wikipedia*

Poland

and west is best, and the twain meet on Poland's eastern border."

Poland's seven neighbors represent an increase from three before the collapse of the Soviet Union in December 1991, none of which exists today—the Soviet Union, Czechoslovakia, and the GDR. For the first time in a millennium, Poland was secure and at peace with all of its neighbors. For the first time in more than a century, it felt safe on its eastern and western borders. With Germany, the Czech Republic, Lithuania, Slovakia, and Ukraine, it has developed particularly close relations. Russia's aggression against Ukraine in 2014–2015 unsettled Poland. It took a leading diplomatic role to try to defuse the tension, but it also called on NATO to increase its presence and maneuvers in the Baltic states and Poland. In 2014 it requested in vain the deployment in the country of two heavy NATO brigades, the equivalent of 10,000 soldiers. Four years later it asked the United States to deploy permanently on its soil an armored division of 15,000 soldiers. It enjoys its best relations among its seven neighbors with its oldest foe—Germany. The latter has proven to be a reliable partner with much to offer.

Poland's foreign policy has shown considerable continuity despite frequent changes of governments. Ties with the United States are of lessening importance as the US focuses its attention more toward Asia and reduces its number of troops in Europe. It has a huge diaspora in America, numbering over 9 million, with the largest concentrations in New York, Michigan, Pennsylvania, and Illinois. Chicago is the largest concentration of Poles after Warsaw. Poland is America's most trusted ally in the area. When the Economist surveyed students at the University of Warsaw in 2001 about their political role models, the top two were Ronald Reagan and Harry Truman. Barack Obama is also popular. More recently, that level of pro-Americanism has cooled. Nevertheless, in 2019 70% of Poles rated America favorably in a poll.

Former foreign minister Radek Sikorski, for a while one of the most popular politicians, with strong anti-Russian and pro-American credentials, noted that "US influence and esteem have diminished in Poland." He was shifted to speaker of the Sejm and eventually dismissed after an illegal wiretap recorded him saying that the Polish-American alliance is "worthless" and could alienate Poland's neighbors.

A think-tank president was more tactful: "We began to realize that for 90% of the problems we have, the solution is in Europe, not in America." No wonder 89% say they want to be in the EU. Seeing clearly that their core interests lie with the EU, Poles regard their relationship with America as less vital. The war in Afghanistan, where 40 Polish soldiers had died by 2014, was unpopular.

Some Poles resent their government's earlier role in aiding the US in its rendition policy and in hosting a secret CIA jail. The government admitted these charges, saying it was part of an effort to build Polish-American trust. Poland became the first country to pay damages ($262,000) to two former prisoners.

Ties are still warm, even though Poland no longer idolizes the US. It has shifted its foreign policy toward greater enthusiasm for the EU and closer ties with Germany and France. Poland plays a key role in NATO's contingency plans to defend the northeastern flank.

Most central Europeans and their governments still have a greater inclination toward pro-Americanism than do their western cousins. The American dream is still potent, and for generations they have gotten positive accounts of the New World from emigres who found a better life there. Many feel that America did the most to win them their independence in 1989, and there remains a residual fear of Germany and especially Russia that could be countered only by American power.

Certainly, most Poles are convinced that only the US can ultimately guarantee their country's security while the EU still struggles to create a defense identity and capability. In his 2007 campaign, Tusk singled the US out as Poland's "most important ally" while at the same time strengthening ties with the countries' neighbors, especially Germany but including Russia. Ambassador to the US Janusz Reiter wrote, "As long as the US is a functioning reality and a united Europe is a dream, we will always choose the reality over the dream." However, current Polish policy is to support both an enlarging NATO and a common EU defense. As former president Bronislaw Komorowski put it, if you live near a "forest full of bandits," it is best to have two locks on the door.

Of course, there were risks involved in Poland's and other central European countries' steady support of the foreign policy objectives of the United States, which sees the European center of gravity shifting toward Asia. They can sometimes feel caught between leading western European nations, which held the keys to the EU, and the US, which provides unaccustomed security. The US and UK are Poland's largest sources of foreign investment, and Germany is its largest market, accounting for over a fourth of its trade. That percentage doubled since Poland joined the EU in 2004.

For the first time, Poland has good relations with Germany and the United States at the same time. Under Donald Tusk, it adopted a more conciliatory tone, which is good for neighborly relations. It has shifted its emphasis from global politics as a junior partner of the United States to a more influential European power with a significant role in the EU and pragmatic relations with Germany and Russia. This

Warsaw Uprising Memorial, Warsaw

is especially true since Donald Tusk was appointed president of the EU's European Council despite his inability to speak French. However, he is fluent in German and his English is passable.

During the Iraq crisis in the spring of 2003, French president Jacques Chirac lashed out at the central European governments' signing of a letter supporting the US in Iraq. They felt degraded to second-class status by Chirac's public statement that "these countries have been not very well behaved and rather reckless of the danger of aligning themselves too rapidly with the American position. They missed a great opportunity to remain silent." One German newspaper called Poland America's "Trojan donkey." Political scientist Andrzej Kapiszewski of Jagiellonian University in Krakow remarked, "Chirac's words were more or less like the words we heard from the Kremlin for the previous 50 years of communism." The fact that France and Germany had allied with Russia over Iraq without consulting with Poland and their other future EU partners was an unpleasant memory for Poles of great powers making deals over their heads and at their expense.

Many Poles believe that they have not fully benefited from their strong support of the US and that the superpower is ungrateful for the sacrifices their government made. Many feel hurt by American requirements that, while Americans enter their country visa-free, Poles must apply for expensive ($160) visas when traveling to the US. They must be interviewed before being granted a visa and are subjected to fingerprinting upon arrival at an American airport.

In partnership with Sweden, Poland inaugurated the EU's Eastern Partnership with six non-Russian republics in eastern Europe and the Caucasus. All are potential EU members in the future. Whereas most European countries had weak and bad relations with Ukraine, Belarus, and Moldova, Poland conducted high-level meetings and an exchange of governmental officials and students on a regular basis. Russia's invasion and annexation of Crimea in March 2014 and subsequent aggression in eastern Ukraine created tension in Warsaw's relations with Russia, compelling Poland to build a stronger common front with its other EU and NATO partners.

As an EU member since May 2004, it argues quietly for an "eastern dimension" to the EU's external policy, supporting that organization's "Good Neighbor Policy" and eastern partnership toward the east. As stable, more prosperous, and accessible countries, they would be better able to resist Russian influence and keep Poland more secure. Poland formed a joint peacekeeping battalion with Ukraine,

Modern fusion: a meal of pierogi and Coca-Cola

POLUKRBAT, which served in Bosnia and Kosovo. Poland ratified a concordat with the Vatican in 1998.

Poland's relations with Russia were satisfactory under President Wałęsa, but they cooled under Kwasniewski because of his support for the proposed enlargement of NATO. The fact that Poland actually received and accepted an invitation in 1997 to join NATO two years later did not help. Russia supplies almost 90% of Poland's oil and 80% of its gas needs; 97% of its imported crude oil comes from that country. But Russia also needs a friendly Poland for many reasons, including the latter's crucial location for Russia's oil and gas pipelines to Germany and elsewhere in Europe. For that reason, Moscow entered an agreement with Germany in 2005 to build a pipeline under the Baltic Sea to Germany, thereby avoiding Polish territory altogether. This North Stream went into operation in 2011, and a second pipeline doubled capacity by 2013. Poles were furious, and this pipeline was opposed by all parties. In response, Poland plans its own pipeline from Norway via Denmark and hopes for German support.

Russian President Vladimir Putin's visit to Poland in 2002 was the first by a Russian leader since 1993 and was hailed as a success. He gave his approval of the EU's eastward expansion and called for constructive work with NATO. Putin made symbolic gestures to try to diminish Polish distrust of Russia. He unexpectedly stopped at a monument honoring 50 victims of the 1956 revolt against Soviet rule and at one in the middle of Warsaw commemorating the main Polish underground army in World War II.

Putin could not bring himself to visit the monument to the 1944 Warsaw uprising, when Soviet troops stood still across the Vistula River while German units crushed the Polish fighters. Nor did he mention until several years later the massacre in the Katyn Forest in western Russia, where Stalin ordered the execution of almost 22,000 Polish officers in 1940 and deported over 10,000 more to be killed in other parts of the USSR. It hesitated for years to release documentation that would enable relatives of the victims to receive some justice.

In 2005 the Polish government risked heating up tensions with Russia by releasing 1,700 highly secret Warsaw Pact files that included a war game during the Cold War that called for massive nuclear destruction of Poland and western Europe. A map showed Soviet forces counterattacking NATO forces in a way that involved dropping nuclear bombs from the Dutch coast to Strasbourg, wiping out cities in Germany, France, and BENELUX. There were also details of the 1968 Warsaw Pact invasion of Czechoslovakia. A further wake-up call came in August 2008, when Russia invaded Georgia. This was a reminder that Poles still live in a potentially dangerous part of the world. Deputy Defense Minister Stanislaw Komorowski referred to the year Poland joined NATO: "In 1999 everybody thought the cold war was over. But last year we had Georgia. An independent country was invaded by our partner—Russia. It changed our perception of the threat."

However, Putin signaled that he wanted good relations with Poland. In September 2009 he went to Gdansk to mark the start of World War II. He also invited a Polish honor guard, along with units from Britain, France, and the United States, to march as representatives of the "anti-Hitler coalition" in Moscow's annual parade commemorating VE Day on May 8, 2010. Russia's then-president Dmitri Medvedev made in December 2010 the first official visit to Poland in nine years, and both countries vowed to open a new chapter in their relations. That pledge was dashed by Russia's invasion of Ukraine.

The Polish government has made it clear that it desires good relations with all of its neighbors to the east but that its own commitment is Europe. Its economic orientation is western, particularly since joining the EU in May 2004. This western approach was reinforced by the slowness of economic reform in such neighbors as Belarus and Ukraine.

Its relations with Lithuania are no longer seriously affected by historic complaints concerning Lithuania's treatment of its Polish minority in the Vilnius area. There are irritants, such as Lithuania's refusal to permit its Polish minority to use Polish

Poland

Newly trendy, renovated Jewish quarter of Kazimierz in Krakow

script on official documents, increasing the number of subjects taught in Lithuanian, and its foot-dragging on restitution of pre-war Polish property. Poles in Lithuania are well integrated in Lithuanian society and were given Lithuanian citizenship immediately after that country won its independence from the Soviet Union in 1991. Lithuania is the only country outside of Poland that offers Polish-language education from infancy to adulthood. The two countries have no border disputes. In 1997 Poland forged a "strategic alliance" with Lithuania. It created a joint battalion, LIT-POLBAT, that is interoperable with NATO and prepared to contribute to the Atlantic alliance's security needs. NATO's contingency plans for defending Poland have been extended eastward and call for Polish soldiers to defend Lithuania and the other Baltic states. Poland warplanes based at a Lithuanian airfield police Baltic airspace for NATO on a rotating basis. In general, Poland's neighbors have to get used to its rise to heavyweight status.

Poland was officially admitted to NATO in March 1999. Two weeks later NATO began its air attacks on Yugoslavia. Poland consistently supported the NATO actions, but the air attacks led to tenser relations with Russia and Belarus, both of which opposed the NATO actions. Poland supported the war against terrorism after the September 11 attacks in New York and Washington. It offered parts of its elite special operations forces, known as

GROM, to fight alongside the Americans in Afghanistan.

Most dramatically, it was one of the few US allies to lend active support in the war effort in Iraq in March-April 2003. Polish intelligence agents had sneaked CIA operatives out of Iraq before the First Gulf War in 1991, and since the end of that war, a second Polish ambassador was dispatched to Iraq to represent US diplomatic interests. Polish construction companies had also built many of the roads in Iraq during the 1970s, so few people knew them as well as the Poles. Opinion surveys revealed that a majority of Poles actually opposed military action in Iraq, but opposition was generally passive; only 2,000 demonstrators gathered in Warsaw to protest the war.

There was a feeling of disappointment that Poland derived too little benefit from its deployment. Its efforts to end the visa requirement for the US were rebuffed, and its military complained that it did not get as much financial assistance as it had expected.

The government accepted the call for help from Washington and sent GROM and FORMOZA (Navy Seal) special forces, antichemical and biological units, and a small naval contingent. Its 200 special forces entered Iraq in the first wave of the invasion in March and helped secure the oil fields in the south. This was the first military combat for Polish soldiers since the 1968 Prague Spring in neighboring

Czechoslovakia, and they performed very well without suffering any casualties.

After the war, Poland assumed command of one of four occupation zones in Iraq, in the upper southern zone between Basra and Baghdad. Its 1,700 troops (down from 2,460) were the fourth-largest contingent. Two-thirds were financed by the United States. It had a total of 9,500 soldiers under its command. It also trained Iraqi security forces. Its request to Germany for a troop contribution to this unit was summarily dismissed in Berlin. By 2006, over 10,500 Polish soldiers had been deployed in Iraq. In the words of the defense minister, "They are the core of the new Polish military. They had not been in a warlike situation for half a century. They go out as civilians in uniform, but they come back as real warriors." Honoring a campaign pledge, Prime Minister Tusk ordered the country's 900 soldiers to leave Iraq by the end of 2008. It left 13 trainers.

Not since Poland's liberation from communist rule in 1989 has it assumed so visible a role on the world stage. In the second half of 2007, it took over command of NATO's 9,000-strong International Security Assistance Force in Afghanistan. It maintained a battalion of about 1,100 troops in Paktika, a dangerous province that borders the Pakistani tribal areas. In 2011 its troop total in Afghanistan was 2,600, NATO's seventh-largest. This deployment became unpopular at home and ended by 2015.

Poland maintains one of the largest armies in Europe, with about 65,000 active forces, as it transforms its military into a smaller, modern, mobile, integrated force. It is being reshaped into a professional force that can quickly deploy to trouble spots or multilateral missions anywhere in the world. The force once included 81,000 conscripts who served for 9 months. But conscription has been scrapped, and the last draftees were mustered out of the armed forces in 2009. It also has a reserve force of 234,000. Poland's army numbers 46,400; its navy 8,000 (who man an array of destroyers, patrol and coastal combatants, mine layers and sweepers, naval air, and four conventional submarines, all in desperate need of being upgraded); and its air forces 17,500. There are 14,100 paramilitaries, including border guards. In 2010 there were only 1,500 women soldiers, but that number is expected to rise.

Poland can afford to spend more than 1.95% of its GDP on defense. This makes it one of NATO's largest military spenders in relative terms and the central European member that meets NATO's goal of 2% of GDP. But the sum is small in absolute terms. In 2013 the government began a major modernization of its armed forces. Personnel and pension costs consumed

Poland

too large a share of its spending. Involvement in Iraq and Afghanistan highlighted the need for upgraded weapons. At least a third of the new funds are allocated to military hardware. About 60% of its equipment is antiquated Soviet kit. That includes MIG-29s, Su-22 fighters, and T-72 tanks. Poland has become NATO's eastern frontier facing the unstable western republics of the former Soviet Union. A further problem is that its largest military bases are located in the western part of Poland, far away from Belarus and Ukraine—and Russia beyond. Nevertheless, the emphasis is on special forces, to be modernized to US levels. Poland got important help from Germany, which donated excess stocks of Leopard 2A4 tanks (128), Mig-29 fighter jets (23), and several hundred support vehicles.

In 2008 the departing Bush administration beefed up the US-Polish military relationship by offering security guarantees and the deployment of an American- manned Patriot missile unit with 196 missiles to defend Warsaw. For three years this battery was operated by American soldiers on temporary duty. But from 2013, it is manned by about 100 permanently stationed US troops. This is the first time American soldiers have been stationed on Polish soil other than on NATO maneuvers. Poland also receives more training and equipment, such as armored Humvees.

On a visit in May 2011, President Barack Obama endorsed a bilateral deal between Poland and the United States allowing the US Air Force to station personnel in Poland. A small air detachment at Lask Air Base flies F-16s and trains Polish pilots to fly F-16 fighter jets and C-130 transport planes. Although small in scope, this is an important symbol of a US military presence in the country.

Poland made the largest ever purchase of American military hardware by a former Warsaw Pact country. To the consternation of the French, who had expected Poland to buy their Mirage fighters, the Poles purchased 48 American F-16 fighter jets at a cost of $3.5 billion. They operate out of Lask and Krzesiny Air Bases. Washington offered a sweetheart low-interest loan to enable the Poles to pay, with no principal payments before 2011. The package includes assembly operations for F-16 engines in Poland, investments in Polish steel mills and shipyards, and high-tech ventures in Poland by Lockheed and dozens of American companies. The contract also included the training of the pilots, which takes place in both the US and Poland using American and Polish instructors. Of a one-time military aid package worth $100 million to modernize the

Polish forces, $40 million is earmarked for extra training of F-16 pilots in the US.

The US already prizes Poland as a place for maneuvers. In 2001–2002 it spent $60 million for such war games in Poland, which is centrally located in Europe and has far fewer restrictions than training areas in Germany. For example, maneuver damage in Germany costs the US $30 million each year, compared to only $25,000 in Poland. It offers perfect military training terrain that includes vast flatlands, swamps, and rugged mountains.

The Polish government was receptive to the idea of an American deployment of 10 silos for interceptor missiles to guard against attacks from the Middle East; NATO supported this. However, Russia considered this to be provocative and has repeatedly threatened to deploy short-range Iskander missiles in Kaliningrad close to Poland's border. Polish public support for the missile system rose from 27% to 41% after the August 2008 Russian invasion of Georgia. Poland saw the interceptor bases as a way of permanently stationing American troops on their soil, and they believed they would have provided it with additional security against a resurgent Russia. The plan was seen as a symbol of America's credibility and commitment to regional defense.

However, President Obama, who was not as focused on eastern Europe as was

his predecessor and who desired to "reset" the American-Russian relationship, was less enthusiastic about the deployment. On September 17, 2009, he dropped the original idea and ordered a less ambitious missile defense system. The Polish and Czech governments were shocked. He was unaware that September 17 was the anniversary for the Soviet Union's invasion of Poland in 1939. Obama's poor timing fueled Poland's fears of being abandoned by its most powerful ally. The headline in the Polish tabloid *Fakt* read, "Betrayal! The U.S. sold us to Russia and stabbed us in the back."

Realizing its error, the American government offered Poland, after much haggling, a battery of Patriot missiles armed with live warheads to be used in NATO exercises and to be deployed for an undetermined time at a military base in Morag, located 35 miles from the Russian exclave of Kaliningrad. The US also pressed NATO to develop contingency plans to defend Poland and, by extension, to protect the vulnerable Baltic states, mainly by means of Polish troops.

Russian aggression in Ukraine accelerated more tangible arrangements. On May 13, 2016, a day after a missile shield site became operational in Romania, the US and Poland officially started construction of an Aegis Ashore missile defense system base in Redzikowo near Slupsk. The system

Christmas caroling party consists of many traditional characters, such as King Herod, the devil, death, and an angel
Courtesy: Embassy of Poland

Poland

A ventilated cabin for smokers in an otherwise smoke-free office building in Warsaw

is ostensibly directed at Iran, but neither Poles nor Russians seem to have illusions about its ultimate significance. Vladimir Putin warned that "people taking such decisions must know that until now they have lived in calm, fairly well-off and in safety" but now "we are forced to think how to neutralize the emerging threats to the Russian Federation."

In 2017, Poland moved to sign a $7.6 billion contract with Raytheon to purchase eight Patriot air defense systems, pending approval by the US Congress. The purchase would enhance the country's military modernization plans, since most of its military hardware still dates back to the Soviet bloc era. Defense minister Antoni Macierewicz left little doubt as to the intent behind the plan, citing "growing aggression and a growing threat from the East." American troops also constitute the bulk of a NATO "tripwire" detachment dispatched to northeastern Poland's Suwalki Gap just south of the border with Russia's Kaliningrad exclave. Some 1,100 troops from the US, United Kingdom, and Romania are one of NATO's enhanced Forward Presence battalion battle groups, with others also deployed in Lithuania, Latvia, and Estonia. Without much ambiguity, NATO described these "multinational, combat-ready forces" as "demonstrating the strength of the transatlantic bond, and making clear that an attack on one ally would be considered an attack on the whole Alliance."

In October 2021, Poland deployed 12,000 troops to its border with Belarus in an effort to cope with a large influx of migrants. This polarized Polish society as ugly clashes with desperate migrants darkened Poland's image as an upholder of human rights.

Poland's role in the world was strongly enhanced by Russia's attack of Ukraine on February 24, 2022. It became the lynch pin of the Western Alliance. Munitions poured into Ukraine through Poland. It was one of the EU's most vocal advocates of tougher action against Russia. It opened its doors to more than a million Ukranian refugees who were allowed to work and attend school. They joined the 1.3 million Ukrainians who already lived in Poland.

Poland and Germany

The Federal Republic of Germany's (FRG) first chancellor, Konrad Adenauer, said in 1956 that Germany would have to do with Poland the same as it had done with France after World War II. But the Cold War prevented the establishment of that kind of special relationship. This changed in 1990, when a reunified Germany could officially renounce any claims to territory Germany had lost to Poland in 1945. German then foreign minister Hans-Dietrich Genscher argued that the reacquisition of that land would have created a "new injustice." But Germany's firm position was that only the government of a unified Germany had the democratic authority to cede formerly German territory forever.

Most Poles were uncomfortable with German unity. Germany was not the only country to have to relinquish eastern territory as a price for peace and reconciliation. Poland itself had to accept the permanent loss of its former eastern provinces in present-day Lithuania, Ukraine, and Belarus (one-half of which belonged to Poland before World War II). In 2004 the European Court of Human Rights ruled that about 90,000 of the 1.2 million Poles displaced from the former eastern territories still have the right to claim compensation. Like Germany, Poland accepts a role as bridge between Russia and the west as the only way to escape its traditional geographic dilemma. Its ex-foreign minister, Bronislaw Geremek (1932—2008), wrote that Poland "is a natural connecting bridge for Western Europe on its way east; and for an Eastern Europe that is opening itself to the West, Poland again is on the way."

Lech Wałęsa expressed grave concerns the day after the Berlin Wall fell on November 9, 1989, and his uneasiness was shared by two out of three Polish respondents in a *New York Times* /CSA survey at the time. Geremek greeted it because Poland would be a neighbor of NATO and the EU and for the first time in almost six decades would share a border with a democratic state. "Poland forever returns to where she has always belonged—the free world." As foreign minister, he took Poland into NATO.

The symbol of the new mutual respect is Geremek himself. A Jew who escaped from the Warsaw ghetto at age 11 and remained in hiding until war's end and whose parents were killed by Germans in the Warsaw ghetto, he was the symbol of a new mutual respect. He accepted the Karl's Prize in Aachen and gave his acceptance speech in German, although he had once vowed never to speak that language. Referring to Poland's future, he said, "The winds of history have normally blown against us Poles. Finally, they are blowing in our favor."

Former German chancellor Helmut Kohl and vice chancellor and federal minister for foreign affairs Hans-Dietrich Genscher knew that, while no European country wanted to thwart German unity, there was uneasiness about the possibility that an economically powerful Germany, 43% larger than before and more populous than any country west of Russia, would dominate Europe. Most European leaders were too polite to express these fears publicly. To minimize these fears, Germany signed landmark treaties with the USSR and Poland. On November 9 it signed a friendship treaty with the Soviet Union that amounted to the closest links the Soviets had with any major western nation. It contains a section affirming that both nations "will refrain from any threat or use of force which is directed against the territorial integrity or political independence of the other side." Neither country would aid an aggressor against the other.

The ink was hardly dry when Germany signed a treaty with Poland on November 14, 1990, fixing their mutual border along the Oder-Neisse Line. The former German land to the east of this demarcation constituted a third of Poland's territory. This treaty inaugurated a policy of reconciliation toward Poland that would prove to be as dramatic for European peace and stability as Franco-German reconciliation since the 1950s in the west. On June 17, 1991, the two countries signed a further treaty on "good neighbors and cooperation." This treaty deliberately imitated the pioneering 1963 German-French reconciliation treaty by establishing a German-Polish foundation to promote youth contacts.

Many cliches and prejudices remain on both sides of the border, but a 2006 poll revealed that 71% of Poles consider Germans to be good neighbors and that their relations have improved since Poland joined the EU in 2004. Two-thirds of Germans have never visited their eastern neighbor and do not know the land or the people. Asked in a 2006 survey what they most associated with Poland, the top answer was "car theft and crime," closely followed by "illegal workers" and "poverty, backwardness." But the German and Polish elites have grown together to a remarkable extent.

Most Poles agree that the most important European partner they have is Germany. Not only was it Poland's most persistent and influential advocate in NATO and the EU, but it is also Poland's largest trading partner (buying 27.8% of Poland's exports and providing 20.2% of its imports) and second-largest foreign investor, after France. Elite Polish fears have been assuaged by the way in which Germany has become Europeanized. Geremek wrote that "Europe provides the appropriate setting for relations with Germany. . . With this, the Polish fear of German hegemony or of political dependence on Germany has vanished."

An important link with both Germany and France is the Weimar Triangle, named after the venue of its first meeting in 1991. Traditionally Poland was politically and culturally oriented toward France. However, this primary tie was no longer feasible for Poland after 1989, given Paris's earlier "empty chair" policy toward NATO and its obvious preference for a "deepening" of European Union integration, as opposed to "widening," which would bring in new members from the east. The best anchor for the pursuit of Polish interests became Germany. But Poland wants to widen its western contacts in order to reduce its possible dependence on Germany. The Weimar Triangle, which brings together the three countries' heads of state and government, ministers, and parliamentary representatives for informal talks on fundamental matters of mutual interest, does just that.

Poland also participates in another informal triangular relationship (called "Trialog" or "Troika") with Russia and Germany. This began in 2009 and 2010 with historians' conferences to discuss such issues as the Hitler-Stalin Pact of 1939. Since 2009 there have been meetings of the planning staffs and state secretaries of the foreign ministries. In Vienna the three countries' ambassadors to the Organization for Security and Cooperation in Europe (OSCE) meet once a month.

A symbol of the partnership at the highest level and of tension at the lower level is the bilingual Europa Universitat Viadrina at Slubice (Poland) and Frankfurt an der Oder (Germany). They are separated only by the Oder River and centuries of misunderstandings. This is the first German university that is truly European. It is based on a partnership between Poznan and Frankfurt an der Oder Universities and reserves 30% of its study places for students from central Europe. Courses are offered in both German (the predominant language of instruction) and Polish, and a few courses are given in English. Its small size (6,500 students) allows for a level of interaction, experimentation, and interdisciplinary synergism unknown in other Polish and German universities.

While the university's concept is daring and cosmopolitan, the twin-city setting reveals that there are still problems in the way the two populations deal with each other. They remain culturally and linguistically separate, even though the border is completely open since December 21, 2007, when Poland joined the Schengen Agreement. More and more persons in Slubice speak German, but almost no one on the German side learns Polish. A fifth (about 8 million) of Poles speak German.

Polish students find that many eastern German students at the Frankfurt an der Oder University have little interest in mingling with them. One western German student explained that those western German students who come from the west select this university because of its multinational character and are far more inclined to learn Polish and make Polish friends. Most eastern German students attend merely because it is close to home. There have been some incidents of Poles being the victims of right-extremist attacks in Frankfurt, and they are therefore somewhat wary of moving freely at all hours of the night. Perhaps a few Polish students wonder whether all have embraced Thomas Mann's plea to the German youth in 1952 to create a European Germany, not a German Europe.

Another innovative institution located on the Polish side of the border, in Szczecin, is a Northeast Multinational Corps consisting of Polish, German, and Danish troops, commanded by a Polish officer. This military cooperation, supplemented by a dramatic increase in German-Polish exercises and interaction (second only to that between the US and Poland) is symptomatic of a new spirit in the Polish-German relations. Together the two countries provide the bulk of NATO forces in the east, even though Poland insists that the US is and will remain its key military partner.

NATO membership gives Poland the confidence to engage its eastern neighbors, especially Russia, and it takes seriously its objective to expand the zone of stability eastward. This serves both German and American interests. Nevertheless, Poland is mindful of a possible Russian resurgence. Therefore, Poland unequivocally supported the admission of the Baltic states to NATO while pursuing better relations with Russia under Prime Minister Tusk. It also values membership in the EU as long as it does not diminish the role of NATO in maintaining security in Europe.

Poles experience some hostility on the German side of the border because their country is a major contributor to a huge black market in labor in Germany. Many Germans (who earn more than three times as much as a Pole in Poland) fear that cheap Polish laborers will take their jobs. Many Polish workers have done this in Berlin, a city with the most construction sites in all of Europe, but with Germany's highest unemployment rate among construction workers. Foreign laborers are willing to work on weekends and accept much lower pay and benefits than are Germans. One reason the May 2005 French referendum failed was the prominence in public debate of a mythical "Polish plumber," who would come to France, work longer hours for lower wages, and drive his French counterpart out of business. These kinds of tensions highlight Germany's problems as a high-wage economy in an age of globalization and bordering on low-wage central Europe.

To limit the effects of an influx of Polish labor, Germany negotiated within the EU a seven-year transition before there would be the free movement of labor; that ended in May 2011. Poles can travel freely in EU member states and can even establish their own businesses there, offering their own often-cheaper labor. About 2 million Poles migrated westward to find

Poland

Before the 1995 denomination, it was easy to be a millionaire in Poland.

work, and half returned home. Over 800,000 Poles live in Britain, and Polish has become the second-most widely spoken language. More children in the UK are born to Polish women than to women from any other foreign country.

After entering the EU in May 2004 and the ending of controls for EU citizens at the border, the already-vibrant cross-border trade jumped. Germans not only buy cheap Polish gasoline, cigarettes, and food but even leave their cars at Polish garages for service and repairs and take advantage of cheaper fees charged by doctors, dentists, and hair dressers.

Germany had been Poland's main advocate for EU membership, and until the Kaczynski twins came to power in 2005, Poles usually made a point of not mentioning World War II explicitly in any dealings with Germany. It has long been the rule in the EU that the war would be mentioned only in connection with the postwar miracle that European integration has brought. The twins seldom missed an opportunity to insult Germany, accusing it of "obvious anti-Polish sentiment that is often racist." They argued at the EU summit in June 2007 that Poland needed more votes in the council because it would have had a population of 66 million, not 39 million, were it not for the war. Poles are bitter about Germany's decision to join Russia in building that underwater pipeline that would avoid Poland. But the Polish defense minister went too far in comparing it with the Molotov-Ribbentrop Pact in 1939. Such statements left their bilateral relations raw. Prime Minister Tusk, who speaks German, never made such references.

Germany opposed Poland's hard stance in 2003 on the new EU constitutional treaty. Poles feared being treated like second-class members and applauded their government's tough stance, especially on the issue of voting rights. The 2000 Nice Treaty had awarded Poland almost as many votes in the EU Council of Ministers (27) as Germany (29), which has twice as many people. The Polish government also favored the inclusion of the word "God" in the preamble.

Seeing itself on the outs with much of Europe, Poland backed down in 2007 and accepted a "double-majority" voting system in the council and votes proportional to its population size, albeit with a delay until 2017. That assumed that the revised constitution, known as the Lisbon Treaty, would unanimously be ratified, as it eventually was. Poland's parliament approved it in April 2008. Then-president Lech Kaczynski delayed it to annoy Prime Minister Tusk and the Civic Platform Party. Such grandstanding is risky politics in eastern Europe, where Euroscepticism was usually not appealing. The EU is widely seen by his own people and other eastern Europeans as a guarantor of stability and progress and a generous provider of funding for modernization. The president ultimately signed it.

Part of the problem was that the untraveled and monoglot twins purged the government and foreign ministry of diplomatic and EU experts. A fourth of Polish embassies were without an ambassador. All this changed after the October 2007 elections. Prime Minister Tusk restored good relations with Germany and its chancellor, Angela Merkel. He also grudgingly accepted Berlin's decision to build a memorial to the millions of eastern Europeans, including Germans, who were expelled after the war. Warsaw had long opposed this project, arguing that it would present Germans as the victims rather than the perpetrators of crimes during the conflict.

To defuse German criticism of lax border controls, Poland accepted the principle of "safe third state," whereby Poland would not allow its territory to be used by illegal immigrants to reach Germany and would take back those illegals who slipped through their controls. This necessitated a severe tightening of its own borders and meant that Poland serves as a kind of filter for migrants from the east heading for Germany.

The situation for the estimated 300,000–500,000 ethnic Germans still living in Poland (mainly in Opole but also in the Mazury and Warmia areas) has greatly improved. They constitute Poland's largest ethnic minority. In 1945, following the brutal German treatment of the Polish population during World War II—especially of Polish Jews, who made up half of all Holocaust victims—3 million Germans were expelled from Poland in accordance with the Potsdam Agreement. Many of their homes and farms were occupied by Poles deported by the Soviet Union from Poland's eastern territories, which were annexed by the USSR. This left Poland a largely (about 96%–98%) homogeneous country for the first time in its history.

Relations with Germany were inflamed again in 2004, when groups representing German deportees threatened to file damage claims against Poland. Reaction in Poland was furious, even though the German government had refused to back these claims. The Sejm passed a nonbinding motion seeking war reparations from Germany. The controversy died down, but it revealed how many raw emotions remain on both sides. There is tension still in the air.

Until 1989 ethnic minorities in Poland faced a policy of enforced Polonization. Mainly for economic reasons, 424,000 people emigrated to the FRG from 1955 to 1974 and another 200,000 after 1975. After 1989, Poland adopted the political standards of the Organization for Security and Cooperation in Europe (OSCE) and the Council of Europe for protecting minority rights. These were written into the 1991 Treaty on Good-Neighborly Relations and Friendly Cooperation between Germany and Poland. This treaty affirms the right to use minority languages and to have non-Polish surnames.

There is a German caucus in the Polish parliament, and since 1990 the German government has provided financial support to the German community, including cultural and language assistance, as well as scholarships. From 1989 to 2000, Germany paid more than €105 million to Germans in Poland as an inducement to remain there. An additional €7 million were provided by the Foundation for the Development of Silesia.

The German government of Angela Merkel claimed in 2009 that it wanted its relations with Poland to be as close as they are with France. Under Civic Platform, those relations were the best they have ever been. In a November 2011 speech in Berlin, Foreign Minister Radoslaw Sikorski said, "I will probably be the first Polish foreign minister in history to say this, but here it is–I fear German power less than I am beginning to fear its inactivity. You

Poland

have become Europe's indispensable nation. You may not fail to lead—not dominate, but to lead in reform." Although PiS leader Kaczynski called this "treason" and the first step toward creation of a German-led "Fourth Reich," the Polish government continued to aspire to make Poland the indispensable partner of Germany and to make it a part of Germanic northern Europe that is punctual, hardworking, and fiscally responsible. Kaczynski's preferences, however, dominate the policies of the government, again controlled by his party since 2015. It is easy to push the anti-German button in Poland.

ECONOMY

The pattern of economic development in Poland after World War II was similar in many respects to that in other countries of the area under Soviet domination. But limited natural resources and popular resistance to forced savings resulting in fewer consumer goods slowed the drive to change from a predominantly agricultural economy to one based on industry.

Centralized industrial and economic planning was adopted when the communist regime came to power. Although there were attempts between 1980 and 1989 to reduce the rigidity of central planning, they failed because of opposition from the entrenched bureaucracy. As a result, Poland continued to suffer from a severe housing shortage, high inflation, and the shortage of many consumer goods.

The country faced severe economic difficulties after the collapse of communism in 1989. A major problem was with agriculture. Although about 85% of all land was privately owned under communism,

government policy had always discriminated against the private peasants in an effort to persuade them to join collective farms. There was some modification of this policy over time, but the communist government did not have sufficient funds to pour into agriculture, even if it had wanted to.

The installation of a noncommunist government in 1989 led to a major change in economic policy and a firm commitment to institute a market economy. A dramatic symbol of this change is that the former ruling Communist Party headquarters building was transformed into the stock exchange. Still, by the fall of 1990, a lot of Poles had mixed feelings about the reform. There were clearly some successes. Poland's currency, the zloty, had been stabilized, bringing an end to the currency black market. All over Warsaw, thousands of stalls had been set up where individuals sold a variety of products from farm produce to cassette tapes. Also, store shelves were again full, and people no longer had to stand in line or pay bribes to obtain certain products. On the other side, official statistics of the state-owned sector showed that production had plunged by 25% since communist rule. In addition, strict wage controls had cut the purchasing power of ordinary Poles. On balance, however, Poles expected to benefit eventually, even if there was some pain at the moment.

Privatization

Some Poles criticized the reform because it was going too slowly. Ten months after it had been initiated, not a single large state-owned company had been privatized. Parliament debated such issues as the rights of employees in private companies and

Ex–European Parliament president Jerzy Buzek

whether shares ought to be made available at a discount to employees. Many Poles were also concerned about foreigners coming in and buying everything.

In 1990 the government announced that it would issue shares in seven state-owned companies and make them available to the public for purchase. It took the government four months to prepare the shares. By that time, it had reduced the number of companies being sold to five. When the shares were offered in January 1991, the deadline for purchase had to be extended because there were not enough takers. Another approach to privatization that was discussed was to issue script or coupons to all Polish citizens, who could use them to purchase shares in companies being privatized. Since there were more than 8,000 state-owned companies, privatization would take time.

Poland got some international assistance in 1991, when western nations agreed to forgive 50% of the $33 billion

Za kilka miesięcy, jeśli tak zadecydujecie, Platforma stworzy rząd, który pracuje, a nie obiecuje. Uprościmy podatki i obniżymy je do 15%.
Wprowadzimy „sądy jednego dnia", skazujące chuliganów w trybie 48 godzin.
Zlikwidujemy przywileje władzy.

Kiedy dostajecie kartę do głosowania, władza naprawdę jest w Waszych rękach.
Użyjcie jej w dobrej sprawie.

Proszę Was o głos

Donald TUSK
Człowiek z zasadami

363

Poland

that Poland had borrowed from foreign governments. The United States was even more generous, forgiving 70% of the $3.8 billion debt it held. The government's ability to reduce the deficit in the 1994 budget to 3.9% of GDP triggered the second phase of a 50% reduction in Poland's $33 billion debt to western governments in the Paris Club. It also led to an agreement between Poland and London Club banks. It reduced the $13 billion debt to western private banks by 45%.

These agreements meant that Poland has become a more attractive place for foreign investment, as evidenced by the fact that foreign investment doubled in 1995 to $2.5 billion. Another factor is that the government moved to make the zloty a hard currency in 1995. Foreign investment continued to grow after that time and reached $6.6 billion in 1997, the highest yearly amount for any central European country since the fall of communism. By 2003 France had become the largest foreign investor in Poland, overtaking the United States and Germany. By 2000 over 50% of Poland's banks were owned by foreigners.

Although a significant percentage of industrial establishments remain in state hands, the rapid growth in the number of private enterprises means that the significance of state enterprises in the overall economy is decreasing. A 1996 study indicated that the private sector was by that time responsible for 60% of national output. According to Poland's privatization office, more than 2 million private companies were established between 1989 and 1997. The lack of local capital and the difficulty of getting credit have meant that the majority of private enterprises are in the areas of wholesale and retail trade, services, and handicrafts. The number of private businesses by 2002 showed how vibrant the entrepreneurial spirit is in Poland. There were 2 million registered businesses, 1 for every 19 Poles.

The most popular form of privatization has been through "liquidation." This means that the companies have been sold or leased to their employees. At least 900 larger companies were privatized in this manner. Another method of privatization has been to transform state-owned companies into joint-stock companies, then sell their shares through negotiations with investors or through a public offering. As of October 1994, 124 large-scale enterprises had been sold in this manner. In December 1994, the state drew up its Mass Privatization Program, involving the privatization of 444 of the remaining large state-owned enterprises. Under this plan, 15 national investment funds (NIFs) were set up as joint-stock companies. The 444 enterprises were then turned into joint-stock companies, with their shares distributed to the

**Poland's national poet:
Adam Mickiewicz**

15 NIFs. The NIFs possess all the rights of owners, including the freedom to sell off companies or assets.

There are also companies that the government did not originally expect to be able to privatize, essentially those that were either too big to close or too sick to sell or the industries were located in single-factory towns. Included in this category were Poland's giant steel mills and coal-mines. Although they were run at a loss, these mines met most of Poland's energy needs and provided an additional 20 million tons each year for export.

The Polish government was faced with the need to restructure its coal and steel industries in order to qualify for EU membership. To meet EU requirements, the Polish cabinet adopted a plan on June 30, 1998, for reforming them. It has the EU's biggest coal reserves, and its coal industry is the second-largest in Europe, after Russia's. Some 25,000 mining jobs were eliminated in 1998, and 105,000 (or 40%) were cut by 2002, leaving 142,000 jobs by 2003. The workers received either generous severance payments or a five-year preretirement leave of absence. Coal production, 137 million tons in 1997, dropped to 112 million tons by 2002. In 2002 the government approved a three-year plan for further cuts, closing seven mines and eliminating a further 35,000 jobs as a step toward privatization, but the trade unions successfully blocked these moves.

However, further reduction has its limits, since Poland relies on coal for 60% of its total energy needs and, with lignite pits, over 80% of its electric power station needs. It will continue to rely on coal because any shift to oil and gas would create an unwanted dependency on Russia. Coal miners remain politically influential, and the ruling Law and Justice Party

made much of its promise to protect the industry. However, there is the prospect of a huge shale gas bonanza, which could transform the country's geopolitical position. If the current estimates are correct, the shale could offer centuries of gas supplies at current usage. But since extraction requires fracking, it is controversial.

This fact makes it almost impossible for Poland to meet the greenhouse gas targets set by the EU and the Paris Climate Accord of 2015. In fact, Poland pressured the EU by making its support for the accord conditional on obtaining some recognition that coal was "the foundation" of its development. It relented and ratified the agreement, perhaps realizing that countries are allowed to set their own targets and that the enforcement of the commitments is very weak. It hopes to develop a capacity to build coal-fired plants that will capture greenhouse gasses underground. It has no nuclear power plants, but it has long-range plans to build two of them on the southern shore of the Baltic Sea by 2024 and 2030. These plans could falter on public opposition. A 2011 poll after the Fukushima disaster found 53% of Poles against nuclear power, but by 2014 a majority favored it. An agreement to get nuclear electrical power from Lithuania was stalled, but that remains a future possibility. It worries about its overdependence on Russia's Gazprom, which supplies 80% of its gas imports. The new liquefied natural gas (LNG) terminal in Swinoujscie is expected to alleviate this greatly.

Poland earned its call to fame by proposing and successfully implementing in 1990 a debt-for-environment swap scheme or eco-conversion. It persuaded several major creditors—the US, France, Italy, Norway, Sweden, and Switzerland—that the best form of debt repayment would be to spend the money (over $500 million) on rectifying the country's abysmal environmental situation. Created in 1992 to administer the funds, the EkoFundusz foundation disbursed money for some 1,400 projects, ranging from remediation of air and river pollution to recycling and protection of water supply. In 2016, Poland became the first country in the world to issue a sovereign green bond. Proceeds from the $796 million five-year bond would be invested in "renewable energy, clean transportation, national parks, landfill rehabilitation and afforestation."

Despite the efforts, Poland's record remains spotty at best. The European Commission threatened it with fines for violating EU's clean air laws. The 2016 World Health Organization's report presented a shocking image of the country's air quality: 33 of the 50 most polluted cities in Europe were in Poland, with some cities exceeding EU norms by almost 20 times.

Poland

Insufficient governmental action and especially a heavy reliance on coal are likely to blame. Moving away from using low-quality coal heaters is often too costly for low-income families who would need state subsidies.

The two largest labor unions are Solidarity, which declined to 700,000 members and left politics after its 2001 electoral disaster, and the ex-communist All-Poland Alliance of Trade Unions (OPZZ). Membership in unions had by 2011 plummeted to about 20% of full-time workers. Both were instrumental in creating a strict labor code that is designed to protect those workers with jobs at the expense of those seeking one. One World Bank study concluded that this code is more geared toward lifetime employment in huge state enterprises than toward the 75% of jobs in the private sector. They compel many investors to sign "social packages" that commit them to maintain employment levels for a specified period of time and to pay "privatization bonuses" to employees, generous wage increases, and often special contributions for a variety of causes. One result was a temporary slowdown of foreign investment, which rose sharply in 2004–2005 in the wake of Poland's accession to the EU. Another is high unemployment, which in 2015 had climbed to 11.5% (twice that, 26%, for those between ages 15 and 24 and a 6-year high). The average workweek had declined to 40 hours by 2001.

The Tusk government, which took power in November 2007, planned to privatize hundreds of businesses and to reduce by half the state-owned sector's contribution to the economy from 20% of GDP to 10%. The sell-off would include tourism, publishing, construction, and, most controversially, the struggling shipyards. The European Commission contended that state subsidies to the country's shipyards, amounting to €1.3 billion, violated competition agreements and had to end and be paid back. But in July 2009, it relented by approving a large state-aid program for the famous Gdansk shipyard. Ukraine's Donbass Group agreed to purchase 83% of it. Selling such an icon to a foreign company sickened former Solidarity activists like Wałęsa, who called it "a crime." "No one can sell his mother." Despite this assistance, the Gdansk yards again faced bankruptcy in 2014. The yards at Gdynia and Szczecin were sold to a Caribbean-registered company.

Agriculture

Agriculture did not receive as much government attention as industry because it was always largely in private hands throughout the entire period of communism. Today, however, agriculture has grown in importance. Economists in 2005 estimated that out of 1.8 million Polish farms, 200,000 to 400,000 are large enough to thrive in the EU market. Poland has Europe's smallest farms, averaging only 17 acres, compared with 59 acres in Spain, France, and Germany. In southern Poland, the average farmer owns just 10 acres. From 1996 to 2002, farm incomes fell more than 30%, and that continues for small farmers. EU farm subsidies are not designed for such little agrarians, who cannot afford concrete floors in their barns and special equipment for slaughtering and milking. Fewer than 20% of rural Poles live off their own farms. Total EU subsidies amounted to €40 billion from 2007 to 2013 and another €42.4 billion for 2014 to 2020.

EU membership alleviated the situation, even though EU farm subsidies were phased in over a 10-year period, starting at 25% of existing EU levels. Ninety percent of Polish farmers applied for the EU's direct payments. Only two-thirds of support payments come from Brussels; the Polish treasury must pay the rest. In the meantime, the main sources of income for more than half of all farm workers are state benefits or jobs in the underground economy. But the EU market and subsidies are creating a rural boom for the 200,000 to 400,000 farmers with larger plots of land, who are gearing up to function in a modern economy.

After joining the EU, demand for Polish produce soared, generating a threefold increase in farm exports. Farm output has climbed 10%. The average Polish agriculture worker saw his income jump by 73% in 2004. Some are making unprecedented profits. Formerly the most skeptical of the EU, farmers are now among its most ardent supporters.

Agriculture and related industries account for only 3.4% of Poland's GDP by 2015, even though farming employs 12.4% of the population. By comparison, 57% of Poles work in the services sector, which produces 65% of GDP, and 32% are employed in industry, creating 32% of the nation's wealth. Poland has more than twice as many farmers as Germany and France combined. Acknowledging the significance of these statistics, the Ministry of Agriculture recommended a "massive reduction" in the rural workforce. Many consolidate their land or slowly disappear from

The Wawel Cathedral of Krakow, Poland. Pope John Paul II was once archbishop here.
Photo by Miller B. Spangler

Poland

farming. The total number of farms has dropped from 4 million at the time communism collapsed to 1.4 million by 2013.

In an economic sense, Poland is becoming two nations. The gap in living standards between the fifth of the population living in villages or farms and their more affluent countrymen in the cities is widening. Life in the countryside is getting richer, as is the whole country—87% of rural families now have cars, 80% washing machines, and 62% computers. But their incomes are still about 30% below urban levels, and 17% live in poverty, compared with 7% in the cities.

As inequality grows, so does crime. Only a tenth of all university students are from rural areas. A further gap is developing between Poles in the western part of the country, who are being pulled more closely to Germany, and those in the eastern part, who trade with economically desperate Belarus and Ukraine, with which the EU rejects visa-free travel. The income difference between Poles on the one hand and Belarusians and Ukrainians on the other is larger than between Poles and Germans and is growing. Poland's economic eyes are focused on the west. Three-fourths of its trade is with the EU and only a tenth is with former Soviet republics. Germany alone accounts for over a fourth of its exports and imports.

Current Economic Situation

While the transition to a market economy has been successful, the current economic picture is mixed. Although it was not hit as hard as others in the region by the global economic downturn of 2008–2009, and its economy kept growing during the crisis, its economy was jolted because its EU trading partners were in trouble: 76% of its exports go to them, and 67.7% of its imports come from them. It was helped by the fact that its economy is not as export-dependent (40%) as many smaller countries because it has a larger domestic market. Also, it has a strong and stable government. A timely $20.5 billion credit line from the IMF in April 2009 helped stabilize Poland's banks and halt the zloty's loss of almost half its value. It experienced no housing bubble.

The economy grew at more than 5% annually throughout the 1990s and continued at 4% annually since joining the EU in 2004. In 2022, after a few sluggish years, it was still growing by 4.9%. Poland's relatively large domestic market also means that it is not as vulnerable when western European partners fall into recession. Productivity increased by 7.7% in 2005, up from 4.1% a year earlier. Labor costs are low by western European standards. Its average hourly wage costs are €7 ($9.10), compared with over €29 in

Germany. Combined with rising productivity, it is exporting well, especially its automotive industry. For example, Fiat Poland is the largest contributor to the export surge, and 90% of the Pandas produced in Poland are exported.

Inflation ran at a red-hot 35% in 1993 but had declined to 10.4% by 2023. It was easy to be a millionaire in Poland when bank bills were denominated as high as 1 million and 2 million zloty. Once hyperinflation was brought under control, a denomination process in 1995 reduced the number of zeros by four, making financial transactions more manageable and the currency (now formally called the new zloty—PLN) more respectable. The zloty soared in value and temporarily became one of the world's strongest currencies. It declined during the global recession and continues to be subject to rapid swings in value. The government is required to join the eurozone but not while the common currency is in crisis. While 80% favored EU membership in 2013, only 30% wanted to adopt the euro. Adoption would require a change in Poland's constitution. The Tusk government made a gamble in 2013 by opening the door to a future referendum on the euro's adoption. Since two-thirds oppose it and a constitutional change would be required, its introduction is unlikely in the immediate future. President Duda strongly advocates against it, too.

Unemployment had declined to 5.2% in 2023. It is double that among youth. This is why so many (2 million) moved west to find work, especially in Britain and Ireland. They send home remittances, worth €9 billion in 2010. More than half returned home. To stimulate foreign investment, the government lowered the top corporate tax rate to 19%.

Since communism's fall in 1989, Poland has increased its number of students fivefold. Almost 60% of 18- to 24-year-olds attend university. Never before in history have Poles been so well educated and multilingual. This has made Poland an alluring place to locate servicing centers for companies' European operations. Per-capita GDP has risen from 43% of the EU average to 63% in 2014. The government ran a 7.9% budget deficit in 2010, but it lowered that to 2.9% in 2023. The public debt was 55% of GDP in 2014. By law the government must introduce spending cuts if it exceeds 55%.

In a 2005 ranking of competitive economies in the world conducted by the Swiss-based International Institute for Management Development, Poland placed 57th out of 60 countries studied because of inefficiency in government and business. The report cited inconsistency in taking political decisions, protectionism, and legal barriers for business. It was singled

out as having the worst telecommunication system of all countries compared, and flight connections are poor. The report concluded that in domestic enterprises employees are unmotivated, managers are unreliable, marketing is inefficient, and there appear to be no ethics in business. In 2015 the World Bank placed Poland 25th in a global ranking of places to do business. Transparency International ranked it 30th best in terms of corruption.

Increasing prosperity is visible, especially in Warsaw and other larger cities. The consumption of durable goods like home appliances and cars has grown impressively. For instance, the number of cars for each 1,000 people has jumped from 139 in 1990 to 580 in 2011, and the proportion of late-model automobiles has increased dramatically. Unfortunately, they drive on some of Europe's worst roads; only 3% of them meet EU rules. Poland had only 186 miles (300 km) of interstate highways, none near Warsaw. In 2011 a new stretch of interstate highway, called the A2, was opened between the outskirts of Warsaw and the German border. A further 92 kilometers has to be built to connect Warsaw to the highway. A quarter of the rail track is judged to be substandard to carry the debt-ridden state railway, PKP.

The infant mortality rate, an important indicator of overall standard of living, was halved in the course of the 1990s to 9 per 1,000 live births and now stands at 5. Poland has one of the EU's lowest fertility rates, with the average woman having only 1.3 children. Life expectancy has risen to 73 years for men and 81 for women. To try to deal with the aging population, the Civic Platform government stopped early retirements and started gradually to raise the retirement age to 67, not only for men, but also for women, 65% of whom are in the workforce. This meant that men had to work two more years and women seven. Reversing this new law became a crucial electoral promise of the conservative Law and Justice Party, and once it won a majority in the parliament, its government returned the retirement age to 65 for men and 60 for women, effective in late 2017. This move reduced the number of people in the workforce, and the government estimated its cost to be over $9.6 billion over four years, or about 2.2% of GDP. While the law is popular, especially among the rural population, many economists worry about its impact on economic growth and the budget deficit. The international ratings agency Moody's warned that, by 2060, "there will be approximately two pensioners for every three working-age persons in Poland," up from the current 1:5 ratio. With a per-capita GDP of over $25,000 in 2014, Poles were nearly six times wealthier on average than they had been at the end of the communist era. GDP per capita in 2015 was 67% of the EU average, compared with only 33% in 1989. Never before have Poles been as wealthy in comparison to western European standards.

Warsaw is in the midst of major expansion, with new ring roads, mass transit, and bridges being built to relieve traffic jams. A 54-story apartment complex, designed by Polish-born Daniel Libeskind, rises in the center of the city. It challenges the ugly Palace of Culture and Science, a weird wedding-cake monstrosity the Russians built after the war to honor Stalin.

Poland's economy is evolving with the times. Gdansk, well-known for its expansive but aging shipbuilding industry, is quickly becoming a new outsourcing hotspot, as a growing number of international corporations vie for its technology- savvy university graduates. Service centers accounted for some 30% of the city's economy in 2016. In Krakow, closing down of some heavily polluting industrial plants was partly offset by an influx of software companies, including Google, IBM, and Motorola, attracted to the city's output of software engineers.

The political battle over control of mass media and the Constitutional Tribunal took on an economic meaning in January 2016, when Standard and Poor's downgraded Poland's credit rating from A- to BBB+, citing threats to the constitutional framework of the country. The move could increase the government's costs of borrowing, and the value of the Polish zloty fell to the lowest point in four years.

European Union

Poland's economic hopes hinge on its 2004 accession to the European Union. The significance of Poland lies in its very size. It alone accounts for nearly half of the GDP of central and eastern Europe and for 40% of the GDP of all 10 EU accession states. At 38 million, its population is larger than all of the other accession states combined. It is the EU's sixth-largest member in terms of population and has the club's seventh-largest economy. It is the largest net recipient of EU funds for modernization: €67 billion ($88 billion) in the seven years to 2013. About $142 billion in the EU's 2014–2020 budget is earmarked for Poland. The resulting infrastructure alters the old image of a backward country. Because of its size and sense of history, Poland was determined that it be recognized from the beginning as a "big country" whose influence will be felt in the club. Thus, the negotiations between Brussels and Warsaw were detailed and hard.

Two-thirds of Polish respondents in 2001 had said they feared they would be "second-class" EU members for years after entering. They were realistic in recogniz-ing that economic costs would outweigh benefits in the short term. Poles felt hurt by the EU's insistence that there must be a transition period of seven years before they are allowed to work freely within the EU area; that was lifted in May 2011. They were allowed to work in Britain and Ireland, and by 2006 an estimated 300,000 worked in the former and another 100,000 in the latter. Of a total of 2 million who had left since Poland joined the EU in 2004, half later returned home.

The sale of Polish land to foreigners is a very delicate and emotional matter. Because Poland was repeatedly invaded in the past, Poles were nervous about losing their land to rich, peaceful invaders from the west; that fear is strongest in western and northern Poland, especially given the fact that land is about a tenth of the price in Germany. The government was able to negotiate a waiting period of seven years for the sale of land in northern and western Poland, which were once mainly German territories, and three years in the rest of the country.

On June 7–8, 2003, Poles nervously engaged in a two-day referendum on their country's entry. The constitution requires that at least 50% of registered voters participate in order for the voting to be valid. The results were an overwhelming victory for those who see Poland's future in the EU—with 59.6% turning out to vote, 78% said yes. Turnout was highest in large cities like Warsaw, where authorities offered free museum tickets to dissuade people from leaving during the weekend. The no votes came from ultraconservative Catholics worried about an erosion of traditional Polish values and from those farmers who realized that the country's 2 million subsistence farms would disappear when faced with EU competition.

The Catholic Church was given credit for enlarging the turnout through a pastoral letter from the pope that was read in churches across the country on the Sunday of the referendum calling on Poles to vote in favor. Pope John Paul II called membership "an act of historic justice." He added, "Poland can make a contribution with its moral and spiritual values and its religious convictions." Indeed, the government said it would insist that the EU's new constitution make reference to "Christian values," not merely to the "Greco-Roman civilization and the Enlightenment," which appeared in the preamble. It had to back down on that issue, as well as nearly equal voting rights as twice-larger Germany. A jubilant President Kwasniewski proclaimed, "We have returned to the European family!"

Like most other new members of the EU, Poland was fearful that countries like Germany and France would be in-creasingly driven by national rather than European interests. But the Justice and Law (PiS) government that took office in October 2005 and then a new president, Lech Kaczynski (1949—2010), introduced a significant shift in policy toward the EU by taking a strongly nationalistic and Euroskeptic turn itself.

That changed noticeably when Donald Tusk became prime minister in 2007. The tactics of the former Kaczynski government had tarnished Poland's reputation within the EU. Critics had argued that Poles were unwilling to play the delicate and intricate game of compromise and diplomacy on which the EU is based. The Tusk government changed that. Partly as a reward, the European Parliament in July 2009 elected former prime minister Jerzy Buzek as its president for a two-and-a-half-year term. He became the first eastern European politician to occupy one of the EU's high-profile posts.

On July 1, 2011, Poland assumed the six-month revolving presidency of the EU's Council of Ministers. It had high hopes of elevating its profile in Europe and deepening relations with the EU's eastern borderlands. But the euro crisis dominated the EU during that time. Since Poland is not in the eurozone, it found that it had little influence in that regard. On the other hand, it was making its mark elsewhere. In October 2014, Prime Minister Kopacz managed to persuade fellow EU members to reduce their ambitious targets for energy efficiency and renewable energy from 30% by 2030 to 27%, reflecting Poland's reliance on coal. Coal provides 70% of Poland's electricity. That is projected to fall to 11% by 2040. Later that year, Donald Tusk became president of the European Council, among the most prestigious positions in the European Union.

Warsaw hosts the headquarters of FRONTEX, the EU border control agency. Poland objects to plans to replace it with a stronger entity to handle migrant issues, since it fears a possible loss of sovereignty.

The massive migrant crisis of 2015 put an enormous pressure on the European Union as its leaders scrambled to find humanitarian solutions that would also be acceptable to their citizens. On September 22, 2015, the Council of the European Union adopted a scheme to relocate 120,000 asylum seekers from Greece, Hungary, and Italy by distributing them over two years among 22 member states. Initially Poland opposed the plan, but it relented in the face of significant pressures, abandoning its regional partners the Czech Republic, Hungary, Romania, and Slovakia that were outvoted and forced to adopt it. PiS objected to the plan, and by April 2016, Poland's deputy foreign minister declared the whole idea "dead."

Poland

The electoral victory of PiS had a cooling effect on Poland's relations with the EU. One of the first decisions of the new prime minister was to remove the flag of the European Union from her press conference hall. In January 2016, the European Commission started a formal rule-of-law investigation, and in April the European Parliament passed a resolution that expressed serious concern over the "effective paralysis" of Poland's Constitutional Tribunal that "endangers democracy, human rights and the rule of law." The EP president, Martin Schultz, compared Law and Justice's moves to a "coup d'etat," which provoked demands for an apology. The Modern Party spokeswoman warned, "by not respecting European values, PiS is ensuring that we will first find ourselves on the fringes of the European Union, and then outside of it."

In March 2017, the PiS government attempted to retaliate by voting against the reelection of Donald Tusk, the Polish president of the European Council and a former rival of Jaroslaw and Lech Kaczynski. Irate over Tusk's criticism of the government's policies, Poland was the only country among the 28 members to oppose him. Tusk was widely seen as the right candidate for EU's tricky and potentially bruising negotiations over Brexit. Facing the defeat, Poland's foreign minister reiterated his party's claim, "We know now that [the EU] is a union under Berlin's diktat."

In mid-2017, the European Commission initiated infringement proceedings against Poland, Czech Republic, and Hungary for refusing to accept migrants as part of the EU redistribution scheme. EU migration commissioner Dimitris Avramopoulos, stated that "relocation is not a choice. It is a moral commitment. It is a legal decision, with legal obligations agreed collectively, which has to be carried out collectively, without exceptions."

CULTURE

Ever since Poland regained its independence in 1918, successive governments have accorded respect to cultural endeavors. This tradition may have its roots in the fact that, in the 19th century, when there was no independent Poland, culture, particularly literary works, provided an important bond of national unity, in spite of the partition of the country among several empires. Eager to win the support of intellectuals, the communists provided lavish government subsidies for various cultural programs.

Moreover, rigid insistence on "socialist realism" was never as strong in Poland as it was in the Soviet Union, even during the time of Stalin. This permitted greater intellectual experimentation than elsewhere in the Soviet orbit. In the post-Stalin period, a cry for greater freedom and a more humane form of socialism originated in Polish literary circles among writers who considered themselves to be loyal communists but who insisted they had the right to describe things as they were—sordid and often heartbreaking. This was in stark contrast to the cheerful distortions of fact by party propaganda.

The Poem for Adults by the communist writer Adam Wazyk, published in 1955, heralded the beginning of the "thaw" in cultural as well as political relations. The party denounced this wave of writing as "revisionist." It was eventually suppressed, as were the publications and free-discussion groups created by students. The politically less controversial fields of graphic arts and music continued to flourish. At least one composer of the younger generation, Krzysztof Penderecki, achieved international fame with his "Passion According to St. Luke."

Poland has produced four Nobel Prize laureates in literature, beginning with Henryk Sienkiewicz in 1905 and Wladyslaw Reymont in 1925. In 2005 the third laureate was Czeslaw Milosz. He had briefly worked for the communist government after the war, accepting plum diplomatic posts in Washington and Paris. But he defected in 1951 and became a professor at the University of California in Berkeley, where he continued to write in Polish. After the collapse of communism, he returned to Krakow. He won his Nobel Prize in 1980 for poems focusing on the complex moral problems of the 20th century. His *The Captive Mind*, published in 1953, is a prose attack on writers like himself, who collaborated with totalitarian rule. Fellow Nobel Prize winner Wislawa Szymborska (1996), who renounced communism in 1957 and later supported Solidarity, said of him, "After a long and fruitful life Czeslaw Milosz has joined the ranks of our greatest poets, among whom he had assured himself a place long ago." Poland tends to make romantic heroes of its poets, but Szymborska was little known abroad until she died in 2012. Her last book to be translated was published in the US under the title *Here*.

Under communism, official statistics stressed the numerical growth of cultural institutions. Poland boasted of 10 philharmonic orchestras, 9 symphony orchestras, and 3 musical ensembles associated with the state-run radio network. No name stands out more boldly in the music world than Frederic (Fryderyk) Chopin, whose 200th birth anniversary was celebrated in 2010. The government invested $100 million in refurbishing sites associated with his life, such as his birthplace at Zelazowa Wola, located 50 kilometers (30 miles) from Warsaw. It created a multimedia museum in a palace in central Warsaw. Chopin left for France in 1830, just before the November Uprising against the Russian occupiers.

Polish theater and cinema always tended to do well in terms of international recognition. They continued to enjoy official support under the communists. The works of Slawomir Mrozek are well known in the west, as well as in Poland. In 2012 *In Darkness*, a touching film about a sewer worker who helped Jews escape during the Nazi occupation of Lwow (now Lviv in Ukraine), was nominated for an Oscar as best foreign-language film. Film director Andrzej Wajda won numerous international awards, including an honorary Oscar for lifetime achievement. Krzysztof Kieslowski is listed among Europe's most influential and analyzed film directors.

Education was traditionally based on a system of eight years of compulsory primary schooling, followed by secondary general and technical schools, which about 75% of the elementary school graduates attended. Access to universities and specialized institutes of higher learning was controlled by entrance examinations. Although the percentage of students going to institutions of higher learning was much higher under communism than it had been in the 1930s, it was still much lower than comparable figures for western Europe. As in the Soviet Union and other communist-governed nations, there was particular stress on the hard sciences and less on humanistic subjects, which were considered less "relevant" to the regime. About half of the students were children of white-collar workers. Only 17.7% were the sons and daughters of peasants.

By 2010 much had changed in Polish education. A third of the 500,000 students in higher education attend one of 325 private universities, all opened since 1989 to meet the pent-up demand for education. They are of widely varying quality. Business schools especially have boomed. Sixty percent of students pay for their own studies. Two-thirds of professors have more than one teaching job, and this fact often adversely affects their help to students.

University education is one of democratic Poland's greatest successes. More Poles are getting it than ever before. In 1988 only 6.5% of Poles had a degree, but by 2014 that had climbed to 27%. The Ministry of Higher Education adopted a plan to create a group of elite universities with more funding. By 2010, 25 out of 106 public universities were receiving 84% of the funding. The premier universities remain the Jagiellonian University in Krakow and the University of Warsaw, and their graduates are well represented among the political and economic elites. For example,

Poland's President Duda, Prime Minister Szydlo, and one deputy prime minister, Jaroslaw Gowin, have all attended the Jagiellonian University.

One development arising out of the declaration of martial law in December 1981 was the growth of an underground culture. Many cultural workers refused to collaborate with the regime and turned to underground publishing. Novels and short-story collections were published unofficially during this period and then hawked from door to door. Some became underground bestsellers. Art shows were held in apartment houses and churches. There were even underground cabarets. Some media, such as film, do not lend themselves to such a culture, however, and they suffered.

Most educated Poles read one of two main national newspapers. *Gazeta Wyborcza* (Electoral Gazette) was created in May 1989 to help Solidarity defeat the communists. It has always seen itself as an ideological warrior for the kind of liberal-democratic regime that Poland has developed into. Its circulation of 400,000 is declining, but it remains the largest of any serious newspaper and gets 40% of the newspaper advertising market. *Rzeczpospolita* is a daily owned by the government and Mecom of Britain. Its slant has moved to the right to capture disgruntled readers.

With the installation of Poland's first noncommunist government in 1989, all of this began to change. The old proscriptions and prohibitions were removed, and artists became free to write and publish what they liked, at least insofar as the government was concerned. Commercial considerations have since become important, however. Not everybody likes the new literature catering to popular tastes that has begun to appear. But almost no one wants to go back to the old system of state control.

Religion

Religion has always played an important role in Polish life, usually as a unifying force. About 95% of all Poles classify themselves as Roman Catholics, and 41% and declining attend mass regularly (down from 55% in 1987). Half that many attend in large cities, such as Warsaw and Krakow. Under communism, the church actually prospered, and Poland was one of the few countries in the world where the number of persons becoming priests and nuns actually increased. As of the early 1990s, Poland had 24,678 priests, up from 20,234 in 1980. That was a ratio of 1 priest for every 1,280 church members, compared to 1 priest for every 1,650 church members in the United States. The average age of a Polish priest is 45, compared with 65 in the EU. In addition, more than 1,000

church and other religious buildings have been constructed in Poland since 1985.

Seminaries were once full, and 1,000 Polish priests served flocks in Germany. However, as secularization grows, interest in becoming a priest, monk, or nun has declined noticeably. In 2004 there were 2,178 in their first year of religious studies; by 2008 that number had declined by 37% to only 1,382. Nevertheless, Poland is the only country in Europe that produces enough priests for its own need. A fourth of all European Catholic priests being trained are Polish.

Undoubtedly the fact that Pope John Paul II was Polish played a role in this. His photograph was to be seen almost everywhere: over shop doors, on placards hanging from rear-view mirrors in automobiles, and on key chains. After John Paul II's death in April 2005, the country was deprived of its most powerful unifying force. Ex-president Kwasniewski said, "He helped us maintain a good opinion about ourselves—sometimes maybe too good an opinion—that we are important." In April 2014 John Paul II was made a saint. The conservative approach to Catholicism of "the Polish pope" is generally shared by the church hierarchy in the country. It contrasts with the approach of Pope Francis, but this did not affect the warm reception he received while visiting Poland in 2016. His open-air mass near Krakow attracted a crowd of 1.5 million.

There was a close connection between Solidarity and the Catholic Church during the 1980s. The church acted as an island of freedom encompassing believers and nonbelievers alike. It was therefore not surprising that one of the first things the new noncommunist government did was to reinstate religious instruction in the schools. The church regained most of its property confiscated by the communists.

Now the church often divides Poles. It has found that the people do not share its positions in many cases. The most important one is abortion, long legal in Poland under communism. In 1990, the church launched a campaign to ban all abortions, and this severely divided the country. In spite of the late Pope John Paul II's personal intervention, polls continued to show that a majority of Poles favor continuation of abortion, at least under specific circumstances.

The legislature began debate on the issue of abortion in 1991. The bill it considered at that time would have barred it in all cases and set a jail term for anyone who performed or had one. That was too strong for parliament, and it refused to take any action. When Pope John Paul II visited Poland in June 1991, he brought up the issue again. Because of this continued church pressure, the Polish Congress of

Physicians adopted a new medical code in 1992 that effectively prohibited physicians from performing abortions except if the mother's life is in danger or if she was raped or if the baby has certain grave genetic defects. This was written into law in 1993 when the Sejm passed a bill setting restrictions on abortion.

The constitution, approved in May 1997, would have legalized abortion again. However, an appeal to the Polish Constitutional Court produced a ruling that the constitution's invoking of God as the "source of truth, justice, goodness and beauty" meant that abortions were illegal. Other potential church-state controversies are over pornography censorship, divorce, contraception, in vitro fertilization, the LGBTQ community and same-sex marriage, all areas where the Church's position is considerably more conservative and restrictive than what exists today in Polish society. Given the dramatic changes in that society, these are, in a sense, societal quarrels rather than strictly church-and-state disputes. This trend was strengthened by the death in 2005 of John Paul II. The Tusk government announced that it would "not kneel before priests."

The society is moving steadily toward a more secular view of life that includes greater separation of church and state and the rejection of church mandates on individual morality. Approximately 95% of all Poles are baptized Roman Catholic and identify themselves as Catholic. However, only 70% believe in heaven, according to a 2009 poll. Just 41% practice their faith regularly by attending mass most Sundays, and that figure is falling. Nevertheless, in contrast to most other European countries, Polish churches seem full. Masses are still often standing room only.

Perhaps the most extreme Catholic views are expressed on Radio Maryja, which has a newspaper, *Nasz Dziennik*. Appealing to less-educated Poles, the nuns in this operation oppose abortion and the EU. Church officials oppose this group, but it still has some political clout.

In 2016, a Catholic grassroots initiative promoted by the church proposed a complete ban on abortion except to save mother's life. Once Jaroslaw Kaczynski and ex-prime minister Szydlo expressed their support for the proposal, a flood of public protest brought thousands of people into the streets. The law of 1993 already is one of the most restrictive abortion laws in Europe. Crowds of protesters, especially young women, demonstrated by brandishing wire coat hangers, symbolic of illegal and dangerous back-alley abortions such a law would likely provoke. Borrowing a page from their Irish counterparts, many also flooded the prime minister's social media account with detailed reports

Poland

of their menstrual cycles, lampooning her stated interest in women's health.

In October 2016, another wave of mass demonstrations ensued, with thousands of women (and men) dressed in black marching through the streets and chanting, "My womb, my choice." Many businesses and offices were closed on "Black Monday," when women went on strike to protest the ban. Foreign Minister Witold Waszczykowski dismissed the protest: "Let them have fun. They should go ahead if they think there are no bigger problems in Poland." Yet, in the end, PiS backed away from the idea and instructed its deputies to vote down the bill. It is unlikely that the issue will disappear.

Poland has one of Europe's lowest fertility rates: 1.4. It also must deal with sexual abuse scandals involving priests. Three-fourths of Poles believe the church should tackle pedophilia openly.

CURRENT ISSUES

Poland under any government has demonstrated that it intends to be a leader, not a follower, among European nations. The Civic Platform government sought to do this without irritating its EU partners. It was conciliatory in tone, although it remained determined to press for Poland's interests in concrete ways. Despite its often-fiery rhetoric and very different perspective on many aspects of domestic and foreign policy, Law and Justice was unlikely to disengage from the European Union. Jaroslaw Kaczynski declared in May 2016 that "today, being in Europe means being in the EU." To be sure, his reasoning may be different than Civic Platform's. "We want to be a member of the European Union, because we want to have an influence on Europe's fate. But our position depends above all on our strength. We have to gain a strong position, become a strong, European nation," he added.

Not only that Poland is being changed by EU membership in the long run, but to some extent the reverse is also true. Poles are more patriotic, religious, and family-oriented than western Europeans. Their reluctance to accept refugees of different ethnic backgrounds, initially seen as disloyal to other member states, became the norm rather than exception throughout the EU. Arguably, for the first time in decades, Poland is a player, not a playground, for European diplomacy. Still, EU's grave concern with the political changes in Poland started in 2015 put the country under much international scrutiny and often scorn. Donald Tusk's elevated position in the EU gave Poland some clout, but his criticism of PiS's domestic policies provoked the PiS government's failed attempt at voting down Tusk's candidacy for reelection as president of the European Council in 2017. The bad blood between the two largest parties spills over into foreign policy.

Brexit provided an important challenge to the Polish government. Among the thorniest issues is the fate of more than 850,000 Poles residing in the UK, who have already experienced a wave of ethnic taunts, discrimination, and vandalized cars and might be pressured to leave. Some $1.2 billion of remittances sent to Poland annually are also at stake. Poland's adamant support for free movement of people is difficult to reconcile with its traditionally strong ties to Britain, for whom that freedom was the principal reason for leaving the EU.

Just as it is fighting for the rights of its citizens abroad, Poland attempts to prevent Syrian and more broadly Asian and African migrants from settling in the country. Cognizant of the need to find some replacement for the 2 million Poles working and living abroad, Poland is far more accommodating toward European migrants. In particular, about 1.3 million temporary work permits were issued in 2016 to Ukrainians, almost none of whom were political refugees.

Russia's land seize in Ukraine has strengthened traditional distrust of Poles toward Russia. Thousands of young people joined patriotic paramilitary groups. The Polish government stated that Poland cannot be safe if Ukraine is unstable; it devoted considerable attention to its eastern neighbor's tribulations and pushed for its closer relations with the EU. Poland remains a strong supporter of economic sanctions against Russia, even though its farmers suffer greatly from the loss of income due to Russia's countermeasures.

The combined challenges of Brexit, the uncertainty over the future role of the EU, the Russian threats, and the realignment of the American foreign policy add to a sense of instability that Poland faces both domestically and internationally. The credit ratings agency Moody's, worried about the economic impact of the pension reform, noted that "concurrent with the ongoing constitutional crisis and tensions with the European Union, this counter-reform reflects a shift in policymaking toward less-predictable and less-orthodox measures that have been associated with the PiS government elected in October 2015."

Despite the tensions both abroad and at home, PiS remained popular within Poland. This positive feeling was sustained by its extravagant welfare policies, especially generous child subsidies. That put PiS in a favorable position in the parliamentary elections held in November 2023. Nevertheless, despite the fact that the United Right alliance got a majority of votes, it fell short of a Sejm majority. The opposition, consisting of the Civic Coalition, Third Way, and The Left, achieved a combined total vote of 54%, and managed to form a majority coalition government. After the elections, the coalition proposed Donald Tusk as its candidate for prime minister. Tusk's cabinet was sworn in on December 13, 2023. In the Senate also, the opposition electoral alliance Senate Pact 2023 won a plurality of the vote and a majority of seats. In these elections the voter turnout was 74.4%, the highest in contested elections, beating previous records set in 1989 and 2019.

Czech Republic (Česká republika /Czechia)

Charles Bridge over the Vltava River, Prague

Area: 30,452 sq. mi. (78,871 sq. km).

Population: 10,827,529 (2023 estimate)

Capital City: Prague (pop. 1,357,326; 2023 estimate).

Climate: It is temperate, transitional between the oceanic (maritime) and continental climate types with warm summers and cold, cloudy and snowy winters. The temperature difference between summer and winter is due to the landlocked geographical position of the country. The average annual temperatures range from 90 °F (32 °C) in July to as low as 0 °F (−17 °C) during February.

Neighboring Countries: Germany (west); Poland (northeast); Slovakia (southeast); Austria (south).

Official Language: Czech.

Other Languages: Slovak, German.

Ethnic Background: 57.3% Czechs, 3.4% Moravians, 0.9% Slovaks, 0.7% Ukrainians, 6.1% other, 31.6% not stated (2021 estimate)

Religion: 11.7% Christianity (9.3% Catholicism, 2.4% other Christian) 1.2% other, 56.9% no religion, 30.1% unanswered (2021 estimate)

Form of Government: Unitary parliamentary republic

Chief of State: Petr Pavel, President of the Republic (January 2023).

Head of Government: Petr Fiala, Prime Minister (November 2021).

National Flag: It consists of two equal horizontal bands of white (at the top) and red with a blue isosceles triangle (or chevron) based on the hoist side. The colors are both symbolic and historic. White and red are the traditional colors of the Czech lands originating from an 1192 Bohemian coat of arms, while blue is the traditional color of Slovakia. After the establishment of an independent Czechoslovakia in 1918, the flag was adopted in 1920. Upon the dissolution of Czechoslovakia in 1992, the Czech Republic kept the Czechoslovak flag while Slovakia adopted a new one. As to symbolism, according to unofficial interpretation, the white represents purity and peace; the red represents courage, hardiness in war and the blood of the patriots shed for the freedom of homeland; and the blue stability, responsibility, and vision.

Public Holidays: January 1 (Restoration Day of the Independent Czech State), September 28 (Statehood Day), October

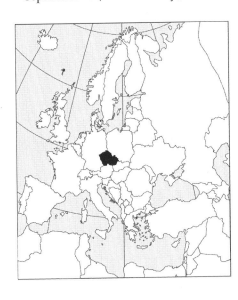

Czech Republic

28 (Foundation of the Czechoslovak Republic in 1918).
Currency: Czech koruna (crown) ((CZK)).
Main Exports: Machinery and transportation equipment.
Main Imports: Machinery and transportation equipment.
Main Trading Partners: Germany (30.1% of exports and 21.5% of imports), Slovakia (10.1% of exports and 4.8% of imports), Poland (7.0% of exports and 8.8% of imports), China (12.9% of imports), Russia (5.8 of imports), France (4.8% of exports) Austria (4.5 of exports). (2022)

Bohemia and Moravia, ca. 1360

Among the countries in central Europe that underwent the difficult transition from decades of communist régime, this land began with a head start. Between the wars its well-educated people lived for 20 years in a successful democratic experiment and enjoyed the highest prosperity in the region. Its democratic lamp flickered for three years after World War II, but then the lights went out. Thanks to the courage of such free men as Vaclav Havel, who refused to live a lie, to a different kind of Soviet leader after 1985, and to the decay of the communist state at home, a "Velvet Revolution" peacefully swept away the ruins of communism, and freedom was rekindled.

The Czech Republic is in a period of self-examination in other respects, as well. Before 1989 many important Czech questions could not be discussed openly; they were "on ice." Before 1939 it was part of a multi-cultural country, with many Germans, Jews, and Hungarians, in addition to Czechs and Slovaks. Now it is smaller, more homogeneous and provincial. Czechs have just begun to question their country's policy before and during World War II, and a passionate controversy has erupted over the circumstances surrounding the 1948 communist takeover.

It is the modern successor state to that ancient region known as Bohemia and Moravia. Most of the countryside consists of rolling hills, except for the Sudeten Mountains in the north, where individual peaks rise to over 5,000 feet. Although most of the land is suitable for cultivation, there are extensive forest areas, the largest being the Bohemian Forest, located in the west, along the border with Germany.

It is today almost exclusively inhabited by ethnic Czechs, except for a tiny remnant of German speakers in the western part of the country, left after the mass expulsions that followed World War II. In addition, the dissolution of the Czech and Slovak Federal Republic in January 1993 left approximately 300,000 Slovaks living in the Czech Republic. Most of these are people from rural parts of Slovakia who

came west seeking employment. They are mainly found in industrial areas in the eastern part of the Czech Republic.

Political Status: Part of the Austro-Hungarian Empire until 1918 (ruled from Vienna); part of Czechoslovak Republic, 1918–1938; part of Nazi Germany, 1939–1945 (incorporated into the Third Reich as Bohemia and Moravia); part of Communist-influenced Czechoslovak Republic, 1945–1948; communist state, 1948–1989; part of democratic Czech and Slovak Federal Republic, 1990–1992.

HISTORY

Ancient Kingdoms

In the early centuries of the Christian era, a subgroup of the Slavs, subsequently known as the West Slavs, settled in the area to the south of the Carpathian and Sudeten Mountains and along the Vltava and Danube Rivers. According to the Frankish chronicle of Fredegar (*The Chronicle of Fredegar*), a Frankish trader named Samo organized them into a unified state at the beginning of the 7th century. This collapsed at Samo's death in 658, however, and the West Slavs reverted back to their tribal organization. It was not until the 9th century that the West Slavs were again brought together under a single government with the establishment of the Moravian Empire.

It was also at about this time that Christianity was introduced into the area. The first missionaries were Roman Catholic monks, and they came mainly from Germany. The language they used for church services was Latin. Somewhat later, the Moravian king, learning of missionary efforts among the South Slavs, requested missionaries from Constantinople.

Two young monks, Cyril and Methodius, came to Moravia and, following Eastern Orthodox practices, began teaching the Slavs in their own language. In the process, they developed a script, later known as Cyrillic, to write the Slavic language.

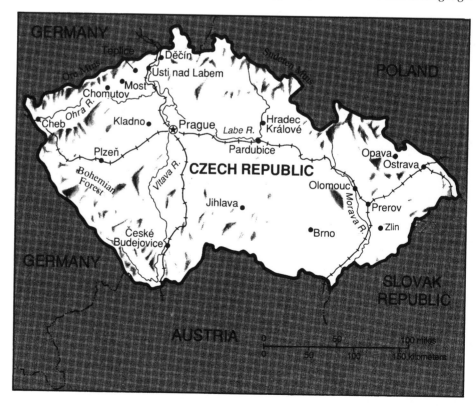

Cyrillic eventually became the basis for the written languages of the eastern and southern Slavs, though for historical reasons not of the Czechs. The reason is that, although the two brothers had great success in converting the people, they were ultimately unable to supplant the western missionaries backed by Rome. After Methodius's death in 885, the Latin form of Catholicism became predominant, and the area came under the sway of Rome. As a result, written Czech uses Roman rather than Cyrillic characters.

At the end of the 9th century, the Moravian Empire came under attack from groups of Magyar (Hungarian) peoples moving into the area from the east. According to Czech historians, the Magyars drove a wedge between the western and southern Slavs and also separated the Czechs from the Slovaks. In the process, the Moravian Empire disintegrated. By the beginning of the 10th century, the center of Czech development had moved westward into Bohemia, while the Slovak lands began a 1,000-year period under the Hungarian crown.

The old Moravian Empire was replaced by the kingdom of Bohemia, ruled by the princes of the Premyslid dynasty, who became powerful in the 10th century. One of the members of this family was the legendary "Good King Wenceslas" (also known as St. Wenceslas). He was murdered by his

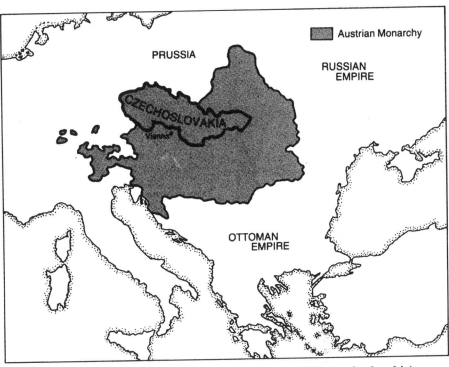

The Austrian monarchy about 1793 (showing pre-1993 Czechoslovakia)

brother, who took the throne as Boleslav I and who brought much of the former Moravian Empire under his rule. But later, under the continued harassment of the Magyars, he agreed to merge the kingdom of Bohemia into the Holy Roman Empire. The Holy Roman emperor recognized the right of the Bohemian nobles to elect their own ruler, who would be the highest authority in Bohemia. At the same time, there was a substantial German migration into Bohemia and Moravia after this, and German influence grew steadily.

Nevertheless, a new line of Czech rulers that came to power in the mid-14th century began to reverse this trend, even managing to assert a growing influence over neighboring states. The "golden age" of Czech history occurred under Charles IV, the king of Bohemia who also became the Holy Roman emperor. For a generation, Prague became the capital of the Holy Roman Empire. Determined to make his capital worthy of its imperial status, Charles IV supported the construction of new palaces and churches. He was also responsible for founding Prague's great Charles University and for the still-standing, famous Charles Bridge across the Vltava River.

The 14th century saw the beginnings of a movement for church reform in Bohemia. Though couched in religious language, the movement was primarily a reaction against the extensive landholdings of the Roman Church and the dominant role of Germans in religious and political

matters. This was also the period of the Great Schism, when two separate popes, one in Rome and one in Avignon, each claimed to be the one true pope.

Jan (John) Hus, the young preacher who led the reform movement, criticized the papacy and accused the clergy of being corrupt. Echoing ideas expressed earlier by John Wycliffe in England, he also maintained that the Bible was the sole authority for Christians, not the teachings of the church.

The Council of Constance, called to heal the breach in the church and end the Great Schism, rejected Wycliffe's and Hus's teachings and ordered Hus to appear before them to answer charges of heresy. Receiving a promise of safe conduct from Holy Roman Emperor Sigismund, Hus traveled to Constance to defend his positions. Upon his arrival, the council refused to meet with him and condemned him to death. Sigismund withdrew his safe conduct, and Hus was burned at the stake in 1415.

Hus became a martyr, even to those Czechs who had not been his followers; he was a national hero who died at the hands of the Germans. Thus, when Sigismund attempted to succeed to the Bohemian throne after the death of the Czech king in 1419, he set off the Hussite Wars, also called the Bohemian Wars or the Hussite Revolution, which lasted from 1420 to 1436. Although the wars were fought in the name of religion, they had great political and social overtones, as well. They

Jerusalem Synagogue in Prague

Czech Republic

Memorial in Bratislava to founding of Czechoslovakia

were an expression of Czech nationalism. The conflict was complicated by the fact that the Hussites (followers of the teachings of reformer Jan Hus) were sometimes divided among themselves and in 1434 even waged war against each other. Ultimately, however, the Hussites prevailed. The church signed a separate agreement with them, allowing them to retain Hussite rituals in return for their acknowledging the pope as head of the church.

Part of the Multinational Habsburg Empire

This agreement failed to endure, partly because the more radical Hussites were repressed and partly because the Czech Catholic nobility resisted the treaty terms during the following decades. In 1462, the pope declared the agreement invalid and requested King Mathias of Hungary to send in troops to enforce his decision. With the support of Czech Catholics, Bohemia was then incorporated into the Hungarian kingdom.

Hungarian rule continued until 1526 when the last Hungarian king was killed at the battle of Mohacs, and the crown passed to Ferdinand of Habsburg. Since Bohemia was included among the possessions of the Hungarian crown, Ferdinand was "elected" king of Bohemia, as well. In 1547, the right of the Czech nobles to elect their king was abolished, and the crown of St. Wenceslas became the hereditary property of the House of Habsburg.

Conflict between the predominantly Protestant Czechs and their Roman Catholic kings continued during the next decades. Although the Protestants were able to obtain promises from the Habsburg rulers allowing freedom of worship, they continued to fear persecution. The situation was further exacerbated when Calvinism began to spread into Bohemia.

Conflict erupted in May 1618 after two Protestant churches were closed. Angry Protestant leaders stormed Prague Castle and, in an act since known as the "Defenestration of Prague," tossed the two royal governors out of a castle window. According to tradition, they landed on a dung heap and were unhurt.

The Czech nobility then met and deposed the Habsburg ruler. Reclaiming their ancient electoral rights, they named Frederick, Elector of the Palatinate, as king of Bohemia. Frederick was both a Calvinist and the head of the Protestant Union of German Princes. This was, therefore, a direct challenge to Habsburg power and marked the beginning of the Thirty Years'

War. Frederick is known in history as the "winter king," for he retained the Bohemian crown only briefly, being defeated in 1620 by a Habsburg army at the Battle of White Mountain.

After the Habsburgs reclaimed the Bohemian crown, they decided to put an end to all dissent within the kingdom. The leaders of the revolution were executed, and other suspected opponents had their property confiscated. More than 30,000 families, including members of the Czech nobility, fled from the terror that gripped Bohemia at this time. The Czechs thus lost an important part of their national leadership. In addition, Roman Catholicism was imposed, and the German language was accorded equal status with Czech. Publications were censored, and books were burned. The Habsburgs first reasserted their hereditary claims to the Bohemian crown, then went further and abolished the Bohemian government entirely. The Bohemian lands were governed by a separate administration located in Vienna until 1749.

The Thirty Years' War ended with the Peace of Westphalia in 1648. During the century that followed, there was a large-scale migration of German peasants into traditionally Czech lands, and this was accompanied by a gradual process of Germanization in education, in culture, and in urban life.

In 1749, Maria Theresia abolished the separate Bohemian administration and merged Bohemia and Austria into a single state. Although it thus lost the last shadow of a separate political existence, the tariff union between Bohemia, Moravia, and

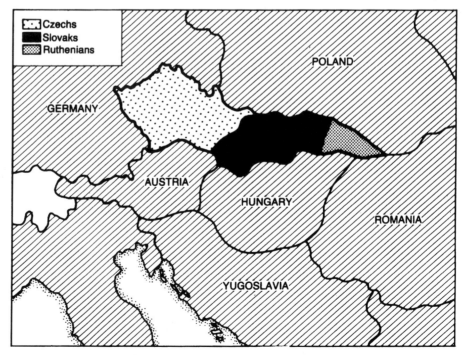

Czechoslovakia, 1918–1938, encircled by hungry neighbors

374

Czech Republic

Austria that followed shortly afterward, benefited Bohemia economically, as it quickly became the most industrially developed part of the empire.

Joseph II (1765–1790), who succeeded Maria Theresia, introduced a series of other changes and reforms whose chief result was to increase the number of German government officials and to create secret police. On the other hand, Joseph II's policy of religious toleration led to a decrease in the influence of the Catholic Church. This period also marked the beginning of a period of Czech cultural revival.

The French Revolution and the Napoleonic era that followed it had a major effect on the power of the Habsburgs, but Bohemia remained largely unaffected. The period of relative tranquility that set in after the final defeat of Napoleon in 1815 was misleading, however. As the Industrial Revolution spread to Bohemia in the first half of the 19th century, it brought a prosperity that encouraged the growth of a new Czech nationalism. Thus, while the Habsburg rulers devoted their energies to maintaining themselves and other royalty in power throughout Europe, their position was being undermined at home.

When rioting erupted in Paris in February 1848 and then spread to Berlin and Vienna, Prague also exploded in turmoil. On March 11, an assembly in Prague demanded freedom of the press, equality of languages, a legislature to represent the Czech people, and the abolition of serfdom. In June, the first Pan-Slav Congress assembled in Prague. It was dominated by Francis Palacky, a Bohemian historian who believed that Czechs could find freedom and remain within the empire at the same time.

While the congress was meeting, riots broke out against the commander of the Austrian forces in Prague. He suppressed the revolutionary movement and set up a military dictatorship. Moderate Czechs continued to press for a new constitution but to no avail. Order was restored throughout the empire under a centralized, absolutist regime.

The creation of the "dual" monarchy in 1867 provided for a national legislature for the Austrian part of the Austro-Hungarian Empire and gave Czechs representation in Vienna for the first time. Between 1867 and World War I, Czech nationalists used this new forum to demand self-government within the Austro-Hungarian Empire. The goal of independence was not actively pursued until the fortunes of war presented the opportunity to sever the centuries-old domination of Austria in 1918. Attainment of this goal was helped by an extensive propaganda campaign carried on by Czechs living in Paris and in the United States.

President Tomas G. Masaryk

Birth of an Independent Czechoslovak State

The first direct contribution to independence was made by the thousands of Czech and Slovak soldiers who refused to fight with the armies of the Central Powers during World War I, choosing instead to surrender to the Russians. These prisoners of war formed a special force, the Czecho-Slovak Legion, which then fought

President Eduard Beneš

on the side of the Russians against Germany and Austria.

When the Russian Bolsheviks (communists) signed the Treaty of Brest-Litovsk in 1918, taking Russia out of the war with Germany, the western allies suggested the transfer of the legion to the western front by way of Siberia and Japan. They became briefly involved in the Russian Civil War after the Bolsheviks attempted to disarm them. Seizing control of the Trans-Siberian Railroad, they made their way eastward through Siberia to Japan.

Although Bohemia remained under Austrian control during World War I, a Czech National Council started to function in early 1916. Located in Paris and composed of such leading personalities as Tomas G. Masaryk, Eduard Beneš (Benešh), and Milan Stefanik, it maintained contact with a resistance organization, the "Mafia," back in Bohemia.

The council's goal, which was close to being achieved by mid-1918, was to win support for the creation of an independent Czechoslovak state. Masaryk was instrumental in gaining American support for this cause. His wife was an American, Charlotte Garrigue, and this gave him connections he otherwise would not have had. Two documents signed in America would be of historic importance in laying the basis for the future Czechoslovak state.

The Pittsburgh Agreement, signed on June 30, 1918, expressed Slovak support for the union of Czech and Slovak lands in return for the promise that Slovakia would have considerable independence within the new state. The Philadelphia Agreement, signed in October by Masaryk and the leader of American Ruthenians, promised autonomy for Ruthenia, the ethnic Ukrainian part of prewar Czechoslovakia (now a part of the Ukraine).

A National Committee representing three parties, the National Democrats, Agrarians, and National Socialists, was set up in Prague in July 1918. This committee, headed by Karel Kramar, proclaimed the Independent Czechoslovak State on October 28, 1918. Two days later, the Slovak National Council voted to be part of the proclaimed state. The Central National Council of the Ruthenians opted to become part of Czechoslovakia on May 8, 1919.

The First Czechoslovak Republic, 1918–1939

The frontiers of the Czechoslovakian state were drawn during 1918–1919, partly as a result of military action and partly by the decisions of the postwar peace conference between the major powers. The borders between the Czechs and Poles and between the Slovaks and Hungarians were contested. The final settlements resulted in confusing and potentially troublesome

Czech Republic

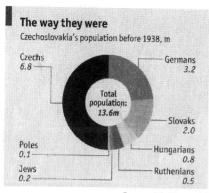

The way they were
Czechoslovakia's population before 1938, m

Czechs 6.8
Germans 3.2
Slovaks 2.0
Hungarians 0.8
Ruthenians 0.5
Jews 0.2
Poles 0.1
Total population: 13.6m

Source: *The Economist*

borders. A large number of Hungarians were included in Slovak territory, and a number of Slovaks resided in Hungary. When Tomas Masaryk died in 1937, his coffin was carried by six soldiers, one for each of the country's nationalities: a Czech, a Slovak, a German, a Hungarian, a Ruthenian, and a Pole.

The resulting Czechoslovakian state included minorities of Poles and Hungarians as well as about three million Germans, living mainly in northern and western Bohemia. Denied the status of one of the "state" peoples, the Germans tended to become culturally identified with Germany during the period that followed World War I. They participated fully in Czechoslovak politics, however, and were represented by several political parties.

The Czechs, who dominated the national government, had their problems with other ethnic groups, as well. Slovaks, in particular, not only felt excluded from the political process but were concerned about their cultural integrity, as well. Throughout the interwar period, there were a number of differences that divided the Czechs and the Slovaks. The conflicts centered on the form and concept of the Czechoslovakian nation. The Czechs were more advanced industrially than the Slovaks. Being in the majority, Czech civil servants dominated the government. The Slovaks insisted that the term "Czechoslovak nation" was no more than a cover-up for Czech-dominated governmental centralization. Some asserted that they had the right to secede from Czechoslovakia.

Ruthenia presented another problem. Czechs were willing to concede that they were a separate people, but they refused to grant them the self-government that they thought they had been promised. The problem was its strategic location. Backward and inhabited by poverty-stricken peasants, Ruthenia nevertheless enabled the nation to have a border with Romania, an important ally.

In spite of these problems, the Czechoslovak Republic was an economically developed country with a democratic pattern of government. Political parties represented a wide range of outlooks. The Communist Party was legal throughout the years of the republic and claimed a substantial following. Although the government was a coalition of parties, the Agrarian Party was continuously a part of the government after 1922.

The top political leadership also provided stability. Masaryk, Czechoslovakia's first president, was reelected in 1927 and 1934. When he died in 1935, Eduard Beneš, who had been foreign minister since 1918, succeeded him. Beneš's policy had been directed toward encouraging strict observance of the Treaty of Versailles. He formed alliances with Romania and Yugoslavia. Later, he turned to France and then to the Soviet Union.

Domestically, government relations with ethnic Germans deteriorated badly during the last several years before 1938. These Sudeten Germans had originally pressed for political autonomy. By 1938, however, most of them had come under Nazi influence and were demanding that territories where they were in a majority be permitted to join Germany. Hitler threw his open support to these demands in the spring of 1938. England and France had rejected the German demand in May but were ready to give in to Hitler by September. Mussolini now proposed a four-power conference to resolve the matter. Hitler and Mussolini, plus Prime Minister Chamberlain of Great Britain and Premier Daladier of France, met at Munich, Germany, at the end of September 1938. Czechoslovakia was not invited. Seeking a solution short of war, France and Great Britain agreed to German annexation of the Sudeten area of Czechoslovakia.

This decision was made despite the fact that France had guaranteed Czechoslovakia's borders by a treaty of alliance in 1924. The Soviet Union also had a mutual-assistance pact with Czechoslovakia that it had signed in 1935, but the Soviet Union was not represented at Munich. The Soviet agreement promised armed assistance if France also fulfilled its commitment. As a result of the Munich Pact, Germany occupied some 10,000 square miles of territory inhabited by 3.5 million people, one-quarter of whom were Czechs.

President Beneš accepted the pact under duress, partly because he was pressed by both France and Great Britain to do so. Czechoslovakia was thus dismembered so that the major powers could gain, in Prime Minister Chamberlain's words, "peace in our time."

The four great powers guaranteed the territorial integrity of the remaining parts of Czechoslovakia. But no one did anything when Hitler announced the annexation of Bohemia and Moravia on March 15, 1939, and sent in German troops to occupy the area. Slovakia became a nominally independent state, while Ruthenia was ceded to Hungary.

Czechoslovakia: "Divided and Reconstructed, 1939–1948"

During World War II, many of Czechoslovakia's leaders left the country. Eduard Beneš, who had resigned on October 5, 1938, became the head of the Provisional Government organized in London in 1940. Klement Gottwald and other important Czech communists sought support in Moscow. Negotiations in March 1945 between Beneš, Gottwald, and Joseph Stalin in Moscow resulted in a decision to create a "National Front" government, consisting of Beneš's government-in-exile plus Gottwald and his communists. Beneš arrived in Košice in March 1945 and there established his new government.

This first postwar government was drawn exclusively from parties belonging to the National Front, consisting of four Czech and two Slovak parties. Their programmatic statement, known as the Košice Program, stipulated that Czechoslovakia's future foreign policy would have an "all-Slav" foundation and would be based on an alliance with the Soviet Union. This declaration was even more meaningful because of the territorial closeness of the Soviet Union after Ruthenia was made a part of the Soviet Ukraine.

For the next three years, Czechoslovakia was governed by the National Front and functioned as a democratic nation. During this period, the Soviet Union was willing to tolerate parliamentary politics as long as the communists held the upper hand on matters of importance. Although the communists seized total power in February 1948, they could have done this at any time from 1945 onward, since they were the strongest party of postwar Czechoslovakia. As it was, they dominated the National Front through their occupancy of deputy premiership, plus the Ministries of Information, Interior, Agriculture, and Education.

The communists received by far the largest number of votes in free elections held in 1946. By the winter of 1947–1948, however, there were signs that their popular support was dropping sharply. It appeared that they were headed for defeat in elections set for May 1948.

The circumstances leading up to the communist coup began with the dismissal of eight police officers in Prague and their replacement by communists. When the minister of interior refused to reinstate the noncommunist officers, 12 noncommunist ministers resigned in the hope that this would force new elections in which the communists would be defeated.

Czechs protesting the 1968 invasion

Photo: Oldrich Skácha

Instead of submitting to elections, the communists threatened to use force, a threat strengthened by the arrival of Soviet deputy foreign minister Valerian Zorin in Prague. Communist "action committees" took control of newspapers and occupied the headquarters of noncommunist parties. Faced with this show of strength and organization, coupled with the fear of a possible civil war, President Beneš accepted a new government formed by Klement Gottwald. When Beneš resigned in June 1948, Gottwald succeeded to the presidency, and Antonín Zápotocký became premier.

Jan Masaryk, son of Tomas G. Masaryk, had been foreign minister under Beneš. At the time of the coup, he was reported to have committed suicide by leaping from a high window of a government building to a stone courtyard below. In 1989, after the fall of the communist regime, it was officially confirmed that he had been pushed.

Czechoslovakia Becomes a People's Republic

After the 1948 coup, Czechoslovakia was a faithful ally of the Soviet Union, imitating the Stalinist pattern of rule at home and supporting Soviet policies abroad. As in other eastern European communist countries, a series of purges occurred between 1949 and 1954, aimed at cleansing the party of individuals who might have a greater loyalty to nationalism than to communism. Both Vladimir Clementis, foreign minister, and Rudolf Slansky, secretary-general of the Czechoslovak Communist Party, were among 11 victims hanged in 1952 after having been found guilty of "Titoism" and "nationalist deviation."

The death of Joseph Stalin in the Soviet Union in 1953, followed by Gottwald's death a few days later, brought no visible change to the government. This was because the domestic scene was stable. Economic growth and an increase in the standard of living made for a relatively placid population. Because no single individual was able to assume all of Gottwald's authority within the party, there began a period of collective rule. Antonin Zápotocký, who had been premier since 1948, succeeded to the presidency, the dominant political position within the Czechoslovak system. Antonin Novotný became party leader. Reflecting a change also carried out in the Soviet Union at this time, Novotný's title was downgraded to first secretary.

The denunciation of Stalin by Soviet leader Nikita Khrushchev in 1956, plus the neighboring Hungarian revolution of the same year, failed to bring any substantial changes. The communist leadership of Czechoslovakia, rendered more monolithic by purges, remained Stalinist even after his death.

President Zápotocký died in 1957 and was succeeded by Antonin Novotný, who retained his position as first secretary of the Czechoslovak Communist Party. This marked the beginning of his political ascendancy and a further period of Stalinist rule in Czechoslovakia, since Novotný was no reformer.

Novotný distinguished himself by opposing nearly every proposal for political innovation and resisting any move toward de-Stalinization within Czechoslovakia. Almost alone among the members of the communist bloc, Czechoslovakia continued to have political prisoners left over from the Stalinist purges of the early 1950s.

One symbol of the Novotný era became a huge statue of Stalin, erected in 1955 on an embankment overlooking the Vltava River in Prague. The statue survived Khrushchev's 1956 de-Stalinization campaign and even the 1961 decision of the 21st Party Congress to remove Stalin's body from the mausoleum on Red Square. It was finally taken down in October 1962.

Perhaps Novotný's proudest achievement was the new constitution he pushed through in 1960. According to the text, Czechoslovakia had become the second

country—after the USSR—to make the transition to "Socialist Republic." Since the name was identical to that of the individual Soviet republics, it has even been suggested that Novotný had in mind the incorporation of Czechoslovakia into the USSR.

Novotný's troubles began after 1960. Domestically, there was a growing intellectual ferment that was pressing for greater cultural freedom. In the economic field, industry began to show the strains of the Stalinist command model. By 1962, the situation had reached crisis proportions. The government was forced to abandon its third five-year plan and to rely on makeshift annual plans for the next three years. Internationally, there was Khrushchev's continuing de-Stalinization campaign.

The events in the USSR reinforced the more liberal, reform elements in the Czech Party. Rudolf Barak, minister of the interior and a member of this faction, was an obvious challenger to Novotný's leadership. Even the events in Moscow were not sufficient to boost Barak to power as long as he lacked firmer support within the party. In 1962, Barak was removed from all positions, arrested, and sentenced to 15 years in jail for embezzlement and "conspicuous consumption." This probably meant that he had been living too luxuriously.

Barak's removal did not end Novotný's troubles. At a party congress in Prague in 1962, the Central Committee decided to conduct an inquiry into the purges of 1949–1954. The result was a declaration that Clementis and Slansky had been wrongfully convicted.

As pressure increased on Novotný, he dismissed the top officials in Slovakia. These included Karol Bacilek, first secretary of the Slovak Communist Party, and Viliam Ďiroký, Slovak premier. Both men had aroused Slovak hatred because of their support for Prague's policies of centralization. Ďiroký was replaced by Josef Lenart, a more popular Slovak, and Bacilek was succeeded by Alexander Dubček. These changes quieted the situation and allowed Novotný to be elected to another term as president of the republic in 1964.

Long before Novotný's term of office expired, however, he fell from power. Numerous popular complaints in 1962–1963 had caused Novotný to pledge economic reforms, but this remained an empty promise. It eventually became clear that political reform would have to precede economic reform. The reason was that the party disagreed over two major issues: how fast economic reforms should be implemented and how much autonomy ought to be granted to Slovakia.

Both surfaced in late 1967 when Dubček accused Novotný of undermining the program of economic reform and of refusing

Czech Republic

Czechs honoring students who died for freedom in 1968, Wenceslas Square, Prague

to meet Slovak demands for more self-government. At the same time, there were protests from the Czechoslovak Writers' Union and demonstrations by students in Prague. This series of events, taken together, would probably have led to Novotný's dismissal, had Soviet party chief Leonid Brezhnev not thrown his support to Novotný during a visit to Prague.

Brezhnev's gesture of support only postponed Novotný's fall. The internecine fighting between Novotný's and Dubček's backers continued to sharpen. Two months later, the Central Committee separated the functions of the presidency from those of the first secretary of the Communist Party. On January 5, 1968, Alexander Dubček took over Novotný's functions as first party secretary of the Czechoslovak Communist Party. A clumsy attempt at a military coup, apparently an attempt to save Novotný, was discovered, and Dubček removed the participants from office. One army general committed suicide, while a second fled the country, eventually making his way to the US.

"Socialism with a Human Face"— An Experiment and Its Consequences

The change in party leadership generated even greater hope that wider political, economic, and social changes would follow. When Novotný finally resigned from the presidency in March 1968, it was clear that Czechoslovakia was proceeding in a new direction. A popular national military hero who had been decorated by both tsarist and Soviet Russia—General Ludvik Svoboda was chosen president. Oldřich Černík became premier and formed a cabinet that supported Dubček.

The party's program for the future was adopted in April under the title of "The Czechoslovak Road to Socialism," also known as the Action Program. The program endorsed important changes, such as an end to most censorship, restrictions on the powers of the secret police, and guarantees for the expression of minority viewpoints. In light of what subsequently happened, it is also important to stress that the Action Program was concerned only with domestic matters, with nothing to suggest any change in Czechoslovakia's policies either toward the Soviet Union or the Warsaw Pact. Dubček also repeatedly declared that the Communist Party had the leading role in the government and that his administration was committed to a continuation of socialism. In Dubček's words, the purpose of the reform movement was to create "socialism with a human face."

These developments raised great anxiety among some of the leaders of neighboring communist countries. The great fear was that, once liberalization was set in motion, it would inevitably get out of control. Moscow also began to express its worries. In May 1968, Czechoslovak visitors to the Soviet Union were advised to beware of counterrevolutionary attacks on the leading role of the party. Two months later, more than 70 writers released a document entitled "Two Thousand Words" calling for "pressure from below" for further liberalization and democratic reform. The Soviet press cited this as proof that counterrevolutionary forces existed in Czechoslovakia. In addition, the Soviet Union added some psychological pressure by delaying the departure of Soviet forces

that were in Czechoslovakia for Warsaw Pact maneuvers.

At the beginning of July, neighboring communist nations suggested a joint meeting to address their concerns. The Czechoslovak government countered with a suggestion of bilateral talks. Rebuffed, Czechoslovakia's communist neighbors held their own meeting in Warsaw in mid-1968. This conference produced a document known as the "Warsaw Letter," which warned that Czechoslovakia could maintain its independence only as a "socialist" (i.e., communist) country. The letter added that reactionary forces were diverting Czechoslovakia from socialism and asked that immediate action be taken to restore censorship of the press and radio and to clamp down on antisocialist political movements.

Prague responded with a letter of its own, arguing that the party was in complete control. It could not take the suggested actions because its authority was based on responsiveness to the will of the people, who desired more freedom of expression. This exchange of letters did nothing to settle the situation, and it may even have inflamed it further. Prague's reply brought a Soviet request for a special meeting with the Czechoslovak leadership.

In the end, two meetings were held, the first in late July and the second in early August. At the second meeting, all the other Warsaw Pact nations were in attendance except Romania. Pressed to modify their program, the Czechoslovak leadership stood firm, though they did agree to a joint statement that made reference to the need to strengthen the forces of socialism against imperialist aggression.

Invasion and Its Aftermath

On the night of August 20–21, military units of the Soviet Union, Hungary, East Germany, Poland, and Bulgaria invaded Czechoslovakia. Within a few hours, they had overrun the country and occupied the leading cities. TASS, the official Soviet news agency, announced that the occupation had been in response to a request for assistance against "counterrevolutionary" forces. None of the Czechoslovak leadership had made any such request, however. In fact, the entire Czechoslovak leadership—Dubček, Černík, and Josef Smrkovsky, president of the National Assembly—had been placed under arrest at the time of the invasion.

The Soviets tried but failed to find Czech collaborators who would confirm the Soviet explanation of the invasion. Instead, the Czech Foreign Ministry publicly denounced the military move as a violation of the Warsaw Pact, and President Svoboda flatly refused to participate in the formation of a Soviet-dominated government.

The deadlock was broken when Svoboda agreed to go to Moscow for direct talks with the Soviet leaders, provided Dubček and the other leaders traveled to Moscow with him and participated in the talks. At the meeting, it was agreed that the Dubček administration would be allowed to remain in office, though it was made clear that Czechoslovak leaders would have to change their political outlook. In October, a treaty was signed that legalized the stationing of Soviet troops within Czechoslovakia for an unlimited time. The Czechoslovak party congress, which had met during the first week of the invasion, was also declared invalid. The liberal Central Committee selected at that time was repudiated. Finally, the Executive Committee of the presidium was created to counteract liberals in the presidium itself.

Retreat from Reform

One element of the reform movement survived, however. At midnight on December 31, 1968, Czechoslovakia became a federal state. With the creation of separate Czech and Slovak republics, the Slovaks had finally achieved their goal of a separate, autonomous state. Basically, the Soviet leadership had decided to try to coopt the nationalistic but more conservative Slovaks.

Dubček's position soon became impossible. On the one hand, he refused to abandon his commitment to reform; on the other hand, he tried to placate conservatives by criticizing anti-Soviet attitudes, denouncing student demonstrations, and reimposing censorship.

None of this saved him. In April 1969, Dubček was demoted from first party secretary to chairman of the Federal Assembly. Gustav Husák, the new first party secretary, was a Slovak who earlier had been a supporter of reform. After the invasion, however, he had switched positions, arguing that the first priority for Czechoslovakia was to live in harmony with the Soviet Union. During the remainder of 1969, most of the rest of the preinvasion reform leadership was either demoted, forced to resign, or dismissed. Removed as chairman of the Federal Assembly in the fall of 1969, Dubček was sent to Ankara as ambassador to Turkey. Eight months later, he was expelled from the Communist Party.

With pro-Moscow conservatives now in control of the party, the Central Committee repealed the resolution condemning the Warsaw Pact Invasion. Czechoslovakia was back in line. In May 1970, a new treaty of friendship was signed with the Soviet Union.

An extensive purge of the party was carried out between 1970 and 1975 that resulted in the dismissal of about 450,000 members—nearly one-third of the total. In general, it was the more liberal members who were purged. Having consolidated his power, Husák announced in 1976 that he was ready to begin a policy of reconciliation. Purged members were invited to apply for readmission to the party. There was one major stipulation, however—they formally had to repudiate the policies and leaders of the Prague Spring. In spite of this precondition, some ex-members were accepted back into the party, and it began to grow again.

The government was reorganized at both the federal and national levels in early 1971. Chief among the changes was that the Federal Cabinet was given the right to veto decisions of the Czech and Slovak national cabinets. In mid-1975, Husák replaced an ailing Svoboda as president of the republic, retaining his position as head of the party. The Czechoslovak power structure thus reverted to the pattern that had existed prior to Dubček's replacement of Novotný as first secretary of the Czechoslovak Communist Party in early 1968. Husák continued to occupy both positions for 12 years, becoming a symbol and instrument of Soviet domination of Czechoslovakia (even though he had once been thrown into jail for "bourgeois nationalism").

In early 1977, a group of Czech intellectuals released a document called "Charter 77," which charged the government with a long list of human rights violations, including the exclusion of young people from institutes of higher education on the basis of their parents' political views. The document also accused the government of systematically violating the right of public expression guaranteed in the Czechoslovak constitution. A number of western newspapers picked up the story, and news of the document soon filtered back into Czechoslovakia. The government's reaction was predictable. Charter signatories were investigated by the secret police, and several were sent to prison. The government never managed to suppress the Charter 77 movement, however, and its attempts to do so only further tarnished its international reputation. The domestic press refused to publish the "Charter 77" declaration.

The Beginning of the End of Communism

After Gorbachev launched his campaigns for glasnost, perestroika, and democracy in the Soviet Union, a more or less public debate began to occur within the Czechoslovak leadership. Individual

presidium members publicly argued over whether loyalty to the USSR required them to support a similar program in Czechoslovakia. It soon became clear that the top leadership was sharply divided over the issue. The hard-liners, whose spokesman was Vasil Bilak, argued that events in the Soviet Union had no relevance for Czechoslovakia. On the other hand, Premier Lubomir Štrougal, who emerged now as spokesman for the moderates, argued the case for Prague's own restructuring.

President Husák remained publicly neutral until just before a visit of Gorbachev to Czechoslovakia in April 1987. He then endorsed a general program of reform. But Husák was a reluctant reformer; no changes were to be implemented until the next five-year plan, scheduled to begin on January 1, 1991.

During his visit, Gorbachev used his public speeches to set forth the rationale for reform. While he did not insist that the Czechoslovak leadership implement a similar program, he had no praise for them. It was becoming clear that Husák, at 74, was no longer able to provide any clear leadership and that the issue of reform was becoming a vehicle to determine the succession.

The issue was resolved in 1987, when Husák voluntarily retired as general secretary while remaining on as president. His successor, Miloš Jakeš, a member of the ruling presidium since 1981, was a compromise choice, a man not associated with either of the two factions within the presidium. Although a member of the party secretariat for over 20 years, Miloš Jakeš had never developed a strong political profile.

His record was rather ambivalent. Originally appointed by Dubček to head the Party Control and Auditing Commission, he transferred his loyalty to the new leadership installed after the Soviet invasion. He subsequently presided over the post-1968 purge of the party that resulted in the expulsion of most liberals and moderates. Many of these same people, who constituted an important part of the country's cultural and technological elite, were also fired from their state jobs and forced either to take menial jobs or emigrate. Given this background, Jakes had a problem establishing credibility in his new job.

Jakes's own public statements after becoming general secretary were nonconciliatory. On at least one occasion, he characterized the Prague Spring as an attempt "to destroy the socialist system." At the same time, his speeches included references to the need for a "fundamental restructuring of all spheres of public life."

His promotion to general secretary did not put an end to the Bilak-Štrougal

Czech Republic

Former president Havel shares a light moment with his private secretary.

Photo by Oldrich Skácha

struggle. It may even have intensified it, since they were now trying to influence a man of untried qualities. Štrougal's speeches in favor of Gorbachev-style reform apparently became embarrassing to the party, and he was forced out as premier in October 1988.

Ladislav Adamec, who succeeded Štrougal was, like Jakeš, a man of the middle. During a trip to Moscow in February 1989, he spoke of the need for political as well as economic reforms. At the same time, Adamec remained willing to carry out the will of the conservative majority on the presidium.

The Velvet Revolution

All of this began to change in the late summer of 1989, as the changes sweeping across central and eastern Europe reached the East Germany. A human hemorrhaging commenced westward. East German vacationers began crossing the newly opened border between Hungary and Austria. Budapest informed the irate East German leaders that the human rights agreements accepted at the Helsinki Conference in 1975 superseded earlier bilateral treaties preventing the free movement of peoples.

The next avenue of escape was through Czechoslovakia. Thousands had taken refuge at the West German embassy in Prague. West German foreign minister Hans-Dietrich Genscher appeared on the balcony overlooking the embassy garden and told the 8,000 weary but ecstatic East German refugees who were crammed into the compound that they would be permitted to travel to West Germany. Genscher described the atmosphere around the embassy at the time as being "on the knife's edge." Stasi provocateurs mingled with the refugees, and there was fear that something could go wrong at any moment, with so many persons squeezed into such a small space surrounded by a nervous and hostile communist regime afraid for its own survival.

Vaclav Havel, then the dissident leader of the 77 movement that spearheaded the Velvet Revolution that ended communist dictatorship in Czechoslovakia, later told former German ambassador Michael Steiner that the revolution in Germany had had an important influence on later events in Prague. Havel and some of his supporters had seen with their own eyes how women with babies had walked right through lines of machine-gun-toting Czech troops surrounding the West German embassy. This convinced Havel that the people were stronger than state power and could overcome it. He saw what normal citizens could accomplish. "Freedom trains" took East Germans through the GDR into the west. The stampede grew when Czechoslovakia opened its western borders. As East Germany was forced more and more to give in to the demands of its people, disaffected Czechs intensified their own demonstrations demanding greater rights.

The culmination came on the evening of November 17, when a crowd of about 3,000 young people gathered at the entrance of Wenceslas Square (Vaclavske Namesti) and began a chant calling for free elections. They were met by a line of riot police plus an antiterrorist squad called the Red Berets, who attacked and bludgeoned them to the ground. Personally ordered by Jakeš, the attack was a fatal error. It ignited the emotions of the Czech people, who responded with 10 days of singing, chanting, and nonstop organizing. This was Prague's so-called Velvet Revolution, and at its end the communists had been elbowed from power. On November 24, with 300,000 people in the streets, Jakeš called a meeting of the Central Committee and submitted resignations for himself and the rest of the presidium.

Karel Urbanek replaced Jakeš as party leader and issued an unequivocal condemnation of the violence of November 17. But it was Ladislav Adamec, the premier, who now stepped into the power vacuum and

began discussions with the opposition, since November 19 organized as the Civic Forum. He continued to play that role for perhaps two weeks. During that time, the party agreed to give up its monopoly of power and to form a coalition government with the opposition. But Adamec wanted to keep a majority of the seats in the hands of the communists. When Civic Forum rejected his proposed cabinet on December 3, Adamec resigned and was replaced by Marián Čalfa. The new cabinet, installed on December 10, contained a majority of noncommunists. Jiří Dienstbier, a founder-member of Charter 77, became foreign minister, while Václav Klaus, an economist committed to creation of a market economy, became finance minister.

As an added benefit, Gustáv Husák now submitted his resignation as president. Václav Havel, longtime dissident, founder of Charter 77, and prominent playwright who never attended a university, was elected president by acclamation on December 29. Alexander Dubček, reform communist leader of the 1968 Prague Spring, was elected leader of the national assembly.

With the new leaders all in place, the country settled in for a period of consolidation that included some dismantling of the old system. In the political and social arenas, the secret police were dissolved, and required courses in Marxism-Leninism were abolished in the universities. The government dropped its system of licensing priests and ministers. Fewer changes were made in the economic sphere. One reason for this is that everybody seemed to be waiting for new elections scheduled for June 6 in order to have a popular mandate.

Presidential Palace guard

One issue, the rivalry between Czechs and Slovaks, resurfaced with virulence. Upon Slovak insistence, the name of the country was changed to the Czech and Slovak Federal Republic.

The first democratic elections since 1946 finally took place in June 1990 and resulted in a victory for Civic Forum and its Slovak partner, Public against Violence. An astonishing 96% of voters participated in the election. After the election, Václav Havel was reelected president, and Marián Čalfa was reappointed premier.

After the June elections, there was a struggle within the leadership of the Civic Forum between free-marketers and advocates for a "third way" between communism and capitalism. The spokesman for the free-marketers was the finance minister, Václav Klaus, while Foreign Minister Jiří Dienstbier was a major spokesman for the opposing viewpoint, which most of the 1968 communists favored. Havel tried to stay above the fray. Klaus won the first round in October 1990, when he was elected chairman of Civic Forum. In February 1991, however, the two factions decided to divide into two separate organizations. They would continue to be associated on a coordinating committee of Civic Forum chaired by President Havel.

Separation of the Republics

One other issue that demanded attention after the June 1990 elections was that of Slovak separatism. Slovaks had always been concerned about maintaining a separate identity, but now individual Slovak leaders began demanding creation of a separate, independent Slovak state. In effect, their argument was that Slovakia could not maintain its separate identity as part of a federation shared with the Czechs.

In December 1990, the Federal Assembly tried to defuse the situation by passing new legislation spelling out in greater detail the separate powers of the Czech and Slovak regional governments. The legislation also gave President Havel special powers to deal with the threat of Slovak separatism.

Although a majority of both Slovak and Czech deputies voiced support for the legislation, Slovak nationalists remained unappeased. When President Havel visited Bratislava in March 1991, he was greeted by thousands of Slovaks shouting abuse. The situation became even worse after Vladimir Mečiar, the Slovak premier, took up the Slovak nationalist cause, at least partly because he feared the effect of Prague's privatization policies on Slovak industry. Mečiar had gotten too far out in front of the political forces, however, and he was dismissed as premier in April 1991. Yet the issue remained alive. The new premier, Ján Čarnogurský, head of Slovakia's Christian Democratic Movement, tried to straddle the issue by supporting continuation of the federation for the time being while favoring an independent Slovakia in principle.

As Slovak nationalism continued to dominate Czechoslovak politics in 1991 and 1992, President Havel was forced to spend more and more of his time on this issue. Acting as a mediator between the Czechs and Slovaks, he brought the two sides together for discussions and, at one point, called for a referendum. Public polls showed that a small majority of Slovaks supported a continuation of the federation, so the Slovak nationalists eventually rejected that suggestion. Havel also proposed some changes in the nature of the federal government, and these were presented to the Federal Assembly in December 1991 in the form of three draft laws, which were never enacted.

After numerous proposals and discussions failed to produce an agreement, it was decided to hold new federal elections on June 5–6, 1992, to resolve the general issue. Slovakia held its own elections to the National Council on the same days. In the elections, the vote split along national and ideological lines. In the Czech Republic, Václav Klaus and his Civic Democratic Party won a convincing victory on a program of anticommunism and reform. In the Slovak Republic, Vladimir Mečiar and his Movement for a Democratic Slovakia won an equally convincing victory with their blend of statism, socialism, and nationalism.

When Klaus and Mečiar met after the election to discuss the formation of a new federal government, the latter made it clear that he would not accept a federal state that could dictate policy to Slovakia. Among his demands were that the Slovak Republic establish its army and currency-issuing central bank and have the independent right to borrow. None of these positions was acceptable to Klaus, and the talks collapsed after six and a half hours.

Because a new federal government had to be formed, Klaus suggested giving a new, temporary federal government the power to act until a referendum could be held to ask citizens whether they wanted to live in a federal state. After further talks, Czech and Slovak negotiators agreed to establish a weak interim federal government whose task would be to facilitate bringing the union to a close. The actual constitutional questions relating to the separation would be resolved in the legislatures of the two republics.

When Václav Havel, still trying to save the federal state, agreed to stand for reelection to the federal presidency, Slovak nationalists blocked his reelection. Havel could have stayed on in a caretaker capacity until October, since the dominant Czech party, the Civic Democratic Party, had vowed to block any other candidate for the presidency. He was unwilling to remain under those circumstances, however, and submitted his resignation instead. Most people saw that as a further step in the dissolution of the federal government. As Havel said, had he stayed, he would have been committed by the constitution to defending a common state that no longer had much purpose.

Further negotiations produced an agreement, signed on August 26, calling for a split into two independent states by January 1. On October 1, the federal parliament rejected a bill legalizing the end of the federation, then voted itself out of existence on November 25.

Having agreed to a peaceful separation into two independent nations, the Czechs and Slovaks nevertheless recognized that their economies would be tightly bound to each other for some time and that it would

Wenceslas Square, central Prague

381

Czech Republic

be wise to retain certain elements of the former union if they could. These would include a common currency and a customs union that would allow for the free movement of goods. In addition, Czechs and Slovaks would not be required to show passports to pass from one country to another.

POLITICAL SYSTEM

The Czechs adopted a new constitution for an independent Czech Republic in December 1992. It created a presidential-parliamentary system such as had existed in the former democratic Czechoslovakia. A bicameral legislature was created. There is a 200-member Chamber of Deputies and an 81-member upper house, called the Senate.

The Presidency

The president of the Czech Republic is the titular head of state. Until 2013 the Chamber of Deputies and the Senate elected the president to a five-year term. The president is now elected directly by the people. If no candidate receives 50% in the first round of voting, the top two compete in a second round two weeks later. Whoever gets the most votes is elected.

The functions of the president are largely ceremonial, unlike the powerful Czechoslovak presidency Václav Havel had taken over in 1990. However, if a president is determined to exercise the office's powers on paper to the fullest, he can have a major influence on the political process. That was the case with ex-president Václav Klaus.

The office bestows a moral authority that derives partly from the expectation that the president will remain above politics and partly from the prestige of the first holder of that office—Havel. He was elected president of the Czech Republic on January 26, 1993. A courageous playwright who had refused to compromise with the repressive communist regime and who

President Milos Zeman

„Občas mi není rozumět, ale mé postoje jsou jasné."

Karel Schwarzenberg
kandidát na prezidenta ČR

Karel Schwarzenberg

had therefore spent many years in prison, Havel embodied as nobody else the spirit of resistance to the totalitarian system.

His 1993 inaugural speech, given from a balcony of Hradčany Castle, was rather somber in tone, in contrast to his first inaugural speech. "The revolutionary times are over," he said. "This is the time of every day, common and hard work. To cultivate our best traditions today is infinitely harder than in times of great historical change and the euphoria that came with it."

Havel was reelected in January 1998. Although he had had a malignant tumor and half of the right lung removed in 1996 after he had been diagnosed with lung cancer, he nevertheless stood for reelection. The voting during the first ballot was by the lower house and the Senate each voting separately. When Havel failed to win the required majority in both houses, a second ballot then followed in which the two houses voted together. Here Havel won reelection by a single vote.

Due to his worldwide reputation, Havel could capture the attention of world leaders. No doubt this helped ensure his country's entry into NATO in 1999 and its front-rank status in negotiations to enter the European Union. All agree that he maintained his modesty, wit, and sense of the absurd. No leader was less corrupted by the trappings of office than he. However, his influence at home dwindled. When his last term ended in February 2003, after three years as Czechoslovak president and a decade as Czech president, a curtain descended on the most extraordinary

political figure to come out of the struggle to overthrow communism. He was the only leader in central Europe who took control in 1989 and successfully navigated the transition from resistance to rule and then survived into the 21st century as a champion of democracy.

Havel died of respiratory illness in December 2011 at age 75. In Moscow 80,000 prodemocracy demonstrators held a minute's silence in his memory. Only 11 months earlier, his fellow dissident, Jiří Dienstbier, had passed away at age 73. Dienstbier left behind the underground newspaper he founded, *Lidove noviny* (The People's News), and a son, Jiří, who is a rising political star.

Former prime minister Václav Klaus squeaked through with a one-vote majority in 2003, thanks to the votes of the communists, whom Havel had excluded from influence during his presidency. In 2008 Klaus was reelected. He is an intelligent but abrasive "political animal" with hard-hitting conservative instincts. He was the most Euroskeptic leader in the EU. In 2005 he called for a scrapping of the EU and its replacement by an "Organization of European States," which would be a free-trade bloc for individual states. Terms such as "state of Europe," "European nationalism," and "European citizenship" should be forgotten. He lambasted multiculturalism as a breeding ground for terrorism. In 2009 he made the entire EU nervous by threatening not to sign the revised Lisbon Treaty. In the end, he signed.

Shortly before leaving office, Klaus pardoned all convicts with prison terms

President Petr Pavel
Source: *Wikipedia)*

Election posters

of less than one year, those sentenced for nonviolent crimes to up to two years, and those aged 70 or older. That totaled 6,000 inmates. He also halted the prosecutions of businessmen and officials charged with fraud and corruption if their trials had already lasted eight years or more. These acts infuriated the majority in the Senate, which voted to charge him with high treason and to impeach him during his last days in office. A court threw out the treason charges. Klaus left the presidency and accepted a position at the Cato Institute in Washington.

His successor as president was Miloš Zeman, a former center-left prime minister. In the second round of voting, he received 55% of the votes and defeated former foreign minister Karel Schwarzenberg. Turnout was 61.3%. Zeman dominated Moravia in the east and northern Bohemia. Schwarzenberg found his main backing from the educated, urban, and rich. Like Klaus, Zeman is a populist and a blunt talker. Both are fiercely combative politicians. A frail Zeman was reelected in January 2018 with 51.4% of the votes and a turnout of 66%.

As the first president to be directly elected, Zeman considers that he had a stronger mandate to expand presidential powers farther than his predecessors. He irritated the foreign minister by interfering in the choice of new ambassadors. He took advantage of the political crisis in the fall of 2013 by appointing his confidant, Jiří Rusnok, as prime minister rather than the center-right leader, Miroslava Němcová, whose three-party coalition

had a slim majority in parliament. Some critics accuse him of undermining parliamentary democracy.

Emerging as a strong opponent of EU's interference in its members' politics, Zeman declared in 2016 that some two-thirds of all migrants were economic and not refugees and therefore should be deported, possibly to "empty spaces" in North Africa or to "uninhabited Greek islands." He also implied that Muslim culture is incompatible with European societies and that the flood of migrants leads to a "wave of jihadis" pouring into Europe. In the January 2023 elections, former chair of NATO's military committee, Petr Pavel, won. He defeated ex-prime minister Andrej Babiš; turnout was 68%. He won by promising to stick with the West and support Ukraine's fight against Russia.

The Prime Minister and Parliament

The constitution grants executive power to the government rather than to the president. The prime minister presides over the government and is the key political figure in the system. Appointed by the president, he must establish that he has the support of a majority of the Chamber of Deputies in order to remain in power. The president appoints members of the cabinet upon the advice of the prime minister. Their names are then submitted to the Chamber of Deputies for approval. The constitution makes it difficult to call early elections. For the first time, in the 2010 elections, a voter not only has the option to vote for his preferred party, but also, he can instead cast votes for his favorite four candidates. This new electoral system cost some prominent politicians their seats in parliament. Turnout was 62.6%.

Since no party ever wins a majority in parliament, coalition negotiations must be

Former Prime Minister Andrej Babis

held after each election. They can sometimes last a very long time. In 2007 after the government lost a vote of non-confidence in parliament, it took seven months of excruciating talks to create a functioning government. It lasted almost three months after the October 2013 elections to get a government created. During the negotiations, a caretaker prime minister manages the basic governmental duties until a new government is in place. It is usually the prime minister of the outgoing government. But in 2007 Jan Fischer, a nonparty technocrat and head of the National Statistics Office, took charge temporarily. His main goal was to conclude the six-month rotating EU presidency in a competent way and then serve only until a new prime minister emerged from the May 2010 elections.

Ex-president Klaus's party, the Civic Democrats (ODS), suffered huge losses in the May 2010 and October 2013 parliamentary elections. It collapsed, winning only 7.7% of the votes (down from 20% in 2010 and 34.4% in 2006) and 16 seats (down 37) in the 200-seat parliament. It placed second in October 2017 with 11.32% and 25 seats. On June 17, 2013, Prime Minister Nečas was forced to resign over a lurid sex, bribery, and spying scandal. Under the constitution the entire government must step down. He quit because the head of his office (and his lover and later wife), Jana Nagyová, had bribed members of parliament and ordered intelligence agents to spy on citizens. One of her surveillance targets was the prime minister's wife, whom he divorced. Nagyová was taken into custody along with eight other officials following the most extensive anticorruption operation since the collapse of communism. They were charged with corruption and misuse of power. Four hundred police raided his office, several ministries, and various lobbyists' residences and found almost €5 million in cash ($6 million) and several pounds of gold.

This temporary ODS-led three-party center-right government quickly introduced budget-tightening policies, following up on measures introduced by the preceding ODS government. It had enacted a 15% flat tax and lowered corporate taxes. It also sought reductions in bureaucracy and state spending and reform of the pension and health systems. The retirement age was being gradually raised from 62 for men and 61 for women to 65 for both by 2030. Fees of about $1.85 for a doctor's visit or a prescription and $4.00 for a day in the hospital were introduced to an outcry of protest. Czechs visit their doctors more often than any other Europeans, and many consider free health care a right, despite the fact that the system is partly financed by payroll deduction.

Czech Republic

The Christian Democrats (KDU-CSL), led by Pavel Belobradek, captured 6.78% of the votes (up by 2.4%) and 14 seats; it had fallen below the 5% threshold in 2010 and had been locked out of parliament. In 2017 it garnered 5.8% and 10 seats.

Two new parties sprang onto the political stage, thanks to voters' disgust at corruption scandals affecting all the established parties. The Alliance of Dissatisfied Citizens (ANO 2011, also meaning "yes"), led by the country's second-richest person, Andrej Babiš, was the surprise winner of the 2013 elections. It garnered 18.65% of the votes and 47 seats to win a place in the center left government. It attracted many of the former voters of the historically dominant Civic Democrats (ODS). An ethnic Slovak and a tycoon worth $2 billion with an agribusiness and media empire (including the two highest-circulation daily newspapers), Babiš was able to shake off accusations that he had been an agent for the reviled communist secret police (StB). If true, these allegations could have legally prevented him from participating in politics. He was a member of the Communist Party. He created ANO to oppose the political class and to fight against the endemic corruption and high taxes. ANO has become a kingmaker. ANO won the October 2017 elections, capturing 78 of the 200 seats and 29.6% of the votes. Promising to curb corruption, Babiš was sworn in as prime minister in January 2018, although he faced charges of fraud. Some voters accepted the argument that he is so rich that he could not be tempted by corruption.

In the October 2021 parliamentary elections, Babiš and his ANO party narrowly

Incumbent Prime Minister Petr Fiala
Source: *Wikipedia*

Czechs protest US antimissile radar.

lost to a conservative five-party coalition—"Together." Its leader, Petr Fiala, was named prime minister.

A second new party to join the seven parties that won parliamentary seats in 2013 is Usvit (Dawn), led by Tomio Okamura, which garnered 6.88% of the votes and 14 seats. Some observers call this party protofascist. It is in the opposition.

Top09, a conservative grouping headed by popular and colorful former foreign minister Karel Schwarzenberg, snatched 12% of the votes (down from 16.7%) and 26 seats (down from 41). It won 5.3% and 7 seats in 2017. He is one of the few politicians not suspected of corruption because he is a wealthy aristocrat. A Habsburg prince whose parents fled Czechoslovakia in 1948 when the communists took power, he grew up in Austria. He was an independent member of the outgoing cabinet nominated by the Greens. An urbane internationalist and ardent supporter of the United States, he hosted the 2009 EU-US annual summit in his noble family's spectacular Hluboká Castle. He was unsuccessful in his bid for the presidency in 2013.

The left parties did better. The Social Democrats (CSSD) did manage to emerge as the largest party. Led by Bohuslav Sobotka, it captured 20.45% of the votes (down from 22%) and 50 seats (a loss of 6). This was a disappointing result, but it was sufficient to form the three-party government with Sobotka as prime minister. He signaled a sharp break from the anti-EU policies of the past. The country is to be put on track to join the euro by the end of the decade. President Zeman and he are

known to have a strong dislike for each other. October 2017 was a disaster—7% and 15 seats.

The only established party that succeeded in holding its own in 2013 was the unreformed and unapologetic Communist Party of Bohemia and Moravia (KSCM). Led by Vojtěch Filip, it won 14.9% of the votes (up 3.64%) and 33 seats (up by 7). It fell in October 2017 to 7% and 15 seats. The Communists are strident opponents of NATO, which they regard as a tool of "American imperialism." Following the NATO air war in Kosovo, the party called for war crimes indictments against President Bill Clinton, British prime minister Tony Blair, German chancellor Gerhard Schröder, and former NATO secretary-general Javier Solana. It is the strongest unreformed communist party in the former eastern bloc and has changed neither its Marxist ideology nor its name. Its 100,000 members are nostalgic for the days when they ruled by force. The main thing it altered was its logo; it is now two cherries instead of a hammer and sickle.

The Communists remain untouchables in Czech politics. No other party will work with them. But their electoral success is a warning that the rapid pace of economic reform had hurt many Czechs and that the standard of living for many had plummeted. The fact that any government must work around the Communists' one-tenth of the total seats almost ensures that any governing alliance is unsustainable. The Czech Republic must find a way out of this stalemate.

Foreign Policy

While the Communist Party controlled Czechoslovakia, it had no independent foreign policy. The Czechoslovak ambassador to the United States once said, "The foreign policy of Czechoslovakia is the foreign policy of the Soviet Union." That all changed in December 1989. The Czechoslovak government established relations with Israel and the Vatican, President Havel gave orders for the curtailment of worldwide arms exports, and the country carried out successful negotiations with the Soviet Union to get Soviet troops withdrawn from Czechoslovakia. The last of the troops left in June 1991.

In other signs of change during this period, both Alexander Dubček and Václav Havel made trips to the United States. Havel gave a major address before a combined session of Congress. Czechoslovakia was also among those nations urging the Soviet Union to drop its insistence that a united Germany either be neutral or hold simultaneous membership in both NATO and the Warsaw Pact. Czechoslovakia wanted a united Germany to be part of NATO.

Czech Republic

After the demise of the Soviet Union in 1991, Czechoslovakia extended diplomatic recognition to the successor republics and opened separate relations with them. It sought good relations with the newly independent Republic of Ukraine. But the Czechoslovak leadership was more attuned to the new Russian political leadership in Moscow, with whom it maintains cordial relations. Its relations with the remaining successor republics have been less extensive, although ties with Ukraine warmed after Leonid Kuchma was elected president in 1994.

American-Czech relations remain good. To facilitate travel to the US, the two governments agreed that Czechs can apply online for a visa waiver that allows them to avoid both the long lines outside the embassy and the odious $160 fee.

Some Czechs remain uneasy about a resurgent Russia. That fear is less of a military attack and more of Russia's economic influence, especially in the energy sector. Three-fourths of its natural gas comes from Russia. A Czech-Russian consortium led by Atomstroy-export, a Russian engineering company, is a major contender to build up to five nuclear reactors. During a visit to the Czech Republic in 2007, ex-president George W. Bush emphasized that "the Cold War is over. The people of the Czech Republic don't have to choose between being a friend to the United States or a friend with Russia. You can be both."

Not all Czechs agree, especially those of the Cold War generation. They find naive President Obama's decision in 2009 to "reset the start button" on US-Russian relations and to cancel the planned antimissile system. The domestic intelligence agency BIS warned that as many as 150 Russian spies were operating in the country. One investigative reporter wrote, "We got rid of those people, and now they are coming back." The nation was gripped by a major spy scandal in 2011 involving Russian prison psychologist Robert Rakhardzho, who became a naturalized Czech citizen, befriended a female army major working on the staff of three top generals, and learned from her gossip and rumors about the officers that could be used to compromise and bribe them. All three and the major had to resign. The plot was spiced by sex and infidelity, creating stories of a Czech Mata Hari, the alluring First World War spy executed in France for her snooping. Former President Miloš Zeman has aroused consternation among allies and some Czechs for condemning sanctions against Russia and dismissing events in Ukraine as "civil war." He contradicted the policies of the prime minister and foreign office. His praise of Russian and Chinese leaders sparked angry demonstrations in the streets.

Former president Vaclav Klaus

The Czech government would welcome greater American investment in the Czech industry, partly to offset the strong investment drive from Germany, but partly also because they would like to see a greater American economic presence. For a while the Czech Republic received the largest amount of foreign investment in central and eastern Europe. In the first decade of the 21st century, foreign direct investment amounted to about 10% of GDP annually.

The Czech Republic's relations with Slovakia were a little uneven as long as Vladimir Mečiar remained Slovak prime minister. They have improved greatly since 1998, when a new government committed to closer cooperation with both the Czech Republic and the west replaced Mečiar.

Despite a relatively low level of public support, the Czech Republic became a full member of NATO in March 1999. Czechs were divided roughly into one-third of the population in favor of NATO entry, one-third against, and one-third undecided. Less than two weeks after joining, NATO air offensive against Serbia began in order to halt the Serbian mistreatment of Kosovar Muslims. Polls showed that Czech public opinion was against the NATO action by two to one. This was because of the Czechs' historically good relations with Serbia and pre-1991 Yugoslavia. Nevertheless, Prague supported NATO military actions against Yugoslavia over Kosovo and granted all of NATO's operational requests for use of Czech air-fields and transit across its airspace and territory. It sent a military field hospital to North Macedonia and pledged $30 million to help Kosovar refugees. However, it did not actively participate.

Havel, in particular, was an outspoken advocate of the NATO actions. The Atlantic Alliance is not only a solid cornerstone for Czech security, even though the republic faces no serious military threat, but also NATO is an important symbol of the extent to which Czechs share the west's democratic values. After the war was over, the Czech government, citing the expense of keeping a larger unit in Kosovo, proposed sending a platoon of 150 members. This would have been the smallest contingent of any NATO country except Iceland, which has no army. However, the government reversed its position after Havel criticized the plan. On June 15, the Czech Chamber of Deputies authorized an 800-member military unit for the peacekeeping duty in Kosovo. In late June 1999, he became the first NATO head of state to visit Kosovo.

Primarily because of the moral example set by Havel, the country has earned a reputation within the EU for promoting human rights at every opportunity, whether it be in Belarus, Moldova, or especially Cuba. Its diplomats are among the first to raise sticky questions about democratic values in other lands. This sometimes earns them the charge that they are acting as mere messengers for the US. But they hasten to remind critics that the government opposes the American trade embargo against Cuba and the Guantanamo Bay detention camp.

NATO tries to persuade the country to bring its armed forces up to alliance standards. It devotes less than 2% of GDP to military spending and has a total active force of 17,932 and 3,100 paramilitary troops. Conscription was phased out by 2007. By that time planners had pared the forces, slimmed down the top-heavy command structure, reduced the number of garrisons from 140 to 50, and trained its officers and soldiers to function in the NATO language—English. The army has 12,656 troops that include a rapid-reaction brigade.

The air force has 5,276 airmen and acquired 38 modern home-built light-combat L-159 jet bombers to replace its aging fleet of Russian-made SU-22 fighters. Its supersonic fleet of MiG-21 fighters reached the end of its operational life in 2005. The government had earmarked $2 billion to replace them with new Swedish- and British-made Gripen combat aircraft by Saab, but the disastrous flooding in August 2002 required that the money be used instead for cleanup. Fierce competition returned between Gripen and US F-16s. In 2004 the Czechs chose to lease 14 new Gripen supersonic fighters from the Swedish government for $754 million. It also acquired transport planes. Its troops in Kuwait and Afghanistan had to be moved in commercial aircraft. Prague deployed 300 troops in Iraq, but it withdrew all of them by 2010. It sent 480 soldiers to Afghanistan and 409 to Kosovo.

Following the September 11 terrorist attacks in New York, the Czech government responded by sending a field hospital to

Czech Republic

Afghanistan to assist in the military operations. However, Czech leaders worried about becoming a terrorist target after receiving reports that the mastermind of the September 11 attacks, Mohamed Atta, had met with an Iraqi intelligence agent and discussed attacking the headquarters of US-financed Radio Free Europe, which had been moved into the communist-era parliament on Wenceslas Square in Prague. Officials asked that it be moved to the edge of the city.

Although a majority of Czechs opposed the 2003 war in Iraq, their government supported the American and British allies. Even during the Cold War, the Czechs were the Warsaw Pact specialists in nuclear, biological, and chemical (NBC) warfare, and they maintain that specialty in NATO. Their NBC forces were deployed to Kuwait to support Operation Enduring Freedom in 2003.

The government expressed its willingness in 2007 to provide a base for an American antimissile radar to help protect Europe and the US against future nuclear weapons states in the Middle East. Then-foreign minister Schwarzenberg argued that "a small country like the Czech Republic has to prove itself as a reliable partner and as a good ally." Despite vehement opposition from Russia, the landmark accord was signed in July 2008, the first such agreement to be reached with a central or eastern European country.

However, there were serious obstacles to realization. Public-opinion polls consistently showed that two-thirds of Czechs opposed it. Many are unsure how exposed they want to be on the international stage, with a resurgent Russia close by. Many

Czechs do not want to alienate Russia. Its ability to harass the country was demonstrated at the time of the signing when it reduced by half its oil shipments to the country for "technical reasons." There are concerns about the health effects of such a large radar, and voters in three villages near the planned base rejected it in a non-binding referendum.

Enough parliamentarians opposed the idea that the Czech government had to drop it. Parallel negotiations had taken place to deal with the legal status of American troops deployed on Czech soil to operate the missile site. Many Czechs do not like the idea of having foreign troops (even Americans) stationed on their soil after many decades of Soviet occupation. The stakes were high for Czech political leaders, who had invested a lot of political capital in this missile project. President Obama abandoned the project in 2009. In 2011 the Czechs did the same, feeling disappointed with the US for leaving them high and dry, even though they risked a lot by provoking Russia's ire.

Czech public opinion and most parties are tepid toward the European Union. Czechoslovakia had been admitted to associate membership in 1991, along with Hungary and Poland. The Czech and Slovak republics retained that status after separation. The Czech government began aligning its foreign policy to that of the EU. For example, when Yugoslavia broke up, the Czechs extended diplomatic recognition to the successor republics only after the EU had done so. In 2007 the Czech Republic joined the Schengen Agreement allowing free passage within EU countries.

EU entry was more complicated than NATO membership and involved more transformation and pain (e.g., in terms of the environment). A new member must incorporate 80,000 pages of EU regulations into their laws; half of them deal with agriculture. With its small agricultural sector (3% of the workforce and 2% of GDP), the Czech Republic had fewer adjustments to make than did Poland. It has a modern economy, with 59% employed in services producing 60% of GDP, while 38% work in industry, creating 37% of the nation's wealth.

Many Czechs found the bureaucracy in Brussels to be arrogant and corrupt. Ex-president Václav Klaus warned that the EU could diminish Czech sovereignty and said it was like dropping a lump of sugar into a cup of coffee. The EU's public criticism of Czech preparations for membership created resentment, and the many trade disputes with EU countries make the union appear hypocritically protectionist.

Entry was powerfully boosted by an EU report concluding that nothing in the decrees permitting the postwar expulsions was incompatible with EU laws, and Germany and Austria announced that they would not veto Czech entry because of the Sudeten issue. In the June 2003 referendum, 55% of voters turned out, and 77.33% voted in favor of entry. An exuberant ex-prime minister Špidla exclaimed, "for me this is the end of World War II, with all its consequences." It became a full member in May 2004.

After the EU constitution was rejected by French and Dutch voters in May and June 2005, the Czechs postponed their ratification of the constitutional treaty. In May 2007 it grudgingly supported the resurrection and revision of parts of the document, now called the Lisbon Treaty, as a basis for reforming the EU. But ratification was again a problem. Although the government was largely in favor of the Lisbon Treaty and the lower house of parliament approved it, the upper house asked the Constitutional Court to determine whether the new reform treaty is compatible with Czech law. The court ruled that it was, and in May 2009 the Senate voted to approve it.

President Václav Klaus, who refused to fly the EU flag over the presidential palace, was a well-known Euroskeptic, and he had doubts about the reform. But a 2008 Eurobarometer poll revealed two-thirds of Czechs believed that their country had benefited from membership. Therefore, Klaus eventually signed the treaty. He concluded that the country would be isolated in Europe if he denied his signature. However, he demanded and received from the EU an opt-out from the treaty's Charter of Fundamental Rights. He argued that it

Peace and quiet reign in the Krkonos̆e mountains AP/Wide World Photo

Street musicians in front of the Presidential Palace, Prague

could have prompted a flood of property claims by Germans expelled after the war. Prime Minister Sobotka, who took office in January 2014, vowed to change the country's anti-EU, antieuro reputation.

The Czech Republic's response to the 2015 migrant crisis rekindled cooperation within the Visegrád Group (or V4) that also includes Hungary, Slovakia, and Poland. Rooted in historical links among those nations since their monarchs first met at Visegrád, Hungary, in the Middle Ages, the group coordinated its members' accession process to the European Union and to NATO from 1991 through 2004. The regional cooperation was put on the back burner for a while once all members were accepted by the EU. Members differed in their approach to Russian aggression, for example, with Poles pushing for far more rigorous sanctions than the Czechs. However, there has been some renewed interest in revitalizing it. Hungary's assertive policies vis-a-vis the EU give it much political clout, and its resistance to taking in migrants was welcomed by its regional partners. This became crucial in September 2015, when the European Union created a scheme for the redistribution of 160.000 migrants from Greece and Italy among EU's member states. Initially, all Visegrád Group members uniformly opposed the plan, but eventually Poland abandoned its allies, leaving the Czech Republic, Slovakia, and Hungary (plus Romania) to vote against the scheme. Ultimately, the plan was adopted by a large majority, and the Czechs were expected to implement it despite their objections. That would mean accepting some 2,900 refugees, or an average of 2 persons per 10.000 citizens, one of the lowest percentages in the EU. By June 2017, the EU declared that it was launching infringement procedures against the Czech Republic, as well as Poland and Hungary, for noncompliance with their obligations on relocation. The Czechs were criticized for

having done nothing to implement the relocation quota policy.

The Czech Republic Germany / Austria

Germany's relations with Poland are markedly better than those with the Czech Republic. Unlike Poland, which did not diminish in size since the fall of communism, the Czech Republic became smaller (from 15 million to 10 million inhabitants), while Germany (its major trading partner and foreign investor) became larger. Thus, its old fears of German predominance are greater. It is small wonder that in the spring of 1990 only 37% of Czechs said they favored German unification. In a 1995 poll asking Czech respondents to decide "from which state you feel threatened," over 40% identified Russia, about 25% Germany, and only about 5% the United States. In 1996 half the Czech public regarded Germany as a danger for the Czech economy.

Also feeding fears of the Germanization of the Czech economy is the fact that 4 of the top 20 firms in the republic are German. This does not include Volkswagen's successful joint venture with Škoda. Some Czechs speak of a *Kalter Anschluss* (a "cold annexation," referring to Hitler's acquisition of Austria in 1938). Also, while Poland militarily resisted Germany at the beginning of World War II, Czechoslovakia did not. This fact affects national consciousness and confidence positively in Poland and negatively in the Czech Republic.

Without question, the greatest obstacle to relations between the two countries involves Sudeten Germans. Pursuant to the decree by Czech president Eduard Beneš on May 19, 1945, approved in article 13 of the Potsdam Agreement of August 2, 1945, from 2 million to 3 million ethnic Germans were deported, and from 19,000 to 30,000 were killed or died in transit. By 2000 only 38,000 Czechs called themselves Germans. Refugees from many parts of eastern Europe poured into western Germany after

the war—from Silesia, Pomerania, East Prussia, and the Sudetenland. The Czech Republic entered the 21st century without ever having rescinded the Beneš decrees.

Many Czechs today admit that some excesses did occur in the course of the expulsions. Witnesses reported lynchings, SS troopers being burned alive or tethered to workhorses and torn limb from limb, and innocent Germans randomly shot or raped. Even in late 1945, after emotions had cooled somewhat, 50,000 people turned out in Prague to watch public executions of Germans as entertainment.

Nevertheless, a majority of Czechs believes that the expulsion of these people (who before 1939 outnumbered Slovaks) was just. After all, 91% of Sudeten Germans had voted for a pro-Nazi party in the 1938 elections. In a 2002 survey, only 1.4% of Czechs (7.2% in the former Sudeten area) favored a renunciation of the decrees. Most would refuse to vote for a political party that would be willing to make any concessions to the Sudeten German demands. When newly elected president Václav Havel offered an apology in 1990 and later used the word "expulsion" in a 1995 speech at Prague's Charles University, he was severely criticized at home.

Recognizing that there was a minority of Sudeten Germans who had remained loyal to Czechoslovakia, then-prime minister Jiří Paroubek recommended in June 2005 that some kind of "gesture" of recognition be made to them, some form of symbolic compensation. This was not intended as an admission of guilt but as a deepening of "the friendship between the Czechs and Germans of today." Many Czechs, including their president, angrily rejected this.

Only a month earlier, tempers among expellees in Bavaria had flared up again when a statue honoring President Beneš was erected in front of the Foreign Ministry in Prague a day before the German chancellor was scheduled to visit the city. Paroubek attended the ceremony. Bavarian ex-minister-president Edmund Stoiber called this a "provocation" and "an attack against good-neighborly relations."

Almost everywhere the Sudeten Germans integrated and over time ceased acting as effective pressure groups in German politics. The exception is the 2 million Sudeten Germans who moved to Bavaria, maintain their Sudeten identity, want to show solidarity with their forebears, support the conservative Christian Social Union (CSU), and are organized in such groupings as the Munich-based *Sudetendeutsche Landmannschaft*. They cannot be ignored in Bavarian politics. Czechs want the creation of conditions whereby they no longer need to worry about this issue. But in 2002 former prime minister

Czech Republic

Zeman raised German hackles by describing the Sudeten Germans as "traitors" and Hitler's "fifth column." The matter was so serious that ex-Chancellor Schröder cancelled a planned visit to Prague. Zeman also found himself embroiled in a dispute with the Hungarian ex-prime minister Viktor Orbán, who demanded that the Beneš decrees, which had also included Hungarians, be revoked.

The Czech Republic must deal with many claims for return of sizable amounts of property. Franz Ulrich von Kinski, the primary heir of the line of Bohemian kings, is among the more than a dozen descendants of Austro-Hungarian nobility who sued the Prague government to recover private property confiscated after World War II. Among his 157 claims is a palace on Prague's Old Town Square that houses part of the Czech national gallery. Also, Prince Hans-Adam II of Liechtenstein has taken Germany to court to retrieve over €1 billion in real estate and artworks illegally expropriated to pay German postwar debts to Czechoslovakia. Prague refuses to return the land, though it offered the return of castles and palaces, which was rejected by Liechtenstein.

Germany believes it is much nicer to be surrounded by countries that are "in the same club," that is, in NATO and the EU. It is therefore not surprising that it was the first ally to propose eastern enlargement of these key western organizations. All Czech governments since 1990 regard integration into the EU as the best means of protecting national sovereignty. They like the fact that Germany, whose economic domination many Czechs fear, is itself fully integrated in the EU. Thus, the Czech Republic can deal with Germany in a multilateral setting. This goes a long way to freeing the smaller republic from its 20th-century nightmare of being caught between two large and formerly aggressive powers, Germany and Russia.

Germany's policy is that negotiations over the Czech entry into the EU would not be hampered by bilateral difficulties stemming from the shadows of history. In order to elevate the "European challenge" over the memories of the past, both governments signed a German-Czech Declaration on Mutual Relations and Their Future Development on January 21, 1997.

This strengthens the foundation created by the Neighborhood Treaty (*Nachbarschafts-vertrag*) of 1992. In Havel's words, the 1997 declaration "frees us."

On February 13, 1998, the countries' leaders signed the Czech-German Fund for the Future. This paved the way for a partial compensation of Czech victims of Nazism and established a forum for a nongovernmental dialogue between Sudeten Germans and Czechs. By 1998 two-thirds of Czechs considered German-Czech relations as "rather good" or "very good." The fruits are obvious—more young Czechs are learning German than any other foreign language; 27% of Czechs claim to speak it. Also, almost a third of all Czech exports are to Germany, and 30% of all direct investments are from German firms.

Austria is a major trading partner with and investor in the Czech Republic. Nevertheless, Czech-Austrian relations are also burdened by the Beneš decrees and the expulsion of Sudeten Germans. Even though most resettled in Germany, some went to Austria. Many Austrians resented Prague's approval of the EU's temporary policy of ostracizing their country after the Freedom Party entered the Austrian government in 2000. They are no doubt mystified at patriotic opposition in Prague in 2008 to erecting a copy of a horseback statue of Field Marshal Radetzky, a Czech who commanded an Austrian army in the 19th century. Like almost all reminders of the Habsburg Empire, the original had been removed in 1918.

Nuclear-free Austria also vehemently protested the Czech construction of a nuclear power plant in Temelin, 30 miles from the Austrian border. It was activated in 2000, and a second reactor was completed 15 months later. The Soviet-designed facility operates with a western control system. After spending $3 billion to $4 billion on Temelin, Czechs were extremely reluctant to close it, despite the sharpest diplomatic conflict with its western neighbors since the end of communism. Czechs are considering building several more reactors at Temelin, and the Russian state nuclear company Rosatom is competing fiercely with Westinghouse and Areva, a French energy company, for the contract.

The EU sided with the Czechs, but Vienna reminded Prague both officially and unofficially that Austria has a veto over any new country seeking membership in the exclusive club, the EU. It chose not to use that prerogative. The crisis was defused when the Czech government agreed to tighten security at the plant. State-run electricity giant CEZ hopes to build up to three new nuclear reactors in the Czech Republic and two elsewhere in the region. Renewable resources account for only 6% of energy the country uses.

The government regards nuclear power as a counter to its overdependence on Russia for oil and natural gas. Russia already provides the Czech Republic with almost 80% of its natural gas and 100% of its gas imports. Dozens of Russian firms, including Gazprom, have invested heavily there.

388

Václav Havel
Photo by Oldrich Skácha

ECONOMY

Czechoslovakia was already an industrialized nation when the communists took over in 1948. The coalition government installed in 1945 had nationalized about 60% of all industry and instituted a land reform aimed at breaking up all large land holdings. Major steps had also been taken toward institutionalizing socialism and state planning. With half of their work done for them, the communists only had to complete the nationalization of industry and adapt state planning to the command model developed by the Soviet Union in the 1930s. This was accompanied by a gradual collectivization of agriculture.

Czechoslovakia's first five-year plan was launched on January 1, 1949. Along with the following two subsequent five-year plans, it placed a major stress on the creation of heavy industry—again a slavish following of the Soviet model. The relative neglect of consumer industries and agriculture produced a lopsided economy that began to resemble more and more an industrialized copy of the Soviet model. Food items, such as meat, became scarce; a severe housing shortage developed in the cities; and the quality of consumer goods declined, as well. These developments obviously had an effect on morale, and as the third five-year plan progressed, even heavy industry began to fall short of its targets. In 1962, with the economy in a severe recession, the third five-year plan was simply abandoned.

A number of Czech economists associated with the Institute of Economics of the Czechoslovak Academy of Sciences had been critical of Stalinist concepts of command planning for a number of years. One of the most prominent and outspoken of these proposed a plan for reordering the economy that became known as the "New Economic Model." A Soviet counterpart,

Yevsei (Evsei) Liberman, had influenced the Czech economist, and his plan, like the Liberman Plan, called for limiting the role of the central planners. Individual enterprises were to be managed on the basis of profitability; worker salaries were to be based in part on individual skills; and there was to be a major stress on upgrading technology.

President Novotný initially opposed the plan. However, as the economy continued to flounder, he gave grudging approval for its initiation in 1967, although he did specify that it leave the party's central policy-making authority intact. But it was a start in name only. As a result of continued opposition by conservatives involved in central planning, it failed to have any significant effect.

In Czechoslovakia, the reformers decided to challenge the conservative leadership and were instrumental in securing the resignation of Novotný as head of the party. Dubček, his successor, fully supported the reform measures, and the economist who initially wrote the plan became deputy prime minister.

Even as the reformers began implementing their "New Economic Model"; however, the Soviets were drawing up their own plans to invade Czechoslovakia. Afterward, the Husák regime condemned the economic reform as a "romantic notion." The central planners again assumed control of the economy. Industry continued to be plagued by outdated technology, declining productivity, and low-level products. Proposals for economic reform were never really put into effect or, if they were, had no effect.

Dismantling the Command Economy

The revolution of 1989 put a new set of leaders in power. Although there was some floundering in the first year, the government began to take the necessary steps to create a market economy. In 1991, the Federal Assembly passed a broad privatization law that committed the government to denationalize all industry. Companies nationalized after 1948 were to be returned to their original owners or their descendants, while remaining companies were to be privatized through a complex system of government-issued coupons or sold to foreign investors. The key individual responsible for the government's plans was Václav Klaus, then finance minister.

As the political debate between Czechs and Slovaks over the future of the common state grew in intensity in 1991, however, Klaus's plans for economic reform were thrust partially aside. In November 1991, the Czech government announced that it had made significant progress in its small-scale privatization program, having sold 12,333 out of 20,786 business units

included in the program. Less progress had been made in large-scale privatization, but the government had held seven auctions, approved five direct sales, and prepared two public tenders.

The government began privatization of large-scale industry through its coupon program in March 1992. Czech citizens were offered books of vouchers for 1,000 crowns (approximately $35), which could then be used to bid for shares. Facilitating the process, approximately 400 investment funds were set up to manage the shareholdings. Though by law they were not permitted to hold more than 20% of the shares of any one company, they eventually ended up holding 70% of the shares on behalf of individual investors. In June 1993, with over 1,000 Czech and Slovak companies privatized, the government sponsored creation of the Prague Stock Exchange to provide a market for the shares.

As of January 1, 1993, almost 1,000 Czech companies had been privatized, and there were 6 million stockholders. A second round of voucher privatization in the latter part of 1994 transferred assets worth an additional $5.8 billion. All told, approximately 80% of all Czechs participated in the two sets of voucher privatizations. In addition, more than 100,000 properties worth an estimated $4 billion were returned to their former owners. By 1997, the process of privatization was essentially complete, and in 2000 an impressive 68% of GDP was generated by the private sector. In 2001 the privatization of the banking sector was completed. A year later the government sold its 51% stake in the country's largest telecommunication company, Český Telecom, the biggest

Everybody loves a bride! Prague.

Czech Republic

private equity deal ever in post-communist central Europe.

Some economists have complained that the voucher system of privatization produced a system whereby ownership was separated from oversight, and the effect of this was that companies were not under strong pressure to restructure in order to become more competitive. Since ownership was widely dispersed and the investment funds were primarily portfolio managers, there was some basis for the worry. On the other hand, companies that have not performed adequately have tended to find it difficult or impossible to raise new capital, and that has provided incentives to become more competitive. A greater worry is that the biggest Czech banks manage the biggest investment funds. That presents not only a potential conflict of interest but also opportunities for favoritism.

In February 1993 the Czech and Slovak parliaments announced that the agreement on a common currency for the two republics had been terminated. After just over a month, each republic issued its own currency. The customs union managed to survive. Trade between the two republics did fall considerably following separation, but it has since recovered. In 2015, Slovakia accounted for 9% of the Czech Republic's exports and 7.4% of its imports. The emphasis of Czech trade policy since 1993 has been to redirect its exports to western Europe. Its growing trade with the European Union members far surpasses any loss of exports to Slovakia. Germany alone buys more than 30% of all Czech exports.

The Czech Republic depends on Russia's Gazprom for 80% of its gas supplies, although it has been able to fend off that giant company's efforts to gain control of its transmission, distribution, and retailing of gas. The Czech Republic has diversified its energy sources by purchasing Norwegian gas and transporting it across Germany. It also has a pipeline that is independent of the one that transports Russian gas to western Europe.

The Czech Republic has been the largest recipient of foreign direct investment in central Europe, equivalent to 10% of GDP throughout the first decade of the 21st century. This has resulted in a significant international presence, including by the US. For example, Hewlett-Packard, Exxon-Mobil, and IBM outsourced operations there. In 2002 the republic was the target for $9.3 billion in foreign direct investment, and it continues to grow. By 2000 over 1,200 foreign investors were manufacturing in the Czech Republic. They benefit from significant cost efficiencies, including relatively low wages. Pay is around a quarter of German levels, but social charges are near western European levels, adding 35% to wages.

Although earnings are growing fast, they are still in line with productivity growth, which at about 4% is well above the eurozone's .4%. Productivity at foreign-owned companies is at the same level as in western Europe. Other advantages are a long Czech 39-hour workweek (1,980 hours per year vs. 1,815 in the US and 1,444 in Germany), more flexibility about working practices, a central strategic location, and the ability to source locally from the republic's excellent supply base. By 2010, 97% of the banking sector was owned by foreign banks. They proved to be among the most stable in the region during the 2008–2010 global economic crisis.

The republic is the fifth-largest car producer in Europe. Perhaps the most famous company to invest in the Czech economy was Volkswagen, which invested $5.5 billion to obtain a 70% interest in the Škoda automobile plant, located in Mlada Boleslav, about 30 miles outside of Prague. In 2003 Škoda's domestic market share slipped below 50%, and around 70% of its production is exported. Car production also received a powerful boost from a Toyota-Peugeot-Citroen joint venture in Kolin (central Bohemia). At full production it will turn out 300,000 vehicles, compared with nearby Škoda Auto's 451,675 in 2004.

In 2006 Hyundai announced plans to invest €1 billion in a new auto manufacturing plant at Nošovice in eastern Czech Republic, completed in 2008. This is the country's largest foreign investment, and it made the Czech Republic one of the EU's three largest automobile-manufacturing countries. In 2008 it produced almost 1 million automobiles and accounted for about 10% of the entire economy. But that magnitude makes the industry very vulnerable to the kind of plunge the western European auto market experienced in 2009. Other companies included Nestle, which took a 43% stake in the chocolate maker Čokoládovny Modřany, and Philip Morris, which obtained a 65% interest in Tabak, the cigarette maker.

Two months after the November 1989 revolution, Foreign Minister Jiří Dienstbier, a former dissident who had worked since 1977 as a furnace-stoker on the Prague subway, announced that Prague would "simply end its trade in arms" without regard to economic consequences. That turned out to be impossible, although the government did manage by 1993 to cut the output of weapons plants to 25% of 1988 levels. Political idealism was no longer a controlling factor. Nevertheless, in 2002 the government decided to buy the manufacturer of the plastic explosive Semtex from the chemicals group Aliachem to reduce the possibility that the explosive would ever again be used in a terrorist action, as it was in 1988,

when it brought down Pan Am Flight 103 over Lockerbie, Scotland.

Agriculture

With only 3% of its workforce engaged in farming, producing 2% of GDP, the Czech Republic faced fewer problems than Poland in meeting the agricultural requirements for entry into the EU. The government launched a program to transform the country's agriculture. In earlier federal legislation, collective farms had been legally transformed into cooperatives, and employees were given the right to ask for their own land. After they had taken legal title to their land, however, almost all owners arranged to lease back the land to the cooperatives. Only 1,120 of those who applied for land received more than 25 acres. Most wanted only a couple acres to work for themselves. This was disturbing from the government's point of view because the large agricultural subsidies allotted to the cooperatives to make them competitive acted as a drain on the national budget.

The federal government sought to deal with this problem by passing a "transformation" law which reduced government oversight over the cooperatives and made their elective bodies responsible for management and decision making. The government hoped that, given the responsibility, the cooperatives would transform themselves. To encourage them in this direction, the government cut agricultural subsidies by one-quarter in 1991. A classic example of the communist-era products making a comeback is Kofola, the Czech cola introduced in the early 1960s to try to counter the appeal of American Coke. It now produces more than in its 1970s heyday and is challenging Coke for the top spot in the Czech and Slovak soft-drink market.

The Overall Economy

The Czech economy remains in transition, but it is quite strong. That is why it weathered the 2008–2009 global economic recession relatively well. In 2005

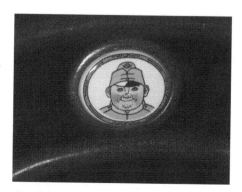

Good Soldier Svejk in a restaurant named after him

the Swiss- based International Institute for Management Development ranked it 36th out of 60 states in terms of competitiveness. The government deficit rose to 5.7% in 2023. Public debt rose to almost 40% of GDP by 2010. Its unemployment rate had fallen dramatically to 2.2% in 2023. Inflation was up to 9.7% and economic growth was 8.6% in 2023. The economy has become so dynamic that businesses face severe labor shortages. Many are acquiring robots. In the post-communist world, its citizens' living standards are exceeded only by those in Slovenia. In the two decades since the fall of communism, per-capita GDP has almost doubled to $20,620 and is 80% of the EU average.

After three years in the doldrums, Czech prosperity was growing steadily again in 2007 and 2008. In 2009 the economy contracted by 4% as a result of the global economic crisis, but it grew by 0.9% in 2023. A real problem is the fact that 80% of GDP is generated by exports, and the bulk of those go to western Europe. Thus, Czechs are vulnerable to the ups and downs of western European economies. It can affect its successful tourist industry, which accounts for 3% of GDP and more than 250,000 jobs. The country has 12 UNESCO sites, including Prague, the world's largest. It possesses over 2,000 castles. Before the Covid pandemic, Prague attracted 8 million tourists each year.

One positive consequence of the kind of prosperity Czechs enjoy since 1989 is that they eat healthier food, have better medical care, and live longer. By 2015 life expectancy for men had risen by 4 years to 74.5 and women by 3 years to 80.6. They eat fewer artery-clogging meaty foods and more chicken, fish, and fresh vegetables. One habit remains constant—while the rest of the world is increasingly turning to wine, Czechs stick to beer, consuming an average of 41 gallons a year. Fed up with a limited choice of mediocre, mass-produced beers, brewers have created over 250 microbreweries. This compares with only one in 1989.

In 2010 drug laws were liberalized, calling only for fines if techno fans and other users are found with amounts limited to personal use. The government wants to distinguish between users and producers. The latter are still outlaws, and the authorities want to clamp down on them. The republic is Europe's largest producer of methamphetamine, and cannabis is mass-produced.

The birth rate is among the lowest in Europe, and the Czech population of 10.5 million is predicted to fall to 8.1 million by 2050 if immigration is restrictive. With more than 230,000 legal immigrants and another 200,000 illegal ones totaling about 4% of the total population, the Czech Republic has twice the percentage of other central European nations. They take jobs most Czechs do not want, such as cleaning, construction, and restaurant work.

The most convenient target for far-right groups who want to blame minority groups for crime and the economic problems at home are the 300,000 Roma (Gypsies). The majority is unemployed and receives taxpayer-funded benefits. Xenophobic, anti-Semitic, and homophobic extremists parade through towns with significant Roma populations and terrorize them and ignite or damage their homes. There are frequent clashes with demonstrators and the police, and Roma sometimes retaliate against their attackers. In 2010 a Czech court banned the far-right Workers' Party for its involvement.

Wages, at $1,400 (€1,160) a month for the average worker in 2015, were sufficiently higher than countries to the east that a sizable black market in labor developed. Despite its economic advance, corruption in business and politics remains widespread. Graft is an important reason EU funds earmarked for infrastructure failed to translate into major road improvements and why projects tend to run hugely over budget. Czech highways, previously superior to those of the neighbors like Poland (who used the EU finds to modernize its infrastructure), are clogged and in dire need for repairs. In 2015 Transparency International ranked the country ninth from the bottom in the EU in terms of corruption. Ex-foreign minister Schwarzenberg described it as a "cancer" that threatens to turn the Czech Republic into "Sicily, minus the sea and oranges."

As of 2023, the Czech Republic has entered a recession and has continued to underperform economically compared to other European Union member states, which show signs of recovery from the crisis caused by the COVID-19 pandemic. The Czech Republic also experienced high debt growth and a decrease in real wages, despite a reduction in the average level of debt in the EU, and recorded the highest inflation rate in the EU during the 2021–2023 inflation spike. Prime Minister Fiala and his government were met with highly negative evaluations by the Czech public.

CULTURE

Prague, the center of Czech culture, is a stunningly beautiful city full of carefully preserved ancient churches with gold-tipped spires, plus baroque, Romanesque, and art nouveau buildings untouched by the bombs of World War II. On the hill above the Vltava River stands Hradčany Castle, residence of the president. St. Vitus Cathedral, Prague's great Gothic cathedral, is part of that same complex, and its spires stand out against the sky. Down the hill from Hradčany and St. Vitus, the 14th-century Charles IV bridge—now a pedestrian walkway closed to traffic—leads across to the old city center. Here, in the old residence quarter of the city, one finds Wenceslas Square (Václavske Namesti) and Old Town (Stare Mesto) Square, with its Jan Hus Memorial.

One must give the old communist government credit. It did put a great deal of money and effort into fixing up the older buildings of Prague in their last years in power. It seemed at the time that scaffolding surrounded half the city's architectural, historical, and religious structures, but visitors to Prague have the benefit of that effort today. Czechs remain divided on a new National Library, designed by Jan Kaplický. Its spotted mound has been called a "jellyfish and a mountain of slime."

Czechs enjoy a rich film tradition. Films, such as *Elementary School* and *Kolya*, are post-Soviet era films that nevertheless fit well within a long-standing Czech tradition of literature and film. Their subtlety and light touch enabled good Czech films to circumvent censorship. As scholar Herb Eagle put it, "You have eccentric characters who are simply incapable of obeying the rules." *Dark Blue World*, and *Divided We Fall* are accurate portrayals of wartime reality. *Dark Blue World* by director Jan Svěrák, describes some of the more than 2.000 Czechs who fled to England in 1939 and served in the Royal Air Force. (Czech fighter ace Josef František, who flew with the Polish 303 squadron, was the highest-scoring RAF pilot during the Battle of Britain.) Since Nazi Germany considered them citizens of the Third Reich, their risks were doubled. If they were captured, they could be executed as traitors rather than interned as prisoners of war. *Divided We Fall* is a powerful film that focuses on the terror of Nazi occupation; it was a finalist for a 2001 Academy Award.

Prague's sprawling Barrandov Studios have produced good films since the 1930s, thanks to its excellent facilities and skilled crews and actors. Its film industry employs 15.000 to 25,000 per year, producing such films in Prague as *The League of Extraordinary Gentlemen, Van Helsing*, and *Amadeus*, which was re-released as *Amadeus: Director's Cut*. The Czechs compete with the Hungarians and Romanians for the lucrative film business, but they do very well because of their considerable skills and low prices compared with London, Paris, and Los Angeles. Prague also lends itself to many different kinds of scenery and can be made to look like almost anywhere. Not having been destroyed in either world war, it offers filmmakers a broad array of architecture, periods, and style. Foreign

Czech Republic

Czech Republic

film crews find inviting hotels, bars, and restaurants after hours.

The fact that such films as *Bridget Jones*, Hugh Grant's *Notting Hill*, Matt Damon's *The Bourne Identity*, and Roman Polanksi's *Oliver Twist* were filmed in Prague also lures tourists by the thousands and attracts world attention to the country. The same could be said of the world's richest top model, Karolina Kurková. However, some tourists are no longer as welcome as they once were, especially young foreign fun seekers, for whom the country is central Europe's cheapest and best fleshpot.

The Czech language gave English such words as "dollar" (tolar), "pistol," and "robot." More importantly, the Czechs have contributed substantially to the world of music and literature. One needs only to recall Antonín Dvořák, composer of the New World Symphony; Vilém Blodek, famous for his comic operas; Leoš Janáček; and Bedřich Smetana, whose music recalls the struggle for nationhood culminating in the creation in 1918 of a new state.

Perhaps the most enduring classic of Czech literature and the most translated book from the Czech language is Jaroslav Hašek's *Dobrý voják Švejk* (The Good Soldier Schweik). This satirical novel follows a lovable and earthy though not very smart dealer in stolen dogs who is drafted into the Austro-Hungarian army during World War I and through excessive zeal combined with ineptitude manages to derail the empire's war effort. Czechs could find a reflection of their own measured responses to external threats in Švejk and his work within the machinery of oppressive power rather than, for example, the Poles' romantic and ultrapatriotic impulse to fight and die at the ramparts sooner than surrender.

Another Czech writer of world renown is Jaroslav Seifert, who was awarded the Nobel Prize in literature in 1984. Seifert was one of the founders of Charter 77, the civil rights group organized to monitor the government's implementation of the Helsinki Accords. His writings were not generally available inside the country until after 1989. Seifert's poetry is not really political, however. A typical example is his "Spring in the Fisherman's Net," which follows:

In the fisherman's cork-fringed net
is spring. Young bulbs abound
on the trees and smile at us
when we look round.
In the fisherman's cork-fringed net
spaced out in three
are the stars; we are acquainted,
one always remembers me
and lights up the pathway home
in the dark at journey's end.
Not so many have the luck

to find in the stars their true girl friend.
In the fisherman's cork-fringed net
the wind is caught. Its laughter is the
laugh all women know
when they talk about men together.
In the fisherman's cork-fringed net
the claws are caught of tender fear.
The same fear that men know
when they talk about women together.
(Tr. by ORBIS; used with permission)

The commercial aspects of culture after 1989 affect music, television, and literature. The literary scene has fallen on hard times. People work and travel more and read fewer books. Internationally known writers from communist times, such as Ivan Klima and Milan Kundera, have few equivalents in today's Czech Republic. Kundera, who is perhaps most famous for his novel *The Unbearable Lightness of Being*, lived as a recluse in France since 1975, where he took French citizenship. He prefers to write in French, and he is the best-known Czech fiction writer since Franz Kafka, who also did not write in Czech and was perhaps more German than Czech.

Kundera's reputation was tarnished in 2008 by a well-documented accusation that, as a 21-year-old student, he had denounced to the Czech police a western intelligence agent working for the Americans. This resulted in a 22-year jail sentence. This sparked a national soul searching in a nation that has always regarded him with ambivalence.

The country's best-known playwright is Václav Havel, whose absurdist plays were seldom seen in the outside world until the fall of communism. As a national hero and president, he did not resume his craft until 2008, when he wrote *Leaving*. This absurdist play deals with a political leader who has lost power but refuses to admit it and refuses to vacate his official residence. Some say that he had in mind his nemesis and successor, Václav Klaus, but Havel denied this. The National Theatre in Prague wanted to produce the play, but Havel insisted that his wife, actress Dagmar Havlová, appear in the lead. "I wrote it for her."

He also published an English edition of his presidential recollections, *To the Castle and Back*, in 2008. He worries about what he calls "post communism," whereby former communists dominate a large part of the economy. However, his admiration for America remains intact. He noted in a 2008 interview with the *Financial Times* that "the U.S., and especially New York, is a sort of a bazaar of the entire world. . . I find the atmosphere appealing. It's a truly free country."

The nation commissioned popular sculptor David Černý to produce a huge

52'x52' display, called *Entropa*, for the entrance of the European Council building in Brussels in 2009. Černý was directed to hire an artist from each member state and produce a work that symbolizes the glory of a unified Europe. However, notorious for his rejection of establishment rules, he faked the hiring of the 27 collaborators and designed it on his own, emphasizing some national stereotypes that needed to be abolished. The Netherlands was covered by a flood with only a few minarets peeping out of the water. Poland had two priests hoisting the LGBTQ rainbow flag, while Slovakia resembled a Hungarian sausage. The Bulgarian government was so enraged about its portrayal (a collection of squat toilets) that its foreign minister summoned the Czech ambassador in Sofia to lodge an official protest. The diplomatic outrage was such that the Czech government felt obliged to apologize for the "work." Černý's many other provocative installations include a sculpture of Sigmund Freud hanging by one hand over a narrow street in Prague and an upside-down statue of St. Wenceslaus, with his apparently dead horse hanging by the feet. Tourists can send text messages to his moving sculpture of two naked men standing in front of Franz Kafka Museum ankle deep in a tub shaped like the country's map—and the figures will "pee" in the water to spell out the text messages.

In June 2009 the government hosted a Holocaust Era Assets Conference to discuss the tracking down of long-lost art collections that were confiscated or acquired under dubious circumstances during the Nazi time. Czech authorities are known to take extraordinary legal measures to prevent the return of looted art from their museums.

Since the 19th century, when the nationalist movement distanced itself from the Catholic Church, which it identified with the foreign domination of the Habsburgs, the country has become more and more secular. This was strengthened by four decades of communist rule. In 2012 the government agreed to pay more than $6 billion over a 30-year period to the churches as compensation for their property confiscated by the communists. In return the state will not have to pay expenses and priests' salaries after 17 years.

Today about 70% of Czechs profess no belief in a particular religious denomination. During the collapse of communism in 1989, the churches presented themselves as an important opposition force, but that did not last. Former pope Benedict XVI tried to reverse the secularization and to remind Czechs of the Christian roots of their country by making a three-day pastoral visit in September 2009. One mass in Brno attracted 120,000 faithful.

A little-known angst that afflicts the Czech Republic is related to the name of the country. In April 2016 the Czech government official announced that they would prefer if their country was referred to as Czechia. This direct translation of the Czechs' own moniker of Česko (CHES-ko) is an attempt to find a shorter, catchier name that would be easier for foreigners to handle than the Czech Republic. Ultimately, this reflects their frustration with the fact that many people around the world do not know much about the country. (Some press reports misidentified the perpetrators of the Boston Marathon bombing as coming from the Czech Republic rather than Chechnya.) The name proposal is not universally loved in the country, though many appreciate its branding potential. Others think the rebranding is intended as a distraction from the real problems of the country, including right-wing extremism and corruption. Many were mystified as to why the government missed the opportunity to popularize the new name immediately by emblazoning it on the jerseys of its 2016 Olympic team instead of ordering them decorated with the formal Czech Republic name. Later that year, the UN accepted "Czechia" as the official short name of the country.

CURRENT ISSUES

In politics, the idealism of the early 1990s has collapsed into cynicism, cronyism, and corruption. But the revolution of November 1989 has not been forgotten. The 25th anniversary of this spectacular event was celebrated by thousands of Czechs who took to the streets to reenact the student protests that led to the overthrow of the hardline communist regime.

Three-fourths of the population admitted in a poll that they have benefited from EU membership. But at election time, the EU is a handy target for parties wanting to profit from voters' dissatisfactions. Only Top09 is unreservedly pro-Europe.

Feuding within the parties weakened and brought down more than a half-dozen prime ministers since EU entry in 2004. Andrej Babiš, a billionaire-turned-prime-minister who is often compared to Donald Trump and Silvio Berlusconi, provided a counterbalance to politics as usual through his insistence on the need to clean up corruption, despite the fact that he faced charges of fraud. He lost his bid for the presidency in January 2023. Czechs face the future with a new prime minister: Petr Fiala leading a 5-party center-right coalition.

Ex-president Miloš Zeman was widely criticized for his pro-Russian views on the crisis in Ukraine. His anti-immigrant rhetoric and unabashedly anti-Muslim barbs make him a difficult partner for the Czech prime minister.

Russia's involvement in its former satellite remains robust. Soon after the US accused Russia of cyberattacks against American corporations, Czech police arrested a Russian national for hacking targets in the US. Perhaps not surprisingly, a few months later, a "highly sophisticated" attack carried out by "experts in a foreign state" broke into dozens of e-mail accounts of the Czech Foreign Ministry, stealing thousands of documents. The officials hinted at Russia as a likely culprit. The Czech Republic also accused Vladimir Putin of supporting and manipulating right-wing populist parties and movements throughout Europe, from Marine LePen's National Front in France to Jobbik in Hungary.

Besides the destabilizing impacts of the migrant influx and Russian influences, Czechs are also worried about the long-term fallout from Brexit. With the accession to the EU in 2004, a large number of Czechs moved to the UK looking for better economic opportunities. One immediate reaction to the Brexit referendum was a sudden wave of racist abuse in the UK, directed mostly at the migrants from eastern Europe. The future of these EU workers residing in Britain remains an important issue. The EU insists on UK's responsibility for equal treatment of EU nationals.

During the Russian invasion of Ukraine in 2022, the Czech Republic took a hard line, advocating for the harshest sanctions against Russia and supporting Ukraine's accession to the European Union. After the invasion, it immediately began supplying Ukraine with weapons and humanitarian aid. Prime Minister Fiala, together with Polish Prime Minister Mateusz Morawiecki and Slovenian Prime Minister Janez Janša, visited Kyiv and met with Ukrainian President Volodymyr Zelensky as a sign of support for Ukraine. It was the first visit of foreign leaders to Kyiv since the beginning of the Russian invasion.

In July 2022, Prime Minister Fiala officially accepted the presidency of the Council of the European Union on behalf of the Czech Republic. He gave a speech in the European Parliament, in which he called for the defense of European values, continued support for Ukraine, and the inclusion of nuclear energy as a renewable resource (which was subsequently approved by a vote of MPs). In October 2022, Fiala presided over the first summit of the European Political Community held in Prague.

Slovak Republic / Slovakia (Slovenská republika)

Slovak women at a street cafe in Bratislava

Area: 18,933 sq. mi. (49,035 sq. km).)
Population: 5,460,185 (2022 census) 5,424,000 (2023 estimate)
Capital City: Bratislava (pop. 475,503, metro 719,537 as of 2021).
Climate: Continental, differing from the mountainous north to the plains in the south. The average temperature ranges from 68 °F (20 °C) in July to 23 °F (−5 °C) in January.
Neighboring Countries: Czech Republic (west); Poland (north); Republic of Ukraine (east); Hungary (south); Austria (west).
Official Language: Slovak.
Other Languages: Magyar, Czech, Ruthenian, German.
Ethnic Background: Slovak 83.8%, Hungarian 7.7%, Romani 1.2%, other 1.9% and unspecified 5.4%.
Religion: Christianity 68.8% (Catholicism 59.8%, Protestantism 7.6%, other Christian 1.4%), other 0.9%, no religion 23.8%, unspecified 6.5%.

Form of Government: Unitary parliamentary republic
Chief of State: Zuzana Čaputová, President (since June 2019).
Head of Government: Robert Fico, Prime Minister (since October 2023)
National Flag: It is a horizontal tricolor of white, blue, and red equal bands, with a coat of arms (a shield) of the same colors at the hoist side. The shield depicts a two-armed white cross on a red field with a blue base. The coat of arms of Slovakia has ancient roots. The two-armed cross was used as early as the 9th century in the Byzantine Empire, long before heraldic symbols were established. From 1189 it was the first coat of arms of Hungary, of which Slovakia was then a part. It was later standardized as a red shield with a white cross rising from three green hills. In the course of the revolutionary days of 1848–49, Slovak nationalists created a coat of arms different from that of Hungary by altering the hills to blue. The choice was based on the fact that white, blue, and red had been recognized as pan-Slavic colors–red standing for the blood that had been shed during battles for their freedom, white representing purity, and peace while blue represented honor.

After the establishment of an independent Czechoslovakia in 1918, its flag was adopted in 1920. Upon the dissolution of Czechoslovakia in 1992, the Czech Republic kept the Czechoslovak flag while Slovakia adopted a new one. Slovaks again made their tricolor official on September 3, 1992. The Slovak shield was added near the hoist on the tricolor with a white fimbriation to separate it from the blue and red stripes.

National Holidays: September 1 (Constitution Day); January 1 (Establishment of the Slovak Republic).
Currency: Euro (€) (EUR) (since January 2009).
Main Exports: automobiles, machinery, and iron and steel.
Main Imports: machinery, automobiles, and mineral fuels.

Main Trading Partners: Germany (21.0% of exports and 14.0% of imports), Czech Republic (12.0% of exports and 9.0% of imports), Austria (5.3% of exports and 9.3% of imports), Poland (7.8% of exports and 7.5% of imports), Russia (7.5% of imports), Hungary (8.7% of exports and 4.6% of imports), France (5.9 of exports), Italy (4.8 of exports), China (7.5 of imports), South Korea (5.7 of imports).

Following Slovakia's "Velvet Divorce" with the Czech Republic in 1993, many pessimists doubted that this poorer partner would survive, let alone thrive. With its large state-owned rust-belt industries and the pollution that accompanies such economic dinosaurs; its sizable Hungarian, Gypsy (Roma), and other minorities who have not always been treated respectfully; and its nationalist and relatively authoritarian politics after 1989 that had tarnished its international image, it seemed to be facing a dismal future. However, its resilience after a period of stumbling inspires hope and some optimism. Slovakia is a "turnaround story."

Most of the Slovak Republic is covered by mountains or hills, but it does possess a single large plain, located to the south and east of Bratislava, the capital. It is also here that the Danube River forms the border for some distance between Slovakia and Hungary. Just north and east of Bratislava, a western spur of the Carpathian Mountains begins. They then stretch east-, northeastward, widening until they cover the entire country from north to south.

The highest mountains are found in the center-north, along the border with Poland. It is here that the steep, rugged peaks of the High Tatras tower over deep valleys dotted with numerous lakes. Gerlachovsky, the tallest peak, is 8,620 feet high. It and the surrounding high terrain form the Tatra National Park. A popular place for vacationing since the 19th century, it is full of spas and holiday resorts. The Carpathian Mountains diminish in height as one moves farther eastward, but they actually run for a couple of hundred miles beyond the Slovakian border, traversing western Ukraine.

As its name implies, Slovakia is mainly a land of the Slovaks. But there are three minorities making up several percent

Slovakia

of the population that have the status of "nationalities." These include Hungarians, mainly in the southeast; Poles in the northeast; and Ukrainians and Ruthenians in the east. The latter also live on the Polish and Ukrainian sides of the border. They enjoyed one day of independence on March 15, 1918, but they show no interest in separatism today. Their most famous countryman was the Pittsburgh-born Andy Warhol. The Hungarians, who number about 560,000, are the largest minority. Carpathian Germans live in the north, the northwest, and central part of Slovakia.

Slovakia has a large number of Roma (Gypsies), estimated at 420,000 or more, much more than the official census figures, notoriously unreliable since many Roma prefer not to identify themselves officially as such. They constitute the fifth-largest Roma population in Europe. They are recognized as a separate nationality. During World War II, when Slovakia had a government that collaborated with Nazi Germany, it was official policy to sterilize Roma. Under the communists, they were offered money if they agreed to sterilization. At the same time, the government attempted to assimilate them, providing them with apartments, jobs, and income, although discrimination continued. Since 1989, assistance to them was reduced.

As in other central European countries, open antipathy toward them continues to exist, and far-right hate groups, such as the Slovenska Pospolitost (Slovak Brotherhood), protest against "Roma terror" and "Roma criminality." In 2004, the government dispatched 2,000 police and soldiers to quell Roma rioting to protest welfare cuts. These were the country's worst riots since 1989, and police had to use water cannons to push the 400 Roma back into their settlement, followed by house-to-house searches.

These actions highlighted their desperate living conditions, shocking poverty, and unemployment. Only one-fifth of Roma men of working age have jobs. Most others are dependent upon welfare. Roma people constitute 80% of Slovakia's long-term unemployed. They die 15 years earlier than the Slovak national average. The poorest Romani live in clusters of wooden shacks without water mains or sewage systems. They are often segregated from "white Slovak" housing and schools. Many Roma children grow up without schooling, and only a quarter start the equivalent of high school, compared with 94% of native Slovaks.

The courts are the most powerful institutions working for desegregation. There are a few Roma representatives in the national parliament. The government's

Bratislava Castle

Photo by Madison Rechenberg

plenipotentiary for Roma communities has traveled to the US to learn about desegregating schools and overcoming entrenched barriers to equality.

Political Status: Part of the Hungarian kingdom of the Austro-Hungarian Empire until 1918; part of Czechoslovak Republic 1918–1938; independent state under German influence, 1939–1945; part of communist-influenced Czechoslovak Republic, 1945–1948; part of communist Czechoslovakia, 1948–1989; part of Czech and Slovak Federal Republic, 1990–1992.

HISTORY

In the 5th century, the forerunners of the Slovaks, then one of a group of west Slavic tribes, moved from the east into the area of modern Slovakia. Other tribes migrated farther west. Together, these various Slavic tribes settled the area to the south of the Carpathian and Sudeten Mountains and along the Vltava and Danube Rivers.

Except for a legendary, short-lived kingdom created by a Frank trader, Samo, in the 7th century, these western Slavic

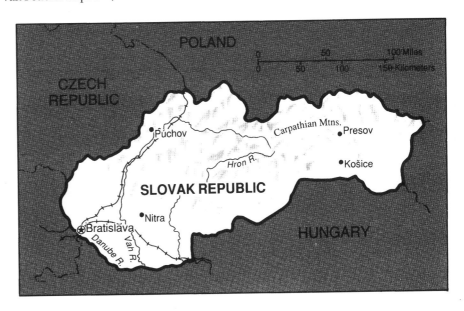

395

Slovakia

peoples continued to be governed by a tribal structure until the 9th century, when the Moravian Empire was established. The seat of this empire was in the western part of modern Slovakia, in the modern Slovak city of Nitra. It was also here that the first Christian church among western Slavs was built in 850. It is likely that the rulers of this first unified state were Slovak tribal leaders, for it was the Slovak lands that were first unified, with the remaining western Slavic lands being added later.

Although the Moravian Empire lasted less than a century, it was important because the western Slavs were converted to Christianity during this time. The first Christian missionaries came from Rome, but Prince Rastislav, who ruled 850–870, requested the Byzantine emperor to send a bishop to "enlighten and instruct his people in the true faith and in their own tongue." Methodius and Cyril, the two Greek Orthodox monks sent by the emperor, introduced a Slavonic liturgy and the first written script for the Slavs, later known as Cyrillic. Because later rulers of the Moravian Empire favored the priests from western Europe, Cyrillic was replaced by Roman letters, but a written Slavic literature dates from this time.

The Moravian Empire began to disintegrate toward the end of the 9th century. First weakened from within by revolts by ambitious Czech nobles desirous of creating their own independent kingdom of Bohemia, the Moravian Empire came under attack from the south and east when Magyar peoples swept into the area, overrunning the Hungarian Plain and gradually extending their control northward to the Carpathian Mountains. Although the Slovak rulers fought a rear-guard action

against the Magyars for some time, all the Slovak lands were brought under Magyar control by about 1000, the date traditionally used to mark the beginning of Christianity in Hungary and the founding of the kingdom of St. Stephen.

The Mongol invasions of the 13th century decimated the population and led king Béla IV to invite a wave of German settlers, valued for their skills in agriculture, mining, and crafts. Given special privileges and essentially self-governing, the German communities continued until the end of World War II, when most (but not all) Germans escaped with the retreating German army or were expelled.

For nearly 1,000 years—until 1918—the Slovaks remained under the Hungarian crown. Since both Magyars and Slovaks were Roman Catholics, and Latin, not Hungarian, was the language used at court and in the churches, Slovaks had no serious complaints. On the other hand, although a few Slovaks managed to rise to high position, most were peasants living on land controlled by members of the Hungarian nobility. When serfdom spread into central Europe in the later Middle Ages, the majority became serfs.

When the last Hungarian king was killed at the battle of Mohacs in 1526, Hungary became a possession of the Habsburgs, whose main seat was at Vienna. This was a positive development for Slovaks because the Habsburgs, being German-speaking, had no reason to favor the Hungarians. When the Turks overran most of Hungary in the 16th and 17th centuries, it was the Slovak lands that remained unoccupied, in effect becoming the main part of the kingdom. For the next 150 years, the seat of the Hungarian

government was Pressburg, better known today by its Slavic name, Bratislava, the present-day capital of Slovakia.

Joseph II of Austria abolished serfdom in the Czech part in 1781 and in Slovakia in 1785. The revolution of 1848 strengthened Hungarian nationalism and ultimately inspired a policy of Magyarization after 1867. The government prohibited the use of the Slovak language in public, decreed that all school education was to be only in Hungarian, and in general did everything it could to suppress a separate Slovak identity.

Yet the revolutions affected the Slovaks, as well. It was in 1848 that an assembly of Slovaks first drew up a demand for political, social, and cultural equality. And even as the Hungarian government attempted to suppress Slovak nationalism, individual Slovak intellectuals worked to counteract the official policy. These included two poets, Ján Hollý (1785—1849) and Ján Kollár (1793—1852), and Ľudovít Štúr (1815—1856), a writer and a political leader. Nevertheless, Slovak culture remained largely suppressed until the collapse of the Austro-Hungarian Empire in 1918.

In spite of this, a Slovak identity did begin to develop, mainly among Slovaks in emigration—in Paris and, particularly, in the United States. The first Slovak newspaper was launched in Pittsburgh in 1886. In 1907 the Slovak League in America unified various Slovak organizations and in 1914 declared the right of self-determination for the Slovak nation. A Slovak who was a general in the French army, Milan Rastislav Štefánik, opened his Paris home to Tomáš Masaryk, whose wife was American, and Eduard Beneš to discuss the creation of a Czech-Slovak state. During World War I, they threw their support behind Masaryk's vision of an independent Czechoslovak state. On October 22, 1915, Slovak and Czech representatives pledged in the Cleveland Agreement to cooperate with each other to create a future state with autonomous status for Slovaks. The Pittsburgh Agreement, signed on June 30, 1918, expressed Slovak support for the union of Czech and Slovak lands in return for Masaryk's promise that Slovakia would have considerable independence within the new state. The independent Czechoslovak Republic was proclaimed in Prague on October 28, 1918. Two days later, the Slovak National Council, meeting in Turčiansky Svätý Martin, a town in central Slovakia, voted to be part of the proclaimed state.

The Independent Czechoslovak Republic

Slovakia remained a part of the independent Czechoslovak Republic until 1939, but that period of cohabitation was not entirely happy. The problem was that

Tatra Mountains at the Slovak-Polish border

Slovakia

the constitution, adopted in 1920, stressed absolute majority rule and emphasized the sovereignty of the state vis-a-vis individual citizens.

In addition, since Czechs and Slovaks were considered to be one people, there were no separate rights for Slovaks, nor was Slovak recognized as a separate language. The lesser-educated Slovaks found themselves at a disadvantage in applying for jobs in the government. Thus, there were fewer than 200 Slovaks among the 8,000-odd civil servants of the central government. In Slovakia, Czechs predominantly staffed the public services. Even in the schools, half the teachers were Czechs.

Although almost all industry was located in the Czech part of the country, no effort was made to develop Slovakia. Even some of the few factories that predated 1918 were allowed to go under. Many Slovaks believed that the Czechs were treating them as a colony. They particularly resented the presence of so many Czechs in important positions throughout Slovakia.

Individual Slovaks who spoke out on this issue often found themselves the subject of official judicial inquiry and action, charged with violating the 1923 law for the protection of the government. This prohibited "agitating . . . against the state because of its . . . constitutional unitary structure." Thus, individuals who advocated federalism—as many Slovak nationalists did—were considered to be guilty of subversion. One of the more prominent cases occurred in 1928, when Professor Vojtech Tuka was arrested and sentenced to 15 years in prison for an assertion in a newspaper article that the original Slovak agreement to join the Czechoslovak Republic had required a referendum after 10 years. In another such incident, the Slovak People's Party newspaper was closed down in 1933 and the editor arrested after 100,000 Slovaks had demonstrated for autonomy in the town of Nitra.

A Slovak provincial administration was actually created in 1927, but this did not satisfy Slovak leaders, who continued to press for full autonomy. The most important of these was Monsignor Andrej Hlinka, leader of the Slovak People's Party, the largest of Slovakia's parties. Other parties that agitated for Slovak autonomy included the Catholic People's Party and the Slovak National Party. In addition, Slovak members of the Social Democrats and the Agrarians were often supporters of autonomy.

In 1937 Masaryk died, and Eduard Beneš became a candidate for the presidency. During his campaign, Beneš sought electoral support from members of the Slovak People's Party by promising autonomy for Slovakia. When Milan Hodža, a Slovak, became Czechoslovak premier at

this time, many Slovaks became convinced that the central government was finally ready to take their interests into consideration. After his inauguration, however, Beneš supported the Slovak government that had existed since 1927 and made no attempt to accord it any greater autonomy.

When a Sudeten German crisis erupted in 1938, Slovaks were beginning to organize their own demonstrations on behalf of autonomy. At the beginning of June, the Slovak People's Party introduced a bill for Slovak autonomy. A few days later, a mass meeting in Bratislava drew 120,000 persons. When Monsignor Hlinka died in August, the situation deteriorated further, for Monsignor Jozef Tiso, his successor as head of the Slovak People's Party, was an even more outspoken advocate of Slovak autonomy.

Meanwhile, the Sudeten German crisis was coming to a head. As pressure from Nazi Germany grew, Premier Hodža resigned on September 22, and President Beneš took charge of the government. He created an all-party coalition with one seat reserved for the Slovak People's Party. Matúš Černák, the man chosen to represent the party, gave President Beneš an ultimatum in October—unless Slovak autonomy was granted within 24 hours, he would resign, and all Slovak delegates would leave the parliament. Černák actually stepped down the next day, but in an anticlimax of sorts, President Beneš submitted his own resignation on October 5. General Jan Syrový, whom Beneš had appointed as premier only days earlier, became the acting president.

The next day, representatives from all of the Slovak political parties and Slovak branches of national political parties—with the exception of the communists and Social Democrats—met in the town of Žilina. After considerable discussion, they voted to merge their several parties to form the Slovak National Unity Party and then drew up a manifesto that announced the formation of an autonomous Slovakian government.

Acting President Syrový accepted the Žilina manifesto and appointed Jozef Tiso as premier of Slovakia. The autonomy of Slovakia was legalized by constitutional amendment, passed by the Prague parliament on November 19. Elections to a Slovak parliament were held on December 18. The Slovak National Unity Party, whose dominant wing was the old Slovak People's Party, ran a single unity ticket and won 97.5% of the vote. The remaining ballots were cast for small German and Hungarian ethnic parties. The Social Democrats and communists were unrepresented because the government had deliberately delayed publication of election procedures until it was too late for these two

Old architecture of Kezmarok

national parties to nominate candidates. Slovakia thus had essentially a one-party government, and this situation continued throughout its existence.

Even after achieving its goal of autonomy, however, Slovak relations with Prague remained poor. The Czechs were stressing the necessity of Czechoslovak unity to guarantee the continued independence of the state. Czechs were also angry at the Slovaks for maintaining contacts with the Carpatho-Germans and for participating in extensive conferences with officials from Hitler's Germany. Emil Hácha, who had been elected Czechoslovak president on November 19, 1938, was extremely upset by these contacts, which he claimed were treasonous. On March 9, he dismissed Jozef Tiso as premier and declared a state of emergency in Slovakia. Several ministers were arrested, but Hácha agreed to allow the deputy premier, Karol Sidor, to reconstitute the Slovak government.

"Independent" Slovakia, 1939–1945

It was at this point that Hitler made his move. On March 12, a Nazi delegation arrived in Bratislava with a message from Hitler urging Premier Sidor to declare Slovakian independence. Sidor refused, but shortly thereafter Monsignor Tiso and Ferdinand Ďurčanský, a second Slovak nationalist, flew to Berlin to meet with Hitler. Here they were informed that Germany would recognize and support a declaration of Slovak independence. Hitler warned them, however, that he "would leave the destiny of Slovakia to the mercy of events," if they decided to remain with Prague.

There had already been reports that Hungary, which had obtained parts of

397

Slovakia

Old-town Bratislava

southern Slovakia in November, wanted to annex the rest of Slovakia. Joachim von Ribbentrop, the German foreign minister, informed Tiso and Ďurčanský that Hungarian troops had begun to mass along the Slovak border. Monsignor Tiso returned to Bratislava on March 14 and immediately addressed the Slovak parliament. Following his report, the parliament unanimously adopted a declaration of Slovakian independence.

Meanwhile, President Hácha, who had requested an interview with Hitler, was invited to come to Berlin on that same day. In fact, the declaration of Slovak independence had already been adopted by the time he arrived in Berlin. Hácha met with Hitler late that evening. After a long harangue, Hitler demanded that Hácha sign an agreement accepting a German protectorate over the remaining parts of the country. Hácha collapsed during the interview but managed to recover enough to sign the capitulation. German troops entered the new Bohemia and Moravia Protectorate on March 15.

The Slovak Republic (or Slovak State) has often been referred to as a "puppet state." The political realities of the time meant that the Slovak government had generally to align its policies with those of Hitler's Germany. It is also true that the Tiso government passed anti-Jewish legislation which, among other things, required Jewish entrepreneurs to sell off 51% of their shares to Slovak partners, set a limit of 4% on the percentage of Jews in public services and the professions, and encouraged Jewish emigration to Palestine. The anti-Jewish legislation was broad

and not essentially different from that in Germany itself.

These laws did not satisfy Hitler, however. In July 1940 he forced the Slovak government to agree to transfer Slovak Jews to a "resettlement" area in German-held Poland. The deportations continued until July 1942. Monsignor Tiso ordered them stopped after the Papal Nuncio informed him that Jews were being murdered in the Lublin area. This new policy remained in force over the next two years. However, when Security Minister Štefan Haššík ordered the disbanding of the labor camps and the repeal of anti-Jewish laws, the Germans assumed direct control of all matters concerning Jews in Slovakia.

The Slovak government deported and killed approximately 50,000 Jews during the war. With only pro forma cooperation from the Slovak government, an estimated 26,650 Jews managed to escape the net and were still in Slovakia in 1945 at the end of the war.

Meanwhile, a sort of Slovak government-in-exile came into being in December 1943 in London. A number of Slovak liberals and leftists, including communists, organized a Slovak National Council and, under the terms of a "Christmas Agreement" signed at the same time, committed themselves to "take over, at an expedient time, all political, legislative, military, and governmental executive power in Slovakia." The Christmas Agreement of 1943 was a broad democratic program that gathered diverse anti-Hitler groups under one umbrella. It contained principles of antifascist resistance and the future organization of a liberated Slovakia. The

Slovak National Council found some support for its plans in Slovakia, particularly among Protestants and some elements of the army and police. It also established some contact with partisan units in the mountains of eastern Slovakia.

In August 1944, communist-led partisans launched the so-called Slovak National Uprising. Its hand forced, the Slovak National Council endorsed the revolt on August 29, constituting itself a provisional government. The insurgents took over large parts of central Slovakia for two months, and there was widespread but not total popular support. Some Slovaks today compare this rebellion to the Warsaw Uprising and argue that it has not been widely recognized in western historiography because of the fact that communists led it. President Tiso, fearing the success of the revolt, requested the help of the German army. The revolt collapsed in October 1944, and German troops remained until they were forced out in 1945. Their presence destroyed any pretense that Slovakia was an independent country.

Reintegration into Czechoslovakia

The vanguard of the Soviet army entered Slovakia on October 18, 1944. Slowed by a subsequent German counteroffensive, it took until April 4, 1945, to clear the rest of Slovakia of German forces. Having reorganized his government-in-exile into a National Front government after consulting Stalin in Moscow, President Beneš arrived in Košice in eastern Slovakia in March 1945 and set up his government. Here the government announced its Košice Program, which spelled out its plans for reconstituting the Czechoslovak state. Under its terms, "the members of the so-called Slovak governments since March 14, 1939, as well as members of the so-called Slovak Parliament" were to be arrested and charged with high treason. The program also called for the suppression of the "Slovak People's Party, and those parties which joined the latter in 1938."

Most of the members of the Slovak government fled to Bavaria at the end of the war. Taken into custody by the US Army, they were extradited at the request of the Czechoslovak government and taken to Bratislava. A National Tribunal appointed to try them sat for nearly a year before rendering its verdict in April 1947. Monsignor Tiso was sentenced to death by hanging, while other members of his government received prison terms. Labor camps were set up in Slovakia, and thousands of persons deemed to "threaten the reconstruction of the state, security, the peace, public order . . . as well as those persons who profess an ideology inimical to the state" were confined in these camps without benefit of trial.

Slovaks try to reason with Warsaw Pact soldiers, 1968.   Photo by Oldrich Skácha

The Continuing Problem of
Slovak "Particularism"

From the point of view of the Czechoslovak government, the crime for which these individuals were punished was fascism, not nationalism. At the same time, Beneš and the others were well aware that Slovak "particularism" was a continuing problem that was not likely to be ended by the imprisonment or even execution of a few leaders. To defuse this issue, therefore, the central government promised that Slovakia would be granted an autonomous status, with a parliament and a cabinet. Adopting this same approach, the communists, at this time the strongest group in the National Front government, organized a separate Slovak Communist Party. The communists did very badly in the 1946 elections in Slovakia, however, and thereafter began to place greater stress on Czechoslovak centralization.

After the communist seizure of power in Prague in early 1948, the new constitution issued three months later created a highly centralized state, with nearly all power centered in the Czech capital. Yet it technically fulfilled the earlier promise of an autonomous status for Slovakia by creating a Slovak National Council with limited legislative powers relating to cultural matters, education, public health, local boundaries, encouragement of agriculture, and local trade.

Two months later, however, the presidium of the Czechoslovak Communist Party negated this theoretical grant of autonomy to Slovakia by calling for a united communist party. Responding to this directive from Prague, the Slovak Communist Party voted to merge itself into the Czechoslovak Communist Party. From this time, the Communist Party organization in Slovakia was merely a branch of the Czechoslovak Communist Party, though it was allowed to keep its separate central committee and regional organization.

The significance of this change became clear in April 1950, when the national government decided to move against religious communities throughout the country. Without informing the Slovak communist leaders, Prague dispatched policemen to dissolve religious orders in Bratislava and deport their members. When Slovak communists protested, they were immediately suspended from their governmental duties. A month later, at the ninth congress of the Slovak branch of the Communist Party, charges of "deviationism" and "bourgeois nationalism" were brought against them, and a general purge followed. Among those dismissed from office were Gustáv Husák, the Slovak premier; Karol Šmidke, chairman of the Slovak National Council; and Ladislav Novomeský, commissioner of public education.

Nine months later, Husák, Šmidke, and Novomeský, plus Vladimir Clementis, a Slovak who had risen to the rank of minister of foreign affairs in the central government, and several lesser-known Slovak communists, were arrested and charged with "nationalist-deviationist tendencies" as part of a general purge of "Titoist" communists in eastern Europe. Clementis, one of the 14 defendants in the so-called Slansky trial held in Prague, was found guilty of bourgeois nationalism and executed in 1952. The others remained in prison for another two years before being given a formal trial in 1954. All were

found guilty. Husák was sentenced to life imprisonment, while the others got lesser sentences. After the trial, there was a widespread purge of Slovak intellectuals from party and government jobs.

Following this purge of leading Slovak communists, leadership in Slovakia was exercised by Viliam Široký, a Slovak of Magyar origin who headed the Slovak branch of the Communist Party, and Karol Bacílek, a Czech who had migrated to Slovakia at the end of World War I. Bacílek replaced Husák as premier. Thus, there were no ethnic Slovaks in leadership roles in Slovakia. Although the Slovak communists had never enjoyed any real popularity among the Slovak people, they were willing to make some concessions to Slovak nationalist aspirations. Their successors were viewed by ordinary Slovaks as outsiders and agents of Prague and were detested for that reason.

With the general alienation of the Slovak population, it is not surprising that the 1956 Hungarian Revolution led to an outbreak of demonstrations in a number of Slovak cities. In response, a frightened Prague government dispatched six divisions of troops to western and central Slovakia to quell the unrest, while Soviet troops were moved in to secure eastern Slovakia. Four years later, the new constitution of the Czechoslovak Socialist Republic abolished the last legal remnants of Slovak autonomy.

Yet the question of Slovak autonomy would not die. Two years later, a party congress in Prague voted to conduct an inquiry into the purges of 1949–1954. This reopened the Slovak issue because Vladimir Clementis was among those found to have been wrongfully convicted. The inquiry's decision on him led Slovak writers and scholars to begin agitating for the rehabilitation of those Slovak communists who had been thrown into prison for "bourgeois nationalism." Although this produced no immediate results, one "bourgeois-nationalist" figure, Gustav Husák, was released from prison in 1960, ostensibly as part of a general amnesty to mark the 15th anniversary of socialist Czechoslovakia.

He and the other victims of the Stalinist trials had to wait another two years for political rehabilitation. When the 12th party congress met in 1962, one of the adopted resolutions voided the earlier convictions and made amends by stipulating that those still alive would be readmitted to the party and given better jobs, while relatives of those executed would receive financial compensation.

Karol Bacílek, the immensely unpopular first secretary of the Slovak branch of the Communist Party, and Viliam Široký, Slovak premier, were also removed at this

Slovakia

time. Both men had aroused Slovak hatred by a consistent policy of cooperating with the Prague government's centralization policies. Josef Lenárt replaced Široký, while Bacílek was succeeded by a Slovak, Alexander Dubček. Czech-Slovak relations now improved, and Antonín Novotný, basking in his new role as a reformer, got himself unanimously elected in 1964 for another seven-year term as president of the republic. The apparent political calm was misleading, however. It soon became clear that there were a number of differing opinions within the party over the progress of reform.

Dubček emerged as the leader of the anti-Novotný forces in late 1967. At a meeting of the party Central Committee, he accused Novotný of undermining the program of economic reform and of refusing to meet Slovak demands for more self-government. Although he had raised the Slovak issue, Dubček placed greater emphasis on economic reform. It was clear that he did not want to be labeled a Slovak particularist. His position was helped by the fact that the Czechoslovak Writers' Union and student demonstrators in Prague joined in the attack against Novotný.

The reformers were not immediately successful, however. The unrest in Prague led to a visit by Soviet party chief Leonid Brezhnev as a gesture of support for Novotný. But the visit was not enough to save the falling president. When the Central Committee convened again two months later, it decided that the functions of the presidency should be separated from those of the first secretary of the Communist Party. On January 5, 1968, Alexander Dubček became the first Slovak to assume the top post in the Communist Party of Czechoslovakia.

Defeat for Reform

The overall purpose of the entire reform movement was to create what Dubček called "socialism with a human face." Dubček was always careful to portray himself as a Czechoslovak leader, though his general plans for political decentralization would have also led to greater Slovak autonomy. Yet the plans of the reformers were not to be. On the night of August 20–21, military units of the Soviet Union, Hungary, East Germany, Poland, and Bulgaria entered Czechoslovakia and, within a few hours, occupied the major cities. In the process, the entire Czechoslovak leadership—Dubček, Cernik, and Josef Smrkovský, president of the National Assembly—was placed under arrest. The Czech Foreign Ministry denounced the invasion as a violation of the Warsaw Pact, and President Ludvik Svoboda flatly refused to participate in the formation of a Soviet-dominated government. The deadlock was broken when he agreed to go to Moscow for direct talks with the Soviet leaders.

At Svoboda's insistence, Dubček and the other leaders accompanied him and participated in the talks. After much discussion, it was announced that there would be no change in the political leadership, though it was clear that they would not be permitted to continue their reform political program. This became even clearer in October, when the two countries signed an open-ended treaty providing for the stationing of Soviet troops within Czechoslovakia.

Compensation for Slovakia

One reform that was of great significance to Slovakia managed to survive the Soviet crushing of the Prague Spring. Since Prague was considered to be the focal point for reform communism, the Soviet leadership dropped its support for a highly centralized Czechoslovak state under Czech leadership and began to favor those conservative Slovak Communists who had earlier been removed for nationalistic tendencies. To win their support, it was decided to grant Slovakia its autonomy by turning Czechoslovakia into a federal state. This reform, put into effect at midnight on December 31, 1968, abolished the old unitary structure and created in its stead a new federal republic consisting of the two separate Czech and Slovak Socialist Republics. During 1969, there was a gradual replacement of the preinvasion reform leadership through demotion, resignation, or dismissal.

Dubček, caught in the middle of all of this, tried to hang on by playing the centralist role. While assuring the liberals that there had been no surrender to the Soviet Union and that reform was still possible, he reassured the conservatives that there was no danger in reform. At the same time, he attempted to convince the Soviet Union that he would not be the source of additional political strife. Dubček found it difficult to be in favor of so many conflicting political views at the same time. In April, Gustav Husák replaced him as party secretary.

Husák was a complex individual himself. Although in many ways a political moderate, he was willing to preside over the end of reform for two reasons: first, because he was favorable to Slovak nationalism and liked the new federal structure; second, because he believed it was paramount for Czechoslovakia to live in harmony with the Soviet Union. Dubček was expelled from the Communist Party in June 1970. This victory for the party's "hard-liners" left Husák surrounded at the center by conservatives who also wanted to recentralize power in Prague. In early 1971, the federal cabinet was given the right to veto decisions of the Czech and Slovak cabinets. Slovak autonomy was once again being eroded.

Husák's own political position was not impaired by this new move toward centralization. He went along with the trend because he was, in fact, in charge of the entire country. In May 1975, he further increased his authority by replacing the ailing Svoboda as president of the republic while remaining head of the party. Husák continued to occupy both positions for the next 12 years. Thus, in a final irony, the man who had once been thrown into prison for "bourgeois nationalism" became both the symbol and instrument of Prague's domination of Slovakia.

Husák became more and more conservative in his later years, so Gorbachev's emergence as a reformer after his election as CPSU general secretary in March 1985 presented him with a problem. After temporizing for some time, Husák announced his retirement as leader of the Czechoslovak Communist Party in 1987, though he retained his position as president of the republic. His successor was Miloš Jakeš. A Czech, Jakeš kept his position as party

Relaxing in Bratislava

Slovakia

leader for two years, until he was forced out in November 1989 as a result of Prague's so-called Velvet Revolution.

Karel Urbánek replaced Jakeš, but it was the premier, Ladislav Adamec, who opened discussions with the opposition. The party now agreed to give up its monopoly of power and to form a coalition government with the opposition. But Adamec wanted to keep a majority of the seats in the hands of the communists. When Civic Forum rejected his proposed cabinet on December 3, Adamec resigned and was replaced by Marián Čalfa. The new cabinet, installed on December 10, contained a majority of noncommunists.

Gustav Husák submitted his resignation as president, thus opening the question as to who his successor should be. Alexander Dubček, leader of the Prague Spring in 1968, and Václav Havel, longtime dissident, founder of Charter 77, and prominent playwright, were both contenders. But the job eventually went to Havel. On December 29, he was elected president by acclamation, while Alexander Dubček was given the compensatory prize of becoming leader of the Federal Assembly.

Renewed Separatism

In the run-up to the June 1990 elections, the issue of democracy versus communism dominated political discussions, but the rivalry between Czechs and Slovaks began to emerge as an issue, as well. Upon Slovak insistence, the name of the country was changed to the Czech and Slovak Federal Republic. As new political parties were organized to contest the elections, separate parties emerged in the two parts of the country. While the Czech reform group was organized as the Civic Forum, the Slovak partner took the name of Public against Violence.

From the beginning Slovaks were concerned about their separate identity. But the issue that led Slovak nationalists to begin demanding the creation of a separate, independent state was economic reform. Many of the Slovak leaders feared that the swift implementation of a market system as advocated by such Czech leaders as Václav Klaus, the new Czechoslovak minister of finance, would have a disastrous effect on the Slovak economy.

The Federal Assembly attempted to defuse the situation in December 1990 by passing new legislation outlining the powers of the Czech and Slovak regional governments. The legislation also gave President Havel special powers to deal with the threat of Slovak separatism.

Although most Slovak deputies afterward expressed their satisfaction with the legislation, the situation continued to simmer. President Havel was mobbed by thousands of Slovaks shouting abuse

when he visited Bratislava in March 1991. Part of the problem was that the Slovak premier, Vladimir Mečiar, had taken up the Slovak nationalist cause. Things improved somewhat after Ján Čarnogurský, head of Slovakia's Christian Democratic Movement, replaced Mečiar in April 1991. Čarnogurský's position was ambiguous, however; although he supported continuation of the federation for the time being, he also said that he favored an independent Slovakia in principle.

Slovak nationalism continued to be the dominant factor in Czechoslovak politics throughout the rest of 1991 and into 1992. President Havel spent more and more of his time on this issue as he tried to act as a mediator between the Czechs and Slovaks, bringing the two sides together for discussions and, at one point, calling for a referendum on the issue. Public polls showed

Vladimír Meciar

that a small majority of Slovaks supported a continuation of the federation. Therefore, the Slovak political leadership eventually rejected such a referendum. Havel also proposed some changes in the federal government, and the Czechoslovak government presented these to the Federal Assembly in December 1991 in the form of three draft laws.

The three draft laws were not passed, but they acted as a catalyst. An ad hoc commission of the Czech and Slovak National Councils (i.e., legislatures) announced on February 9, 1992, that its members had drawn up a draft agreement on a future common state that would be submitted to their respective legislatures. The draft agreement listed foreign policy, defense, monetary, credit, interest and currency policies, and budgetary regulations

as falling within the powers of the federation. Czechs and Slovaks would be equally represented in the federal bodies. It also specified that either republic could withdraw from the common state "only on the basis of the will of the majority of its citizens expressed in a referendum."

When the presidium of the Slovak National Council met on February 12 to consider the draft, it was turned down. Two weeks later, the Slovak National Council adopted a resolution requesting its deputies to submit their views on the draft to the presidium and instructed the Presidium to compile a comprehensive report on the comments that the deputies submitted. The resolution further recommended that the presidium meet with the presidium of the Czech National Council "to jointly assess . . . the possibility of concluding the treaty."

When these maneuvers failed to produce an agreement, it was decided to hold new federal elections on June 5–6 to resolve the issue. Slovakia held its own elections to the National Council on the same days. The Christian Democratic Movement, the party of Slovak premier Ján Čarnogurský, now split into two factions. The more radical faction that had been pushing for an independent Slovakia formed a new party, the Slovak Christian Democratic Movement. It announced that they would run a separate slate of candidates in the June elections. With the radicals gone, the Christian Democratic Movement reaffirmed its support for a common state.

In the June 1992 elections, the vote split along national and ideological lines. Essentially, the Czechs cast their votes for reform and anticommunist candidates, while the Slovaks supported nationalists and leftists. In the Slovak Republic, Vladimir Mečiar and Mečiar's Movement for a Democratic Slovakia won with their blend of statism, socialism, and nationalism. In the Czech Republic, Václav Klaus and his Civic Democratic Party won an equally convincing victory on a program of anticommunism and reform.

When Mečiar and Klaus met after the 1992 election to discuss the formation of a new federal government, Mečiar made it clear that he would not accept a federal state that could dictate policy to Slovakia. He demanded that the Slovak Republic be authorized to establish its own army, its own currency-issuing central bank, and the independent right to borrow. He also indicated that he intended to reverse some of the recent national policies as they applied to Slovakia, including restoring subsidies to state industry, increasing social benefits, and slowing privatization. None of those positions was compatible with development of a free market. The talks collapsed after six and a half hours.

Slovakia

Because a new federal government had to be formed, Klaus suggested giving a new, temporary federal government the power to act until a referendum could be held asking citizens whether they wanted to live in a federal state. After further talks, Czech and Slovak negotiators agreed to establish a weak interim federal government whose task would be to bring the union to a close. The actual constitutional questions relating to the separation would be resolved in the legislatures of the two republics. Further negotiations produced an agreement, signed on August 26, calling for a split into two independent states by January 1.

The process suffered a setback on October 1, when the federal parliament rejected a bill legalizing the end of the federation. After further negotiations, however, the federal parliament voted itself out of existence on November 25.

By that time, the two national legislatures had begun acting as though the federation had already disappeared; this was particularly true in the case in Slovakia. Mečiar had said in June that he wanted to slow down privatization, and he began submitting bills to the Slovak legislature to accomplish that purpose. The Slovak government called for the renegotiation of several privatization agreements and stopped the sale of a number of companies. As a result, only 5.3% of Slovak industry had been privatized by the end of 1992, as compared to 25.2% for the Czech Republic.

On January 1, 1993, the Czech and Slovak Federal Republic disappeared, and in its place, there emerged an independent Slovak Republic and an independent Czech Republic. The separation was peaceful, but all of the celebrations were in Bratislava, the capital of Slovakia. There was no ceremony to mark the occasion in Prague. In the speech he gave to mark the event, Prime Minister Mečiar attempted a note of conciliation. "Two states have been established," he said. "Living together in one state is over. Living together in two states continues."

Early Independence

After achieving independence for Slovakia, Prime Minister Mečiar reiterated the positions he had enunciated in 1992. In his New Year's Day address, he rejected both free-market economics and a ban on former communists in top government positions. He also surrounded himself with reform communists who had been active in the Prague Spring. Mečiar's commitment to democracy and pluralism was not very firm. For example, the government tightened its control on the press and on television after independence, dismissing individuals suspected of oppositionist tendencies. It also began to restrict the language rights of its Hungarian minority. In 1993 the government began taking down Hungarian-language signs in border areas and formally announced that Hungarian names for Slovak towns could not be used in Hungarian-language broadcasts.

Mečiar's greatest changes were in the area of economics, however. In the first months after independence, privatization came to an end for all but the smallest firms. At the same time, the government increased credits to state industry, thereby enlarging the budget deficit and contributing to the collapse of the common currency arrangement with the Czech Republic. There was a drop of almost 50% in exports to the Czech Republic and an even greater drop in imports. Significant deposits had also been switched from Slovak to Czech banks.

Former President Andrej Kiska

Former Prime Minister Peter Pellegrini

Mečiar undoubtedly expected that his halting of privatization and increasing of credits to state industry would have a positive effect on employment and the overall economy. In fact, they had the opposite effect. Mečiar's party split in 1994, when the economic situation worsened and unemployment grew to an estimated 14.4%. Among those withdrawing from the party were Mečiar's foreign minister, Jozef Moravčík, and the deputy prime minister, Roman Kováč. That left the Movement for a Democratic Slovakia without a parliamentary majority. Mečiar was finally ousted on March 11, when he lost a parliamentary vote of confidence. Moravčík, who had led the rebellion against him, replaced him. Although a former member of the Movement for a Democratic Slovakia, Moravčík promised to revive the reform process.

New elections were scheduled to take place on September 30, 1994, so Moravčík did not have much time to make a record for himself. Nevertheless, he managed to accomplish a number of important things during the next six months, including legislation extending protection for Hungarian language rights. He opened negotiations with Hungary for a treaty to settle border questions and to improve the treatment of each other's minorities. He invited Gyula Horn, the Hungarian prime minister, to Bratislava for an official visit. He restored Slovakia to international respectability.

None of that seemed to matter when the people cast their ballots on September 30 and October 1. The essential problem was that Moravčík's supporters were a disparate group of Movement for a Democratic Slovakia rebels, conservative Christian Democrats, and the Democratic Left Party (i.e., the successor to the old Communist Party), which had very little in common other than their opposition to Mečiar. Moreover, Mečiar's Movement for a Democratic Slovakia was still the best organized and financed of all the political parties. Nor did it hurt that his supporters in parliament, in attacking the new government by every means at their disposal, were viewed as heroes by most of those negatively affected by the reforms—in particular Slovakia's 15% unemployed, the peasantry, and the retired.

While no party won an outright majority, Mečiar's Movement for a Democratic Slovakia came in first with 35% of the vote, winning 61 of the 150 parliamentary seats. He found it extremely difficult to create a working majority coalition. Finally, Mečiar announced on November 3 that he had negotiated a "voting pact" with the right-wing Slovak National Party and the left-wing Association of Slovak Workers that would allow him to form a government. Although not then a formal alliance, this voting majority pushed legislation through the parliament, sacking the attorney general; dismissing the board of the National Property Fund (thus suspending privatization); blocking the sale of all state-owned companies approved by the previous government; and bringing radio, television, and the state intelligence service under the control of Mečiar's party.

This trend continued and intensified. In 1995, Mečiar launched a series of public attacks on President Kováč, and these continued in 1996 and 1997. Mečiar also called for Kováč to step down. When this did not work, he attempted to get the parliament to dismiss the president. These moves failed because Mečiar lacked the two-thirds majority in the legislature necessary to force out the president.

One of the more bizarre aspects of this struggle between Prime Minister Mečiar and President Kováč occurred in August 1995 and involved the president's son, Michal Kováč Jr. Michal Jr. was mysteriously abducted in Bratislava and carried across the border into Austria, where he was later arrested on a German warrant. Most observers believe that the Slovak security service was responsible for the abduction, though no one has been able to provide any evidence that Mečiar was directly involved. However, President Kováč had rejected Ivan Lexa, the head of the security service, for the post of privatization minister in 1993. It is widely believed that he may have arranged the kidnapping because he held a grudge against President Kováč. The president said later that accusations and attacks against him had begun in 1993, though he never publicly claimed that there was a political motive behind the abduction. One other thing that ties Mečiar to the kidnapping is that he granted pardons to all persons involved after he took over as acting president in March 1998.

Mečiar never hesitated to use appeals to Slovak nationalism to consolidate his support. In 1995, this led him to push through a new language law aimed at restricting the rights of minorities, particularly the Hungarian minority, to use their national language. This made it illegal for radio or television broadcasts, advertising, and official government information to be in anything other than Slovak. In August 1997, Mečiar carried his antipathy to Hungarian speakers even further when he officially suggested to Gyula Horn, the Hungarian prime minister, that ethnic Hungarian speakers be repatriated to Hungary. As he put it at a party rally in Bratislava, "those people who do not want to be Slovak citizens [should] go to Hungary and live there." Subsequently, the Slovak National Party and the Slovak Workers' Party, the two junior parties in the ruling coalition, endorsed Mečiar's proposal, characterizing it as a "possible and constructive solution."

POLITICAL SYSTEM

The independent Slovak Republic came into being on January 1, 1993. It is a parliamentary democracy, with the leading political office that of the prime minister. Adopted by the Slovak National Council (renamed in 1992 the National Council of the Slovak Republic) in July 1992, Slovakia's constitution formally designates the country as the Slovak Republic. It created a 150-seat assembly as the nation's legislature. The Slovak Republic is a young democracy with many parties competing for parliamentary seats. For example, in the 2010 elections, 18 parties entered the race. In order to reduce the number of parties and enable a more stable coalition government to be created, the constitution requires that a party win at least 5% of the total vote to qualify for any seats in the assembly; in 2010 this reduced the number of parties in parliament to six. Voters choose from party lists, and seats are distributed according to proportional representation.

The Presidency

The constitution bestows on the assembly the right to elect the head of state, to be known as the president of the republic. The legislature amended this constitutional provision on January 14, 1999, to provide for the election of the president by direct popular vote. The bill stipulated that, if no presidential candidates receive more than 50% of the votes in the popular

Former prime minister Róbert Fico

vote, a runoff between the two candidates with the most votes would take place two weeks later.

While still prime minister, Vladimir Mečiar wanted to be elected president. He tried to capture the presidency in 1998 and 1999. He failed both times, losing in 1999 to Rudolf Schuster, who became the first popularly elected president. Even his second defeat did not drive Mečiar from the political arena as many had hoped. He recognized that about the only thing holding

Parliament in Bratislava

Slovakia

President Zuzana Čaputová
Source: *Wikipedia)*

Presidential palace, Bratislava

the government coalition together was opposition to himself and his policies.

He tried again in 2004, winning the first round with 33% of the votes. A relative unknown came in second—Ivan Gašparovič, his one-time lieutenant and parliamentary speaker, who had broken with him in 2002. In the second round, Gašparovič won 60% of the votes to Mečiar's 40%. Mečiar lost his cool in a TV debate, reminding voters of what a bully and loose cannon he can be. Gašparovič won reelection in 2009, reaching his term limit in 2014.

The decisive electoral victory in 2014 of Andrej Kiska was shocking, considering his total lack of political experience and the popularity of Prime Minister Robert Fico, who also sought the presidency but was rebuffed. Kiska ran as an independent whose call to fame was his business enterprises, as well as the philanthropic work he started once he sold his business. He created the Good Angel Foundation helping families in need. As president, he has donated his salary every month to 10 families selected by various charities. He came strongly in favor of sanctions against Russia for its intervention in Ukraine.

In 2019 Zuzana Čaputová became the country's first female president. A former anti-corruption lawyer with no previous political experience, she made justice and the rule of law her top priorities.

Parties and Parliamentary Elections

The September 2002 elections were very important both for Slovakia and for NATO and the EU. If the favorite, Vladimir Mečiar, had won, it was certain that the country would not have been admitted to these elite organizations. The United States

Agency for International Development (USAID) and nongovernmental organizations from the United States substantially helped campaigns to encourage Slovaks to vote for the moderate democratic parties that would be welcome in the Western community of nations. The results were a great relief, as 70% of eligible voters turned out to reelect the existing government.

Although Mečiar's Movement for a Democratic Slovakia (HZDS), renamed in 2000 as the HZDS-People's Party, did well in the 2002 elections, no party would form a coalition with it. His erratic behavior during the campaign did not help him. When a television reporter asked him, a former boxer, how he financed the $1 million in improvements to his luxurious home, he punched the man in the face.

Asked the same question during a TV discussion, he stormed off the stage. Mečiar had been placed under arrest in 2000 after he had refused to cooperate with investigators in connection with charges that he had paid $350,000 in bribes, called "illegal bonuses," to cabinet members when he was head of the government. Investigators also asked him about the kidnapping of the son of the Slovak president in 1995.

Mečiar's voters tended to be easterners, rural folk, pensioners, and low-paid workers longing for the social benefits, simple lives, and guaranteed jobs communism once offered them. They are gradually diminishing. At the polls in 2010, HZDS was eliminated failing to win its way into parliament. It disappeared from the political scene.

The radical right-wing Slovak National Party (SNS), led by firebrand Ján Slota, is another party destined for extinction. Slota himself was excluded from the cabinet, in part because he is widely

considered a racist who cannot control his intemperate tongue. He once said that the best way of dealing with the country's 420,000 Roma (Gypsies) was with "a long whip in a small yard." His other favorite target is the Hungarian minority. He once recommended that Slovaks "get in tanks and level Budapest." It experienced disaster in 2012, winning only 4.55% of the votes (down from 5%) and thereby not qualifying for any seats.

Emerging as the big winner in March 2012 was Robert Fico's left-leaning *Smer-SD* (Direction—Social Democracy), which increased its votes to 44.4% (up from 34.8%) and 83 seats (up from 62). This was the first time in the history of independent Slovakia that any party won an absolute majority. A lawyer and former communist youth activist, he had joined the Communist Party shortly before the Soviet system collapsed. He had resigned in 1999 from the Party of the Democratic Left, the successor party of the Slovak Communist Party, after a disagreement on policy. He subsequently joined with several of the more pragmatic members of his former party to create a new center-left party, *Smer*. Although a committed socialist, he retains a populist and nationalist streak that bothers many people. In October 2011 he supported the then ruling SDKU-DS Party by voting in favor of contributing to the European Financial Stability Fund. However, his price was early elections in March 2012, in which *Smer* won a landslide victory. Fico pledged to raise taxes on the rich, to abolish the 19% flat tax, and to introduce progressive taxation. He delivered on these promises in 2013, nine years after Slovakia became the first central European country to implement flat tax.

Main Street, Bratislava

The former ruling Slovak Democratic and Christian Union (SDKU-DS) was battered in the 2012 elections. Led by Mikuláš Dzurinda, it had won power in 2002 by promising to lead Slovakia into Europe and make it rich. Its reforms were dramatic and won praise throughout Europe, leading to full EU membership in May 2004. It introduced a 19% flat tax for profits and incomes, thereby encouraging foreign investments, which poured into the country. It brought about a more flexible labor code and American-style welfare reforms. It reformed the pension system, introducing new personal accounts run by private companies for 9% of wages. The retirement age was raised to 62, and incentives for working longer were created. Health care was reformed, and unemployment fell.

The SDKU government's measures laid the groundwork for the country's continuing economic growth. But it failed to prepare Slovaks for the pain caused by the transition. Its reforms were good for the country but hard on many individual Slovaks, especially in the eastern part of the country.

In June 2010, Slovaks were again ready for SDKU leadership. The prime minister was Iveta Radičová, an Oxford-educated sociology professor nicknamed the "Tatra Tigress." She was the country's first woman prime minister and one of the rare female politicians in the region. Party leader Mikuláš Dzurinda became foreign minister. Radičová's strongest legacy was her determined anticorruption effort, but a terrible scandal, known as "Gorilla," helped bring her government down. An intelligence report was leaked suggesting that members of her government might have been pocketing commissions from public-procurement and privatization deals. The party was massacred in the March 2012 elections, winning only 6% of the votes (down from 15.4%) and 11 seats (down from 28). Dzurinda resigned as party leader, and Radičová announced that she was leaving politics.

A party led by Béla Bugár represents the large Hungarian minority, Most-Hid (derived from the Slovak and Hungarian words for "bridge"). It seeks to bridge the ethnic divide. In 2012 it won 6.9% of the votes (down 8.1%) and 13 seats, a loss of

1. Bugar had earlier led the now-deflated Hungarian Coalition Party (SMK), which failed to clear the 5% hurdle.

The Christian Democratic Movement (KDH), led by former European commissioner for education Ján Figeľ came in second, garnering 8.2% of the votes (up slightly from 8.5%) and 16 seats (a gain of 1). It focuses on the rule of law and fight against crime. Richard Sulík led Freedom and Solidarity (SaS), a zealously laissez-faire party, into parliament, capturing 5.9% of the votes (down from 12.1%) and 11 seats (down from 22). Finally, a new party, OL'aNO (Ordinary People and Independent Personalities), led by Igor Matovič, captured 8.55% of the votes and 16 seats.

The election of March 2016 resulted in a political earthquake. Held at the height of the concerns and political divisions related to the refugee crisis, it brought a far-right party into the parliament for the first time since World War II. Corruption and problems in public sectors, especially health care and education, were also prominent concerns. Robert Fico's *Smer-SD* (Direction) ran on a strongly anti-immigration platform and retained its leading position, but with only 28.28% of votes, it lost the majority, since its parliamentary representation was greatly diminished from 83 to 49 in the 150-seat parliament. The second-place party, the center-right Freedom and Solidarity (SaS), significantly increased its presence by winning 12.1% of the vote and nearly doubling the number of seats from 11 to 21. The conservative Ordinary People Party (OL'aNO) received 11% of the popular vote and 19 seats, while the Slovak National Party (SNS) won 8.6% of votes and 15 seats. A new center-right party, We Are Family, received 6.6% of votes and 11 seats; the Slovak-Hungarian Most-Hid got 6.5% of votes and 11 seats; and the new Network (Siet, self-styled as #SIET) Party of Radoslav Procházka came in with 5.6% of votes and 10 seats.

The game-changing aspect of the election was the success of the extreme-right Kotleba-People's Party Our Slovakia (LSNS) that won 8% of popular vote and 14 seats in the parliament. Its leader, Marian Kotleba, came from a neofascist movement, rails against immigrants and minorities, had freely professed his admiration for the fascist Slovak State and its head Jozef Tiso, and helped organize mass rallies in which his supporters carried banners that read "Slovakia is not Africa." Unlike other recently successful ultranationalist parties, such as the Hungarian Jobbik or the Danish People's Party, LSNS did not even try much to scrub its image clean to improve its electoral chances. Kotleba is the governor of one of eight regions in Slovakia, and besides the "hordes of Muslim

Slovakia

immigrants" and "Gypsy extremists," he also protests the EU, the euro, and NATO.

In the end, Robert Fico's third cabinet included his *Smer-SD* (over half of the portfolios), the nationalist SNS, the Slovak-Hungarian Most-Hid, and one member of the Network. It was a rocky arrangement from the start. The rank-and-file of Most-Hid and the Network decried their leaders' apparent "betrayal" because they joined the government with *Smer*, seen as the primary culprit in the widespread corruption of the health system or the weak education system, something the leaders had promised they would not do. The SNS had already been a coalition partner of the Social-Democrats in 2006, which then led to *Smer*'s temporary expulsion from the socialist party group in the European Parliament for cooperating with nationalists. SNS's relations with Most-Hid had also been tense, since the nationalists often accuse Slovak Hungarians of disloyalty.

On March 15, 2018, in the wake of the political crisis following the murder of Ján Kuciak, Fico delivered his resignation to then-President Andrej Kiska, who then formally charged Deputy Prime Minister Peter Pellegrini with the formation of a new government.

A new party, Ordinary People and Independent Personalities, won the March 2020 parliamentary elections with 25% of the votes, compared to 18% for Smer-SD. The victorious party ran on an anti-corruption platform. Its leader, Igor Matovič, soon stepped down and was replaced by Eduard Heger, who, as Prime Minister from 1 April 2021 to 15 May 2023, lead an unstable four-party ruling coalition.

During the 2023 parliamentary election, Fico ran on a campaign to cease military support to Ukraine in the Russo-Ukrainian War and expressed interest in beginning peace talks. His party Direction—Social Democracy (*Smer*), won the most votes in the election, with 22.95% of the vote and winning 42 seats. Fico formed a coalition with Voice—Social Democracy (*Hlas*) and the Slovak National Party and began his fourth term as prime minister on October 25.

Foreign Policy

Slovakia's most important foreign relations are naturally those with the Czech Republic. Having agreed to a peaceful separation into two independent nations, the Czechs and Slovaks nevertheless recognized that their economies would be tightly bound to each other for some time and that it would be wise to retain certain elements of the former union if they could. These would include a common currency and a customs union that would allow for the free movement of goods. In addition, Czechs and Slovaks would not be required

Just married in Bratislava

to show passports to pass from one country to another.

Although the common currency collapsed after less than two months, the customs union has survived. Trade between the two new republics fell off considerably following separation. It has since stabilized, but the decline in trade had a negative effect on both economies.

Czech-Slovak relations are on the mend. Former prime minister Mikuláš Dzurinda worked assiduously to improve relations with all of Slovakia's neighbors and Serbia while in office from 2002–2006. One reward came in October 2005, when Slovakia was overwhelmingly elected to a seat on the UN Security Council for 2006–2007. This prestigious post made the country more visible in the world.

Of special importance are Slovakia's relations with Hungary, which had been especially bad under ex-prime ministers Mečiar and Fico. There was disagreement over the Gabčíkovo-Nagymaros Dam on the Danube River. Slovakia built the part it had agreed to construct, but Hungary backed out of an earlier joint agreement that it also build a part; the World Court in The Hague ruled that both sides share responsibility and should cover each other's losses, but there has been no resolution of the conflict.

The more important issue was Mečiar's attitude toward ethnic Hungarians. A Slovak chauvinist, he appeared to believe that allowing Slovakia's 560,000 ethnic Hungarians to use Magyar in areas where they constitute a significant percentage of the

population would somehow diminish the Slovak language. His actions to limit such use prevented good relations with Hungary. In fact, it was never forbidden to use Hungarian. The question was whether to require all civil servants to speak Slovak. There are Hungarian-language schools and generally a good system of minority schools, although Bratislava never granted the right to a Hungarian-language university. Unlike the older generation of ethnic Hungarians, younger ones are more likely to speak Slovak, though not well.

The Slovak parliament endorsed the Beneš decrees in 2007, which had been directed against both the German and Hungarian populations in 1945–1948. Plans for a joint Slovak-Hungarian history textbook were put on hold and later scrapped. Some Hungarian schoolbooks still refer to Slovakia as "Upper Hungary." The Fico government went out of its way to needle Hungary.

In September 2009 it enacted a new language law that criminalized the public use of Hungarian in areas where Hungarians do not constitute at least 80% of the local population. Hefty fines (up to $8,000) were levied against those who use a minority language in "official business," including with police officers, teachers, or doctors. Even Hungarian-language schools must conduct their administration in Slovak. It had to be the most visible language on all signs, monuments, and even grave stones. All cultural events not in Slovak were required to provide simultaneous Slovak translations. Even Hungarian ex-president László Sólyom was prevented in August 2009 from crossing the Slovak border to unveil a statue of St. Stephen. This violated the EU's rules on freedom of movement. The latter had been the first king of Hungary and has allegedly a bad reputation in Slovakia for having been an avid promoter of Hungarian identity.

Payback time came when a populist, Viktor Orbán of the Fidesz Party, won the Hungarian elections in April 2010. His first piece of serious legislation was to grant Hungarian citizenship to the 2.5 million Hungarians living outside of Hungary. The then-Slovak government retorted that Slovaks who fail to report such dual citizenship would be fined more than $4,000 and would probably automatically lose their Slovak passport. Ex-prime minister Iveta Radičová later announced her government's intention to scrap the law. Her coalition generally sought smoother relations with its southern neighbor. Economic relations are excellent.

Relations have improved with countries east of Slovakia, such as Russia, Bélarus, and Ukraine. One factor operating here is the tendency among Slovak nationalists to stress pan-Slavic cooperation. More

Street art in Bratislava

gas heading west. It depends on gas imports from Russia, so it rejected pleas that it reverse the gas flow into Ukraine. But it helped its neighbor by opening a pipeline to supply it.

In 2016, Slovakia reached a deal with Russia's Gazprom. In exchange for dropping its ardent opposition to Gazprom's controversial Nord Stream 2 pipeline under the Baltic Sea, Slovak gas transport capacity would be used as part of the project. This apparently will help Slovakia recover some of the losses due to the rerouting of the major gas pipeline. Until then, the country will continue to earn some $450 million a year in transit fees for the gas transported over its territory from Russia and Ukraine to western Europe.

Desperate for reliable power, it is exploring new ways to reopen its nuclear reactors, which it had to shut down as a condition for entry into the EU. Austria is a fierce critic of Slovakia's Jaslovské Bohunice nuclear power plant.

The focus of the Slovak government since 1998 was on building relations with western Europe that would eventually earn it invitations to join NATO and the European Union. That did not necessarily mean that Slovakia's relations with eastern countries were neglected.

In 2002 came the sought-after invitation to join the EU. Slovaks went to polls in May 2003 and overwhelmingly approved their country's entry into the EU—92.46% voted for EU membership, and only 6.2% were against. Their leaders were shocked that only 52.1% turned out to vote, but the referendum, the first ever to succeed since independence, was not binding. Parliament had the final say, and the vote there was 129 to 10. Those lawmakers opposed were the communists, who had previously supported joining, but they argued that the terms negotiated for entry should have been more favorable.

Former prime minister Dzurinda was very pleased, saying that it was the "first time in the history of our country when we had decided about our path ourselves. We're entering a completely new era as a part of a united Europe." The daily newspaper *Sme* noted, "After integration Slovakia will no longer be the West of the East, but the East of the West." Formal entry occurred in May 2004. One year later it ratified the ill-fated European constitution. In July 2007 a Slovak diplomat, Miroslav Lajčák, assumed the position of Bosnia's high representative; this powerful post always goes to a representative of an EU country. However, the government opposes the majority of its fellow EU countries by not recognizing Kosovo's independence.

Slovakia completed its EU integration in January 2009 by becoming the 16th

importantly, however, Slovakia encouraged a rebuilding of trade ties eastward.

Prime Minister Fico took a positive approach to Russia, stressing that Slovakia wants good relations. He opposed sanctions against Russia for its invasions of Ukraine in 2014–2015. He desired to avoid any changes in the "economic dimension." Slovakia gets almost all of its gas and oil from Russia. The Transpetrol pipeline (owned 51% by Slovakia and 49% by Russia's Yukos) crosses Slovakia to bring Russian crude oil to central Europe. The government had to declare a state of emergency in 2009, when a shortage of gas threatened the country with blackouts. Of its imports of gas, 99.5% comes from Russia.

Nevertheless, it decided in 2013 to cooperate with the EU by reexporting some of the Russian gas back into Ukraine in order to help that vulnerable country. This required that it build a final stretch of pipeline needed to deliver the new supply. Slovakia is a major thoroughfare for Russian

Slovakia

member state to adopt the euro. This came just in the nick of time to help cushion its economy during its worst global economic downturn since the end of communism. However, the government felt the wrath of Brussels when it refused in 2010 to contribute to the eurozone bailout of Greece, a country one-third richer than Slovakia with a reputation for tax avoidance, spend-thriftiness, and corruption.

The bailout was very unpopular in Slovakia, which was struggling to reduce its own budget deficit and to bring endemic corruption under control. Voters had no sympathy for a $1.1 billion lifeline to Greece when their own senior officials, including the president, were experiencing a 24% pay reduction. The government did agree to participate in the broader $440 billion eurozone bailout fund, and in 2011 a majority in parliament voted again to contribute to the eurozone's stability fund. But it staunchly opposed in 2015 forgiving any portion of the Greek debt. Polls show that the EU remains popular.

One of the obligations of membership is that it must secure its eastern border with Ukraine, where more than 40,000 illegal immigrants cross each year. This is a favorite route for smugglers because the heavily forested and mountainous border is difficult to police, and it is a short journey to the Austrian or Czech frontiers. An added problem is corruption. An estimated 10% of police are on a retainer from criminal gangs.

Eastern ties were temporarily affected by the NATO air war against Yugoslavia. Interviewed during the NATO summit in Washington in April 1999, ex-prime minister Dzurinda said that Slovakia was acting as a "de facto ally" of NATO. After his return to Bratislava, the government gave NATO permission to use "any Slovak means of transportation" in connection with its air campaign against Yugoslavia. Such statements infuriated the Russian and Bélarussian governments, both of which had been adamant in their condemnation of NATO actions against Yugoslavia. At its Prague summit in November 2002, NATO formally invited Slovakia to join the alliance, an invitation the government accepted without hesitation. It became a NATO member in April 2004.

In February 2005, a crowd of 4,000 Slovaks waited in the snow in Bratislava's central square for two hours to cheer President Bush's talk of freedom and praise for their country as a model for emerging democracies. During the same visit, the presidents of the United States and Russia held a summit meeting. Presidents Dzurinda and Bush got along very well having several things in common: Both are joggers, our prime minister had run the New York City marathon in 2001 and had cycled around the USA in 2005. Both of them have two daughters.

Prime Minister Fico changed the tone of US-Slovak relations. He favored a more accommodating approach to Russia, and he promised not to "rely on only a one-sided relationship with the USA, but to base our policy on European foreign policy." However, he was aware that most central Europeans are convinced that the US remains their ultimate security guarantor, including against Russia. That is why Slovakia's commitment to the transatlantic alliance is not questioned and why he claimed that he is pursuing a foreign policy of continuity. Fico opposed the planned US missile-defense shield that was to be built

in Poland and the Czech Republic. "We are not happy with rockets and radars in Europe." President Obama canceled those plans in 2009.

Slovakia maintains an active military force of 16,531, including conscripts who serve for six months. The army has 7,322 troops that include a rapid-reaction battalion. The 4,190-man air force flies old Soviet MiGs. Slovakia has cancelled all its defense contracts with Russia. It dispatched 196 peacekeepers to Cyprus, 147 to Kosovo, 34 to Bosnia, and 245 to Afghanistan. It supported the American-British war effort in Iraq in 2003 and deployed to Kuwait a nuclear, biological, and chemical (NBC) team that was incorporated in a Czech NBC unit; it also sent 110 demining engineers to Iraq itself. Polls showed that three-quarters of Slovaks opposed this deployment. That made it easier for Fico, who called the war "unjust and wrong," to withdraw the country's tiny contingent from Iraq in 2007. In January 2014 Slovakia agreed to help the US by accepting three Uighurs from the Guantanamo prison.

ECONOMY

Privatization was instituted as a national policy after the fall of communism, but the actual implementation was always in the hands of the Slovak government. Much of Slovakia's industry was built during the communist era. It is large-scale and has had difficulty competing during the transition to a market economy. There is, for example, an extremely large arms industry. Fears about the fate of its heavily subsidized plants helped fuel the Slovak separatist movement that resulted in the breakup of Czechoslovakia in 1993. Privatization was always a much more controversial policy in Slovakia than in the Czech Republic, and Vladimir Mečiar brought it to a halt after Slovakia achieved its independence.

Back in power, Mečiar reinstituted subsidies and raised governmental salaries and pensions. In effect, he returned Slovakia as much as he was able to the economic policies of the communist era. There were also some privatizations, but their purpose was to turn economic assets over to his supporters and allies. Slovakian economic statistics tended to look good because Mečiar kept communist-era factories running, even when there were no customers for their goods. This eventually produced large budget and current-account deficits that threatened future growth. A study of the Slovakian economy issued by the Organization for Economic Cooperation and Development (OECD) in 1999 concluded that Slovakia was on the verge of a crisis and that it needed to implement policy changes in order to sustain growth levels.

In 1999 the new government of Mikuláš Dzurinda approved a plan designed to stabilize the economy and to enhance foreign investment. The difficulty was implementing it. The Dzurinda government was a somewhat-unwieldy coalition whose chief common goal had been to defeat Mečiar. All parties were committed to bringing Slovakia into NATO and the EU, but they disagreed about specific policies. The government raised prices on such things as electricity in order to cut the budget deficit. Currently 90% of all electric power is produced by Slovenské elektrárne, a state-owned company. Slovakia has nuclear power plants that generate electricity. Renewable resources account for 7% of its total energy.

Central controls kept prices for consumers artificially low, but this had to change after Slovakia joined the EU. All banks and insurance companies were state-owned. But during the two prime ministerial terms of Dzurinda from 1998, all state-owned banks, the main insurer, the gas industry, the oil pipeline operator, and Slovak Telecom were privatized.

The global economic crisis that began in the fall of 2008 and affected all advanced economies was bound to hurt Slovakia, whose dependence on auto sales and exports to Germany is strong. The finance minister moaned, "We are totally dependent on exports, mainly to Germany." After all, Slovakia is the world's biggest per-capita car producer. Its GDP contracted by 4.7% in 2009. The GDP of Germany, its main customer, fell at the same time. Slovakia's economy had boomed until the recession.

Although unemployment was only about 3% in prosperous Bratislava, whose citizens' per-capita income is about 90% of the EU average (compared with 70% in Slovakia as a whole), unemployment is closer to 20% outside the capital, the highest rate in central Europe. In the depressed eastern part of the country, unemployment rises to a distressing 40%.

In 2022, economic growth was 3.8%, inflation was 2%, and the budget deficit was 4.9% of GDP Slovakia got the nod from the European Commission that it could join the eurozone in January 2009. The prospect of joining was an incentive for the government to pursue sound economic policies. It is a remarkable turnaround for a country that was once a backwater to become the first country from the old Warsaw Pact to adopt the euro.

Foreign investment is healthy. One result is that the economy is dominated by foreigners, who control most banks and important industries. This stimulates growth, which increases tax revenues and reduces the budget deficit. EU membership, relative cheap labor, and a lowering of the corporate tax rate to 19% in 2003 make Slovakia an attractive target for investment. It has the region's lowest wages. In 2007 the average monthly wage was €450 ($585). Slovakia's wages are about 20% of western European and German levels. More than half of Slovaks indicate in polls that they cannot save money from their incomes because they have to spend 47% on food and a third on housing.

Induced by generous subsidies, US Steel agreed to invest $480 million to revamp Slovakia's largest mill in Košice on the southeastern edge of the country. The Zdeno Veľký Steel Mill had been built in the 1950s to supply Czechoslovak weapons plants and industry throughout the Soviet bloc. After 1989 it had invested millions in up-to-date equipment from the west in order to make itself internationally competitive. Its extensive efforts to find new markets for its steel paid off initially, but its very success proved its undoing. In 1992, the EU imposed strict trade limits on steel imports from eastern Europe, including Czechoslovakia. US Steel's investment saved it. When the EU challenged in 2004 the subsidies it had received, US Steel agreed to return $32 million to the Slovak state. In 2013 the government again offered US Steel energy and environmental concessions to persuade it to save 11,000 jobs by not selling its plant in Košice.

Foreign investment was so hot by 2005 that industrial and prime office rents in Bratislava were already higher than in nearby Vienna. Despite a fall in real estate values during the recession (up to 40% for residential housing in 2009), many Slovaks are buying housing on the Austrian side of the border because it is much cheaper than in or around the Slovak capital.

In 2003 South Korea's Samsung Electronics Slovakia (SESK) was inaugurated in Galanta, 70 kilometers from Bratislava, where 3,000 local workers are employed. It is the company's bridgehead to central and eastern European markets and the largest manufacturing plant of Samsung in Europe. The Hungarian oil and gas company MOL and Whirlpool have invested. Hewlett-Packard, Dell, and IBM have also outsourced operations in Slovakia; Dell located its largest European headquarters in Bratislava, employing 2,100 people.

The capital was also the base for SkyEurope, central Europe's first low-cost airline. When the divorce with the Czech Republic occurred in 1993, Slovakia was deprived of a national carrier. SkyEurope accounted for half the air traffic at Bratislava Airport and operated 79 routes in 19 countries. However, in 2009 it went bankrupt because of the global economic downturn. In 2007 the final link in the Vienna-Bratislava Autobahn (freeway) was completed. The Freedom Cycling Bridge links the Bratislava region with Austria. These connections came just in time for Slovakia's joining the EU's Schengen open-border regime.

Slovakia is becoming the Detroit of central Europe. Volkswagen already owns a major Škoda plant outside of Bratislava in which it has invested €2.4 billion ($3.29 billion) over two decades. It is the country's largest private employer, with 9,400 workers. It is also Slovakia's largest exporter. Some 99.7% of its annual production of 420,000 units is exported, 40% of which is to Germany.

A joint venture of Toyota, Peugeot, and Citroen built a new automotive plant in Trnava, western Slovakia. In 2004 Slovakia lured South Korean Hyundai affiliate Kia Motors, as well as more investment from Peugeot and Citroen. When all these

Ultra-right demonstrating in Bratislava

Slovakia

plants became fully running in 2007, they produced 850,000 cars a year, the most of any central European country and the most per capita in the world. Slovakia hopes to be producing 1 car for each 6 citizens, most for export; 50,000 Slovaks were in the automobile industry in 2005. Some fear that this is too much dependence on the automotive sector, since it already constitutes 26.5% of industrial output and 30.7% of industrial exports, rising to 50%. Indeed, the downturn in western Europe's car market in 2009 dragged Slovakia's auto industry down with it.

To supply the assembly plants, a rapidly growing parts industry is developing. In 2005 there were 140 automotive suppliers. Ten South Korean components makers announced investments in that year. The proximity of US Steel in Košice provides a ready source of high-quality steel. An American components producer, Johnson Controls, opened 10 locations in the country and by 2015 was employing 6,100 people.

Privatization in the area of agriculture was almost fully implemented prior to Slovakia's independence because the federal government had strenuously pursued agricultural transformation. Federal legislation legally transformed collective farms into cooperatives and stipulated that employees had the right to ask for their own land. Most Slovak peasants opted to remain a part of the cooperative structure, however, with only a tiny minority requesting their own land. Even those few who asked for their own acres mostly wanted only a couple of acres to work for themselves. Agriculture is an area where the government feels little need to make changes.

The Slovak Arms Industry

In the decade from 1978 to 1988, Czechoslovakia was the world's eighth-largest weapons exporter and the global leader in per-capita terms. More than 100 plants produced various types of weaponry, ranging from Skorpion machine pistols to L-39 jet trainers, exported to Czechoslovakia's Warsaw Pact partners and developing countries. Most of these plants were located in central Slovakia, which became the center of Czechoslovakia's heavy arms industry. By 1989, military production represented nearly 60% of total industrial production in Slovakia and employed more than 100,000 people.

"These plants were put up in green meadows," says Josef Fučík, head of the department for conversion of military production in the federal ministry of economics in Prague. "It was a quick fix in the '50s to give modern jobs to Slovakia. Now the bill has come due." The town of Martin, 230 kilometers north of Bratislava, was the site of a tank plant that employed 11,000; nearby Dubnica built armored personnel carriers, while Považská Bystrica, down the road, produced jet engines.

Two months after the 1989 revolution, Foreign Minister Jiří Dienstbier announced that Prague would "simply end its trade in arms" without regard to economic consequences. That turned out to be impossible. With so many jobs dependent on arms production, the bulk of them in a depressed region of Slovakia, the government had to modify its plans. Still, it pledged to cut the output of weapons plants to 25% of 1988 levels by 1993. Slovak politicians strenuously opposed the cuts, and this became a major issue in the push for Slovak independence. They did everything they could to frustrate the policy in the interim period and then reversed the policy in 1993.

While the government halted all efforts to convert arms factories to civilian production, it did not find it easy to carry out its stated policy of keeping its arms industry intact. There was, for example, no domestic demand for tanks, since Slovakia is obligated by the terms of the Conventional Forces in Europe (CFE) Agreement to destroy some of its current tanks. In the past, three-quarters of all arms exports went to former Warsaw Pact allies. Those sales disappeared as these countries cut their military budgets. The Soviet Union, once Czechoslovakia's largest customer, cancelled almost all purchase orders in 1991 when it would have been required to pay for such purchases in hard currency. Its subsequent collapse had a psychological effect in Czechoslovakia, but it had already ceased to be a major arms purchaser prior to that.

There have been some sales to developing countries, but Slovakia is at a disadvantage because it produces mainly heavy battlefield weapons, not the small arms and specialized explosives most in demand in the developing world. Worse, all of Slovakia's major weapons systems are produced on license from Russia, which in many cases is competing in the same markets with more advanced weapons systems.

Efforts made before independence to convert parts of Slovak heavy industry to peaceful purposes were not very successful. An exception was the conversion of the ZTS Martin ("Turčianske Strojárne" factory, located in the city of Martin), a tank manufacturer. It negotiated an agreement with the German firm Hanomag to manufacture earthmoving equipment. The company also began working under license from the Italian manufacturer Lombardini to produce tractor engines and other machinery. In this instance, military production was reduced to one-quarter of overall manufactures.

CULTURE

There has always been a separate Slovak culture. Part of the Hungarian kingdom from the 11th century, Slovaks were a peasant people heavily influenced by Hungarian culture. Their language was codified in mid-19th-century by Ľudovít Štúr, a linguist and patriot who created a literary standard from a variety of local dialects. His disciple, Janko Matúška, wrote the text of what later became the national anthem, "Nad Tatrou sa blyska" ("Lightning over the Tatras"). Its traditional folk tune and references to the beloved alpine mountains reflected and reinforced the bond Slovaks have with their country. Ardent Magyarization (Hungarization) slowed down the development of literature, but by the 1870s, such writers as the poet Pavol Országh Hviezdoslav and novelists Svetozár Hurban-Vajanský and Martin Kukučín promoted Slovak realism.

Slovakia is particularly known for its unique and lively folk music and dances, performed in brightly colored traditional dress. Folk art and crafts have been supported and propagated by ULUV, the Center for Folk Art Production, that organizes exhibitions around the world.

Slovakia has changed greatly in recent years, however, and many parts of the country are now urbanized and industrialized. Bratislava became the seat of the European Music Academy and sponsors many music and theater festivals.

The works of individual Slovak artists and craftsmen compare favorably with that of other Europeans. However, because many Slovaks live in small towns or in the countryside itself (only 54% live in urban areas), Slovak art often has more of a peasant quality about it. There is also not as large an audience for art, so artists tend to be more marginalized.

Religion

The old communist regime was extremely hostile to religion, and it went out of its way to make its practice difficult. The regime particularly restricted the Catholic Church, to which most Slovaks belong, probably because it is part of an international organization. Since the 1989 revolution, the Catholic Church has revealed that it maintained an underground church in Slovakia during those years. This involved such things as secretly providing theological training in private apartments and homes and ordaining hundreds of individuals as priests, who then continued to work in their regular jobs while performing their priestly functions in secret.

As this underground church has emerged, people were surprised to learn of the double lives some of these individuals had been living. As an example, five faculty members at the communist-run Košice University were actually Jesuit priests, including the dean of the School of Civil Engineering. It also turns out that a large percentage of the priests belong to religious orders like the Dominicans, Jesuits, and Salesians, all of which were banned by the communists. There were even some married men ordained as priests, plus some women who became deacons. The church is now attempting to sort out all of these anomalies. Smaller Greek Catholic (Uniate) religious communities exist especially in the mountainous northeast among the Ruthenian (Rusnak) ethnic minority that numbers some 33,000.

CURRENT ISSUES

Together with Hungary, Czech Republic, and Romania, Slovakia voted against the 2015 EU scheme to redistribute some 160,000 migrants from Greece and Italy among the member states. Immigration became a major political hot-button issue, even though in reality only 330 people requested asylum in Slovakia in 2015 and only 8 were granted it. Still, Slovakia argued that the very Schengen system is at stake, since the refugees allocated to a country that was not their first choice would simply keep moving. Slovak politicians warned that placing refugees in their country would provoke a strong anti- EU backlash.

The anti-Muslim and xenophobic atmosphere benefitted greatly the nationalistic SNS and especially the extreme-right LSNS Party, bringing some neofascists and ultra-nationalists to the parliament. The migrant crisis is likely to reignite the not-so-latent anti-Roma sentiments in the country that has done too little to accommodate this most neglected minority in Europe.

Robert Fico's government collapsed in March 2018 in the wake of the murder of investigative journalist Ján Kuciak and his fiancé, who were uncovering evidence of corruption and organized crime. Slovaks took to the streets in numbers unseen since the 1989 Velvet Revolution. Eighty-five percent of Slovaks regard corruption to be a widespread problem.

The country's turmoil brought the first female president to power in 2019: Zuzana Čaputová, an anti-corruption lawyer. Robert Fico started his fourth mandate as prime minister in 2023.

Slovakia's future will be influenced by the neighboring Russo-Ukrainian War. Former Prime Minister Eduard Heger warned that soaring electricity costs leave Slovakia in danger of collapse. The EU must step in even though it is a significant producer of nuclear and hydroelectric energy.

Republic of Hungary (Magyarország)

Parliament on the Danube, Budapest

Area: 35,920 sq. mi. (93,030 sq. km).
Population: 9,678,000 (2023 estimate).
Capital City: Budapest (pop. 1,752,286; 2019 estimate).
Climate: It is continental, with generally long, warm summers with low overall humidity but frequent rain showers and cold snowy winters. Average annual temperature is 9.7 °C (49.5 °F). The average high temperature in summer is 23 to 28 °C (73 to 82 °F) and average low temperature in the winter is −3 to −7 °C (27 to 19 °F).
Neighboring Countries: Slovakia (north); Ukraine (east); Romania (southeast); Serbia, Croatia (south); Slovenia, Austria (west).
Official Language: Hungarian.
Recognized minority languages: German, Serbian, Croatian, Slovak, Romanian, Armenian, Bulgarian, Greek, Romani, Rusyn, Slovenian, and Ukrainian.
Ethnic Background: 87.9% Hungarians (Magyar), 2.2% Roma, 1.5% Germans, 1.1% others, 7.3% unanswered. (2022 census)
Religion: 42.5% Christianity (29.2% Catholicism, 9.8% Calvinism, 3.5% other Christian), 1.3% others, 16.1% no religion, 40.1% unanswered. (2022 census)
Form of Government: Unitary parliamentary republic.
Chief of State: Katalin Novák (since May 10, 2022. Resigned on February 10, 2024).
Head of Government: Viktor Orbán, Prime Minister (since April 2010).
National Flag: It is a horizontal tricolor of crimson red (at the top), white (in the center), and dark green (at the bottom). It was officially adopted in this exact form for the flag of Hungary in 1957. The flag's form originates from national republican movements of the 18th and 19th centuries, while its colors are from the Middle Ages. They were mentioned in a 1608 coronation ceremony, but their association with the monarchs of Hungary may go back to as early as the 13th century. The flag colors are the same as those found in Hungary's tradiional coat of arms. The white is said to symbolize Hungary's rivers, the green stands for its mountains, and the red for the blood shed in its many battles.
Public Holidays: May 15 (National day—Memorial Day of the 1848 Revolution), August 20 (State Foundation Day), October 23 (National day—1956 Revolution Memorial Day).
Currency: Forint (HUF).
Main Exports: Telecommunications equipment, machinery and transport equipment, cars, broadcasting equipment, video displays, vehicle spare parts and ignition engines.
Main Imports: Machinery and transport equipment, motor vehicles & parts, plastics, pharmaceuticals, iron & steel.
Main Trading Partners: Germany (25.1% of exports and 24.6% of imports), Austria (4.5% of exports and 5.8% of imports), Romania (5.3% of exports), China (8.0% of imports), Slovakia (5.1% of exports), Poland (4.3% exports and 5.8% imports), Czech Republic (5.0% of imports), Italy (5.7 of exports), Netherlands (4.9 of imports). (2022)

Hungarians captured the world's attention and admiration in 1956, when they rose up against an alien unwanted master and courageously fought with stones and their bare hands against the well-armed occupation troops and their tanks. This heroic struggle failed, but it helped persuade the communist rulers to liberalize the regime and to permit reform that was daring when compared to what was allowed elsewhere in the Soviet Empire. When the old European order crumbled in 1989, Hungary was more prepared for the new order than any other central or eastern European country. In a remarkable bookend to this process, in the fall of 2016, Hungary's prime minister, Viktor Orbán, used the anniversary of the 1956 uprising to provide a powerful rebuke to what he presented as another empire trying to control his country—only this time it was the European Union. "We sent the Soviets home and cleared Hungary of the consequences of dictatorship. Now we want to remain a European nation and not become an ethnic group in Europe."

The Republic of Hungary lies in the Middle Danube Basin. Two great rivers, the Danube and the Tisza, cross the rolling plains that cover most of the country. The Danube—one of Hungary's few natural frontiers—provides part of the border between Hungary and Slovakia, then turns sharply southward, passes through Budapest, and divides Hungary. Contrary to legend, its waters are not blue but are usually brown because of the presence of silt from upstream areas.

To the east of the river lies the Hungarian Plain, a vast fertile land that explains why Hungary was called the granary of the Austro-Hungarian Empire. The northeast section along the Slovak border is covered with forested mountains, abundant with wildlife. Here one can find limestone caverns and Europe's largest stalactite caves. Most importantly, the northeast contains Hungary's famous wine-producing centers, Eger and Tokaj. West of the Danube, plains turn into hills where the easternmost part of the Alps reaches into western Hungary.

Hungary

St. Stephen on Heroes Square, Budapest

Although there are several theories concerning the origins of the Hungarians, it is generally agreed that they are a Finno-Ugric people. They speak a language distantly related to Finnish and Estonian, although Hungarians cannot understand those tongues. In early historic times, they were first found inhabiting a part of the Russian Plain west of the Ural Mountains. Apparently suffering attacks from even more aggressive neighbors, several Hungarian tribes migrated westward, crossed the Carpathian Mountains, and settled the broad plain that spreads out from the Danube River east and south of the present-day city of Budapest.

Political Status: Independent, 1918–1945; communist state, part of Soviet bloc, 1945–1990.

Hungary c. 1350

HISTORY

Origins of the Hungarian State

Initially led by Arpad, for whom the first dynasty of Hungary was named, the Hungarians did not immediately settle down in central Europe. They terrorized most of the surrounding people until the 10th century, when the German emperor Otto I defeated them. Although there was earlier Christian missionary work among the Hungarians, Stephen I of the Arpad dynasty "converted" the whole nation on Christmas Day, 1000 AD when he accepted a cross and crown sent by Pope Sylvester II. After his death, the church proclaimed him a saint in 1083.

The Crown of St. Stephen later became the symbol of highest authority. It represented the "unity" of all lands claimed by

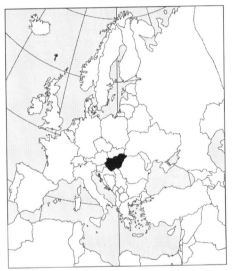

Hungary, including those not inhabited solely by Hungarians. During the 10th century, Slovakia was conquered; by 1003 Transylvania was under the crown, and a century later, Croatia, Slavonia, and Dalmatia were united with Hungary. By the late 14th century, the kingdom of Hungary contained extensive areas inhabited by Saxons (Germans), Slavs, Vlachs (Romanians of Wallachia), and Szekelys (Transylvanian Magyars—the Hungarian word for "Hungarians"—living in the Carpathian Mountains).

During the Middle Ages, Hungary was not isolated from the rest of Europe. At the end of the 12th century, a dynastic connection with France was established when King Béla III married the daughter of the French king; the marriage settlement showed that Hungary's national treasury equaled that of France. Hungary's early constitutional development resembled England's. The Hungarian king was forced to sign a document called the Golden Bull in 1222, which guaranteed the rights of the nobility, similar to the English Magna Carta.

A Mongol invasion in 1241 devastated Hungary and resulted in the loss of one-half of the population. However, the Mongols remained only for a year, so their occupation did not influence Hungary as it would Russia.

The Arpad dynasty ended in 1301, and for two centuries foreign nobility ruled Hungary. In the 15th century, one of Hungary's greatest kings, Mathias Corvinus, ascended the throne. An enlightened Renaissance monarch, he reformed the country's administrative and judicial systems, reorganized the army, founded

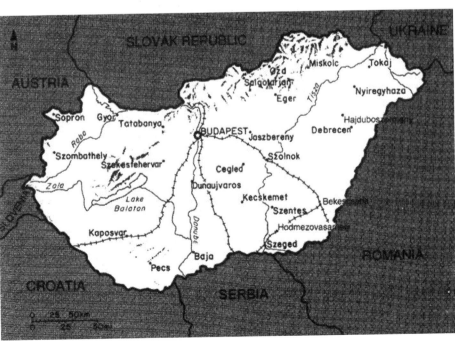

413

Hungary

universities, and preserved Hungary's position as an important European power.

A Part of the Multinational Habsburg Empire

Hungary's defeat by the Ottoman Turks in 1526 was a turning point in the nation's history. After a period of civil war, the Turks incorporated the central part into their empire, while the Habsburgs claimed the western part. A third region, consisting of Transylvania and 16 neighboring counties, became a self-governing principality. This area eventually became known as Transylvania and was the center of Hungarian culture over the next two centuries. It gave Hungary such heroes as Stephen Bocskay and Gábor Bethlen. Transylvania was a model of religious tolerance among the states of Europe. Its princes, backed by armies, spread the principle throughout the rest of Hungary, forcing its adoption as the law of the land.

Transylvania was the easternmost country to participate in the great spiritual movement of the 16th century called the Protestant Reformation. By the end of that century, 90% of all Hungarians were Protestant. In 1699, however, most of Hungary, Transylvania, and Croatia passed from Turkish to Austrian hands by the Peace of Karlowitz. This led to the suppression of Protestantism, which had been tolerated by the Turks as a protection against the influence of the Roman Catholic Habsburgs. Even so, enough survived that the Protestants of Hungary and Transylvania still constitute the largest such grouping in central and eastern Europe.

Francis Rakoczy led a rebellion in 1703 against Habsburg domination. Although it was suppressed, it was a foretaste of the nationalist movement that shook the empire a century later. In 1740 it was Hungary that threw its support behind Maria Theresia when Frederick II of Prussia challenged her claims to the traditional Habsburg territories, guaranteed by the Pragmatic Sanction. Maria Theresia was crowned queen of Hungary at Pressburg (Bratislava), and it was Hungarian support that allowed her to retain all of the Habsburg territories with the exception of Silesia. Under Maria Theresia, Hungary had its own Diet, or National Assembly, composed of a House of Magnates and a House of Deputies.

Failed Revolutions

In the 1830s and 1840s, Hungary's political climate became infused with the spirit of nationalism and reform. Radicals, such as Lajos Kossuth, began giving speeches in the Diet advocating independence from Austria. But even more moderate leaders advocated self-government within the empire. As the revolutionary movement

Rise Hungary! Revolution in 1848.

Budapest: March 22, 1919. The pouring rain does not deter the celebration of Hungary's communist revolutionaries.

spread in 1848, the Diet actually passed a program known as the April Laws, which, while retaining the Habsburgs as the ruling dynasty, made Hungary internally independent.

This did not satisfy the radicals, and in 1849, under Kossuth's leadership, they declared Hungary's complete independence. The revolution was successful at first, since the Hungarian army had gone over to the side of the rebels. It failed in the end, however, when Tsar Nicholas I offered a Russian army to Austria to help put down

the uprising. The next several years were a period of rigid centralization, as Vienna attempted to prevent any such revolutionary outbreaks in the future.

During the years of suppression, an increasing number of Magyar leaders came to realize that complete independence was impossible and that a change in Hungary's status could come only within the context of continued Habsburg rule. Their chance came in 1866, when Austria stumbled into a war with Prussia. After Prussia had defeated Austria, Francis Deak, a moderate

Admiral Horthy

Kalvin Square in Budapest, 1930s

Composer Béla Bartók recording folk songs, 1907

leader, presented a plan that became the basis for the Compromise of 1867, which created the dual monarchy. Franz Josef became kaiser of Austria and king of Hungary. Under such a system, Austria and Hungary each had its own constitution and parliament, but there were common ministries for finance, foreign affairs, and war. The Compromise of 1867 provided the basis for relations between Austria and Hungary until 1918. It also ushered in the most prosperous era of Hungary's history up to that time, despite growing nationalist tensions.

Hungary supported the Central Powers (Germany and Austria) in World War I. At the beginning of the war, Hungarian leaders signed the so-called Truce of God, under which they agreed to refrain from quarreling over domestic issues during the war. By 1916, however, the truce was broken, as opposition to the war increased, and extremists began a propaganda campaign against the war. Two years later, one of these leaders, Michael Károlyi, became head of the government in a war-weary defeated country. In 1918 this government proclaimed Hungary a republic, but it lasted only five months.

The Hungarian communists were made up mainly of soldiers who learned about Marxism while prisoners of war in Russia. They had no political experience, nor had any of them held any important post in the Hungarian labor movement during the prewar period. Released at the end of the war, they formed the main body of the Hungarian Communist Party, which was founded in November 1918. As their message of peace and prosperity began spreading among the mass of unemployed workers and soldiers, the government attempted to suppress the activities of the party by imprisoning its local leaders. Among them was Béla Kun, who had been

a prisoner of war in Russia, fought in the Russian Civil War on the communist side, then organized the Hungarian section of the Soviet Communist Party, and played a leading role in founding its Hungarian counterpart.

While in prison, the communists managed to come to an agreement with some prominent members of the Social Democratic Party, the strongest political group in the country at this time. This led to a merger of the two parties. When the Károlyi government resigned on March 20, 1919, because it was unwilling to accept the diminished territories proposed

by the allies, the merged party under Béla Kun was able to come to power the next day without a violent revolution.

Béla Kun became the head of the new communist government, which took the name of the Hungarian Soviet Republic. It immediately nationalized all banks and all enterprises with more than 20 workers. All titles and ranks of the nobility were abolished. Private property was also abolished, and the state took over the great estates of the Hungarian nobility.

The young Soviet republic collapsed in 1919, when Romania sent in troops to enforce the terms of the peace treaties ending

Hungary

Street book vendor in Budapest

World War I. Béla Kun fled the country. The Romanian army occupied Budapest until November 1919, when its western allies persuaded it to withdraw.

Interwar Years

During the time that Béla Kun held power a number of prewar politicians who had been loyal to the old regime had set up an opposition government. Their small army, under the command of Admiral Miklós Horthy, entered Budapest in late 1919, set up an anti-Bolshevik government, and asked to be recognized by the allies. However, the allies refused. Instead, they demanded creation of a provisional government that would hold elections.

This led to the creation of a coalition government that included the Smallholders Party, the National Democratic Party, and the Social Democrat Party. Elections were set for January 1920. During the months before the elections, bands of terrorists roamed the country, attacking Jews, Social Democrats, members of trade unions, and anyone they suspected either of having communist sympathies or of opposing the return of the conservatives to power.

Because of the terrorism that had prevailed during the campaign, the first postwar parliament was not representative of the country. The Social Democrats decided to boycott the elections because of the attacks on them. The new parliament first took up the question of whether Hungary was still a monarchy. King Charles had renounced all power in 1918 but had not abdicated. The parliament's decision was that Hungary would continue to be a kingdom but without a king. A regent would

be elected to act as head of state. Admiral Horthy was named regent of Hungary in March 1920, and he retained that title and position until October 1944. King Charles died in Spain in 1922.

The Treaty of Trianon, signed on June 4, 1920, legalized the loss of territory that had taken place since 1918. Hungary thus emerged from World War I losing almost three-fourths of its prewar territory and about two-thirds of its population. Among the various losses, Slovakia and Ruthenia went to the recently created Czechoslovakia, while Croatia, Slavonia, and most of the Vojvodina became part of the newly created Kingdom of Serbs, Croats, and Slovenes, which in the later 1920s became Yugoslavia. In addition, Transylvania and part of the Banat went to Romania. Since boundary lines could not follow ethnic divisions, a large Hungarian population was left in each of the lost areas.

After 1920, Hungarians used the word "dismembered" to describe Trianon Hungary. This was intended to produce the image of a broken state that for 1,000 years had been held together under the legal and patriotic symbol of the Crown of St. Stephen. The treaty has had long-lasting effects. It was the underlying reason for Hungary's entry into World War II.

Even today some Hungarians talk about it, and the fate of Hungarians outside of Hungary's borders is still a major foreign policy issue. In 2005, on the 85th anniversary of the treaty, Hungarians on the street were asked their opinions of it. One pensioner said, "It was shameful. It's still a current issue—the West doesn't want to give us justice." A journalist agreed that "it's absolutely a current issue. Sixty-two

percent of our land was taken away, families were torn apart. They took away our railway lines." A 24-year-old librarian responded, "Wow! That's a delicate subject. . . . But for the sake of peace, we have to try and forget."

The enduring hostility toward the Trianon Treaty was demonstrated in January 2011, when Hungary assumed the six-month rotating presidency of the EU. The presiding country traditionally commissions a cultural project to adorn the EU's Justus Lipsius building. The Hungarian government put down a 200-square-meter floor decoration that included a map of central Europe in 1848, with borders clearly showing the full expanse of greater Hungary before the treaty. Those frontiers encompassed the territory of several states that are now members of the EU. Among the first legislative acts of the new Fidesz government in 2010 were to declare June 4 a day of national unity in commemoration of the Treaty of Trianon and to offer Hungarian citizenship and passports to ethnic Hungarians residing abroad. Noting this, many foreign observers regarded the floor map as evidence that the dream of undoing the treaty is still alive. Most Hungarians consider the treaty to be grossly unfair.

Overall, the interwar period was peaceful, at least on the surface. A conservative government led by Stephen Bethlen, a Protestant aristocrat from Transylvania, held power from 1921 to 1931. Desiring a return to the "good old days" but without the Habsburgs, Bethlen ignored the need for land reform and had no understanding of worker and peasant problems. Internationally, the "Little Entente" isolated Hungary. This was an alliance consisting of Hungary's neighbors, Czechoslovakia, Romania, and Yugoslavia—all of which had obtained Hungarian lands as a result of the Treaty of Trianon and intended to keep them.

The worldwide economic depression of the 1930s and Hungary's continuing desire to regain lost lands led the nation down a disastrous path to alliance with Nazi Germany. Government leadership changed five times between 1931 and 1939, but the conservatives remained in control. Anti-Jewish measures were enacted, which affected even the political leadership. The last of the five premiers, the patriotic statesman Count Pál Teleki, committed suicide as a dramatic protest against the invasion of Yugoslavia by Germans crossing Hungarian soil.

World War II

Diplomatic activity preceding World War II resulted in Hungary's regaining southern Slovakia and Ruthenia; northern Transylvania was recovered in 1940. Hungary signed the Tripartite Pact of the

Hungary

Axis powers in November 1940, and in spite of a treaty of "eternal friendship," which lasted less than two years, between Yugoslavia and Hungary, German troops crossed Hungary to invade Yugoslavia. The next question was whether Hungary should join in the German war on Russia. On the pretext that Russian planes had bombed Košice, Premier László Bárdossy sided with the military and published a declaration of war against Russia in mid-1941 without the consent of the parliament. War was later declared against the United States, although that country had made no territorial claims whatsoever against Hungary. It is possible that the "Russian aircraft" were really German planes on which Russian markings had been painted.

Parliamentary institutions and political parties functioned until late in the war. There was no German occupation until March 1944, prompted by the advance of the Red Army. Until then Hungary's 800,000 Jews had lived in comparative safety, hoping to survive the horrors all around them. A pro-German government dissolved political parties and increased the persecution of Jews to a level not previously experienced in Hungary. With Admiral Horthy and other Hungarian authorities cooperating fully, over 430,000 Jews were deported to Auschwitz between May and July 1944. Others fell victim to roving bands of Hungarian Nazi Arrow Cross militia. The over a half-million Hungarian Jewish victims constituted a tenth of all Holocaust victims. Because of Horthy's role in this, there were large protests in 2013 when a statue of him was unveiled in central Budapest. In 2013 Deputy Prime Minister Tibor Navracsics issued an unprecedented admission of wartime guilt: "The perpetrators were Hungarians; it was Hungarians who fired the shots and it was Hungarians who died."

In the fall of 1944, Horthy and his advisers came to the conclusion that the Axis powers could not win the war. Seeking a separate armistice, Hungary sent a diplomatic team to Moscow and announced on October 15, 1944, that it had requested an armistice with the Soviet Union. Horthy's proclamation was poorly timed. The Germans were able to take control of the capital, seize him, and force him to retract his proclamation. He was then compelled to abdicate.

The Hungarian commander-in-chief, General Béla Miklós, joined with the Soviet army when it crossed Hungary's borders. With Soviet support, committees of national liberation were set up in the Soviet-held areas, and a provisional government was formed in Debrecen. When Soviet forces besieged Budapest, the pro-German puppet government fled in January 1945.

2002 election poster beside an old East German Trabant

The provisional government concluded an armistice in Moscow in January 1945.

The government of Hungary was based on a coalition of political parties that included three larger parties, the Hungarian Independence Front, the Social Democratic Party, and the Communist Party, and two smaller parties, the Small-holders Party and the National Peasant Party. According to the terms of the armistice, Hungary was to return to its 1938 frontiers, and this provision was contained in the Peace Treaty of February 10, 1947. The agreement also provided for an Allied Control Commission, with Soviet marshal K. E. Voroshilov as its chairman.

Hungary Becomes a People's Republic

By a decree of March 1945, the Provisional government started an extensive land reform program that was accomplished under the direction of Imre Nagy, the communist minister of agriculture. New elections were set for late 1945. In these elections, probably the freest elections Hungarians had ever experienced, the Small-holders Party received 57% of the vote. The Communist Party and the Social Democratic Party each received 17%. Zoltán Tildy, leader of the Small-holders, became prime minister. He was elected president after the National Assembly proclaimed Hungary a republic in early 1946. Ferenc Nagy succeeded Tildy in the office of prime minister. Although the Small-holders had won a majority of the vote in the election, the government consisted of a coalition. Imre Nagy became minister of the interior.

It is inaccurate to describe the process by which the communists came to dominate the Hungarian government as a "seizure" of power. In reality, this was achieved quite slowly and cautiously over a three-year period. The Communist Party and the Social Democratic Party were merged in mid-1948 to form the Hungarian Workers' Party (HSWP). A communist sympathizer replaced Tildy in that year, and communists dominated the cabinet.

The final move was made in February 1949 with the establishment of the Hungarian Independent People's Front, a combination of all parties and mass organizations. The front presented a single list of candidates that received 96.5% of the vote in the May 1949 elections. The newly elected National Assembly proclaimed Hungary a people's republic and adopted a constitution reflecting Hungary's official position as a member of the Soviet bloc.

The Stalinist Period

The years from 1949 to 1953 were called the "Stalinist period." Political control was wielded by Mátyás Rákosi, a dedicated communist since 1918. He became secretary-general of the Communist Party in 1944, deputy prime minister until 1952, and prime minister from 1952 until 1953.

Under his supervision, reorganized secret police, some of them former fascist Arrow Cross members, prosecuted 1.3 million persons between 1950 and 1953, opened concentration camps holding more than 40,000 inmates, purged the party, and imprisoned half of the 850,000 Communist Party members. The police attacked the few remaining rich landowners, undermined the churches, and kept a close watch over social life in general. The most dramatic event of this period was the trial

417

Hungary

Soviet tanks guard the street intersection leading to the Danube Bridge in Budapest on November 5, 1956.

AP/Wide World Photo

of László Rajk, a "home communist" and one-time minister of the interior and foreign affairs. Accused on falsified evidence of conspiring with Yugoslavia's Tito, he was executed in 1949. This was followed by a purge of the party membership that eliminated all those suspected of having nationalist or anti-Rákosi sentiments. In the process, several thousand party members were also imprisoned.

By 1949, the new regime had introduced the Stalinist model of economic planning, with its emphasis on central decision making and heavy industry. All industry employing more than 10 workers had been nationalized, and a program for the collectivization of agriculture had been initiated.

Lacking most raw materials, Hungary had never placed any great stress on heavy industry. It had concentrated on the development of agriculture based on the processing of its products and the manufacture of consumer goods. The new emphasis on heavy industry in the first five-year plan produced spectacular growth totals in the beginning. Heavy industrial production increased fivefold, and the engineering industry showed a sevenfold increase in productivity over 1938.

By 1953, however, serious shortages had begun to appear in both raw materials and fuel supplies. A serious disproportion had begun to appear between heavy and light industry. Agriculture was beginning to stagnate under the combination of collectivization accompanied by a decline in investment. Wages and salaries had risen less rapidly than consumer prices. The result was a 20% decline in the general standard of living between 1948 and 1953.

The New Course and Revolution

There had been some muted criticism of these developments even before Stalin's death in March 1953, but the dictator's passing brought these out into the open. Imre Nagy took the lead. He challenged Rákosi's handling of the economy, accusing him of forcing the tempo of industrialization all out of proportion to the country's resources. Rákosi was forced to step down as chairman of the council of ministers, although he retained his position as head of the Hungarian Workers' Party. Nagy was named in his place.

In his first speech to parliament in 1953, Nagy presented a program that later became known as the New Course. It included an emphasis on consumer goods instead of heavy industry; abolition of collective farms when such was desired by a majority of the workers; and the release of many political prisoners, including János Kádár.

Continued disputes over these new policies, particularly in agriculture, coupled with a failure to gain support of important party members, led to Nagy's resignation in 1955. András Hegedüs replaced him, and Hungary returned to the old policies of heavy industrialization and collectivization. After the unkept promises of the New Course and a disappointing return to earlier policies, protests from writers and scholars began to be heard in the autumn of 1955. The following summer, the Petöfi Circle, named after a revolutionary poet killed in 1849, was formed. It provided a forum for debate among those who were critical of the government.

In an effort to appease the critics, the Soviet Union brought increased pressure on the Hungarian party to dismiss Rákosi. He resigned in mid-1956 and was replaced by Ernő Gerő. This did not quiet the discord. A number of party leaders who had been executed in the purges of 1949 were reburied with honor; the funerals turned into a mass demonstration against the government. A few weeks later, the students of Szeged University in the city of that name organized a noncommunist youth organization.

By late 1956, news of the Szeged students and of the antigovernment activities in Poland reached Budapest. This prompted students and writers to draw up a resolution and to hold a public demonstration expressing sympathy for the Polish cause. Their plan was to march to a statue of General József Bem, a Polish soldier who had fought with the Hungarians against the Austrians and Russians in 1848–1849. The resolution demanded the evacuation of Soviet troops from Hungary, the return of Nagy as chairman of the council of ministers, free elections, and freedom of speech and press. This was not so much in opposition to communism as it was in favor of the development of some form of socialist democracy.

Although planned only as a demonstration, the October 23 events turned swiftly into a mass revolution. This was due to poor judgment of officials and the emotions generated by the mass activity. The minister of the interior responded to news of the planned demonstration by first banning it but then agreeing not to interfere. That evening, the huge crowd that had gathered in front of parliament began calling for Nagy, who addressed them briefly and then asked them to disperse.

Later in the evening, two specific events triggered an uprising. First, Secretary Erno Gero gave a tactless and accusing speech, during which he denounced the demonstrators. Then the radio station director refused to broadcast the resolution. Fighting first broke out between the demonstrators and the secret police and quickly spread into the working-class districts. A gigantic statue of Stalin in the center of Budapest was toppled; because only the boots remained, the site was popularly called Boot Square.

During the night Soviet tanks appeared, and fighting erupted between Soviet troops and revolutionaries, who were by then supported by parts of the Hungarian army. The unrest spread even further into the countryside, where workers' councils and revolutionary councils were organized to replace the local communist administrations.

On October 24, Nagy replaced Hegedüs as chairman of the council of ministers, and the next day, János Kádár replaced Erno Gero as first secretary of the Hungarian Workers' Party. Russian archives opened after the collapse of the Soviet Union in 1991 reveal that the Soviet presidium (later called Politburo) decided unanimously on October 30 not to use military force. Anastas Mikoyan, who was in Budapest at the time as a Soviet representative of the

Hungary

CENTURY OF
THE MILLENNIUM

Nov. 5, 1956 *Russia brutally quashes the Hungarian Revolution and supports the countergovernment of Janos Kadar, a member of the former cabinet. Later, as premier, he would walk a line between supporting Soviet policies and initiating liberal reforms at home* **More Nov. 5** news Muslim students storm the U.S. embassy in Tehran in a bid to force a trial of deposed Reza Shah Pahlevi (1979). **Tomorrow** Battle For Patriation Is Over (1981).

The Globe and Mail

Cloudy, Mild
High Here 65

TORONTO, MONDAY, NOVEMBER 5, 1956.   5 Cents Per Copy   44 PAGES

HUNGARY CRUSHED
UN Demands Russia Withdraw, Approves Canadian Suez Plans; Paratroops Landing in Egypt

Canadian Appointed As Police Force Chief

Soviet Might Batters Budapest Rebel Force

'Hands Off,' Soviet Says—

Call Session On UN Force, PM Indicates

Assembly Condemns Russia For Its Military Intervention

Gaitskell Offers Deal
Police Disperse Anti-Eden Mob

London Reports Invasion Starts Near Port Said

65 More Miners Found, Survivors May Total 101

President Asks Soviet Call Its Troops Back

---

presidium of the Central Committee, accepted political changes and negotiated an agreement with Nagy and Kádár for the withdrawal of the Soviet army from Hungary. Mikoyan's agreement was obviously based on the premise that Nagy and Kádár, as communists, were committed to the maintenance of communist control in Hungary. However, Nagy, in announcing the Soviet troop withdrawal agreement, also promised to abolish the secret police and to bring representatives of noncommunist parties into the government.

The United States government did not help matters by talking loosely of "liberation" and a "rollback" of communism, when it was not in a position to do anything about the lamentable situation. This gave

Hungarians false hopes of outside rescue that were bound to be disappointed. President Eisenhower said privately during his 1956 reelection campaign, "Poor fellows, poor fellows. I wish there were some way of helping them."

The Kremlin decided that things might spin out of control in Hungary and in the rest of the Soviet Empire. Reports reached Budapest on November 1 that Soviet troops had stopped their withdrawal and, reinforced by additional Soviet tanks of the latest design, were actually heading back toward Budapest, a half-million strong. Nagy responded by announcing Hungary's withdrawal from the Warsaw Pact (the military organization of eastern Europe presided over by the Soviets),

committing Hungary to a policy of neutrality and appealing for help from the United Nations.

Soviet troops attacked Budapest on November 4, 1956. At the same time, Kádár, now in eastern Hungary, having left Budapest on the evening of November 1–2, proclaimed the establishment of a "revolutionary government of peasants and workers" to replace the "fascist" Nagy government. Although there was a great deal of resistance by the Hungarian people, a basically unarmed people were no match for Soviet tanks, and the revolution was ruthlessly suppressed. Around 2,800 Hungarians and 700 Soviet soldiers died in the violence. Kádár was back in power with the backing of Soviet troops.

About 200,000 refugees poured into western countries, including the US, making Cleveland, Ohio, the second-largest Hungarian city. They joined the many Hungarian immigrants who had already settled in the US. They included the poor Jewish tailor parents of Bernard Schwartz, who was born in the Bronx and became famous in Hollywood under the name of Tony Curtis (1925—2010). Among the refugees to the US was the commander-in-chief of the revolutionary forces, Béla Király. He taught history at Brooklyn College and authored and published many books on Hungary and the region. He returned to Hungary in 1989 to serve in his liberated homeland's parliament. He died in 2009 at age 97. At least 225 Hungarians accused of taking part in the revolution were executed. This included Nagy, who was arrested, refused to confess to being a fascist counterrevolutionary, and was hanged in 1958. His rehabilitation and reburial in 1989 in the presence of some 100,000 people signaled a significant turn toward decommunization. However, the only high-ranking official put on trial for the wave of repression after the Hungarian uprising, former interior minister Béla Biszku, kept appealing his original 2014 conviction for war crimes until his death in 2016 at the age of 94.

Politics after 1956

Kádár was in a difficult position after 1956 because he lacked the support of the party and the people. Within the party, those opposed him who favored internal reform and who accused him of selling out the revolution. Large segments of the population, including the students, writers, and workers who had played such a large role in the revolution, viewed Kádár as a Soviet puppet. He was in power only because he had the support of Nikita Khrushchev, the man who had suppressed the revolution. During the first two years after the uprising, Kádár repressed the various social groups and political parties

Hungary

that opposed his government. Hundreds of people associated with the revolution were imprisoned.

In 1959–1960, there appeared the first indications that the government was willing to allow a relaxation of its tight control. Partial amnesty was declared, and several hundred political prisoners were released. After 1961, Kádár adopted policies intended to win popular support. The "People's Courts" that had convicted the revolutionaries were abolished, and Rákosi and Gero were expelled from the party in 1962. This demonstrated Kádár's desire to break completely with the Stalinist policies of the past. Although he became chairman of the council of ministers in addition to first secretary of the party, there was no return to the so-called cult of personality of which Stalin had been accused after his death.

In 1962, Kádár reported to a party congress that collectivization had been completed the previous year and that 90% of all farmland was now organized into cooperative and state farms. Most industrial products were from socialist enterprises. In foreign policy, Kádár expressed complete support for the Soviet policy of peaceful coexistence, for its actions in the Cuban missile crisis, and for its position in the disputes with China.

The congress, in turn, adopted Kádár's "one nation" policy, which declared, in effect, that the government was willing to cooperate with anyone who was not actively opposed to the Communist Party. In this respect, it was willing, he said, to recruit competent, nonparty members for government service. Further liberalization was evident by 1963, when a general amnesty was declared, freeing additional political prisoners numbering in the thousands. Travel restrictions were lowered, and tourism increased.

Kádár's popularity greatly increased as a result of these changes, and that was a considerable help when Khrushchev fell from power in November 1964. Although now "on his own," Kádár managed to hold on to power, though he did have to relinquish the office of chairman of the council of ministers in 1965. Julius Kallai got that position, while Kádár remained first secretary of the party.

Kallai was chairman of the council of ministers until 1967. He was replaced by Jenő Fock, who held the position until 1975. Fock's resignation came shortly after the 11th congress of the Hungarian Socialist Workers Party (HSWP). His resignation "for reasons of health" almost certainly reflected the Soviet leadership's dissatisfaction with the relatively freewheeling style of economic management in Hungary under the "New Mechanism." His successor as chairman of the council of ministers

A fiddler celebrates two significant events of 1989—President Bush's visit and the opening of Budapest's McDonald's.
Photo by Jon Markham Morrow

was György Lázár, who held the position until 1987.

The 11th congress of the HSWP tightened party regulations by introducing a ban on "propagating dissent," almost certainly a gesture meant to appease their Soviet comrades. In another gesture, this time aimed at Hungarian workers, the congress endorsed the reduction of the workweek to 44 hours by 1980.

Although he held no state office after 1965, Kádár continued to be the key leader in the political system. He tended to run a rather collegial Politburo, though he did not hesitate to dismiss those members who got too far out of line. In general, he preferred technocrats rather than political types. He recognized that they were needed to carry out his economic reforms, and they were also less likely to be rivals for power. He always tried to limit the personal power of his associates.

Károly Grósz replaced the ailing György Lázár as chairman of the council of ministers. Former party boss in Budapest, Grósz had often been mentioned as a potential Kádár successor. The matter was decided in May 1988 at a special HSWP conference. It had become clear in the months leading up to the conference that Kádár intended to retire. For the first time, there was something of a campaign for the office of party leader. Grósz, who had previously had a reputation as a hard-liner, put himself forward as an aggressive and energetic pragmatist who supported further reform. He also adopted an open style reminiscent of that of Gorbachev.

Grósz succeeded Kádár as general secretary. As it turned out, however, this was

not just a succession but rather something approaching a revolution in the party. Two well-known advocates of radical reform, Rezső Nyers and Imre Pozsgay, were added to the Politburo.

Nyers, a member of the Economic Institute of the Hungarian Academy of Sciences and a former minister of finance, had been one of the principal authors of the 1968 reform. In the early 1980s, he wrote an article for *Magyar Hirlap*, the Budapest daily, in which he advocated a larger political role for the parliament. In 1985, when the party established multiple candidacies and moved to give a larger role to parliament, it was implementing most of what Nyers had advocated in his article.

Pozsgay, chairman of the Patriotic Peoples' Front since 1982, attempted to give this umbrella organization new life and more influence. He had also argued that the party ought "to withdraw from its present relationship with the state and society and to establish a new relationship." In addition, he was on record as supporting the creation of autonomous interest groups, including independent trade unions under certain circumstances.

Speaking to the party conference following his election as general secretary, Grósz promised that he would seek "to expand democratic procedures within the party to match some of the 'practical advantages' of Western multiparty systems." Later, in a televised address to the Hungarian people, he admitted past mistakes on behalf of the party and promised a new approach "in public life, in production, in human sectors and other fields." Gorbachev was quick to put his stamp of approval on the new general secretary, calling him "a principled communist and authoritative leader" and wishing him "big successes . . . in tackling the task of improving and renovating his socialist society on Hungarian soil."

Grósz continued as chairman of the council of ministers until November 1988, when he turned the office over to Miklós Németh. A 40-year-old economist, Németh had been added to the Politburo in May 1988. Known as a strong advocate of change, he was described by János Lukács, another Politburo member, as a "young, dynamic workhorse."

Németh's appointment was further evidence that the reformers were in charge, although they still retained their alliance with the moderate Grósz. Having placed their supporters in all of the key positions, they turned their attention to institutional reform.

There was some question about where all of this was leading. The situation became even more muddled in December 1988, when Imre Pozsgay spoke out publicly in favor of a multiparty system.

One week later, Grósz rejected Pozsgay's suggestion, but that actually marked the beginning of a struggle within the party over the issue. The matter was largely resolved in February 1989, when the party announced further details of proposed constitutional changes. A multiparty system was to be formally established, and additional political parties were to be permitted to operate freely. The draft also provided for the creation of a new executive presidency. Among other things, the president would be commander-in-chief of the armed forces. Free elections were scheduled for 1990.

Although the program had not formally gone into effect, independent political groups immediately began to form. In March 1989 the first of those, the Democratic Forum, had its first convention in Budapest. In addition, the Small-holders Party and the Hungarian Social Democratic Party—both part of the first government coalition (along with the Communist Party) in 1945—were revived and began to operate as independent groups.

However, the HSWP's commitment to multiparty elections was too much for conservatives still within the party. To resolve the issue, Grósz proposed at a plenum of the Central Committee in April 1989 that the Politburo "lay down its powers and hold a new secret ballot on its composition." In the subsequent voting, four remaining conservatives were removed from the Politburo. The size of the Politburo was thus reduced from 11 to 9. In a separate move, János Kádár was dropped from the Central Committee, and his title of honorary president was abolished. He died soon afterward.

As a sign that Hungarian leaders had had a genuine change of heart, they were prime movers in one of the most dramatic postwar developments right before the very eyes of a stunned world public—German unification. In late summer a human hemorrhaging westward commenced, as East German vacationers began crossing the newly opened border between Hungary and Austria. Budapest informed the irate East German leaders that the human rights agreements accepted at the Helsinki Conference in 1975 superseded earlier bilateral treaties preventing the free movement of peoples.

In June the party went through yet another leadership shake-up. The Politburo and the office of general secretary were both abolished. A four-member presidium, with Rezső Nyers as president, replaced them. Károly Grósz was made a member of the presidium, but he lost most of his power. The winds of change continued to blow strongly in 1989. In October, the party dropped its old name and became the Hungarian Socialist Party.

The Early Post-communist Era

In March 1990, in the first free elections since 1945 were held. Voters repudiated both the communist-reformist Hungarian Socialist Party and the resurrected communist Hungarian United Workers Party. No single party received a majority, but the conservative Democratic Forum came in first with approximately 42% of the vote. It therefore won the right to organize the new government. A coalition was formed with two smaller parties, the Independent Small-holders and the Christian Democrats, with József Antall, leader of Democratic Forum, as prime minister. Together the three parties controlled more than 60% of the seats in the new parliament. The main opposition party was the left-liberal Alliance of Free Democrats, with Federation of Young Democrats and the Hungarian Socialist Party reduced to a tiny remnant on the left.

Antall remained prime minister for the next three and a half years, until his death in 1993. During that time, he came to dominate Hungarian politics almost completely, giving the country a political stability that distinguished Hungary from most of its eastern European neighbors.

In the beginning, the greatest problems the new government faced were related to the economy. Its early focus was on establishing policies that would move Hungary more rapidly toward a market economy. This task appeared easier in Hungary because, of all the central and eastern European nations, the communists had already moved the country the furthest along this path. Nevertheless, state-owned enterprises still constituted 90% of the productive sector.

First of all, the government drew up a long list of laws and regulations aimed at fostering private initiative, encouraging direct foreign investment, and developing private capital markets. It also committed itself to reducing the state sector to less than 50% by 1995.

All over central Europe, there were heated discussions about how best to privatize a former communist-controlled economy. In Hungary, the government opted for a company-by-company privatization, based on finding western companies that would either take over the company entirely or come in as a partner, providing capital and technical expertise. Under this plan, foreign investment increased rapidly, and a good number of companies were able to find foreign partners or purchasers. Small and medium-sized companies were privatized locally, some to groups of employees.

In general, the process was relatively slow. Many of the newly privatized companies also found it difficult to compete, so salaries remained low, and unemployment grew significantly during this time. As a result, the government came under criticism by those who argued that it was moving too slowly and by others who feared that it was dissipating the nation's wealth. Some of this showed up in the local elections in October 1990, when the parties of the government coalition lost badly. In Budapest, the two major opposition parties won over 50% of the vote. In most places, independents won, however, possibly indicating distaste for the political partisanship that had come to dominate debate.

None of this threatened the coalition's majority in parliament, however. In fact, the government coalition had regained much of its popularity in the country by the beginning of 1992, and Antall, though still not particularly popular, was conceded to be the most effective leader in central Europe.

POLITICAL SYSTEM

The Hungarian republic is a multiparty parliamentary democracy. The legal system was based on the 1949 constitution substantially modified in October 1989 and adopted in 1990. It was superseded by a new constitution (called the Basic Law) on January 1, 2012. This retains a parliamentary form of government with guarantees for basic human rights. Supreme power is vested in parliament. The Constitutional Court, composed of judges appointed by the National Assembly for nine-year terms, could overturn parliamentary decisions and governmental decrees deemed unconstitutional. For example, it ruled in December 2011 that several provisions of the government's new media law were unconstitutional.

However, in March 2013, the parliament voted to deny the court the ability to reject constitutional amendments except on procedural grounds. It can base its rulings only on the 2012 constitution, not on two decades of prior precedent. It also allows the government to reintroduce measures previously rejected by the court. This weakened it. The mandatory retirement age for judges was lowered from 70 to 62; critics contend that this change enabled the ruling Fidesz Party to pack the court. The court can no longer review the substance of constitutional changes.

The newly adopted constitution came into force despite a wave of protests that it was destroying the crucial checks and balances. The day after it was enacted in 2012, about 30,000 Hungarians protested noisily in front of the Budapest opera house, crying "Viktator! Viktator!" This was a reference to Prime Minister Viktor Orbán's seeming determination to concentrate all power in the hands of his Fidesz Party, which had a two-thirds majority in

Hungary

the parliament and already controlled the presidency, the state prosecutors' office, the state audit office, and the national media council. The duration of the appointments seems to entrench the ruling party. Critics claim that it eliminates the independence of the central bank and the judiciary. Critics say that Orbán, always a committed noncommunist, is in effect recreating one-party rule. The EU especially, but also the Council of Europe and the IMF, put heavy pressure on the Hungarian government to change the objectionable parts of the new Basic Law. Orbán seemed not to care. He retorted that his government is willing to examine some details but that it made good on its campaign promises to do away with the old order and complete the transition from communism.

President

Hungary has a largely ceremonial president of the republic as chief of state. The National Assembly elects the president for a term of five years. He has the power to sign or reject laws, formally appoints the prime minister and cabinet, and decides the dates of elections to the National Assembly.

Under the current Constitution of Hungary adopted by the Fidesz–KDNP government coalition in 2011, the President must be elected in a secret ballot by the Members of Parliament, no sooner than sixty but no later than thirty days before the expiry of the mandate of the previous office-holder, or if his or her mandate terminated prematurely, within thirty days of the termination. The constitution authorizes the Speaker of the National Assembly to set the date for the election.

A presidential candidate needs the written nomination of at least one-fifth of the Members of Parliament (40 MPs), who may not nominate more than one candidate; it is thus mathematically impossible for there to be more than four candidates. In the first round of the election, a two-thirds majority of all incumbent MPs is required to elect the president. If this condition is not fulfilled, a second round is held between the two candidates who received the highest and second-highest numbers of votes in the first round. A simple majority of the voting MPs is then sufficient. Since 1990, there have been no more than two candidates in any presidential election held in Hungary.

In May 2012 János Áder was elected a new president. Áder is a lawyer and former member of the European Parliament. He was also a founding member of the ruling Fidesz Party.

In March 2016 he surprised his party and the prime minister by rejecting and

Prime Minister Viktor Orbán

sending to the constitutional court a bill that was to give Hungary's central bank a wide latitude to conceal its spending. Ader asserted that the bill was "not in line with the constitutional provisions on the handling of public funds."

Ader's predecessor as president from 2010 to 2012 was Pál Schmitt, a former Olympic fencing gold medalist, diplomat, minister in the communist government, and member of the European Parliament. He resigned when it was revealed that he had plagiarized some of his 1992 doctoral thesis. The granting Semmelweis University stripped him of his doctor's title, saying that his paper did not meet the professional and ethical standards for a thesis. A panel determined that it contained passages copied from two other authors. Almost 200 pages had been borrowed.

An indirect presidential election was held in Hungary on March 10, 2022. The incumbent president of the Republic János Áder was ineligible to run due to term limits. There were only two candidates. The governing alliance, Fidesz-KDNP nominated Katalin Novák, the former minister for Family Affairs and an ally of Hungarian Prime Minister Viktor Orbán, as its presidential candidate. The opposition alliance, United for Hungary nominated Péter Róna, a lawyer and economist as its presidential candidate. Katalin Novák became the first female President of Hungary after winning an absolute majority. Nevertheless, she resigned on February 10, 2024, after coming under mounting pressure for pardoning a man convicted of helping to cover up sexual abuse in a children's home.

The National Assembly

The National Assembly is a single chamber parliament with a total of 199 seats. Its members are elected for a four-year term in an election that is part proportional, part constituency. Deputies can be elected in one of three ways: directly from one of the single-member constituencies; by being included on a county list of party candidates; or by being included on a national list; there are regional and party-list seats. According to the electoral reform that went into effect for the April 2014 elections, a greater proportion of the MPs are elected in the single-member constituencies. Critics claimed that some of those districts were gerrymandered. There are no longer runoff elections; there is only a single round of voting. The reforms favor large unified parties like Fidesz. European monitors concluded that Fidesz enjoyed an "undue advantage" in the elections; this included biased media coverage. In order to limit the number of parties in parliament and thereby to maintain greater political stability, a party must win at least 5% of the votes in order to receive any parliamentary seats. All citizens over age 18 may vote. For the first time in 2014 Hungarians living outside the country were allowed to vote.

The National Assembly is the fulcrum of power, with the prime minister as the country's political leader. He is the head of government and the individual responsible for government policy. He is nominated by the president and confirmed by the National Assembly. He can be removed if he loses a constructive vote of

President János Áder

confidence in the National Assembly. This means that a government can be voted out of office only if a replacement can immediately secure a parliamentary majority. This positive no-confidence vote, taken from Germany's Basic Law, helps ensure greater stability.

In 2005 parliament passed a law opening communist-era secret service files, which contain thousands of documents, tapes, and more than 50,000 names. Unlike other former Warsaw Pact countries after the fall of communism, Hungary did not reveal the names of secret police collaborators and the information they had accumulated about citizens. Critics claim the law violates the protection of personal data enshrined in the constitution. In 2011 the rules on access to earlier state security archives were changed, permitting persons who were spied upon to remove their own files. This eliminates part of the evidence of the past.

Parties and Elections

Hungary is moving ever closer to a two-party system. A sharp political polarization exists between rightist and leftist parties and between a relatively well-off western Hungary, which favors Fidesz (Federation of Young Democrats), and a poorer and less populous east, which traditionally votes for the ex-communist Hungarian Socialist Party (MSZP). Also fishing successfully for votes is the far-right, anti-immigrant, and anti-Semitic Jobbik (Movement for a Better Hungary).

In 2004 Ferenc Gyurcsány, one of Hungary's richest-men-turned-champion-of-the-poor, became prime minister for the Socialist Party. With the party's popularity declining and new elections on the horizon, the party needed a more appealing prime minister. Although he was a former communist youth league leader, his selection marked a clear break by the socialists from a generation of leaders who came to power as reform-minded communists in the 1980s and who created the Socialist Party out of the wreckage of the Communist Party in 1990.

Strident partisanship and pent-up political emotions erupted in September and October 2006. The trigger was a secret speech Gyurcsány delivered to his party members in the parliament after the June 2006 general elections and the disastrous fall local elections, in which the ruling socialists lost 19 of 23 cities. He later argued that he was trying to motivate his party to accept austerity measures and public-sector restructuring by saying, "No country in Europe has screwed up as much as we have. . . We lied morning, noon and night." A recording of this talk, which the prime minister said was exaggerated for

dramatic effect, was leaked to the main radio station and aired to a stunned public. Gyurcsány never recovered from this blunder.

Sensing a golden opportunity to topple the government, the Fidesz opposition, supported by then-president Solyom, demanded Gyurcsány's resignation and called on its supporters to demonstrate against the government. What followed was the worst political violence the country had experienced since 1956. An estimated 30,000 to 40,000 demonstrators, some carrying national flags and singing patriotic songs, took to the streets, burned cars, surrounded the parliament, and temporarily took over the state TV station, forcing it off the air.

Similar violence accompanied the 50th anniversary of the 1956 uprising only a month later. The protesters were so aggressive that police fired rubber-coated bullets and used tear gas and water cannons to disperse them. At one point, demonstrators even commandeered two World War II-era tanks on display and drove them toward the police. The fact that the ruling socialists grew out of the old Communist Party made this occasion particularly volatile. Fidesz refused to attend the ceremony. In fact, its parliamentarians followed Viktor Orbán out of the debating chamber every time Gyurcsány rose to speak.

Orbán, who had studied a year at Oxford courtesy of the George Soros Foundation, had been Hungary's youngest freely elected prime minister when winning the post in 1998 at the age of 35. Now, going after Gyurcsány, he played on voters' anxiety and created hopes that could not be fulfilled. But his poll ratings shot up, while those of Gyurcsány steadily declined. The socialists found themselves without a majority. With social tensions rising and the

global economic recession hurting Hungary badly, Gyurcsány saw no alternative to resigning in March 2009. He grabbed headlines again in September 2012, when he went on a hunger strike to protest a new law, later declared unconstitutional, requiring voters to register online at least 15 days before an election.

He was replaced as prime minister by his economics minister, Gordon Bajnai, a 41-year-old independent and former economics professor and businessman. His cabinet was composed of both socialist politicians and unaffiliated experts. He offered an olive branch to the opposition parties to try to break the political deadlock: "The country has no money left for fighting." His government introduced economic austerity, raised the pension age from 62 to 65 beginning in 2012 (2010 average: 59.7 years), lowered benefits by about 8%, and abolished the 13th-month pension payment.

Bajnai had only a year to turn the country around before the April 2010 elections. The socialists were trounced. In 2014 they were the second-largest party at the head of a left electoral alliance, led by Attila Mesterházy and composed of his Socialist Party (MSZP), Together 2014 (E14), Democratic Coalition (DK), and the Liberal Party, led by Gábor Fodor. The alliance captured only 38 seats.

The stunning victor of the 2010 and 2014 elections was the Federation of Young Democrats (Fidesz). Led by Viktor Orbán, who served as prime minister from 1998 to 2002, it won 44.5% of the votes (down from 52.73% in 2010) and 133 seats. This gave Fidesz more than two-thirds of all parliamentary seats, and it claims a solid mandate for reform. The supermajority enabled it to introduce a new constitution on January 1, 2012.

Crown of St. Stephen

Hungary

Orbán solidified his dominance in the April 2018 elections, judged by international observers as "free but not fair." Blasting migrants, Soros, the EU, and the UN, he won a third term with half the votes and 134 seats. Jobbik, which is moving to the center, won 25 seats; the socialists, 20; DK, 9; and LMP, 8. Turnout was 69%.

It consolidated its power so resolutely that critics accuse it of seeking to destroy the checks and balances in the political system and achieve absolute control. Orban reduced the constitutional court's jurisdiction over financial matters and restricted the authority and salary (by 75%) of the independent central bank president, who refused to abide by the government's demand not to raise interest rates. He rejected the IMF's and European Council's continued help in stabilizing the country's finances and instead levied a one-time "crisis tax" on large companies, thereby unnerving foreign investors. He practically forced citizens to transfer their pensions from private to state funds in order to be able to tap that money for his government's economic program. He forced banks to take losses on foreign-denominated mortgages. A majority of mortgages are denominated in Swiss francs, leaving tens of thousands of homeowners struggling as the forint loses value. They can now pay what they owe at an artificially low exchange rate, and the banks must absorb the losses.

Most controversially the Fidesz government introduced a media law that attracted indignant criticism, both at home and abroad. It places all media under the supervision of a new Media Council, whose members are appointed by the government. Journalists are required to reveal all their sources if requested by the authorities or courts. All reporting must be "authentic," "accurate," "balanced," and not in breach of "human dignity." These terms are undefined, but alleged transgressions can result in sizable fines. Plans for an internet tax had to be abandoned due to popular protests. This was a rare U-turn for Orbán.

By vetoing in 2016 the bill that was to allow Hungary's central bank (MNB) to shield its transactions from public scrutiny, President Áder echoed his compatriots' uneasiness about potential abuses of the state institution for political purposes. For example, in 2014 the bank endowed an educational foundation with some $900 million, more than Hungary's entire state budget for higher education. The bank's governor and a close ally of Prime Minister Orbán stated that the foundation would provide alternatives to "the already obsolete doctrines and mistakes of the neoliberal school of economics." Fund transfers from the bank and their future uses would

Ultra-right Jobbik at a protest in Budapest

no longer be subject to public oversight. This raise concerns after the bank made a number of unusual purchases, including fine arts; a majority stake in the country's main stock exchange; some prime real estate; weapons; a large number of books written by the bank's governor; villas now owned by people connected to him; and trips to Africa, allegedly to study libraries and elections.

This is a particularly touchy subject in the country where corruption is so vast that Transparency International described it in 2015 as "centralized" and "systematically pursued." Dismissing American criticism, Orbán declared that "checks and balances are a U.S. invention that for some reason of intellectual mediocrity Europe decided to adopt."

Over time, Orbán moderated his nationalist appeal, dropping his earlier anti-Semitic rhetoric. In 2013 a Jobbik politician, Márton Gyöngyösi, said in the parliament that Hungarian Jews should be catalogued and screened as potential security risks. His remarks were met with a wave of revulsion and condemnation. Almost 600,000 Hungarian Jews perished in the Holocaust. Hundreds of Jobbik supporters protested the convening in Budapest of the World Jewish Congress in May 2013. Critics thought that Orbán was slow to react, but he stated publicly that Gyöngyösi's remarks were "unworthy of Hungary" and that anti-Semitism is "intolerable." He became the first Hungarian leader to acknowledge that Hungarians had played a role in the extermination of their Jewish compatriots.

A biographer, Paul Lendvai, argues that Orbán is constructing an authoritarian state. He describes Orbán as "a

A line forms at the House of Terror, opened April 2002 to document communist Repression.

master tactician, a gifted populist, a radical and consummate opportunist, and a ruthless power politician who believes not in ideas but in maximizing his power without any compunction, giving vent to Hungarian nationalism or tapping into fear and prejudice." He is still a fiery populist who spouts chauvinistic, anti-EU polemics and criticism of "unbridled capitalism." He arouses passions across the political spectrum and polarizes an already-divided society.

He aroused indignation by declaring his preference for "illiberal" democracy, to which former German chancellor Angela Merkel shot back, "I cannot understand the word illiberal in connection with democracy." Many fear that he has departed from the principles of the EU by praising such authoritarian rulers as Vladimir Putin. Anywhere else in Europe, his rhetoric would be intolerably nationalist. But in Hungary it sounds more moderate because of a radical right-wing party that came out of nowhere to become the nation's second-largest party in 2014 and to force Fidesz to reposition itself as a mainstream center-right party—Jobbik.

Jobbik (Movement for a Better Hungary) won 20.5% of the votes in 2014 (up from 16.67%) and 23 seats. Its young (31 years) leader, Gábor Vona, a former history teacher, tapped into growing nationalism to catapult his party from the fanatical fringes to the corridors of the parliament. He appeals mainly to rural, unemployed, disenchanted young, voters who have been hit hardest by the recession. His anti-Semitic and anti-Roma rhetoric made these groups scapegoats for the hardships the nation is suffering. It railed against "Israeli colonizers" and had Roma in mind when it said, "No work, no support." It vowed to ban immigrants from diluting Hungarian purity and to revise the 1920 Trianon Treaty, which deprived Hungary of two-thirds of its prewar territory. In order to attract more voters, the party has toned down its antisemitism and anti-Roma rhetorics, though it traded some of it for a more anti-Muslim attitude, less costly politically. It has remodeled itself to be a modern, trendy, and youthful party. This has worked well for it. Moreover, in April 2015 Jobbik won its first direct by-election in the city of Tapolca, defeating Fidesz, as well as the socialists. The party's success can be attributed to a good local campaign and its conscious efforts to scrub its image.

Its shock troops called themselves "Magyar Garda" (Hungarian Guard). They had uniforms reminiscent of those worn by Hungarian Nazis during the war, the Arrow Cross, which had lent a bloody hand in the Holocaust. Its Nazi rhetoric evokes Hungary's glorious past. In 2009 the Magyar Garda were outlawed, but

they are still active. Their bouncers at rallies now wear slightly different outfits and call themselves "New Hungarian Guard." Orbán and Fidesz vow not to cooperate with Jobbik and to defend Hungary from this rowdy party. However, Orbán's close relations with Russia's Putin and the accusations of corruption leveled by the US have turned some supporters away and into the arms of Jobbik.

In an attempt to stop Orbán's dismantling checks and balances in the April 2022 parliamentary elections, the six major opposition parties held a two-round primary to choose a single opponent—Péter Márki-Zay. He promised to overhaul the constitution in a referendum. The results were disappointing—Fidesz won 54% of the votes and 135 seats. It retained its two-thirds supermajority. The opposition United for Hungary alliance got a mere 34% and 56 seats. Orbán won a fourth consecutive term in office, becoming the EU's longest- serving leader, after 12 years in power. "We won so big you can see it from the moon."

Foreign Policy

During communist rule, alignment with the Soviet Union had been a basic component of foreign policy. For example, Hungary followed the lead of the USSR in breaking relations with Israel in 1967, and it joined the Soviet boycott of the 1984 Los Angeles Summer Olympics. It also supported the Soviets in quarrels with the People's Republic of China.

On the other hand, Hungary always maintained a more independent position vis-a-vis the Soviet Union than either Bulgaria or Czechoslovakia. Hungarians were frank about their desire for better relations with the west. Although they participated fully in the Council of Mutual Economic Assistance (CMEA, or COMECON), and the Soviet Union remained their single largest trading partner, they also pushed to increase their trade with the west and were the first to call for reform of CMEA.

The first noncommunist government since 1945 brought changes in Hungary's foreign policy. The biggest immediate one was that Budapest negotiated an agreement with the Soviet Union calling for the removal of all Soviet troops by July 1991. Hungary was also instrumental in the demise of the Warsaw Pact. When the Hungarian government announced that it intended to leave the communist alliance, Moscow, apparently fearing that other members would join the exodus, proposed that the military aspects of the organization be terminated as of April 1, 1991. The Warsaw Pact plus the CMEA, Hungary's other formal tie to Moscow, were formally dissolved on July 1, 1991.

Its relations with Russia are now among equals. Orbán defied an EU ban and

welcomed Putin on an official visit to Budapest in February 2015. Thousands of Hungarians went into the streets to protest this event in the midst of a Russian invasion of Ukraine. He supported the EU sanctions against Russia, but he claimed they hurt Europe worse than Russia. He fears a collapse of Ukraine, where 200,000 ethnic Hungarians live.

West Germany's trade with Hungary grew steadily to about 30% of all Hungarian trade with the west in 1985. This made it Hungary's second-largest trading partner, after the Soviet Union. There was also extensive cooperation between the two countries designed to facilitate the transfer of technology. Approximately 350 cooperative agreements were signed between West German and Hungarian firms before 1989.

Austrian entrepreneurs have also been active investors. According to the Hungarian government, approximately 1,880 joint ventures were established between foreign investors and local partners in the first 18 months of the new democratic regime. More than 60% of the investors were either Austrian or German.

American-Hungarian relations have been relatively good since 1973, when the two countries signed an agreement settling claims for damages to American property during World War II. The US government returned the St. Stephen's Crown, in American custody since World War II, to Hungary in 1978. However, not until 2005 did the US government apologize for the 1945 looting by its soldiers of a train loaded with valuable items stolen from Hungarian Jews during the war. In early 1945 the "Hungarian gold train" had pulled out of Budapest with retreating German forces, and it was abandoned near Salzburg, Austria. In May the advancing American troops found 24 of its 46 cars, and some helped themselves to many of its contents. Most of the goods but not all were turned over to the Intergovernmental Committee for Refugees, which auctioned the items to benefit Holocaust victims. Sued by the survivors, the US government agreed to an apology and settlement of $25.5 million.

The United States granted Hungary "most-favored nation" trade status, and relations became even warmer after 1989. In general, it has been a strong supporter of multilateral economic assistance to Hungary. After coming to power in May 1990, the noncommunist government established diplomatic relations with Israel and the Vatican.

Hungary was admitted to membership in the Council of Europe in November 1990, the first central or eastern European nation to seek and receive admittance. It became an associate member of the EU in

Hungary

The Hilton Hotel's mirrored facade reflects the Gothic spires of Matthias Church in Old Budapest, site of the coronation of Charles IV as king of Hungary in 1916.

Courtesy: *Jon Markham Morrow*

December 1991, along with Poland and Czechoslovakia. In 1997, the EU extended an invitation for Hungary to begin negotiations leading to full membership. The center-left government set up an efficient EU communications office and organized public meetings around the country. In an April 2003 referendum, 84% of voters supported entry.

The government had foreseen that participation in the voting might be a problem, so it struck the 50% turnout requirement from the law; in the end only 46% voted. The people of Budapest greeted the positive results with bursts of fireworks over the Danube and the playing of Beethoven's Ninth Symphony, the EU anthem. Officials waxed lyrical about their country's "writing its name in history," and one newspaper ran the headline, "Europe, Here We come!" Then-prime minister Péter Medgyessy announced, "History begins again today, after an interruption of 60 years." Formal EU membership came in May 2004. Then-foreign minister László Kovács rejoiced, "Finally Hungarians will be treated as equals in Europe."

EU membership brings challenges. Hungary assumes an enormous burden in securing borders with seven countries, three of whom are not yet EU members. This became especially important after 2007, when it joined the Schengen Agreement for free movement within the EU. It has not maintained the financial discipline to adopt the euro any time soon. Its parliament had already ratified the ill-fated EU constitution before French and Dutch voters turned it down in May and June 2005. Hungary's political leaders were disappointed because

the document's clause on protecting minorities, which could have helped ethnic Hungarians in neighboring countries, was lost. Its most visible EU role was the six-month rotating presidency from January through June 2011. This was a modest success culminating on the last day in the completion of negotiations with Croatia concerning its entry into the EU in 2013.

Hungary was also invited in 1997 to become a member of NATO. This was approved by popular referendum in November. Hungary was formally admitted in March 1999. The beginning of NATO's air war against Yugoslavia, coming as it did only days after Hungary had become a formal member of NATO, presented the government with a particular problem. There are several hundred thousand ethnic Hungarians living in the Vojvodina region of Serbia; their welfare is only one of the reasons Hungary keeps an uneasy eye on neighboring Serbia.

Hungary did not participate in the air war, but it did grant NATO full access to its airspace, and gave approval for the passage of foreign peacekeeping troops through Hungary and even their stationing in the country to support humanitarian aid missions. In addition, the Hungarian parliament approved a 350-member guard battalion to join the peacekeeping forces in Kosovo, where it helps protect the KFOR headquarters in Priština (Prishtina). In January 2000 NATO closed its military base in Pécs, which had been used to supply its peacekeeping troops in Bosnia and Herzegovina, as part of its efforts to streamline its Bosnian operations.

Despite the fact that three-fourths of Hungarians opposed the American-British

war in Iraq in 2003, the government defied France and Germany by signing an important open letter supporting the war effort. It provided an airbase at Taszár—where the US could train several hundred Iraqi exiles for use as intermediaries between an American invasion force and civilians and soldiers in Iraq. Hungary balked, however, at American suggestions that 28,000 Iraqis receive police training in Hungary. When a miffed French president Jacques Chirac condescendingly called Hungary and other central European governments "not well brought up" and scolded them for not following his lead, then-prime minister Medgyessy retorted in immaculate French that he was "too well brought up" to respond to Chirac's gibes and diatribes.

Budapest sent 300 mainly logistic soldiers to Iraq. A former Hungarian ambassador to Washington explained the rationale: "The Hungarian interest is not what happens in Iraq per se. It's that the transatlantic relationship remains as strong and unharmed as possible, and that the United States remains a European power." Former Secretary of State Colin Powell was awarded the Grand Cross. Hungary withdrew its forces after the January 2005 Iraqi elections, largely in response to polls showing that more than 60% of Hungarians wanted their troops out. It maintains 243 peacekeepers in Kosovo, 160 in Bosnia and Herzegovina, and 360 soldiers in Afghanistan, including several companies of combat soldiers in Kandahar.

In 2004 Hungary began a shift away from a conscript army to a professional force. It also had to modernize and equip its armed forces better. It had one of the lowest rates of defense spending (1.8% of GDP) and had done the least among all the new NATO allies.

One western diplomat noted, "Hungary is not a military nation. They haven't won a battle since around 1456. And there's very little support for military spending." Nevertheless, the government increased the defense budget by 16%, much of it for technical improvements and restructuring. It created uneasiness in NATO corridors when its new chief of the secret services, Sándor Laborc, was sent to fill the rotating post of chairman of NATO's intelligence committee for a year. Laborc had spent six years at the KGB's academy in Moscow in the 1980s.

Hungarian military strength has increased since 2016 due to force development programs and military reforms. This consistent development paid off, as its Defense Forces have moved up to 54th place out of 150 countries surveyed in Global Firepower's annual military force assessment in 2023. Hungary has maintained its position this year, and the Global Firepower (GFP) 2024 index ranks it as one of the strongest armed forces in Central Europe.

Following the 2015 refugee crisis and the subsequent coming to power of the Law and Justice (PiS) Party in Poland, the two governments were drawn closer by their Euroscepticism and the opposition to mandatory quotas for the relocation of migrants imposed by the EU. In addition, Viktor Orbán's friendly personal relations with PiS leader Jarosław Kaczyński facilitated coordination of foreign policies, as Poland's new government looked to Orbán for pointers on how to deal with criticism from the EU over its own, Orbán-inspired, illiberal reforms. PiS copied several domestic moves of Fidesz, including muzzling the media and attempting to control the constitutional court. In January 2016, Kaczyński and Orbán met privately in Niedzica in southern Poland (the site of a medieval Hungarian castle guarding the ancient border between the two countries) to consult without the need to worry about public scrutiny associated with official visits. At another meeting that year, both leaders profusely praised each other and declared their mutual trust to be so strong that they could "steal horses together . . . and one particularly large [horse stable is] called the EU."

The cooperation with Poland also reflects Hungary's interest in revitalizing regional cooperation of the Visegrad Group that also includes the Czech Republic and Slovakia. Rooted in historical links among those nations since the Middle Ages, the group coordinated its members' accession process to the European Union from 1991 through 2004. Hungary's GDP per capita (PPP) is the lowest among the "V4," but its assertive policies vis-a-vis the EU give it much political clout. This became crucial in September 2015, when two decisions by the Council of the European Union created a scheme for the redistribution of 160,000 migrants from Greece and Italy among EU's member states. Hungary refused to participate in the quota system that would have actually relieved its own asylum-seeker burden, and thus it had to process by itself the migrants already in its territory. Initially, the Visegrad Group members uniformly opposed the plan, but eventually Poland abandoned its allies, leaving the Czech Republic, Slovakia, and Hungary (plus Romania) to vote in vain against the scheme that was adopted by a large majority. Except for Hungary, they were all expected to implement the plan despite their objections.

The unity of the V4 has come under much strain when Hungary and Poland engaged in a series of policies clearly intended to defy the authority of the EU. Their increasingly "illiberal" drift worries the Czech and Slovak governments

"Danube Swabians"— German Hungarians

that value their EU links more than their partners' attempts at a "cultural counter-revolution." They certainly don't support Poland's and Hungary's interest in renegotiating EU treaties.

Hungary and Germany

Germany was wholly supportive of Hungary's entry into the EU. Hungary is a politically stable country with only three governments in the 1990s (compared with eight in Poland, a record in central Europe) and a privatization program that was almost complete by the end of the 20th century. It enjoys good relations with its seven neighbors, each of which has a Magyar minority.

Unlike the Poles and Czechs, Hungarians show no dislike for Germans, although they bear some animosity toward Austria, which ruled them for a half-century. There were about 370,000 Germans in Hungary at the end of the war in 1945, and most of the almost 200,000 who were driven out settled in West Germany. They integrated well and did not form the kind of influential irredentist political organizations as did the Sudeten Germans. The laws that had allowed such forced removal were repealed in the early 1990s, and the parliament's president, Katalin Szili, apologized to Germany in 2007, "Forgive us! Never again!" There are still 62,000 persons in Hungary who claim German nationality, but only 34,000 of them speak German as their mother tongue.

In May 1989 Hungary played a crucial role in German unification by opening its border with Austria to East Germans wanting to escape from the GDR. József Antall, the country's first conservative prime minister after the collapse of communism, claims that "I was always an unconditional supporter of German unification. . . I am proud to be able to say today that German unity depended on Hungarian independence." Ex-foreign minister Gyula Horn, who died in 2013, played an important role in these events. A survey of

elite Hungarian opinion in May 1990 confirmed the same sentiments. Germany was widely regarded as a mediator between eastern and western Europe and an advocate for the interest of central Europe.

There is no uneasiness about the fact that Germany is the country's most important trading partner—in fact, about a quarter of Hungary's foreign trade is with Germany. In 2014, Germany invested some $20.5 billion in Hungary, a third of which went into the auto industry. Building on his party strong links to Bavaria's CSU, Orbán declared in 2015 that "today Bavaria's borders are defended in Hungary." This sentiment was particularly welcomed by Horst Seehofer, CSU leader and Bavaria's minister president (prime minister), an ardent critic of Chancellor Angela Merkel's immigration policy.

Treatment of Hungarian Minorities

One problem that Hungary has with its neighbors is over minorities. Significant Magyar-speaking populations are in Romania, the Czech and Slovak Republics, Carpathian Ukraine, and the former Yugoslavia. Romania, with between 1.7 and 2 million ethnic Hungarians, has the most, but there are at least 600,000 in Slovakia, mainly in the area of the southern plain. There are fewer in Serbia, and they are chiefly in the autonomous province of Vojvodina.

The "Yugo" Magyars became a particular problem for Hungary after Serbia terminated the autonomy status of Vojvodina in 1989. This put these Magyars directly under Belgrade's rule. With the withdrawal of Croatia and Slovenia from the collapsing Yugoslavia in 1991–1992, these Magyars became hostages to Hungary's actions because Serbia accused Hungary of assisting the Croatians.

Partly because of this concern, Hungary supported the dispatch of UN peacekeeping troops, taking the position that the UN ought to be given a greater role in protecting human and minority rights. In his address to the Security Council in 1992, Géza Jeszenszky, the Hungarian foreign minister, argued that "protecting human and minority rights is more than a legal and humanitarian issue—it is an integral part of international security. Therefore, a firm assertion of these rights by the UN Security Council is indispensable." In 2002 Vojvodina's autonomy was restored.

Hungary had a running controversy with Romania concerning Romanian treatment of ethnic Magyars during the latter years of the Ceaușescu regime. But the matter became more low-key after his fall. Under Ceaușescu, Hungarians feared that the Romanians were attempting to "denationalize" Hungarians in Transylvania, and that feeling continued to some extent

Hungary

after 1989. However, the Hungarian Democratic Federation of Romania, the party that represents ethnic Hungarians, became part of the government coalition in 1997. Hungary and Romania signed an agreement recognizing each other's borders and providing for the opening of a Hungarian consulate in Cluj.

Relations with Slovakia deteriorated after Vladimir Mečiar became prime minister. A former communist who discovered the power of nationalism in building popular support, Mečiar supported legislation requiring the use of Slovak even in areas where Hungarians were in a majority. In 1997 he suggested that ethnic Hungarians should migrate to Hungary if they were not willing to become good Slovaks.

Adding to the mutually bad relations is the quarrel over Hungary's abandonment of a 1977 agreement to construct jointly a series of dams and hydroelectric power stations on the Danube at Gabčíkovo-Nagymaros. The Slovaks obtained a decision from the International Court of Justice in 1997 that Hungary had broken international law in abandoning the 1977 agreement. Mečiar's defeat in the 1998 Slovak elections has changed that situation, and now the two countries are on speaking terms again. In 1998 Hungarians entered the Slovak governing coalition.

Orbán once suggested that Hungary would not support Slovakia's entry into NATO unless Bratislava gave benefits to the half-million Hungarians living there. He infuriated the Czechs by implying that the Beneš decrees, by which tens of thousands of Hungarians had been expelled

Franz Liszt

Béla Bartók

from Czechoslovakia and had their property expropriated, were incompatible with EU membership and should be revoked. All these remarks seemed to raise some central European ghosts of the 19th century. Nervousness rose even higher in 2007, when the Slovak parliament endorsed the Beneš decrees. Then, in July 2009, Slovakia enacted a new language law directed against Hungarian speakers that fined people up to $7,000 for breaking rules promoting the use of Slovak in public.

Minorities make up about 10% of Hungary's population. There are 200,000 to 220.000 German Hungarians called "Danube Swabians," 100,000 to 110,000 Slovaks, and 80,000 to 90,000 Croatians. Like other countries in the region, Hungary has a large Roma (Gypsy) minority numbering 600.000 to 650,000 and constituting about 8% of the total population. Roma face discrimination in Hungarian society, but the government attempts to ameliorate their lives. Like Slovakia and the Czech Republic, it has introduced preschool programs that help Roma children learn the country's language. It also partly finances boarding schools, such as the Gandhi College in Pécs, which attempt to prepare Roma for university study. There is a Roma station—Radio C—that serves as a vehicle for the many tribes to speak to each other. It is the first independent Roma radio station in central Europe.

There has been some progress. In the June 2004 European Parliament elections in Hungary, a woman became the first Roma ever to win a seat in that body. In 2008 the National Gallery sponsored an exhibition of contemporary Romany art. This was an especially significant gesture at a time when an outlawed small but loud-mouthed Magyar Garda (Hungarian Guard) dressing up in black paramilitary uniforms with nationalist insignias was parading around denouncing "Roma crimes" and ranting about "safeguarding

national culture and traditions." Few Roma are in doubt about who the targets of such rhetoric are.

Magyar Garda played on old stereotypes of Roma as petty criminals and drains on the social welfare system at a time of economic turmoil. In 2008 alone, seven Roma were killed, and six more murders followed the next year. Over 30 Molotov cocktail attacks were launched against their homes, prompting the Roma to start protecting their neighborhoods through nighttime patrols. In 2013 a Budapest court sentenced three neo-Nazis to prison for life without parole (and a fourth for 13 years) for murdering six Roma and wounding several others on a spree of racist violence lasting 14 months.

Roma people constitute a large proportion of the public-works labor force created by the government's policy that limited the amount of time the jobless have to find a job or lose unemployment benefits. As such, they were prominently represented among the workers constructing the controversial antimigrant concertina wire fence between Hungary and Serbia.

Orbán denounced the Magyar Garda, but his outspoken nationalism angers almost all of Hungary's neighbors. He is a populist who curries favor at home with his appeals to the sensitive subject of 5 million ethnic Hungarians who live outside the country's borders. He spoke of "the spiritual and cultural reunification of the Hungarian people."

Without discussing it with Hungary's neighbors, he enacted a "status law" that offered special favors in obtaining work permits to the 2.5 million Hungarians in Romania. He later had to calm Romania's government, which feared that Budapest harbored ambitions to get back Transylvania, which he called "part of Hungary's living space in the Carpathian Basin," by offering all Romanians three-month work permits. The same law irritated the Slovaks.

In 2003 it was significantly watered down so as not to give offense to neighboring countries. Gone were the claims that Hungarians living abroad form part of a "single Hungarian nation" and the promise of special work permits with all benefits enjoyed by Hungarians. There were still "Hungarian certificates," but they could not serve as official travel or identity documents. In 2004 a Romanian-Hungarian Reconciliation Park in the Transylvanian city of Arad near the Hungarian border was opened.

In a 2004 referendum a majority of voters voted in favor (by 51.5%) of granting citizenship to the roughly 2.5 million ethnic Hungarians living abroad. However, since turnout was under 50%, it was not adopted. The issue had divided the country and angered its neighbors.

Prime Minister Orbán proclaimed his party's 2010 election victory as a "worldwide victory for Hungary. . . As of right now, the yardstick will be that which is in Hungary's interest. And Hungarians outside our borders are fully empowered to engage in the nation's work." It was not clear at the time if that included the right to vote for the estimated 2 million persons of Hungarian descent living outside the country. It did in 2014, and many voted for Fidesz. But the offers to ethnic Hungarians of both citizenship and passports were among the first legislative acts to be adopted by the Fidesz-dominated parliament. The new 2012 constitution enshrines this grant of citizenship to Hungarian minorities outside the country.

ECONOMY

The economy that the post-communist government inherited in 1990 was one that had been moving away from an orthodox communist command economy for a good number of years, though it still retained some aspects of that original pattern. The deviation began in the 1960s under the leadership of János Kádár. For the first six years following the Soviet intervention to put down the Hungarian Revolution, Kádár enforced the old policies of heavy industrialization and collectivization that the regime had tried to get away from after the death of Stalin in 1953. The results were predictably unsatisfactory.

In 1963, with the economy in extreme stress and performing badly, Kádár took note of a reform proposal by a Professor Liberman at the University of Kiev. Intrigued, Kádár decided to try out some of Liberman's ideas. To encourage individual enterprise, the Hungarian government granted a one-year tax exemption to new artisan-type enterprises and guaranteed them access to supplies of raw materials. The result was an immediate increase in the number of working artisans in the villages, a welcome reversal of the longtime trend of migration to the cities. The reform also led to increased service facilities in the cities, as tailors and repairmen and mechanics set themselves up in their own shops. Journalists dubbed the new emphasis on more plentiful consumer goods "goulash communism." The party's calculation was that citizens with full bellies would be less inclined to revolt.

In 1966, a more extensive economic reform began to be discussed. This program, which eventually became known as the "New Economic Mechanism," went into effect in 1968. The New Economic Mechanism postulated the continuation of

central planning but proposed a change in the nature of that planning. Instead of concentrating on a minute, day-to-day control over the economy, central-planning experts would concentrate on long-range goals.

Day-to-day management of the economy was delegated to the managers of individual enterprises, who were enjoined to go forward with the plan based on market demand. Although industry would remain state-owned, the state's control would be exercised indirectly by general credit and interest policies and, in the case of individual enterprises, by means of loans provided to finance technological innovations. Wages were to be established by individual factories though within guidelines set by the central planners. Most important of all, the government gradually relinquished its control over prices. Before the reform began, there were over 1 million administered prices; by 1970, the figure had dropped to just over 1,000.

The New Economic Mechanism differed from Czech economic proposals of the same time period in envisioning a continued positive role for the central planners. It was also not accompanied by a parallel discussion of possible political reforms. It therefore managed to survive the Soviet invasion of Czechoslovakia. Kádár's condemnation of the Czech experiments and his participation in the invasion of Czechoslovakia were crucial.

The New Economic Mechanism had beneficial effects throughout the economy, but this was particularly true with regard to agriculture. The end of artificially low prices for farm products and the accompanying increase in average earnings in the countryside enhanced incentives and led

to a significant growth in production. The change was spectacular. In the mid-1960s, Hungary was a net importer of agriculture products. By the end of the 1960s, it had become a net exporter. In 1990, approximately 30% of Hungary's exports were food products.

The Hungarian government instituted some further economic changes in 1984 that amounted to a strengthening of the New Economic Mechanism. In 1985, approximately three-quarters of all enterprises became eligible for a new type of management system that gave them almost complete autonomy. In addition, a new set of financial rules was issued whereby efficient companies were permitted to pay higher wages and were actually encouraged to get rid of unnecessary employees.

The plan called for state subsidies to be eliminated, and those inefficient enterprises that could not make it on their own were to be allowed to go bankrupt. Only one major company experienced bankruptcy at this time, however, and all of its viable parts, along with employees, were taken over by other companies.

Following the change in political leadership in 1988, a further reform of the economic program was adopted. Its objective was to create "a genuine commodity, monetary, capital and labor market." A long-range plan, it contemplated several years of austerity and at least two to three years of little or no growth before a turnaround would occur.

The most important change had to do with Hungary's small private sector. This sector, which constituted only 4%–5% of the overall economy in 1988, was to be encouraged to grow until it became approximately 30% of the overall economy.

Hungary

Hungary joined the International Monetary Fund, the Bank for International Settlements, and the International Bank for Recovery and Development (the World Bank) while the communists were still in control. That same government also established a realistic exchange rate for the forint, its national currency.

Hungary deliberately reoriented itself toward world markets. In the 1970s, it began negotiating with western companies for the opening of manufacturing facilities in Hungary. The most famous product was probably Levi's jeans, which Hungary exported throughout eastern Europe and the Soviet Union.

In the 1980s, a number of other western companies began operating in Hungary. Among those was McDonald's, which opened its first store in downtown Budapest in 1987. Although fast-food restaurants were still a foreign concept in central and eastern Europe, the government began opening its own fast-food outlets in 1984 under the English name of City Grill. They proved to be so popular that a state catering firm signed a contract with McDonald's to franchise the real thing.

On the negative side, Hungarian borrowings to finance the importation of western technology had raised its hard-currency debt to approximately $8 billion by 1981. When the Polish economy collapsed, western bankers began to worry about Hungary's debt, as well. Arguing that it had a relatively well-managed market-oriented economy, the government was able to retain its access to western credit. By 1989, debt servicing consumed 38.5% of Hungary's hard-currency earnings. Its economic situation improved in the early 1990s, and for several years Hungary became the largest

recipient of foreign investment in central and eastern Europe.

The Post Communist Era

Hungary's greatest problem was privatizing industry. Foreign investment, particularly joint ventures, made a contribution, but it became a political issue as opposition parties asserted that the government had sold the country's patrimony to outsiders. The potency of the argument was revealed by a 1994 poll of workers indicating that only 4% strongly favored foreign investment, while 40% were opposed.

Much of this was perception, since foreign investments still constituted less than 10% of GDP. In addition, the number of Hungarian-owned small firms continued to grow rapidly even as the state sector contracted. The private sector accounted for over 50% of GDP as early as 1994.

At that time, the state-owned sector still included most of the country's energy, chemical, and pharmaceutical industries and nearly all banks, though there were plans to reduce state ownership to 2%. In addition, enterprises that were to remain under state control had been transferred to a new state holding agency, the State Property Company, and it was intended that even these would be partially privatized by having the State Property Company issue stock that would be sold to the public. In the 21st century, Hungary has officially completed its transition to a market economy, and over 92% of its GDP is generated by the private sector.

Hungarians are better off economically than they have ever been. They experienced a rude setback in 2008–2009 as a result of the global downturn. Credit froze around the world in October 2008, and

Hungary found itself unable to finance its budget deficit. The government was compelled to secure a $27 billion rescue package from the IMF, the World Bank, and the European Union. The value of its currency, the forint, fell. About 70% of all household and business debt is denominated in foreign currencies, especially the soaring Swiss franc. Hungarians who had taken out loans and mortgages in foreign currencies in the boom years discovered that they had to pay back far more than they had borrowed. By law the banks must accept repayment in devalued forints.

The economy shrank by about 6% in 2009, a far cry from the previous steady GDP growth Hungary had experienced of almost 5% per year since 1998. It was 0.2% in 2023. The Orbán government hoped to kick-start growth through a flat-rate income tax of 16%, with generous tax breaks for families, and a reduction in business taxes from 19% to 10% in 2013.

Per-capita GDP was 62% of the EU aver-age in 2005 (up from 52% in 2000), compared with 47% for Poland and 72% for Slovenia. Inflation was 9.5% in 2023. At 55% Hungary has the EU's lowest employment rate. Unemployment stood at 3.8% in 2018. It is much higher for young Hungarians, a situation aggravated by the lowering of the school-leaving age from 18 to 16. Many youth are leaving to find work elsewhere in western Europe. But it may be lower since it is estimated that the black economy may account for one-fifth of GDP. Its productivity growth, at 6.3% in 2005, was one of Europe's highest. Real wages went up by more than 17% from 1999 to 2002 and 13% in 2018. The minimum wage had risen by 72%. In 2004, average gross monthly wages were €580, compared with €530 in the Czech Republic and €500 in Poland. One in three Hungarians lives on or below the poverty line; that figure is far higher for the Roma minority.

The budget deficit got out of control, but it had been brought down to 4.1% in 2023. Both main parties indulged in populist spending while in power. It must maintain it at 3% if it aspires to adopt the euro. At 80% of GDP in 2014, its public debt is over the limit of 60% to qualify for the euro, but it is coming down. The new constitution contains a ceiling for public debt of 50% of GDP. It remains burdened by an oversized public sector that consumes about half of the GDP.

By 2015, 75.7% of Hungary's exports, most of which are advanced capital goods, went to EU countries. Its main trading partner by far is Germany, which provides a fourth of its exports and imports. It is dependent upon Russia for over 80% of its gas supplies. In 2006 Hungary broke with the EU's planned Nabucco pipeline

Hungarian patriot Lajos Kossuth cheered in New York, 1851

Hungarian-Croatian bilingual school in Hungary

project to join Gazprom's Blue Stream pipeline, which brings oil under the Black Sea from Russia to Türkiye and one day on to Hungary. However, in 2009 Hungary signed on to the plan to transport Iraqi gas through Nabucco's pipeline, circumventing Russia.

Foreign investment is slowing down. By 2005 it had attracted €48 billion in foreign direct investment, making it the second-leading FDI per-capita country in central and eastern Europe after Poland. However, by 2010 foreign investors were sparking resentment among parts of the population. The ruling Fidesz Party stoked this by railing against privatization and foreign investment. The right-wing press is filled with conspiracy theories about global capitalism and greedy foreign financiers. Fortunately, the country's banks, most of them foreign, did not collapse during the recession.

During the 1990s major investors included such American firms as General Motors, General Electric, Ford, Compaq, Alcoa, and Ameritech; German companies like Deutsche Telekom and in 2008 Daimler, which chose Kecskemet, Hungary, for a new €800 million assembly plant, its first in central Europe; Japanese companies,

such as Suzuki; and Austrian firms Julius Meinl and Kleiner Bauder. General Motors invested $193 million in a joint-venture project with Hungary's Raba Factory to produce 200,000 engines and assemble an estimated 15,000 Opel Astra automobiles a year. The first Opel Astra rolled off the assembly line in 1992. Suzuki, a Japanese automobile company, began manufacturing Suzuki Swifts at its plant in the town of Esztergom in 1992. Ford paid $80 million for a plant to produce electronic components for cars. The auto industry accounts for 10% of GDP.

General Electric purchased Tungsram, Hungary's lighting manufacturer, in 1989. Other American companies investing in Hungary include the Digital Equipment Corporation, Schwinn Bicycle Company, Cartier, Apple Computer, and US West. General Electric, Alcoa, and Oracle have outsourced some of their operations to Hungary.

In addition, the Swiss have entered into joint ventures in pharmaceuticals and food. IKEA, the Swedish-based furniture group, opened a store in Budapest. Austrian and German firms were among the first large investors. In 1990, for example, nationals of these two countries sponsored more than 60% of all joint ventures, although more recently most investment has come from other countries. The EU member countries are the source of 60% of foreign direct investment, the highest in central and eastern Europe. In the 1990s, the largest single investor in Hungary was the United States, which had provided a third of the $25 billion invested by foreigners in that country. But by 2003 the US had fallen to the third place in central and eastern Europe behind Germany and the Netherlands.

Another success story is the growth in local start-up firms, particularly high-tech firms. One such example is Graphhisoft, a

firm started in the early 1980s, which today is one of the world's top five companies making computer-aided design software for architects, with subsidiaries in 12 countries. Another is Cygron, a firm that produces artificial-intelligence software. Cygron was having trouble marketing its Data-Scope software internationally, however, so in 1998 it sold out to MindMaker, a California-based company owned by József Király, an expatriate Hungarian.

High-tech continues to be a growth industry in Hungary, largely because of the abundance of talent stemming from an education system that emphasizes mathematics and science. International companies that have built major research and development facilities in Hungary include Ericsson, Nokia, Motorola, and Siemens. By 2015, 64.9% of the workforce was employed in the services sector, which produces 70% of GDP; 27% were employed in industry, producing 30% of GDP. The percentage of GDP generated by the private sector has steadily risen from 18% in 1990, 55% in 1994, and 80% the end of the century to 92% today. Tourism accounts for 10% of GDP and rising. The former flag carrier airline, Malev, went bankrupt and stopped flying in 2012. Those visitors who do not understand the difficult Hungarian language can keep informed through the English-language weeklies *The Budapest Sun* and *The Budapest Times*.

Hungary's unemployment data came under some criticism after the Orbán government introduced in 2011 a controversial law restricting the number of days one could collect unemployment benefits to 30, after which time they needed to find a job—or could be employed at a lower wage with the public-works "workfare" program. The program, reminiscent of those in the post-Depression era in the US, pays less than a regular job would but still more than unemployment benefits. This, in principle, should encourage people not to rely on state benefits but has not been found as a successful way to create normal employment. Some 260,000 public-works beneficiaries in 2015 provided a variety of usually menial jobs, including constructing the controversial razor-wire fence along the Hungarian-Serbian border. Because the government reports these workers as "employed," the overall unemployment figures may be skewed. Either way, in 2015 Orbán allocated $964 million to the program, and by 2018 it was predicted to cost 1.6% of GDP while employing some 9% of the labor force.

Agriculture remains an important part of the economy, although it accounts for only 5.2% of employment and 3% of GDP. Significant changes have taken place in this sector, as well. Collective farms had already been given considerable autonomy

Franz Liszt performs for Franz-Josef I, emperor of Austria and king of Hungary.

Hungary

under the communists, and numerous small businesses had also grown up in conjunction with them. Agriculture has been privatized, though legal conflicts about the ownership of land slowed the issuance of deeds in some cases. A major problem is with eastern Hungary, where a higher percentage of people subsist on small farms and where, in some areas, unemployment tops 20%. The government is addressing this problem by offering tax breaks to industry willing to relocate here.

A new major highway was constructed that run from Budapest to the Romanian border. Since 2015 it connects Hungary with Romania as the first border crossing on a motorway between the two countries.

One worrisome problem is the quality of Hungary's health care, despite the fact that it spends 7% of its GDP on it. Its people are among the sickest in Europe. They go to the doctor an average of a dozen times a year, twice the western European rate. A practice that has especially become a subject of public debate is the tipping of doctors. Without it treatment is often slow or denied. Many Hungarians think the tipping system demonstrates that doctors are not concerned with and accountable to their patients. The former socialist government reduced the number of hospital beds by a fourth and closed three hospitals in 2006. Ultimately the health system should be changed so that the patients pay some of their costs and the culture of bribery is eliminated.

Hungarians have one of the lowest life expectancies in the EU (71 years for men and 79 for women—10 to 12 years fewer for Roma). This is not helped by the fact that almost a quarter of the population is considered to be obese. A special tax was levied on packaged junk foods and sugary drinks to bring this figure down. They also have the third-worst record in Europe (behind Lithuania and Russia) for suicide, with men four times more likely than women to kill themselves.

Despite all the international condemnation of Viktor Orbán, the country continues to attract foreign investment and performs well economically. Several automotive companies announced the construction of new plants, including Mercedes-Benz, which invested $1.1 billion in a new facility in Kecskemét. Over 500,000 cars have been produced since its opening on March 29, 2012. The Mercedes-Benz plant in Hungary contributes to a great extent to the growth of the compact car segment.

Electronics, car parts, and pharmaceutical products also contributed to rise in foreign trade. Inflation has been falling, tax reform provided more money for purchases and bank savings, S&P upgraded Hungary's credit rating to BBB-, and unemployment shrunk dramatically to a historic low of 4.9%.

To encourage investment in real estate, the government introduced a scheme reducing VAT for buyers of newly built houses to 5% from the standard 27%. On the other hand, it discontinued another program that guaranteed foreign investors EU residency if they bought $280,000 of government bonds. The offer drew in a large number of mostly Chinese and Russian investors.

Natural Resources

Hungary is relatively short of natural resources, which means that it is heavily dependent on imports. In the past, the Soviet Union provided it with approximately 90% of its oil, iron ore, and timber needs, plus a high proportion of other raw materials; Russia currently provides for three-quarters of Hungary's gas and oil needs. Hungary's main domestic fuel source is a low-quality brown coal. Unfortunately, its reserves are not extensive, and coal production has started to decline.

For this reason, the government made a commitment to develop nuclear energy. There are currently three plants in operation, two of them completed in 1987. Its major power plant is in the town of Paks, which produces 40% of Hungary's electricity. Russia drew plans to modernize four Soviet-built power units at Paks, and it has a contract to provide nuclear fuel to the plants. In 2014 Russia agreed to lend Hungary €10 billion ($13.6 billion) to build two new 1,200-megawatt blocks at the plant. Orbán agreed to this deal without a tender and without parliamentary approval. The EU rejected the deal because of these violations, as well, out of concern with its members' continued dependence on Russian energy. Still, Hungary declared that it would continue working with Russia's Rosatom on the project. By 2017, the EU relented and approved the deal, provided that Hungary sells at least 30% of the plant's future output on the open market. For his part, Russian president Putin offered to increase his country's financing for the project from 80% to 100%. The EU launched a similar investigation over non-public bidding by the Chinese, related to the proposed fast-rail link between Budapest and Belgrade.

There are reminders that safety was not a high priority under the former communist regime. In October 2010 three towns along the Danube were flooded by 200 million gallons of red toxic sludge from the storage reservoir of an aluminum plant in Ajka, 100 miles southwest of Budapest. The torrent swept cars, people, and animals away; damaged houses and bridges; and forced hundreds of residents to evacuate. Nine persons died, and 150 were injured in what is regarded as the worst natural disaster in Hungarian history. The soil covering 16 square miles of this agricultural region has to be replaced. The images of horrified victims trying to dig themselves and their possessions out of the stinging muck were broadcast around the world.

The International Commission for the Protection of the Danube River has long predicted that there are dozens of accidents waiting to happen along this vital waterway. The Soviet Union made Hungary the east bloc's main producer of aluminum. Hungary has considered itself ahead of its neighbors in cleaning up after the Soviet era. One rarely sees the kind of rusting, polluting factories and abandoned trash dumps one used to see along back roads. The government of Viktor Orbán responded very quickly, temporarily taking over the polluting company and detaining the CEO for questioning. This kind of forceful hands-on approach, with a sharp eye on public opinion, is the prime minister's style. One bank chief economist

Hungarian folk art in Szentendre   Photo by Madison Rechenberg

noted, "He has to be a kind of tough guy. . . this is what local people want."

In a similar fashion, the government's tough approach to the Dutch beer maker Heineken drew some support among the Hungarians resenting multinational corporations' sway in their own country. In an apparent act of retaliation for a legal victory by Heineken over a local brewery in the mostly Hungarian Transylvania, Fidesz MPs proposed outlawing the use of "totalitarian symbols" for commercial purposes. This would affect Heineken, whose logo features a red five-point star, a prominent communist symbol.

CULTURE

The Magyar language is not related to any of Europe's major languages except Finnish and Estonian, and even these languages are mutually incomprehensible. Hungarian culture is therefore distinct from that of its neighbors. There is also a strong international culture, since most educated Hungarians are fluent in at least one foreign language. Hungarian plays have to be translated before they can go abroad, but one such play, *Cats* Play by István Örkény, was popular when it was produced in the United States in the 1970s.

In 2002 the first Hungarian writer ever was honored with the Nobel Prize in literature. Imre Kertész was a Holocaust survivor whose novels concentrate on his experiences in Auschwitz and Buchenwald. His works were almost unknown in his own country, since he refused to conform to the communist rule. He led a solitary life in Hungary and eked out a living translating German-language works. Only two of his novels were translated into English prior to the award—*Fateless* and *Kaddish for a Child Not Born*, both of which are semiautobiographical novels. Kertész was a harsh critic of his native Hungary for its role in sending Jews to their deaths and for what he saw as latent anti-Semitism. He died in 2016.

Unlike Germany and Austria, Hungary has not come to terms with the fact that its art museums contain many works illegally taken from Jewish collectors during World War II. The heirs of a wealthy banker, Baron Mór Lipót Herzog, filed a lawsuit in the US District Court in Washington to get back over 40 works, including a stunning collection of El Greco paintings, worth $100 million. But a Hungarian court ruled in 2008 that the government is not required to return the paintings.

Hungarians are also noted for their films, many of which would be classified as new wave or art films. Only about 20 Hungarian films are made in a year, however, so theaters show many foreign films. One particularly successful Hungarian producer in recent years, István Szabó, made the films *Colonel Redl* and *Hanussen*, both of which were released in the United States. Both deal with the cultural area of the old Austro-Hungarian Empire and were released with a German soundtrack. His film *Mephisto* won an Oscar. The Hungarian film *Sunshine* was an Oscar runner-up.

Composers Franz Liszt and Béla Bartok were Hungarians. Many musicians fled abroad after the failure of the 1956 revolution, and many of those were associated with the Philharmonia Hungarica. Although often mistaken for a touring orchestra from Budapest, it actually had its home base in western Germany. But Hungary produced a new generation of musicians in time, and soloists developed a strong reputation at home and abroad. One of the 20th century's most renowned cellists, János Starker, who taught at Indiana University, died in 2013. A child prodigy, he survived Nazi internment.

Emigres, such as the pianist Peter Frankl and conductor Arpad Joó, were invited back to Hungary for guest performances. One American singer was made an honorary citizen of Budapest posthumously in 2011—Elvis Presley, who had endorsed the unsuccessful 1956 Hungarian uprising. The city also named a park after him.

Under communism, the government supported cultural activities and spent an estimated $27 million to renovate the State Opera House in Budapest in the 1980s. The arts were heavily subsidized, with the average ticket to a full opera or first-class concert costing about $2. The government also sponsored numerous "folk festivals" throughout the country. Things have changed little in this area since 1990. Although the price for such things as a seat at the opera has increased considerably, high culture still continues to be subsidized.

Most of Hungary's universities are public, but it had one of Europe's most international and successful private universities, Central European University in the heart of Budapest's old town. Its 1,700-strong student body, from all over the world was composed entirely of graduate students focusing on social sciences, public policy, and business. It was founded in 1991 by George Soros, who was born in Hungary but made a fortune as a currency speculator and hedge-fund manager in the United States. He provided most of the funding and an astonishing $840 million endowment for this unique university. The CEU opened its new building in 2016 at a cost of $38 million.

In 2017, the CEU became a focal point of an international confrontation after the Orbán government passed an education law banning colleges that offer academic credentials from another country while not having a campus in that country. The move is seen as aimed squarely at the CEU, which is registered in both the US and Hungary and would now have to open a campus in America. Its staff would also need additional permissions if they came from a non-EU country. The move provoked a series of mass protests in Hungary and letters from several hundred western scholars, including 17 Nobel laureates. It also contributed to the European Parliament's resolution demanding that Hungary be punished under article 7 of the Treaty of the EU. This would be a colossal setback for Hungary, especially if the "nuclear option" were applied that suspends a country's voting rights. CEU was moved to Vienna. Taking its place will be the only Chinese university operating inside the EU. It is scheduled to open its doors in 2024.

The government passed a law in 2021 handing control of the eleven main state universities to foundations that answer to Orbán.

The government had a cruel surprise in 2013 for students receiving state-funded scholarships. They must work for two years in Hungary for every year of subsidized study. This law, unique in Europe, was met with broad opposition and street protests.

In 2016, Prime Minister Orbán announced a plan to spend more than $780 million to transform Budapest's main park, Liget, into a cluster of several major museums. The massive architectural project is intended to boost the capital city's attractiveness to international tourists and increase their number from the current 3 million a year. In the process, some of the spectacular buildings vacated by the museums would be restored to their precommunist glory and house state institutions, such as the Supreme Court. The royal castle (now the National Gallery of Art) overlooking the city and the Danube from Buda's Castle Hill will also be renovated to recapture its Versailles-like splendor, and the prime minister's office will be moved next to the castle. Besides economic calculations, Orbán's plans have political underpinnings, as the eradication of communist imprints and the visionary remaking of the city is likely to create a lasting legacy for the leader of Fidesz. Critics decry the cost of the undertaking, the loss of green spaces, and the government's legal maneuvering that makes it impossible to block the project in court.

Religion

Church-and-state relations were quite bad for many years under communism. However, they began to improve at the beginning of the 1970s, after Cardinal Mindszenty, who had been residing in the

Hungary

American Embassy from 1956 onward, agreed to go into exile; he died in Vienna in 1975. His successor, László Lékai, was named a cardinal in 1976. János Kádár summed up his position on religion at a press conference in Paris in late 1978: "We have ever considered it most important that honest religious citizens, doing a fair day's work building our country, should not be faced with irreconcilable problems of conscience by the confrontation of state and church. As the result of protracted, patient work settling the relationship between the state and the churches, a religious citizen can now, at the same time, be committed to social progress and socialism, and be a faithful son of his church."

Cardinal Lékai died in 1986. Negotiations for appointment of his successor and new bishops dragged on before the government finally gave its approval to the appointment of Cardinal László Paskai. The government had insisted that the church take action against one of its priests, Father György Bulányi, who was preaching the incompatibility of Christianity and service in the military. The church, which had its own problems with Father Bulányi, was nevertheless unwilling to repudiate him completely.

Church-and-state relations improved dramatically after Grósz became general secretary. For example, the government rehabilitated József Cardinal Mindszenty and extended an invitation for the pope to visit Hungary. One of the first acts of the new noncommunist government, installed in May 1990, was to reopen diplomatic relations with the Vatican. It followed this up by dismantling all government controls over religion. The Christian Democrats were part of the government coalition from 1990 to 1994. The government sparked an outcry in 2012 by reducing the number of recognized religious organizations from over 300 to only 14 "historical" churches (raised to 18 as protests erupted). Small Christian and Muslim organizations would no longer have been recognized although they continue to function. The Constitutional Court annulled this law in 2013.

By the 21st century, Hungary's Jewish population was approximately 100,000, the third-largest in Europe though only a small part of the 800,000 who lived in Hungary prior to World War II. The communist rulers blamed the Holocaust almost exclusively on the Nazis, aided by a few Hungarian "extremists." Before 1989 Jews kept a low profile, although the government permitted them to run a school and the only rabbinical seminary in eastern Europe. After the fall of communism, the local Jewish population opened two Jewish schools. Jewish publications, cultural associations, and youth groups have begun expanding, and Budapest's 4,000-seat synagogue has been renovated. Jews are represented at all levels of political life. Every Jewish child is entitled to free tuition from kindergarten to university in schools run by Jewish institutions. Jewish religious and cultural activity is reviving, especially in Budapest. As *the Washington Post* reported, "it all amounts to the revival of what was one of Europe's largest and most prolific Jewish communities." In 2004 a Holocaust Memorial Center was opened in the capital around a restored synagogue on Páva Street, which had been used in 1944 as an internment camp. The main far-right party, Jobbik, recently reduced its anti-Semitic rants in favor of anti-Muslim rhetoric. Still, at least some of the venom directed at George Soros and the NGOs and academic institutions he supports is rooted in the perception that his agenda is motivated by some international conspiracy, a usual anti-Semitic slur (Soros is Jewish).

CURRENT ISSUES

The center-right Fidesz government of Prime Minister Viktor Orbán has centralized power to an extent unprecedented since the collapse of communism. Its landslide victories in national and local elections cement Orbán's position as the country's undisputed boss. He faced the April 2022 parliamentary elections and won a fourth consecutive term in office, becoming the EU's longest-serving leader, after 12 years in power. There is widespread unease abroad about Orbán's weak commitment to democracy, liberalism and checks and balances. His "illiberal democracy" calls for a strong state, high social discipline, and limited public dissent. The opposition contends that Hungary has become a dictatorship.

The EU is concerned, but it cannot easily discipline members. The prime minister tries to be conciliatory and reassuring with his critics, but his public pronouncements are not encouraging. The country's political landscape has been redrawn. Democracy and the rule of law are in danger. Corruption is so vast that Transparency International calls it "state capture."

The rising tensions between Hungary and the European Union promise a rocky road ahead. The larger issue—and the reason for the European Parliament's call for article 7 sanctions against the country—is the erosion of EU's accomplishments regarding "fundamental values of democracy, fundamental rights and the rule of law," as part of the drift toward "illiberal democracy." Hungary's minister for human resources added to the fire by declaring in 2017 his willingness to "use all legal means at our disposal to stop pseudo-civil society spy groups, such as the ones funded by George Soros." Accusing Soros of trying to flood Hungary with Muslim migrants, Orbán forced the philanthropist to move his Central European University to Vienna and his other operations to Berlin.

The European Commission, already angered by the Hungarian government's expensive "Stop Brussels" anti-EU propaganda campaign, launched legal action against Hungary. Its vice president snapped at Orbán, "everyone is entitled to their opinion but you are not entitled to your own facts." A prominent EU parliamentarian, Guy Verhofstadt, added, "you want to keep the EU funds, but you don't want our values. . . You have violated every single one of them."

Many of these issues came to the fore when the enormous wave of migrants flooded Hungary in 2015. It generated a lot of strong emotions and will continue to have a powerful impact on politics. By August, some 140,000 refugees entered the country; in just one week that month, 2,500 crossed the border into Hungary, mostly from Serbia, a non-EU country. Hundreds choked Budapest's Keleti (eastern) railroad station, hoping in vain to catch a train to Germany. It was later discovered that some of the terrorists who committed the mass killings in Paris in November 2015 passed through the station.

Required by the Schengen Agreement to protect the zone's external border, Hungary found it very difficult to maintain order. Declaring immigration as a threat to European civilization, Orbán announced that his country would build a 175-kilometer (109 miles) razor-wire fence to seal off the border with Serbia. It soon sent police detachments and military units to monitor the border. Violent clashes with the migrants ensued as some of them threw rocks and water bottles at the police, who used force and tear gas. Hungary described those acts as a "terrorist attack." Frustrated with their situation, several hundred migrants left the Keleti station on foot, walking among a largely silent crowd of Hungarians toward their destination—the Austrian border and then Germany. The march, as well as the clashes and harsh police actions, were widely covered by international media, and Hungary's policy met with widespread condemnation. However, Orbán resolutely maintained his stance. Hungarian courts held well over 2,000 trials for border crimes, with an astonishing 99% conviction rate.

Orbán also refused to participate in the EU's relocation scheme for 160,000 migrants in Italy and Greece, pushed for by

Germany. Instead, he sneered at Germany for being "rich and weak." To strengthen his hand, Orbán decided to hold an October 2016 referendum playing on the sovereignty theme by asking, rather leadingly, "Do you want the EU, even without the approval of the Hungarian parliament, to be able to prescribe the mandatory resettlement of non- Hungarian citizens in Hungary?" His plans backfired when not enough voters showed up at the polls (44.04%), although nearly all of those who did vote against the EU.

By June 2017, the EU lost patience. Singling out Hungary, Poland, and Czechia, the European Commission noted that these countries "have not done anything" to admit any of the refugees relocated from Italy and Greece.

Over time, the uproar among other EU members gave way to a grudging approval of Orbán's approach to handling border control, as other countries rushed to find their solutions to the problem the organization as a whole was unsuccessful at solving. Fences and stronger border controls sprang up throughout the region. In March 2017, Hungary started constructing a second row of barriers. They are accompanied by metal shipping containers that house asylum seekers while their applications are being processed. This time, other EU members' responses have been muted. This suggests that Orbán may be right when he says about his policies, "What we did then has not only become widely accepted, it is the norm to be followed."

Realistically, there are limits to Hungary's ability to thumb its nose at the EU, since at least 3% of the country's GDP comes from the EU's money for infrastructure projects. However, Orbán has also been cultivating his close personal relations with Vladimir Putin and spoke highly of Donald Trump's approach to immigration and Muslims. Hungary is Putin's strongest ally in the EU; Orbán insists that Russia is no threat to the EU or NATO and is highly critical of sanctions against Russia. The Bratislava-based GLOBSEC Policy Institute (formerly the Central European Policy Institute) produces a Vulnerability Index to evaluate the Visegrad countries' susceptibility to "hostile foreign influence." By far, Hungary had the highest level of vulnerability to Russian influences. Disturbingly, the Hungarian national security committee identified various links between Hungarian far-right groups, such as the neo-Nazi National Front Movement, and Russian officials.

Orbán paints a picture of the world in which the identity and well-being of Hungarians are in jeopardy due to the EU's over-bearing and perhaps totalitarian designs that include the refugee policy that is "a Trojan horse of terrorism" and that allows Muslim migrants to threaten the Europeans' "Christian identity."

At least one crucial reason for Orbán's tough stance, besides his ideological predilections, is the growing challenge from the right by Jobbik. As the popularity of that party grows, Fidesz keeps a wary eye on its influence among the electorate. With the relative weakness of the political left in Hungary and its politics moving to the right, a convergence of sorts is developing in which Jobbik seeks to scrub its extremist image to appear more respectable to center-right voters, while Fidesz tries to neutralize Jobbik's challenge by adopting some of its rhetoric and ultra-nationalism.

Hence the government financially supported such controversial projects as the monument to a pro-Nazi wartime politician who promoted the expulsion of Hungarian Jews, nearly a half-million of whom perished in death camps. The controversy notwithstanding, this may be good politics among as many as 25% percent of Hungarians holding anti-Semitic views. Such views frequently percolate in public discourse. Fidesz knows that it has scored some important points that improve its chances of electoral success.

In the April 2022 parliamentary elections, Orbán enjoyed a landslide victory winning a fourth consecutive term in office and a supermajority that might make him even bolder in the future.

The Former Yugoslavia (Jugoslavija)

Serb Parliament, Belgrade, with election billboard of ex-president Boris Tadic

Few European regions have so concerned the world since the collapse of communism as the former Yugoslavia. It was always the most liberal and independent communist regime. Most observers were therefore optimistic about the prospects for this multiethnic and multinational federation as the last decade of the 20th century dawned. However, fate took a different course. Bloody ethnic strife seized the headlines, and the word "genocide" reappeared in the daily news for the first time since World War II. Events in this bleeding ex-state prompted NATO to fire its first shots in anger, and international peacekeepers are the only ones in certain parts of the area who can keep hostile ethnic groups from each other's throats.

On April 27, 1992, after four of the six republics that had been integral parts of the Socialist Federal Republic of Yugoslavia—Slovenia, Croatia, Bosnia and Herzegovina, and Macedonia—had declared their independence, the remaining two, Serbia and Montenegro, proclaimed themselves the successor state as the "new" Federal Republic of Yugoslavia. This rump state was renamed Serbia and Montenegro in 2003. Then, voters in Montenegro opted for independence in a May 21, 2006, referendum. Kosovo (Kosova in Albanian) declared its own independence from Serbia on February 17, 2008, which Serbia still refuses to accept. Serbia's only remaining "autonomous" region is Vojvodina. It was originally granted the autonomous status because a large minority (approximately 300,000) of the population is ethnically Hungarian. That special status was eliminated in 1990–1991 but restored in 2002, and its own officials rule there with some oversight from Serbia. Thus ended the great experiment of uniting most southern Slavs ("jug" means "south") within one country.

436

The Former Yugoslavia

HISTORY

The Slavic-speaking peoples of the Balkan Peninsula are classified as South Slavs. They are one of three branches of the Slavic peoples, the other two being the East Slavs (Russians, Ukrainians, Belarusians) and the West Slavs (Poles, Czechs, Slovaks). The Slavic language is a branch of the Indo-European family of languages. When the Slavic peoples first appeared in history, they were found mostly in the area of the Pripet Swamps in what are now the republics of Belarus and Ukraine.

The South Slavs began migrating into the area of the Balkans sometime in the 6th century. At first, they were dominated by two Turkic peoples also present in what became the Balkans, the Avars and Bulgars. When the Avar and Bulgar khanates crumbled in the first quarter of the 7th century, however, the Byzantine emperor signed an alliance with two of the stronger Slavic tribes, the Serbs and Croats. Supported by this alliance, the Slavic peoples either pushed the Turkic peoples out of the Balkans or submerged them in their greater numbers. By the end of the 7th century, Slavic language and culture was dominant throughout most of the northern Balkans. The exceptions were in the east, where the Vlach (also called Wallachians, ancestors of modern Romanians) were in a majority, and in mountainous areas of the west, where the native Illyrian people (ancestors of the modern Albanians) managed to keep their culture alive.

The Serbs and Croats eventually gave their names to the areas of the Balkans they now occupy, while a third tribe, the Slovenes, who had actually been the first of the Slavic tribes to enter the Balkans,

The Former Yugoslavia

settled further west. In 748, the Slovenes were incorporated into the Carolingian Empire and converted to Roman Catholicism. They remained a part of western culture from that time onward. The Croats were also incorporated into the Carolingian Empire for a short time at the beginning of the 9th century and converted to Roman Catholicism. At the end of the 11th century, they came under the control of the kingdom of Hungary.

The first Serb state rose about the middle of the 9th century, when a number of south Serbian tribes united to oppose expansion from the Bulgar state to the southeast. Vlastimir, the ruler of this state, sought the support of the Byzantine emperor against the Bulgars. In the process, he submitted himself to the overlordship of the Byzantine emperor.

One effect of this is that Serbia became open to Byzantine cultural influences, the most important of which was Orthodox Christianity. In addition, the two missionaries from Thessalonica, Cyril and Methodius, had created a script for the Slavic language based on Greek letters. They worked in different locales: North Macedonia, Bulgaria, and Moravia in the present-day Czech Republic. They started a literacy movement in the town of Ohrid, now in North Macedonia. The Cyrillic alphabet was adopted by Serbia, along with Orthodox Christianity. In the process a great cultural divide was created in the Balkans that ran through the middle of the Slavic settlements. Henceforth, Serbs (along with Bulgarians, Montenegrins, and Macedonians) were on one side of that divide, and the Croats and Slovenes were on the other.

In spite of Byzantine assistance, Vlastimir's kingdom eventually fell under Bulgarian control. As a result, the Serb church became a part of the Bulgarian Orthodox Church. The area of Serbia next came under the control of a Macedonian kingdom created at the beginning of the 11th century. Then the Byzantine empire overthrew the Macedonian kingdom in 1018 and tried to extend its control over the area of the eastern Balkans. This led to short lived kingdoms arising in Herzegovina and Montenegro to challenge the Byzantine control. Toward the end of the 11th century, yet another kingdom rose in the area of Novi Pazar, only to be supplanted by a revived Bulgarian kingdom after the capture of Constantinople by soldiers of the fourth crusade in 1204.

A new Serbian kingdom rose in the area of the city of Skopje beginning in 1282. It was called the Nemanjić Empire after the name of the dynasty. The founder of this dynasty was Stefan Nemanja. This kingdom reached its height under its ninth ruler, Stefan Dušan, who ruled from 1331 to 1355. During his reign, Serbia was an empire for the only time in its history. Although this kingdom eventually extended its control over a large part of the northern Balkans, its greatest significance was probably cultural. The Nemanjićs were committed to the Orthodox Church. It was during this time that the Serbs managed to separate from the Bulgarian Orthodox Church and establish an autonomous Serbian Orthodox Church. The founder was St. Sava, one of Stefan Nemanja's sons, who helped establish the Serbians' identity and religion. The seat of the church was later moved to Peć. In 1375, it was raised to a patriarchate.

Equally important, the Nemanjićs managed to create a Serbian "high culture" based on religious cohesion. They fought the influence of Roman Catholicism and worked to suppress Bogomilism, a religious heresy centered in Bosnia. They were also responsible for construction of many churches and monasteries, which have come to signify the essence of medieval Serbian Orthodoxy. Among the most renowned of these churches are the Mileševa (about 1235), Peć (1250), Morača (1252), Sopoćani (about 1260), and Dečani (1327). Many of these churches are decorated by frescoes, the most important being those of the Raška school. In addition, this period produced a number of literary works, including a biography of Stefan Nemanja. A close partnership between church and state created a culture that was both courtly and religious. This continued to define the best of what it meant to be Serbian long after the kingdom itself was no more.

This kingdom came to an end in the 14th century, when Turkish armies defeated the Serbs in the Battle of Kosovo, which took place on June 28, 1389 (June 15 by the old calendar). The leader of the Serbian forces was Prince Lazar. A Serbian assassin, Milosh Obilić, who made his way into the Turkish camp pretending to be a deserter, killed the Turkish sultan, Murad I. He stabbed the sultan with a poisoned dagger. However, Murad's son managed to rally his forces and defeat the Serbians. Taken prisoner during the battle, Prince Lazar was beheaded.

For 70 years, Serbs were required to pay an annual tribute and to serve in the Turkish armies. However, they were allowed domestic autonomy. In 1459, the sultan placed all of Serbia under Turkish rule. All lands became his property, and all Serbs became bond slaves of the land. A new kind of elite military force was created out of conscripted Christian boys from the Balkans. Called Janissaries ("New Troops"), they almost always converted to Islam and became famous and respected warriors. They became property of the sultan and over time grew into one of the most influential power institutions in the empire. The patriarchate of Peć was suppressed for a time, but it was restored in 1557. Henceforth, Serbian culture lived on only within the Serbian Orthodox Church.

The Road to Serbian Independence

Turkish rule continued for another three and a half centuries before the Serbs raised the banner of rebellion. Under the leadership of Karadjordje (Karageorge or "Black George"), the Serbs revolted against the Turks in 1804. This revolt was suppressed in 1813, but a more successful one broke out two years later under the leadership of Miloš Obrenović.

In 1817, Serbia won the right to have its own national assembly. Miloš became prince of Serbia and promptly had his great rival, Karadjordje, murdered. This was the beginning of a feud between the Obrenović and Karadjordjević families that continued into the 20th century, frequently disrupting the political life of the country.

After the Russo-Turkish War of 1828–1829, Serbia was given the status of an autonomous principality. It was technically still under Turkish suzerainty, but it was effectively a Russian protectorate.

In 1876, Serbia became the cause of another war between Russia and Türkiye after it declared war on Türkiye. When it became clear that Serbia would not be able to stand against the Turks, Russia intervened in 1877. Russia defeated the Turks and forced Türkiye to recognize the independence of Serbia (and Romania) in the Treaty of San Stefano. The great powers revised the Treaty at the Congress of Berlin in 1878, but the resulting Treaty of Berlin included recognition of Serbian independence.

In 1885–1886, Serbia fought a war against Bulgaria after that nation and eastern Rumelia united in 1885. The conflict began when Prince Milan demanded that Bulgaria cede some of its territory to Serbia. Prince Alexander of Bulgaria defeated Serbian forces, and it was only Austria's threat to enter the war on Serbia's side that produced an armistice. Serbia then recognized the union of Bulgaria and eastern Rumelia.

In 1903, a palace revolution led by forces loyal to the Karadjordjević family led to the murder of the Obrenović family and the ascension of the Karadjordjević dynasty to the throne. In a change of foreign policy, the new king set out in earnest to create a Greater Serbia by bringing as much of the Balkans as he could under his control. This brought Serbia into conflict

The Former Yugoslavia

WESTERN BALKANS, 1560–1680

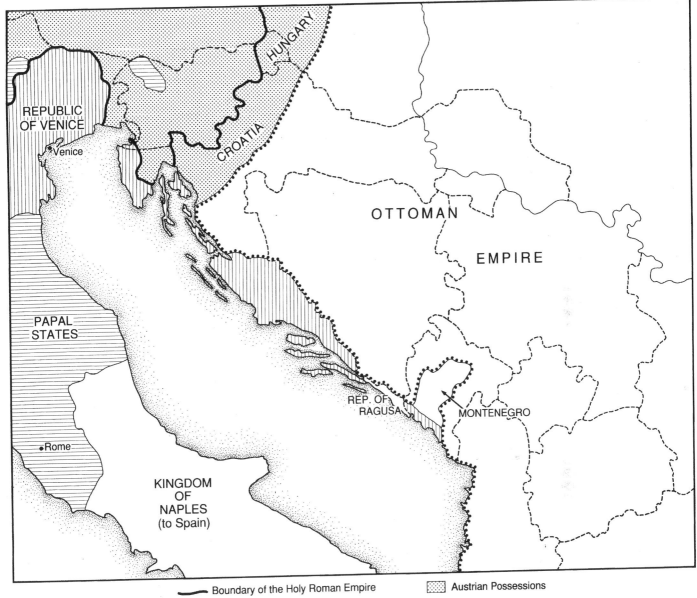

—— Boundary of the Holy Roman Empire   ▨ Austrian Possessions

OTTOMAN (Turkish) EMPIRE at its greatest extent.

MONTENEGRO, an area of virtually inaccessible mountains, never conquered by the Turks.

REPUBLIC OF VENICE, ruled by an elite of wealthy merchant families. Dominated the Adriatic Sea from bases in Dalmatia.

REPUBLIC OF RAGUSA (Dubrovnik), a small city-state which flourished as an important cultural center, developing distinctive local styles of architecture and sculpture and establishing Croatian as a modern literary language.

These boundaries were essentially stable for over a century, as the Austrian Habsburgs resisted further Turkish advances into central Europe.

KINGDOM OF NAPLES, ruled by the Spanish Habsburgs as a separate kingdom.

PAPAL STATES—In these territories the pope was the secular ruler. Other church territories were ruled by bishops or abbots, who were princes of the Holy Roman Empire.

AUSTRIAN POSSESSIONS—A collection of separate kingdoms, duchies, and counties ruled by the Austrian branch of the House of Habsburg.

HOLY ROMAN EMPIRE—During this period all emperors were from the Austrian Habsburgs.

1680–1740

The Ottoman Empire attempted to expand into central Europe, but the Turkish army was held at the gates of Vienna in 1683 and then forced back, liberating the entire central basin of the Danube River; the new Austro-Turkish border stabilized in 1739.

AUSTRIAN MILITARY FRONTIER—Refugee Serbian communities were settled along the border in Croatia and Slavonia (not to be confused with the present republic of SLOVENIA) by the Austrian government. A military constitution to defend the Slavonian borderland was granted in 1702 and later extended to Croatia and Transylvania.

KINGDOM OF THE TWO SICILIES—After changing hands several times, the kingdom of Naples and the kingdom of Sicily were combined in 1735 under a junior branch of the House of Bourbon.

439

The Former Yugoslavia

WESTERN BALKANS, 1740–1797

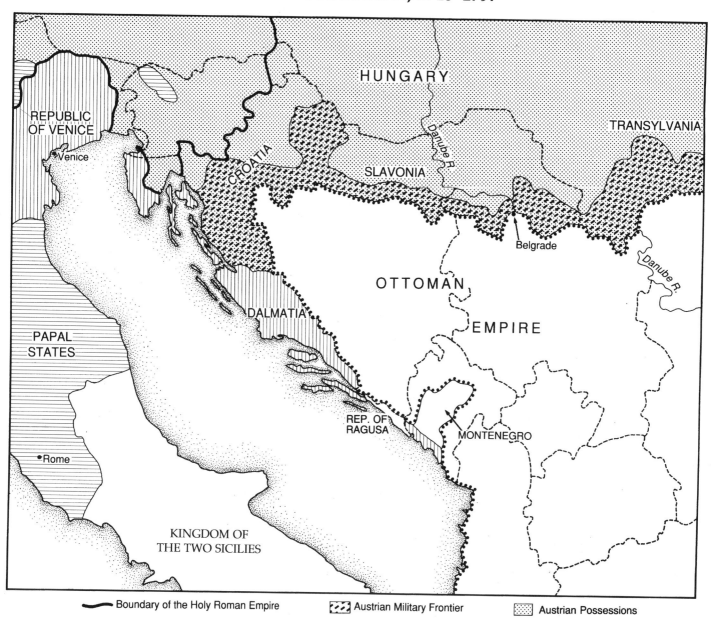

Boundary of the Holy Roman Empire   Austrian Military Frontier   Austrian Possessions

The Ottoman Empire was no longer a threat, and Austria was occupied in central Europe with the rise of Prussia and the partition of Poland. Boundaries were basically stable during this period.

1797–1815

During the Napoleonic wars, political boundaries and country names changed frequently.

The Venetian territories were carved up in 1797, the largest part going temporarily to Austria.

The Holy Roman Empire became extinct in 1806.

In 1809 France briefly annexed all of the eastern Adriatic coast, as well as Ragusa and nearly all of present-day Slovenia.

By 1809 all territories ruled by the Roman Catholic Church had been acquired by secular states.

Meanwhile, Montenegro won a small expansion of its boundaries.

The Former Yugoslavia

WESTERN BALKANS, 1815–1860

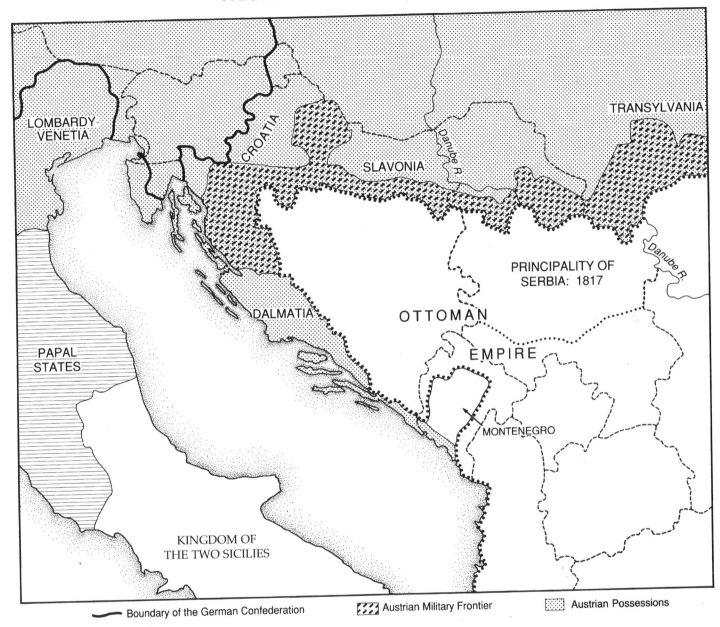

— Boundary of the German Confederation   ▨ Austrian Military Frontier   ░ Austrian Possessions

In the post-Napoleonic settlements, Austria (re)gained all of the Venetian territories, plus Ragusa, as well as those church territories within its borders. The military frontier was maintained, becoming a separate crownland in 1849 with special privileges for the Serbian settlers.

GERMAN CONFEDERATION—Created to replace the Holy Roman Empire with the same eastern and southern boundaries.

The Pope was restored as ruler of central Italy, but all other former Church territories remained secularized.

SERBIA—The Serbs had been fighting for their independence since 1804, achieving in 1817 recognition as an autonomous principality under Ottoman overlordship.

These boundaries were essentially stable during this period.

The Former Yugoslavia

THE ETHNIC/RELIGIOUS MIXTURE

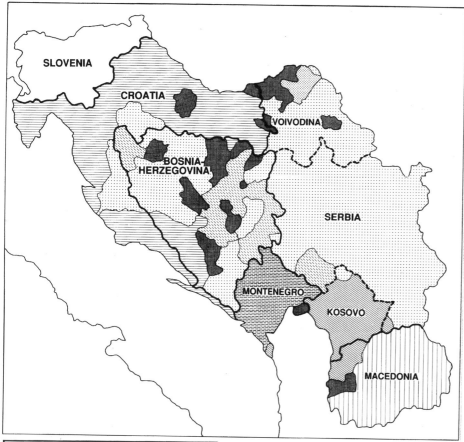

As of the 2002 census

- Slovenes
- Croats
- Serbs
- Bosnians (Muslims)
- Montenegrins
- Macedonians
- Hungarians
- Albanians
- Ethnic mixture

The last king of Serbia,
Peter I

almost-impassable mountains allowed the Montenegrins to resist repeated Turkish attempts to conquer the area. Although the Turks and later the Venetians did occupy parts of Montenegro, it was never completely controlled. The Congress of Berlin recognized its independence in 1878. During the years before World War I, the Montenegrins, like some of their neighbors, were advocates of South Slav nationalism. They lent military support to the cause in 1878 against the Turks and took part in the Balkan Wars of 1912–1913.

World War I

A Bosnian Serb student named Gavrilo Princip assassinated the Austrian archduke Franz Ferdinand in Sarajevo on June 28, 1914. Princip belonged to Young Bosnia, a nationalist organization influenced by the Black Hand. When on trial, he declared himself to be "a Yugoslav nationalist, aiming for the unification of all Yugoslavs."

Austria responded to the murder with an ultimatum to Serbia, demanding in part that Austrian officials be permitted to participate in the investigation of the crime. When the Serbian government accepted only part of the terms of the ultimatum, Austria-Hungary declared war on Serbia. Montenegro sided Serbia. Because of a multitude of cross-alliances, France and Russia came into the war on the side of Serbia, while Germany entered as an ally of Austria-Hungary. Britain entered when Germany violated Belgian neutrality, and World War I began. Bulgaria and Türkiye later entered on the

in 1878 as part of the Treaty of Berlin, but it had not formally annexed them. Serbia, supported by Russia, threatened to go to war against Austria in 1908, but Russia was forced to back down in 1909, and Serbia was left in the lurch.

It then began putting together an alliance of Balkan countries that led to the First and Second Balkan Wars in 1912–1913. Serbia obtained additional territories as a result of these conflicts. However, Austria frustrated Serbia's attempts to gain access to the Adriatic Sea coast, among other things by sponsoring creation of an independent Albania. In 1914, Serbia played an important role in the origins of World War I by sponsoring the Black Hand, a Serbian nationalist organization formed in 1911 with the goal of unifying all Serbs (its actual formal name was Unification or Death). The group orchestrated the assassination of Archduke Franz Ferdinand, heir to the Austrian throne.

Montenegro

Montenegro experienced centuries of independence, while the surrounding areas seethed under Turkish control. The

with the Austrian Empire, since Serbia also laid claim to Austrian lands occupied by South Slavs.

Relations worsened after Austria formally annexed Bosnia and Herzegovina in 1908. Austria had obtained these lands

The Former Yugoslavia

The last king of Montenegro, Nicholas I

side of Germany and Austria-Hungary, while Romania entered as an ally of France, Britain, and Russia. Thus, almost all of the Balkans became involved in the war. The US entered the war in 1917 siding with France, Britain, and Russia.

Austrian armies reached Belgrade by December 1914 but were repelled by a counterattack. Bulgaria's entry in 1915 helped shift the equation against Serbia. The Serbian army retreated to the Adriatic coast and then to the island of Corfu. In 1918, Allied forces made their way into the Balkan Peninsula. The Serbian army joined with the Allies in defeating Bulgaria, then liberated Serbia.

A New Nation Is Born

During the war, discussions were held on creating a separate state for South Slavs who had been part of the Austro-Hungarian Empire. Serb leaders hesitated at first because their longtime vision was of a single greater Serbian kingdom that would include all areas inhabited by Serbs. The remaining South Slavic leaders had something else in mind. They wanted a decentralized South Slavic state organized along federal lines that would allow a large amount of autonomy to the individual ethnic groups. Representatives of the two points of view signed the Corfu Pact in 1917 in which they agreed to create a South Slav state after the war under the Karadjordjević dynasty.

Although basically South Slav, what became Yugoslavia consisted literally of what was left over after France, Great Britain, and the US redrew a new map of eastern Europe after World War I. On December 4, 1918, the Kingdom of the Serbs, Croats, and Slovenes was proclaimed in Belgrade, with Prince Alexander of Serbia as regent. Serbia (including North

Macedonia and Kosovo), which had been independent before the war, formed the core of this new kingdom. The kingdom of Montenegro, also independent before the war, was unconditionally annexed by Serbia prior to the proclamation of the new South Slavic State. To this was added territories from the former Austro-Hungarian Empire—Croatia, the Vojvodina, Bosnia and Herzegovina, and Slovenia—plus strategic points taken from Bulgaria along the Serbian-Bulgarian border.

Politics of the Interwar Period

The political structure of this new kingdom was supposed to be decided by the Constituent Assembly elected in 1920. In 1921 it adopted a constitution creating a centralized government. The necessary votes came from the Serbian parties and smaller ones that had "sold" their votes in return for promises of special favors. This led the Croatian Peasant Party to boycott the assembly because of its opposition to the centralized system.

The period 1921–1928 was one of conflict between the Serbs and Croats over the question of centralism versus federalism. The Serbs prevailed by using increasingly harsh tactics, including the arrest of the Croat opposition leader and dissolving his party. Outraged, the Croatian deputies withdrew from parliament, swearing not to return until they had been granted a federal system in which Croatia would no longer be controlled from Belgrade. The demands of the Croats were unacceptable to the Serbian leaders and also to King Alexander.

Taking advantage of a decade of disagreement between the Serbs and Croats, the king abolished the constitution and proclaimed a royal dictatorship. He later changed the name of the country to the Kingdom of Yugoslavia, which did not alter the fact that Serbs, Croats, and Slovenes lived and fought with each other within the boundaries of the kingdom. Alexander's mistake was in thinking he could create a Yugoslav nationalism by decree.

The combatants at the start of World War I, 1914

The Former Yugoslavia

He was assassinated while making a state visit to France in 1934 by Macedonian and Croatian terrorists. The assassin was an agent of the Internal Macedonian Revolutionary Organization, while the Ustaše, a Croatian separatist group, also was implicated in the plot.

From 1934 to 1941, a three-man regency ruled the country, with Prince Paul as first regent. Internal affairs were left to the premier, who governed with the support of a specially organized party, the Yugoslav Radical Union. Parties in opposition formed an alliance and demanded a new constitution that would set up a government capable of dealing with the discontented Croats. When the extent of the Serb-Croat split was revealed in 1938 elections, the government sought talks with the Croatian leadership. The result was an agreement creating an internally self-governing Croatia.

In international relations during the interwar period, Yugoslavia was most concerned about protecting its borders against the ambitions of neighboring states and the great powers who wanted to use the conflicts among the Balkan states to extend their own influence. Both the "Little Entente" and the "Balkan Entente" were supposed to serve these purposes. In 1920–1921 Yugoslavia formed an alliance with Romania and Czechoslovakia, the "Little Entente," which was directed primarily against Hungarian ambitions to revise the Treaty of Trianon. France backed the "Little Entente" through treaties with Czechoslovakia (1924), Romania (1926), and Yugoslavia (1927).

After a series of conferences from 1930 to 1933, Greece, Türkiye, Romania, and Yugoslavia signed the Balkan Pact (February 1934) guaranteeing the territorial status quo against aggression by any Balkan state. In practice, this meant that the pact was directed against Bulgaria. Several months later, the signatories adopted the Statutes of the Balkan Entente that set up a permanent council provided for regular meetings and extensive economic and political cooperation. Both alliance systems disintegrated by the end of the 1930s.

The rise of Germany and Italy, the inability of the League of Nations to deal with acts of aggression, and the appeasement policy of Britain and France made Yugoslavia search for new means of ensuring its security. Accordingly, it signed a pact of friendship with Bulgaria (1937) and a nonaggression and arbitration pact with Italy in the same year. This moved Yugoslavia closer to the Axis powers.

During the late 1930s, Prince Paul repeatedly appealed to the British for arms and economic assistance in order to ward off an increasingly militant Germany. His requests fell on deaf ears. Germany, Italy,

Assassination: King Alexander of Yugoslavia at Marseilles, France, October 1934

and Japan signed the Tripartite Pact in September 1940, which bound their nations into a military alliance. Yugoslavia was greatly alarmed, especially when Germany became insistent that Yugoslavia also sign that pact.

Prince Paul resisted and stalled for time. He wanted to transfer a whole and sovereign nation to his nephew, King Peter, then only 17 and soon to be of age. Notwithstanding the fact that they had ignored

Prince Paul of Yugoslavia

Paul's pleas for assistance, the British were totally opposed to any action by Yugoslavia that would strengthen the hand of the Axis powers.

Feeling the noose tightening around his multiethnic nation, Prince Paul instructed his ministers to draw up three conditions for signing the pact which he felt certain Hitler would never accept: (1) that the sovereignty and territorial integrity of Yugoslavia would be respected; (2) that no military assistance would be requested of Yugoslavia and also no passage of troops through the country in the event of war; and (3) acknowledgment of Yugoslavia's interest in a free outlet to the Aegean Sea through Salonika, Greece.

Hitler surprised Prince Paul and the Yugoslav government by readily agreeing to its terms (with no thought of respecting them), and the pact was reluctantly signed. However, Hitler omitted the second clause denying German troops access to Yugoslavia's transportation system.

The apparent alliance with the Axis powers infuriated many Yugoslavs, particularly the independent-minded Serbs. It embittered the British, with whom Prince Paul had always been close. Accordingly, Great Britain was instrumental in staging a coup d'etat in March 1941 that resulted in the overthrow of Prince Paul's government. The new regime made the King Peter a temporary puppet. It sent a discouraged Prince Paul into poverty-stricken exile, wrapped in the undeserved mantle of a Nazi sympathizer when, in truth, he hated Nazi Germany.

World War II

Certain Yugoslav officials and army officers bitterly opposed the government's decision to sign the Tripartite Pact and, thus, apparently to join the Axis side in 1941. Following the military coup, the army announced a policy of neutrality and continued Prince Paul's policy. The Nazis saw through this transparent plan and attacked Yugoslavia 10 days later, after which Germany dissolved Yugoslavia. Germany retained part, while other areas were distributed to friends and supporters.

Croatia was enlarged and placed in the hands of Ante Pavelić, a Nazi ally. Slovenia was divided between Germany and Italy; Macedonia was occupied by Bulgaria; parts of Bosnia and Dalmatia went to Italy; a small piece in the north was given to Hungary; and German administration was imposed on Serbia. A puppet government was established in Belgrade.

From 1941 to 1944, Yugoslavia was ravaged not only by struggles against the Nazi occupation but also by civil war between the Chetnik and Partisan resistance forces, as well as between Partisans and Ustasha forces in Croatia. The Chetniks were bands of officers and men drawn from the remnants of the Royal Yugoslav Army. Loosely organized and generally undisciplined, they were pro-Serbian and anticommunist. The Partisans, led by Josip Broz (known by his revolutionary *nom de guerre* simply as Tito) and the Yugoslav Communist Party, tried to form an organization with a broader, national following.

The Communist Party had been one of the largest parties in the Constituent Assembly elected in 1920. Its goal was the establishment of a Yugoslav Soviet Republic. In 1921, however, the government banned the party after the murder of the minister of the interior, although there was no evidence linking the party to the assassination. The party remained illegal throughout the interwar period, which meant that its members were forced to operate underground.

Tito was one of its early leaders. The son of a Croat peasant and a Slovene mother, he had been inducted into the Austrian army during World War I and was taken prisoner of war by a Russian detachment at the age of 23. He escaped from prison in Russia and joined the Bolsheviks, fighting with them in the Russian civil war. After he returned to Yugoslavia, he became the secretary of the Zagreb branch of the Communist Party of Yugoslavia. When the party was declared illegal in 1921, he was arrested and sentenced to five years of hard labor.

By 1937, he was the secretary-general of the party, which he reorganized and purged in accordance with the latest dictates from Moscow. After the Germans occupied the country, he used his control of the party organization to create guerrilla units called "Partisans" for use against the Germans.

At first, Partisans and Chetniks attempted to fight side by side. But it soon became evident that, while they were both struggling to free Yugoslavia from Axis control, their image of the country's future was totally different. The Chetniks were fighting for the return of the monarch and a Serb-dominated government. The Partisans were fighting for a federally organized, socialist republic. There was also a disagreement on general military strategy. The Partisans wanted all-out resistance, while the Chetniks, afraid of German reprisals, wanted to wait for the arrival of the Allies.

Eventually the Chetniks and Partisans were fighting each other as hard as they fought the common enemy. In order to combat the Partisans and prevent the Germans from killing Serbs, the Chetniks began to collaborate with the German occupiers. Evidence of collaboration resulted in a loss of Allied support for them. The British sent a military mission to aid the Partisans several months before there was a similar move by the Soviets. The western powers thus formally recognized the Partisans' contribution to the war effort and Tito's leadership.

Under Tito's direction, the Anti-Fascist Council for National Liberation of Yugoslavia (AVNOJ) was formed in 1942 to function as a government in liberated territories. A year later, at the town of Jajce in Bosnia, AVNOJ elected a provisional government that named Tito premier and marshal of Yugoslavia. AVNOJ thus replaced the nominal authority of the government-in- exile, located in London, and it forbade King Peter, successor to Prince Paul, to return. The British then persuaded the king to appoint Dr. Ivan Shubashich (Šubašić) as premier of the exiled government on the assumption that Shubashich, who had been governor of Croatia until 1941, was a man who could negotiate with the Partisans.

In October 1944 Soviet and Partisan forces liberated Belgrade. It is significant that, by the time Red Army forces arrived in Belgrade, the Partisans were in firm control of large parts of Yugoslavia. Tito and Shubashich signed an agreement providing for a regency council to act in the king's name; free elections within three months of liberation; and a legislature consisting of AVNOJ until an assembly could be convened. The "Big Three"—the US, the USSR, and Great Britain—approved this arrangement at the Yalta Conference in February 1945, and the king was thus forced to accept it. Three regents were chosen in March 1945—a Serb, a Croat, and a Slovene. None was a communist, but all had Tito's approval.

Tito formed a new government in which he was premier and Shubashich was foreign minister. The cabinet included representatives from each of the six areas of Yugoslavia and the government-in-exile. Before the elections for a constituent assembly took place, Shubashich resigned, protesting the government's refusal to allow "collaborators" to vote. This term was loosely applied to anyone who opposed the government. The elections were boycotted by the opposition parties—the Serbian Radical Party, Agrarian Party, Democratic Party, and Croat Peasant Party—in protest against the atmosphere of intimidation created by what had become a very active secret police. As a result, the people could vote only for the Communist People's Front list of candidates.

Yugoslavia Becomes the Socialist Federal Republic of Yugoslavia (SFRJ)

The Constituent Assembly that was elected declared Yugoslavia to be a federal people's republic. When a new constitution was adopted in early 1946, the assembly changed its name to the People's Assembly. This body consisted of two houses, a Chamber of Nationalities and a Federal Chamber. The Chamber of Nationalities had 30 representatives from each of the 6 federal republics, plus 15 from the autonomous province of Kosovo and 20 from the autonomous region of Vojvodina. In theory, therefore, it served a function somewhat similar to that of the US Senate. The Federal Chamber was the "popular body," with 1 representative for every 50,000 inhabitants.

The People's Assembly was not designed as a deliberative body, however.

Marshal Josip Broz-Tito, leader of the Partisans in World War II

The Former Yugoslavia

It met only twice a year, on April and October 15, and then only to rubber-stamp government decisions. More power resided with the presidium of the People's Assembly, since the presidium appointed and dismissed cabinet ministers and had law-making authority when the assembly was not in session. As with all communist regimes, however, real power rested with the Communist Party.

Although the government remained in theory a "people's front," the policies it instituted during this period were based on Soviet models. Larger estates were expropriated, and a beginning was made on the establishment of collective farms. In 1947, the government launched its first five-year plan. In industry, emphasis was placed on electrification, chemicals, and metallurgy. Foreign trade was oriented toward the eastern bloc nations.

The Soviet-Yugoslav Dispute of 1948

Yugoslavia had been considered such a loyal satellite that the new Communist Information Bureau, or Cominform, set up in September 1947, had established its headquarters in Belgrade. But a quarrel began over the issue of joint Yugoslav-Soviet companies. Two joint companies were actually set up, for air transport and river shipping. But the way they were operated appeared so disadvantageous to the Yugoslavs that they refused to allow any further joint companies to be formed. This led to a bitter dispute between Tito and Stalin and resulted in the curtailment of Soviet aid and a reduction of trade between Yugoslavia and the east.

The dispute marked the first time a ruling communist party had defied Moscow's authority and still remained in power. The disagreement pointed to the question of the power relations between the two countries. Tito's challenge to Moscow was possible because his political survival did not depend on Stalin's support. Unlike the communist leaders of other eastern European countries (except Albania), Tito had not come to power by the might of the Soviet army but because of his personal following in the Partisan movement, which had the leading role in liberating Yugoslavia at the end of the war. In fact, there were no longer any Red Army troops on Yugoslav soil in 1948.

After the war, the Yugoslav communists had thought of themselves as Moscow's most faithful followers. Tito's desire to follow the correct line was evident in the enthusiasm with which he modeled Yugoslavia's economy and constitution on those of the Soviet Union. It was in recognition of Tito's importance that Stalin set up the Cominform headquarters in Belgrade.

In light of this background, the real dispute was not Yugoslav departure from the official Moscow communist line or

A sample of an Ex-Yugoslav banknote

any other one issue. It was the refusal to be controlled by Moscow in matters that affected the interests of Yugoslavia. The question was how two communist parties and their leaders should conduct their mutual relations when each was also responsible for the interests of his own state.

Stalin's opposition to any communist power that was not under his personal control was shown by his attitude toward the plans for a Balkan federation authorized by Tito and supported by Dmitrov, the Bulgarian communist leader. The Bulgarians even agreed that, after federation, Yugoslavia should annex the part of Macedonia that was within Bulgaria. By 1947, the plans included the possibility of bringing Albania, Romania, and Greece into some kind of union, and there were hints of a Balkan-Danubian Federation involving Hungary.

Sensing an increase in Tito's power if there were federation, Stalin abruptly reversed his early support for the plan. When the Bulgarian leadership expressed hope for a customs union as a step toward federation, *Pravda*, the Moscow official newspaper, responded with an article stating that the Balkan states did not need any kind of customs union or federation. At a meeting in the Kremlin in 1948, Stalin and Foreign Minister Molotov took both Bulgaria and Yugoslavia to task—the Bulgarians for planning a customs union with Romania and the Yugoslavs for providing assistance to the Greek communists and for sending troops into Albania without Moscow's approval.

There were also other issues involved. The Yugoslavs were critical of the Soviet failure to send aid to the Partisans during the war and of Stalin's instructions to play down the role of the Communist Party in the resistance movement. They could not forget that Stalin had opposed setting up the AVNOJ as the supreme authority in 1943. The Yugoslavs were also angry at the Soviet Union for its failure to press Yugoslavia's claim to Trieste against Italy at the close of the war, presumably because Stalin did not want to antagonize the Allies by bringing up the claim.

In response, Stalin accused the Yugoslavs of directing propaganda against the Soviet Union and of having an "unduly large" peasant membership in their Communist Party. There were also accusations that the party was being run "undemocratically." Another charge was that the Yugoslavs treated the Soviet military advisors and civilian experts as foreigners.

The Yugoslavs requested that the dispute be settled by two-party discussions. Instead, the Soviets called a meeting of the Cominform and issued a statement in mid-1948 indicating that the member parties backed the Soviet position. The Yugoslav Communist Party was expelled from the Cominform, Stalin denounced Tito, and his name became a symbol of "nationalist deviationism" among communist leaders who courted Moscow's favor. Despite its economic and diplomatic isolation, however, Yugoslavia survived and established a precedent for other challenges to Soviet authority that followed after Stalin's death.

Relations with the US improved after Tito's expulsion from the Cominform, but they remained correct rather than cordial.

Politics after 1949

Yugoslavia began to search for new trading partners, for a new foreign policy that would demonstrate its independence, and for a new statement of principles that would explain the changes introduced in the Yugoslav system after the break with Moscow. In domestic politics, the two themes that were developed were decentralization and economic democracy. The first step came in 1950 with the creation of "workers' councils" in all state-owned economic enterprises. At the same time, the former economic ministries that had directed the economy were abolished and replaced by national coordinating councils made up of representatives from each of the republics. Thus, the central directive role of the state was reduced, while the participatory role of the workers was enhanced at the local level.

Beginning in 1952, producers' councils were created at the local and republic

The Former Yugoslavia

Belgrade University Library

levels. In 1953, the constitution was modified to incorporate the concept of workers' self-management, and a national Council of Producers was created as a second national legislative body to replace the Chamber of Nationalities. The Chamber of Nationalities was not abolished, however, but was partially amalgamated into the Federal Chamber. What was different about the national Council of Producers, as well as the local and republic producers' councils, was that representation was on the basis of occupation, and persons voted where they worked.

Decentralization was considered to apply primarily to economic decision making. In the political arena, other constitutional changes were made to create a more obvious central political authority. The old executive structure of a "presidium of the National Assembly" and a Council of Ministers was abolished and replaced by

a "president of the republic" with true executive powers, assisted by a Federal Executive Council. Marshal Tito became the new president. The Communist Party also changed its name at this time and became the League of Communists of Yugoslavia. However, it was not willing to give up its monopoly of political power.

Milovan Djilas, a vice premier and president of the National Assembly, published a series of articles in the communist newspaper *Borba* in late 1953, in which he argued, among other things, that "no class or political movement can claim the exclusive right to represent society as a whole or to proclaim their ideas as objective truth." For this, he was expelled from the Politburo and Central Committee and forced to resign his government offices. Later he would be imprisoned for more critical things he would write. The most famous was his study of the way the new

communist elite had become a privileged dominant class. It was appropriately entitled *The New Class*.

A new constitution was adopted in 1963 that extended the concept of worker's self-management to that of "social self-management." In a move toward greater economic democracy, more authority was given to local communes, to the governments of the republics, and to the organs of self-management in the economy. These changes compounded Yugoslavia's problems with regionalism, however, and reopened conflict between the liberals and conservatives, as well as between the wealthier and poorer republics. The less-developed republics, such as Serbia and Montenegro, argued that the changes benefited only the developed republics. Croatia and Slovenia, on the other hand, argued that the changes did not go far enough and that they were still subsidizing the rest of the country.

One of the foremost opponents of the reforms was Alexander Ranković, then vice president of Yugoslavia, strongman of the Serbian party organization, influential in the security police, and once considered a likely successor to Tito. The decision to expel him from the Central Committee in 1966 was a decisive victory for the reformists, this time backed by Tito.

Although the decision was a blow to Serb nationalists, it did not eliminate the basic anxiety of the remaining republics over Serbian domination of Yugoslavia. In order to provide the individual republics a greater stake in the general affairs of the country, a group of amendments was adopted in 1967 giving a stronger voice to the Chamber of Nationalities and in general increasing the role of the individual republics in decision making at the center.

There was another series of amendments in 1971 that, in addition to establishing a collective presidency to handle the matter of the succession after Tito, made a number of economic changes. Worker councils were given greater authority to determine how the surplus funds of their enterprises were to be allocated. Private individuals were guaranteed the right to work with their own "means of production" and to employ workers on a contractual basis.

In 1974, a new constitution introduced a system of elections to the various legislative assemblies based on delegations drawn from occupational and interest groups. It also provided that the federal legislature—the Assembly of the Socialist Federal Republic of Yugoslavia—be made up of an equal number of delegates from each of Yugoslavia's six republics. Elections to the federal legislature were indirect. Assemblymen of the individual republics, themselves representing local occupation and interest groups, selected delegates to the federal legislature.

The Former Yugoslavia

One purpose of the new system was to give the League of Communists of Yugoslavia (LCY) greater control over the elected representatives. Under its self-managing socialism, Yugoslavia had created a degree of economic democracy; politically, however, the LCY retained its monopoly of power.

The 1970s saw a number of purges within the party. The most prominent was the mass sacking of the Croatian wing of the LCY in 1971–1972 because of alleged nationalistic deviations. Between 1972 and 1974, there were additional purges within the Serbian wing, this time because of an overly liberal attitude toward dissent within LCY ranks. Despite these mass firings, there remained a large core of veterans, both in the LCY and the government, who had remained more or less continuously in office since 1945.

The core of the problem was that the LCY attempted to withdraw from direct control of the economy while retaining an overall political ascendancy. The economic reforms devolved considerable authority to the republic level, to regional banks, and to individual enterprises. The result was to create a tremendous stake in control over local economic activity. This often encouraged local decisions at variance with national political policy, in particular the commitment at the national level to redistribute funds to poorer areas of the country for the purpose of financing industrialization. After Tito's death in 1980, it also acted to frustrate attempts of the new national leadership to control growing inflation through a national austerity program. What Yugoslavs discovered was that, after control over the economy had been shifted to the republic and autonomous provincial level, the federal government no longer had the tools to manipulate the economy.

Foreign Policy: Communist Era

Yugoslavia was a "friend" of the west so long that it was easy to forget that its leaders remained communists and that its relations with the west were the result of Stalin having expelled it from the communist bloc. Nevertheless, this break led Yugoslavia to sign a five-year Treaty of Friendship and Assistance with Türkiye and Greece in 1953 that was subsequently known as the Balkan Pact. The following year, it was converted into a defensive alliance. Yugoslavia also settled an outstanding issue with Italy that had been left over from World War II, the disposition of Trieste, by agreeing to divide the disputed land.

In addition, it built up its international prestige by actively courting the nonaligned nations of Africa and Asia. These nations accepted Yugoslavian leadership in the nonaligned movement because Tito

The May 5, 1980, edition of *Politika* announces Tito's death

had given Yugoslavia what they thought of as the best of all possible worlds—following a course of socialist development though free of Soviet control, and receiving aid from the west but without becoming an economic adjunct to capitalism.

Yugoslavia thus positioned itself between the two blocs. It was never an ally of the United States, and it welcomed the resumption of diplomatic relations with the Soviet Union in June 1953, after the death of Stalin. Thereafter, Yugoslav-Soviet relations alternated between periods of calm and storm, depending on the extent of control Moscow was attempting to exercise over Yugoslavia.

Soviet leaders Bulganin and Khrushchev visited Belgrade in 1955, and in the subsequent communique, they acknowledged that what Yugoslavia was doing was their own business. In turn, Tito agreed to support Soviet policy on arms limitation, the division of Germany, and the admission of the People's Republic of China (PRC) to the UN.

There were further improvements in Yugoslav-Soviet relations following Khrushchev's denunciations of Stalin in 1956, the dissolution of the Cominform in that same year, and the dismissal of Vyacheslav Molotov as Soviet foreign minister. All of these moves indicated a Soviet acceptance of the possibility of different paths toward socialism. By June 1956, the two sides announced that they had achieved a "complete normalization" of relations on party and state levels.

But this was only a brief interlude. The actions of the Soviets and the apparent willingness to deal with Yugoslavia on an independent basis created false hopes of liberalization in Poland and Hungary. Hungary embarked upon a liberal and more independent course. The result was a harsh Soviet military invasion in the fall of 1956. Subsequent Soviet attacks on "revisionism" reopened the old conflict between Tito and Moscow. It was not until 1960–1961 that a new attempt to smooth relations was made, probably to counteract the effect of increasing difficulties between the Soviet Union and China.

In 1968–1969, Soviet-Yugoslav relations suffered once again under the impact of an international crisis. Tito had spoken out in favor of programs of liberalization that were taking place in Czechoslovakia. When the Soviet Union and its Warsaw Pact allies intervened militarily in that country, Tito voiced his condemnation of this move in the strongest terms. He rejected the Brezhnev Doctrine, the Soviet explanation for the move, as no more than an attempt to justify a violation of the sovereignty of a communist state by invoking the higher interests of socialism.

In 1971, Leonid Brezhnev paid a visit to Yugoslavia for the first time since the invasion of Czechoslovakia. During the meeting with Tito, the Soviet leader disavowed the existence of any doctrine of limited sovereignty and, to Tito's satisfaction, endorsed the view that each country had the right to develop socialism according to its own experience. The reaffirmation of the 1955 Belgrade Declaration opened the door to better relations between the two countries.

One major issue between Yugoslavia and the Soviet Union in the 1970s was the latter's desire for a European Communist Conference. Yugoslavian participation was extremely important because without the Yugoslavs several of the western European communist parties would have refused to attend.

Yugoslavia's price, exacted at a 1974 preparatory meeting in Warsaw, was that the meeting was to be open to the public, that it would not become a forum for attacking parties that had declined to attend, and that all decisions were to be by consensus. Yugoslavia was supported in this stand by Romania and by the delegates representing the Italian, Spanish, and French parties.

The conference finally took place in the summer of 1976 in East Berlin. Although it endorsed the main lines of Soviet foreign policy, the Soviets were not happy with other parts of the concluding document, which reiterated the Yugoslav-Romanian formula for interparty relations of "voluntary cooperation" based on the principles of equality, sovereignty, noninterference in internal affairs, and respect for different roads to socialism.

Soviet-Yugoslav relations remained at about the same level until December 1979, when the Yugoslavs condemned the Soviet invasion of Afghanistan, and relations turned cool. Yugoslavia did sign a 10-year economic agreement with the Soviet Union in 1980. As a result of the second oil crisis in 1979, Yugoslavia was finding it harder and harder to compete in western markets. The agreement seemed to offer the promise of a long-term market for Yugoslav goods. The Soviets paid in convertible rubles, however. As the Yugoslav government learned, convertible rubles were of little value if the Soviet Union was not producing the things Yugoslavia was willing to import. Belgrade eventually built up a huge credit of several billion rubles that it was unable to use.

Relations improved after Gorbachev came to power in 1985. The Yugoslavian people welcomed him enthusiastically when he visited in March 1988. He traveled and spoke around the country. In retrospect, the visit took on a greater significance because of his assertion, in the agreed joint statement at the conclusion of the stay, that every country had a right to pursue its chosen variant of communism. This statement, which was essentially a repudiation of the Brezhnev Doctrine, paved the way for the 1989 revolutions in central and eastern Europe.

Post-Cold War

US-Yugoslav relations were always based on the premise that Yugoslavia espoused a nonexpansionist communism. Therefore, it was a more benign form and offered an alternate pattern of development that might influence other communist countries in central and eastern Europe. Because of this strategic role assigned to it, the US supported a unified, federal Yugoslavia.

The 1989 collapse of communism ended this strategic role for Yugoslavia. In fact, it was exposed as a badly run communist state. Reformers in the western part of the country argued first for radical reforms, only to have their projects blocked by the Serb leadership. They then abandoned communism and carried out democratic elections. In Serbia, however, the communists changed the name of their party but managed to keep political control. Since they continued to obstruct real reform at the federal level, the democratic reformers eventually opted for independence.

The US government never understood the dynamics of what was going on in Yugoslavia and continued to support a unified Yugoslavia even after it had become clear that such a Yugoslavia would be dominated by a Serbia that had not shed its communist policies. For example, even after Slobodan Milošević had destroyed the autonomy of Kosovo and Vojvodina, had instituted a boycott of goods from Slovenia, had organized Serbs in other parts to oppose their republics' policies, and had undermined the economic policy of the Yugoslav government at the national level, Secretary of State James Baker announced in the summer of 1991 that the United States would not support a breakup of Yugoslavia "under any circumstances."

Thus encouraged, Milošević, supported by the Yugoslav People's Army—the last stronghold of communism at the national level—launched his war against Croatia and threatened one against Bosnia and Herzegovina. Even in November 1991, when Serbia's aims had become clear to the world and the EU had decided to institute economic sanctions against Serbia and Montenegro, the two aggressors, the US decided to levy economic sanctions against both sides, aggressors and victims.

This was a classic case of a policy outliving its usefulness. The EC extended recognition to Slovenia and Croatia on January 15, 1992. The US waited another three months before following suit. Ambassador Warren Zimmermann remained in Belgrade, however, and Washington continued to maintain good relations with the Serb-dominated Yugoslav government. All of this ended when, with US backing, the UN voted to impose economic sanctions against Serbia and Montenegro in May 1992. The US government had begun to press Serbia on its treatment of Albanians in Kosovo. On March 23, Zimmermann traveled to Prishtina to open an exhibition organized to mark the 50th anniversary of the Voice of America. While there, he held talks with representatives of Albanian parties.

The Former Yugoslavia

Yugoslavia after Tito

Speculation about the internal and international outlook for Yugoslavia centered on the question of what would happen to the country when President Tito disappeared from the scene. The aging leader and his associates were aware of the problem. They decided to establish a system of post-Tito government designed to keep the country together in spite of deep-seated animosities among the various nationalities.

The Constitution of 1974, while making Tito president for life, provided for several collective bodies, including a rotating presidency of the supreme governing council, representative of the major national units. This body began to function when Tito, struggling for months against a terminal illness, gave up his position as chief of state. The collective leadership thus gained experience in running the state without Tito at the helm. When he finally died in May 1980, his funeral became the occasion for a glittering assembly of heads of state and other dignitaries, ranging from kings to leaders of communist states.

The new leadership functioned with modest success until 1988, although it was unable to reverse growing economic difficulties. When the government attempted to bring inflation under control, it ran up against the mandate of the 1974 constitution that all significant federal decisions had to be decided by consensus. It proved to be impossible to come up with an ant inflation policy that the leaderships of the six republics and two provinces could agree on. The result was stalemate at the center. The government was reduced to muddling through.

By 1988, the annual rate of inflation was 200% and growing. Worried about their dropping standard of living, workers launched a series of strikes. Intellectuals, losing confidence in the system, began to demand changes. In less-developed areas of the country, there was also growing dissatisfaction among individual ethnic groups who had come to believe that the system was treating them unfairly. Among the most disaffected were the ethnic Albanians of the autonomous province of Kosovo.

Greater Serbian Domination Threatens the Union

Up to that moment, one might have described the situation as serious but not threatening. What turned it into a crisis was the emergence of a new Serbian leader, Slobodan Milošević, who launched a broad movement to reassert Serbian leadership. Arguing that the promotion of regionalism was the root cause of Yugoslavia's problems, he demanded control over the police, judiciary, and economy in the two autonomous provinces of Vojvodina and Kosovo. In addition, he demanded a radical increase in Serbia's power within the Yugoslav Federation.

To achieve these goals, Milošević began mobilizing the Serbian masses. In Vojvodina, 100,000 Serbs besieged the provincial parliament in September 1988, forcing the resignation of the entire Vojvodina leadership and their replacement by Milošević loyalists. The same tactics were also tried against Kosovo, and demonstrations and counterdemonstrations continued over the next several months.

Meanwhile, inflation continued to grow, and the worsening economic situation, coupled with the growing ethnic problems, led to a collapse of the Yugoslav government on December 30, 1988. Finally, Ante Marković, president of the Federal Executive Council, decided to take advantage of loopholes in the law and propose an economic stabilization program. Approved by the federal parliament on December 20, 1989, it went into effect on January 1, 1990. The program consisted of making the Yugoslavian dinar convertible by pegging it to the German mark, allowing interest to rise to market levels, and removing price controls from most goods. The price of certain items, including various raw materials and energy, were frozen. The program worked. By March, inflation had sunk from over 2,000% to 8.4%.

Political developments continued to move in a direction that threatened the future of the united Yugoslav state. In January, an emergency congress of the League of Communists was held, among other things, to discuss the creation of a multiparty system. There was a serious split. On one side were the hard-liners, led by Slobodan Milošević of Serbia; on the other were those pushing for a multiparty system, led by Ciril Ribičič of Slovenia. The congress actually passed a resolution favoring creation of a multiparty system, but the Slovenian delegation walked out, thus bringing it to a halt. They were particularly incensed about an economic boycott against Slovenia that Serbia had instituted in November.

Thus, while Milošević was threatening in Serbia to colonize the province of Kosovo, Slovenia was moving toward creating a multiparty democracy and suggesting that it saw no future for itself in Yugoslavia. In the April 1990 elections, Slovenes split their votes, electing Milan Kučan, candidate of the communists, as president while giving control of the legislature to the Demos, a coalition of conservative political parties that had campaigned on a platform of independence within a year. A month later, Croatia held its own multiparty elections, which were won by the Croatian Democratic Union, which campaigned on a platform of making a confederation of sovereign states out of Yugoslavia.

North Macedonia and Bosnia and Herzegovina held their own free, multiparty elections in November 1990. Montenegro and Serbia were scheduled to hold multiparty elections in December 1990. In Serbia, Milošević decided to consolidate his control by transforming the Serbian branch of the League of Communists of Yugoslavia (LCY) into the Serbian Socialist Party. Thus, the old LCY, already a minority in all of the republics other than Montenegro and Serbia, ceased to exist as a national party except in the Yugoslav army, where the leadership remained communist. This was a strange action by someone who claimed to stand for a strong, unified country. In fact, Milošević was a Serbian nationalist who was only interested in a united Yugoslavia if he could dominate it completely. Otherwise, he would tear it apart and seize what other pieces he could.

A look at the policies he pursued bears that out. Appealing to Serbian nationalism, he demanded greater control in the two autonomous provinces of Kosovo and

Slobodan Milosevic at The Hague

Vojvodina, eventually destroying their autonomy completely. In 1990, his agents began organizing Serbian nationals living in the other republics, fomenting them to demand secession of their areas from their republics and union with Serbia. He personally declared that he would rectify boundaries and reclaim Serbian lands if the federation broke up. The other republics had always reacted negatively to the idea of a Serbian-dominated Yugoslav government, which reminded them of the period after World War I when Serbs dominated the new Yugoslavia. Milošević's Serbian chauvinism and his destruction of the autonomy of Kosovo and Vojvodina convinced many non-Serbs that he intended once again to assert Serbia's control over all of Yugoslavia. At least three separate actions he took in 1990–1991 contributed to that perception.

In December 1990, in the lead-up to Serbian elections, Milošević undermined the financial stability of the national government by illegally siphoning off $1.5 billion from the Yugoslav National Bank. The money was taken in the form of a "loan" authorized by a vote in the Serbian legislature. Both the assembly session and the removal of the money were kept secret from Yugoslavia's federal government. He then used the money to pay for pensions and salaries, which he had raised in the run-up to Serbian elections. The increases were undoubtedly a factor in the elections, which he and his Serbian Socialist Party won handily.

The other republics were outraged when they learned of Milošević's actions. Since the $1.5 billion was half of the new money the Yugoslav National Bank had assigned for circulation in 1991 in all six republics, his action seriously undermined the federal government's economic stabilization program.

Milošević's second stunt was to organize a boycott of Slovenian products and to begin levying a tariff on all items brought into Serbia from that republic. This effectively negated the concept of a united Yugoslavia. His third move in his program of rule or ruin was to block election of a new federal president in May 1991. The outgoing president was Borisav Jović, a Serb. Under Yugoslavia's system of rotating presidencies, the incoming president was the man who had held the vice presidency for the previous year, Stipe Mesić, a Croat.

To be sure, Milošević was not the sole offender. In 1990, when the leaders of Slovenia and Croatia began pushing for a change in the structure of the Yugoslav Federation to create greater autonomy for the individual republics, they passed laws declaring their laws to be superior to federal law and also created republic militias. The sad thing is that this quarreling

In economically torn Montenegro, a youngster holds up a sign, "We wait for you, where are you, Slobo" (Serbian leader Slobodan Milosevic), during an antigovernment demonstration in Titograd (now Podgorica).

The Former Yugoslavia

completely undermined the economic stabilization program of the federal government. Only the Yugoslav People's Army (JNA) remained united at this point, although there were clear signs that this unity was very frail and depended on the army's not getting involved in the quarrels between the individual republics.

The army also had its own problems. The most important was that there was strong sentiment within the military to preserve a united Yugoslavia, even if it meant using force against a part of the Yugoslav people. A second problem was that 70% of the officers were Serbs, and a good percentage of them were attracted to Milošević's program. A third factor was that the army was the one remaining place where the LCY continued to exist. A final factor was that, while the officers were mainly Serbian, ordinary soldiers were conscripts who came from throughout Yugoslavia. Many feared, therefore, that the army would begin to disintegrate if it intervened against an individual republic and if it were perceived as doing so on behalf of either Serbia or the LCY.

Yugoslavia Falls Apart

On May 19, 1991, the Croatian government held a referendum on independence. After a favorable vote, the Croatian Assembly adopted a declaration of independence on June 25. The Slovene government adopted its own declaration of independence on the same day. Both governments reiterated, however, that they remained willing to join a looser Yugoslav confederation in which the central government would handle foreign policy, defense, and such economic matters as a common currency.

Meanwhile, the Yugoslav People's Army reacted to the declarations by sending an invasion force into Slovenia. That republic was selected because it had moved to take control of its international border with Italy and Austria. The JNA was not expecting much opposition, but the Slovenians fought back valiantly. Meanwhile, the rest of the world, which had encouraged the army action by asserting that they would not support a separate Slovenia or Croatia "under any circumstances," began calling for a cease-fire. At the same time, army desertions by non-Serbs were a problem.

This led to an agreement with Slovenia that it could staff the control posts if it would turn the revenues over to the central government. Other aspects of the agreement were that the JNA would return to the barracks; Slovenia and Croatia would suspend their declarations of independence for three months; and Serbia would allow Stipe Mesić to be elected president. The latter aspect of the agreement was important in a military as well

as a political sense because the president was also the JNA commander-in-chief.

The agreement brought peace to Slovenia but not to Yugoslavia. One of the first actions of President Mesić was to arrange a cease-fire—the third—on July 2. That same day, in an interview that appeared on Belgrade television, General Blagoje Adžić, chief of the JNA general staff, angrily repudiated the cease-fire and thereby his own commander-in-chief. He then added that the army "accepted the challenge of total war that had been imposed on it" and would soon end it with a complete victory. The next day, an armored column left Belgrade for Croatia.

After Slovenia and Croatia had begun moving toward independence, Slobodan Milošević called upon Serbs in other republics to remain loyal and not to allow the Yugoslav union to be destroyed. In Croatia, Serbs organized Serbian governments in two different parts of Croatia and declared these regions to be independent of Croatia. Hoping to conciliate the Serb leaders, the Croatian legislature passed a law guaranteeing protection for minority ethnic groups within the republic. However, the new Croat constitution described the new republic as being for Croats. This heightened Serb fears by reawakening memories of World War II. Arguing that Serbs could secede from Croatia if Croatia could secede from Yugoslavia, Croatian Serbs held a referendum on July 7 affirming their intention to remain a part of the Socialist Federal Republic of Yugoslavia.

War against Croatia

President Milošević gave a speech on July 6, 1991, in which he told Serbs to be ready to defend themselves. He also gave Serb leaders in Croatia generous access to Serbian radio and television. The first fighting in Croatia began on July 7, 1991—the same day as the referendum—when Croatian Serbs attacked Croatian territorial defense forces near the town of Tenja.

As soon as fighting broke out, the Yugoslav People's Army (JNA) sent in its own units "to keep the peace." However, its targets were always Croatian territorial units. There were no reports whatsoever of any Serbian territorial units being in conflict with JNA forces. The fighting remained small-scale for some time, since President Franjo Tudjman had ordered Croatian units not to attack the JNA, and the JNA had its own instructions not to initiate battles but only to intervene when new fighting occurred. Gradually, however, the JNA's control of Croatian territory spread, as Serb territorial forces launched new battles in area after area.

The problem for Croatia was that Serbs insisted on living in a state controlled by Serbs. But Croatians were not entirely free

of this mentality of expansion. The Republic of Bosnia and Herzegovina, which lies between Serbia and Croatia, has an extremely mixed population, with 44% Bošnjak (Muslim), 33% Serbs, and about 17% Croats. President Tudjman admitted in July 1991 that members of his government had held secret talks with Serbian leaders about carving up Bosnia between Serbia and Croatia, leaving a small Muslim rump that neither wanted. Word of these talks did not help Croatia's image.

Croatia was saved by the fact that Serbia and the JNA were even more bloody-minded. In August 1991, Milošević revealed his plans for a reconstituted Yugoslavia. They called for carving up Croatia and incorporating about a third of the territory into the new state, even though Serbs constituted only about 12% of Croatia's population at this time.

Meanwhile the JNA, which up to this time had contended that it was acting as a neutral buffer between the two sides, began bombarding Croatian cities with artillery and aircraft. In late August, much of the city of Vukovar was destroyed. By this time, perhaps 20% of the republic had fallen under JNA or Serb militia control. On September 18, Zagreb, the capital, came under fire from aircraft and artillery.

Up to this moment, the Croatian government had been carrying out a "passive defense" and refusing to challenge the JNA directly. But it now retaliated against the JNA actions by cutting the oil lines that ran across Croatia to Serbia and laying siege to Yugoslav army barracks in Croatia. The Yugoslav navy implemented a siege around Croatia's Dalmatian ports. It later bombarded, first Split, then Dubrovnik, with artillery shells and missiles, damaging them considerably. Dubrovnik was rebuilt with international assistance after the war ended.

Croatia got some indirect assistance from other republics when Bosnia and Herzegovina and North Macedonia publicly declared their neutrality and ordered their citizens to ignore conscription notices from the JNA. The Serbian and Montenegrin political response was to order general mobilization in both of those republics. Even in Serbia, however, many young men went into hiding rather than serve.

The European Community (EC, later the EU) had put itself forth as a peacemaker even before the war began. Subsequently it negotiated cease-fire after cease-fire, only to see each new one broken. It threatened Serbia with an economic embargo without effect. It arranged for a peace conference to begin at The Hague on September 7, 1991. The EC then appointed former British foreign minister Lord Carrington as chairman of the European peace conference and sent him to Yugoslavia. He met with Presidents Milošević and Tudjman, plus General Kadijević, the Yugoslav defense minister. The three agreed that the JNA ought to return to its barracks, that the Croatian national guard should be demobilized, and that all irregular militias should be disbanded. Nothing actually happened, however, and the war went on. Kadijević's chief of staff, the radical General Adžić, ignored him.

On October 3, the Serbs took control of the federal presidency. Branko Kostić, Montenegrin representative to the SFRJ presidency and vice president, called a meeting of the presidency and submitted a declaration of a state of emergency. With President Mesić absent and the Slovenian representative to the presidency boycotting the meeting, the proposal was passed with Kostić's own vote plus the three votes controlled by Serbia (and its two formerly autonomous regions).

By this time, it had become clear to almost everyone just what Serbia was attempting to do. After the October 3, 1991 meeting, characterized by President Gligorov of North Macedonia as "illegitimate and unconstitutional," both North Macedonia and Bosnia and Herzegovina withdrew their representatives to the presidency. North Macedonia's representatives to the federal legislature withdrew from that body, as well.

The three-month moratorium on the independence declarations of Croatia and Slovenia—agreed to at Brioni—expired on October 7, 1991. Freed of that limitation, the Croatian and Slovenian governments severed all ties with the Socialist Federal Republic of Yugoslavia. By this time, the JNA and Serb militias occupied approximately a third of Croatia. The Yugoslav air force marked the day with an attack on the presidential palace in Zagreb at the very moment that President Tudjman was in conference with Stipe Mesić, the federal president, and Ante Marković, the federal prime minister. As the *Economist* put it, "the attack put to rest any pretense that there is real life left in the Yugoslav federation."

Up to this time, Montenegrin troops had not been directly involved in the war. Now, however, they entered Croatia from the south, conquering the area up to Dubrovnik and establishing a land siege around that city. They were joined by JNA troops, who had pushed their way down from the north.

Serbia rejected an EU plan for a more loosely structured Yugoslavia and demilitarization of areas with minorities. It insisted that it could not abandon Serb minorities outside Serbia. It would not agree to any plan that did not permit minorities to switch the regions where they were in a majority from one republic to another. The exasperated EC instituted economic sanctions against Serbia and Montenegro. The United States, for its own reasons, instituted economic sanctions against all of Yugoslavia, including Croatia and Slovenia.

The last vestige of a united Yugoslavian government disappeared in December 1991, when Ante Marković, the prime minister, resigned because 81% of the proposed budget for 1992 was earmarked for the army. The Yugoslav legislature, dominated by Serbia after representatives of Slovenia, Croatia, and North Macedonia had withdrawn, had already expressed its lack of confidence in Marković, a Croat from Bosnia and Herzegovina.

International Recognition for Independent Republics

By this time, Germany and Austria had begun to make a public case for recognition of Slovenia and Croatia. Some other EC members, particularly France and Britain, continued to oppose recognition until Germany announced that it would proceed unilaterally if the EC took no action. British prime minister John Major then threw his support to Germany, and France grudgingly gave in. In December, the EC announced that, on January 15, 1992, its members would implement recognition of those Yugoslav republics that requested it and deserved it.

General Veljko Kadijević, the Yugoslav defense minister, resigned on January 8, citing ill health. That gave Serb radicals control of the JNA. But Slobodan Milošević, president of Serbia, had by this time switched positions, and he and the EC reached agreement on a new cease-fire and peacekeeping plan modeled on the suggestions he had put forth in November. The JNA would pull out of the three Serb enclaves in Croatia and be replaced by a peacekeeping force from the United Nations. The UN troops would disarm local militias and organize local police. Croatia would not have control over the enclaves, but neither would Serbia. The future of the enclaves would be determined at subsequent talks. The cease-fire—the 50th—went into effect on January 3. Five days later, the UN Security Council voted to send 50 UN observers to Croatia to report on the feasibility of the plan.

By January 15, 1992, four republics—Slovenia, Croatia, North Macedonia, and Bosnia and Herzegovina—had requested EC recognition. It recognized only the first two, largely for political considerations. EC governments were worried that recognition of Bosnia and Herzegovina would bring war to that republic. The Serbian Democratic Party, the main spokesman for Serbs in Bosnia and Herzegovina, opposed separation from Yugoslavia and threatened to lead a secession of Serb-dominated areas. Serbs formed their own "Serbian Republic of Bosnia and Herzegovina" and began arming themselves.

National Library, Sarajevo, gutted by incendiary shells, August 25, 1992

The Former Yugoslavia

War in Bosnia

Because of this development, the EC advised the government of Bosnia and Herzegovina to hold a referendum on independence to establish that a majority actually wanted to break free from Yugoslavia. The referendum was held in March 1992 and produced a two-thirds majority in favor of independence. Serbs, who had boycotted the referendum, threw up barricades throughout the capital city of Sarajevo that evening, and it appeared that a major civil war was ready to break out. However, President Alija Izetbegović defused the situation by meeting with the Bosnian Serb and Croatian leaders. The Serbs agreed to dismantle their barricades, and the other two political factions agreed to joint patrols by the Yugoslav People's Army and the Bosnian police.

On March 18, 1992, the leaders of the three communities agreed on a plan for restructuring the state, creating "three constituent units, based on national principles and taking into account economic, geographic and other criteria." The plan would have created three autonomous units within the governmental structure, one for Muslims, one for Croats, and one for Serbs. Control in each municipality would have been by that national group which was in an "absolute or relative majority."

Since the three communities have always lived side by side and many families are mixed, the agreement would have been difficult to implement. In any case, it was never given a chance. The radical Serb leaders who wanted a single Greater Serbia forestalled that possibility by launching a war of conquest in April.

In essence, the Yugoslav army, overwhelmingly dominated by Serbs, split into two parts. Those with any ties to Bosnia or other non-Serb lands remaining in Bosnia joined the Muslim-Croatian army.

The rest of the army removed itself to Serbia and Montenegro. Units left behind in Bosnia were provided with tanks, artillery, and all the equipment of a modern army. General Ratko Mladić became the military commander of this force, while Radovan Karadžić exercised political leadership. The Yugoslav army continued to provide support and resupply from Serbia. Thus, the Yugoslav army, having learned from its involvement in Croatia that it could not afford to be seen as being present, created a proxy to continue its war for a Greater Serbia.

Within three months, this Serbian army in Bosnia had managed to capture approximately 70% of the territory. It also laid siege to the capital, Sarajevo. In the process it directed an unceasing bombardment into this once-beautiful medieval city in an effort to crush resistance. With the west continuing to enforce the arms embargo it had instituted at the beginning

President Slobodan Milosevic of Serbia, left, shakes hands with President Franjo Tudjman of Croatia, as President Alija Izetbegovic of Bosnia and Herzegovina, right, looks on following the signing of the Balkan Treaty at the Elysee Palace in Paris, December 14, 1995. Behind them applauding, from left, are Spanish premier Felipe Gonzalez (hidden), President Clinton, French president Jacques Chirac, and German chancellor Helmut Kohl.

AP/Wide World Photo

454

Waiting for the school bell in Serbia

of the fighting, the lightly armed Bosnian army was no match for the tanks and artillery of the Serbs. The siege and the shelling went on, gradually reducing large parts of the city to ruins.

Meanwhile, Serbs used their control of the Yugoslav legislature to pass new laws establishing customs zones in Serb-inhabited areas of Croatia and parts of Bosnia and Herzegovina. In the case of Croatia, they also decreed that Yugoslav, not Croatian, law would apply in Serb areas occupied by the UN peacekeeping force. In addition, the legislature passed a law on the new Yugoslavia that required that "the new community be made up of nations and republics that want to remain in Yugoslavia." They implemented this by giving representation in the Yugoslav legislature to Serbs living outside of Serbia.

Montenegro held its own referendum in March 1993, and the people voted overwhelmingly to remain in a Yugoslav Federation. A union of two parts, one with a population of 9.98 million and the other with only 620,000, was rather odd. But that was what was left of the old Yugoslavia.

The claim that there was a "Federal Yugoslavia" that was superior to and separate from the Republic of Serbia ceased to have any validity on June 1, 1993, when Milošević ousted Dobrica Ćosić as president and replaced him with Zoran Lilić, a puppet who lacked real standing either domestically or internationally. After his dismissal, Ćosić said, "The federal state, if

it is a state at all, is practically under the protectorate of Slobodan Milošević and the Serbian government."

The embargo instituted against Serbia for its support of the war in Bosnia hurt the republic economically but not to such an extent that it was willing to end its war of conquest for a Greater Serbia. Serbs actually gave President Milošević's party an increased percentage of the vote in the 1993 elections. With the government's almost total control over the news media, it was easy to convince Serbs that they were the aggrieved party, particularly since the leadership of the Serbian Orthodox Church supported the government on this issue.

Peace Negotiations and the Dayton Accords

The change came in August 1994, when the Yugoslav government publicly withdrew support from Bosnia's Serbs after they had rejected a new UN peace plan that would have ceded them 49% of Bosnia. Serbia then announced that it had "sealed" its border with Bosnia and would not permit the export of anything except food, clothing, and medicine. After much negotiation, Belgrade agreed to allow 135 civilian observers to monitor the 370-mile frontier with Bosnia. This brought an easing of sanctions against Serbia in September.

In spite of widespread reports of violations on the part of Serbia, the UN

continued to look to Milošević as a possible negotiating partner. It attempted to win Milošević's cooperation by offering a further relaxation of sanctions in return for his recognition of Croatia and Bosnia. He made it clear, however, that he would not recognize the independence of either republic until an overall settlement was reached. In the interim, Serbia continued to provide at least some limited support to the Bosnian and Croatian Serbs.

Milošević's position began to change in May 1995, when the Croatian army recaptured western Slavonia, an area that had been held by Croatian Serbs since their declaration of a separate Serb state in 1991. As it became clear that the Croatian army intended to launch an invasion three months later of the Krajina, the remaining Croatian Serb enclave in the center of Croatia, the Serbian government not only did nothing, but also there is some evidence that it allowed the Croatian Serbs to know that they could expect no support from Serbia. As a result, when the invasion began, the Croatian Serb government of Milan Martić collapsed, and nearly all Croatian Serbs (about 500,000) fled eastward even before the arrival of Croatian troops.

Milošević also stood by as a Croatian army entered Bosnia and then, in cooperation with the Bosnian army and the separate Bosnian Croat forces, gradually increased their control of Bosnian territory to just over 50%. It appears clear that the sanctions against Serbia were having their desired effect and that he concluded that his dream of a Greater Serbia could not be achieved under the then-prevailing circumstances. Most of the Bosnian Serbs must have come to the same conclusion, for they now agreed to give Milošević the power to negotiate on their behalf.

Milosevic posters in Belgrade, 2005

455

The Former Yugoslavia

This led to the Dayton peace talks that concluded successfully with a formal signing ceremony in December 1995. It brought a suspension of the economic sanctions against Serbia and a promise that they would be permanently removed if Serbia continued to support the peace process.

The Serbian economy was operating at an extremely low level by this time. Exhausted by the war, the people hoped that the peace agreement would lead to renewed growth. Outside economists suggested that Serbia should launch a major privatization program such as had already been carried out nearly everywhere else in central and southeastern Europe. None was pleased with the outcome. The end of the economic sanctions brought few dividends, and Milošević actually revoked some privatization and free-market measures.

Election Unrest in Serbia

Elections to the Yugoslav legislature took place in November 1996. Because of the disarray of the opposition parties at this level, there was never any doubt that the parties of the government coalition would win a majority of the seats. Over two-thirds of the seats were indeed won by the two parties led by Milošević and his wife, Mirjana Marković.

Two weeks later, however, municipal elections took place throughout Serbia. In a surprise, the opposition won control over 32 municipalities, including Belgrade and such industrial cities as Kragujevac and Niš. Milošević had always had strong support in these cities. But the dismal state of the economy, the unemployment rate of almost 50%, and the fact that even those who were employed often had to wait months for their money had turned the workers against him.

The situation changed completely after the government moved to invalidate opposition victories in 14 of Serbia's 19 largest cities. Beginning on November 20, huge crowds of up to 100,000 demonstrators gathered daily in the middle of Belgrade to demand that the opposition be permitted to take their seats. Gradually, the demonstrations spread to other cities in Serbia.

Because the United States and several EU governments had made it clear that they would favor reimposing economic sanctions if Milošević used force to suppress the opposition, the government tried to buy off the demonstrators by economic measures, such as reducing the cost of electricity and promptly paying pensioners.

None of this worked, however, and the demonstrations continued.

The government next tried to shut off all information about the demonstrations by closing down or seizing all private radio and television stations. Radio Free Europe countered this by picking up the broadcasts of the banned stations and rebroadcasting them over RFE frequencies. The demonstrations continued until February 1997, when Milošević finally gave in and agreed to honor the opposition victories. The confrontation lasted for 78 days.

The victories temporarily introduced a small amount of political pluralism into Serbian life, but it was not destined to survive very long. Within a few months, *Zajedno*, the opposition political coalition, collapsed when its two main leaders began quarreling over which of them would stand for the Serbian presidency in the approaching election. Taking advantage of the disarray, Milošević was soon able to install his own man as mayor of Belgrade and to reassert control over regional television. Seemingly politically invincible at this time, he would see less than four years later that he would have to answer for his long misrule of a disintegrating Yugoslavia.

Divided Kosovo seen at divided Mitrovica: The Serb side greets visitors with a Serbian flag.

Milo Djukanović (Montenegro), Nikola Špirić (Bosnia and Herzegovina), Jadranka Kosor (Croatia), Borut Pahor (Slovenia), Hashim Thaci (Kosovo) . . . leaders of the western Balkans (minus Serbias).

Republic of Slovenia (Republika Slovenija)

The island in Lake Bled with its ancient church

Area: 7,827 sq. mi. (20,271 sq. km.)

Population: 2,119,675 (2023 estimate)

Capital City: Ljubljana (pop. 288,359; 2023 estimate)

Climate: Mediterranean southwest of Ljubljana; Alpine in the north; continental in the rest of the republic. Average annual temperature in the Mediterranean climate type is 53,6 F (12°C), in the lower regions of central Slovenia it is between 46.4 F (8°C) and 33.8 F (1°C), while at the highest peaks it never exceeds 32 F (0°C).

Neighboring Countries: Austria (north); Hungary (northeast); Croatia (west and south); Italy (west).

Official Language: Slovenian.

Recognized regional languages: Hungarian, Italian, Serbian and Croatian.

Ethnic Background: 92.0% Slovenes, 3.8% Bošnjaks, 1.1% Kosovars, 0.8% Serbs, 2.3% other (Croats, Hungarians, Italians, Romani). (2021 estimate)

Religion: 77.8% Christianity (73.4% Roman Catholicism, 3.7% Orthodox Christian, 0.7% other Christian), 3.9% other, 18.3% no religion. (2018)

Form of Government: Unitary parliamentary republic

Chief of State: Nataša Pirc Musar, President (2022).

Head of Government: Robert Golob, Prime Minister (April 2022).

National Flag: It is a tricolor of equal horizontal bands of white (top), blue, and red, with the coat of arms of Slovenia over the white and blue bands at the hoist side. The coat of arms, separated by a red fimbriation from the white and blue stripes. is a shield with the image of Mount Triglav, Slovenia's highest peak, in white against a blue background and beneath it there are two wavy blue lines representing the Adriatic Sea and local rivers. Above it all there are three six-pointed golden stars arranged in an inverted triangle which are taken from the coat of arms of the Counts of the city of Celje, the great Slovene dynastic house of the late 14th and early 15th centuries. The flag's colors are considered to be Pan-Slavic, as defined by the Prague Slavic Congress of 1848. The initial symbolic interpretation was that the white stands for nobility and frankness;

the blue for faithfulness, honesty, impeccability, and chastity; and the red for courage, generosity, and love. The existing Slovene tricolor was raised for the first time in history during the Revolution of 1848.

Public Holiday: June 25 (Independence Day)

Currency: Euro (€) (EUR) (since January 1, 2007).

Main Exports: Automobiles and vehicle parts, electric machinery, pharmaceuticals and other chemical products, and furniture.

Main Imports: Machinery and transport equipment, chemical products, mineral fuels, and metals.

Main Trading Partners: Switzerland (21.0% of exports and 15.3 of imports), Germany (14.5% of exports and 10.5%

Slovenia

of imports), Italy (10.6% of exports and 10.5% of imports), China (11.9% of imports), Austria (6.7% of exports and 6.7% of imports), Croatia (8.4% of exports and 4.0% of imports), France (3.4% of exports). (2022)

The Republic of Slovenia was the first of the former Yugoslav republic to gain its independence and to enter both the European Union and NATO in 2004, as well as to adopt the euro in 2007. In the first half of 2008, it became the first ex-communist land to occupy the EU's rotating presidency.

Because of their relative prosperity, social stability, and strong cultural and economic links with the west, Slovenes are inclined to consider themselves as central Europeans rather than as a Balkan people. The country likes to offer itself to the west as an economic and diplomatic "bridge to the Balkans."

This relatively prosperous country includes the northeastern part of the Istrian Peninsula, which gives it a short coastline on the Adriatic Sea. Koper is its major port and maritime gateway to the world. The Julian Alps run along most of the border with Italy, while the Karavanke Mountains mark the border with Austria. Somewhat farther south and southeast are the Kamnik Mountains.

The Sava River forms a wide valley between the Julian Alps and the Karavanke Mountains, then flows across the republic in a southeasterly direction. A second major river, the Drava, originates in Austria (where it is known as the Drau), then enters the republic north of the Kamnik Mountains. It flows in a southeasterly direction before crossing into Croatia. Except for the mountainous area, most of Slovenia is covered by often steep, heavily forested rolling hills, with the exception of the plateau area of gray karst limestone east of Trieste. Only half the size of Switzerland, Slovenia could be called a "one-hour country" because everything—mountains, beaches, the capital city—can be reached in about 60 minutes. Travel writer Jan Morris once wrote, "When God devised Slovenia, he smiled."

Over 90% of Slovenia's population belongs to the majority ethnic group. About 3,000 Italians live along the coast in the western part of the republic. At least 100,000 Slovenes live in northeastern Italy, including 17% of the population of the province of Trieste, 12% of Goriza, and 5% of Udine. Approximately 8,500 Hungarians live in the northeastern part of Slovenia, but most of the minorities are people who came from other parts of former Yugoslavia in search of work, mostly from Bosnia and Herzegovina, Croatia and Serbia. Slovenia was Yugoslavia's most economically advanced part. Large numbers of Muslims fleeing the war in Bosnia and Herzegovina entered Slovenia between 1992 and 1995, and some remained.

HISTORY

The Slovenes migrated into the area of the western Balkans in the 6th century, the first of the Slavic peoples to enter the region. In 627 AD, a Slavic kingdom, called Karantanija came into existence in the Sava River Valley. It lasted about 120 years, then was incorporated into the Carolingian Empire in 748. It was at this time that the Slovenians were converted to Roman Catholicism.

In the 9th century, the Carolingian Empire was divided, and Slovenia became part of the eastern, German-dominated area. In the 10th century, it was incorporated into the Holy Roman Empire, where it remained through several changes of rulers. Eventually it passed to the Habsburgs in the 14th century after they had established their capital at Vienna. Periodic attempts at Germanization shrank the realm of Slovenian culture. However, most of the Slovenian heartland remained intact, thanks to the efforts of native Roman Catholic priests.

Slovenian peasants were eventually made serfs, along with those in other parts of the empire. This produced a number of uprisings in the 15th and 16th centuries. But things remained very much the same until the 18th century, when Maria Theresa and her son Joseph II attempted to improve the lot of the people by granting them personal freedom.

After the collapse of the Austrian Empire in 1918, Slovenian leaders supported the creation of the Kingdom of Serbs, Croats, and Slovenes. This was renamed the Kingdom of Yugoslavia in 1929. Slovenia was partitioned during World War II, with Italy taking the southwest, Hungary a small piece of land north of the Mura River called Prekomurje, and Germany the northeast. This spawned a Slovenian resistance movement, the most significant of which was the communist-led Liberation Front. By the end of the war, the partisan army had grown to 37,000 fighters.

The war and its bloody aftermath claimed at least 100,000 Slovene lives. Thousands had been sent to labor and concentration camps, deported, or held hostage. In the spring and summer of 1945, Tito's partisan forces systematically killed an estimated 100,000 alleged Axis collaborators, Chetniks, and other unwanted persons in Slovenia. Many of them had attempted to surrender to British forces in southern Austria, but they were sent back. Slovenes were shocked in 2009 to see TV images of mass graves, such as Huda Jama (Bad Cave); this is only one of around 600 such postwar gravesites. During the communist era it was impossible to talk about this issue. But the TV pictures have caused some Slovenians to question the national myth that Tito was a beneficent savior, despite the fact that his postwar victory brought added Adriatic territories to Slovenia and Croatia.

After the defeat of Germany in 1945, Slovenia became one of the constituent republics of the People's Republic of Yugoslavia. In 1947, it received some additional territory from Italy as part of the Paris Peace Treaty. Trieste remained Italian, but its hinterland became a part of Yugoslavia. In 1954, some of the former Free Territory of Trieste (Zone B) was transferred to Slovenia. After Slovenia entered the European Union (EU) in May 2004, Trieste once again was reunited with its former hinterland.

Slovenians are a hardworking people with good leadership. They did well economically until about 1980. But Yugoslavia never recovered from the oil shock of 1979, and the wealthier parts of the country found themselves called upon to provide more assistance to badly run and ailing large-scale industry in eastern

International business students in Lake Bled

Slovenia

Yugoslavia. By the middle of the 1980s, political leaders in Slovenia and Croatia were pushing for a change in the economic system, but the Serbian leadership opposed them. Slovenia and Croatia proposed a loosened form of federation that would give them economic independence. This was unacceptable to Serbia. Independence Faced with this stalemate at the national level, Slovenia and Croatia began to push for internal changes. By the spring of 1990, Slovenia had ended the political monopoly formerly held by the Slovenian Communist Party and created a de facto pluralistic system. In April 1990, multiparty elections resulted in a legislature dominated by the six-party Democratic United Opposition, or Demos.

Demos, a coalition of conservative political parties, had campaigned on a platform of independence within a year. At the same time, Milan Kučan, candidate of the communists, was elected president. Shortly thereafter, the communists became the Party of Democratic Renewal and endorsed independence, as well. On July 2, 1990, parliament adopted a "declaration of sovereignty" by an overwhelming 187 votes to 3. In September,

it took control of the "territorial defense force" (TDF), which had been first created in 1968 and which constituted an embryonic independent Slovene army. A referendum on independence was held on December 23, 1990. Of those voting, 88.5% opted for independence, "unless it proved possible to negotiate a looser Yugoslav confederation." Parliament adopted its own endorsement of the declaration on December 26. It voted in February 1991 that republic law would henceforth take precedence over laws of the Yugoslav Federation.

Slovenia began managing its own borders and customs facilities, and in May 1991 it started retaining all draftees within its own borders and incorporating them in the republic's TDF. Approximately 22,000 Yugoslav People's Army (JNA) troops were stationed on Slovene territory at the time. Even though they confiscated about 70% of the TDF's military equipment, much of it remained in Slovenian hands.

All attempts to negotiate a new union failed due to Serbian stonewalling. Serbia instituted a boycott of goods from Slovenia. Finally, Slovenia and Croatia declared their independence on June 25, 1991. The "Ten-Day War" began.

On June 27, the JNA commenced military operations after the republic took charge of the border posts with Austria and Italy. Many Slovene soldiers left their JNA units and defended their own free republic, and the republic's territorial force swelled to as many as 60,000 lightly armed recruits and reservists. The Slovenes fought back, and they managed to capture some tanks and other equipment. They resisted the takeover of further border stations and blocked many roads and JNA barracks, taking about 8,000 soldiers captive and only later releasing them. The population practiced mass civil disobedience and sabotage. In 10 days, the fighting was over, with fewer than 100 dead and 300 wounded on both sides, compared later with 10,000 dead in Croatia and 200,000 in Bosnia.

Yugoslav leaders were clearly unprepared for a war in Slovenia. In many ways they had little desire to fight for the breakaway republic. Serbs have no historical or ethnic claims to it, and few Serbs lived there. They were also aware that a much bigger battle was about to begin in Croatia, cutting off any JNA troops left in Slovenia. Therefore, they agreed to a cease-fire and withdrew all their troops by October. Slovenia was free.

Meanwhile, the west attempted to dissuade the Slovenians and Croatians from radical actions. It refused, as US secretary of state James Baker put it, to recognize their independence "under any circumstances." It was soon appalled by the bloodshed in Croatia and began to offer mediating services.

Some of the European nations, especially Germany and Austria, even began talking about extending recognition to Slovenia and Croatia. After two cease-fires had broken down, the third held. In a compromise imposed by negotiators from the EC (now EU), Slovene agents were authorized to collect federal customs duties at the disputed customs posts, while Slovenia agreed to suspend application of its declaration of independence for three months. This brought an end to the war in Slovenia, but it actually only moved the venue of the war to Croatia. Slovenia activated its declaration of independence as of October 7.

By December, with the war in Croatia still going on, most European nations were fed up with Serbia and the JNA leadership. Germany now pressed the EC to recognize the two republics, and this was finally agreed to, effective January 15, 1992. Secretary of State Baker refused to follow suit, however, in effect continuing support for the hardline, Serbian nationalist, and ex-communist leadership of Serbia. Anything seemed better to Baker than to see one more part of Europe falling apart. This changed only after the Yugoslav army began to spread its destruction throughout most of the rest of former Yugoslavia. The United States then changed its mind and sponsored UN economic sanctions against Serbia.

POLITICAL SYSTEM

A new constitution, approved in December 1991, established a parliamentary democracy. The European Union later required some changes, such as restrictions in the original text on foreigners' right to purchase land in Slovenia. Its criminal code came into effect in 1995. Like every other democratic European country, it has no death penalty. The court system is headed by a Constitutional Court. Its members are nominated by the president and approved for nine-year, nonrenewable terms by the National Assembly.

The role of the president is largely ceremonial, although ex-president Milan Kučan, a former communist leader, carved out an important role for himself in the area of foreign affairs. He won the presidency in 1992 and was easily reelected in 1997. One factor in his good showing was that he strongly supported Slovenia's entry into the European Union and NATO.

He was not allowed by the constitution to run for a third term, and in 2002, he was succeeded by Janez Drnovšek, who resigned as prime minister to assume the presidency. Mortally ill, Drnovšek resigned in January 2008 and died one month later. In the election that had taken place in November 2007, Social Democrat Danilo Turk defeated Christian Democrat Lojze Peterle in the second round of voting by a whopping 69.2% to 30.1% margin. Turk was a former professor and diplomat, living in New York for 13 years as the country's ambassador to the UN and then, from 2000 to 2005, serving as the deputy UN secretary-general.

Turk lost his bid for reelection in November 2012 to Borut Pahor, a former prime minister. Pahor had been a member of the European Parliament with a reputation for achieving compromises. He has a degree in international studies at the University

President Nataša Pirc Musar
Source: *Wikipedia*

459

Slovenia

Ex-president Borut Pahor

Prime Minister Robert Golob
Source: *Wikipedia*

of Ljubljana. During his student days, he earned the money to pay for his studies by being a male model. For that he gained the nickname "Barbie Doll" among his political rivals.

At the 2022 Slovenian presidential election, Nataša Pirc Musar announced her candidacy for President of Slovenia as an independent candidate. Although Pirc Musar has not been a member of a political party, she was endorsed by former presidents of Slovenia Milan Kučan and Danilo Türk and supported by the Pirate Party, the Youth Party, and the European Greens.

In October, she came second in the first round of the presidential elections, becoming one of the two contenders in the runoff. In the second round of the presidential elections in November 2022, Pirc Musar defeated Slovenian Democratic Party candidate Anže Logar and was elected the first female president of Slovenia.

The president proposes a prime minister to the National Assembly after consulting with parliamentary groups. The prime minister, the official head of government, presides over the cabinet and is responsible for government policy. He must be affirmed in office by a positive vote of the National Assembly and may be removed by a negative vote of confidence. This is the most powerful office in the Slovene political system.

Slovenia has a bicameral legislature composed of two houses, the National Assembly and the National Council. The National Assembly, composed of 90 members, is the "popular" house, equivalent to the British House of Commons. It is directly elected for a four-year term. A party must win at least 4% of the total votes to qualify for seats. One seat each is reserved for the Italian and Hungarian minority groups, and these representatives can veto any legislation that specifically affects their communities.

The upper house, the National Council, is elected for five years. It has a total of 40 members, 22 of them representing local interests; 12 evenly divided between employers, employees, and the self-employed; and 6 representing nonprofit activities, such as education and culture. Its powers are limited to delaying legislation.

Being small, the country has no states or provinces. It is broken down into 193 local units called *občine*, or municipalities or townships. Parliament or 40,000 voters can sign a petition demanding referenda, which are held frequently. For example, in June 2011 voters rejected the gradual raising of the retirement age to 65, and in December 2015 they rejected same-sex marriages. Yet, they were legalized in July 2022.

Parliamentary Elections

The country faced its first-ever early elections in December 2011. The strongest party in the election was the new Positive Slovenia Party (LZJ-PS), led by Zoran Janković. However, he failed to be elected prime minister by parliament. Therefore, former prime minister (until 2008) Janez Janša, leader of the Slovenian Democratic Party (SDS), became prime minister again. He had once been a freedom fighter, journalist, and critic of Yugoslav defense excesses. His arrest in 1988 had helped spark massive street protests in Ljubljana and pave the way for independence. He looked back, "That changed my destiny." He was a defense expert and former defense minister in the early 1990s.

Janša was accused and convicted of having taken bribes from Patria, a state-run Finnish arms company, and of having accumulated €200,000 ($265,000) in assets without declaring them or revealing their origin. At first he refused to step down. But faced with street demonstrations involving thousands against the political elite and government corruption, his coalition partners forced him to resign in March 2013. He was sent to jail.

He was replaced by 43-year-old Alenka Bratušek. She was Slovenia's first female leader. After losing the July 2014 election but still as prime minister, she tried to appoint herself the EU's energy commissioner, but she did not pass her confirmation hearing before the European Parliament by a huge margin, due to insufficient experience.

The winner of the July 2014 elections was a party founded only a month earlier. The Party of Miro Cerar (SMC) bore the name of the constitutional law professor Miro Cerar, a well-known TV commentator on legal matters. Modest and law-abiding, his party won over a third of the voter and 36 of the 90 seats. It led the government, with coalition partners the Democratic Party of Pensioners of Slovenia (DeSUS) and Social Democrats (SD). In 2015, it changed its name to Modern Center Party (thus retaining the acronym SMC). Cerar resigned in March 2018, although he remained untainted by the political scandals and rampant corruption that plagues the country. His successor was Marjan Šarec.

In the June 2018 parliamentary elections, Janša's SDS won the most votes (25%), but he could not construct a coalition despite the popularity of his antimigrant platform. Slovenes were shaken in 2015, when a half-million refugees traversed the country on their way to Germany. Šarec put together a fragile, five-party, center-right minority government supported by the hard left.

At the parliamentary elections held in Slovenia on April 24, 2022, the ruling

Former Prime Minister Marjan Sarec

Former Prime Minister Janez Jansa

Slovenian Democratic Party (SDS), led by Prime Minister Janez Janša, conceded and was defeated by Robert Golob and his Freedom Movement (GS). the Freedom Movement won 41 seats in the 90-seat National Assembly. Turnout was 70%, a substantial increase compared to the previous two elections (51.71% in 2014 and 52.63% in 2018).

Two center-left parties, the Social Democrats and The Left, announced they would join a government led by Golob, giving him a majority in the legislature. They formed a three-party center-left coalition government and on May 25, 2022, Golob was appointed Prime Minister of Slovenia by the National Assembly.

The defeat of Janez Janša has been described internationally as a defeat of right-wing populism since Janša was a supporter of former US president Donald Trump and an ally of Hungary's Prime Minister Viktor Orbán.

Foreign Policy

The Slovenian government ardently aspired to become part of the west. It joined NATO's Partnership for Peace in 1994, and full membership in NATO followed in April 2004. It had received an invitation to join at NATO's Prague summit in November 2002. The government, all political parties, and the influential Catholic Church were solidly in favor of membership, but political leaders had to make a persuasive case to the people, many of whom were skeptical of NATO's utility for the country. When voters went to the polls in March 2003 to vote on both NATO and EU entry, two-thirds supported NATO membership, but 93% gave their approval of EU membership.

Slovenia has little firepower to offer the military alliance. Slovenia ended conscription and since 2003 its armed forces are organized as a fully professional standing army. Its Commander-in-Chief is the President of the Republic of Slovenia. Currently there are approximately 7,300 active troops and approximately 1,500 in reserve, reduced from 55,000 personnel during conscription.

Slovenia sends peacekeepers to Bosnia and to Kosovo. In 2010 it took over NATO command in Skopje, North Macedonia. It does offer NATO valuable geography advantages, such as a land connection to Hungary, which was isolated from its NATO partners until Slovakia became a member of the alliance. Since Slovenia joined NATO, Italy's air force patrols its airspace.

It signed an association agreement with the European Union in 1996 and became a full member in May 2004. Over two-thirds of its trade is with EU members, and 90% of its foreign investment comes from Germany, Italy, Austria, and France.

In Slovene campaign for dual membership, the government adopted the slogan "At home in the EU, safe in NATO." As the results were announced, political leaders gathered to celebrate in Prešeren Square in the center of Ljubljana. By joining the EU and adopting the euro in 2007, Slovenes confirmed both their independence and their alignment with western Europe. They demonstrated that at last they were a nation free to choose for itself.

In January 2008 it became the smallest country except Luxembourg and the first ex-communist nation to assume the revolving six-month EU presidency. This was not easy for such a small country. One western diplomat quipped, "It's a little bit like taxiing a 747 with a bicycle." It immediately faced a practical problem—since it has very few diplomatic missions in the world, its successor to the presidency, France, agreed to provide representation in 110 countries where Slovenia has none. The year before, Slovenia had helped out its predecessor, Portugal, by representing it in North Macedonia and Montenegro. Slovenia needed no help in Washington because it got the former Yugoslav embassy when the diplomatic buildings were parceled out among the parts of the former federation in December 2001. Bosnia and Herzegovina received the one in London, while Croatia got the embassy in Paris. The consulate in Paris went to North Macedonia, and the ambassador's residence there was kept by Serbia.

Because of its wealth, Slovenia has a developed economy, and it may end up as a net contributor to the EU budget rather than a recipient of structural funds (subsidies). The country enjoys a high level of prosperity and stability. Slovenia's per-capita GDP reached 92% of the EU average in 2022. The nominal GDP in 2023 was 68.108 billion USD, and nominal GDP per capita (GDP/pc) in 2023 was USD 32,350.

Membership also forced it to cancel its free-trade agreements with the Balkan states, with which it had maintained trade surpluses. But Slovenian companies have become big investors in the former Yugoslavia; two-thirds of its FDI are in the region. With their old contacts, a shared history, and similar language, they are natural partners. Slovenian and Croatian companies are active in the attractive market some call the "Yugosphere." Slovenia plays an important role in the Balkans as a bridge between them and EU and NATO.

In 2010 both countries joined Serbia to form a new joint company, called Cargo 10, out of their three separate railways. The idea is to bolster Corridor 10, a pan-European rail and road network linking central and southeastern Europe, by shifting freight to rail.

Its top priority as holder of the EU presidency in 2008 was to keep the momentum of enlargement alive for its Balkan neighbors, including Croatia and Serbia. It skillfully coordinated the EU's response to Kosovo's declaration of independence on February 17, 2008. It supported both Kosovo's desire to secede from Serbia and Belgrade's prospects for one day entering the EU. It also helped end two years of drift in the EU's dealings with Russia by supporting the European Commission's effort to negotiate a long-term partnership accord with Moscow. In all of these matters, Slovenia's contribution was modest but useful.

Its relations with Croatia are not the best. Their rivalry is demonstrated in the cliches they have of each other: Slovenes are haughty and humorless, while Croatians are lazy, lawless, and too nationalistic. They have never fought a war against each other. But their disputes reflect issues that are left over from the breakup of Yugoslavia and hinder relations between all the former six republics. The two had a long-standing disagreement concerning an alleged debt of about $400 million owed by a Slovenian bank to Croatians in the earlier Yugoslav era. This dispute was settled as a precondition for Croatia's entry into the EU in July 2013.

There are problems concerning the operation of the jointly owned Krško nuclear power plant, located close to the Croatian border and licensed to operate until at least 2023 and perhaps two decades longer. They quarrel over two small stretches of land, one near the Slovenian town of Piran and the other along the southeastern border with Croatia, near Zagreb. They

Slovenia

Ljubljana Old Town

argue over the use of the name "Teran" for wine produced on both sides of the border.

Most important, they disagree over territorial jurisdiction in the Adriatic Sea. Slovenia has a minuscule coastline of only 47 kilometers, compared with Croatia's 1,700 kilometers, and it has no direct access to international waters. They reached an accord in 2001, but Croatia declined to ratify it. Slovenia's hopes to negotiate a free corridor were foiled in 2003, when Croatia announced plans to declare an exclusive economic zone within its territorial waters. This also affected fishing rights. Slovenia responded angrily by temporarily recalling its ambassador from Croatia and threatening to withhold its support for Croatian entry into the EU and NATO. When Croatia postponed its plan to declare the exclusive zone, Slovenia backed away from its threat concerning NATO, which Croatia entered in April 2009. While it seems that Croatia, with its long Dalmatian coastline, should be able to relinquish a sea lane to Slovenia, the matter is complicated by the possibility that there might be oil and gas under those waters.

In September 2004 there was a border incident in which a Slovenian group led by a member of parliament was arrested by Croatian border guards for refusing to show identity cards. The whole affair was filmed by a TV crew and aired the same night on Slovenian television. It came just before parliamentary elections. Then-prime minister Rop was accused of overreacting, for example by threatening Croatia's admission to the EU. The daily newspaper *Delo* called the government's response "stupid, unnecessary, inadequate and irresponsible."

The disagreement flared up again on January 1, 2008, when Croatia proclaimed a 57,000-square-kilometer fisheries protection zone in the Adriatic against Italy's and Slovenia's wishes. While EU officials urged Croatia not to enforce that proclamation, there was quiet frustration that Slovenia seemed to be using its role as temporary president to have the dispute moved up on the EU agenda and to slow down Croatia's accession talks in order to force Zagreb to back down.

For a long time, Slovenia refused to budge on the EU, blocking Croatia's entry until a compromise could be reached on this maritime dispute. Some critics found this a dangerous precedent in the Balkans. But in June 2010, Slovene voters in a referendum narrowly approved (51.5%) their government's November 2009 agreement (accepted by parliament in April 2010) with Croatia not to allow the 18-year dispute to stall Croatia's EU accession negotiations. Zagreb agreed not to claim disputed areas during the talks and to submit the complicated issue to binding arbitration. In gratitude, Croatia's newly elected president, Ivo Josipović made his first state visit to Slovenia in April 2010. In the end Slovenia did not stand in the way of Croatia's membership in the EU.

The dispute continued, despite the June 2017 decision by the Permanent Court of Arbitration in The Hague. Slovenia received three-quarters of the disputed Piran Bay and the right to use a small corridor of Croatia's territorial waters to reach the high seas. Several land areas were also delineated. However, in the meantime Croatia rejected the arbitration as "irrevocably compromised" when a Slovenian arbiter

was accused of colluding with the Slovenian government. Croatia's then president Kolinda Grabar Kitarović declared that to her country the arbitration "does not exist," and she vowed to ignore the ruling. With both countries eager to use the disputed waters for economic and military purposes, there will be further pressure to accept the arbitration's outcome.

Slovenia's relations with the United States are "good" but not close. It was the first central European country to have visa-free travel to America. Since Tito's Yugoslavia was much less isolated from the west and never dominated by the Soviet Union, some individual members of the Slovenian government had much closer private ties. For example, former president Drnovšek traveled to the United States in 1994 to receive an honorary degree from Boston University. It was an irritant in US-Slovenian relations in 1993–1995 that he was a consistent critic of Western inaction in Bosnia. US-Slovenian relations improved after the Dayton Accords was signed in 1995. Slovenia strongly supported NATO actions against Serbia over Kosovo in 1999.

Things were not so harmonious during the 2003 war in Iraq, which four-fifths of Slovenes opposed. Slovenes desired to stay out of armed conflicts far from home. The government was in a difficult position. It decided to sign the so-called Vilnius Declaration with nine other mainly eastern European countries and to grant an American request to allow airplanes with aid, refugees, and wounded to use its airspace but not those carrying troops and military supplies. It was the only signatory of the Vilnius Letter not to send troops to Iraq. It publicly corrected an error made by the US, which had listed Slovenia as a partner in the war against Iraq. By 2007, however, it had 4 instructors in Iraq training Iraqi forces and 50 in Afghanistan. By dispatching more peacekeeping soldiers to Kosovo in March 2007, it had more troops abroad in NATO missions per capita than any other ally. To express his thanks in June 2008, outgoing US president George W. Bush made the first stop on his last trip to Europe in Slovenia.

Ljubljana Old Town

One of the most delicate matters the Slovene government had to deal with was the status of the 25,671 residents from other former Yugoslav republics, mainly Serbs, Croats, and Bosnians but also some Albanians, Montenegrins, and Macedonians, who found themselves living in Slovenia without citizenship. After independence in 1991, ethnic Slovenes were automatically granted Slovene citizenship. People from other ethnic backgrounds were required to apply for such citizenship. When

25,671 failed to do so, they were deleted from the national population register without public warning or announcement.

Referred to as "erased" people, they thereby lost their basic right to permanent residency that is a precondition for the permission to work and receive health care and pensions. In 1999 the Slovenian Constitutional Court ordered the government to restore their rights. A subsequent referendum on the question rejected the court decision by a vote of more than 90%, but a further court decision invalidated the referendum.

With the EU looking on approvingly, the government admitted in 2004 that it had made a mistake and proceeded to restore citizenship for the erased. This upset many ethnic Slovenes, who feared that thousands will be entitled to sue for millions of euros in back benefits and damages. A non-binding referendum in April 2004 produced a large margin of votes

against the erased. Then-prime minister Janša pounced on the matter, angrily claiming that many of the erased were former Yugoslav military officers who had fought against Slovenia's independence. Some observers called this issue an election "gift" for Janša, without which "he never would have been elected." He halted the return of rights to the erased. But in 2010 parliament adopted (48 to 30) an amendment to the act dealing with the erased that resolved the injustices they suffered. Those without permanent residence permits can obtain them. Parliament endorsed a declaration in 2011 saying that they have a right to organize themselves based on their ethnicity and that they can foster their culture, language, and contribution to a multicultural society.

Slovenia's leaders are aware of the importance of the western Balkans for their country. It allocates 80% of its bilateral development aid to the region. It is

Slovenia's second-most important market, accounting for 17% of exports and 6.5% of imports. Most (67.4%) of the foreign direct investments in the area are made by Slovene companies.

Recognizing that importance, Slovenia organized and hosted a regional conference in March 2010 at Brdo pri Kranju. It was attended by all prime ministers in the area except the Serbian, who refused to go since Kosovo was participating under its independence name, the Republic of Kosovo. The EU's most senior officials were disappointingly absent. The meeting was long on symbolism and short on substance. However, the picture of former adversaries sitting together, reaffirming their EU intentions, and cooperating to benefit the entire region sent a significant signal. The conclusion was "Everyone needs everyone."

As elsewhere throughout the region, the defining experience of 2015 for Slovenia became the migrant crisis. Not only was Slovenia on the "Balkan migratory route," but together with Hungary it was also the first Schengen Area member on that route. Thus, it was Slovenia's responsibility to control the entry into the area since there were no further passport checkpoints within it, leaving other countries open to unchecked entrants. When Hungary closed off its border with Serbia and then Croatia, the stream of migrants on their way to Austria and Germany shifted to flood Slovenia's meager border forces and humanitarian personnel. By mid-October, nearly 400,000 migrants had entered the country, at a rate of several thousand per day (the record number was 12,000). Tempers flew as thousands of people at a time were caught between the Slovenian and Croatian borders. At one point, frustrated migrants burned a few dozen tents with humanitarian supplies. On a number of occasions, Croatian police escorted large groups of refugees from a train station to the border, where the migrants rushed through the river to enter Slovenia with or without registering at the border checkpoint. The situation could easily reignite regional tensions. Slovenia directed its military and even hired private security guards to maintain order.

EU's slow and inadequate response irritated many Slovenes, disappointed that their little country was left with managing the crisis on its own. It was also upset when Austria declared it would construct a fence on its southern border, potentially stranding thousands of people within Slovenia. By November, Slovenia started building its own razor wire fence on the border with Croatia without, however, closing the border altogether. This changed by March 2016, when Slovenia and Croatia announced that they would no longer

Slovenia

allow the transit of most refugees through their countries as part of a decision to seal off the Balkan route after Türkiye agreed to take back all refugees ejected by Europe. Only migrants who already had the proper paperwork in advance would be allowed to enter.

ECONOMY

When Slovenia broke away from Yugoslavia in 1991, it had a fairly modern commercial and industrial base, and it has continued performing well. It has sustained stable annual economic growth, low unemployment, and a strong trade balance. Slovenia is no longer largely agricultural. By 2015, only 2% of GDP was generated by agriculture, although 8.3% are employed in that sector. The harvesting of forestry products provides an additional income for many rural inhabitants. Crops include wheat, corn, rye, oats, potatoes, rapeseed, sugar beets, and fruit. Livestock (cattle, sheep, pigs, poultry) is also raised throughout the republic. Agriculture is highly mechanized, and the standard of living in the countryside approximates that of its neighbor, Austria. Still, the government is concerned that Slovenian farmers will have difficulty competing as members of the European Union.

Slovenia has developed a modern economy, with 60.3% of its workforce employed in services (producing 66% of GDP) and 30.8% in industry (32% of GDP). It has a significant steel industry that produces approximately three-quarters of 1 million tons annually. It also manufactures trucks, automobiles, furniture, domestic appliances, and medicine. Other industrial products include cement, sulfuric acid, cotton, and woolen fabrics, plus such processed agricultural products as sugar.

It produces its own coal, has some hydroelectric stations that yield almost a third of its electricity, and generates about a third of its electricity from atomic power. In June 2008 it had to shut down a nuclear power station because of a water leak. The government quickly apologized for initially telling its neighbors that it was only a drill, and the EU issued its first continent-wide radiation alert. All other energy must be imported, including 40% of its natural gas from Russia.

The economic dislocations associated with its declaration of independence and the resulting loss of the former Yugoslav market led to a three-year recession, but the economy began growing again in 1993 and has continued growing ever since. Slovenia launched a Privatization Act in 1992 that has been a success. Its program used a system of vouchers. This process applied only to larger firms. Most Slovenian companies were small, and they were "socially owned," in line with Yugoslavia's system of worker self-management. Such firms were privatized through a form of internal share distribution (i.e., all shares were distributed to the employees and management). Larger firms, on the other hand, were privatized using public share offerings. In that case, 20% of the shares were transferred to the Slovene Development Fund, which sold the shares to authorized investment firms in which the public had invested their privatization vouchers.

The Slovene Development Fund also assumes outright ownership of firms in financial or organizational disorder. They are reorganized and rehabilitated, then prepared for sale to the public. This was the one group of firms where foreign direct investment was possible as a form of privatization. That was one of Slovenia's problems as it contemplated membership in the European Union. The country had to respond to EU criticism of the slow pace of economic liberalization, especially in privatizing major state-owned enterprises, such as telecommunications and big banks. In 2007 it sold shares in the second-largest bank, NKBM. It had to jettison a lot of rules that once prevented foreigners from investing in the economy. By the time of EU entry, most of its largest companies remained domestically owned, and only a third of banking assets were in foreign hands. The state still had 40% of corporate capital in its possession, a high percentage for a market economy.

It had to make other changes, as well. Its banking and insurance sectors were still

dominated by government-owned companies that had to be merged and sold. The same was true for telephones and electricity. Telekom Slovenia remained in majority state hands, but 49% of its shares were offered for sale in 2008. Its wireless arm, Mobitel, was the first operator to introduce advanced third-generation phone service in eastern Europe. Mobile (91%) and Internet (over 50%) penetration rivals the most developed western European countries. In 2011 Slovenia ranked 35th out of 142 countries in terms of number of international patents.

Tourism accounts for 8%–10% of GDP and 10% of employment. Because of the violent breakup of Yugoslavia, many tourists were frightened away for several years. The bustling modern port of Koper has become the largest and best Adriatic port in the EU and is the gateway of choice for many foreign goods entering the community. It can handle container traffic, 200,000 new cars each year, and everything from bulk minerals to agricultural produce. Its importance will increase once the government achieves its plan to build a new rail line connecting Koper and the city of Divača. Despite protests from its national carrier, Adria Airways (which ceased operating in 2019), the no-frills easyJet airlines won permission to land in Ljubljana, thereby sharply increasing the air traffic into the country.

The economy is open and is 50% dependent upon exporting. Such a country is bound to be vulnerable to the kind of global downturn that affected the entire world in 2008–2009. The recession presented a severe test. Up to then Slovenia's economic performance had been good. Real GDP had grown 4% annually since 1994, and in 2021 it was 4.1%, the best for a decade. In 2021 the budget deficit was 1.9% of GDP. Total public debt rose from 22% of GDP in 2008 to 64% in 2013. This relatively low debt helped qualify Slovenia for the euro in 2007.

A former finance minister said this relative success was aided by the fact that "ours was a softer form of socialism than in many other places in Europe." Transparency International ranked Slovenia in 2009 as the least corrupt among ex-communist countries (27th), tied with Estonia. Inflation was 7.6% in 2023, and unemployment of 9.7% in 2013 was below the eurozone average. There was a serious downturn in the auto and construction industries. Property prices, which roughly doubled between 2003 and 2007, declined. There is an underground economy that is estimated to be more widespread than the EU average.

Some of its economic problems are similar to those found in richer western European countries: high taxes (a top rate of 41%, lowered from 50%), generous public benefits, a pay-as-you go pension system that must eventually be reformed to remain solvent. This is especially true given the country's high wages by regional standards, costly public services, rigid labor laws that provide Europe's most protected employment, large and influential trade unions, and low fertility rate. The population is rapidly aging. Life expectancy for men is 76.1 years and 82.8 years for women.

Slovenia's economic problems arise from the fact that it resisted privatization for so long and is still hesitant. The state's dominance of the economy led to poor governance and crony ties between business and government and state banks and other parts of the economy. Firms are weighed down by debt. When recession came, the banks were stuck with €7 billion ($9.6 billion) in nonperforming loans. This discouraged foreign investors from putting their money into the country, and economic growth slowed.

The biggest economic problem it faces is a banking crisis. Equity in the three largest banks, which are state-owned, has been dangerously diminished, since a fifth of their total loans are nonperforming. Two of its banks failed stress tests in 2014. Bank assets amount to an oversized 130% of GDP. Moody's cut Slovenia's credit rating to junk status. The government seeks to deal with these problems by recapitalizing the banks to the tune of €3 billion euros ($4.1 billion), privatizing them, and spinning off bad loans into a "bad-bank." It succeeded in avoiding a bailout from its eurozone partners.

CULTURE

Slovenian culture reflects the fact that this is an overwhelmingly Roman Catholic country. However, it differs from Croatia, which is also Roman Catholic, in that it is much more western in orientation. Driving through the beautiful countryside, it is almost impossible to differentiate this area from Austria across the border. Towns and cities are clean and prosperous-looking, and the people dress much as they do elsewhere in western Europe. Only the signs in Slovenian make it clear what country you are in. Slovenia has the second-lowest urbanization rate in the Balkans, with half of the population living in rural areas. Only Bosnia and Herzegovina has a lower rate of people living in the cities—40% (while Bulgaria has 74%).

There is not a great deal of literature in Slovenian that is known outside the country. Much of what exists is religious in nature. The Freising manuscripts, dating from about 1000, are the earliest works available. Slovenian came into wider use during the Reformation, when Protestants translated the Bible and also produced some tracts in the language. The Slovenians eventually rejected Protestantism. In the 18th century, a Roman Catholic version of the Bible appeared in Slovenian, and this was followed by grammars in the early 19th century. Slovenian came into common use only after the middle of the 19th century.

Relations between the government and the Roman Catholic Church are strained, partly based on differing interpretations of the constitution's definition of the role of the church in public life. It has been pressing for return of all of its property nationalized during the period of communism and for the reintroduction of religious instruction in the schools. Much of its earlier property has been returned. The government has continued to emphasize the separation of church and state. In Reporters without Borders' 2014 survey of media freedom in 180 countries, Slovenia placed 34 overall but 1st in the Balkans.

Slovenia is the 8th highest-ranked country out of 144 in the world for gender equality, according to the 2016 Global Gender Gap Index. Nevertheless, there was no female representation on the boards of 71% of the 101 largest Slovenian companies.

In March 2015, Slovenia became the 31st country in the world, the eighteenth in Europe as well as the first former communist country where the parliament passed a law allowing same-sex couples to marry and adopt children. (By contrast, next-door Croatia went as far as amending its constitution to define marriage specifically as a union between a man and a woman.) However, by December a grassroots initiative spurred by a group called Children are at Stake led to a referendum, in which almost two-thirds of voters repealed the law. The Church of Slovenia strongly supported the rejection. Center-right prime minister Janez Janša explained his concern for a small country with the population growth of just 0.1%: "It's not possible to build the future of Slovenia with same-sex couples."

Actually, between 2006 and 2017, Slovenia recognized a more limited form of registered partnerships for same-sex couples, which gave same-sex partners access to pension and property rights.

Finally, same-sex marriage has been legal in Slovenia since 9 July 2022 in accordance with a ruling from the Constitutional Court of Slovenia. The court ruled that the ban on same-sex marriages violated the Constitution of Slovenia and gave the Parliament six months to amend the law to align with the ruling, even

Slovenia

though the decision took effect immediately after publication.

Slovenia tries to overcome its identity crisis of sorts: It is routinely confused with Slovakia, also a small post-communist and Slavic country that split from a larger entity (Czechoslovakia). A number of high-profile foreign politicians have misspoken, referring to one instead of the other. Rumor has it that, in some European capitals, staff from the embassies of both countries meet regularly to swap the mail each was sent by mistake. Because their flag looks so much like that of Slovakia, too (and of Russia), Slovenes have been debating changing it. In 2003, the parliament sponsored a competition for an alternative. The winning design has 11 horizontal blue, white, and red stripes linked in the middle to form four triangles that symbolize the country's Triglav Peak and its reflection in water. However, public opinion has not been supportive of the change, and the parliament has yet to follow up on the idea. In the meantime, Slovenia's tourism board pushes a campaign emphasizing that Slovenia is the only country in the world with the word "love" in its name: S-LOVE-nia.

Slovenes were happy about their tiny country's superb performance in the 2014 Winter Olympics in Sochi. Tina Maze won Slovenia's first-ever Winter Olympic gold medals, taking home two in skiing. In all, Slovene athletes mounted the medal podium eight times. Slovenia's great contribution to the world of skiing includes its Elan brand that pioneered side-cut carving skis, which boosted interest in downhill skiing at the time of the explosive growth of snowboarding. Cycling has become a passion. In 2021 Tadej Pogačar won the Tour de France for the second year in a row.

A famous Slovene, who became the first foreign-born naturalized First Lady of the United States, was born in Novo Mesto as Melanija Knavs and grew up in the nearby town of Sevnica. She later became a model and Germanized her last name to Melania Knauss, in due time becoming the third wife of the American billionaire Donald Trump. Her proud compatriots from Sevnica produced a variety of chocolates, beauty creams, salamis, and wine under the "First Lady" label (the Trumps hired a Slovenian law firm to prevent anyone from using Melania's name for commercial purposes).

CURRENT ISSUES

For all their eagerness to join the EU and be well integrated within Europe, Slovenes were disappointed by the organization's poor response to the migrant crisis of 2015–2016. Former prime minister Miro Cerar pointedly observed that the crisis threatened the existence of the EU unless a long-term solution was found. In the absence of a convincing collective strategy, each country started looking after its own interests, leaving its partners in a lurch. Still, Slovenia earned the respect of its partners with its measured response in this situation.

As Slovenia celebrated 30 years of its independence in June 2021, it remained one of the newest countries (though not cultures) in Europe. With its stable, democratic political system, Slovenia represents one of the success stories of central and eastern Europe. Slovenia's per-capita GDP (PPP) is higher than that of half of the EU and anywhere in the Balkans. Economic growth in 2023 was 0.6%, one of Europe's fastest. Its unemployment was the lowest since 2009.

Janez Janša, nationalist prime minister, was defeated in the April 2022 parliamentary elections after three terms in office. Robert Golob's Freedom Young party won 34% of the votes to Janša's 24%. Golob commands a comfortable 53 of 90 seats. The government should serve a full term. Golob faces difficult challenges: reducing dependence on Russian gas (90%) and oil (30%); coping with the fallout from the war in Ukraine; and creating a more liberal society. By 2015, Slovenia ranked 63rd of 157 countries in happiness, as indicated by the World Happiness Report. It remains a relatively wealthy country with current account surpluses and a level of government indebtedness that will remain below the eurozone average.

Republic of Croatia (Republika Hrvatska)

Official Language: Croatian.

Recognized Minority Languages: Serbian and Bosnian (both of the same linguistic basis as the Croatian).

Ethnic Background: 91.6% Croats, 3.2% Serbs, 5.2% others (2021 estimate).

Religion: 87.4% Christianity (79.0% Catholicism, 3.3% Orthodoxy, 5.1% other Christian), 2.3% other, 6.4% no religion, 3.9% undeclared (2021 estimate)

Form of Government: Unitary parliamentary republic

Head of State: Zoran Milanović, President (since February 2020).

Head of Government: Andrej Plenkovic, Prime Minister (since October 2016).

National Flag: It is a horizontal tricolor consisting of three equal size horizontal bands of red (top), white and blue, with the Croatian coat of arms in the center. The coat of arms is a shield depicting the red and white checkerboard of Croatia. Above the shield there is a crown composed of the shields of Croatian various regions. From dexter to sinister they are the historical arms of Croatia, Dubrovnik, Dalmatia, Istria and Slavonia. The red-white-blue tricolor has been used as the Croatian flag since 1848, and the Pan-Slavic colors are widely associated with romantic nationalism. The white color is defined as a symbol of the nobility and frankness;

Area: 21,851 sq. mi. (56,594 sq. km).

Population: 3,823,000 (2023 estimate)

Capital City: Zagreb (pop. 767,131; 2021 estimate)

Climate: is Mediterranean in the west; mild continental in the central and east parts of the country. Average monthly temperature ranges between 27 °F (−3 °C) in January and 64 °F (18 °C) in July.

Neighboring Countries: Slovenia (north); Hungary (northeast); Serbia (east); Bosnia and Herzegovina (east and south); Montenegro (southwest).

467

Croatia

Croatian Serbs flee after the fall of Krajina, 1995.

the blue of faithfulness, honesty, impeccability, and chastity; and the red of courage, generosity, and love. When the SFR Yugoslavia was created, Croatia's flag had a five-pointed red star with a yellow border in place of the coat of arms. The star was replaced by the coat of arms in May 1990, after the first multiparty elections. The current flag and the coat of arms were officially adopted on 21 December 1990.

National Holiday: May 30 (National Day); June 25 (Independence Day since 2020).

Currency: Euro (€) (EUR) (since 2023)

Main Exports: Fuels, machinery, ships, electricity and electrical transformers, chemical products, packaged medicaments, food, and textiles.

Main Imports: Transport equipment, fuels, chemical products, and packaged medicaments.

Main Trading Partners: Italy (12.2% of exports and 13.8% of imports), Bosnia and Herzegovina (10.3% of exports and 3.42% of imports), Germany (11.3% of exports and 12.4% of imports), Slovenia (11,5% of exports and 10.7% of imports), Austria (5.3% of exports and 5.17% of imports), Hungary (11.2% of exports and 7.31% of imports), Serbia (6,3 of exports and 3.48% of imports), US (3.72%

of exports and 7.56 of imports), China (3.6% of imports). (2022)

Existing at the edge of great empires, Croatia has been subject to different influences throughout its history. But it has always cherished its own ancient heritage and retained its own style of life and culture. The Republic of Croatia declared its independence from Yugoslavia in June 1991. After a bitter six-month war against Serbia and the Yugoslav People's Army (JNA), it received international recognition by the members of the European Community (now EU) in January 1992.

Croatia has a long coastline on the Adriatic Sea. In the north and east, the chief topographical features are the Sava and Drava River Valleys, plus the Croatian-Slavonian Mountains, a mountainous ridge that separates the two valleys. The Drava River forms the border with Hungary, while the Sava forms the border with Bosnia and Herzegovina. Most of the rest of Croatia consists of either mountains or uplands.

The Great Kapela Chain traverses the northwest. Somewhat farther south, the Velebit Range begins, followed by other Dinarian Alps, which run along the border with Bosnia and Herzegovina. The long Croatian coastline consists of the Istrian Peninsula, Dalmatian Islands, and a fairly narrow strip of the mainland reaching down as far as Montenegro. This is essentially a narrow coastal plain backed by mountains. Along with the Dalmatian Islands, it became a major summer resort area for western Europeans.

This region was once the ancient Roman province of Dalmatia and includes such historic cities as Split, where the emperor Diocletian lived after his retirement from 305 to 313. The nucleus of the town is actually the Palace of Diocletian. Another important city is Dubrovnik, founded in the 7th century and famous for its late-Renaissance buildings. Its picturesque streets, which are narrow and winding, are closed to motor vehicles. Serving as a backdrop to HBO's Game of Thrones further helped popularize the city.

Prior to independence, Croats represented 78.1% of the population, and Serbs, the largest minority with about 600,000, constituted another 12.2%. A further 2.2% listed themselves as Yugoslavs, and 1% as Muslims. The civil war in 1991—1992 resulted in a major shift in populations, however. Croats were pushed out of areas controlled by Croatian Serbs, and many Muslim refugees from Bosnia made their way into Croat-controlled areas of the republic. Another major change occurred in the summer of 1995, when about 300,000 Serbs fled the Krajina as Croatian soldiers recaptured that area. Only about 120,000

returned, and 85,000 were still registered in 2006 as refugees, chiefly in Serbia.

Today, Serbs number a little over 200,000 (4.5%) and are found in significant numbers only in larger cities, in the eastern part of Croatia, and in East Slavonia (the easternmost part of Croatia, along the Danube). There are frequent bus connections from Belgrade, but transportation links remain poor. Regular air links were never restored, and travelers driving east from Zagreb saw few signs guiding their way toward Belgrade. Croatia does more than twice as much trade with Slovenia as it does with Serbia, which is four times larger. Only 5% of its exports flow to Serbia, and only 1% of its imports come from there.

Visa requirements between the two countries were suspended. Some Serbs returned, but the young and more educated find better prospects in Serbia or elsewhere. If a third of residents in a region are Serbs, they can demand Cyrillic script on street signs and official correspondence, something that irritates Croat nationalists. Ethnic Croats are returning in even lower numbers. There is little work to be found. For example, in Vukovar, where some of the fiercest fighting had taken place, unemployment was officially 37%, twice the national average. But there is a good sign—at the town hall, Serbian and Croatian flags fly side by side.

The government is working hard to reach out to Croatian Serbs, and bilateral relations with Serbia have thawed noticeably; they are proper without being close. President Josipović signaled his determination in 2010 to improve relations with both neighboring Serbia and Bosnia and Herzegovina. Former Serbia's president, Boris Tadić, had visited Zagreb in 2007 and apologized to Croats for war crimes committed by those "acting on behalf of my people." Much has been done to return property to those who fled, even evicting Bosnian Croats who settled in Serbs' houses. There were difficult problems, such as the fact that both Serbia and Croatia accused each other in The Hague war crimes tribunal of genocide during the 1991–1995 Balkan War. However, the court ruled in 2015 that neither was guilty of genocide, that is, "the intent to destroy a group," despite 20,000 dead.

The governments of Croatia, Bosnia, Montenegro, and Serbia have agreed to try to settle the remaining refugee issues. Montenegro became the first ex-Yugoslav entity to agree to pay war compensation, offering Croatia $460,000 for cattle its soldiers appropriated. In 2006 an excellent locally produced film, *Vukovar: The Final Cut*, was made. It tells the story of the devastating siege of this eastern Croatian city in 1991. The most encouraging thing about it is that it was a joint Serbian-Croatian production.

HISTORY

During the great migrations from the area of the western Carpathian Mountains in the 7th century AD, Croats, a Slavic people, settled in Dalmatia. Along with the Slavonians, they constituted the western division of the Serbo-Croatian migration, while the Serbs formed the eastern portion.

At this time, the Croats were ruled according to tribal institutions. The first primitive form of the Croatian state started to take shape at the beginning of the 8th century. Small in numbers but militarily powerful, they conquered neighboring areas and mixed with other Slavs and the original Romanized population. While the Slovenians were being incorporated into the Carolingian Empire, the Croats fell under the domination of the Byzantine Empire beginning in 877.

Rebelling against this outside control, they formed the first united Croatian Kingdom in 910. Its ruler was Tomislav, and the kingdom he founded lasted for about two centuries. In wars waged against Bulgaria and Hungary during this time, Croatia enlarged its control over additional parts of the Dalmatian coast. Many Croatian nationalists regard this period of history as the golden age of their country. They built up a large navy and for a time at the end of the 10th century even exacted tribute from Venice.

This kingdom came to an end in 1091, when a dispute arose among rival claimants to the throne, and an appeal was made to King Ladislas I of Hungary to resolve the matter. Related to the royal house of Croatia, Ladislas took control of Croatia for himself instead. Although an insurrection broke out after Ladislas's death, it was put down by his successor, Koloman, who was crowned king of Croatia and Dalmatia in 1102. Koloman reorganized the administration of Croatia. He granted it autonomy in domestic affairs and placed it under a royal official called a "Ban." The Ban was sometimes a member of the royal house of Hungary and sometimes a Croatian nobleman.

Habsburg and Hungarian Rule

Croatia came under Habsburg rule in 1526, when the Turks killed the last Hungarian king at the battle of Mohacs. His heir and successor as king of Hungary was Ferdinand Habsburg, ruler of Austria. A year later, the Croatian Diet ratified the change in rulers by electing Ferdinand king of Croatia.

Not long after that, the Turks overran most of Croatia, with only the area around Zagreb remaining free. Recognizing the necessity of defending the southern border against the Turks, the Habsburgs created an area of forts and watchtowers known as the "Military Frontier." Since most of the area had been depopulated as a result of Turkish military incursions, the Habsburgs persuaded individuals to move to the area by granting them land in return for military service. Most of these settlers were Orthodox Serbs and Wallachians (also called Vlachs), who had fled from areas farther to the south and east to escape the yoke of the Turks.

The Habsburg rulers managed to free most of Croatia from the Turks by 1699. The Treaty of Carlowitz, signed in that year, acknowledged this. The newly freed areas of Croatia regained domestic autonomy, including their own Diet, or legislature. However, the Habsburg rulers continued to exercise direct control over the area of the Military Frontier because of its strategic significance. The separate military government for the Military Frontier was not finally abolished until 1881. The tradition of the frontier remained long after 1881, however. It was mainly the descendants of the Orthodox Serb and Wallachian settlers of the old Military Frontier who refused to accept Croatian independence in 1991 and organized a separate "Serbian Republic of the Krajina," with the goal of remaining united with their fellow Serbs in Serbia and Bosnia.

The tie of Croatia to its Habsburg rulers was peculiar because it was through their title as kings of Hungary. From Croatia's point of view, their loyalty was to the individual who was king of Hungary, not to either Hungary or, for that matter, Austria. The Croatian nobility therefore opposed centralizing tendencies of Habsburg

Ancient Roman gate at Pula

rulers during the 18th century. When they were no longer able to resist directly, they gradually merged themselves more and more into the Hungarian kingdom in order to take advantage of the fact that the Habsburgs had recognized Hungary as a free and independent kingdom under its own laws. Thus, in 1790, Croatia requested that it be permitted to send three deputies to the Hungarian Diet, which would be responsible for regulating all Croatian affairs.

Having escaped the centralizing tendencies of the Habsburg rulers, Croatia found itself more and more tied to Hungary, a link that it would take 100 years to undo. The process began in 1809, when Austria ceded a strip of territory on the Adriatic to Napoleon, who organized it into the Illyrian provinces. They lasted only four years, and Croatia reverted back to Hungary thereafter. However, Croat nationalists trace the rise of national feeling to this short-lived government, which brought Croats, Slovenes, and Serbs together for a short time.

The rise of national feeling can also be traced to the beginning of literary works in the Croatian language. It was Ljudevit Gaj (1809–1872) who produced the first such works, although he edited a journal called *Illyrian News*, in which he advocated the union of all South Slavs.

Another equally important development came in 1843, when Hungary attempted to establish Hungarian as the official language in Croatia. This incensed the Croats, but Hungary compounded the problem in 1848, when the parliament passed legislation that would have incorporated Croatia into the administrative system of Hungary. The Croats now allied themselves with the Habsburg monarchy and, under the command of their Ban, Baron Joseph Jelačić, a Croat force of 40,000 men helped to put down the Hungarian revolution. As a reward, Austria's 1849 constitution designated Croatia and Slavonia as an Austrian crownland separate from Hungary, assigning it also the port of Fiume.

This arrangement was reversed 18 years later, when Austria signed the famous *Ausgleich* ("compromise") with Hungary, which transferred Croatia back to Hungary. Croatia remained affiliated with Hungary until 1918. In 1868, Hungary signed an agreement with Croatia giving it provincial autonomy, its own parliament, and the right to use Croatian as its official language. Many Croats were dissatisfied with this arrangement, however, so Croat national feeling continued to grow. As anti-Hungarian sentiment grew, so did a sense of solidarity with fellow Slavs. Croats therefore greeted enthusiastically Serbia's victories in the two Balkan Wars of

Croatia

1912–1913. Many still dreamed of a Croat kingdom under the Habsburgs, but the dream of a united Yugoslavia increasingly found supporters. When it became clear that Serbia was on the winning side in World War I, the stage was set for a union of South Slavs.

Croatia Joins Yugoslavia

Croatia was included in the new Kingdom of Serbs, Croats, and Slovenes formed on December 1, 1918. In 1921, a constitution was adopted that created a unitary central government. Since Serbs made up about 40% of the overall population, their party, the Radical Party, tended to dominate this new kingdom. When Stjepan Radić, leader of the Croatian Peasant Party, protested this, the government responded by arresting him and banning his party. The period from 1921 to 1928 was one of constant conflict over the issue of centralism versus federalism, with Croatian nationalists advocating creation of a federal state.

When a Montenegrin assassinated Radić inside the parliament building in 1928, the Croatian deputies withdrew from the assembly, threatening not to return until a federal state had been created in which Croatians were not dominated by Serbs. King Alexander I opposed the idea of a federal state, and in 1929, he abolished the constitution and took power himself. After he had proclaimed his royal dictatorship, he changed the name of the country to Yugoslavia.

A Macedonian associated with the Croatian dissidents assassinated Alexander in 1934. Since Alexander's son, Peter, was only a child, Alexander's cousin Prince Paul was named regent; he ruled until 1941. In 1939, he attempted to solve the problem of nationalist dissent by creating an internally self-governing Croatia.

The Opera House, Zagreb

Paul was deposed in March 1941 after he allied Yugoslavia with Germany. The denunciation of the alliance brought a German invasion in April 1941 and German occupation of the country between 1941 and 1945. Hitler permitted an "independent" Croatia to be proclaimed in April 1941. The head of this entity was Ante Pavelić, leader of a fascist organization called Ustasha. The Pavelić regime was characterized by brutality and violence, much of it targeted against local Serbs. One of the problems the Croatian government has with Serbs today is that they remember the murderous actions of a previous Croatian government and are unwilling to trust the current one.

There were many Croats who opposed this Ustasha government. One was Josip Broz Tito (born of a Croat father and Slovene mother), leader of the Partisan forces against the Germans. During the war, Tito and his communist Partisans organized local committees throughout Croatia as they liberated individual areas from German or Ustasha control. Toward the end of the war, these committees were combined into a council of national liberation. After Zagreb was liberated, this council proclaimed itself the People's Government of Croatia. When Yugoslavia was reconstituted as the People's Republic of Yugoslavia in 1945, the People's Republic of Croatia joined as one of the six constituent republics.

Marshal Josip Broz Tito, who ruled Yugoslavia from 1945 to 1980, ruthlessly suppressed all nationalist agitation within the country. Franjo Tudjman was one of Tito's generals. In the early 1970s, he and Stipe Mesić, the last president of Yugoslavia, were among Croatian communist leaders imprisoned on charges of nationalistic deviations.

Croatian nationalist groups began to reemerge in the late 1980s. Most of these eventually joined to form the Croatian Democratic Union, which won the republic elections in April 1990. Franjo Tudjman, leader of the party, was elected president at the same time. The political program of the movement only called for increased autonomy within a more confederal Yugoslavia.

It was Yugoslavia's tragedy that a Serbian nationalist, Slobodan Milošević, rose to power within the League of Communists of Serbia at this same time. Milošević not only opposed all political concessions to Croatia but also deliberately sabotaged economic reform. He therefore created a political stalemate that was also destroying the economy.

Croatia Wins Independence

On May 19, 1991, the Croatian government held a referendum on the question of independence. After a favorable vote, the Croatian Assembly adopted a declaration of independence on June 25. The government reiterated, however, that it was willing to continue discussions on a looser Yugoslav confederation, with the central government confined to foreign policy, defense, and a common currency.

When Croatia began moving toward independence, the Serbs within the republic, egged on by Milošević and a press dominated by Serbs, organized two autonomous regions. Despite a new law passed by the Croatian legislature guaranteeing protection for minority ethnic groups, Croatian Serbs held their own referendum on July 7 reaffirming their loyalty to the Socialist Federal Republic of Yugoslavia.

Like Slovenians, Croatians agreed to suspend their declarations of independence for three months. Serbia, in turn, agreed to allow a Croatian, Stipe Mesić, to be elected president. The latter agreement was important in a military as well as a political sense because the president was also the commander-in-chief of the Yugoslav People's Army (JNA).

The agreement brought peace to Slovenia but not to Croatia. One of the first actions of President Mesić was to arrange a third cease-fire on July 2. General Blagoje Adžić, chief of the JNA General Staff, angrily repudiated it—and thereby his own commander-in-chief—in an interview that appeared on Belgrade television. He stated that the army "accepted the challenge of total war that had been imposed on it" and would soon end it with a complete victory. The next day, an armored column left Belgrade for Croatia.

On July 6, 1991, Milošević gave a speech in which he told Serbs to be ready to defend themselves. He also gave Serb leaders in Croatia generous access to Serbian radio and television. The first fighting in Croatia began on July 7, when Croatian Serbs allied with Milošević attacked Croatian territorial defense forces near the town of Tenja. Once the fighting had begun, the JNA intervened "to keep the peace," though its targets were always Croatian territorial units. Since President Tudjman ordered Croatian units not to attack the JNA, the fighting remained small-scale for some time. The JNA did not initiate battles at this time and only advanced when new fighting would break out. Gradually, however, its control of Croatian territory spread as Serb territorial forces launched new battles in area after area.

Croatian Serbs insisted on living in a state controlled by Serbs. But the Croatians were not entirely free of this mentality. The Republic of Bosnia and Herzegovina, which lies between Serbia and Croatia, has an extremely mixed population, with 33% Serbs and about 17% Croats. In July, President Tudjman admitted that members of

470

his government had held secret talks with Serbian leaders about carving up Bosnia between the two, leaving a small Muslim rump that neither wanted. Word of these talks hurt Croatia internationally.

Croatia was saved by the fact that Serbia and the JNA were even more bloody-minded. In August, Milošević revealed his plans for a reconstituted Yugoslavia that called for carving up Croatia and incorporating about a third of the territory into the new state, although Serbs constituted only 12% of Croatia's population.

Meanwhile the JNA, which up to this time had contended that it was acting as a neutral buffer between the two sides, began bombarding Croatian cities with artillery and aircraft. In late August, much of the city of Vukovar was destroyed. By this time, perhaps 20% of the republic had fallen under JNA or Serb militia control.

On September 18, 1991, Zagreb, the capital, came under fire from aircraft and artillery. At about the same time, the Yugoslav navy instituted a blockade of Croatia's Dalmatian ports. Soon it began attacking them, beginning with the city of Split. Up to this moment, the Croatian government had been carrying out a "passive defense" and refusing to challenge the JNA directly. Now it cut oil lines across Croatia to Serbia and laid siege to Yugoslav army barracks in Croatia. Croatia also began getting some indirect assistance from other republics when Bosnia and Herzegovina and North Macedonia adopted a position of neutrality and ordered their citizens to ignore conscription notices from the JNA. Even in Serbia, however, many young men went into hiding rather than serve.

The three-month moratorium on Croatia and Slovenia's independence declarations—agreed to at Brioni—expired on October 7, 1991. Freed of that limitation, the Croatian Assembly approved a resolution severing all ties with the Socialist Federal Republic of Yugoslavia. By this time, the JNA and the Serbs occupied approximately a third of the country. The Yugoslav air force marked the day with an attack on the presidential palace in Zagreb at the very moment that President Tudjman was in conference with Stipe Mesić, the federal president, and Ante Marković, the federal prime minister. As the *Economist* put it, "the attack put to rest any pretense that there is real life left in the Yugoslav federation."

By this time, it had become clear to almost everyone just what Serbia was attempting to do. But it took almost three months more before Britain and France could be persuaded to abandon the ideal of a united Yugoslavia. Even then, the American government refused to abandon that ideal. But the European Community (now EU) announced in December that it

Franjo Tudjman

would recognize Slovenia and Croatia as of January 15. The fighting continued up to that date but tapered off afterward. Under the terms of the eventual cease-fire, a United Nations Protection Force (UNPROFOR) was deployed in and along the boundaries of the three Serb-controlled areas within Croatia, the self-declared, independent "Serbian Republic of the Krajina." The declaration of independence was only pro forma, however. The goal of the Serbians was to unite with Serbia and the Serb-occupied areas of Bosnia in a "Greater Serbia."

Croatia subsequently made three attempts to reintegrate the Serb-occupied territory into Croatia, twice in 1993 and once in March 1994. On each occasion, the Serbs launched artillery attacks on Zagreb and other Croatian towns. In addition, UNPROFOR opposed Croatian efforts to restore control over Serb-held areas.

In January 1995, with the Croatian Serbs still armed and in control of one-third of the country and continuing to act as a separate government attached to Yugoslavia, President Tudjman decided that the UN-PROFOR mission had failed and that it was time for it to leave. He then informed the United Nations that the UNPROFOR mandate would not be renewed when it expired in March. What worried him was that the "Contact Group" (US, Russia, France, Great Britain, and Germany), negotiating with the Bosnian Serbs, had accepted their demand that they be permitted to confederate with Serbia. Tudjman expected that the Croatian Serbs would make the same demand, and Krajina would be lost forever. He also recognized that, although the Croatian Serbs were heavily armed, their mini-state was economically unviable on its own and was only surviving because of continuing support from Serbia by means of a thin corridor several hundred miles long across the northern part of Bosnia. Removal of the

UNPROFOR troops would give Croatia the chance to cut that lifeline to Serbia.

Tudjman's decision was an enormous gamble, for it ignored the possibility that Serbia might reintervene directly if he moved against the Croatian Serbs, and they started to lose. This was what bothered the Contact Group, which put him under heavy pressure to reverse his decision. What finally occurred was a sort of compromise. Tudjman agreed that he would permit half of the 12,000 UNPROFOR troops to stay, while the UN agreed to provide another 500 troops to police the border between Serb-held parts of Croatia and Bosnia and Serbia.

Two months later, Croatia sent its troops into the eastern section of Croatian-Serb-held Krajina, known as western Slavonia, and managed to recapture the area in just 40 hours. Although the Croatian Serbs retaliated with rocket attacks against Zagreb and other Croatian towns, Croatia held on to the pocket. Several thousand Serbs fled the area, making their way either to the remaining part of Krajina or to Serb-held Bosnia. Approximately two months later, Croatian forces overran the remaining section of Serb Krajina in just four days, between August 4 and 8. They met very little resistance; in fact, the Croatian Serb forces just seemed to melt away. As the Croatian forces entered from the west, as many as 150,000 Serbs fled eastward into Bosnia, many making their way across Bosnia into Serbia. The refugees included the 16,000 militiamen who had made up the Serb Krajina army.

The Recovery of Eastern Slavonia

President Tudjman next set his sights on eastern Slavonia, the remaining part of Croatia still held by Serbs. After shifting a significant part of his forces to the eastern part of the country, he made a public demand for its return.

The purpose of these actions was to ensure that eastern Slavonia was included on the agenda of the upcoming peace talks. But he also made it clear that he would use force if diplomacy failed. "The world," Tudjman was quoted as saying, "should not deceive itself into thinking that Croatia will be prepared to postpone a settlement of this issue indefinitely."

In the end, no force was necessary. On November 12, 1995, the Croatian Serbs agreed during the Dayton peace talks to accept Croatian sovereignty over eastern Slavonia after a transition period of one to two years. The transition period actually lasted three years. It was not turned over to Croatian control until January 1998. During that interregnum, a transitional administration set up by the UN Security Council governed the territory. Some UN peacekeeping forces were already there

Croatia

from the previous UN mission to Croatia, and others began arriving in January 1996. The United Nations hoped that, with a sufficiently long transition, the majority of Serbs living in the area could become reconciled to living under Croatian control and would remain.

In that sense, the operation appears to have been a failure. Although Croatia requested that UN police remain in eastern Slavonia after Croatia took official control on January 15, this did little to convince Serbs to stay. At least 10,000 Serbs left the area in the month preceding the final transfer of authority. Most went to Serbia.

The Croatian government must bear some of the responsibility for this outflow because it made clear that Croats expelled from the area during the war would be resettled with government assistance. At the same time, the 60,000 Serbs who had lived in other parts of Croatia before the war were refused permission to return to those areas. In addition, hardline Croatian nationalists did their best to instill fear in the Serbs by distributing pamphlets threatening to kill those Serbs who chose to remain.

The raising of the Croatian flag over the area does not mean that the area has been totally reintegrated into Croatia. About half of the Croatian population formerly resident in the area has returned, mainly due to lack of housing and job possibilities. Meanwhile, only half of the Serb refugees were resettled in other parts of Croatia, with the support of international funds. Contrary to general predictions, these transfers of population have been peaceful, with no clashes between Serbs and Croats. Moreover, Serbs are no longer fleeing across the eastern border into Serbia or applying for asylum in western Europe.

UN War-Crimes Tribunal in The Hague

Croatia had to face up to the fact that some Croatians were involved in atrocities that occurred during the Balkan wars in the 1990s and have to answer for their deeds. This creates tensions between the prodemocratic leadership after Tudjman's death and some nationalist veterans. Under Tudjman, Croatians were portrayed exclusively as victims in the 1991 war of independence and the conflicts thereafter. Some citizens resent the democratic government's willingness to shed light on possible atrocities committed by Croatians. When ex-prime minister Ivica Račan decided in July 2001 to hand over two prime suspects to the UN war-crimes tribunal in The Hague, several cabinet ministers resigned, and thousands of people went into the streets to protest. But Račan made the pragmatic argument that failure to hand over suspects would bring international sanctions on Croatia.

In March 2000 General Tihomir Blaškić, the former Croatian commander in Bosnia who had given himself up to the UN tribunal in 1996, was sentenced to 45 years in prison for war crimes. In March 2003, a Croatian court sentenced former general Mirko Norac to 12 years in prison for killing Serb civilians in 1991. He had surrendered in 2001 on the condition that he not be transferred to The Hague. In June 2007 Norac again went to trial, along with another retired general, Ramim Ademi, on further charges of atrocities against ethnic Serbs.

In April 2003 Croatian police arrested a Bosnian Croat, Ivica Rajić, long sought by the international court for killing Muslims in Bosnia. At the same time, a case entered a Croatian court that would have been unthinkable a few years earlier:

Nevenka Tudjman, daughter of the late president, went to trial on charges of graft and abuse of power. In October 2006 a commander who had a seat in parliament, Branimir Glavaš, was detained on war-crimes charges.

The government was rescued from its riskiest prosecution, that of General Janko Bobetko. Like Norac, he was a hero in the eyes of most Croats for creating and commanding an armed force that succeeded in recapturing the one-third of the country occupied by the Serbs since 1991. His failure to prosecute any subordinates who may have committed war crimes made him potentially guilty of them. As an 83-year-old diabetic with serious heart problems, his indictment in 2002 touched a raw nerve. In April 2003 he died, and his funeral became a rally for the nationalist right.

There were doubts that the Croatian Democratic Union (HDZ), the successor to Tudjman's party, which took over the government in December 2003, would continue cooperating with The Hague. It had been openly critical of the tribunal. But ex-prime minister Ivo Sanader moved the party from Catholic nationalism to centrist conservatism, and he pledged full cooperation. In March 2004 two retired army generals were sent to The Hague. They were indicted for commanding forces that murdered and intimidated ethnic Serbs so they would flee Croatia. In April Zagreb transferred six Bosnian Croats to the tribunal. In July 2004 the tribunal sentenced former Croatian prime minister Milan Babić, who had testified against Slobodan Milošević, to 13 years in prison for inflaming an ethnic-cleansing campaign that led to the expulsion of tens of thousands of Serbs. In June 2007 a Croatian Serb, Milan Martić, was convicted of murder, torture, and the ordering of two days of indiscriminate cluster bombing of Zagreb in May 1995.

Not until December 2005 did Spanish police apprehend the much-wanted General Ante Gotovina, while dining in a four-star hotel restaurant in the Canary Islands. Regarded by many Croatians as a hero, he was implicated in the killing of about 150 Serb civilians and in the expulsion of 150,000 Serbs during Croatia's offensive in 1995 to recapture land seized by Serbs. His passport indicated that he had globe-trotted through three continents while an international manhunt took place. The EU had refused to open membership talks with Croatia until he was caught and delivered to the court. This delay quelled any illusions that Croatia would sail smoothly into the union. It also deprived Croatians of the notion that, unlike Serbs, they had dealt effectively with the tainted moral legacy of their own "homeland war" from 1991 to 1995.

"Gotovina Hero!" Call to free a Croatian general on trial in The Hague for tolerating the murder of Serb POWs

The trial began in March 2008 and was broadcast live in Croatia. It lasted two years. The tribunal did not dispute Croatia's right to retake its land in Krajina. But it charged General Gotovina and his two codefendants, Generals Ivan Čermak and Mladen Markač (all three heroes at home) for knowingly shelling civilian targets, allowing their forces to go on violent rampages, terrorizing civilians and looting and burning Serbian homes. The US had taken a keen interest in the trial because Croatian officials argue that American military advisers helped plan the operation and directed drone aircraft over the battle zone to gain real-time intelligence used by Croatian forces. Gotovina's chief defendant was Greg Kehoe, an American who was a former prosecutor at the tribunal and head of the office that built the criminal cases against Saddam Hussein.

In November 2012 Generals Gotovina and Markač were dramatically acquitted and returned home to a hero's welcome, with the crowds chanting, "Victory!" The court had become convinced that there had been no organized plan for "ethnically cleansing" the Serbs and that the generals' targets had been legitimate military ones. They could not control the bands that murdered and looted. Croats were ecstatic, while Serbs were furious at this decision. Gotovina may even enter politics as a conservative politician close to the Catholic Church.

Former leader Franjo Tudjman, who died in December 1999, remains a Croatian hero. A beautiful suspension bridge leading into Dubrovnik is named "Dr. Franjo Tudjman." The tribunal had been close to indicting him. He would have been charged with leading a "joint criminal enterprise" that included expelling Serbs. Prosecutors were aided by the extensive records he had kept, and they quoted from his speeches calling Krajina Serbs "a cancer on the underbelly of Croatia."

When convicting in May 2013 six Bosnian Croats of persecuting and murdering Muslim civilians during the war, the court cited Tudjman and his defense minister, Gojko Šušak, as members of a "joint criminal enterprise." They had sent money, vehicles, weapons, and senior military personnel to run operations in Bosnia. "These crimes were not committed in a random manner by a few undisciplined soldiers" but were the result of a planned military campaign to remove the Muslim population and establish a territory for Croats only.

In May 2009 a Croatian court convicted an opposition legislator, Branimir Glavaš, of war crimes. He was the first senior politician to be held responsible for wartime atrocities against Serbs. Because of his legislative immunity, he was not incarcerated.

Prime Minister Andrej Plenkovic

Croatia had to deal with Serbia's January 2010 accusation at the International Court of Justice that it had committed genocide when it expelled the Serb population in 1995. This is a belated response to a similar Croatian lawsuit against Serbia in 1999. In 2015, the ICJ decided that, while mass killings and torture were committed during the war, they did not amount to genocide directed by one state against the other. That does not preclude some individuals' responsibility for genocidal actions but absolved both governments of this charge.

POLITICAL SYSTEM

The Republic of Croatia is a parliamentary democracy with a multiparty system. The fulcrum of power had always rested with the president. With the death of President Franjo Tudjman in December 1999, that changed, and the presidency became less powerful. Croatia has no vice president. According to the constitution, in case of the incapacity or death of the president, the speaker of the parliament assumes the president's powers temporarily. He then calls new elections 60 days after the president leaves office.

Parliament (Hrvatski Sabor) is unicameral after the Chamber of Representatives and Chamber of Counties were abolished in April 2001. It has 151 members elected directly for a term of four years. The country is divided into 10 territorial electoral units, each sending 14 members to parliament. Two additional units totaling 12 seats are reserved for nonterritorial constituencies: One is for expatriate Croats, including 300,000 Croats in Bosnia and Herzegovina, and the other is for representatives of minority groups, including Serbs, living within Croatia. The leader of the coalition of parties that can maintain a majority in parliament is the prime minister, who is the most powerful figure in the political system.

At the local level there are 20 county governors and assemblies.

The Presidency

Tudjman's authoritarianism and occasional abuse of human rights was a source of international concern. In 1996, his regime angered human rights activists when it sponsored two new laws whose effect was to limit basic freedoms guaranteed in the constitution. Under the first law, anyone desiring to establish an organization to monitor the actions or to supplement the work of government ministries needed the government's permission. The second law made it a crime to insult "the dignity and authority of leading officials."

Using these new laws, the government attempted in 1996 to close down two of four remaining independent newspapers, the *Feral Tribune* and the *Novi List*. Partly in response, the Council of Europe voted to postpone indefinitely Croatia's entry into that body. This led the Croatian government to pass a new press law in October that set out certain press guarantees. Croatia was admitted to the Council of Europe shortly thereafter. Pope John Paul II visited Croatia in 1998, an event exploited by Tudjman as a validation of his rule, even though the purpose of the pope's visit was religious.

Tudjman was succeeded by Stipe Mesić on January 24, 2000. The new president subsequently won much of the credit for dismantling the quasi-authoritarian Tudjman regime and for clearing Croatia's way back into Europe, about which he rhapsodized, "Croatia's future is a united Europe which must be a synonym for democracy, tolerance, the promotion and respect of human rights and the rule of law. Croatia, which will be based on these foundations, will have no problems in finding its rightful place in the European Union." In fact, all parties and political leaders made EU entry their top priority. Mesić was reelected in January 2005. One populist candidate whom he defeated was Boris Mikšić, a Croat American millionaire businessman, who returned to Croatia after three decades in the United States.

A prominent politician in the last years of the former Yugoslavia and its last rotating president, Mesić said that his chief goal was to speed up Croatia's integration into the European Union and NATO. The fact that he promised to abandon support for Croatian separatists in Bosnia

Croatia

and Herzegovina, to support the return of ethnic Serbian refugees who fled Croatia during the period of the war, and to cooperate with the war-crimes tribunal in The Hague—all three policy reversals of Tudjman positions—bolstered the chances for such integration.

In October 2002 he had become the first head of state to appear as a witness at the UN tribunal in The Hague. He accused the former Serbian leader Slobodan Milošević of engineering the breakup of Yugoslavia, plundering the Yugoslav treasury and National Bank to aid Serb rebels in Croatia and to finance a Serb army, using that armed force to seize Croatian territory, and generally provoking warfare that created "rivers of blood." He also confirmed that an important meeting had taken place in March 1991 between Milošević and Tudjman. They discussed carving up Bosnia and Herzegovina and dividing it between themselves. Not surprisingly Milošević lashed back, calling Mesić a criminal and accusing him of ordering the torching of Serb villages.

In January 2010 Ivo Josipović, a professor of international law and renowned composer, was elected president by a landslide, receiving 60% of the votes in the second round, with a turnout of almost 50%. Josipović, a Social Democrat, appealed to the voters' loss of patience with corruption, which was one of the major themes in the election. He promised to serve "without compromise in the fight against corruption and organized crime." He was narrowly defeated (50.4% to 49.6%) for reelection in January 2015. Turnout was 58.5%. The victor was Kolinda Grabar-Kitarović of the center-right bloc. Her experience was impressive: NATO assistant secretary-general, ambassador to the US, and minister of foreign and European affairs. Since the president has a say in foreign policy and is head of the army, this background served Croatia well. In response to the migrant crisis of 2015, she supported the hardline approach adopted by Hungary and called for using the Croatian military to control the border. These ideas were not particularly popular in the society largely sympathetic to the plight of the refugees. Grabar-Kitarović was the country's first female president, and her good looks gained her the nickname "Barbie."

Parliamentary Elections

Former president Tudjman took advantage of the euphoria that swept Croatia following the recovery of Krajina to call for national parliamentary elections that took place in October 1995. They resulted in an absolute majority for his party, the Croatian Democratic Union (HDZ). With new parliamentary elections scheduled to take place in 2000, western governments

and institutions began to put pressure on Tudjman to modify Croatia's electoral laws. The message was that, unless he did so, Croatia would not be considered for membership in any of the various Euro-Atlantic structures. In May 1999, therefore, he instructed the HDZ to hold a series of meetings with the leaders of six opposition parties to hash out a newly agreed election law.

As a result of these meetings, the HDZ agreed to relinquish exclusive control over Croatian Television and allow it to become a public broadcaster. In addition, agreement was reached on abolishing the system of separate voting lists for Croats living abroad. What this meant in practice was that such Croats would still be able to vote in Croatian elections, but it would no longer be as easy to elect a solid bloc of deputies to the Croatian parliament as voters in Herzegovina had done in the past. This change, made at the behest of the international community—which would have preferred that Bosnian Croats not be permitted to vote in Croatian elections—turned out to be meaningless in practice. The HDZ ensured a strong Herzegovinian vote by placing a number of hardline Croatians on the HDZ's parliamentary list for Croats in Bosnia and Herzegovina.

The elections, which took place on January 3, 2000, resulted in a victory for the political opposition. The new prime minister was Ivica Račan, leader of the Social Democratic Party. He had once headed the League of Communists of Croatia prior to independence, but he shifted to the center-left.

Račan tried to introduce democratic reforms and to prepare his country for EU and NATO membership. The EU and the US made it clear that a crucial part of this process involves bringing war-crimes suspects to court. Therefore, Croatia turned over several suspects to the war-crimes tribunal in The Hague despite the political risks at home. In September 2000, Račan forced seven generals, all former Tudjman supporters, to retire when they criticized their government's crackdown on war criminals and accused Račan of betraying the country's interests and honor to the west.

The Račan coalition turned its back on Tudjman's publicly stated wish to reduce the Serb population in Croatia to 5% of the total population, compared with 12% before independence. It attempted to persuade the 200,000 ethnic Serbs who fled to Serbia and the additional 30,000 who sought refuge in Bosnia to return to their earlier homes in Croatia. Some did so. Property disputes and the lack of jobs remain the main obstacles. Returning refugees often find their former houses occupied by others who themselves are refugees.

President Zoran Milanović

Račan improved relations with Croatia's neighbors, especially Bosnia. Serbs and Croats no longer need visas to visit each other's country, and air and train service between the two has been restored and improved. However, most Croats were concerned about living standards and jobs after almost four years of difficult but necessary reforms. They were willing to turn back to the Croatian Democratic Union (HDZ) in parliamentary elections in 2003.

Former HDZ leader Ivo Sanader had purged the party of some of the hardline nationalists. Some were implicated in war crimes. He claimed that the party is no longer nationalist at all but rather a center-right Christian Democratic Party. A former theater director from Split, he had been a head of Tudjman's office. He had studied in Austria, speaks four languages, and made it clear that foreign policy was his priority. He embraced a decidedly pro-American policy and in April 2009 led Croatia into NATO.

In July 2009 he unexpectedly resigned from politics. He gave no explanation, but he faced increasing questions about how he had gotten to be so rich while in office. He is suspected of siphoning more than €10 million from state-owned companies. He fled to Austria, but he was extradited to Croatia, where he was tried and eventually sentenced to 8.5 years for the misuse of funds.

He was replaced as prime minister by his deputy, Jadranka Kosor, the country's first female prime minister. She studied law at Zagreb University and was a successful journalist when she entered politics in the mid-1990s. She promised to pursue Sanader's policies, especially fighting the economic recession, resolving the border dispute with Slovenia, and overcoming the deadlock over EU membership. It was during her tenure that the EU formally accepted Croatia's EU membership. Sanader made a clumsy attempt at a comeback and was expelled from the HDZ in January 2010. In 2012 he was sentenced to 10 years in prison for corruption.

Kosor pursued her agenda with some success, and she bolstered her country's credibility with the EU and the US. She unblocked accession talks with the EU by temporarily resolving a disagreement with Slovenia over the latter country's access to the sea. They agreed not to let this long-standing dispute stand in the way of Croatia's bid for EU membership. Afterward they will submit the issue to an EU arbitration committee. With the EU's strong urging, she also embraced anticorruption with a vigor many had thought impossible. It "is the basis for everything." "This is a fight at all levels," she proclaimed and instituted a policy of zero tolerance. Although many Croatians want to see corruption curbed, she was not rewarded with popularity. Her approval rating stood at only 35% at the end of 2009.

She locked horns with President Josipović. Like many in her HDZ Party, which still has high-level supporters who honored former wartime leader Franjo Tudjman, she was furious when the president appeared in the Bosnian parliament in April 2010 and apologized for Croatia's role in the Bosnian war. He said he was "deeply sorry" that his country had "contributed to the suffering of people and divisions which still burden us today." The prime minister protested that the president should cooperate with the government in the field of foreign policy, not veer off and try to make it himself.

In December 2011 Kosor's HDZ Party suffered a crushing defeat after ruling 17 of the preceding 20 years. A coalition of three parties, HDZ won only 23.8% of the votes (down from 36.6% in 2007) and 47 seats (18 fewer). This was the first time HDZ was not the strongest individual party in parliament. It moved to the opposition benches.

Emerging as the landslide victor was Zoran Milanović's Social Democratic Party (SDP), the leading party in a four-party center-left coalition with the humorous name of Kukuriku (Cock-a-doodle-doo). It captured 40% of the votes (up from 31.2%) and 81 seats (up from 63). He became prime minister.

The Croatian Democratic Assembly of Slavonia and Baranja (HDSSB), led by Vladimir Šišljagić, won 2.9% of the votes and six seats (up two). A new party, Labour, led by Dragutin Lesar, garnered 5.1% of the votes and six seats. The 300,000 ethnic Croats living in Bosnia were allowed to vote, together with another 100,000 Croatian citizens living abroad.

The November 2015 parliamentary election was dominated by headlines related to the ongoing migrant crisis, but there were also other pressing issues high on the voters' minds. Top among them were six years of stagnant or shrinking economy, a high unemployment rate (third-highest in the EU), and the lack of improvements to the business environment or the tax system. While Prime Minister Milanović and his Social Democrats won much praise for their empathetic approach to the refugees, in the end the economic issues helped tip the scale in favor of the HDZ. The results of the election were inconclusive: The conservatives of the HDZ won 59 seats, while the SDP and its allies came in second, with 56 seats. Neither won the 76 needed to control the parliament. Under the circumstances, HDZ approached a new party created in 2012, an alliance of independent candidates called Most (Bridge) that won 19 seats on its call for fiscal responsibility and administrative efficiency. Most's parliamentary delegation is dominated by municipal mayors, professors, and other professionals, and its real appeal was that it offered an alternative to the two mainstream parties.

After lengthy negotiations, a new HDZ-Most cabinet with several other independents was created in January 2016. It was led by Croatian Canadian businessman Tihomir Orešković, with leaders of HDZ (Tomislav Karamarko) and Most (Božo Petrov) as deputy prime ministers. Much of the attention of this self-styled "Tim's Team" was consumed by infighting and multilateral attempts to hold no-confidence votes against Karamarko (for an alleged conflict of interest) and against Orešković, as well as by the latter's attempts to force his deputies to resign. This was unfortunate, as Croatia's problems, such as the economy and the refugee issue, were pushed to the back burner.

On June 16, 2016, the opposition succeeded in pushing through a vote of no confidence in the government of Tihomir Orešković. The parliament dissolved itself in July, and then-President Grabar-Kitarović called for new parliamentary elections to be held on September 11, 2016.

In the run-up to the elections, a scandal broke out when the leader of Social Democrats, former prime minister Zoran Milanović, was secretly taped during a meeting with war veterans, disparaging Bosnia as a failed state and declaring that "miserable" Serbia "wants to rule half the Balkans." He also warned that, in case Bosnian Serbs attempt to split from Bosnia, Croatia might move in to protect Bosnian Croats. This resurfacing of virulent nationalism in the most recently admitted member of the EU took many people aback, both in Croatia and abroad. While the SDP was widely expected to win the elections, a part of the electorate changed its minds.

The elections were won by the Croatian Democratic Union (HDZ), led this time by Andrej Plenković. With 36.27% of popular vote, HDZ obtained 61 seats in the 151-seat parliament, while the coalition led by Social Democrats received 33.82% of votes and 54 seats. Milanović announced his temporary withdrawal from politics. Plenković formed a government in coalition with Most (9.91%, 13 seats) plus 8 additional deputies representing national minorities. About half of the ministers were reappointed from the previous government. Most leader Božo Petrov became speaker of the parliament. However, he stepped down only a few months later when another crisis hit in April 2017 and HDZ demanded his resignation, while Prime Minister Plenković dismissed three ministers supported by Most.

Foreign Policy

Croatia likes to think of itself as a western nation, and Franjo Tudjman once argued to reporters that Croatia is not part of the Balkans. Most Croatians would agree with him. But he never managed to bring Croatia into the European mainstream, partly because many Europeans remained suspicious of his sometimes-dictatorial ways and partly because of his occasional incursions into Byzantine diplomacy. During the war between 1991 and 1995, for example, he held conversations with Belgrade on at least two occasions concerning a possible division of former Yugoslav territories into a Greater Croatia and a Greater Serbia.

Tudjman feared that the west's inaction was permitting Serbia to create a Greater Serbia on its own, leaving Croats squeezed into a small part of the western Balkans. That would explain—but not justify—why he intervened in Bosnia in 1993 to support radical Bosnian Croat leaders who favored the partition of Bosnia between Croats and Serbs. Later he sent an army of up to 10,000 Croatian soldiers into Bosnia to assist the Bosnian Croats.

He negotiated an agreement with Belgrade in January 1994 that was touted as a first step toward normalizing relations. In actuality, it was a cynical agreement between Croatia and Serbia to cooperate in the division of Bosnia. But carving separate Serb and Croat territories out of Bosnia would have created a precedent for a partition of Croatia, as western diplomats carefully pointed out to Tudjman. Thus, when the west produced its own ultimatum in February 1994, demanding that the Serbs withdraw their artillery from the environs of Sarajevo, he changed his position and threw his support behind a Croat Muslim federation in Bosnia associated with Croatia.

Tudjman's commitment to the Croat Muslim federation was halfhearted and,

Croatia

at best, tactical. He always defended the right of Bosnian Croats to hold Croatian citizenship and to vote in Croatian elections. While he was alive, they continued to do so. As he commented to Secretary of State Madeleine Albright when she visited Croatia in August 1998, "the main problem between the United States and Croatia is the problem of Bosnia. . . Croatia . . . is obliged by its constitution to take care of Croats outside the Republic of Croatia."

Under Tudjman, Croatia continued to have troubled relations with its neighbors. For example, UN peacekeepers had to control Croatia's Prevlaka Peninsula, a two-mile strip of land that lies on Croatia's southernmost border with Montenegro. This grants access to Boka Kotorska Bay, Montenegro's only deepwater seaport and naval base. The Yugoslav army occupied the peninsula during the war. Until December 2002 it had not been possible to return the territory to Croatian control because of Belgrade's objection. Serbia-Montenegro and Croatia signed a landmark border agreement, ceding the peninsula to Croatia. The agreement demilitarizes the area, permits Serbian and Montenegrin naval vessels to traverse the channel into the bay without stopping, and prohibits military maneuvers in the area. It calls for joint sea police patrols.

Likewise, Yugoslavia always insisted on keeping the border crossing between Croatia and Montenegro at Debeli Brijeg closed, even though the Montenegrin government had requested that it be opened. Montenegro opened the border crossing briefly in November 1998 for the Roman Catholic All Saints holiday, then attempted to open it on a regular basis in 1999. At that moment, Yugoslav army troops intervened and closed the crossing. Yugoslav soldiers and Montenegrin police began jointly manning it in April 1999. Croatia signed an agreement with the Bosnian government in September 1998 granting Bosnian nationals free access to the Croatian port of Ploče. In 2018 an agreement was in place to construct a bridge linking a tiny corner of Croatia in the south to the rest of the country. This is the first time a project funded largely by EU money has been awarded to a Chinese company.

The US government signed several accords with Croatia dealing with trade, science and technology, education, and nontechnical military assistance. It engaged in intelligence cooperation with Croatia in the mid-1990s. It provided encryption gear to each of the country's regular army brigades, maintained listening posts to intercept telephone calls in Bosnia and Serbia, and flew intelligence-gathering drone aircraft from a base near Zadar along the Adriatic. Tudjman's son Miro claimed, "We had a partnership," but US

officials confirm only that it had a "liaison relationship" with Croatia and other nations in the region. The US also furnished some funds for its democratization projects. In spite of these gestures, however, Croatia's relations with the United States have been troubled.

For example, when Croatia applied to become a member of NATO's Partnership for Peace program in 1998, American ambassador William Montgomery informed Croatian officials that Croatia would first have to make greater efforts toward democratization, allow the return of those Serbian refugees who wished to come back to Croatia, and give more support to the Dayton peace process before its membership could be considered. Washington was particularly concerned by what it perceived as Tudjman's lack of support for the Bosnian Croat federation in Bosnia, often expressed in terms of inadequate backing for the Dayton Accords. When he expressed the desire to establish closer ties with the European Union, he received much the same reply.

Tudjman always made it clear that, although he wanted Croatia to become a member of NATO and the EU, he was unwilling to change his own policies to achieve those goals. He reiterated this stance in January 1999 during his state-of-the-nation address. He said that foreign powers were making accession to NATO and the EU difficult with their "efforts to alter the political landscape in Croatia and force us into undesirable integrations."

Under Tudjman, the European Union refused to negotiate any major accords with Croatia. It did agree to admit Croatia to the Council of Europe in 1996. The problem for the EU was always Croatia's human rights record, in particular the numerous accusations of discrimination against Serbs living in Croatia.

A report by the Organization for Security and Cooperation in Europe, drawn up in March 1999, said of Croatia, "there has been no progress in improving respect for human rights, the rights of minorities and the rule of law." Under pressure from the United States and the European Union, the report continues, Croatia has made commitments to freedom of the press. But Croatian Television, the main source of news for most Croatians, "remains subject to political control by the ruling party."

Post-Tudjman Foreign and Defense Policy

With Tudjman's death in December 1999 and his party's repudiation at the polls in January 2000, Croatian foreign policy changed in the direction urged by the European Union and the United States. Former president Stipe Mesić strongly supported Croatia's membership in the EU

and NATO, and he took policy positions that contributed to bringing that about. Specifically, he promised to cooperate with the war-crimes tribunal at The Hague, to support the return of ethnic Serbian refugees who fled Croatia during the war, and to abandon support for Croatian separatists in Bosnia and Herzegovina.

Croatia began negotiating a "stabilization and association agreement" with the EU that placed it higher on the list of countries seeking membership in that elite European club. After Slovenia, Croatia became the strongest candidate in former Yugoslavia for accession. It applied in 2003 and became an official candidate in 2005. By continuing to hand over wanted war criminals to The Hague, the Sanader government helped the country take a giant step toward EU membership. Accession talks resumed after the indicted war criminal Ante Gotovina had been captured and handed over to the International War Crimes Tribunal in 2005.

It received €436 million in EU aid ($675 million) through 2009. The EU urged it to crack down harder on corruption and to tighten its "unrestricted" cooperation with the war-crimes tribunal. The European Parliament gave the same message, but it issued a positive report of Croatia's progress. In January 2012, 66% of voters approved of Croatia becoming the 28th EU member in July 2013. It was supported by all main political figures, academics, institutions, and the Catholic Church. The small turnout of only 43.5% was due to worries that Croatia would have to bail out such countries as Greece and that a country with only .8% of the EU population would have no effective say in EU matters. It is now a full EU member.

Croatia received some rewards for its changed foreign policy. It was admitted to NATO in April 2009. Then-prime minister Sanader was delighted: "Croatia is going where it belongs. Croatia is going back home [to the west]." Support at home for such membership has increased to over 60%, a welcome reversal of earlier opposition. But NATO is regarded by many Croatians as merely confirmation of western integration and a symbolic threshold a country has to cross to get to the real prize—EU membership.

Here worrisome problems developed. As its maritime border dispute festered, Slovenia had demonstrated that it would not approve of Croatia's entry without a compromise that respects its demands. However, the two countries agreed in 2010 not to let the dispute block Croatia's EU entry and to submit it to the Permanent Court of Arbitration in The Hague. Soon, Croatia decried the process as "irrevocably compromised" when a Slovenian arbiter was accused of colluding with the

Croatia

Slovenian government. Even though the court itself dismissed these concerns, Croatia announced it would not feel bound by the results of the arbitration. When the court's decision was announced in June 2017, Slovenia received three-quarters of the disputed Piran Bay and the right to use a small corridor of Croatia's territorial waters to reach the high seas. Several land areas were also delineated. Croatia's president Kolinda Grabar-Kitarović declared that "Croatia will neither accept nor reject the arbitration's ruling" because "the tribunal doesn't exist."

Corruption continues to show its ugly face. Transparency International ranks Croatia 50th out of 168 countries in terms of corruption. Croatians and EU officials were shocked by a stunning rise in gangland-style killings. The homegrown "mafia" that profited during the wars in the 1990s had become bolder. Gangs invest in legitimate businesses and in prime real estate, but they use the old methods to get their way—murders, beatings, and threats.

However, both former prime minister Kosor and former president Josipović declared war on corruption, and Kosor booked some solid successes. Tough new laws enforced by many new police and judicial appointments have helped. Among the high-profile investigations was an indictment of a former deputy prime minister, and an ex-defense minister was indicted. Although the chief impetus for this comes from the EU, most Croatians support these efforts, which must be taken seriously. The main problem is public procurement; the EU cannot allot funds that are siphoned off by crooked politicians and organized criminals. It has learned in the case of Romania and Bulgaria, which entered the EU in 2007, that its leverage dissipates after a country joins. If Croatia's crackdown fails, then the hopes of other Balkan countries to enter will be jeopardized.

Croatia's armed forces are subject to an arms limitation regime established under the Dayton Peace Accords. Its total active military force has been reduced to 18,600. The military is being transformed into a small professional force that can be deployed with NATO anywhere in the world. Conscription has been abolished. The army has 11,390 soldiers, and there are 3.000 paramilitary armed police. This force is backed by 21,000 reservists. Its navy of 1,850 sailors mans one conventional submarine and seven patrol and coastal combatants, and it conducts joint exercises with the US Navy. The air force has 3,500 personnel and flies 24 combat aircraft (12 of them MiGs) and 32 helicopters. It has 10.000 paramilitary forces. Alongside this transformation is a reduction of the three secret service agencies to two—one military and

Riding with tradition in Klis

Photo by Roman Payerhin

the other civilian under strong civilian and parliamentary oversight.

In February 2003 it was one of 10 countries in central and eastern Europe to sign a letter supporting the American-British policy toward Iraq. It sent a 50-member military police unit to Afghanistan and supplied rifles and ammunition to the new Afghan army. By 2010 it had 290 troops fighting in Afghanistan with no "caveats" (restrictions). It offered the UN an infantry company of about 100 soldiers to perform peacekeeping in the Middle East. Its positive commitment to the work of the UN was rewarded in 2007 when it was elected to serve a two-year term on the UN Security Council. The government generally pursues a pro-American policy. The United States and Croatia marked 30 years of bilateral ties in 2022. Since October 23, 2021, Croatia has been a participant in CBP's Visa Waiver Program, which permits Croatian citizens to visit the United States for business or tourism for up to 90 days without a visa.

Croatia's foreign policy profile was elevated in 2019 when Foreign Minister Marija Pejčinović Burić was named secretary general of the European Council.

ECONOMY

Croatia has much excellent farmland in the northeastern part of the country, but farming is carried on throughout the republic. Corn is the chief grain crop, followed by wheat. Other commercial crops include plums, used in the production of slivovitz (a dry, usually colorless brandy); grapes, which are processed into wine and other brandies; sugar beets, flax, hemp, and fruits.

The raising of livestock also plays a significant role, divided about equally between cattle and sheep. Pigs and poultry are also important farm products. Croatia still has significant forest areas, so timber products provide employment to many rural inhabitants.

Manufacturing is well developed. It is mostly light industry that concentrates on manufacturing goods for sale to consumers. Croatia also produces extractive products, such as petroleum, coal, and bauxite. Fishing is a major industry for people along the Dalmatian coast. Its Adriatic port, Rijeka, has deep waters and is therefore capable of handling large ships. The World Bank provided the primary funding

477

Croatia

for a €215 million development project of the port.

The most profitable of all is tourism, which provides nearly a fifth of Croatia's GDP. But this sector languished for a while after the wars during the 1990s.

Political instability in the area and the threat of renewed fighting were important deterrents. With the many justly famous resorts along the Dalmatian coast coming back to life again, tourism is booming. The country has become one of the travel industry's hottest new destinations, and tourism is becoming Croatia's chief foreign currency earner. In 2014 alone, it hosted more than 11.6 million visitors. Tourism struggled during the 2009–2010 economic recession, but the decline was temporary, and in 2016 a record 16.3 million tourists visited Croatia. Serb tourists, who used to flock to the coast, were aggressively courted. Most guest beds are in small guesthouses and private rooms, limiting expansion opportunities for large-scale tourism but also helping preserve the spectacular coast from excessive development. While red tape and poor business conditions stand in the way of tourism expansion, Croatia's popularity is growing, not least because it is an attractive alternative to conflict-ridden Mediterranean destinations, such as Tunisia and Egypt. One consequence of EU membership is that Russian and Turkish visitors now need visas.

The war left a stagnant economy and thousands of refugees, particularly in the area of Zagreb. The demobilization that began with the end of the war also contributed to an already-massive unemployment problem. Exports covered barely half of commodity imports. In 2010 it had a relatively large foreign debt amounting to 90% of GDP. Taxes are too high. Judicial and administrative reforms are urgently needed, although some successes have been achieved. With only 3.8 million people, the country has a backlog of 1.2 million cases, including issues over title deeds. The public sector spends more than half of GDP and is weighed down by inefficient state-owned industries. Privatization and transformation from a planned economy to a market economy was slow and unsteady.

Croatia was hit hard by the 2009 global recession and 2020 pandemic but weathered the crises better than some of its neighbors. Its banks are relatively stable, causing one banker to rejoice, "God must be Croatian since the country is not encumbered by dangerous financial instruments and while its banks have no toxic assets." It did not have to turn to the IMF for standby credit.

By the standards of the region, Croatia is relatively rich. It has an open economy with an accommodative foreign policy, highly dependent on international trade in Europe. EU structural funds amounting to €14 billion ($19 billion) were available to Croatia to 2020. Its Gross Domestic Product (GDP) per capita was recorded at 16610.32 US dollars in 2022. GDP growth was an admirable 0.9%, and the budget deficit was 3.4% in 2023. Croatia's GDP per capita is expected to reach 17009.00 USD by the end of 2024.

CULTURE

The 9th century Church of St. Cross in Nin, the first Croatian capital, is often referred to as "the smallest cathedral in the world." The Plaque of Baska, dating to 1100, holds a Croatian inscription in the Glagolitic script. Marko Martulia (b. 1450) was particularly known for his writings in Latin, but he also wrote a poem in Croatian verses (Judita, 1521). Rudjer Bošković (b. 1711) is world famous as a forerunner in the field of modern physics. Dubrovnik, Renaissance cradle of artists, scientists, nobles, merchants, and sailors, existed as an independent city republic for centuries. Now restored after the destruction of the recent war, it is once again a mecca for tourists.

The Opera House, Zagreb

Roman Catholicism has always been a part of Croatian tradition, as well. It permeates and largely defines the culture. For example, it was Bishop Josip Juraj Strossmayer who carried out a reorganization of the University of Zagreb in 1874. This tradition became somewhat secularized in the 19th century through the writings of such cultural figures as Franjo Rački, the Croatian historian. Even today, part of the definition of being a Croat continues to be membership in the Roman Catholic Church. Most Croats regard the pope as the highest moral authority. The Vatican was among the first to recognize Croatia's statehood in January 1992.

In June 2003 the pope made his 100th pilgrimage abroad by visiting Croatia for five days. He beatified a 20th-century Croatian nun, Sister Marija Petković, who had founded the Daughters of Mercy and devoted her life to helping children throughout the world. He assured the people that he remembered their "sufferings caused by the war, which are still visible on your faces," but he urged Croats to move past their turbulent history. The following month the Croatian Catholic Church demonstrated its power by rejecting plans to introduce yoga classes for teachers. It said that such a scheme would introduce "Hinduist religious practices dressed up as exercises into Croatian schools."

The Catholic Church scored a major victory in December 2013, when two-thirds voted to ban same-sex marriage. The debate deeply polarized the country, where LGBTQ rights parade in 2012 attracted 10,000 persons without incident.

Linguistically, Croatian does not differ greatly from Serbian. Borrowed words in the vocabulary tend to come from German or Latin rather than from Greek or Turkish, as in the case of Serbia. Another difference is that Croatian uses the Roman alphabet, while Serbian uses the Cyrillic alphabet.

Although not quite a religion, Croats treat their soccer with much fervor and zeal. The national team's excellent performance at the 1998 FIFA World Cup championship—the first one for the newly independent Croatia and just a short while after the war—brought the patriotic and nationalistic feelings to a frenzy when the team came in third, beating the heavily favored Germans. The March 2013 World Cup qualifying match between the Croatian and Serbian national soccer teams in Zagreb provided a reminder that healing from the Balkan wars will take time. Anticipating problems, the only Serbs allowed to attend were officials and journalists. Deafening boos accompanied the Serbian national anthem. Croat fans unfurled banners proclaiming such things as "we defended our homes." They chanted "Vukovar, Vukovar" and "Kill the Serbs." Later that year a Croatian soccer player, Josip Joe Šimunić, was fined $4,300 for making Nazi chants over the loud speaker after the national team qualified for the World Cup. He shouted to the fans, "For the homeland!" to which the crowd responded "ready!" That had been the call used by Croatian pro-Nazi Ustasha during World War II. A more uplifting moment for Croats in 2014 was Marin Čilić's stunning tennis victory in the US Open.

Sports are not immune to other societal maladies either. In 2015, the president of Dinamo Zagreb soccer club and a few others were arrested for partaking in organized crime, embezzling $17.3 million and failing to pay $1.8 million in taxes.

One of Croatia's little-known gifts to men's fashion throughout the world is the necktie, or kravata. It came from the cravats worn by Croat soldiers in the French army during the Thirty Years' War, 1618–1648.

CURRENT ISSUES

The change of government in 2015 was primarily a result of the public's foul mood. Polls had found that very few voters thought Croatia was going in the right direction, and most found corruption to be widespread in business and in government. That somber mood continues, as the popularity of politicians sinks. The fact that former prime minister Ivo Sanader

Croatia

Honey stand in Trogir

Photo by Roman Payerhin

was sentenced to a lengthy prison term for corruption was a clear warning.

Croatia's chief EU negotiator, Vladimir Drobnjak, stated that joining the EU on July 1, 2013 was "the exclamation mark on our statehood and our international recognition." The country had entered NATO in April 2009, but EU membership was the highest prize many Croats longed for. A failure to qualify for membership would have been a devastating omen for the other western Balkan countries that are in line to join. Still, Croats are ambivalent about membership. Rightly or wrongly, many blame the EU for their economic woes.

On January 1, 2023, Croatia finally achieved its long-held ambition to become the twentieth member of the single currency. The switch from the kuna will bring benefits. Croatia relies on the single currency area for more than half its external trade, two-thirds its direct investment and 70% of its tourists.

Also, as of January 1, 2023, Croatia is officially a Schengen member state.

As the European governments scrambled in 2015 and 2016 to find a solution to the migrant crisis, Croatia's approach was refreshingly friendly, surely a reflection of many of its citizens' recollection of their own experiences as refugees escaping the ravages of war on tractor-drawn wagons. Almost all migrants were there only in transit to other countries, primarily Germany, since Croatia does not yet serve as a major magnet for those looking for a better life. It has a high unemployment rate and a struggling economy with limited benefits to foreigners; it is also not an easy place for assimilation of primarily Muslim newcomers. The country was shocked in 2015 by the beheading of its citizen Tomislav Salopek, taken hostage by ISIS in Egypt and murdered when its demands for the release of female Muslim prisoners in Egypt were not met.

The welcoming mood changed markedly after Hungary closed its border with Serbia and the refugees switched to next-door Croatia as an obvious alternative. Then Hungary started building a barrier on Croatia's border, too, and Slovenia limited migrant entries from Croatia. Zagreb got nervous over a possibility that, with those bottlenecks in the north and west, the migrants might stay in Croatia. At its peak, the massive inflow of migrants cost the country some $284,000 a day. Immense lines overwhelmed border officials.

Croatia closed all but one of its eight border crossings from Serbia, and chaos erupted when the refugees broke the police barricades. Then-prime minister Milanović declared, "They will get food, water, and medical help, and then they can move on. We have hearts, but we also have heads."

There are few easy answers to the crisis. In November 2015, Croatia started allowing in only Afghan, Iraqi, or Syrian migrants, implying that others are less in need of this chance. In March 2016, Slovenia and Croatia decided to close off their borders to migrants, in an effort to stop them from using the Balkan route to enter Europe. Only those with an entry permit or actually intending to apply for asylum in Croatia are to be allowed.

The crisis will continue to reverberate in Croatia's politics but not necessarily more so than the deeper worries about the country's inability to reap as many benefits from joining the EU as could have been expected. Its unemployment figures are among the worst in Europe, though better than in non-EU regional neighbors, such as Serbia and North Macedonia.

Some political forces demonstrate that virulent ultra-nationalism may not be buried altogether too deeply under the surface. This was visible in April 2018, when a Croatian parliamentary delegation cut short a visit to Serbia after the far-right leader of the Serbian Radical Party and convicted war criminal Vojislav Šešelj stamped on the Croatian national flag and shouted insults. Serbian president Aleksandar Vučić called this behavior "inadmissible." Still, the rowdy nationalism of soccer fans notwithstanding, EU's accession process has already helped stabilize Croatia's future, as well as that of Serbia, and helped normalize their mutual relations.

Republic of Serbia (Република Србија) (Republika Srbija)

Belgrade, view from the Bridge of Brotherhood and Unity, also known as "Brankov Bridge"

Area: 29,913 sq. mi. (77,474 sq. km) excluding Kosovo.

Population: 6,647,003 (2022 census; excluding Kosovo); 6,707,000 (2023 estimate)

Capital City: Belgrade (pop. 1,197,714 city, 1,383,875 urban)

Climate: It is continental, with marked contrasts between winters and summers. In the north, winters are cold and summers are hot and humid, with well-distributed rainfall patterns. In the south, summers and autumns are drier, and winters are with heavy snowfall in the mountains. Average annual temperatures range from around 32 °F (0° C) in January to 72° F (22° C) in July.

Neighboring Countries: Hungary (north); Romania, Bulgaria (east); Kosovo, North Macedonia, and Albania (south); Montenegro (southwest); Bosnia and Herzegovina, Croatia (west).

Official Language: Serbian.

Recognized minority languages: Hungarian, Slovak, Albanian, Romanian, Bulgarian, Rusyn, and Macedonian.

Ethnic Background (excluding Kosovo): 84.4% Serbs, 2.6% Hungarians, 2.2% Bosniaks, 1.2% Roma, 9.6% other and unidentified (2022 census) .

Religion (excluding Kosovo): 86.6% Christianity (81.1% Orthodoxy, 3.9% Catholicism, 1.6% other Christian), 4.2% Islam, 8.0% other and unidentified, 1.2% no religion. (2022)

Form of Government: Unitary parliamentary republic.

Chief of State: Aleksandar Vucic, President (May 2017).

Head of Government: Ana Brnabić, Prime Minister (since June 2017).

National Flag: It is a tricolor consisting of three equal horizontal bands of red, blue, and white, with the lesser coat of arms, centered vertically and shifted to the hoist side. By generally recognized symbolism of Pan-Slavic colors the red stands for the blood shed for the country, blue for commitment and loyalty, and white for purity and honesty. The coat of arms of the Republic of Serbia was officially established in 1882. Its two-headed eagle is a symbol taken from Byzantium. It is understood that one of its heads is turned toward the heavenly kingdom, while the other is turned towards the earthly kingdom. The same tricolor, in altering variations, has been in use since the 19th century. The current form of the flag was officially adopted in 2004 and slightly redesigned in 2010.

Public Holiday: February 15 (Statehood Day).

Currency: Serbian Dinar (RSD).

Main Exports: Automobiles, base metals, furniture, processed food, machinery, electrical machinery and equipment, chemicals, sugar, rubber and rubber goods, clothes, and pharmaceuticals.

Main Imports: Chemicals and chemical products, fuel and oil, basic metals, machinery and equipment and motor vehicles and parts, pharmaceuticals. (2023)

Main Trading Partners: Italy (7.2% of exports and 6.6% of imports), Germany (13.7% of exports and 11.4% of imports), Bosnia and Herzegovina (7.5% of exports and 3.1% of imports), Russia (4.1% of exports and 7.5% of imports), China (12.1% of imports), Romania (4.4% of exports), Hungary (5.4% of exports and 5.6% of imports), Türkiye (5.2 of imports), Croatia (4.2% of exports), Montenegro (4.0 of exports), Poland (3.0% of import). (2022)

POLITICAL SYSTEM

The collapse of the Socialist Federal Republic of Yugoslavia in 1991–1992, after four of the six republics declared their independence and withdrew, left behind a

Ex–president Boris Tadic with ex–US secretary of state Condoleezza Rice

Serbia

Ex–prime minister, Vojislav Kostunica

rump Federal Republic of Yugoslavia composed of Serbia and Montenegro, the largest and the smallest republics in the former union. The majority of Montenegrins also wanted out, but intense pressure from the European Union (EU) persuaded them to remain in a loose association with Serbia for at least three years until 2006. In 2002 the EU's foreign policy chief Javier Solana convinced Serbia's and Montenegro's leaders to accept a change in the name and the structure of their federation. The word "Yugoslavia" was consigned to history, and in 2003 the remaining federation was officially renamed the State Union of Serbia and Montenegro.

Most powers were devolved to each of the two parts, and very little authority, except foreign and defense policy and a single armed force, remained in the hands of the federal president and government. The new union had weak joint institutions. A federal parliament had limited authority, elected a weak federal president and had some say in foreign policy. Each republic retained its own economic system and currency. Montenegro officially adopted the euro in 2002, as did Kosovo (except in Serb-populated areas), while Serbia retained the dinar.

The Serbian enclaves in Croatia all collapsed, and the "Republika Srpska" (RS) in Bosnia and Herzegovina was reintegrated into Bosnia as the Dayton Accords were implemented. That left Serbia and its two autonomous provinces of Vojvodina and Kosovo, plus the Republic of Montenegro. The latter declared its independence on June 3, 2006, following a successful referendum in which 55.5% of Montenegrins voted to break the formal link with Serbia. Kosovo followed suit on February 17, 2008.

In the earlier cases of Slovene, Croat, and Bosnian declarations of separation, Serbia resisted by military means. In the case of Montenegro, Serbia accepted the inevitable and declared its own independence on June 5, 2006. The last shred of the Yugoslav Federation disappeared without bloodshed. Then-Serb prime minister Vojislav Koštunica refused to congratulate the newly independent republic. No Serb officials or Serbian members of the Montenegrin parliament attended Montenegro's independence ceremonies. But Serb president Boris Tadić saw the new development as an opportunity to demonstrate that separation in the former Yugoslavia can now be peaceful and that "we can maintain the historical good relations between us." He assured his neighbors that "Montenegro will have a reliable friend in Serbia" and that "Serbia will be the closest friend."

Belgrade parliament in flames, October 5, 2000

481

Serbia

Election billboard for ex-president Boris Tadic: "The Future Right Now"

Montenegrin independence triggered a complicated separation and the official resignation of Svetozar Marović, the independence-minded Montenegrin who had become federal president in 2003. The joint federal parliament was abolished. The armed forces had to be split up beginning with a reshuffling of the top ranks in the army and military intelligence service. Each side named its own top commander. Thousands of soldiers were relocated to their home countries, but each republic kept the military facilities on its own territory. Dividing dozens of embassies, diplomatic residences, and other common assets may take years.

Under federation, there were common Foreign Affairs and Defense Ministries. Those were now divided, and each republic named separate foreign and defense ministers. According to an earlier agreement when the former state of Serbia and Montenegro was created, Serbia inherited membership in the United Nations and other international organizations. Montenegro had to apply as a new UN member and was quickly admitted on June 28, 2006. Both also revised their constitutions to reflect their new independent status. Serbia adopted a hastily written new 206-article constitution in October 2006. It was approved nearly unanimously in parliament but only narrowly by voters in a referendum.

Its preamble states that Kosovo is an "integral" part of Serbia that can never be taken away. However, that was not to be. On February 17, 2008, Kosovo declared its independence, supported by the United States and 20 (later 23) EU countries. Serbia vows never to accept this, and it has largely succeeded in clinging to control over Serbs remaining in Kosovo, especially those in the north, around Mitrovica. In a February 2012 referendum, 99.7% of voters in Mitrovica refused to recognize

Kosovo's political institutions. (See separate chapter on Kosovo.)

It is not easy for many Serbs to accept their country's reduction in size. Not since World War I has their area of influence been so small. While the Montenegrins and Kosovars were in a triumphant mood, Serbs suffered a sense of loss. It seemed like yet other defeats for their country. Serbs need time to absorb this new reality. In the long term, this development could be a blessing by freeing Serbia from the kinds of ethnic and constitutional struggles that have distracted it and weakened its efforts to become a respected and full member of the new Europe. Serbia can now focus on its own problems and its future as an ultimate member of the European Union.

Milošević's Last Years in Power

Serbia's control until 2000 was evident in 1997, when Slobodan Milošević, the long-time president of Serbia, had himself elected president of Yugoslavia. The fact that this suddenly became the most important political office during the remainder of his rule until October 2000 proved that it was not a constitutional state. His second term as president of Serbia ran out in 1997, and he was forbidden by the constitution to stand for a third term. He therefore decided to move to the federal level and get himself elected as president of Yugoslavia. Since the election of the president by the Yugoslav legislature and his Socialist Party (along with the SNP, a pro-Yugoslav party from Montenegro) was in firm control there, it was not difficult for him to arrange for his election as president of Yugoslavia in July 1997.

This was a reminder of the dual nature of the post-communist regime: There was a federal structure, with a president, parliament, prime minister and government in Belgrade. There were the same institutions at the republic level in both Serbia and Montenegro. Below these two levels were municipalities, which elected their own governments. Beside these three layers of government were the provinces of Vojvodina in the north and Kosovo in the southwest. Both could play a part in Yugoslav government if they chose, but both had their own institutions, as well.

The president of Yugoslavia had always been a ceremonial position without much power. But Milošević was not content to fill a ceremonial position. First, to maintain his control over Serbia, his political base, he had to get a loyal lieutenant elected as president of Serbia. This proved to be more difficult than he had anticipated. It took three elections, but he managed to have his own man, Milan Milutinović, installed as president of Serbia in December 1997. Milutinović had previously been foreign minister of Yugoslavia. His term as Serb

president ran until the end of 2002. Almost immediately after leaving office, he was sent to the UN War Crimes Tribunal in The Hague to face charges for alleged crimes. His trial began in July 2006, and he was acquitted in February 2009 of charges that he ordered a terror campaign in Kosovo.

A New Political System

A dramatic change in the nature of the regime came with the heady days following the October 2000 elections. All evidence pointed to a clear victory by Vojislav Koštunica and his 18-party Democratic Opposition of Serbia (DOS). Nevertheless, Milošević, who had gained plentiful experience in manipulating elections and whose followers controlled the ballots and the polling places, claimed that Koštunica had not won a majority and that there would have to be a second round of elections.

Koštunica refused, realizing that any delay would have enabled Milošević to find a way to rig the elections, as he had done in the past. A powerful human swell propelled by a populist coalition of workers, students, and intellectuals took to the streets to support Koštunica. Inflamed workers took over the offices of factories, hospitals, banks, and mines. Crowds stormed the parliament and state-run television station. Milošević had had huge powers of patronage, but its beneficiaries had become hated figures in the eyes of the populace. The sheer magnitude of spontaneous "people power" forced Milošević to concede victory, especially since the army refused to use force against the protesters, as he had ordered. The revolution was bloodless. Koštunica, who had systematically won over key leaders of the police and army, proclaimed, "For a long time, we lived in an order in which democracy never existed. It exists now!"

This model of peaceful revolution worked so well that it was studiously copied by Georgian president Mikhail Saakashvili and his followers to overthrow a corrupt and authoritarian regime in that Caucasus country in 2003. They even sent representatives to Belgrade to learn the techniques that had been so successful in October 2000, and they adopted the same slogan: "He's finished!" The Ukrainian democratic opposition also applied the model to prevent a stolen election in December 2004.

Milošević's miscalculations were monumental. He thought the Serbian people would support him forever, but the economic devastation he had brought to Serbia had changed many minds. Under his rule the standard of living had plummeted, and Serbs could see no way out of the economic morass as long as he remained in power. Koštunica's promise of

Serbia

"a normal life in a normal country" was alluring. Unlike the late Croatian leader Franjo Tudjman, Milošević failed to recognize the post-Cold War realities and demonstrably turned his back on the west. American pro-democracy assistance to unseat Milošević was substantial.

The newly elected Koštunica emerged from the revolutionary euphoria to face daunting problems. He could not be sure of the ultimate loyalty or limits of the army and security forces, whose leaders had been installed by Milošević. The economic situation was depressing in the extreme. A decade of sanctions and mismanagement, intensified by the NATO air war against Serbia to end a genocidal policy against Kosovo Albanians in the spring of 1999, had left the economy in shambles, the environment severely blighted, and half of the people with no or little work. For a decade, the economy had shrunk at the rate of 7% per year. Average wages were $38 per month.

An estimated 70% of the economy operated in illegal or semilegal forms. Gangsterism had flourished in the 1990s, fueled by war profiteering, sanctions breaking, and a corrupt system of import permits. The underworld took full advantage of the country's isolation from law-governed states. Milošević's cronies gained control of most of the country's businesses, an estimated 750 apartments in Belgrade, and pirated huge sums of money to enrich themselves. In 2000 the US Treasury Department estimated that at least $1 billion had been spirited out of Yugoslavia through banks in Cyprus. Koštunica was one of the few prominent politicians who had no benefit from the underworld. Belgrade politicians were notorious for collecting illegal fees of up to $3,000 for licenses to open street kiosks and for skimming 40%–50% of the value of city contracts in illegal fees.

Despite this dismal outlook, Koštunica, the federal president, went into the

President Aleksandar Vucic

December 23, 2000, parliamentary elections with an 80% popularity rating. His coalition won big, and his rival and nominal ally, Zoran Djindjić, became Serbia's prime minister. Tragically, he was assassinated on March 12, 2003.

The restoration of the Serbian monarchy is highly unlikely despite a ceremony in 2001 returning Serb citizenship to Crown Prince Alexander II, a former British army officer and banker, and his wife and three sons. The ceremony took place in a suite of London's Claridge's Hotel where he had been born 55 years earlier and which Prime Minister Winston Churchill had declared to be Yugoslav soil. He is the son of Serbia's last reigning monarch, Petar II, who died in 1970 and was buried in Libertyville, Illinois, outside Chicago, the second-largest concentration of Serbs in the world. Alexander ordered that the coffin of Petar II be removed from the floor of St. Sava Monastery and be flown to Belgrade for reburial in the family crypt. Serbia held a state funeral for Petar II on May 26, 2013.

Alexander was granted the right to reclaim family properties. He moved back to

the family's ancestral palace in Belgrade in July 2001. At first Alexander was emphatic that he would not reclaim the throne or challenge the country's republican constitution unless royal sentiment became stronger. But in December 2003 he said that the time was right for the restoration after he received the support of the Orthodox Church.

Presidential Elections

Serbia elected its president in June 2004, unencumbered by the earlier 50% turnout rule, which was abolished after only 38.8% showed up to vote in November 2003. In the second round of voting, ultranationalist Tomislav Nikolić, then a member of the Serbian Radical Party (SRS, whose official leader, Vojislav Šešelj, went on trial for war crimes in The Hague in 2007), came in second, with 45% of the votes. He was beaten by Boris Tadić of the Democratic Party (DS), who captured 53.5%. Tadić was supported by the urban elites of Belgrade and by voters in the western-oriented northern province of Vojvodina. Nikolić, whose nickname is "the undertaker" because he had once managed a cemetery, found his votes in the ethnic rural heartlands in the center and south of Serbia.

This result was repeated in 2008. Tadić framed the election as a referendum on joining the European Union and escaping from international isolation. Turnout in the runoff was an astounding 61%, the highest since Milošević was removed from power in October 2000. In a close finish, Tadić came out on top, winning 50.5% of the votes to Nikolić's 47.8%. The majority voted for the long-term prospect of joining Europe. Since the overthrow of Milošević in October 2000, the reform parties have governed Serbia even though they are weakened by internal divisions.

Tadić, a former psychology professor, appealed to the international community to help ease Serbia's political isolation and to pave the way for negotiations to enter the EU. "Today we need support from the West because the citizens of Serbia voted for a pro-Western way." One week after his 2004 inauguration, he traveled to Washington to deliver a simple message: "We are ready to retake our traditional place in the constellation of Western democracies." He acknowledged that the government lacked full civilian control of the security forces, which survived Milošević's fall. Appealing to the strong Serbian nationalist sentiments, he defended the view that Kosovo remains part of Serbia. "Kosovo is not lost. If Kosovo is ever lost for the Serbs, it will also be lost for Europe."

In May 2012 Tomislav Nikolić surprisingly defeated Tadić for the presidency in a close run-off election, 50.21% to 46.77%. Once an extreme nationalist who had been

Drumming up votes for Kostunica

Serbia

a close ally of Milošević, Nikolić left the Radicals (SRS) and formed a new party, the Serbian Progressive Party (SNS). He now supported European integration and good relations with the neighbors. He put aside his pro-Russian sympathies and worked hard to move his nationalist party toward the political center. Tadić had achieved much on the international stage, but he had the misfortune to be in power when the economy stagnated and unemployment climbed to 24%. In early 2017, Nikolić warned of a possible military conflict with Kosovo after Kosovars refused entry to a Serbian train painted in the colors of the Serbian flag and with huge signs reading "Kosovo is Serbia" in 21 languages.

An evolution similar to Nikolić's occurred in his associate, Prime Minister Vučić, who decided to run for the presidency in 2017. He followed Nikolić from the Serbian Radical Party into the Serbian Progressive Party. Once a fanatical nationalist who desired the creation of a Greater Serbia, Vučić has left his vituperative talk behind and speaks calmly. He is pro-European, seeks good relations with the United States, and calls Croatia a friend. It was he who was the driving force to normalize relations with Kosovo, which opened the door to official accession negotiations with the EU. However, he refuses to renounce his country's special relations with Russia and China. His electoral promises were to fight corruption and lawlessness and to move toward economic liberalization. With support from President Nikolić, who decided not to seek reelection, Vučić won in April 2017 with 56.01% of votes in the first round, eliminating the need for a second round. His closest competitor, independent candidate Saša Janković, came in a distant second with only 16.63%.

Vučić participated in the 2022 general election as the presidential candidate of the Serbian Progressive Party. He won 58% of the popular vote in the first round, and secured his second mandate as president of Serbia.

Vučić's election provoked widespread street demonstrations throughout the country, especially by young Serbs. Worried about his tight grip on power and control of the media in the runup to elections, critics accused Vučić of an authoritarian bent. In turn, the government declared that the protests were fomented by western intelligence agencies, political opposition, or the liberal financier George Soros, though no evidence was provided.

In a bold move, Vučić designated Ana Brnabić as the new prime minister, and she was easily approved by the parliament, dominated by his party. Brnabić became the first female and the first openly gay prime minister in Serbia. Her western

education and LGBT background was likely to allay EU's concerns about the direction of Vučić's rule. At the same time, her choice of several ministers suggested a nod to Russia. She was reelected in April 2022.

Parliamentary Elections

Parties seeking seats in parliament must win at least 5% of the total votes. This 5% rule does not apply to those parties representing ethnic minorities. Parliamentary elections are important because the prime minister wields much more power than any president. The good news in the five elections to 2014 was that well over half of the voters chose democratic parties over more radical and nationalist ones that seek to undo the revolution of October 2000 and block Serbia's integration with Europe.

The extreme nationalist Serbian Radical Party (SRS) emerged as the strongest party in the 250-seat parliament in 2003 and 2007. Its leader was an indicted war criminal in The Hague, Vojislav Šešelj, whose trial began in November 2007. Heading the ticket in 2007 and 2008 was his stand-in, Tomislav Nikolić, who lost in presidential elections in 2004 and 2008. He called for an end of western-style reforms, a termination of growing military cooperation with NATO, a questioning of the attempt to join the EU, and a return to the notion of "Greater Serbia," though as a long-term project and without going to war. Nikolić almost snagged the position as parliamentary speaker in 2007, but he was removed from that post almost immediately.

By autumn 2008 the Radical Party was imploding as a result of an internal war between the anti-European hardline wing of the jailed Vojislav Šešelj and the allies of the more pragmatic pro-European supporters of Tomislav Nikolić. The latter was expelled with 17 of his backers and created his own party in October 2008, the Serbian Progressive Party (SNS). The SNS came to power after the 2012 election when it formed a coalition government with the Socialist Party of Serbia. It has remade itself as a modern center-right party that has dropped its militant rhetoric and anti-EU stance. It attracts right-leaning voters without offending the EU or US. Even the Serbian Orthodox Church has started to turn its back on nationalist hard-liners. For a few years after 2012, the old Radicals were a marginal rump party with no representation in parliament. However, the ultranationalists came roaring back in the early elections of April 2016. Their fortunes were boosted by the acquittal two weeks earlier of their founder and moving spirit, Vojislav Šešelj, by the International Tribunal for the former Yugoslavia (ICTY), hardly a week after it sentenced Bosnian Serb leader Radovan Karadžić to 40 years.

Prime Minister Ana Brnabic

The party received 8.60% of popular vote and won 22 seats, making it the third-largest in the parliament.

The SNS and its leader, Aleksandar Vučić, emerged from the March 2014 early elections as the undisputed power in Serbia. They won an absolute majority, garnering 48.3% of the vote (up from 24.4%) and 157 of 250 parliamentary seats (up from 73). His predecessor as prime minister, Ivica Dačić, called this a "political tsunami." Even Vučić admitted that the result went beyond the party's wildest dreams. The opposition was routed.

Vučić repeated this strategy in 2016, calling for early elections for April (they were not due until 2018). He declared that his country needed "four more years of stability so that it is ready to join the European Union." His Serbian Progressive Party-led coalition won 48.25% of the popular vote, losing some seats but still retaining 131, a majority in the 250-seat parliament. Never since the dark days of Milošević, whom Vučić once served, was so much power in one man's hands. He enjoyed an approval rating of 58% just before the 2016 elections.

Like the Radicals, Milošević's old Socialist Party of Serbia (SPS) reaps votes from workers who have lost their jobs after privatization; middle-class professionals who cannot find steady employment in the new Serbia; and resentful Serbian refugees from Bosnia, Croatia, and Kosovo. By the 2008 parliamentary elections, however, the party, led by Ivica Dačić, was determined to reinvent itself as a mainstream center-left social democratic party that can share power with other democratic parties. He became prime minister from 2012 to 2014. It is a paradox that SPS has proven

Belgrade. Parliament of The Republic of Serbia

to be a key party in moving the country into Europe. He said he wants Serbia and its people no longer to be viewed abroad as "lepers." In the 2014 elections, it won 13.5% of the votes, while in 2016 it only received 10.95% (29 seats) in coalition with several smaller parties.

The former ruling Democratic Party (DS) got 19 seats in 2014 (down from 67) and 16 in 2016. A new association, It's Enough—Restart (also known in English as Enough Is Enough), captured 6% of popular vote and 16 seats in 2016. A party representing the Hungarian minority won six seats in 2014 and four in 2016. There is no strong unified opposition in parliament.

All of the important parties now favor Serbia's EU membership. The EU helped this by an offer to Serbia of a prized Stabilization and Association Agreement (SAA). Fearing that the EU door might close if the opportunity were lost, then-president Tadić signed it on April 29, 2008. The risk that Tadić ran in accepting the bid was dramatized by the fact that he received death threats for signing it. In December 2009 a trade agreement with the EU demonstrated that the path to membership was open.

Tadić accepted an important precondition on the insistence of the Netherlands and Belgium—that the government demonstrate its full cooperation with the war-crimes tribunal in The Hague. In addition, 17 European nations announced that they would no longer charge Serbs for visas. In July 2009 Serbs (except those living in Kosovo), Montenegrins, and North Macedonians were granted visa-free travel throughout the EU.

In 2007 Serbia's government renewed its commitment to cooperate fully with The Hague tribunal, and the latter said that Belgrade had, in fact, increased its efforts to search for suspects. Therefore, the EU restarted talks leading to eventual membership. At its Riga summit in November 2006, NATO had come to the same conclusion. It reversed its long-standing prerequisite that Serbia must hand over Mladić and Karadžić before being admitted to its Partnership for Peace (PfP) program. Both organizations helped create a choice for Serbs—to cling to the illusion that Kosovo's independence could be overturned or to begin accession talks with the EU and other western organizations. Four elections demonstrated that the latter option was the preferred one. Serbia became an official candidate for EU membership in March 2012. Official membership negotiations began on January 1, 2014.

As prime minister, Vučić was generally successful in negotiating the minefield between the EU demands for greater transparency, privatization of state assets, reducing the deficit, and normalization of relations with Kosovo on the one hand and the preferences of Serbian public opinion in these regard on the other. His party's electoral victory in 2016 suggests a promising level of societal support for meeting the requirements of EU accession, though the success of ultranationalists revealed an important countercurrent and the EU worries about now-president Vučić's grip on power and his government's warm ties to Russia.

In the 2022 parliamentary election, SNS lost its parliamentary majority while opposition parties returned to the National Assembly. The United for the Victory of Serbia alliance, which placed second, was dissolved shortly after the election. Ana Brnabić, who has been the prime minister since 2017, and her third cabinet were inaugurated in October 2022. Brnabić's cabinet has been involved in the North Kosovo crisis and was faced with anti-government protests from May to November 2023, which were triggered after two mass shootings, the Belgrade school shooting and in the villages near the cities of Mladenovac and Smederevo.

On May 3, 2023, a school shooting occurred at Vladislav Ribnikar Model Elementary School in Belgrade. The shooter was identified as a 13-year-old male student. He opened fire on his fellow-students and staff, resulting in the deaths of ten individuals, including nine students and a security guard. Six others, five students and a teacher, also sustained injuries. The shooter surrendered willingly and was taken into custody. However, due to his age being below 14, which falls below Serbia's age of criminal responsibility, he could not face legal charges. His father legally owned the firearms used in the incident. Since the apprehension, the shooter has been placed under the care of a psychiatric hospital located in Belgrade. Meanwhile, legal actions have been initiated against his parents.

The attack occurred one day before the other mass shooting in Serbia. Both shootings caused mass protests in the country, named Serbia Against Violence.

Despite initially being organized by the Democratic Party (DS), Do not Let Belgrade Drown (NDB), Party of Freedom and Justice (SSP), Movement of Free Citizens (PSG), People's Party (Narodna stranka), and Together opposition parties, no party signs were reported to be seen at the protests. The People's Movement of Serbia (NPS) and Ecological Uprising (EU) joined as organizers in August 2023, while the People's Party was excluded as an organizer in the meantime. The protests grew larger and lasted until November 2023.

The protestors met in front of the country's parliament before marching in silence through the Belgrade streets near Serbian government offices demanding institutional accountability and the resignation of the Minister of Internal Affairs, the head of the Security Intelligence Agency (BIA), the Minister of Education, and the Council of the Regulatory Authority for Electronic Media, as well as cancelling programs that promote violence and shutting down media and tabloids that publish false news and violate the Journalistic Code. In response, Prime Minister Brnabić accused them of "politicizing" the shootings. "Serbia Against Violence" protests were also held in the cities of Novi Sad, Kragujevac, Kraljevo, and Čačak.

The cooperation between the parties organizing the protests gradually increased,

Serbia

and led them to the creation of an electoral alliance in anticipation of the next elections. DS, Together, and Serbia Center (SRCE) signed a cooperation agreement, establishing greater cooperation between the parties. Green–Left Front, ZLF (founded on July 14, 2023) prepared framework principles of cooperation between the parties which was revealed in September 2023 as the Agreement for Victory.

Formed out of the Serbia Against Violence protests, Serbia Against Violence (abbr. SPN) became an opposition coalition of political parties. SPN is profiled as a pro-European coalition that is opposed to the Serbian Progressive Party. Its representatives have declared support for anti-corruption and environmental measures, increasing pensions and salaries, investing in education, health care, and public transport, and introducing progressive taxation. Formalized in October 2023, SPN took part in the parliamentary, Vojvodina provincial, Belgrade City Assembly elections and elections for city assemblies in other cities, all of which were held on December 17, 2023.

2023 Serbian parliamentary election

Parliamentary elections were held in Serbia on December 17, 2023. The ruling Serbian Progressive Party (SNS) decision to have early parliamentary elections in 2023 is a repeated winning strategy used in the 2014 and 2016 elections. Initially, they were scheduled to be held by April 30, 2026. President Vučić, after announcing that early elections could be held either in 2023 or 2024, called them in November 2023. Along with the parliamentary elections, the Vojvodina provincial and local elections were held in 65 cities and municipalities, including the capital, Belgrade.

In these parliamentary elections, there was a total of 6,500,666 registered voters who could vote at 8,273 polling stations. Citizens chose one of 18 electoral lists, on which 2,817 candidates were proposed for 250 seats in the parliament. The electoral threshold in Serbia is a minimum of 3% of votes. According to Electoral Committee of the Republic (RIK) data, 3,820,746 people voted.

In this year's parliamentary elections, the ruling Serbian Progressive Party entered the race with traditional coalition partners under the slogan "Serbia must not stand still" (Srbija ne sme da stane), while the Socialist Party of Serbia "Ivica Dačić–Prime Minister of Serbia," a faithful partner of the SNS, ran independently.

On the other hand, nine opposition parties (organizers of the protests since May 2023) gathered in a coalition called "Serbia against violence" (Srbija protiv nasilja), organized in October.

Former prime minister Zoran Djindjic
The Economist

A separate coalition was formed by the Serbian party Zavetnici and the Serbian movement Dveri, while Miloš Jovanović's New Democratic Party of Serbia and Vojislav Mihajlović's Movement for the Restoration of the Kingdom of Serbia came out with a list called "Hope for Serbia" (Nada za Srbiju).

The Liberal Democratic Party of Čedomir Jovanović, the Serbian Radical Party of Vojislav Šešelj, and the People's Party of Vuk Jeremic also entered the parliamentary race.

Former President of Serbia Boris Tadić and his Social Democratic Party formed a coalition with Saša Radulović's movement Enough is Enough (Dosta je bilo).

A debutant in the elections, the conspiracy theorist doctor Branimir Nestorović entered the election race; and on the ballot, there were also the Union of Vojvodina Hungarians (Savez vojvođanskih Mađara), the Russian Party, Serbia in the West (Srbija na Zapadu) coalition, as well as the Albanian Democratic Alternative.

Residents of Serbia could also vote for the list Party for Democratic Action (PDD) of Šaip Kamberi, Justice and Reconciliation Party of Usama Zukorlić, SDA Sandžak, Coalition for Peace and Tolerance, which was made up of minority parties.

The electoral campaign was met with an increase in political tensions, polarization, and voter intimidation. Candidates campaigned on issues such as fighting against crime and corruption, decreasing inflation, and the Ohrid Agreement.

The President of Serbia, Aleksandar Vučić, despite not being a candidate and no longer being president of the Serbian Progressive Party, he mainly represented it during the campaign. He recently stepped down as party leader, becoming, as he said, an ordinary member. Nevertheless, his name was on the election list, and it

was the most frequently mentioned and seen during the election campaign.

After the Republic Election Commission (RIK) processed the results from eight polling stations where voting for the parliamentary elections was repeated, it announced the convincing victory of the coalition list led by SNS "Aleksandar Vučić–Serbia must not stand still." The SNS list won 46.75 %, or 1,783,701 votes. It means that this party and its coalition partners will have around 129 mandates, which is enough for a majority in the 250-seat Serbian Parliament.

The opposition list "Serbia against violence" won 23.66%, or 902,450 votes (64 mandates).

The Socialist Party of Serbia, won 6.55%, or 249,916 votes, suffering from its worst result since the 2007 election.

The NADA coalition won 5.02%, or 191,431 votes, and "We–The Voice from the People" of doctor Branimir Nestorović won 4.69% or 178,830 votes, thus gaining representation in the Parliament.

In the new convocation of the Serbian Parliament, there will be minority parties, but there will not be the "National Gathering"(Nacionalno okupljanje) coalition of the Dveri movement and Zavetnik party, who participated in the elections together, and who were represented in the assembly until now. They won 2.76% of the votes.

According to the RIK report: the Union of Vojvodina Hungarians won 1.7% of the votes; the Serbian Radical Party 1.46%; and the list of Saša Radulović and Boris Tadić 1.18% of the votes; the People's Party list won 0.88%; the list led by Usame Zukorlić and Tomislav Žigmanov 0.76% of the votes; the list "SDA Sandžak–Sulejman Ugljanin" received 0.57%; the list "Political struggle of Albanians continues–Shaip Kamberi" received 0.35% of the votes; and the Together for Future list won 0.18%; the Russian Party won 0.3% of the votes; the list of Čedomir Jovanović 0.24%; 0.14% voted for the "Serbia in the West" list; while the "Albanian Democratic Alternative" list received 0.08% of the votes.

One of the biggest surprises of the election was the large drop (from about 12% to about 6%) in support for the Socialist Party of Serbia, which has been in the country's political life since the 1990s. Its leader Ivica Dačić, the former Minister of Foreign Affairs, said he would offer to resign from the position of party president.

The NADA coalition, i.e., the block of parties gathered around the New Democratic Party of Serbia, won 13 mandates, which its leaders assessed as a success.

Another big surprise of the parliamentary elections was the list headed by dr Branimir Nestorović.

The return of Legija, in custody a half-year later

Nestorović is a pediatrician and at the beginning of the corona virus pandemic he was a member of the state Crisis Staff, but then he left it, and he gained popularity when he started expressing views that were contrary to Serbia's health policy, opposing vaccination and protection measures. Nestorović and his associates made forming the majority in the Assembly of the City of Belgrade depend on them.

The reports of domestic and international monitoring organizations, including the mission of the Organization for Security and Cooperation in Europe (OSCE), indicated that there were electoral irregularities in the elections, mostly in the Belgrade region.

The OSCE Office for Democratic Institutions and Human Rights (ODIHR) concluded that the elections were well organized, but that SNS had a systematic advantage in the election and abused public funds. The domination of the President of the State Aleksandar Vučić in the campaign, despite the fact that he was not a candidate in the elections, gave his party an unjustified advantage undermining the chances of the opposition. In addition, a number of earlier recommendations to improve oversight mechanisms and introduce a campaign expenditure limit remain unaddressed, which reduces transparency and increases opportunities for high campaign spending.

The observation mission of the CRTA (Center for Research, Transparency and Accountability) announced that on the day of the elections, organized migration took place, which affected the outcome of the Belgrade elections. Testimonies about this were also recorded by Radio Free Europe.

Part of the MEPs called for an independent investigation of all reported irregularities during the elections. The European Union and the United States of America have called on the authorities in Serbia to investigate the allegations of international observers.

Serbian President Aleksandar Vučić retorted that "there will be no international investigation when it comes to elections" and that he "doesn't care what the foreign media and foreign governments say about it."

The government led by the Serbian Progressive Party denied that there were major electoral irregularities, with the assessment that these were the "cleanest elections so far." Prime Minister Ana Brnabić pointed out that citizens voted for implemented projects and for success.

Mass protests began a day after the election by the coalition Serbia against violence, which accuses the government of allegedly forging the results, especially in the Belgrade elections, and requests holding new elections according to fair and democratic standards. The government rejected all their claims and stated that the opposition bloc did not provide evidence, nor did it file complaints with the official election bodies.

The protests were peaceful, until Sunday, December 24, when the leaders of the opposition bloc invited supporters to storm the Belgrade City Assembly building, claiming that they had won in Belgrade and that power belonged to them.

Today it houses the City Assembly of Belgrade.

Demonstrators broke the doors and windows of the historic Belgrade building, so that the police had to react, arresting several dozen people, and proceedings were initiated against some of them. Both policemen and demonstrators were

The mansion "Stari dvor" was the royal residence of the Obrenović dynasty.
injured.

Serbia

The ProGlas Initiative, which gathers university professors, actors, and other celebrities, joined the opposition and also demanded a repetition of the elections at all levels.

This initiative was active in the election campaign, claiming to be non-partisan and inviting people to vote. After the protest of the opposition, ProGlas also organized a meeting in the center of Belgrade, asking for a re-vote, which the government refused. The leaders of the coalition Serbia against violence also addressed the crowd. From that protest, a message was sent to the citizens to send ProGlas photos and videos that can be used to prove election irregularities by January 13, in order to submit a request to the Constitutional Court to annul the election results. The citizens were also told that the Christmas and New Year holidays would be used to "regroup," without specifying what that meant.

The Serbian Progressive Party (SNS) convincingly won the extraordinary elections for the Assembly of Serbia and this party will continue to rule Serbia unchallenged, confirmed the official body for the implementation of the elections.

Milošević's Extradition to the War-Crimes Tribunal

Milošević, of all people, threw his hat into the ring to challenge the DOS after the 2000 elections. As the only candidate, he won reelection as leader of his Socialist Party, which was in disarray. More moderate members had already quit the party and formed two separate leftist parties. Also dreaming of a comeback was Milošević's wife's, Mirjana Marković's, Yugoslav Left Party. This charade ended in April 2001, when Milošević was arrested after a gun battle with his heavily armed bodyguards and indicted on corruption charges. Western countries demanded that he be sent immediately to The Hague to be tried by the UN international war-crimes tribunal.

Koštunica and Djindjić were divided on this question—the former opposed and the latter in favor. Djindjić paved the way to extraditing Milošević by revealing evidence of mass graves of Kosovo Albanians killed by Milošević's forces in 1999. The revelations provoked disgust in the minds of many ordinary Serbs; three-fourths of them believed by June 2001 that Milošević should be tried for war crimes. The prime minister found the economic carrot the West held out to be essential for his impoverished country. The prospect of $1.2 billion in economic and reconstruction assistance was linked to Milošević's extradition. Djindjić later asked, "How much would it have cost this country if this had not happened?"

Facing resistance from Koštunica and the Montenegrin faction in the governing coalition, the prime minister and the cabinet majority issued a decree that it would cooperate with the UN and hand over Milošević. When the latter's hand-picked Constitutional Court judges ruled the decree to be unconstitutional, Djindjić resorted to one of Milošević's own earlier measures that permitted the Serbian cabinet to ignore any federal law it did not like. Without informing Koštunica or anyone else, the cabinet simply ordered the extradition on June 28, 2001, the anniversary of the 1389 Battle of Kosovo and the 1914 assassination of Archduke Franz Ferdinand in Sarajevo. Within three hours Milošević was in a plane bound for The Hague. There he was charged with 66 counts of war crimes and genocide in Croatia, Bosnia, and Kosovo. He was the first head of state ever to be taken to court on allegations of genocide, the most serious of all war crimes.

On March 31, 2002, the cabinet issued further arrest warrants for four additional Milošević associates who had been indicted for war crimes. Economic motives were again at play, as the US froze $40 million in assistance until the Yugoslav government demonstrated its willingness to cooperate with the tribunal. A former prime minister, Zoran Živković, revealed in 2005 that CIA agents took part in dozens of failed attempts by Serbian police in 2003 to capture the Bosnian Serb wartime commander Ratko Mladić. A key war-crimes suspect shot himself outside the parliament building in protest. Dealing with Serb war crimes remains highly emotional and dangerous, as many Serbs regard themselves as victims of the wars and see The Hague tribunal as biased against them.

Many other top leaders found themselves in custody, including the leader of the nationalist Serbian Radical Party, Vojislav Šešelj, whose trial lasted for over eight years, from 2007 to 2016. He went on a month-long hunger strike in 2006 to win the right to conduct his own defense; he failed to have the three judges hearing his case replaced. He was charged with contempt of court in 2009 for frequently disrupting the proceedings, threatening the court, and revealing the names of protected witnesses. While in custody, he also kept publishing a variety of books and pamphlets, often titled in a way that combined a name of someone he attacked (such as an ICTY judge) with profanities or insults. Former Bosnian Serb president Biljana Plavšić was sentenced to 11 years in a Swedish prison, but she was released early in October 2009. Top suspects, such as General Ratko Mladić and former Bosnian Serb leader Radovan Karadžić, were eventually also brought before the court (see below). In June 2007 Serbian and Bosnian Serb police worked jointly to arrest one of Mladić's top aides, Zdravko Tolimir. Further US aid has been conditioned on Serbian cooperation in apprehending them.

Western demands were strengthened in June 2004, when a commission of the Republika of Srpska government finally admitted that Serbian forces had been responsible for the deaths of up to 8,000 Muslims in Srebrenica in 1995. In December 2003 a Bosnian Serb general was convicted in The Hague of commanding a two-year sniper and artillery terror campaign against the citizens of Sarajevo. Croats and Bosnian Muslims have been tried and convicted. In 2003 three Kosovo Albanians were indicted for the first time, and in 2005 the indicted then Kosovo prime minister, Ramush Haradinaj, submitted himself for trial in The Hague, but he was acquitted.

Prominent witnesses were called to testify against Milošević, such as former Slovenian president Milan Kučan, Croatian president Stipe Mesić, and former NATO commander Wesley Clark. Clark testified that he has spent over 100 hours with Milosevic and was convinced that the former Serb leader was "the motivating force in most if not all" of the events in four Balkan wars in the 1990s. These were only a few of the 1,400 witnesses Milošević said he wanted to call to the stand, including former president Bill Clinton, ex-prime minister Tony Blair, and German ex-chancellor Gerhard Schröder. Despite Milošević's antics in court, including seeking to discredit every witness against him, the prosecution built a strong case against him. There was no "smoking gun" to prove that he directly ordered atrocities, since he put very little on paper and often met his subordinates alone. But there was much circumstantial evidence. His main objective in The Hague was to perform for his audience in Serbia, where the proceedings are televised, and to hammer away at his view that the Serbs were the main victims of an international plot to smash up Yugoslavia and that he was the chief peacemaker rather than the cause of the bloody wars.

As a way of fighting back, members of the country's military police arrested one of Serbia's deputy prime ministers, Momčilo Perišić, and an American diplomat at a Belgrade restaurant on charges of passing to the Americans sensitive military information. The incident, which former prime minister Djindjić called a "first-rate scandal" and "a blow to the country's international credibility," was a part of the army's effort to block the flow of evidence to The Hague. The government later apologized to the US for holding the diplomat incommunicado for 15 hours and for roughing him up. Nevertheless, military prosecutors charged him in September 2002 for spying for the US Perišić denied the allegations and correctly claimed to be the victim of a power struggle.

Facing the threat of penalties by the US and the EU, the Serb government decided in 2005 to cooperate with the UN war, crimes tribunal and to surrender indicted suspects. Its nervous efforts sparked controversy by treating the indictees as national heroes. For example, Koštunica called General Vladimir Lazarević's decision to come out of hiding "patriotic, highly moral and honorable." The retired general was blessed by the leader of the Serbian Orthodox Church and was accompanied to The Hague by the justice minister. The government's sincerity was also called into question when Foreign Minister Vuk Drašković said that Serbian security forces knew the whereabouts of General Mladić and were protecting him.

The government vigorously denied reports in June 2009 that Mladić had been filmed recently engaging in a normal social life. This severely damaged the claim that Serbian officials do not know Mladić's whereabouts. In February 2010 the police raided the Belgrade home of the Mladić family and found a large cache of Swiss francs, euros, and dollars that could be used to pay for his food and protection. They also found 18 of his diaries, comprising 3,500 handwritten pages, recounting in detail his activities in the war. War-crimes prosecutors in The Hague asked that these diaries be admitted into evidence against his former boss, Radovan Karadžić. The government rejected the Mladić family's request that he be officially declared dead since he had not been seen in public since 2005. It would not be long, as it turned out, that Mladić was finally apprehended.

After over a dozen Serbs and Bosnian Serbs had been sent for trial, the EU agreed in April 2005 to begin "stabilization and association" negotiations with both Serbia and Montenegro as a step toward eventual membership. That agreement was withdrawn in May 2006, when Serbia had failed to meet a deadline for capturing Mladić. This decision exasperated the government, which had been more aggressive in its attempts to capture the war criminal, whom some Serbs still consider a hero. It cracked down on the network of military veterans suspected of aiding the general. In December 2005 a Serbian court convicted 14 former Serb militia members of massacring 200 Croatian POWs.

Koštunica exclaimed, "Never in our history has the entire state and nation been made to suffer because of one officer." He warned that his country could break with the west if a more conciliatory international approach is not taken. He pointed to a grim development—the ultranationalist Radical Party had by 2006 become the largest party, with 40% support in the polls.

In June 2005 a video was shown on Serbian television that galvanized the government's cooperation with The Hague tribunal. It had been provided by the court's prosecution and was the first graphic portrayal of what had happened in Srebrenica in 1995. It begins with a Serb Orthodox priest blessing camouflaged paramilitary troops called Scorpions. Later, troops are shown taking six young men out of a truck and killing them. In the video, shot by a Scorpion, one can clearly hear the troops insulting the scared Muslims. Only a month earlier, an opinion poll had revealed that over half of Serb respondents did not believe the Srebrenica massacre had ever occurred.

The government acted quickly. Koštunica said the film showed "brutal, callous and disgraceful crime against civilians." President Tadić said in an emotional television statement that the images were proof of the "monstrous" crimes committed in Serbia's name during the Balkan wars of the 1990s. He added that the perpetrators had been freely walking the streets, but now they must face justice. Ten former members of the elite Scorpions were immediately arrested for the crimes, and five were arraigned on murder charges at the end of 2005.

Their trial began in February 2006. In the first trial inside Serbia that involved the Srebrenica massacres, four were convicted and jailed in April 2007. In November Serbian war-crimes prosecutors indicted 14 more ex-Yugoslav soldiers and paramilitaries for torturing and killing 70 Croat civilians in late 1991. In June 2008 police arrested outside of Belgrade one of the four most-wanted fugitives, Stojan Župljanin, a Bosnian Serb police commander accused of atrocities against Bosnian Muslims and Croats.

In February 2007 the Hague court ruled that Serbia was not responsible for genocide in Bosnia because it had not aimed to "destroy in whole or in part the Bosnian Muslim population." However, the court decided that Srebrenica was a genocidal event and that Serbia is to be blamed for failing to use its "known influence" to stop it. Bosnia had brought this charge in 1993 and was disappointed that Serbia is not required to pay it reparations. Although Serbia escaped being labeled a genocidal country and having to pay billions of euros in claims, Bosnia did obtain what it called "a recognition of Serbia's guilt."

In 2013 two close aides of Milošević—Jovica Stanišić and Franko Simatović—were acquitted. Although they were involved in forming, directing, and paying special secret combat units in Bosnia, that was not considered to make them criminally liable for the crimes the units committed. Their three-year trial did, however, reveal many of the inner workings of the Milošević era. The tribunal has refused to hold any member of his regime individually accountable for the many atrocities Serbs committed.

In an effort to win favor from the EU and to improve its relationship with its neighbors, parliament in March 2010 narrowly passed (with 127 of 250 votes) a resolution condemning the July 1995 Srebrenica massacre. The word "genocide" could not be used because it was rejected by the reformed Socialist Party (formerly Milošević's), on whose votes the government depends. Also, most Serbs do not believe the war had been one of genocide. Instead, the carnage was called a "crime."

It offered "condolences and apology to the families of victims because not enough was done to prevent the tragedy." It committed itself to Bosnia's territorial integrity. Following The Hague 2007 ruling, it did not accept blame for the killings. The close vote revealed the continuing lack of consensus in Serbia on the character of the 1990s Balkan wars.

Nevertheless, the resolution makes it impossible to pretend that the massacre never happened or that the number of dead had been grossly exaggerated. In July 2010 President Tadić paid homage to the 8,000 victims. Tadić had flown a few months

Serbia

earlier to Croatia to discuss with the Croatian president the mutual withdrawal of charges that each had practiced genocide against the other. In November 2010 he visited Croatia again to apologize at the site outside of Vukovar, where 200 Croats had been massacred. In 2015, the International Court of Justice ruled that the violence committed by Serbian forces against Croatians during the 1990s was not genocide (it also dismissed the countersuit). The court asserted in a 153-page document that, although there was proof of large-scale killings, there was not enough proof of intent. Individuals could still be charged with genocide, but Serbia would not be required to pay restitution to Croatia.

In 2014, the governments of Serbia and Bosnia cooperated to arrest 15 perpetrators of a notorious 1993 massacre in Bosnia. And in 2015, 20 years after the massacre, 8 men were arrested in Serbia on suspicion that, as Bosnian Serb policemen, they were involved in the murder of about 1,000 men in a warehouse in the village of Kravica outside Srebrenica.

Death of Milošević in 2006

On March 11, 2006, after 5 years of incarceration and courtroom antics in The Hague, Milošević was found dead in his cell at age 64. Dutch prosecutors cited his autopsy to pronounce that he had died of a heart attack. His worshipers and family cried "murder," claiming that he had been poisoned or denied proper medical treatment for his heart ailment.

Milošević's Socialist Party demanded a full state funeral, but President Tadić dismissed that as "inappropriate." After much bargaining, the authorities agreed to a private funeral in Serbia and a public display in Belgrade. Tens of thousands gave him a hero's farewell. Some carried banners declaring, "Slobo is a hero and heroes never die!" and "The Tribunal kills!"

His casket was placed under a canopy in front of the parliament building, where mobs had stormed in October 2000 to end his corrupt presidency. Up to 80,000 paid their respects there. His burial took place at a family residence in his home town of Požarevac, 35 miles southeast of Belgrade, where about 15,000 gathered. No government officials were present at either ceremony, nor was any member of his family; all had fled abroad and are under indictment.

His vision of a "Greater Serbia," which he had manipulated to propel himself to power, is dead. However, his emotional send-off reinforced the sense of victimhood in many Serbs. It also provided an unwanted boost to the Radical Party, which is more intensely nationalist than his own Socialist Party had been. His shrunken party split into Milošević loyalists, who

Serbian Orthodox priests in Belgrade

favor cooperation with the Radicals, and others who want to put his defeats and corruption behind them. The latter group succeeded in reinventing itself as a moderate center-left party and entered the government in July 2008.

Assassination in Belgrade

Prime Minister Zoran Djindjić was a philosophy professor with a razor-sharp mind. The son of an army officer, he had spent much of his youth in Germany studying philosophy and forging close lasting ties with that country. He was unsentimental, pragmatic, and modern. For example, he wanted Kosovo's future resolved within a few years and insisted that "all options" should be open. He was also ready to see Montenegro go its own way if that was what its people wanted. His priorities were to eliminate the vestiges of Milošević's rule in Serbia and to steer his country into the European Union, the negotiations for which had begun in 2002. "We must find a solution mainly by finding our place in Europe, not by seeking historical rights or national interests."

On March 12, 2003, Djindjić stepped out of his armored car outside the main government building in Belgrade and was gunned down. As turbulent as Balkan politics had been, this was the first political assassination in the region since World War I. He was mourned, as hundreds of thousands of Serbs attended his funeral and paid their respects with flowers and tears. This was the largest crowd since Tito's death in 1980.

With those shots the reality of post-Milošević Serbia came into clear focus. It became grimly visible to what extent Serbia had been taken over by gangsters, how deeply the ex-dictator's legacy had taken root, and how close this nation was to sliding back into chaos or the status of a failed criminal state. The dictator's overthrow in 2000 had left in place much of the evil he

had fostered. To avoid bloodshed and gain the clout he needed to unseat Milošević, Djindjić had cut a deal with certain gangland and paramilitary leaders, most notably the Red Berets' former leader, Milorad Ulemek (a.k.a., Luković), more commonly known as Legija, a nickname derived from his service in the French Foreign Legion in the 1980s. Djindjić would not go after some of the thugs, who were exerting influence within the army, police, and security organizations and directing mafia activities, such as drugs, human trafficking, and prostitution, if they would help him bring down the Milošević regime.

It was Legija's men who had rejected orders from Milošević to crack down on the opposition and who had later agreed to arrest Milošević and to bundle him off to The Hague. Thus, the revolution that had occurred was part popular uprising and part internal power coup. Each leader, including Djindjić, had his own ties to different sections of the security services and had to live in uneasy coexistence with unsavory elements. When the prime minister started putting pressure on the gangsters and making preparations to arrest them, they organized a plot, "Stop the Hague," and killed him.

During the Milošević era and well into the democratic transition, this interlocking network between organized crime, corrupt security chiefs and judges, and ultranationalist politicians reigned. One TV editor described it this way: "Politics was criminalized and crime was politicized." Especially during the Milošević era, they dominated Serbia, operating extortion rackets and drug rings, kidnapping businessmen who spoke out against them, terrorizing politicians, even murdering former president Ivan Stambolić. This ended with the assassination of Djindjić.

Nebojsa Čović, who acted as prime minister for a few days, stated unmistakably what was at stake: "We have to decide who really rules this country—the mafia and its assassins, or its elected leaders." Under a new prime minister, former interior minister Zoran Živković, who had been an imposing and vociferous critic of Milošević, the government cracked down with a vengeance. A state of emergency was declared until April 22, the army was ordered to swear its loyalty and take over for the police, civil liberties were temporarily suspended, and airports and train and bus stations in Belgrade were closed.

A police sweep, called Operation Sabre, resulted in over 10,000 arrests, and 4,500 were jailed, while charges were filed against 3,700. One of those charged was popular singer Svetlana Ražnatović (better known as Ceca), the widow of the infamous warlord Željko Ražnatović (known as Arkan), who had been assassinated three years earlier. Police said she had links to the Zemun drug cartel, named after a Belgrade suburb, which had been implicated in the assassination. The authorities sent bulldozers to flatten the large shopping center that served as Zemun's criminal headquarters.

Having failed to prosecute the underworld bosses, 35 judges were forced into retirement; not a single senior official of the Milošević era had been tried in Serbia for war crimes. The Red Berets' former leader Legija went into hiding, and he was tried in absentia. He surrendered in May 2004, and in June he joined a dozen other murder suspects being tried in Serbia's special court for organized crime and war crimes, set up in 2003. The court has made steady progress in the war on organized crime. Two weeks after his arrest, assailants tried to kill Djindjić's sister, and his mother and other relatives received death threats to be carried out if Legija is convicted. He got 40 years in 2005 for the Stambolić murder and for attempted assassination of ex-foreign minister Vuk Drašković. In February 2007 a Belgrade court convicted Ulemek-Legija and six of his men for killing four of Drašković's associates while trying to murder him in 1999.

While on the run, Legija produced a novel, *Iron Trench*, about a Serbian soldier lying critically wounded in a ditch during the war in Bosnia. Blatantly anti-Muslim in tone, it nevertheless questions what was gained by the war. Although there is some question about the book's true authorship, it quickly sold 70,000 copies. The acclaim received by *Iron Trench* and by Radovan Karadžić's novel *The Miraculous Chronicle of the Night* reflects the somewhat-legendary status these nationalist figures still enjoy. Two more books by Legija appeared in 2005.

Red Berets' deputy chief Zvezdan Jovanović was arrested two weeks after Djindjic's murder and confessed to having been the triggerman. He had waited for three days to take his shot. He said he did it to stop suspects from being delivered to The Hague. After a three-and-a-half-year trial in Belgrade's new special court for organized crime, Legija and Jovanović were sentenced in May 2007 to 40 years in prison, Serbia's maximum penalty. The Supreme Court rejected their appeal in October 2009. Eleven other defendants were convicted also, five in absentia. The verdict said that the motives were to halt Djindjić's pro-western policies, to bring Milošević's allies back into power and to stop further extraditions to The Hague.

The crackdown also led to the discovery of former Serbian president Ivan Stambolic's body, a bitter foe of Milošević who had been missing since August 2000, when he had been abducted while jogging in a Belgrade park. Arguing that Milošević had given orders for the "permanent removal" of Stambolić, police charged Jovanovic and eight others with the murder; the eight were jailed in July 2005. They also issued arrest warrants for Mrs. Milošević, Mirjana Marković, and their son Marko, who are suspected of involvement in the killing.

Both had fled the country for Russia. Some of the charges against Mirjana were dropped in July 2008 as a condition for the Socialist Party's entry into the government. The results were breathtaking. Acting President Nataša Mićić proclaimed on national television, "We have dismantled Milošević's criminal apparatus and severed a spiral of crime that has ravaged our country for more than a decade." Only time can tell if the entire cancer has been extracted and whether Djindjić's own prediction after a previous assassination attempt will be true: "You can shoot me, you can even kill me, but this country and its democratic system will still function."

Under circumstances almost too bizarre to be true, Radovan Karadžić was arrested in Belgrade in July 2008 after 13 years on the run. The 63-year-old former president of Bosnian Serbs was disguised so thoroughly that he could move around Belgrade freely. He was sporting a huge bushy, white beard; flowing gray hair with a black dyed spot on the top; and oversized horn-rimmed glasses (see photos in the chapter on Bosnia and Herzegovina). The trained psychiatrist was living under the assumed name of Dr. Dragan Dabić, handing out business cards proclaiming himself as a "bioenergist," delivering lectures at conferences on alternative medicine, publishing articles in Serbia's *Healthy Living* magazine, counseling on Christian Orthodox spirituality, and giving treatments for impotence and depression.

His chances of remaining free had been considerably reduced since a major political shift occurred in Serbia after the May 2008 elections. They put power into the hands of President Boris Tadić, who was determined to lead his country into the EU, and took it away from former nationalist prime minister Vojislav Koštunica. Karadžić was arrested within two weeks of a change of guard in the Serb intelligence services.

Tensions were high after Tadić received death threats, and journalists were attacked by far-right nationalists. Thousands of Karadžić's Radical Party supporters gathered in downtown Belgrade in an attempt to prevent his extradition to The Hague. They turned violent, smashed shops, and attacked and injured more than a dozen policemen. Undaunted, Serbian authorities whisked the fugitive away several hours later before dawn and brought him to a penitentiary in Scheveningen, Netherlands. Karadžić appeared in his first public court hearing on July 31, 2008, which signaled the beginning of the legal proceedings against him. His trial resumed in March 2010, after he had exhausted his stalling tactics.

He lost his case in March 2016; was convicted of genocide, war crimes, and crimes against humanity; and was sentenced to 40 years in prison. While he was found guilty of 10 out of the 11 charges with which he was originally charged, he maintained that all of his actions were to protect Serbs during the Bosnian conflict.

Only two key fugitives remained on the run. In May 2011 Ratko Mladić was captured after more than 15 years in hiding. In 2010 the government had raised its reward for his capture from €1 million to €10 million and intensified its hunt in Belgrade. However, it suffered a setback when a Belgrade municipal court invoked the statute of limitations and acquitted 10 persons accused of having helped hide him.

Authorities ultimately found him after pressuring his diminishing network of supporters and cutting off his financial lifeline. He was found hiding in a darkened house in a Serbian farming village. He had worked on construction crews to remain solvent. The shrunken ailing figure gave up without resistance even though he was armed. Polls showed that a majority of Serbs opposed extraditions to The Hague, and the ultranationalist Serbian Radical Party organized a rally opposing his delivery to the international court. Once there Mladić refused to enter a plea, calling the charges "obnoxious." He showed the same kind of obstructionist behavior Milošević had. In late 2016, prosecutors demanded a life sentence for him, arguing that anything less would be "an insult to the victims, living and dead, and an affront to justice."

In July 2011 Goran Hadžić, who had commanded Serb forces in Croatia and was held responsible for the three-month siege and destruction of Vukovar, was apprehended in a forest north of Belgrade after seven years in hiding. He had been president of the Serb Krajina splinter republic during the war. He was penniless. In 2013 two Bosnian Serb police chiefs, Mićo Stanišić and Stojan Župljanin, were given 22-year sentences for ethnic cleansing. The court originally rendered surprising verdicts acquitting two close Milošević aides, Jovica Stanišić and Franko Simatović, but their three-year trial revealed many of the inner workings of the Milošević period. (In 2015, UN appeals judges ordered a new trial for those two, citing legal errors in the original process.) It also overturned the conviction of the most senior Yugoslav army officer, General Momčilo Perišić.

Serbia

Ivo Andric

This followed the acquittal on appeal of Croat general Ante Gotovina, a decision that enraged Serbs.

In 2015, a former Serbian general who had been imprisoned since 2001 for his role in the Srebrenica massacre, Radislav Krstić, was awarded £50,000 in compensation from the British government after his throat had been cut by "Islamic extremists" while he was in his cell in a British prison. He was later transferred to a Polish prison to complete his 35-year sentence.

Foreign Policy

Even though the United States did not recognize the new Yugoslav government in 1991, it continued to staff an embassy in Belgrade over the next several years. The stated purpose was to maintain contacts with Belgrade in order to try to persuade it to agree to a negotiated peace settlement in Bosnia. After the end of the Bosnian war in 1995, American-Serbian relations improved because Washington was counting on Milošević's continued support of the Dayton Accords to make them work. Gradually many of the sanctions against Yugoslavia were removed, and it appeared that Yugoslavia was about to shed its pariah status. That was put on hold in February 1998 after Serbia launched a series of punitive attacks on Albanian villages in Kosovo.

When those attacks did not bring satisfactory results from Serbia's point of view, Belgrade sent in additional units of paramilitary police and army units, which continued Milošević's policy of "pacification" of the province. This resulted in the destruction of many Kosovar villages and forced several hundred ethnic Albanians to become refugees in their own country. NATO countries intervened on behalf of the Kosovars.

At the beginning of the air war against Yugoslavia in March 1999 Belgrade broke off diplomatic relations with the NATO states, and most international organizations broke ties with Belgrade. As hundreds of thousands of Albanians were pushed out of the province, they came to fill refugee camps in North Macedonia and Albania, in the process threatening to destabilize those countries. All of its immediate neighbors supported NATO's demand that Serbia restore Kosovar autonomy and stop its policy of ethnic cleansing, and they favor NATO's occupation of the province. Greece voiced opposition.

Yugoslavia could not find many friends among its neighbors until Milošević was removed from power in October 2000. Once Vojislav Koštunica had assumed the reins of power in Belgrade, he announced, "I expect support from Europe for the democratic changes in Serbia and for its return to where it has always belonged—Europe." The west responded without hesitation, quickly dropping economic sanctions and bringing Yugoslavia back into most international institutions with incredible speed but with many conditions.

He quickly restored diplomatic relations with the US, Germany, France, Britain, and Yugoslavia's neighboring nations. Underscoring his promise of a new era of cooperation with Serbia's Balkan neighbors, he traveled to North Macedonia for talks with other regional leaders. There he admitted that Serb soldiers and police had committed large-scale murder in Kosovo. North Macedonia's late president Boris Trajkovski rejoiced, "we are living in truly historic times." Koštunica also became the first leader of Yugoslavia to visit non-Serb Bosnian territory since the Bosnian war began in 1992. He met the three members of Bosnia's collective presidency at the Sarajevo Airport in October 2000. As Serbian prime minister, he sent his defense minister to Albania, the first since 1947. This marked the end of the cold war between Tirana and Belgrade.

Within three weeks of Koštunica's election in 2000, Yugoslavia joined the Balkan Stability Pact, funded by the EU. On November 1, Yugoslavia was readmitted to the UN after an eight-year suspension of voting rights. By 2013 a former Serb foreign minister, Vuk Jeremić, had become UN General Assembly president. He stirred up anger by suggesting that the war-crimes tribunal in The Hague had unfairly singled out Serbs in its prosecutions. He also arranged for a Serb choir to sing a song, "March on the Drina," in the plenary hall, which had become an unofficial anthem among Serb soldiers who committed massacres in Bosnia and elsewhere in the 1990s.

Several delegates reminded Koštunica that UN membership obligates Serbia to cooperate with the UN war-crimes tribunal in The Hague and to turn Milošević over for trial, something the new president, a legal scholar and moderate Serb nationalist, had said he would not do. Immediately afterward, his country was welcomed back into the OSCE, from which it had been suspended in 1992. In March 2003 the Council of Europe welcomed Serbia back into the organization after Serbia accepted a series of conditions concerning cooperation with the war-crimes tribunal.

Serbia will always play a crucial role in the Balkan geopolitical situation. If it is poor, turbulent, and aggressive, the rest of the area will be insecure and unsettled. Like the rest of the democratic world, Washington was pleased by the change and courted Koštunica assiduously until it tired of his resistance to cooperating with the war-crime trials in The Hague. It supported the Serbian government of Zoran Djindjić with financial assistance and diplomatic encouragement and continued that assistance for his successors.

The US backed the lifting of the UN arms embargo on Serbia and Montenegro, which maintained united armed forces until separating in June 2006. Signaling its desire for good military ties with Serbia in May 2006, the US sent two F-16 fighter jets to Batajnica Air Base near Belgrade for a courtesy visit. Arms shipments are subject to limits established under the Dayton Peace Accords and subsequent agreements with Bosnia and Herzegovina and Croatia.

Serbia's armed forces have shrunken greatly since the Balkan wars. In 2010 its total active military force counted 29,125 soldiers. Of these, the army has 12,260, including 1,800 conscripts. The air force and air defense have 4,262, including 477 conscripts. They fly Soviet-era MiG aircraft. The navy has about 3,000 personnel (including 900 marines) who man 4 conventional submarines; 3 frigates; and an assortment of patrol and coastal combatants, mine sweepers, and support ships. Training command has 6,212 soldiers, and the department of defense, 6,391. Conscripts serve nine months. Its reserve force numbers 50,151.

Major military reform is underway, and civilian service for those who do not wish to be soldiers was introduced. In 2006 Serbia and Montenegro had to sort out their military bases and personnel. Each kept the facilities on its own territory, and soldiers were free to resettle in their own countries.

Serbia signed a landmark border agreement in 2002, ceding to Croatia the Prevlaka Peninsula, which controls access to Boka Kotorska (Kotor Bay), Montenegro's main deep seaport. The agreement demilitarizes the area, permits Serbian and Montenegrin naval vessels to traverse the channel into the bay without stopping

Serbia

A sample of a Serbian banknote

or conducting military maneuvers in the area, and calls for joint sea police patrols. As a result of Montenegro's declaration of independence in June 2006, Serbia lost its direct access to the sea.

In 2003 Serbia requested admission to NATO's Partnership for Peace program as a first step toward NATO membership. This would help it reform its armed forces. But the uncertainty in 2004 about Belgrade's willingness to cooperate with The Hague caused NATO and the EU to delay cooperation, and discussions over Serbian offers in 2003 to dispatch troops and police to Afghanistan and Iraq were postponed. NATO's invitation was reissued in November 2006.

The annual March commemoration with sirens blaring honoring the victims of the 1999 NATO air war to break Serbia's hold over Kosovo reveals the continued ant western sentiment in Serbia over the war. Opinion polls demonstrate that only a small percentage of Serbs support their country's integration into NATO. Ex-foreign minister Vuk Drašković noted, "Until NATO bombed us, most Serbs saw the West as the last great hope, the last love, the last illusion." Now reformers face a difficult challenge to convince disillusioned Serbs that the US, NATO, and the EU have their best interests in mind.

Since 2002 Serbia's leaders express the wish to join the EU, and the EU opened the way in 2003 dependent upon the commitments to reform and overcome ethnic strife. This process was put on hold until Belgrade's cooperation with the war-crimes tribunal was clarified; the accession process was resumed in 2007. It culminated in the signing of a Stabilization and Accession Agreement on April 29, 2008. In November 2009 the Netherlands unblocked the path to membership. The next month visa-free travel to Europe was granted, and Serbia formally applied to join. In 2011 Serbia and the EU reached a deal that would pave the way for membership in the World Trade Organization. Serbia is attempting to manage a delicate balance between seeking EU membership and supporting its historically,

Russia. Prime Minister Vučić maintained that "Serbia is on the European path, and we will not give up on that path." But it refused to support EU sanctions imposed against Russia over Ukraine. In May 2014, the "Russian 100" rescuers flew in from Moscow within hours of an appeal from Serbia to help during massive floods. Later that year, 70 years after the Red Army liberated the city from the Nazis, Vladimir Putin was a guest of honor in Belgrade at a military parade.

In November, Russian paratroopers held one-day exercises with Serbian soldiers, and Russian patriarch Kiril blessed a statue of Tsar Nicholas II outside the Serbian presidency building. Perhaps most importantly, Russia's refusal to recognize Kosovo prevents that new country from being accepted into the United Nations, where Russia wields veto power in the Security Council. Clearly, Russia remains Serbia's best ally. Some of the connection remains emotional, though there is certainly much geopolitics involved, too. With Montenegro's admission to NATO in June 2017, Russia's interests in the region tie it to Serbia even more firmly. All 40 grateful residents of a mountain hamlet called Adžinci, some 200 miles south of Belgrade, unanimously decided to rename their village Putinovo ("Putin's Village"). Putin returned in January 2019 and basked in the warm feelings Serbs have for Russia. Tens of thousands were bused into Belgrade to demonstrate for him.

In 2016, Serbia announced signing a deal with the Russian-dominated Eurasian Economic Union. It is not altogether clear what economic advantages Serbia would derive from the deal, since it already has free-trade agreements with the main members of the EAEU: Russia, Kazakhstan, and Belarus. Given Russia's political goal for the EAEU to recreate some of the Soviet economic space so as to counterbalance the influence of the European Union, Serbia's relations with the EU may suffer.

Kosovo

The EU does not demand that Belgrade recognize Kosovo, but it requires and

sponsors talks between the two countries on technical issues. For instance, they reached an agreement on auto license plates. In February 2012 they agreed on common border controls and Kosovo's right to participate in regional conferences. Germany insists that Serbia give up its claims to Kosovar territory if it wants to join the EU. On a visit to Belgrade in 2011, German chancellor Angela Merkel made clear that Serbia can either join with Kosovo or not join without Kosovo. In March 2012, after a last-minute agreement with Romania over protecting the rights of Romanian-speaking Vlachs in Serbia, Serbia was granted official EU candidate status.

No major Serbian politicians or parties accept Kosovo's declaration of independence on February 17, 2008. When it happened, some government leaders joined the hardline nationalist Radical Party to mobilize as many as 200,000 Serbs in the streets of Belgrade to protest. Free rail and bus tickets were given to bring in people from all over the country. Then-prime minister Koštunica declared, "As long as we live, Kosovo is Serbia!" After hearing fiery speeches, mobs peeled off to loot shops and attack the American, Croatian, Bosnian, and Turkish embassies. At least 100 broke into the US embassy when it was closed and set fire to some of the rooms. They were quickly extinguished, but not before a young demonstrator perished in the blaze. In September 2015, nine people accused of setting the fire received suspended sentences of a few months.

The UN Security Council unanimously condemned the violence, which was not limited to Belgrade. In the northern Kosovo town of Mitrovica, 5,000 demonstrators confronted UN police guarding the bridge separating the Serbian and Albanian communities. Two border stations were burned when they tried to hoist Kosovo's flag. The Serb government did everything it could to prevent Kosovo Albanian rule from taking effect in the new country's Serb-inhabited enclaves. Its foreign minister and diplomats traveled the world in a vain attempt to dissuade countries from recognizing independent Kosovo, as over half of UN member states, including 23 EU members, have done.

The government used all legal and democratic means to prevent Kosovo from gaining membership in the UN and other international bodies, such as NATO, the World Bank, or the IMF. At the UN it moved to have the International Court of Justice give an advisory opinion on whether Kosovo's declaration of independence was legal. The nonbinding decision was rendered on July 22, 2010, and was unambiguous—Kosovo's declaration of independence was legal and did not violate international law.

493

Serbia

In March 2011 the two countries began high-level talks in Brussels, coordinated by the EU's top diplomat, Baroness Catherine Ashton. They aimed first to deal with practical problems, such as allowing planes heading to Kosovo to overfly Serbian airspace or to permit exports from Kosovo to pass through Serbia. On December 10, 2012, traffic began moving over border crossings.

Knowing that Serbia would never again be able to rule hostile Kosovo Albanians, Serb leaders signed a historic agreement with the Priština government on April 19, 2013. They accepted the authority of the Kosovo government over all of Kosovo, and Kosovo granted a large measure of autonomy to Serbs living in Mitrovica in the north. Kosovo's armed forces cannot be deployed there. Serbs in Kosovo are given limited authority over health care and education, as well as representation in top police posts and courts in areas where they predominate. There is an understanding that neither government will stand in the way of the other's admission to the EU.

Very importantly, the agreement does not require Serbia to recognize Kosovo as an independent state. The two sides could not agree on a timetable for implementing the accord. The US supported the agreement but played no direct role in the negotiations. (See the separate chapter on Kosovo.)

Former prime minister Zoran Živković announced during his 2003 visit to Washington, "Serbia is looking for an ally in the United States, and in return Serbia can offer to be a reliable partner in the Balkans." After all, the second-largest concentration of Serbs in the world is Chicago. American leaders are aware that a deeply felt Serbian nationalism inspires continuing anger over the support the US provided to Kosovars. They seek a good relationship with Serbia. A growing number of Serbian military officers attend command staff and war colleges in the US, and from 2006 the Ohio National Guard helped train the Serbian army. Between 2015 and 2021, Serbia increased its military spending by 70% to $1.4 billion. It has excellent relations with NATO, whose members surround it, and America trains Serbian troops.

Current president Joe Biden visited Serbia in May 2009 to offer it "a strong, new relationship." He said his country does not expect Serbia to recognize Kosovo's independence. But it does expect it to cooperate with the EU and others in Kosovo and to "look for pragmatic solutions that would improve the lives of all the people in Kosovo." Ex-secretary of state Hillary Clinton followed in October 2010, telling the Serb president that dialogue with Kosovo would "have a positive impact

on the relationship between Serbia, your neighbors, Europe and the United States." Still, many Serbs rooted for Donald Trump, her rival during the US presidential election in 2016, unwilling to forgive her husband's role in NATO's bombing of Serbia.

Türkiye has also become an active partner with Serbia, entering agreements to abolish visas and to establish free trade and seeking reconciliation between Bošnjaks and Serbs in Bosnia. A new, EU-sponsored initiative is a highway link from Niš in Serbia through Kosovo and on to Tirana and Durrës on the Albanian coast. The construction of this important link, will improve economic cooperation in the region.

Serbia continues to insist that the seizure of property by Kosovo prevents many Serbs from returning to the region. Serbia describes those people as IDPs, or Internally Displaced Persons, emphasizing its refusal to recognize Kosovo as a foreign territory.

For Serbs, Kosovo remains the "mother of all problems." A 2019 poll revealed that 70% of Serbs reject any compromise over Kosovo.

ECONOMY

The country still has what must be called a socialist market economy, although considerable progress is being made to liberalize and privatize the economy. But it is neither a capitalist nor a totally government-directed economy. There are three basic parts. One is a small market-oriented one that generates most of the growth. There is the large, unreformed socialist system, and finally there exists an "underground" economy that generates an estimated 30% of GDP and much of the employment. Only half of working-age people participate in the workforce, compared with the 66% EU average.

Economic collapse played a large role in the dissolution of Yugoslavia in the 1990s. The country had been a leader among the socialist states in economic decentralization, but it remained a socialist state. Fast economic growth in the 1970s had brought better living conditions but a multitude of problems, as well. Mounting inflation became more and more of a problem, and the foreign trade deficit began to grow. Not wishing to put an end to the economic growth, the leadership rather reluctantly responded with things like import restrictions and a ceiling on wage increases. Eventually it was also forced to begin devaluating the currency. The great increase in energy prices in 1973–1974 and again in 1979 eventually proved too much for the Yugoslav economy, and it, like most of the world, slipped into recession.

While Yugoslavia's economy drifted during the 1980s, inflation grew year after year until, by the end of 1988, it had gotten out of control completely, soaring to an annual rate of 2,500%. The situation frightened the political leadership, and in desperation it turned to Ante Marković, an exponent of the free market. He was installed as president of the Federal Executive Council in March 1989.

Even then, there was stiff opposition to his stabilization program, but he managed to get it adopted after several months. It went into effect on January 1, 1990. Within three months, the dinar had been stabilized, and inflation had been brought down to single digits. In addition, currency reserves were up, and the foreign debt had been reduced to $16 billion. Foreign investment also began pouring into the country, and individual Yugoslavs started several thousand privately owned businesses.

With the stabilization program so successful, politics reasserted itself. The second phase of Markovic's program called for beginning the privatization of state-owned industry, instituting radical changes in the federal tax structure, and making banks more independent of the government. But elections were scheduled in the various republics, so the politicians demanded that the national wage freeze be lifted instead. It was Slobodan Milošević who most strongly opposed the privatization policy. Lacking support in the republics, the national stabilization program was put on hold.

Meanwhile, free elections in Slovenia and Croatia brought a repudiation of the old communist leadership and their replacement by nationalist leaders, who began talking of the need to replace the federation by a loose confederation of sovereign nations. Domestically, these new leaders adopted free-market economic policies. This contrasted with the position of Milošević, who argued for a strong centralized Yugoslavia and against free-market economic policies.

Caught between the two forces, the economic stabilization program of the Marković government collapsed. By the beginning of 1991, inflation was again running at an annual rate of 120%, and the dinar had to be devalued by 30%. By April 1991, strikes were breaking out all over the country, as thousands of enterprises were unable to meet their payrolls. Things were bad all over the country, but Serbian industry, the largest and most inefficient in the country, was worst off. Unemployment in 2014 was 26% and rising (up from 14% in 2008) as industrial production continued to plummet. Thus, an economic stabilization plan that had been working was completely destroyed by national and political rivalries.

War in Bosnia and Kosovo had a terrible effect on the Serbian economy. The cost of Milošević's financial support for the Bosnian and Croatian Serbs was an estimated 40% of Serbia's GDP. This produced a hyperinflation that effectively destroyed the Serbian currency by the end of 1993 and caused the GDP to drop by two-thirds, or to about $10 billion. This prompted a currency reform in 1993. A new dinar linked to the German mark was introduced, and this temporarily stopped the hyperinflation. The dinar remains weak.

When Serbia accepted the Dayton Peace Accords, signed in December 1995, the west rewarded it by "suspending" the economic embargo and promising to remove it entirely if the peace agreement held. The Serbs now had a chance to get their economy back on track once again. There was, in fact, some improvement in 1996 and 1997. A major effect of the air war in 1999 was that a great deal of Yugoslavia's infrastructure was destroyed.

Under former prime minister Djindjić's and his successor's stewardship from October 2000 to the end of 2003, Serbia made impressive economic progress. It reduced public spending, sold state assets, and regularized taxation. Its privatization law of 2001 won international praise, and privatization is advancing quickly. In 2006 the mobile phone network was privatized, and the oil sector was to follow. Although much industry is still publicly owned, there is a significant private sector. In agriculture, 84% of the land is in private hands. The purchase and sale of land is permitted, and there exists a free market in agricultural products.

A major problem is that investors had fear because the rule of law is weak. Nevertheless, the US government removed the remaining barriers to economic cooperation and trade with Serbia, and America has become the country's largest investor. In 2003 US Steel bought the ailing Smederevo steelworks. At first, US Steel Serbia suffered heavy losses, but the cash investment eventually paid off; it is now Serbia's largest exporter. Fiat cars are second. The American tobacco giant Philip Morris purchased a Serbian cigarette factory and became the largest foreign investor in the country.

Serbia survived massive layoffs in a major car factory in Kragujevac, the hub of ex-Yugoslavia's motor industry. In 2009 Fiat announced it would begin making 200,000 cars every year in Kragujevac as part of a joint venture that by 2013 had invested €1.2 billion ($1.65 billion) and created 3,800 jobs. It purchased a 67% share in the country's main automaker, Zastava,

which had once produced what one author called "the worst car in history," the Yugo. It took over the management and is bringing technology and introducing stricter quality control. In 2009, Yura, a South Korean auto parts maker, set up a plant in Kragujevac, which employs 1,000. Serbia is one of the main hubs for China's Belt and Road Initiative. Chinese investments in Serbia amount to 20% of total FDI in the entire western Balkans.

Serbia closed insolvent banks. This strengthened those that remained, so that when the global economic downturn hit Serbia in 2008, prompting a run on its banks and the withdrawal of 20% of their deposits, all 33 banks were able to meet their obligations, with the help of the central bank and EU. In 2005 Microsoft opened a software center in Belgrade, a year in which 7,000 new firms were registered. Making an impressive comeback is Serbia's arms industry, which in 2011 accounted for 4% of exports and was the fastest-growing industry after agriculture.

In 2008 the Russian state-owned gas monopoly Gazprom purchased a controlling share (51%) of the Serbian state oil monopoly NIS. It thereby incorporated Serbia into the South Stream gas pipeline that would have run under the Black Sea, through Bulgaria, and into western Europe. This would have been a blow to the EU's plans to build its own Nabucco pipeline that would be outside Russian control. Serbia would have become a hub for Russian energy supplies and strengthen Russia's dominance of the European energy market. A huge gas storage facility was also promised. Serbia was bitterly disappointed when Russia canceled its plans for the South Stream pipeline project in December 2014.

Gazprom invested about $725 million toward modernizing Serbia's energy infrastructure. Russia will take three metric tons of spent fuel from the closed Vinča nuclear reactor and thereby keep this nuclear material out of terrorists' hands. To diminish reliance on Russian gas slightly, Serbia's state-owned gas supplier, Srbijagas, signed a contract with HEAT, an Austrian company, to build a stopgap gas supply line. Serbia gets over 21% of its energy from renewable resources. Serbia has one of Europe's largest reserves of lithium, and essential ingredient of electric car batteries.

A major burden for Serbia was the presence of 94,000 refugees, a huge number for a country of 8 million people. In 2012 Serbia joined other Balkan nations in raising $395 million ($303 million from the EU) to help house 74,000 people who are still living as refugees. This was the largest displacement in Europe since World

War II, until the problem was further aggravated by the overwhelming influx of Middle Eastern and African migrants in 2015 and 2016. Even though almost all were only passing through Serbia on their way north, mostly to Germany, the financial and logistical effort was considerable for the small country. It took a great toll on Serbian economy, with the need for supplying food, shelter, medical supplies, and medical treatment to the migrants.

The country's important challenge is to recover from the global economic crisis, which hit the country just when it had barely recovered to prewar levels. One banker noted, "Serbia's had 20 years of crisis . . . so the worst is already behind us." In the longer term, it must establish a truly modern, competitive free-market economy and get the economy firmly out of the hands of organized criminals.

American drug enforcement officials praised Serbia in 2010 for seizing a 2.7-ton shipment of cocaine from South America and arresting 11 Serb and Montenegrin suspects. Many Balkan gangs operate in Latin America. More action can be expected as Serbia and Croatia have intensified their collaboration. In May 2010 they announced plans for a regional center to combat organized crime, and the following month they signed a defense cooperation agreement. In March 2014 authorities arrested Darko Šarić, one of the most feared and wanted drug traffickers in the Balkans, who had been on the run since 2009. In 2015 he was sentenced to 20 years in prison.

Construction of a new Belgrade waterfront ("Belgrade on Water") generated a lot of social protest when several buildings were demolished to make room for one part of the ambitious urban redevelopment project. To that end, city officials also destroyed a refugee center. The officials hoped the new cityscape would enhance Belgrade's Savamala District's reputation as "New Berlin" for its busy and trendy nightlife. The lack of transparency and societal consultations, combined with the opulent look and price tag of the project (almost $4 billion) upset a lot of locals. The waterfront boasts the highest skyscraper in the Balkans (a glass tower twisted in the middle), as well as condominiums, offices, hotels, and restaurants; it was developed by an Abu Dhabi firm.

Currently, the World Bank classifies Serbia as a middle-income country and its economy functions on the principles of the free market. In 2022, GDP in Serbia reached USD 9,538 per capita, or 63.56 billion USD for the whole country. Serbia was ranked 86 among the major economies. Inflation in Serbia in 2022 was around 11.98%. Its economic growth slowed in the

Serbia

first half of 2023 as decelerating private and public investment as well as elevated inflation hurt consumption and weighed on economic activity. Full-year economic growth was expected at 2%, with risks of decreasing. The nominal GDP in 2024 is projected to reach $81.694 billion, which is $12,400 per capita.

CULTURE

The collapse of Yugoslavia left Serbia with a more homogenous ethnic identity. What is left is essentially Serbian culture, characterized by the Serbian language, written in a 30-character Cyrillic alphabet, and the Serbian Orthodox religion.

Serbia also includes more than 300,000 ethnic Hungarians, who are concentrated in Vojvodina, where they constitute the largest minority, with 14% of the residents. Vojvodina has a total population of 2 million. It is the wealthiest part of Serbia and home to 60,000 Slovaks. The province has six official languages, including Ruthenian, Slovak, and Hungarian, and schooling is in their own language. Latin letters are widely used. It has its own provincial government with a prime minister. In the beginning of 2010, a new autonomy statute went into effect for Vojvodina. In 2012 it elected its own parliament. Although some nationalists said this could ultimately lead to independence, about two-thirds of its population are Serbs, who have no interest in independence.

Approximately 70,000 Albanians constitute the majority in the Preševo Valley within Serbia. The Sandžak area in southwest Serbia has a predominantly Muslim but non-Albanian population. A little over half of the approximately 236,000 Sandžak Muslims are Bošnjaks. Most Albanians are Muslim, although there is a small minority that is Roman Catholic and even a few who are Orthodox. Hungarians are usually Roman Catholic or Protestant. There is also a Romanian-speaking Wallach minority.

In 2017, Serbia unveiled a memorial in Jarek to Germans expelled and killed after World War II. Some 550,000 Danube Swabians lived in Yugoslavia before the war, and about half of them supported Hitler's Nazi Germany; some participated in wartime atrocities. After many escaped with the retreating Germans, some 140,000 stayed and suffered retribution, from expulsion to abuse and starvation in concentration camps to murder. Only some 4,000 remain in Serbia today.

Serbs can be justly proud of the picturesque Serbian Orthodox churches and monasteries that date from a great blossoming of culture during the Middle Ages. In January 2010 hundreds of thousands marched in a somber funeral procession in Belgrade to mourn the death of popular patriarch Pavle. Known for his modesty and humility, he had since 1990 led the 7-million-member church through the country's post-communist adjustment and ethnic conflicts. Irinej Gavrilović was elected to replace him. Stating that "the Serbian Orthodox church had always been present in the life and deeds of the great Nikola Tesla," church officials continue to push for the remains of Nikola Tesla to be moved to St. Sava's Cathedral and out of his museum. The great physicist is a national hero in Serbia; many oppose this idea.

The nation also has an admirable literary tradition. In 1961 Ivo Andrić, a former Yugoslav diplomat, was awarded the Nobel Prize in literature. His epic novel *The Bridge over the Drina* describes the long and troubled relationship between Muslims, Catholics, Orthodox Christians, and occupiers in his native city of Višegrad in Bosnia.

World-renowned tennis champion Novak Djoković and his wife, Jelena, created a foundation that focuses on early childhood development in Serbia. They estimate that half of Serbian children do not have enough brain stimulation between the ages of zero and six. Djoković was appointed UNICEF ambassador in 2011 to help raise awareness of low preschool enrollment in Serbia. His foundation raised $1.4 million at its first benefit dinner in 2012 and $1.7 million the following year.

In the drowsy farm village of Medju, near the Romanian border, the American Olympic swimmer and later popular Tarzan actor Johnny Weissmuller was born in 1904. Although his family emigrated to the US when he was a baby, his birthplace honors him with a bronze Tarzan statue. About 20 kilometers (12 miles) away is another village, Žitište, where a bronze statue of Rocky Balboa, made famous in the many Sylvester Stallone Rocky boxing films, also was erected. In 2008 another village unveiled what it claims is Europe's first statue to the late Jamaican reggae star Bob Marley. Such monuments to Hollywood icons and pop culture are springing up all over the Balkans.

The strangest manifestation of lingering ethnic tensions occurred in October 2014 at a soccer game between Serbia and Albania in Belgrade. A brawl was caused by a drone flying overhead bearing the flag of Greater Albania. Soccer games remain venues for displays of sometimes-rabid nationalism. As elsewhere, the brawls are typically provoked by soccer hooligans.

CURRENT ISSUES

Enthusiasm for enlarging the EU to include the Balkans has cooled somewhat. The European Union insists on "debalkanizing" the Balkans, meaning establishing fixed borders and more stability. It may take years for Serbia to achieve its main strategic goal—full EU membership. Serbia officially applied for membership in the EU in December 2009, and received candidate status in March 2012. Following a positive recommendation of the European Commission and European Council in June 2013, negotiations to join the EU started in January 2014. When negotiations began polls indicate that over 60% favor joining the EU. However, this is a long way off because it will require a compromise on Kosovo, something that 70% of Serbs oppose.

Once the International Court of Justice ruled in July 2010 that Kosovo's declaration of independence was legal, Serbia moderated its tone and agreed to meet with high-level Kosovo officials to seek solutions to practical problems. But it made clear that its opposition to Kosovo's independence has not changed. It is a bitter pill because Kosovo had historically been the cradle and heart of the Serbian nation, and some of its most treasured religious architectural gems remain there as pointed reminders.

However, most Serbian leaders know that Kosovo's independence cannot be reversed. The government restored full relations with the EU and returned its ambassadors to those countries that have recognized Kosovo. Those include all but five EU members. A major hurdle was cleared when an agreement to improve relations was signed with Kosovo in April 2013. Among others, it created an association of Serb-majority communities in Kosovo and integrated all Kosovo police forces into one Kosovo Police (eliminating Serb-specific units). Very importantly for Serbia, both sides agreed not to "block, or encourage others to block, the other side's progress in their respective EU paths." Serbia continues what it calls the "Belgrade-Priština dialogue."

Ohrid Agreement

The efforts to bring about to normalization of Kosovo–Serbia diplomatic relations an agreement was achieved known as the Ohrid Agreement. It was mediated by the European Union. On February 27, 2023, it was verbally accepted by Kosovo Prime Minister Albin Kurti and Serbian President Aleksandar Vučić, and a plan for its implementation was agreed on March 18,

Serbia

2023. Reaching an agreement with Kosovo is a requirement for Serbia to join the EU.

The agreement was initially known as the "Franco-German proposal," because it was drafted by French and German diplomats based in the region and was inspired by the "two-Germanies" model from the Cold War. On December 5, 2022, a draft proposal was presented by the EU to both Kosovo and Serbia at the EU-Western Balkans summit in Tirana. In February 2023, Serbian President Aleksandar Vučić and Kosovo Prime Minister Albin Kurti met in Brussels to discuss the agreement, and they accepted the EU's draft. Josep Borrell, EU Foreign Minister, said that no further discussion was needed regarding the plan itself and that future negotiations would be dedicated to its implementation. Kurti and Vučić met again on March 18, 2023, at Ohrid (North Macedonia) and verbally accepted a roadmap for implementing the agreement.

Relations with Kosovo remain tense. This was stoked in January 2023 when Priština required Serbs to replace Serbian-issued car license plates and IDs.

In September 2023, tensions between Serbia and Kosovo escalated threatening to undermine the ongoing dialogue process with the European Union, when a clash between armed group and Kosovo police broke out in the predominantly by Serbs inhabited village of Banjska in northern Kosovo near the Serbian border. Serb militants blocked a bridge in Banjska, and the clash broke out when Kosovo police came to the scene to investigate the issue. The incident resulted in the death of Kosovo police officer Afrim Bunjaku. Another police officer was injured. Afterward, the area was put under siege and the attackers were neutralized. Three of the armed ethnic Serbs were killed and several others who were injured had been detained.

Kosovo's Prime Minister Albin Kurti accused Serbia claiming that organized criminal groups with political, financial, and logistical support from Belgrade were behind the attack. Serbian President Aleksandar Vučić addressed the public and responded that those armed individuals who attacked Kosovo police were not from Serbia but from local Kosovo Serbs. He condemned the killing of the Kosovo police officer and accused Kurti of trying to drag Serbia into a conflict with NATO. According to him, the Kosovo police officer was killed because NATO forces did not intervene.

Although at first it appeared to be a simple clash between the police and a group, the incident revealed that it had the potential to affect the relations between the two

countries and the balance in the region. Although there was no evidence that Serbia was behind the attack, it was changed on September 29, 2023, when Milan Radoičić, former Vice President of the Serbian List, a party of Kosovo Serbs, claimed responsibility for the incident. He was detained in Serbia following this development to be released on judicial control conditions. Serbia's statements that it would not extradite Radoičić to Kosovo put Serbia, which was already in a difficult situation due to the events, in even more trouble.

Serbia was also hampered by another development, namely it was revealed that the ammunition used during the attack came from Serbia.

It is not likely that any sanctions would be imposed on Serbia within the framework of these events. Serbia's recent efforts to harmonize itself with the EU institutions within the framework of its balance policy and Vučić's diplomatic moves have prevented it. The incident has affected Serbia's dialog with Kosovo. However, the EU, which wants to retain as much room for maneuver in the region as possible, will not take any steps to punish or squeeze Serbia in the near future.

The 2022 Russian invasion of Ukraine sent shock waves through the Balkans. Dependent on Russian oil and gas and sharing strong historical sympathies for Russia, Serbia refused to impose any sanctions on Russia. This infuriated its western partners. In one poll, 60% of Serbs blame America for the war, and only 26% blame Russia. However, Serbia condemned Russia at the United Nations General Assembly and Human Rights Council.

Open Balkan Initiative

The Open Balkan is an initiative created by North Macedonia, Serbia, and Albania, with the objective of closer regional cooperation and connectivity. Initially, it was referred to as the Advanced Regional Cooperation Initiative or "Mini Schengen Zone," aiming to promote and secure the four EU freedoms: free movement of people, goods, capital, and services.

The idea of an economic area between these countries appeared in the early 1990s, but it was eventually abandoned due to the Yugoslav Wars. The signs of it reappeared in 2018 as a way to improve political relations. It was brought up by Prime Minister Edi Rama who took it from the former Prime Minister of Albania Fatos Nano. Besides Edi Rama, the initiative was launched by the President of the Republic of Serbia, Aleksandar Vučić, and then Prime Minister of the Republic of North Macedonia, Zoran Zaev. The plans

for the area were declared and the first agreements signed in 2019 under the name "Mini-Schengen," and on July 29, 2021, it was established as the "Open Balkan" initiative (OBI).

This economic and political zone has a total area of 50,940 sq mi (131,935 sq. km.) and an estimated total population of almost 12 million. Its administrative centers are the cities of Belgrade (Serbia), Skopje (North Macedonia), and Tirana (Albania); the official languages are Albanian, Macedonian, and Serbian; and the current currencies are the Albanian lek, the Macedonian denar and the Serbian dinar.

So far, the members of OBI are the three founding countries, but the initiative has an open-door policy for the other countries in the region. The three potential members were expected to be Montenegro, Bosnia and Herzegovina, and Kosovo, but their official reactions to the initiative until now are unfavorable. Former President of Montenegro, Milo Đukanović, considered the initiative redundant, that it overlapped with the Berlin Process, and that it was launched because the European Union was delaying the accession negotiations of the Balkan countries. After the political changes in Montenegro, Jakov Milatović, the current president, believes that inclusion in the OBI could be a measure to facilitate the relations between Montenegro and Serbia.

While expressing personal support for the initiative, former Chairman of the Council of Ministers of Bosnia and Herzegovina, Zoran Tegeltija, said that Bosnia and Herzegovina still lacked a consensus about it for "political reasons."

In September 2020, Kosovo agreed to join the Mini-Schengen Area as part of the Kosovo and Serbia economic normalization agreements, but so far has not signed any agreement with any of the founding countries, and even opposed the whole initiative. Prime Minister of Kosovo Albin Kurti said that "Kosovo does not want to join in because Serbia is not treating it as an equal side and independent country." Serbia treats Kosovo as a unilaterally declared state which, according to Resolution 1244 of the United Nations Security Council, is legally part of Serbia until a final solution is reached.

The member states consider the Open Balkan as a platform for promoting and developing the region's capacity, developing economies, and creating a regional and single market without limitations, barriers, and borders. Besides trade opportunities, declared goals include, for example, student exchanges, mutual recognition of degrees and work permits, cooperation in disaster prevention, and food security.

Serbia

From a political point of view, Open Balkan aims to accelerate the European integration of the West Balkan countries and contribute to each of the countries in the initiative to become a member of the European Union.

At the series of summits that followed many declarations and agreements were signed establishing the legal framework and foundations for concrete activities: the Agreement on conditions for free access to the labor market in the Western Balkans, the Agreement on the interconnection of schemes for electronic identification of the citizens, the Agreement on cooperation in the field of veterinary, phytosanitary, and food and feed safety, and many others. At the summit held on September 2, 2022, in Belgrade, for instance, several agreements on the exchange of food products, energy, cinematography, as well as cooperation in emergencies, were signed.

The signed trilateral agreements have already given concrete results and benefits for the citizens. There are many new initiatives in sight: Establishment of common agency for attracting investments in Open Balkan; Promoting the region as an attractive tourist destination; Establishment of a regional theatre fund; Organizing regional youth exchange, schools, and festivals; and Reducing and eliminating the fees and taxes arising from the procedure of cross-border movement of people, goods, and services.

The Open Balkan initiative is nominally supported by representatives of the European Union and the United States of America. Nevertheless, it receives little active support from the EU, possibly because the eventual duplication with the Berlin Process, which also aims to lead the region towards EU membership, cannot be ruled out.

The Open Balkans initiative should be seen as complementary to the Berlin process, and its added value comes from the fact that it was not imposed from outside but originated from the region itself. The countries of the Western Balkans need to be closely involved in the decision-making processes and activities of the European Union.

Bosnia and Herzegovina (Bosna i Hercegovina)

Sarajevo lives again!

Neighboring Countries: Serbia (east); Montenegro (southeast); Croatia (west and north).

Official Languages: Bosnian, Serbian, Croatian (all of the same linguistic basis).

Other Language(s): Albanian.

Ethnic Background: 48.4% Bošnjak (Bosniak), 32.7% Serb, 14.6% Croat, 4.3% other.

Religion: 50.7% Muslim, Christian (30.7% Orthodox, 15.2 Catholic), 1.1% atheist, 2.3% other.

Form of Government: Federal parliamentary directorial republic.

Chief of State: Željko Komšić (chairman of the tripartite Presidency of the Republic of Bosnia and Herzegovina since July 2023)

Head of Government: Borjana Krišto (Prime Minister—Chair of the Council of Ministers since January 2023).

National Flag: It consists of a medium blue field with a yellow right-angled triangle with its base at the top of the background. A row of seven full five-pointed white stars and two half stars runs along the side of the hypotenuse of the triangle. The flag was established by the United Nations in 1998,

Area: 19,780 sq. mi. (51,229 sq. km).

Population: 3,428,000 (2023 estimate)

Capital City: Sarajevo (pop. 275,524 city; 419,957 urban; 555,210 metro). (2013 census)

Climate: Continental in the north and Mediterranean in the southwest. Although close to the Mediterranean Sea, the country is chiefly cut off from its climatic influence by the Dinaric Alps. The coldest month in the mountainous Bosnia is January, with an average temperature of about 32° F (0° C), and the warmest month is July, which averages about 72° F (22° C). Herzegovina, closer to the coast, can be oppressively hot in summer. Along the Neretva River valley, the coldest month is January, with an average temperature of about 42° F (6° C), and the warmest month is July, with an average temperature of about 78° F (26° C).

Bosnia and Herzegovina

and designed so that it could not be symbolically linked to a single ethnic, religious, or political group. The three points of the triangle stand for the three main ethnic groups, "constituent peoples" of Bosnia and Herzegovina: Bosniaks, Croats, and Serbs. The triangle could also be seen as representing the approximate shape of the territory of Bosnia and Herzegovina. The stars, representing Europe, are meant to be infinite in number. The colors of the flag—white, blue, and yellow, are usually associated with neutrality and peace. They are also colors traditional in Bosnian culture and history, while the blue background is evocative of the flag of the European Union.

Public Holiday: Mart 1 (Independence Day)

Currency: Convertible mark (KM).

Main Exports: Furniture, oil and mineral fuels, iron and steel, iron and steel articles, aluminum, electrical energy, electrical machinery, wood, industrial machinery, footwear, inorganic chemicals.

Main Imports: Oil and mineral fuels, industrial machinery, plastics, motor vehicles and parts, electrical machinery, iron and steel, aluminum, pharmaceuticals, iron and steel articles, copper.

Main Trading Partners: Croatia (14.9% of exports and 9.9% of imports), Italy (11.1% of exports and 12.3% of imports), Germany (14.8% of exports and 10.5% of imports), Serbia (13.2 of exports and 10.7 of imports), Austria (9.5% of exports), China (8.1 of imports). (2022)

Shortly before his death in 1897, Bismarck had predicted, "one day the great European War will come out of some damned foolish thing in the Balkans." That happened on July 28, 1914, when Gavrilo Princip, a Bosnian Serb nationalist, assassinated the Austrian archduke and his wife in Sarajevo. The shots of Sarajevo sounded the end of an almost-50-year absence of major wars among European great powers. Group rivalry and bloodshed are not new to Bosnia, the most ethnically diverse part of the entire volatile Balkans. In the last decade of the 20th century, this precarious republic offered Europeans the grisly spectacle of the worst human barbarity since World War II. Blood and belonging outweigh all other values.

The Republic of Bosnia and Herzegovina (Bosna i Hercegovina—BiH) is the independent successor state to the Socialist Republic of Bosnia and Herzegovina that was part of the Socialist Federal Republic of Yugoslavia until 1991. It is roughly triangular. It also has a tiny, 13-mile section of coastline on the Adriatic Sea but no harbor. Almost all of the country is mountainous. Herzegovina, the name that applies to the southern part of the republic, is derived from Herzog, a Germanic title for "duke," taken by a local ruler in the 15th century.

The name "Bosnia" is derived from the Bosna River, a tributary of the Sava River. Its 168-mile course is almost entirely within the republic. It originates in Herzegovina in the south, flows northeast through Bosnia and flows into the Sava River at the border. The Sava River, in turn, forms the northern border with Croatia.

A second river, the Drina, forms a large part of the border with Serbia. It is also a tributary of the Sava River. Another two rivers flow from south to north across the republic, the Vrbas River to the west of the Bosna and the Una River in the extreme northwest. The source of all of these rivers is the mountain chain known as the Dinarian Alps, which runs in a northwest-southeastern direction across the western part of the republic.

Individual peaks soar to over 7,500 feet, though wide valleys running in the same direction separate the ridges. The center of the republic is a piedmont region with an average height of 1,500 feet, while the Sava and Drina River Valleys produce lowlands in the east. About half of the land is arable. Most of the remainder is covered by forests of pine, beech, and oak.

The exception is the area of Herzegovina in the south. A native proverb says, "Bosnia begins with the forest, Herzegovina with the rock." The mountains of Herzegovina are of gray Karst limestone, filled with crevices, sinkholes, and pits, and they overwhelm the viewer with their barren desolation. Most of this area has very little population. It is only possible to live in the fertile river valleys that cut through the mountains and in some up-land hollows where there is arable soil. Bosnia's weather is generally mild, with cold winters. In Herzegovina, on the other hand, summers are often oppressively hot.

The population of Bosnia and Herzegovina consists of three main ethnic groups: Bosniaks, Serbs, and Croats, no single group being in the majority, and is the most diverse of the republics of the former Yugoslav Federation. The term "Bošnjak" has replaced "Muslim" as an ethnic term. This avoids confusion with the religious term "Muslim," a believer in Islam.

The differentiation on which the concept of the three "nations" of Bosnia and Herzegovina is based is religion and culture, not ethnicity. The Muslims there are a Slavic people who converted to Islam during Turkish rule. The language they speak is now referred to as Bosnian. No one now refers to "Serbo-Croatian" as a language anymore. Bosnian, Serbian, Montenegrin and Croatian are essentially dialects of the same language. Serbs are mainly adherents of the Serbian Orthodox Church, while Croats are almost all Roman Catholics.

HISTORY

Slavic-speaking peoples settled the present-day area of Bosnia and Herzegovina as early as the 7th century AD. It first emerged as a separate political entity toward the end of the 12th century, when a nobleman named Kulin managed to gain control of most of the lands along the Bosna River, who became known as the Ban of Bosnia. Kulin's principality did not last long, but one of the things he did was to convert to Bogomilism and make it the state religion.

Bogomilism had originated two centuries earlier, farther to the east in Bulgaria. By the 12th century, it had become well established in Bosnia. It shared many common characteristics with Catharism or Albigensianism, in particular a belief in a Manichaean dualism. Its distinguishing belief was that the world is governed by two principles, good and evil, the first spiritual and the second material. The physical world, being material, was viewed as the realm of the devil. Both the Roman Catholic and Greek Orthodox Churches condemned this dualism as heretical, so Bogomils found themselves rejected by both west and east.

Early in the 13th century, the Roman Catholic Church dispatched a papal legate to the area to institute a purge of the local clergy. Somewhat later, Dominican missionaries were sent in to fight the heresy. They came with military force provided by the Hungarian monarchy. These forces brought Bosnia under Hungarian control. In 1299, the Hungarian king granted Bosnia as a fief to a Croatian aristocrat named Pavle Šubić. The latter brought in Franciscan missionaries to help stamp out the Bogomils.

Šubić passed the principality on to his son, Mladen, but the local nobility overthrew the latter in 1322. Stephen II Kotromanić, a native Bosnian, replaced him as a Ban. Kotromanić was succeeded by his nephew, Stephen Tvrtko, who expanded the principality greatly during his lifetime, annexing part of Dalmatia to the west and part of modern-day Montenegro to the south. Tvrtko eventually took the title "Stephen I, King of Serbia, Bosnia, Dalmatia, Croatia, and the Littoral."

His younger brother succeeded Tvrtko and was crowned as Stephen II in 1391. By the time of his death seven years later, the Turks had launched an invasion of Bosnia, and the kingdom began to disintegrate. It soon broke down into several principalities, most of them paying a yearly tribute to the Turks. The ruler of one of these principalities opted to become a vassal of the Holy Roman emperor instead. For this the title of Herzog (duke) of St. Sava was bestowed on him. Over time, this title became attached to the land instead of the ruler and in its modern form is Herzegovina.

After the Ottoman Turks conquered Constantinople in 1453, the Turks decided to take control of the Balkan Peninsula directly. The new invasion of Bosnia began in 1460. Some parts tried to hold out against the Turks. However, many of the Bogomil leaders saw the Muslim Turks as being preferable to the Hungarian Roman Catholics, still trying to stamp out Bogomilism, and allied themselves with the Turks. Afterward, most of these Bogomils converted to Islam.

These new converts adopted the dress, title, and etiquette of the Turkish court while retaining their lands, their language, and most of their old customs. They also became the local military caste, which gave them a rank just below that of the Turkish governor. They remained loyal to the Ottoman Empire, and some of them even rose to the highest offices in the empire. One of those was Semiz Ali Pasha, who became grand vizier in 1561. His successor, Sokollu Mehmed Pasha (Mehmed-paša Sokolović), also came from Bosnia. Meanwhile, most of the peasants remained Orthodox Christians.

Little changed until the 17th century, when the Austrian Empire, then still known as the Holy Roman Empire, began to push down into the Balkans. Prince Eugene of Savoy burned Sarajevo in 1697. A portion of the seacoast area of Herzegovina plus a part of Bosnia that bordered on the Sava River passed to Austria in 1718. Türkiye took the Bosnian territory back in 1739, but it reverted to Austrian control in 1791.

In the first half of the 19th century, an estrangement began to develop between the Muslim aristocrats of Bosnia and the Ottoman government, primarily over the issue of traditional privileges. There were several revolts between 1820 and 1850 that led the regime to strip the aristocracy of most of its privileges. The peasantry was also growing dissatisfied as a result of increasing tax obligations, and this led to other rebellions.

Things came to a head in July 1875, when a revolt among Christian peasants soon spread throughout the country and turned into a war specifically against Turks. The revolt next spread to Herzegovina, then to Bulgaria. Serbia and Montenegro declared war against the Ottoman Empire in July 1876.

Austro-Hungarian Rule

Russia and the Austro-Hungarian Empire had been rivals in the Balkans throughout the 19th century. Alexander II,

the Russian tsar, opened negotiations with the Austro-Hungarian government immediately after Serbia entered the war against Türkiye. The agreement the two sides signed at Reichstadt stipulated, among other things, that Austro-Hungary would receive territorial concessions in case of a change in the status quo in the Balkans. When Serbia subsequently began losing its war against Türkiye, Russia entered the conflict as Serbia's ally in July 1877.

Having won against Türkiye, Russia negotiated a treaty under which Türkiye recognized the independence of Serbia and Romania and agreed to the establishment of a large Bulgarian state. However, when the Austro-Hungarian government heard about the terms of the Treaty of Stefano, it was outraged. The creation of a large Bulgarian state clearly constituted a change in the status quo, but the treaty made no mention of corresponding territorial concessions to Austro-Hungary. Vienna then threatened Russia with war. German chancellor Otto von Bismarck had to step in to preserve the peace. His solution was a congress of European nations that he would host in Berlin.

The Congress of Berlin in 1878 awarded Austro-Hungary administrative control of Bosnia and Herzegovina. The territory was not formally annexed at this time because the prime minister in Vienna, a Hungarian, did not want any more Slavs in the empire. This was a technicality, however. From this moment onward, Bosnia and Herzegovina became a part of the Austro-Hungarian Empire. In 1908, after a successful revolt of the Young Turks against the Ottoman Empire, Vienna formally annexed Bosnia and Herzegovina.

The "damned foolish thing in the Balkans" that Bismarck had predicted occurred on July 28, 1914, with the assassination of the Austrian archduke in Sarajevo. Austria held Serbia responsible for this act and, ultimately backed by Germany, made unacceptable demands on Serbia. By the first week of August, Europe was locked into a war. Four devastating years later, the Austro-Hungarian Empire was in collapse following its defeat in World War I. The Serbs, with Allied blessing, claimed all of the South Slavic lands for a new Kingdom of Serbs, Croats, and Slovenes, which was proclaimed on December 4, 1918. In 1929, this new state changed its name to Yugoslavia.

Incorporation into Yugoslavia

The area of Bosnia and Herzegovina was submerged within this centralized state of South Slavs—the Kingdom of Serbs, Croats and Slovenes, later renamed Yugoslavia. Bosnia and Herzegovina was at this time both poor and rural, with no strong local political leaders. Serbs tended

Bosnjaks mourn death of Alija Izetbegovic.

to look to Serbia, while Croats looked to Croatian leaders outside of Bosnia. The people of the republic were satisfied to be part of Yugoslavia, even though Bosnia remained primarily rural. After World War II it became one of the six constituent republics of Yugoslavia. When things began falling apart in the late 1980s, its political leadership had its own ideas about what should be done.

Political discussions remained within the League of Communists of Bosnia and Herzegovina, the monopoly party, until 1990, when new elections were scheduled. After it authorized the formation of additional political parties, the old system collapsed. Three new parties won the November 1990 elections: the Muslim Party of Democratic Action, which gained 86 assembly seats; the Serbian Democratic Party, which won 70 seats; and the Croat Democratic Union, which got 45 seats. These three political parties subsequently formed a coalition, and they elected Alija Izetbegović, leader of the Party of Democratic Action, as president of the republic. During the communist era, he had been imprisoned for his Islamic convictions, and he died in October 2003, a hero among his Bošnjak people.

Bloody Road to Independence

The political leadership of Bosnia and Herzegovina mainly stood aside in 1990–1991 as the quarrel between the Serbs on one side and the Croats and Slovenes on the other grew more heated. It favored continuation of a united Yugoslavia, but it also wanted economic reforms, repudiation of the communist leaders, and a more

Bosnia and Herzegovina

Sarajevo market 10 years after the 1994 atrocity

decentralized political structure. When Croatia and Slovenia declared their independence on June 25, 1991, Bosnian leaders once again urged calm on both sides. After the Serbs and the Yugoslav People's Army began their war against Croatia, however, the Bosnian leadership began to prepare for the breakup of the country. It was unwilling to remain in a truncated Yugoslavia dominated by Serbia.

Bosnian representatives stopped participating in the institutions of the Yugoslav federal government on October 3, 1991, after Serbian and Montenegrin leaders took control of the Yugoslav presidency. On December 20, the Bosnian government voted to ask the European Community (EC, now EU) for recognition as an independent state. The government was divided on the issue, with the Muslims and Croats voting for independence and the Serbs insisting that Bosnia and Herzegovina remain part of the larger Yugoslav federal state. The Serbs then threatened to form their own "Serbian Republic of Bosnia and Herzegovina" encompassing those territories where they were in a majority.

On March 18, 1992, the leaders of the three communities agreed in principle to restructure the state, creating "three constituent units, based on national principles and taking into account economic, geographic and other criteria." The effect would have been to create three autonomous units within the governmental structure, one for Muslims, one for Croats, and one for Serbs. Control in each municipality would have been exercised by that national group which was in an "absolute or relative majority." The agreement

would have been extremely difficult to implement since the three communities had always lived side by side, and many families were mixed. Its main value, therefore, was more as a way to forestall a civil war rather than as a practical blueprint.

In April, the EU and the United States recognized the independence of Bosnia and Herzegovina. Although gratifying in the abstract, it had a negative side. The Serbian Democratic Party withdrew from the coalition, its two Serbian members of the presidency resigned, and Serb leaders announced the formation of a "Serbian Republic of Bosnia and Herzegovina" which intended to remain part of Yugoslavia.

The Yugoslav Army was still stationed in Bosnia at that time. It announced that it would move its forces to Serbia and Montenegro. In fact, it divided its forces, leaving in Bosnia all those who had any connection with Bosnia or other non-Serb states. These forces, provided with tanks, artillery, and all the equipment needed to fight a modern war, became the army of the Bosnian Serbs.

With a UN arms embargo making it impossible for the Bosnian government to obtain any significant weaponry, Bosnia found itself completely outgunned. Within three months, the Bosnian Serbs controlled 70% of the Bosnian territory. The Bosnian Croats, who were receiving military assistance from Croatia, dominated most of the rest. Serbs surrounded the capital, Sarajevo, with heavy weapons and snipers and besieged the city for three years. While periodically engaging in diplomatic discussions in Geneva, they continued their shelling. By the time it was over, about 10,500

Sarajevo people, including 1,500 children, were dead. Meanwhile, the west continued its arms embargo against Bosnia.

Convinced that Bosnia had lost the war, UN negotiators tried to get the leadership to agree to a partition that would have left the Serbs in control of half of the territory. But the Bosnian government refused to sign, and the siege went on. Convinced that the west intended to allow Serbia to succeed in creating a "Greater Serbia," the Bosnian Croats, encouraged by the Croatian government, switched sides and attempted to enlarge the area they controlled at the expense of the Bosnian government.

A change came in February 1994, when western public opinion, appalled by a particularly atrocious shelling of Sarajevo that killed 66 people and injured 200 others, caused western governments to take action. This produced a NATO ultimatum that the Serbs remove their heavy artillery pieces from a 12.5-mile zone around Sarajevo. The Serbs refused, whereupon the UN proposed a compromise. The Serb guns could remain where they were, and the UN Protection Force (UNPROFOR) would dispatch peacekeepers to these locations, in theory to ensure that the Serbs did not resume their bombardment of Sarajevo.

The Serbs agreed to accept UN peacekeepers at their artillery sites. This was a mistake because the compromise placed the UN forces in a situation where they could become hostages, should a new war of wills erupt between the UN and the Serbs. The compromise temporarily ended the shelling, however, and an overland route to Sarajevo, closed for two years, was also reopened. Sarajevo began to return to something approaching normality.

The NATO ultimatum to the Serbs paid yet another dividend. In this new atmosphere, the Bosnian Croats were persuaded that they could hold more of Bosnia by joining a US-sponsored Bosnian-Croat federation than by continuing on their own. A separate federation government was subsequently set up and has continued to exist.

These two successes did not bring an end to the war. Forced to stop their artillery barrages of Sarajevo, the Serbs merely intensified their attacks against other besieged Bosnian government enclaves, including the towns of Tuzla and Goražde. The UN protested these new attacks, but the Serbs continued with the artillery barrages until NATO once again used force, shooting down four Serbian jets over Bosnia. Bosnian Serbs still controlled 70% of Bosnia and continued their pressure on the rest.

Diplomatic Activity to Achieve Peace

The United Nations released a new peace plan in July 1994 that again proposed a division of the country, giving the

Bosnia and Herzegovina

Bosnian Serbs 49% of Bosnia. Reversing his earlier stance, President Milošević of Serbia endorsed the new peace plan, then broke publicly with Bosnian Serb leaders and "sealed" the border between Serbia and Bosnia when they rejected it. He also agreed to allow the placement of 135 civilian monitors along the 370-mile border to verify that aid to the Bosnian Serbs had stopped. Although almost no one believes that Serbia really ended all support for the Bosnian Serbs at this time, the amount of assistance did diminish.

Reacting to this additional pressure, the Bosnian Serbs attempted to sabotage the peace plan by launching attacks on the UNPROFOR peacekeepers. By firing on planes attempting to land at Sarajevo Airport, they managed to shut down the UN food airlift and end all commercial flights into the capital. The first UN reaction was to do nothing, presumably because of a fear that any action against the Bosnian Serbs would bring Serbia formally back into the war. In fact, Sir Michael Rose, commander of UNPROFOR in Bosnia, threatened to call in air strikes against Bosnian government forces at the beginning of August after the Bosnian army tried to drive back Bosnian Serb forces just north of the Sarajevo.

A disagreement between the US and other members of the "Contact Group" also broke out in August 1994, when Washington began urging an end to the military embargo against the Bosnian government. The US government stopped enforcing the embargo in November after the UN General Assembly adopted a resolution urging the Security Council to lift the arms embargo on Bosnia. This was the second such General Assembly resolution, an earlier one having been passed in 1993. Since France and Great Britain, both permanent members of the Security Council with the power of veto, opposed lifting the embargo, however, no action was taken.

At the end of December 1994, ex-president Jimmy Carter mediated a four-month "cessation of hostilities" between the Bosnian Serbs and the Bosnian government. The truce held for a while, but both sides used it mainly to strengthen their forces. It came to an end at the beginning of April 1995, when the Bosnian government struck preemptively in an attempt to disrupt Bosnian Serb communications facilities.

The Bosnian Serb response was to seize their heavy artillery pieces from UN-supervised storage areas and begin a new artillery barrage on Sarajevo. They also renewed their siege of the city, cutting it off from the outside world. General Rupert Smith, UNPROFOR commander in Bosnia, demanded a stop to the artillery barrage and a lifting of the siege. When the Bosnian Serbs did not respond, he called

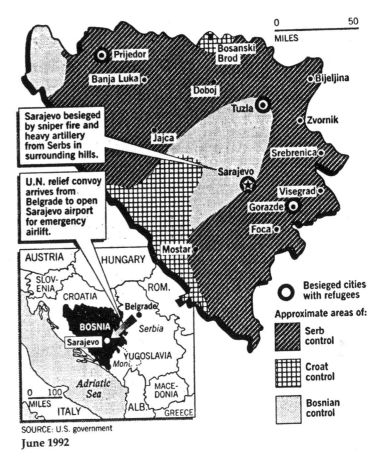

SOURCE: U.S. government

June 1992

Bosnia and Herzegovina

Calendar of Radovan Karadzic (middle) with Serbian heroes on sale in Bosnia Serb sector

for a NATO air strike on an ammunition dump near Pale, the Bosnian Serb "capital." The Bosnian Serbs then launched a mortar barrage on the city of Tuzla that resulted in 70 civilian deaths. When General Smith ordered a second NATO air strike, the Bosnian Serbs took 350 UNPROFOR peacekeepers hostage. It was now the UN that blinked.

General Bernard Janvier, the overall UN military commander in former Yugoslavia, and Yasushi Akashi, the UN's special representative in former Yugoslavia, over-ruled General Smith's recommendation to continue the NATO bombing; they took away his authority to call in air strikes. UNPROFOR, they announced, would not take sides.

Anxious to win release of the UNPRO-FOR hostages, the UN agreed to hand back several hundred tanks, howitzers, and mortars to the Bosnian Serbs in June 1995. The so-called weapons collection points ceased to exist. This eliminated the UN hostage situation, but the Serbs, with their heavy weapons back, began shelling Sarajevo again, killing nine civilians lining up for water on June 24. Meanwhile, the UN "safe-haven" cities of Žepa, Sre-brenica, and Goražde were once more cut off by surrounding Serb forces and were being slowly starved out. Even UN peacekeeper forces stationed in these cities could not be resupplied.

Considering the situation on the ground in Bosnia to be unacceptable, the governments of France and Great Britain now decided to up the ante. Recognizing that the lightly armed UN peacekeeper force was incapable of defending itself, they decided to create a heavily armed 12,500-man rapid-reaction force separate from the UNPROFOR. These troops began arriving

in Bosnia in July, but the new force came too late to prevent the fall of Srebrenica on July 11, then Žepa on July 22.

Women, children, and older men subsequently made their way from the fallen enclaves to Bosnian government-controlled areas, but more than 8,000 Bosnian men remained missing. Later, it became clear that most had been shot, their bodies dumped into mass graves, shortly after

being taken prisoner by General Mladić's forces. He bears a major responsibility for these deaths since he was in charge of the sieges of both Srebrenica and Žepa and personally toured Žepa on July 27, 1995. He gave an interview at the time to the weekly newspaper *Svet*, in which he boasted, "By autumn we'll take Goražde, Bihać and in the end Sarajevo, and we'll finish the war in Bosnia." On the eve of the Srebrenica massacre, he defiantly asserted on Bosnian Serb TV that the time had come to avenge centuries of conquest by the Ottoman Muslims.

The Tide Turns: Dayton

This turned out to be the high-water mark for the Bosnian Serbs, however. The events associated with Srebenica and Žepa, plus the continued shelling of Sarajevo, appalled the international community, which now began calling for some decisive action. On August 30, NATO demanded that the Bosnian Serbs pull back their artillery from around Sarajevo.

When General Mladić refused, NATO launched air strikes against Bosnian Serb command posts, ammunition dumps, and radar sites. NATO continued its bombing until September 2, then gave the Bosnian Serbs until September 4 to begin removing their artillery. Mladić again refused, whereupon the air strikes were resumed on September 6. The bombing continued

A Bosnian Serb soldier holds a refugee child.

AP/Wide World Photo

504

Bosnia and Herzegovina

A chat in a Mostar cemetery

for another two weeks before the Bosnia Serbs relented and began removing their heavy weapons from the vicinity of Sarajevo.

At least three brigades of Croatian army troops entered Bosnia in early September. Operating in conjunction with Bosnian Croat and Muslim forces, they launched an offensive that gradually reduced the amount of land held by Bosnian Serbs from 70% to about 50%.

Meanwhile, things were beginning to happen on the diplomatic front. The first breakthrough occurred on August 29, 1995, when Karadžić agreed that President Milošević was empowered to negotiate on behalf of the Bosnian Serbs. Next, the US government invited the foreign ministers of Serbia, Bosnia, and Croatia to a meeting in Geneva. On September 8, the three foreign ministers agreed to a statement of principles for peace in Bosnia. This, in turn, paved the way for the Dayton peace talks, which resulted in an accord signed by the presidents of the three republics on November 21, 1995. Estimates of the toll of the devastating three-and-a-half-year war vary from about 100,000 (according to the Sarajevo-based Research and Documentation Center) to a quarter million killed; of those, about 66% were Bošnjaks, 26% ethnic Serbs, and 8% ethnic Croats; 1.8 million were uprooted.

The agreement provided for the division of Bosnia between a Bosnian Serb entity and a Bosnian-Croat federation. The two sub entities were to have their own presidents and their own legislatures. But there would still be a central government with a group presidency, a two-house legislature, a court, and a central bank.

The agreement also called for a NATO force of 60,000 members to keep the peace; it began arriving at the end of the year. The various opposing forces then withdrew to agreed positions and the situation began to stabilize. However, it was only a truce, not a reconciliation. When the Serb-occupied suburbs of Sarajevo were turned over to Bosnian government control in March 1996, almost all Serbs fled.

This attitude persisted during the runup to internationally monitored elections that took place on September 14, 1996. The Dayton Accords had specified that individuals were to be permitted to return to their previous place of residence to vote. Those—mostly Muslims—who tried to do this were turned back from both the Serb and Croat controlled areas. The elections also reflected this division, with people in each area permitted to vote only for candidates representing the dominant national grouping.

The inaugural session finally took place in the Serb-controlled town of Lukavica. Here a new council of ministers was named, with Muslim and Serb cochairs: Haris Silajdžić, representing the Muslim-Croat Federation, and Boro Bosić, representing the Republic of Serbia. Silajdžić characterized the creation of the joint institutions for Bosnia as being "the victory of democracy over dictatorship" and spoke optimistically of "the reintegration of Bosnia and Herzegovina with Europe." Others at the ceremonies were not nearly as optimistic.

Dayton was a diplomatic success since it stopped the fighting. But it left behind a broken country with two ethnically divided entities that were supposed to be held together by a weak central government. That country was largely ungovernable, although the absence of central authority is not immediately noticeable since the regional governments deal with the day-to-day problems. Dayton was a temporary solution that needs to be reworked, but that did not happen.

Bosnia as an International "Protectorate"

The collective presidency for all of Bosnia held its first meeting on September 30, 1996. The session had to be held in a hotel at the edge of Sarajevo because Krajišnik, the Serb member, refused to meet in a government building downtown, citing security concerns. He then did not show up to take a formal oath of office in October because he was unwilling to swear allegiance to a united Bosnia. The newly elected national legislature, scheduled to meet for its first session in October, was postponed for the same reason. It finally met in January 1997, after it was agreed to dispense with the oath. As these events made clear, the international community could create joint institutions, but it could not force cooperation among the still-quarreling factions, even with the offer of large amounts of foreign assistance.

As a result, the six nations that oversaw the Bosnian peace effort—the United States, France, Germany, Italy, Great Britain, and Russia—decided in December 1997 to authorize a high representative to make decisions on behalf of Bosnia whenever the divided Bosnian government was unable to do so. He stepped in to resolve such issues as media licensing, housing, and tariff laws. When the joint legislature found itself deadlocked on such issues as a common license plate, passport, currency, flag, and national emblem, the high representative made the selections for the Bosnians.

It was also his office that was responsible for the creation of a new currency. As a preliminary step, the German mark was accepted in 1997. On June 22, 1998, the Bosnian government began issuing a new currency, the marka, whose value was equal to one German mark. The marka began circulating almost immediately in the area of the Croat and Muslim Federation, but it was ignored in the Bosnian Serb area. Its value is now pegged to the euro. Bosnia and Herzegovina received the former Yugoslav embassy in London when the diplomatic buildings were parceled out among the parts of the former federation in December 2001.

Whenever Bosnian elected officials attempted to obstruct the Dayton Accords,

Bosnia and Herzegovina

A column of Bosnian policemen, Sarajevo

AP/Wide World Photo

the high representative did not hesitate to dismiss them. There thus exists a sort of international protectorate over Bosnia, whose goal is to create a situation where separatism and particularism will be harder and harder to maintain. This has proved to be an extremely difficult task.

The goal of the high representative's office is to create the circumstances whereby as many as possible of the 2.2 million displaced persons and refugees could return to their former homes, as stipulated in the Dayton Accords. About 1.2 million fled abroad, while 1.2 million were displaced within Bosnia. From 40,000 to 70,000 found their way to St. Louis, the largest Bosnian community in the US. A start was made in 1997, when top officials in the Muslim and Croat federation agreed to allow 120,000 refugees to return to 156 villages in central Bosnia under the control of the other nationality. This was surprisingly successful.

In 2004 the 1-millionth Bosnian refugee had returned home. A year later, half of them had returned to their prewar homes, where they are a minority. Some of them have sold their reclaimed properties. Over 90% of claims by lawful owners to get their property back have been settled. Not all returnees go back to where they originally came from. Only 400,000 were known to be still waiting to go home, and the

number of returnees is trailing off. Some will never return. Many former Serb residents of Sarajevo are wary of returning. Elderly Bosnians are particularly inclined to go back to their earlier homes to finish out their years where they had always lived. Because of the lack of jobs, younger Bosnians go either to Sarajevo or abroad if they can. A 2004 survey by the UN Development Program revealed that more than half of young people would leave Bosnia if given a chance. Legal changes across Bosnia provide more protection for minorities and more input into local government. In 2012 Bosnia joined other Balkan nations in raising $395 million ($303 million from the EU) to help house 74,000 people who are still living as refugees. This remains the largest displacement in Europe since World War II.

There has been much rebuilding in formerly ethnically cleansed areas, and most infrastructure has been rebuilt. Some of it was financed by foreign sources, including the Arab world. Saudi Arabia spent over $500,000 on religious and humanitarian projects, in part in order to spread its rigid interpretation of Islam in a country where most Muslims are not conspicuously pious. Some western efforts to rebuild mosques in Serb cities, such as Banja Luka, in order to reintegrate Bosnian Muslims

driven out during the war and reestablish Islamic religious life led to riots. In 2016, the beautiful Ferhadija Mosque in Banja Luka was reopened in the presence of religious and political leaders, including Türkiye's prime minister. The mosque had been blown up and razed to the ground with bulldozers, together with 15 other mosques in the city, to erase any traces of Islam there. A 2001 ceremony that was to start the reconstruction was interrupted by a violent Serb mob that killed one attendee and injured dozens, forcing NATO troops to evacuate foreign dignitaries by helicopters.

Such violence, which is much diminished, merely underscored how hard it is to diminish the extreme nationalism that separates Bosnia's ethnic groups. But there have been signs of progress. The main Bosnian Serb party, the Serb Democratic Party (SDS), says it has abandoned its dreams of a "Greater Serbia," and the leading Croat party, the Croatian Democratic Union (HDZ), has also given up its earlier hopes for union with Croatia.

Military Forces

Neither Croatia nor Serbia poses a military threat to Bosnia. Bosnia's armies have therefore been reduced to small numbers, as have the foreign peacekeepers in the country. In 2005 the US maintained only 150 troops in Bosnia to help local authorities adopt defense reforms and hunt down war-crime suspects. Even such a symbolic presence was important because the local populations regard the United States as the ultimate key to maintaining stability and order in the country. By 2007 all 150 had been withdrawn. In 2003 Bosnia became the first country in the Balkans to ratify a deal with the US exempting Americans on its soil from prosecution in the newly created International Criminal Court.

About 1,000 Russian peacekeepers served under American command and, because of the historically close ties between Serbs and Russians, were able to achieve some compromises from Bosnian Serbs that other nationalities could not. In addition to soldiers from most NATO countries, there were peacekeepers from such far-flung countries as Morocco, the Baltic states, and Albania. The result of the peacekeepers' presence was enforced peace for the local population and for the foreign troops. In the four years of warfare before the Dayton Accords, more than 1,000 UN peacekeepers had been killed or wounded in Bosnia; after Dayton there was not a single US or NATO casualty from hostile action.

On December 2, 2004, in "Operation Althea," the EU took over the NATO-led mission, renaming it EUFOR. SFOR ceased to exist. It already commanded the

506

Bosnia and Herzegovina

Reconstructed Ferhadija Mosque in Banja Luka

Photo Bojana Dujković

conditions for joining NATO's Partnership for Peace (PfP), Bosnian Serb, Croat, and Bošnjak leaders agreed in 2003 to a joint command of their armed forces. Bosnia now has a state defense minister and general staff to command the two armies. They also agreed in 2004 to reduce their combined number of active soldiers from 19,800 to 11,100 in 2010. There were some disagreements, such as the three presidents' failure to confirm a decision on which military installations would belong to the central government. This is a major barrier to joining NATO.

In addition to a unified military command that is now in place, they are facing the daunting task of unifying the complex networks of their intelligence services. Separate armies have been abolished, and the process of integration is well underway. Bosnia deployed 36 soldiers to Iraq, 10 to Afghanistan, and 7 to Kosovo. At the end of its Riga summit in 2006, NATO formally invited Bosnia to join its PfP program.

POLITICAL SYSTEM

The government of the state of Bosnia and Herzegovina (BiH) was remade as a part of the Dayton Accords. It called for the creation of a Bosnian government composed of two entities: the Federation of Bosnia and Herzegovina (which includes both Bošnjaks and Croats and is usually referred to simply as "the Federation") and the Republika Srpska (RS—Republic of the Serbs). These two entities divided the territory of Bosnia on a 51%–49% basis. Each has a high degree of autonomy, its own rules, its own complete administration, its own army, and its own customs and tax regimes. Their relative influence on the functioning of the state and on the lives of its citizens is bigger than that of the central government; that makes the country a confederation. In 2004 the central state began collecting customs duties.

300-strong peacekeeping force in North Macedonia, as well as the police mission in Bosnia once run by the UN. But NATO continues to work with the EU in Bosnia. It provides planning and assets, as well as reserve forces, if there should be an upsurge of ethnic violence, which by 2005 was no longer expected. Both have the authority to arrest alleged war criminals. NATO maintains a small mission in Sarajevo led by an American general to assist with defense reforms, counterterrorism, and war criminals. It shares a headquarters building and facilities with EUFOR.

In the transfer of command to the EU, the American troops were replaced by Finns. Nevertheless, about 80% of EUFOR's 7,000 troops previously served in the NATO force. They simply switched their badges. They are a lighter-weight force. The deployment of EUFOR was merely one part of an overall strategy to stabilize the Balkans. NATO's departure signified the end of Bosnia's "postwar" era and the beginning of a more conventional "political and economic transition." It underscores

European and American confidence that peace is irreversibly secured. By 2010, only a couple of hundred EU troops and 11 American soldiers remained, down from 2,500 the year before.

A defense committee attached to the central government provides some coordination for funding to the two separate armies that exist. Since 2002 the United States refuses to provide military assistance to the armies in Bosnia unless such help goes through the defense committee and therefore funds projects in which all three groups participate and cooperate with each other.

When the Dayton Accords were signed in 1995, the two political entities kept the armed forces they had at the time and had to accept an arms-limitation regime. Some people referred to "two and one-half armies," since Bosnian Croats maintained most forces separate from their joint army with the Bošnjaks.

The defense law called for joint institutions at the level of Defense Ministry and general staff. In order to satisfy the

Former Prime Minister Denis Zvizdic

507

Bosnia and Herzegovina

Party activists drumming up votes in Sarajevo, 2006

In 2005 it began collecting a value-added tax of 17% in an attempt to bring a lot of the underground economy into the open.

Together, they elect a Bosnian government with its own three-person presidency, composed of a Bosnian Serb, a Bosnian Croat, and a Bošnjak. After the October 2022 elections, they were Milorad Dodik (Serb), Denis Bećirović (Muslim), and Željko Komšić (Croat). Bakir Izetbegović, who was defeated by Bećirović in 2022, is the son of Bošnjak national hero, Alija Izetbegović, and is a moderate politician who advocates integration with Europe.

Željko Komšić President of the Presidency of Bosnia and Herzegovina
Source: *Wikipedia*

Since 2002 each serves a four-year term and can be reelected. The chair of the presidency rotates every eight months. This is mostly a ceremonial role except for control of the small armed forces. They have proven that they can sometimes cooperate constructively.

There is a two-chamber legislature. The lower house is the House of Representatives. The upper is the House of the Peoples; two-thirds of its members are elected from the Federation and one-third from the RS. A valid majority must include the support of at least one-third of the members representing each entity. The national government is the Council of Ministers. One of the 10 ministers is chosen as prime minister. It should be noted that each of the two entities can also conduct foreign policy.

The prime minister serves four years, and the position no longer rotates on an eight-month basis. His powers are limited. For example, the earlier prime minister, Adnan Terzić, fired Bosnia's foreign minister Mladen Ivanić in June 2005, but the latter simply refused to go. An obstacle to EU entry is a 2012 decision by the European Court of Human Rights rejecting the constitutional provision that only Muslims, Croats, and Serbs can be presidents. The court ruled that this violates the rights of other minorities in Bosnia.

There is a self-governing district, Brčko, under the sovereignty of the central state government and under international supervision. It belongs to neither of Bosnia's two entities. This city controls the narrow passage between the eastern and western parts of Bosnia and had been run by the Serbs. It became a neutral district jointly administered by Serbs, Croats, and Muslims. It had a majority Muslim population

prior to the beginning of the Bosnian war. It is Bosnia's only truly multiethnic city and one of the few cities in Bosnia where the three main ethnic groups work and attend school together. In March 2009 all three sides endorsed a deal over its future.

The center has its own court and central bank. In addition to these central institutions, the Federation and RS have their own elected parliaments, presidents, and prime ministers. Each of 10 cantons has its own powerful assembly and local government. International authorities supervise elections at all levels. There is considerable frustration in dealing with the many levels of administration and overlapping jurisdictions. Voters are faced with a bewildering electoral task. For example, in the October 2010 elections, 54.9% of eligible voters turned out to select a parliament for their weak central state, parliaments for the two parts of the country, cantonal legislatures, and several presidents. Every party and national camp can block reform projects in the central parliament. No one expected anything to change in their troubled country.

In an attempt to create a more efficient and stronger state, the US and its European partners convened a meeting in Washington of the nine top Serbian, Muslim, and Croatian leaders from Bosnia. Under intense American and European pressure, the nine signed a Commitment to Pursue Constitutional Reform aiming at a constitution that would have only one president. The package failed to win the necessary two-thirds support in parliament. This disappointing failure left both

Borjana Krišto, Chairwoman of the Council of Ministers of Bosnia and Herzegovina
Source: *Wikipedia*

Reconstructed bridge at Mostar: Muslim side on left and Croat side on right

the EU and US without a clear plan for strengthening the political system to ensure that Bosnians are ready for self-rule. The reform agenda is in bad shape.

The Bošnjak-Croat Federation, which is supposed to control 51% of Bosnia, is still in some ways a fiction. Power is concentrated in the two separate Croat and Bošnjak entities. In particular, Herzeg-Bosna, the Croatian half of the Federation—which according to the terms of the Dayton Accords was supposed to have been disbanded in January 1996—continued to exist. For a while it operated in some manner as an integral part of the Republic of Croatia. Croatian currency, stamps, uniforms, telephone area code rates, and even customs levies were used throughout Herzeg-Bosna. Bosnian Croats were permitted to vote in parliamentary elections in the Republic of Croatia.

They now receive less support and encouragement from the more democratic Croatian governments that took office after Franjo Tudjman died in 1999. They can have automatic citizenship in the more prosperous Croatia, and many, especially the young, take it and move there, leaving only about half of Bosnia's prewar Croat population of about 830,000 behind. Most Bosnian Croats possess Croatian passports. Thus, unlike their Bosnian compatriots, they got the right to work and study anywhere in the EU after Croatia became a member of the EU in July 2013. This

created two classes of citizens. Croat flag, and coats of arms are prominently displayed throughout the area, and even the official flags of cantons include the characteristic Croat red-white checkerboard.

Croatia's leaders made a strategic decision that accession to the EU is more important than Greater Croatia. Croatia's president, Ivo Josipović, appeared in the Bosnian parliament in April 2010 and apologized for Croatia's role in the Bosnian war. He said he was "deeply sorry" that his country had "contributed to the suffering of people and divisions which still burden us today." Serbian leaders have made a similar decision by renouncing Greater Serbia. Bosnia's borders are no longer contested.

Bosnian-Croat connections with the Bošnjak half of the Federation are improving, but they remain limited. One symbol intended to heal the rupture is the bridge at Mostar, destroyed in the fighting in November 1993. It was renamed New-Old Bridge and reopened with much fanfare in July 2004. It was carefully reconstructed with funds from the World Bank and other donors in the identical style using the same methods and materials employed by Turkish architects five centuries ago. It remains to be seen whether this historical treasure will ultimately bring together Croats, who make up about 60% of the population, and Bošnjaks (approximately 40%) in the city of 100,000 that is the only

truly mixed Bosnian city. In the meantime, they live on separate sides of the bridge and do not interact much. The schools are divided on strictly ethnic lines.

The tense October 2010 elections for the central parliament and the three-man presidency demonstrated once again the deep ethnic divisions that persist. As again citizens voted along ethnic lines. Bošnjak and Croat voters elected leaders who want to unify the country and take it into the EU, which makes greater centralization a condition for membership. Nevertheless, some Bosnian Croat leaders say that if the division in two states continues, they will request a third state for Croats.

Bosnian-Serb-backed Milorad Dodik, their prime minister, was reelected as the Bosnian Serb president. However, his Party of Independent Social Democrats (SNSD) won only 38 of 83 seats in the Bosnian Serb parliament and had to seek support from coalition partners. It lost even more heavily in the October 2014 elections. Increasingly authoritarian, Dodik remained president, and he won again in 2018. He harvested many votes by saying that he might organize a referendum to demand independence; he often repeats this threat. "Srpska forever" is his answer to what he calls "an impossible state." Independence is inevitable, he argues: "It is our political right to decide on our status." He has argued that, if Montenegro and Kosovo can break away from Serbia, then his state can sever from Bosnia. The Bosnian Serb strategy seems to be to chip away at the Dayton Accords until foreign powers lose interest and patience and let Bosnian Serbs go their own way.

Bosnian Serbs seem as resolved as ever that they should preserve their separate identity and withhold their loyalty from the unified state, even though the constitution does not permit secession. They refuse to let go of their own police force, and that was the chief obstacle to beginning accession talks with the EU. Finally, the intransigent leaders accepted a watered-down version of police reform in June 2008.

In return, the EU's stabilization and association agreement with Bosnia, which began the process toward membership, went into effect. The EU is about the only thing all sides agree upon. Sarajevo publisher Damir Uzunović remarked, "We will be the last country in the region to join the EU because they can't do anything else with us." But Carl Bildt, foreign minister of Sweden, said in July 2009 that Bosnia's politicians must recognize that their interminable disputes are causing them to fall behind their neighbors on the path to the EU. For example, they were temporarily excluded from a decision to offer some Balkan countries visa-free travel to most EU states, but that was granted in 2010.

Bosnia and Herzegovina

US soldiers would stay in Bosnia and Herzegovina (until 2008).

are not goading on ethnic brothers in Bosnia, and there is a high representative on guard. Most important, an overwhelming majority of Bosnians want nothing to do with violence.

Office of the High Representative

The entire political system has since Dayton been overseen by the UN high representative, who is always a European. Paddy Ashdown of the UK was a powerful activist in this post. In 2004, he fired six Serb police officers and three other officials for failing to arrest war-crimes suspects. This was backed by the US government, which froze the assets of the Serb Democratic Party and forbade its leaders from entering the United States. Subsequent to that crackdown, the Bosnian Serb government rendered seven Bosnian Serb indictees to The Hague. In 2005 he sacked the Croat in the tripartite presidency, Dragan Čović, for refusing to resign in the face of serious corruption charges.

Ashdown was again at loggerheads with the RS government in June 2005, when it rejected plans to reform the police, a key EU demand before it can open accession talks. The divided country has 15 police forces that cooperate with each other only voluntarily. Reform is essential because each is under the control of old political cliques, and it will take a long time to change that. Ashdown called this the "nexus of politics, crime and the police." The Bosnian Serb government objects to any reform that would strip it of control of its own police.

In this lamentable situation, the UN high representative became the central legislative power. He could unseat elected officials and impose legislation directly if the fractious parliamentarians could not act. This is a role the UN had never wanted to play. Originally the high representative was supposed only to promote compliance with the Dayton Accords. But he exercised near-dictatorial power. Polls indicated that Ashdown was twice as popular with voters as even the favorite Bosnian politicians. If Bosnian officials did not make changes he thought necessary, then he made them himself. If the

To enact the reforms the people and the EU need, the Muslim member in the three-headed presidency, Bakir Izetbegović, argued for a more centralized state. For example, such a strong government could complete the country's part of a 210-mile superhighway linking Budapest to the Adriatic Sea. As it is, local bickering has prevented all but a 12-mile stretch from being completed inside Bosnia. Milorad Dodik absolutely rejects such a powerful center and threatens to secede unless the RS is left free to be run as a quasi-sovereign state. He emphasizes, "Bosnia is divided, not just on the surface, but essentially." To underscore such autonomy, his government announced plans to open offices in European capitals and Washington.

Silajdžić counters by condemning Dodik's RS as a "genocidal" creation that must be scrapped.

Ethnic tensions continue in all aspects of life, and a maze of rival ethnically controlled bureaucracies are rife with corruption. Real power is often exercised behind closed doors far from the democratic process and public scrutiny. As long as administrative structures are weak, elections can do little to foster responsible government. Political stalemate will probably leave the country underdeveloped. For 15 months until January 2012, the country was without a central government. The only good news was that few experts believed there would be war or large-scale violence. Unlike 1992, Serbia and Croatia

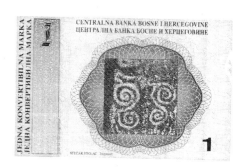

Convertible mark, Bosnia's currency

Bosnjak student (right) with her French classmate at the College of Europe

Bosnians did it, the EU regarded it as a plus for the country. If Ashdown had to do it, it was a minus. For instance, he threatened to fire Bosnian Serb leaders in 2004 if they failed to recognize the evidence and admit to responsibility for the Srebrenica massacre in 1995. They did it. Now they try harder to find and apprehend indicted war criminals.

The high representative has no formal authority over the many international agencies involved in the transition; 55 of them are organized in the Peace Implementation Council (PIC), which oversees international strategy in Bosnia. NATO, the EU, and the UN have separate responsibility for military and civilian administration. This could leave civilian authorities powerless in the face of violence, but the possibility of such violence has diminished considerably. Few people expect a renewal of international or ethnic hostilities.

Both Europeans and Americans had hoped that this position could be phased out and that the European Commission could open a mission in the country and oversee its transformation in a less imperial way. Ashdown was criticized for his assertive style. A 2005 report on the Balkans spearheaded by former Italian prime minister Giuliano Amato concluded that "the powers and activities of the high representative . . . have blocked the development of self-government," adding that the post had "outlived its usefulness." "There is a danger that it . . . takes up so much oxygen that elements of civil society could be stunted." Most expert observers agree.

Ashdown's replacement, Christian Schwarz-Schilling, a German politician with deep experience in Bosnia,

announced in 2006 that he would be the last high representative and that the UN-mandated post would be abolished in June 2007. He promised in the meantime to use its powers only if there is a threat to peace or in dealing with war-crimes suspects. He offered to apply kinder and gentler forms of persuasion.

However, real authority was not transferred to elected authorities. After a year

of no progress toward state restructuring and interethnic integration, the sixth high representative was sent to Bosnia in July 2007: Slovak diplomat Miroslav Lajčák. His mandate to overrule national authorities was to last only until June 2008. But he displayed determination to keep the government functioning. When the Bosnian Serb president hindered the central government from making necessary decisions by refusing to have his ministers attend sessions, Lajčák allowed the government to make decisions even when some ministers were absent. Dodik was furious. Not surprisingly, Lajčák was vilified by the Serb and Bosnian Serb news media.

When Lajčák became Slovak foreign minister in January 2009, he was replaced by Valentin Inzko, an Austrian diplomat with Slovene origins. He is the fourth man sent to be the last in his job. Inzko was instructed to remain only in a much weaker capacity as the EU's special representative, with no legal powers. With only about 200 EU troops and 11 US soldiers remaining, there was little muscle behind him. Nevertheless, the existing political gridlock required that he exercised his authority. For example, in April 2011 he infuriated Croats by suppressing an election-commission ruling that had paralyzed Federation politics.

The high representative has been so demeaned that none of the parties, especially the Bosnian Serbs, pay any attention to his

Srebrenica lives on, 2006

Bosnia and Herzegovina

efforts. To find a way out of this mess, the EU and US launched a diplomatic effort in October 2009, part of what is called the "Butmir process," to discuss the future of the office. The EU wanted to shut it down, but American diplomats worry that Bosnia could fall apart without foreign supervision. The effort failed. No consensus was reached, and the Office of the High Representative was not closed. The OHR can still fire elected officials and unilaterally impose law. His mandate is extended year after year. In August 2021, Hans Christian Friedrich Schmidt, a German politician, replaced Valentin Inzko as the High Representative for Bosnia and Herzegovina.

The UN Tribunal for War Crimes

"Ethnic cleansing" was a Serb policy practiced from the beginning of the war. In areas under their control, the Serbs systematically destroyed mosques and, less systematically, Roman Catholic churches. They also either destroyed or seized the homes of Muslims and Catholics, forcing them to flee these areas. Some 750,000 Muslims plus a smaller number of Catholic Croats were forced out of these areas. Many atrocities occurred particularly during the first year of the war while the Serbs were consolidating control over the 70% of the country they controlled until the Dayton Accords.

The reports of atrocities were so widespread and well documented that the United Nations decided to set up a warcrimes tribunal. The International Criminal Tribunal for the former Yugoslavia, established at The Hague, began operating in 1994.

Of all the evidence it collected, some of the most important came from a Serb defector, Čedomir Mihajlović, a former member of the Serb secret police. The documents include a directive from Serbian state security services in Belgrade concerning the running of concentration camps in Bosnia. This refuted Serbian government assertions that it was not directly involved in the war. At the same time, the Belgrade press in a series of articles denied the legitimacy and identity of Mihajlović, portraying him as a great international fraudster.

Another document, also from Serbian state security services, gave explicit instructions to the Serbian paramilitary commander known as Arkan (later assassinated in Belgrade). It concerned the eviction and killing of Muslims in the Bosnian town of Bijeljina, which was cleansed of Muslims at the beginning of the war. In 1995, Richard Goldstone, chief prosecutor for The Hague tribunal, named Radovan Karadžić, leader of the Bosnian Serbs, and Ratko Mladić, commander of the Bosnian Serb army, as suspected war criminals.

Indictments were returned against them in July 1995. A number of other indictments were issued.

In 2002 NATO troops tried and failed to capture Karadžić. They missed catching him in Pale by only two hours in 2004. The intensification of NATO's efforts to apprehend war criminals reportedly drove Karadžić, Mladić, and others into hiding in Serbia. A disguised Karadžić was finally caught in Belgrade in July 2008 and sent to The Hague for trial.

The search for alleged war criminals was also seen as necessary to bring "balance" after US troops seized six Arabs in Sarajevo in January 2002 on charges of plotting to attack the US embassy and other American facilities in Bosnia; all six had close ties with al Qaeda. Two Bosnian court orders had forbidden that the men be turned over to the Americans, but the government, pressured by the US embassy, permitted it anyway.

In 2002 US troops arrested a Bosnian Muslim suspected of having links to al Qaeda for spying on an American base. During the war from 1992 to 1995, Bosnia had been a magnet for foreign Muslims wanting to fight for Islam. In July 2007 the former wartime army chief of staff Rasim Delić went on trial in The Hague for failing to prevent beheadings, rapes, and other war crimes by "El Mujahid," a unit of mostly Arab Islamic volunteers. Many mujaheddin, or holy warriors, were expelled, but some remained, married Bosnian women, and received citizenship and passports as an expression of gratitude. In 2007 the citizenship of hundreds of them was revoked in response to a request by the US.

Foreign intelligence agencies have long warned that Islamic militants were organizing themselves in the area between the cities of Zenica, Tuzla, Sarajevo, and Travnik in order to use Bosnia as a launching pad for terrorist attacks in Europe. Police say that they hide explosives in lemons and tennis balls and seek to establish training camps in the hills near Sarajevo. A joint US-Croatian intelligence report in 2006 claimed that so-called white Muslim terrorists are being recruited in Bosnia. These fighters with European features would be able to infiltrate western European cities and targets more easily than Middle Eastern Muslims.

In 2007 and 2008, the Bosnian government conducted a broad review of foreign-born residents who had come during the 1992–1995 war, married local women, and remained despite repeated calls by the US and international organizations for their deportation. About 70% of them are of Arab or South Asian origin. The Dayton Peace Accords require all combatants "not of local origin" to withdraw, but hundreds ignored that. In 2007 the government "denationalized" at least 500 people. Deportations began, while others left on their own. In February 2010 about 600 police raided Gornja Maoča, a village of Muslim hardliners in the northeast of the country. It sheltered foreign-born mujahideen war veterans whom the authorities suspected of spreading religious hatred.

Bosnia's war left a spiritual legacy. There is a resurgence of Muslim piety, and a more radical strain of Islam has taken root since the 1992–1995 war. More women cover themselves in a Muslim way of dress. Mosques are full. Sarajevo presents a more pronounced Muslim face to the world. Several hundred Bosnians are thought to have joined the fighting in Iraq and Syria.

By 1999, two generals faced trial: Radoslav Krstić, a Bosnian Serb army commander, and Tihomir Blaškić, commander

Street scene in Sarajevo, 2003

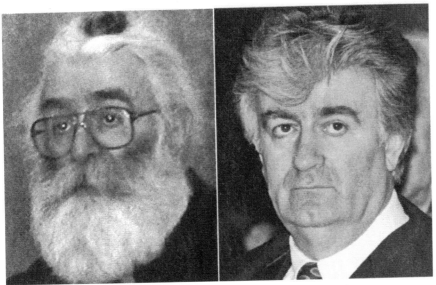

Karadzic, in disguise and as the Bosnian Serb president

Source: *The Economist*

of the Croat forces in southern Bosnia between 1992 and 1994. Radislav Brdjanin, a member of the Bosnian Serb parliament, was arrested, while Momir Talić, another Serb general, was arrested in August 1999 while on a visit to Vienna.

The case against the Croat general Tihomir Blaškić was concluded in March 2000. At first found guilty of ordering a series of attacks on Muslim villagers in Bosnia while his forces were attempting to secure the area for Croatia, Blaškić was sentenced to 45 years in prison. Four years later his sentence was radically reduced on appeal to nine years after most of the convictions against him were dropped. Even more significant, the decision indirectly indicted the government of Croatia. "The Republic of Croatia did not content itself with merely remaining a spectator on the sidelines or even seek simply to protect its borders," the court ruled. "It intervened in the conflict, pitting Muslims and Croats of central Bosnia against each other."

A steady stream of indictments and convictions followed in 2001. Krstić was convicted of genocide at the "safe haven" of Srebrenica and sentenced to 46 years in prison. This was the tribunal's first conviction of genocide. In 2004 the tribunal confirmed its judgment that what happened during the war in Bosnia was genocide. The judge told five more Bosnian Serbs who were convicted of war crimes, "you participated in this hellish orgy of persecution." In July 2009 two Bosnian Serb cousins, Milan and Sredoje Lukić, were sentenced for war crimes, including locking Muslims in two houses and burning them alive, killing at least 119.

Indictments were also brought against high-ranking Muslims for war crimes.

Minister for Refugees Sefer Halilović gave himself up to the tribunal to face charges of having commanded Muslim soldiers who murdered villagers and dumped their bodies in the Neretva River. He was acquitted. In 2006 two Muslim army commanders—Enver Hadžihasanović and Amir Kubura—were convicted at The Hague for failing to restrain foreign Muslim volunteers who murdered Bosnian Croats and Serbs. In 2008 former commander Rasim Delić was sentenced to three years for failing to prevent atrocities committed by foreign Islamist fighters against captured Serb soldiers.

In February 2003 Biljana Plavšić, known earlier as the "Iron Lady" for her ruthless leadership, virulent nationalism, and anti-Muslim utterances, was sentenced to 11 years despite her expression of remorse and the fact that former US secretary of state Madeleine Albright had testified that Plavšić had been instrumental in carrying out a peace plan. The only woman indicted for war crimes, she said she had been driven by "blinding fear" that Serbs would be victims but instead had become "victimizers" in their defensive zeal. After the war she had undergone a pragmatic conversion. While serving a war-crimes sentence in a Swedish prison, she published a book about the Bosnian war. She was released early in October 2009.

In April a Muslim commander who had tried to defend Srebrenica and who is therefore a hero among many Bosnian Muslims, Naser Orić, was delivered to the war-crimes tribunal on charges of atrocities against Bosnian Serbs. In July 2006 he was found guilty of failing to prevent the murder and torture of Serb captives and sentenced to two years, time served. He

was immediately released and got a hero's welcome when he returned to Sarajevo.

He was one of seven Muslims indicted. Even former Bošnjak leader Alija Izetbegović was being investigated for war crimes by the tribunal when he died in October 2003, a hero in his land. A Bosnian Serb commander, Momir Nikolić, pled guilty to the massacre of up to 8,000 Muslim men and boys at Srebrenica and became the first former Bosnian Serb officer to agree to provide testimony. Mass graves continue to be found in Bosnia. In 2004 Bosnian Serb government officials admitted their people's culpability for the massacre. Nevertheless, in June 2004 High Representative Ashdown dismissed 60 leading Bosnian Serb politicians, including the parliamentary speaker, interior minister, police, mayors, and members of parliament, for failing to arrest Radovan Karadžić.

In 2003 Bosnian Serb general Stanislav Galić was sentenced to 20 years for ordering his troops to fire on civilians going about their daily lives during the 44-month siege in Sarajevo. His forces dug into the surrounding hills and rained sniper and artillery fire down on pedestrians, buses, streetcars, funerals, marketplaces, and soccer fields, killing 10,500 people (including 1,800 children) and wounding 50,000 more.

A special court was created in Sarajevo in March 2005 that took over cases from the UN war-crimes tribunal and is monitored by that body. It was initially staffed mainly by international prosecutors and judges, and their Bosnian counterparts gradually took over. Bosnia was the first country in the region entrusted with trying such cases independently.

Not until June 2004 did a Bosnian Serb government commission admit that Bosnian Serb forces were responsible for the Srebrenica massacre. This was followed in November by an official Bosnian Serb government apology after reviewing the commission's findings. It added a commitment to arrest those responsible for the atrocities.

In March 2005 the Bosnian Serb government launched a publicity campaign urging citizens to help it track down war-crimes fugitives. It brought the blunt message "Either they go to The Hague or we go to hell." A month later Bosnian Serb authorities announced that they were investigating nearly 900 officials of their own government to determine whether they might have had a role in the massacre.

For those who still had doubts about the Srebrenica massacre, a video was shown on Serbian television in June 2005 that had been provided by the war-crimes tribunal prosecution in The Hague. It was the first graphic portrayal of what had happened

Bosnia and Herzegovina

in Srebrenica in 1995. It begins with a Serb Orthodox priest blessing camouflaged paramilitary troops called Scorpions. Later, troops are shown taking six young men out of a truck and killing them at close range. In the video, shot by a Scorpion, one can clearly hear the troops insulting the scared Muslims. Nine faces of suspects could be recognized. Only a month earlier, an opinion poll in Serbia had revealed that over half of Serb respondents did not believe the Srebrenica massacre had ever occurred.

The video revived bitter wartime memories of Serbs executing Muslims. Ten former members of the elite Scorpions were immediately arrested for the crimes, and five were arraigned on murder charges at the end of 2005. Their trial began in February 2006. In the first trial inside Serbia that involved the Srebrenica massacres, four were convicted and jailed in April 2007.

In June 2007 a major catch was made—Zdravko Tolimir. The Bosnian Serb army's head of intelligence and General Mladić's right-hand man, he was one of the main suspects in the Srebrenica massacre. Tolimir, who insisted that he had been fighting against "terrorist groups," was given a life sentence in 2012 and died in the United Nations detention center in The Hague in 2016.

Some Bošnjaks responded to the ruling by demanding special status that would separate Srebrenica from the Bosnian Serb area. Bosnian Serb Prime Minister Milorad Dodik rejected this. But he designated the town of 10,000, in which Muslims are now a minority, a "region of economic and social concern" and ordered enhanced infrastructure investment that might lure some former residents back.

Dodik had already signaled sensitivity to this massacre by attending the 2003 memorial service for the approximately 8,000 victims of the Srebrenica massacre. He spoke of "respect for the dead" and reconciliation and peace. Local Bosnian Serb police provided security for the commemoration, attended also by former president Bill Clinton. Shortly thereafter the federal president of Serbia and Montenegro, Svetozar Marović (a Montenegrin) offered a landmark apology to Bosnia for the 1992–1995 war, followed in 2004 by Bosnian Serb government apologies. Such utterances would have been inconceivable only a few years earlier. Every year tens of thousands from all over Bosnia visit Srebrenica, now in the Serb half of Bosnia, to honor the victims. Many take part in the annual three-day hike to Srebrenica to retrace the route taken by the 8,000 men and boys. To commemorate the 20th anniversary of the massacre, more than 10,000 people participated in the 70-mile "March of Peace" hike in July 2015. A long column snaked through the hills while retracing the paths that Muslims used trying to escape from the Bosnian Serb forces.

After The Hague ruling, survivors of the Srebrenica crime filed a lawsuit against the UN and the Dutch government. The latter had already accepted "political responsibility" for the UN mission's failure to protect Muslims and donates about $20 million in aid to Bosnia each year. One-third of that sum is reserved for projects related to rebuilding Srebrenica.

Call to prayer:
Muslim worshipers in Sarajevo

In an effort to win favor from the EU and to improve its relationship with its neighbors, the Serbian parliament in March 2010 narrowly passed (with 127 of 250 votes) a resolution condemning the July 1995 Srebrenica massacre. The word "genocide" could not be used because it was rejected by the reformed Socialist Party (formerly Milošević's), on whose votes the Serbian government depends. Also, most Serbs do not believe the war had been one of genocide. Instead, the carnage was called a "crime." It offered "condolences and apology to the families of victims because not enough was done to prevent the tragedy." It committed Serbia to Bosnia's territorial integrity. Following the 2007 Hague ruling, it did not accept blame for the killings. However, the resolution makes it impossible for Serbs to pretend that the massacre never happened or that the number of dead had been grossly exaggerated.

Srebrenica remains an unhealed wound. Ahead of the 20th anniversary of the massacre, the United Nations Security Council voted on a draft resolution that would have described it as "a crime of genocide." Ten UNSC members voted in favor, four—including China that has veto power—abstained, but the resolution was vetoed by Russia. It described the draft as divisive and "anti-Serb," even though both the International Criminal Tribunal for the Former Yugoslavia and the International Court of Justice had already recognized the massacre as genocide.

The commemoration of the anniversary itself on July 17, 2015, was solemn and brought together dignitaries from all around the world. While about 1,000 bodies

SARAJEVO. — Rathaus. - Vijećnica.

Sarajevo City Hall, 1912

still remain unidentified, 136 recently identified bodies were buried at the memorial cemetery in Srebrenica-Potočari. Yet, emotions got raw when the prime minister of Serbia, Aleksandar Vučić, attempted to join the ceremony. Greeted with whistles and then pelted with rocks and bottles, Vučić and his entourage were rushed out of the area. Seeing the leader of the country that once supported the perpetrators of the massacre was too much for the families of victims, though the prime minister's gesture was appreciated by some.

Former Bosnian Serb president Radovan Karadžić was arrested in Belgrade in July 2008 after 13 years on the run. The 63-year-old was disguised so thoroughly that he could move around Belgrade freely. He was sporting a huge, bushy, white beard; flowing gray hair with a black dyed spot on the top; and oversized horn-rimmed glasses. The trained psychiatrist, who did an internship at Columbia University in New York City, was living under the assumed name of Dr. Dragan Dabić, handing out business cards proclaiming himself as a "bioenergist," delivering lectures at conferences on alternative medicine, publishing articles in Serbia's *Healthy Living* magazine, counseling on Christian Orthodox spirituality, and giving treatments for impotence and depression.

While on the run, Karadžić wrote a novel, *The Miraculous Chronicle of the Night*, a somewhat-autobiographical tale set in Sarajevo in the 1980s. Born in Montenegro, Karadžić had moved to Sarajevo as a teenager. The hero is an engineer who, like Karadžić, was imprisoned when Tito died in 1980. It was a bestseller at Belgrade's international book fair and was on the short list for Serbia's top literary award, the Golden Sunflower, in 2004. It was his fourth publication after going into hiding. His other works include a children's book, a play, and a selection of his poetry.

At The Hague he faced charges of 11 counts of genocide and crimes against humanity. Like Milošević before him, he insisted on defending himself. He tried to rest his case on a fictitious promise of immunity by US negotiator Richard Holbrooke in 1996 if he would disappear from public life. Holbrooke vigorously denied the allegation, and the court rejected the motion.

After he had run out of stalling tactics, he launched his rambling defense in March 2010 by brushing aside the accusations against him as "myths." His was a "holy cause" that aimed to prevent Bosnian Muslims from establishing an Iran-type Islamic state and expelling all Christians. What happened at Sarajevo was not a siege at all, just a case of combatants fighting each other. He dismissed the massacre at Srebrenica as merely a case

of people dying during four years of fighting. The notorious concentration camps were normal "investigation centers." The true victims were the Serbs.

His defense came to the end in March 2016, when he was convicted of genocide, war crimes, and crimes against humanity and sentenced to 40 years in prison, despite his lengthy defense and bizarre claims that he had tried to be a "true friend to Muslims" and to make them feel safe. UN high commissioner for human Rights Zeid Ra'ad Al Hussein observed that the verdict exposed Karadžić as "the architect of destruction and murder on a massive scale."

In February 2010 Serb police raided the Belgrade family home of Ratko Mladić and found, among other things, 18 of his diaries, comprising 3,500 handwritten pages, recounting in detail his activities in the war. War-crimes prosecutors in The Hague asked that these diaries be admitted into evidence against Karadžić.

In May 2011 General Mladić was captured after more than 15 years in hiding. Polls showed that a majority of Serbs opposed extraditions to The Hague. Many Serbs consider the tribunal to be nothing more than an anti-Serb kangaroo court.

Once there Mladić refused to enter a plea, calling the charges "obnoxious" and the tribunal a "satanic court." He engaged in obstructionist behavior. In 2014 he refused to testify in defense of his wartime leader, Radovan Karadžić. He, too, was charged with genocide and crimes against humanity. In late 2016, prosecutors demanded a life sentence for him, arguing that anything less would be "an insult to the victims, living and dead, and an affront to justice."

In 2012 the first woman was convicted of war crimes by a Bosnian local court. A former female Bosnian Muslim soldier admitted to killing Croat civilians and prisoners during the 1990s war.

ECONOMY

Prior to 1992, industry contributed just over half of the GDP. Bosnia and Herzegovina is still mainly agricultural. Herzegovina, with its warmer climate, has traditionally specialized in semitropical crops like pomegranates, lemons, olives, rice, and tobacco. Farther north, the chief crops are cereal grains and soybeans, supplemented by potatoes, melons, grapes, plums, mulberries, and figs. Cattle, sheep, pigs, and poultry are raised throughout the republic.

Before the war, Bosnia and Herzegovina was a major manufacturer of military equipment. It also manufactured Volkswagen automobiles, and there was some textile manufacturing in the larger cities. The majority of its industry was extractive.

It produces coal, iron, copper, manganese, lead, mercury, bauxite, and silver, as well as marble and building stone. Asphalt and lignite are found in the southern part of Herzegovina. Timber is another major industry.

Three and a half years of war left most of Bosnia and Herzegovina in ruins, particularly most of its cities. At the same time, much of the countryside was rendered unusable because of the millions of land mines scattered by the various factions. The economy has begun to revive somewhat, but much of this is associated more with money coming into the economy because of the presence of foreign troops, plus international aid efforts, rather than a domestic economic revival.

Bosnia received more than $14 billion in aid from 1996 to 2007. It came from 17 foreign governments, 18 UN agencies, 27 IGOs, and 200 NGOs. The magnitude of aid it received can be seen in the fact, that from 1995 to 2002, its per-capita development aid was €246 ($320), compared with €23 for the south and east Mediterranean; €9 for Belarus, Ukraine, and Mol-

Convertible mark, Bosnia and Herzegovina's currency dova combined; and €4 for the

Bosnia and Herzegovina

former Soviet republics in Central Asia. This inpouring of funds helps explain the construction boom, but they have diminished drastically in recent years. The IMF granted it a standby credit of $1.5 billion in 2009.

Except for the expenses associated with the SFOR (replaced by EUFOR) and the cost of relief efforts, much of this aid has been funneled through the Bosnian government and its two "national" entities. A considerable portion of this was reportedly siphoned off to individuals through massive corruption. In 1999, for example, the antifraud unit of the Office of the High Representative publicly charged that up to $1 billion had disappeared from public funds or had been stolen from international aid projects and that this malfeasance had occurred as a result of fraud carried out by the various entities of the Bosnian government.

No one denies that corruption and cronyism are rampant in Bosnia. Another effect of all the foreign aid money pouring into the country has been to distort salary schedules throughout the economy. As an example, a driver for the United Nations earns $600 a month; a doctor at Sarajevo's Kosovo hospital is paid half that much. The average monthly take-home wage after taxes in 2013 was €421 ($550). As a result, many professionals have abandoned their positions to take unrelated jobs that pay more money. Wages are about 50% higher in industrial clusters. They do work primarily for German companies.

Unemployment in 2014 stood at 44% overall and over 60% for youth. It is higher in the RS than in the Federation. However, the World Bank estimates that only 16%–20% have no work at all. The reason is that the thriving underground economy is probably worth more than 40% of GDP. Because of this "gray economy," which functions behind the backs of the tax authorities, Bosnia is a land of considerable hidden wealth. This provides grounds for greater confidence in the country's economic potential.

An unexpected way to employ at least some of the jobless is in call centers. Some of the tens of thousands of young Bosnians who spent the war or some postwar time in Germany and speak German are attractive as service representatives. Their salaries are considerably lower than in western Europe but very attractive within Bosnia, besides providing some employment in the first place.

To try to bring some of the hidden wealth out into the open, Bosnia levied a uniform 17% VAT in July 2005. Bosnia then was poorer than it was before the war. Production, which fell by 80% during the war, remains sluggish. Until the global economic downturn in 2009, which hurt Bosnia,

GDP growth was healthy (5.4% in 2008); it shrank by 2.9% in 2009 but grew by about .8% in 2010. Inflation fell from over 6% in 2000 to 1% in 2009; it remains low under a currency board system that pegs the convertible mark to the euro at rate of about 2:1. GDP per capita was $6,400 in 2010.

About 20% live below the poverty line and another 30% just above it. Those figures would be even worse except for the fact that an estimated 250,000 Bosnians left the country for permanent settlement elsewhere, 170,000 through official resettlement programs. Remittances from Bosnians working abroad amounted to 23% of GDP, but they dipped during the recession, as did foreign direct investment. Unable to find work at home, thousands of young Bosnians continue to leave every year in search of a better life. Over half of the young want to emigrate, and three-fourths believe the economy is going downhill. It is the professionals who are most likely to leave. They seek their fortunes abroad. Between 1998 and 2000, an estimated 30,000 university-age youths emigrated because of the dismal economic prospects; there are eight universities in the country. Politicians are widely considered to be corrupt, and organized crime is chronic.

The largest problem is that Bosnia has barely begun the transition from a centralized economy to a market-oriented one. In the Muslim-Croat Federation, only 1.4% of state-owned property had been privatized. The US government was so frustrated at the lack of progress that it ended a major aid program aimed at easing the transition to a market economy. All over Bosnia, larger industry technically remains in state hands, although nearly all of it is closed and has been that way since the beginning of the war.

Few international donors and investors see a future in reviving rusting industrial works. Foreign investment is discouraged by corruption; excessive red tape; and the facts that ownership rights are unclear, contract law is difficult to enforce, and the courts are slow and inefficient. In 2015, the World Bank ranked Bosnia 75th out of 189 countries in terms of "ease of doing business" but 175th for "starting a business" and 171st for "dealing with construction permits." Although western European investors see few tempting opportunities, Daimler-Chrysler announced in 2003 that, in the following 10 years, it would invest in the reconstruction of Bosnian industries, especially aluminum, electrical, and mining operations. Other German companies are attracted by Bosnia's location and labor pool. Retailers from neighboring Croatia and Slovenia have moved into the Bosnian market. Still, by 2016 the largest investments have come from Serbia, Austria, the UK, and Switzerland.

The most popular sectors of the economy are manufacturing, banking, and telecommunication, as well as trade and financial services. In 2014, the total value of foreign direct investment reached $320 million. But without more foreign capital, alternative sources of employment will be difficult to find outside the underground or illegal sector.

Another unresolved problem is that most industry was integrated before the war on a Yugoslavia-wide basis, with raw materials coming from other republics and finished products shipped to customers throughout the country. Not only have most of those links disappeared, but also economic ties between the Muslim, Croatian, and Serb parts of Bosnia have largely disappeared.

The many governments claim 50% of GDP. This makes it difficult for the government to become creditworthy. Most Bosnians' everyday lives have not improved since the war. Sarajevo's wartime scars have largely disappeared, but one sees more war damage outside the city center.

Bosnians of all ethnic groups were hurt by the world recession that struck in 2008–2009. To try to cope with the economic down turn, the Muslim-Croat Federation has reined in state spending (which constitutes almost half of GDP) by cutting public salaries and veterans benefits by 10%. The latter cuts unleashed street clashes between police and veterans, who received $200 to $665 per month for their earlier military service. Nevertheless, few people speak today about a renewed outbreak of violence, and few diplomats expect it. For most Bosnians, it is economic worries and jobs that are most pressing. This is a sign of progress.

A new and somewhat-controversial development has been the influx of wealthy tourists and investors from the Persian Gulf region. Attracted by the country's Muslim heritage, as well as its thermal springs, skiing opportunities, and development potential, Arab companies started building holiday complexes, shopping malls, and private villas. Because most purchases are made by intermediaries, no precise data are publicly available. However, just one project started in 2016 by a developer from Dubai includes at least 3,000 villas, apartments, a hospital, and a sports stadium, for an estimated total of $2.7 billion. Besides the wealthy, such projects are also intended for middle-class buyers seeking an affordable respite from the conflicts in their region. Some Bosnians worry about the potential influence of the more fundamentalist cultures in the gulf.

Bosnia and Herzegovina is ranked by the World Bank as an upper-middle-income country that has accomplished much since the mid-1990s. In December

2022, the GDP per capita in Bosnia and Herzegovina reached 6,976.00 USD. It is expected to continuously increase from 2023 till 2028 by a total of 2,635.8 U.S. dollars (+33.89 percent).

CULTURE

One of the most important cultural elements in Bosnia and Herzegovina is that approximately 44% of the population is Muslim. Now called Bošnjak, they are a Slavic people who converted to Islam.

Various attempts were made to stamp out the Bogomilist "Bosnian Church" as heresy, beginning in the 13th century. However, the church still existed in the late 15th century, when this area was overrun and incorporated into the Ottoman Empire. Most of the Bogomil aristocracy allied themselves with the Turks and assisted them in their conquest of the area. They converted to Islam, impelled by opportunistic motives and their hatred of the Roman Catholic Hungarians, who had waged religious war against them for the previous two centuries. Their descendants are the modern Bosnian Muslims who fought for their existence against efforts by Serbs in Bosnia and Serbia to wipe them out through a process of ethnic cleansing.

Bosnian Serbs are predominantly Orthodox Christian, while Bosnian Croats are largely Roman Catholic. In June 2003 Pope John Paul II made his second trip to Bosnia and celebrated mass for 45,000 pilgrims at the Petrićevac monastery, which had been destroyed by Serb saboteurs in 1995. During World War II, a Catholic priest from Petrićevac, near Banja Luka, had led Croat fascists armed with knives and hatchets to a nearby village, where they butchered 2,300 Serbs, including 500 women and children. The pontiff asked for God's forgiveness for "so much suffering and bloodshed" inflicted by Roman Catholics and others. He beatified Ivan Merz, a theologian in the early 1900s who would be Bosnia's first saint.

With the rise in investment and tourism from the gulf states, Arab presence has become more pronounced. In 2011, Qatar created in Sarajevo its Al Jazeera Balkans television station broadcasting in regional languages. (Russian, Turkish, and western broadcasters are also present.) Some hotels catering to gulf tourists are alcohol free, and some building developments are specifically constructed for the Arabs. Arab religious charities have been active in the country for two decades. Many restaurants, hotels, and physicians advertise in Arabic. In 2017, Bosnia waived visa requirements for Saudi citizens who have a Schengen visa or visa to any EU country. Joining the wealthy Muslims are

thousands of refugees from Afghanistan and the Middle East. Most are on their way to western Europe.

In 2006 an internationally acclaimed Bosnian film, *Grbavica*, won the Golden Bear Award (the top honor) at the Berlin International Film Festival. Directed by young Bosnian documentary filmmaker Jasmila Žbanić, it is an extraordinary movie about a Muslim medical student raped by a Serb during the Bosnian war. She gives birth to a girl. After it opened in Sarajevo, the Bosnian parliament voted to recognize raped women as war victims and give them financial assistance.

It is remarkable that the starring role of the mother was played by Mirjana Karanović, Serbia's best-known film actress. Until very recently it would have been unthinkable for a Serb to play the victim of Serbs in Bosnia. The film was shot in Sarajevo, a city that remains largely segregated. Segregated schools still exist, and intermarriage, which was once commonplace in large cities, has become rare. Serbs live outside the town in an area called "new Sarajevo," while Muslims dominate the city proper. Before the film opened in Belgrade, Karanović predicted that it would be received peacefully. "We Serbs are in a crisis of spirit. We don't know who our heroes are and who are the villains."

The most acclaimed film to come out of Bosnia in 2011–2012 was *In the Land of Blood and Honey*, a love story of a Serbian soldier and a Bosnian woman, that was written, directed, and coproduced by actress Angelina Jolie. It was done by a team of actors from all over the former Yugoslavia, most of whom had experienced the war firsthand.

A telling sign of how difficult any reconciliation remains is the tale of the Bruce Lee statue in Mostar. The Chinese American star of kung-fu films was an unlikely symbol of unity in the region. Yet, when the Mostar Youth Movement sought something that all the ethnicities had in common, the martial arts legend beloved throughout Yugoslavia in the "good days" before its collapse became a promising compromise choice. Even the location of the statue became an issue, however, as the fighting figure could not be facing in the direction of either of the primary foes in the city—the Bošnjaks or the Croats. Unveiled in 2005, the life-size bronze statue was promptly vandalized and had to be removed for exhibition elsewhere. It was finally reinstalled in Mostar in 2011, an unexpected embodiment of bridges between cultures.

On the other hand, it is also in Mostar that the annual soccer tournament is held that brings the various communities together. The Eid tournament is a friendly

competition of "imams, friars, and priests" from the Muslim, Catholic, and Orthodox faiths. Inclusion is also visible elsewhere. EU accession commitments helped in 2016 with the adoption of amendments to the Law on the Prohibition of Discrimination that now specifically includes sexual orientation and gender identity.

CURRENT ISSUES

Although the Dayton Accords brought an end to the fighting, they did not reunite the country. The follow-through the west had hoped would lead to sustainable peace, cooperation, and economic recovery has not yet succeeded, although some progress has been made. Most Serbs in Serbia and within Bosnia do not want to divide Bosnia and attach its Serb half to Serbia. However, the Bosnian Serb government and its leader, the increasingly authoritarian Milorad Dodik, who was reelected in 2022, often threaten to hold a referendum on independence, especially after Kosovo declared its independence from Serbia in February 2008. He has strengthened relations with Russia and assures his support against the "liberal West."

Poisonous ethnic tensions continue to pervade every sphere of life. Few anticipate a renewal of violence, and the virtual absence of revenge killings is very encouraging. But the Dayton structure is unwieldy and increasingly unworkable. It has resulted in a Byzantine system of government that produces endless blocking and gridlock among the community leaders. It took 15 months after the October 2010 elections to create a central government and appoint a prime minister, Vjekoslav Bevanda, a Bosnian Croat. Progress is almost impossible.

Elections confirm that the leaders of the parties responsible for the war are still very much in charge in their respective enclaves. Ethnic nationalism remains strong, although the leaders on the top are sometimes able to cooperate with each other. Three nationalist political parties remain in power in separate ethnic enclaves. A top UN official lamented that creating normal government and life in Bosnia is "like trying to build a house where ashes are still burning."

A positive sign of people power was the formation in June 2013 of a human chain by thousands of persons around the Bosnian parliament in Sarajevo for 14 hours to protest the deadlock on the 13-digit identification numbers assigned at birth to each citizen. Bosnian Serbs demand that the numbers specify their region, while Croats and Muslim Bošnjaks prefer random numbers in order to move away from ethnic divisions. About 1,500 furious legislators,

Bosnia and Herzegovina

government employees, and foreign bankers were trapped inside.

In February 2014 protest riots broke out in the northern city of Tuzla over massive lay-offs. They quickly spread across the country and became violent. Chanting slogans against "criminals" in government and urging them to "resign today," protestors were venting their anger against inactive, self-serving, and corrupt politicians, who had achieved nothing in countering the widespread poverty and unemployment. Several government offices, including the presidential headquarters in Sarajevo, were set on fire. Many citizens organized assemblies to discuss new forms of government. They demanded a new government of experts, the young, and the uncorrupt. They have lost patience with such forms of corruption as the need to bribe officials to get a job as a hospital cleaner (some $2,700) or about $13,700 to secure a position at one of the main telephone companies.

It is difficult to judge how much influence the US have; it has only a handful of troops there, and the EU's military contingent in Operation Althea has declined.

Although it is not yet a "failed state," public services are suffering from the gridlock. The economy is stagnant, and unemployment is extremely high, at 44% (over 60% for youth). Bosnia is a center for the trafficking of narcotics and women. Organized crime is chronic and deeply rooted. Bosnia is a persistent drain on western aid and defense budgets. Its central government is weak and ineffective, and the two parts of the Federation cannot make decisions on essential matters. It must also change its constitution to allow smaller minorities to compete for posts now reserved for Muslims, Serbs, and Croats.

Bosnia and Herzegovina has one of the lowest total fertility rates in the world, with only 1.36 births per woman in 2020. That is far below the replacement level and may spell trouble for the country in the future.

Bosnia and Herzegovina is an increasingly uncongenial hideout for war criminals. Crimes against individuals are no more common in it today than in Switzerland. Thus, it is relatively safe. There is no threat from outside the country. With dramatic political changes in Serbia and impressive economic reform and EU membership in Croatia, there is more competition for western aid monies. Western aid to Bosnia will continue to be reduced, but the country remains reliant on international assistance. However, there is far too little foreign investment.

The bloody ethnic fighting is not likely to be renewed. Bosnia's borders are no longer challenged, and there is a single customs and border-police service. Over 1 million refugees and victims of ethnic cleansing have returned to their homes or reclaimed their property.

All Bosnians now carry the same passport, can move around the country freely and safely, and were granted visa-free travel to EU states in 2010. Bosnian Croats now enjoy full EU rights. Free and peaceful democratic elections have been held repeatedly at all levels of government, even though the outcome has not always been welcome.

Bosnia won a two-year seat on the UN Security Council for 2010–2011. NATO presented it with a membership action plan (MAP) and invited it to join its Partnership for Peace program. The goal remains to integrate the region into Europe, and the EU is key to that aspiration. But it is hard to foresee any real economic recovery as long as the politics of ethnic animosity and corruption continues to divide the people and prevent necessary reforms.

A fresh controversy erupted in 2017, when the Muslim member of Bosnia's presidency, Bakir Izetbegović, announced that Bosnia would appeal the 2007 decision of the International Court of Justice that cleared Serbia of genocide during the Bosnian war. Serbian officials reacted angrily, describing the decision as "very dangerous." Major powers counseled caution. The ICJ rejected the request because it did not come from all three members of the presidency. The presidency's Serb chairman, Mladen Ivanić, had been opposed to the appeal, seeing it as unconstitutional and likely to renew conflict among the ethnic groups.

In the land where two decades ago some 100,000 people died in fraternal slaughter, the best hope for a better future lies with the membership in the European Union. The pressure and promise from Brussels have already helped bring the hostile parties together. Milorad Dodik, the leader of the Serb Republic in Bosnia, fears that his entity would be weakened, and he keeps threatening a referendum on leaving BiH altogether, though in March 2017 he stated publicly on television that "there will be no referendum on secession. . . My political attitude, as well as of my party (SNSD) is far from that plan. There is no plan of secession on the agenda of the RS." Either way, High Representative for Bosnia and Herzegovina Valentin Inzko warned in 2016 that any RS attempt at secession would provoke international intervention. Serbia's forthcoming EU membership would render these fears obsolete, since regional integration within the EU could promote easier contacts between RS and Serbia proper.

Bosnia and Herzegovina formally applied for EU membership in February 2016, after the organization agreed to drop its demands that Bosnia's electoral rules be first changed to allow members of minorities other than the three main ethnic groups to run in elections. In exchange for EU funds—some $1.1 billion over three years, plus another $560 million for infrastructure upgrades—and further integration, Bosnia's political forces pledged their collective commitment to greater economic development and reform. With Slovenia and Croatia already members and Serbia an increasingly solid candidate, Bosnia and Herzegovina has a strong incentive to pursue the integration, with its associated benefits and responsibilities.

On the understanding that several steps were taken, the Commission recommended Bosnia and Herzegovina for candidate status in October 2022. The European Council granted Bosnia and Herzegovina the status of candidate country in December 2022. A year later, in December 2023, the European Council decided it would open accession negotiations with Bosnia and Herzegovina, once the necessary degree of compliance with the membership criteria is achieved. The Council also invited the Commission to report on progress in March 2024 at the latest, in order to make a decision.

Perhaps the greatest hope for Bosnia and Herzegovina will come from the young generation. After a year of protests, in 2017 high school students in Jajce won the right to study in an integrated school rather than one in which various ethnic groups were separated. The existing "two schools under one roof" policy means that students are taught by teachers from their ethnic group following separate school curricula. This often happens in the same building, though students may have different shifts or use separate entrances and even restrooms. While many more schools still need desegregation, the students in Jajce observed, "We don't hate each other and the fact that politicians are trying to instill this hatred in us is wrong." Their signs are remarkably astute: "We are here to create the future, not to repeat the past." Nevertheless, half of young Bosnians want to leave.

Montenegro (Crna Gora)

Ethnic Background: 45.0% Montenegrin, 28.7% Serb, 12.0% Bosniak, 4.9% Albanian, 4.9% undeclared, 4.5% other (as of 2011 census)

Religion: Christianity (72.1% Orthodox, 3.4% Roman Catholic), 19.1% Islam, 5.4% other

(The results of the 2023 census will be published by MONSTAT successively in the second half of 2024, after data entry, processing and control.)

Form of Government: Unitary parliamentary republic

Chief of State: Jakov Milatović, President (since May 2023).

Head of Government: Milojko Spajić, Prime Minister (since October 2023).

National Flag: It is red, with the coat of arms of Montenegro in the center, and golden borders. The coat of arms portrays a crowned, double-headed golden eagle holding up a *globus cruciger* and a scepter in his claws. Atop a scepter there is a golden cross. The *globus cruciger* is depicted in blue and has a golden waist and cross. The chest of the eagle holds a breast shield displaying a golden *lion passant* against a blue sky background. The lion stands on a green field.

The double-headed eagle as a symbol originates from the Byzantine Empire. According to traditional belief, he is a messenger of God's word he transmits to the kings on earth by traveling up and down, between heaven and earth, on the Tree of Life. One head stands for the material world whereas the other stands for the divine symbolizing both earthly and church powers working together. Accordingly, the earthly ruler, the representative of God on Earth, should exercise both power and justice.

The lion passant depicted on the inescutcheon of the flag is a universal symbol of strength, kingship, pride, and sovereignty. The gold crown atop the eagle heads, the scepter, and the orb are also symbols of power and authority, as well as royal history. The gold surrounding the red color on all edges also shows the royal heritage that it once had. The cross atop the scepter and the crown shows that the country subscribes to Christianity. Finally, the red color of the flag's field symbolizes the blood shed in the quest for independence.

The flag was officially adopted in 2004, when Montenegro was still a constituent of the State Union of Serbia and Montenegro, and it was kept as a national flag after country's independence in 2006.

Public Holidays: May 21 (Independence Day), July 13 (Statehood Day), November 13 (Njegoš's Day).

Currency: Euro (€) (EUR)

Area: 5,333 sq. mi. (13,812 sq. km.).

Population: 633158 (December 2023 census preliminary data)

Capital City: Podgorica (pop. 180,000; December 2023 census preliminary data) Cetinje–the Old Royal Capital

Climate: It is Mediterranean in the southern lower areas, with dry summers and mild, rainy winters, and continental in the mountainous north. Average January temperatures range from 46 °F (8 °C) at the city of Bar on the southern coast to 27 °F (–3 °C) in the northern mountains. Mountainous regions receive some of the highest amounts of rainfall in Europe.

Neighboring Countries: Bosnia and Herzegovina (northwest); Croatia (west); Serbia (northeast); Kosovo (east); Albania (south).

Official Language: Montenegrin

Languages in official use: Serbian, Montenegrin, Bosnian, Albanian.

Montenegro

Former pesident Filip Vujanovic

Main Exports: Aluminum and aluminum goods, mineral oils, fuels, wood and wooden goods, charcoal, iron and steel, electricity, and beverages.

Main Imports: Mineral fuels, oils, machinery, mechanical devices and tools, electrical machinery and equipment, pharmaceutical products.

Main Trading Partners: Serbia (24.5% of exports and 20.0% of imports), Italy (5.8% of exports and 6.2% of imports), Türkiye (6.2% of exports), Kosovo (6.1% of exports), Bosnia and Herzegovina (8.6% of exports), Switzerland (11.6% of exports), Germany (9.2% of imports), Greece (5.9% of imports), China (9.8% of imports), Croatia (5.5% of imports). (2021)

Montenegro is a Mediterranean country located in the west-central Balkans at the southern end of the Dinaric Alps. Its names—both Montenegro (from Venetian Italian) and Crna Gora (in Montenegrin)—denote "Black Mountain," in reference to a landscape of once deep-dark forested mountains. Mount Lovćen (5,738 feet; 1,749 meters), near the Adriatic Sea, was its historical center and stronghold in the centuries of struggle with the Turks. Alone among the Balkan states, Montenegro was never subjugated. The old proper Montenegro, in the southwest, is mainly a karstic region of arid hills, with some cultivable areas—e.g., around Cetinje and in the Zeta valley. The eastern districts, which include part of the Dinaric Alps (Mount Durmitor), are more fertile and have huge forests and grassy uplands. The drainage system of Montenegro flows in two opposite directions. The Piva, Tara, and Lim rivers follow northern courses and are part of the Black Sea basin, while Morača and Zeta rivers are southern ones and are part of the Adriatic basin. Its Adriatic coastline has a

good, deepwater port, the port of the city of Bar. Skadar (Shkodër) Lake, the largest bird sanctuary in Europe, forms part of the border with Albania. The rugged interior is largely uninhabited and is an ideal habitat for wolves and bears.

The country's attractions include spectacular mountains, medieval villages, beautiful sandy beaches, a coastline dotted with churches and fortified towns such as Kotor and Herceg Novi, Durmitor National Park with its limestone peaks, glacial lakes, and 1,300m-deep Tara River Canyon.

Montenegro's administrative capital is Podgorica, though its cultural center is the historical capital and old city of Cetinje.

Montenegro has an upper-middle-income economy, and ranks 49th in the Human Development Index.

Durmitor National Park with the Tara River Canyon, the walled city of Kotor, and *Stećci* Medieval Tombstone Graveyards are natural and cultural World Heritage Sites in Montenegro.

The Constitution adopted in 1992 declared Montenegro as "an ecological State," defining the country's strategic commitment to adopt and apply the highest standards and norms in the field of environmental protection, nature conservation and economic development on the principles of ecologically sustainable system.

Montenegro is a member of the United Nations, NATO, the World Trade Organization, the Organization for Security and Co-operation in Europe, the Council of Europe, the Central European Free Trade Agreement, and it is a founding member of the Union for the Mediterranean. It has

The city of Kotor depicted by Jovana Ivanović, a young architect.

Montenegro

also been in the process of joining the European Union since 2012.

For much of the 20th century, Montenegro was a part of Yugoslavia, and from 2003 to 2006, it was a constituent of the state union of Serbia and Montenegro.

HISTORY

The forerunners of today's Montenegro are the medieval principalities of Doclea (Duklja) and Zeta. The first mention of Doclea dates back to the 10th century, while its successor, the Principality of Zeta, emerged in the 14th and 15th centuries. From the late 14th century to the late 18th century, large parts of southern Montenegro were ruled by the Venetian Republic and incorporated into Albania Veneta (Venetian Albania). The name Montenegro was first used to refer to the country in the late 15th century.

From the creation of the first state (Doclea) on its present-day territory until its integration into the state of Yugoslavia, Montenegro was led and shaped throughout history by four dynasties: Vojislavljević (1018–1186), Balšić (1360–1421), Crnojević (1451—1530), and Petrović Njegoš (1696—1918). The territory of Montenegro was ruled by the Serbian Nemanjić dynasty from 1186–ca1360.

During the Turkish rule, the country experienced centuries of independence while the surrounding areas seethed under Turkish control. The almost-impassable mountains allowed the Montenegrins to resist repeated Turkish attempts to conquer the area. Although the Venetians and later the Turks did occupy parts of Montenegro, it was never completely controlled. Under the rule of the House of Petrović-Njegoš, it was first a theocracy and later

**Poet, Bishop, Ruler—
Petar II Petrović Njegoš**

Djukanovic wins the 2006 elections.

a secular principality. The Great Powers recognized Montenegro's independence at the Congress of Berlin in 1878. In 1910, the country became a kingdom.

During the years before World War I, the Montenegrins, like some of their neighbors, were advocates of South Slav nationalism. They militarily supported to the cause in 1878 against the Turks and took part the Balkan Wars of 1912–1913. After World War I, from 1918, it was part of all three consecutive Yugoslavias. Following the breakup of Yugoslavia in 1990s, the republics of Serbia and Montenegro together proclaimed a federation initially called the Federal Republic of Yugoslavia, reconstituted and renamed a State Union of Serbia and Montenegro. At the referendum held on May 21, 2006, the citizens of Montenegro voted for independence from the state union with Serbia with a total of 55.54% of votes. Independence was declared on June 3, 2006. On June 28, 2006, Montenegro became the 192nd member of the United Nations, and on May 11, 2007, the 47th member of the Council of Europe, and on June 5, 2017, the 29th member of NATO.

The Road to Independence

Yugoslav president Slobodan Milošević, appointed Montenegrin Momir Bulatović as prime minister of the Federal Republic of Yugoslavia in 1998 (the country then still consisted of Serbia and Montenegro). Bulatović had just lost the Montenegro presidency to Milo Djukanović, who started distancing himself from Milošević, so the appointment apparently was to help Bulatović control the freshly elected president of Montenegro. Instead, Djukanović stated that Bulatović's new government was "illegitimate, illegal and un-Yugoslav" and that he would recognize neither Bulatović nor his cabinet.

Djukanović appointed 20 of his supporters to represent Montenegro in the 40-member federal Yugoslav upper house. The effect of these appointments was to deny Milošević the necessary two-thirds majority he needed to change the 1992 constitution to increase his powers.

Djukanović also publicly condemned Milošević's policy toward Kosovo and

expressed his support for the restoration of Kosovar autonomy. In June 1998, the Montenegrin parliament passed a resolution demanding that Milošević immediately end the violence in Kosovo. After endorsing the demands of the international Contact Group, the resolution also stated that all Montenegrin troops were to be removed from Kosovo and returned to barracks in Serbia or Montenegro if Milošević chose not to accept the Contact Group demands. Separately, Djukanović reiterated that Montenegro did not want to participate in the war in Kosovo. Such policies won much international approval and helped Montenegro gain a reputation as a kind of democracy under Serbian dictatorship. Thus, it received international assistance, while Serbia was subjected to sanctions.

The Montenegrin government was particularly concerned about the large numbers of Kosovar refugees who had made their way across the border into Montenegro to escape Serb military actions. By July 1998, there were already 18,000 of them in Montenegro, and more kept arriving every day. Unlike Serbia, Montenegro was attempting to help the refugees as much as possible. It also permitted the UN High Commission for Refugees to operate in the republic. As large numbers continued to come, however, the Montenegrin government began deporting some of them to Albania. In September 1998, for example, it transported some 3,200 Kosovars. By that time, the refugees already in Montenegro constituted 11% of the population, and the government concluded that it simply could not handle more. But by April 1999, the number had grown to 55,000. Montenegrins were also still caring for 25,000 refugees from the wars in Croatia and Bosnia. Refugees thus constituted 15% of its population in 1999.

Milo Djukanovic

Montenegro

Study break at Podgorica University

The Montenegrin government consistently condemned Serbia's policies in Kosovo and was friendly to the west. But once NATO began its air war against Yugoslavia, its targets included airports and military targets in Montenegro, as well as in Serbia. Podgorica's civilian airport became one such target because the Yugoslavian military had a wing of its airplanes located there.

Because of Montenegro's opposition to Milošević's goals, it became the target of Yugoslav government actions. When NATO's air war over Kosovo began in the spring of 1999, Milošević removed the military commander in Montenegro because he was considered to be friendly to President Djukanović. His successor was a Milošević loyalist. In April, Milošević also attempted to take over control of the Montenegrin paramilitary police on the pretext that they should come under national control during wartime. Djukanović resisted that action, but the NATO bombing of targets in Montenegro aroused the instinctive patriotism of many Montenegrins and created some supporters for Milošević's cause.

NATO's air war ended in June 1999 after Milošević's capitulation, but the hostilities between Belgrade and Podgorica continued. Anti-Milošević demonstrations throughout Serbia, which followed the end of the war, put him on the defensive. However, he temporarily survived these efforts to force him out of power, and he renewed his attempts to regain control over Montenegro. On his part, Djukanović moved to reestablish friendly relations with Albania and Croatia and to reopen the border with those countries. In April 2000, Albania and Montenegro signed an agreement on economic, trade, and cultural cooperation during a visit by the Albanian foreign minister to Podgorica. One border crossing was opened, with another to follow.

The Montenegrin government set up its own customs and trade regime in September 1999. Two months later, the German mark (followed later by the euro) was made the official currency as the government attempted to shield the Montenegrin

economy from the inflation raging next door. Milošević's response was to declare an embargo on all trade with Montenegro. Political relations remained tense. Djukanović announced that Montenegro would not participate in the 2000 federal elections because "the federal state does not exist."

This did not yet mean a final breakup of Yugoslavia. The advice Djukanović got from abroad—both from the United States and most western European countries— was that he should take no precipitous actions, lest they lead to war with Serbia. At the same time, polls in Montenegro indicated that Montenegrins were split on the question of independence: 41% favored it in 2004, 39% opposed it, and 20% were undecided. Most Montenegrins have relatives in Serbia and want to maintain close and friendly ties with it. Such polling figures argued for caution on Djukanović's part.

In October 2000 the situation changed dramatically in Serbia, when voters threw Milošević out of the Yugoslav president's office and elected a democratically oriented opposition politician, Vojislav Koštunica. The Montenegrin government had boycotted the election and had asked its people to do the same. Koštunica's election raised expectations that the two republics could reconcile their differences. Koštunica insisted that Montenegro must remain linked to Serbia, which would lose its access to the Adriatic and Mediterranean Seas without it. But he stated that he favored drawing up a new constitution that would·make Montenegro feel more equal with Serbia. He was willing to allow the Montenegrin people to decide in a referendum if they wanted to become independent. In 2002 he supported dropping the term "Yugoslavia" altogether and renaming the state "Serbia and Montenegro." Within two weeks of his election, he traveled to Podgorica to reassure President Milo Djukanović and to offer him

Caution, "school," in Cyrillic

the prime ministership in his new government. The latter declined.

The March 2002 agreement brokered by the EU to rename Yugoslavia and to restructure its federal institutions prevented a referendum for three years. It was finalized a year later and included EU promises of economic and political assistance. But this agreement could be reconsidered after the three years had elapsed. In 2004 the Montenegrin government already started talks with Serb officials about possibly dissolving the union. It worried about suffering economically and being dragged down with Serbia, which faced international criticism over its lack of cooperation with the war-crimes tribunal in The Hague.

The US and European countries made public their opposition to Montenegrin independence. Even though Montenegro already enjoyed what many observers

Podgorica, University of Montenegro Campus

Photo courtesy UCG

Montenegro

Ex-Prime Minister Dusko Markovic

would call independence, western leaders worried that even a referendum on the subject could set off another round of secession and violence in the Balkans. Djukanović called early parliamentary elections in October 2002 and won a clear parliamentary majority with 39 of 75 seats; he took over the post of prime minister. His close political ally and deputy leader of his pro-independence Democratic Party of Socialists Filip Vujanović won a landslide victory for the presidency in May 2003, capturing 63.3% of the votes. He promised to move his land toward mainstream Europe and to organize a referendum on Montenegro's independence in three years.

After the government announced a referendum in 2006 to decide the question of independence, the Serb prime minister rejected Podgorica's proposal that the two entities retain close links but be recognized as independent. Montenegro aspired to both NATO and EU membership as an independent state. The EU decided to take a "twin-track approach," allowing both republics to negotiate with it separately but in tandem. It issued a feasibility study in April 2005 concluding that accession talks could begin.

Serb prime minister Koštunica had noted pessimistically, "This looks like a marriage doomed to divorce." He was right. The deal officially sanctioned the existence of separate economies with different currencies (the dinar for Serbia and the euro for Montenegro) and conflicting legal systems.

In July 2004 the Montenegrin parliament adopted a new flag, national anthem, and a statehood day as part of the drive for independence. A traditional folk song was adopted as the national anthem, aptly named "Oh, the Bright May Dawn." Both Serbia and Montenegro raced to approve new anthems before the Athens Olympics because fans in both republics had developed the embarrassing habit of drowning out the Yugoslav anthem with jeers and boos whenever it was played at national sports events. Serbia and Montenegro's last joint international appearance was an athletic event: It fielded a combined team in the world soccer championship in Germany in June 2006 and was quickly eliminated.

The referendum was memorable for several reasons. There was a complete absence of violence in this highly divided society, in which at least a third of its residents declare as Serbs, with another 50,000 Albanians. International observers certified that the voting was fair. With voter turnout at 88%, the result was clear, with 55.5% voting yes and 45.5% no. That did not stop the Serb members of parliament from boycotting the session on June 3, 2006, when independence was formally proclaimed. This made Montenegro the world's 192nd sovereign state and completed the process of federal Yugoslavia's disintegration.

Djukanović dominated the news media, but a televised debate was held before the polling that gave voters one last chance to compare the arguments for and against. In that debate, the leader of the opposition to separation, Predrag Bulatović, accused Djukanović of trying to establish a "private state." The latter helped finance the return of thousands of the 16,000 Montenegrin expatriates (equal to 3% of the total voter turnout), including several hundred New Yorkers, to vote for independence. Serbian railways also provided free tickets to mostly anti-independence Montenegrins in Serbia to return home and vote no. The Albanian minority solidly supported severance from Serbia. When the preliminary results were announced, Podgorica was alive with the thunder of fireworks and celebratory gunfire. Crowds rushed into the main streets, honking horns and waving the national flag.

INDEPENDENCE

In the earlier cases of Slovene, Croat, and Bosnian declarations of separation, Serbia resisted by military means. This time it accepted the inevitable and declared its own independence on June 5, 2006. The last shred of the Yugoslav Federation disappeared without bloodshed.

Montenegro's then-prime minister Milo Djukanović, a resourceful politician who was the only Balkan leader to cling to power throughout Yugoslavia's breakup, argued that the move toward separate statehood is "a river so strong that it cannot dry up." He presented his country's choice as "between Montenegro joining the EU as an independent, modern state with a clear sense of identity, or joining as a junior partner in an unbalanced, dysfunctional union with big brother Serbia, constantly fearful of losing our identity. The truth is that the imposed union between our two states does not work properly, and its continued existence would delay the integration of both states into the EU."

There can be no doubt that the two countries' political cultures had diverged significantly in the eight years following Djukanović's split from Serbia. He had

Milo Djukanovic addresses a rally.

Montenegro

kept his country out of the Kosovo war as well as he could and tried to make amends to the international community for what federal Yugoslavia had done.

His statement reveals how important the EU is in both Montenegro's and Serbia's hopes for the future. A key argument in favor of independence was that Montenegro might be able to join more quickly than its former partner, which is burdened by the requirement to capture war criminals and deliver them to The Hague. It was the EU that insisted that the threshold for victory be 55%, not a mere 50%, and after the referendum it appealed to the two countries to arrange a Czechoslovak-style "velvet" divorce. But it also warned both sides that EU membership is not inevitable and that there would be no shortcut to joining. Nevertheless, the prospect of EU membership was an essential part of the independence package. It initialed an agreement with the EU in 2007 and began the process of accession. In December 2010 it won formal candidate status.

Former Serbian prime minister Vojislav Koštunica refused to congratulate the newly independent republic. No Serb officials or Serbian members of the Montenegrin parliament attended Montenegro's independence ceremonies. But Serbian president Boris Tadić saw the new development as an opportunity to demonstrate that separation in the former Yugoslavia can now be peaceful and that "we can maintain the historical good relations between us." He assured his neighbors that "Montenegro will have a reliable friend in Serbia" and that "Serbia will be the closest friend."

Although there is diminishing tension in the air, the issue of Montenegrin sovereignty never stirred the same kind of deep passion in Serbia as does Kosovo. In fact, at the time of the referendum, 60% of Serbs favored independence from the much poorer Montenegro, only one-eighth its size with a tenth of its population.

The Process of Separation

Montenegrin independence triggered a complicated separation and the official resignation of Svetozar Marović, the independence-minded Montenegrin who had become federal president in 2003. The joint federal parliament was abolished. The armed forces had to be split up, beginning with a reshuffling of the top ranks in the army and military intelligence service. Each side named its own top commander. Thousands of soldiers were relocated to their home countries, but each republic kept the military facilities on its own territory. Dividing dozens of embassies, diplomatic residences, and other common assets may take years.

Under federation, there were common Foreign and Defense Ministries. Those were now divided, and each republic named separate foreign and defense ministers. Under an earlier agreement when the former state of Serbia and Montenegro was created, Serbia inherits membership in the United Nations and other international organizations. Montenegro had to apply as a new member and was admitted on June 28, 2006. By its first anniversary as a sovereign state, it had joined the United Nations, the World Bank, the IMF, and NATO's Partnership for Peace (PfP).

Both also revised their constitutions to reflect their new independent status; Montenegro requires a two-thirds majority in parliament to change its constitution. In the wording of its declaration of independence, Montenegro sees itself as a "multiethnic, multicultural and multireligious society . . . based on the rule of law and market economy." Its national strategic goal was integration in the European Union and NATO. In November 2006 NATO invited both Montenegro and Serbia to join its Partnership for Peace program, which is an initial step toward full membership.

In May 2016, NATO ministers signed the Accession Protocol, which gave Montenegro an official "invitee" status in anticipation of joining NATO in 2017. Montenegro supported the NATO-led operation in Afghanistan from 2010 to the end of 2014 and later the mission to train the Afghan security forces. This is a dramatic change for a country that suffered NATO bombardment during the 1999 war in Kosovo, so thousands of nationalists and Serbs took to the streets protesting this decision. Russia reacted adamantly to the news, demanding that the government organize a referendum, through which anti-NATO elements could derail the project. Russia saw it as an unwelcome assertion of independence by Montenegro right next to Russian ally Serbia but primarily as NATO's arrogant spreading of its influence soon after Russia's intervention in Ukraine prevented that country's further drift westward.

Certainly, it is not the size of Montenegro's military that worries Russia. Montenegro has a small force of some 2,350 active-duty soldiers, including the army, the navy, and the air force. There are some paramilitary forces, which include Ministry of Interior personnel and special police. Then the chairman of the Russian parliament's defense committee Admiral Vladimir Komoyedov snapped dismissively, "They are ready to admit even the North Pole to NATO just for the sake of encircling Russia." Russian projects in Montenegro will now be abandoned. Nevertheless, then-prime minister Djukanović saw the matter as an issue of sovereignty, as well as greater autonomy from Serbia, and was determined to see the process through. In 2018 Montenegro sent a platoon to the large NATO drill in Norway, and it also deployed troops in Afghanistan.

On June 5, 2017, Montenegro joined NATO by depositing its documents of accession in the presence of ex-Prime Minister Duško Marković and ex-Minister of Foreign Affairs Srdjan Darmanović. All 28 members' parliaments had ratified the entry, even though there was some worry about President Trump's support

Source: *International Herald Tribune*

Montenegro

for Montenegro's membership in light of his desire to forge closer cooperation with Russia. Stressing that the collective security pledge of NATO had helped keep Europe safe for nearly 70 years, Secretary-General Jens Stoltenberg emphasized that Montenegro joined "with a seat at the table as an equal, with an equal voice in shaping our Alliance, and its independence guaranteed." This was a major moment for the small republic that had faced down Russia's pressure and opted clearly for a political and military orientation toward the west.

POLITICAL SYSTEM

The president is directly elected by universal suffrage for a five-year term. It is a parliamentary democracy, and the most powerful political position is that of the prime minister, whose party or coalition must command a majority in parliament for its most important legislation. A party must win at least 3% of the total votes in order to qualify for any parliamentary seats.

Two leaders emerged in the lead-up to independence after a half-decade of struggle. Under the leadership of President Momir Bulatović, Montenegro had been a loyal supporter of Milošević's policies until 1997. But Bulatović was challenged for the presidency by his prime minister, Milo Djukanović, who accused him of being a puppet of Milošević. Djukanović won and subsequently began to take an independent line toward Milošević.

The 1998 parliamentary elections were essentially a rerun of the battle between Djukanović and Bulatović for the presidency, with the additional factor that Milošević did everything in his power to help Bulatović defeat Djukanović and take control of the legislature. When all of the results were in, however, the coalition led by Djukanović had won 49.5% of the vote, while Bulatović's Socialist Party had captured only 36%.

Montenegrins gradually distanced themselves from Serbia's war policies, and in 1997 the ruling party of reformed communists split in two. Ultimately the separate groups developed into two political blocs: one pro-independence and the other pro-union with Serbia.

Presidential Elections

Filip Vujanović of the Democratic Party of Socialists (DPS) was elected president of Montenegro in May 2003. He was re-elected in April 2008 and again in April 2013, winning 51.2% of the votes. The loser in 2013, Miodrag Lekić, refused to accept the results. He claimed that it was unconstitutional for Vujanović to run for a third term, even though the Constitutional Court had approved it in February 2013.

President Jakov Milatović
Courtesy: *The Office of the President of Montenegro*

His reelections helped cement the country's westward political and economic course since independence.

The following presidential election were held in 2018 and won by Đukanović, with 53.9% of the vote in the first round. President, Đukanović was eligible for re-election in 2023, since his first presidential term (1998–2003) was served before the successful 2006 Montenegrin independence referendum.

The 2023 presidential elections were held on March 19. Since no candidate received most of the vote, a second-round vote was held on April 2. In the first round, Đukanović, leader of the populist DPS, received 35%, coming first. Jakov Milatović, candidate of the newly formed centrist Europe Now! Movement, running on an anti-corruption platform, outperformed the polls, gaining 29% of the votes, and faced Đukanović in the second round. Andrija Mandić, one of the leaders of the right-wing populist DF, secured 19% of the votes, finishing third in the first round. After the first round, Mandić called his supporters to vote for Milatović in the second round. Thus, the second-round runoff resulted in Milatović defeating Milo Đukanović in a landslide, becoming the first elected president not being a member of the Đukanović's DPS since the introduction of the multi-party system in 1990, winning 58.88% of the popular vote.

Parliamentary Elections

Vujanović's predecessor in office and Montenegro's most influential politician, Milo Djukanović, had assumed the more powerful post of prime minister in November 2002. The prime minister is responsible to the 81-seat parliament, the Skupština. Djukanović's Democratic Party of Socialists (DPS) has dominated Montenegrin politics since independence.

In November 2006 Djukanović stepped down as prime minister to make way for

a less centralized, less autocratic rule. He stayed on as leader of his DPS party and remained extremely influential in the country. He was replaced by his own Party companion, former justice minister Željko Šturanović, who was favored because he was free of some of the murky maneuverings in which his party had been involved as Yugoslavia came unraveled and Serbia was subject to international sanctions. Although diagnosed with lung cancer, he remained in power until February 2008, when he handed the keys to the prime minister's office back to the 46-year-old Djukanović, who remained very close to then President Vujanović.

Djukanović decided to have the next elections 18 months early, in March 2009, in order to strengthen his position in the midst of the global recession that was bound to hurt Montenegro and his government. Turnout was a respectable 66.2%. For the sixth time, he emerged as prime minister, a post he had first occupied at age 29 in 1991.

Early elections were again held in October 2012. Djukanović's three-party Coalition for a European Montenegro, led by his DPS, captured 45.6% of the votes and 39 seats, a loss of 6. This fell short of a solid parliamentary majority, so the DPS had to rely on the support in parliament of minority groups. Other parties clearing the 3% hurdle were Democratic Front, led by ex-foreign minister Miodrag Lekić, which garnered 22.8% of the votes and 20 seats (down 7); the Socialist People's Party of Montenegro, which won 11% of the votes and 9 seats (down 7); a new party, Positive Montenegro, which got 8% of the votes and 7 seats; and the Bosniak Party, which captured 4% of the votes and 3 seats (up 1). Much of Djukanović's power stems from the fact that the opposition is divided. Since independence no government has been voted out at the ballot box.

Voters clearly showed their preference for familiar leadership in time of economic distress. In December 2010 Djukanović had passed the reins to his deputy prime minister and finance minister Igor Lukšić, who in his mid-30s was Europe's youngest head of government. He is regarded in Brussels and Washington as a reformer. An economist by training, he aimed to open up the country and to lead it into the EU and NATO. After Djukanović again assumed the prime ministership in December 2012, Lukšić became deputy prime minister for the second time, as well as foreign minister.

The elections in October 2016 occurred in a highly charged atmosphere stemming from the 2015 street protests against Djukanović's hold on power and alleged corruption, as well as the impending NATO membership. There were also

Montenegro

verbal clashes in the parliament, with the opposition Democratic Front drowning out Djukanović's speech with epithets. On the day of the election, the authorities arrested 20 Montenegrins and Serbs, including the former head of Serbia's special police, charging them with attempting a coup to attack the parliament. Serbian authorities arrested more people and seized uniforms and money apparently intended for use in Montenegro. Djukanović later implied Russian involvement in the alleged plot, implicating by extension the pro-Russian and anti-NATO Democratic Front. Two leading opposition parliamentarians were accused of involvement.

The election itself brought few surprises. The Democratic Party of Socialists, who ran on the slogan "Safe step!" won 41.4% of votes and 36 seats. Together with Social Democrats (5.2%, 2 seats), and the ethnic parties of the Bošnjak, Albanian, and Croat minorities (an additional 4 seats), the governmental coalition won 42 of the 81 seats. The Democratic Front won 20.3% and 18 seats.

Soon after the election, Milo Djukanović resigned as prime minister again, and his party selected Duško Marković to replace him. It would be Marković who attended the official ceremony admitting Montenegro to NATO in June 2017. Demanding new elections by 2018 and protesting the charges against their two colleagues, almost all opposition members decided to boycott parliamentary sessions.

The following parliamentary elections, the fifth since Montenegro gained its independence in 2006, were held on August 30, 2020. They were held simultaneously with the local elections in five municipalities and were organized in special conditions, due to the COVID-19 pandemic in Montenegro.

The period of the pre-election campaign was marked by the high polarization in the electorate. Several corruption scandals connected with the members of the ruling party triggered 2019 anti-government protests, while a controversial religion law sparked another wave of protests. OSCE election observers stated that "The abuse of state resources gave the ruling party an unfair advantage" and that the governing party benefited from a lack of independent media.

The election resulted in a victory for the opposition parties. Even though DPS came out as the single strongest party, winning 35.06% of the votes (–6 seats), the three opposition coalition lists agreed to unite and jointly form the government. Opposition coalitions, For the Future of Montenegro, Peace is Our Nation and the United Reform Action, won 41 of the 81 seats in the Parliament of Montenegro, while the ruling DPS, together with the Liberal Party,

won 30 seats, going into opposition after thirty years in power.

The leaders of three coalitions, Zdravko Krivokapić (For the Future of Montenegro), Aleksa Bečić (Peace is Our Nation) and Dritan Abazović (United Reform Action), agreed to form an expert government, and to continue to work on the European Union accession process. Their program also included fight against corruption, overcoming society polarization and economic crisis, and work on changing the disputed Law on Religious Communities. They also welcomed the minority parties of Bosniaks and Albanians in Montenegro wishing they also take part in the government.

By signing the Agreement, they guaranteed that the new government will not initiate any procedures to change the national flag, coat of arms or anthem, i.e. that it will respect the current Constitution of Montenegro, that there will be no political revanchism, also that the new government will pass all laws in accordance with European standards and implement all reforms related to European integration of the country, that it will depoliticize main state institutions in order to ensure an uncompromising fight against corruption and crime, and that the new government will respect all current international obligations, including the country's membership in NATO and abandoning all initiatives to de-recognize Kosovo's independence, which previously was advocated by some members of the new parliamentary majority (e. g. Democratic Front, major constituent of For the Future of Montenegro coalition). Krivokapić said that Montenegro will not be under influence of Serbia or Russia, but that his government will establish better diplomatic relations with both countries, also naming accession of Montenegro to the European Union, as the main priority of the new ruling coalition.

On September 23, the deputies of the new majority in parliament officially supported Zdravko Krivokapić as the new prime minister-designate, as well as electing Aleksa Bečić new President of the Parliament of Montenegro. The new leaders announced the new government as reformist, pro-European and dedicated to Montenegrin national interests. The new government was elected on December 4, 2020.

Reviewing political developments in Montenegro, the Serbian pro-government tabloids have unanimously criticized the coalition agreement between the new parliament majority, for agreeing not to discuss changing national symbols of Montenegro, the de-recognition of Kosovo, or the country's withdrawal from NATO, during the new government term.

On March 3, 2022, President Djukanović asked Deputy Prime Minister Abazović to

form a new government following a no-confidence vote in early February against Prime Minister Krivokapić. On April 28, Montenegro's parliament approved a new government composed of a broad coalition of both pro-European and pro-Serb parties, with Abazović as Prime Minister.

The DPS agreed to support a minority government, which was formed on 28 April 2022 by URA, the Socialist People's Party (SNP), the Social Democratic Party (SDP) and Civis and some ethnic minority parties. Abazović declared that the new government's main focus will be the reforms required by the EU so that Montenegro can ask to speed up its accession process in light of the new situation created by the Russian invasion of Ukraine, as well as the fight against corruption, more sustainable investments and development, protection of the environment, and better care for children and youth.

However, Abazović became closer to Serbian president Aleksandar Vučić and prioritized "regional cooperation" over European integration, saying that Vučić-backed initiatives such as Open Balkan would bring Montenegro closer to European living standards. Minister of European Affairs Jovana Marović resigned from the government and the URA for reasons including Abazović refusing to consider the risks of Open Balkan. After an agreement between Montenegro and the Serbian Orthodox Church on August 3, 2022, the DPS withdrew its support, announcing a no-confidence vote against Abazović's government. On August 20, 2022, the no-confidence vote passed. After several unsuccessful attempts at forming a new government over several months, Djukanović dissolved the Parliament on March 16, 2023, three days before the presidential elections which he lost to Jakov Milatović of Europe Now! movement. Abazović remained in power as a caretaker prime minister pending the formation of a new government.

Parliamentary elections were held on June 11, 2023. The Europe Now! movement won a plurality of seats (24 of the 81) while the DPS led Together! coalition came in second (21 seats). For the first time, the DPS failed to win most seats since the introduction of multi-party politics in 1990. Voter turnout was a low 56%.

After months of negotiations, on October 19, a coalition agreement was reached between Europe Now!, For the Future of Montenegro, Democratic Montenegro (excluding URA), the Socialist People's Party of Montenegro (as DEMOS was unable to get seats in Parliament), Civis, the Albanian Forum, and the Albanian Alliance. Milojko Spajić, the leader of Europe Now!, ruled out a coalition with the DPS and URA. It was agreed that Spajić would serve

Prime Minister Milojko Spaić
Source: *Wikipedia*

as Prime Minister, and Andrija Mandić the leader of For the Future of Montenegro would be President of Parliament, with his coalition providing a support role until the end of 2024. Beginning in 2025, the government will be reshuffled, and the two parties of For the Future of Montenegro that gained seats in the legislature will be granted one vice-presidential seat each as well as four ministries. The proposed composition of the new government was approved on October 31, 2023.

ECONOMY

Montenegro has an upper-middle-income economy and Montenegro hopes to attract foreign investors to utilize the country as a regional base for the entire Balkans. In addition to the privatization of the large aluminum works KAP (aluminum being the country's main export), Hungary's Magyar Telecom purchased a 51.1% share of the fixed-line telecommunications company *Telekom Crne Gore*. Among the other large investors are Belgium's Interbrew, Greece's Hellenic Petroleum, and Japan's Daido Metal. Anybody willing to invest €500,000 or more is entitled to citizenship. This is how exiled former Thai prime minister Thaksin Shinawatra became a Montenegrin citizen. Many hope he will invest much more of his billions in the country.

Net foreign direct investment in 2015 was nearly $650 million, an increase of about 80% over the previous year. Most of the FDI goes into finance, tourism, energy, health care, and real estate; it comes mainly from Switzerland, Norway, Austria, and Russia. Montenegro hopes that

its lowest corporate and personal income tax in Europe, at 9%, will lure more. Personal income tax rates are between 15.5% and 23.5%, and the VAT is 17% (7% for port-related items). It takes only four days and three documents to register a limited liability company.

With its appealing Adriatic coastline, it is no surprise that tourism offers so much promise and that large cruise ships and high-end yacht traffic steers into its waters. Over 1 million tourists visited the country in 2010. It accounts for almost a fifth of GDP and provides more than 22,000 jobs, many of them seasonal. Of course, this industry is vulnerable to the ups and downs of the world economy. Tourism will grow steadily within the next decade, making Montenegro one of the world's fastest-growing tourist destinations.

In a controversial move, Montenegro signed a deal with Swiss-Egyptian company Orascom to turn a former Italian fascist concentration camp on the island Mamula in the Adriatic into a luxury resort. Because it was a place of suffering for the Montenegrins during World War II, opponents accused the government of gross insensitivity. The company is investing $17 million to do the renovations to the largely decrepit structure.

Long-term prospects for tourism depend on the level of security in the country.

Its location makes it also attractive to drug smugglers, and the Montenegrin government is concerned about the increase in organized crime in the region. In early 2016, reacting to six clashes between armed criminal gangs, it sent an antiterrorist police squad to defuse the situation.

The country already uses the euro, although the EU made it known in October 2007 that its use is technically incompatible with EU law. But Montenegro was not asked to abandon the common currency. The government defended itself by arguing that its adoption in 2002 was a necessary step toward independence and future EU membership.

On October 15, 2007, it signed a stabilization and association agreement with the EU, and in December 2010 it won official candidate status. In its report, the European Commission praised "important progress" in bringing its legal framework and state institutions up to EU standards.

But it said that "the fight against corruption and organized crime remains a major challenge." Montenegro opened EU accession negotiations in June 2012 and has laid the groundwork for its entry into NATO in 2017. It became a member of the World Bank and IMF in 2007.

From December 19, 2009, Montenegrins enjoy visa-free travel to most EU states. EU membership remains the government's

Nikšić, the house of Đurići by Vojo Stanić

Photo: Lazar Pejović

Montenegro

top foreign policy priority. A 2009 poll confirmed that EU membership is desired by 72% of Montenegrins.

A new tunnel for cars through the mountains between Podgorica and the coast cuts travel time to as little as 40 minutes. This tunnel changes the dynamics of coastal tourism. In addition to tourist income, the country receives remittances from its expatriates totaling 1.3% of GDP; if unrecorded transfers are included, one could add 50%–100%. In addition to the tourists, thousands of Bosnians, Serbs, Kosovars, and Albanians pour into the country to work in construction, agriculture, and the tourism industry.

The main challenge was emerging from the global recession of 2008 and one of Europe's worst economies. Average monthly salaries were only €995 ($1055.591) per month in August 2023. By 2006 the economy was growing by 6.5% per capita annually, and the boom continued until the onset of the global crisis in 2009, which saw growth fall to –5.3%. However, growth bounced back to 3.2% in 2012. According to Trading Economics global macro models and analysts ' expectations, GDP per Capita is expected to reach $8189.00 by the end of 2024. The average unemployment rate from 2008 to 2023 was 17.69%. It has dropped to 11.80% in September 2023. Labor remains relatively inexpensive, which is appealing to investors.

One of the big challenges for Montenegro is to succeed in the privatization process. A case of privatization that left serious consequences on Montenegrin economy as well as on Russia-Montenegro relations was the privatization of KAP (Kombinat Aluminijuma Podgorica), an aluminum factory and bauxite mine. KAP provided more than half of Montenegro's industrial production, accounted for 80% of its exports and constituted as much as 40% of its GDP. The government had tried hard and unsuccessfully to sell the conglomerate to Alcoa of the US and Alcan of Canada. In 2005 a majority package of shares of the KAP was sold to the Russian oligarch Oleg Deripaska. After the collapse in global aluminum prices in 2009, the government was forced to buy back nearly 30 percent. However, CEAC (Central European Aluminum Company) still controlled the company's management and led KAP into debt. In addition to buying back half of Deripaska's KAP stake after the price collapse in 2009, the Montenegrin Government also provided guarantees for a 132 million Euro loan that Deripaska took from Hungary's OTP bank and Russia's state-controlled VTB bank. The whole case ended up at the arbitration tribunal of the Vienna-based UN Commission on International Trade Law (UNCITRAL) with Deripaska filing a suit against Montenegro

in front of the arbitration court for 93 million euros. Deripaska's lawsuit was eventually rejected by the court but the company, which once employed 5,000 workers ended up in bankruptcy in 2013, with 180 million Euros of debt.

Other challenges include the small elite that profited from privatization and became rich, powerful, and very influential in the government. Along with an influx of Russian, British, and Irish investors, they doubled the price of houses in only a year, but by 2009 property prices plunged more than 50%. Nepotism is rampant; without connections it is difficult to get ahead.

Corruption and organized crime are also deeply rooted problems. In 2010 a Serbian-Montenegrin gangster, Darko Šarić, was indicted in Serbia for organizing a 2.7-ton cocaine shipment from South America that was seized by Serbian drug authorities. Montenegro freed three of his alleged accomplices when Serbia failed to provide evidence against them, thereby damaging relations between the two countries. Šarić vanished, until he was apprehended in Latin America in 2014 and eventually sentenced in Serbia to 20 years in prison.

Montenegro protested that it is battling corruption with some success and has adopted an action plan to address EU concerns. Freedom House in New York cited improvement, and Transparency International gave Montenegro a better rating than any other western Balkan country except Croatia and Slovenia.

The Russian invasion of Ukraine (2022) affected global inflation adding heavily to the inflationary pressures building up in the euro area during the post-pandemic recovery and pushing up consumer prices, especially for energy and food. In Montenegro

Our Lady of Philermos

costs keep climbing, triggering inflation rates that far outpace wage growth.

It could be expected that a stabilization in food prices and a continued revival in public investment leave real GDP growth relatively stable in 2024.

Still, the key issue in the future prosperity and well-being of Montenegrin society is how attractive Montenegro will be as a country to attract inward investment.

CULTURE

The most important influences that shaped the Montenegrin culture came from Slavic, Ottoman, Central European, and Mediterranean cultures (notably parts of Italy, like the Republic of Venice).

The traditional culture of Montenegro is also related to the tribal life in which the national identity was nurtured and maintained. Increasing integration into the Yugoslav state during the 20th century, including the general provision of public education, led to the end of the tribal tradition, but the awareness of tribal affiliation remained in Montenegrin social life.

An example of the traditional folk dance of the Montenegrins is the Oro, the "eagle dance" that involves dancing in circles with couples alternating in the center and is finished by forming a human pyramid of dancers standing on each other's shoulders. The most significant artistic achievements in Montenegro are related to the Christian (both Orthodox and Catholic) and Islamic traditions.

Both the Latin and Cyrillic alphabets have equal status, and both could be seen in public use in the country. However, the former is increasingly popular.

Montenegro has many significant cultural and historical sites, including heritage sites from the pre-Romanesque, Gothic, and Baroque periods. Among the most notable structures are the Romanesque cathedral of St. Tryphon in Kotor, the 16th-century Husein-Pasha Mosque in Pljevlja, and the Baroque church ofvv Our Lady of the Rocks on an islet in the Bay of Kotor. The area of Kotor was recognized in 1979 by UNESCO as a World Heritage site. However, ahead of all there is the archeological site of Red Rock Cave (Crvena stijena), one of the most significant prehistoric sites in Europe with more than 20-meter-thick cultural layers formed in the period from the Middle Paleolithic to the Bronze and the Iron Age.

Medieval monasteries contain many artistically important frescoes which date back as far as the 10th century. A 13th-century fresco depicting the life of St. Elias, located in the Morača monastery, is perhaps most notable.

The city of Cetinje is the former royal capital and cultural center of Montenegro.

Montenegro

It is the location of several national institutions of culture, and of the official residence of the President of Montenegro.

The National Museum of Montenegro at Cetinje within its rich collection houses also one the most important of all Christian treasures—Our Lady of Philermos, a Byzantine icon of the Theotokos, dated to the 11th or 12th century. Yet, in tradition, it is believed that it was painted by St Luke in 46 AD. Originally kept at Phileremos Monastery in Rhodes and then in Malta, the icon has long been venerated as the patroness of the Knights Hospitaller and the Sovereign Military Order of Malta.

Fine arts has produced some world-renowned pieces. Milo Milunović used aspects of post-Impressionist technique to depict the landscape of Montenegro, while in the post-World War II period Petar Lubarda used Expressionist techniques to portray his homeland. Miodrag Dado Djurić is the most prominent representative of contemporary figurative art. In the late 20th century, a younger generation of artists blended international trends and styles with Montenegrin imagery and political concerns. At the beginning of the 1990s, new forums for art exhibitions were created, such as the Montenegro Cetinje Biennial.

In 2024, Montenegro celebrates the hundredth birthday of Vojo Stanić, the great master of Montenegrin fine arts. Stanić is one of the most prominent contemporary Montenegrin painters. He graduated from the Academy of Sculpture in Belgrade in 1951, but then he turned to painting which allowed him to express better his visions of the world that surrounded him. Stanić is a painter of the Mediterranean. His paintings are small theatrical stories from everyday life along with elements of surrealism and fantastic. They often represent human weaknesses reviving the spirit of the Renaissance comedies. Stays in Paris in 1958

Kino (Cinema) by Vojo Stanić

Photo Lazar Pejović

A prominent painter Vojo Stanić celebrates his hundredth birthday in 2024. Photo courtesy CANU

and Rome in 1973 and 1974 influenced the formation of his style, which did not change or adapt to trends in painting; he ignored abstract art claiming that "the human figure is the supreme motive of all art."

Stanić is a subtle analyst whose work has a special meaning derived from a complete philosophical system that problematizes two classical spheres: anthropological and cosmological, artistically transcribed by a layered fable, characterization, allegorical scenes and a multitude of symbols, often mysterious, intensified by the enigmatic grotesque of critical or, in turn, visionary projections of reality.

This fascinating artist affirmed Montenegrin culture with exhibitions in Rome, London, Vienna, Moscow, New York, Oslo, Shanghai, Dubai, Monaco, Venice, Berlin, Beijing, Belgrade, Zagreb, and numerous other places. Stanić represented Yugoslavia with his works at the Venice Biennale in 1997.

Montenegrin literature includes works written in Montenegrin and other languages in the area of modern Montenegro

from the 9th century till the contemporary period.

Oral literature, which over time also acquired its written form, had its roots in folklore transmitted by folk singers (guslars).

Important monuments of the oldest Montenegrin literature include *Andreaci's Charter* from the beginning of the 9th century, *Miroslav's Gospel* (12th century), *The Chronicle of the Priest of Doclea* (13th century), and the first printed book by the Southern Slavs *Octoechos of the First Tone* (15th century).

Andrija Zmajević is remembered as the first baroque poet and theologian, while the greatest Montenegrin poet, Petar II Petrović Njegoš, is equal in fame to Milton and Dante among the Southern Slavs.

Among the leading classics of Montenegrin literature are the novelists Stjepan Mitrov Ljubiša, Marko Miljanov, Mihailo Lalić, Ćamil Sijarić, and among poets those are Risto Ratković, Aleksandar Leso Ivanović, Radovan Zogović, and Vito Nikolić.

Montenegro

Fountain by Vojo Stanić

Photo Lazar Pejović

In the 1990s, contemporary Montenegrin literature gave a strong impetus to the renewal of Montenegrins' national consciousness and aspirations to rebuild their country and integrate into European trends.

CURRENT ISSUES

Europe's second-newest country faces serious challenges, even as it has reached one of its goals by joining the North Atlantic Treaty Organization in 2017. Already, the independence-referendum campaign in 2006 and the results revealed deep divisions within its society. Citizens identifying themselves as Montenegrins, Albanians, or Muslims overwhelmingly voted for independence. The third or more who claimed to be Serbs voted against it. Montenegro must work very hard to heal the wounds of the campaign and create a setting in which the Serb population can play a constructive role in the country's political life. The tension is even further induced by the Orthodox Church, with the Montenegrin and Serbian communities denying each other canonical legality.

Over time the intensity of the internal identity debate has declined, although foreign relations with Serbia remain frosty. When in October 2008 Montenegro officially recognized Kosovo's independence, thousands of pro-Serb Montenegrins protested in the streets of Podgorica, storming the parliament and chanting "Kosovo is Serbia!" Serbia expelled the country's ambassador, but it soon accepted him back when it realized how little such a move had accomplished.

With its membership in NATO and the drive to join the European Union, Montenegro opted to itself firmly within the European structures, which pits it against Russia and its regional allies. As the investigation into the planned coup of 2016 progressed, charges of Russian involvement match that country's designs and interests in the broader Balkan neighborhood. With Montenegro's accession, NATO controls the entire Mediterranean coast of Europe, further complicating Russia's connections to its closest ally in the region, Serbia. With North Macedonia's accession to NATO, Serbia became militarily landlocked and difficult to reach. Nevertheless, many Montenegrins have historical affection for Russians.

Montenegrins see the ultimate solution to most of their problems in membership in the EU, which uses its influence to accelerate reform. The process has begun, but the road ahead is long. All parties and three-fourths of the people support this effort.

In 2020, Montenegro legalized same-sex partnerships.

In April 2024, Montenegro will organize the ESG Adria Summit, a leading regional event dedicated to green transition, sustainable development, and responsible corporate governance.

Republic of Kosovo (Republika e Kosovës) (Република Косово / Republika Kosovo)

Map of Kosovo

Area: 4,203 sq. mi. (10,887 sq. km).

Population: 1,768,000 (2023 estimate)

Capital City: Prishtina (pop. urban 161,751, municipality 198,897). (2011 estimate).

Climate: It is predominantly continental with Mediterranean and Alpine influences. The summers are hot, and the winters, cold and snowy. The average temperature ranges between 0 °C (32 °F) in January and 22 °C (72 °F) in July.

Neighboring Countries: Serbia (north); Montenegro (northwest); Albania (southwest); North Macedonia (south).

Official Languages: Albanian, Serbian.

Recognized Minority Languages: Bosnian, Turkish, Romani.

Ethnic Background: 92% Albanians, 4% Serbs, 2% Bosniaks, 1% Turks, 1% Romani

Religion: 93% Islam, 6% Christianity, 1% others.

Form of Government: Unitary parliamentary republic. Kosovo is recognized by 102 member states of the United Nations. Nevertheless, it is claimed by Serbia as the Autonomous Province of Kosovo and Metohija (under UN Security Council Resolution 1244).

Chief of State: Vjosa Osmani-Sadriu, President (since April 2021).

Head of Government: Albin Kurti, Prime Minister (since March 2021).

National Flag: It consists of six white stars strung in an arc above a golden map of Kosovo on a blue field. According to an official interpretation, the stars symbolize Kosovo's six major ethnic groups: Albanians, Serbs, Bosniaks, Turks, Romani, and Gorani. The white and blue colors of the flag are usually associated with neutrality and peace, and the gold one with prosperity and power. The blue background is evocative of the flag of the European Union.

Public Holidays: February 17 (Independence Day), April 10 (Constitution Day).

Currency: Euro (€) (EUR), Serbian dinar (RSD) in Serb-majority areas.

Main Exports: Metals and mineral products, plastics and rubber, machinery, appliances and electric materials, prepared food, beverages and tobacco, and textiles.

Main Imports: mineral fuels and oils, machinery, mechanical and electrical equipment, vehicles and automotive parts, plastics and plastic articles, pharmaceuticals, prepared food, beverages and tobacco, metals and chemical products.

Main Trading Partners: US (16.3% of exports), Italy (8.0% of exports and 5.9% of imports), Albania (14.7% of exports and 5.7% of imports), Germany (8.2% of exports and 13.1% of imports), North Macedonia (11.5% exports), Serbia (6.5% of imports), Türkiye (12.5% of imports), China (9.7% of imports), Switzerland (7.4% of exports). (2021)

The youngest country in Europe, Kosovo is located to the southwest of Serbia. Over 90% of its people are ethnically Albanian. This is a mountainous region. The highest mountains, the Albanian Alps (in Serbian, the Mokra Gora), are located in the northeastern part of the country. A second mountain, the Šar, arises in the southwest along the North Macedonian border. It contains the Sharr Mountain National Park, established in 1986, Kosovo's only national park. There is a plateau region in the center, with lower mountains rising again to the east.

Kosovo has two plain regions: the Metohija/Dukagjin basin is located in the west,

Kosovo

and the Plain of Kosovo is in the east. The chief rivers are the White Drin, running toward the Adriatic Sea, with tributaries like the Erenik, the Sitnica, the South Morava in the Goljak area, and the Ibar in the north. Its largest lakes are Badovac, Batlava, Radonjic, and Gazivoda. About 39% of the country is forested, and 52% is considered agricultural, of which 31% is covered by pastures and 69% is arable.

Kosovo is a young country in several respects. It declared its independence on February 17, 2008, and its first constitution came into effect the following year on June 15. It is the seventh state to emerge from the Yugoslavia that dissolved in the 1990s. Unlike most European nations, Kosovo had a booming birth rate, and half of its population is under age 25. It has Europe's youngest population. However, fertility is falling. In 1950, the rate was 7.8 children per woman, but by 1990 it had fallen to 3.6. Now it is 2.2, just over the level needed for a stable population. Ethnic Albanians boycotted the 1991 census, so estimates of Kosovo's total population vary from 1.8 million to 2.5 million. Over 90% are Albanians. Any new census, in order to be accurate, would require cooperation between Albanians and Serbs living in the country.

The prime minister at the time of independence and again in 2008, President Hashim Thaçi noted that "a Kosovo identity does not exist." Very few Serbs would

call themselves "Kosovar." Most Kosovars are secular Muslims who consider themselves to be Albanian. For them, religion has always been secondary to being Albanian. They are proud that language and nationality, not religion, are the defining societal elements.

Orthodox Serbs constitute the largest Christian minority, but their church is riven by political and doctrinal divisions. Dozens of their churches were destroyed after the 1999 war, and an empty hulk of the unfinished, abandoned cathedral looms in Prishtina. However, there are many intact beautiful monasteries, such as those in Gračanica, Dečani, and Peja (Peć).

Conversions to Christianity have become common, and there are an estimated 65,000 Catholics. Downtown Prishtina is the location for the first cathedral in the world named after Mother Teresa. The world-famous nun had been born into an Albanian family in Skopje, North Macedonia. It was ready for services in 2010. Of the 15,000 or so Protestants, one pastor estimates that only 2,000 attend church regularly.

A contest was held to design the new flag, and the only ground rules were that it reflects the multiethnic population. However, many entries ignored that and submitted variations of the red and black Albanian flag that had served as the nation's colors until independence. The banner that was ultimately adopted had the colors

of the European Union (blue and gold), with six white stars to represent the two largest ethnic groups—Albanians (about 90%) and Serbs (5%)—and four additional smaller communities.

The Long Road to Independence

The interest of earlier political leaders in the individual Yugoslav republics to retain the maximum amount of scarce investment funds for local use led to grievances upon which local nationalism then fed. The autonomous region of Kosovo in the Republic of Serbia became particularly disaffected. It is the homeland of ethnic Albanians, who in the 21st century constitute over 90% of the province's population (after half the Serbs who had lived there fled following the 1999 war). Half of the 100,000 Serbs living in Kosovo are in the north, bordering on Serbia proper, with the part of the city of Mitrovica north of the Ibar River as their main city. A good number of its residents are Serbs displaced from other parts of Kosovo. The other half are in enclaves scattered across the land and bordering on Norh Macedonia. Altogether, the Serbian minority is predominant in about 15% of the country's territory.

Kosovo has undeveloped industry but considerable mining potential. It was always one of the poorest parts of Yugoslavia. Its unemployment rate was perennially the highest (around 50%), but many Kosovars find work in the underground "black" economy, behind the backs of the tax collectors.

At the beginning of the 1980s, dissatisfaction with the local situation produced a wave of nationalist agitation. Riots began in Kosovo in March-April 1981, led by youths from the University of Prishtina (in 1981 renamed Kosovo University). Eventually, thousands of demonstrators joined in clashes with police and openly propounded nationalistic slogans. Originally limited to the capital city of Prishtina, the demonstrations spread to other parts of Kosovo and then to the neighboring

Ibrahim Rugova (1944–2006)

Damage by precision bombing in Belgrade, still visible in 2005

Unarmed and isolated, the Albanian political leadership opted for a program of passive resistance and noncooperation. Perhaps they were lucky. Ibrahim Rugova, the man they elected as president of their "republic" in 1991, was firmly committed to a policy of nonviolence. He persuaded his people to go along with him. Rugova and his "government" collected their own taxes and used the monies to set up schools where the children could be educated in their own language and clinics where the people could receive medical assistance. Withdrawing into their own Albanian world, their only contact with Serbs was when they were stopped, and often harassed, by heavily armed Serbian police. Meanwhile, ordinary Serbs lived in their own villages, guarded by Serbian soldiers. Thus, even while a war went on for nearly three years in neighboring Bosnia, Kosovo remained quiet.

Milošević's War against the Ethnic Albanians in Kosovo

After remaining quiet throughout the Bosnian war, Kosovo finally exploded in 1998. The reasons can be traced to the actions of younger, more radical Albanians who had grown more and more frustrated by the failure of Ibrahim Rugova's passive resistance program to bring about any easing of the Serb repression. (Rugova was later nicknamed "Balkan Gandhi.")

In 1997, a new, more violent leadership arose to challenge the very idea of nonviolence. This organization, calling itself the Kosovo Liberation Army (KLA, also known by its Albanian initials, UCK),

Republic of North Macedonia (where another 374,000 ethnic Albanians live).

The university was closed on April 2, 1981, and the Yugoslav regime began a policy of "rooting out Albanian nationalism" and purging local organizations of Albanian nationalist elements. The university had undoubtedly become a hotbed of Albanian nationalist sentiment, but the underlying cause of the agitation was almost certainly economic. While there were demands for the creation of a separate Albanian Republic of Kosovo, there was no strong sentiment to merge the province with Albania. It is generally conceded that the standard of living of the people of Kosovo was higher than that of Albanians in Albania. They also had more freedom and, unlike the Albanians, were permitted to practice their religion. For these reasons, only a tiny minority supported union with Albania in the early 1980s.

The abolition of Kosovo's autonomous status in early 1989 was followed by Serb attempts to stamp out all manifestations of Albanian nationalism. Among other things, the Serbs fired all Albanian teachers and issued new regulations requiring that all instruction be given only in the Serbian language. This policy extended also to Kosovo University.

Serbia's reestablishment of control over Kosovo left a sullen populace, but it also forced the main Albanian political party, the Democratic League of Kosovo, to respond in a more radical manner than it might otherwise have done. It declared the Republic of Kosovo to be independent in 1991; this was confirmed by a popular referendum. It elected its first government in 2002.

The Serbian government's reaction was to carry out a massive purge throughout the province, dismissing Albanians from all important posts in the province. It also ordered arbitrary arrests, seized property, and tolerated (possibly even encouraged) widespread police brutality. Although Serbs were only 10% of the population, they now filled all governmental offices and all significant positions in hospitals, universities, businesses, and schools.

The Republic of Kosovo never received any international recognition, and the large number of Yugoslav army units stationed throughout the province until mid-1999 acted as a guarantee of continued Serbian control. Yet, in a real sense, it is possible to trace the slow birth of the Republic of Kosovo from 1991 onward. The Albanians slowly constructed a parallel government and society over the next couple of years.

Wagon train, June 1999: A long line of ethnic Albanians traverse a mountain road in northern Albania on the way back to Kosovo.

Kosovo

Don't kill my freedom. Surrender the weapons.

had actually been in existence since 1992. But it played no significant role until it managed to obtain weapons from Albania during the collapse and civil war that raged there in 1997.

This collapse of Albanian governmental authority led to a flood of all kinds of military equipment, as troop units dissolved and military warehouses were ransacked. It was mostly guns and other small weaponry that made their way across the mountains into Kosovo. However, when they arrived, some KLA leaders began to dream about driving the Serbs out of the province and creating an independent Kosovo. They could not know that their dreams would be realized within a little more than a year, prompting Tim Judah, Balkan correspondent for the *Economist*, to describe the KLA as "one of the most successful guerrilla movements in modern history."

Some recognized that they were still too lightly armed and too badly trained to achieve that on their own. But they hoped that a series of attacks on the Serbs might help stir up world opinion and publicize the plight of the Kosovar Albanians. They clearly expected President Milošević to order retaliatory actions against them, although it is not certain that they expected the ferocity with which the retaliatory actions were carried out.

In late 1997 the KLA began launching guerrilla attacks against Serb military targets in Kosovo. In January 1998, KLA rebels killed two Serbian soldiers. Responding to these attacks, the Serb government dispatched combined police and paramilitary units from the Ministry of Interior "to restore order." The Serbs rounded up thousands of Albanians and questioned them, often under torture. On March 6, they launched a series of "punitive raids" against Albanian villages. Armed with mortars, helicopter gunships, armored vehicles, and heavy artillery, they shelled individual villages that had been identified as centers of rebel support. One such

target was the Drenica region, where two days of heavy Serb assault resulted in the deaths of more than 80 villagers, including many women and children.

The killings led the United States, United Kingdom, Germany, France, and Italy to agree to place an embargo on sales of arms to Yugoslavia. But Belgrade rejected demands that Serbia pull its special paramilitary forces out of Kosovo and open talks with the Kosovar Albanian political leadership. Continued pressure did elicit a suggestion from the Serbian government that it was willing to open talks with Kosovo and that the issue of "self-rule" could be on the agenda. Since the Serbian government had branded the KLA as a terrorist organization, however, Milošević made it clear that no discussions could be carried on with representatives of this organization.

In a curious coincidence, the Kosovar Albanians had presidential and parliamentary elections scheduled for March 22, 1998. Amazingly, they managed to carry them out in the midst of the Serb occupation. Moreover, more than 80% of Albanian voters participated, even though the Serbs condemned and tried to stop them. In fact, voting could not be carried out in several villages that were under tight Serb police control.

Since Ibrahim Rugova was overwhelmingly reelected as president, Serbia had its "negotiating partner" whenever it desired to settle the dispute peacefully. Moreover, Rugova was an individual firmly committed to a policy of nonviolence. But the Serbs did not really want to talk.

In April 1998 Milošević sent paratroop units to Kosovo to seal the frontier with Albania. In May, the units' mission was enlarged to include the Kosovar Albanian villages in the vicinity of the Albanian border. Since the inhabitants of these villages were considered to be supporters of the KLA, Yugoslav soldiers began clearing the area by burning the villages and forcing the inhabitants to flee. Initially the number

Three people, One heart, One Kosovo. Support the return of refugees.

Statue of Zahir Pajaziti, one of KLA's first founders, in Prishtina

of dead remained small, although the refugees figure had grown to perhaps 20,000 by the end of May.

The KLA was also active during this time, organizing attacks on Serbian soldiers and attempting to establish control over parts of Kosovo. For a time, they claimed to dominate one-third of Kosovo, but this was misleading. Lightly armed and badly trained, they usually were forced to flee when they came into direct contact with units of the Yugoslav army.

NATO Gets Involved

Still, their occasional successes and their claim that they would not accept anything less than independence for Kosovo made it difficult for the various NATO members who wanted to see an end to the fighting and killing there. NATO made it clear again and again that it would go no further than to put pressure on Serbia to restore Kosovar autonomy. On the other hand, as long as the KLA continued to demand independence, NATO would stand aside and do nothing. That is what happened for another two months.

Meanwhile, the number of Kosovar refugees continued to grow until it reached an estimated 300,000 by September. This finally produced a UN Security Council resolution demanding that Serbia withdraw part of its forces from Kosovo. Following up on this, US envoy Richard Holbrooke negotiated a deal in mid-October 1998 that led to a ceasefire. Shortly

Kosovo

Map of Kosovo with Serbian town names and arrows showing escape exits for Albanian Kosovars before and after the 1999 war

went on. By mid-March 1999 an estimated 80,000 ethnic Albanian Kosovars had been forced to flee their homes as more Serb troops were moved into Kosovo.

In the end, Milošević refused to sign the Rambouillet Accords, but the Kosovars did. Accordingly, NATO began an air war against Yugoslavia on the night of March 24, 1999, with raids on airfields and arms factories in and around Belgrade and on other targets in Kosovo and Montenegro. President Bill Clinton announced that the purpose of the bombing was to protect unarmed ethnic Albanian citizens from Serb attacks by getting Milošević to agree to the Rambouillet Accords.

Meanwhile, Milošević launched what was obviously a long-planned program of ethnic cleansing in Kosovo. By the end of April there were an estimated 917,000 refugees. Approximately 357,000 fled to Albania, while a further 130,000 were admitted to North Macedonia. Montenegro, which opposed Milošević's policy toward Kosovo, had taken in another 72,000. Some of the remaining refugees had already been moved to such countries as Germany, Austria, Norway, Greece, Romania, Türkiye, and the United States. As the refugees continued pouring out of Kosovo, the camps and the rescue workers were overwhelmed.

Yugoslav forces continued to expel ethnic Albanians from their villages, which were then destroyed. Estimates of those killed by Serbian forces ran from a low of 10,000 to a high of 100,000, but no one really knows. It appeared, however, that Milošević had decided to create facts on the ground by expelling all or nearly all ethnic Albanians. In May 2010 Serb war-crimes prosecutors uncovered the third mass grave containing the bodies of hundreds of ethnic Albanian civilians killed during the 1999 war, then transported to Serbia to hide the atrocities. Three other such graves were discovered in Kosovo itself. Hundreds have been exhumed and returned home for burial.

As NATO continued its bombing, additional voices were raised about the need for ground troops to put a stop to the ethnic cleansing. Several NATO members did begin moving troops into the area on a contingency basis. But everyone recognized that it would take weeks for any nation to have troops ready to go in, even if a political decision to that effect were made.

That decision was rendered unnecessary when Milošević accepted NATO's terms on June 3. It took another six days before a firm agreement was reached and another several days before NATO forces began entering Kosovo. Kosovar Albanian refugees began trickling back in even before all Serbian forces had left the province and before NATO could certify

thereafter, the first of 2,000 unarmed civilians began arriving in Kosovo under a mandate from the Organization for Security and Cooperation in Europe (OSCE) to monitor the truce.

The ceasefire lasted for approximately three months, but it began to break down in January. In many cases, it was KLA guerrillas who began the process by ambushing one or two Serb policemen. Either the Serb paramilitary forces or units of the Yugoslav army would then retaliate, usually destroying one or more villages and often killing many of the inhabitants.

A particularly atrocious killing in January 1999 threatened to disrupt the entire peace process—45 ethnic Albanians were found dead in the village of Rečak (Račak in Serbian). William Walker, head of the OSCE's verification team, blamed the killings on the Serbs after he had visited the site. Milošević's reaction was to order Walker expelled from Kosovo. He later

backed down, but attitudes hardened all around from this moment.

Western officials now proposed a new round of talks, to be held at Rambouillet, in France. Germany, Great Britain, France, the United States, and Russia hosted the talks. Representatives of Milošević and three factions from Kosovo were presented with a draft settlement plan. Basically, it would have guaranteed Kosovo autonomy under a sort of NATO protectorate for three years, after which the final status of the province would be decided. Neither side accepted the plan during the first round of negotiations, although the Kosovar delegation did offer a pledge to sign the Rambouillet Accords after it had held consultations in Kosovo.

Milošević, on the other hand, said that he could accept Kosovo autonomy but could not agree to the stationing of NATO forces there. Meanwhile, fighting was on the increase even as the negotiations

Kosovo

that it was safe to do so. Many were villagers intent on planting their crops before it was too late.

However, most refugees took longer to return. When they did, they found destroyed houses and villages with little of value left. Some international assistance was available for rebuilding, but they faced a hard task rebuilding their lives. Meanwhile Serb families streamed northward with their goods, either to Serbia proper, to Montenegro, or to Serbian enclaves in northern Kosovo or elsewhere in the province protected by NATO peacekeepers.

Milošević was indicted as a war criminal in May 1999, and that became another complication. One effect was to increase public support for NATO's actions. Another was to make it even less thinkable that the Kosovars should in any way be put back under Serb rule as long as Milošević remained in control in Yugoslavia. Many

feared that Milošević would cling to power even more tenaciously since its loss might mean an international trial followed by prison.

In Serbia Milošević moved quickly to repair most of the war damage resulting from the NATO bombing, although the visitor to Belgrade can still see evidence of the damage done by NATO's precision-bombing attacks. Not until June 2003 was the last debris from the bombed bridges over the Danube cleared away so that large ships could pass.

Since the war Bill Clinton is a hero in Kosovo, with a street and businesses named after him and an honorary degree from Kosovo University in Prishtina. In 2009 an 11-foot gold-colored statue of him was unveiled in gratitude on one of Prishtina's main streets. In general, the US is still glorified in Kosovo, as a replica of the Statue of Liberty on top of the Victory

Hotel in Prishtina demonstrates. A survey in 2010 revealed that 98% of respondents said they approve of America and Americans.

One is frequently reminded of this. In October 2008 and May 2009 ex-secretary of defense Robert Gates and vice president Joe Biden visited the country. Gates pledged to maintain US military presence and train and equip Kosovo soldiers until a united Kosovo state was stable. Thousands of Kosovars lined the road from the airport into Prishtina, cheering and waving the Stars and Stripes and signs reading "Kosovo loves you" and "Thank you, USA" to give Biden a hero's welcome. Biden proclaimed, "We are back. We will stand with you." He called Kosovo's independence "irreversible." But he stressed the importance of continuing to reach out to the Serb minority, and he visited the Serb monastery of Dečani to pay his respects.

In October 2010 ex-secretary of state Hillary Clinton also got a hero's welcome. She waded into the crowds at her husband's statue and popped into a neighboring clothing shop named "Hillary." She assured the people that "status, sovereignty and territorial integrity of Kosovo are not up for discussion," and she told the Serbian president the same thing a day later. She pledged continuing support for Kosovo and its quest for full membership in NATO and the EU. She urged Kosovars to protect the rights of the Serb minority, and she visited a 14th-century Serbian Orthodox religious shrine in Gračanica, just outside of Prishtina. She encouraged the Serbian and Kosovar governments to open talks about practical issues. That happened in March 2011, when they launched their first formal direct talks.

Kosovo after the Fall of Milošević

The breaking of Milošević's hold on power in Serbia brought rejoicing throughout Serbia and the west. But it created difficulties for Kosovar Albanians. For most of the world, NATO's bombing in 1999 was a humanitarian rescue mission, but for most ethnic Albanians, it was the culmination of a national liberation struggle. Milošević's authoritarianism and status as an indicted war criminal were their strongest arguments that independence was both inevitable and morally necessary. With him gone and with the Serbian government's continuing insistence that Kosovo is a province of Yugoslavia, Kosovars found what little international support they had for independence to have evaporated. Western governments had always opposed independence on the grounds that it might destabilize North Macedonia. UN resolution 1244 declared at the end of the war that Kosovo belonged to Yugoslavia.

Former President Jahjaga (top left), President Thaçi, and Prime Minister Mustafa (middle and right bottom)

At most, the international community supported substantial autonomy, but that was not what most Kosovars wanted. One diplomat explained, "The Albanians never really believed us when we said independence was out."

One of the reasons western leaders and the EU tried so hard to keep Serbia and Montenegro together was that the total collapse of the former Yugoslav federation would have made it impossible to contain Kosovars' separatist demands. The new Serbian constitution still classifies Kosovo as part of Serbia. This infuriated many Kosovo Albanians. Their tense relations with UN officials in Kosovo encouraged Serbs there to organize in 2003 a union of Serb municipalities and to assert that, if Kosovo becomes independent, the 40,000 Serbs in the northern area would secede and join Serbia proper. This was an outcome international officials wanted to prevent. But it became harder and harder to avoid dealing with Kosovo's final status.

Revenge killings of Serbs also weakened international sympathy, as did deadly raids in 2000 by a new Liberation Army of Preševo, Medvedja and Bujanovac (known by its Albanian initials UCPMB) across the eastern border into Serbia's Preševo Valley, where 70,000 ethnic Albanians live and constitute the majority. UCPMB wanted to unite them with Kosovo. Its guerrillas, well-armed from hidden KLA caches, operated across a three-mile buffer zone between Serbia and NATO troops (primarily the 1,700 American soldiers deployed in Kosovo) to ambush Serb policemen. Former Serbian president and prime minister Vojislav Koštunica, who had publicly and sharply opposed the NATO air war against Serbia in 1999, needed to court western support and therefore avoided the kind of brutal response that Milošević would have ordered. He did complain that NATO did not adequately guard the border to Serbia and had done too little to disarm the KLA fighters completely.

Indeed, out of fear of casualties, the 31 western countries sending protection forces to Kosovo hesitated to root out the KLA, which maintained a shadow presence in the province, aggressively. Nevertheless, what was different was that NATO and Serbia were now cooperating to prevent another Balkan conflict. Belgrade restrained its response to the Preševo raids, and NATO tried to cut off the flow of weapons to the guerrillas. In spring 2001 NATO permitted Serbian soldiers to move into the five-kilometer buffer zone along the border to interdict KLA infiltration. KLA activists redirected their raids across the North Macedonian border, where that nation's Albanian population is concentrated. The intruders were beaten back by North Macedonian military forces.

Ramush Haradinaj has already been acquitted twice by The Hague tribunal.

Local elections in Kosovo in October 2000 revealed just how badly the KLA had squandered the popularity it once enjoyed. Its officials had seized property and businesses and often behaved arrogantly toward people who only a year ago had viewed them as liberators. The party it had formed, the Democratic Party of Kosovo (PDK), led by Hashim Thaçi, who in February 2008 became the prime minister who declared Kosovo's independence, was humiliated at the polls. The PDK lost in most of the 27 municipalities it had controlled since July 1999. The big winner in the election, which tested the mood in the province, was the nonviolent Democratic League of Kosovo (LDK), led by the reclusive scholar Ibrahim Rugova. It captured more than 60% of the votes, with almost 60% participating. Whereas the west had

forced the KLA to disband and disarm, voters forced it to abandon its political role temporarily.

The predominance of Rugova's LDK was again confirmed in the 2001 and October 2004 elections to create a provincial government. The UN, represented from June 2004 to June 2006 by no-nonsense Danish diplomat Soren Jessen-Petersen, could hand over to it many of the political powers the UN had wielded since 1999 while retaining the right to veto any decision by local institutions. In the 2004 voting for seats in the 120-seat provincial assembly, 33 parties participated, and turnout was 53%. Rugova's party won 45% of the votes, while Ramush Haradinaj's Alliance for the Future of Kosova (AAK) came in third with 8% of the votes and nine seats. Together they formed a governing coalition,

Kosovo Serbs in Mitrovica like Russian prime minister Putin and rock music, 2008.

Kosovo

North Macedonian magazine *Forum* notes Kosovar Albanians' gratitude to America.

with Haradinaj as prime minister. Kosovo Serbs boycotted the election, but they are guaranteed a quota of at least 10 seats.

The Kosovo government's challenges are great. It remains a deeply impoverished land with extensive war damage, strong tensions among the various ethnic groups, and a high level of corruption and organized crime. Criminal gangs, operating under the guise of Albanian nationalist militias, traffic in drugs, weapons, and women. In 2008, Transparency International, a Berlin-based anticorruption watchdog, ranked Kosovo as the world's fourth-most-corrupt economy, after Cameroon, Cambodia, and Albania. Bribery is commonplace.

An indigenous police force of 7,000, created and trained by 2,000 UN police officers from around the world and by EU specialists in the European Union Rule of Law Mission in Kosovo (EULEX), have helped to decrease serious crime. Official unemployment rate in Kosovo averaged 27.1% in the decade to 2022, and it is even higher among Kosovars under age 30, who constitute 70% of the total population. But the underground economy provides work for some of these. Stylish new cafes and shopping malls in Prishtina partly disguise the fact that the average month's pay is only €250 ($350). One sees building, especially of private housing, going on everywhere in Kosovo. However, corruption and the pressing need to improve the rule of law discouraged foreign investors from putting their money into the moribund economy.

That the 14,000 remaining foreign peacekeepers (declining over time to 4,000), including 1,600 Americans, were still needed to maintain order was demonstrated in March 2004, when the worst outburst of violence occurred since the 1999 war. It began after a Serbian youth from a village near Prishtina was allegedly injured in a drive-by shooting. According to an Albanian youth who escaped, a gang of Serbs then chased three Albanian boys into the fast-flowing Ibar River, which divides the two communities of Mitrovica, where they drowned. In revenge Albanian mobs drove some 4,100 Serbs in scattered enclaves from their homes and killed 19 and injured more than 900. Orthodox clergy claim that around 25 churches and monasteries were destroyed, triggering revenge attacks against mosques inside of Serbia.

NATO troops were unprepared and took two days to quell the violence and evacuate besieged Serbs. They rushed in 2,000 reinforcements to bring their total troop level to about 20,000. EU, NATO, US, and Serbian government officials were furious. Ex-prime minister Bajram Rexhepi called it a "disaster" and promised to rebuild the houses and churches. Then-Serb prime minister Koštunica called the events

a "pogrom." After the violence, Serbs boycotted Kosovo's institutions, including the government. It was followed by a 35% drop in the rate of refugees returning to Kosovo after fleeing in 1999.

The September 11, 2001, terrorist attacks in the US significantly reduced Kosovo's claim to the world's, especially America's, attention and funding. Nevertheless, a start had been made on training a national army, and 60 countries dispatched civilian or military personnel; more than $2 billion have been spent since 1999 to help the province. The sustained investment of money and soldiers has paid off. The country now has 105 banks with ATMs available. About 6,000 Serbs have returned to their homes in Kosovo, and their language can be heard in the major cities.

Finally Albanian extremists are being taken to court. This is a sensitive issue because many Kosovo Albanians regard all former guerrillas as heroes. In 2002 an international court in Kosovo sentenced five former guerrillas to prison for abducting and beating four fellow ethnic Albanians. This was the first time any former KLA members were convicted of such crimes. In 2003 the UN war-crimes tribunal in The Hague for the first time indicted four ex-KLA guerrillas for acts committed during the 1998–1999 war; four had been delivered to The Hague by 2004. One of them, Fatmir Limaj, was a member of the Kosovo parliament and later transport minister.

In April 2003 the UN administrator took the unprecedented step of branding

an Albanian rebel group as terrorist—the Albanian National Army (ANA)—which, unlike previous Albanian groups, had a cell structure. In 2005 the tribunal in The Hague completed the first trial of a Kosovo Albanian by convicting Haradin Bala of murder and torture. A major problem with trying Kosovo Albanians was the difficulty of finding witnesses willing to risk their lives by testifying. Such intimidation is the greatest single threat to the rule of law in Kosovo.

In March 2005 even Kosovo's prime minister Ramush Haradinaj surrendered to UN authorities. In the 1990s roughly 300,000 Kosovars, about a sixth of the total population, settled in Switzerland. He was one of them for almost a decade, where he was a nightclub bouncer. He returned to Kosovo, where he rose to be the most visible KLA commander, losing two brothers and sustaining three wounds himself in the conflict. Unlike Rugova, a pacifist, Haradinaj is a war hero. After the war, he founded the AAK, and following the October 2004 elections, he became Europe's youngest prime minister at age 36. He was the most charismatic and effective leader Kosovo had had in its five years of quasi-independence under UN administration. He displayed a mixture of energy, discipline, and attention to detail, and he knew how to get results.

The Serbian government was furious about his appointment, and investigators from the war-crimes tribunal soon appeared to question him about allegations

Former Kosovo prime minister Agim Çeku building a bridge to Serbia

Source: *European Voice*

Kosovo

of abuse toward Serbs. His decision to go to The Hague came as a surprise. In order to prevent the kind of disastrous unrest that had happened a year earlier, NATO temporarily increased its troop strength by 1,000. Haradinaj was permitted to return to Kosovo immediately to await the beginning of his trial in 2007.

In the autumn of that year, he was freed of all charges and returned to Kosovo as a national hero. The decision was changed in 2010, and he was ordered to be retried because witnesses had been intimidated, and that invalidated the trial. Kosovo is a land of tight clans; silence and loyalty are matters of life and death. Haradinaj submitted to his rearrest and transport back to The Hague. In December 2012 he was acquitted again, to the fury of many Serbs. A damning report by American prosecutor Clint Williamson for the EU in 2014 supported claims that senior KLA leaders had ordered heinous crimes of ethnic cleansing and murder during the war against Serbs and Roma.

Haradinaj was first replaced as prime minister by Bajram Kosumi. Then in March 2006, the Kosovar assembly elected by a vote of 65 to 33 the popular former KLA commander and subsequently head of the Kosovo police force Agim Çeku. He made it clear that there was no other possible solution to Kosovo's status than independence. But he reached out to Serbs by switching into Serbian during his acceptance speech and called on all minorities to participate in the region's political life and consider it their home.

Serbians strongly opposed his appointment and consider him a war criminal. When he accepted an invitation from the Bulgarian parliament in June 2009 to discuss Kosovo's integration into international organizations, Serbia demanded that he be arrested on an Interpol arrest warrant and extradited to Serbia on charges that he had allegedly ordered the murder of 669 Serbs during the Kosovo war. Çeku vigorously denied the charges and emphasized that he had never been indicted by the International Criminal Tribunal in The Hague. But he was detained and interrogated for 72 hours before being released. It was an embarrassment for Sofia, which recognizes Kosovo's independence, albeit with reservations.

Negotiations on Kosovo's Status

The violence of March 2004 created a renewed sense of urgency over Kosovo. The UN had avoided starting final status talks for fear of inflaming Kosovo's political atmosphere and that of its neighbors. But the population was losing patience. In July 2004 the Kosovo parliament adopted constitutional changes that include the right to call a referendum on independence from Serbia and to transfer control for international relations and public security from the UN mission to the Kosovo government. UN officials denied that Kosovo has the authority to do this.

A tentative first step toward an agreement had already been taken in Vienna in October 2003, with second-echelon government officials from Kosovo and Serbia reading prepared statements to each other in the presence of UN, EU, and NATO dignitaries. The Serb government suspended these "Vienna talks" in December 2004, when Haradinaj became prime minister of Kosovo. Although talks between government officials were discontinued after the March 2004 violence, communications continued between leading figures on both sides outside of Kosovo. The Greek government played a particularly useful role in facilitating these contacts.

On May 27, 2005, the UN Security Council set a diplomatic process in motion. A UN envoy assessed the situation in advance of a "status envoy" in the fall to arrange negotiations between Kosovo's Albanians and Serbia. The Kosovo government showed that it was implementing reforms ranging from financial transparency to security guarantees for the Serb minority. The US, Britain, France, Germany, and Russia agreed that Kosovo should have "conditional independence." Serbs would have to make the best of it. The conditions were that the rights of the Serb and other minorities must be protected, that there would be no return to the pre-1999 situation, and that there would be no "Greater Albania" linking all ethnic Albanians in one state. The goal was "final status" talks on independence.

Negotiations under the chairmanship of UN special envoy Martti Ahtisaari were to open in the Kinsky Palace in Vienna in January 2006. But they had to be postponed for a month because of the death of Kosovo's key negotiator, President Ibrahim Rugova. He died at age 61 of lung cancer days before the scheduled negotiations were to begin. His people gave him a lavish state funeral. Thousands honored his flag-draped coffin that was transported through the streets of Prishtina. Four presidents and representatives of over 40 countries attended the ceremony, including US secretary of state Condoleezza Rice.

Rugova was replaced as chief negotiator and largely ceremonial president by law professor and close colleague Fatmir Sejdiu, who was elected by the Kosovo assembly. He is a political moderate, and he pledged to achieve independence, to guarantee minority rights, and to make Kosovo "at peace with itself and its neighbors."

Kosovo investigative reporter Alban Bokshi

The Serbian government responded in anger. Then-prime minister Koštunica said Belgrade would not accept an imposed solution in Kosovo. He attended the June 28, 2006, anniversary of the famous 14th-century Battle of Kosovo in Gračanica, where he declared, "No one is on firmer, truer ground in the talks on Kosovo's final status than Serbia." Moderate Serbian president Boris Tadić, who became the first Serbian leader to visit Kosovo since the end of the 1999 war, asserted that "independence for Kosovo is unacceptable for me. I will never endorse it." However, other Serbs hinted that they could accept "more than autonomy but less than independence."

Nobody underestimated the difficulties involved. No Serbian leader wants to go down in history as the one who gave away Kosovo, which many Serbs regard as their historical birthright. Yet many Serbs were aware that they would not be able to prevent independence.

The hard problems remain: the divided city of Mitrovica, the return of all refugees, the security of Serbian enclaves, and the serious social and economic crisis. There developed a widespread conviction that the Kosovo issue must finally be solved in order to avoid "prolonging the pain and increasing the risks for the region," in former UN envoy Jessen-Petersen's words. The International Crisis Group had reported in 2005 that Kosovo stood on the edge of renewed conflict.

After lengthy negotiations between the Kosovo and Serbian governments, EU envoy Martti Ahtisaari drew up a plan in 2007 that envisioned a decentralized Kosovo government with the authority to sign international treaties and the responsibility to protect minorities and Serb religious sites and to prepare the return of Serb refugees. This would be conditional independence under temporary international guidance. The governmental system and its checks and balances are highly complex, with a "double majority" in parliament where minority interests are concerned and with Albanians having to submit to Serb local rule in some communities. For his skillful mediation and negotiation, Ahtisaari was awarded the Nobel Peace Prize in 2008. Receiving his prize, he asserted that "Kosovo is independent, and it will remain independent. The progress there is irreversible."

Conditions are not ideal for democracy in Kosovo: The economy is in terrible shape; unemployment is high; and organized crime and corruption are, as in the rest of the Balkans, too prevalent and extend to the highest political levels. But Kosovars have elected their leaders for many years, they have changes of government, their legislative assembly has acted responsibly, and on the whole, they have

shown respect for the rights of minorities. At the local level, Serbs choose their own leaders. They have a free media and vigorous opposition politics. They were ready to take control of their own governance on February 17, 2008.

Russia threatened to use its veto in the UN Security Council to prevent independence unless it was approved by Serbia. The US and most EU countries supported the Ahtisaari plan, but they tried to avoid a clash with Putin's Russia. If he used his UN veto, the UN representative in Kosovo would legally be obligated to annul any declaration of independence. Therefore, the matter was postponed until later in 2007. Then-prime minister

Agim Çeku proposed November 28, 2007, the Albanian national holiday, as a good day to proclaim independence, but he stated that his government did not want to act without the backing of Washington and Brussels.

Independence

A UN-sponsored troika process, consisting of representatives of the EU, US, and Russia, made one last effort, but it failed to reach a compromise. The process ended in December 2007. A joint EU-US statement declared that the UN Security Council was not in a position to agree on the way ahead. It endorsed the view that the potential for a negotiated solution had been

Kosovo

Former president Atifete Jahjaga

exhausted and that the EU stood ready to play a leading role in implementing a settlement defining Kosovo's future status in a careful and coordinated manner.

Kosovars yearned for independence, and they maintained a positive attitude. Several annual surveys by Gallup International from 2006 on revealed that they are among the five most optimistic nations of the world; another Gallup poll in 2009 found that Kosovars were the most satisfied among seven western Balkan countries. That optimism paid off on February 17, 2008, when Kosovo declared its independence from Serbia. The outcome was freedom for the entire province with certain conditions, including protections for Serbs and other minorities, supervision by the EU, and protection by NATO and other foreign troops for years. Gratitude for America's support was strong and visible, with demonstrators unfurling giant American flags and chanting "Thank you, USA," and "God bless America."

As a gesture of conciliation, then Prime Minister Thaçi addressed the parliament on February 17, 2008, in both Albanian and Serbian, and he pledged to protect Serbs' rights. But the Serbs would have none of it. With the support of the government in Belgrade, Kosovo Serbs set fire to two border posts between northern Kosovo and Serbia and completely destroyed them. NATO troops were forced to intervene. The Serb minister for Kosovo stated that these attacks were "in accordance with the general government policies." In Belgrade, the news was received with despair and anger. About 2,000 furious Serbs converged on the US embassy and set it on fire. One protester perished in the flames. The Serbian government formally proposed that Kosovo be divided along ethnic lines, but the chief EU envoy, Pieter

Feith, was clear: "This country . . . should not end up even with soft partition."

The violence continued in March, when UN police officers raided a UN courthouse in Mitrovica that had been seized by Serbs. The latter responded by shooting guns and throwing rocks and grenades. One Ukrainian officer was killed, and dozens were hurt. This was part of a Serb campaign to make Prishtina's rule over northern Kosovo impossible. This area already had parallel institutional structures linked to Serbia, and pensions and pay come from Serbia.

Kosovo's new constitution went into effect on June 15, 2008. It is a pro-EU document built around the western-backed "settlement package." It ceded final authority to an EU-led International Civilian Office, led by the international civilian representative (ICR). The post involved sweeping powers. After four years, this office was shut down on September 10, 2012. The EU fully supported Kosovo's progress under its Stabilization and Association Process, meaning ultimate EU membership for both it and Serbia. The constitution gave no role to the UN.

The main thrust of the new constitution is decentralization of power and the maximum feasible autonomy at the local level. Kosovo is composed of 30 municipalities, which form the basic territorial units of local self-government. In communities with Serbian majorities, the Albanian minority must be governed in local matters by Serbs. Serb-majority municipalities have the authority to provide secondary health care; offer higher education; oversee cultural affairs, including the protection and promotion of the religious and cultural heritage; be involved in the selection of local station police commanders; and receive funds from institutions in Serbia. These were embedded in a Kosovo-Serb agreement in April 2013.

In the first elections held after the independence of the newest country in the world, voters elected their local governments in November 2009. The big news was the turnout: 45% in all of Kosovo and 20% in the Serb enclaves. Fearing a Serb boycott, the government and diplomatic community were delighted that so many Serbs voted and ran for office, even though they largely ignore the state centered in

Kosovo farmers on market day in Mitrovica

542

A graffiti-covered monument—24 meters wide and 3 meters high to celebrate Kosovo—a newly free nation

Prishtina. In the other Serb enclaves outside the north, Serbs have grudgingly accepted the new state, even though they reject independence from Serbia.

To protect the rights of minorities in the single-chamber Assembly of Kosovo, a "double majority" is required on all issues that affect minorities. This means that two-thirds of the whole assembly and two-thirds of the representatives of the minorities (especially Serbs), who are guaranteed at least 20 of 120 seats (100 of which are directly elected by the people for four-year terms), must approve. Depending on the size of the government, two or three of the ministers are required to be from the minorities. The judiciary is independent. The assembly elects the president for five years and approves the government.

Because Russia, which has a veto in the UN Security Council, supports Serbia's rejection of Kosovo freedom as "illegal" (on the grounds that it has not been approved by the Security Council), the UN was unable to withdraw completely, as it had planned to do. UN resolution 1244, adopted in 1999 after the Kosovo war, required the UN mission to stay until a new resolution decides the status of the territory; Russia blocked such a new resolution. A perplexed UN secretary-general Ban Ki-Moon said that a "UN umbrella" would remain. Nobody knew exactly what this meant. Its future role in the new state was unclear as it shrank to 10% of its former size but did not disappear. UNMIK shrank in significance, but it remained an intermediary in Kosovo's international dealings. It directly administered Serb-claimed Mitrovica, which has come to symbolize the ethnic divide. Diplomats, especially Americans, continue to wield influence.

In December 2008 the UN handed over responsibility for civilian law enforcement, customs, and judiciary to the EU and local authorities in Prishtina. Handing off the supervisory role to the EU was problematic. The EU's police and justice (EULEX) presence was by 2009 in place all across Kosovo. By 2015 it counted about 1,600. This was the largest civilian mission in the EU's Common Foreign and Security Policy. Through it Kosovo was the biggest recipient per capita of EU foreign assistance; two-thirds of such aid came from the EU, whereas the US was the largest bilateral donor.

Evaluations of EULEX's success differ. In October 2012 a committee report of the European Parliament called it "disastrous." It pointed to organized crime, intimidation, corruption, and inefficient and politically influenced justice. These have hurt EULEX's reputation. To be fair, all state-building efforts show mixed results at best.

NATO's KFOR remains to maintain the fragile peace. But it decided in 2009 to reduce its numbers from the roughly 14,000 troops from more than 30 countries (including about 1,600 Americans) to around 4,000 in 2019, calling this a "purely deterrent presence." They are backed by a new lightly armed Kosovo Security Force under NATO guidance. It is to develop into what then-prime minister Thaçi called "a multi-ethnic force in the service of the country and all of its citizens," including Serbs.

The defiant Serb minority greeted the new constitution by announcing that it had set up its own elected 43-seat parliament in Mitrovica within Kosovo. Serbs had done the same thing in Croatia and Bosnia in the early 1990s. Of the 43 assembly members,

35 come from the north of Kosovo, even though two-thirds of Kosovar Serbs live in enclaves elsewhere in the country. Serb municipal elections had been in May, an act that the UN and EU had branded as illegal. The new assembly convened on a highly symbolic day: June 28, the anniversary of the epic Kosovo battle in 1389. Its first act was to declare that Kosovo remains "an inseparable part of Serbia" and that its secession was "illegal." In February 2012 Serbs in northern Kosovo, feeling betrayed, organized a referendum and voted 99.74% to have nothing to do with the rest of the Albanian-dominated country.

Serbia pretended that Kosovo was not independent. For example, in March 2010 its then-president Boris Tadic refused to participate in a Balkan summit meeting in Slovenia unless Kosovo's representatives attended under another name than "Kosovo-UNMIK." This would have implied that Kosovo was not independent, so Kosovo's leaders refused to back down. Tadić stayed home. One other participating state, Bosnia and Herzegovina, does not recognize Kosovo's independence, but its leader attended anyway (albeit leaving the room when the Kosovar prime minister gave his speech).

The Kosovo government pretended to be sovereign all over the country. But the area north of the Ibar River was still ruled de facto by Serbia and used its currency, the dinar. Serbia consolidated its grip over Serbian-settled areas, especially in the north. To the Kosovo Albanians' chagrin, their future was still tied to Serbia.

All this amounted to a depressing mess for Kosovars. The international reaction was mixed. While 108 countries, including the United States; 23 of 28 EU members (after Croatia's EU entry in July 2013); neighbors Montenegro and North Macedonia; and large Muslim countries starting with Saudi Arabia had recognized independent Kosovo by 2010, such EU countries as Spain, Greece, Romania, Slovakia, and Cyprus, as well as Russia, China, India, Egypt, and Brazil, had not. Nearly half of the UN's 193 members had not yet recognized it in 2015. Until it is a UN member or is supported by two-thirds of its members, a country cannot belong to the Universal Postal Union, required for international postal service. It cannot have a phone prefix or its own Internet domain name. Kosovo rents dialing codes from Slovenia and Monaco. In 2013 Kosovo got welcome legitimacy from Facebook, which offered Kosovars the option of identifying themselves as citizens of Kosovo rather than of Serbia. In December 2014 the International Olympic Committee granted full recognition to Kosovo, which can now send its own team to the games. These were viewed as diplomatic coups.

Kosovo

Russia and China have a veto in the Security Council on Kosovo's joining the UN. Serbia persuaded the General Assembly to submit the question of Kosovo's independence to the International Court of Justice for a nonbinding advisory ruling on its legality. On July 22, 2010, the UN's highest court ruled 10–4 that Kosovo's declaration of independence did not violate international law. This ruling did not go as far as to say that Kosovo was legal under international law, thereby leaving the question of legitimacy to other sovereign states which decide to recognize Kosovo. Nevertheless, Kosovo claimed a victory, and the ruling prompted some countries to recognize its independence. Prime Minister Thaçi made a point to be in Washington when the decision was announced. He met with Vice President Joe Biden, who reaffirmed America's "full support for an independent, democratic, whole and multiethnic Kosovo, whose future lies firmly within European and Euro-Atlantic institutions." He compared Thaçi with George Washington, a reference he may regret in the future.

Serbia's former president Boris Tadić admitted that the decision was a "heavy blow" to his country. Serbia immediately asserted again that it would never recognize what it calls a false state and that the decision did not establish a legal basis for an independent Kosovo. It threatened to follow up with requesting a UN General Assembly resolution calling for new talks on Kosovo's status. This infuriated European and American diplomat. Twenty-one countries maintain embassies to the Republic of Kosovo. But over time, more will be opened.

Belgrade has sent out conciliatory signals and agreed to EU-led talks with Kosovo as a condition for becoming an official candidate country. Serbia made some concessions, such as agreeing to Kosovo's participation in regional summits. Some technical agreements were reached, such as one dealing with auto license plates. The two countries have committed themselves to resolving outstanding issues peacefully, and they have launched constructive direct talks to deal with practical problems. The violence and ethnic cleansing that many observers had predicted have not taken place. A mass exodus of Serbs has been averted. However, tens of thousands of Kosovars are leaving through Serbia and Hungary to seek better lives elsewhere. Kosovo today is mostly peaceful.

Serb leaders signed a historic agreement with the Prishtina government on April 19, 2013. They accepted the authority of the Kosovo government over all of Kosovo, and Kosovo granted a large measure of autonomy to Serbs living in Mitrovica in the north. Kosovo's armed forces cannot be deployed there. Serbs in Kosovo are given limited authority over health care and education, as well as representation in top police posts and courts in areas where they predominate. There is an understanding that neither government will stand in the way of the other's admission to the EU.

Very importantly, the agreement did not require Serbia to recognize Kosovo as an independent state. They agreed to exchange "liaison officers." The US supported the agreement but played no direct role in the negotiations.

Tensions between ethnic Albanians and Serbs are low despite such incidents as the July 2010 shooting and wounding of a Serb member of Kosovo's parliament outside his home in northern Mitrovica. More serious were clashes in July 2011. In response to Serbia's embargo on Kosovo goods, Kosovo slapped import taxes on Serbian products and sent special police units into the Serb-inhabited north to seize two border crossings from Serbia. In the scuffle, a Kosovar policeman was killed, and one of the border points was torched by Serbs. NATO sent several hundred peacekeepers to bring the clash under control. Serb ex-president Tadić called for calm and said the protesting Serbs were "hooligans."

Conflict broke out again in October 2011, when Kosovar Serbs blocked roads leading into the northern enclave to prevent Kosovo police and customs officials from getting to the two border crossings. NATO peacekeepers and EU police were again sent in to restore order.

Most of Kosovo's Serb police officers, who had been exhorted by Serbia to resign, have returned to work. Serbia's most pro-EU government ever, led by ex-president Boris Tadić, assigned new people to deal with Kosovo. Supported by the US, Germany, France, and the UK, Kosovo was admitted to the IMF and World Bank in May 2009, despite a Serbian letter of warning sent to all 185 members.

A major test of the peace process was local elections in November 2013. They proceeded smoothly in all parts of the country except in Mitrovica in the north, where OSCE monitors and NATO soldiers were on hand to try to maintain order. Although the Serbian government had called on Serbs in the north to vote in the elections, masked Serbian hard-liners wielding bats attacked three of the polling sites there, smashed ballot boxes, and fired tear gas, forcing their closure after election officials fled.

Mitrovica remains a tinder box: In January 2016, a leader of a Kosovo Serb political party, Freedom, Democracy, Justice, was sentenced by the local EULEX court to nine years in prison. Oliver Ivanović was found guilty of encouraging the murder of nine ethnic Albanians by ultranationalist "Bridge Watchers" in Mitrovica in 1999. The sentence provoked a furious reaction in Serbia.

Tensions escalated again in 2017 over the arrest of former prime minister and KLA commander Ramush Haradinaj in France on a Serbian warrant. While he was later released, Kosovars saw the attempt as a provocation. Soon afterward, a train that was to restore rail communication between Belgrade and the Serb city of Mitrovica in Kosovo, caused a major crisis. It had been painted with the colors of the Serbian flag, Orthodox symbols, and written in 21 languages "Kosovo is Serbia." The provocation worked in that Kosovo authorities moved to block the train, which, however, stopped before entering Kosovo. Then Serb president Nikolić accused Kosovo of seeking a war and warned that Serbia would send its military to defend Serbs in Kosovo if need be. The affairs were a serious setback to the slow but perceptible progress in mutual relations.

POLITICAL SYSTEM

What did take place on November 7, 2007, was a final parliamentary election to legitimize the government that would declare independence soon thereafter. After Rugova had died almost two years earlier, his center-right League of Democratic Kosovo (LDK) lost its traditional position as largest party. The winner was the center-left Democratic Party of Kosovo (PDK), one of two parties that have their roots in the Kosovo Liberation Army (KLA). It is led by former KLA leader Hashim Thaçi. The seventh of nine children from a farming family in the Drenica region of Kosovo, he studied history and politics in Switzerland. He had been a ruthless and much-feared commander, who ordered arrests, assassinations, and purges within the rebel ranks. However, as prime minister until December 2014, he was pragmatic and willing to compromise with the Serbs, who still regard him as a reviled figure. He shows tolerance, championing, for example, civil rights for the LGBTQ population. In 2016, he became the president of Kosovo.

The other party is the center-right Alliance for the Future of Kosovo (AAK), led by former KLA commander and prime minister Ramush Haradinaj, who was temporarily cleared of war crimes shortly before the election. Thaçi had often clashed with the pacifist Rugova, and he faced rivalry with Haradinaj. But all of these large parties favored independence and cooperated to make that happen on February 17, 2008. Thaçi said soon after taking office, "We can't wait until all states are ready to recognize us." They formed a grand coalition.

The first national elections after independence took place on December 12, 2010. Because of polling irregularities and fraud, there had to be a revote in five municipalities on January 9, 2011, but this did not change the outcome. The election took place under a shadow cast by reports that Thaçi had been involved in drug, weapons, and human-organs trafficking and amid controversies about how the early elections had come about. Former president Fatmir Sejdiu resigned in October 2010 after the Constitutional Court ruled that he could not serve as both national president and party leader of the LDK. He pulled his LDK out of the governing coalition, creating a leadership crisis in the party. Haradinaj's recall to The Hague left his AAK in turmoil. Seeing a chance to win reelection while the opposition was in disarray, Thaçi brought about the fall of his own government in a no-confidence vote he engineered. He then called for new elections. Many Kosovars considered this maneuver illegitimate. The PDK emerged victorious, and it got the most votes in June 2014. But no coalition government could be formed until December 2014. Finally, it joined the Democratic League of Kosovo (LDK) to form a government with Prishtina mayor and economics professor Isa Mustafa as prime minister. In the opposition are the Alliance for Kosovo's Future (AKK); the VV; and a new party, Civic Initiative for Kosovo (NISMA).

Parliament elected Atifete Jahjaga as president in April 2011. A woman police commander with no political experience, she was the first female leader in the country. In February 2016, in the third round of voting, the parliament elected Hashim Thaçi as the new president of Kosovo. Certainly, the most influential politician in Kosovo, Thaçi is tainted by allegations

Change of command, KFOR

President Vjosa Osmani-Sadriu
Source: *Wikipedia*

of abuses while a commander of the KLA and of participation in various enterprises of organized crime, apart from his political activity. For the crimes during the struggle for independence he was one of the four accused who were transferred to The Hague after their indictment was confirmed in November 2020. They have all pleaded not guilty to all counts. Thaçi has been held in detention in The Hague since 2020, when he stepped down as president after war crimes and crimes against humanity charges against him were confirmed by a pre-trial judge at the Kosovo Specialist Chambers.

After Hashim Thaçi had to resign, then Speaker of the Assembly, Vjosa Osmani-Sadriu, served as acting president between November 2020 and March 2021. At the indirect elections for President of Kosovo held by the parliament of Kosovo on April 3 and 4, 2021, Osmani successfully ran on an anti-corruption platform and an intention to normalize relations between Kosovo and Serbia. She was elected after three rounds of voting winning 71 votes out of 120. Osmani became the second woman to hold the position of the president of Kosovo. Before taking the oath of office, she resigned from the leadership of Guxo!, a center-right political party in Kosovo she had formed in November 2020.

Kosovo Parliamentary Elections 2017

Parliamentary elections of June 2017 were provoked by a vote of no confidence in Prime Minister Mustafa's government. Each party in the victorious coalition of PDK, AAA, and a new Initiative for Kosovo (NISMA) was led by a former KLA commander, so the media proclaimed the victory of "ex-warriors." The coalition won 33.74% of votes and 39 seats

in the 120- seat legislature. It appeared likely that its lead candidate, Ramush Haradinaj, would become prime minister again. Only a few months earlier, in January, he had been detained by French border police on an old Serbian arrest warrant for alleged atrocities during the war for independence. After much international outcry, France decided to release him three months later, noting that he had been already acquitted by The Hague tribunal twice. However, the party that claimed it had the biggest electoral mandate was Vetevendosje (Self-Determination), a nationalist party that ran by itself rather than in a coalition and still won 27.49% of votes, doubling their representation from 16 to 32 seats. Since the Democratic League of Kosovo (LDK) coalition won 25.53% and 29 seats, it was not altogether clear what combinations of these forces would be able to form a government. Ramush Haradinaj declared that his coalition would ally with the 10 small ethnic parties and a few LDK parliamentarians to obtain a majority.

The only Islamic party to compete in this largely secular country wins very few votes. Many Serbs shun the polling altogether, especially in Mitrovica, but it is relatively high in central Kosovo enclaves. The United Serbian List got 5.2% of the votes and 6 seats.

Kosovo Parliamentary Elections 2019

In July 2019, Prime Minister Ramush Haradinaj had to resign after being summoned for questioning by the KSC in The Hague, Netherlands. The Kosovo constitution requires the President to designate a new candidate to either form a government, or hold new elections in between 30 and 45 days after consultation with political parties or coalitions who hold a majority in the Assembly.

President Hashim Thaçi asked the PANA Coalition to propose a new candidate to form a coalition government. However, other political parties opposed it. Subsequently, at an extraordinary session held on August 22, 2019, MPs voted to dissolve parliament, with 89 of the 120 voting in favor, necessitating elections within 30–45 days.

New parliamentary elections were held in Kosovo on October 6, 2019. The main opposition parties, led by Vetëvendosje and the Democratic League of Kosovo (LDK), received the most of the votes. Vetëvendosje leader Albin Kurti became Prime Minister, forming a governing coalition with the LDK on an anti-corruption platform. The government was formed on February 3, 2020. Kurti is the second Prime Minister who had not been a fighter of the Kosovo Liberation Army during the 1990s.

The coalition soon collapsed because the LDK filed a no-confidence motion on

Kosovo

Prime Minister Albin Kurti
Source: *Wikipedia*

25 March 2020 due to disagreements over how to handle the coronavirus pandemic. It was the first time a Kosovo government had fallen in such a manner. While the Kurti cabinet continued in office as a caretaker government, the LDK leader Avdullah Hoti attempted to form his government.

Although Hoti's eligibility to be Prime Minister had been questioned by Kurti and Vetëvendosje, the Constitutional Court ruled that after the party that won the elections failed to form again a new government, another party could, and Hoti might be approved as Prime Minister in a parliamentary vote.

Hoti was elected Prime Minister on June 3, by a vote of 61–24, with one abstention. However, on December 21, the government did not receive the support of the majority of the Assembly because the Constitutional Court ruled that the vote of Etem Arifi of the minority Ashkali Party for Integration in favor of Hoti was invalid. Arifi had been convicted of fraud. As a result, early elections were called, with the Hoti government continuing as a caretaker.

Kosovo Parliamentary Elections 2021

New parliamentary elections were held in Kosovo on February 14, 2021. The results were a landslide victory for Vetëvendosje led by Albin Kurti and its coalition partner, Vjosa Osmani, former speaker of the parliament of Kosovo. The alliance won more than 50% of the total votes, the highest share since the first elections held in 2001. Their nearest competitors, the Democratic Party, finished in second place, trailing by more than 33%.

The specificity of the 2021 elections was the record number of 102,100 non-resident citizens who acquired that right and participated via postal voting.

The two newly created minority parties, Romani Initiative and United Community, which had been backed by the Serb List, won two and one seat, respectively. However, the parties faced accusations of strategic voting organized by the Serb List to gain control of seats outside the ten reserved for Serbs. The investigation prompted by the Election Panel discovered many irregularities, including a suspicious 49% increase in the Bosnian minority vote compared to the 2019 elections, with a large share of those votes having been cast in Serb-dominated areas rather than in their communities. The result of the investigation caused the loss of one of the two seats won by the Romani Initiative and the seat won by the United Community. That was confirmed by the Supreme Court.

ECONOMY

Kosovo has one of the most underdeveloped economies in Europe. It was the poorest province of Yugoslavia and received substantial development subsidies from the Yugoslav federation. Additionally, in the 1990s a combination of bad economic policies, international sanctions, inadequate external trade, and ethnic conflict and war severely damaged the economy. Its imports exceed its exports tenfold, and this drives up the country's relatively huge current account deficit, which in 2008 amounted to 23% of GDP. Its agriculture is antiquated and unproductive. It imports most of its food, including such staples as meat and milk. The country is again producing its own wine, especially in the Rahovica area, where it was made as early as 28 BC.

However, there are pockets of apparent prosperity in Prishtina. Kosovo looks more like a poor part of the rich European continent than a developing country. Many families have members abroad who send money home, and they rely on it. Such remittances account for an estimated

Former prime minister Isa Mustafa

15%–20% of GDP. In 2008 they outweighed foreign direct investment by €550 million to €350 million. In addition, generations of Kosovars were guest workers in Europe, and their pensions constitute a huge infusion into the economy. The service sector constitutes 60% of the economy. The best-paying jobs are with international organizations.

Over 40% are still officially counted as unemployed (56% of the youth). With 25,000 young people entering the workforce annually, the economy would have to grow by 7% in each of 15 years in order to bring joblessness under control. GDP growth in 2011 was 5.5%. The underground economy is large and provides unreported and untaxed work for many. To lure foreign investment, the country has the lowest tax burden in Europe: 10% for both the highest personal income and for corporate profits.

International assistance is crucial and accounts for around 34% of GDP. By 2008 the EU had pledged €2 billion and the US $350 million. Serbia pledged €120 million to the Serb enclaves in Kosovo. In July 2008 a donor's conference in Switzerland raised €1 billion ($1.3 billion). Kosovo is a newborn nation with the expected economic uncertainties. In many ways it had to start from scratch.

Its one big economic advantage is that Kosovo is rich in all kinds of minerals. It took 70% of former Serbia's mineral deposits (and 90% of its coal) with it when it broke free in 2008. Despite irritating daily power cuts lasting for hours, there are 14 billion tons of lignite coal reserves (the world's fifth-largest proven reserves of this low-grade coal). There are already two large coal-fired electrical power plants, named Kosovo A and Kosovo B. The former has the dubious distinction of being the worst single-point source of pollution in Europe and despite plans to shut it down in 2017, it is still partially operating. Kosovo B needs revamping to conform to EU standards, and a new power station is under development. Electricity demand is increasing by 7% each year, and a staggering 44% of electricity entering the distribution network is either stolen or not paid for.

There are also vast deposits of nickel, lead, zinc, cadmium, bauxite, and even some gold. Halloysite, an aluminosilicate clay mineral used as a raw material for porcelain and bone china, has been discovered. It is only one of five known exploitable deposits of this very high-value clay; one of the other four is in Utah. The problem is that its extraction infrastructure is old and in need of large investments. That is why mining has been stalled since 1999. Its most important mining complex is Trepča. However, it is politically explosive because it is run jointly by ethnic Serbs and Albanians, and its mines and processing factories are spread between the Serb-dominated north and the Albanian-dominated south. Geological surveys show that 88% of Kosovo's mineral wealth is the southern part of the land.

Kosovo's economy remains weak. The private sector that has emerged since 1999 is mainly small-scale. The industrial sector is weak, and the electric power supply remains unreliable. This is a critical constraint on the economy. Free-trade agreements have been signed with Croatia, Bosnia and Herzegovina, Albania, and North Macedonia. UNMIK introduced an external trade regime and customs administration in September 1999, when it established customs border controls in Kosovo. All goods imported into Kosovo faced a flat 10% customs duty fee. In 2009 Kosovo replaced its UN-issued customs stamps with its own. However, Serbia, which is one of its most important trading partners, refused to accept the new stamps. Neither country backed down, so that crucial trading relationship has suffered. As a whole, the EU is Kosovo's biggest trade partner and is responsible for a third of its imports and over half of its exports.

Kosovo's biggest export is scrap metal from old cars. The euro is the official currency although the Serb enclaves still use the dinar. The chief means of entry to this landlocked country, apart from the main highway leading northward from Skopje, North Macedonia, and the new super-highway leading from northern Albania to Prishtina, is Prishtina International Airport Adem Jashari. The airport was privatized in May 2010, and taken over by Limak Kosovo International Airport J.S.C with a 20-year contract under the model of Build-Operate-Transfer. The KEDS energy company was privatized in 2013 as well. It is owned and operated by a private sector firm, Calik Limak consortium. Kosovo Telecom, previously known as the Post and Telecommunications of Kosovo (PTK), is still controlled by the government. It includes Vala, the largest mobile operator in Kosovo. The plans to sell state telecommunications assets set off another skirmish with Belgrade, which claims ownership of Kosovo's public-sector companies and infrastructure.

The massive unemployment rate among the youth has major consequences for the future of the country. Many young people are leaving Kosovo, mostly for the European Union countries. In 2014, the largest percentage (40%) of illegal migrants detected while crossing into Hungary were from Kosovo. With the rapid increase of the number of migrants from the Middle East, Kosovars found themselves out of luck. Kosovo is seen as a "safe country" by most EU members, and its citizens are not eligible for political asylum. Germany rejected virtually all applications for asylum from Kosovars in 2014.

Corruption and Crime

A key for improving the economy and attracting investment, in addition to solving the "status question," has been the strengthening of a rule of law and the gradual diminution of violence, organized crime, and corruption. The latter exist at a high level. For example, in April 2010 the offices of Transport Minister Fatmir Limaj, a former KLA fighter and close political ally of then-prime minister Thaçi, were raided by EULEX police and prosecutors for evidence relating to fraud in road-construction contracts. Members of his family were caught at Prishtina's airport trying to leave the country with suitcases containing millions in cash. Large public companies, such as the Kosovo Energy Corporation (KIK), are routinely looted by their executives, most of them political appointees. The government is under growing pressure from European and American diplomats to crack down on such corruption. In July 2010 EU police arrested the central-bank governor on corruption charges.

Criminal relationships permeate even political parties and institutions. Criminal gangs, operating under the guise of Albanian nationalist militias. Its economic weakness has produced a thriving black economy in smuggled gasoline, cigarettes, and cement, among other commodities. In 2016, Transparency International, a Berlin-based anticorruption watchdog, ranked Kosovo as Europe's fourth-most-corrupt economy, after Ukraine, Russia, and Moldova. Still, its 95th place in the world out of 176 countries that year was actually an improvement over 2011, when it was number 112. Bribery is commonplace, and money laundering is practiced on a large scale.

In 2010 a devastating report was published by the parliamentary assembly of the Council of Europe alleging that then Prime Minister Thaçi, a former KLA commander, had directed a mafia network that, in the chaos of war's end in 1999, had taken over the heroin trade and engaged in kidnappings of Serbs and others. The most damaging claim was that some Serb prisoners-of-war had been taken to Albania, had their organs removed for export, and were then murdered. It is claimed that Albanians were also kidnapped to settle old scores. Thaçi rejects the claims as "lies." Nevertheless, the EU announced plans to set up in 2016 an international tribunal in The Hague focusing exclusively on crimes believed to have been committed by Kosovo's Albanian rebels during the war against ethnic minorities and political opponents. The tribunal would be part of the Kosovo judicial system but would have international judges and be housed in a former Europol building. The issue is extremely sensitive in Kosovo since many former KLA fighters occupy prominent posts in the government and are seen as heroes; witnesses against them may feel intimidated in Kosovo.

Separate charges of organ trafficking were the focus of a 2010 trial in Prishtina against seven men, including Israeli, Turkish, and Kosovar citizens, who lured poor people from eastern Europe to remove their organs and sell them for up to $200,000 to patients around the world, often bilking the victims of their promised reward of up to $26,000. A US prosecutor, John Clint Williamson, was hired to investigate the charges, and a panel of American, Polish, and Kosovar judges was created to try seven additional defendants, including a senior official in the Health Ministry. In May 2013 five Kosovars, including a urologist and anesthesiologist, were found guilty of organ trafficking and sentenced to 3 to 8 years in prison.

Allegations against Thaçi had been investigated before and were found to be baseless. However, they continue to haunt Kosovo. Doubts remained. KFOR documents from about 2004 had pointed to Thaçi as one of the three main organized criminals in the region. The information had been kept secret in the interest of international stability. The charges have shaken the country and damaged his authority, both at home and abroad. They are a test of the young country's legal institutions and rule of law. They are bound to hamper Kosovo's efforts to enter the EU. One scholar at a think-tank, Kosovar Stability Initiative, said, "It was bad before. Now it is worse. Kosovo can't afford this."

Corruption discourages foreign investment. It has inspired a new kind of business school, the American University in Kosovo (AUK), founded in 2003 in the hilly eastern outskirts of Prishtina, to produce graduates imbued with the university's honor code: Each student publicly vows not to "cheat, steal or plagiarize" and to "show respect to all."

Because of the many weapons in the hands of civilians, law enforcement inefficiencies, and widespread devastation following the Kosovo war, both revenge killings and ethnic violence surged significantly. The number of reported murders rose 80% in 2001. Reported arsons rose 140%. The number of reported serious crimes resembles more the patterns of other European cities.

Police action has improved greatly. By 2008, recorded murder rates had declined steadily, falling by 75% since 2003 to under

Kosovo

3 per 100,000 people. This is a figure comparable to that of Switzerland, Ireland, or Finland. Landmines laid by both the Serbs and KLA during the Kosovo war, as well as unexploded NATO ordnance, remain a problem.

CULTURE

Because of its history and geography, the culture of Kosovo represents a blend of different cultural spheres especially of the Western and Eastern cultures. The society of Kosovo has undergone considerable changes over the past centuries, especially during its existence within Yugoslavia, one of the most notable being the increasing level of secularity. The national identity evolves more upon the language and culture, than the religion.

The architecture that can be seen in Kosovo dates back to the Neolithic period including the Copper, Bronze and Iron Ages, Antiquity and the Medieval period. It reflects the influence of different civilizations and religions, evidenced by the structures that have survived to this day. The monasteries and churches from the 14th century are the Serbian Orthodox legacy. Architectural heritage from the Ottoman period includes mosques and hammams (Turkish baths) from the 15th, 16th, and 17th centuries. Historical architectural structures of interest also include kullas (tower houses) from the 18th and 19th centuries as well as a number of bridges, urban centers, and fortresses.

The literature of Kosovo is written in Albanian, Serbian, Bosnian, and Turkish. During the Ottoman rule, when Kosovo was a part of the broader Ottoman literary culture, it produced several prominent writers (Pjetër Bogdani, Pristinaşi Mesihi, Prizrenli Suzi Çelebi, Aşık Çelebi, Tahir Efendi Jakova). However, the Ottoman authorities banned the written use of the Albanian language. This policy was further continued during the Serb rule, from 1912 until the outbreak of World War II.

Albanian literature in Kosovo was set off by poet Esad Mekuli (1916–1993), who founded the literary periodical *Jeta e Re* in 1949. The novelist Adem Demaçi, who spent twenty-eight years as a political prisoner of the Yugoslav government, also played an important role in the life of the periodical. *Jeta e Re* was later published as a book. Demaçi also helped publishing of the successful collections of poetry *Njifyell ndër male*, 1953 (A Flute in the Mountains), and *Kânga e vërrinit*, 1954 (Song of the Lowland Pastures) by Martin Camaj who became a renowned Albanian folklorist, linguist, poet, and writer.

In 1974, when more freedom and equality were given to Kosovo Albanians by the Yugoslav constitution, the literature bloomed in Kosovo in the following decade. The leading prose writers were Anton Pashku, Rexhep Qosja, Nazmi Rrahmani and Teki Dervishi. Inventive and experimental poetry has flourished in the works of Din Mehmeti, Besim Kokshi, Azem Shkreli, Rrahman Dedaj, Ali Podrimja, Eqrem Basha, and Sabri Hamiti.

Contemporary culture, due to the fact that Albanians make up the majority of Kosovo's population, tends to be Albanian with minor variations.

CURRENT ISSUES

The July 2010 decision by the highest UN court confirmed that Kosovo's declaration of independence did not violate international law. In April 2013 Kosovo signed the historic Brussels Agreement with Serbia recognizing Kosovo's authority over the entire land. In January 2014 Kosovo began talks on an EU Stabilization and Association Agreement, an important step toward membership. Nevertheless, UN and EU membership remains a distant dream.

In 2016, Kosovo was accepted into the European soccer federation UEFA (against Serbia's objections) and then into the worldwide association FIFA. This allowed it to participate in the 2018 soccer World Cup under its own name and colors. It was less successful in trying to gain membership in UNESCO, the UN cultural agency, where it fell three votes short of the required two-thirds majority among member states. UNESCO membership would have been an important step toward international recognition. A hugely symbolic consolation came at the 2016 Olympic Games in Rio de Janeiro, where Kosovo was allowed to compete for the first time. Majlinda Kelmendi made history by winning the country's first Olympic gold medal (in judo).

Kosovo remains at the mercy of its two main ethnic groups and their political leaders. An agreement between Serbia and Kosovo regulating energy and telecommunications and the disputed Mitrovica Bridge led to outbursts in the parliament, where the opposition opened up several tear-gas canisters and used whistles to protest what they see as giving too much power and influence to ethnic Serbs within Kosovo. Police investigated the disturbances, and a new security body scanner had to be purchased after this unparliamentary event. Kosovo's constitutional court took up the issue to determine whether the agreement violated the constitution.

A similarly heated confrontation occurred when the government attempted to pass a border demarcation agreement with Montenegro, a precondition to joining the EU. The opposition decried the proposal as tantamount to losing some 8,200 hectares (32 square miles) of Kosovo territory, as compared to the 1974 internal borders within Yugoslavia. Both governments and the US insisted that there were virtually no differences. In the end, the ferocity of the protests in and outside the parliament had as much to do with the general dissatisfaction with the government as it did with the territorial pride. The two presidents were engaged in talks about a partition and land swaps: Serbia would take the north of Kosovo in exchange for giving up part of the Preševo Valley, where 60,000 ethnic Albanians live. The United States supported that.

During the talks in November 2020, then President Hashim Thaçi, a former top KLA leader, was indicted for war crimes by the Kosovo Specialist Chambers. This is a newly established body in The Hague, part of Kosovo's judicial system that operates under Kosovo law. Thaçi was replaced by Vjosa Osmani.

High unemployment, especially among the youth (60% among 15 to 24-year-olds) and the overall perception of corruption in politics added much heat to the confrontation, quite unlike a similar border demarcation with Macedonia in 2008. (In a 2016 survey by Transparency International, 65% of Kosovars named corruption as one of their country's three biggest problems.) The conflict makes any future border agreement with Serbia difficult. In the end, the government postponed any decision.

One effect of the crisis was that the EU quickly decided to scupper the much-anticipated waiving of visa requirements for citizens of Kosovo, only a few months after promising it. Kosovars, including Serbs and other minorities living within the country, were the only people in the Balkans who did not enjoy visa-free travel in the European Union. In 2016, this finally seemed about to change, when the EU recognized Kosovo's improved border controls, introduction of biometric passports, and readiness to accept back its citizens rejected for asylum in the EU. The change would have reduced the incentives to enter the EU illegally (thus undercutting well-developed smuggling networks) and provided a safety valve against the frustration of the unemployed youth. Even if eventually implemented, it will generate new security concerns, as the number of supporters of violent jihad is growing in Kosovo.

With its violent past, criminal networks, and poor control over weapons in the country, Kosovo must be on watch against the growing radicalization of its youth in this largely secular country. The influx of charities and other NGOs from the gulf countries has introduced a more radical strain of Islam into the country. By mid-2015 it boasted the highest per-capita number of jihadi recruits in any European country—some 232, or 125 per 1 million citizens. In 2015, the authorities cut off access to a reservoir that supplies half of the city of Prishtina, leaving tens of thousands of people without water. The closing was in response to a threat that ISIS members might poison the major water supply. Five men with links to ISIS were arrested and charged with terrorism.

It will take years of hard work to qualify for EU membership. Five EU member states—Spain, Cyprus, Romania, Greece, and Slovakia—still do not even recognize Kosovo. But it is Kosovo's best chance because the EU links Serbia's and Kosovo's chances of EU accession to reconciliation between them. They have to sort out their relations first. An important element of this process could be the 2013 Brussels agreement between them that stipulated, among other things, that "neither side will block, or encourage others to block, the other side's progress in their respective EU paths."

Obstacles abound. Mutual distrust remains high, and conflict may flare up at a slightest provocation. That is unfortunate, since some signs of progress had been visible. For example, both countries reached an agreement paving the way to Kosovo receiving an international calling code, +383, separate from Serbia's +381. And yet this part of the Balkans remains a tinder box. When Albania's prime minister Edi Rama declared that the lack of progress in accession of western Balkans to the European Union may result in "a little union" of Albanians, former Kosovo president Hashim Thaçi added on April 19, 2017, that "all Albanians in the region will live in a single country in order to proceed further with the integration into the European family."

Fears of renewed ethnic strife and a Balkan-wide war that such a vision of Greater Albania would entail sparked an international outcry, starting with Serbia. Thaçi remained interested in that idea, and the major successful parties of the June 2017 elections, Vetevendosje and Ramush Haradinaj's AAK, are supportive.

Serbia can count on Russia's continued support in blocking Kosovo's attempts to join the UN. Grateful, in 2011 Kosovo Serbs declared Vladimir Putin an "honorary citizen of Kosovo." A leader of the Democratic Party of Serbia stated in 2015, "Crimea is Russia and Kosovo is Serbia." On the other hand, at that time Kosovars found a powerful ally in ex-German chancellor Angela Merkel. She said that Serbia has two options: It can either join the EU with Kosovo, or not join the EU without Kosovo.

Just days before Kosovars celebrated the 10th anniversary of their independence on February 17, 2018, a rare moderate proponent of ethnic coexistence, Oliver Ivanović, was murdered in the Serb section of Mitrovica. Tension is always present.

The left-wing Self-Determination Movement, led by Prime Minister Albin Kurti, won the February 2021 parliamentary elections. The next parliamentary elections will be held in Kosovo no later than 2025, if the full four year term of the incumbent Assembly is completed.

Republic of North Macedonia (Република Северна Македонија; Republika e Maqedonisë së Veriut)

View of Skopje, Church of St. Kliment

Area: 9,928 sq. mi. (25,713 sq. km).

Population: 1,836,713 (2021 census); 1,820,000 (2023 estimate)

Capital City: Skopje, (pop. 526,502 city; 488,103 urban; 607,007 metro). (2021)

Climate: Mediterranean in the south and mild, temperate continental in the north. The temperatures recorded throughout the year range from −4 °F (−20 °C) in winter, to 104 °F (40 °C) in summer. The average annual temperature is 53 °F (11.5 °C), whereas the plains experience higher temperatures, 59 °F (15 °C). The warmest month is July, which has an average temperature of 72 °F (22.2 °C) and the coldest is January, with an average temperature of 33 °F (0.3 °C).

Neighboring Countries: Albania (west); Greece (south); Bulgaria (east); Kosovo (north); Serbia (north).

Official Languages: Macedonian, Albanian.

Official Regional Languages: Turkish, Romani, Serbian, Bosnian, Aromanian.

Ethnic Background: 58.4% Macedonians, 24.3% Albanians, 3.9% Turks, 2.5% Roma, 1.3% Serbs, 0.9% Bosniaks, 0.5% Aromanians, 1.0% Other, 7.2% undeclared. (2021)

Religion: 60.4% Christianity (46.1% Orthodoxy, 14.3% Other Christian), 32.2% Islam, 0.1% Other, 0.1% No religion, 7.2% undeclared. (2021)

Form of Government: Unitary parliamentary republic.

Chief of State: Talat Xhaferi, President (since January 28, 2024).

Head of Government: Dimitar Kovačevski, Prime Minister (since January 2022).

National Flag: It depicts a stylized rising yellow sun on a red field, with eight broadening rays streaming forth from the center to the edges of the field. The flag was officially adopted in 1995. Its contemporary "golden sun" design is inspired by the national coat of arms of the country and represents "the new sun of liberty" referred to in the Macedonian national anthem *Denes nad Makedonija* (Today Over Macedonia). Nevertheless, the use of the sun emblem on the Macedonian flag represents the country's ancient heritage. In the art of the classical period, it was commonly included in depictions of the gods. It was also found in a golden box in a Macedonian tomb. The box held human ashes, which are believed to belong to a member of Macedonia's ruling family slightly before the reign of Alexander the Great. The sun has been a symbol of Macedonia ever since, although political concerns have prevented the modern Macedonian flag from depicting a sun of the same style as the ones found in ancient art.

Red and yellow, along with black and gold, have always been considered the traditional colors representing Macedonia.

Public Holidays: August 2 (Republic Day), September 8 (Independence Day).

Currency: Macedonian Denar (MKD).

Main Exports: Iron and steel, clothing and accessories, and food products.

Main Imports: Machinery, petroleum, and iron and steel.

Main Trading Partners: Germany (45.1% of exports and 8.6% of imports), Greece (3.9% of exports and 11.2% of imports), Serbia (4.6% of exports and 6.2% of imports), Italy (3.7% of exports and 3.8% of imports), Bulgaria (5.0% of export), Kosovo (4.6% of exports), Hungary (3.1% of exports), UK (15.8% of imports), China (7.8% of imports), Türkiye (6.3% of imports). (2022)

When one first hears the word "Macedonia," one's imagination flies back to the

550

4th century BC, when Alexander the Great ruled the world from this starkly beautiful mountainous region. Modern North Macedonia has little, if anything, to do with that particular past, however. The only re-Hellenized part of Alexander's home kingdom is to be found across the border in Greece, whose northernmost province also bears the name "Macedonia." North Macedonians in the Republic of North Macedonia formed the southern tier of unified Yugoslavia.

In September 1991 they became the only citizens of that collapsed state who were able to gain their independence peacefully. The North Macedonians overwhelmingly voted "yes" in a referendum on independence. They were also the first people in the world to establish "preventive peacekeeping," whereby they persuaded the United Nations to establish a stabilizing presence before the outbreak of ethnic violence. This is a small, multiethnic country that is determined to maintain its self-rule without the bloodshed that has stained the former Yugoslav republics to the north.

Macedonia is located in the southwestern Balkans. The valley of the Vardar River, commonly referred to as the Vardar Plain, dominates the center of the republic. This lowland area is the only place in the Balkans where the mountains can be traversed both north-south and east-west.

The Vardar River begins in the northwestern part of the republic and flows north and east until it reaches Skopje, the capital that was rebuilt after a devastating earthquake destroyed most of it in 1963. It continues southeastward down through North Macedonia, hemmed in by mountains to the west and east, then crosses into Greece. At the Greek border, it becomes the Axios River. Flowing through Greek Macedonia, it flows into the Gulf of Salonica. This provides North Macedonia with a natural outlet toward the south, although this is dependent on the status of relations with Greece. This passage was closed between February 1994 and October 1995 as a result of a Greece embargo instituted against North Macedonia in an attempt to force it to change its name.

The east-west route connects the Albanian port of Durrës with Bulgaria in the east. Albania's long isolation means that the western route has been little used in recent times.

A chain of mountains (really a series of ridges) running in a southwest-northeast direction dominates the western part of North Macedonia. Fairly wide valleys are located between the ridges. A second chain of mountains, the Šar, runs westeast along the border with Serbia. In the center, the Crna Gora (Black Mountains) reach down into North Macedonia from Serbia, stopping just north of Skopje. Another mountain, the Osogovske Planini (Osogovo Mountain Chain), marks most of the border with Bulgaria.

Ethnic North Macedonian speakers represent 64.18% of the total population. North Macedonian belongs to the family of South Slavic languages. Ethnic Albanians, the largest minority, make up 25.17% of the total. Ethnic Albanians live mainly in the western part of the republic. Other minorities include Turks (4%), Romani (Gypsies, 2.3%), Serbs (2%), and Vlachs (1%), who are related to Romanians and have their own language. Almost all Serbs live in the northeastern part, near the city of Kumanovo and villages on Mount Skopska Crna Gora, near the capital of Skopje.

HISTORY

The name "Macedonia" is an ancient one, going back to the 4th century BC and earlier. There was also a larger North Macedonia that was part of the Ottoman Empire from 1371 to 1912. It was an area of mixed populations. The Turks ruled non-Islamic peoples through their religious structures, and most North Macedonians are Orthodox Christians. Thus, the Turks made no differentiation between Greek- and Slavic-speaking individuals.

In 1913, this historic North Macedonia was divided up by Greece, Bulgaria, and Serbia after they had wrested it from the Ottoman Empire in the First Balkan War. Greece carried out a Hellenization of the territories it obtained. Therefore, North Macedonian speakers are almost exclusively found inside the Republic of North Macedonia. There are North Macedonian speaking minorities in western Bulgaria, which always treated North Macedonians as Bulgarians; in Greece, where an estimated 50,000 are not officially recognized; and in Albania and Serbia. North Macedonians tended to become amalgamated in the larger Bulgarian population. Serbia treated the North Macedonians as Serbs until World War II. During the war, North Macedonians fought with the Partisan Movement of the communist leader, Marshal Tito. After the war, he turned Yugoslavia into a federal republic, and the Socialist Republic of North Macedonia became one of the six constituent republics.

Independence

The failure of unified Yugoslavia to solve its economic problems led to a slow disintegration. North Macedonians never took the lead in this process, but like the Slovenians and Croatians, they supported abandonment of communist economic policies. In 1990, the legislature asserted North Macedonia's sovereignty, and elections resulted in the first noncommunist government.

By the beginning of 1991, North Macedonians supported a major reformation of Yugoslavia, although they continued to favor some form of union. When Serbia and Montenegro reelected their communist leaders, the stage was set for a confrontation. It was the new Slovenian and Croatian leaders who made the strongest case for change. But it was the Serbian stonewalling that eventually convinced North Macedonians that they could not remain part of a Yugoslavia dominated by Serbia. In September 1991, therefore, North Macedonians followed the lead of Slovenia and Croatia and voted in a referendum for a "sovereign and independent" republic.

On October 3, 1991, Branko Kostić, Montenegrin representative to the Yugoslav collective presidency, called a meeting in his role as vice president and proposed declaring a state of emergency. Since the president, Stipe Mesić, was not present, and the Slovenian delegate was boycotting the meeting, Kostić got his resolution passed with the support of the three votes controlled by Serbia (Serbia, plus its two formerly autonomous regions of Vojvodina and Kosovo). As a result, the North Macedonian delegate to the presidency withdrew from subsequent meetings, and the North Macedonian Assembly condemned Kostić's actions as unconstitutional and invalid. The North Macedonian government then condemned the war against Croatia, declared its neutrality, called upon North Macedonian soldiers to return to North Macedonia, and requested the Yugoslavia People's Army to withdraw its local forces. Not wanting to drive North Macedonia into an alliance with Croatia, Belgrade agreed to have all of its troops out of North Macedonia by April 15, 1991. The North Macedonian delegates to the Yugoslav legislature also stopped attending parliamentary sessions in November.

In January 1992, the North Macedonian Assembly passed two amendments to the constitution demanded by the EC (now EU) as a price for recognition. The first stated that North Macedonia does not have any territorial claims against its neighbors. The second stated that North Macedonia will not interfere in the internal affairs of the neighboring sovereign countries. Other related actions included repealing the two sections of the constitution that provided for participation in federal organs, including the presidency, and recalling all North Macedonians in the diplomatic staff. In addition, the assembly approved the formation of a North Macedonian national army of 25,000–30,000 troops. International diplomatic recognition was slow in coming. That, too, is now an accomplished fact, although it required some concessions on the part of the North Macedonian government.

North Macedonia

Soldier on a Horse, Skopje

Photo: Marin Gavrilovski

There have always been serious concerns about a possible political destabilization caused by one or more of North Macedonia's neighbors trying to interfere in domestic politics. Those fears were brought once more to the fore in October 1995, when there was an attempt on ex-president Gligorov's life. A car bomb was set off at the side of the road just as his official limousine passed en route to his office. The driver was killed, and several bystanders were injured. Gligorov himself was hit in the head by a piece of shrapnel and had to be hospitalized. No group took credit for the attempt on the president's life. Speculation as to who was responsible includes Bulgarian extremists or North Macedonian nationalists who objected to concessions that he made to Greece relating to the flag and constitution.

POLITICAL SYSTEM

North Macedonia is a multiparty democracy with a presidential-parliamentary system of government. The most important political figure is the president of the government, referred to in most democracies as "prime minister." He must command a majority in parliament. The first free parliamentary elections took place in 1990.

The Presidency

The president is elected directly for a term of five years. If a candidate fails to win a majority of votes in the first round of elections, a runoff is held two weeks later between the top two candidates. To be valid, the turnout for this second round must be at least 50%. The position is largely, though not entirely, ceremonial. He has the right to veto legislation, although parliament can repass the legislation over his veto. Perhaps his chief power is that, because he is elected by the entire nation, he can exercise a sort of national leadership.

Boris Trajkovski was president from December 1999 until February 2004, when he was killed in a tragic small-plane crash while flying in thick fog to an international investment conference in Mostar, Bosnia. He is widely credited with easing tensions and finding a compromise between the North Macedonian majority and Albanian minority, thereby preventing a serious outbreak of violence in 2001 from degenerating into a civil war. He fought off calls within his own party to take a tough line toward the Albanian rebels. The election of his successor was refreshingly free of nationalist rhetoric.

Under the constitution, a deceased president is replaced by the parliamentary speaker, who has to hold new elections within 40 days. Elected president in April 2004 was Prime Minister Branko Crvenkovski of the Social Democratic Union of North Macedonia (SDSM). As prime minister, he had advocated reconciliation, saying "a man who cannot forgive is not a man." In the second round, with a turnout of 53.7%, Crvenkovski captured 62.7% of the votes to 37.3% for Saško Kedev of the Internal North Macedonian Revolutionary Organization-Democratic Party for North Macedonian National Unity (VMRO-DPMNE). Kedev claimed fraud, but the OSCE judged the elections to have been "generally consistent with international standards." In his swearing-in ceremony, Crvenkovski vowed to press on with efforts to achieve reconciliation with North Macedonia's ethnic Albanian minority and to prevent any resumption of violence.

In April 2009, Gjorgje Ivanov of the conservative governing party VMRO-DPMNE was chosen as president—a man who had never before run for public office. In the second round, he received twice as many votes as his Social Democratic opponent, Ljubomir Frčkoski. The election did not spark the chaos and violence that was witnessed in the preceding year. Ivanov was a law professor at the University of Skopje. He pledged in his campaign not to bend to Greek pressure over the country's name: "I go to bed with North Macedonia in the evening and wake up with North Macedonia in the morning." He is known in the public as a sharp-tongued political commentator who had made a name by opposing the Ohrid Agreement and who is unpopular with ethnic Albanians. He was reelected in April 2014 with 55.3% of the votes.

Ivanov's decision to stop investigations of former prime minister Gruevski and

President Stevo Pendarovski

552

Prime Minister Zoran Zaev

55 other officials investigated for involvement in electoral fraud and a wiretapping scandal provoked an outburst of street protests throughout the country in April and May 2016. Nicknamed the "Colorful Revolution," the demonstrations were supported by several opposition parties and brought out thousands of protesters who demanded the resignation of Ivanov and the interim prime minister Dimitriev. The president maintained that the preemptive pardoning would serve "the state interests." The chief investigator observed wryly, "If the president intends to continue pardoning people who are charged, he will be very busy." Russia accused the west of fomenting the revolution.

Presidential elections were held in North Macedonia in 2019. President Gjorge Ivanov was constitutionally barred from seeking a third term in office, having previously been elected in 2009 and 2014. The first round of the elections was held on April 21, and three candidates were on the ballot: Stevo Pendarovski supported by the ruling coalition led by the Social Democratic Union of Macedonia, including the Democratic Union for Integration; Gordana Siljanovska-Davkova of the leading opposition party VMRO-DPMNE, and Blerim Reka, an independent candidate supported by Albanian opposition parties Alliance for Albanians and Besa Movement. In the first round Pendarovski received the most votes but not enough for an absolute majority. In the second round held on May 5, Pendarovski defeated Siljanovska-Davkova with 54% of the vote.

Next presidential elections are scheduled to be held in North Macedonia on April 24, 2024.

Parliament

Parliamentary elections occur every four years. North Macedonia has a 120-seat parliament (Sobranie), 85 of which are elected in single constituencies on the basis of the majority principle. The remaining 35 are selected by proportional representation. This latter system was instituted in 1994 as a concession to the smaller political parties.

Early parliamentary elections took place in June 2008 after Greece had prevented its entry into NATO because of the 17-year dispute over the country's name. In addition, the Democratic Party of Albanians had pulled out of the governing coalition when its demand was not met that the newly independent Kosovo be recognized. Prime Minister Nikola Gruevski gambled on a snap election and won a parliamentary majority in a landslide victory. The results were a reminder that North Macedonia remains a multiethnic country despite the power-sharing compromise that had prevented a civil war only a few years earlier. There was little voting across ethnic lines. The polling was marred by violence in the Albanian areas, where one man was killed and nine wounded in gun battles. OSCE monitors also commented that the poll did not fully meet international standards.

Fourteen parties contested the 2014 parliamentary elections. Emerging as the winner of the 2008, 2011, and April 2014 elections was the VMRO-DPMNE, which in 2014 won 43% of the votes and 61 seats (up 5). Nikola Gruevski, a former World Bank economist, amateur boxer, and stage actor, remained prime minister.

Despite the fact that Gruevski had a parliamentary majority and could not be "held hostage" by an Albanian party, his VMRO-DPMNE has in the past formed a governing coalition with the Union for Democratic Integration (DUI). Led by Ali Ahmeti and the strongest party among ethnic Albanians, it garnered 13.7% of the votes (up from 12.8%) and 19 seats (up 4). A former factory worker who lived in Swiss exile, Ahmeti enjoys hero status among Albanians for playing a crucial role in the peace process and keeping a lid on tensions in conflict areas. He was hurt by allegations, which he vehemently denied, that he had been an informer for Serbian intelligence.

DUI's participation in the previous government had shown just how much North Macedonian politics had changed. More than half of the DUI legislators are former members of the Albanian National Liberation Army. The defense minister, Talat Xhaferi, is a former Albanian rebel fighter. Some North Macedonian veterans were outraged at his appointment. However, unlike Kosovo Albanians, who declared

**Former prime minister
Nikola Gruevski**

outright independence and their own state, Ahmeti's followers fought for their Albanian rights within the North Macedonian state to be recognized and respected.

The other major Albanian party, the Democratic Party of Albanians (DPA), again did poorly, winning only 5.9% of the votes (down from 8.5%) and 7 seats (down from 11). It is in the opposition.

The main opposition party was the center-left SDSM, led by Zoran Zaev. In the past, it was the largest grouping under an umbrella called Sun-Coalition for Europe. SDSM won 25.3% of the votes and 34 seats (down 8). It is the successor party to the League of Communists of North Macedonia and was the ruling party for the first six years after independence.

One reason for parties' desire to be included in the government is that being out of power means to be without patronage. For example, within days of Gruevski's taking office in July 2006, 544 managers and top officials in state companies were sacked or sidelined, and hundreds of civil servants were replaced by VMRO or DPA loyalists.

One of the government's priorities was the prosecution of ex-government ministers for corruption. Usually acts of corruption are prosecuted only when the opposition wins an election. It promptly charged or arrested the former economics minister, the head of the state health care fund, and the directors of a state-owned printing company. Others were put under investigation. For the first time in North Macedonia's history, a member of the government structure was charged by his own party. State Secretary for Defense Ljupčo Popovski was accused of accepting bribes worth more than €20,000. The fact that only the Ministry of Economy can issue trade licenses and permits keeps the door to bribery open.

The Berlin-based Transparency International estimated that corruption scares

North Macedonia

off many foreign investors. A 2004 report by the European Commission concluded, "The high level of corruption and the mistrust towards institutions it generates remain major deterrent facts to growth and investment, and beyond this, to the success of many reforms which have been initiated to accelerate the transition of the country towards a modern democracy and economy."

A major governmental crisis developed in 2015 after the leader of the Social Democrats, Zoran Zaev, who was charged with "conspiring with a foreign intelligence service to topple the government," demonstrated that then-prime minister Gruevski was involved in massive wiretapping of some 20,000 opposition figures, journalists, clerics, activists, some government officials, and foreign diplomats. This way, the government was able to influence elections, courts, and the media. In May, tens of thousands of protestors took to the streets, demanding that the increasingly conservative and even authoritarian Gruevski resign. By June, with much assistance from the EU, North Macedonia's major parties reached the "Pržino Agreement" to hold early elections, preceded by Gruevski's resignation. He did resign in January 2016, but North Macedonia's Constitutional Court rejected the plans for elections in June due to numerous continuing irregularities. The investigation conducted by courageous prosecutor Katica Janeva faces many obstacles, including witness intimidation and murder. The biggest blow was the preemptive pardon in April 2016 by President Gjorge Ivanov of dozens of suspects investigated by Janeva.

Finally, after delays, the elections took place in December 2016. The VMRO-DPMNE coalition came in first with 39.4% of votes and 51 seats (a loss of 10), but the Social Democrats did very well, receiving 37.9% and 49 seats, a large increase of 15 seats. With the minimum difference between the two, it was not clear for several months which party would form the government. Further complicating the situation was the refusal by President Gjorge Ivanov to give the mandate to form a government to Zoran Zaev and his Social Democrats because they were allied with ethnic Albanian parties. Ivanov insisted that the ethnic Albanians' demands to establish Albanian as the country's official second language would destroy North Macedonia's independence and unitary status because of Albania's meddling. When the coalition elected an ethnic Albanian, Talat Xhaferi, as the new parliament speaker, tempers boiled over, and on April 27, 2017, a group of some 200 people stormed the parliament building and physically attacked the parliamentarians. Among the 77 injured was Zaev, who

was hit on the head and had to be escorted out with bloodied face and clothes. The attackers waived North Macedonian flags, and some wore ski masks; they chanted demands for new elections. The EU threatened sanctions if the president did not stop blocking the new government, but Ivanov refused to even meet with EU enlargement commissioner Johannes Hahn. Ivanov's supporters from the VMRO-DPMNE Party organized daily protests, including thousands of people carrying cardboard shields painted in national colors to symbolize the defense of their national identity. The party was facing a loss of power after 10 years in government.

In the end, on May 31, 2017, Zoran Zaev became the prime minister, and his SDSM party entered into a coalition with two ethnic Albanian parties, the Democratic Union for Integration (DUI) and the Alliance for Albanians. Besa (Oath), the second-largest ethnic Albanian party, did not join the cabinet but promised to support it. There was no doubt that rebuilding a semblance of normalcy in North Macedonian politics would take a long time.

Early parliamentary elections were held in North Macedonia on July 15, 2020. It was originally scheduled for November 2020, but Prime Minister Zoran Zaev called early elections because, in October 2019, the European Council failed to come to an agreement on starting talks with North Macedonia on joining the European Union. The election date was set for April 12, but it was postponed until July due to the COVID-19 pandemic in North Macedonia.

The election resulted in an extremely divided parliament, with the pro-EU SDSM-led coalition winning a plurality of votes and seats. The nationalist conservative VMRO-DPMNE-led coalition came as a close second, lagging by only two seats and less than 1.5% of the vote. Large gains were also seen by the BDI and the Alliance for Albanians–Alternativa coalition, both representing the ethnic Albanian minority. The Left, a socialist party, entered parliament for the first time with two seats, and the Democratic Party of Albanians lost one seat. Turnout was down roughly 15% mainly due to the COVID-19 pandemic.

A coalition had to be formed as neither of the two largest parties hold enough seats to form a majority on their own, and mathematically, any coalition will have to include at least one of the two largest Albanian minority parties.

On August 18, the SDSM and BDI announced that they had reached an agreement on a coalition government as well as a compromise on the issue of an ethnic Albanian Prime Minister. Under the deal, SDSM leader Zoran Zaev will be installed as Prime Minister, and will serve in that

position until no later than 100 days from the next parliamentary elections (Rotation government). At that time, the BDI will propose an ethnic Albanian candidate for Prime Minister, and if both parties agree on the candidate, that candidate will serve out the remaining term until the elections. The coalition of the SDSM-aligned parties, BDI, and the Democratic Party of Albanians was approved by the parliament in a 62–51 vote.

While in service as a prime minister, Zoran Zaev signed the Prespa agreement with Greece, resolving a long-standing dispute over the country's name, which led to the accession protocol of North Macedonia to NATO. He was also one of the initiators of Mini Schengen Zone (Open Balkan Initiative), an economic zone of the Western Balkans countries intended to guarantee "four freedoms." Zaev agreed with the major opposition party VMRO-DPMNE on early elections due to halted EU talks and resigned in January 2020, but after the election, he began his second term as the head of the government. He formally stepped down again after the local elections in October 2021, and was succeeded by Dimitar Kovačevski in January 2022.

Dimitar Kovačevski, a politician and economist, served as prime minister of North Macedonia from January 2022 to January 2024. He previously served as deputy finance minister from 2020 until his appointment as prime minister.

A member and currently president of the Social Democratic Union of Macedonia, Kovačevski previously served as deputy finance minister from 2020 until his appointment as prime minister in 2022 after the resignation of Zoran Zaev.

On January 25, 2024, Kovačevski resigned. Starting from January 28, 100 days before the parliamentary elections scheduled for May 8, 2024, a technical government by the Pržino Agreement will lead the country.

On 25 January 2024, Xhaferi resigned from the post of the President of the Assembly, following the resignations of the government of Dimitar Kovačevski, in preparation to be elected as the president of a technical government which, by the Pržino Agreement, will lead the country in the 100 days before the parliamentary elections scheduled for 8 May. The technical government was organized by Talat Xhaferi (or Talat Džaferi) who served as the President of the Assembly of the Republic of North Macedonia from 2017 to 2024. He has previously served as Minister of Defense from 2013 to 2014.

After the resignation of the government of Dimitar Kovačevski, Talat Xhaferi (or Talat Džaferi) resigned from the position of Speaker of the Assembly on January 25, 2024, in preparation for being elected

North Macedonia

Prime Minister Talat Xhaferi
Source: *Wikipedia*

as the President of the technical government that, according to the Pržino Agreement, will lead the country. in the 100 days before the parliamentary elections scheduled for May 8. 2024. Talat Xhaferi was previously the Minister of Defense from 2013 to 2014, and the President of the Assembly of the Republic of North Macedonia from 2017 to 2024.

Ethnic Politics

North Macedonian nationhood has been contested throughout history. National identity is therefore weak and insecure. Regional identity tends to be stronger, and many North Macedonians identify with their neighbors, such as Serbs to the north, Albanians to the north and west, and Bulgarians to the east. The government has a national strategy to strengthen a sense of North Macedonian identity, but it runs into resistance from Greece and domestic Albanians.

A major issue faced by any government is the ethnically mixed nature of North Macedonian society. As North Macedonia moved to open up its political system following the collapse of communism, nationalist-minded Albanians began making increased demands for greater political and cultural autonomy. One aspect is the question of whether it should be possible to display the Albanian flag on government buildings where ethnic Albanians constitute the majority of the population and have taken control of the municipal government. The previous administration had made display of the Albanian flag illegal in 1997 by passing a law regulating the public display of national symbols. When the mayor of the city of Gostivar installed

an Albanian flag over the city hall in July 1997, the national government responded by dispatching police forces to the city with orders to remove the flag. The resulting clashes between ethnic Albanians and police left 3 dead and at least 50 persons injured. Approximately 320 persons were arrested. Today one sees only Albanian flags in predominantly Albanian areas.

Former prime minister Georgievski's government, which supported improved interethnic relations, pushed through an amnesty law in 1999. Ex-president Gligorov vetoed the law, but it was then passed over his veto one month later. This ended the jail terms of some 900 persons who had been convicted for violating the 1997 law on the public display of national symbols. Among those freed were the mayors of Gostivar and Tetovo.

Another pressing issue for ethnic Albanians is the protection of their language and the lack of possibilities for higher education in Albanian. They regard their ability to use their language in official dealings and in education as an important part of their identity as a nation. However, given the diversity of the country's population, North Macedonians believe there has to be one official language—Macedonian—to prevent the country from splitting apart. The government established Albanian-language classes at the pedagogic faculty of Skopje University, but for several years it rejected demands by ethnic Albanians for their own university. In response, Albanians set up their own Albanian-language university at Tetovo, a majority-ethnic-Albanian city of a quarter million inhabitants. Although the only available facility was a cluster of shabby, reinforced-concrete apartment buildings, this new university quickly grew until it had 300 faculty and 6,000 students.

The government refused to give the university official accreditation, arguing that an Albanian-language university would stoke nationalist sentiments among ethnic Albanians. But under intense international pressure, ex-prime minister Georgievski's government grudgingly endorsed creation of an Albanian-language university. The war in Kosovo and disagreements within the government coalition put this matter on further hold until 2000, when the right to such a university was granted. Tetovo's Albanian-language university officially opened in 2001, although in 2002 it was still not completely legal. There is another private university in Tetovo, Southeastern European University, which offers instruction in Macedonian, Albanian, and English. The University of Skopje gives Albanian-language courses in the education school. Instruction in North Macedonian is offered at two universities: the University St. Cyril and Methódius (named after

the founders of the pre-Cyrillic Glagolitic alphabet, who once resided in North Macedonia) in Skopje and the University St. Climent Ohridski in Bitola.

In February 2001 ethnic violence broke out for a half-year that was so serious that only NATO intervention and important constitutional changes could save the country from civil war. An Albanian rebel group calling itself the National Liberation Army (NLA) attacked police stations and other government facilities controlled by Slavs. They subsequently seized villages in the mountains and expanded their military action to the outskirts of the capital. They demanded more rights for Albanian speakers, but the North Macedonian government (which contained members of the Albanian minority) regarded the actions as a scarcely disguised attempt to separate Albanian areas and unite them with neighboring Kosovo, from where most of the rebels' weapons came. NATO and EU countries feared that the warfare could get out of control, draw peacekeepers out of Kosovo, and perhaps even spill over North Macedonian borders and destabilize the entire region. Therefore, they became intensely involved with the settlement of the crisis by bringing both sides to the negotiation table. The result was the 2001 Framework Agreement, known as the Ohrid Accords, discussed below.

In Operation Essential Harvest, a NATO force of 4,500 collected more than 4,000 rebel weapons, while the North Macedonian parliament approved of constitutional changes designed to meet the Albanian demands for greater civil rights, protection of their language, and greater representation in North Macedonia's government service, including the police. They agreed on a law for local self-government by devolving powers to municipalities. Very important was the promise of amnesty for rebels taken captive. It was hoped that this would sufficiently defuse the tensions so that North Macedonian police and refugees could return to the rebel heartland in the north and persuade fighters in the hills to come down and resume their civilian lives without fear of arrest. Not until March 2002 did that amnesty take place. To reward the country, the World Bank and EU organized a one-day pledge conference that produced €515 million in assistance to North Macedonia.

About 700 NATO troops remained in the country to supervise the peace plan. Many North Macedonians found the settlement too generous to the minority and tended to blame the troubles on NATO's gentle treatment of armed ethnic Albanians in Kosovo. The settlement did prevent a larger war, but it did not put an end to the tensions that had led to the conflict in the first place. Many ethnic Albanian villages

North Macedonia

and neighborhoods still remained off-limits to the police, and violent incidents were a daily occurrence and went unchallenged by the local police.

Ohrid Peace Accords

The DUI had achieved recognition in the western-brokered Ohrid Peace Accord, signed in 2001. It made Albanian an official language in areas where Albanians represent more than 20% of the population. Street signs in Skopje are in Albanian, as well as North Macedonian. Albanians were granted the status of full partners in the country, hitherto denied. Proportional employment of the ethnic Albanians in the administration was a key provision. All of these steps have meant that there is less interethnic hatred than in neighboring Kosovo. Most Albanians in North Macedonia want to prevent, not rekindle, violence.

The Ohrid Agreement did not bring complete stability to an insecure country. In September 2003 ethnic Albanian gunmen kidnapped a policeman. A police operation was launched to track down the perpetrators, resulting in the death of two ethnic Albanian guerrillas and the temporary exodus from some villages near the Kosovo border. The fighters were part of the Albanian National Army (AKSH), which talks of "Greater Albania" encompassing all ethnic Albanians. They spend most of their time, however, smuggling cigarettes. At the end of 2003 the government offered lottery prizes to persons who surrender guns to the authorities. An estimated 170,000 illegal weapons remain in private hands; only 900 were turned in.

The Ohrid Agreement was put to a test again in November 2004 when hard-liners among the Slav majority managed to have a referendum scheduled that would have prevented the granting of autonomy to the Albanian minority. It was in response to a government law redrawing municipal districts to make ethnic Albanians a dominant force in 16 out of 83 (reduced in number from 123) municipal districts. Especially controversial were provisions that widened Skopje's city limits to include several Albanian-dominated districts. This pushed the city's population to over 20% Albanian, thereby qualifying the capital as a bicommunal, bilingual city.

Envoys from the US and EU went to North Macedonia to campaign against the referendum, making it clear that rejecting the Ohrid Agreement would be a step back into the dangerous politics of ethnic conflict. The government pled with voters to boycott the polling. If 50% of eligible voters do not vote in a referendum, then any result is invalid. That is exactly what happened. Only 26% voted, so the constitutional changes to devolve power were

back on track. On November 10, 2004, three days after the failed referendum, politicians from all sides reassembled at Lake Ohrid to recommit themselves to the reconciliation process.

In May 2004 the government charged a former interior minister, Ljube Boškoski, with staging the killing of seven South Asian migrants two years earlier in a bizarre attempt to win for the government a free hand to deal harshly with the country's ethnic Albanian minority. He allegedly arranged for the seven to be smuggled from Bulgaria into North Macedonia and murdered. The crime scene was changed to make it seem as if they were armed Islamic militants heading for western Europe. In March 2005 he was indicted by the war-crimes tribunal in The Hague but was eventually acquitted. This was the first such indictment in North Macedonia.

In May 2015, governmental armed forces engaged in an "antiterrorist operation" killed 14 people in an Albanian neighborhood of the town of Kumanovo. The operation was aimed at an unspecified group "from a neighboring country," apparently militants from the former National Liberation Army of ethnic Albanians. Eight policemen also died. The event raised fears that the violence from 2001 might be reignited.

Foreign Relations

North Macedonia opted for independence because it believed that Serbia would dominate any federation with Croatia and Slovenia gone. Nevertheless,

it wants to maintain good economic relations with Serbia and all other neighboring countries. It also favors a common market among the former republics. North Macedonia has good relations with Bulgaria and Türkiye, fairly good relations with Albania, and increasingly good relations with Greece.

The European Union did not extend recognition to North Macedonia at the time it recognized Slovenia and Bosnia and Herzegovina. Greece, an EU member and North Macedonia's most important neighbor from an economic standpoint, objected to its use of the name "Macedonia" and to the 16-pointed star it had on its flag. Athens insisted that North Macedonia had to change its name before it could be recognized. It feared that an independent North Macedonia could exert some influence on its own citizens in Greek Macedonia and make territorial claims, even though North Macedonia had signed an agreement with Greece disavowing any such claims.

Greece finally dropped its objections to North Macedonia's admission to the United Nations in April 1993, provided it would agree to use the clumsy name "Former Yugoslav Republic of North Macedonia," or FYROM for short. On that basis, North Macedonia received general recognition and UN membership. It was also understood that North Macedonia's flag would not be flown at the United Nations. North Macedonians disliked the name FYROM.

When ex-president Trajkovski visited Washington in February 2002, he

Папата Јован Павле Втори ја прогласи Мајка Тереза за блажена

Со церемонија на плоштадот Свети Петар во Рим

Born in Skopje, Mother Teresa achieved sainthood.

requested that his country be called North Macedonia: "We are only struggling for our name." In his first foreign policy act in his second term, in November 2004, President Bush officially recognized the republic as Macedonia. The timing was not accidental. It was announced at the time of a referendum on the Ohrid Agreement and was intended to induce moderate Slav North Macedonians not to undo the reforms. The State Department called it a reward for the ethnic progress that has taken place. North Macedonians were delighted, and Greece's protests were more restrained than earlier.

Greece managed to keep the European Union, which used FYROM, from extending diplomatic recognition to North Macedonia until December 1993. The United States, which had sent 500 American troops to North Macedonia in July 1993 as part of a 1,000-troop United Nations presence, had refrained from recognizing North Macedonia for the same reason. The EU move allowed the United States to reverse itself and extend diplomatic recognition to North Macedonia in February 1994.

Greece's reaction was to announce an embargo on all imports and exports to North Macedonia, other than food and medicine. The EU attempted to get the trade blockade removed. When Athens refused, the EU brought Greece before the European Court of Justice. The embargo continued until October 1995. Greece agreed to lift the embargo after the North Macedonian parliament gave in to Greek demands and voted to change the flag and constitution. The new flag consists of an eight-ray golden sun on a red background.

Athens continued to assert that the name "Macedonia" applied only to its own northern region and that the former Yugoslav republic must find another name for itself. It made this issue a condition for North Macedonia's future EU membership. The UN mediated talks between the two states to resolve the disagreement. Greece proposed the name "Makedonija-Skopje," but the North Macedonians said no.

They even waved a red flag by naming Skopje's international airport after Alexander the Great. This act prompted Greece to postpone the country's entry into NATO in April 2009, even though more than 120 countries, including the US and Russia, had already accepted the name "Macedonia." In December 2011 the International Court of Justice in The Hague ruled that Greece was wrong in vetoing North Macedonia's bid to enter NATO in 2008 because of the name dispute. However, it refused to instruct Greece not to exercise such a veto in the future. The government was angered by being locked out from the Atlantic Alliance.

Athens proposed adding words like "upper" or "new" to the name, and it rejected a last-minute compromise of "Republic of North Macedonia (Skopje)." Greek prime minister Alexis Tsipras found it "not unreasonable" for the word "Macedonia" to be used in a compound name for the country. The North Macedonian government also did not object to a qualifier to be added. But emotions are high on this subject. Hundreds of thousands demonstrated in Greece against the very idea in February 2018.

Prime Minister Gruevski did not make things easier in July 2008, when he demanded Greek recognition of a Slavic North Macedonian ethnic minority in the officially homogeneous Greece. Despite these name problems, Greek-Macedonian relations improved after 1995, and their economic relations flourish. In particular, normal transportation and economic and diplomatic communication have been established.

In January 2019 an agreement was finally reached. In June 2018 the two governments agreed on the name "North Macedonia" and on North Macedonia's entry into NATO and the EU. North Macedonia agreed to "claim no relation to the ancient Greek civilization of Macedonia." It held a referendum in September to adopt the deal, but only 37% participated. A two-thirds majority in parliament accepted it in the face of violent street protests. The deal barely squeaked through the Greek parliament in January 2019. Despite the fact that 70% of Greeks opposed it, the agreement went into effect.

Greece has sought to expand its economic presence in North Macedonia since 1995. By 1998 it had become North Macedonia's third-largest trading partner. In August 2001 it sent 150 troops to North Macedonia as part of a NATO commitment to disarm ethnic Albanian rebels. It has become the biggest investor in North Macedonia. It owns the oil refinery there and has built a pipeline from Thessaloniki to Skopje. The country's largest bank, a leading supermarket chain, and a mobile-phone operator are all controlled by Greek interests.

North Macedonia signed a trade and cooperation treaty with the EU in 1996. In its June 2003 summit in Greece, the EU agreed that North Macedonia would be among the Balkan countries that should join. It already signed a Stabilization and Association Agreement (SAA) with the EU. Entry into the EU is an issue on which there is a consensus; 87% supported it in a 2004 poll. The official application for membership was the very last document President Trajkovski signed before his fatal flight in 2004. Finally, in 2005 the EU granted it the official status as a candidate

for entry. This news was greeted by other Balkan countries that hope to join. The EU provided €210 million ($300 million) in assistance from 2007 to 2009 but said North Macedonia must do more to control corruption. Although North Macedonia has EU candidate status, it still has no date for the start of accession negotiations. However, it is making some progress in the reforms the EU requires. From December 19, 2009, its citizens have visa-free travel to most EU states. The euro crisis temporarily made enlargement a low priority.

North Macedonia is a member of the Council of Europe and the OSCE. It is actively taking part in the Partnership for Peace program. It became a full member of NATO on March 27, 2020. Even prior to belong to the alliance, North Macedonia has sent 4% of its forces on NATO missions, almost 10 times the proportion Greece has provided.

Its active military force numbers 8,000 soldiers, including conscripts who serve six months. All but 1,200 are in the land forces. There are 800 in the army air force with 4 combat aircraft and 12 armed helicopters and 400 in a marine wing that operates five river-patrol craft. There is a total of 4,850 in the reserves and 7,600 paramilitary police (7,600 of whom are armed). North Macedonia deployed 40 support soldiers to Iraq under US command and has 165 troops in Afghanistan, including special forces and medical personnel. It provided a helicopter transport unit for EU peacekeepers in Bosnia and Herzegovina. It hopes to increase its foreign deployments.

North Macedonia found itself drawn more and more deeply into the problems caused by continuing Serbian repression in the neighboring Serbian province of Kosovo. North Macedonia's involvement actually began as early as July 1993, when the United Nations authorized a 1,000-troop UN force for North Macedonia in an attempt to keep North Macedonia from being drawn into the fighting then consuming much of the rest of ex-Yugoslavia. When the military campaign against the Kosovo Liberation Army, which Serb forces launched in early 1998, began to create large quantities of ethnic Albanian refugees and reports of Serb atrocities against ethnic Albanians, NATO countries intervened diplomatically and eventually got Serbia to agree to a cease-fire. It went into effect in October 1998. It was to be monitored by 2,000 civilian "verifiers" stationed throughout the province of Kosovo.

Concerned about the need to rescue the civilian monitors should renewed fighting break out in the province, NATO opened discussions with the North Macedonian government about the placement of a NATO rapid reaction force in North

North Macedonia

Macedonia. A French-led coalition of 1,800 European soldiers began arriving in North Macedonia in December 1998. Three months later, the mission of the rapid-reaction force had changed, and its numbers had grown to 12,000 soldiers.

When in 1999 Serbia launched a systematic campaign in Kosovo aimed at driving a significant portion of the ethnic Albanians out, North Macedonia became one of two primary destinations for these refugees. Belgrade added to the flood by arranging to have trainloads of refugees transported to the North Macedonian border. By 1999, approximately 400,000 Kosovo Albanians had found refuge in North Macedonia. Some were able to stay with relatives.

North Macedonia, not a rich country, was ill-equipped to handle such numbers of refugees. The UN and NATO forces originally sent there for other purposes were reassigned to help with this task. North Macedonia also began receiving assistance from various international aid organizations. The next couple of months proved to be an unusually difficult time for the country as it grappled with the large number of refugees. Slobodan Milošević's capitulation in June and the NATO takeover of Kosovo solved that problem. Most of the Kosovar refugees left the camps in North Macedonia and made their way back home.

The United Nations, NATO, and EU continued to maintain a significant presence in the country. North Macedonia got the former Yugoslav consulate in Paris when the diplomatic buildings were parceled out among the parts of the former federation in December 2001.

On March 31, 2003, the EU launched its first military mission, named Concordia, when it assumed from NATO the command over about 320 peacekeeping troops and 80 civilians in North Macedonia. They were drawn from all current or pending EU member states. A German admiral was in overall command, and a French general directed operations on the ground. The force used NATO plans and equipment. In an operation called Promixa, the EU provided about 200 police officers to work alongside the local police in areas affected by the 2001 conflict.

Despite its support for the UN's and NATO's Kosovo policy, North Macedonian Slavs were nervous about the negative impact an independent Kosovo could have on North Macedonia's own assertive Albanian minority. In 2017, Albania's prime minister Rama and Kosovo's former president Thaçi each suggested that, if their countries are not admitted to the EU, they may form their own "union." That hinted at a "Greater Albania," a nation-state combining all 6 million Albanians.

This, as well as Kosovo's independence in February 2008, could influence the dreams of some North Macedonian Albanians. Armed Kosovars who crossed North Macedonia's borders in an unsuccessful attempt to "liberate" the Albanian minority had strengthened these concerns in April 2001, although North Macedonian troops drove them out.

When North Macedonia officially recognized Kosovo in October 2008, Serbia expelled the North Macedonian ambassador in an attempt to punish it and 50 other countries for not supporting Serbia's position. Realizing several months later that it had painted itself into a disastrous diplomatic corner, Belgrade dropped its punitive measures.

ECONOMY

North Macedonia is overwhelmingly agricultural, with most people living in the Vardar River Valley or the valleys interspersed between ridges in the west. Because of the limited farmland available, many young workers live and work in other western countries. The chief crops are wheat, barley, corn, tobacco, cotton, rice, sunflowers, sugar beets, and a growing wine industry. Cattle raising is also important.

Almost all industry is concentrated in the Skopje area. Heavy industry consists of steel and chemicals. Light industry includes textiles, furniture, porcelain, and chinaware.

By 1996, 750 companies, accounting for 40% of GDP, had been privatized. Another 250 were privatized during 1996, while an additional 200 companies were privatized between 1997 and 1999. North Macedonia began privatizing its banks in 2000.

The economy declined by approximately 23% between 1990 and 1996. It bottomed out in 1996, but then it began growing in 1997 and has continued.

The country's economy sputtered as a result of the global economic downturn in 2008–2009, and it took some time for North Macedonia to work itself out of it. Exports of metals, textiles, and agricultural produce have slumped; unemployment has risen; and remittances have shrunk. Unable to borrow money abroad for a stimulus policy, the government was forced to cut public spending.

In 2014 growth was 3.8%, and inflation was –0.3%. On the flip side, the trade deficit widened. There was a corresponding increase in North Macedonia's current account deficit, which may be somewhat smaller than official statistics show. Not all remittances, estimated to be almost 5% of GDP, from North Macedonians working abroad get counted in the statistics. Total

foreign debt was 34% of GDP and rising in 2013, still among the lowest in the region. The budget deficit was about 3% of GDP.

In 2023, the Republic of North Macedonia was considered to be an upper middle-income country that has made great steps in reforming its economy over the last decade. More efforts are still needed to generate economic growth and improve living standards for all.

GDP growth is therefore likely to remain modest, at around 2 per cent in 2023, before accelerating to 3 per cent in 2024 on the back of an expected global recovery.

Unemployment Rate in Macedonia decreased to 12.80 percent in the third quarter of 2023 from 13.10 percent in the second quarter of 2023. However, more North Macedonians are working than the statistics would indicate. The "gray economy" is estimated to account for half of GDP. Many workers take jobs secretlyv in order to be classified officially as unemployed. That way they qualify for free state insurance.

Average net salaries were $641 (€880; MKD 36,134) per month in 2023. The country is tempting for investors. Greece is currently the fourth-largest source of foreign investment in the North Macedonian economy, accounting for about 10% of total inflows. Approximately 300 Greek companies employ about 20,000 North Macedonians. In 1999 the government allowed the Greek company Hellenic Petroleum to purchase Okta, North Macedonia's only state oil refinery. The country must import 30% of its energy needs. The country relies on the Greek port of Thessalonica for its oil. Two-thirds of landlocked North Macedonia's trade moves through that port. A pipeline connects the port with the Okta refinery.

Energy is in critically short supply since Bulgaria shut down two reactors at its Kozloduy nuclear power plant. North Macedonia produces only about three-fourths of its electricity needs and is compelled to purchase expensive imports from Germany, Austria, and the Czech Republic. North Macedonia has been the recipient of significant amounts of international aid as a result of the war in Kosovo and the ensuing refugee crisis.

North Macedonia attracts 350,000 foreign tourists each year, who account for about 3% of GDP. The industry employs 16,500 people, which is important for an economy desperate for jobs. Turks are on top, constituting 14% of all tourists.

It found the funds for a radical makeover of downtown Skopje, which visitors often found to be characterized by ugly concrete blocks and empty places. The center had been flattened by an earthquake in 1963. Fifteen new structures and an arch

Statue of Mother Teresa in front of her birthplace in Skopje

Photo courtesy: *Marin Gavrilovski*

archaeological sites more carefully after illicit plundering and selling. Poverty has inclined thieves to loot ancient Greek and Roman tombs, especially in search of jewelry.

Religion is the second defining influence. The majority of North Macedonians are Orthodox Christians. The church was part of the Serbian Orthodox Church until 1967, when it broke away and formed the Macedonian Orthodox Church. The Serbian Orthodox Church has never accepted the split, however, and does not recognize the Macedonian Orthodox Church. Approximately a quarter of the population is Muslim. Most of these speak Albanian as their first language.

To assert the country's ancient cultural roots, the government is taking steps, dubbed "antiquization" by the critics, that risk sacrificing the support the country has in the world. The project is nearing completion. North Macedonia named the main highway to Greece after Alexander the Great and the national sports stadium after Alexander's father, Philip. It also erected a huge 12-meter-high (40-foot) statue of Alexander on a 10-meter (34-foot) pedestal in the central square of Skopje. Its official name is Warrior on a Horse, but nobody is fooled by who the warrior is. Part of the grandiose Skopje 2014 urban facelift project, it is surrounded by additional warriors and a fountain, with music, roaring lions, and lights that change color. The square is full of other statues, including two saints, Cyril and Methodius, who invented the first version of the Cyrillic alphabet; Byzantine Emperor Justinian, who was born near Skopje; and 19th-century North Macedonian heroes. There is a new neoclassical archaeological museum, the parliament is topped by new glass cupolas, and a new foreign ministry is finished with a classical temple-style portico.

All of this enrages Greece, which charges that North Macedonia is appropriating key symbols of Greek identity. Many Albanians in North Macedonia also dislike what is being done. Therefore, a new square in the predominantly Albanian section of the city was built with a statue of the medieval Albanian hero Skanderbeg. A 30-meter statue of Mother Teresa went up on the main square. Even North Macedonians have mixed feelings, asking "How much does all this cost?"

In an unexpected way, North Macedonia became involved in the 2016 presidential elections in the United States. Much controversy surrounded the alleged use and misuse of "fake news" that each campaign accused its opponents of deploying. And yet there was a source of such news, and it was located in a small city of Veles, where scores of teenagers

of triumph shot up along the banks of the Vardar, and old buildings were renovated. Winding through the city are 220 retro red double-decker buses from China.

Not only is North Macedonia's glorious past but also a painful memory of the fate of the country's 8,000 Jews in World War II are commemorated. The country was occupied by Bulgaria, which protected its own Jewish population. On March 11, 1943, Bulgarian troops rounded up and deported 7,148 Jews to the Treblinka death camp. Only 12 lived to tell the story. Today only about 200 Jews remain in the country. The government could find few

Jews and their heirs to compensate for the crime, so it created a memorial fund that built a Holocaust Museum in the old Jewish quarter, a five-minute walk from the Alexander statue.

CULTURE

There is a separate North Macedonian culture. Although some North Macedonians deny it vehemently, aspects of it are similar to that of Bulgaria. There is a more middle-class and cosmopolitan culture associated with the city of Skopje. North Macedonia must guard its rich

North Macedonia

designed, copied, pasted, and—yes—faked a lot of news designed to be catchy and sensational—and to generate income from Google ads. Without much interest in American politics and even fewer scruples, the youngsters often provided a starting point for an ever-broadening circle of "news" that were replicated and soon cited as true. The town of 55,000 was the location of at least 100 pro-Trump websites, many of which peddled concocted stories about the pope's alleged endorsement of the Republican candidate or Hillary Clinton's criminal indictment. One of the entrepreneurs earned some $16,000 from his two websites in four months, in a country where the average monthly salary is less than $400. The resulting affluence provided luxury goods in the town whose best times may have been long gone.

CURRENT ISSUES

A major test that faced the government was the migrant crisis, placing North Macedonia on the frontline of attempts to control the wave of migrants streaming into Europe through Greece. After numerous clashes in 2015, in April 2016 North Macedonian police used tear gas and rubber bullets to disperse hundreds of migrants trying to break through a fence from the border camp of Idomeni in Greece. Tempers flared as the deal the EU reached with Türkiye came into force, and most of the 12,000 people faced likely removal back to Türkiye—or a prolonged stay in the camp. Earlier that year, North Macedonia started refusing entry to Afghan migrants that constitute about a third of all asylum seekers in Europe, declaring that Afghans are only economic migrants not eligible for asylum. This was a reaction to the refusal by Croatia to accept the Afghans for that very reason, who were then moved to Serbia and eventually back to North Macedonia.

The attempt to prevent further Afghan migrants from entering North Macedonia gathered some support from EU member states, some of whom sent their police forces to help it control its border. EU border agency Frontex began patrolling the border between North Macedonia and Greece to prevent migrants from entering.

As of 2023, for the first time since 2015, more refugees and migrants are using the Central Mediterranean route from North Africa to Italy than Balkan route to reach Western Europe.

It is fortunate that North Macedonia has not relapsed into all-out ethnic civil war, as many had predicted, and that fighting has not spilled over into neighboring countries. But periodic ethnic tensions, erupting again in 2015, remind one that North Macedonia still lacks complete stability, police control, and confidence between the two ethnic communities. It continues to need western intervention to keep them in check.

The ethnic divide remains as entrenched as ever, although North Macedonians elected governments that try hard to reduce tensions. The country's leaders vowed to continue the policy of ethnic reconciliation. In July 2004 the government adopted a long-delayed plan to grant more powers to local councils. This was the most difficult step in implementing the 2001 Ohrid Agreement. The move to give Albanians more control over municipalities in which they form majorities sparked violent clashes.

North Macedonia is still subject to private vendettas, politically motivated murders, and the illegal activities of rebel armies and smuggling rings.

The sorry spectacle of thugs storming the parliament and assaulting and bloodying its members shocked the nation. Ex-President Ivanov's stonewalling the attempts to create a functioning government left a bad taste in the mouths of supporters of democracy, especially among the representatives of the European Union, whose job is to evaluate whether North Macedonia is making progress toward meeting the standards of the EU.

North Macedonia's deep divisions and months of political wrangling marred by violence provided an unwelcome vignette of a country in trouble. Adding insult to injury was the US Republican congressman Dana Rohrabacher, chair of the Subcommittee on Europe, Eurasia, and Emerging Threats. Speaking to an Albanian TV channel, he declared that North Macedonia "is not a country" and should be divided between neighboring states because "they will never be able to live together in the future." He proposed that "Kosovars and Albanians from North Macedonia should be part of Kosovo and the rest of North Macedonia should be part of Bulgaria or any other country to which they believe they are related."

In its outraged response, the North Macedonian Foreign Ministry stated that he stokes "nationalistic rhetoric." Within two weeks, Rohrabacher publicly retracted these statements and declared that "Macedonia is a legitimate country with the right of self-determination and sanctity of borders." This time, he noted "the meaningful support that the North Macedonian military has provided over the past 20 years to the United States, to NATO, and to associated multilateral defense organizations, in peacekeeping and related refugee operations in Afghanistan, Iraq, Bosnia, and Kosovo." No doubt this is the image of North Macedonia its citizens would prefer to be able to project in the future.

EU membership talks were given fresh impetus in 2022 by the desire to provide a bulwark against greater Russian influence in the Balkans. Parliament approved a proposal to resolve the longstanding dispute with Bulgaria over history and language. This opened the way for EU accession talks. EC President Ursula von der Leyen called this "a big step on your path toward a European future, your future."

North Macedonia, Serbia, and Albania are the founding members of the Open Balkan Initiative (OBI). More details of the OBI are given in the chapter on the Republic of Serbia.

Republic of Albania (Republika e Shqipërisë)

Muslims at noon prayers in front of Et'hem Bey Mosque, central Tirana

Area: 11,100 sq. mi. (28,748 sq. km).
Population: 2,793,592 (2022 estimate)
Capital City: Tirana (Tiranë). (pop. 557,422).
Climate: Mediterranean, with wet winters and hot, dry summers on the coast; continental in the interior. It is characterized by four distinct seasons. The average monthly temperatures range from −1 °C (30 °F) during the winter to 21.8 °C (71.2 °F) in the summer.
Neighboring Countries: Montenegro (north); Kosovo (northeast); North Macedonia (east); Greece (south).
Official Language: Albanian.
Recognized Minority Languages: Greek, Macedonian, Aromanian.

Ethnic Background: 82.6% Albanian, 0.9% Greek, 16.5% other. (2011)
Religion: 59% Islam, 17% Christianity, 9% no religion, 15% undeclared (2020)
Form of Government: Unitary parliamentary republic
Chief of State: Bajram Begaj, President (since July 2022).
Head of Government: Edi Rama, Prime Minister (since 2021, 3rd Cabinet).
National Flag: It consists of a red field with a silhouetted black two-headed eagle in the center. The Albanians see the eagle as a symbol of the sovereignty of their state while the red color stands for bravery, strength, valor, and bloodshed. Like the symbol of the Byzantine Empire to which Albania once belonged, its black eagle is double-headed. It was taken from the coat of arms of the House of Kastrioti of the 15th century, accepted as one of the most ancient symbols used by Albanian leaders. The Albanian national flag has been in use since the country proclaimed its independence from Ottoman rule in 1912.
Public Holiday: November 28 (Independence Day).
Currency: Lek (ALL).
Main Exports: Textiles, leather footwear, footwear parts, construction materials and base metals, minerals, fuels, and electricity, food, beverages, and tobacco (2022).
Main Imports: Refined petroleum, machinery and equipment, cars, medicaments, electricity, and metals (2022).

Main Trading Partners: Italy (43.2% of exports and 21.7% of imports), Greece (5.2% of exports and 7.8% of imports), Kosovo (7.8% of exports), Türkiye (12.1% of imports), China (8.2% of imports), Germany (6.6% of exports and 6.2% of imports), Spain (4.8% of exports); (2022).

Albania is a small, largely mountainous land located along the eastern shores of the Adriatic Sea. Its forbidding mountains, combined with a language of mysterious origins totally different from any other in Europe, have served to isolate this small nation throughout much of its history. During the communist era, this isolation was strengthened by an eccentric and self-absorbed regime that had major difficulties getting along with other communist countries, let alone with the rest of the outside world. Its transition to democracy has been especially rough. In 1997 it fell into chaos closely resembling a Hobbesian state of nature, according to the country's justice minister. The future will reveal whether this starkly beautiful land with generous people will enjoy stability, democracy, prosperity, and community with the rest of Europe.

In spite of its small size, Albania has a widely varied climate, the major factor being the mountains. About one-seventh of its land area consists of a series of small plains running north to south down along the coastline. Here the climate is hot and humid in the summer and relatively warm in most winters. Semitropical crops, such as citrus, can be produced, but other crops include figs, wine grapes, and olives. Farther inland, the plains are at increasing elevations and are correspondingly cooler—the average temperature in July is 63°F (17.2°C) in these regions. Here the chief crop grown is grain. As the elevation rises even more, the green foliage of rolling

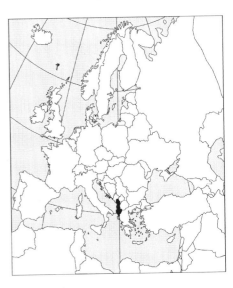

Albania

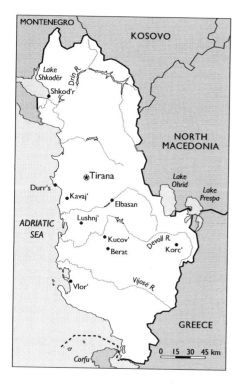

pastures gives way to sparse evergreens and scattered brush. Gray and brown craggy peaks rise steeply to the sky. The air is thin, cold, and clear. This is the home of the eagle, where few sounds interrupt the stillness.

In this setting, the people continue the isolated life they have experienced for centuries. There are some settlements that have little or no contact with the rest of Albania because of their inaccessibility. The few towns that exist are usually the result of a need for a place to trade agricultural goods. Fishermen ply the cool waters of Lake Shkodër in flat-bottomed boats. Although there is mineral wealth, it is almost impossible to extract it profitably because of the lack of transportation.

Most of the Albanians of today are remote descendants of the Illyrians, an ancient people of the Indo-European group. At one time, they were to be found throughout most of the Balkan Peninsula, but they were either gradually absorbed or driven out as successive waves of Slavs moved into the area. They are now found only in the western part of the Balkans. Even so, they spill across borders and are in Kosovo, Montenegro, North Macedonia, and Greece. There are also colonies of Albanians in Italy, but that is the result of past migrations and recent illegal immigration. In addition, there are about 600,000 persons of Albanian descent living in the United States.

Southern Albania (known in Greece as North Epirus) has a significant Greek minority, estimated by Albania to be 3%

of the total population, or 90,000, and by Greece to be 200,000. There are also some North Macedonians who live on the Albanian side of the border. Because of the poor economic conditions in Albania, however, most of the men of this area actually live and work in Greece, with only the women and children left behind.

HISTORY

Early Albanian Governments

The Kingdom of Illyria came into being in the 3rd century BC, centered around an ancient city on the site of present-day Shkodër. Conquered by the Romans in 167 BC, the area remained a part of the Roman Empire for the next five centuries. When the empire dissolved in the 4th century AD, Illyria became a part of the Eastern Roman—later Byzantine—Empire.

As the Slavs arrived in the Adriatic region in the 6th and 7th centuries, most of the Illyrians were absorbed; the rest settled along the southern Adriatic coast where Albania is now located. During the centuries that followed, Albania was conquered and reconquered by various eastern and western armies. The most lasting influence was that of the Serbs and the Venetians (Italians).

The Albanians were conquered by the Ottoman Turks in the 15th century and incorporated into their empire. Although the Albanians had put up stiff resistance to the Ottoman conquest, once they had been absorbed politically, they allowed themselves to be absorbed culturally, as well. Albania was the only part of the Balkan Peninsula where the majority of the population converted to Islam.

Albanian nationalism was awakened by the decisions of the major powers at the Congress of Berlin, which was held after the Russian-Turkish war of 1877–1878. The great powers awarded to Montenegro and Greece territories the Albanians claimed as their own.

They formed the League of Prizren to protest the division of lands they felt should not be given to neighboring countries, but this effort was not successful. They also demanded local control within a reformed Turkish Empire rather than independence that would have put them at the mercy of other foreign powers. Both Italy and Austria-Hungary had been showing interest in the area. Although the Turks supported the league in its protest against the expansion of neighboring states, they rejected the demand for local control. The Turks suppressed the league in 1881 and banned the use of the Albanian language in 1886.

The league was a means of expressing the first national feelings of the Albanians in their native land. When it and Albanian liberty were crushed, Albanian

communities living in Italy and the United States took up the national movement. Turkish oppression continued, and there was a series of rebellions from 1909 to 1912 that resulted in Albanian control of almost all of what is now that country.

The remaining Turkish power was eliminated in the First Balkan War of 1912. On November 28 of that year, a national assembly met at Vlorë and proclaimed Albania's independence. Ismail Qemali headed the first provisional government.

The Birth of a Modern Albania

The Treaty of London ending the First Balkan War (1912) left the question of Albania to an ambassadorial conference of the major powers. They agreed with the demand for independence, but as might have been expected, they redrew the map of the region. Shkodër, demanded by Montenegro, was left to Albania; Kosovo, inhabited by a large number of Albanians, was given to Serbia, creating a problem that lingers to this day. In the south, the powers gave part of northern Greece to Albania, but with Greek support, the people revolted.

The great powers also provided a hand-picked ruler for Albania—William of Wied, a German prince. Italian-supported Essad Pasha, successor of Ismail Qemali, was actually the most important man in

Albanians under the Turks (1910) and as an independent kingdom (1912)

Albania

Albania's medieval hero Skanderbeg (George Castriot)
Photo by Adam Nowakowski

Complaining that Zog was misusing Italian money and miffed at being denied military use of Albania's ports, Benito Mussolini sent an invasion force that swept Albania on April 7, 1939. Zog fled to Greece and then to London with his queen of only 354 days, Hungarian countess Geraldine Apponyi de Nagi-Appony, an American heiress, and their 2-day-old son, Leka.

Victor Emmanuel, figurehead king of Italy, became king of Albania. Italy mounted an invasion of Greece through Albania. It was repulsed by Greek and Yugoslav armies that were able to occupy much of Albania until a German attack in 1941.

Albania saved virtually all of its 200 native Jews and 400 Jewish refugees. It was one of the only European countries to end the war with more Jews than before. Partisan groups also rescued American service personnel who had crash-landed in the country.

Albania Reborn as a People's Republic

Resistance groups were organized in 1941–1942 by communists and noncommunists. The Albanian Communist Party was founded in 1941 with Yugoslav help. Among its leaders was Enver Hoxha, a young man educated in France and Belgium and considered one of the "intellectuals" in the party. It set up the National Liberation Movement (LNC), which for a time included the clan chief Abaz Kupi and his guerrilla fighters.

Another resistance group, the Balli Kombëtar National Front, had an antiroyalist and strongly nationalistic outlook. The two groups came close to joining in 1943, but the LNC, on the advice of the Yugoslav communist leader Tito, backed out. Soon the two groups were fighting each other. A provisional government headed by Enver Hoxha was formed in October 1944, moving to Tirana as the government of Albania upon withdrawal of the German forces.

Albania was proclaimed a people's republic in 1946. The absence of competing

the country. The years 1912–1914 were turbulent. There were rebellions in the north and south, where borders were disputed. General dissatisfaction reigned throughout the country. Prince William fled at the outbreak of World War I.

Four years of utter anarchy followed, with the armies of Serbia, Montenegro, Greece, Italy, France, Austria, and Bulgaria occupying parts of Albania. At the end of the war, Italy occupied Albania, with Serbia holding the northeastern region and Korçë in the possession of the French.

On December 25, 1918, delegates from all parts of Albania met at Durrës to elect a provisional government and to send a delegation to the Paris Peace Conference to present a demand that Albania's 1913 borders be restored. Greece, Italy, and to-be-Yugoslavia had made a secret deal to divide Albania among them. This was firmly rejected by US President Woodrow Wilson. His action, combined with the determination of the Albanian leaders, saved the tiny nation.

In order to understand events that followed World War I, it is necessary to remember that Albania was still a primitive country. Although unique and interesting culturally, it was backward. There was no written Albanian language and no education system. There were only a few miles of road and one bridge. There was no industry in the whole country. Albania was divided into many localities along social, religious, and geographic lines, and the

basic unit of power was the clan. Government control was at best scanty.

A parliamentary and cabinet system of government emerged in 1920. Italy, preoccupied with its own problems, reluctantly recognized Albania's government. The major powers finally resolved the border questions in 1926. Two political parties were organized: the Progressive Party, dominated by Muslim leaders, and the Popular Party, headed by a liberal Greek Orthodox bishop Fan S. Noli, who had a US college degree.

Ahmed Bey Zogu, one of the leaders of the Popular Party, became Albania's premier in 1922 when he stayed to defend the capital against a revolt after the rest of the government had fled. Two years later, he resigned and fled to Yugoslavia when an angry band of demonstrators marched on the capital. Noli, his successor, hoped to introduce a reform program that would drag Albania into the 20th century. This could not be done without massive outside aid or internal unity. Noli could muster neither. Zogu returned with the support of Yugoslav troops; the National Assembly proclaimed Albania a republic and elected him president for seven years.

Ruthless and determined, Zogu had a constituent assembly proclaim Albania a "democratic, parliamentary and hereditary kingdom" in 1928, with himself as King Zog I. He sought financial assistance from Italy. By the mid-1930s, this ripened into Italian control of Albania's economy.

King Zog I

Albania

Enver Hoxha

political parties and assistance from Yugoslavia's communists enabled Hoxha to assume power with relative ease. After World War II, the Yugoslavs desired to assume the role the Italians had before the war. An economic treaty was forged in 1946 providing for a customs union, coordination of economic planning, currency equalization, and the formation of "joint companies." Yugoslav advisers appeared in greater numbers, and there was even talk of union between the two nations.

The Yugoslavian embrace was apparently too stifling for Hoxha, but there was little he could do about it at the time. In the meantime, the Yugoslavs threw their support to Koçi Xoxe, who as minister of

the interior controlled the police and security forces. What saved Hoxha was the Soviet-Yugoslav split that occurred at this time. Accusing Xoxe of being a supporter of Tito, Hoxha had him and his followers purged at the first congress of the Albanian Party of Labor (APL) in November 1948; Xoxe was later executed.

Hoxha clearly dominated the APL, but he was not without his critics. The next major challenge came in the early 1950s, this time from moderates who objected to dislocations caused by a policy of industrialization and collectivization. After 1953, they also began calling for de-Stalinization as was occurring in Russia. The spokesmen for this point of view were two members of the politburo, Bedri Spahiu and Tuk Jakova. With Stalin dead and the Soviet leadership moving cautiously toward de-Stalinization, Hoxha could not simply purge these critics.

He actually made a gesture toward the moderate wing of the party in 1954, when he gave up the position of chairman of the council of ministers, though he turned it over to one of his own supporters, Mehmet Shehu. A year later, he managed to have both Spahiu and Jakova expelled from the politburo. Yet another challenge came in 1956 at the party's third congress, but it came from middle-ranking bureaucrats and military officers. Hoxha crushed it easily.

The last contest occurred in 1974–1975. It appears not to have been a direct challenge to Hoxha but rather to some of his policies. Now wielding absolute power,

Hoxha purged the dissenters. Between July and December 1974, he removed the entire top level of the military establishment, including the defense minister, Beqir Balluku, who was also a member of the politburo. His dispute with the military was apparently over the extent of party control in such areas as military training and discipline. He followed this ouster with a purge of the nation's top economic and managerial elite when they challenged the role of the party in their areas.

An ailing and tired Hoxha died in early April 1985 at the age of 77. Ramiz Alia, whom Hoxha had groomed as his successor, took his place. Alia, born in 1925, had been a longtime associate of Hoxha, though it was only in 1982 that he became the designated successor.

Alia belonged to the first generation of Albanian communist leaders, although he was 17 years younger than his mentor. He became a member of the party in 1943, when it was still only an aspirant to power, and became a full politburo member and a member of the powerful secretariat in 1961. When he was appointed president of the presidium of the People's Assembly (titular head of state) in 1982, he retained all of his party posts. Thus, he was already a member of the secretariat at the time of Hoxha's death and only had to assume the additional duty of first secretary.

Although no one challenged Alia for the office of first secretary, it soon became clear that the other members of the politburo considered him to be not more than a first among equals. Since the politburo was dominated by hard-liners, he was extremely cautious in initiating changes for the first few years. No additions were made to the politburo, even though that body had three fewer members than in 1982. Alia did make two lesser appointments—the addition of one person to the secretariat and the replacement of the chairman of the state planning commission.

At the ninth congress of the Albanian Party of Labor in 1986, Alia had fulsome praise for Hoxha, to whom, he said, Albania owed boundless gratitude. At the same time, the new five-year plan adopted at the congress put much more stress on foreign trade than in the past.

The Collapse of Communism

A slow and extremely cautious movement away from the old Hoxha system in general accompanied the new emphasis on trade. But it remained glacial until March 1990 when Alia, responding to the recent extraordinary changes elsewhere in central and eastern Europe, launched his own campaign of "democratic" change. Among other things, Alia promised contested elections by secret ballot, including

Enver Hoxha makes a point to elderly villagers, while Ramiz Alia (left) listens attentively.

Albania

within the Albanian Labor Party; limits on terms of office; a decentralization of decision-making authority to district officials and individual enterprises; some price decontrol; and the introduction of economic incentives in industry and agriculture.

Subsequent changes were, in some ways, even more significant. In April 1990, the assembly approved a law lifting criminal penalties for attempts to escape across the frontier. This was followed in May by a new law explicitly granting citizens the right to travel abroad. The assembly also lifted the old laws outlawing the practice of religion and declared religious belief to be a matter of individual conscience. Finally, it created the office of justice minister and gave it the task of creating a new system of courts and defense attorneys. None of this represented a basic reform of the system, however, for there was no change in the monopoly role of the party.

The May 1990 law granting citizens the right to travel abroad raised expectations among the Albanian populace, which were subsequently frustrated by Albanian officialdom. Toward the end of June, some 5,000 Albanians took refuge in a dozen foreign embassies in Tirana and demanded to be allowed to leave the country. After several days, the Albanian authorities gave in to the demands, and the refugees were allowed to leave. Over the next four months, an additional 25,000 persons were issued passports and left the country legally.

In the cities, demonstrations began occurring periodically, and some people took to wearing crosses and shouting anticommunist slogans in the streets. Occasionally, violence erupted when officials of the secret police ripped the crosses off people's chests.

Meanwhile the government continued its program of liberalization. Collective farmers were told that they could have private plots and that they would be permitted to sell excess produce in local open-air markets. Cultural controls were

also relaxed. At Enver Hoxha University in Tirana, a disco began playing rock music every Saturday night. The prohibition against individuals owning private automobiles was also lifted, though that change had little practical significance, since almost no private individual could afford to own one.

These gestures on the part of the party leadership only emboldened people to demand more. Nearly all of the protests were in the cities and overwhelmingly made up of young people, particularly young men. In December 1990, about 2,000 students at Enver Hoxha University organized a protest demonstration demanding greater democracy. After three days, the ruling Party of Labor, meeting in emergency session, gave in and endorsed "the creation of independent political organizations" and scheduled new elections for February 1991. Albanian communists, like their fellow party members in eastern Europe and the Soviet Union, had been persuaded to give up their monopoly of political power. The next day, the first oppositional political party, the Democratic Party, was organized. Approximately 80,000 people attended the rally for the new party.

By January 1991, three additional oppositional parties, the Republicans, the Forum for Human Rights, and the Ecological Party, had come into being. Charging that an election date of February 10 would not give them adequate time to prepare, they demanded that the elections be postponed until a later date. The government gave in and rescheduled them for March 31.

The period January-March 1991 was filled with demonstrations, political rallies, additional student strikes, and some violence. Oppositional newspapers also began appearing. At Enver Hoxha University, students decided that Hoxha's name should be stricken from the university's official title and organized a strike that later was turned into a hunger strike. The authorities allowed it to continue for 12 days and then surrounded the university with special troops. Demonstrations in support of the students erupted in urban areas across Albania. In two cities, Tirana and the port city of Durrës, statues of Hoxha were toppled. The government again backed down and agreed to remove Hoxha's name from Tirana University.

Ramiz Alia, under attack from hardline party members, decided to dismiss Adil Çarçani, the hardline chairman of the council of ministers, and assume personal control of the government apparatus by creating a "temporary presidential council." Fatos Nano was named head of the new government—an economist who had been made deputy chairman of the council of ministers in January. Alia's actions made clear what up to that time had been

only suspected: The communist Party of Labor had split into two factions, orthodox Marxist-Leninists, who wanted to stamp out dissent, and reformers, who supported Ramiz Alia.

Meanwhile, thousands of Albanians again began fleeing the country, first to Greece and then, at the beginning of March, in commandeered ships to Italy. Many appeared to be fleeing the violence and bloodshed that were accompanying the street demonstrations. The government declared martial law in the port city of Durrës in an attempt to stop the exodus, but about 12,000 Albanians eventually made it out of the country anyway. They were not well received in Italy, however, and many later returned home.

The March 31, 1991, elections were something of an anticlimax. The political opposition won in the cities, but the Party of Labor, managing to retain its hold over the countryside, won two-thirds of the seats in the People's Assembly. Ramiz Alia lost his own race in the city of Tirana but was reelected chairman of the presidium of the People's Assembly on April 30. Fatos Nano was reappointed chairman of the council of ministers.

As it turned out, the new mandate lasted just over one month. After two weeks of verbal sparring between the government and the political opposition, a group of newly formed, independent trade unions called for a general strike. With almost total worker support, it made clear, as nothing else could, that the party's claim to be the party of the workers was a fraud. During the three and a half weeks it continued, the general strike brought industrial production to a complete halt and established conclusively that the party had lost control of the cities. On Skanderbeg Square in central Tirana, where demonstrators had torn down a huge statue of Enver Hoxha in February, 50,000 demonstrators battled police with rocks, bottles, and fire bombs on May 29, leaving the front steps of the Palace of Culture on the square shattered and fire-blackened.

The opposition demanded the resignation of the communist government and the formation of a new interim government that would include representatives of the opposition parties. Workers demanded that their wages be doubled and the 48-hour workweek be reduced. The party acceded to all demands in the first week of June. Fatos Nano, in submitting his resignation as chairman of the council of ministers to the legislature, warned of food shortages and the threat of famine. "You have no idea how bad the situation is," he told the legislators.

The new cabinet was sworn in on June 12, 1991. Its head was Ylli Bufi, a member of the Party of Labor but whose training

Albania

This once-isolated nation had built bunker fortifications (which are still in place).

was as an engineer, not a party apparatchik. His reputation was that of an open-minded reformer. Half of the 24-member cabinet was selected by the communists, while another 12 members came from the opposition. In theory, this government of national unity was supposed to be a government of technicians, with members selected as individuals, without reference to party. In fact, 7 of the 12 opposition cabinet seats went to members of the main opposition party, the Democratic Party. The other 5 seats were allotted to the smaller Republican, Social-Democratic, and Agrarian Parties. Sali Berisha, head of the Democratic Party, was one of the opposition leaders entering the cabinet.

The 10th national congress of the Party of Labor was scheduled to take place on June 10–12. Prior to the beginning of the congress, President Ramiz Alia submitted his resignation as head of the party, and Xhelil Gjoni, the new party secretary, delivered the keynote address. The speech probably shocked some of the delegates with its attacks on Enver Hoxha's collectivization of agriculture and his "brutal pursuit of 'class struggle,' under which intellectuals and churchgoers were persecuted and jailed, some merely for listening to foreign radio broadcasts or reading the Bible." The congress had its surreal moments, such as when Hoxha's widow, Nexhmije, asserted that, if her husband were still alive, he would be a supporter of democracy and Albanian membership in the European Union. At the conclusion of the congress, the party voted to become the Socialist Party of Albania, hoping apparently that a change in name might help to stem a further decline in popular support.

Tumult in the Post communist Era

The task of the new government was not an enviable one. Shops were empty, and the people were angry. Industrial production was down drastically, and exports were down by 50% over the previous year. In the countryside, communists and anti-communists quarreled about whether to break up the collective farms, while peasants held off on planting.

The government tried to solve the land problem first. In July 1991, the legislature passed a law authorizing peasants to obtain small parcels of land from the collective farms. That helped, although communists in the legislature insisted on a clause to forbid peasants from selling any of their newly acquired land. In addition, because the legislation was passed so late in the crop year, a good percentage of the land never did get planted. The fall harvest would be much smaller.

The new government did get some good news, however. The aid already being provided from Italy, the United States, and Türkiye would continue and be expanded. The EU offered a trade and cooperation agreement that would allow additional sales to the EU of such Albanian products as chromium and make Albania eligible for technical assistance. In addition, the EU promised Albania 50,000 tons of wheat.

None of this was enough, however. The food situation grew worse over the summer, and unemployment continued to grow, reaching over 35% by August. As a result, an estimated 10,000 Albanians commandeered a freighter, the Vlora, and sailed for Italy. Five months earlier, the Italian government, faced with 24,000 refugees on its hands, had tried to persuade them to return to Albania. About half went willingly. Most of the rest remained in Italy, unemployable because they were unskilled. This time, the Italian government decided it would use different tactics. When the Vlora arrived, its passengers were taken in hand by riot squads and locked up in a sports stadium. Five days later, most were given $40 in cash, a T-shirt, and a pair of jeans and were flown back to Albania. If the treatment was rather brisk and perhaps a little harsh, the Italian government accompanied this with an offer of $85 million in food aid and another $50 million to purchase imported materials to keep the factories running.

Grateful for the aid, Tirana agreed to try to stop future mass departures by placing its ports under military control and instituting joint coastal patrols with Italian warships. Barbed wire was later strung around the port of Durrës to keep would-be stowaways out of the port area.

The government announced a privatization program in September that called for 25,000 state businesses to be sold. But this brought protests from the unions that up to 100,000 jobs would be lost as a result. They demanded that the government guarantee unemployed workers 80% of their usual salary, and this was actually written into law in November 1991. The average worker's salary was less than $30 a month. Even so, there was a question where the government would get the money to pay the unemployed workers. The budget deficit was already over 20% of GDP and climbing.

Meanwhile, in the countryside, the people had gotten tired of waiting for the government to make up its mind about the collective farms, and they had begun sharing out land and livestock on their own. These "spontaneous privatizations" produced a sort of anarchy in the countryside as looters stripped farm buildings of floors, window frames, roof tiles, and even bricks. There were also reports of embittered ex-farm directors dynamiting greenhouses and farm buildings on their way out and farmers burning fields they claimed as their own rather than let a rival family have them.

Ylli Bufi visited the United States in November and thus became the first Albanian prime minister to visit Washington. Shortly after his return, however, the Democratic Party pulled out of the government coalition, and it fell. Its head, Sali Berisha, accused the Socialists of hindering economic and political reforms. The charges were true. The Socialists were wary of market-economy solutions to problems and did force the Democrats to compromise with them. But the real reason for the pullout was that new elections were supposed to take place in May 1992, and the Democrats wanted them to occur as early as February. When the People's Assembly refused to agree to move up the elections, the Democrats withdrew from the cabinet. The Democrats wanted to fight the elections from outside the government. This coincided with new food riots that broke out in December 1991, apparently triggered by a comment by Bufi that food reserves would last only a week.

Bufi submitted his resignation as chairman of the council of ministers and was replaced by Vilson Ahmeti. Ahmeti was to preside over a caretaker government that would prepare for new elections. On December 23, President Alia announced that the elections would be moved up after all and would take place on March 22, 1992.

The period between December and March was a trying time for Albania. With the population barely surviving on foreign humanitarian assistance, there were once again attempts to flee the country, followed by food riots as thousands of people stormed warehouses and seized what goods they found there. With anarchy spreading, it became unsafe to go out at night, as armed groups of young men roamed the streets attacking people.

During the election campaign, there were also disturbing signs that Albanians were being given an exaggerated idea of what the world could do for them. For example, one journalist quoted "ragged peasants in the countryside" as saying that Albania's Democratic Party leaders and US secretary of state James Baker "will be bringing them shoes and food." A common shout at election rallies was "America will save us."

The Democratic Party won 62% of the vote in the March 22 elections, giving them an absolute majority in the People's Assembly. Including the votes of the Republican and Social Democratic Parties, the opposition actually got three-quarters of all votes cast. The big losers were the Socialists, with 25% of the vote, down from 67% a year earlier. Since the Democrats had made it clear that they would remove Ramiz Alia as president if they and their allies won a two-thirds majority in the People's Assembly, Alia saved them the trouble and submitted his resignation on April 3. The People's Assembly then elected Sali Berisha, leader of the Democratic Party, as the new president of the republic.

Sali Berisha, a French-trained cardiologist and Hoxha's erstwhile personal physician, had very little political experience when he became president. Similarly, Aleksandër Meksi, his chairman of the council of ministers, had graduated from Tirana University with a degree in engineering. Most of his subsequent experience was with the Institute for Cultural Monuments and the Institute of Archaeological Excavations as a "restorer and student of monuments of medieval architecture." These two men took control of a country that was and still is the poorest in Europe, that was suffering from a breakdown in political and economic life, and that had an unemployment rate approaching 50%. The electoral campaign also raised exaggerated hopes among the populace.

Political Trials

The economy did begin to grow again in 1993, but most people saw no improvement in their own situation. As a result, support for the government began to wane. Under extreme pressure to turn matters around, President Berisha adopted an authoritarian approach, thereby antagonizing some of the members of his own Democratic Party. This led to the expulsion of five MPs, including Gramoz Pashko, a former deputy prime minister, while two other party members resigned. Meanwhile, the Social Democratic Party, completely reorganized by Fatos Nano, a

Chicken salesman at Tirana market

young economist who had served as chairman of the council of ministers for a short time in 1991, began gaining in popularity and appeared to have a good opportunity to win new parliamentary elections scheduled for 1996.

Perhaps for that reason, the government brought charges against Fatos Nano for misappropriating state funds in early 1994 and put him on trial. The charges related to the administration of Italian aid money provided during the time that Fatos was chairman of the council of ministers. It was easy to show that the program had been administered incompetently, but the government was unable to provide any evidence that Nanos benefited financially. Nevertheless, the court found him guilty and sentenced him to 12 years in prison.

In June 1994, Ramiz Alia, Albania's last communist leader, was also brought to trial and was found guilty of abuse of power and other charges. He was sentenced to nine years in prison. Nine other former top communists were found guilty at the same time and given sentences ranging from three to nine years. Enver Hoxha's widow was imprisoned. Some of these individuals were undoubtedly guilty of the crimes with which they were charged. There is some irony in Alia's conviction, however, since it was he who permitted Albania's first multiparty elections that swept him from power in March 1992.

These various trials had a chilling effect politically. They also led to growing fears that Berisha was becoming just another in

a long line of authoritarian Albanian rulers. That latter perception may help explain the severe defeat Berisha suffered in 1994 over approval of a new constitution. The draft constitution, drawn up by a parliamentary committee with advice from western experts, lost in parliament when it failed to win the two-thirds majority necessary to pass it. This was mainly because of opposition by defectors from Berisha's own party. Rather than working for a compromise in parliament, Berisha decided to submit the draft constitution to the people in a popular referendum. Campaigning throughout the country for its adoption, Berisha turned the referendum into a vote of confidence in himself. The result was that the constitution was rejected by a 54% vote. Ismail Kadare, an Albanian writer, commented afterward, "Albanians were not against the constitution but against the style of the propaganda. The television propaganda was frantic. It annoyed everybody and recalled the days of Communism."

Unlike most central and eastern European nations, Albania as of 2008 had not opened up the secret files that were kept on citizens during the communist era. In any case, since the secret service burned many files during the transition year to democracy, there are large gaps in them. It is estimated that more than 100,000 people are still serving long jail sentences, performing forced labor in chrome and copper mines, or suffering banishment with their families to remote mountain regions.

Albania

Anarchy

Parliamentary elections took place on May 26, 1996, but there were such crude irregularities in the run-up to the election, including clubbing of opposition supporters by the police, polling stations packed with Berisha people, and charges of ballot stuffing, that independent observers found them rife with fraud. The opposition, which won only a handful of seats, refused to take their seats in parliament, and they maintained their boycott over the next nine months.

Things came to a head in January 1997, when an "investment" scheme that had promised savers interest rates of 50% a month collapsed. This was, it developed, only one of at least nine such pyramid schemes that had been operating in the country and which collectively had managed to skim off at least $1 billion in Albanian savings. The government moved to close down the schemes, but it was too late. Six weeks of rioting and unrest led to the collapse of nearly all authority. The whole southern part of the country passed out of government control, and even parts of the army went over to the opposition. Almost 1,500 people were killed.

Berisha tried everything—the threat of force, a promise partially to reimburse what people had lost—but it was to no avail. Finally, Berisha dismissed Aleksandër Meksi, chairman of the council of ministers, on March 1, 1997, and, after consultations with the various opposition parties, replaced him with Bashkim Fino, a 35-year-old Socialist from the southern town of Gjirokastër. Fino headed a caretaker cabinet, made up of representatives of all major political parties, charged with holding new parliamentary elections by June.

These concessions had no immediate effect on the revolt in the south. Although the Socialists appeared to be well poised to benefit from the political unrest, they, in fact, had little or no control over the insurgents in the south. The rebels' two nonnegotiable demands were Berisha's resignation and reimbursement for money lost in the collapsed pyramid schemes. In early March, Berisha arranged for his reelection as president by the parliament, but that act turned out to be irrelevant. By March 13, when the new government was sworn in, the country had disintegrated into anarchy, and the government had lost control even in Tirana, the capital.

All over the country, the people had armed themselves by breaking into or taking over military depots, and a civil war appeared to be eminent. As the government lost control, about 300 prisoners were released from the Central Jail in Tirana, including Fatos Nano, the leader of the Socialist Party, and Ramiz Alia, the last communist ruler of Albania. On March 16, President Berisha granted amnesty to both men, plus 49 others who had been released.

By early April, Fino had begun to assert some authority in most parts of Albania, and an armed force of 6,000, assembled under the auspices of the Organization for Security and Cooperation in Europe (OSCE), was arriving at major ports. The OSCE force was led by Italy, which also provided 2,500 of the troops. The force quickly moved to ensure, first, the distribution of aid, then, the establishment of stability to allow new elections in June 1997, won by the Socialist Party.

A New Constitution, a Rejected Monarchy

The Socialists and their allies immediately announced that they would use their two-thirds majority to amend the constitution to create a parliamentary republic. The new parliament convened on July 23, 1997, although the Democrats boycotted the session in a protest against plans to change the constitution. Sali Berisha submitted his resignation as president on the same day.

Albanians had the opportunity in 1997 to choose another kind of chief of state: a monarch. In 1993 Leka, the son of the last king, had returned to Albania, but he was quickly thrown out. Four years later, he returned in the wake of the pyramid-scandal chaos, accompanied by his mother, former queen Geraldine, and they were received courteously. He persuaded then-president Berisha to hold a referendum on the restoration of the monarchy. It was the only former communist state to hold a referendum on restoring a monarchy. Leka lost, but a surprising 30% of Albanians voted in favor. Most Albanians regarded him as a historical irrelevance. A few months before her death in 2002, Geraldine resettled in Albania with her son, who still called himself "king," and his family. The 6'8" (2.02 meters) Leka, known as the tallest Albanian, received a parliamentary pardon and lived his last nine years in Albania. He stayed out of politics and died in December 2011. His funeral ceremony was attended by the country's top political leaders. There are pretenders: Prince Leka II and his wife, Princess Ella, an actress.

Fatos Nano immediately took charge of the country. This took the form of a purge of the judiciary, security forces, and the military of those the Socialists labeled "incompetent political appointees." In fact, these were, in the main, persons who had some connection with the Democratic Party, and they were replaced by persons associated with one of the parties of the government coalition. The Democrats accused the government of appointing its loyalists to all government jobs, and there was undoubtedly a great deal of that. On the other hand, a number of persons appointed to positions in the media were persons of professional ability with no particular ties to the Socialist Party. In addition, most mayors retained their positions, even though many were members of the Democratic Party.

The Democratic Party boycotted the parliament and the parliamentary commission drawing up the new constitution because it did not want to give the process any legitimacy by participating. Parliament approved the document on October 21, 1998. When the constitution

Girls march in central Tirana carrying signs declaring "I respect the other's opinion."

President Ilir Meta

was submitted to a popular referendum in November 22, 1998, the Democratic Party boycotted this vote, as well. This may have had some effect, since only 50.57% of the electorate turned out to vote on the constitution. However, 93.5% of those who did turn out to vote cast their ballots in favor of the new constitution. It went into effect November 28, 1998.

Kosovo War

In March 1999 thousands of ethnic Albanians began streaming across the border from Kosovo, particularly after NATO began an air war against Yugoslavia in late March. Serbian president Slobodan Milošević's response to the bombing was to launch what was obviously a long-planned program of ethnic cleansing in Kosovo Province that resulted in an estimated 357,000 refugees fleeing across the border into Albania during the month of April. When the Kosovars began coming in, Albanians provided what assistance they could, freely sharing what they had and often taking them into their own homes.

But this is, after all, the poorest country in Europe, and there was no way Albania could have handled the situation alone. Thus, it soon found itself playing host to thousands of NATO troops (who had come in to help the refugees and also offer protection against possible Serb invasion), plus international aid groups who arrived to help the refugees. Fortunately, Milošević's acceptance of NATO's terms in early June brought an end to the bombing. Soon afterward most of the refugees began making their way back to Kosovo.

Albania's assistance to the Kosovar refugees was rewarded by a wave of international economic assistance that began to flow into Albania in the summer of 1999. Thus, in May, a group of inter-

national aid donors meeting in Brussels pledged Albania $200 million to help it cope with the refugees and to continue economic reform. In June, the World Bank approved two loans, the first a structural adjustment credit of $45 million to help the government complete privatization efforts and strengthen the judiciary and the second a $24 million loan designed to improve irrigation.

Also in June 1999, Germany pledged $20 million, while the IMF granted a new loan for $12.9 million and increased credits also available under a 1998 agreement by $13.1 million. In December 1999, the World Bank extended yet another $13.65 million loan. This helped finance the reconstruction of two roads damaged by NATO vehicles and refugee convoys during the Balkan campaign earlier in the year. The first connects Durrës with Kosovo, and the second links Berat with Çorovodë.

The Albanian government remained nervous about violence in Kosovo spilling over into Albania. Albanian sentiments are obvious. During a soccer match in Belgrade, Serbia, in 2014, a drone passed overhead bearing the flag of Greater Albania. When Albanian players tried to protect it, a skirmish broke out. This stunt prompted the postponement of what would have been the first visit to Belgrade by an Albanian prime minister in 70 years.

POLITICAL SYSTEM

Albania's constitution, approved in November 1998, establishes a parliamentary democracy. The "supreme organ of state power" is a 140-member People's Assembly, which is elected for a four-year term. Beginning with the June 2009 elections, proportional representation from party lists in 12 constituencies is the electoral

Former prime minister Sali Berisha

Prime Minister Edi Rama

system used. The threshold for receiving seats in parliament is 3% for parties and 5% for alliances. Using their two-thirds majority in the People's Assembly, the Socialists and their allies changed the way government operates even before this was incorporated in the new constitution. The office of the presidency has become a ceremonial position without political authority. The president is elected by parliament for a five-year term and is expected to remain above political partisanship.

In July 2007 Bamir Topi assumed the title. He won the three-fifths majority required only after four rounds of voting. A 50-year-old biologist, he is Albania's first head of state never to have belonged to the Communist Party. He is also one of the few senior politicians not to have been seriously tainted by scandal.

As a result of a series of confrontations between the major political forces in Albania (discussed below), the next presidential election took a threat from the European Union that Albania's application for membership will be disregarded unless a fair election is held and the office of presidency remains above the fray. It still took four rounds of voting to elect the new president, Bujar Nishani, then the interior minister on behalf of the Democratic Party of Albania. The main opposition party, the Socialists, boycotted the election. A graduate of the Skanderbeg Military Academy, Nishani holds a master's degree in European studies.

The presidential election of April 2017 occurred in a similar atmosphere, though with the main adversaries switched. This time, it was the Democratic Party that was boycotting the parliament and thus not available to vote for the president, while the Social Democrats tried to pressure them

Albania

President Bajram Begaj
Source: *Wikipedia)*

to rejoin the political dialogue. Therefore, nobody offered any candidate for the first three rounds of voting, each closing within minutes. Finally, in the fourth round, the parliament elected its speaker and former prime minister, Ilir Meta of the Socialist Movement for Integration, as the new president. He received 87 votes of the 89 parliamentarians present in this normally 140-members body.

The next indirect presidential elections which have taken place from May 16 to

June 4, 2022, failed in the first, second, and third rounds due to all parties disagreeing on a candidate.

Bajram Begaj, a graduate of Tirana's Faculty of Medicine who became an active medical officer in 1998 and had a long career in the army, ultimately serving as the Chief of General Staff of the Albanian Armed Forces from July 2020 to June 2022, was elected as the president of Albania on the fourth round. Although politically independent, he was officially nominated by the governing Socialist Party and was elected in the parliament by 95,12% of votes. Begaj was sworn in on July 24, 2022. He is the fifth president in the history of Albania to have a military background.

The office of prime minister, which replaced the position of chairman of the council of ministers, is the fulcrum of authority. The Democratic Party helped quiet the domestic situation when it ended its 10-month boycott of the parliament in July 1999. The youthful former weight lifter Ilir Meta, who had served earlier as deputy prime minister, became prime minister in October 1999. He promised to bring Albania closer to the European Union and to continue his effort to set reforms in motion and to improve the economy.

Meta was forced to resign in January 2001 because of serious feuding within his Socialist Party. It started when party leader Fatos Nano accused Meta's government of corruption and incompetence and challenged his right to rule. The left won the June 2001 elections. This was the Socialists' second straight win, a rarity in the Balkans.

The next prime minister in 2002 was Pandeli Majko, who had occupied that post earlier. In July 2002 he was replaced by Fatos Nano, and Ilir Meta became foreign minister. Much of Nano's and Meta's time and energy was devoted to feuding with each other. A rebellious group in the Socialists' parliamentary party refused to support the government, thereby paralyzing the legislature.

Nano and Berisha faced off again in the July 2005 elections, in which Nano, who suffered from a mounting "fed-up factor" in the minds of voters, sought a third straight election win. Berisha came out on top. Albania is the only Balkan country that has failed to conduct an election accepted by the international community. This time it agreed to work closely with the OSCE mission in Tirana to revise its electoral law, redraw constituency boundaries, and update the voter registers.

The OSCE declared the 2005 elections to have been only partly in compliance with international standards. There was little fraud but allegedly considerable intimidation and vote buying. The appearance of fairness is important. In 2004 the EU had postponed talks over membership because of failure to deal with organized crime and corruption in the police and judiciary. Nano challenged the results for 60 days before conceding victory on September 1, 2005.

Even the June 2009 parliamentary elections, in which a deputy and two activists were killed in campaign scuffles, were declared by the OSCE to have failed to meet the highest international standards, despite "tangible progress." It determined that, in 22 out of 66 polling centers, vote counting was "bad or very bad." An investigation of one ballot box found that most of the votes had been cast by persons who were either out of the country or did not have a valid identity document. Also, civil servants at 30% of the polling places were allegedly threatened with dismissal if they did not vote for the Democratic Party (DP).

Claiming in 2009 that their victory would be proven if the ballot boxes were opened to inspectors, the Socialists vowed to boycott parliament until a partial recount could take place. They maintained that they did not want to change the result but rather to ensure that future elections are free of fraud. The resulting prolonged paralysis prevented parliament from passing laws that require a three-fifths majority. These include many reforms needed to meet EU standards. This lamentable situation revealed the country's divisive politics and weak judiciary, which did not intervene.

In February 2010 the Council of Europe urged Albania's leaders to end their standoff. In May the European Parliament

Election for mayor in Tirana: "Come with us"

Albania

summoned the party leaders to Strasbourg to issue an even sterner warning: The EU accepts only well-functioning democracies as members. Either resolve the issue, or Albania's bid could be suspended. In December 2010 it was granted visa-free travel within the 25-nation EU Schengen Area.

In January 2011 the feud between the two main parties, which had been simmering for months, burst into violence when 20,000 gathered in the streets of Tirana to protest deeply rooted corruption. Four protesters were shot dead. The unrest was sparked when then-deputy prime minister Ilir Meta resigned after a private TV station aired a video supposedly showing Meta asking a colleague to influence the awarding of a power station contract. He was tried and acquitted.

In June 2013 the Socialists and their electoral partners (ASMI), composed of 37 parties, won a landslide victory. Led by Tirana's colorful former mayor Edi Rama, they captured 57.6% of the votes (up from 41.4%) and 83 seats (up from 65). It formed the government with Rama as prime minister. The new ruling cabinet was mostly young and included six women, including the defense minister; with further changes, half of the cabinet was female. Ilir Meta was Rama's chief coalition partner. In his campaign Rama drew heavily on quotations from a book of Barack Obama's speeches.

The electoral alliance (APMI), composed of 25 center and center-right parties driven by the right-of-center DP, captured 39.5% of the votes (up from 30.6%) and 57 seats (up from 46). It was led by Sali Berisha,

former president, prime minister, personal physician of Enver Hoxha, and the man who had dominated Albanian politics since 1991. Voters had grown tired of Berisha after eight years and had had enough of a string of scandals on his watch. He became leader of the opposition, to be replaced later by Lulzim Basha.

At first, the path to the parliamentary elections in 2017 looked as tortuous as ever. The Democratic Party boycotted the parliament from February to mid-May, did not register for the election, and set up a giant wedding tent ("Freedom Tent") literally in the middle of a normally busy boulevard in downtown Tirana. Placed right in front of the prime minister's building, the protesters used enormous loudspeakers to lambast the government and bombard the city with loud music. As mentioned above, election of the country's president developed into a farce due to the boycott. Finally, thanks to a resolute intervention of EU and US officials, both sides of the conflict agreed to a truce of sorts, with the DP receiving several ministerial portfolios in a transitional cabinet. Prime Minister Rama could not resist temptation and tweeted jokingly a fake ad: "TENT for rent, for events, weddings, and protests! Used for three months, in good technical condition . . . full options, even with view from the Prime Ministry!!"

The election itself went off relatively smoothly and retained Edi Rama and the Socialists in power. While the turnout was unusually low (46.8%), the results were quite clear. The Socialist Party received 48.3% of votes and 74 seats, thus becoming

a majority party by themselves. The Democratic Party won 28.8% and 43 seats. Lulzim Basha "froze" his leadership position in the party following its weak showing in the election. The usual kingmakers, the Socialist Movement for Integration (LSI), previously led by Meta, got 14.3% votes and 19 seats. Prime Minister Rama let it slip that dealing with the LSI in the past was like handling "temperamental children," so he relished an opportunity to steer Albania toward the European Union membership all by himself. This, however, remains a tough task.

Next regular parliamentary elections were held in Albania on April 25, 2021. They took place during the COVID-19 pandemic.

A total of 46 political parties, of which 5 parties are running for the first time, were registered with the Central Election Commission. Voters had the opportunity to choose between 12 electoral lists, of which 3 were coalitions, while in some constituencies five independent candidates also participated. The largest opposition party, the PD, formed the Partia Demokratike–Aleanca për Ndryshim (PD-AN) coalition by joining forces with twelve smaller parties. They won 39.43% of the vote, 59 seats. The LSI, also in opposition, formed a coalition of its own called Shqipëria—Shtëpia Fituese (ShQF) winning 6.81%, 4 seats. The ruling party PS (Socialist Party of Albania), decided to run in the elections alone but with the inclusion of some candidates from other allied parties. The Socialists came first by winning 48,67% of the vote, 74 seats. On April 27, Edi Rama claimed "the most beautiful victory" and thanked "for trusting me to lead a third term."

On April 28, 10 members of the Democratic Party's leadership called for Lulzim Basha's resignation as a leader, alleging the loss of the elections.

The next parliamentary election will be held in Albania by June 2025.

Foreign Policy under Communism

Because of Albania's small size, foreign affairs have always played an extremely important role. Between 1945 and 1948, it was Yugoslavia that played "big brother" and attempted to dominate Albania. When Enver Hoxha rebelled, he had no choice but to throw Albania into the arms of the Soviet Union. This marriage lasted as long as Stalin was alive. Hoxha had no difficulty switching his loyalty to the new Soviet leadership in 1953, at least for a while. The country entered the Council for Mutual Economic Assistance (CMEA), the Soviet-dominated economic organization for eastern Europe, in 1949 and the Warsaw Pact in 1955. Almost all foreign trade was with the USSR and other members of the CMEA.

Old part of the medieval city of Gjirokastër in southern Albania
Photo by Martha Grenon

Albania

Born in Skopje of Albanian parents, Mother Teresa is honored in Tirana.

Signs of a Soviet-Yugoslav reconciliation in 1955 made Hoxha apprehensive. He feared that the Soviets might accept his removal as the price for Yugoslavia's renewed friendship. But the situation was saved for Albania by an international crisis—Soviet intervention in Hungary in 1956, which led to a decided cooling in Russian-Yugoslav relations.

The Soviet leader Nikita Khrushchev continued to push "de-Stalinization" after 1956, which was at cross-purposes with Hoxha's desire to retain absolute, one-man power. He was also disturbed by Moscow's proposal in the CMEA for an "international socialist division of labor." It appeared that Albania's role would be to furnish the CMEA with foodstuffs and raw materials. That would mean the death of Hoxha's cherished industrialization program. It became evident that China was also becoming disgruntled with the Soviets' leadership. Hoxha decided to become a Chinese protege. By late 1959, Albanian speeches were already assuming a Chinese slant on political issues. The Chinese were

delighted to have at least vocal support in their disputes with the Russians.

The new direction of Albanian policy became clear at a meeting in Bucharest, Romania, in 1960, when the Albanian delegation backed the Chinese. The next occasion for a confrontation came in November 1960 at a Moscow conference of 81 communist parties. In spite of, or perhaps because of, Soviet pressure in the intervening months—including a denial of wheat deliveries at a time when famine threatened Albania—Hoxha attacked Soviet leader Khrushchev in language that outdid even the Chinese criticism.

The dispute was brought into the open in 1961, when Khrushchev attacked the Albanian party, which in turn denounced him. Diplomatic relations between Moscow and Tirana were broken in 1961. After the break Albania also ceased to participate in CMEA or the Warsaw Pact. When the Chinese countered with an attack on Yugoslavia, the style of the dispute was set until the later open rupture between Moscow and Beijing in 1963.

Albania accepted Chinese "guidance" in party and state affairs after its break with the Soviet Union in 1961 and between 1960 and 1975 received approximately a half-billion dollars in interest-free credits from China. With almost 2,000 Chinese technical experts, Albania was able to set up some 30 new industrial projects, chiefly for the production of energy, irrigation, and processing of raw materials. Albania was even exporting modest amounts of oil to Greece, with which it had concluded a trade agreement for the first time since World War II.

When the Soviet Union and its allies invaded Czechoslovakia in 1968, Albania officially announced its formal withdrawal from the Warsaw Pact. Concerned about its security, it also launched an effort to improve relations with neighboring countries. For the first time since 1948, Albania began to cultivate better relations with Yugoslavia. This policy began to bear fruit in 1970. Trade between the two countries increased; Yugoslav tourists were permitted to enter Albania, and cultural exchanges between the University of Tirana and the Albanian-language University of Prishtina in Kosovo Province were approved. The two countries raised their diplomatic staffs to embassy level shortly thereafter.

The presence of 1.6 million ethnic Albanians living in Yugoslavia, so often in the past a basis for disagreements between the two countries, for a time helped contribute to a healing, as cultural contacts between the ethnic Albanians on both sides of the border increased in frequency. Relations worsened again in 1976, however, as a new wave of unrest and Albanian "unity" activity began in Kosovo.

A number of violent demonstrations occurred among the students at Prishtina University in 1981, accompanied by demands to exclude Kosovo from Yugoslavia's program of cultural cooperation with Albania when the program came up for renewal in 1984. In retaliation, Tirana accused Yugoslavia of practicing a policy of "cultural genocide" against ethnic Albanians living within its borders and broke off talks on a new cultural exchange agreement in 1984. Yugoslavia continued to be Albania's chief trading partner, but the level of trade dropped after 1984 and then stagnated.

Economic factors probably played a role in this development, but political factors were clearly dominant. The Serbian government's subsequent actions against ethnic Albanians in Kosovo, in particular the termination of that province's autonomy in 1989, diminished the possibility of improved relations between the two countries. The situation was further compounded in 1991, when Albania extended diplomatic recognition to the self-proclaimed independent "Republic of Kosovo."

Albania's relations with the People's Republic of China soured in the late 1970s because of a change that occurred in China's foreign policy at this time. Hoxha disapproved of the warming trend in Chinese-American relations that had begun in the early 1970s. But he was particularly angered when the People's Republic extended an invitation to Marshal Tito to visit China. Albania launched an anti-China campaign in 1977, and this led to a break in Chinese-Albanian relations in 1978. China discontinued all economic and military assistance to Albania and withdrew all of its technical experts.

Diplomatic relations were resumed in 1979, but they did not regain their earlier warmth, largely for ideological reasons. This time the reason was the economic reform that Deng Xiaoping launched when he came to power in 1978. Hoxha disliked Deng's move and considered him to be a revisionist. Relations began to improve after Hoxha's death in 1985, however. Today, Albania's relations with the People's Republic of China are good. In 2009 a Chinese delegation made its first high-level visit to Albania since ties had been severed in the mid-1980s. Its main interest is in securing raw materials, including chrome and copper.

Albania continued to reject diplomatic relations with either the United States or the Soviet Union as long as Hoxha was alive. However, it did come out of its self-imposed isolation to a limited extent in the early 1980s. There was an improvement in relations with Greece, Italy, and France, and Albania opened talks with Great Britain and West Germany in an attempt to

Good neighbor policy: Albanian student with his Greek classmate at the College of Europe

Post-communist Foreign Policy

The wave of political change sweeping across central and eastern Europe in the last months of 1989 did not affect Albania directly, but it did change the world in which it operated. Prefacing his remarks with a specific reference to recent international developments, Alia told the Central Committee in April 1990 that "the problem of the reestablishment of diplomatic relations with the United States of America and the Soviet Union is on the agenda." Albania resumed diplomatic relations with Moscow soon afterward. The first contacts between American and Albanian diplomats occurred in May 1990, but diplomatic relations were not officially renewed until March 1991.

After a government of national unity including members of the political opposition was installed in early June, Albania found additional doors opening to it. It was admitted to the European Bank for Reconstruction and Development in September and the IMF and World Bank in October. Membership in these organizations made Albania eligible for technical assistance and also loans.

Albania's relations with the United States also improved after the change in government in June 1991. Washington supported Albania's applications for membership in international organizations and promised it humanitarian economic assistance. Ylli Bufi, former Prime Minister of Albania, traveled to the United States in November, the first Albanian leader to come to Washington. Although the visit was technically private, Bufi did meet with Arnold Kanter, former US undersecretary of state for political affairs.

Relations with the United States underwent a major change after Sali Berisha was elected president in 1992. Journalist Flora Lewis, who visited Albania in 1993, reported that there is "a constant flow of American military personnel coming and going to give advice and check the

resolve bilateral differences that prevented the establishment of diplomatic relations.

British-Albanian differences were over an Albanian gold reserve placed in London prior to World War II and British demands that Albania pay compensation for sinking a British ship off the Albanian coast in 1946. The sticking point in Albanian-West German relations was Albania's demand for $2 billion in reparations from Bonn for damage done in Albania during World War II. Germany was unwilling to concede the principle of reparations, but it did suggest the possibility of a loan or credits to finance a major industrial plant in Albania.

This process speeded up after Enver Hoxha died in April 1985. His successor, Ramiz Alia, though committed to a general continuation of Hoxha's policies, supported a policy of opening up more to the rest of the world. An agreement on border demarcation was signed with Greece. In general, diplomatic contacts increased with western European and third-world countries.

At the same time, the Albanian Party of Labor continued to reject party-to-party relations with other communist countries during this period, and the only ones represented by an ambassador in Tirana were Romania, North Korea, and the People's Republic of China. Albania did sign a major trade agreement with East Germany, which agreed to provide Albania with industrial technology, including agricultural machinery, in return for Albanian chrome ore. A further cautious breakthrough

occurred in 1987, when Albania reestablished diplomatic relations with Canada and West Germany.

In 1988 Albania and Bulgaria agreed to elevate their diplomatic relations to the ambassadorial level. Albania also agreed to attend a foreign ministers' conference on the Balkans hosted by Yugoslavia. The foreign ministers of Albania, Yugoslavia, Romania, Bulgaria, Greece, and Türkiye met in Belgrade in February 1988. Their talks covered a number of issues, including trade, regional economic interests, communications, and creation of a nuclear-free and chemical-weapons-free Balkans. Not much of a concrete nature was accomplished, but they did agree to meet again. For Albania, the very fact of its participation represented a breakthrough.

Albania

situation." Since Albanians feared that the Yugoslav war might spread first to Kosovo and then to Albania, they saw America as a protector. The United States made no commitments to Albania at this time, though the Clinton administration, worried about the war spreading in Kosovo, did express its disquiet to the Serbian government.

Albania said that it would resist any attack from across the border, but its weapons, almost entirely Soviet or Chinese-made versions of Soviet weapons from the 1950s and early 1960s, would be almost useless against well-armed Serbian forces. This is one reason President Berisha, visiting NATO headquarters in Brussels in 1992, said that Albania would like to join the western alliance. That would come 17 years later, in April 2009, when it formally joined NATO. This was a moment of enormous symbolic and psychological importance; Albania belongs to the west.

Albania's relations with the Vatican expanded when, in 1993, John Paul II became the first pope to visit Albania since the Middle Ages. Only about 10% of the population is Roman Catholic, but the pope got a warm welcome. President Berisha greeted the pontiff. Their two speeches made an interesting dialogue about the Balkans. John Paul II, addressing a rally in Tirana, advised, "Do not let the sense of nation that you feel strongly at this moment degenerate into the kind of intolerant and aggressive nationalism that claims its victims still today and fuels ferocious hatreds in several parts of the world, some not far from here."

Then-president Berisha's speech touched on the same theme. "The Holy Father," he said, "has come to the Balkans today at a time when not far from us, in Bosnia and Herzegovina, criminal demons are committing massacres and ethnic cleansing, are exterminating an entire people. We can never permit the ethnic cleansing of Albanians from their territory, and we insist that the region's crisis will never be resolved without a solution of the question of Albanians in Kosovo." Berisha asserted

in 2009, "That is the greatest accomplishment of my country after independence."

Tirana became even more outspoken in its support for Albanians outside its borders. This prompted North Macedonian accusations of meddling. There were, in fact, two separate issues involved here. The first was the dream of a "Greater Albania" uniting all 6 million Albanians in a single government. A few nationalists espouse this viewpoint, but they represent only a small fraction of the population. The second, and more significant, issue was Kosovo, where Albanians make up 95% of the population. President Berisha's fear was that the Bosnian war could spread to Kosovo. He was convinced that, if that happened, Albania and probably North Macedonia could be drawn in, as well.

President Berisha was influenced by Albanian nationalists, who acknowledged that their dream of a Greater Albania depended on a major upheaval in the Balkans. Worried by the war in Bosnia, Berisha increased his government's contacts with more radical ethnic Albanians in North Macedonia—those who favored joining Albania—presumably to be ready to act should the war spread. When in 1995 it became clear that this was undermining the main party of ethnic Albanians who were part of the governmental coalition in North Macedonia, however, Berisha reversed the policy. He reduced ties with the radicals and reiterated his support for North Macedonia's current borders.

Albanian relations with Greece are primarily governed by the fact that there are significant numbers of ethnic Greeks living in southern Albania. The Greek government, which refers to southern Albania as North Epirus, claims the right to speak on behalf of ethnic Greeks living in Albania. In recent years, the situation was exacerbated by the Orthodox bishop of the Greek province of Epirus, who put pressure on Athens to use force to protect the rights of ethnic Greek minorities in Albania. The Greek government was never willing to go that far, but it did threaten in

1995 to expel Albanian citizens living and working in Greece.

Greece and Albania signed an agreement in April 2009 delineating their continental shelf and maritime borders in the Ionian Sea. Another factor affecting Albanian-Greek relations was that Greece was one of Serbia's strongest supporters during the Bosnian war. But Greece is also a strong proponent of Albanian membership in the EU. Tirana formally applied in 2009, and the accession process has begun.

Albania's relations with both the United States and western Europe cooled considerably. The United States was particularly critical of irregularities in the parliamentary elections in 1996 and several times called for new elections. By 1997, Washington had taken the position that Berisha's resignation was essential. When, therefore, Berisha appealed for the European Union and NATO to send peacekeeping troops to restore order after his government had lost control, the word he received was that the first step toward restoring order had to be his own resignation.

After Fatos Nano became prime minister in 1997, Washington officially promised to provide financial support for the reconstruction and democratization of Albania. Other countries extended offers of economic assistance, including Germany, which pledged $18 million in 1997. Albania's relations with Greece also improved at this time.

Rexhep Meidani, who replaced Berisha as president, did not differ greatly in his position on Kosovo. In 1998, for example, he gave an interview in which he endorsed an interim policy of autonomy but added, "for me the final solution is quite clear; . . . the Albanians can no longer live under the Serbian regime." But Meidani went on to make clear that he favored an independent Kosovo, not a "Greater Albania." As prime minister, Ilir Meta also dismissed such dreams: "Greater Albania is a project that doesn't exist even in our minds." However, not all politicians are willing to ignore such an idea. President Meidani endorsed the Rambouillet Agreement in March, then the NATO bombing campaign that followed Yugoslavia's rejection of the agreement.

Kosovo's declaration of independence on February 17, 2008, was cause for jubilation there and in Albania proper. The old idea of a "Greater Albania" binding all 6 million Albanians in one nation-state was seldom mentioned. Only 1 out of 10 Kosovo Albanians said in polls that they wanted to belong to Albania, but that possibility is being increasingly discussed. Of course, there are cultural links, fostered by the electronic media. Language binds them, although southern Albanians speak a Tosk dialect, which predominates in books and newspapers, while Kosovars speak the Geg dialect.

The two countries, along with the Albanian enclaves in North Macedonia and Montenegro, will become natural trading partners when the transportation links between them are improved. There is no cross-border rail connection. That is why a $1.4 billion-dollar project to improve the road from the northern Albanian port of Durrës to Prishtina, completed at the end of 2009, is so important: That trip now takes less than three hours. A donor conference sponsored by the World Bank and the EU raised more than €1 billion for Kosovo in June 2008. Part of this sum was used to improving the connecting roads. The Central European Free Trade Agreement (CEFTA), as well as a bilateral trade accord, is in place to facilitate regional trade.

The warmth of American-Albanian relations was demonstrated by the hero's welcome former President George W. Bush received in June 2007, when he became the first sitting US president ever to visit the country. Albanians lined the road leading into Tirana wearing cardboard Uncle Sam hats and cheering him. He was awarded the nation's highest honor, the Order of the Flag medal; was put on a new line of commemorative postage stamps; and had the street in front of the parliament building named after him. The prime minister declared him to be "the greatest and most distinguished guest we have ever had in all times." The good feelings toward America had been strengthened by President Woodrow Wilson's support of Albanian independence and opposition to carving up Albania 95 years earlier and by US willingness to defend Albanians in Kosovo and that country's independence.

Military

The number of American and other NATO troops in Albania began to increase greatly in March 1999, particularly after Serbian forces began driving ethnic Albanians out of Kosovo more or less simultaneously with the beginning of the NATO bombing campaign. With large numbers of refugees pouring over the border, numerous international aid missions also moved in to provide assistance. While offering whatever help it could to refugees from Kosovo, Albania welcomed both the NATO troops and the international aid missions. After the war, Albania consistently advocated an independent Kosovo, without which there could be no long-term stability. Despite the distrust that exists in the relationship with Serbia, Tirana tries to maintain discourse and a constructive tie with it.

It hoped that such timely assistance to NATO allies could pave the way for Albania's membership in the alliance,

Eating well in a Tirana restaurant
Courtesy: *Austin Caskill Jr.*

which seemed unlikely for many years. The reasons were that its democracy was not yet sufficiently stable, and its armed forces were not ready. But the restructuring of its military was completed in 2010. Conscription was 12 months before it was abolished. A fully professional army is taking shape. There is stiff competition among young Albanians to join the new force. Albania has reduced its active-duty soldiers to 14,295 under one command. The separate navy and air force are being combined with the army, and there are 500 paramilitary forces. Bases in Durrës and Vlorë operate mainly patrol and coastal combatants and mine-warfare vessels. All fixed-wing aircraft, including the 26 aged MiG aircraft, were grounded. When one of them crashed in September 2004, killing the pilot, critics demanded that the entire MiG fleet stop flying out of Tirana's international airport and be sent to a museum. That has happened. Instead, it is building a helicopter-based force for transporting ground forces, conducting medical evacuations, and engaging in combat; it possesses 16 helicopters and 10 reconnaissance and utility planes. It is developing a niche capability in demining.

In 2010, it deployed about 350 soldiers with NATO forces in Afghanistan and with the Americans in Iraq. In Afghanistan, its 140 soldiers participate in a medical team with North Macedonia and Croatia and take part in training the Afghan army. All of its 250 troops in Iraq have been withdrawn, but it helped guard the airport at Mosul with the 101st Airborne Division. It has 13 peacekeepers in Bosnia and Herzegovina and 63 in Chad. Albanians had traveled to Syria and Iraq to fight for the terrorist Islamic State.

Albania was 1 of 10 former communist countries to sign the so-called Vilnius Letter expressing support for the Iraq war at an "important" time. It opened its airspace, land routes, and territorial waters to allied nations during the war. It also offered access to its military bases, which the US did not need. Albania signed an

agreement with the US to shield American soldiers serving in Albania from prosecution by the International Criminal Court.

After the war, American leaders expressed their gratitude by promising to help Albania gain full membership in NATO, which occurred in April 2009. They offered high-level training and exercises designed to help improve its military capabilities and sent a number of military experts to work in Albania's Defense Ministry. They helped promote an Adriatic Charter to improve relations between Albania, North Macedonia, Croatia, and the rest of Europe. In September 2003 Albania, North Macedonia and Croatia agreed to a Common Declaration on defense.

Ex-secretary of defense Donald Rumsfeld said, "I value the relationship that the United States has with Albania. It's important to us." The US supported Albania's successful bid to join NATO, along with Croatia, in April 2009. Partly in gratitude, Albania agreed in December 2008 to accept five Uighur detainees (Muslims from western China) from Guantanamo prison. It was the first country to accept detainees who were not its former residents. They became celebrities in Tirana, appearing on TV chat shows and giving interviews.

In the fall of 2004, Albania discovered to its own amazement that it possessed several hundred canisters of lethal military chemicals, the same kind of sulfur mustard Saddam Hussein had used against Iranians and his own Kurdish population in the 1980s. At a time in 1979 when Albanian dictator Hoxha had alienated himself from all patron countries, he tried to control his own population by stirring up hysteria over an imagined attack by a combination of enemies, including Yugoslavia, the Soviet Union, the US, and China. He ordered the country's biggest public-works project ever—the construction of 750,000 concrete bunkers, one for every four Albanians at the time. Most are still there. He also purchased large quantities of weapons, and he ordered the poison gas from China and had it stored in a remote bunker in the mountains. When he died in 1985, the cache was forgotten until it was discovered in 2004.

Albania garnered international praise for immediately disclosing the stockpile's existence. The US assumed responsibility for constructing a custom-made mobile incinerator to be towed along steep mountain roads to the very door of the bunker and to destroy the chemicals there. It helped install fences and surveillance gear to protect the stocks. It also offered $20 million to finance the project. This was the first time the US offered to do this outside the former Soviet Union. Aware that this gave Albania the opportunity to strengthen its ties with the west

Albania

Street in Kruje

Photo by Adam Nowakowski

and to demonstrate that it is a partner in the struggle against terrorism, former Defense Minister Pandeli Majko called its actions a "psychological" break with the past. "After the Cold War, we have passed from a phase of irresponsibility and entered a phase of responsibility and transparency." Widespread rejection, underscored by street protests involving thousands, prevented the government from accepting an American appeal in 2013 that Albania help destroy Syrian chemical weapons on its own soil.

However, a disastrous explosion at a military depot near Tirana Airport on March 15, 2008, highlighted a problem that sets Albania apart from its new Atlantic allies. The country was sitting on about 100,000 tons of excess outdated ammunition in unstable condition of Chinese and Soviet origin stored in various depots throughout the country. The blast could be heard as far away as the North Macedonian capital of Skopje, 100 miles distant, and the tremors were felt far beyond Tirana. A massive ball of fire shot up from the site, and shrapnel and shell fragments rained down on homes, businesses, and vehicles. The fire raged for 14 hours, and 26 persons died, 10 more disappeared, and about 300 were injured; more than 5,500 homes and businesses were damaged or destroyed. The defense minister was sacked, and damaged homes were rebuilt with government subsidies. Nineteen former officials were given prison sentences

in 2012 for gross mismanagement in the incident; nine were cleared.

ECONOMY

Before Enver Hoxha's death in 1985, Albania billed itself as the world's first "true socialist economy." One reason for this claim was that 100% of the "means of production" had been nationalized under Hoxha. Until 1990, this extended even to motor vehicles, which could be owned only by the state. Citizens were permitted to own bicycles, however. That proud boast lost all of its glitter long before the defeat of the Socialist Party of Albania in the 1992 elections. But the truth behind that boast continues to give government ministers headaches as they work to privatize the economy and move Albania toward a market economy.

Albania launched its first five-year plan in 1951 with a goal of a rapid development of industry and national self-sufficiency, including agriculture. Growth during the first two five-year plans was fairly rapid, since Albania was starting from almost nothing. It slowed thereafter, but this can largely be blamed on the halt in Soviet economic aid after the break in relations in 1961. There was fairly rapid growth between 1966 and 1970—reflecting the assistance that the country got from China—but there was a slowdown after 1970.

Albania achieved full collectivization of agriculture in 1967 and followed this up by a reduction in the size of peasants' private plots. Albanian agriculture regularly achieved only about 50% of its assigned production targets in the late 1960s and early 1970s. This sector also suffered from the loss of Chinese assistance after the Albanian-Chinese diplomatic break. As a result, the government abandoned its long-term goal of self-sufficiency and began to develop foreign trade.

Albania is still the least developed country in Europe, but the regime's policy of industrialization did produce substantial changes in a number of areas. For example, Albania has significant resources of chrome, iron, coal, copper, and petroleum, and there was significant development in these areas during the years of communism.

By the late 1980s, Albania had the capacity to produce over 800,000 tons of chrome a year, making it the world's third-largest producer of that vital metal at the time. In the 1970s, Albania constructed an oil refinery with an annual capacity of 1 million tons and began exporting crude oil and refined petroleum products to Italy, Greece, Germany, Switzerland, and Romania. Other exports included electric power, copper, coal, textiles, and food products.

Red tape and too much control from Tirana had created a situation of slow growth that the bureaucrats were unable to reverse. Severe shortages developed, particularly of raw materials, modern machinery, and consumer goods. Food items, such as meat and cheese, had to be

A sample of Albanian banknote

rationed, though staples, such as bread, sugar, and milk, remained adequate until 1990. Fruits and vegetables were also still freely available at that time.

In 1990, however, Ramiz Alia promised to institute a number of economic reforms aimed at decentralizing decision making and creating some economic incentives in industry and agriculture. Though developments elsewhere in eastern Europe were an important influencing factor, the state of the Albanian economy played the more important role in the political developments in 1990–1991. A common complaint, both of people demonstrating in the cities and of others who fled the country, was the lack of any hope for their own future. Part but not all of that pessimism was caused by the failure of the communist system itself.

The other serious, long-term problem was for years Albania's rate of population growth, which was higher than its rate of economic growth. That has changed. A birth rate of 2.1 children per woman is the replacement rate. Albania, along with Kosovo and the Albanian minority in North Macedonia, is among the few European countries that not only maintain but also exceed that rate. Steady 6% growth in the economy now sustains that continued increase in population. Over 50% of its population is under 30. However, this does create pressure on farmland, since many Albanians are still farmers.

Economy in Post-Communist Era

Since 1992, all Albanian governments have been committed to the privatization of state-owned industry and the creation of a market economy. However, they have not been able to make much progress in the area of privatization because of the dire state of the economy. When the government removed subsidies on state industry in 1991, about half of industry closed down or laid off workers and went on short hours.

With social discipline breaking down, Albania entered a period of anarchy. The Berisha government managed to reverse that trend and to restore order in the cities, though roving bands of robbers continued to operate in parts of the countryside. Meanwhile, industrial production continued to drop, with many plants working at 5% capacity by 1993. The situation then stabilized, and the economy began growing again in 1993. For the next couple of years, Albania had one of the fastest-growing economies in Europe, though it started from a very low baseline.

In 1994, the government launched a major program of privatization, selling off all (1,800 in total) small state-owned enterprises with fewer than 300 employees and less than $500,000 in assets. Many

new small and medium-sized private companies were also started, creating an estimated 100,000 jobs. By 2005, the private sector accounted for almost 80% of output, much of it in the underground economy. Privatization continues. Germany's Hochtief won a concession to manage Tirana's Mother Teresa Airport.

An estimated 850,000 or more Albanians (approximately one-fourth to one-third of the population) work abroad, at least 600,000 in Greece and 200,000 in Italy. When Greece went into a dire recession, some of them returned home. Some lose their residence permits if they lose their job. Albanians have mostly integrated well, and their children often speak better Greek than Albanian. Many need language classes if they return to Albania.

Those abroad include more than 10,000 professionals, including university professors and researchers. Their absence raises fears that Albania will lack the skilled professionals it needs to complete the transition to a market economy and handle the administrative demands made by EU integration.

On the plus side, Albanians living abroad used to remit €1 billion (about $1.45 billion) a year, equivalent to about 11% of GDP. That declined by half in 2010. Remittances made it possible for the government to stabilize the value of the lek, and it contributed heavily to the success of privatizations. Remittances also helped maintain the country's high growth rate (6% annually for six years leading up to 2008, one of the highest in the Balkans) until the global economic downturn in 2009, when economic growth was an estimated 2.5%. It was one of the few European economies that did not shrink in that recession

year, and it needed no bailout. Along with the proceeds of organized crime, they also reduce poverty, contain social tensions, fuel a building boom (until the world recession temporarily turned the boom into a bust), support many families, and offset a large trade deficit. Tourism adds another €750 million to the economy. Albania is becoming one of Europe's most intriguing destinations.

Albania taps an unusual source of assistance. Because of past migrations from this poor land, about 600,000 persons of Albanian descent live in America. They were heavy contributors to Albania's Democratic Party in the run-up to the 1992 elections, and for a while they invested in their old homeland. Some even returned to offer their foreign skills. Most of this consisted of Albanian Americans providing capital to Albanian relatives to set up or buy businesses. Much was invested in pyramid schemes that began to collapse in early 1997.

For a while, the news from the countryside was a little better. The old collective form of farming basically disappeared as a result of the legislature's 1991 decision to allow peasants to obtain their own parcels of land. The peasants themselves carried out most of the implementation of that decision, and they did so in a haphazard manner. The peasants were unable to agree among themselves about who owned what lands. As a result, only about half of the agricultural land was planted in 1991.

Most of the quarrels over land ownership were resolved by 1992, and about 80% of the land was in private hands, although the distribution of land deeds was a much slower process. This had a negative

Class outing

Albania

City of Shkoder

Photo by Adam Nowakowski

economic effect, for peasants without land deeds are unable to use their land as collateral for borrowing. There has been a mass migration from desperately poor rural areas into the cities. Albania now imports most of its food, including fresh produce from Greece and North Macedonia. However, it is the world's largest exporter of sage (grown wild) and one of Europe's major exporters of medicinal herbs.

The collapse of several pyramid "investment" schemes in January 1997 led to a complete loss of confidence in the government and banks in general. By March the government had lost control of almost all of the country. It was estimated that a third of Albania's capital reserves evaporated in the collapse, and the resulting anarchy set the country back even further. Since Albania was already receiving one-third of its annual budget of $960 million from the European Union, Italy organized a rescue operation that involved moving Italian and other troops into Albania to restore order.

The value-added tax was raised from 12% to 20% in 1998. The tax rate on corporate profits and personal income was made a flat 10% to lure foreign investors and make businesses more willing to pay their taxes. In general, taxes remain a problem because as much as 30% of the economy is underground, meaning that economic activity occurs behind the backs of the tax collectors. Tax evasion also stems from many citizens' conviction

that government officials are corrupt and would only pocket their tax money.

They have a point. Bribes are paid to register companies, obtain permits and licenses, and avoid harassment by tax authorities. According to the World Bank, 77% of companies bribe officials. In 2008 Transparency International ranked Albania 105th out of 180 countries in terms of corruption perception. This was lower than all other former communist countries in the Balkans. This is one reason foreign direct investment lags behind the rest of southeastern Europe. The judiciary has a bad reputation as corrupt, poorly trained, and heavily politicized. The EU has particularly focused on judicial reform as a condition for completing a stabilization and association agreement. The central government made a start toward making earnings visible to the tax officials by paying its own employees through banks. Until recently, officials all the way up to the prime minister were paid in cash.

Some economic progress has been made. In 2005 Albania was the only country in southeastern Europe where economic output exceeded 1989 levels. Inflation by 2007 was 2.9%, in 2015 it was 1.9%. GDP per capita doubled between 1999 and 2005. While in 2008 it was still only $3,670, a tenth of that in Greece, in 2014 its GDP per capita (PPP) of $11,100 was only about half that of Greece. Albania is no longer Europe's second-poorest country after

Moldova; it is the fifth and with an average income more than twice that of Moldova.

Not all is rosy, of course. One must often bribe to receive adequate health care. Unemployment was 17.7% in 2015, higher for women and in the countryside, where much of the population is employed in subsistence farming. There is a wide gap between a minority of well-off and the struggling underclass. Half of the wealth is controlled by a fifth of the population. That is why so many live and work outside the country. A sign of a pocket of affluence is the existence of the University of New York Tirana (no connection with NYU), which offers what is described on a sign in the lobby as "the only real European and American education" in Albania.

The efforts to privatize large state-owned companies, to build better roads, to collect more taxes, and to overcome the chronic power and water shortages continue. By 2007 only one-sixth had running water, and less than a fifth had uninterrupted electricity. City dwellers suffered power cuts of at least 6 hours a day, rising to about 12 hours in the countryside. However, those shortages have eased as generating capacity has increased. As more and more Albanians move into the cities and furnish their homes with modern appliances, demand for electricity is growing at three times the European average. Hydropower units produce 90% of its electricity, but droughts reduce water levels in dams that feed the antiquated hydropower plants. An estimated 30% of power supply is lost in transmission. The problem is aggravated by the shutdown of two nuclear reactors in Bulgaria, which cut electricity exports by two-thirds and drove up energy prices all over the Balkans, including Albania. That reflects itself in slower economic growth and fewer foreign investments.

Problems remain that make it very difficult to attract foreign investment. The budget deficit rose from 3.7% in 2008 to 5.4% in 2014. Political polarization and widespread corruption continue to be problems. A report by the International Crisis Group estimated in 2003 that almost half of the GDP was accounted for by criminal activity. However, there is widespread tolerance for it. Many saw criminal wealth as "progress."

The country has become a transit route and warehouse for international traffickers of drugs, cigarettes, immigrants, and women and children for prostitution or begging in the rest of Europe. The Albanian and Italian navies cooperate in trying to stop them from crossing the Adriatic, but few were caught. In 2005 the government forbade the use of speedboats, the favored transportation used by traffickers to get people out of the country. Through stricter border controls and revenge killings of traffickers by the victims' families, trafficking of women has been significantly reduced.

The country's role as a major transit point for human trafficking from the east to western Europe has been greatly diminished. However, a 2015 report noted that there has been a dramatic increase in the number of Albanian child slaves smuggled into the United Kingdom. Brought into the country in trucks across the English Channel, these children have been forced to work primarily in prostitution; fewer in forced labor; and some pressed into domestic servitude, begging, and petty crime.

Restricted economic opportunities generate other criminal activities. Albania is a major regional producer and trafficking channel for cannabis. In 2016, over 2.5 million marijuana plants were seized and destroyed by the police, up from 90,000 in 2013. Attempts to smuggle cannabis to Italy and Greece have intensified, with dozens of powerboats or trucks involved. A single powerboat stopped on its way to Italy carried some 900 pounds of marijuana.

CULTURE

In 1964, Hoxha launched an ideological and cultural revolution aimed at eliminating religion, the influence of family and sectional loyalties, and prejudices toward women. Albania became the only country in the world to prohibit all religious practice. All churches and mosques were closed, and most religious leaders were imprisoned. In addition, a major effort was made to end the traditional Islamic seclusion of women and to bring them into the workplace. Three years later, Albania became the world's first officially atheist country.

The party relaxed some of its controls beginning in 1970, but the cultural revolution resumed in 1973. Now the targets were young people, the military, and the technicians. The party reorganized the education system to make it stricter. Party officials who had advocated a moderate line were purged. Intellectuals were sent to factories and collective farms to do manual labor. This did not succeed in changing the basic culture of the country, but it enforced a surface conformity. It is not even clear that closing all of the mosques and churches reduced the number of believers, although it did succeed in driving religion underground.

The prohibition against all public religious rituals left a void, and the regime attempted to fill this by creating a new calendar of secular festivals. National holidays, such as Albanian Independence Day (November 28), formed the core of the new calendar, but days were also set aside for honoring the worker and a number of agricultural festivals.

In April 1990, the regime rescinded laws prohibiting the practice of religion. In November, the party voted to return all houses of worship to their respective religious communities. Most churches and mosques had been converted into gymnasiums, movie theaters, and warehouses, and others had been allowed to fall into disrepair. Therefore, implementation was slow. About 40 churches had been turned over to religious authorities by April 1991, and this process continues into the 21st century.

A much more serious problem in rebuilding the church is the shortage of priests. There were fewer than 10 Greek Orthodox priests in the country in April 1991 and only 32 Catholic priests. All were elderly, and most had spent long years in prison. The head of Albanian Catholics, the Apostolic administrator of Durrës, was a 76-year-old man who lived in total retirement in a small village in the north of the country.

On March 21, 1991, a symbolic mass was said in Shkodër Cathedral, though the building was not really in a condition to be used. Its two towers had been demolished in 1967, its portal was boarded up, and inside the yellow plaster was peeling everywhere. In another symbolic act, Mother Teresa, an ethnic Albanian born into a prosperous family in nearby Skopje, North Macedonia, came to Shkodër in March 1991. She attended the first mass at Shkodër Cathedral and founded a convent nearby. The three nuns in residence opened an orphanage for unwanted Albanian children. Mother Teresa had founded her own order in India and adopted Indian citizenship. Her adopted country rejected Tirana's request in 2009 to send her remains from Calcutta to Albania for reburial.

The Islamic community has taken back its remaining mosques, but they are also in a dilapidated condition. One mosque, the Xhamia e Plumbit, an 18th-century mosque that stands before the gates of Shkodër, had been rehabilitated somewhat and is currently in use. Muslim clerics suffered a treatment similar to Christians, and they are also elderly men who have served long terms in prison. Muslim and Catholic leaders condemned the proposed 2009 law to make Albania the first Balkan country to legalize same-sex marriage.

Perhaps the only Albanian writer with an international reputation is Ismail Kadare, who lives in both Albania and France. He graduated from Tirana University and went to Moscow to study at the Maxim Gorky Literature Institute. Since he mastered the technique of writing his 30 books in a manner that could be read in two different ways, he was not sent to labor camps or executed during the communist era, as were other critical authors. In fact, his career flourished in Hoxha's regime, and he belonged both to parliament and the regime-sponsored Writers Union. He was one of the few Albanians allowed to travel abroad. His fiction offers rare insights into life under tyranny. His best novels are said to be *The Three-Arc*. The two elements that defined traditional Albanian culture were religion—primarily Islam—and the way of life associated with the peasantry of the Balkans.

Albanian communist films were extremely popular in Mao's China, as they provided a window into the world while also packing a dollop of Stalinist values. With a growing nostalgia for some elements of the Cultural Revolution, many Chinese return to watching those films online. At the same time, in 2017 Albania's Institute for Communist Crimes announced its push for outlawing TV broadcasts of most communist-era films as "a massive brainwashing tool" and "an ethical and aesthetic catastrophe" for the youth.

After 1945, the Albanian Party of Labor introduced its own double agenda, an economic goal of industrialization and a social goal of creating the "new socialist person." Industrialization raised the urban population and led to increased mechanization of the countryside. In addition, because of its need for trained technicians, the regime set up many new technical schools that eventually produced an educated urban elite. Albania is still basically a rural and peasant society, however, with over half the people living in villages where clan or feudal relationships persist.

Albania remains heavily clan-oriented. A negative aspect of this is the ancient rite of Kanun ("blood must be paid with blood") to settle feuds between families. This is found in northern Albania and Kosovo, mainly in remote mountain villages, but also sometimes in cities. The odious practice had been outlawed during the 40-year communist reign of Enver Hoxha and almost completely disappeared. But it erupted again after the collapse of communism ushered in a new atmosphere of lawlessness. It is estimated that 20,000 people have been trapped by such feuds since 1991, with 9,500 killed and about 1,000 children deprived of schooling. The only safe place for a male (even a child) marked for death is within the confines of his home, which is off-limits. Women and children are spared, but even those men who escape abroad are sometimes hunted

Albania

down and murdered. These blood feuds are the subject of Joshua Marston's remarkable 2012 film *The Forgiveness of Blood*, which was received positively in Albania.

In an attempt to reduce the negative aspects of this, the chiefs of the best-known families in the north met in 2005 and adopted a new "code of honor" for vendettas to replace the one in effect for more than six centuries. The main improvement is that families have the right to exact vengeance only on the perpetrator of a wrong, not on every male family member bearing the same last name as the wrongdoer. The innocent should be spared.

If this works, it would be an enormous relief for more than 800 families with more than 2,000 children who live cloistered lives in Albania and Kosovo out of fear of being killed in a private vendetta. This change comes as Albanian authorities are intensely working on resolving the problem. They are drafting laws with severe sanctions, including the seizure of property, for those who commit such murders. Changes in the penal code include sentences of 25 years to life in prison for those who kill in a blood feud. That has helped diminish the practice. According to the minister for corruption and humanitarian problems, "vengeance is also a crime." Helping to change Albanians' image of conflict are dozens of pop stars coming out of the Albanian diaspora.

CURRENT ISSUES

The EU's summit in Greece in June 2003 gave it and other Balkan nations the assurance that they can also join someday. The Stabilization and Association Agreement (SAA) talks had stalled because of lack of progress in the critical area of justice and home affairs. But in June 2006, it signed an SAA with the EU, and it formally applied for admission in 2009. In December 2010 Albanians were awarded visa-free travel throughout the 25-nation EU Schengen Area. In June 2014 it became an official candidate. In April 2018 the EU announced that both Albania and North Macedonia could begin formal accession talks. An elated Prime Minister Edi Rama called this a "new chapter in our history of long efforts, struggles, defeats and results for the last three decades to reach our European dream."

By 2020, the EU plans on spending approximately $730 million to improve the country's infrastructure. It will take several more years to secure full membership. Many members doubt that Albania is ready, given unsolved problems of corruption and inadequate legal institutions.

The EU told the country's leaders that, if they are interested in membership, they must push through key reforms rather than feuding with each other and boycotting parliament. Albania must tackle corruption head on. In 2008 Transparency International ranked it among Europe's 10 most corrupt countries, and in 2016 it was still the 7th worst. Prime Minister Edi Rama has made the elimination of corruption one of his two top priorities (the other one is unemployment). He initiated programs, such as an online anticorruption portal. The portal allows users to anonymously record any instances of corruption that they encounter. Thousands of reports have been logged, and a few dozen have been referred to prosecutors. Another program, implemented in March 2015, sends text messages to citizens after they visit state-run hospitals, asking whether they were asked to pay a bribe in order to receive treatment. Such programs slowly improve the situation. While its rankings in Europe remain dismal, Albania did improve its worldwide standing from 110th out of 175 countries in 2014 to 83rd out of 176 in 2016.

Albania's EU dream also depends on its economic performance. In 2015, the World Bank ranked it as the worst (189th) in the world in the handling of construction permits. It was told to reform its electoral practices, improve the standards of state administration, and upgrade electrical generation and the transportation system.

There has been progress in the economic area. The government has made notable advances in privatization. Road improvement has been impressive, although there is still much work to be done. Tirana, one of the least appealing examples of communist taste and neglect, got a facelift while Prime Minister Edi Rama was its dynamic mayor. No city in Europe has changed as much in the quarter-century to 2018 as Tirana. More than a third of Albania's population lives there, and it generates half of the country's GDP.

The old politburo quarter, off-limits earlier to the common people, underwent a radical transformation, becoming the hottest spot for night life, with cafes, restaurants, and a nightclub. Even Enver Hoxha's former residence now houses a coffee bar. Bicycle lanes were created in Tirana and other towns. Rama admitted, "Of course, Tirana will never become Paris or Rome, but that doesn't mean we shouldn't make the effort." The United Nations awarded him a prize for environmental development. Remittances from about 1 million Albanians working abroad are important economic stimuli, and some foreign investors have returned.

Improving Albania's economy and environment is a joint concern for the country and its European neighbors. Albanians were one of the top five nationalities—besides Syria, Afghanistan, Iraq, and Pakistan—pouring into Greece and the European Union during the massive migration wave of 2015. However, the EU soon decided that Albania does not qualify as an "unsafe country," therefore its citizens cannot claim the right to political asylum. As economic migrants, they have to return to their country with its high unemployment. Not surprisingly, Albanians are very eager to join the EU. In a poll administered in 2016, over 90% supported the idea.

There is no doubt that a possibility of gaining EU membership is the most powerful carrot and the stick the international community has in Albania. The preelection crisis of 2017 would have certainly dragged on for far longer and perhaps developed into a more dangerous confrontation if it had not been for the EU intervention. Prime Minister Rama stirred up a lot of emotions and negative reactions when he warned that, in the absence of a realistic path to EU membership, Albania may seek a "little union" with Kosovo or other Albanian-population areas. This clear hint at "Greater Albania" spooked neighbors and other countries alike and generated vehement denouncements from Serbia and Russia, both of which insist there is a western and Albanian conspiracy to place all ethnic Albanians in one country. Kosovo president Thaçi's warm reaction, combined with his push for a referendum that would support a union (or rather merger) with Albania, plus his attempts to create a Kosovar army, added fuel to the fire.

North Macedonia, in particular, erupted as the VMRO-DPMNE party mobilized crowds fiercely opposed to North Macedonian Albanians' (and, they surmised, Albania's) influence in their country. The European Union walks a thin line between being able to pressure Albania with the promise of membership on the one hand and trying to maintain the standards of accession on the other. An EU member, Greece, protested loudly against the placement in Tirana's Skanderbeg Square of stones from various parts of the Balkans, including a Greek region of Filiates. The Greeks strongly objected to what they saw as "tangible proof of the central support for irredentist tendencies against the countries bordering Albania, given that the names of regions of various Balkan states are literally etched in stone." Symbols matter a lot in this part of the world.

Albania has also counted on the United States. In the wake of the abortive coup in Montenegro, Prime Minister Rama made an ardent plea to the Trump administration not to abandon his country in the face of a possible Russian interference.

A crucial test of Albania's ability to progress toward EU standards is the justice reform that was passed in 2016 but remained still languishing by the summer of 2017. Many officials in the justice sector and politicians are suspected of corruption, so making headway has been slow. Some 800 judges and public prosecutors need to be vetted, and a "decriminalization law" is to screen out politicians and public servants who had past or pending criminal convictions.

Costs of a failure to reach a higher level of development may also include a growing frustration among Albania's youth. An increasing number of young people join the ranks of jihadi organizations abroad. In 2017, a former Muslim imam was sentenced in absentia for recruiting men to fight with rebel groups in Syria. Almir Daci, who apparently fought in Syria himself, received a sentence of 15 years in prison for recruiting at least 25 men in eastern Albania. A theology teacher was arrested after she made statements supportive of ISIS.

Albania's desire to join NATO was fulfilled in April 2009. Then-prime minister Berisha had asserted in 2007, "We are determined to take any decision, adopt any law, undertake any reform that would make Albania suitable to receive the invitation to join the Western military alliance." Its dispatch of soldiers to Afghanistan, Iraq, and Bosnia gained it powerful advocates for membership. But Albania is full of antiquated weapons and ammunition left over from the communist era that had to be destroyed in a safe way.

Its communist past becomes an attraction of sorts to tourists, and the government decided in 2017 to open up the mysterious Sazan Island off the coast of Vlorë. Crisscrossed by antinuclear tunnels and reinforced with bunkers, this former military stronghold had been off-limits even to Albanians.

Albania has progressed from a failed state to an imperfect but functioning democracy. It was one of the few European countries not to have experienced a recession in recent years. Nevertheless, it remains one of Europe's poorest countries. Corruption is rife, and organized crime and trafficking plague the land. The country faces heady challenges.

Since 2011, Albania was subjected to an enormous hacking attack. It was the most disruptive in Europe on a NATO country since 2007, when Russia assailed computer networks in Estonia. Albania has been the weakest NATO country since it joined in 2009. It was one of the 14 formerly communist states to sign up. A secretive Iranian group called Mujahadeen Khalz (MEK) is the most likely suspect. Prime Minister Edi Rama called the assaults "absolutely the same as a convention aggression only by other means."

Albania, Serbia, and North Macedonia are the founding members of the Open Balkan Initiative (OBI). More details of the OBI are given in the chapter on the Republic of Serbia.

Romania (România)

Sinaia Monastery

Area: 92,046 sq. mi. (238,397 sq. km).

Population: 19,051,562 (January 2023 estimate)

Capital City: Bucharest (pop. 1,739,297 city and municipality). (2023 estimate)

Climate: Continental, with four distinct seasons and a moderate rainfall. The average annual temperature is in the low 50s F (about 11 °C) in the south and in the 40s F (about 8 °C) in the north.

Neighboring Countries: Moldova, Ukraine (northeast); Bulgaria (south); Serbia (west); Hungary (northwest).

Official Language: Romanian.

Recognized minority languages: Hungarian, Vlax Romani, Ukrainian, Turkish, German, and Russian.

Ethnic Background: 89.3% Romanians, 6.0% Hungarians, 3.4% Romani, 1.2% others.

Religion: 84.8% Christianity (73.4% Romanian Orthodoxy, 6.2% Protestantism, 4.5% Catholicism, 0.7% other Christian), 0.5% others, 9.0% undeclared, 5% no data.

Form of Government: Unitary semi-presidential republic.

Chief of State: Klaus Iohannis, President (elected November 2014).

Head of Government: Marcel Ciolacu, Prime Minister (since June 2023).

Public Holidays: January 24 (Day of the Unification of the Romanian Principalities); December 1 (National Day of Romania).

National Flag: It is a tricolor consisting of three vertical bands of equal width, colored blue, yellow, and red. The colors are said to symbolize various aspects of Romanian history and culture. They were the colors used in the insignia of Moldavia and Walachia, two principalities that later joined to form Romania. Their local flags were likewise based on ancient heraldic banners. Walachia also chose a naval ensign with horizontal stripes of red, blue, and yellow, colors later selected for the Romanian national flag. The first flag that became the basis for the modern Romanian tricolor was

Romania

Dacia, c. 110 AD

Wallachia, Moldavia, Transylvania, c. 1555

and Bulgaria. One hundred miles from the Black Sea, the river turns north and eventually east again, flowing through Romania to the Black Sea. The area between the river and the sea in this region is known as Dobruja and has been the object of many disputes in the past. Romania's seaports, Constanța and Mangalia, lie on the Black Sea. Recently canals have been completed through Dobruja and Bulgaria, making transit along the Danube to the Black Sea shorter by more than 100 miles. In 2013 a second bridge over the Danube was opened between Vidin on the Bulgarian side and Calafat in Romania.

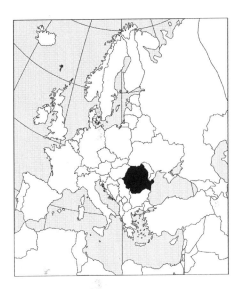

produced during the Revolutionary 1848. After its modifications throughout history, it was finally defined by the constitution in 1998 simply as three vertical bands of blue-yellow-red. The symbolic interpretation of the colors states that the blue represents freedom, the yellow represents justice, and the red stands for fraternity.

Currency: Romanian Leu (plural: lei) RON.

Main Exports: Vehicles, machinery, mechanical appliances, iron and steel, cereals.

Main Imports: electrical machinery and equipment, vehicles and automobiles, minerals, fuels, and oil, pharmaceuticals, medical equipment and supplies, grain.

Main Trading Partners: Germany (19.8% of exports and 17.8% of imports), Italy (10.1% of exports and 8.2% of imports), Hungary (7.4% of exports and 6.5% of imports), Bulgaria (3.9% of exports and 7.0% of imports), France (6.0% of exports), Poland (5.9% of imports).

In the first half of the 20th century, Romania's capital city of Bucharest earned a reputation as the "Little Paris of the East" because of its wide boulevards and stylish villas. Communism and a self-serving ruling communist dynasty under Nicolae Ceaușescu from 1965 to 1989 changed that and much else. Under his regime the increasingly impoverished Romanian people were forced to make every sacrifice in order to secure the country's independence from Moscow and to fulfill the megalomaniac dreams of its repressive leader. It is now a country with much work to do to catch up with the rest of democratic Europe. Balkan in geography, Orthodox in religion, Latin in language and temperament, and European in ambition, Romania is the Balkans' largest nation.

The dominant feature of Romania's geography is the chain of mountains that

separate Moldova and Muntenia (formerly a part of Wallachia) from Transylvania in the west. This has been most commonly described as a giant reverse "S" composed of the eastern and southern Carpathians. They extend westward as far as the magnificent cliffs of the Iron Gate, located on the banks of the Danube River, where it flows through the Alps. This mountain range continues through Bulgaria, where the bottom of the "S" forms the massive Balkan Range. About one- fourth of Romania is covered by forests, which are an important source of wood and timber products.

The Danube flows eastward for more than 200 miles from the Iron Gates, forming the 290-mile border between Romania

Romania

Peles Castle, Sinaia, built by Carol I

The other geographical feature is a plain that begins in the southwest, just south of the Iron Gate, and broadens as one travels eastward. By the time one gets to Bucharest, the "valley"—for it is actually the northern side of the Danube River Valley—has widened to about 80 miles. East of Bucharest, it widens out into a broad plain, which becomes the delta of the Danube River. This plain is the chief grain-growing region of Romania. Although mountains dominate the center and north of the country, much of this area actually consists of mountain valleys or plateaus. It is thus agriculturally productive.

Although most of the population is ethnic Romanian, minorities constitute approximately 12%. The two historic provinces of Moldova and Wallachia are overwhelmingly ethnic Romanian, but Transylvania has significant Hungarian and German minorities. Estimates of minorities vary considerably, but Hungarians are about 6.0% of the population, Germans .3%, Ukrainians .3%, Russian .2%, and Turkish .2%. Romani (Gypsies) officially are 3.4%, but that percentage may be as high as 10%. The census allows citizens to say what they are, and some Roma categorize themselves as "Romanian." Other minorities include Jews, Armenians, Serbs, Turks, Bulgarians, and Greeks.

Political Status: Independent states in the east and south from the 13th century; Turkish control from the 15th and 16th centuries in the south and east; increasing Russian influence in the 19th century; independent in 1878 after Russian-Turkish conflict. The western sector was under the Hungarian Crown in the Middle Ages, under independent princes in the

16th century, and under Habsburg control and later part of Austria-Hungary until 1918, when it became a part of Romania. Communist state, part of the Soviet bloc, 1945–1989.

HISTORY

Origins of the Romanian State

The Romanians trace their earliest history back to an unknown time when their ancestors, the Dacians, formed a state in the Danube area. Conquered by the Roman Emperor Trajan (Marcus Ulpius Traianus) in 106 AD, Dacia became a province of Rome, remaining under its rule until the Emperor Aurelian (Lucius Domitius Aurelianus) withdrew Roman forces in 271. Although the Latin heritage of the present-day Romanians is reflected in their name and language, they are not completely distinct from their Slavic neighbors. This is because the Dacians were subjected to Slavic influence during the centuries that followed the Roman withdrawal. Some Romans remained and with the Dacians formed the modern Romanian nation.

Not much is known about the life of the Dacians until the 13th century. Possibly they found safety from the invasions of the barbarians from central Asia by moving high into the Carpathian Mountains, living in pastoral isolation.

There are three major areas that constitute Romania today: Muntenia (former Wallachia), Moldova, and Transylvania. The first became an independent state in the 13th century, and Moldova did the same in 1359. Transylvania, which had been inhabited by the ancient Dacians, was under the Hungarian Crown

during the Middle Ages, under independent princes (but still responsible to the Hungarian monarch) during the time the surrounding area was part of the Turkish Ottoman Empire in the 16th and 17th centuries, under the Habsburgs after 1687, and under Hungarian (Magyar) control after 1867. It finally became part of Romania after World War I.

The Turkish Ottoman Empire gained control of Wallachia and later Moldova in the 15th and 16th centuries. They were not incorporated into the empire but were allowed a measure of independence in choosing their princes, called Hospodars.

At the beginning of the 18th century, the Turkish rulers started to select puppet Greek princes. Until the 19th century, Wallachia and Moldova were nominally under Ottoman rule, which was not always rigid and was often shared with other powers. In addition to Turkish control of their internal affairs, the Romanians were also subjected to the cultural influence of the French, economic domination by the Greeks, and political intervention of the Russians.

The Treaty of Adrianople, signed in 1829, recognized Russian interest in the two principalities. In it the Turkish sultan agreed that rulers elected by the two states could not be removed without Russian consent. It further provided that Russia could briefly occupy the area. During this occupation, which lasted from 1829 to 1834, the principalities were governed by a Russian commander, Count Pavel Kiseleff (Павел Дмитриевич Киселёв), who helped prepare the Organic Statutes, which became the basic law of Moldova and Wallachia.

According to the statutes, the two principalities would be separate, each with

Carol I

its own assembly of wealthy landowners, who would in turn elect a prince. The forces of nationalism and revolution soon undermined this system of separation. As the revolutions of 1848 spread across Europe, some echoes were felt in Romania, as well. In Wallachia, revolutionaries forced the ruler to abdicate and set up a provisional government, which proclaimed as its goal the unification of all Romanians into a single state. Russia then intervened to suppress the revolution, but the goal was finally accomplished 13 years later.

Russian occupation of Moldova and Wallachia in 1853 was one of the causes of the Crimean War, which followed in 1854–1856. Under the terms of the Treaty of Paris, which ended the conflict, Moldova and Wallachia were placed under the joint protection of France, Great Britain, and Austria. After the Paris Peace Conference, these powers decided that each Romanian principality was to have a separate assembly and prince. On matters of common concern, the parliaments could meet together.

This attempt to keep the two principalities separate was reversed in 1859, when both chose Alexandru Ioan Cuza to be their prince. Two years later, he proclaimed the unified Romanian state, with Bucharest as the capital. He made efforts toward land reform, freeing the peasants from their feudal obligations. But the peasants were not given enough land to live on, and they remained indebted to the landlords. Cuza was ousted in a military coup staged in 1866 by both conservatives and liberals, who favored installation of a member of European royalty as ruler in Romania.

They selected Karl of Hohenzollern-Sigmaringen (a distant relative of the king

Ferdinand I

of Prussia) as prince of Romania. Romania subsequently became an independent state as a result of the Russo-Turkish War of 1877–1878 and was then declared to be a kingdom. He took the title of King Carol I (Karol I) of Romania in 1881, the title he used until the end of his reign in 1914. Shortly after Carol was installed as prince, a new, democratic constitution was adopted, which led to the creation of two political parties—the Liberal Party representing the middle class and the Conservative Party representing the landowners. These two political parties essentially alternated in power throughout Carol's reign. The large peasant class had no voice in government.

Under the terms of the Treaty of Berlin, signed after the Russo-Turkish War of 1877–1878, the province of Bessarabia (returned to Romania by the Treaty of Paris in 1856 and called "Basarabia" in Romanian), reverted to Russia. Romania was compensated by receiving the region of northern Dobruja from Türkiye.

The Balkans were relatively quiet during the rest of the 19th century, but that changed soon after 1900. A revolution in Serbia in 1903 brought a new dynasty to the throne, while Bulgaria declared its independence from the Ottoman Empire in 1908. That was partly a reaction to the "Young Turk" revolution carried out in the Ottoman Empire in 1908. Although people in the Balkans feared that the "Young Turk" revolution would strengthen the Ottoman Empire in the long run, the short-term effect was to weaken the Ottoman Empire and make it vulnerable to attack from without.

This is essentially what happened in 1912, when the First Balkan War erupted. In that war, Montenegro, Serbia, Bulgaria, and Greece attacked and defeated the Ottoman forces, then they seized almost all of the Ottoman Empire's remaining territories in the Balkans. Then the three of the victors (Serbia, Bulgaria, and Greece) fell to quarreling over the spoils, which led Bulgaria to go to war against Serbia in the Second Balkan War in 1913. Romania, which had avoided involvement in the First Balkan War, now allied itself with Serbia against Bulgaria. For its efforts it obtained the southern Dobruja from Bulgaria.

Romania remained neutral during the first two years of the First World War, but British and French promises of Bukovina, Transylvania, and other Hungarian lands lured it into the war on the Allied side. The war did not go well for Romania. When its troops invaded Transylvania, German forces counterattacked and then pushed on to Bucharest, which they occupied on December 6, 1916. Romania sued for peace in early 1918, but as the tide turned against

Germany, it reentered the war. Romania was thus on the winning side at the peace conference. It was in a particularly good position to press territorial demands, since its troops had occupied Transylvania and Bessarabia near the end of the war.

Romania after World War I

The peace settlement at the conclusion of the war gave Romania Bukovina (formerly part of Austria), plus Transylvania and part of the Banat (both formerly Hungarian territory). Romania also took Bessarabia back from Russia by the simple expedient of sending in troops after the Bessarabian parliament declared the Moldovan Democratic Republic and voted in 1918 to unite with Romania. (This lasted until 1939, when Russia repossessed Bessarabia.) It also kept southern Dobruja, which it had taken from Bulgaria in the Second Balkan War.

Romania had thus doubled in size. Now its chief task was assimilating all of the people living in these new territories. The areas that created the most trouble were Transylvania and Bessarabia. Transylvania had a large Szekler population related to the Magyars of Hungary that rejected assimilation. In addition, the Hungarian government rejected Romania's claim to the area and encouraged the Szekelys to retain their Hungarian identity. In spite of vigorous opposition from Transylvania, Romania adopted a new constitution that gave the country a highly centralized government.

Bessarabia had been a subject of dispute with Russia since the beginning of the 19th century. In 1812, Russia acquired the territory from the Ottoman Empire. The Treaty of Paris transferred southern Bessarabia to Moldova in 1856. Russia took it back in 1878 at the conclusion of the Russo-Turksh War. After 1918 Romania had Bessarabia back, though it could hope to keep it only as long as the new revolutionary Soviet government in Russia remained weak. Moreover, although Bessarabians spoke Romanian, the province also included numerous other minority groups who had no reason to want to be part of Romania.

Romania had internal problems, as well. Perhaps its greatest was the need for land reform. Eventually, the government broke up many of the larger estates in such areas as Transylvania and distributed smaller parcels of land to the peasants. This allowed more peasants to support themselves. But most peasants, then almost 80% of the population, continued to live in poverty. Romania embarked on a program of industrialization financed by taxes levied on the peasantry.

King Ferdinand, who had succeeded his uncle to the throne in 1914, reigned until 1927. His son, Carol II, did not take the

Romania

throne immediately because he preferred to live in Paris with the attractive Madame Lupescu. As a result, Michael, Carol's young son, was nominal ruler from 1927 to 1930, with Nicholas, Carol's brother, as regent. Carol II finally returned to Bucharest in 1930 and persuaded parliament to revoke the law excluding him from the throne. Well known for his many romantic escapades, he renounced his throne twice to pursue his amorous adventures. He earned his nickname, "the playboy king."

From 1930 to 1940, King Carol actively promoted the disintegration of the traditional political parties by playing party leaders against each other and, in the process, strengthening his own power. By 1938 Romania was a royal dictatorship.

During the late 1920s, a group called the League of the Archangel Michael was organized. In accordance with its biblical name, it was supposed to do battle with the devil. In Romania, the devil turned out to be anyone who opposed the league, which was fascist and anti-Jewish in outlook. Its name was later changed to the Iron Guard, by which it was better known outside Romania. After his return, King Carol subsidized the group, and it became the largest fascist party in the Balkans.

In the 1937 elections, the National Peasants Party received the largest vote, but the king refused to ask its leader, Iuliu Maniu, to form a government. Instead, the leader of the fascist National Christian Party was named premier. His dismissal in 1938 marked the beginning of Carol's dictatorship. A new constitution was drafted; the Iron Guard was outlawed; and the Front of National Rebirth, Romania's fascist party, replaced political parties.

In the 1920s and early 1930s, succeeding governments had supported the League of Nations and "Little Entente" as ways to preserve the balance of power in the Balkans. From 1936 onward, however, Romania cultivated closer ties with Hitler's Germany. In spite of this, Romania lost in the first year of World War II the territories acquired after the First World War. Russia took Bessarabia back, as well as northern Bukovina. Hungary got northern Transylvania, while Bulgaria took back Southern Dobruja.

An Ally of Nazi Germany

Carol II abdicated in September 1940 and fled Romania. He ultimately settled in Portugal, died in 1953, and a half-century later in 2003 his remains were returned to Romania where they were interred in the town of Curtea de Arges with national honors. General Ion Antonescu formed a government backed by the Iron Guard. Two months later, on November 23, 1940, Romania joined the Axis powers. The cooperation between General Antonescu

Carol II with son Michael in 1936

and the Iron Guard did not last long. With Hitler 's blessing, he suppressed an attempted revolt by the Guard in January 1941. Hitler's concern for stability in Romania was greater than his support for "like-minded" parties whose activities disrupted the country of an ally.

From early 1941 until mid-1944, the country was governed by Antonescu's military dictatorship, with the backing of German troops. Romania participated in military operations against the Soviet Union after Germany invaded that country, and it made heavy contributions to the Axis war effort, including liquidating Jews. There were several pogroms, including one in Iasi in 1941, where as many as 12,000 Jews were murdered. Before the war Romania (including Bessarabia) had 1 million Jews; only about 6,000 remain. In October 2009 a monument was unveiled in Bucharest honoring the 300,000 Jews and Roma who perished in the Holocaust. Nevertheless, some Romanians still admire Marshal Ion Antonescu because he had fought against the Soviet Union to recover Romanian territory.

In 2016, the government approved legislation to speed up restitution claims from

the Jews whose property had been seized by the Romanian fascist regime and later nationalized by the communists. With only about 11,000 Jews remaining in Romania from their prewar population of some 800,000, Holocaust survivors don't have much political clout. While tens of thousands of claims were submitted by the deadline in 2003, more than 40,000 remained unanswered by 2016.

Although there was only a very weak anti-Nazi movement in Romania, it was the first Axis satellite to defect at the close of the war. On August 23, 1944, King Michael (Carol's son), backed by the National Peasants Party, the Liberal Party, the Socialist Party, and the Communist Party, ousted the Antonescu government. Romania then declared war on Germany. Negotiations that had started in Cairo were ended in September in Moscow with the signing of an armistice.

The Romanian People's Republic Is Born

Prior to World War II, the Romanian Communist Party had been weak and unpopular. Outlawed in 1924, its pro-Russian attitude and advocacy of self-determination for Bessarabia and Transylvania were contrary to prevailing opinion. The government quickly suppressed a communist-sponsored railroad strike in 1933 and arrested dozens of party members.

During the 1930s and 1940s, there were two groups of Romanian communists: the "home" communists, who were behind bars in Romania, and the "Muscovites," who had fled to the Soviet Union to avoid being jailed and persecuted. In the early postwar period, the power struggle between the two groups became the most significant feature in domestic politics. The "Muscovite" communists—Ana Pauker ("Red Ana"), Vasile Luca, Teohari Georgescu, and Emil Bodnăraş—returned to Romania in 1944.

In October, the communists joined with the Social Democratic Party, the Union of Patriots, and the Ploughmen's Front to form the National Democratic Front. The first objective of this union of parties was to launch an attack on the National Peasants Party, headed by General Constantin Sănătescu, which controlled important posts in the government. Nicolae Rădescu replaced Sănătescu.

Early in 1945, the communists started a campaign to publicize a program that they hoped would bring them to power: agrarian reform, a new government, and the return to Romanian administration of that part of Transylvania transferred to Hungary during World War II. There was a communist-supported demonstration in early 1945, in which several people were killed. A few days later, Andrei Vyshinsky, one of Molotov's deputies in the Soviet Foreign Ministry, demanded the resignation of the Rădescu government. He further specified that a National Democratic Front government, led by Petru Groza, should be put in power. Rădescu could offer no resistance, since Romanian troops had been ordered out of Bucharest.

Nicolae Ceausescu

The new government included noncommunists as well as communists, but the important Ministry of the Interior, which controlled the police, was given to Teohari Georgescu, one of the "Muscovite" communists. Northern Transylvania was returned, and a land reform program was started. General Ion Antonescu was executed in mid-1945.

The Soviet Union recognized the new government headed by Groza. The United States and Britain did not, however. In a compromise, a special commission was created to advise King Michael, titular head of state, which included representatives of the National Peasants Party and the Liberal Party. This new, "broadened" government then set the time for new elections.

The enlarged government took office in early 1946 and was recognized by the western powers the following month. Elections, in which women could vote

for the first time, were held in November 1946. In the months before the elections, the communists pressured some of the other parties into running a common list of "government" candidates. The result was a victory at the polls for this bloc.

A peace treaty signed on February 10, 1947, formally returned Transylvania to Romania. It specified that other frontiers were to follow the line of January 1, 1941. This meant that Bessarabia and northern Bukovina remained part of the Soviet Union, and southern Dobruja stayed with Bulgaria.

The communists eliminated opposition from other political parties outside the National Democratic Front in 1947. Ion Mihalache, Iuliu Maniu, and other leaders of the National Peasants Party were arrested and sentenced to life imprisonment on charges of conspiring with American intelligence officers. The National Peasants Party was outlawed, and government officials from the Liberal Party who had agreed to a common list of candidates in the elections were dismissed in late 1947. The left-wing Social Democrats, who had also joined in the common list of candidates, were absorbed into the Communist Party, which now became the United Workers Party. It retained this name until 1965, when it again became the Communist Party of Romania. Having neutralized all opposition, the communists removed the last remnant of the old system by forcing King Michael to abdicate at the end of 1947.

A new constitution was adopted in 1948, and the Romanian People's Republic was officially born. The story of internal politics in the following years involved a struggle for power between the "home" and "Muscovite" communists. Initially the "Muskovite" group controlled the government; Ana Pauker was foreign minister, Vasile Luca was minister of finance, and General Emil Bodnăraş was minister of war.

A "home" communist, Gheorghe Gheorghiu-Dej, had helped organize the railroad strike in 1933 and was arrested and sentenced to 12 years in prison. He escaped in August 1944 and in October 1945 became secretary-general of the Communist Party. This meant that he was titular head of the party, while Ana Pauker and her associates were in control of the government. During the postwar years, he consolidated his power and gained sufficient support from within party ranks to remove Pauker, Luca, and Georgescu from their party and government posts in 1952.

The subsequent official Romanian explanation of this purge is an example of rewritten history. The move was described as the beginning of Romania's independence from foreign domination. The fact is that there was no real change in Romanian foreign policy or

A TV picture shows the Ceausescus upon their capture.

Romania

in Romania's relations with Russia until the late 1950s and early 1960s. Also of significance was the execution in 1954 of Lucrețiu Pătrășcanu, a moderate national communist who had been removed from office in 1948. This event took place two years after the supposed beginning of Romania's new national course.

A more probable explanation of the 1952 purge was that the victory of the "home" communists resulted from an internal power struggle in which Gheorghiu-Dej had the support of General Bodnăraș and probably Moscow. The reason for dismissing Pauker and her followers was their supposed responsibility for economic failures.

In addition to his party post, Gheorghiu-Dej became chairman of the Council of Ministers in 1952. Holding the highest party and government offices, he had become the real ruler of Romania. The death of Stalin in 1953 brought upheavals in the communist world, and Gheorghiu-Dej adapted to these changes. He continued to exercise the primary power in Romania until his death in 1965.

Following Stalin's passing, the Soviet leadership adopted the principle of collective leadership. Gheorghiu-Dej obediently resigned his party post, retaining for himself the position of chairman of the Council of Ministers. Gheorghe Apostol, the trade union chief, became first secretary of the Communist Party. However, Gheorghiu-Dej soon realized that the party post was more important than the government position, so he took it back in 1955, giving up his government position instead. Chivu Stoica became the new chairman of the Council of Ministers. Two further changes occurred in 1961. Gheorghiu-Dej decided that it would be convenient for him to have a government post, so he added the title of president of the Council of State (ceremonial head of state). He also concluded that Stoica was becoming too ambitious, so he replaced him with Ion Gheorghe Maurer.

The Ceaușescu Era Begins

In 1965 Gheorghiu-Dej died unexpectedly at the age of 63. There was no designated successor, so his offices were divided among his subordinates. Nicolae Ceaușescu was Gheorghiu-Dej's deputy in the party secretariat, and he managed to obtain the top party post, that of secretary-general.

Ceaușescu had joined the Romanian Communist Party in the 1930s through its youth organization. A protege of Gheorghiu-Dej, he became a full member of the party politburo in 1955 at the age of 37. Over the next 10 years, he occupied himself as a member of the Central Committee Secretariat. His special area of responsibility was party organization and cadres, a

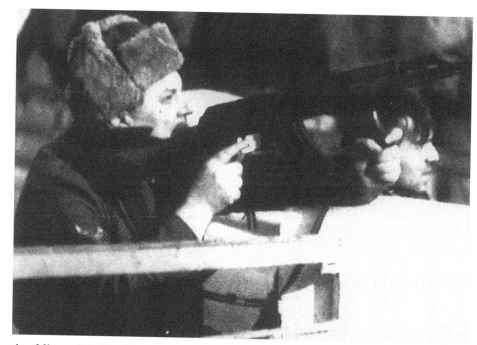

A soldier points his rifle at enemy positions during street fighting in Bucharest.

position that allowed him to exercise extensive control over party appointments. In 1965, however, he was only one of three individuals who wielded power in a collective leadership.

It was under these circumstances that the ninth congress of the Romanian Communist Party met in July 1965. The congress approved a new constitution—the one in force until the revolution of 1989—and a new set of party laws. Its adoption was largely symbolic. It did not change the system in any important respect, though it did announce that Romania was no longer a "people's republic" and that it would be known as the "Socialist Republic of Romania." It made explicit that it was the Romanian Communist Party that exercised all leadership within the state. It placed a general emphasis on national independence. At the same time, it abolished the Szekler autonomous region, which had originally been set up in Transylvania to give the Hungarian-speaking minority a modicum of self-government.

The National Assembly elected Ceaușescu to succeed Chivu Stoica as president of the Council of State. He was on his way toward establishing his preeminent authority within the country. Over the next several years, Ceaușescu also became chairman of the National Defense Council, supreme commander of the armed forces, and chairman or honorary chairman of a number of party and state commissions and committees. The culmination of all this came in 1974, when the constitution was amended to create the position of president of the republic.

Of course, it was filled by Ceaușescu. This accumulation of offices was accompanied by the development of a full-blown "cult of personality" around Ceaușescu. In speeches and in the press, he began to be referred to as the "hero of heroes" and the years of his rule as "the years of light." In later years, he was given credit for everything that happened in the country.

More ominously, he also placed his family in important positions of power in the government and party. Three of his brothers held senior posts in the government, one on the Council of Ministers, while his wife, Elena, was first deputy chairman of the Council of Ministers, member of the Permanent Bureau of the Political Executive Committee (Romania's equivalent of a politburo), and chairman of the National Council for Science and Technology. She became the regime's chief censor. Finally, his son Nicu was first secretary of the Union of Communist Youth and a candidate member of the Political Executive Committee. Nicu's wife was also a member of the Central Committee.

Ceaușescu trained an oversized omnipresent secret police organization, called Securitate, composed of handpicked privileged agents who were fanatically loyal to him. They kept the general populace in a constant state of terror. One in 30 citizens worked as informers for the Securitate. It is estimated that of the half-million political prisoners sent to the infamous Râmnicu Sărat Prison in the 1950s, before the Ceaușescu era, one-fifth died of the harsh conditions. In 2013 former prison commander Alexandru Vișinescu was

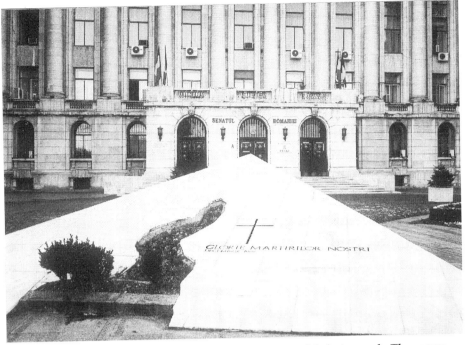

Palace on Revolutionary Square, where Ceausescu gave his last speech. The monument reads: "The glory of our martyrs." In 2004 the Senate moved from this building to the Palace of the Parliament.

put on trial. This was the first case of its kind in Romania to reexamine the culture of impunity.

Ceaușescu used public funds to finance such grandiose schemes as his creation of a grand avenue and presidential palace, which he had been building in the middle of Bucharest. The construction of this extravagant structure nearly bankrupted the country, consuming an estimated third of GDP at one point. It employed 20,000 construction workers, and it required so many megawatts of power that Bucharest suffered electrical shortages for years. Today it houses both parliamentary chambers it is the second-largest office building in the world, after the Pentagon.

His many homes had golden bathroom fixtures and other objects of splendor. Ceaușescu also continued the grand program, launched in 1988, of transforming the countryside by razing half of Romania's villages by the year 2000 and moving the inhabitants into new high-rise buildings in "agro-industrial" centers.

Ceaușescu's Fall

All of this was swept away at the end of 1989 in a violent uprising that ended in Ceaușescu's and his wife's deaths by firing squad on December 25. Proud of his independence from Moscow, Ceaușescu had rejected Gorbachev's policy of reform and made every effort to isolate his countrymen from events going on elsewhere in central and eastern Europe. In November 1989, he had reaffirmed his policies at

a party congress and had been reelected head of the party for a further five-year term. It was probably this act of reaffirmation that was responsible for his downfall. His policies had caused a significant decline in Romanians' standard of living over the previous decade.

The revolt actually began as an ethnic dispute in the city of Timisoara, in the western part of Romania, when a Hungarian Reformist priest was arrested. Grossly exaggerated reports in the west spoke of up to 60,000 deaths. In the end it was only 100 deaths but still a tragic massacre. It spread to Bucharest, the capital, when Ceaușescu called a mass meeting for December 21 to denounce the events in Timisoara. Instead, the people began shouting "freedom" and "democracy," and Ceaușescu stalked off. That afternoon, the streets were full of people demonstrating against him. In the evening, his wife ordered the secret police to begin firing on the people and had the Securitate burn the victims. General Milea, the defense minister, refused to obey a similar order to the army. He committed suicide the next morning after Ceaușescu called him a traitor. But the army now joined the revolution. Ceaușescu and his wife fled the capital, but they were captured, driven around the countryside in a tank for two days, taken to a remote military base, tried in a hastily prepared military court, and summarily executed. In July 2010 their bodies were exhumed to try to solve the mystery of where they were actually buried.

The Securitate fought on for a few days more, often resorting to underground tunnels and weapons caches. But the army gradually managed to restore order. In the meantime, a group calling itself the National Salvation Front emerged as the new political leadership in the country. In 1999 the Securitate files began to be opened in an effort to heal the wounds of communism. In 2007 they were turned over to the Independent National Council for the Study of the Securitate Archives. Historians estimate that there were a half-million Securitate officers and millions of informers (1 out of 30 Romanians) who spied on their fellow countrymen. In 2006 the Institute for the Investigation of the Crimes of Communism was established to look into the activities of the secret services. No senior communist or Securitate official had ever been put on trial until 2014, when the former commandant of the notoriously brutal Râmnicu Sărat Prison was put on trial. One out of five died behind bars. Securitate agents have proved to be pervasive and resilient, with extensive political and business connections.

In general, many of the "new democrats" who rushed forward to promote capitalism had actually been from the privileged Communist Party elite (called nomenclatura) that had promoted communism before the revolution. Many of these former communists control much of Romania's wealth today. The Romanian edition of Forbes' rich list in December 2009, the 20th anniversary of Ceaușescu's fall, provided details of how 85% of the richest 100 people in Romania are from the former nomenclatura.

The New Regime

The Front, at first made up almost exclusively of former establishment figures who had fallen out with Ceaușescu, was enlarged within a few days to take in various noncommunist elements. It then began referring to itself as the Council of National Salvation. In the third week of January, it announced that multiparty elections would take place in May and that it intended to run its own candidates. This brought condemnation from the leaders of the three largest opposition parties. After a series of negotiations, the council agreed to make room for representatives of other parties. On February 1, it brought the representatives of 29 other political parties into the government coalition. By this time, it had grown to approximately 180 members. It also underwent a name change and became the Provisional Council for National Unity. A new 10-member Executive Committee, headed by acting president Ion Iliescu, came into existence at this time.

Meanwhile, having reorganized itself as a political party, the original National

Romania

Salvation Front announced that it, not the council, would field candidates in the upcoming May 20 elections. As its candidate for president, it nominated Ion Iliescu. Most of the leadership of the front had been members of the old Romanian Communist Party, and the local branches of the National Salvation Front set up at the time of the revolution were largely made up of ex-officials. Thus, while the old Communist Party structure had collapsed, a large percentage of its membership transferred their loyalties to the National Salvation Front.

Eventually, some 80 political parties came into existence, though only 3 of them had any significant political support in the country. Two of these, both parties that were outlawed when the communists took over, were the Liberals and the Peasant Party. The third, the Hungarian Democratic Union, represents the interests of ethnic Hungarians. Although the opposition attacked the National Salvation Front because of its high component of ex-communists, there was, in fact, little to differentiate between them as far as programs were concerned. All said that they were committed to the creation of a multiparty democracy and a market economy.

In the May 1990 elections, Ion Iliescu was elected president with approximately 83% of the vote, while the National Salvation Front took 66% of the seats in the National Assembly. Election observers announced that there had been some irregularities in the voting, but overall the election had been free.

For approximately six months, the policies of the new government remained unclear as factions within the front debated whether Romania would move toward a free market or attempt to develop some sort of mixed economy, with the government continuing to play an important role. Petre Roman, the new chairman of the Council of Ministers (prime minister), called for a transformation to a market economy within two years. Others talked about a gradual transition that would safeguard jobs and wages. The Peasants Party and the National Liberal Party, the two main opposition parties, had argued for a rapid transition to a market economy and privatization of land and industry. Their showing in the May 1990 elections strengthened the hand of those who argued for a mixed economy.

Still some progress was made. Over the summer, legislation was passed encouraging the creation of small businesses and authorizing the government to turn state enterprises into privately owned companies. Other legislation authorized the government to sell apartment houses built after 1948. Longtime bureaucrats found it easy to frustrate the intent of these laws.

A larger issue was that the democratic credentials of the government came into question after it encouraged miners to attack a group of antigovernment demonstrators on University Square in Bucharest in June 1990. Six individuals were killed in the resulting violence, and the headquarters of some of the opposition political parties were ransacked. Antigovernment rallies continued over the summer. As a result, the Romanian government found itself boycotted by potential donor countries, in spite of its desperate need for economic assistance.

In October, Petre Roman submitted to parliament another package of land, banking, and tax proposals, which he said were intended to speed Romania's transition to a market economy. Among the proposals was that prices of nonessential goods and services would be freed, though the government would continue to subsidize the price of energy, fuel, and rent for another year and control the price of basic foods and services. Although Romanians were talking about these proposals as radical and likely to contribute further to the spiral of inflation that had hit the country, they were actually yet another example of gradualism that would leave the underlying problems unsolved.

The government did take one set of actions of a positive nature. It redistributed almost a third of the country's arable land to private farmers. The result was an unusually good grain harvest and an increase in meat and fresh products in the unregulated farmers' areas.

It began converting the National Bank into a western-style central bank in December 1990. The bank was to give up all of its retail operations and confine itself to issuing currency and controlling monetary policy. The Foreign Trade Bank, which formerly performed certain central bank functions, gave up its monopoly over foreign exchange. Private banks were also authorized at this same time. Eight private banks came into existence within the next six months, the first being the Banca Comercială Ion Tiriac SA (renamed Tiriac Bank), founded by a Romanian expatriate, the ex-tennis player Ion Tiriac.

Although Roman's economic reforms had the support of international economists, their implementation led to a drop in the standard of living of most Romanians, as inflation outpaced wage increases. The matter became serious in September 1991, when 52,000 coal miners in western Romania went on strike over pay and prices. Several thousand made their way to Bucharest, where they demanded the resignation of Petre Roman. The demonstrations soon turned violent. Before they were over, three persons had been killed, and hundreds had been wounded.

President Klaus Iohannis

President Iliescu, whose relations with his prime minister had been bad for some time, fired Roman and promised the miners that he would form a new "government of national openness." With so much violence and disappointment, many Romanians now refer to this time as the "stolen revolution."

Roman afterward charged that Iliescu and his allies had called on the miners to demonstrate and that it was all a communist plot to remove him and reverse his economic reform. There is no evidence of that. It appears, rather, that Iliescu took advantage of the miners' protest to get rid of Roman. It does not seem to have been a policy matter either, for the man Iliescu named as Roman's replacement, Theodor Stolojan, had at one point been minister of finance in Roman's government and later was his minister for privatization. A strong believer in reform, he pledged his new government to a continuation of Roman's economic policies. His was a government of national unity.

In the lead-up to the September 1992 elections, the National Salvation Front split over whether to support Iliescu. The pro-Iliescu faction became the Democratic National Salvation Front, while Roman's wing organized itself as the Front for National Salvation. Iliescu won in the second round, taking 61.4% of the votes. In 2018 Iliescu was indicted for crimes against humanity committed during the revolution.

POLITICAL SYSTEM

The revolution of 1989 overthrew the old communist regime and installed a revolutionary regime, whose stated goals were the creation of a multiparty democracy and a market economy. Free elections occurred in May 1990. The new government gave itself 18 months to draw up a constitution, and it accomplished that

Romania

Palace of the Parliament, housing both the Chamber of Deputies and the Senate; the largest legislative building in the world

when the new constitution was approved in a popular referendum on December 8, 1991. It lacked specific guarantees of rights for minorities that ethnic Hungarians had demanded. This was rectified in September 1996, when Romania signed a new treaty with Hungary that included a section wherein each side promised to treat its minorities according to high "European standards." Minorities are guaranteed seats in parliament.

In 2003 90% of Romanian voters supported amending the constitution to promote market and democratic reforms necessary for entry into the European Union (EU). The government was so afraid that the required minimum of 50% of eligible voters would not turn out to vote, thereby invalidating the referendum, that government officials, doctors, party members, and even priests were enlisted to go door to door in some regions to encourage people to vote. In areas with snow, voting officials carried ballot boxes directly to people's houses and asked them to vote on the spot. They set up special voting booths at railway stations and made loud-speaker announcements that travelers could vote there, even if their identity cards had expired. The final participation was 55%.

Romania has a bicameral parliament. Since both chambers are elected in the same way by the people, both have the same legitimacy. The method was changed for the November 30, 2008, elections and is now a "mixed member proportional representation system." Some members are elected through party lists, and others are elected individually. New multimember constituencies called "electoral colleges" (colegii electorale) were drawn up. If a candidate wins more than 50% of the votes in the constituency on the first round, he or she gets a seat. In those constituencies left over in which no candidate wins 50% the first round, the seats are distributed according to proportional representation. This means that a party wins a percentage

of seats based on the percentage of votes it wins. A party must win at least 5% of the votes nationwide to win any seats, although special rules apply to parties representing national minorities.

The Senate has 137 members. The Chamber of Deputies, or lower house, has a differing number of seats from election to election. From 2000 to 2004, it had 344 seats, thereafter 332. In the Chamber of Deputies there is 1 representative for every 70,000 inhabitants; in the Senate, 1 for every 160,000. In a November 2009 nonbinding referendum, an overwhelming majority of voters favored abolishing one of the two parliamentary chambers and reducing the number of members.

Many sets of presidential and parliamentary elections have taken place in an orderly fashion. Most observers now concede that Romania has completed the transition to a multiparty democracy. No single party or coalition commands a majority.

The Presidency

The president, who is popularly elected, exercises overall executive power. He is expected to set general policy and act as spokesman for the nation. In addition, he has specific responsibilities in the areas of foreign affairs and defense. He nominates the prime minister, who must be confirmed by the Grand National Assembly, and other senior officials. He has some supervision over the judicial system and controls the security services. Laura Stefan of the Romanian Academic Society think-tank described his powers in this way: "The president deals with big issues, deciding how things should move forward, but he doesn't actually do anything directly." Presidential and parliamentary elections are normally held at the same time. Among the democratic-era presidents were Emil Constantinescu of the Democratic Convention Alliance (1996–2000) and Ion Iliescu of the Party of Social Democracy (1990–1996 and 2000–2004).

In December 2004 Traian Băsescu, a former oil tanker captain, transport minister, and mayor of Bucharest, unexpectedly and narrowly defeated the sitting prime minister, Adrian Năstase. A no-nonsense politician with an unpolished brand of charisma, He championed a government anticorruption drive; a successful Romanian entry into the EU; and, in his words, "making Romania a democratic country in real terms."

Nevertheless, most politicians came to loath him as confrontational, devious, authoritarian, threatening, and divisive. He bullied and manipulated opponents and allies alike. Due to his rough governing style, he made very few friends in the political establishment. Parliament voted 322 to 108 to impeach Băsescu. He was accused of using the secret services, which the president controls, to discredit his many political enemies (for which no proof was found) and of creating political deadlock. This was the culmination of months of recriminations, mudslinging, and feuding that included a live call-in TV show on which the president and prime minister called each other a liar.

In the May 19, 2007, referendum, 74% of voters voted for the president to remain in office; turnout was only 44%. This result did not end the bickering that has been an obstacle to reforms. His triumph was marred by a scandal. On the day of the voting, he was accosted by a female journalist who tried to film an impromptu interview with him on her cell phone. He lost his temper, insulted her, and grabbed her phone, telling her she could have it back later. Unaware that it was still recording, he complained to his wife about the "aggressive, stinking gypsy." He later apologized for that indiscretion.

Nevertheless, he won reelection in 2009 against ex-foreign minister Mircea Geoană by the thinnest of margins: 50.33% to 49.66%. Geoană's greatest drawback was his cozy ties with the tycoons who

Romania

Prime Minister Viorica Dancila

dominate big business and media. Although international observers concluded that the vote largely met their standards, Geoană alleged fraud and filed a complaint with the Constitutional Court, which can invalidate election results. The court unanimously rejected the complaint.

In July 29, 2012, he had to endure yet another referendum seeking his impeachment. The new center-left government of Victor Ponta accused him of allegedly abusing his power and intervening too actively in economic policy. Băsescu had little public support, since his approval rating had plummeted to 17%, in large part because he backed austerity. A crushing 87.5% voted against him. Ponta temporarily suspended Băsescu and appointed an interim president. However, since the turnout was only 46.2%, less than the required 50%, the Constitutional Court

ruled the referendum to be invalid and reinstated Băsescu. The EU warned Prime Minister Ponta against using the power of decree to change the rules for referenda, to weaken the court, and to undermine the rule of law. Ponta still demanded that Băsescu step down on the grounds that the massive vote against him left him discredited. He refused and stumbled along in office until his term expired in 2014.

In the November 2014 presidential elections, the upset winner over Prime Minister Victor Ponta was a member of the tiny German minority in Transylvania and a Protestant, Klaus Iohannis, mayor of the tourist city of Sibiu. He won 54.5%. Turnout was 62%, the highest in 18 years. He is a former physics teacher who ran an anticorruption campaign. Nearly 400,000 emigrants were allowed to vote in their embassies, and the overwhelming majority of them cast their votes for Iohannis.

Declaring that "you cannot fight corruption with white gloves," Iohannis has been a strong supporter of the DNA anticorruption agency, which helped provide it with some real teeth—in 2014 its prosecutors charged 1,100 people in court and won an unusual 90% of cases. The president also exerted a lot of pressure on members of the parliament to vote down a bill granting politicians immunity from prosecution. In 2017, he opposed attempts by the Grindeanu PSD-ALDE government to decriminalize certain acts of corruption. Later, even though he vowed only to appoint a new prime minister that is a person of integrity, his approval of Mihai Tudose for the post was met with mixed reviews, since Tudose is well known for having plagiarized his dissertation.

Prime Minister Marcel Ciolacu
Source: *Wikipedia*

Klaus Iohannis was re-elected president of Romania by a landslide in 2019.

Parliament and Prime Minister

The prime minister chooses his cabinet, which must also be confirmed by the Grand National Assembly. The prime minister articulates specific policies, maintains liaison with the legislature, and oversees the day-to-day operations of government. Many parties compete for seats, and they change their names frequently.

The corruption watchdog Transparency International ranks Romania as the most corrupt EU country after Bulgaria (and 70th in the world). Bribery is endemic, including for securing medical treatment or favors from teachers or professors. The government appointed a respected nonparty justice minister, Monica Macovei, to take corruption by the horns. Bribery and kickbacks have long greased Romanian hands, but the EU made it clear that its timely entry into the club would depend on how well it dealt with this endemic problem. Legitimately worried about backsliding, it also implemented a post accession monitoring program.

Macovei introduced the biggest judicial shake-up in the country's history. New law requires that officials and their families must publish their assets and incomes on the Internet. This includes villas, cars, gifts, and other perks. Not desiring to do this, a third of all judges and prosecutors quit in the first year. Forty border police, nine members of parliament, four members of the Tăriceanu government, and the deputy prime minister were charged.

As a result of making such a disclosure on a form required by the EU, former prime minister Adrian Năstase was charged with graft in a landmark case. He tried to explain his acquisition of three apartments,

Building opposite Bucharest University with a banner for the Social Democrat Party

Young Romanian diplomats with their American professor in Bucharest

jewelry, and cash worth more than $1 million as gifts from his wife's dead aunt. His nickname, "Seven House Năstase," and his well-heeled lifestyle visibly above his official salary had long raised questions about his commitment to bringing corruption under control.

His Social Democratic Party (PSD) is both a party and an economic elite. Its leading supporters sold the best state assets, mostly to themselves at discounted prices, and then proclaimed a free-market revolution. Although the PSD was back in power, Năstase was again indicted on corruption charges, along with four accomplices, in 2009. He was sentenced to two years in prison in 2012 for illegally raising $2 million for a failed presidential campaign against Băsescu, becoming the first ex-prime minister to be sent to prison. He was the "big fish" conviction the EU had long asked for. Four others received six-year terms.

Năstase reportedly attempted to commit suicide at the time he was arrested, but a policeman lunged toward him, causing him to shoot himself in the neck rather than his head. He was carried away on a stretcher. Năstase claimed to be the victim of a politicized judiciary. A Romanian anticorruption specialist noted, Romania "is becoming a country where the powerful have to account for what they've done." In March 2013 he was released from prison after only nine months, during which time he wrote three books. This way, he took advantage of a remarkable law passed to help those prisoners willing to write (or perhaps have someone ghostwrite and smuggle into the prison) a publication. Those who do can have their sentence reduced by one month for each book.

Trials are now randomly assigned to judges by a computer so that those charged cannot steer their case into the

court of a friendly judge. Millions of dollars have been invested in computerized databases for police and courts, and the hiring of prosecutors and judges is done on the basis of open competition rather than cronyism. A secret police unit, which was suspected of blackmailing prosecutors and judges, has been closed down.

These new laws enabled the soft-spoken female judicial chief to face down tycoons and politicians accustomed to justice ministers who take orders rather than give them. Unhappy with the effect a public-sector pay cut could have on their €600 salaries (equivalent to an emergency doctor or university professor), the judges went on strike in September 2009, saying that the conditions under which they have to work are a "humiliation" that would be made worse by the cuts. They vowed to hear only "urgent cases." Given the independence they have been granted from politicians, there was little the government could do about this. The EU, which has pressured Romania to improve its judicial system to fight corruption, had watched with concern this rare strike.

The fragile government fell in March 2007, and a minority government, composed of Călin Tăriceanu's Liberals and the Hungarian ethnic party, was formed. In April Monica Macovei was dropped from the new cabinet for not being "a team player." Her activities had come too close to too many politicians. She had suffered a vote of no confidence in the Senate, and her reforms were incomplete. Romania was already under fire from the EU for not fighting corruption sufficiently. But in May 2007 the government finally created the Agency for Integrity, which the EU required of it. Its head until August 2008, Daniel Morar, quickly became intensely disliked by most politicians and the media.

Nevertheless, now that Romania is a full member, the EU has lost its most powerful against it, and the elites feel like they are off the hook. In its July 2008 report on corruption, the EU wrote of regression on all fronts, of all high-level corruption trials having been rebuffed by courts, and of the absence of a single verdict on a prominent corruption case.

The sincerity of its anticorruption efforts was not helped by a newspaper sting operation in February 2011, whereby a journalist with *Romania Libera* sent a text message to all 460 members of parliament suggesting a meeting with representatives of a fake United Arab Emirates investment fund to discuss a possible deal. A fourth of the parliamentarians expressed interest in the proposal; only 10 answered that they were forbidden from accepting such offers. An advisor to President Băsescu concluded that "the fight against corruption is the key to everything that is going on now in Romania," and it is a cause of the political paralysis that prevails.

Mass street protests in 2012, sometimes violent, caused the rapid downfall of two prime ministers: Emil Boc and Mihai-Răzvan Ungureanu. The latter survived in office only 78 days. In May 2012 he passed the prime ministership to Victor Ponta, leader of the Social Democratic Party, which dominates the Social Liberal Union (USL). This is an awkward alliance of liberals and social democrats. He presented himself as a modernizer in the mold of Tony Blair. He vowed to reverse the "social injustices" of the austerity policy. At 39, he was the EU's youngest head of government.

Ponta's center-left USL alliance won by a landslide in 2012. His only disappointment was not having gained a two-thirds majority. This would have given his party the parliamentary votes to change the constitution.

In June 2015 Romania's anticorruption agency announced that it was investigating Prime Minister Ponta for potential money laundering, forgery, and tax evasion prior to his taking office. His family members were also under investigation. President Iohannis asked him to resign, but Ponta vowed to stay on until the parliament (controlled by his party) dismissed him. The parliament promptly voted to preserve his immunity a few days before his corruption trial. However, following a deadly nightclub fire in Bucharest in November that killed 32 people and injured more than 160 others, some 20,000 people took to the streets, blaming the government for the incident and demanding that the prime minister step down. It became an indictment of the whole political system, where permits and safeguards took a back seat to money and political

Romania

interests. Faced with the massive protest, on November 4 Victor Ponta announced his resignation by stating, "I am doing this because, in all the years I have been in politics, I put up resistance during conflict with political adversaries, but I have never fought against the people." In 2018 all charges against him were dropped.

Protests continued, however, in the atmosphere reminiscent of previous mass mobilizations, including the 1989 overthrow of the communist regime. A new government full of technocrats was appointed, led by Dacian Cioloș, a former EU agriculture commissioner. His task became to steer the country until the next election, scheduled for late 2016.

The legislative election of December 11, 2016, included both the Chamber of Deputies and the Senate. It was based on the party list proportional representation principle again rather than the winner-take-all plurality system used in 2008 and 2012. The turnout was again a dismal 39.44%, and many parties were brand new or new coalitions of older parties. The Social Democratic Party (PSD), led by Liviu Dragnea, won 45.5% of votes and 154 seats in the 329-seat lower house and 67 out of 135 seats in the Senate. The National Liberal Party (PNL), led by Alina Gorghiu, received 20% of the popular vote, 69 seats in the Chamber of Deputies, and 30 in the Senate. The third-largest party was a freshly created Save Romania Union (USR) that won 8.9% of votes, 30 seats in the Chamber of Deputies, and 13 in the Senate. The Hungarian UDMR received 6.2%, the Alliance of Liberals and Democrats (ALDE) won 5.6%, and the center-right People's Movement Party (PMP) won 5.4%. Because PSD leader Liviu Dragnea was legally prohibited from becoming prime minister due to a criminal conviction for electoral fraud, he selected Sorin Grindeanu as his stand-in. ALDE joined the government with the PSD. Henceforth began a bizarre series of developments.

Just as the National Anticorruption Directorate was getting to more and more officials, on the night of January 31, 2017, Grindeanu's government issued a decree decriminalizing corruption by officials if the amount involved was less than about $48,000. The law would have stopped ongoing investigations of corruption offenses, freed officials convicted of corruption (supposedly to reduce prison overcrowding), and prevented further investigations related to those offenses. Massive protests of up to 500,000 people throughout the country ensued, probably the largest in Romania's history and certainly since the fall of Ceaușescu. Protesters noted that many prominent politicians, including Liviu Dragnea, would benefit from the decree. Under pressure, the

government relented and withdrew the ordinance. Later, it tried again by submitting it to the Senate. Widespread popular protests continued, and the international community expressed its disapproval. Protesters coordinated their mass gatherings through social media, using #rezist, which became a symbol of the movement. In May, a Senate committee dropped the proposed legislation.

Irate, Dragnea sought to remove Grindeanu, ostensibly for not passing his party's initiatives, such as a tax cut and salary raises for public employees, but he refused to leave. In the end, just six months after placing him in power, the PSD held and succeeded in passing a vote of no confidence in its own prime minister due to his "contempt for democratic rules . . . immaturity and political irresponsibility." Former prime minister Victor Ponta saw the vote as "an atomic war."

A new cabinet was formed, led by Mihai Tudose, a former two-time minister of economy. He was in office from June 2017 to January 2018. His selection did not satisfy crusaders for integrity because the one thing he is known for is having plagiarized his doctoral dissertation in 2010. In 2016 he asked for his degree to be annulled but continued to list his doctorate on the official website of the parliament. In January 2018 he was replaced as prime minister by Viorica Dăncilă, who was in office until November 2019, to be succeeded by Ludovic Orban who served as prime minister until December 2020.

Instability returned to politics; the country had five prime ministers in as many years. In the December 2020 elections, the Social Democrats captured 30% of the votes, the PNL 26%, and the

ultra-conservative Alliance for the Unity of Romanians (AUR) a surprising 9%. American-educated Florin Cîțu became prime minister. He was in office until November 2021, and was succeeded by Nicolae Ciucă. Ciucă served as prime minister until June 2023.

Marcel Ciolacu, the leader of the Social Democratic Party, currently serves as the Prime Minister of Romania. Ciolacu led the party to victory in the 2020 Romanian parliamentary election but was not able to form a majority coalition in the new convocation. Other parties opposed to the PSD formed a new coalition on December 23 and formed the new government pushing Ciolacu's PSD into opposition. However, in 2021, following the political crisis that led to the collapse of the Cîțu Cabinet, he managed to bring the PSD back to the government, forming a cabinet with its former rival, the National Liberal Party, thus forming the National Coalition for Romania.

Next parliamentary elections are scheduled to be held in Romania on or before December 2024.

Foreign Policy in the Communist Era

Romania first obtained the freedom to develop its own independent foreign policy in 1958, when Soviet troops were withdrawn from the country. From then on Romania prohibited the permanent stationing of foreign troops on its soil. But the issue over which it split with the Soviet Union, its desire to industrialize, first became an issue in 1961–1962. It was at this time that the Soviet Union proposed the creation of a supranational planning group within the Moscow-dominated Council for Mutual Economic Assistance (CMEA, also known as COMECON) to

Central Square, Brasov, one of seven former Austrian cities

Timisoara Opera Square

decide which country should produce how much of what. The Soviets wanted an international division of labor that would allow some countries to emphasize industrial production, while others (notably Romania and Bulgaria) were intended to be a source of raw materials and agricultural products. The Soviet-Chinese dispute gave Romania the chance to defy Moscow. The first sign of opposition came in 1963, when Romania refused to support the creation of the CMEA group.

In 1964, the Romanian Central Committee issued a statement that has been described as a "Declaration of Independence" in economic as well as political matters. In the economic area, it asserted the right to develop its own natural resources. In political affairs, it rejected the idea that any communist party was superior to another, claiming the right of each party to develop its own policies. Its attitude toward the Warsaw Pact military alliance was similar to its view of CMEA.

Romanian leaders successfully resisted Soviet attempts in 1966 to strengthen the Warsaw Pact by creating a permanent eastern European political authority and by increasing the integration of the various military units from each country. When the Soviet Union and other Warsaw Pact allies intervened in Czechoslovakia in 1968, Ceausescu criticized the invasion and pledged to resist any Soviet incursion into Romanian territory. Romania maintained this critical attitude toward the Soviet Union from that time onward. It always rejected Warsaw Pact maneuvers on Romanian soil and refused even to attend the annual meeting of Warsaw Pact nations in 1971.

Relations improved somewhat in the middle of the 1970s. But in 1979 Ceausescu publicly aired his differences with the Soviet Union over Soviet Middle Eastern policy (especially the diplomatic isolation of Israel) and Soviet demands that Warsaw Pact allies increase their military expenditures.

In 1980, Romania openly, if indirectly, criticized the Soviet invasion of Afghanistan. Ceausescu attacked countries that "gravely threaten the cause of people's independence." The Romanian position became even clearer in 1981, when it abstained on a United Nations vote demanding the withdrawal of foreign troops from Afghanistan. All of the Soviet Union's eastern European client states voted against the resolution.

He also took an independent position with regard to Soviet SS-20 missiles and Theater Nuclear Force (TNF) negotiations. In 1983, after the Soviets withdrew from the TNF talks in Geneva, Ceausescu issued a public call for both the Soviet Union and the United States to stop deploying nuclear missiles and to resume arms control negotiations. Another example of Romania's independence was the Soviet decision to boycott the 1984 Summer Olympics. Every other Soviet "ally" joined in the move, but Romania sent its athletes to Los Angeles and brought back 32 medals, including 20 golds, to place third in the total number of medals won.

Romania's relations with the Soviet Union became more complex after the Soviet Communist Party's 27th congress in 1986. Ceausescu forthrightly condemned Gorbachev's programs for economic reform, but at the same time, Romania's economic ties to the Soviet Union actually increased. Gorbachev finally paid a visit to Romania in 1987. The Soviet press gave the visit low-key treatment, but the Romanian press was far more enthusiastic. Several economic agreements were signed, but it was clear that political differences remained.

Under Ceausescu, relations with other countries were basically determined by those countries' ties with the Soviet Union. Thus, the primary thrust of Romanian foreign policy in those years was to establish close links with those countries opposed to an expansion of Soviet power. A second, related interest was Romania's desire to expand its trade with the west. Neither of these principles involved a turning away from communism. Domestically, Romania remained among the most orthodox of communist nations.

During those years, it maintained its closest relations with the People's Republic of China. The reasons for this are clear. In addition to a common ideology, the two nations strongly opposed Soviet domination of the communist world. Romania consistently supported the Chinese arguments in the Sino-Soviet quarrels. In addition, there was a regular exchange of high-level diplomatic missions between the two countries and an extensive promotion of cultural contacts and trade.

Relations with western Europe and the United States developed on another basis during those years, with trade perhaps being the most important factor. Romania never made the mistake of thinking it could ignore its geopolitical position entirely or that it could depend on any country other than itself in case of extreme Soviet displeasure. It was nevertheless the first central or eastern European nation to establish diplomatic relations with the Federal Republic of Germany.

Ceausescu and Relations with the United States

Until about 1985 it went out of its way to encourage better relations with the United States. The breakthrough dated from 1967, when Richard Nixon, visiting various European capitals, stopped in Bucharest and was personally received by Ceausescu. Two years later, then-president Nixon decided to pay a state visit to Romania as part of a round-the-world trip. He thus became the first American president to make a state visit to a communist country. Nixon suggested the visit to "needle our Moscow friends," but he wanted to show his appreciation for the way he had been treated in 1967. The visit took on a symbolic importance beyond that, however.

First of all, a Romanian Communist Party conference, to which the Soviet leadership had been invited, had to be rescheduled in order to make the visit possible. Originally scheduled to attend the conference, Brezhnev and Kosygin canceled out of the rescheduled conference. Second,

Romania

as reported by a New York newspaper, Nixon received "a warm reception from hundreds of thousands of flag-waving Romanians in the largest and most genuinely friendly welcome of his global tour." President Nixon asked Ceaușescu to act as a channel of communication to the Chinese. The subsequent breakthrough in American-Chinese relations, therefore, owed something to the Ceaușescu connection.

The Nixon trip to Romania was followed by a Ceaușescu visit to the United States the following year. Lasting two weeks, it had an obvious political component, but its major emphasis was economic. He met with a number of American businessmen and signed a contract for a $10 million aluminum sheet-rolling mill and an agreement for an exchange of researchers and university teachers. Ceaușescu visited the United States twice after that time, in 1973 and again in 1978.

On the American side, President Gerald Ford stopped in Bucharest in 1975. The US accorded Romania "most favored nation" trade status, meaning that the US conducted normal trading relations with it. The United States also sponsored Romanian applications for membership in such international organizations as the International Bank for Reconstruction and Development (World Bank) and the International Monetary Fund (IMF).

Beginning in the 1980s, the United States became increasingly critical of Romanian internal developments. This was accompanied by occasional threats to withdraw "most favored nation" status unless the Romanian government made certain internal changes. One instance was a tax on Jewish emigration that Romania had instituted. Under the Reagan administration, the American government focused increasingly on Romanian treatment of Christian evangelicals.

The matter came to a head in 1987, when the US Senate voted to suspend Romania's "most favored nation" status for six months to signal that it disapproved of Romania's human rights record. To put an end to such recriminations, Ceaușescu responded by voluntarily renouncing all such trade concessions.

Romania's actions did not put an end to American criticism of Romania's human rights record, however. Several times in the last two years of Ceaușescu's rule, Washington criticized his program to transform the countryside by razing villages and replacing them with high-rise "agro-industrial" complexes. The basis for the criticism was that the program, although billed as an economic measure, was being implemented almost exclusively in areas where there were Hungarian and German ethnic minorities. A major goal of the program appeared to be the destruction of

those centers of non-Romanian culture so that their inhabitants could be assimilated into the majority Romanian culture.

Post-Cold War

Romania's foreign policy changed after the overthrow of Ceaușescu in December 1989 and the creation of a new government committed to democracy and a market economy. But it shifted less than one might have thought. The new leadership attempted to establish a friendly relationship with all nations, and in general it succeeded. Even the Soviet Union welcomed the overthrow of Ceaușescu and followed this up with friendly gestures, such as opening the border between Moldova and Romania for a day so that relatives could visit back and forth.

The repudiation of communism after the failure of the August 1991 coup against Gorbachev, followed by the subsequent collapse of the Soviet Union, obviously changed that relationship with Moscow. Romania quickly moved to establish diplomatic relations with the successor republics, but the changes were more in form than in substance. With the notable exception of the newly independent Republic of Moldova, Romania's main interest in the successor republics was economic, as it struggled to hold on to export markets.

Romania's relations with Moldova are complicated. Except for that part east of the Dniester (Nistru) River (always inhabited largely by Russians and Ukrainians and still hosting Russian troops), Moldova had been part of Romania prior to 1940. A majority of the people living there speak Romanian, although the Cyrillic alphabet was used until 1989. In the wake of the Soviet Union's collapse, the clocks were changed from Moscow to Bucharest time, and a new flag identical to Romania's was

Roma roadside peddler of fuel funnels
Photo by Roman Payerhin

introduced. In Transdniester today the population mix is approximately 60% Russian and Ukrainian and 30% Moldovan. In general, they get along well. Most Russians and Ukrainians speak only Russian, but unlike in Estonia and Latvia, that has not caused major problems. Loose talk in the midst of the 2014 Ukraine crisis about Russia's alleged right to protect Russian speakers everywhere in the former Soviet Union has Moldovans on edge.

In August 2004 Romania promised to supply Moldova with electricity in the event that Transdniester cut its power supplies. To show his support for the Romanian-speaking neighbor, newly elected president Băsescu chose Moldova for his first foreign trip. In theory, Bucharest supports the reincorporation of Moldova, though on a purely voluntary basis. Reunification is no longer a central political issue, and a 2009 poll revealed that only 15% of Moldovans would support it if a referendum were now held. It is mainly intellectuals and the young who feel the most Romanian and would accept a union with Romania. Many see Romania as a promising symbol of European integration. This is an emotional issue in Moldova.

Moldovans who can prove that their forebears were Romanian before 1940 can acquire fast-track Romanian citizenship and passports. Half the poor country's population qualifies. Out of 4 million inhabitants, about 2 million have received Romanian citizenship. This allows them to travel and work in EU countries. Because Romanian officials could process only about 20,000 applications each year, they opened two consulates to keep up with the crushing demand.

Because Romania offers so many passports to Moldovans, it could not complain in 2010 when the Hungarian government passed a law permitting the many Hungarians in Romania to have dual citizenship. EU membership complicates the relationship with Moldovans. The Romanian government promised a special regime for Moldovans living within 30 kilometers (19 miles) of the border.

It was predominantly young Moldovans who rioted in April 2009, when the Communist Party claimed victory in the first round of parliamentary elections, allegedly through fraud. The communist government accused "certain forces" from Romania of having masterminded the outburst, expelled the Romanian ambassador, and imposed a visa requirement on Romanian visitors. Bucharest made a rare public rebuke of the EU by demanding a tougher line toward Moldova. The tension seemed to have quieted down by the time the communists lost power in July 2009.

The United States welcomed the overthrow of the Ceaușescu regime, and its early attitude toward the new government was extremely favorable. Among other things, Secretary of State James Baker arranged a short visit to Bucharest in the spring of 1990. But the United States was also critical of some of the actions of the new government. It decided after the death of six demonstrators in June 1990 that all assistance to Romania would be put on hold.

Washington went along with inclusion of Romania in the aid consortium for eastern Europe. But it was not until Petre Roman visited Washington in 1991 that one could speak of a noticeable thawing of relations. Relations warmed further in 1992, as the administration began to give the Romanian government good marks for such things as allowing greater press freedom, holding democratic elections, and bringing the intelligence services under legislative control. This trend culminated in the granting of "most favored nation" trading status to Romania in 1993. On the occasion of his October 2003 visit to the US and meeting with the American president, ex-president Iliescu stated that "the United States today is an exceptional partner and a friend of Romania."

President Băsescu aspired that Romania become a regional power, like Poland, which requires close ties with the United States and Britain. He had even spoken of a "Bucharest-London-Washington

Prosperous farmers in Bran

axis." This is especially important given the Black Sea's geostrategic significance. Half of the oil that flows into western European markets comes via that waterway, as does much of the illegal traffic in drugs, people, and arms. His slogan was, Securitize the Black Sea basin and democratize the states around its shores, three of which—Ukraine, Moldova, and Georgia—are trying to wriggle free of Russian tutelage. Georgia failed in 2008, and Ukraine, in 2014.

Băsescu was aware that France had been an important supporter of Romania's entry into the EU. However, he became irritated by France's criticism of such close Anglo-Saxon ties and warned Paris to stop lecturing his country about what foreign policy it should pursue: "We have no lessons to receive." He was particularly irked by the French foreign minister's insult that he lacked "a European reflex." This crack was made only a month before French voters rejected Europe's new constitution.

The European Union and NATO

All Romanian governments supported the country's efforts to join the European Union. In 2003 Minister of European Integration Hildegard Puwak stated unmistakably, "We have always shared the same values as the European people. We feel as part of the European family. Acting on this European dream, we have focused all our national resources toward preparing for EU accession." That dream came true on January 1, 2007.

The EU and the US government warned Romania frequently about its widespread corruption, which endangers development. The newspapers are full of stories about scandals of all kinds. Ordinary Romanians, whose per-capita income in purchasing power terms is only 28% of the EU15 average (compared with a 45% average in central Europe), complain about having to pay off bureaucrats and about large companies that pay few taxes. Transparency International's Corruption Perception Index in 2009 ranked Romania among the bottom three among EU members. Both Romania and Bulgaria must still account to the EU on how they are fighting corruption, but the union has lost its most powerful leverage: membership.

Romania recognizes that its enthusiastic support for US policy can cause tension with the EU. It was outraged when Romania defied the EU by being the first country to sign an agreement promising not to surrender American citizens to the newly created International Criminal Court (ICC). That accord was never ratified. In 2003 it raised eyebrows in Brussels when it gave a $2.5 billion contract without a tender to the American company Bechtel to build an interstate highway across Transylvania.

Romania obviously enjoys the EU's largess; among central European countries, Romania is the largest recipient of EU funds, after Poland. There are signs everywhere that the road on which one is driving was financed by the EU. An EU project lasting until 2007 involved the construction of a major highway linking the towns of Nadlac and Sibiu, which will ultimately be incorporated into the Budapest-Sofia-Athens highway. The European Investment Bank lent Romania €131 million to rehabilitate and furnish about 1,400 preuniversity schools all over the country.

Romanian leaders regard NATO membership as the key to solving many of the country's economic and diplomatic problems. Ex-president Iliescu viewed it as allowing his country "to be integrated into the civilized world." Romania enjoyed strong French support when it first applied for membership in NATO, but it was turned down in 1999 chiefly because of American refusal. The alliance had longstanding worries about democratic reform, corruption, and military readiness. It also singled out Romania's treatment of minorities, particularly of the Roma. Romania was the first country to join NATO's Partnership for Peace in the hope of enhancing its prospects for full membership later. It supported NATO actions over Kosovo and agreed to allow NATO planes limited access to the country's airspace. To increase its own firepower, Kosovo purchased American military hardware, including F-16 jet fighters. It also accepted 6,000 refugees from Kosovo. However, fearing destabilization of Serbia and the wider Balkans, it did not recognize Kosovo's independence after its February 2008 declaration.

Romania's and neighboring Bulgaria's value in NATO eyes skyrocketed in the wake of the September 11 terrorist attacks in the US. Indeed, the strategic significance of the entire Black Sea region grew because it became a staging area for the war effort in Afghanistan. In the words of ex-foreign minister Mircea Geoană, "September 11 transformed the Black Sea into a natural springboard." His country regarded itself as a "de facto NATO ally" in the struggle against terrorism. For this reason, both Türkiye and Greece supported the candidacies of Romania and Bulgaria on the grounds that NATO's southern flank has become strategically crucial for combating traditional threats, as well as "new threats," such as terrorism; transborder crime, and trafficking in weapons, drugs, and human beings, including illegal immigrants and women often destined to involuntary prostitution. The government denies any knowledge of rumors that the US maintained a secret CIA prison on its territory.

Romania

Romania and Bulgaria joined NATO in April 2004. Romania already hosted such NATO maneuvers as the information and communications "Combined Endeavor 05" in May 2005 with 1,200 soldiers and 43 partner nations involved. Their admittance provides a geographic bridge between northern and central Europe and Greece and Türkiye. It provides the US and its NATO partners a foothold much closer to the current areas of danger to Europe and North America: the unstable Caucasus and the troubled Transcaucasian region of the former Soviet Union, including Chechnya, the Middle East, and central Asia, all located across the Black Sea. In April 2008 it hosted the largest-ever NATO summit, which extended membership to Croatia and Albania. Of the 5,000 officials who attended, 1,500 were from the US.

Romania cooperated closely with the U.S. to demonstrate what it can contribute as military partners. It unconditionally offered its airspace and use of all port and land facilities, and it refurbished airstrips for allied use. It sent its "Carpathian Hawks" battalion to perform peacekeeping duties in Kabul and guard duty at the US base at Kandahar. Its specialized mountain unit served in the mountainous area helping the US-led force hunt down the remnants of the Taliban and al Qaeda. In 2003 it used its own C-130 transport aircraft to carry its troops to Afghanistan; in 2010 it had 990 soldiers in the ISAF command in that country. It also has tripled its soldiers assigned to peacekeeping missions. It has made available to American troops a military base in Constanța that serves as staging ground for troop rotation in the Balkans. It sent 57 peacekeepers to Bosnia and 151 to Kosovo.

It joined the 10 new democracies in eastern and central Europe in signing the Vilnius Letter supporting the US-British war effort in Iraq in 2003.

Romania opened its airspace to allied aircraft heading to the war in Iraq and permitted 1,000 American soldiers to use the Mihael Kogălniceanu (widely known as MK) Airbase and the nearby Black Sea port of Constanța as a bridge for troops and equipment from the US and Germany to the Middle East. Negotiations were completed in 2006 to make these bases permanent, and the first American troops came in 2007; there is a permanent party of about 100 at MK, with 2,000 soldiers rotating through at any given time. It sent a chemical and biological warfare unit to Kuwait. Its intelligence service also foiled Iraqi attempts to use Romania as a staging ground to organize terrorist attacks on Israel and western Europe. It declared 10 Iraqi diplomats and 31 others as persona non grata and expelled them. It deployed

Bran Castle in Transylvania. Despite the legend, Dracula was never here.

a mechanized infantry battalion with 800 soldiers to Iraq. Fearing for its credibility as a NATO and EU member, it refused to withdraw them in 2005 when several US allies did so. This is despite polls in 2005 showing that 55% of Romanians want their troops to come home. It was among the last 3 of 38 allies to withdraw its remaining troops from Iraq in July 2009. However, it left 13 trainers in the country.

As the US starts moving its European bases farther east, it views both Romania and Bulgaria as its anchors in the southeast, much as Poland is in the north. Romania also has the advantage of being one of the few countries in the region that has no outstanding disputes with any of its Black Sea neighbors and partners. Until the annexation of Crimea, it had been improving its relations with Russia after an icy decade following the collapse of communism. For the first time since its birth in 1859, Romania has no great regional or global power as its immediate neighbor.

Having boosted its military budget to 2.4% of GDP, a higher percentage than most western European countries, to speed up the restructuring process, in 2015 Romania spent nearly $3 billion, or 1.71% of GDP, on the military. The country's military has 60,000 active-duty forces (down from ca. 300,000 in 1989), plus some 15,000 civilians. Of those, 43,000 serve in the land forces; 7,150 in the navy that man seven principal surface combatants, as well as patrol and mine warfare vessels; and 9,700 in the air force. By law, military contractors must perform 80% of the production in Romania.

In 2010 the Supreme Defense Council approved a US proposal to base missile

interceptors in the country. Moscow was extremely upset despite assurances from the Romanian president that none would be directed against Russia. In May 2016, the US opened the $800 million NATO Aegis Ashore ballistic missile defense facility at Deveselu Air Base, near the city of Caracal in southern Romania. SM-3 missile interceptors are defensive and ostensibly not intended against Russia, but Russians dismiss such claims. A military official declared that "they are 200, 300, 1,000 percent aimed against us. They are moving to the firing line." A similar site has been under construction in Poland.

Romania embarked on a policy to modernize its equipment and reduce the ranks of its top-heavy armed forces. Conscription was abolished in 2006 in favor of a professional force. It offered to provide 1 of the 13 EU "battle groups," each with 1,500 troops intended to act on very short notice ahead of forces from other such bodies as the UN.

Greatly concerned about Russia's territorial ambitions in Ukraine and beyond, Romania started considering reinstatement of conscription. In particular, it worries about a possible intervention in the Russian-controlled Transnistria region of Moldova, a country with which Romanians share many traits. As a result, Romania has been at the forefront of a push for tougher sanctions against Russia for its 2014 annexation of Crimea.

ECONOMY

At the end of World War II, Romania was still an overwhelmingly agricultural economy with over three-quarters of the workforce employed in farming. Bucharest, center of what industry there was, was large and relatively modern. There were only three other cities in the country with populations of over 100,000 persons. The political elites who had dominated the government during the interwar period had been committed to a policy of industrialization, but except for the petroleum industry, they were not notably successful.

Immediately following World War II, a land reform act set an upper limit of 123 acres (50 hectares) on all individuals. This also provided for the expropriation of all real property of individuals alleged to have been fascist collaborators. The collectivization of agriculture was begun in 1949. In theory it was voluntary, but peasants who refused to join a collective found themselves required to deliver a set amount of produce to the state at an artificially low price.

Collectivization was completed in 1962, although subsequently there was further amalgamation of collective farms that brought together single villages into new multivillage cooperatives. Under the communist regime, the state purchased, processed, and distributed most agricultural products. It ran town and city markets, where individuals and state and collective farms could market some of their produce. Agricultural output increased considerably during the period 1970–1977 but largely stagnated after that. This was particularly true for animal production. From 1979 onward, Romanians had trouble finding beef and pork in the markets. One reason for this was the government's decision to place a greater emphasis on exporting agricultural products as part of its program to pay off the foreign debt.

Romania dropped four zeros from its money in 2005.

All but 9.4% of the land was controlled by the state. The privately held land (nearly all located in mountainous areas deemed unsuitable for extensive cultivation) plus the private plots of individual collective farmers provided over half of the country's potatoes, fruit, meat, milk, and eggs. In fact, the small private sector produced an estimated one-third of Romania's total agricultural production.

In spite of its shortcomings, collectivization, with its emphasis on mechanization, did bring about major changes in the countryside. The old, traditional farming methods were largely supplanted, and productivity accordingly increased. Excess agricultural workers were drawn into the industrial workforce.

Starting from a relatively low base in 1948, Romania introduced an industrialization program using the Stalinist command model. This resulted in one of the fastest growth rates in the world. The

driving force behind the Stalinist command model was the very high investment level. Up to 35% of gross national product was determined by the state. This results in a rapid growth rate if one is dealing with a situation in which there is a surplus of labor and adequate raw materials, as was the situation in Romania in the 1950s and 1960s. On the other hand, a high investment level means that there is less left over for consumption, and living standards will necessarily remain low. This was the case for postwar Romania.

Under communism, Romania's industrialization program concentrated on the creation of heavy industry rather than consumer goods. The major industries built or expanded during this period include oil refineries, chemical plants, and various sorts of metal-working and machine-building enterprises. In later years, a major area of emphasis was electric power generation.

Two huge hydroelectric stations, the Iron Gate II project with Yugoslavia and the Turnu-Măgurele project with Bulgaria, were constructed during the 1980s. Romania's first nuclear power plant was completed in the second half of the 1980s. These new sources of energy were designed to promote a continued growth in industry in general and the metallurgical sector in particular. Two other projects the government pursued in the 1980s were an expansion of the Galati steel complex and construction of a new steel complex at Călărași.

In the final years under Ceaușescu, Romania had largely exhausted the possibilities of the Stalinist demand model and had reached the point where both labor and raw materials were scarce. In fact, many of the raw materials had to be imported. Instead of moving toward decentralized decision making and placing greater emphasis on quality as opposed to quantity, he stubbornly clung to the command model.

The situation was exacerbated by Ceaușescu's determination to pay back

Îmi place
să vin aici,
în zilele senine.
Dacă văd 1 avion,
înseamnă
că o să mă întâlnesc
cu cineva cunoscut
în ziua aceea.
Dacă văd 2,
o să-mi meargă bine
toată săptămâna.
Iar dacă nu văd
nici unul...
mă duc
la McDonald's™.
i'm lovin'it.

i'm lovin' it

Romania

the foreign debt of approximately $13 billion that he had run up during his industrialization spree in the 1970s. To accomplish that, he instituted a harsh austerity program and cut Romania's hard currency imports by more than two-thirds. Romania also began to reorient its trade toward the CMEA countries, in particular with the Soviet Union. Between 1980 and 1989, the proportion of Romania's trade with other members of the CMEA grew from a third to just over a half. The government was also able to pay off its hard currency debt by the beginning of 1989 but only by dropping Romania's standard of living to perhaps the lowest in Europe. During his last years, food was rationed, cities were unlighted at night, and gas and electricity were available only on a limited basis.

The first sign that the Romanian people were losing their patience came in 1987, when riots broke out among workers in Brasov. They were triggered by a new government decree announcing additional penalties for workers who failed to fulfill production quotas. They were met by tanks, police dogs, and tear gas. For several days, Brasov was off-limits to all foreigners.

The government did not have difficulty putting down the riots, but the blows to Ceaușescu's credibility and to the regime's legitimacy were more severe. Once again, workers had risen up in protest against a so-called workers' state. One indication of this loss of credibility was that, for the first time, some prominent Romanians dared to criticize the regime publicly. One such was Silviu Brucan, former ambassador to the United States and the United Nations, who urged the government to recognize the legitimacy of the workers' grievances. Several government ministers also dared to defend themselves against charges that they were responsible for the widespread shortages.

In spite of these signs of growing domestic opposition, Ceaușescu held to his policy of austerity and used the funds thus accumulated to pay off Romania's foreign debt. In April 1989 it had paid off the last of its foreign loans and was debt-free.

Economy in Post communist Era

The answer of the Romanian people came in December 1989, when they rose up and brought down the entire regime. Romania installed a noncommunist government committed to multiparty democracy and a market economy since the beginning of 1990. But the individuals making up the new government in 1990 were badly divided among themselves as to the proper path to follow. They had been in power for about a year before taking any action to begin transforming the economy. They also made decisions during that first year that temporarily eased

the lot of the Romanian people, but they had negative longer-term consequences.

One of those decisions was to use part of Romania's foreign currency reserves, then about $1.8 billion, to import food for domestic consumption. The government continued the policy in 1991. However, by that time, it had used up most of its foreign currency reserves and turned to financing consumption through an enlarged budget deficit. In effect, Romania was living beyond its means after 1989 and could not afford to do it any longer. International aid helped to close the gap, but the standard of living declined further after 1992.

Economic statistics for this period look awful. For example, industrial production decreased by over 40% after 1989 and then remained at that lower level. Part of this drop resulted from the disruptions of the revolution itself, but there were larger causes, as well. Domestically, shortages of energy and raw materials played an important role. Internationally, Romania lost a significant part of its export market when the Soviet Union collapsed. It also lost a major source of raw material imports.

Romanian workers were unhappy about the economic situation, but they were also extremely fearful about change. Freeing prices had produced a virulent inflation that had eroded wages, while talk of privatization of state firms raised the specter of future unemployment. Surprisingly, polls taken during this period indicated that a majority of the Romanian people continued to favor both privatization and the development of a market economy.

The news from the countryside was also negative. The breakup of the collective and state farms gave land to the peasants, but they had no farm machinery to work the land. In the early 1990s, it was common to see peasants using milk cows for plowing. They have since replaced the milk cows with oxen. Much of the land was fragmented. Many of the former collective farm bosses ended up with large holdings and enjoy annual subsidies from the EU's Common Agricultural Program (CAP). Romanian agriculture is likely to remain at a relatively primitive level for a number of years. In 2009 it imported 70% of its agricultural products. The extent to which Romania has not yet developed a modern economy is shown by the fact that 29% of the workforce in 2015 was still employed in the agricultural sector (producing 6% of GDP), compared with 42.4% in services (52% of GDP) and 29% in industry (42% of GDP).

Under the EU policy of concentrating rural holdings, millions of Romanians will have to leave the land within the next decade. Romanian law encourages larger plots and cooperation among landowners, who are required to sell their holdings

Romanians counted the days
until EU entry.

if they do not cultivate their land within three years. Foreign companies are also purchasing Romanian agricultural assets. The giant American enterprise Cargill bought Olpo Podari, the largest Romanian sunflower oil maker. Cargill already owned about 10% of the country's silo capacity after acquiring Comcereal in 2005. A bright spot is the wine industry, which ranks sixth in Europe in production. However, Romanians prefer plum brandy and beer, and they consume an average of only 20 liters of wine every year, compared with the European average of 37.

Because of the severe deterioration in the infrastructure that occurred during the last several Ceaușescu years, a great deal of money had to go into rebuilding rather than into new growth. The government did launch a voucher privatization program in 1995 that began the process. Citizens received vouchers valued at $325 that they were able to use to purchase shares in 3,905 companies to be privatized. Very little information was made available on the companies, however, so the public had scant ability to choose intelligently. In addition, since very few companies were considered to be profitable, few citizens bothered to turn in their vouchers. Finally, the state retained 40% of the shares, which meant that it retained effective control of the privatized companies.

In 1997 the government proclaimed what it described as the "test of fire" for reforms. Responding to IMF criticism of the slow pace of liquidation or privatization of money-losing enterprises owned

Romania

by the state, it announced the closure of 17 enterprises, including 3 refineries that had originally been built for export markets that never materialized. The decision was a necessary one, but it meant that 30,000 people lost their jobs. Similar actions with regard to money-losing coal mines produced layoffs for 32,000 miners. These various reforms produced the desired result; by 1998, the private sector had grown from 52% of GDP in 1996 to 62% of GDP. However, in 2008, more than 40% of the workforce was still on the state payroll.

Privatization continued. Many large companies were liquidated, including the Min-vest mining company, the hard coal pits in the Jiu Valley, and the lignite mines in Ploiesti. Some were reopened after reorganization, and others were offered for privatization. In 2005 the state sold 50% plus one share of the Banca Comerciala Romana (BCR) and the Romanian Savings Bank (CEC). The state-owned oil company Petrom, whose sales are equal to about 4% of GDP, was privatized in 2004. It had been a vast off-budget reserve of cash, cheap credit, and patronage.

In 1999 Renault took over the Dacia car plant in Mioveni with the intention of producing the modern-day equivalent of the Yugo, a €5,000 car that people in the region could afford. This put Romania on the region's auto industry's map. The last Dacia sedan rolled off the assembly line in 2004, and the carmaker began making the no-frills, low-cost (€7,700, or $10,600) Logan sedan, which Renault also makes and sells in other countries. It has simple, reliable technology. Its sales in 2013 surged 211%. The company exports 85% of its production, but the home market has great potential: There are just 167 cars per 1,000 people. The Renault connection saved Dacia and the whole Romanian auto industry during the great recession of 2008–2010. Dacia employs 8,000 Romanians and is one of the country's largest investors. In 2009 Ford announced that it had bought a state-owned plant in Craiova to build its new Transit van.

Its labor costs are low (€1.76 per hour in 2004 vs. €5.29 in Poland and the EU average of €25.30). But by 2008 wages and income were growing by 25% every year. In 2013 the average monthly pay after tax was €400 ($575). GDP per capita in Romania and Bulgaria was less than 50% of the EU average.

With business-friendly incentives and a good training system in a countrywide network of technical colleges and universities left over from the communist era, it hopes to attract even more foreign investment. American multinationals like Hewlett-Packard and Oracle have already entered. In 2008 Nokia, the world's largest

cell phone manufacturer, closed its German plant and relocated in Cluj, Romania, where wages are one-tenth of those in Germany. About 5,000 foreign companies are located in Timisoara alone.

By 2000, the portion of Romania's GDP generated by the private sector was 60%. Foreign investors are taking a greater interest, although Romania continues to attract far less foreign investment per capita than the central and eastern European average. One reason is corruption. In 2005 the World Yearbook of Competitiveness ranked Romania 55th among 60 states in terms of economic competitiveness.

Inflation continues to come down from its 2001 rate of 40% to 2.8% in 2021. The energy sector contributes 20% to the nation's GDP. Faced with depleting local oil fields, expected to run out soon, the newly privatized oil and gas concern Petrom, Romania's largest company, is active in central Asia, particularly Kazakhstan, while a smaller company, Rom-petrol, is extracting crude oil in Ecuador. There are prospects for oil and gas drilling offshore. That is why Romania took Ukraine to the International Court of Justice in 2004 to try to end a long-running dispute over Black Sea exploration rights. Romania also began exploration of its shale gas reserves in an attempt to achieve energy independence. Such activity faces stiff protests by environmental groups.

Despite its deep suspicion of Russian domination of energy supply routes through Gazprom, it gets 86% its gas imports from Russia. The SE Europe Pipeline from Georgia also crosses Romania. A pipeline is being constructed in Romania that will carry Caspian and Russian crude oil from Constanța to refineries in western Europe and also via deep-sea tankers to the US. Constanța is the entry point for 60% of Romania's imports. It is also the locale for the country's only nuclear power plant. Using Canada's Candu technology, it will have five units; two units function already. When completed, the complex

will provide 10% of the country's energy (compared with 30% hydropower) and will export electricity.

By 2000 the overall economy was still only three-quarters as large as it had been in 1989. But it became the EU's fastest-growing economy in 2008, after an eight-year boom averaging over 6% annually. The average monthly wage was climbing 25% per year, higher in towns, but in the countryside people struggled to subsist. The information-technology sector was booming, and the use of mobile phones and the Internet was rising fast. The banking system was functioning normally, and credit card use was growing quickly. Mass media were thriving, and a lively free press and 68 TV stations now exist.

The budget deficit in 2021 was 6.6%. Total foreign debt was 47.3% of GDP. Both are within the range to qualify for the euro. The government had planned to adopt it in 2015, but it has been postponed indefinitely because of the euro crisis. In the meantime, it benefits from keeping its own currency. This gives it the flexibility to set its own interest rates, control liquidity, rein in its deficit more easily, and sell its exports more competitively. Two-thirds of its sales go to the eurozone.

As a step toward the euro, Romania reformed its currency, the leu (plural: lei), in July 2005 by dropping four zeros from the eye-popping numbers on its money. However, as much as half of its economy is still underground, unreported, and untaxed. To encourage citizens to pay their taxes and to lure foreign investment, the government introduced a 16% flat tax on corporate profits and personal income in 2005.

Thanks to robust growth (4.2% in 2021) and to the employment abroad of over 3 million Romanians (one-fifth of the workforce), unemployment is low. In 2014 it was below 5%, less than half the EU average; it is only 2% in Bucharest and Transylvanian boom towns, creating a tight labor market, especially for skilled labor. Wages are increasing. Italy, Spain, and France are the

Romania dropped four zeros from its money in 2005.

Romania

favorite foreign countries for Romanians because of similarities in climate, culture, and language. Romanians can reach some fluency in a Romance language after a few weeks of study.

The emigration of doctors, engineers, and information-technology specialists is a serious problem, especially for health care. In 2012–2013 alone, 30% of resident doctors left the country; since joining the EU, it has lost 14,000 doctors. This is especially dramatic in rural areas. With starting salaries of only €350 ($490) per month, they cannot be retained in Romania.

Romania has one of the weakest health-care systems in the EU. It spends only $1.9 billion annually on health and has the highest rate of "avoidable deaths" in Europe: almost half. Every year dozens of people are prosecuted for corruption in the health sector. Perhaps the most egregious case was Hexi Pharma, a company that diluted hospital disinfectants so much (some by 90%) that they were no more effective than dishwater, jeopardizing thousands of patients. The company's owner died in a single-car accident, smashing into a tree a day before he was to face prosecutors in May 2016.

Until the 2009 downturn, Romanians abroad sent home about €3 billion in remittances each year. In spite of their EU membership, Romanians did not enjoy the unrestricted right to work in all the partner countries until 2014. Since the downturn was felt all over Europe, the migrant workers were not only able to send fewer remittances home, but a few of them also returned to join the tight job market. About 3 million remained abroad, however, and this helped keep unemployment low in Romania. In 2015, Romanians were the second-largest national group emigrating permanently to OECD countries. The country's 370,000 migrants placed it behind only China and ahead of Poland and India.

To deal with the crisis, the government borrowed $26 billion from the IMF, the EU, the World Bank, and the European Bank for Reconstruction and Development. It also introduced a painful austerity policy that aimed to cut the budget deficit from 7.2% of GDP to 5.9% by the end of 2010. It stood at 1.2% in 2012. Public-sector wages were cut by one-fourth, and pensions and benefit payments, by 15%. Thousands of "privileged pensions" were scrapped, and up to 100,000 public-sector jobs were slashed. The VAT was raised from 19% to 24%.

The government's most imaginative tax-raising measure was to bring witches and soothsayers into the labor code in 2011. Some Romanians believe they have extrasensory perception since Transylvania sits atop one of the globe's most powerful magnetic fields. They now are supposed to pay 16% income tax and contribute to health and pension plans. Parliament is even considering requiring them to issue receipts and to subject them to fines or prison if their predictions do not come true. No wonder many witches went to the banks of the Danube and dumped toxic mandrake in order to cast spells on the president and parliament.

CULTURE

The Romanians take great pride in their Latin origin, although over the centuries they have also been subject to Hungarian, Slavic, and Turkish cultural influences. Romania's Hungarian minority constitutes almost 7% of the total population and is located primarily in the Tisa Plain and in Transylvania. Although they speak a Magyar dialect, the Szeklers are distinguishable from the Hungarians on historic grounds. They have been in Transylvania since the Middle Ages, when they were frontier guards for the Magyar settlements. The Hungarian Magyars recognized them as a free people of noble birth and as one of the privileged nations of Transylvania, along with the Saxons (Germans) and the Magyars. Roma and other minorities make up 3.6% of the population.

Most Romanians (87%) belong to the Romanian Orthodox Church, but Roman Catholicism and Calvinism are strong among the Hungarian population. The old communist constitution guaranteed freedom of religion with qualifications. For instance, the organization of "religious cults" was regulated by law. The church could not operate schools other than seminaries. The church budget was under state control, and its officials had to be acceptable to the state. The secret service (Securitate) also thoroughly infiltrated the clergy. For example, Metropolitan Daniel, who was elected on September 12, 2007, had been permitted to travel abroad. This would have been impossible for anyone who did not cooperate with the Ceaușescu regime.

The Iliescu government adopted a "hands-off" attitude toward religion, neither supporting nor interfering. The subsequent Constantinescu government took a more specifically proreligion stance, although it was primarily symbolic. For instance, icons of the Romanian Orthodox Church lined Constantinescu's office shelves, and he made a point of having an Orthodox priest say a prayer at political meetings. A 2005 opinion poll found that the church is the public institution most trusted by Romanians—87% placed it on the top of their list. Of the other institutions, 72% mentioned the army, 59% the mass media, and 48% the presidency, while 63% distrust the trade unions, 67% the judiciary, and 73% the parliament. Given its honored place in society, it is appropriate that the world's tallest Orthodox church (400 feet, or 120 meters) is scheduled to be finished in 2024: the People's Salvation Cathedral. Located next to the Palace of the Parliament, it will dwarf that eyesore of the Ceaușescu era.

There has been considerable movement from rural to urban areas since World War II. The population is now about 55% urban and 45% rural. The more recent exodus of as many as 3 million to 4 million (1 out of 5) Romanians, including from the villages in the poorest regions in the south and east, to find work abroad has led to immense social dislocation in those areas. Bucharest is still by far the largest city, containing more than one-fifth of Romania's city dwellers. It

Romania has Europe's largest Roma population. Roma entertaining passers-by in neighboring Serbia.

is modern and a center of cultural expression. In the countryside, folk music, art, and colorful costumes are noticeable.

Moviegoers can admire the Romanian countryside in the many films that are now shot there. Its two major studios, Castel and Media Pro Pictures, are reporting dramatic growth in their business. The biggest undertaking by 2003 was the American Civil War epic *Cold Mountain*, starring Nicole Kidman and Jude Law. Director Anthony Minghella had entire farms built, complete with planted tobacco and corn. One battle scene required 1,000 Romanian extras. With its low labor costs, Romania is ideally suited for such movie making.

On the other hand, residents of the village of Glod have threatened to kill or sue Sacha Baron Cohen, who used them and their village for his fictitious portrayal of Kazakhstan in *Borat*. The locals greatly resent what they see as a humiliating presentation of their personae and their impoverished village; they insist they were deceived and abused by Cohen.

Free primary education is compulsory for eight years, and there are universities in Bucharest and in 20 other cities. As a sign of close historic ties with France, a section of the University of Bucharest offers entire curricula and degree programs in French; it does the same in English. Romania is the only country where more secondary-school pupils study French than English. A major change since communism is that almost a third of university students attend more than 40 private universities.

Romania has made a cultural mark on the world through its composers, such as George Enescu and Ciprian Porumbescu; sculptors like Constantin Brancusi; and painters, including Nicolae Grigorescu and Nicolae Tonitza. In a new "Park of Totalitarianism" in Bucharest, other works are displayed that not everybody would consider to be art but as parts of Romanian history. It contains statues and busts from the Communist era of such leaders as Ceaușescu, his predecessor Gheorghe-Gherorghiu Dey, and even Vladimir Lenin himself.

In 2009 Herta Müller won the Nobel Prize in literature. Her award coincided with the 20th anniversary of the fall of communism in Romania. She became the 12th woman to receive the prize. She was largely unknown both abroad and outside of literary circles in Romania and Germany. Born in 1953, she grew up in the German-speaking city of Nițchidorf in the Banat region of Romania. Only the mayor and the policeman spoke Romanian. Her ancestors were Banat Swabians from southern Germany.

Thanks to Romania's minority rights even during communism, she was schooled in German and wrote in German from the very beginning of her literary career. As a university student, her thoughts and ideals collided with the rigid communist regime, and she joined an organization calling itself the Action Group Banat to seek freedom of speech. Hounded by the Securitate, which spied on them and planted bugs in their home, she emigrated to Berlin in 1987 with her then-husband, Richard Wagner, also a German-language writer.

Her 20 books deal with the challenges of living in a dictatorship. Among her four novels translated into English are *The Land of Green Plums* and *The Appointment*. Her last book in 2009, published just before she received the prize, is a masterpiece about life in Soviet labor camps: *Everything I Own I Carry with Me*.

One questionable form of commercial activity has been cleaned up—adoptions by foreign parents. The Ceaușescu dictatorship had encouraged procreation and prohibited birth control, so 100,000 abandoned children lived terrible lives in crammed, understaffed, and ill-equipped orphanages. Since the dictator's fall, 50,000 babies have been sent abroad for $20,000 to $50,000 each.

After the EU demanded a change of this corrupt adoption system, Romania declared a moratorium on foreign adoptions in 2001 and adopted new laws in 2004 making the moratorium permanent. Adoption is considered a "last resort," and Romanian couples are given priority. Only foreign couples able to prove their direct kinship with a child are eligible. There were still about 30,000 children in orphanages in 2006, some of them living in appalling conditions. But the numbers declined after the moratorium went into effect because the financial incentives for offering children for adoption had disappeared. The EU funds day-care centers and foster care within Romania as an alternative to adoption.

In 2003 Romanian authorities acted decisively in another social situation. They ordered that a 12-year-old Gypsy girl, the daughter of the head of Romania's Roma (Gypsies), be separated from a 15-year-old boy she had been forced to marry and that all intimate relations between them cease until they are old enough to be legally married. The wedding sparked a national debate about forced marriages among Roma adolescents. They were both ordered to attend school.

No one knows the size of the Roma population in Romania. Census figures are 535,000, but many observers believe that as many as 2.5 million is a more accurate figure. There are 10 million to 12 million in all of Europe. They cannot always communicate with each other since their language, originally related to Sanskrit, has splintered into dozens of mutually incomprehensible dialects. Communism largely put an end to their traditional nomadism. Many have no birth certificates, and some never set foot in a school, which shuts them out of the modern job market. Only 17.2% attend preschool, compared with 67% of other children, and one in two attends primary school. A mere one-fifth receives secondary education. This may belong to that part of Roma culture that hurts their image. They are clannish, strongly patriarchal, and poorly educated, and young Roma are forced to marry at a very young age and have large families.

Many engage in organized begging using their children to soften up passersby. Rightly or wrongly, many Romanians blame them for much of the crime that occurs. More than half of them live in extreme poverty, compared with a rate of 9.3% among the rest of the population; 90% are below the poverty line. They lag far behind the general population in life expectancy, infant mortality, employment, and literacy. Polls in 2008 showed how much discrimination they face: Four out of five Romanians would not want Roma neighbors, and a majority would not want their child to be in a classroom with Roma. There are few positive role models. Largely because of such discrimination, highly educated and successful Roma usually choose not to reveal their ethnic background.

Much of western Europe is hostile to itinerant Roma, but few were as determined to stop the tide as France. In 2010 the government ordered police to clear 441 illegal squatter camps, "with priority" to Roma camps. About 8,000 were given a resettlement grant of €300 ($410) apiece and sent home before their camps were bulldozed. EU justice commissioner Viviane Reding compared these actions to Nazi atrocities committed during World War II, and the European Commission condemned the deportation.

In a controversial move, in 2013 parliament acted decisively to prevent Bucharest from "going to the dogs." It authorized the capture and killing of tens of thousands of stray dogs after three people, including a Japanese tourist and a four-year-old boy, died from canine attacks.

CURRENT ISSUES

There are growing calls for a restoration of the monarchy. One poll showed that a popular vote on it was favored by 70% of the public. It is not clear who would be the new monarch.

Despite many difficult problems, they live freer and more prosperous today than ever before. They kept up their faith in the future by glancing at a huge digital electronic clock in the middle of a busy

Romania

Bucharest traffic island called "Europe Square." It ticked off the days until Romania joined the EU on January 1, 2007.

Romania has considerable potential if it can stay the course in modernizing and reforming its economy. Privatization has been largely completed. It receives support from the European Union, and it can look forward to ever-increasing economic integration with the rest of Europe. However, the EU will continue to monitor Romania's poor record in reducing corruption, a major scourge on the country. The decision to accept Romania and Bulgaria into the EU before they cleaned up their acts in terms of corruption and respect for the law continues to haunt the organization, since progress has been very slow and painful.

Romania still has a long way to go, though a variety of approaches have been tried. In 2016, a new digital initiative called the "Museum of Corruption" displayed online cases and sometimes odd objects of corruption as pieces of art that can be browsed on the virtual "walls" of the museum. Those include, among others, sheep, whiskey and fish, mineral water, and even a bridge.

The unpopular president Băsescu left office in 2014 and was replaced by anti-corruption advocate Klaus Iohannis. Several forces have been unleashed that may yet alter the tarnished image of Romania. One is the National Anticorruption Directorate that inexorably though slowly chips away at the corrupt political class. Another is the reform-minded segment of the population who does not mind braving the elements to take to the streets in remarkably successful campaigns of public protests, serving as a check on the politicians.

The country's friends hope it can finally turn the tide to have political and legal reforms to match its impressive strides in the economy. The latter is performing well, buoyed by funding from the EU as well as good business infrastructure and low wages that attract foreign investment. The quest for reforms is helped by the continuing—though not unconditional—goodwill of the EU and NATO, for whom this large country with its strategic location remains an important partner.

The citizens of Romania are likely to remain watchful, too. After the deadly nightclub fire, protesters carried posters declaring starkly, "Corruption kills." Interestingly, some of the protesters were carrying the Romanian flag with a hole cut out in the middle, intentionally harkening back to the 1989 revolution when the communist coat of arms was frequently cut out from the flags to quickly restore their national character. Clearly, not all of the aspirations of that revolution have been fulfilled yet. By 2022, the country had five prime ministers in five years. After weeks of political paralysis, former general Nicolae Ciucă formed a coalition government with the Liberals (18%) and the Social Democrats (38%), which will rotate the premier's job.

The Ukraine war brought unreliable energy supplies and a tide of Ukrainian refugees.

In February 2024, President Iohannis approved the deployment of NATO's Response Force in Romania for 2024. In a letter addressed to parliament he said that he approved the entry, stay or transit through Romanian territory of the NATO Response Force to prepare or conduct military operations in 2024. He pointed out that "The international environment is becoming less predictable against the backdrop of concurrent crises in 2023. In the context of great power strategic competition and the reassessment of geopolitical approaches to international politics, the scale of conflict at the regional and international levels has increased."

Romania and Bulgaria will become part of the Schengen area from March 31, 2024, which allows free movement between member states for 400 million citizens.

Next presidential elections will be held in Romania in either mid- or late November 2024. As the Romanian Constitution allows a maximum of two presidential terms (consecutive or not), incumbent President of Romania Klaus Iohannis, first elected in 2014 and then re-elected in 2019, is not eligible for re-election. His second (and last) term will normally end in December 2024.

Republic of Bulgaria (Република България)

Rila Monastery

Area: 42,854.9 sq. mi. (110,993 sq. km).

Population: 6,385,000 (2023 estimate)

Capital City: Sofia (pop. 1,248,452; 2021 estimate).

Climate: It is predominantly continental but influenced by the Mediterranean in the country's south. The average annual temperature is 51 °F (10.5 °C).

Neighboring Countries: Romania (north); Türkiye, Greece (south); Serbia, North Macedonia (west).

Official Language: Bulgarian.

Recognized Minority Languages: Turkish.

Ethnic Background: 84.57% Bulgarian, 8.40% Turkish, 4.41% Romani, 1.31other, and 1.31% undeclared (2021 census).

Religion: 71.5% Christianity, 10.8% Sunni Muslim, 0.1% other, 12.0% other, 5.2% no religion, 12.4% unanswered (as of 2021)

Form of Government: Unitary parliamentary republic.

Chief of State: Rumen Radev, President (since January 2017).

Head of Government: Nikolai Denkov, Prime Minister (since June 2023).

National Flag: It is a tricolor flag consisting of three equal-sized horizontal bands of white, green, and red. This flag was adopted when Bulgaria gained independence after the Russo-Turkish War of 1877–1878. At times throughout history, it has been supplemented with state emblems. The initial design of the flag was re-established by the 1991 Constitution of Bulgaria and was confirmed in a 1998 law. The choice of colors in the Bulgarian flag is based on the pan-Slavic tradition of using the established symbolism of white, blue, and red, which in this case has been modified by replacing blue with green. The official interpretation states that white signifies peace and prosperity, whereas the green depicts agriculture and wealth, and the red stands for the independence struggle and military courage.

Public Holiday: March 3 (Liberation Day), September 22 (Independence Day).

Currency: Lev (BGN)

Main exports: machinery and transport equipment, refined fuels, iron and steel, clothing, and agricultural products (fruit, wine, cigarettes, dairy products, and meat).

Main Imports: Mineral fuels, oils, distillation products, electrical and electronic equipment, machinery and vehicles.

Main Trading Partners: Germany (14.9% of exports and 12.2% of imports), Italy (7.5% of exports and 6.6% of imports), Romania (10.1% of exports and 7.5% of imports), Greece (6.6% of exports and 5.3% of imports), Türkiye (6.1% of exports and 7.8% of imports), France (3.6% of exports), Belgium (3.2% of exports), Russia (7.6% of imports), China (5.4% of imports).

One of the last countries to win its independence from the Ottoman Empire in 1878, Bulgaria has stood on its own two feet longer than most of its neighbors. Since Russia had played a key role in helping the country win its freedom, this was one of the few countries in eastern and central Europe in which the population harbored genuinely positive sentiments toward Russia and Russians during the 20th century. One of Sofia's main avenues is still called Boulevard of the Tsar Liberator, on which one can sip coffee in a Viennese cafe. Its western ambiance points to that part of Europe on which Bulgarians' sights and yearnings are fixed.

Sitting in that cafe in Sofia, Croatian author Slavenka Drakulić reflected on the concept of "Europe." She wrote in her book *Cafe Europa: Life after Communism*, "What does Europe mean in the Eastern European imagination? It is certainly not a question of geography. . . It is something distant, something to be attained, to be deserved. It is also something expensive and fine: good clothes, the certain look and smell of its people. Europe is plenitude: food, cars, light, everything—a kind of festival of colors, diversity, opulence, beauty. It offers choice: from shampoo to political parties. It represents freedom of expression. It is a promised land, a new Utopia, a lollipop. And through television, that Europe is right there, in your apartment, often in colors much too bright to be real."

Bulgaria

The Republic of Bulgaria is a relatively small, square-shaped country bordering on the Black Sea to the east and bounded by the Danube River to the north. The Black Sea coast not only has beautiful sandy beaches that are now being developed, but it is also the site of the major tourist center of Varna. Stretching from west to east is the Balkan Range (Stara Planina) separating the fertile Danubian Plain in the north from the Thracian Plain in the south.

In the exact center of the country there is the Kazanlik "Valley of Roses," where fragrance and beauty combine with commercial value in the production of rose oil. The southwest is dominated by the rugged Rila Mountains—which include Mount Musala, the highest peak in the Balkans—and by the snow-capped Pirin Mountains. South of Plovdiv, Bulgaria's second-largest city along the Maritsa River, lie the Rhodope Mountains, where hundreds of mineral springs can be found.

In the 7th century, an Asiatic people called the Bulgars crossed the Danube River and settled in the area known today as the Republic of Bulgaria. Within two centuries after their conquest of the region, the Bulgars had become completely absorbed into the native Slav population, adopting their language and culture.

Cyril and Methodius, two brothers who were missionaries, devised an alphabet in order to translate the Bible and religious writings into the Slavic language of the people. They had been born in Thessalonica, sons of a noble Byzantine family of Slav-Bulgarian lineage. All Slavs at the time ultimately adopted their alphabet. Their Bible contributed to the conversion of the Bulgarians to Christianity, which became the official state religion in 863. The conversion of all non-Christians began. The invention and dissemination of books and literacy in the Bulgarian language spoken at the time was of prime importance for the cultural history of Bulgaria and eastern Europe in general. The Bulgarians' conversion thus brought them their first literary language and early contact with the Byzantine Empire.

Political Status: Bulgarian state 681–1018; Byzantine rule 1018–1185; Second Bulgarian state 1185–1396; part of Ottoman Empire, 1396–1878; autonomous principality, 1878–1908; independent, 1908–1944; Communist state, part of Soviet Empire, 1945–1990.

HISTORY

The beginning of the Bulgarian state dates from 681, when Bulgaria was united under the leadership of Asparukh, its first khan (leader). His successors as khans embarked on a policy of elevating Bulgaria to a status equal in territory, population, and economic and military strength to the great European political giants of the day, such as the empire of the Franks. By 852 Bulgaria's borders had been extended to include what is now Hungary, Romania, Moldova, North Macedonia, and northern Greece. It was a European superpower.

Khan Boris converted to Christianity in 863 under the auspices of the Greek Church. Tsar Simeon, who died in 927, was responsible for the establishment of an independent Bulgarian patriarchate. Now religiously separate from Constantinople, subsequent tsars fought constant wars against it, particularly as they expanded the territory under their control until they governed most of what are now large parts of Albania, Serbia, North Macedonia and Greece. In time, an individual

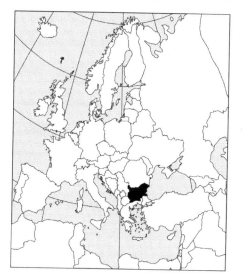

tsar might even challenge the political authority of the Byzantine Empire.

It was in response to just such a challenge that the Byzantine emperor Basil II (976–1025) destroyed a Bulgarian army and, indirectly, the Bulgarian state. According to tradition, Samuel, the Bulgarian tsar, sent a large army toward Constantinople, intending to lay siege to the city. Basil II's forces met the Bulgarian soldiers before they could reach Constantinople.

In the succeeding battle, Basil II defeated the Bulgarians, also taking many prisoners. To teach Samuel a lesson, he ordered 14,000 of the Bulgarian prisoners to be blinded, then sent them back to Samuel. It is said that Samuel died of shock on seeing what had happened to his men. Basil II then converted Bulgaria into a province of the Byzantine Empire.

Between the 12th and 14th centuries (1185–1393), a second Bulgarian kingdom existed. Its most famous tsar was Ivan Assen II (1216–1241), who dominated the whole region. The Bulgarian liberation insurrection in 1185 had been sparked by heavy special taxes imposed on the Bulgarian lands to meet exorbitant expenses for the wedding of the Byzantine emperor with a juvenile Hungarian princess. The initial economic motives of the rebellion were quickly forgotten, however, as the restoration of the Bulgarian state became the primary objective. After incessant warfare and a brilliant victory in 1230, Bulgaria had achieved the situation in which it had found itself in the 10th century: Its territory encompassed almost the entire Balkan Peninsula.

Bulgaria

Russian Orthodox church in Sofia

The Bulgarians went on to defeat hordes of Tatars, which until then had been invincible. These Asians had engulfed all states west of the Ural Mountains, including Russia, and had conquered Hungary. They attacked Bulgaria in order to secure their flank before invading western Europe. Their humiliating defeat in 1241 ended once and for all their hopes of conquering western Europe. Bulgaria's territorial expansion fostered successful economic and cultural development. The Bulgarian patriarchate was fully restored in 1235 and became the only Eastern Orthodox religious institution that enjoyed the backing of a well-established political power. It thus achieved great authority in the entire east.

Bulgaria was the first land to be conquered by the expanding Ottoman Turks, under the leadership of Sultan Murad I. This was devastating for the Bulgarians because of the especially long Turkish occupation. Its domination was particularly heavy because Bulgaria, then called by its three historical provinces—Moesia, Thrace, and Macedonia—was geographically so close. The Turks then defeated the Serbs at Kosovo in 1389. Four years later, Bulgaria was formally incorporated into the Ottoman Empire, where it remained until 1878. The empire's inhabitants were organized into administrative units on the basis of their faith, with a religious leader as head of each unit. The Turks thereby used the Orthodox Church to administer the Bulgarians.

The Birth of Modern Bulgaria

The liberation of Bulgaria from Turkish control was the product of a war between Russia and Türkiye that ended in Turkish defeat. The Russians had arguably envisioned a single, large Bulgarian state. This was stipulated in the resulting Treaty of San Stefano on March 3, 1878, the date still celebrated as national liberation day.

The Austrians and British objected, however, and Russia was forced to permit a rewriting of the treaty at the Congress of Berlin. The result, signed in 1878, was that the western portion of Bulgaria was returned to Türkiye, while the remaining area was divided into two parts, separated by the Balkan Mountains. This is why Bulgarians call the Congress of Berlin "the catastrophe." The northern part became Bulgaria and was established as a self-governing territory with the right to select its own prince. The portion south of the mountains became the autonomous Turkish territory of East Rumelia. The division did not last, however; in 1885, the East Rumelians merged with the rest of Bulgaria without a shot being fired. The nation as a whole remained a self-governing autonomous principality until it declared its complete independence from the Ottoman Empire in 1908.

There were three main problems that Bulgaria faced in the period following Ottoman rule. The first concerned territory. The Great Bulgaria envisioned in the Treaty of San Stefano had included much of the territory the Bulgarians had lived in at the time of their greatness in the 10th century. The Treaty of Berlin had reduced those territories by nearly two-thirds. The union of East Rumelia and Bulgaria in 1885 partially solved the problem but still left Bulgaria with claims to additional territory. It was this question that led to Bulgarian participation in the two Balkan wars of 1912–1913, to an alliance with Germany and Austria in World War I, and to an alliance with Germany in World War II.

The second problem was the status of neighboring Macedonia. In the 19th century, it was still part of the Ottoman Empire. Most outsiders assumed that they must be either Serbians or Bulgarians, and the Bulgarian and Serbian governments took this same position, each claiming the Macedonians as separated brethren.

To complicate the situation more, Greece also claimed the area, arguing that Macedonia was historically Greek. As a result of this Greek-Serbian-Bulgarian rivalry, until World War I, each state waged a constant battle to increase its influence through a variety of means, including political propaganda; school subsidies; Orthodox Church authority; and, worst of all, terrorism.

The third problem was the nature of Bulgaria's relationship with Russia. On one hand, there had been a great deal of popular affection for Russia as the liberator of Bulgaria from Turkish rule. On the other hand, this affection had been mingled with a fear that the price of Russian friendship might be Bulgarian servitude.

Bulgaria was the only nation in the Balkans to join the Central Powers (Germany and Austro-Hungary) in World War I. It had done so in order to win back territory lost in the Treaty of San Stefano in 1878, and Germany promised what Bulgaria wanted. But this resulted in not only defeat in 1918, but also a loss of even more territory. During the interwar period, Bulgaria denounced as excessively harsh the terms of the treaty settling the war and the boundaries of the southern Balkans.

From 1919 to 1939, Bulgarian history was troubled. There were political plots from left- and right-wing groups, assassinations, mass murders, and constant acts of individual terrorism. One of the most important groups in the country, especially in the years between 1923 and 1934, was the Internal Macedonian Revolutionary Organization (VMRO). This was a terrorist group fighting for Macedonian self-government and undermining any political leaders who pursued policies inconsistent with this goal.

The early post-World War I years were dominated by Alexander Stamboliyski, a colorful, strong-willed leader of the Agrarian Party. During the period he was prime minister, which lasted until 1923, reforms in the tax structure, legal system, and landownership were carried out. The land reforms were not as drastic as they were elsewhere in the Balkans, since Bulgaria was basically a peasant society with few large landholdings. While Stamboliyski was in office, the Communist Party of Bulgaria was the second-largest party in the

VMRO active in Bulgaria today

Bulgaria

country. After a right-wing military regime came to power in 1923, the party was banned, and its leaders, one of which was Georgi Dimitrov, had to go into exile.

After 10 years of VMRO terrorism and government inefficiency, a military coup was launched in 1934. Colonel Kimon Georgiev, the leader of the Zveno group—an organization of reform-minded intellectuals and politicians—became prime minister. In less than a year, he was out of office. His powers went to King Boris III, who ruled Bulgaria as a royal authoritarian from 1935 until his death in 1943.

Bulgaria joined the Axis in 1941, but it refused to declare war on the Soviet Union when that nation was invaded by Germany. During 1941, as a by-product of a German attack on Yugoslavia, Bulgaria occupied almost all of Macedonia and part of Serbia and also took over western Thrace, a part of Greece.

Bulgaria was the only state in the region in which not a single Jew was deported or killed. In agreement with its German ally, the Bulgarian government adopted anti-Jewish laws in March 1943. But the speaker of the parliament used his influence to prevent the second step—the deportation of Bulgarian Jews. His supporters and the general population launched mass protests against the deportation order issued by the government. Thus, the entire 50,000-strong Jewish community was saved.

But the story is more complicated and troubling, as Bulgarian American filmmaker Jacky Comforty shows in his award-winning documentary, *The Optimists*. Bulgarian Jews suffered terrible abuse. They were prevented from studying in universities, removed from teaching and government jobs, banished to deserted places within the country, and denied diplomatic protection abroad. In their occupation areas, Bulgarian soldiers rounded up 7,500 Macedonian Jews and 4,000 Jews from Thrace and delivered them to the Germans for deportation.

It is rumored that because he opposed Bulgarian military participation on the eastern front, King Boris III was poisoned by the Germans and died in 1943, three days after visiting Hitler in Germany. His six-year-old son Simeon succeeded him. A three-man regency exercised state power. Under the administration of Prime Minister Ivan Bagrianov, a less pro-Axis policy was adopted. Thousands of political prisoners were released. In 2001 Simeon II was to become prime minister in a radically different Bulgaria.

Bulgaria announced in 1944 that it was ready to seek a separate peace with the Allies. However, the Soviet Union declared war on Bulgaria a few days later, and the Soviet army entered the country.

Sofia, looking toward Sveta Nedelja Square around "Holy Sunday Church"

Photo: Miller B. Spangler

Bulgaria Becomes a People's Republic

Technically, a native resistance group calling itself the Fatherland Front overthrew the government at this time. This was a "popular front" grouping that had come into existence during World War II with the assistance and under the sponsorship of the Communist International (Comintern). An undoubted factor in this sponsorship was that Georgi Dimitrov, the Bulgarian communist who had fled the country in 1923, was now secretary-general of the Comintern.

The communist role in the Fatherland Front was very strong, but it was a genuine "popular front," encompassing the Agrarian Union, one wing of the Social Democrats, and Zveno. The prime minister of the new government was Colonel Kimon Georgiev, a member of Zveno. The communists were a minority in the cabinet, but they controlled the key Ministries of Justice and Interior. This gave them control over both the police and the courts, and they used this to institute a systematic purge of opposition figures.

Since all of the parties of the Fatherland Front were pro-Russian and united in their hatred of the "German collaborators" who had frozen them out of power in the past, there was strong support among the other parties for these actions. Those executed included the 3 regents, former prime ministers Bagrianov and Bozhilov, 26 former cabinet ministers, and 68 deputies from the wartime assemblies. In addition, special "People's Courts" were set up throughout the country, and thousands of additional individuals were sentenced to death and executed.

Having eliminated the "German collaborators," the communists next turned to

their partners in the Fatherland Front. Under the terms of the Declaration of Europe, signed by the "Big Three" at Yalta in February 1945, free elections were to be held throughout eastern Europe. Determined to establish their own political dominance, the communists demanded a common Fatherland Front list of candidates with a prearranged ratio giving them half of the seats in the new assembly.

Zveno, more a military faction than a political party, accepted these terms. The Agrarian Union and the Social Democrats did not. The communists thereupon produced their own Agrarian collaborator, Alexander Obhov, and managed to get him elected head of the party by packing the congress of the Agrarian Union. Similar tactics were used against the Social Democrats. The elections, which took place in November 1945, produced an 86% majority for the Fatherland Front.

Georgi Dimitrov, who had been elected president of the Central Committee of the Bulgarian Communist Party at a party congress in March 1945, returned to Sofia in the midst of the election campaign. Although clearly the preeminent leader of the party that dominated the government, he did not enter the government at this time. One reason may have been that the American and British governments challenged the validity of the November elections and demanded that the true leaders of the Agrarian Front and Social Democrats be brought back into the government. This became the subject of the Moscow Conference of December 1945, but American and British pressure was of no effect.

By the summer of 1946, the communists felt strong enough to campaign against Zveno, the remaining independent

Varna Old Town

Photo by Roman Payerhin

element in the Fatherland Front. An attack was launched in the communist press against the founder of Zveno, General Velchev, who held the position of minister of war. Velchev eventually was forced to resign from the cabinet. Colonel Georgiev remained as prime minister until the autumn, when he, too, was forced out.

Bulgaria was still technically a monarchy up to this point. However, a plebiscite, held in September 1946, resulted in a vote in favor of a republic. A month later, new elections were held for a Grand National Assembly, which was charged with preparing a new constitution.

The Fatherland Front won those elections, and Georgi Dimitrov took the office of premier (subsequently renamed "chairman of the council of ministers") in the new government. Some legal opposition continued for a while, however, since the independent factions of the Agrarian Union and the Social Democrats had both run candidates in the elections and had managed to get a few of their candidates elected. They were permitted to make speeches in the assembly, but this was soon replaced by a campaign of intimidation. Things came to a head in June 1947, when Nikola Petkov, leader of the independent faction of the Agrarian Union, was arrested on the floor of the assembly—even though his parliamentary immunity should have protected him. Charged with preparing for a coup d'etat, he was found guilty and sentenced to death.

Somewhat later, Georgi Dimitrov addressed a specific warning to the few Social Democrats remaining in the assembly. "As you remember," Dimitrov informed them, "from this rostrum I many times warned your political allies from Nikola Petkov's group. They did not listen to me. They took no notice of all my warnings. They broke their heads, and their leader is now under the ground. You should now think it over, lest you share their fate." The following July, Kosta Lulchev, head of the Social Democrats, was arrested, along with six of the nine remaining deputies from that party, and he was subsequently sentenced to 15 years imprisonment.

The Dimitrov government presented Bulgaria with a new constitution in December 1947. As might have been expected, it was modeled closely after the 1936 "Stalin Constitution" of the USSR. Bulgaria now became a "people's republic," while its government became almost a carbon copy of the Soviet model, except that the legislature consisted of one house only. Bulgaria had no need for a separate house representing different nationalities such as existed in Russia and Yugoslavia. Like the Soviet Union, theoretical sovereignty rested with the legislature, but the actual decision making was carried out by a presidium and a separate council of ministers. Reflecting the fulcrum of power, Georgi Dimitrov took the position of chairman of the council of ministers for himself.

Internecine Struggles

Having eliminated the opposition, the communists turned against each other. The charge was "nationalist deviation," and the ostensive cause was Yugoslav leader Tito's break with the Soviet Union in 1948. It turned into a struggle between communists who had served an apprenticeship in the Soviet Union and those who had remained behind. It was largely directed from Moscow. Stalin apparently became convinced that he could not trust any of the "native" communists.

The most significant of that group was Traicho Kostov, who had risen to the position of vice chairman of the council of ministers in charge of economic affairs and who was widely considered to be Dimitrov's probable successor. The list of charges eventually filed against him was rather extensive, but the most serious was that he had kept secret information on Bulgarian economic matters from Soviet representatives, not realizing, as *Rabotnichesko Delo*, the communist party newspaper, phrased it, that "secrets and commercialism do not exist in our dealings with the Soviet Union." Kostov was sentenced to death and executed in late 1949. Several of his associates, including the finance minister, the foreign trade minister, the director of the national bank, and the commercial attaché in Moscow, were sentenced to long terms in prison. Other leading native communists were tried, sentenced, and eliminated. In addition, a purge of the party ranks resulted in about 20% of the membership being expelled from the party.

In the midst of the purge, Georgi Dimitrov died while on a trip to the Soviet Union. His immediate successor was Vasil Kolarov, but he died six months later in 1950 and was in turn replaced by Vulko Chervenkov. The latter was Dimitrov's brother-in-law and had spent many years in the Soviet Union. Known as an arch-Stalinist, he was almost certainly responsible for the severity of the purge of the "native" communists. By using the weapon of "nationalist deviation," he eliminated all possible rivals and consolidated his own power position.

The purges had one final result. At the Kostov trial, an attempt was made to portray the defendant as an American agent who had been encouraged in his actions by Donald Heath, the head of the US legation in Sofia. This was followed by the arrest of five Bulgarians employed by the US legation and a subsequent "spy trial" of other alleged American agents. Finally, the US government had enough. In 1950, it broke off diplomatic relations with Bulgaria.

Chervenkov was the most ruthless of Bulgaria's postwar rulers, but he did not get to enjoy his power for very long. After Stalin's death in 1953, his old patron

Bulgaria

was dead. Nikita Khrushchev's rise to power threatened Chervenkov's position. Khrushchev was determined to heal the breach with Tito of Yugoslavia, and Chervenkov had distinguished himself as an enemy of Tito. In 1954, he gave up the position of general secretary of the Central Committee—the top party position—although he managed to retain the leading state position, that of premier. Chervenkov actually managed to hold on to most of his power for another two years, but he was never able to overcome his Stalinist past. When Khrushchev launched his attack against Stalin in 1956, Chervenkov found himself accused of Stalin's chief crime—promoting a "cult of personality"—and was again forced to accept a demotion, this time to deputy chairman of the council of ministers.

The Beginning of the Zhivkov Era

The man who got Chervenkov's party position in 1954—changed at this time from general secretary to first secretary—was Todor Zhivkov. His first membership in the Bulgarian Communist Party dates back to 1932, and he had been one of the organizers of the partisan underground in the Sofia area during World War II; he commanded the partisan regiments in and around Sofia at the time of the 1944 Fatherland Front seizure of power. Lacking close ties to the "Moscow" communists, who had returned to Bulgaria to take charge of the party, Zhivkov spent the next four years in various subordinate positions.

His breakthrough came in 1948, when he became first secretary of the Sofia City Committee and, simultaneously, a member of the party Central Committee. From this time, his rise was more rapid. He became an alternate member of the politburo in 1950 and a member of the secretariat. A year later, he was admitted to full politburo membership. Thus, when Chervenkov came under attack in 1954 as a Stalinist, Zhivkov was able to move into the position of first secretary of the Central Committee, a position he held until November 1989.

Zhivkov's rapid rise after 1948 would indicate that he got his start as Chervenkov's protege, and his actions after 1954 would bear that out. It was not until Chervenkov had been further demoted in 1956 that Zhivkov made his own bid for greater power. In 1957, he increased his control by removing some of his opponents, but it was not until 1962 that he consolidated his position by taking the additional title of chairman of the council of ministers (now renamed premier). At the same time, he severed his last connection with Chervenkov and had him dismissed from the government. The break was over foreign policy. Zhivkov favored closer relations

with Yugoslavia and, in general, wanted to bring Bulgarian foreign policy closer into alignment with Soviet foreign policy under Khrushchev. After Chervenkov's dismissal, Zhivkov publicly endorsed Soviet policies in the Cuban missile crisis of 1961, made moves toward establishment of better relations with Yugoslavia, and totally supported the Soviet Union in its disputes with China.

One of the problems Zhivkov had to face was the trend toward a more relaxed and liberal leadership that had started prior to the time he became premier. Detention camps had been closed, and limits were placed on the secret police. Writers and scholars were given more freedom to express their views. In some cases this new freedom was used to criticize the government. Zhivkov's position was not secure enough to tolerate such criticism. He had eliminated his rivals from the top level of the party, but he still faced the opposition of lesser members who had been supporters of Chervenkov.

Other problems were created by popular discontent with a shortage of food, consumer goods, and housing. Economic reform was needed to stifle criticism, but it would have met with opposition from the "dogmatists" and those who profited from the present setup. Zhivkov's only alternative was to end the brief period of liberalization and to reimpose restrictions. Even though this was a step backward, it was not a return to the repressive atmosphere of the Stalinist days. Meanwhile, Zhivkov tried to shore up his own position by tying himself closely to his Soviet benefactor, Khrushchev. When the latter lost power in November 1964, Zhivkov's position became precarious, and his gestures of loyalty toward the new Soviet leadership could not disguise the loss of support that he experienced at this time.

A few months later, the inner turmoil of Bulgaria was underlined by the most unusual event in its postwar history. In April 1965, a plot to overthrow the government was discovered in Sofia. The coup had been planned for the April 14 meeting of the politburo, at which time the plotters intended to arrest leading party members and to occupy important areas to prevent Soviet military action within Bulgaria. Soviet military spies discovered the plot, and the coup was quickly prevented. It was not until mid-May, however, that the Bulgarians received their first official explanation of the plot. It was declared to be an unimportant event caused by a small group of pro-Chinese plotters. This was not the case. The conspirators were not insignificant people but rather were former World War II freedom fighters, Bulgarian communists, high-ranking army officers, and top-level party members. It is probable

that they wanted to remove Zhivkov in the hope that a new leadership would bring a new course of independence for Bulgaria in its relations with the Soviet Union.

After the attempt failed, one Central Committee member committed suicide, others were tried secretly, and there was the usual purge of anyone with questionable loyalty. A renewed pledge of allegiance to the Soviet Union was required. Shaken by the events of 1965, Zhivkov initiated a series of reforms, particularly in the economy. They were designed to allow some decentralization of decision making. But the entrenched bureaucracy and conservatives opposed them so strenuously that they were phased out in 1968. Although he had initiated them, Zhivkov's support was never more than half-hearted, so it did not reflect adversely on him when they were discontinued.

Zhivkov continued as premier until 1971, when a new constitution created the position of president of the State Council. When he gave up his previous position, it went to Stanko Todorov. Zhivkov was named president of the State Council. This relieved him of many day-to-day duties connected with running the government but still gave him a government post as titular head of state. Todorov was subsequently replaced as premier by Grisha Filipov, who continued to hold that position until 1986.

By this time, Zhivkov was 75, and the politburo had gotten old along with the secretary-general. The example of Gorbachev's significant personnel changes since coming to power a year earlier began to create strong pressure on Zhivkov to step down and allow a new generation of leadership to take over. As a result, a significant reshuffle occurred among Bulgaria's senior government and party leaders, though Zhivkov managed to retain his own hold on power. Filipov retired as premier and was replaced by Georgi Atanasov, still in his 40s.

At the party congress in 1986, Zhivkov was reelected to another five-year term. There were no changes made in either the politburo or secretariat, though there was a fairly significant turnover in membership on the Central Committee. About 80 out of 250 members were retired and replaced by younger individuals from the city and regional party organizations.

Perestroika Comes to Bulgaria

In January 1988, the Bulgarian Communist Party held a special party conference whose purpose was to discuss the progress of perestroika in Bulgaria. What was outlined was a relatively cautious approach to reform modeled closely on developments in the Soviet Union. Enterprises were to operate under a form of self-management with the right to set prices, salaries, and production goals, but all of this would be within general guidelines set in Sofia. There was also a suggestion that terms of office of higher party officials might be limited, though implementation was not to begin until the next party congress in 1991.

A new political shake-up of sorts occurred in July 1988, when Zhivkov ousted three men from the politburo who had been strong supporters of reform. It appears that Zhivkov might also have been concerned about his own political survival. One of those removed, Chudomir Alexandrov, a young technocrat in the mold of Gorbachev, had been tipped by many as the next leader of the party. In any case, the result, according to Stephen Ashley, head of Bulgarian research at Radio Free Europe, was "to reduce the Politburo to a tight clique of former partisans and Zhivkov's long-standing proteges."

In spite of Zhivkov's purge, pressure for change continued to build within the country. Domestically, Bulgarian industrialization had brought into existence a significant and growing "middle" class of technicians, engineers, teachers, doctors, and other better-educated individuals. They wanted a larger role in decision making and resented the interference of political operatives in their areas of expertise. Internationally, the Bulgarians had always looked to the Soviet Union for leadership and so were inevitably affected by the wave of changes occurring there. Zhivkov's own first reaction was to go along with Moscow's reforms, and for a while glasnost and perestroika became the new watchwords in Bulgaria. Local newspapers were suddenly filled with unprecedented debates, and "independent associations" were authorized by law.

But when a human-rights group was formed to monitor rights abuses, Zhivkov considered this to be too great a challenge. Moving to isolate the group, he expelled those who happened also to be members of the Bulgarian Communist Party. Another leading communist, Svetlin Rusev, lost his seat on the Central Committee when he organized an independent environmental committee to protest pollution in the city of Ruse.

Perhaps the greatest challenge came in November 1988, when a group of 100 leading intellectuals formed the Club for the Support of Perestroika and Glasnost. Once again, Zhivkov reacted by arresting the leaders and expelling them from the party. In effect, he had rejected glasnost and perestroika and opted for repression and the status quo. While pleasing some people, such actions alienated intellectuals and set the stage for Zhivkov's own eventual departure.

That came in November 1989 in a palace coup organized by Zhivkov's foreign and defense ministers in a sort of counterpoint to the revolutionary ferment then sweeping across eastern Europe. Petar Mladenov, the man who engineered the coup, had been Zhivkov's foreign minister for the previous 19 years. During that time, he had kept his mouth shut and was awarded by promotions that eventually put him in the politburo. After Gorbachev launched his policy of perestroika, however, Mladenov became attracted to the new ideas, in particular as they applied in the international arena.

Increasingly, however, he found his efforts frustrated by actions Zhivkov was taking for domestic reasons. Thus, in May 1989, only four months after Mladenov had signed a new international human-rights accord in Vienna, Zhivkov launched a new campaign encouraging the emigration of ethnic Turks. When Mladenov organized a 35-nation environmental conference in Sofia in October and invited an independent Bulgarian group, Eco-Glasnost, to participate, Zhivkov had his secret police rough up Eco-Glasnost members in a park in Sofia. Mladenov was embarrassed and his attempt to polish up Bulgaria's image was largely negated.

Mladenov first submitted his resignation, and when it was not accepted, he decided that Zhivkov had to go. Cautiously, he began sounding out other politburo members. This brought a promise of support from Dobri Dzhurov, the defense minister. Dzhurov, a World War II partisan colleague of Zhivkov and longtime politburo member, had been revolted for years by Zhivkov's behavior and incessant efforts to advance the career of his son Vladimir. His support was particularly important because he could guarantee the loyalty of the army. Mladenov also got promises of support from Georgi Atanasov, the

premier, and Andrei Lukanov, the minister for foreign economic relations.

Meanwhile, a wave of change was beginning to sweep across eastern Europe, and this strengthened Mladenov's case further. Even Zhivkov realized by this time that some concessions were necessary. In a statement published in the party newspaper on October 29, Zhivkov conceded the failure of earlier Bulgarian reform efforts and promised to introduce changes along Soviet lines. He had very little credibility left by that time, however.

The Communist Regime Crumbles

The pivotal politburo meeting took place on November 9. Mladenov made a motion calling for Zhivkov's resignation and proposing himself as general secretary. He won on a vote of five to four. The next day, Gorbachev put his stamp of approval on the change by sending Mladenov a highly complimentary, congratulatory message.

One of Mladenov's first actions as general secretary was to reinstate 11 former party members who had been purged because of their membership in a dissident organization called the Independent Discussion Club for the Support of Glasnost and Perestroika. He followed this up with a statement pledging support for greater diversity and promising that, in the future, street rallies by antigovernment groups would be allowed. That same week, Eco-Glasnost was granted official recognition, making it a legal organization.

Mladenov next called a meeting of the Central Committee for November 16. Here, Zhivkov and three of his supporters were removed from the politburo, while a fourth was dropped as a Central Committee secretary. A half-dozen other men were also dismissed, including two nonvoting members of the politburo. In addition, the Central Committee recommended that Mladenov take over Zhivkov's other post as head of state.

The next day, the National Assembly met to implement the recommendation of the Central Committee. At the same time, it also repealed a law making it a crime to say anything likely "to create dissatisfaction with the government and its undertakings" and declared an amnesty for persons convicted under the old legislation. Speaking afterward, Mladenov told the legislature that he favored political and economic restructuring and that the National Assembly "should play a democratic alternative to the administrative command system that reigned before." Later, he told journalists, "personally, I am for free elections." Another interesting aspect of the proceedings was that a number of the members of the assembly rose to give anti-Zhivkov speeches. All of this was broadcast to the nation via live television.

The Bulgarian National Theater

Bulgaria

The Saint Kliment Ohridski University, Sofia

AP/Wide World Photo

Mladenov clearly wanted controlled change. But news of the events happening elsewhere in eastern Europe reverberated through Bulgaria, and popular demands began to mount. Mladenov visited Moscow at the beginning of December 1989. Asked there by journalists what his reaction was to the decisions of the Czechoslovak and East German communist parties to give up their constitutional monopoly of power, he first suggested that he would leave that up to the Bulgarian people to decide. He then added that, although he could not predict how the issue would be resolved, "I foresee changes in the Constitution."

Back in Bulgaria, popular demonstrations, which had begun occurring on an almost-daily basis, grew larger in size, and their demands became more far-reaching. A new umbrella organization, the Union for Democratic Reform, was also formed to coordinate the actions of the opposition. Responding to these pressures, Mladenov called another meeting of the Central Committee on December 8. Six more members of the politburo were ousted, plus 27 members of the Central Committee.

This second purge in a month only seemed to whet the appetite of the opposition. Two days later, 50,000 of them gathered for another prodemocracy rally in the middle of Sofia. All of this was fully covered by the controlled press and state television. The next day, Mladenov went on television to promise that the monopoly on power of the Bulgarian Communist Party would be abolished, and there would be free elections in the spring. "We need to adopt the principle of a multiparty system," he said.

Mladenov's promises did not placate the opposition. On December 14, when the National Assembly took up a bill to scrap article 1 of the constitution, which guaranteed the party's leading role, 20,000 demonstrators surrounded the legislature and began shouting for an immediate end to the party's monopoly on power. When Stanko Todorov, the assembly's chairman, told them that article 1 had already been suspended but that it could not be repealed for a month because of another constitutional provision, he was met by cries of "we do not believe you," "resign," and "Berlin, Prague, Sofia." The next day, the assembly unanimously passed a declaration affirming that article 1 would be stricken from the constitution at its next session in January. Mladenov also announced that roundtable discussions with opposition leaders would begin the following week.

In a new development, ethnic minorities organized a mass rally against government persecution at the end of December. That same day, the Central Committee met and voted to reverse Zhivkov's policy of assimilation, calling it "a grave political error." Under the new policy, ethnic Turks could take back their old names and speak Turkish in public. The government

subsequently adopted this policy. For the first time, this led to a demonstration of another sort, as thousands of anti-Turkish Bulgarian nationalists gathered outside the National Assembly chanting, "Bulgaria for the Bulgarians," and demanding that the government's action be rescinded. In a curious reversal of past developments, the communists and the democratic opposition now came together to reaffirm the new policy.

When the National Assembly met on January 15, 1990, and voted to delete article 1 from the constitution, the action came as a sort of anticlimax. Roundtable discussions between the communists and the opposition, a coalition of 13 new parties, movements, and groups collectively referred to as the Union of Democratic Forces (UDF), began in January. At the beginning of February, Mladenov offered to form a coalition government with the opposition. When this offer was refused, Andrei Lukanov replaced Georgi Atanasov as premier.

At a hastily called party congress, the party voted to change its name to the Bulgarian Socialist Party. This was accompanied by a general restructuring of the party. The old power position of general secretary was abolished and replaced by a chairman. In another change, the congress also endorsed the creation of an executive presidency. The National Assembly voted these changes into law at the beginning of April. Mladenov was elected president,

612

Let's finish what we've started (Simeon Movement), 2005.

and Alexander Lilov became the new chairman of the Bulgarian Socialist Party.

Multiparty elections took place in June 1990, and the Bulgarian Socialist Party won with almost 53% of the vote. The UDF got only about a third of the seats in the assembly, with the rest going to a third party, the Movement for Rights and Freedoms, which represented approximately a half-million Turkish speakers, plus independents. Although the Socialists won in the overall vote, their main support came from the countryside. The UDF actually won in the urban areas. For this reason, the UDF thought of itself as having won the election, and it refused to cooperate with the Socialists.

Before the Socialists could get their new government installed, President Petar Mladenov came under attack for remarks he had made in December 1989 ordering tanks to be used against the Bulgarian people. He resigned on July 6. After almost a month of stalemate, the Bulgarian Assembly named Zhelyu Zhelev president. He had led the democratic opposition in the June elections and had spent 17 years under house arrest under the former regime. He was a compromise candidate backed by all the parties.

Meanwhile the Socialists, divided between conservatives and reformers, were having difficulty getting a government organized. They first offered to form a coalition government with the UDF. When the opposition refused, it took the Socialists three months to get their new government chosen and approved. Andrei Lukanov was reappointed premier in September, but his tenure turned out to be short. By November, thousands of Bulgarians were demanding his resignation. He won a vote of confidence in the assembly, but the demonstrations continued. One issue was an unpopular austerity plan put into effect by the government and widespread shortages of food, gasoline, and consumer goods. But a greater issue was a lack of confidence in a government led by an ex-communist.

The Post Communist Era Begins

Lukanov finally stepped down on November 29, 1990, after the Confederation of Independent Trade Unions began a general strike aimed at forcing him out of office. His successor, Dimitar Popov, was chosen on December 7. Popov, a nonpolitician who had been head of Sofia's municipal court before becoming prime minister (the term replacing "premier"), was apparently selected to stand above the parties and lead a coalition government that could be supported by all factions.

Although originally considered to be a caretaker government, Popov submitted a far-reaching program in January 1991 that began moving Bulgaria toward a free market. Price controls were loosened, interest rates were increased, a new landowner-ship law was passed, and proposals were submitted to reform the banking and tax laws and begin the privatization of state-owned enterprises. Prices rose tenfold, interest rates soared to about 50%, and unemployment began edging up. On the positive side, shop windows and market stands began filling up, and food became plentiful, though things like medicines, fertilizers, toilet paper, sugar, petroleum products, and pesticides remained scarce. Polls indicated that Bulgarians had become more optimistic, apparently convinced that their present sacrifices would pay dividends later.

Parliamentary elections were set for October 1991. In the lead-up to the elections, the Union of Democratic Forces broke into four factions, and numerous new political parties came into being. Only three parties had crossed the 4% threshold, the UDF with 34% of the vote, the Bulgarian Socialist Party with 33%, and the Movement for Rights and Freedoms with 7.5%. This gave the UDF 111 seats, the BSP 106 seats, and the MRF 23 seats.

President Zhelev designated Filip Dimitrov, head of the UDF, to form a cabinet on November 5. Since it lacked a parliamentary majority, Dimitrov offered to form a coalition with the MRF. The MDR, an ethnic Turkish party that mainly represents Bulgaria's Muslim population and is reputedly led by a number of ex-security officials from the communist era, refused to enter the cabinet. But it agreed to support the government in the National Assembly. In the end, the 14-member cabinet contained a number of "technicians" chosen for their expertise and belonging to no party. Only 8 of the 14 were members of the parliament.

In his opening policy statement, Prime Minister Dimitrov set forth long- and short-term goals. His long-term goal would be to replace the previous system; his short-term goal would be to stabilize

One for all, all for one; Bulgarian Coalition (Socialists)

the country's economy and curb inflation. His specific policies included amending the Foreign Investment Act passed by the previous government, privatization, the reform of banking, tax reform, and amending the Land Act.

This was the last significant victory for the Union of Democratic Forces, however. Although Prime Minister Dimitrov managed to make an important start on most of his short-term goals, the economic pain they engendered produced a split in the

Entrance to the presidential palace, Sofia

Bulgaria

President Rumen Radev

Union of Democratic Forces, which in turn led to the fall of his ministry later in the year. He subsequently served as Bulgaria's ambassador to the United States and United Nations.

POLITICAL SYSTEM

Bulgaria has a parliamentary type of government. A popularly elected president is a figurehead who represents the nation. The president is considered to be the spokesman for the nation, but he has little power. He is commander-in-chief of the armed forces. The prime minister is the fulcrum of political power. He is formally nominated by the president and confirmed by the 240-member National Assembly. He presides over the cabinet and oversees day-to-day affairs of government. He thus is responsible for implementation of policy.

The Presidency

Presidential elections take place every five years. In November 1996 Petar Stoyanov, then a little-known lawyer, defeated the incumbent, Zhelyu Zhelev, winning 60% of the vote. His landslide victory was seen as a vote of no confidence in the ruling Socialists. He accused the Socialists of isolating Bulgaria from the rest of Europe, and he argued that Bulgaria had to implement sweeping reforms such as had been so successful in central Europe. He favored bringing Bulgaria into the European Union and NATO.

In 2001 Stoyanov was voted out of office in an election with 55% turnout. The new president was Georgi Parvanov, former history professor and member of the Socialist Party. He pledged to strive for membership in the EU and NATO. He earned respect for his ability to keep fractious coalition governments focused on the reforms required for EU entry. He was decisively reelected in 2006, winning 76%

of the votes in the second round against the leader of the nationalist and racist Ataka (Attack) Party, Volen Siderov, who campaigned against the large Muslim and Roma minorities. In November 2011 Rosen Plevneliev of the GERB party captured the presidency with 52.56% of the votes. He declared administrative reform and energy independence as his top priorities.

In the presidential election of November 6, 2016, voters were offered for the first time an option to cast the ballot for "None of the above." President Plevneliev declined to run for a second term. The election was won by a career military officer and former commander of the Bulgarian Air Force, Major General Rumen Radev. His candidacy was supported by the Socialists. In the second round, he won 59.4% of the vote against 36.2% for Tsetska Tsacheva, the candidate of the ruling center-right GERB Party. Radev, who once studied at the US Air War College, had been known for his antimigration and pro-Russia views, including his strong criticism of western sanctions against Moscow. He successfully rode the wave of resistance to immigration, declaring that he would not allow Bulgaria to turn into a "migrant ghetto." Soon after his inauguration in January 2017, he was already sharply criticized by the previous head of state, Plevneliev, for proposing a law that would disenfranchise Bulgarians living abroad and for focusing on Türkiye's interference in Bulgaria's politics while down-playing Russia's meddling. Humiliated by the crushing defeat of his party's candidate, Prime Minister Borisov resigned, leading to the creation of a caretaker government and new parliamentary elections.

In November 2021, President Rumen Radev won a second presidential term.

Parliamentary Elections

A hybrid proportional voting is used. In order to keep fringe parties out of 240-seat parliament and thereby maximizing the likelihood that stable governments can be created and maintained, a threshold of 4% was established. This means that a party must win at least 4% of the votes nationwide to become eligible for a parliamentary seat. In a new system adopted for the July 2009 elections, 209 of the 240 seats are distributed according to proportional representation. This means that a party gets a percentage of those 209 seats in accordance with the percentage of votes it wins nationwide. The other 31 seats are awarded to the winner in each of 31 voting constituencies. Whoever gets the most votes, wins the seat. Thus, every Bulgarian has a representative from his or her constituency.

In June 2001 elections were held following a bizarre political development: the

Former Prime Minister Boyko Borisov

astonishing rise of former King Simeon II, who had become tsar in 1943 and was only six years old when he was forced to leave after a rigged plebiscite that abolished the monarchy. He never abdicated. He thus represents a link to a more prosperous past, when Bulgaria was known as the Switzerland of the Balkans. He spent nearly 55 years in exile, becoming a businessman in Spain; learning eight languages; and cultivating a refined, courteous manner. He has friends and relatives in royal houses all over Europe and the Middle East.

He spent Christmas 1998 in Sofia, when he also met with Prime Minister Kostov, although the conversation apparently had no political overtones. According to the Bulgarian press, he briefed Simeon on the costs of maintaining the two palaces, three hunting lodges, and two country houses that the government had decided to turn back to Simeon, in line with a decision of the Constitutional Court in June 1998. Simeon thus became one of the richest men in Bulgaria. He subsequently donated a small castle and surrounding park, located on the outskirts of Sofia, to the city's municipality. Of perhaps greater political interest, in December 1998 the Bulgarian government requested the Constitutional Court to invalidate the 1946 referendum that abolished the monarchy.

He moved back to Bulgaria in April and created his party, the National Movement of Tsar Simeon II, only 11 weeks before the elections. He was greeted with enthusiasm. One diplomat said, "It's as if he landed from another planet like some kind of messiah." He generated a wave of sentiment for the precommunist past that fueled expectations that he could create a prosperous future. His real name is Simeon Saxe-Coburg-Gotha, but he Bulgarized it to Simeon Sakskoburggotski. His aides addressed him as "Your Majesty," but most Bulgarians simply call him "Simeon." He himself did not run for a parliamentary seat.

Bulgaria

Parliament

Prime Minister Nikolai Denkov
Source: *Wikipedia*

He promised to transform Bulgaria within 800 days by attracting foreign investment, cutting taxes, and rooting out corruption. Because so many voters identified him with the Bulgarian nation, his opponents could not easily attack him. His party took about 40% of the votes, but it failed to win a parliamentary majority. He formed a coalition government with the center-right Union of Democratic Forces, the Socialist Party, and the Turkish Movement for Rights and Freedoms (MRF). Simeon, who became prime minister, was the first monarch to regain power in Europe in an election since Louis Napoleon a century and a half earlier. Within months his popularity had declined markedly as doubts grew about his ability to solve

Simeon's 800 days run out!

Bulgaria's problems. After his 800 days had ticked off, he and his government had yet to fix many of the problems they promised to solve. He lost power in 2005, and the party faded.

Despite some impressive economic and diplomatic gains, some Bulgarians had not yet seen the benefits from economic reforms by the time new elections took place on July 5, 2009. This was especially true since Bulgaria had been hard hit by the global economic crisis. Citizens had been embarrassed by the EU's unrelenting criticism of the failure to stem corruption. The results contained a pointed protest message.

The favorite had in 2009 won decisively: GERB (Citizens for the European Development of Bulgaria). It is a populist center-right party committed to fighting crime and corruption and led by Sofia's charismatic and rough-talking ex-mayor Boyko Borisov, who became prime minister. He is a former black-belt karate champion and national karate team coach, ex-police general, and bodyguard to both ex-communist leader Zhivkov and later to King Simeon.

His government was brought down in February 2013 by weeks of sometimes-bloody street protests that claimed seven deaths, including six self-immolations. They began in response to unusually high electricity prices, austerity measures, and low living standards. But they turned into general antigovernment and anticorruption protests, made worse by charges of government wiretapping. As many as 100,000 demonstrators gathered on a single evening, and 76% of the population supported them.

In the May 2013 parliamentary elections, GERB received the most votes. However, it could not find coalition partners, so it was in the opposition until new elections took place in October 2014. GERB captured 32.7% of the votes and 84 seats. It formed a minority coalition under Prime Minister Borisov. Left Bulgaria got 15.4% and 39 seats.

In third place with 14.8% of the votes and 38 seats was the Movement for Rights and Freedoms (MRF), an ethnic Turkish party led by Ahmed Dogan. It is often criticized by anticorruption campaigners, especially since Dogan boasts publicly of his ability to channel state funds and wield political power. The MRF has held the balance of power in most post-communist governments.

The nationalist and far-right party National Union Attack (Ataka), led by Volen Siderov, was the biggest loser. It grabbed 4.5% of the votes and 11 seats. Its votes are sometimes needed by the prime minister. Because it campaigns on a racist platform by targeting immigrants and the Turkish and Roma minorities, other parties are hesitant to deal or coalesce with it. Ataka demands the scrapping of Turkish-language news bulletins on public TV and radio, which are guaranteed by law. Four more parties cleared the 4% hurdle and won seats: Reformed Bloc (23), Patriotic Front (19), Bulgaria without Censorship (15), and Alternative for Bulgarian Revival (11). Parliament is unstable and fractious.

The government was unprepared for the massive influx of Syrian refugees, and Ataka took full advantage of the public alarm that the country is being overwhelmed. Ataka prodded the government to construct a controversial 30-mile,

615

Bulgaria

10-feet-high fence along the border with Türkiye and to add 1,500 new border guards to stop the flow. One of its parliamentarians referred to the desperate Syrians as "terrible, despicable primates," and the party's Alfa Television uses such terms as "savages," "scum," and "mass murderers" to refer to them.

The 750,000 Turkish speakers, 10% of the total population, face some residual resentment in the wider Bulgarian society because of what many regard as the unwelcome consequences of earlier Turkish colonial oppression and deportations carried out in 1913. Turkish speakers, by contrast, are inclined to remember most vividly the deportations of Turks in the late 1980s by Bulgarian Communist authorities.

Since 2013 daily street protests have broken out. The previous Socialist prime minister had made the mistake of naming a rich oligarch with dubious business practices, Delyan Peevski, to head the national security agency. Although the appointment was quickly withdrawn, it was too late. Tens of thousands of protesters took to the streets in Sofia, Varna, Burgas, and other cities calling for more transparency, less corruption and organized crime, an end to the rule of local oligarchs, and the government's resignation. In Sofia the marchers met at the presidential palace and slowly walked to the parliament. One day they blockaded the legislative building, trapping 100 lawmakers and ministers for more than 8 hours. Polls showed that a majority of citizens supported the protests. The protests were skillfully orchestrated by social media. Due to huge investments in high-speed broadband, Bulgaria has become one of Europe's most online countries.

After the crushing defeat of GERB's candidate Tsetska Tsacheva in the November 2016 presidential election, Prime Minister Borisov resigned, prompting the need for a caretaker government and a new election. The election, held in March 2017, brought Borisov back to power for the third time. GERB won 32.7% of votes and 95 of the 240 seats, while its main rival, the Bulgarian Socialist Party, received 27.2% and 80 seats, regaining most of the losses from the previous election. The nationalist United Patriots (including the Bulgarian National Movement—IMRO, National Front for the Salvation of Bulgaria, and Attack) won 9.1% and 27 seats, similarly to the mostly ethnic Movement for Rights and Freedoms (MRF) that came with 9% and 26 seats. The parliament was rounded up by the populist Volya (Will), with 4.2% and 12 seats. Borisov's government is a coalition of the center-right GERB and the United Patriots.

Prime Minister Boyko Borisov, and his populist conservative party GERB, have led Bulgaria consecutively since 2016. Borisov's third government was embroiled in numerous corruption scandals during its time in office, specifically surrounding the allocation of EU funds, infrastructure projects, and government subsidies.

Scandals culminated in protests on July 9, 2020, with the aim of removing Borisov's government and Chief Prosecutor Ivan Geshev. These protests would continue daily until after the government's term concluded on April 16, 2021. The protests saw the rise to prominence of several so-called "parties of change," consisting mainly of new political parties which opposed Borisov, and many of whom joined in with the protests.

The following elections took place on April 4, 2021, and were scheduled as regular elections following four years after the 2017 election.

The period of 2021–2023 Bulgarian political crisis was a time of instability in Bulgaria, which has seen the country face five elections over two years: April 2021, July 2021, November 2021, October 2022, and April 2023.

The first two elections failed to form a governing coalition, but the November 2021 election saw Kiril Petkov create an unstable government that lasted only 7 months. The October 2022 snap elections resulted in another gridlock, leading to the April 2023 elections. These were initially scheduled to be held before November 2026. Still, as no government was approved by the 48th Parliament, President Rumen Radev announced in January 2023 that he would call a snap election. The elections were held on April 2, 2023.

The results saw a close race between GERB—SDS and PP–DB. the GERB—SDS placed first with 69 seats, closely followed by PP–DB which won 64. Also, V, DPS, and BSPzB made it into the parliament, as well as ITN after having fallen out in the 2022 elections.

President Radev subsequently handed a mandate on May 29 to the PP–DB to form a government, which nominated

Former tsar and prime minister Simeon dumped in 2005

616

McDonald's in Bulgarian Cyrillic
Photo by Roman Payerhin

Nikolai Denkov for prime minister. However, Radev recommended Denkov return the mandate due to a video's release, an alleged recordings from an incriminating PP meeting. That sparked protests and criticism from PP–DB, arguing the president's requirement was unconstitutional. GERB—SDS agreed to restart negotiations with PP–DB to form a "government of experts." Denkov announced on June 2 that the two parties had reached an agreement on the composition of a cabinet with certain modifications that removed "inflammatory political figures." Parliament voted to approve the new GERB—SDS–PP–DB government on June 6, 2023, with Nikolai Denkov as prime minister.

Foreign Policy

Some Bulgarians admired the Russian people and looked to Russia for assistance and leadership. The Bulgarian government banned a domestic communist party in 1923, and it established diplomatic relations with the Soviet Union in 1934. When Bulgaria became a communist state after 1945, the first principle of Bulgarian foreign policy became loyalty to the Soviet Union. Georgi Dimitrov, the new Bulgarian leader, had been a loyal servant of Stalin since the 1920s.

After 1948, Bulgaria's traditional rivalry with Yugoslavia reinforced this orientation. Following Tito's quarrel with Stalin, Bulgaria replaced Yugoslavia as the principal country through which Soviet influence was projected in the area of the southern Balkans.

This relationship with the Soviet Union was reflected not only in Bulgaria's relations with its neighbors but in its relations with the United States, as well. As the Cold War began, Bulgaria joined the Soviet Union in making extravagant attacks on the United States. As a result, diplomatic relations, broken by the US in 1950, were not renewed until 1959. Formal but cool relations continued until the 1970s, when Bulgaria became interested in exporting to the United States.

The government agreed to end jamming of Voice of America radio broadcasts and also signed a consular convention which accorded greater protection for Americans in Bulgaria. Deputy Prime Minister Ivan Popov paid a visit to the United States in 1974, and it appeared that American-Bulgarian relations would continue to improve. But the Soviet Union renounced its trade agreement with the United States in 1975 over the issue of Jewish emigration, and the Bulgarians followed suit, abandoning their efforts to expand trade. Thereafter, American-Bulgarian relations simply mirrored the state of American-Soviet relations. For example, when the Soviets announced a boycott of the 1984 Olympic contests in Los Angeles, Bulgaria was the very first country to indicate that it would not participate either.

There was an evolution toward greater independence in Bulgaria's relations with the Soviet Union in the 1980s. The first signs came in 1984–1985, when the Soviet Union instituted a political-economic boycott of western Europe after arms negotiation talks had failed to resolve the issue of intermediate range ballistic missiles in Europe. Interested in obtaining new technology from western Europe to reverse several years of declining growth rates, the Bulgarian government was unwilling to go along at first. After some pressure from Moscow, it went along with a political freeze, but it did everything it could to maintain its economic ties to western Europe. Gorbachev's rise to power was welcomed in Bulgaria, and his foreign policy of cooperation with the west found particular support.

Bulgaria instituted a political opening to the west in 1987, when Zhivkov paid an official visit to West Germany. Bulgaria, he told his hosts, wanted to expand its economic relations with Bonn and the European Community (now EU). Even then, West Germany was Bulgaria's largest trading partner outside of the Moscow-dominated Council for Mutual Economic Assistance (CMEA, also known as COMECON). Since that time, Germany has been unified, CMEA and the Soviet Union have collapsed, and Bulgaria has lost most of its markets in eastern Europe and the former Soviet Union.

Bulgaria and Greece had no diplomatic relations whatsoever until 1964. Relations remained cool for another 10 years, becoming cordial only after 1974. They were particularly good during the years of the left-wing Greek government of Andreas Papandreou. In the late 1990s, Greece announced that it supported Bulgaria's application for membership in NATO. In the 21st century, Greece has been a key supporter of Bulgaria's efforts to enter NATO and the EU.

Post-Cold War Policy

Relations with Yugoslavia followed the pattern of Soviet-Yugoslav affairs. There was one additional complication—the traditional rivalry over Macedonia. Sofia never recognized Macedonian as a separate language, and on occasion it felt called upon to speak out on behalf of "Bulgarians" living in the Yugoslav Republic of Macedonia. The death of Tito in 1980 brought no change, for better or worse. The collapse of Yugoslavia in 1991 when Croatia and Slovenia seceded, coupled with the subsequent decision of the Republic of Macedonia to seek recognition as an independent country, changed that situation.

Bulgaria was the first state that extended diplomatic recognition to the Republic of North Macedonia in 1991. The Bulgarian government recognized the existence of a Macedonian "state" but never officially conceded that Macedonian is a separate language. However, the two countries' prime ministers declared in 1998 that they would sign documents in both official languages.

Romania is the one nation with which Bulgaria has maintained consistently friendly relations over the years. Romania was the only one of Bulgaria's neighbors that was also a member of the Soviet bloc. The two nations have continued to cooperate since 1989. Ex-communists continued to play important political roles in both societies, and both were at first denied economic assistance by the EU and the United States. Thanks to an EU mediating role, Bulgaria and Romania built a second bridge along their 290-mile shared border along the Danube. It connects the two countries at Vidin in western Bulgaria and Calafat in Romania. Traffic over the earlier bridge between Ruse in Bulgaria and Georeiu in Romania had doubled from 2000 to 2004. Bulgaria has distanced itself from Russia, once its patron, but it continues to cultivate economic relations with the successor states to the old Soviet Union, in particular Russia and Ukraine.

Bulgaria

Bulgaria became a member of the Central Europe Free Trade Agreement (CEFTA) in 1998. This links Bulgaria economically with the Czech Republic, Hungary, Poland, Romania, Slovakia, and Slovenia. By 2002 the members of the CEFTA had entirely phased out tariffs among themselves. CEFTA was also seen as a stepping stone to the European Union. At its December 2002 Copenhagen summit, the EU granted Bulgaria a "roadmap" that led to full membership January 1, 2007.

The EU also earmarked €1.5 billion in pre-accession assistance, but most of it was frozen as punishment for not having reduced corruption. Now that Bulgaria has officially joined, that aid could rise to the equivalent of 3.7% of GDP, 1.7% of that for agricultural subsidies, if only the country could meet the EU's anticorruption standards. In 2009 the EU agreed to release $27 million in farm subsidies and $129 million to help modernize Bulgaria's agriculture once it was convinced that the government had adopted financial controls to protect against corruption and fraud.

European integration and infrastructure development are closely linked. One sees signs everywhere that the roads on which one is driving were built or improved with EU funding. The EU is helping fund an interstate highway linking Sofia to the Greek border and ultimately to Athens in the south and Budapest in the north. A rail line connecting Athens via Sofia to Vienna, Prague, and Nuremberg is also under construction, as is one that would connect Sofia and North Macedonia's capital of Skopje.

The EU demands that combating corruption be the first priority. In a 2008 report of 180 countries, the Berlin-based Transparency International ranked Bulgaria 57th (down from 64th in 2007) in terms of overall corruption. In 2009 it was still ranked among the three worst offenders in the EU. Bulgaria's geographical location on the Black Sea and along the Turkish border makes it easy prey for all kinds of smugglers and organized criminals; many in the EU see it as a hub between the Middle East and Europe for trafficking in people, weapons, and drugs.

Bulgarians generally regard customs officials, the police, judges, prosecutors, health-care administrators, politicians, and businessmen as persons who respond to bribes. A 2006 poll revealed that three-fourths regard customs officials as the worst. The problem is systemic and has deep roots. The first business groups to emerge from the country's transition from communism specialized in trading, mixed with smuggling and organized crime. They recruited former secret service agents to help them. After two decades, it is extremely difficult to untangle all these elements.

The Bulgarian and Romanian flags flying with the EU colors

Suspicions were strengthened by the killings in 2003 of a series of high-profile business leaders, including Bulgaria's richest man, Ilya Pavlov, a day after he had testified in the murder trial of five men charged with assassinating former prime minister Andrei Lukanov. Two years later the country's most prominent banker, Emil Kyulev, was gunned down in broad daylight in the middle of Sofia. In April 2008 Georgi Stoev, an investigative writer of books on mafia activities, was murdered in the capital.

In January 2010 another prominent investigative journalist and radio presenter who wrote about organized crime groups

Mountain hike

was shot dead in the light of day in downtown Sofia. A murky figure who dealt with both the police and the crime groups (known as mutri, or "mugs" and often led by former security service officers), Boris "Bobi" Tsankov was a colorful and controversial figure who was always short of cash to support his flamboyant lifestyle and fancy cars.

Over the past decade, there have been more than 200 contract killings in Sofia and Black Sea resorts. This extends even to soccer: In the dozen years to mid-2007, no fewer than 15 club owners or backers have died violently. Three presidents of the Lokomotiv Plovdiv team were gunned down within two years from 2005 to 2007. While this is on a level with western European countries, what stands out is that courts have been unable to issue convictions in these or other corruption cases. No murderer or high-level official has been found guilty, and there have been few arrests.

It is the climate of impunity and the fact that all ministries leak information and EU funds to mobsters that worry the EU and others. One consultant called the promised $15 billion in EU aid the "mother lode" for the corrupt. With the EU breathing down its neck, Bulgaria started to improve the situation in 2006 by dismissing 40 police officers for corruption and making trafficking in humans a crime. But the

Bulgaria

problems continue. In 2008 the economy minister, the head of the highways agency, and the interior minister (who admitted to meeting personally with crime bosses) resigned. In July 2008 the parliament was even deliberating impeaching President Parvanov over alleged links with a suspected criminal group.

The EU admitted Bulgaria on January 1, 2007, "on faith" and promise—rather than evidence—that the country would tackle its problems with corruption and the rule of law once within the organization. But the European Commission sent both Bulgaria and Romania early-warning letters informing them that they are lagging in such fields as judicial reform and the fight against corruption. Bulgaria was chided for "insufficient progress in tackling organized crime." The country is being subjected to an unprecedented EU monitoring regime. Sensing that this criticism was coming, the Bulgarian government made an unusual request in May for legal expertise from the commission to help deal with the country's biggest corruption scandal at that time: The economy and energy minister and an investigator were accused of obstructing a high-level investigation in order to protect friends.

Suspecting that some former secret police agents in the dismantled State Security (Държавна сигурност) are involved with organized crime, parliament approved a law in 2006 to open up Cold War files in order to unmask such persons and to determine who once collaborated with the intelligence service. It is the last central European country to do this. At a lower level, investors complain often of administrative obstacles, demands for kickbacks, and inefficiency in the judicial system.

The EU does not fully trust the Bulgarian government with information and funds. The sad truth is that many Bulgarians also have little trust. In one 2009

Eurobarometer poll, over 80% said they did not trust their government, parliament, and courts, but almost 75% said they trust the EU. Its problem at this point is that it no longer has as much leverage against Bulgaria as it once had before the country joined. Many EU officials point to the Bulgarian case as evidence why the enlargement process should be slowed down. The most it can do is to admonish and to reduce or withhold financial assistance, but this can hit Bulgaria hard.

The EU also casts a wary eye on Bulgarians nominated by Sofia for top posts. In 2010 the government nominated former foreign minister Rumiana Jeleva to be the new EU commissioner for humanitarian aid and crisis response. After reading press accounts of her and her husband's business activities, she was questioned pointedly in the European Parliament hearings about her financial interests and competence for the job. It was decided that she did not have a firm enough grasp of her portfolio to serve. Her nomination was withdrawn, and World Bank vice president Kristalina Georgieva was put forward instead. In the previous year, another ex-foreign minister and later ambassador to France and UNESCO Irina Bokova was chosen without controversy as director general of the UN Educational, Scientific, and Cultural Organization in Paris. Bokova was the daughter of a top newspaper editor in the communist era, when she entered the foreign service. She is a popular member of the Socialist Party, the successor party of the Bulgarian Communists.

Defense Policy

When fighting erupted in Kosovo in March 1999, the Bulgarian government endorsed NATO policy on Kosovo and gave limited permission for NATO forces to transit the country en route to Kosovo, even promising logistical support in such

a case. Bulgaria's aspiration to become a full member of NATO was fulfilled in April 2004. The alliance had long-standing worries about democratic reform, corruption, and military readiness. It also singled out Bulgaria's treatment of minorities, particularly of the Roma.

The chances that Bulgaria would be admitted to NATO skyrocketed in the wake of the September 11 terrorist attacks in the US. Indeed, the strategic significance of the entire Black Sea region grew because it is a staging area for the war effort in Afghanistan. In the words of Romanian ex-foreign minister Mircea Geoană, "September 11 transformed the Black Sea into a natural springboard."

The Bulgarian government considers itself an ally against terrorism. For this reason both Türkiye and Greece supported the candidacies of Romania and Bulgaria on the grounds that NATO's southern flank has become strategically crucial for combating traditional threats, as well as "new threats," such as terrorism; transborder crime; and trafficking in weapons, drugs, and human beings, including illegal immigrants and women destined to often involuntary prostitution. Bulgaria is a target of terrorism. In July 2012 an Israeli tourist bus was bombed at the Burgas Airport, killing five Israeli tourists and wounding three dozen more. Investigators concluded that Hezbollah was behind the bloodbath.

The government was so desirous of NATO and EU entry that, when a UN investigation revealed the extent of Bulgaria's arms sales to unsavory regimes, the government closed many of its arms industries. This was a serious financial blow to cities that depend on weapons production. By 2001 foreign arms sales had dropped by 90% from the peak years under communism. In 2002 it uncovered and halted illegal exports of weapons parts to Syria, thereby improving its image as a country that does not sell arms to blacklisted states. However, in 2008 the American military was caught off guard and was alarmed by the shipment of three planeloads of small arms and ammunition to Iraqi Kurds.

Bulgaria cooperated closely with the US to demonstrate what it can contribute as military partners. It unconditionally offered its airspace and use of all port and land facilities, and it refurbished airstrips for allied use. It sent peacekeepers to Kabul. Ex-foreign minister Solomon Passy stated that his country had from the beginning acted on the proposition that "if you want to become a member of NATO, behave as if you are one." He said the bases would be "an invaluable investment in the security of the region and in Bulgaria's future prosperity."

Bulgaria

In 2006 the US and Bulgaria signed a 10-year agreement permitting the use of three bases near the Black Sea for transport and training activities. They are Novo Selo Training Area, Bezmer Air Base in the southeast, and Graf Ignatievo Airfield in central Bulgaria. Up to 3,000 American soldiers are stationed there at any time. Fearing that the US could use these bases to attack other countries, such as Iran, a majority of Bulgarians registered their opposition in a 2006 poll.

Bulgaria joined NATO in April 2004. This was received with rejoicing. A diplomat at the Foreign Affairs Ministry, Angel Bandjov, exclaimed, "Finally we are back where we belong, and there is no way back to criminality, totalitarian dictatorship and Russian claims. We still have many things to reform and many efforts to make, but the watershed is passed."

Its admittance provides a geographic bridge between northern and central Europe and Greece and Türkiye. It provides the US and its NATO partners a foothold much closer to the current areas of danger to Europe and North America: the unstable Caucasus and the troubled Transcaucasian region of the former Soviet Union, including Chechnya, the Middle East, and central Asia, all located across the Black Sea.

It joined the 10 new democracies in eastern and central Europe in signing the Vilnius Letter supporting the American-British war effort in Iraq in 2003. It rejected an intemperate outburst from French president Jacques Chirac criticizing all 10 for missing a good opportunity to remain silent and warning of consequences for joining the EU. President Parvanov stated, "Bulgaria insists on mutual respect." Some Bulgarians were reassured by Defense Secretary Donald Rumsfeld: "Let me be clear, those countries have not been invited as junior partners, allowed to join the grownups' table so long as they sit quietly. No, they have been invited to lead." Many analysts in and out of Bulgaria say that Chirac's remarks were a serious miscalculation and had the effect of uniting eastern and central European countries against France and the French position toward Iraq.

Bulgaria opened its airspace to allied aircraft heading to the war in Iraq and permitted American soldiers to use the previously closed Sarafovo Military Base near the Black Sea port of Burgas as a bridge for troops and equipment from the US and Germany to the Middle East. This airport had operated since September 11 as a de facto American base with approximately 200 American soldiers stationed there. The US plans to shut down many of its remaining bases in Germany and establish smaller bases farther east filled with

rotating troops without their families and posed to strike quickly. It views both Romania and Bulgaria as its anchors in the southeast, much as Poland is in the north.

Bulgaria deployed an infantry battalion of 460 troops to Iraq under Polish command. By March 2005, eight soldiers had been killed, one of them by American troops in a friendly fire incident. In July 2004 militants beheaded two captured Bulgarian truck drivers. Most of its troops, the 334 light-infantry battalion, were withdrawn from Iraq at the end of 2005; by 2009 all remaining 155 had been pulled out. Opinion polls revealed that more than 60% opposed their country's military commitment to Iraq. Bulgarian soldiers remain part of the peacekeeping forces in Kosovo, Bosnia, and Afghanistan. It was among the first countries to recognize Kosovo's independence in February 2008.

Bulgaria boosted its military budget above 2% of GDP to speed up the restructuring process. In 2005 the country began restructuring its military forces. By 2010 it had 34,975 active-duty troops. Conscripts serve nine months. At that time there are also 302,500 reservists, plus 34,000 paramilitaries. The army numbered 16,278; the navy, 3,471, who man one conventional submarine, four frigates, and an assortment of patrol and coastal combatants and mine warfare vessels; and 6,706 in the air force, flying Soviet-era MiGs and combat helicopters. In 2008 it auctioned off some of its Second World War-era tanks, including German Panzers and 140 Soviet T-34s. In 2006–2007 it had smelted down 2,500 Soviet-era models. It bought American F-16 fighter jets.

NATO's Membership Action Plan (MAP) for Bulgaria required it to reduce its military from 250,000 to below 100,000 by 2004. Hundreds of senior officers were retired, and a corps of younger leaders has been trained to move into command roles; 2,175 of them are certified as competent in English.

Like Romania, Bulgaria cheered the fall of Slobodan Milošević in Serbia in 2000. A democratic Yugoslavia benefits Bulgaria. Both countries were seriously hurt by the economic sanctions levied against that pariah state (now lifted), as well as by the destruction of the Danube bridges in Serbia, which until 2003 cut off their river connection with western Europe. The Foreign Affairs Ministry calculated that the sanctions and bridge destruction had cost the country $6 billion. It lost a third of its tourist income in the wake of the 1999 bombing campaign against Serbia and was working to recoup that and more. It reached an agreement with Serbia to build a highway between Sofia and Niš.

Bulgarians experienced a serious foreign policy blow in May 2004, when a Libyan court tortured and sentenced five Bulgarian nurses to death by firing squad after convicting them of deliberately infecting hundreds of Libyan children in 1999 with blood products contaminated with HIV in order to conduct experiments. The Bulgarian government called the verdicts "unfair and absurd." Independent medical studies concluded that the infections at the hospital had predated the nurses' arrival by several years. Its western partners, the EU and the US, supported the Bulgarian position. The

Bulgaria

verdict was later overturned, but a retrial resulted again in death sentences.

In an effort to show solidarity to the nurses in May 2005, ex-president Georgi Parvanov toured the hospital that had seen the HIV outbreak and visited the nurses in prison. The president refused to pay "blood money" to the victims' families, arguing that it would amount to an admission of guilt. As the retrial of the nurses was about to begin in May 2006, a Bulgarian newspaper published cartoons satirizing Libya's leader, Colonel Qaddafi, and its judicial system. They were sent to 100 newspapers worldwide and drew a sharp protest from the Libyan government.

Finally, in July 2007, after more than eight years in prison, the five returned home to an emotional welcome. More than anything, their freeing was the result of patient EU negotiations. Although the parties claim that no direct payments were made to Libya, up to $400 million was donated from various sources, including the US, to a fund to be given to the families of the infected. There were also promises of improved aid and trade ties between the EU and Libya.

ECONOMY

Bulgaria was still predominantly an agricultural society at the end of World War II. Using the Stalinist model, the government started the first of its five-year plans in 1949. The emphasis was always on the industrial sector, and this resulted in a transformation of the Bulgarian economy.

A powerful internal migration from rural to urban areas, especially Sophia, continues unabated. Today, 95% of the GDP is attributable either to industry, construction, or services.

Agriculture

In spite of this significant shift, agriculture continues to play an important role in the Bulgarian economy. Although the population has become predominantly (70% and rising) urban, 6.4% are farmers, and a fourth are still employed in agriculture- related jobs. In 2015 they produced only 6% of GDP.

Bulgaria placed a heavier emphasis on the development of agriculture than did the other central and eastern European countries. Collectivization, begun in 1948, was carried out more quickly than elsewhere. By 1950, 43% of the land had been collectivized; by 1960 this figure reached 100%. This is even more surprising when one considers that Bulgaria is a mountainous country, and much of the land is not suitable for intensive cultivation. Extensive wineries have been established in the hills, and they produce good wines that are reasonably priced by western standards.

Originally some 3,200 collective farms were set up, roughly corresponding to the number of villages in the country. These were then merged into 930 economic units beginning in 1960. A further consolidation began in 1969, when Bulgaria launched what it termed agro-industrial complexes (AICs). The AICs became the model for subsequent Soviet experiments of this

nature. There were 281 such AICs in the country, and they had their own factories for the processing of the harvests.

After the victory in the 1991 elections of parties committed to creation of a market economy, the government launched a new economic program that included liquidation of the AICs. In a two-step process, peasants were granted immediate ownership of the private plots they cultivated under communism, while the remainder of the land was made available for their use on a temporary basis. A complicated land reform law enacted by the Socialists resulted in over 1.7 million conflicting claims, so that by 1997 less than 10% of the remaining land had been privatized. As a result, the average size of a private plot had grown to just less than three acres, while the remaining land being worked by the peasants, which had been transferred on a temporary basis only, could neither be used for collateral nor be sold.

The process of the privatization of agriculture is still incomplete. The consumer faces severe shortages and very high prices. The National Statistical Office determined in 2000 that the average Bulgarian family has to devote 43% of its in-come for food. Its food and drink industries faced major challenges to meet EU quality norms.

Industry and Trade

In the 1990s, the situation in industry has been, if anything, worse than that of agriculture. The reason is that almost all of Bulgaria's industry was created after World War II, and it was composed mainly of large monopoly units that operated on the basis of orders from Sofia. Moreover, many factories were specifically set up to produce goods for export to the Soviet Union or other members of the CMEA. By 2015 the services sector employed 62.2% of the population and produced 63% of GDP, while the industrial sector employed 31.3% and created 30% of GDP. The largest foreign exchange earner and one of the country's biggest employers is the tourist industry, which accounts for 13% of GDP. It is Bulgaria's fastest growing industry.

In 1989, over 80% of Bulgaria's foreign trade was carried on with other communist states. Most of those markets evaporated with the collapse of communism. The disarray in the Soviet economy was particularly painful for Bulgaria since over 50% of Bulgaria's foreign trade was with the Soviet Union alone. Short of hard currency, the Soviet Union canceled 70% of its Bulgarian orders at this time.

The Bulgarian governments in power up to 1997, though verbally committed to creating a market economy, basically managed to do so only in the area of retail trade. By 1995, only 34 enterprises

Steel worker protesting in Sofia, 2009

621

Bulgaria

classified as either medium and large had been privatized.

Privatization and Investment

Under plans drawn up by the government of Prime Minister Lyuben Berov, profitable state enterprises were to be turned into joint stock companies, with stock then sold to the public. Unprofitable state enterprises were to be broken up and absorbed as part of other groups. The Bulgarian Socialist Party, which won the 1994 elections, partially implemented these plans, but they so were marred by wide-scale corruption that most privatized enterprises ended up in the hands of the old communist elite. When the new owners proceeded to strip the privatized enterprises of their remaining assets, a near collapse of the economy resulted, causing such a revulsion against the Socialists that they were driven from power in 1997.

The caretaker government of Stefan Sofiyansky, installed in 1997, reversed the policies of the previous government and put an end to the downward plunge of the economy. In particular, he closed down most of the major state-owned money-losing enterprises and cut out all energy subsidies, thus forcing prices up to world market levels. That restored some of the confidence in the Bulgarian lev and caused inflation to drop drastically, from 243% in February to 12% in March.

The government of Ivan Kostov, installed in May 1997, built on this beginning. Most importantly, he got the Bulgarian parliament to pass a law creating a currency board within the Bulgarian National Bank to keep its money stable. It made it impossible for the National Bank to continue to fuel inflation. In particular, the value of the lev was pegged to the German mark (now to the euro), overseen by an independent "currency board." Further, the National Bank was required to maintain 100% foreign reserves backing for all currency in circulation. It is forbidden to finance government budget deficits. The effect of these measures was to restore confidence in the domestic currency and to reduce inflation to negligible amounts.

These moves restored international confidence in the Bulgarian economy, and this, in turn, led to increased foreign investment. The international financial institutions also resumed lending to Bulgaria. The IMF, World Bank, and EU provided crucial loans during the 2008–2009 global recession. Foreign investment surged in 2004 to the equivalent of 10% of its GDP. To help keep the money coming, the personal and corporate tax was cut to 10% in 2008, the lowest tax rate for business in southeastern Europe.

The government also began a policy of privatization aimed at completing

Bulgaria's transition to a market economy. Bulgaria's banks were the first to be privatized, with international bankers playing a leading role. Next came several large privatization deals negotiated with foreign investors. Then, in 1998, the Bulgarian parliament passed a new privatization plan that provided for the sale of more than 1,000 state companies. This list was later extended so that 71.1% of state-owned assets had been sold by 2004, earning the country more than $2 billion. One of the most courageous and difficult decisions was to sell a controlling 59% stake in the Neftochim refinery complex at Burgas on the Black Sea to Russia's Lukoil in 2001.

By 2004 the economy was largely in private hands, with the state's share at only 21.1%. Housing has been successfully privatized. In Sofia, 95% own their own homes, while the rest pay horrendously high rents by the standards of the local population.

The country's privatization agency concentrates on the sale of infrastructure sectors excluded from previous privatizations, such as hydroelectric power stations, thermoelectric power stations, regional companies for electric power distribution, coal-mining enterprises, enterprises for the maintenance of power equipment, and even companies running water supply and sewage systems.

In 2008 a dispute flared over what responsibility the state should assume for the failing Soviet-era Kremikovtzi steel company near Sofia, which employs 8,000 workers. It was a huge source of pollution and urgently needed refurbishing, which

the owners (the state, 25%, and Global Steel of India, 75%) claimed they could not pay. Thousands of angry workers staged protests, clashed with police, and blocked roads in central Sofia in October 2008 and again for an entire week in April 2009, demanding that the government find an investor for the sprawling plant. On May 15, 2009, gas supply (main fuel for the factory's operations) was cut off, the coke production plant–one of the most controversial symbols of the company–has been shut down permanently. In 2011 the factory was sold to an SPV financed by First Investment Bank. Since then, the terrain was partially cleared and opportunities for redevelopment are being sought.

Energy and Performance

Coal supplies 38% of its electricity. That is a major reason the country's air is the most polluted in Europe, containing the highest concentrations of carbon monoxide and sulfur dioxide. Another 7%–9% of its electricity is derived from hydroelectric power. It has banned fracking, even though this makes it more energy-dependent on Russia. Bulgaria had become a key link in the transit of Russian gas to western Türkiye, Greece, and the rest of the Balkans. Burgas is home to the region's largest oil refinery.

Bulgaria has long been the leading electricity exporter in southeast Europe and was the fourth-largest in Europe. Its Kozloduy nuclear complex on the Danube provided more than 40% of its own electrical needs, and it covered about 80% of the electricity deficits in the region, especially in Greece (40%) and Serbia (30%).

Modern hotel and art gallery in Varna

Photo by Roman Payerhin

622

Bulgaria

In 2002 the EU strong-armed it to close the two oldest and smallest of the units at Kozloduy that used Chernobyl-era technology. Two additional Soviet-era reactors were decommissioned at the end of 2006 as a result of an EU threat to delay accession talks. Two other more modern units not considered a risk remain in operation. These shutdowns cut electricity exports by two-thirds and led to severe power shortages and soaring energy prices all over the Balkans, but especially in Albania, Montenegro, Greece, and Serbia.

The country plans to restore its role as the biggest electrical power exporter with two large projects. The construction of a second nuclear complex at Belene on the Danube, 30 miles (50 kilometers) from Kozloduy, envisaged in 2010 is still in 2024 an ongoing project. It built a coal-fired power plant at Maritsa East One in the southeast which started operating in 2011.

In January 2023 the energy minister, Rosen Hristov, set out an energy strategy which includes plans for two new reactors at Kozloduy and two at Belene. The strategy outlines the continued use of coal until 2030 before reducing its use to zero by 2038.

Bulgaria cooperated with an international team of nuclear specialists in 2003 to recover 37 pounds of highly enriched uranium (enough for a small bomb) from a nuclear research facility and transport it to Russia for conversion into less dangerous atomic fuel. The operation was funded by the US, and special Bulgarian police secured the facility and transported the uranium to the airport for shipment to Russia.

In 2009 Bulgarians got an ice-cold eye opener about their close ties with Russia when the latter shut off the flow of natural gas through pipelines in Ukraine in a dispute over pricing. This left many Bulgarians, who get all their gas from Russia, without heat in the midst of a bitter cold snap. The incident revealed how vulnerable Bulgaria is to Russia, which can use its energy dominance to get its way. It sparked renewed antigovernment riots in the freezing streets, led by protesters carrying signs reading, "We are tired of living in the EU's poorest and most corrupt country."

In an attempt to limit its 90% dependence on one source of energy supplies, Bulgaria has entered a variety of agreements.

In 2008 it signed on to Russia's 900-kilometer (600-mile) South Stream pipeline project, which would have made Burgas a European gateway for Russia's natural gas deliveries. Russia cancelled it in 2015. It signed up to the consortium building the ITGI pipeline that seeks to circumvent Russia and deliver gas from Azerbaijan to the EU. It also joined the Nabucco pipeline project pushed by the EU and US to bring Iraqi gas around Russia into Europe. That, too, was scrapped.

To a window shopper in Sofia, things are going well, with the stores full of western consumer goods and restaurants and cafes doing a brisk business. Many people are well dressed. But per-capita GDP has risen from 33% to only half of the EU average since joining the EU. This is the lowest in the EU and below that of neighboring Romania. According to projections, it will take more than two decades for Bulgarians to achieve incomes of two-thirds of the EU average.

Bulgaria was hit hard by the global economic downturn of 2008–2010. Inflation was down from 600% per month to under 6% in 2006, but rising food and fuel costs and wage increases of almost 25% annually in 2007 and 2008 drove it back to over 14% in 2008; in the 2009 recession, it declined again to 1.5%. Inflation stood at 2.5% in 2021 The economy grew annually by about 5% from 2000 to 2007 and by 5.5% in 2008. After the economy had contracted by almost 18% from 1995 to 1997, it was impressive to have successive years of healthy growth. In 2009, however, growth plummeted to –5% but rose to 3.7% in 2013.

Unemployment had declined from 20% in 2001 to below 6% in 2008 as foreign investment has picked up and the tourism and IT sectors have expanded. The rate in formerly booming Sofia and Varna was below 3%. However, it rose to 14% nationwide in 2013, more if one added in the large Roma community and long-term elderly unemployed. Real estate values fell sharply, and the construction boom is temporarily over. This added to the jobless rolls. Average salaries had increased from $168 per month in 2003 to €400 ($500) in 2014, but 22% live below the official poverty line. Remittances from the 1.2 million Bulgarians who work outside the country exceeded €1 billion ($1.30 billion) in 2008, worth around 5% of GDP. Many of them lost their jobs abroad because of the global economic crisis, and some returned home and pushed up the jobless rate. Bulgaria's economic woes were made worse by the currency and debt crises in Greece, its neighbor and most important trading partner. A third of its banks are owned by Greeks.

Thanks to five straight budget surpluses (2.5% of GDP in 2021), its national debt was halved to below 30% of GDP between 2001 and 2006, and by 2008 it stood at only 15%. They also gave the government some maneuvering room in dealing with the economic crisis in 2009. Its economic performance outstripped many of the new central and eastern European member states that joined the EU in 2004. In 2003 the World Economic Forum ranked Bulgaria 64th out of 102 states in terms of competitiveness. It also moved up from 62nd to 52th place out of 175 countries in the UN human development rating.

While the country slowly adjusts to a free-market economy, a lively

Bulgarian student (center) with other European classmates at College of Europe, Bruges. She is now a diplomat.

Bulgaria

underground economy thrives behind the backs of the tax collectors. Estimates are that two-thirds of imports enter the country by dubious means, that a half-million Bulgarians live from this flourishing "shadow economy," and that one-fifth of the GDP is derived from it. Adoption of the euro has been postponed indefinitely.

CULTURE

Bulgaria was still mainly a peasant society when the communists came to power in 1945 and began to transform it. They got rid of the private farms and herded the peasants into either collective or state farms. Some of the traditional peasant culture died as a result, but much of it survived. The Bulgarian Communist Party had greater success in the cities, though not in the way it had hoped. The workers who came to the cities to work in the new industry abandoned most of their traditional peasant ways.

The party's attempts to create communist intellectuals through its emphasis on education actually produced the new elite that overthrew the communists. Many students are enrolled at state institutions, and at one point 27,900 students are studying in 9 private universities. Perhaps the most famous is the American University of Bulgaria at Blagoevgrad. Much of its funding came from the USAID. After Bulgaria entered the EU in 2007, that funding ended. The US also has a debt to Bulgaria: John Atanasoff, who was born in Bulgaria in 1903, emigrated to America and was credited with inventing the first electronic digital computer.

The problem for Bulgaria will continue to be to keep its well-educated and enterprising young at home. By some estimates, the country has lost a quarter of its population since the fall of communism in 1989, falling from about 9 million then to 6.4 million now. The dismantling of the Bulgarian bureaucracy, which had employed 60% of the citizens and majority of educated people during the communist era, created youth unemployment of over one-third and stoked such emigration. A brain drain hampers the country's efforts to catch up economically. This problem is compounded by a "baby bust," which means that the population is declining by .7% annually, Europe's fastest rate.

To deal with the consequences of these demographic problems, the country successfully persuaded about 500,000 Bulgarians living in Moldova and Ukraine to return home. They were offered a fast-track process to acquire Bulgarian citizenship after five years.

There was disappointing news after entering the EU in 2007 that Bulgarians would not be free to move around within the community for a period of up to seven years. In the past, Bulgarians working abroad have preferred Spain, Germany, Italy, and Greece. Not all EU15 countries opened their doors to them, but that barrier ended in January 2014.

Religion is being accorded a greater role, and the government has become officially neutral. Anti-Turkish legislation was quickly withdrawn when democracy came, and the Turkish-speaking minority may now use Turkish in public. They are also permitted to take back their former Turkish names. There are about a half million ethnic Turks in the country, most of whom are Muslim. Their largest concentrations are in the southern and northeastern parts of the country. The party that represents Turks, the MRF, has held the balance of power in most post-communist governments.

Fears of jihadi terrorism led in 2016 to the Patriotic Front party coalition's push for a ban on wearing niqab in public. This Muslim women's head covering that leaves only a small slit around the eyes visible is not popular among Bulgaria's Muslims, who mostly wear a head-scarf (hijab). Yet, there are some small Salafist Roma communities where it gained popularity.

The poorest minority is that of the Roma (Gypsies), estimated to number 4 million to 12 million in all of Europe and about 800,000 in Bulgaria, or approximately 11% of the population. The official figure is 350,000. They were forced to stop their nomadic ways in the 1950s, and 84% live below the poverty line. Fewer than a fifth are believed to attend primary school, and a quarter are illiterate. In some places their unemployment rate is over 90%. In 2005 they demonstrated in Sofia, where the leaders of eight central European nations were meeting to launch a 10-year program to end prejudice and discrimination. Bulgaria's government has a daunting task to overcome centuries of discrimination against them and to integrate them into the nation's life. Over a quarter of Roma schoolchildren learn in classrooms separated from others. About a fifth of Roma families have a member who works abroad, and some manage to go abroad regularly for seasonal jobs. Successful individuals often leave their communities and try to hide their ethnicity.

In the lead-up to the November 2011 presidential and local elections, anti-Roma protests flared when a young Bulgarian was killed by a car driven by an associate of a notorious Roma mob boss. They rapidly spread to other cities, where young people in the streets chanted anti-Roma slogans. Sensing an opportunity to win votes, Ataka ("Attack") members wore black T-shirts bearing the slogan "I do not want to live in a gypsy country" and waved banners proclaiming "Gypsy crime—a danger for the country."

The Bulgarian Orthodox Church was accorded a special position even under the old regime. It has begun to speak out and take a more active role. Its membership is estimated at 3 million. There are up to 60,000 Roman Catholics in the country, plus an even larger and growing number of Protestants, divided into Pentecostals, Congregationalists, Seventh-Day Adventists, Methodists, and Baptists. They no longer suffer persecution. There are also several other identifiable minority groups, including Armenians.

CURRENT ISSUES

Bulgarians joke that they did not feel the economic crisis because they have always been in crisis. With one out of five living below the poverty line, it will be a decade or more before ordinary Bulgarians begin to experience a modicum of prosperity and have euros in their pockets.

Bulgaria entered NATO in April 2004 and continues to be a cooperative supporter of American policy. In 2015 a US Marine Corps unit of 155 troops with tanks and artillery was sent to Bulgaria on behalf of NATO in connection with the fallout of Russia's involvement in Ukraine. Similar units were then dispatched to other NATO border countries in central and southern Europe.

Bulgaria joined the EU in January 2007, but it still finds itself under close scrutiny. If it fails to take energetic and effective measures against corruption and organized crime, it will continue to lose important EU subsidies and respect. Kristalina Georgieva, a Bulgarian economist, serves as the 12th managing director of the International Monetary Fund (IMF) since 2019.

Bulgaria and Romania will become part of the Schengen area from March 31, 2024, which allows free movement between member states for 400 million citizens. Its construction of the 100-mile fence along the border with Türkiye, which picked up pace in 2015, proves its determination to stem the flow of migrants from the Middle East and also establishes its credentials as a reliable future member of the Schengen System. It is a bitter irony that, only two decades earlier, the Bulgarians dismantled the old communist Iron Curtain fence stretching along the same route in two rows separated by a 1,500-foot minefield.

The resolute resistance to immigration belies the existential threat that comes with the shrinking population. Since 1990, the percentage of mortality has been exceeding the natality. Authorities estimate that by

2030 the total population of Bulgaria will decrease from the current 6.4 million to 6.1 million by 2040 and 5.2 million in 2050. It is the world's fastest-shrinking country. The problem is most severe in the countryside and in the neglected northwest. To some extent, depopulating is ravaging much of eastern Europe. Social provisions for the aging population will certainly be affected without an influx of young immigrants contributing to the economy.

A majority of Bulgarians back efforts to defeat corruption and crime. There are frequent street protests, which are a constant reminder of how much Bulgarians are dissatisfied with the way they are ruled.

The culture of impunity is weaker, although convictions are still rare. Critics contend that the crackdown on corruption has brought paralysis in public administration. One expert said, "Before, the administration did nothing without a bribe. Now they simply do nothing." No wonder the UN World Happiness report in 2017 ranked Bulgaria 105th of 155 globally and the third-lowest in Europe, after Ukraine and Albania, still a clear improvement over its 129th place a year before.

In October 2018, a grisly murder stunned this nation, where corruption is endemic but murder is relatively rare. Investigative journalist and host of an anticorruption news show Viktoria Marinova, who had just reported on a major fraud case involving the misuse of EU subsidies, was raped and murdered. Bulgarians say they have little trust in law enforcement and the judicial system.

In November 2021, incumbent President Rumen Radev won a second presidential term.

The year 2022 was one of political turmoil in a deeply divided country. The Russian invasion of Ukraine bears some of the blame. Many Bulgarians have pro-Russian sympathies and for a while were supportive of Russia's war. The conflict inflated energy prices and interrupted trade and tourism in the Black Sea. It also prompted NATO to deploy 3,000 additional troops on Bulgarian soil. The government expelled 70 Russian diplomats. Forming a stable ruling coalition after two elections was not easy. Some pro-Moscow parties competed for votes.

Websites and Bibliography of Key English-Language Books

WEBSITES
The UN, the EU, the OECD, NATO, and Other

Aktion Euro. https://www.aktion-euro.de. Site for the euro currency.

Carnegie Endowment for International Peace. https://carnegieendowment.org/.

Central Intelligence Agency. https://www.cia.gov/index.html. Includes useful CIA publications, such as The World Factbook and maps.

Council of the European Union. https://europa.eu/european-union/about-eu /institutions-bodies/council-eu_en.

Delegation of the European Union to the United States. https://eeas.europa.eu /delegations/united-states-america_en.

EUobserver. https://www.euobserver.com. EU news.

Euractiv. https://www.euractiv.com. European news.

European Commission. https://ec.europa.eu/commission/index_en.

European Parliament. http://www.europarl.europa.eu/portal/en.

European Policy Institutes Network. https://epin.org.

European Union. https://europa.eu.

Library of Congress, Collection: Country Studies. https://www.loc.gov/collections /country-studies/about-this-collection/. Coverage of more than 100 countries.

Link to Your Roots. https://www.hamburg.de/bkm/eculture/7361886/netzwerk bildung/. A database to help Americans trace their European roots.

North Atlantic Treaty Organization. https://www.nato.int/.

Organization for Economic Co-operation and Development. https://www.oecd .org/about/.

Organization for Security and Co-operation in Europe. https://www.osce.org/.

United Nations. https://www.un.org/en/.

United Nations System. https://www.unsystem.org/.

US Department of State. https://www.state.gov/. Includes country reports.

The World Bank. https://www.worldbank.org/. News and publications with links to other financial institutions.

World Trade Organization. https://www.wto.org/.

XE Currency Converter. https://www.xe.com/currencyconverter/. The most up-to -date foreign currency values.

Newspapers, Journals, and Television with Good Coverage on European Affairs

BBC. https://www.bbc.com/.

Chicago Tribune. https://www.chicagotribune.com/. Named best overall US news paper online service for newspapers with circulation more than 100,000.

Christian Science Monitor. https://www.csmonitor.com/. Named best overall US newspaper online service for newspapers with circulation under 100,000.

City Paper. http://www.citypaper.lv/. Published in Tallinn, Estonia; includes coverage of all Baltic states.

CNN. https://www.cnn.com. Latest news with external links.

C-SPAN. https://www.c-span.org. Includes C-SPAN International.

Economist. https://www.economist.com. British weekly news magazine.

Financial Times. https://www.ft.com. Authoritative British newspaper.

Foreign Affairs. https://www.foreignaffairs.org. One of the best-known international affairs journals.

New Europe. https://www.neweurope.eu/. Weekly newspaper focusing on EU affairs.

New York Times. https://www.nytimes.com. Respected US newspaper; now owns International Herald Tribune, published as New York Times Global Edition.

Politico. https://www.politico.eu/. Formerly European Voice; weekly news on EU and European affairs.

Washington Post. https://www.washingtonpost.com. Respected US newspaper.

Central and Eastern Europe

Association for Slavic, East European, and Eurasian Studies. https://www.aseees. org/. Provides links to Slavic resources.

Baltic Review. https://baltic-review.com/.

Baltics Worldwide. http://www.balticsworldwide.com.General information on the Baltics.

Baltic Times. https://www.baltictimes.com/. English-language weekly covering news in all three Baltic republics.

Center for Russian, East European, Eurasian Studies. https://www.ucis.pitt.edu /crees/. (Full index on central Europe and former USSR.

Bibliography

EIN World News Report: Central Europe News Monitoring Service. https://world.einnews.com/region/centraleurope?from=centraleurope. Contains updated information and news.

Eurasianet. https://www.eurasianet.org. News for Eurasia.

European Stability Initiative. https://www.esiweb.org. Berlin-based, working to restore stability to southeastern Europe.

Legal Information Centre for Human Rights. http://www.lichr.ee/home/?lang=en.
Open Society Archives, Central European University. https://www.ceu.edu/category/open-society-archives.

Washington, DC, Embassies. https://www.embassy.org/embassies. A site with links to all embassy websites in Washington, DC.

Country Sites

Sweden

Business Sweden. https://www.business-sweden.se/Export/.

Embassy of Sweden. https://www.swedenabroad.se/en/embassies/usa-washington/.

Sveriges Riksdag. https://www.riksdagen.se. Swedish parliament site.

Sweden. https://www.sweden.se. Official country site.

Norway

Norway Post. www.Norwaypost.com. Norwegian newspaper in English.

Norwegian Government Security and Service Organisation. https://www.regjeringen.no/en/id4/.

Norwegians Worldwide. https://nww.no/. Cultural ties with Norway.

Royal Norwegian Embassy. https://www.norway.no/en/usa/.

Sons of Norway. https://www.sofn.com. Norwegian heritage and culture, especially in the United States.

Denmark

Berlingske. https://www.berlingske.dk. Respected Danish newspaper.

Embassy of Denmark. http://usa.um.dk/.

Finland

Finnish Institute of International Affairs. https://www.fiia.fi/en/.

Project Finland. http://www.projectfinland.org. Colorful, interactive site introducing American children to their Finnish counterparts.

This Is Finland. https://finland.fi/. Government institutions, current events, and culture; sponsored by the Finnish Ministry for Foreign Affairs.

Iceland

Embassy of Iceland. http://www.iceland.org/us.

Estonia

EESTI.EE. https://www.eesti.ee/en/. Estonian government portal.

Embassy of Estonia. https://washington.mfa.ee/.

Latvia

Ministry of Defense. https://www.mod.gov.lv/en.

Ministry of Economics. https://www.em.gov.lv/en/.

Ministry of Foreign Affairs. https://www.mfa.gov.lv/en/.

Lithuania

ELTA. http://www.elta.lt/en. Lithuanian news agency.

Ministry of Foreign Affairs. http://www.urm.lt/default/en/.

Statistika. http://www.std.lt. Lithuanian statistical data including census figures.

Kaliningrad

NewKaliningrad. https://www.NewKaliningrad.ru. Opposition website.

Germany

American Institute for Contemporary German Studies. https://www.aicgs.org/.

Berlin.de. https://www.berlin.de/en/news/. News of Berlin.

Deutscher Budestag. https://www.bundestag.de/en. German parliament online.

Bibliography

Deutschland.de. https://www.deutschland.de/en. Site of the monthly magazine *Deutschland*, with general news.

Embassy of Germany. https://www.germany.info/.

German Council on Foreign Relations. https://dgap.org/en.

German Studies Association. https://www.thegsa.org/.

Germany: Simply Inspiring. https://www.germany.travel/en/ms/german-heritage/home.html. Site to discover America's German heritage.

Die Linke (The Left) Germany. https://en.die-linke.de/welcome/.

Statisches Bundesamt. https://www.destatis.de/EN/Home/_node.html.

Austria

Advantage Austria. https://www.advantageaustria.org/us/Oesterreich-in-den-USA.en.html. US-Austrian trade site.

Austrian Embassy. https://www.austria.org.

Keele University, Professor Kurt Richard Luther. https://www.keele.ac.uk/spire/staff/luther/. Site of Austria specialist Kurt Richard Luther on diverse political topics relating to Austria.

Poland

The Chancellery of the Prime Minister. https://www.premier.gov.pl/en/contact.html.

Ministry of Foreign Affairs. https://www.gov.pl/web/diplomacy.

Ministry of National Defense. https://www.gov.pl/web/national-defence.

National Security Bureau. http://en.bbn.gov.pl/.

Panstwowa Komisja Wyborcza. https://www.pkw.gov.pl. State Election Commission, official election results in Poland.

Polish News Bulletin. http://www.pnb.pl.

President of the Republic of Poland. https://www.president.pl/en/.

Sejm Rzeczypospolitej Polskiej. http://opis.sejm.gov.pl/en/index.php. Polish parliament.

Senat Rzeczypospolitej Polskiej. https://www.senat.gov.pl/en/. Polish senate.

Czech Republic

Ministry of Foreign Affairs. https://www.mzv.cz/jnp.

Prague Post. https://www.praguepost.com. Prague English-language newspaper.

Slovak Republic

Government Office of the Slovak Republic. https://www.government.gov.sk. With photo gallery.

National Council of the Slovak Republic. https://www.nrsr.sk/web/.

Hungary

Embassy of Hungary. https://washington.mfa.gov.hu/eng.

Budapest Sun. http://www.budapestsun.com/. Hungarian English-language newspaper.

Ministry of Foreign Affairs and Trade. https://www.kormany.hu/en/ministry-of-foreign-affairs-and-trade.

Serbia

B92. https://www.b92.net/eng. Serbian site in English with news, photos, and analyses.

The Government of the Republic of Serbia. https://www.srbija.gov.rs/.

Ministry of Foreign Affairs. http://www.mfa.gov.rs/en/.

Tito's Home Page. https://www.titoville.com/. A site with information about Tito.

Montenegro

EIN World News Report, Montenegro News Monitoring Service. https://world.einnews.com/country/montenegro.

Visit Montenegro. https://www.visit-montenegro.com/. Montenegrin tourism.

World Trade Organization: Montenegro. https://www.wto.org/english/thewto_e/acc_e/a1_montenegro_e.htm.

Slovenia

Republic of Slovenia. http://www.gov.si/en.

Republic of Slovenia Government Communication Office. http://www.ukom.gov.si/en/.

Croatia

Ministry of Foreign and European Affairs. http://www.mvep.hr/en/.
Government of the Republic of Croatia. https://vlada.gov.hr/en.

Bosnia and Herzegovina

Government of Federation of Bosnia and Herzegovina. http://www.fbihvlada.gov
  .ba/english/.
Ministry of Foreign Affairs. http://www.mvp.gov.ba/default.aspx?pageIndex=1.
Government of Republic of Srpska. http://www.vladars.net/eng/Pages/default
  .aspx.

Kosovo

Office of High Representative in Kosovo. http://www.ohr.int.

North Macedonia

Economic Chamber of Macedonia. http://www.mchamber.org.mk/Default
  .aspx?mId=1&lng=2. Macedonian economic, political, cultural, and historical
  information.
Government of the Republic of North Macedonia. https://vlada.mk/node
  /14652?ln=en-gb.
New Balkan Politics. http://www.newbalkanpolitics.org.mk/. Online political magazine on North Macedonian affairs.
Virtual Macedonia. https://www.vmacedonia.com/. Macedonian tourism.

Albania

Albanian Daily News. https://www.albaniandailynews.com/. English-language
  newspaper.

Romania

Ministry of Tourism. http://turism.gov.ro/.
Romanian Government. http://gov.ro/en.
Romania Online. http://www.rol.ro. Includes photos.
Romania.org. http://www.romania.org. News and culture in Romania.

Bulgaria

Novinite. https://www.novinite.com. English-language Sofia news agency.

NORDIC EUROPE: GENERAL

Albright, Madeleine. *Fascism: A Warning.* New York: HarperCollins, 2018.
Archer, Clive, and Stephen Maxwell, eds. *The Nordic Model: Studies in Public Policy
  Innovation.* Brookfield, VT: Gower, 1980.
Arter, David. *Scandinavian Politics Today.* New York: St. Martin's Press, 1999.
Ash, Timothy Garton. *Homelands.* New Haven: Yale University, 2023.
Booth, Michael. *The Almost Nearly Perfect People: The Truth about the Nordic Miracle.*
  London: Jonathan Cape, 2013.
Connery, Donald S. *The Scandinavians.* New York: Simon Schuster, 1966.
Derry, T. K. *History of Scandinavia: Norway, Sweden, Denmark, Finland and Iceland.* Min-
  neapolis: University of Minnesota Press, 1980.
Einhorn, Eric S., and John Logue. *Modern Welfare States: Politics and Policies in Social
  Democratic Scandinavia.* Westport, CT: Greenwood Press, 1990.
Erikson, Robert, et al., eds. *The Scandinavian Model: Welfare States and Welfare Research.*
  New York: M. E. Sharpe, 1987.
Forshaw, Barry. *Death in a Cold Climate: A Guide to Scandinavian Crime Fiction.* London:
  Palgrave Macmillan, 2011.
Griffiths, Tony. *Scandinavia: A History from the Napoleonic Era to the Third Millennium.*
  London: Hurst, 2004.
Gstohl, Sieglinde. *Reluctant Europeans: Norway, Sweden, and Switzerland in the Process
  of Integration.* Boulder, CO: Lynne Rienner, 2002.
Helle, Knut, ed. *The Cambridge History of Scandinavia.* Vol. 1, Prehistory to 1520. Cam-
  bridge, UK: Cambridge University Press, 2003.
Ingelbritsen, Christine. *The Nordic States and European Unity.* Ithaca, NY: Cornell Uni-
  versity Press, 1998.
Ingstad, Helge, and Anne Stine Ingstad. *The Viking Discovery of America: The Excavation of a Norse Settlement in L'Anse aux Meadows, Newfoundland.* New York: Check-
  mark Books, 2001.
Lansen, Lene, and Ole Waever. *European Integration and National Identity: The Challenge of the Nordic States.* New York: Routledge, 2001.

Bibliography

Logue, John, and Eric S. Einhorn. *Modern Welfare States: Scandinavian Politics and Policy in the Global Age.* New York: Praeger, 2003. A new edition of their 1989 study.

Oberg, Jan, ed. *Nordic Security in the 1990s.* New York: St. Martin's Press, 1992.

Turner, Barry, and Gunilla Nordquist. *The Other European Community: Integration and Cooperation in Nordic Europe.* New York: Martin Robertson, 1982.

Wendt, Franz. *Cooperation in the Nordic Countries: Achievements and Obstacles.* Atlantic Highlands, NJ: Humanities, 1981.

SWEDEN

Bucken-Knapp, Gregg. *Defending the Swedish Model: Social Democrats, Trade Unions, and Labor Migration Policy Reform.* Lanham, MD: Lexington Books, 2009.

Esping-Andersen, Gosta. *Politics against Markets: The Social Democratic Road to Power.* Princeton, NJ: Princeton University Press, 1985.

Hadenius, Stig. *Swedish Politics during the 20th Century.* Stockholm: Swedish Institute, 1985.

Heclo, Hugh, and Menrik Madsen. *Policy and Politics in Sweden: Principled Pragmatism.* Philadelphia: Temple University Press, 1987.

Koblick, Steven, ed. *Sweden's Development from Poverty to Affluence, 1750–1970.* Minneapolis: University of Minnesota Press, 1975.

Lesser, Wendy. *Scandinavian Noir.* Farrar, Straus and Giroux, 2020.

Lorenzen, Lilly. *Of Swedish Ways.* New York: Barnes and Noble, 1978.

Lundqvist, Lennart J. *Sweden and Ecological Governance: Straddling the Fence.* Manchester, UK: Manchester University Press, 2004.

Metcalf, Michael. The Riksdag: *A History of the Swedish Parliament.* New York: St. Martin's Press, 1988.

Miles, Lee. *Sweden and European Integration.* Brookfield, VT: Ashgate, 1997.

Milner, Henry. *Sweden: Social Democracy in Practice.* Oxford, UK: Oxford University Press, 1989.

Misgeld, Klaus, Karl Molin, and Klas Amark, eds. *Creating Social Democracy: A Century of the Social Democratic Labor Party in Sweden.* Translated by Jan Teeland. University Park: Pennsylvania State University Press, 1994.

Oakley, Stewart. *The Story of Sweden.* London: Faber and Faber, 1976.

Persson, Inga, ed. *Generating Equality in the Welfare State: The Swedish Experience.* Oxford, UK: Oxford University Press, 1991.

Ruin, Olof. Tage Erlander: *Serving the Welfare State, 1946–1969.* Translated by Michael F. Metcalf. Pittsburgh, PA: University of Pittsburgh Press, 1990.

Samuelsson, Kurt. *From Great Power to Welfare State: 300 Years of Swedish Social Development.* London: George Allen and Unwin, 1968.

Scott, Franklin D. *Sweden: The Nation's History.* Minneapolis: University of Minnesota Press, 1977.

Sundelius, Bengt, ed. *The Committed Neutral: Sweden's Foreign Policy.* Boulder, CO: Westview Press, 1989.

Tilton, Tim. *The Political Theory of Swedish Social Democracy: Through the Welfare State to Socialism.* Oxford, UK: Oxford University Press, 1990.

NORWAY

Archer, Clive. *Norway outside the European Union: Norway and European Integration from 1994 to 2004.* New York: Routledge, 2004.

Archer, Clive, and Ingrid Sogner. *Norway, European Integration, and Atlantic Security.* Thousand Oaks, CA: Sage, 1998.

Derry, T. K. *A History of Modern Norway: 1814–1972.* New York: Oxford University Press, 1973.

Heidar, Knut. *Norway: Center and Periphery.* Boulder, CO: Westview Press, 2000.

Hoidal, Oddvar K. *Quisling: A Study in Treason.* Oxford, UK: Oxford University Press, 1989.

Holst, Johan Jergen. *Norwegian Foreign Policy in the 1980s.* Oxford, UK: Oxford University Press, 1988.

Jonassen, Christen J. *Value Systems and Personality in a Western Civilization: Norwegians in Europe and America.* Columbus: Ohio State University Press, 1983.

Lovoll, Odd S. *Norwegian-American Studies.* Northfield, MN: St. Olaf College, 1989.

Osterud, 0yvind, ed. *Norway: The Transformation of a Political System.* Special issue, West European Politics 28, no. 4 (September 2005).

Overland, Orm, ed. and trans. *From America to Norway: Norwegian-American Immigrant Letters,* 1838–1914. Vol. 1. St. Paul: University of Minnesota Press, 2012.

Popperwell, Ronald G. *Norway.* New York: Praeger, 1973.

Princess Martha Louise. *Princess Martha Louise's Wonderful World.* 2007.

Bibliography

Ramsey, Natalie R., ed. *Norwegian Society*. Oslo: Universitatsvorlaget, 1977.

Selbyg, Arne. *Norway Today*. New York: Oxford University Press, 1986.

Skard, Sigmund. *The United States in Norwegian History*. Westport, CT: Greenwood Press, 1976.

Strom, Kaare, and Lars Svasand, eds. *Challenges to Political Parties: The Case of Norway*. Ann Arbor: University of Michigan Press, 1997.

Su-Dale, Elizabeth. *Culture Shock! Norway: A Guide to Customs and Etiquette*. Minneapolis: Scandisc, 1995.

DENMARK

Arenson, Theo. *The Family of Kings*. London: Castles, 1976.

Fitzmaurice, John. *Politics in Denmark*. New York: St. Martin's Press, 1981.

Holbraad, Carsten. *Danish Neutrality: A Study in the Foreign Policy of a Small State*. Oxford, UK: Oxford University Press, 1991.

Johansen, Hans Christian. *The Danish Economy in the Twentieth Century*. New York: St. Martin's Press, 1987.

Korneliussen, Niviak. *Crimson*. Translated by Anna Halager. London: Virago, 2018. Deals with Greenlandic society.

Lundbak, Henrik. *Danish Unity: A Political Party between Fascism and Resistance*. Copenhagen: Museum Tusculanum Press, 2003.

Miller, Kenneth E. *Denmark: A Troubled Welfare State*. Boulder, CO: Westview Press, 1991.

Oakley, Stewart. *A Short History of Denmark*. New York: Praeger, 1972.

Petrow, Richard. *Better Years: The Invasion and Occupation of Denmark and Norway, April 1940–May 1945*. New York: Morrow, 1975.

———. *The Story of Denmark*. New York: Praeger, 1972.

ICELAND

Baring-Gould, Sabine. *Iceland: Its Scenes and Sagas*. London: Hurst, 2005.

Durrenburger, E. Paul, and Gísli Pálsson. *The Anthropology of Iceland*. Iowa City: University of Iowa Press, 1989.

Gislason, Gylfi. *The Problem of Being an Icelander: Past, Present and Future*. Reykjavik: Almenna Bokofelagio, 1973.

Karlsson, Gunnar. *Iceland's 1100 Years: The History of a Marginal Society*. London: Hurst, 2001.

Kent, Hannah. *Burial Rites*. New York: Little, Brown, 2013.

Laxness, Halldor. *Independent People: An Epic*. New York: Vintage Books, 1996.

Magnason, Andri Snaer. *On Time and Water*. New York: Open Letter, 2021.

Magnusson, Sigurdur Gylfi. *Wasteland with Words: A Social History of Iceland*. London: Reaktion Books, 2010.

Olafsdottir, Audur Ava. *Butterflies in November and Miss Iceland*. Grove Press, 2020.

———. *Animal Life*. New York: Black Cat, 2022.

The Saga of King Hrolf Kraki. New York: Penguin Books, n.d.

Sjon. *Codex 1962*. Translated by Victoria Cribb. New York: MCD/Farra, Straus and Giroux, 2018.

Smiley, Jane. *The Sagas of Icelanders*. New York: Viking, 2000.

Thorhallsson, Baldur, ed. *Iceland and European Integration*. New York: Routledge, 2004.

Tomasson, Richard F. *Iceland: The First New Society*. Minneapolis: University of Minnesota, 1980.

FINLAND

Arter, David. *Politics and Policy-Making in Finland*. New York: St. Martin's Press, 1987.

Austin, Daniel F. C. *Finland as a Gateway to Russia*. Brookfield, VT: Ashgate, 1996.

Engman, Max, and David Kirby, eds. *Finland: People, Nation, State*. Bloomington: Indiana University Press, 1989.

Jakobson, Max. *Finland in the New Europe*. Westport, CT: Praeger, 1998.

Jutikkala, Eino, and Pirinen Kauko. *A History of Finland*. New York: Praeger, 1974.

Koivisto, Mauno. *Landmarks: Finland in the World*. Helsinki: Kirjayhtyma, 1985.

Maude, George. *The Finnish Dilemma*. London: Oxford University Press, 1976.

Nickels, Silvie, ed. *Finland: An Introduction*. London: George Allen and Unwin, 1973.

Paasi, Anssi. *Territories, Boundaries and Consciousness: The Changing Geographies of the Finnish-Russian Border*. New York: Wiley, 1997.

Penttila, Risto E. J. *Finland's Search for Security through Defence, 1944–89*. New York: St. Martin's Press, 1990.

Puntila, L. A. *The Political History of Finland 1809–1966*. London: Heinemann, 1975.

Rinehart, Robert, ed. *Finland and the United States*. Washington, DC: Institute for the Study of Diplomacy, 1993.

Bibliography

Sahlberg, Pasi. *Finnish Lessons: What Can the World Learn from Educational Change in Finland?* New York: Teachers College Press, 2011.

Singleton, Fred, and Anthony F. Upton. *A Short History of Finland.* Cambridge, UK: Cambridge University Press, 1995.

Tiilikainen, Teija H. *Europe and Finland.* Brookfield, VT: Ashgate, 1998.

Wuorinen, John H. *A History of Finland.* New York: Columbia University Press, 1965.

BALTIC REPUBLICS: GENERAL

Clemens, Walter C., Jr. *Baltic Independence and Russian Empire.* New York: St. Martin's Press, 1991.

———. *The Baltic Miracle: Complexity Theory and European Security.* Lanham, MD: Rowman & Littlefield, 2000.

———. *The Baltic Transformed.* Boulder, CO: Rowman & Littlefield, 2001.

Gerner, Kristian, and Stefan Hedlund. *The Baltic States and the End of the Soviet Empire.* New York: Routledge, 1993.

Hansen, Birthe, and Bertal Heurlin, eds. *The Baltic States in World Politics.* New York: St. Martin's Press, 1998.

Hiden, John, and Patrick Salmon. *The Baltic Nations and Europe: Estonia, Latvia and Lithuania in the Twentieth Century.* New York: Longman, 1991.

Krickus, Richard J. *The Kaliningrad Question.* New York: Rowman & Littlefield, 2002.

Landgren, Signe Maria. *The Baltic States: New Participants in the European Security Debate.* Stockholm: SIPRI, 2000.

Lieven, Anatol. *The Baltic Revolution: Estonia, Latvia, Lithuania and the Path to Independence.* New Haven, CT: Yale University Press, 1993.

Manning, Clarence. *The Forgotten Republics.* New York: Philosophical Library, 1952.

Misiunas, Romuald J., and Rein Taagepera. *The Baltic States: Years of Dependence, 1940–1990.* Berkeley: University of California Press, 1993.

Palmer, Alan. *Northern Shores: A History of the Baltic Sea and Its Peoples.* John Murray, 2005.

Rubulis, Aleksis. *Baltic Literature.* Notre Dame, IN: University of Notre Dame Press, 1970.

Smith, Graham, et al., eds. *The Baltic States: Estonia, Latvia and Lithuania.* New York: Routledge, 2002.

Thomson, Claire. *The Singing Revolution: A Political Journey through the Baltic States.* London: Michael, 1992.

Trapans, Jan Arveds, ed. *Toward Independence: The Baltic Popular Movements.* Boulder, CO: Westview Press, 1991.

ESTONIA

Egremont, Max. *The Glass Wall Lives on the Baltic Frontier.* Picador, 2021. In the US by Farrar, Straus, and Giroux.

Howell, Margie, ed. *Estonia and Russia, Estonians and Russians: A Dialogue.* Stockholm: Olof Palme International Center, 1996.

Laar, Mart. *War in the Woods: Estonia's Struggle for Survival 1944–1956.* Washington, DC: Compass, 1992.

Poom, Ritva, et al. *Estonian Short Stories.* Chicago: Northwestern University Press, 1995.

Raun, Toivo U. *Estonia and the Estonians.* Updated 2nd ed. Stanford, CA: Hoover Institution Press, 2001.

Rausing, Sigrid. *Everything Is Wonderful: Memories of a Collective Farm in Estonia.* New York: Grove Press, 2014.

Smith, David J. *Estonia: Independence and European Integration.* New York: Routledge, 2002.

Taagepera, Rein. *Estonia: Return to Independence.* Boulder, CO: Westview Press, 1993.

Tammsaare, A. H. *Truth and Justice* (a five-part novel about Estonian history).

Thomson, Claire. *Culture Smart! Estonia: A Quick Guide to Customs and Etiquette.* London: Kuperard, 2007.

LATVIA

Angrick, Andrej, and Peter Klein. *The "Final Solution" in Riga: Exploitation and Annihilation, 1941–1944.* New York: Berghahn Books, 2008.

Dreifelds, Juris. *Latvia in Transition.* New York: Cambridge University Press, 1997.

Ezergailis, Inta Miske. *Nostalgia and Beyond: Eleven Latvian Women Writers.* Lanham, MD: University Press of America, 1997.

Kauffmann, Jean-Paul. *A Journey to Nowhere: Detours and Riddles in the Lands and History of Courland.* Translated by Euan Cameron. London: MacLehose Press, 2012.

Pabriks, Artis, and Aldis Purs. *Latvia: The Challenges of Change*. New York: Routledge, 2001.

Plakans, Andrejs. *The Latvians: A Short History*. Stanford, CA: Hoover Institution Press, 1995.

Purs, Aldis, and Artis Pabriks. *Latvia: State and Society*. New York: Routledge, 2002.

LITHUANIA

Ashbourne, Alexandra. *Lithuania: The Rebirth of a Nation, 1991–1994*. Lanham, MD: Rowman & Littlefield, 1999.

Briedis, Laimonas. *Vilnius: City of Strangers*. Vilnius: Baltos Lankos/CEU Press, 2009.

Daumantas, Juozas. *Fighters for Freedom: Lithuanian Partisans versus the USSR, 1944–1947*. New York: Manyland Books, 1975.

Lane, Thomas. *Lithuania: Stepping Westward*. New York: Routledge, 2002.

Vardys, V. Stanley, and Judith B. Sedaitis. *Lithuania: The Rebel Nation*. Boulder, CO: Westview Press, 1996.

CENTRAL AND EASTERN EUROPE HISTORY: GENERAL

Frucht, Richard, ed. *Encyclopedia of Eastern Europe: From the Congress of Vienna to the Fall of Communism*. New York: Garland, 2000.

Held, Joseph, ed. *The Columbia History of Eastern Europe in the Twentieth Century*. New York: Columbia University Press, 1992.

Judson, Pieter M., ed. *Constructing Nationalities in East Central Europe*. 6th ed. New York: Berghahn Books, 2004.

Palmer, Alan. *The Lands Between: A History of East-Central Europe since the Congress of Vienna*. New York: Macmillan, 1970.

Pridham, Geoffrey, and Attila Agh, eds. *Prospects for Democratic Consolidation in East-Central Europe*. Manchester, UK: University of Manchester Press, 2001.

Ramet, Sabrina P., ed. *Eastern Europe: Politics, Culture, and Society since 1939*. Bloomington: Indiana University Press, 1998.

Roberts, Andrew. *The Storm of War: A New History of World War II*. New York: HarperCollins, 2011.

White, Steve, Judy Batt, and Paul G. Lewis, eds. *Developments in Central and East European Politics*. Durham, NC: Duke University Press, 2003.

Wolchik, Sharon L., and Jane L. Curry. *Central and East European Politics: From Communism to Democracy*. Lanham, MD: Rowman & Littlefield, 2008.

THE COMMUNIST ERA

Applebaum, Anne. *Iron Curtain: The Crushing of Eastern Europe 1944–1956*. New York: Doubleday, 2012.

Ash, Timothy Garton. *The Magic Lantern: The Revolution of '89 Witnessed in Warsaw, Budapest, Berlin and Prague*. New York: Vintage Books, 1993.

d'Encausse, Helen Careere. *Decline of an Empire: The Soviet Socialist Republics in Revolt*. Translated by Martin Sokolinsky and Henry A. La Farge. New York: Newsweek Books, 1978.

Fischer-Galati, Stephen, ed. *Eastern Europe in the 1980s*. Boulder, CO: Westview Press, 1981.

Gaddis, John Lewis. *The Cold War: A New History*. New York: Penguin Books, 2006.

Naimark, Norman, and Leonid Gibianskii. *The Establishment of Communist Regimes in Eastern Europe, 1944–1949*. Boulder, CO: Westview Press, 1997.

Rupnik, Jacques. *The Other Europe: The Rise and Fall of Communism in East-Central Europe*. New York: Pantheon, 1989.

Schnitzer, Martin. *U.S. Business Involvement in Eastern Europe: Case Studies of Hungary, Poland and Romania*. New York: Praeger, 1981.

Shore, Maraci. *The Taste of Ashes: The Afterlife of Totalitarianism in Eastern Europe*. New York: Crown, 2013.

Triska, Jan F., and Charles Gati, eds. *Blue Collar Workers in Eastern Europe*. Winchester, MA: Allen and Unwin, 1981.

Volgyes, Ivan. *Politics in Eastern Europe*. Chicago: Dorsey Press, 1986.

POSTCOMMUNIST CENTRAL AND EASTERN EUROPE

Agh, Attila, and Gabriella Ilonszki, eds. *Parliaments and Organized Interests: The Second Steps*. Budapest: Hungarian Centre for Democracy Studies, 1996.

Barany, Zoltan, and Ivan Volgyes, eds. *Legacies of Communism in Eastern Europe*. Baltimore, MD: Johns Hopkins University Press, 1995.

Biscop, Sven, and Johan Lembke, eds. *EU Enlargement and the Transatlantic Alliance: A Security Relationship in Flux*. Boulder, CO: Lynne Rienner, 2007.

Bibliography

Bremmer, Ian, and Ray Taras, eds. *Nations and Politics in the Soviet Successor States.* New York: Cambridge University Press, 1993.

Brown, J. F. *Surge to Freedom: The End of Communist Rule in Eastern Europe.* Durham, NC: Duke University Press, 1991.

Buckley, Mary. *Post-Soviet Women: From the Baltic to Central Asia.* New York: Cambridge University Press, 1997.

Bugajski, Janusz. *Nations in Turmoil: Conflict and Cooperation in Eastern Europe.* 2nd ed. Boulder, CO: Westview Press, 1995.

Cottey, A., and D. Averre, eds. *New Security Challenges in Post-Communist Europe: Securing Europe's East.* Manchester, UK: Manchester University Press, 2002.

Crawford, Keith. *East Central European Politics Today.* New York: Manchester University Press, 1996.

Dawisha, Karen, and Bruce Parrott, eds. *The Consolidation of Democracy in East-Central Europe.* New York: Cambridge University Press, 1997.

DeBardeleben, Joan, and John Hannigan, eds. *Environmental Security and Quality after Communism.* Boulder, CO: Westview Press, 1994.

Derleth, J. William. *The Transition in Central and Eastern European Politics.* Upper Saddle River, NJ: Prentice Hall, 2000.

Dimitrova, Antoaneta L., ed. *Driven to Change: The European Union's Enlargement Viewed from the East.* Manchester, UK: Manchester University Press, 2004.

Einhorn, Barbara. *Cinderella Goes to Market: Citizenship, Gender, and Women's Movements in East Central Europe.* London: Verso, 1993.

Ekiert, Grzegorz, and Stephen E. Hanson, eds. *Capitalism and Democracy in Central and Eastern Europe.* Cambridge, UK: Cambridge University Press, 2003.

Freedom House. *Nations in Transit 2008: Democratization from Central Europe to Eurasia.* Washington, DC: CQ Press, 2008.

Gardner, Hall, ed. *Central and Southeastern Europe in Transition.* Westport, CT: Praeger, 2000.

Gartner, Heinz, et al., eds. *Europe's New Security Challenges.* Boulder, CO: Lynne Rienner, 2001.

Gould, John A. *The Politics of Privatization: Wealth and Power in Postcommunist Europe.* Boulder, CO: Lynne Rienner, 2011.

Graubard, Stephen R., ed. *Eastern Europe . . . Central Europe . . . Europe.* Boulder, CO: Westview Press, 1991.

Hamilton, F. E. Ian, Kaliopa Dimitrovska Andrews, and Nataša Pichler-Milanović, eds. *Transformation of Cities in Central and Eastern Europe: Towards Globalization.* Washington, DC: Brookings Institution Press, 2005.

Heenan, Patrick, and Monique Lamontagne, eds. *The Central and Eastern Europe Handbook.* London: Fitzroy Dearborn, 1999.

Heller, Agnes, and Ferenc Feher. *From Yalta to Glasnost: The Dismantling of Stalin's Empire.* Cambridge, UK: Basil Blackwell, 1990.

Higley, John, and Gyrgy Lengyel, eds. *Elites after State Socialism.* Lanham, MD: Rowman & Littlefield, 2000.

Hitchcock, William I. *The Struggle for Europe: The Turbulent History of a Divided Continent 1945–2002.* New York: Doubleday, 2003.

Holman, Otto. *Integrating Central Europe: EU Expansion and the Double Transformation in Poland, the Czech Republic and Hungary.* New York: Routledge, 2002.

Hupchick, Dennis P. *The Balkans: From Constantinople to Communism.* New York: Palgrave Macmillan, 2002.

Hupchick, Dennis P., and Harold E. Cox. *A Concise Historical Atlas of Eastern Europe.* New York: St. Martin's Press, 1996.

Katzenstein, Peter J., ed. *Mitteleuropa: Between Europe and Germany.* Providence, RI: Berghahn Books, 1997.

Kostadinova, Tatiana. *Political Corruption in Eastern Europe: Politics after Communism.* Boulder, CO: Lynne Rienner, 2012.

Kotkin, Stephen. *Uncivil Society: 1989 and the Implosion of the Communist Establishment.* New York: Modern Library, 2009.

Jansky, Libor, Masahiro Murakami, and Nevelina I. Pachova. *The Danube: Environmental Monitoring of an International River.* New York: United Nations University Press, 2004.

Jeffries, Ian. *Eastern Europe at the Turn of the Twenty-First Century: A Guide to the Economies in Transition.* New York: Routledge, 2002.

Johnson, Lonnie R. *Central Europe: Enemies, Neighbors, Friends.* New York: Oxford University Press, 1996.

Kovrig, Bennett. *Of Walls and Bridges: The United States and Eastern Europe.* New York: New York University Press, 1991.

Lampe, John R., ed. *Creating Capital Markets in Eastern Europe*. Baltimore, MD: Johns Hopkins University Press, 1992.

Larrabee, F. Stephen. *NATO's Eastern Agenda in a New Strategic Era*. Santa Monica, CA: Rand, 2004.

Lewis, Paul G. *Political Parties in Post-Communist Eastern Europe*. New York: Routledge, 2001.

Mahncke, Dieter, Wayne C. Thompson, and Wyn Rees. *Redefining Transatlantic Relations: The Challenge of Change*. Manchester, UK: Manchester University Press, 2004.

Marer, Paul, and Andras Kves, eds. *Foreign Economic Liberalization: Transformations in Socialist and Market Economies*. Boulder, CO: Westview Press, 1991.

Mason, David S. *Revolution in East-Central Europe: The Rise and Fall of Communism*. 2nd ed. Boulder, CO: Westview Press, 1996.

Mazower, Mark. *The Balkans*. New York: Modern Library, 2000.

Meyer, Michael. *The Year That Changed the World: The Untold Story behind the Fall of the Berlin Wall*. New York: Scribner, 2009.

Michnik, Adam. *In Search of Lost Meaning: The New Eastern Europe*. Berkeley: University of California Press, 2011.

Michta, Andrew A. *America's New Allies: Poland, Hungary, and the Czech Republic in NATO*. Seattle: University of Washington Press, 1999.

Millard, Frances. *Elections, Parties, and Representation in Post-Communist Europe*. New York: Palgrave Macmillan, 2004.

Ramet, Sabrina Petra. *Nihil Obstat: Religion, Politics, and Social Change in East-Central Europe and Russia*. Durham, NC: Duke University Press, 1998.

———, ed. *Rocking the State: Rock Music and Politics in Eastern Europe and Russia*. Boulder, CO: Westview Press, 1994.

Remington, Thomas F., ed. *Parliaments in Transition: The New Legislative Politics in the Former USSR and Eastern Europe*. Boulder, CO: Westview Press, 1994.

Rose, Richard, and Neil Munro. *Elections and Parties in New European Democracies*. Washington, DC: CQ Press, 2003.

Roskin, Michael G. *The Rebirth of East Europe*. 4th ed. Upper Saddle River, NJ: Prentice Hall, 2002.

Rothschild, Joseph. *Return to Diversity: A Political History of East Central Europe since World War II*. Rev. ed. New York: Oxford University Press, 1999.

Rueschemeyer, Marlyn, ed. *Women in the Politics of Postcommunist Eastern Europe*. Armonk, NY: M. E. Sharpe, 1998.

Rywkin, Michael. *Moscow's Lost Empire*. Armonk, NY: M. E. Sharpe, 1994.

Sarotte, Mary Elise. *The Struggle to Create Post-Cold War Europe*. Princeton, NJ: Princeton University Press, 2009.

Sebestyen, Victor. *Revolution 1989: The Fall of the Soviet Empire*. New York: Pantheon, 2009.

Shlapentokh, Vladimir, and Munir Sendich, eds. *The New Russian Diaspora: Russian Minorities in the Former Soviet Republics*. Armonk, NY: M. E. Sharpe, 1994.

Smith, Graham, et al. *Nation-Building in the Post-Soviet Borderlands: The Politics of National Identities*. New York: Cambridge University Press, 1998.

Stark, David, and Lszl Bruszt. *Postsocialist Pathways: Transforming Politics and Property in East Central Europe*. New York: Cambridge University Press, 1998.

Stokes, Gale. *Three Eras of Political Change in Eastern Europe*. New York: Oxford University Press, 1997.

———. *The Walls Came Tumbling Down: The Collapse of Communism in Eastern Europe*. New York: Oxford University Press, 1993.

Toman, Michael A., ed. *Pollution Abatement Strategies in Central and Eastern Europe*. Baltimore, MD: Johns Hopkins University Press, 1994.

Tongeren, Paul van, Hans van de Veen, and Juliette Verhoeven, eds. *Searching for Peace in Europe and Eurasia: An Overview of Conflict Prevention and Peacebuilding Activities*. Boulder, CO: Lynne Reinner, 2002.

Turnock, David, ed. *Eastern Europe and the Former Soviet Union*. New York: Oxford University Press, 2000.

Weigel, George. *The Final Revolution: The Resistance Church and the Collapse of Communism*. New York: Oxford University Press, 1992.

GERMANY

Adenauer, Konrad. *Memoirs, 1945–1953*. Chicago: Regnery, 1966.

Alba, Richard, Peter Schmidt, and Martina Wasmer, eds. *Germans or Foreigners? Attitudes toward Ethnic Minorities in Post-Reunification Germany*. New York: Palgrave Macmillan, 2003.

Bibliography

Anderson, Jeffrey, and Eric Langenbacher, eds. *From the Bonn to the Berlin Republic: Germany at the Twentieth Anniversary of Unification.* New York: Berghahn Books, 2010.

Ardagh, John. *Germany and the Germans: After Unification.* Rev. ed. New York: Penguin Books, 1991.

Aust, Stefan. Baader-Meinhof: *The Inside Story of the R.A.F.* New York: Oxford University Press, 2009.

Balfour, Michael. *Germany: The Tides of Power.* New York: Routledge, 1992.

Barbieri, William A., Jr. *Ethics of Citizenship: Immigration and Group Rights in Germany.* Durham, NC: Duke University Press, 1998.

Bark, Dennis L., and David R. Gress. *A History of West Germany.* Cambridge, MA: Basil Blackwell, 1989.

Beevor, Antony. *Berlin: The Downfall 1945.* New York: Penguin Books, 2002.

Bessel, Richard. *Germany 1945: From War to Peace.* New York: Harper, 2009.

Boehm, Philip, trans. *A Woman in Berlin: Eight Weeks in a Conquered City.* New York: Metropolitan Books, 2005.

Bracher, Karl D. *The German Dictatorship: The Origins, Structure, and Effects of National Socialism.* New York: Praeger, 1970.

Brandt, Willy. *My Life in Politics.* New York: Penguin Books, 1992.

Broadbent, Philip, and Sabine Hake, eds. *Berlin Divided City, 1945–1989.* New York: Berghahn Books, 2010.

Buse, Dieter K., and Juergen C. Doerr, eds. *Encyclopedic History of Modern Germany.* 2 vols. Hamden, CT: Garland, 1997.

Cecil, Lamar. *Wilhelm II.* 2 vols. Chapel Hill: University of North Carolina Press, 1996.

Childs, David. *The Fall of the GDR: Germany's Road to Unity.* London: Pearson Longman, 2001.

Clark, Christopher. *Iron Kingdom: The Rise and Downfall of Prussia, 1600–1947.* Cambridge, MA: Belknap Press, 2006.

Clay, Lucius. *Decision in Germany.* Garden City, NY: Doubleday, 1950.

Conradt, David P. *The German Polity.* 7th ed. New York: Longman, 2000.

Conradt, David P., Gerald R. Kleinfeld, and Christian See, eds. *Power Shift in Germany: The 1998 Election and the End of the Kohl Era.* New York: Berghahn Books, 2000.

———, eds. *Precarious Victory: The 2002 German Federal Election Its Aftermath.* New York: Berghahn Books, 2004.

Craig, Gordon A. *From Bismarck to Adenauer: Aspects of German Statecraft.* New York: Harper and Row, 1965.

———. *The Germans.* Rev. ed. New York: Penguin Books, 1992.

———. *Germany 1866–1945.* New York: Oxford University Press, 1978.

Crawford, Alan, and Tony Czuczka. Angela Merkel: *A Chancellorship Forged in Crisis.* Chichester, UK: John Wiley and Sons, 2013.

Dalton, Russell J. *Politics in Germany.* 2nd ed. New York: HarperCollins, 1993.

Darmstaedter, Friedrich. *Bismarck and the Creation of the Second Reich.* New Brunswick, NJ: Transaction, 2008.

Edinger, Lewis, and Brigitte Nacos. *From Bonn to Berlin.* New York: Columbia University Press, 1998.

Elias, Norbert. *The Germans.* New York: Columbia University Press, 1996.

Erb, Scott. *German Foreign Policy: Navigating a New Era.* Boulder, CO: Lynne Rienner, 2003.

Evans, Richard J. *The Coming of the Third Reich.* New York: Penguin Books, 2008.

———. *The Third Reich in Power.* New York Books: Penguin, 2008.

Fest, Joachim. *Hitler.* New York: Random House, 1975.

Fisher, Marc. *After the Wall: Germany, the Germans, and the Burdens of History.* New York: Simon Schuster, 1995.

Friedrich, Jorg. *The Fire: The Bombing of Germany, 1940–1945.* New York: Columbia University Press, 2006.

Fulbrook, Mary. *Anatomy of a Dictatorship: Inside the GDR, 1949–1989.* New York: Oxford University Press, 1999.

———. *A Concise History of Germany.* Cambridge, UK: Cambridge University Press, 2004.

———. *History of Germany 1918–1990: The Divided Nation.* London: Blackwell, 2003.

———. Ash, Timothy. *The File: A Personal History.* New York: Random House, 1997.

———. *In Europe's Name: Germany and the Divided Continent.* New York: Random House, 1994.

Gedmin, Jeffrey. *The Germans: Portrait of a New Nation.* Washington, DC: AEI Press, 1995.

Genscher, Hans-Dietrich. *Rebuilding a House Divided: A Memoir by the Architect of Germany's Reunification.* New York: Broadway Books, 1998.

Bibliography

Giersch, Herbert, Karl-Heinz Paque, and Holger Schmieding. *The Fading Miracle: Four Decades of Market Economy*. Cambridge, UK: Cambridge University Press, 1992.

Glaessner, Gert-Joachim, and Ian Wallace, eds. *The German Revolution of 1989: Causes and Consequences*. Oxford, UK: Berg, 1992.

Gordon, Thomas and Greg Lewis. *Defying Hitler: The Germans Who Resisted Nazi Rule*. New York: Penguin Books, 2019.

Green, Simon. *The Politics of Exclusion: Institutions and Immigration Policy in Contemporary Germany*. Manchester, UK: Manchester University Press, 2004.

Green, Stephen. *Reluctant Meister: How Germany's Past Is Shaping Its European Future*. London: Haus, 2014.

Griffith, William E. *The Ostpolitik of the Federal Republic of Germany*. Cambridge, MA: MIT Press, 1978.

Grosser, Dieter, ed. *German Unification: The Unexpected Challenge*. Oxford, UK: Berg, 1992.

Gunlicks, Arthur. *The Lander and German Federalism*. Manchester, UK: Manchester University Press, 2003.

Hamilton, Daniel S. *Beyond Bonn: Crafting U.S. Policy toward the Berlin Republic*. Washington, DC: Brookings Institution Press, 1994.

Hamilton, Richard. *Who Voted for Hitler?* Princeton, NJ: Princeton University Press, 1982.

Hampton, Mary, and Christian See, eds. *Between Bonn and Berlin: German Politics Adrift*. Lanham, MD: Rowman & Littlefield, 1998.

Hancock, M. Donald, and Henry Krisch. *Politics in Germany*. Washington, DC: CQ Press, 2009.

Hancock, M. Donald, and Helga Welsh, eds. *German Unification: Process and Outcomes*. Boulder, CO: Westview Press, 1992.

Herspring, Dale R. *Requiem for an Army: The Demise of the East German Military*. New York: Rowman & Littlefield, 1998.

Hockenos, Paul. *Joschka Fischer and the Making of the Berlin Republic*. New York: Oxford University Press, 2008.

Holborn, Hajo. *The History of Modern Germany*. 3rd ed. Princeton, NJ: Princeton University Press, 1982.

Jacobsen, Annie. *Operation Paperclip: The Secret Intelligence Program to Bring Nazi Scientists to America*. New York: Little, Brown, 2014.

Jahner, Harald. *Aftermath: Life in the Fallout of the Third Reich, 1945–1955*. Allen Lane, 2021.

Jarausch, Konrad, and Volker Gransow, eds. *Uniting Germany: Documents and Debates*. Providence, RI: Berghahn, 1995.

de Jong, David. *Nazi Billionaires: The Dark History of Germany's Wealthiest Dynasties*. New York: Marine Books, 2022.

Kamphner, John. *Why the Germans Do It Better*. Atlantic Books, 2020.

Keithly, David M. *The Collapse of East German Communism: The Year the Wall Came Down, 1989*. Westport, CT: Praeger, 1992.

Klusmeyer, Doublas B., and Demetrious G. Papademetrion. *Immigration Policy in the Federal Republic of Germany*. New York: Berghahn, 2009.

Koehler, John O. *Stasi: The Untold Story of the East German Secret Police*. Boulder, CO: Westview Press, 2000.

Kohl, Walter. *Leben oder Gelebt Werden: Schritte auf dem Weg zur Versohnung*. Munich: Integral Verlag, 2011. An estranged son writes a damning portrait of Helmut Kohl.

Lange, Thomas, and Geoffrey Pugh. *The Economics of German Unification: An Introduction*. Williston, VT: Edward Elgar, 1998.

Langenbacher, Eric. *Between Left and Right: The 2009 Bundestag Elections and the Transformation of the German Party System*. New York: Berghahn Books, 2010.

———, ed. *Launching the Grand Coalition: The 2005 Bundestag Election and the Future of German Politics*. New York: Berghahn Books, 2007.

Lankowski, Carl. *Germany and the European Community*. New York: St. Martin's Press, 1992.

Larson, Eric. *In the Garden of Beasts: Love, Terror, and an American Family in Hitler's Berlin*. New York: Crown, 2011.

Leaman, Jeremy. *The Political Economy of Germany under Chancellors Kohl and Schroder: Decline of the German Model?* New York: Berghahn Books, 2009.

Leithner, Anika. *Shaping German Foreign Policy: History, Memory, and National Interest*. Boulder, CO: First Forum, 2009.

Lieven, Anatol, and Dmitri Trenin, eds. *Ambivalent Neighbors: The EU, NATO, and the Price of Membership*. Washington, DC: Brookings Institution Press, 2003.

Livingston, Robert Gerald, and Volkmar Sanders. *The Future of German Democracy*. New York: Continuum, 1994.

Bibliography

Longhurst, Kerry. *Germany and the Use of Force: The Evolution of German Security Policy, 1990–2003.* Manchester, UK: Manchester University Press, 2005.

MacGregor, Neil. *Germany: Memories of a Nation.* New York: Alfred A. Knopf, 2014.

Maier, Charles S. *Dissolution: The Crisis of Communism and the End of East Germany.* Princeton, NJ: Princeton University Press, 1997.

Mann, Golo. *The History of Germany since 1789.* New York: Praeger, 1968.

Markovits, Andrei S., and Simon Rich. *The German Predicament: Memory and Power in the New Europe.* Ithaca, NY: Cornell University Press, 1997.

Marsh, David. *The Germans: The Pivotal Nation: A People at the Crossroads.* New York: St. Martin's Press, 1990.

Marton, Kati. *The Chancellor: The Remarkable Odyssey of Angela Merkel.* New York: Simon & Schuster, 2021.

Mazower, Mark. *Hitler's Empire: How the Nazis Ruled Europe.* New York: Penguin Books, 2008.

McAdams, A. James. *Judging the Past in Unified Germany.* Cambridge, UK: Cambridge University Press, 2001.

Merkl, Peter H. *The Origin of the West German Republic.* New York: Oxford University Press, 1965.

Millar, Peter. *1989: The Berlin Wall: My Part in Its Downfall.* New York: Acadia, 2010.

Moorhouse, Roger. *Berlin at War.* New York: Basic Books, 2011.

Muller, Jan-Werner. *Another Country: German Intellectuals, Unification, and National Identity.* New Haven, CT: Yale University Press, 2000.

Mushaben, Joyce. *The Changing Faces of Citizenship: Integration and Mobilization among Ethnic Minorities in Germany.* New York: Berghahn Books, 2008.

Neitzel, Sonke, and Harald Welzer. *Soldiers: German POWs on Fighting, Killing, and Dying.* Translated by Jefferson Chase. New York: Vintage Books, 2013.

Newnham, Randall E. *German Foreign Policy: Navigating a New Era.* Boulder, CO: Lynne Rienner, 2003.

Niven, Bill. *Facing the Nazi Past: United Germany and the Legacy of the Third Reich.* New York: Routledge, 2001.

Opp, Karl-Dieter, Peter Voss, and Christiane Gern. *Origins of Spontaneous Revolution: East Germany, 1989.* Ann Arbor: University of Michigan Press, 1995.

Padgett, Stephen, ed. *Adenauer to Kohl: The Development of the German Chancellorship.* Washington, DC: Georgetown University Press, 1994.

Phillips, Ann L. *Power and Influence after the Cold War: Germany in East-Central Europe.* Lanham, MD: Rowman & Littlefield, 2000.

Plato, Alexander von, Almut Leh, and Christoph Thonfeld, eds. *Hitler's Slaves: Life Stories of Forced Labourers in Nazi-Occupied Europe.* New York: Berghahn Books, 2010.

Pommerin, Reiner. *The American Impact on Postwar Germany.* Providence, RI: Berghahn Books, 1995.

Pond, Elizabeth. *Beyond the Wall: Germany's Road to Unification.* Washington, DC: Brookings Institution Press, 1993.

Pulzer, Peter. *German Politics, 1945–1995.* New York: Oxford University Press, 1995.

Reeves, Richard. *Daring Young Men: The Heroism and Triumph of the Berlin Airlift, June 1948–May 1949.* New York: Simon and Schuster, 2009.

Rohl, John C. G. *Kaiser Wilhelm II, 1859–1941: A Concise Life.* Translated by Sheila de Bellaigue. Cambridge, UK: Cambridge University Press, 2014.

Ruge, Eugen. *In Times of Fading Light: The Story of a Family.* Translated by Anthea Bell Minneapolis, MN: Graywolf Press, 2013.

Sarotte, Mary Elise. *The Collapse: The Accidental Opening of the Berlin Wall.* New York: Basic Books, 2014.

Schneider, Peter. *Berlin Now: The Rise of the City and the Fall of the Wall.* New York: Penguin Books, 2014.

Schoenbaum, David. *Hitler's Social Revolution: Class and Status in Nazi Germany 1933–1939.* Garden City, NY: Anchor Books, 1967.

Schulze, Hagen. *Germany: A New History.* Cambridge, MA: Harvard University Press, 2001.

Schweitzer, Carl-Christoph, et al., eds. *Politics and Government in Germany, 1944–1994: Basic Documents.* 2nd rev. ed. Providence, RI: Berghahn Books, 1995.

Sinn, Hans-Werner. *Can Germany Be Saved? The Malaise of the World's First Welfare State.* Cambridge, MA: MIT Press, 2007.

Smyser, W. R. *How Germans Negotiate: Logical Goals, Practical Solutions.* Herndon, VA: United States Institute of Peace Press, 2003.

Snyder, Timothy. *Bloodlands: Europe between Hitler and Stalin.* New York: Basic Books, 2010.

Sperling, James, ed. *Germany at Fifty-Five: Berlin Ist Nicht Bonn?* Manchester, UK: Manchester University Press, 2004.

Steinberg, Jonathan. *Bismarck: A Life.* Oxford, UK: Oxford University Press, 2011.

Steiner, Andre. *The Plans That Failed: An Economic History of East Germany, 1945–1989.* New York: Berghahn Books, 2010.

Stent, Angela E. *Russia and Germany Reborn: Unification, the Soviet Collapse, and the New Europe.* Princeton, NJ: Princeton University Press, 1999.

Stephan, Alexander. *Americanization and Anti-Americanism: The German Encounter with American Culture after 1945.* New York: Berghahn Books, 2007.

Stern, Fritz. *Five Germanys I Have Known.* New York: Farrar, Straus and Giroux, 2007.

Sturmer, Michael. *The German Empire: 1871–1919.* New York: Weidenfeld and Nicolson, 2000.

Szabo, Stephen F. *The Diplomacy of German Unification.* New York: St. Martin's Press, 1992.

———. *Germany, Russia, and the Rise of Geo-Economics.* London: Bloomsbury Academic, 2015.

———. *Parting Ways: The Crisis in German-American Relations.* Washington, DC: Brookings Institution Press, 2004.

Taylor, Frederick. *The Berlin Wall: A World Divided, 1961–1989.* New York: HarperCollins, 2007.

———. *The Downfall of Money: Germany's Hyperinflation and the Destruction of the Middle Class.* New York: Bloomsbury Press, 2013.

Thompson, Wayne C. *In the Eye of the Storm: Kurt Riezler and the Crises of Modern Germany.* Iowa City: University of Iowa Press, 1980.

———. *The Political Odyssey of Herbert Wehner.* Boulder, CO: Westview Press, 1993.

Thompson, Wayne C., Susan L. Thompson, and Juliet S. Thompson. *Historical Dictionary of Germany.* Metuchen, NJ: Scarecrow Press, 1994. Contains many entries, a lengthy chronology, and a bibliography.

Timmins, Graham. *Politics of New Germany.* New York: Routledge, 2006.

Turner, Henry A. *Germany from Partition to Reunification.* New Haven, CT: Yale University Press, 1992.

Turner, Lowell. *Fighting for Partnership: Labor and Politics in Unified Germany.* Ithaca, NY: Cornell University Press, 1998.

Ullrich, Volker. *Eight Days in May: How Germany's War Ended.* Allen Lane, 2021.

Uris, Leon. *Armageddon: A Novel of Berlin.* London: Corgi, 1963.

Vaizey, Hester. *Born in the GDR: Living in the Shadow of the Wall.* Oxford, UK: Oxford University Press, 2014.

Wallander, Celeste A. *Mortal Friends, Best Enemies: German-Russian Cooperation after the Cold War.* Ithaca, NY: Cornell University Press, 1999.

Wawro, Geoffrey. *The Franco-Prussian War: The German Conquest of France in 1870–1871.* Cambridge, UK: Cambridge University Press, 2003.

Weitz, Eric D. *Weimar Germany: Promise and Tragedy.* Princeton, NJ: Princeton University Press, 2007.

Wolf, Markus. *Man without a Face: The Autobiography of Communism's Greatest Spymaster.* New York: Times Books Random House, 1997.

Yoder, Jennifer A. *From East Germans to Germans? The New Postcommunist Elites.* Durham, NC: Duke University Press, 1999.

AUSTRIA

Bader, William B. *Austria between East and West 1945–1955.* Stanford, CA: Stanford University Press, 1966.

Beller, Steven. *A Concise History of Austria.* New York: Cambridge University Press, 2007.

Berg, Matthew Paul. *The Struggle for a Democratic Austria: Bruno Kreisky on Peace and Social Justice.* New York: Berghahn Books, 2000.

Bischof, Gunter, Anton Pelinka, and Michael Gehler, eds. *Austria in the European Union.* New Brunswick, NJ: Transaction, 2002.

Bischof, Gunter, Anton Pelinka, and Oliver Rathkolb, eds. *The Kreisky Era in Austria.* New Brunswick, NJ: Transaction, 1993.

Bischof, Gunter, and Fritz Plasser, eds. *The Changing Austrian Voter.* New Brunswick, NJ: Transaction, 2008.

———, eds. *The Schussel Era in Austria.* Contemporary Austrian Studies, vol. 18. New Orleans, LA: UNO Press, 2008.

Bischof, Gunter, Fritz Plasser, and Barbara Stelxl-Marx, eds. *New Perspectives on Austrians and World War II.* Contemporary Austrian Studies, vol. 17. New Orleans, LA: UNO Press, 2009.

Bluhm, William T. *Building an Austrian Nation: The Political Integration of a Western State.* New Haven, CT: Yale University Press, 1973.

Bibliography

Fichtner, Paula Sutter. *The Habsburgs: Dynasty, Culture and Politics*. London: Reaktion Books, 2014.

Fitzmaurice, John. *Austrian Politics and Society Today*. New York: St. Martin's Press, 1991.

Gruber, Helmut. *Red Vienna: Experiment in Working-Class Culture, 1919–1934*. Oxford, UK: Oxford University Press, 1991.

Hamann, Brigitte. *Hitler's Vienna: Dictator's Apprenticeship*. New York: Oxford University Press, 1999.

Herzstein, Robert E. *Waldheim: The Missing Years*. New York: Arbor House W. Morrow, 1988.

Johnson, Lonnie. *Introducing Austria: A Short History*. Riverside, CA: Ariadne, 1992.

Johnson, William M. *The Austrian Mind: An Intellectual and Social History*. Berkeley: University of California Press, 2000.

Krzyzanowski, Michal, and Ruth Wodak. *The Politics of Exclusion: Debating Migration in Austria*. New Brunswick, NJ: Transaction, 2008.

Luther, Kurt Richard. *Austria 1945–1995*. Brookfield, VT: Ashgate, 1998.

Luther, Richard, and Wolfgang C. Muller, eds. *Politics in Austria: Still a Case of Consociationalism?* Portland, OR: Frank Cass, 1992.

Mitten, Richard. *The Politics of Antisemitic Prejudice: The Waldheim Phenomenon in Austria*. Boulder, CO: Westview Press, 1992.

Pelinka, Anton. *Austria: Out of the Shadow of the Past*. Boulder, CO: Westview Press, 1999.

Pelinka, Anton, and Fritz Plasser, eds. *The Austrian Party System*. Boulder, CO: Westview Press, 1989.

Rady, Martyn. *The Habsburgs*. New York: Basic Books, 2020.

Schorske, Carl F. *Fin de Siecle Vienna: Politics and Culture*. New York: Vintage Books, 1981.

Segar, Kenneth, and John Warren, eds. *Austria in the Thirties: Culture and Politics*. Riverside, CA: Ariadne, 1992.

Spaulding, E. Wilder. *The Quiet Invaders: The Story of the Austrian Impact upon America*. Vienna: Osterreichischer Bundesverlag, 1968.

Steininger, Gunter Bischof, and Michael Gehler, eds. *Austria in the Twentieth Century*. New Brunswick, NJ: Transaction, 2008.

Steininger, Rolf. *Austria, Germany and the Cold War*. New York: Berghahn Books, 2008.

Sully, Melanie A. *The Haider Phenomenon*. New York: Columbia University Press, 1997.

Vocelka, Karl, and Heller, Lynne. *Die Private Welt Der Habsburger: Leben und Alltag einer Familie*. Graz; Wien; Köln. Verlag Styria, 1998.

Wodak, Ruth, and Anton Pelinka, eds. *The Haider Phenomenon*. New Brunswick, NJ: Transaction, 2001.

POLAND

Batalion, Judy. *The Light of Days (Women in the Resistance)*. William Morrow, 2021.

Begley, Louis. *Wartime Lies: A Novel*. New York: Fawcett Columbine, 1991.

Bethell, Nicholas. *Gomulka, His Poland and His Communism*. Harmondsworth, UK: Penguin Books, 1972.

Brumberg, Abraham, ed. *Poland, Genesis of a Revolution*. New York: Random House, 1983.

Bukowczyk, John J. *Polish Americans and Their History: Community, Culture, and Politics*. Pittsburgh, PA: University of Pittsburgh Press, 1996.

Davies, Norman. *God's Playground: A History of Poland*. Vol. 2, *1795 to the Present*. New York: Oxford University Press, 2005.

———. *Heart of Europe: The Past in Poland's Present*. New ed. New York: Oxford University Press, 2001.

———. *Rising '44: The Battle for Warsaw*. London: Pan Books, 2004.

Garton Ash, Timothy. *The Polish Revolution: Solidarity*. 3rd ed. New Haven, CT: Yale University Press, 2002.

Glazyca, George, and Ryszard Rapacki. *Poland into the 1990s: Economy and Society in Transition*. New York: St. Martin's Press, 1991.

Grabowski, Jan. *Hunt for the Jews: Betrayal and Murder in German-Occupied Poland*. Bloomington: Indiana University Press, 2013.

Gross, Jan T. *Neighbors: The Destruction of the Jewish Community in Jedwabne, Poland*. Princeton, NJ: Princeton University Press, 2001.

Halecki, O. *A History of Poland*. New York: Dorset Press, 1992.

Haltof, Marek. *Polish National Cinema*. New York: Berghahn Books, 2002.

Bibliography

Jasiewicz, Krzysztof. *Polish Politics after the 1997 Parliamentary Elections: Back to a Polarized Polity?* Washington, DC: National Council for Eurasian and East European Research, 1998.

Karpinski, Jakub. *Countdown: The Polish Upheavals of 1956, 1970, 1976, 1980.* Translated by Olaga Amsterdamska and Gene M. Moore. New York: Karz-Cohl, 1982.

Kochanski, Halik. *The Eagle Unbowed: Poland and the Poles in World War II.* Cambridge, MA: Harvard University Press, 2012.

Kurski, Jaroslaw. *Lech Walesa: Democrat or Dictator?* Boulder, CO: Westview Press, 1993.

Lukowski, Jerzy, and Hubert Zawadzki. *A Concise History of Poland.* Cambridge, UK: Cambridge University Press, 2001.

Michta, Andrew A. *The Soldier-Citizen: The Politics of the Polish Army after Communism.* London: Macmillan, 1997.

Nagengast, Carole. *Reluctant Socialists, Rural Entrepreneurs: Class, Culture, and the Polish State.* Boulder, CO: Westview Press, 1993.

Olson, Lynne. *For Your Freedom and Ours: The Kosciuszko Squadron: Forgotten Heroes of World War II.* London: Arrow Books, 2003.

Pisarska, Katarzyna. *The Polish American Community's Lobbying for Poland's Inclusion into NATO.* Lodz, Poland: Mediton, 2003.

Sanford, George. *Poland: The Conquest of History.* Amsterdam: Harwood Academic, 1999.

Sutherlin, John W. *The Greening of Central Europe: Sustainable Development and Environmental Policy in Poland and the Czech Republic.* Lanham, MD: University Press of America, 2000.

Taras, Ray, and Marjorie Castle. *Democracy in Poland.* 2nd ed. Boulder, CO: Westview Press, 2003.

Thompson, Kenneth W. *The Presidency and Governance in Poland.* Lanham, MD: University Press of America, 1997.

Walesa, Lech. *The Struggle and the Triumph: An Autobiography.* Translated by Franklin Philip. New York: Arcade, 1994.

Wolczuk, Kasia, and Wolczuk, Roman. *Poland and Ukraine: Maintaining a Strategic Partnership through a New Iron Curtain?* Washington, DC: Brookings Institution Press, 2003.

Zaborowski, Marcin. *Germany, Poland and Europe.* Manchester, UK: Manchester University Press, 2005.

Zamoyski, Adam. *The Polish Way: A Thousand-Year History of Poles and Their Culture.* New York: Hippocrene Books, 1994.

THE CZECH REPUBLIC

Bryant, Chad. *Prague: Belonging in the Modern City.* Cambridge, MA: Harvard University Press, 2021.

Agnew, Hugh. *The Czechs and the Lands of the Bohemian Crown.* Stanford, CA: Hoover Institution Press, 2004.

Beneš, Edward. *Memoirs of Dr. Edward Beneš.* London: Allen Unwin, 1954.

Fawn, Rick. *The Czech Republic: A Nation of Velvet.* New York: Routledge, 2005.

Fogel, Daniel S. *Managing in Emerging Market Economies: Cases from the Czech and Slovak Republics.* Boulder, CO: Westview Press, 1994.

Golan, Galia. *Reform Rule in Czechoslovakia: The Dubcek Era, 1968–1969.* Cambridge, UK: Cambridge University Press, 1975.

Havel, Vaclav. *The Art of the Impossible: Politics as Morality in Practice.* New York: Alfred A. Knopf, 1997.

———. *To the Castle and Back.* New York: Knopf, 2007.

Heimann, Mary. *Czechoslovakia: The State That Failed.* New Haven, CT: Yale University Press, 2009.

Innes, Abby. *Czechoslovakia: The Short Goodbye.* New Haven, CT: Yale University Press, 2001.

Journalist M. *A Year Is Eight Months.* Garden City, NY: Doubleday, 1971.

Kaplan, Karel. *The Short March: The Communist Takeover in Czechoslovakia 1945–1948.* New York: St. Martin's Press, 1987.

Keane, John. *Vaclav Havel: A Political Tragedy in Six Acts.* New York: Basic Books, 2000.

King, Jeremy. *Budweisers into Czechs and Germans: A Local History of Bohemian Politics, 1848–1948.* Princeton, NJ: Princeton University Press, 2005.

Klima, Ivan. *My Crazy Century.* Translated by Craig Cravens. New York: Grove Press, 2013.

Kraus, Michael, and Allison Stanger, eds. *Irreconcilable Differences? Explaining Czechoslovakia's Dissolution.* Lanham, MD: Rowland and Littlefield, 2000.

Bibliography

Kusin, Vladimir V. *From Dubcek to Charter 77*. New York: St. Martin's Press, 1978.

Leff, Carol Skalnik. *The Czech and Slovak Republics*. Boulder, CO: Westview Press, 1996.

Littell, Robert, ed. *The Czech Black Book*. New York: Praeger, 1969.

Mamatey, Victor S., and Radomir Luza. *A History of the Czechoslovak Republic, 1918–1948*. Princeton, NJ: Princeton University Press, 1973.

Musil, Jif, ed. *The End of Czechoslovakia*. Budapest: Central European University Press, 1995.

Paul, David W. *Czechoslovakia: Profile of a Socialist Republic at the Crossroads of Europe*. Boulder, CO: Westview Press, 1981.

Sayer, Derek. *Prague: Capital of the Twentieth Century*. Princeton, NJ: Princeton University Press, 2013.

Scherpereel, John A. *Governing the Czech Republic and Slovakia: Between State Socialism and the European Union*. Boulder, CO: First Forum, 2009.

Skilling, H. Gordon. *Czechoslovakia's Interrupted Revolution*. Princeton, NJ: Princeton University Press, 1976.

Tampke, Jurgen. *Czech-German Relations and the Politics of Central Europe*. New York: Palgrave Macmillan, 2003.

Wheaton, Bernard, and Zdenek Kavan. *The Velvet Revolution: Czechoslovakia, 1988–1991*. Boulder, CO: Westview Press, 1992.

THE SLOVAK REPUBLIC

Beneš, Edward. *Memoirs of Dr. Edward Beneš*. London: Allen Unwin, 1954.

El Mallakh, Dorothea H. *The Slovak Autonomy Movement, 1935–1939: A Study in Unrelenting Nationalism*. Boulder, CO: East European Quarterly, 1979.

Fogel, Daniel S. *Managing in Emerging Market Economies: Cases from the Czech and Slovak Republics*. Boulder, CO: Westview Press, 1994.

Golan, Galia. *Reform Rule in Czechoslovakia: The Dubcek Era, 1968–1969*. Cambridge, UK: Cambridge University Press, 1975.

Heimann, Mary. *Czechoslovakia: The State That Failed*. New Haven, CT: Yale University Press, 2009.

Henderson, Karen. *The Politics of Slovakia: Voters, Parties and Democracy 1989–2004*. New York: Routledge, 2006.

Innes, Abby. *Czechoslovakia: The Short Goodbye*. New Haven, CT: Yale University Press, 2001.

Journalist M. *A Year Is Eight Months*. Garden City, NY: Doubleday, 1971.

Kaplan, Karel. *The Short March: The Communist Takeover in Czechoslovakia 1945–1948*. New York: St. Martin's Press, 1987.

Kirschbaum, Stanislav J. *A History of Slovakia*. New York: St. Martin's Press, 1995.

Kraus, Michael, and Allison Stanger, eds. *Irreconcilable Differences? Explaining Czechoslovakia's Dissolution*. Lanham, MD: Rowland and Littlefield, 2000.

Kusin, Vladimir V. *From Dubcek to Charter 77*. New York: St. Martin's Press, 1978.

Leff, Carol Skalnik. *The Czech and Slovak Republics*. Boulder, CO: Westview Press, 1996.

Mamatey, Victor S., and Radomir Luza. *A History of the Czechoslovak Republic, 1918–1948*. Princeton, NJ: Princeton University Press, 1973.

Mikus, Joseph A., and Kathryn Day Wyatt, trans. *Slovakia, A Political History: 1918–1950*. Milwaukee, WI: Marquette University Press, 1963.

Musil, Jif, ed. *The End of Czechoslovakia*. Budapest: Central European University Press, 1995.

Paul, David W. *Czechoslovakia: Profile of a Socialist Republic at the Crossroads of Europe*. Boulder, CO: Westview Press, 1981.

Scherpereel, John A. *Governing the Czech Republic and Slovakia: Between State Socialism and the European Union*. Boulder, CO: First Forum, 2009.

Skilling, H. Gordon. *Czechoslovakia's Interrupted Revolution*. Princeton, NJ: Princeton University Press, 1976.

Steiner, Eugen. *The Slovak Dilemma*. Cambridge, UK: Cambridge University Press, 1973.

Wheaton, Bernard, and Zdenek Kavan. *The Velvet Revolution: Czechoslovakia, 1988–1991*. Boulder, CO: Westview Press, 1992.

HUNGARY

Batonyi, Gabor. *Hungary*. New York: Routledge, 2006.

Benzinger, Karl P. *Imre Nagy, Martyr of the Nation*. Lanham, MD: Rowman & Littlefield, 2008.

Bibliography

Braun, Aurel, and Zoltan Barany, eds. *Dilemmas of Transition: The Hungarian Experience.* Lanham, MD: Rowman & Littlefield, 1999.

Cartledge, Bryan. *The Will to Survive: A History of Hungary.* London: Timewell Press, 2006.

Ferge, Zsursa. *A Society in the Making: Hungarian Social and Societal Polities, 1945–75.* White Plains, NY: M. E. Sharpe, 1980.

Gati, Charles. *Failed Illusions: Moscow, Washington, Budapest, and the 1956 Hungarian Revolt.* Stanford, CA: Stanford University Press, 2006.

Gough, Roger. *A Good Comrade: Janos Kadar, Communism and Hungary.* London: I. B. Tauris, 2006.

Halpern, L, and Charles Wyplosz, eds. *Hungary: Towards a Market Economy.* New York: Cambridge University Press, 1998.

Hare, P. G., H. K. Radice, and N. Swain, eds. *Hungary: A Decade of Economic Reform.* Winchester, MA: Allen and Unwin, 1981.

Held, Joseph, ed. *The Modernization of Agriculture: Rural Transformation in Hungary.* New York: Columbia University Press, 1980.

Kenez, Peter. *Hungary from the Nazis to Soviets.* New York: Cambridge University Press, 2009.

Kerly, Bla K., ed. *Lawful Revolution in Hungary, 1989–1994.* New York: Columbia University Press, 1996.

Korda, Michael. *Journey to a Revolution: A Personal Memoir and History of the Hungarian Revolution of 1956.* New York: HarperCollins, 2006.

Kourig, Bennett. *Communism in Hungary: From Kun to Kadar.* Stanford, CA: Hoover Institution Press, 1979.

Kun, Joseph C. *Hungarian Foreign Policy: The Experience of a New Democracy.* New York: Praeger, 1993.

Lendvai, Paul. *The Hungarians: A Thousand Years of Victory in Defeat.* Princeton, NJ: Princeton University Press, 2004.

———. *Hungary: Between Democracy and Authoritarianism.* London: C. Hurst, 2013.

Lessing, Erich. *Revolution in Hungary: The 1956 Budapest Uprising.* London: Thames and Hudson, 2006.

Marton, Kati. *Enemies of the People: My Family's Journey to America.* New York: Simon and Schuster, 2009.

Molnar, Miklos. *A Concise History of Hungary.* Cambridge, UK: Cambridge University Press, 2001.

Sebestyen, Victor. *Twelve Days: The Story of the 1956 Hungarian Revolution.* New York: Pantheon, 2006.

———. *Budapest.* W & N, 2022.

Slyon, Lzszl, and Georg Brunner, eds. *Constitutional Judiciary in a New Democracy: The Hungarian Constitutional Court.* Ann Arbor: University of Michigan Press, 1999.

Sugar, Peter F., ed. *A History of Hungary.* Bloomington: Indiana University Press, 1994.

Swain, Nigel. *Hungary: The Rise and Fall of Feasible Socialism.* New York: Verso, 1992.

Thorpe, Nick. *'89: The Unfinished Revolution: Power and Powerlessness in Eastern Europe.* London: Reportage Press, 2009.

THE BALKANS AND FORMER YUGOSLAVIA: GENERAL

Barnett, Neil. *Tito.* London: Haus, 2006.

Bennett, Christopher. *Yugoslavia's Bloody Collapse: Causes, Course and Consequences.* New York: New York University Press, 2000.

Borowiec, Andrew. *Yugoslavia after Tito.* New York: Praeger, 1977.

Bugajski, Janusz. *Ethnic Politics in Eastern Europe.* London: M.E. Sharpe, 1995.

Cohen, Lenard J. *Broken Bonds: The Disintegration of Yugoslavia.* 2nd ed. Boulder, CO: Westview Press, 1995.

———. *Serpent in the Bosom: The Rise and Fall of Slobodan Milošević.* Boulder, CO: Westview Press, 2002.

Cviig Christopher. *Remaking the Balkans.* London: Pinter, 1995.

Dragnich, Alex N. *Yugoslavia's Disintegration and the Struggle for Truth.* New York: Columbia University Press, 1996.

Dunn, William N., and Josip Obradovic. *Workers' Self-Management and Organizational Power in Yugoslavia.* Pittsburgh, PA: University of Pittsburgh Press, 1978.

Djilas, Milovan. *Wartime.* Translated by Michael B. Petrovich. New York: Houghton Mifflin Harcourt, 1980.

Lampe, John, & Mark Mazower (eds.). *Ideologies and National Identities: The Case of Twentieth-Century Southeastern Europe.* Budapest: CEU Press, 2003.

Fischer, Bernd J., ed. *Balkan Dictators: The "Strongmen" of South-Eastern Europe.* London: Hurst, 2005.

Bibliography

Gallagher, Tom. *The Balkans after the Cold War: From Tyranny to Tragedy.* New York: Routledge, 2005.

——. *The Balkans in the New Millennium: In the Shadow of War and Peace.* New York: Routledge, 2005.

Gerolymatos, Andre. *The Balkan Wars.* New York: Basic Books, 2003.

Glenny, Misha. *The Balkans: Nationalism, War and the Great Powers, 1804–1999.* New York: Viking, 2000.

——. *The Fall of Yugoslavia: The Third Balkan War.* 3rd rev. ed. New York: Penguin Books, 1996.

Hall, Richard C. *The Balkan Wars, 1912–13: Prelude to the First World War.* New York, 2000.

Jeffries, Ian. *Former Yugoslavia at the Turn of the Twenty-First Century: A Guide to the Economies in Transition.* New York: Routledge, 2002.

Jelavich, Barbara. *History of the Balkans: Twentieth Century.* Vol. 2. New York: Cambridge University Press, 1983.

Kaplan, Robert D. *Balkan Ghosts: A Journey through History.* New York: Vintage Books, 1996.

Kurspahić, Kemal. *Prime Time Crime: Balkan Media in War and Peace.* Herndon, VA: United States Institute of Peace Press, 2003.

Lampe, John. *Yugoslavia as History: Twice There Was a Country.* 2nd ed. New York: Cambridge University Press, 2000.

Little, Alan, & Laura Silber. *The Death of Yugoslavia.* London: Penguin Books, 1995.

Lydall, Harold. *Yugoslavia in Crisis.* New York: Oxford University Press, 1989.

Mazower, Mark. *The Balkans: A Short History.* London: Weidenfeld and Nicolson, 2000.

Meier, Viktor, and Sabrina Ramet. *Yugoslavia: A History of Its Demise.* New York: Routledge, 1999.

Merrill, Christopher. *Only the Nails Remain: Scenes from the Balkan Wars.* Lanham, MD: Rowman & Littlefield, 1999.

Meyer, Edward C. *Balkans 2010.* Washington, DC: Brookings Institution Press, 2002.

Morrison, Kenneth & Elizabeth Roberts. *The Sandžak: A History.* London: Hurst & Co. 2013.

Morton, Jeffrey S., et al., eds. *Reflections on the Balkan Wars: Ten Years after the Break-up of Yugoslavia.* New York: Palgrave Macmillan, 2004.

Naimark, Norman M. *Fires of Hatred: Ethnic Cleansing in Twentieth-Century Europe.* Cambridge, MA: Harvard University Press, 2000.

Oliver, Ian. *War & Peace in the Balkans: The Diplomacy of Conflict in the Former Yugoslavia.* London: IB Tauris, 2005.

Pavlowitch, Stevan K. *Hitler's New Disorder: The Second World War in Yugoslavia,* London: Hurst & Co., 2008.

Pond, Elizabeth. *Endgame in the Balkans: Regime Change, European Style.* Washington, DC: Brookings Institution Press, 2008.

Ramet, Sabrina P. *Balkan Babel: The Disintegration of Yugoslavia from the Death of Tito to the Fall of Milošević.* 4th ed. Boulder, CO: Westview Press, 2002.

——. *Nationalism and Federalism in Yugoslavia, 1962–1991.* Bloomington: Indiana University Press, 1992.

——. *The Three Yugoslavias: State-building and Legitimation, 1918–2005.* Indiana University Press, 2006

Resic, Sanimir, and Barbara Tournquist-Plewa, eds. *Balkans in Focus: Cultural Boundaries in Europe.* Lund, Sweden: Nordic Academic Press, 2002.

Rusinow, Dennison. *The Yugoslav Experiment 1948–1974.* London: Hurst & Co., 1977.

Rusinow, Dennison. *Yugoslavia: Oblique Insights and Observations.* Pittsburgh: Pittsburgh University Press, 2008.

Schrenk, Martin, Cyrus Ardalan, and Nawal A. El Tatawy. *Yugoslavia: Self-Management Socialism and the Challenges of Development: Report of a Mission Sent to Yugoslavia by the World Bank.* Baltimore, MD: Johns Hopkins University Press, 1979.

Sell, Louis. *Slobodan Milošević and the Destruction of Yugoslavia.* Durham, NC: Duke University Press, 2002.

Shay, Shaul. *Islamic Terror and the Balkans.* New Brunswick, NJ: Transaction, 2008.

Sher, Gerson S. *Praxis: Marxism Criticism and Dissent in Socialist Yugoslavia.* Bloomington: Indiana University Press, 1977.

Silber, Loura, and Allan Little. *Yugoslavia: Death of a Nation.* New York: Penguin Books, 2000.

Sirc, Ljubo. *The Yugoslav Economy under Self-Management.* New York: St. Martin's Press, 1979.

Stanković, Slobodan. *The End of the Tito Era*. Stanford, CA: Hoover Institution Press, 1981.

Stavrianos, L. S. *The Balkans since 1453*. New York: New York University Press, 2000.

Tomasevich, Jozo. *War and Revolution in Yugoslavia, 1941–1945: Occupation and Collaboration*. Stanford, California: Stanford University Press, 2001.

Ullman, Richard H., ed. *The World and Yugoslavia's Wars*. New York: Council on Foreign Relations, 1996.

Vuic, Jason. *The Yugo: The Rise and Fall of the Worst Car in History*. New York: Hill and Wang, 2010.

Wingfield, William Frederic. *A Tour in Dalmatia, Albania, and Montenegro. 1853*. Reprint, New York: Cosimo Classics, 2007.

Zimmermann, Warren. *The Origins of a Catastrophe*. New York: Random House, 1996.

SLOVENIA

Benderly, Jill, and Evan Kraft, eds. *Independent Slovenia*. London: Macmillan, 1994.

Burgher, Bob. *Culture Smart! Slovenia: A Quick Guide to Customs and Etiquette*. London: Kuperard, 2006.

Cox, John K. *Slovenia: Evolving Loyalties*. New York: Routledge, 2005.

Ferfila, Bogomil, and Paul Phillips. *Slovenia*. Lanham, MD: University Press of America, 2000.

Gow, James, and Cathie Carmichael. *Slovenia and the Slovenes: A Small State and the New Europe*. London: Hurst, 2000.

Šabič, Zlatko, and Charles Bukowski, eds. *Small States in the Post-Cold War World: Slovenia and NATO Enlargement*. New York: Praeger, 2002.

CROATIA

Bartlett, Will. *Croatia: A Crossroads between East and West*. New York: Routledge, 2002.

Curtis, Benjamin. *A Traveller's History of Croatia*. Northampton, MA: Interlink Books, 2010.

Drakulić Slavenka. *As If I Am Not There: A Novel about the Balkans*. New York: Viking, 2000.

———. *Cafe Europa: Life after Communism*. New York: Penguin Books, 1996.

Goldstein, Ivo. *Croatia: A History*. London: Hurst, 1999.

Irvine, Jill A. *The Croat Question: Partisan Politics in the Formation of the Yugoslav Socialist State*. Boulder, CO: Westview Press, 1993.

Tanner, Marcus. *Croatia: A Nation Forged in War*. New Haven, CT: Yale University Press, 2001.

Ugrešić Dubravka. *The Culture of Lies: Antipolitical Essays*. Translated by Celia Hawkesworth. University Park: Pennsylvania State University Press, 1998.

SERBIA

Anzulović, Branimir. *Heavenly Serbia: From Myth to Genocide*. New York: New York University Press, 2000.

Bujošević, Dragan, and Ivan Radovanović. *The Fall of Milošević: The October 5th Revolution*. New York: Palgrave Macmillan, 2003.

Cox, John K. *The History of Serbia*. Westport: Greenwood Press, 2002.

Djukić Slavoljub. *Milošević and Markovic: A Lust for Power*. Montreal: McGill-Queen's University Press, 2001.

Gordy, Eric D. *The Culture of Power in Serbia: Nationalism and the Destruction of Alternatives*. University Park: Pennsylvania State University Press, 1999.

Gow, James. *The Serbian Project and Its Adversaries: A Strategy of War Crimes*. London: Hurst, 2003.

Judah, Timothy. *The Serbs: History, Myth, and the Destruction of Yugoslavia*. New Haven, CT: Yale University Press, 1997.

LeBor, Adam. *Milošević: A Biography*. New Haven, CT: Yale University Press, 2004.

Macdonald, David Bruce, ed. *Balkan Holocausts? Serbian and Croatian Victim-Centered Propaganda and the War in Yugoslavia*. Manchester, UK: Manchester University Press, 2003.

Pavolwitch, Stevan K. *Serbia: The History behind the Name*. London: Hurst, 2002.

Ramet, Sabrina & Vjeran Pavlaković. *Serbia since 1989*. Boulder, CO: Westview Press, 2006.

Thomas, Robert. *The Politics of Serbia in the 1990s*. New York: Columbia University Press, 1999.

———. *Serbia under Milošević: Politics in the 1990s*. London: Hurst, 1999.

Bibliography

BOSNIA AND HERZEGOVINA

Andrić, Ivo. *The Bridge on the Drina*. Chicago: University of Chicago Press, 1977. First published 1995 by Harvill (London).

Bose, Sumantra. *Bosnia after Dayton: Nationalist Partition and International Intervention*. London: Hurst, 2002.

Chandler, David. *Bosnia: Faking Democracy after Dayton*. 2nd ed. Sterling, VA: Pluto, 2000.

Cousens, Elizabeth M., and Charles K. Cater. *Toward Peace in Bosnia: Implementing the Dayton Accords*. Boulder, CO: Lynne Rienner, 2001.

Donia, Robert J., and John V. A. Fine. *Bosnia and Herzegovina: A Tradition Betrayed*. Yonkers, NY: Labyrinth, 1994.

Friedman, Francine. *Bosnia: A Polity on the Brink*. New York: Routledge, 2002.

———. *The Bosnian Muslims*. Boulder, CO: Westview Press, 1995.

Mahmutćehajić, Rusmir. *Bosnia the Good: Toleration and Tradition*. Budapest: Central European University Press, 1997.

Malcolm, Noel. *Bosnia: A Short History*. New York: New York University Press, 2000.

Rohde, David. *Endgame: The Betrayal and Fall of Srebrenica, Europe's Worst Massacre since World War II*. Yonkers, NY: Labyrinth, 1997.

Sacco, Joe. *Safe Area Goražde*. London: Jonathon Cape, 2007. A graphic nonfiction account of the Bosnian war. Text with comic-like illustrations but good firsthand reporting.

Sells, Michael A. *The Bridge Betrayed: Religion and Genocide in Bosnia*. Berkeley: University of California Press, 1996.

Smith, David James. *One Morning in Sarajevo: 28 June 1914*. London: Weidenfeld and Nicolson, 2008.

Stewart, Rory, and Gerald Knaus. *Can Intervention Work?* New York: W. W. Norton, 2011.

Stover, Eric, and Gilles Peress. *The Graves*. Yonkers, NY: Labyrinth, 1998.

Šehić, Faruk. *Under Pressure*. Istros Books, 2019.

Vulliamy, Ed. *The War Is Dead, Long Live the War: Bosnia, the Reckoning*. London: Bodley Head, 2012.

MONTENEGRO

Andrijašević, Živko M. & Šerbo Rastoder. *The History of Montenegro from Ancient Times to 2003*. Podgorica: CICG, 2006.

Bieber, Florian (ed.). *Montenegro in Transition: Problems of Identity and Statehood*. BadenBaden: Nomos Verlagsgesellschaft, 2003.

Djukanović, Bojka. *Historical Dictionary of Montenegro*. Lanham, MD: Rowman & Littlefield, 2023.

Fleming, Thomas. *Montenegro: The Divided Land*. Rockford, Illinois: Chronicles Press, 2002

Morrison, Kenneth. *Montenegro: A Modern History*. New York: I.B. Tauris, 2009.

Morrison, Kenneth. *Nationalism, Identity and Statehood in Post-Yugoslav Montenegro*. Bloomsbury Academic, 2018

Roberts, Elizabeth. *Realm of the Black Mountain: A History of Montenegro*. Ithaca, NY: Cornell University Press, 2007.

Stephenson, Francis Seymour. *A History of Montenegro*. London: Harold & Son, 1916.

Treadway, John D. *The Falcon and the Eagle: Montenegro and Austria-Hungary, 1908–1914*. West Lafayette, Ind, 1983.

Warren, Whitney. *Montenegro: The Crime of the Peace Conference*, New York: Brentano's 1922; Classic Reprints 2010, 2019

KOSOVO

Campbell, Greg. *The Road to Kosovo: A Balkan Diary*. Boulder, CO: Westview Press, 2000.

Clark, Howard. *Civil Resistance in Kosovo*. Herndon, VA: Pluto, 2000.

Daalder, Ivo H., and Michael E. O'Hanlon. *Winning Ugly: NATO's War to Save Kosovo*. Washington, DC: Brookings Institution Press, 2001.

Duijzings, Ger. *Religion and the Politics of Identity in Kosovo*. New York: Columbia University Press, 2003.

Hammond, Philip, and Edward S. Herman. *Degraded Capability: The Media and the Kosovo Crisis*. Herndon, VA: Pluto, 2000.

Judah, Tim. *Kosovo: War and Revenge*. New Haven, CT: Yale University Press, 2000.

Kostovicova, Denisa. *Kosovo: The Politics of Identity and Space*. New York: Routledge, 2005.

Latawski, Paul, and Martin A. Smith. *The Kosovo Crisis and the Evolution of Post-Cold War European Security*. Manchester, UK: Manchester University Press, 2003.

Malcolm, Noel. *Kosovo: A Short History*. New York: Harper Perennial, 2000.

Maliqi, Shkelzen. *Kosovo: Separate Worlds: Reflections and Analyses*. Prishtina: MM, 1998.

Mertus, Julie A. *Kosovo: How Myths and Truths Started a War*. Berkeley: University of California Press, 1999.

O'Neill, William G. *Kosovo: An Unfinished Peace*. Boulder, CO: Lynne Rienner, 2002.

Rezun, Miron. *Europe's Nightmare: The Struggle for Kosovo*. Westport, CT: Praeger, 2001.

Schnabel, Albrecht, and Ramesh Thakur, eds. *Kosovo and the Challenge of Humanitarian Intervention*. New York: United Nations University Press, 2000.

Smith, Martin A., and Paul Latowski. *The Kosovo Crisis*. Manchester, UK: Manchester University Press, 2003.

Vickers, Miranda. *Between Serb and Albanian: A History of Kosovo*. New York: Columbia University Press, 1998.

NORTH MACEDONIA

Brown, Keith. *The Past in Question: Modern Macedonia and the Uncertainties of Nation*. Princeton, NJ: Princeton University Press, 2003.

Cowan, Jane K., ed. *Macedonia: The Politics of Identity and Difference*. Herndon, VA: Pluto, 2001.

Peltifer, James, ed. *The New Macedonian Question*. New York: Palgrave Macmillan, 2001.

Phillips, John. *Macedonia: Warlords and Rebels in the Balkans*. New Haven, CT: Yale University Press, 2004.

Poulton, Hugh. *Who Are the Macedonians?* Bloomington: Indiana University Press, 1994.

Ripiloski, Sasho. *Conflict in Macedonia: Exploring a Paradox in the Former Yugoslavia*. Boulder, CO: Lynne Rienner, 2011.

Sokalski, Henryk J. *An Ounce of Prevention: Macedonia and the UN Experience in Preventive Diplomacy*. Herndon, VA: US Institute for Peace, 2003.

Szajkowski, Bogdan. *Macedonia*. New York: Routledge, 2006.

ALBANIA

Biberaj, Elez. *Albania: A Socialist Maverick*. Boulder, CO: Westview Press, 1990.

Costa, Nicholas J. *Albania: A European Enigma*. Boulder, CO: East European Monographs, 1995.

Fischer, Bernd J. *Albania at War: 1939–1945*. London: Hurst, 2003.

Hall, Derek. *Albania and the Albanians*. New York: Pinter, 1994.

Hamm, Harry. *Albania: China's Beachhead in Europe*. London: Victor Gollancz, 1977.

Hoxha, Enver. *The Artful Albanians: The Memoirs of Enver Hoxha*. Edited by Jon Halliday. London: Chatto and Windus, 1986.

Kola, Paulin. *The Search for Greater Albania*. London: Hurst, 2003.

Lemel, Harold W., ed. *Rural Property and Economy in Post-Communist Albania*. New York: Berghahn Books, 2000.

Marmullaku, Ramadan. *Albania and the Albanians*. London: Hurst, 1975.

Pano, Nicholas C. *Albania*. New York: Routledge, 2006.

Pettifer, Kames & Miranda Vickers. *The Albanian Question: Reshaping the Balkans*. London: IB Tauris, 2009.

Prifti, Peter R. *Albania since 1944*. Cambridge, MA: MIT Press, 1978.

———. *Land of the Albanians: A Crossroads of Pain and Pride*. Tirana: Horizont, 2002.

Rejmer, Margo. *Mud Sweeter than Honey: Voices from Communist Albania*. Maclehose Press, 2021.

Vickers, Miranda. *The Albanians: A Modern History*. New York: I. B. Touris, 2001.

Vickers, Miranda, and James Pettifer. *Albania: From Anarchy to Balkan Identity*. New York: New York University Press, 2000.

Winnifrith, Tom, ed. *Perspectives on Albania*. New York: St. Martin's Press, 1992.

Ypi, Lea. *Free: Coming of Age at the End of History*. Allen Lane, 2022.

ROMANIA

Braun, Aurel. *Romanian Foreign Policy since 1965*. New York: Praeger, 1978.

Glajar, Valentina, and Domnica Radulescu, eds. *"Gypsies" in European Literature and Culture*. New York: Palgrave Macmillan, 2008.

Graham, Lawrence S. *Romania: A Developing Socialist State*. Boulder, CO: Westview Press, 1982.

Grumeza, Ion. *Dacia: Land of Transylvania, Cornerstone of Ancient Eastern Europe*. Lanham, MD: Hamilton Books, University Press of America, 2009.

Kaplan, Robert D. *In Europe's Shadow: Two Cold Wars and a Thirty-Year Journey through Romania and Beyond*. New York: Random House, 2016.

King, Robert R. *History of the Romanian Communist Party*. Stanford, CA.: Hoover Institution Press, 1980.

Moscovici, Claudia. *Velvet Totalitarianism: Post-Stalinist Romania*. Lanham, MD: University Press of America, 2009.

Nelson, Daniel N., ed. *Romania after Tyranny*. Boulder, CO: Westview Press, 1992.

———, ed. *Romania in the 1980s*. Boulder, CO: Westview Press, 1981.

Papadimitriou, Dimitris, and David Phinnemore. *Romania and the European Union: From Marginalization to Membership?* New York: Routledge, 2006.

Radulescu, Domnica. *Black Sea Twilight*. London: Transworld/Doubleday, 2010. A second novel based on the author's life in and escape from Romania.

———. *Train to Trieste*. New York: Alfred A. Knopf, 2008. Novel translated into nine languages about the author's escape from Romania.

———. *Country of Red Azaleas*. New York: Twelve, 2016.

Rady, Martyn. *Romania in Turmoil: A Contemporary History*. New York: I. B. Touris, 1992.

Roper, Steven D. *Romania: The Unfinished Revolution*. New York: Routledge, 2005.

Shen, Raphael. *The Restructuring of Romania's Economy: A Paradigm of Flexibility and Adaptability*. Westport, CT: Praeger, 1997.

BULGARIA

Bell, John D., ed. *Bulgaria in Transition*. Boulder, CO: Westview Press, 1998.

Bristow, John A. *The Bulgarian Economy in Transition*. Brookfield, VT: Edward Elgar, 1996.

Crampton, Richard J. *A Short History of Modern Bulgaria*. New York: Cambridge University Press, 1987.

Dellin, L. A. D., ed. *Bulgaria*. New York: Praeger, 1957.

Dimitrov, Vesselin. *Bulgaria: The Uneven Transition*. New York: Routledge, 2002.

Giatzidis, Emil. *An Introduction to Post-Communist Bulgaria: Political, Economic and Social Transformation*. Manchester, UK: Manchester University Press, 2002.

Jones, Derek C., and Jeffrey Miller, eds. *The Bulgarian Economy: Lessons from Early Transition*. Brookfield, VT: Ashgate, 1997.

Saxe-Coburg-Gotha, Simeon. *A Unique Destiny: The Memoir of the Last Tsar of Bulgaria, Prime Minister of a Republic*. Guilford, CT: Stackpole Books, 2021.

Todorov, Tzvetan. *The Fragility of Goodness: Why Bulgaria's Jews Survived the Holocaust*. Princeton, NJ: Princeton University Press, 2001.

Zhivkov, Todor. *Modern Bulgaria: Problems and Tasks in Building an Advanced Socialist Society*. New York: International, 1974.

Zloch-Christy, Iliana, ed. *Bulgaria in a Time of Change: Economic and Political Dimensions*. Brookfield, VT: Avebury, 1996.

Graphic Material Credits

—Kaja Kallas, Prime Minister of Estonia, photo **p. 252**: https://commons.wikimedia.org/wiki/File:Prime_Minister_of_Estonia_Kaja_Kallas_2023.jpg

—Edgars Rinkēvičs, President of Latvia, photo **p. 278**: https://commons.wikimedia.org/wiki/File:Edgars_Rink%C4%93vi%C4%8Ds_as_president-elect,_2023-05-31_(cropped).jpg

—Evika Siliņa, Prime Minister of Latvia, photo **p. 280**: https://en.wikipedia.org/wiki/Evika_Sili%C5%86a#/media/File:Jauniev%C4%93l%C4%93t%C4%81s_Ministru_prezidentes_Evikas_Sili%C5%86as_preses_konference_(cropped).jpg

—Gitanas Nausėda, President of Lithuania, photo **p. 301**: https://commons.wikimedia.org/w/index.php?curid=81426065

—Olaf Scholz, Chancellor of Germany, photo **p. 440**: https://en.wikipedia.org/wiki/Olaf_Scholz#/media/File:Olaf_Scholz_in_2023_(cropped).jpg

—Karl Nehammer, Chancellor of Austria, photo **p. 538**: https://commons.wikimedia.org/wiki/File:Karl_Nehammer_2023.jpg#/media/File:Karl_Nehammer_2023.jpg

—Gustav Klimt, The Kiss (1907–1908), photo. 546: https://commons.wikimedia.org/wiki/File:The_Kiss_-_Gustav_Klimt_-_Google_Cultural_Institute.jpg

—Donald Tusk, Prime Minister of Poland, photo **p. 591**: https://commons.wikimedia.org/w/index.php?curid=142330161

—Petr Pavel, President of Chechia, photo **p. 640**: https://commons.wikimedia.org/w/index.php?curid=131513000

—Petr Fiala, Prime Minister of Chechia, photo **p. 642**: https://commons.wikimedia.org/wiki/File:Petr_Fiala_(51940875566).jpg#/media/File:Petr_Fiala_(51940875566).jpg

—Zuzana Čaputová, President of Slovakia, photo **p. 677**: https://commons.wikimedia.org/w/index.php?curid=113569762https://en.wikipedia.org/wiki/Zuzana_%C4%8Caputov%C3%A1#/media/File:%D0%97%D1%83%D0%B7%D0%B0%D0%BD%D0%B0_%D0%A7%D0%B0%D0%BF%D1%83%D1%82%D0%BE%D0%B2%D0%B0_(02-11-2021).jpg

—Nataša Pirc Musar, President of Slovenia, photo **p. 767**: https://upload.wikimedia.org/wikipedia/commons/7/7a/Nata%C5%A1a_Pirc_Musar_%282023-05-19%29.jpg

—Robert Golob, Prime Minister of Slovenia, **p. 769**: https://commons.wikimedia.org/w/index.php?curid=132630657

—Željko Komšić, President of the Presidency of Bosnia and Herzegovina, photo **p. 850**: https://commons.wikimedia.org/w/index.php?curid=128782766

—Borjana Krišto, Chairwoman of the Council of Ministers of Bosnia and Herzegovina, photo **p. 851**: https://upload.wikimedia.org/wikipedia/commons/6/64/Borjana_Kri%C5%A1to_%282023-12-05%29_%281%29_%28cropped%29.jpg

—Milojko Spaić, Prime Minister of Montenegro, photo **p. 878**: https://upload.wikimedia.org/wikipedia/commons/f/f1/Milojko_Spaji%C4%87_%282023-12-20%29.jpg

—Vjosa Osmani-Sadriu, President of Kosovo, photo **p. 907**: https://commons.wikimedia.org/wiki/File:Vjosa_Osmani1.jpg

—Albin Kurti, Prime Minister of Kosovo, photo **p. 908**: https://en.wikipedia.org/wiki/Albin_Kurti#/media/File:Albin_Kurti_(2023-02-18).jpg

—Talat Xhaferi, Prime Minister of North Macedonia, photo **p. 923**: https://upload.wikimedia.org/wikipedia/commons/e/e4/Talat_Xhaferi_-_2023_%28cropped%29.jpg

—Bajram Begaj, President of Albania, photo **p. 948**: https://commons.wikimedia.org/w/index.php?curid=133593698

—Marcel Ciolacu, Prime Minister of Romania, photo **p. 983**: https://commons.wikimedia.org/w/index.php?curid=144187848

—Nikolai Denkov, Prime Minister of Bulgaria, photo **p. 1021**: https://commons.wikimedia.org/wiki/File:Nikolai_Denkov_full_portrait_2021.jpg

—The **coat of arms** of the respective countries have been taken from Wikipedia Public Domain graphics: https://en.wikipedia.org/wiki/Sweden#/media/File:Great_coat_of_arms_of_Sweden.svg
https://en.wikipedia.org/wiki/Norway#/media/File:Coat_of_arms_of_Norway.svg
https://en.wikipedia.org/wiki/Denmark#/media/File:National_Coat_of_arms_of_Denmark.svg
https://en.wikipedia.org/wiki/Iceland#/media/File:Coat_of_arms_of_Iceland.svg
https://en.wikipedia.org/wiki/Finland#/media/File:Coat_of_arms_of_Finland_2.svg

https://en.wikipedia.org/wiki/Estonia#/media/File:Coat_of_arms_of_Estonia
.svg

https://en.wikipedia.org/wiki/Latvia#/media/File:Coat_of_arms_of_Latvia.svg

https://en.wikipedia.org/wiki/Lithuania#/media/File:Coat_of_arms_of_Lithu
ania.svg

https://en.wikipedia.org/wiki/Kaliningrad_Oblast#/media/File:Coat_of
_Arms_of_Kaliningrad_Oblast.svg

https://en.wikipedia.org/wiki/Germany#/media/File:Coat_of_arms_of_Ger
many.svg

https://en.wikipedia.org/wiki/Austria#/media/File:Austria_Bundesadler.svg

https://en.wikipedia.org/wiki/Poland#/media/File:Herb_Polski.svg

https://en.wikipedia.org/wiki/Czech_Republic#/media/File:Coat_of_arms_of
_the_Czech_Republic.svg

https://en.wikipedia.org/wiki/Slovakia#/media/File:Coat_of_arms_of_Slova
kia.svg

https://en.wikipedia.org/wiki/Hungary#/media/File:Coat_of_arms_of_Hun
gary.svg

https://en.wikipedia.org/wiki/Yugoslavia#/media/File:Emblem_of_Yugosla
via_(1963%E2%80%931992).svg

https://en.wikipedia.org/wiki/Slovenia#/media/File:Coat_of_arms_of_Slove
nia.svg

https://en.wikipedia.org/wiki/Croatia#/media/File:Coat_of_arms_of_Croatia
.svg

https://en.wikipedia.org/wiki/Serbia#/media/File:Coat_of_arms_of_Serbia.svg

https://en.wikipedia.org/wiki/Bosnia_and_Herzegovina#/media/File:Coat_of
_arms_of_Bosnia_and_Herzegovina.svg

https://en.wikipedia.org/wiki/Montenegro#/media/File:Coat_of_arms_of
_Montenegro.svg

https://en.wikipedia.org/wiki/Kosovo#/media/File:Emblem_of_the_Repub
lic_of_Kosovo.svg

https://en.wikipedia.org/wiki/North_Macedonia#/media/File:Coat_of_arms
_of_North_Macedonia.svg

https://en.wikipedia.org/wiki/Albania#/media/File:Coat_of_arms_of_Albania
.svg

https://en.wikipedia.org/wiki/Romania#/media/File:Coat_of_arms_of_Roma
nia.svg

https://en.wikipedia.org/wiki/Bulgaria#/media/File:Coat_of_arms_of_Bul
garia.svg